HARCOURT BRACE JOVANOVICH

New York Chicago San Francisco Atlanta Dallas *and* London

Anatole G. Mazour
John M. Peoples

THIRD EDITION

Men and Nations

A WORLD HISTORY

Anatole G. Mazour is Professor Emeritus of History at Stanford University, Stanford, California, having taught there for twenty-five years. He has also taught at the University of California, Miami University, Carleton College, the University of Chicago, and the University of Nevada. Dr. Mazour received his M.A. from Yale University and his Ph.D. from the University of California. He is the author of several books, including *Russia: Past and Present; Finland Between East and West; The Rise and Fall of the Romanovs;* and *Russia: Tsarist and Communist.*

John M. Peoples recently retired after teaching world history and other social studies courses at Alameda High School, Alameda, California, for thirty-five years. Dr. Peoples received both his M.A. and his Ph.D. from the University of California.

Maps by Harold K. Faye

Copyright Acknowledgments

Quoted Material
Excerpt on page 642 from *The Revolt of the Masses* by José Ortega y Gasset. Reprinted by permission of W. W. Norton & Company, Inc. and George Allen & Unwin Ltd.

Illustrations
Pp. 25, 32, Photo F. L. Kenett, © George Rainbird Ltd.; 55, *both*, Jewish Symbols in the Greco Roman Period, by Erwin R. Goodenough, Bollingen Series XXXVII, vol. II, Symbolism in the Dura Synagogue © 1964 by Bollingen Foundation, reproduced by permission of Princeton University Press: Plates VII and XVI; 163, *both*, copyright the Archeological Survey of India; 405, © The Frick Collection, New York; 439, © Münchner Stadtmuseum; 455, © Aldus Books, London; 473, Reproduced by permission of the publisher, Horizon Press, from *The World of Atget,* copyright 1964; 668, © Museum of Modern Art, New York, Purchase; 703, *bottom right,* 708, *top left, top right, bottom,* 725, *center right,* Robert Capa, © Magnum; 789, *bottom right,* Copyright 1973 by Herblock in the Washington *Post;* 797, *top right, bottom left,* Margaret Bourke-White, Time/Life Picture Agency, © Time Inc.; 802, *bottom left,* Walker, Time/Life Picture Agency, © Time, Inc.

CONTENTS

MAPS

xiv

When this Roman head was carved—about 100 B.C.—the world was very different from what it is now. Yet the qualities of sternness, determination, and strength which it reflects are timeless. In the same way, the forces that shaped Roman history are still at work today. Studying them can illuminate not only what has gone before, but also what lies ahead.

History and You

History is the yesterday of mankind; it is the memory of men. Without a knowledge of yesterday, without any memory, there is no guide to tomorrow. A society without history lacks direction. But men who are conscious of their past can improve their future. They know that the forces that have shaped the past are similar to those that shape the world they live in, and to those that will determine the future.

This book is a record of the past. Even as you read it, your world will change. You will live in the present, and see it become the future. The one certain thing in history is that conditions change. Most Americans believe that the changes can become progress—movement toward a goal, a better world in which mankind can live securely, meaningfully, nobly. But without a guide, without direction, changes may be aimless and meaningless.

This book tells you, a student of history, the story of men and nations. It is more than a record of events. For those who have imagination, it is a dramatic account of what happened to actual men and women as they strove and searched for a good life. And it tries to tell not only what happened, but why it happened.

In order to understand the story better, ask yourself questions as you read it. If you read thoughtfully and critically, asking questions and trying to find answers, you will discover that history has often been shaped by certain forces. You can learn to discover these forces by asking yourself questions like these:

1. How has geography influenced the course of history? Have men simply adjusted to their environment, or have they tried to modify it? As an example, you will see that the history of Greece was influenced by the fact that the Greek peninsula is cut into many small regions by mountains and long inlets from the sea.

2. How have people worked and earned their living? In other words, how have they organized their economy? What roles were played by farming, trade, and manufacturing? How was income distributed?

3. How have men been governed? Has political power been held by a few people, or by many? Have individual men had rights and liberties?

How have rights and liberties been gained, protected, or lost? In what way were laws made and enforced? How have they worked in practice, and for whose benefit? Why and how have men changed their form of government?

4. How have men gained knowledge, and how have they passed it on to their descendants? Have they had a formal system of education? Who has been educated? Has there been any connection between the number of people educated and the form of government? Have men learned much or little from other peoples? Have science and invention played an important part in their lives?

5. How have different religions arisen, and how have they influenced people's lives? You will read, for example, that the original religious beliefs of the Romans were influenced first by the Etruscans, then by the Greeks, then by various other peoples. Finally Roman religion was replaced by Christianity. Why did these changes take place, and how did they affect Roman life?

6. How have the arts—literature, painting, sculpture, architecture, and music—reflected the people who created them and the times in which they were produced? What arts have flourished and why?

7. How have men and nations settled their conflicts? Have they tried to reach peaceful solutions, or have they gone to war? Did the wars settle the issues that caused them? Did they create other problems?

8. Throughout history, civilizations, national states, and political regimes have risen and fallen. What forces led to their rise, decline, or fall? Did men learn from the experiences of the past, or did they seem to repeat earlier mistakes?

If you try to find answers to such questions as these, you will be learning about the many forces that have worked together to make the world what it was and what it is. You will learn about the power of ideas, such as the democratic belief that every human being has worth and dignity that must be respected. You can watch ideas like this appear, develop gradually, become strong, and finally be accepted by enough people to be put into practice. You will see other ideas decline and die out.

Men have been pondering questions and ideas like these since earliest times. As you seek your own answers, you will be discovering what kind of person you are and want to be; you will be shaping your own role in the future world of men and nations.

A. G. M. and J. P.

xvi

USING THIS BOOK

Men and Nations has been created to present the basic facts and ideas of world history as clearly as possible. This is the way it has been organized:

The Unit

There are ten units, which group the chapters into broad historical periods. Each unit opens with a large illustration, symbolizing its contents, and with a list of the chapters it contains. (See, for example, page 2.)

The Chapter

The forty-one chapters of *Men and Nations* are organized around definite periods or topics. Like the units, each begins with a single illustration symbolic of its contents. After an introduction there is a list of the *chapter sections* into which the chapter is divided. (See pages 4 and 5.) A chapter may contain from two to six sections, each numbered. At the end of each section is a *checkup* to test your knowledge of the material you have just read.

Chapter Review

Every chapter ends with a review of its contents. First there is a *time line,* which presents in graphic form the most important events—with their dates—discussed in the chapter. It is followed by a *chapter summary* and by several *questions for discussion* and *projects.* (See page 16.)

Unit Review

Each of the ten units ends with a two-page review, "Study in Depth." Here you will find a number of *individual projects* and *group projects* that relate to the unit. Here, too, you will see a list of books for further reading about the unit. (See pages 78 and 79.) Books useful throughout the course of study are listed in the *basic library* on page xviii.

Maps

The 115 maps will give you the location of every place mentioned in the text as well as show you topography, the size of empires, the thrust of invasions, and the extent of alliances. Each map is placed as close as possible to the relevant text. Of special interest is the map on page 1, which presents some basic regions of the world that will be important in your reading throughout the book.

Charts

Important sequences of events or ideas are summarized in chart form for easy reference. (See, for example, page 53.)

Illustrations

The hundreds of illustrations show you how people and places looked throughout man's history. Most of them date from the period they represent, and thus reflect how men of the past saw themselves.

Picture Features

Some works of art are especially illuminating as historical witnesses. Sixty-one such works are given special attention in the series called "History Through Art." These picture features range from one of the earliest known portrait carvings through pungent caricature of the 1700's to abstract painting of the present day.

Chronology of Historical Events

A series of integrated time charts shows you what was happening in widely separated areas of the world at the same time. This chronology enables you to obtain an overview of the broad sweep of history that textual narrative alone cannot give.

Atlas

At the back of the book, a series of maps presents all the countries of the contemporary world.

Index

The index provides a quick way of locating any topic discussed in the book, any place located on a map, and anything shown in an illustration. Pronunciations of difficult words are also included.

BASIC LIBRARY

REFERENCE BOOKS

Bartlett, John, *Familiar Quotations*. Little, Brown.

Bowle, John, ed., *The Concise Encyclopedia of World History*. Hawthorn.

Boyd, Andrew, *An Atlas of World Affairs*. Praeger.

Copeland, Lewis, and Lawrence Lamm, eds., *The World's Great Speeches*. Dover.*

Deffontaines, Pierre, ed., *The Larousse Encyclopedia of World Geography*. Odyssey-Golden.

Encyclopædia Britannica. Encyclopædia Britannica.

Espenshade, E. B., *Goode's World Atlas*. Rand McNally.

The Harper Encyclopedia of Science. Harper & Row.

Information Please Almanac. Macmillan.

Langer, William L., ed., *An Encyclopedia of World History*. Houghton Mifflin.

Long, Luman, ed., *The World Almanac and Book of Facts*. Newspaper Enterprise Association.

Oxford Economic Atlas of the World. Oxford Univ. Press.

Palmer, R. R., ed., *Historical Atlas of the World*. Rand McNally.

Peterson, Houston, ed., *Treasury of the World's Great Speeches*. Simon & Schuster.*

Seldes, George, *The Great Quotations*. Lyle Stuart.

Seltzer, L. E., ed., *The Columbia-Lippincott Gazetteer of the World*. Columbia Univ. Press.

Shepherd, W. R., *Shepherd's Historical Atlas*. Barnes & Noble.

Steinberg, S. H., ed., *The Statesman's Year-Book*. St. Martin's.

Webster's Biographical Dictionary. Merriam.

Webster's Geographical Dictionary. Merriam.

GENERAL WORKS

Bowle, John, *Man Through the Ages*. Little, Brown.

Bullock, Alan, ed., and others, *World History: Civilization from Its Beginnings*. Doubleday.

Cottrell, Leonard, *The Horizon Book of Lost Worlds*. American Heritage.

Eisen, Sydney, and Maurice Filler, eds., *The Human Adventure: Readings in World History*, Vols. 1 and 2. Harcourt Brace Jovanovich.*

Hughes, Paul L., and Robert F. Fries, eds., *European Civilization: Basic Historical Documents*. Littlefield, Adams.

Life eds., *The Epic of Man*. Time-Life.

Linton, Ralph and Adeline, *Man's Way: From Cave to Skyscraper*. Harper & Row.

Muller, Herbert J., *Uses of the Past: Profiles of Former Societies*. New American Library.*

Stearns, Raymond P., *Pageant of Europe*. Harcourt Brace Jovanovich.

Van Loon, Hendrik, *The Story of Mankind*. Pocket Books.*

Wells, H. G., *The Outline of History*. Doubleday.

* Paperback.

BOOKS IN SPECIAL FIELDS

Bach, Marcus, *Major Religions of the World*. Abingdon.

Blow, Michael, *Men of Science and Invention*. American Heritage.

Bolton, Sarah K., rev. by B. L. Cline, *Famous Men of Science*. Macmillan.

Britten, Benjamin, and Imogen Holst, *The Wonderful World of Music*. Doubleday.

Browne, Lewis, *This Believing World: A Simple Account of the Great Religions of Mankind*. Macmillan.*

Champion, S. G., and Dorothy Short, eds., *Readings from World Religions*. Fawcett.*

Clough, Shepard B., *The Economic Development of Western Civilization*. McGraw-Hill.

Fitch, Florence M., *Their Search for God*. Lothrop, Lee & Shepard.

Gaer, Joseph, *How the Great Religions Began*. New American Library.*

Gardner, Helen, *Art Through the Ages*. Harcourt Brace Jovanovich.

Gombrich, E. H., *The Story of Art*. Phaidon.

Gorsline, Douglas, *What People Wore: A Visual History of Dress from Ancient Times to Twentieth-Century America*. Viking.

Hall, A. Rupert and Marie B., *A Brief History of Western Science*. New American Library.*

Janson, Horst W., *History of Art: A Survey of the Major Visual Arts from the Dawn of History to the Present Day*. Harry N. Abrams.

Jupo, Frank, *Adventure of Light*. Prentice-Hall.

Landström, Björn, *The Ship: An Illustrated History*. Doubleday.

Ley, Willy, *Watchers of the Skies: An Informal History from Babylon to the Space Age*. Viking.

Life eds., *The World's Great Religions*. Golden Press.

Macy, J. A., *The Story of the World's Literature*. Washington Square.*

Montgomery, E. R., *The Story Behind Great Inventions*. Dodd, Mead.

——, *The Story Behind Great Medical Inventions*. Dodd, Mead.

Muller, Herbert J., *Freedom in the Western World: From the Dark Ages to the Rise of Democracy*. Harper & Row.

Neal, Harry A., *Communication: From Stone Age to Space Age*. Messner.

Preston, R. A., and others, *Men in Arms: History of War and Its Interrelationships with Western Society*. Praeger.

Smith, Huston, *The Religions of Man*. Harper & Row.*

Snyder, Louis L., and Richard B. Morris, eds., *A Treasury of Great Reporting*. Simon & Schuster.*

Tunis, Edwin, *Oars, Sails, and Steam*. World.

——, *Weapons: A Pictorial History*. World.

——, *Wheels: A Pictorial History*. World.

Watterson, Joseph, *Architecture*. Norton.

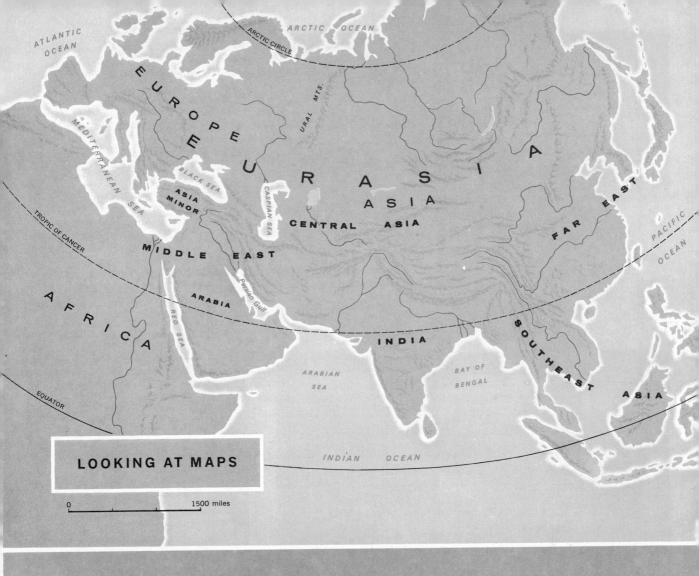

ATLANTIC OCEAN

ARCTIC OCEAN

ARCTIC CIRCLE

EUROPE

EURASIA

MEDITERRANEAN SEA

URAL MTS.

BLACK SEA

ASIA MINOR

CASPIAN SEA

ASIA

CENTRAL ASIA

FAR EAST

PACIFIC OCEAN

TROPIC OF CANCER

MIDDLE EAST

ARABIA

Persian Gulf

RED SEA

AFRICA

INDIA

SOUTHEAST

EQUATOR

ARABIAN SEA

BAY OF BENGAL

ASIA

LOOKING AT MAPS

INDIAN OCEAN

0   1500 miles

The many maps in this book will help you to get your bearings in time and space—they will show you *when* certain events occurred and, particularly, *where* they occurred. Some of the maps show a whole continent, such as Africa or Europe. Other maps show only a specific nation or part of a continent. Throughout this book you will find references to parts of continents. Such geographic divisions as Western Europe or North Africa are fairly easy to locate. Other regions, however, are more difficult to identify. The continent of Asia, for example, is so large that its main regions have separate names. The map above shows you what parts of Asia are referred to by these names.

People do not always use the same name for the same region. The name "India," for example, is sometimes used to refer to a specific country and sometimes to the whole peninsula of southern Asia. Over the years names have also changed. For ancient and medieval times, for example, the name "Near East" is generally used to describe Egypt and the countries of southwestern Asia. Today, many people use the name "Middle East" instead. Also, as certain parts of the world gain new prominence, some names, such as Southeast Asia, are used more and more. Your study of world history will have greater meaning if you watch for these names as you read this book and look at its maps.

1

THE BEGINNINGS

A king, seated at upper left, banquets with his guests while servants, below, bring animals and other supplies for the feast. This inlaid panel was made in Sumer over 4,000 years ago. The Sumerians were probably the first people in the world to develop a civilization.

2

OF CIVILIZATION

Mankind Gradually Developed Civilized Communities

The history of mankind can be compared to the life story of an individual in many important ways. From the time a child is born, he begins continuously to learn. He learns much more before the start of his formal schooling than he will ever learn again. Yet this education is carried on without the benefit of reading or writing. It is the result of experience, which teaches the child to recognize and name thousands of objects, and to recognize those that are harmful and those that are useful. It is a process of learning to think by sorting out facts and impressions and arranging them in useful ways.

As a child becomes older, he learns to organize his thoughts and also to record his experiences. This recording may be done partly through curiosity and partly as a useful source for future reference. There may be composition papers, arithmetic tests, results of experiments, perhaps a diary. These are reliable written records to check on what he was learning, and when. But it would be impossible for anyone to keep a complete record of how he learned the thousands of things he knows, both before and after he could write.

So it is with the story of mankind. Some 5,000 years ago—not so long as the life span of the human race goes—men learned how to preserve and pass on their knowledge by recording it in written form. Since that time we have written records of much that has been learned and done. Almost all

Stonehenge, built in England in prehistoric times

of this book deals with the period since men began to write. This period is called *historic time,* and the collected records represent the history of man.

However, men were living on earth for hundreds of thousands of years before they invented writing. During these years—*prehistoric time,* or time before written history—they learned much. Some things were as important as anything that has been learned since. For example, men found out how to make fire, grow crops, and work metal. Without this knowledge, life as we know it could not exist.

We do not know much about the life of man during the long centuries of prehistoric time. What little we do know has been pieced together from studying things that he left behind him. This knowledge is summarized, very briefly, in the first chapter of this book. It covers an important period in the story of mankind. If you remember that during this early period man had not yet learned to read or write, his accomplishments seem remarkable. Already, in a period which we regard as the childhood of mankind, man began to demonstrate his most valuable gift—intelligence.

THE CHAPTER SECTIONS:

1. Prehistoric man made vital discoveries in the Stone Age (1,750,000–4000 B.C.)
2. The first civilizations began in four great river valleys (4000–2000 B.C.)

Prehistoric man made vital discoveries in the Stone Age

Archeologists (ar·kee·AHL·uh·jists), the scientists who study prehistoric man, are able to make educated guesses about dates in prehistoric time, and can tell us many things about early man. They do so by studying three kinds of remains: (1) the bones of early man, from which they can reconstruct his size and appearance; (2) the bones of animals found near him; and (3) the weapons, tools, and other utensils found with him. Archeologists call these tools and weapons artifacts— that is, things made by human skill. Because the most numerous artifacts that have survived are of stone, the period of man's development which they represent is called the Stone Age.

The Old Stone Age

Although prehistoric men left no written records, archeologists know that human forms appeared on earth hundreds of thousands of years ago. For a long time, human progress was slow. Archeologists call this earliest period of man's story the Old Stone Age, or Paleolithic (pay·lee-oh·LITH·ik) Age. (The word *paleolithic* comes from the Greek words *palaios,* meaning "old," and *lithos,* meaning "stone.")

Earliest man. Recent discoveries of bones have led scientists to believe that manlike creatures appeared in Africa some time between 500,000 and 1,750,000 years ago. (Even older bones have been found, but further specimens and research are necessary before scientists can determine their relation to man.) Remains of a very early form, called East Africa man, have been found in eastern Africa south of Lake Victoria. It seems likely that these early men moved gradually from Africa to Asia and Europe. Although in many ways these creatures bore little resemblance to modern man, they walked erect and had the physical characteristics of human beings. It is also thought that they used stones and pieces of wood as tools and weapons.

We know little of man's development during most of these hundreds of thousands of years. His way of life was much like that of the animals. He hunted, as did the hunting animals, and, like many other animals, he gathered edible berries and roots. But three important characteristics helped set man apart from the animals and enabled him to progress. First, his erect posture allowed him to use his hands to hold weapons for hunting and defense. Second, he could speak, so that he could give and receive information through language. Third, he had a large brain to make use of the information and to gather more.

The Ice Age. During the past 1½ million years, man's history and that of the earth itself have been

5

greatly influenced by extremes of climate. Four times within this era, the earth has undergone periods of extremely cold weather. Four times the northern polar icecap (a permanent ice sheet near the North Pole) moved south and was joined by glaciers—large, slowly moving masses of snow and ice—that formed in the mountain ranges. Each of these four glacial periods lasted from 10,000 to 50,000 years. Together they are known as the Ice Age.

It is difficult to imagine the great extent of these glacial ice sheets. Today, ice covers about one twelfth of the earth's land surface. During the third and longest glacial period, ice covered about one third of the earth's surface, and in some places was several miles thick. Large areas of northern North America, Europe, and Asia were under ice (see map, opposite page).

The Ice Age affected the earth in various ways. Men and animals migrated to warmer southern regions. Many kinds of animals disappeared entirely. The grinding, chiseling effect of the moving ice made great changes on the surface of the earth. While much of the northern half of the earth was covered with ice, the rest of the earth received unusually large amounts of rainfall. Rivers and lakes rose. Inland seas formed. Many regions which had been deserts began to produce vegetation and support animal life. On the other hand, the level of the seas dropped by as much as 200 to 400 feet, because so much water was frozen in the icecaps. As the sea level fell, underwater ridges became uncovered and formed land bridges, linking some of the continents and islands that are today separated by water.

In the interglacial periods—the intervals between the four glacial periods—the icecap and glaciers gradually melted and receded. Men and animals moved back toward the north. We are now living in a warm era after the fourth glacial period, which ended between 10,000 and 25,000 years ago.

Java and Peking men. Archeologists are just beginning to learn about the manlike creatures whose remains have been found in Africa. They have slightly more information about two forms of prehistoric men who lived about the middle of the Ice Age, from 500,000 to 750,000 years ago. Their remains have been found at two widely separated places in Asia: on the island of Java, off the coast of Southeast Asia; and in a cave near Peking, China (see map, opposite page).

Although complete skeletons of these early men have not yet been found, archeologists have made scientific guesses about their appearance on the basis of the bones that have been excavated. These early men were not handsome by our standards. They were short, squat, and powerfully built. They had powerful jaws with sharply receding chins. Their low foreheads had heavy eyebrow ridges.

No artifacts were found with Java man, but in one cave with the remains of Peking man there were crude stone hand axes. This tool was really little more than a stone with a natural shape that fitted the hand. Early men improved on this natural shape by chipping away pieces of stone to make a crude point or cutting edge. This method of making tools and weapons was typical of the Old Stone Age. Peking man also knew how to use fire.

Neanderthal man. Further traces of man belong to a much more recent period of the Old Stone Age. In caves in Germany, archeologists first found the remains of this later kind of man. The caves were in a gorge known as the Neanderthal (nee·AN·dur·tahl), so he is called Neanderthal man. He lived, probably, from about 70,000 B.C. until sometime around 40,000 B.C.° He was short and powerfully built, with a heavy jaw, thick eyebrow ridges, and a large nose.

Neanderthal people made better tools than the men who preceded them. They lived in caves, wore clothes made of animal skins, and knew the use of fire.

Neanderthal men differed from earlier men in another way. Apparently, earlier men had let their dead remain where they died; Neanderthal people buried their dead. What is more, they buried with them tools, weapons, and even food. They must have expected these offerings to be of use to the dead person after his death. Clearly, this practice shows a belief in some sort of life after

(*continued on page 9*)

° B.C.: an abbreviation of "*Be*fore the birth of *C*hrist."

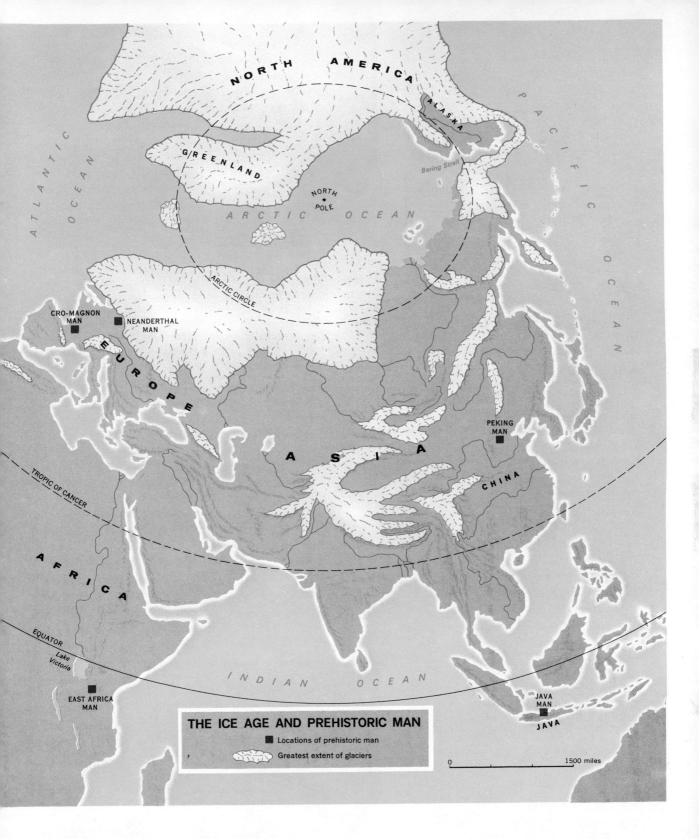

THE ICE AGE AND PREHISTORIC MAN

■ Locations of prehistoric man

🌊 Greatest extent of glaciers

0 _____ 1500 miles

Prehistoric people left no written records, but their progress can be reconstructed from their remains. The stone hand ax below right was an effective cutting tool for Paleolithic man. The bone disk below left may have been used as a button. It was carved, originally, from the flat part of a bone like the one below center. Archeologists have determined that the Neanderthal skull above belonged to a 40-year-old arthritic man who was killed in a rock fall. In the Neolithic tomb at bottom, the body was buried with pots containing offerings of grain and meat. The Neolithic cave paintings at left are from Africa. Above, two men appear to be herding cattle. The giraffe below is skillfully painted with just a hint of an outline.

death. Such a belief is basic and common to most religions. We do not know exactly what Neanderthal people believed, but we are sure that they had some kind of religion.

Like earlier forms of men, Neanderthal man disappeared. We do not know why. Glaciers had again advanced southward and covered much of Europe and North America. He may have died out from the cold, or he may have been overcome by men who were stronger physically and more alert mentally. It is also possible that he was absorbed by the more advanced types of men that followed him.

Cro-Magnon man. Around 40,000 B.C.—just about the time Neanderthal man disappeared—a new kind of man moved into Europe, perhaps from Africa or Asia. The new kind of man was better equipped to survive than Neanderthal man, for he was stronger and more intelligent, and had better tools and weapons.

Archeologists call this new kind of man Cro-Magnon man, from the name of a cave in southern France where his remains have been found (see map, page 7). But the France of 40,000 B.C. was very different from the France of today. It was quite cold. The polar icecap of the fourth glacial period extended far south into Europe. We know Europe was cold because with Cro-Magnon man's bones were found the remains of plants and animals that live only in a cold climate.

In addition to climate, plants, and animals, we know much more about Cro-Magnon people themselves than about any of the other early men. For one thing, more of their remains have been found. Then, too, these men themselves have "told" us more. They could not write, but they could draw and paint. Cro-Magnon men were probably the first real artists. In the caves of southern France and Spain where Cro-Magnon men lived, the walls are covered with their paintings of the animals they hunted. Among the animals they painted were the woolly mammoth and the reindeer. Their paintings are excellently drawn and are full of life and movement. The Cro-Magnons also made small clay and limestone statues of animals and carved figures on bones and antlers.

Physically, Cro-Magnon men were almost the same as modern men. They lived on earth for many thousands of years. By the end of the Old Stone Age, however, the Cro-Magnon type no longer existed. In appearance, man had become as he is today.

The Middle Stone Age

Archeologists call the period from about 8000 B.C. to about 6000 B.C. the Middle Stone Age. It is also called the Mesolithic Age (from the Greek *mesos,* meaning "middle," and *lithos,* meaning "stone"). After the fourth glacial period ended, extensive forests appeared in many parts of the world. The larger animals died out and smaller ones became the basis of man's food supply. The stone tools that were made in this period are distinctive because they are much smaller than those of the Old Stone Age.

Man made much progress during the short Mesolithic period. He domesticated, or tamed, the goat. He also domesticated the dog, which proved valuable in hunting smaller game. He invented the bow and arrow as well as fishhooks, fish spears, and harpoons made from bone and antler. Mesolithic man also learned to fit a handle to the hand ax. By hollowing out logs, he made dugout canoes so that he could fish in deep water and cross rivers without swimming.

The New Stone Age

About 6000 B.C., in certain parts of the world, basic changes occurred in man's way of life. The period that began then is called the New Stone Age, or Neolithic Age. (Its scientific name comes from the Greek words *neos,* "new," and *lithos,* "stone.")

In the Old Stone Age and Middle Stone Age, stone was chipped to produce an edge or a point. In the New Stone Age, men discovered a better way. They learned that stone could be polished to a fine edge and a sharp point on a flat piece of sandstone. They learned to use many kinds of stone as well as wood. With the new methods and materials, they could make special tools: awls, wedges, saws, drills, chisels, and needles.

Although archeologists named the New Stone Age after the artifacts produced then, other

9

changes were far more important. Earlier people had been wanderers, following migrating animals. Neolithic people settled down in villages. They could do so because of two important developments: (1) the domestication of several additional kinds of animals and (2) agriculture.

The food supply of Paleolithic and Mesolithic hunters had been uncertain. It might fail for a number of reasons: poor luck in hunting; migrations or famines among animals; or the mysterious cycles of increase and decrease that affect animal populations. Domesticated animals provided a much more certain food supply. Mesolithic man had tamed dogs and goats. Neolithic man learned to raise cattle, horses, sheep, and pigs. Some of these animals supplied power for pulling plows and wheeled vehicles; the wheel was another invention of Neolithic man. Most of the animals provided a ready source of food. Cows, goats, and sheep were living producers of milk, from which cheese could be made. When they were slaughtered, they provided meat, and hides for leather.

Of even greater importance than the increased number and use of domesticated animals was Neolithic man's greatest innovation—agriculture. It is not quite clear how people learned that seeds could be planted and made to grow year after year. In any case, man somehow learned to plant wheat, barley, rice, and millet. He also learned to use fertilizer, invented the plow, and developed methods of storing grain.

Man's shift from food hunting to food producing was so important that it has been called the Neolithic Revolution.° The new sources of food permitted Neolithic men to settle permanently in one region and to build homes. And, in turn, the establishment of permanent settlements was probably the reason for the great inventiveness of Neolithic men. There was more time to work on tools, more time for art and social life. Neolithic men built furniture, made pottery, and wove cloth. More people could live together in communities. They developed rules to regulate their living, thus creating the first organized governments.

CHECKUP

1. Name three kinds of remains that tell us about prehistoric men.

2. What were some of the effects of the glacial periods? What happened during the interglacial periods?

3. What was the greatest difference between Paleolithic and Neolithic times? What changes were made possible by this difference? Why?

4. IDENTIFY: historic time, prehistoric time, archeologists, artifacts, East Africa man, Java man, Peking man, Neanderthal man, Cro-Magnon man.

2 The first civilizations began in four great river valleys

Man had made much progress by the end of the Stone Age. He learned, among other things, to fashion tools and weapons, make fire, create artistic works, tame animals, and grow his own food. All these accomplishments are things that only man can do. Like his erect posture, his ability to speak, and his large brain, they help set him apart from animals. We use the word *culture* to describe the sum total of these basic human activities. We also use the word *culture* when speaking of the way of life of a specific group of people, such as an Indian tribe.

Using the word *culture* in the second sense, we can speak of Neolithic culture, meaning a Stone Age society based on farming. However, it should be remembered that not everyone developed this way of life during the Neolithic Age. Not all areas of the world had soil and climate suitable for farming. In some regions, where there were pasture lands covered with grass, men maintained a herding culture, moving their flocks and herds from one place to another. They were nomads; that is, they wandered about in small groups or tribes and never settled down permanently. Among the important pasture areas of early man

° **revolution:** Although this word is most commonly used to describe the overthrow of a government, it is also applied to drastic changes in men's lives.

10

were the plains of Mongolia in east-central Asia and the area north of the Caucasus Mountains between the Black and Caspian seas.

Moving into the river valleys

During Paleolithic times, men lived in small groups wherever game was plentiful and wherever they could find natural shelter. But Neolithic farmers gathered in larger settlements in areas which offered certain natural benefits, such as rich land for agriculture.

There were many small districts on earth where they settled together, but the results were of special significance in four great regions: (1) the Nile River Valley in Egypt, (2) the valley of the Tigris and Euphrates (yoo·FRAY·teez) rivers in southwestern Asia, (3) the Indus River Valley in northwestern India,° and (4) the valley of the Yellow River in northern China (see map, page 12).

In these four river valleys, men first attained the advanced form of culture known as *civilization*. All people, no matter how primitive, belong to some sort of culture. Only when a culture becomes highly developed is it called a civilization. Most civilizations have at least these characteristics: (1) advanced technical skills, such as the use of metals; (2) highly developed forms of group living, usually cities, with some sort of government; (3) division of labor; and (4) intellectual achievements, such as a calendar and a system of writing.

The rest of this chapter traces the general background of the earliest civilizations. You will read detailed accounts of them in the three chapters that follow.

Learning to use metals

The discovery of metals was probably accidental, rather than a thought-out attempt to meet a need. Perhaps someone happened to build a fire on a vein of ore that contained copper; afterward he noticed bright, shining lumps of metal in

° **India:** The Indus Valley is actually in the modern-day country of Pakistan. However, this country is part of the subcontinent of India. The term *India* covers the history of the entire region until 1947 A.D., when Pakistan became a separate nation.

HISTORY THROUGH ART

Prehistoric Ivory Head

A Cro-Magnon artist carved this head of a woman from ivory about 40,000 years ago, during the Old Stone Age. Found in France, it is less than 1½ inches high. From works like this, we learn that some prehistoric peoples had a sense of beauty not unlike our own. Such works show, too, that not all prehistoric societies were concerned solely with the day-to-day struggle for existence. This head is one of the earliest known attempts at human portraiture. It may have been a household charm or—as its small size suggests—an object of worship that could be easily carried from place to place.

the ashes. Then men learned to heat ore in order to extract the metal—a process called smelting.

Sometime around 4000 B.C., men in both the Nile Valley and the Tigris-Euphrates Valley were producing copper by smelting. Copper could be hammered into weapons, tools, utensils, and jewelry. Molten copper could also be poured into molds to harden in the shape of a tool or a weapon. Metal objects made in this way are called castings.

Copper tools and weapons were used for several thousand years. They were not entirely satisfactory, mainly because copper was too soft to

11

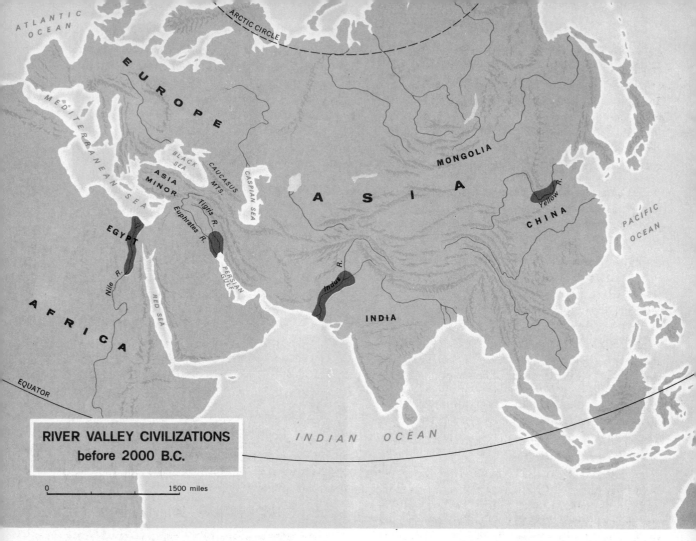

RIVER VALLEY CIVILIZATIONS
before 2000 B.C.

0   1500 miles

hold a sharp edge, or to do heavy work. In time, a better metal came into use. This was bronze, a mixture of copper and tin. This mixture, or alloy, is harder than copper. Since some copper ore contains tin, the discovery of bronze may also have been accidental. Bronze was made into jewelry and weapons in Egypt and the Tigris-Euphrates Valley by 3000 B.C., and was in wide use by 2000 B.C. It was also used at an early date in India and China.

Iron is a stronger material than either copper or bronze. Some early peoples laboriously hammered fragments of iron from fallen meteorites and used these as edges on tools and weapons, but this was not real iron working.

Iron ore is found in more places and in larger amounts than either copper or tin. Yet its use came much later than the others, for the smelting process is more difficult. One important step was the invention of the forge, a kind of furnace where great heat could be produced by forcing a draft of air through fire. Another device was the bellows, which was used by iron workers to produce the draft of air.

After the ore had been softened by the extreme heat of the forge, the hot metal had to be hammered. This process eliminated the impurities which, if left in, would weaken the iron beyond use. You can see that it was not by accident that man learned to produce iron.

We do not know when, where, or by whom the process of making iron was invented. It may have originated separately in several different areas. Some scholars believe that Negro smiths in central Africa learned to smelt iron quite early. Wherever this knowledge originated, it spread slowly. As you will read later, iron was first used extensively by the Hittites, a people of Asia Minor.

Irrigation, government, and cities

The valleys of the Nile, Tigris-Euphrates, Indus, and Yellow rivers have a feature in common that greatly influenced their early histories. Once a year, these river systems rise and flood their valleys. Except during these periods, however, there is little, if any, rain; the rest of the year is hot and dry.

This problem of climate meant that the farmers of the valleys had to get water to their crops during the dry season by building systems of irrigation—that is, creating artificial means such as ditches and canals. The floods of three of these river systems—the Tigris-Euphrates, the Indus, and the Yellow—are violent. Farmers in these valleys also had to build dikes to control flooding in the high-water months.

Farming in these river valleys, then, depended on irrigation and flood control. Large irrigation and flood-control projects cannot be built by individuals working alone. People had to learn to work together in groups. It took teamwork to build ditches and canals for irrigation and dikes to control floods. Historians believe that government may have originated in such cooperation; as people worked together, they developed governments through their efforts to plan, direct, and regulate their work.

The first valley dwellers had moved into their valleys in small groups, or tribes. Each group settled in a village along the river. They lived together in the village and went out to work the surrounding land.

In time, more and more people banded together to work on group projects and for common defense. Some of these village communities grew to become cities. Another reason for the growth of cities was an increase in population, made possible

by improved farming methods. Living in cities stimulated the exchange of ideas and the creation of great palaces, temples, and various other kinds of public buildings.

Division of labor

As methods of farming improved, not everyone had to work in the fields in order to produce enough food for all. This development led to important changes in the way men lived.

Some men were able to specialize in work other than farming. Experts at tool and weapon making could devote all their time to this work. They traded their products for food and other things they needed. Thus a class of skilled workers, called artisans, appeared. Merchants and traders also came into being. They made their living by buying goods from farmers or artisans and selling the goods to anyone who needed them. Traders carried ideas as well as goods. They transported not only things to sell, but, for example, systems of counting to show how many articles were bought and sold.

Trade became increasingly important as the river-valley civilizations developed. Egypt, for example, lacked good supplies of tin and iron. Its people traded for them, exchanging surplus food and other products.

Working out a calendar

Metal tools and weapons, the growth of cities, and specialization of labor were all important aspects of mankind's progress. However, it is not only material progress that creates a civilization. Many of the greatest advances come from intellectual creations. One important example of such an intellectual advance was the development of the calendar.

The people in the great river valleys developed workable calendars early in their history. Because these people were farmers, the changes of the seasons were important to them. They had to know, for example, when the annual floods would start and stop. One way was to regard the time from flood to flood as a year, and to divide it according to the phases of the moon. The time from new moon to new moon would be a month; twelve

Stone Age Man Today

Scientists learn about prehistoric men not only by studying their remains but also by observing people of the present who live in similar ways. Primitive people must spend a large proportion of their time finding and preparing food. The woman above, an Indian of the Brazilian rain forest, makes flour from the manioc plant. In a much harsher environment, the Bushmen of Africa often live close to starvation. At right, a man returns from a day of hunting with a small antelope slung over his shoulder. Below, a family gathers at a fire in front of their grass hut.

of these months, called lunar months, would equal a year. The trouble is that a lunar month is only about 29½ days long. Twelve "moons" equal only 354 days, not the approximately 365¼ days that are in a year. A calendar based on lunar months was unsatisfactory because months came earlier each year. As you read more detailed accounts of river-valley civilizations in the next three chapters, you will see how early people coped with this problem.

As you know, the letters B.C. with a date are an abbreviation of "*Before the birth of Christ.*" The letters A.D. with a date stand for the Latin phrase *Anno Domini,* meaning "in the year of our Lord," or "since the birth of Christ." Of course, no ancient man ever dated anything B.C. A moment's thought will tell you why.

This method of reckoning time with B.C. and A.D. is used only in those parts of the world where most of the people follow the Christian religion. Moslems, Chinese, Jews, and Hindus have other ways of counting the years. For example, the Christian year 1900 A.D. corresponds with the Moslem year 1318 and the Chinese year 4597.

Inventing writing

With the many changes of late Neolithic times, life became increasingly complex. Men in settled communities developed rules for living together and for protecting property. They worked out agreements as to who should do what work, and how, and when. Governments grew up, and with them came taxation to pay the costs of government. Trade developed, and with it transactions between buyers and sellers. The old methods of transmitting information orally became inadequate. Kings wished to record the events of their reigns; fathers wished to leave lasting instructions to their sons.

What was needed was written language. It could be a storehouse of ideas, just as a granary was a storehouse of food. Although its development was a long and complex process, it may be summarized in four chief steps:

(1) *A picture represents a thing.* Thus a picture of a tree would stand for the word "tree." Picture signs of this sort are called *pictograms.*

You can see that pictograms would have disadvantages. It is easy to show a tree or a man or a horse. But how would you represent an idea such as truth or life after death?

(2) *A picture stands for an idea.* As time went on, man began using symbols to stand for ideas. Suppose he was a farmer and gained his livelihood from orchards. In this case he might use a tree drawing to represent "abundance." Picture signs of this sort are called *ideograms.*

(3) *A picture stands for a sound, usually a syllable.* In using pictograms and ideograms, a great many pictures are needed. Fewer are required if a certain symbol can represent a sound, not just one meaning. Thus the tree symbol could stand not only for "tree" but also for the syllable "trea" in the word "treason." Signs of this sort are called *phonograms.*

(4) *A sign represents a single consonant or vowel.* These signs, or letters, form an alphabet, the final state in the development of writing. Over the years, two things happened to the tree symbol: it became simplified so that it was easier to draw; it came to stand for the beginning sound of the phonogram, not the whole sound. Thus a simplified version of the picture—the letter *T*—came to represent just the initial sound of "tree." This story of the development of the letter *T* is an imaginary one, but it illustrates how man invented alphabets.

Not all early forms of writing went through each of these steps; but whatever form early systems of writing took, their appearance marked the end of prehistoric time and the beginning of historic time.

CHECKUP

1. How did the need for irrigation and flood control help to develop governments?
2. Why was a calendar necessary?
3. Why was written language needed? What were the four chief steps in developing an alphabet?
4. IDENTIFY: culture, nomads, civilization, castings, alloy, forge, artisans, lunar month.
5. LOCATE: Mongolia, Caucasus Mountains, Nile River, Tigris River, Euphrates River, Indus River, Yellow River.

CHAPTER REVIEW

Chapter 1   Mankind Gradually Developed Civilized Communities   (1,750,000 B.C.—2000 B.C.)

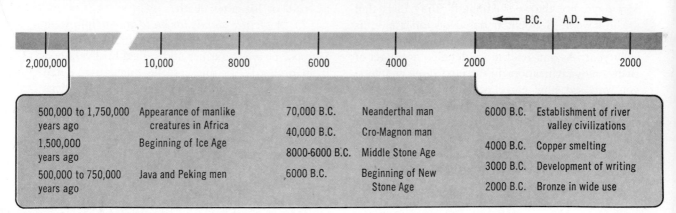

500,000 to 1,750,000 years ago	Appearance of manlike creatures in Africa	70,000 B.C. Neanderthal man	6000 B.C. Establishment of river valley civilizations
1,500,000 years ago	Beginning of Ice Age	40,000 B.C. Cro-Magnon man	4000 B.C. Copper smelting
500,000 to 750,000 years ago	Java and Peking men	8000-6000 B.C. Middle Stone Age	3000 B.C. Development of writing
		6000 B.C. Beginning of New Stone Age	2000 B.C. Bronze in wide use

CHAPTER SUMMARY

Man's long past generally is divided into two main periods. The long era before the invention of writing —which took place about 5,000 years ago—is called prehistoric time. The period since then is known as historic time. Because prehistoric men left no written records, archeologists have reconstructed their story from human and animal remains and from tools and weapons.

Manlike creatures appeared in Africa hundreds of thousands of years ago, during the Old Stone Age. Early men differed from other creatures in three important ways: They could stand erect, they could speak, and they had large brains.

Various forms of man appeared and disappeared during the Old Stone Age, during which ice sheets often covered the earth. Java and Peking men were relatively primitive types; Neanderthal people made better tools, lived in caves, and buried their dead. Cro-Magnon men left paintings in the caves of southern France and Spain where they lived.

During the Middle Stone Age, man domesticated the goat and dog and invented the bow and arrow and other specialized tools.

About 6000 B.C. there began the New Stone Age, during which basic changes occurred in man's way of life. Neolithic men domesticated more animals and learned how to farm. They settled in permanent villages and then went on to create the first organized governments.

Neolithic culture led to the first civilizations, which grew up in four river valleys: those of the Nile, the Tigris-Euphrates, the Indus, and the Yellow rivers. Men learned to use metals and to cooperate in building irrigation and flood control systems. The first cities grew up, and division of labor became possible.

Intellectual advances, such as the development of the calendar and writing, enabled man to deal more effectively with the increasing complexity of life in civilized communities.

QUESTIONS FOR DISCUSSION

1. Explain why the Old and New Stone Ages were not so much fixed periods of time as periods of culture. Why have men in various areas passed through prehistoric stages at different times?

2. Why do you think it took prehistoric man thousands of years to make a few important discoveries, whereas today many discoveries are made in a very short span of time?

3. The Neolithic Revolution led to a division of labor that has expanded greatly in modern societies. What are some of the advantages and disadvantages of such specialization?

4. What do you think was the greatest contribution of prehistoric man to civilization? Justify your answer.

5. How did environment determine life in the four great river valleys? Is man still influenced by environment in earning his living?

6. Climate had a greater influence on the life of ancient man than it has today. Explain.

PROJECTS

1. Draw pencil sketches of some of the stone tools used by prehistoric man.

2. Make a chart showing the achievements of man in the Old Stone Age, Middle Stone Age, and New Stone Age.

3. Draw a map of the four great river valleys.

4. Draw a map showing the locations of the various types of prehistoric men.

16

The Egyptians Built a Civilization in the Nile Valley

Your study of world history will soon become a meaningless jumble unless you find clear answers in your mind to two questions about each event and idea that you will study: Where did it happen? When did it happen? Questions of this sort, in historians' terms, are questions of *place* and *time*.

For example, in this chapter you will study the civilization of the ancient Egyptians. Some questions involving *place* might be: Where did this civilization exist? What was the land like? Questions involving *time* might include: When did this civilization flourish? What else was going on in the world at the time?

You can find answers to your questions about the place where something happened by consulting the many maps that appear in this book. You can answer your questions about the time when things happened by using the chapter time lines and the tables of dates that appear in the text. The relationships between the two elements, place and time, are shown in the chronology at the back of the book. Charts like these will help you a great deal in understanding what was happening in many different parts of the world at about the same time.

The Egyptians developed a civilization about 3000 B.C., or about 5,000 years ago. How can the human mind form a clear picture of things that happened as long ago as those in ancient Egypt?

The pyramids at Giza

What do periods of a thousand years and more really mean?

You might try answering these questions by thinking about the meaning of the word *generation*. A generation has usually been considered to be about thirty years, or the average time necessary for a person to grow up and start raising a family. You may have a family Bible that records the birth dates of three generations—a period of about a century. But suppose that you had a record of each generation of your family going back to the time when men learned to write, about 5,000 years ago. It would list only 166 generations. In these terms, a long time span is not too hard to imagine.

This chapter deals chiefly with the period from about 3000 B.C. to about 300 B.C.—a long time in man's history. This covers a span of 2,700 years, or some ninety generations. Therefore the chapter ends only about seventy-six generations ago.

History will mean more to you, and become more interesting, if you always remember that it happened to real people—in part, to your own ancestors. In this chapter you will see men tilling the fertile soil of the Nile Valley, building huge pyramids, and creating works of art that we still admire today.

THE CHAPTER SECTIONS:

1. Egypt enjoyed many natural advantages in climate and geography (6000–3000 B.C.)
2. Ancient Egypt, sheltered from invasion, had a long history (2900–332 B.C.)
3. The culture of ancient Egypt reached impressive heights (2900–332 B.C.)

1 Egypt enjoyed many natural advantages in climate and geography

Of all the ancient river-valley civilizations, that of Egypt is probably the best known today. Its ancient landmarks, such as the Sphinx and the pyramids, are known to almost everyone in the civilized world. And, of course, Egypt still exists as a nation (the Arab Republic of Egypt), which you can read about in magazines and in the daily newspapers.

The Egypt of ancient times probably looked very much like the Egypt of today. Egypt is a large country, but most of it is a sandy desert. Here and there is an oasis—a place where irrigation or an underground spring provides enough moisture to make the ground fertile. But the bright green of growing crops can be seen only in one long, narrow strip. This strip is the valley of the Nile River, which flows northward from the mountains of east-central Africa to the Mediterranean Sea (see map, page 20).

This Nile River, so important to the life of man in the valley, is about 4,000 miles long. Along its length there are six great cataracts where the river is forced into narrow channels cut through rock. The Nile Valley averages about 12 miles in width. Throughout its length, desert plateaus rise from the edge of the valley as high as 200 feet above the valley floor.

"The gift of the Nile"

Many centuries after the early period of Egyptian history, a Greek historian named Herodotus (hih·RAHD·uh·tus) wrote of his travels in Egypt. "All Egypt," he said, "is the gift of the Nile." Herodotus wrote accurately, for he was describing a remarkable feature of Egyptian geography. Each year, from June to October, rains and melting snow from the mountains at the source of the Nile cause the river to overflow its banks and spread out over the flatlands of the lower Nile Valley. The crest of the flood occurs at the beginning of September. As the flood recedes, the gentle slope of the land allows the water to drain off gradually, leaving behind a layer of fertile soil, or silt, which the river has carried along in its flood.

From earliest times, Egyptian farmers have planned their work according to the flood. They know that it will come every year, and about when it will start. They harvest their crops before it begins, then wait for the water to soak the hard, dry earth before it drains off and leaves its new,

This wall painting, found in the tomb of a farmer, shows him and his wife sowing, plowing, and harvesting in the underworld. Around them flow canals containing the water on which all Egyptian farming depended. Date palms grow along the canals, bottom. At the top of the painting are hieroglyphics and scenes from the Book of the Dead.

19

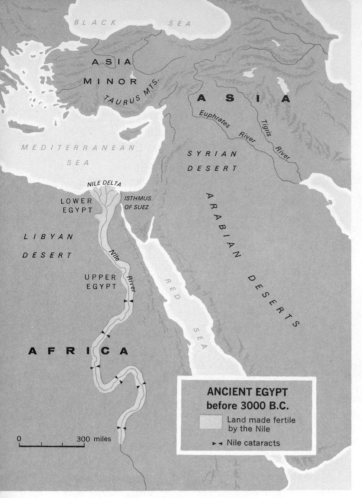

ANCIENT EGYPT
before 3000 B.C.

Land made fertile
by the Nile

►◄ Nile cataracts

0   300 miles

Other natural advantages

The Nile Valley had other natural resources besides the amazingly fertile soil. There was the climate, for example—a climate well suited to farming. It is frost-free the year round, with a large proportion of sunny days.

An interesting and important feature of the climate was, and is, the prevailing wind. The deserts bordering the Nile Valley form a hot, low-pressure area, drawing winds from the region of the Mediterranean Sea. These winds blow steadily southward, or upstream. A boat can go upstream with the wind by using a sail. It can also drift downstream, against the wind, carried by the river current. This fact was most important to the ancient Egyptians. The Nile became a pathway of travel and trade.

One feature of the Egyptian climate has had great importance for archeologists. Because it is so dry, objects that normally disintegrate fairly quickly in damp climates have instead been preserved for centuries. Thus manuscripts of papyrus (see next page), wooden artifacts of all sorts, and even pieces of fabric have come down to us in excellent condition.

There were some other natural resources. Deposits of clay, granite, sandstone, and limestone were available for building. The ancient Egyptians needed these materials, for there were few forests to furnish lumber. There was a little copper, iron, gold, and a few precious stones. With few mineral resources, Egypt developed an agricultural economy and has remained chiefly a farming country to the present day.

Finally, there was one other natural advantage—the valley's location. The Nile Valley is surrounded by deserts or seas. These furnished a natural protection against invaders. The natural barriers were broken in only one place—at the Isthmus of Suez.

Notice on the map on this page how the Isthmus of Suez joins Egypt, on the continent of Africa, with western Asia. The land between the Tigris and Euphrates rivers in Asia was the location of another early civilization. The Isthmus of Suez was a link, a land bridge, between the two continents and their civilizations. Throughout his-

fertile soil. There is little or no rainfall, and the flood moisture is sufficient for only one planting. Early in their history, however, the Egyptians learned to irrigate the land by diverting water from the Nile and carrying it to the fields in short canals. Then they could plant and harvest two and even three crops a year.

You can easily see the importance of this regular behavior of the Nile. Each year the soil of the valley is renewed. Because of this, the land of the Nile Valley has been farmed continuously for more than 6,000 years, and is still fertile.

Where the Nile flows into the Mediterranean Sea, it divides into several branches and spreads out over a wide territory. Here it drops much of the soil it carries, forming a region of islands and marshes. This region is called the Nile Delta, because it is shaped like the Greek letter Δ, delta.

tory it has been the route for traders, for the exchange of ideas, and for invading armies.

Early steps toward civilization

The long valley of the Nile, especially at the northern end where the river flows through the delta into the Mediterranean Sea, has been inhabited since earliest times. Paleolithic remains have been found there. A Neolithic culture developed sometime around 6000 B.C. The people of the Nile Valley soon began to take other steps along the road to civilization. They learned to use copper to make needles, chisels, and jewelry. In time they discovered how to make bronze, the stronger alloy of copper and tin. They may have invented the potter's wheel, a rotating disk that made it easier for a potter to make a round vessel. They also developed the *kingdom,* one of the earliest forms of organized government.

Egyptian writing. Along with the other major developments of Egyptian civilization came writing. By about 3000 B.C., the Egyptians had worked out a system of writing called hieroglyphic (hy·ur·uh-GLIF·ik). The word comes from the Greek *hieros,* "sacred," and *glyphe,* "carving." There were more than 600 hieroglyphic signs, used mainly by priests for religious inscriptions and other formal writings. Hieroglyphics were a combination of ideograms and phonograms. The Egyptians did not develop a true alphabet, but they did progress toward one. They had twenty-four signs with only one letter each—all consonants. They had some eighty signs containing two consonants. There were no signs for vowels.

The Egyptians gradually simplified hieroglyphic writing. One system was a kind of handwriting known as hieratic (hy·uh-RAT·ik). An even simpler script was called demotic. Throughout their history, however, the Egyptians continued to use hieroglyphics to carve official records on public buildings. This use of the ancient, traditional symbols resembled our own use of Latin inscriptions and Roman numerals on important buildings.

At first, Egyptians carved hieroglyphics on rock, a long and difficult process not suited to ordinary use. Searching for a better writing material, they used what they found near them. A reedy plant called papyrus grew in the marshes near the Nile. The Egyptians cut papyrus into long, thin slices, which they placed together, moistened, and pounded to form a mat with a smooth surface. This product was also called papyrus, from which we get our word *paper.* Egyptians made papyrus in pieces from 5 to 18 inches wide. They joined these to make long strips which could be rolled up. An ancient Egyptian "book" is actually a roll of paper. Some Egyptian papyrus rolls were over 100 feet long.

Egyptians wrote on papyrus with ink made from vegetable gum, water, and soot. Vegetable gum is a sticky juice given off by certain trees and plants. It dissolves in water and hardens in air. The Egyptians diluted the gum with water before mixing it with soot. For a pen, they used a sharpened reed.

Solving the hieroglyphic puzzle. Modern scholars learned to read the language of the ancient Egyptians through a clever bit of detective work. In 1798 A.D., a French army under Napoleon Bonaparte invaded Egypt. The following year an officer found a stone slab along the shore of the Rosetta branch of the Nile Delta. It was carved with writing of three kinds: hieroglyphic, demotic, and Greek.

Scholars guessed that all three inscriptions had the same meaning. Twenty-three years after the Rosetta Stone was found, a French scholar, Jean François Champollion (shan·paw-LYAWN), solved the mystery. Beginning with the Greek, which he could read, he deciphered the hieroglyphic inscription (honors granted by the priesthood to the ruler) and established the principles by which all other hieroglyphics could be read.

CHECKUP

1. What natural resources were found in Egypt?

2. Describe Egyptian writing materials; Egyptian books.

3. What is meant by the statement "All Egypt is the gift of the Nile"?

4. IDENTIFY: oasis, potter's wheel, hieroglyphic, Rosetta Stone.

5. LOCATE: Nile Delta, Isthmus of Suez.

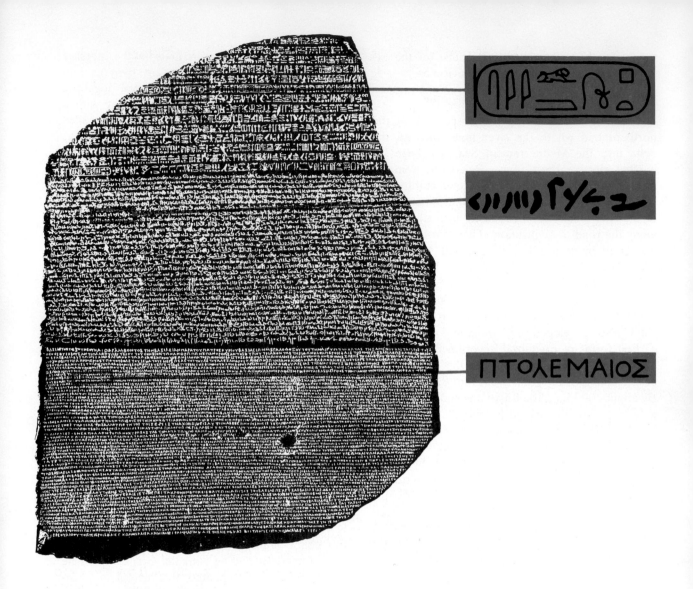

The Rosetta Stone

Written in hieroglyphics, demotic script, and Greek (from top to bottom), the Rosetta Stone provided the key to the language of the ancient Egyptians. The Greek text was translated almost immediately after the stone was discovered. It contained a resolution of Egyptian priests in honor of the young monarch Ptolemy V when he ascended the throne in 196 B.C. Further progress was hampered by the belief that hieroglyphics were secret symbols whose key could not be learned.

Jean François Champollion decided when he was eleven years old that he would be the decipherer of hieroglyphics. He obtained reproductions of every available Egyptian text and, over a fifteen-year period, compiled from them all the forms of the hieroglyphic signs, with their simplified hieratic and demotic equivalents. One helpful clue was the Egyptian practice of enclosing the name of a god or royal personage in a cartouche, or oblong outline. Thus the name "Ptolemy," illustrated above, could be matched with its demotic and Greek equivalents. After several more years, Champollion was able to determine the meaning of each individual hieroglyphic symbol.

2   Ancient Egypt, sheltered from invasion, had a long history

Solving the puzzle of Egyptian writing provided the key to the story of the ancient Egyptians. Now scholars could read the inscriptions carved on temples and other buildings; now the papyrus rolls could be translated. The history of this ancient people began to emerge.

A united kingdom

Over the centuries, early Egyptian settlements were united to form the two kingdoms of Upper Egypt and Lower Egypt. (Upper Egypt lay farthest south from the Mediterranean Sea, along the upper Nile River; Lower Egypt lay to the north, nearest the sea.)

Then, about 2900 B.C., a ruler traditionally known as Menes (MEE·neez) united all Egypt into one kingdom. As a symbol of his new power, he wore a double crown, which combined the white crown of Upper Egypt with the red crown of Lower Egypt. This crown remained a symbol of royal power throughout Egypt's long history. Menes and his successors put down rebellions, gained new territory, regulated irrigation, and promoted trade and prosperity.

Much of the power of these rulers came from the fact that they were religious leaders as well as political leaders. They were regarded as gods. They took the title *pharaoh,* which means "great house." The pharaoh was so awe-inspiring and so greatly feared that it was not proper for his subjects to call him directly by his name. That is why they called him by the word for the palace in which he lived.

The pharaoh's position as god placed him far above common mortals. He was head of the government, judge, high priest, and general of the armies. He was a complete *autocrat*—that is, he alone had the power to make, enforce, and interpret laws. Although the pharaoh had absolute, or unlimited, power, it was his duty to protect and care for his people.

Menes founded a *dynasty,* or family of rulers. In a dynasty the right to rule is hereditary—that is, it is passed on within the family, usually from father to son. This hereditary rule ends only when a family is overthrown or dics out (so that there is no one left to inherit the throne). In over 2,500 years, beginning with the time of Menes and continuing to about 300 B.C., there were no fewer than thirty Egyptian dynasties. This long period is divided into four eras: the Old Kingdom, the Middle Kingdom, the Empire, and the Decline.

The Old Kingdom

The Old Kingdom, from about 2800 to 2250 B.C., was probably the greatest period of all Egyptian history. Many important discoveries in science and the arts took place then. It was then that the largest pyramids, which are regarded as symbols of Egyptian civilization, were built. (For this reason the period of the Old Kingdom is sometimes called the Pyramid Age.)

In the early dynasties there were only two main social divisions: (1) an upper class, consisting of the pharaoh, the royal family, and the priests and officials who helped govern the country, and (2) a lower class, consisting of everyone else. The majority of this lower class consisted of peasants, or farmers.

From his capital at Memphis, the pharaoh appointed all government officials and priests. At first he claimed all the land. Farmers paid him one fifth of the crop as rent; if they failed to do so, their irrigation water was cut off. They also owed him services, such as a period of duty in the army or work on the irrigation system or on public buildings like the pyramids.

As time passed, officials in the upper class gradually became a hereditary group of nobles. Toward the end of the Old Kingdom, the pharaohs grew weaker and the nobles grew stronger. For 250 years after the end of this period, the country was torn by civil wars as rivals claimed the throne.

The Middle Kingdom

In about 2000 B.C., a strong new line of pharaohs reunited Egypt, beginning a period known as the Middle Kingdom. They restored order and

Tomb Statue of an Official

To preserve his identity in the hereafter and to assure the continuance of life after death, the family of an Egyptian nobleman had this wooden figure carved and buried with him. Chancellor Nakhti was an official during the Old Kingdom. Although he was an old man when he died, he is depicted here in the prime of life, untouched by old age, because that is how he wanted to appear for all eternity. Thus the statue is not an accurate picture of Nakhti at his death, but rather an idealized likeness of him.

He is portrayed with shaved head, his face animated by deep-set eyes. The sculpture was carved out of wood and painted brick red to represent the chancellor's deeply tanned skin. The dry climate of Egypt preserved the carving for over 4,000 years.

prosperity, but good times lasted only for a while. The problems of making all the decisions and seeing that they were carried out were too great for all but the strongest and ablest rulers. There was too much power in the hands of one man, and too much responsibility for one man to bear.

Gradually, as had happened in the Old Kingdom, the pharaohs lost some of their powers. The chief minister gained the power of supervising minor officials, such as tax collectors. Governors of provinces became powerful and, in time, made their positions hereditary. Priests were important not only as conductors of religious ceremonies but also as healers of disease. They performed many governmental duties and became wealthy. The position of priest also became hereditary. Thus the power of the pharaoh was weakened by the rise of a hereditary class that was made up of nobles and priests.

The Middle Kingdom ended in disorder around 1780 B.C. The country was weakened by rivalries, conflicts, and the division of power. Then, about 1730 B.C., Egypt was invaded for the first time in many centuries. An Asiatic people called Hyksos crossed the Isthmus of Suez and conquered the Nile Delta. The Hyksos army, with its horses and chariots, was far better equipped than that of the Egyptians. The Hyksos ruled parts of Egypt for about 150 years, but added little to its culture.

The Empire

Eventually, the nobles of Upper Egypt rebelled against the Hyksos and drove them from the country. Then Egypt was again united, under a

Funeral Mask of a Pharaoh

In sharp visual contrast to the simple wood sculpture of Chancellor Nakhti is this gold funeral mask of the Empire Pharaoh Tutankhamen. The mask, made of beaten gold inlaid with semiprecious stones and colored glass, has the richness and detail befitting a pharaoh. Because Tutankhamen was only eighteen when he died, there was no need to idealize his funeral mask. It is, in fact, a very accurate likeness of him.

The pharaoh is wearing the royal burial headdress and a decorative beard, which is a symbol for the god Osiris, lord of the dead. The fine-featured mask wears an expression of complete peace and glows with youth— a youth that Tutankhamen had just lost and would soon recover, greatly enhanced, in the company of the gods.

succession of strong pharaohs who ruled from Thebes far up the Nile. The period in which they ruled—from about 1550 B.C. to about 1085 B.C. —is called the Empire.

The new line of pharaohs regained much of the authority held by earlier pharaohs. They took power away from the nobles and priests. For a time, at least, the pharaohs were once more autocratic rulers. They kept strict control over the government and all the officials, and created a strong army and navy. They adopted the horse-drawn chariots of the Hyksos and began to use iron weapons.

The Hyksos invasion had terrified the Egyptian pharaohs, who realized that their homeland could be invaded. They were determined that it would not happen again. Since a defense line at the Isthmus of Suez had proved inadequate to stop the Hyksos, the Egyptians had to find a better one. None existed south of the Orontes River in Syria,° a fact which led the Egyptians to conquer territory along the eastern end of the Mediterranean up to the Orontes (see map, page 27). They also conquered Ethiopia in Africa, rounding out their southern defense.

Like many other peoples, however, the Egyptians found it easier to conquer an empire than to hold and rule it. Usually they allowed the native prince of a conquered region to act as gov-

° **Syria:** This term has had various meanings throughout history. In its broadest sense, it refers to the whole region between the Euphrates River and the eastern end of the Mediterranean Sea, south of Asia Minor. In its narrower sense, as used above, it includes only the northeastern part of this territory.

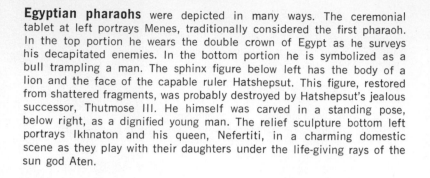

Egyptian pharaohs were depicted in many ways. The ceremonial tablet at left portrays Menes, traditionally considered the first pharaoh. In the top portion he wears the double crown of Egypt as he surveys his decapitated enemies. In the bottom portion he is symbolized as a bull trampling a man. The sphinx figure below left has the body of a lion and the face of the capable ruler Hatshepsut. This figure, restored from shattered fragments, was probably destroyed by Hatshepsut's jealous successor, Thutmose III. He himself was carved in a standing pose, below right, as a dignified young man. The relief sculpture bottom left portrays Ikhnaton and his queen, Nefertiti, in a charming domestic scene as they play with their daughters under the life-giving rays of the sun god Aten.

ernor. To be sure of his loyalty and obedience, they took his son back to Egypt to be trained at the palace at Thebes while he was held as hostage. But only the ablest pharaohs could hold the empire together. Whenever the government of Egypt became weak, some part of the empire revolted and tried to break away.

Famous pharaohs of the Empire. Some of the pharaohs of the Empire have become famous. One of these is believed to be the first woman in history about whom a great deal is known. Her name was Hatshepsut (ha·CHEP·soot), and she ruled from about 1500 to 1480 B.C. It was unusual for a queen to rule as pharaoh, but Hatshepsut was unusually able. She was more interested in the welfare of her country than in war and conquest. She tried to make Egypt prosperous by increasing trade and governing wisely and efficiently. She ordered the construction of temples to the gods and other kinds of public buildings.

Hatshepsut first ruled with her husband and half brother, Thutmose II (thoot·MOH·suh). This marriage illustrates a strange custom of Egyptian rulers. Since the pharaoh was a god, it was not proper for him to marry an ordinary human being. He usually married his sister or half sister. After Thutmose II died, his place was taken by his son, Thutmose III. Hatshepsut continued to rule. When she died and Thutmose III came to power, he had her name removed from all the public monuments erected at her order.

When he became the sole ruler, Thutmose III proved to be an able ruler and general. He extended the boundaries of the empire to its greatest limits, as shown on the map on this page. From the Euphrates River to the Mediterranean coast, from Asia Minor to Ethiopia far up the Nile River, Thutmose ruled as pharaoh. His system of government was so good and his armies so powerful that Egypt remained secure for years after his death.

Amenhotep's religious revolution. A third famous pharaoh, Amenhotep IV (ah·mun·HOH·tep), who ruled from about 1375 to 1358 B.C., was not a famous conqueror, nor even a very good ruler. He is famous because he brought about a social and religious revolution in Egypt.

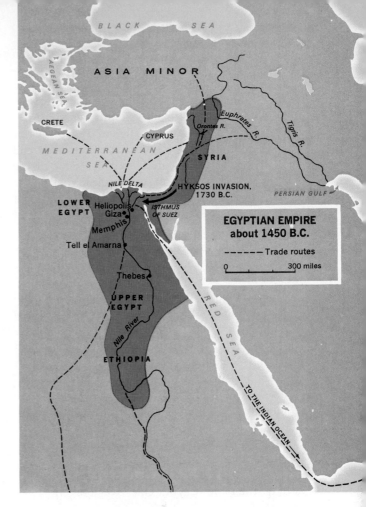

Amenhotep was interested in a new kind of religion. He believed that the sun god, Amen (AH·mun), was the only god, not just the first among many gods. This belief in one god only is known as monotheism (MAHN·uh·thee·iz·um), from the Greek words *monos,* meaning "one" or "single," and *theos,* meaning "god." Belief in many gods is called polytheism, from *polys,* meaning "many," plus *theos.* Amenhotep believed that Amen was a kindly god who loved and cared for his people.

Amenhotep changed the name of the sun god from Amen to Aten, to show that the god had a new nature. He changed his own name from Amenhotep, which meant "Amen is satisfied" to Ikhnaton (ik·NAH·tun), which meant "he who is beneficial to Aten."

The priests of Amen had become so powerful that they interfered in all affairs. To help break

27

their power, Ikhnaton moved his capital from Thebes, where the great temple of Amen was located, to a new city, Tell el Amarna, which he built. At first he allowed other gods to be worshiped, but later only Aten could be worshiped.

Reaction to Ikhnaton's religion. The priests of the other gods were displeased. Their rich and easy living was being destroyed by order of the pharaoh. The priests of Amen, the old sun god, were greatly disturbed. The rich revenues that formerly came to them at their great temple of Thebes now went to the new god in the new city. Appointments to high positions, which formerly went to the priests of Amen, now went to believers in the new god.

The priests of Amen and of the other gods began to cause trouble. Because they had a strong hold on the people, they were able to stir up opposition to the pharaoh. Soon Ikhnaton learned that he could not change people's religious beliefs by decree. The bitter struggle between pharaoh and priests caused much disorder in Egypt. When Ikhnaton died, the priests of Amen re-established their power. They forced his successor, Tutankhamen (toot·ahnk·AH·min), to move the capital back to Thebes.

After the death of Ikhnaton, there were few strong rulers in Egypt. One, Rameses II, ruled from about 1292 to 1225 B.C., and held Egypt and the empire together. He was the pharaoh of the Hebrew oppression, which you will read about in the next chapter.

The Decline

Beginning about 1100 B.C., Egypt grew steadily weaker. The empire was gradually lost, and foreign invaders—including the Assyrians and the Persians—came into Egypt itself. Even during these times, however, dynasties of Egyptian pharaohs continued to reign, although many were merely figureheads. It was not until Alexander the Great conquered Egypt in 332 B.C. that native rule came to an end.

CHECKUP

1. How did the ruler of Egypt get his title? What does it mean?
2. Why was there opposition to Ikhnaton's religious reforms?
3. Explain this statement: "The Egyptians found it easier to conquer an empire than to hold and rule it."
4. IDENTIFY: Menes, autocrat, dynasty, Hyksos, Hatshepsut, Thutmose III, Rameses II.
5. LOCATE: Upper Egypt, Lower Egypt, Memphis, Thebes, Orontes River, Ethiopia, Tell el Amarna.

③ The culture of ancient Egypt reached impressive heights

The culture of a group of people, as you have read, refers to their way of life. It is often difficult to summarize the culture of a people whose history extended over many centuries, as did that of the Egyptians. However, the culture of ancient Egypt was remarkably stable, with little change from one century to another. Change did occur, of course, but it came about very gradually. This stability resulted partly from favorable surroundings, particularly the regular Nile floods and Egypt's protected geographic location.

Farming and trade

Farm land in Egypt was organized in large estates. Farming was done by peasants, who cultivated with crude hoes or wooden plows. Even these primitive methods produced good crops, often three a year, because of the rich soil, warm climate, and irrigation. The peasants kept only part of the crop. The rest went for rents and taxes, which were paid in such products as grain, cattle, and wine.

The Nile floods set the schedule for the year's work. In November, when the flood had subsided, peasants cultivated and planted the land. The growing season lasted until May, when crops were harvested before the floods began again in June. Wheat and barley were the chief grain crops. Flax was grown to be spun and woven into linen. Cotton was an important Egyptian crop, just as it is today, and was woven into cloth.

Ancient Egypt produced more food than its people required. The surplus was traded with other peoples for products that Egypt needed. Egyptians were among the first of all peoples to build seagoing ships. These ships sailed into the Mediterranean and Aegean seas, the Red Sea, and even the Indian Ocean. Merchants also traveled overland in caravans, riding donkeys and camels into western Asia and deep into Africa (see map, page 27).

Social classes

Egyptian society, as you have read, was divided essentially into two classes: an upper class consisting of the royal family, nobles, and priests, and a lower class including everyone else. Most of this class consisted of peasants, who supplied labor for agriculture and government projects. There were also some artisans, merchants, traders, and scribes (clerks), but they were comparatively few in number. The conquests of the Empire period provided large numbers of captives who became a third class, that of slaves.

Within the lower classes, it was possible for people to improve their status, although, in general, Egyptian social classes were rigid. However, an exceptionally intelligent and ambitious peasant might occasionally become a noble or priest. Slaves, at first despised by all, gradually rose until they merged with the peasants.

An attractive feature of Egyptian society was the favorable status of women. A woman could own property in her own right and could pass it on by inheritance to her daughter. Women were the equals of their husbands in social and business affairs. In many ways, Egyptian women were better off than women in other cultures until quite recent times.

Architecture and engineering

When you think of Egypt, it is likely that the first things that come to your mind are the pyramids and the Sphinx. They still stand after nearly 5,000 years. Pyramids were built as tombs for the pharaohs. During the period of the Old Kingdom, Egyptians believed that only the pharaoh, a god, was sure to have a life after death. (He might, however, grant immortality, or eternal life, to a chosen few of his favorites.) It was important that the pharaoh's burial place should be in keeping with his splendid position, and also that his remains, and the objects provided for his well-being in the afterlife, should be protected and preserved.

There are about eighty pyramids still standing, most of them in groups along the west bank of the Nile. The best known group, at Giza, includes the Great Pyramid, built for Pharaoh Khufu (KOO·foo) about 2600 B.C. This gigantic structure is more than half a mile around at the base and rises to a height of 450 feet. It consists of over 2 million blocks of stone averaging $2\frac{1}{2}$ tons each.

The building of the pyramids obviously required skillful engineering. Egyptian architects and engineers were among the ablest in the ancient world. They built ramps, or sloping walkways, along which enormous stones were pushed or pulled to raise them above the ground. Levers were also used for moving heavy objects.

The Egyptians built huge temples, too. When any large building is erected, there must be a satisfactory method for framing large openings and supporting heavy roofs. For this purpose, Egyptian architects used the post-and-lintel construction method—vertical posts, or columns, supporting horizontal beams called lintels. Since both the columns and the lintels were usually of stone, they were quite heavy and required advanced engineering skill to be hoisted into place.

The arts

Like their architecture, the other arts of the Egyptians were of high quality. Sculpture ranged in size from huge stone figures such as the Sphinx, weighing thousands of tons, to small, lifelike statuettes of kings and sacred animals, beautifully shaped from copper, bronze, stone, or wood.

Egyptians decorated many of their buildings with paintings showing everyday life—craftsmen at work, farmers harvesting grain, and people enjoying banquets. Egyptians developed a distinctive way of representing the human figure, with the head in profile, the shoulders full on, and the feet

(continued on page 32)

30

The people of ancient Egypt led active lives in which religion played a major role. Pharaohs built temples such as the one at left to honor the gods. The massive post-and-lintel portal is decorated with hieroglyphics proclaiming the monarch's devotion to the god. At the top is a sacred scarab. All Egyptians hoped for life everlasting and the favor of the gods. In an illustration from *The Book of the Dead,* below, a dead man and his wife look on as the jackal-headed funeral god weighs the man's soul against the feather of truth. The fierce Eater of the Dead is at right, ready to devour the soul if the scales do not balance.

For pharaohs and peasants alike the Nile was the main thoroughfare for travel and commerce. The boat above is a model of a vessel used for fishing and spearing water fowl. These products, like everything else in Egypt, were taxed. Since money had not yet been invented, taxes were paid in produce and labor. Record keeping was a complicated procedure, requiring a keen mind and years of specialized training. As keepers of tax rolls and other records, scribes were important and powerful in Egyptian life. In fact, such positions were originally reserved for the sons of pharaohs. The scribe above sits cross-legged, writing on his lap.

Pendant of Tutankhamen

Like many other peoples, the ancient Egyptians used symbols in depicting their gods and traditions. On the right of the necklace above is the serpent goddess, symbol of Lower Egypt, wearing the crown of the north. On the left is the vulture goddess, who represented Upper Egypt, wearing the crown of the south. (Note that these same symbols appear on the headdress of Pharaoh Tutankhamen on page 25.) The two figures are protecting the sacred eye, which symbolized both Amen-Ra and Horus. The pendant, found on the mummy of Tutankhamen, is made of gold inlaid with precious stones.

in profile. They did this not because they were unskilled but because they felt it was important to depict the complete body. In spite of a certain stiffness, the paintings are vivid and colorful representations of the Egyptian enjoyment of life.

Science

The Egyptians invented a lunar calendar at an early date. As you have read, such a calendar was not entirely satisfactory. Then, somewhere in the Nile Valley, someone noticed that a very bright star began to appear above the horizon just before the floods came. This was the star we now call Sirius, the Dog Star. The interval from one rising of Sirius to the next was 365 days. The ancient Egyptians based their year on this cycle, dividing

it into twelve months of thirty days each. This system left them with five extra days, which they used for holidays and feasting.

Numbering the years was no great problem. At first, years were known by an outstanding event: the year of the great flood or the year the locusts swarmed over the fields. Later, people used the reigns of pharaohs: the first, second, or twentieth year of the reign of a certain pharaoh. Using this method, we can trace back the yearly record in Egypt to about 2780 B.C. Some historians believe that this is the earliest recorded date in history which can be firmly established in terms of our own system of dating.

Early in their history, the Egyptians recognized the need for exact measurements and a system of mathematics. They developed a number system based on 10, similar to the decimal system we use today. In arithmetic, they used fractions as well as whole numbers. They used geometry to fix the boundaries of fields after the floods subsided and to lay out canals and irrigation ditches.

The Egyptians also made discoveries in medicine. They knew a great deal about the anatomy of the human body and used this knowledge in treating illness and in embalming bodies. *The Book of Healing Diseases,* written during the period of the Old Kingdom, classified diseases according to symptoms and prescribed treatments. Some of the treatments were only magic spells, but many others were more scientific, specifying herbs and drugs.

Education

It would have been impossible for the Egyptians to gather and pass on all their knowledge without a system of education. Egyptian education was partly religious. Schools were usually in temples. Most education was aimed at training scribes. For a fee, a scribe would read or write for those who could not. He might also be employed by a wealthy man to keep accounts. He might even rise high in government service.

A great center for advanced study, stressing astronomy and religion, was located at Heliopolis (hee·lee·AHP·uh·lis). It was famous throughout the ancient world. It is thought that Moses, who led the Hebrews out of Egypt, was educated at Heliopolis. Much later, when Egypt was ruled by foreign kings, Heliopolis remained known throughout the Mediterranean world. Many famous Greeks crossed the Mediterranean to study there.

Religion

Religion was outstandingly important in Egyptian life. The Egyptians worshiped natural forces such as the sun and moon. In early days each village and district had its local god or gods. In time some of these were accepted and worshiped throughout the country. Each god had an animal as his symbol. Among the sacred animals were the cat, the bull, the crocodile, and the scarab (a beetle).

Amen-Ra (often called simply Amen or Ra), the sun god, was first in importance. He was the source of life and goodness, lord of all other gods, the giver of victories. His temples were filled with gifts of thanks, and his priests became wealthy and powerful. Osiris, god of the Nile River and of fertility, was loved the most. He was lord of the Realm of the Dead and judged who should be rewarded with eternal life. The wife of Osiris was Isis, the moon goddess. She was mother of the universe, queen of the world and the heavens. Horus, god of the rising sun, was the son of Osiris and Isis.

The afterlife. At first, Egyptians believed that only the pharaohs and a few others chosen by the pharaohs had a life after death. Later, Egyptians believed that everyone, and animals as well, could enter the hereafter. They thought that the spirit would be happier if the body were preserved. Therefore, they worked out a way of preserving the body by mummification—that is, embalming it so that it would dry and keep for centuries.

The mummy was placed in a tomb and provided with clothing, food, jewelry, tools, weapons, and even servants in the form of sculptured or painted figures. These were necessary for the long journey to the Realm of the Dead. The number and richness of the articles in the tomb measured the importance of the dead person. On this final journey the soul was beset by serpents and demons. To guard against these hazards, the Egyptians put in the tomb *The Book of the Dead,* a collection of hymns, prayers, and magic chants that formed a kind of guide to the afterlife.

When the soul reached the Realm of the Dead, it entered the Hall of Truth, where Osiris sat in judgment. Here the soul had to testify to the kind of life it had lived on earth. It had to take an oath that it had not lied or murdered or been proud and haughty.

When the soul had testified and taken the oath, it was weighed on a great scale against a feather, the symbol of truth. If the scales balanced, it had spoken truly, and could enter into the presence of the sun god and eternal happiness in the "field of content." But if its sins outweighed the feather, it was thrown to a horrible monster called the Eater of the Dead. Thus, good character and a good life were very important to Egyptians because they were believed to be rewarded in the world of the hereafter.

Egyptian tombs. Because of the precious articles buried with the dead, Egyptian graves were constantly being robbed. The pyramids built during the Old Kingdom were opened and their contents stolen. During the Middle Kingdom and Empire, the Egyptians cut elaborate secret chambers into cliff walls, but thieves robbed most of these tombs, too. In 1922 A.D., however, archeologists discovered the previously unopened grave of Tutankhamen, Ikhnaton's successor. This rock-cut tomb dated from the 1300's B.C. Its rich store of gold, jeweled objects, furniture, and household items was intact and has taught us much about ancient Egypt.

CHECKUP

1. What were four important agricultural products of the ancient Egyptians?
2. Why did the Egyptians build the pyramids? What techniques did they use in constructing them?
3. Name and identify four principal deities of the Egyptians.
4. IDENTIFY: post-and-lintel construction, *The Book of Healing Diseases,* scarab, *The Book of the Dead.*
5. LOCATE: Red Sea, Indian Ocean, Giza, Heliopolis.

33

CHAPTER REVIEW

Chapter 2   The Egyptians Built a Civilization in the Nile Valley   (6000 B.C.—332 B.C.)

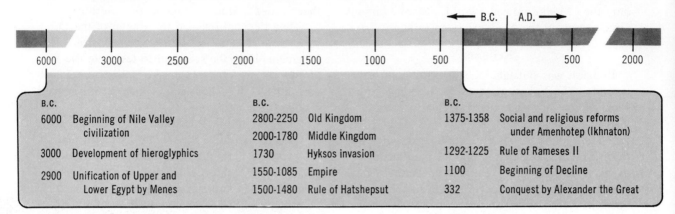

B.C.		B.C.		B.C.	
6000	Beginning of Nile Valley civilization	2800-2250	Old Kingdom	1375-1358	Social and religious reforms under Amenhotep (Ikhnaton)
		2000-1780	Middle Kingdom		
3000	Development of hieroglyphics	1730	Hyksos invasion	1292-1225	Rule of Rameses II
		1550-1085	Empire	1100	Beginning of Decline
2900	Unification of Upper and Lower Egypt by Menes	1500-1480	Rule of Hatshepsut	332	Conquest by Alexander the Great

CHAPTER SUMMARY

Many natural advantages aided the development of civilization in Egypt. The fertile soil of the Nile River Valley was annually renewed by the predictable flooding of the river. In addition, Egypt had a frost-free climate, prevailing upstream winds that encouraged trade and travel, some natural resources, and surrounding deserts and seas that protected the valley.

Great advances took place within this security: agriculture supported by irrigation, the use of copper and bronze, the development of the kingdom—one of the earliest forms of organized government—and the invention of hieroglyphic writing.

Menes traditionally united all Egypt into one kingdom about 2900 B.C. He and the pharaohs who followed him were complete autocrats, and were religious as well as political leaders. During the next 2,500 years, Egypt was ruled by over thirty dynasties. This long period was divided into four eras: the Old Kingdom, the Middle Kingdom, the Empire, and the Decline.

The Old Kingdom was probably the greatest period in Egyptian history; it was then that the largest pyramids were built. At the end of the Middle Kingdom, the Asiatic Hyksos invaded. During the period of the Empire, Egypt conquered land along the eastern end of the Mediterranean Sea to prevent other invasions. Outstanding rulers during this period included Hatshepsut, Amenhotep—who tried to change the religious beliefs of the Egyptians—and Rameses II.

The culture of ancient Egypt was impressive. Farmers produced a surplus of food. Architectural monuments included the great pyramids and huge temples. Other achievements included fine sculpture and painting, a lunar calendar, medical discoveries, and a famous school at Heliopolis.

Religion was extremely important in Egyptian life. The Egyptians worshiped natural forces through animal symbols. They believed in an afterlife with rewards and punishments based on whether a person's life on earth had been good or evil.

QUESTIONS FOR DISCUSSION

1. What was the greatest contribution of ancient Egypt to civilization? Justify your choice.

2. Already in the early Egyptian dynasties, two social classes had emerged. Is the establishment of social classes part of human nature, and will it therefore always occur in a society? Explain.

3. What are the chief differences between an autocracy, such as prevailed in ancient Egypt, and a democracy as it exists in the United States? Do you think there are any advantages of an autocracy over a democracy?

4. Why did ancient Egypt decline? What are some reforms that could have been made in ancient Egypt to keep it powerful even longer?

5. Explain the reasons for the importance of a scribe in ancient Egyptian society.

PROJECTS

1. Write a letter to Pharaoh Amenhotep giving him reasons why his religious reforms will fail.

2. Draw a map of the ancient Near East, showing in color the Egyptian Empire at its greatest extent, and the routes of Egyptian trade both by land and by sea.

3. Make a chart listing the various developments that took place in Egypt during the Old Kingdom, Middle Kingdom, and Empire.

4. Draw a cartoon contrasting the wealth of a pharaoh with the poverty of a peasant.

34

Many Different Peoples Ruled the Fertile Crescent

While one great civilization—the Egyptian—dominated the Nile Valley for thousands of years, a number of civilizations rose and fell in an area of western Asia called the Fertile Crescent.

How did the Fertile Crescent get its name? Look at the map on page 37. Note the light green strip of land that begins at the Isthmus of Suez. It extends northward along the eastern end of the Mediterranean Sea and swings over in a half-circle south of the highlands of Asia Minor and Armenia. Then it curves southeastward, following the valley of the Tigris and Euphrates rivers, and ends at the Persian Gulf. Because its shape is somewhat like that of the new moon, it is called a crescent—a word that describes the first-quarter moon. Parts of this crescent of land were fertile.

Like Egypt, the Fertile Crescent was surrounded by deserts and mountains. One great difference in geography, however, made the history of the two areas quite different. The deserts and highlands around the Fertile Crescent were not so barren as those around Egypt. There was enough grass and other plant life to support tribes of herdsmen. These wanderers were wild, fierce, and toughened by their way of life. They envied the richer, easier life of the valley people. At various times the people of the Fertile Crescent grew weak. Then the herdsmen moved in, conquered, and settled down.

The story of ancient Egypt was the story of a

Head of an unknown Persian prince

single people living in one place. Sometimes they expanded their territory, and at other times they were conquered by enemies from outside. But throughout ancient times, Egypt was the home of people living in essentially the same land as their ancestors.

The situation was quite different in the Fertile Crescent. Here people were on the move. They came into the region from outside, made conquests and extended their empires, and then in turn were overthrown by new invaders.

Migration is one of the most important factors in history. Sometimes it is forced on a group, as when their crops fail or they fear attack by an enemy; you have already read about how people migrated to warmer climates during the Ice Age. Sometimes people migrate to conquer new land, seize wealth, or overthrow their hostile neighbors.

One type of migration often produces the other.

The history of the Fertile Crescent became the story of a succession of migrating peoples. Each ruled the area or a part of it for a time. Each in turn was conquered by another people who were stronger and usually less civilized.

THE CHAPTER SECTIONS:

1. Sumerian civilization arose in the Tigris-Euphrates Valley (3000–2300 B.C.)
2. The Babylonians, Hittites, and Assyrians conquered empires (2300–612 B.C.)
3. The Chaldeans and Persians ruled large areas (612–331 B.C.)
4. The seagoing Phoenicians traded and established colonies (1000–700 B.C.)
5. The Hebrews contributed basic ideas to Western civilization (2000–586 B.C.)

1   Sumerian civilization arose in the Tigris-Euphrates Valley

The earliest civilization of the Fertile Crescent developed in one of the great river valleys mentioned earlier—that of the Tigris and Euphrates rivers.

The Tigris-Euphrates Valley

The Tigris and Euphrates rivers both rise in the highlands of Armenia. The Tigris, the easternmost of the two rivers, flows about 1,100 miles to the Persian Gulf; the Euphrates, the westernmost river, flows about 1,700 miles before reaching the Persian Gulf. At one point the two rivers come within 20 miles of each other, then flare out until the valley between them is more than 150 miles wide. They then flow together and create a delta at the Persian Gulf. In ancient times the rivers entered the gulf separately and farther inland (see map, opposite); silt deposits over the centuries extended the shoreline 125 miles into the gulf.

The Tigris has the greater volume of water; it cuts a deep channel, lowering the water level below that of the land and making irrigation difficult. The Euphrates, too, creates problems for those who live along its banks. Its current is fast and violent, carrying five times the amount of silt the Nile does. Because this silt builds up the river

bed, the river often floods the plain. Canals and dikes have to be dug, not only to bring water to the fields but also to carry away the surplus.

The flood of the Tigris and the Euphrates, unlike that of the Nile, is unpredictable. It may come anytime between the beginning of April and the early part of June. Not only is the time unpredictable but the volume of water cannot be estimated. It is no wonder that the inhabitants of the valley regarded nature as hostile and the gods controlling it as unreasonable and changeable. Their world was quite different from that of the Egyptians, who saw only goodness in nature.

Various terms have been applied to certain regions of the Tigris-Euphrates Valley. Mesopotamia (meaning "between rivers") is the name the Greeks gave to the northern part, above the neck where the two rivers come within 20 miles of each other. The southern part, below the neck, has usually been known as Babylonia. The entire valley is today part of the nation of Iraq.°

° The name *Mesopotamia* is sometimes used to refer to the entire Tigris-Euphrates Valley, from the Persian Gulf in the south to the mountains of Asia Minor and Armenia in the north.

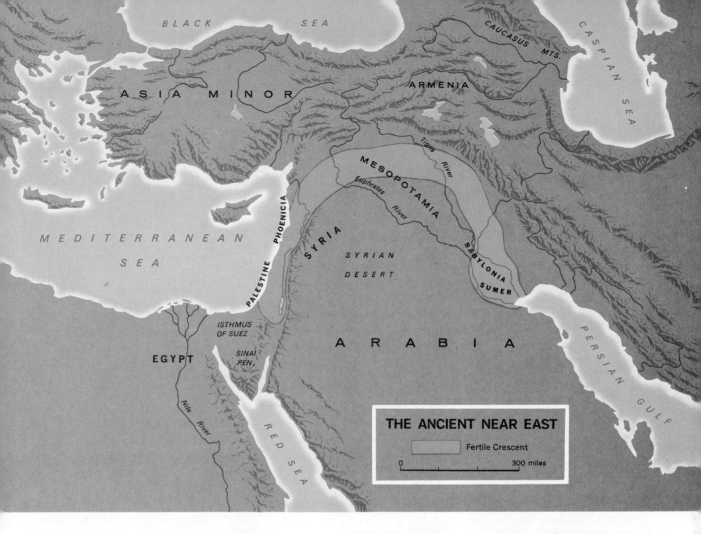

THE ANCIENT NEAR EAST

Fertile Crescent

0   300 miles

Sumer and its people

The lowest part of the Tigris-Euphrates Valley (that is, the southern portion of Babylonia) was formed by the rich soil that the rivers poured into the Persian Gulf century after century. This area, called Sumer, was especially fertile. Some historians think that it was the location of the Garden of Eden which the Bible describes. Here Neolithic men settled and grew crops.

Two groups of people moved into Sumer from the east and mingled with the original inhabitants to create a people and culture known as Sumerian. By 3000 B.C., they were using metal and had developed a kind of writing.

The Sumerian culture was at least as rich and as highly developed as that of Egypt, for the Sumerians were even more original and inventive than the Egyptians. In fact, evidence seems to show that civilization probably began in Sumer.

City-states

Early in their history, the Sumerians developed a kind of government called the *city-state*—a town or city and the surrounding land it controlled. The people believed that each city-state belonged to a god or gods. A priest managed the god's land and interpreted the god's will to his people. He directed worship and governed the city.

The Sumerian city-states were seldom united under a single government. There was much rivalry among them, particularly over land boundaries and water rights. Failure to unite weakened the Sumerians and, although able and civilized in many ways, they were finally conquered by less

The Sumerians left ample evidence of their advanced civilization. Of great importance are the many examples of cuneiform writing, most of which record business transactions. The tablet above, with its neat wedge-shaped indentations, is a deed for the purchase of a house. The great architectural achievement of the Sumerians was the ziggurat, a temple that might be almost 150 feet high. The typical ziggurat had four straight sides built in layers, surmounted by a shrine. There the god of the city was said to alight from his "boat of heaven" to receive sacrifices. The drawing at right, based on excavations in the Fertile Crescent, suggests what a ziggurat may have looked like. The round-eyed figures above right represent Sumerian men, dressed in kiltlike garments, and a woman with a robe draped over her shoulder. Their hands are clasped in worship, and they probably stood originally in a shrine on top of a ziggurat.

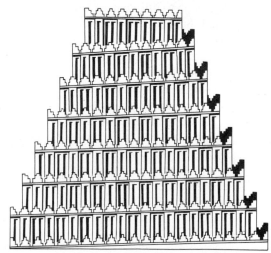

civilized but more warlike people, as you will see.

The Sumerians had three distinct social classes. At the top was a privileged class of nobles, including priests and government officials. Next came a group of merchants and artisans. At the bottom were peasants and slaves.

Sumerian writing and writing materials

Sumerian writing looked quite different from Egyptian writing. While Egyptian hieroglyphics were developed by scribes who carved characters on stone, Sumerian writing originated as marks pressed into clay tablets. Because scribes used a pointed stick, called a stylus, most of the signs were combinations of wedge shapes. The Latin word for "wedge" is *cuneus,* so we call the writing of the Sumerians cuneiform (kyoo·NEE·uh·form) writing. There were about 600 cuneiform signs— pictograms, ideograms, and phonograms.

The papyrus reed did not grow in Sumer, so the Sumerians did not learn paper-making, but continued throughout their history to write on clay. They rolled out a lump of soft clay, made their wedge-shaped marks on it, and then allowed the tablet to dry until it was hard, after which it would last indefinitely. It might shatter, but the pieces could always be fitted together.

The puzzle of cuneiform writing was solved in much the same way as that of Egyptian hieroglyphics. Centuries after the high point of Sumerian culture, a ruler of Persia named Darius the Great suppressed a rebellion led by nine chiefs, whom he then punished. To discourage other rebellions, he ordered the story to be carved in both pictures and writing on a limestone cliff at Behistun, a village in what is now western Iran.

The Behistun Rock, as the cliff is called, shows Darius passing judgment on the nine rebel chiefs, who are standing with their hands bound behind them. The writing is in three languages, all written in cuneiform: Old Persian, which was partly known to modern scholars; Elamite, a native language of the region; and Babylonian, which closely resembled Sumerian. A brilliant Englishman, Henry C. Rawlinson, deciphered the Old Persian cuneiform, and scholars soon worked out the other two languages.

HISTORY THROUGH ART

Sacred Sumerian Animal

Peering through the branches of a flowering shrub stands a Sumerian animal created about 4,500 years ago. Scholars identify him as either a ram or a goat, but are not sure what he represents. He may be a sacred animal used in religious rites to insure the fertility of the fields—a constant problem because of the unpredictable nature of the Tigris and Euphrates rivers. He may possibly be the "ram caught in the thicket by his horns," which Abraham, as described in the Bible, sacrificed instead of his son Isaac. (It is interesting to note that Abraham is thought to have originally lived in Sumer.) In any case, the animal, which stands twenty inches high and is made of gold foil, lapis lazuli, silver, and mother-of-pearl over a wood core, is vivid proof of the wealth and considerable skill of the Sumerians.

39

Farming and trade

Most of the Sumerian people were farmers and raised crops of grain, vegetables, and dates. Their domestic animals included cows, sheep, and goats, as well as oxen to pull plows and donkeys to pull carts and chariots. Sumerians developed a dairy industry very early. They wove fine woolen goods and raised flax for linen.

Theoretically, all the land belonged to the god of the city-state, and most of it was worked in his behalf—that is, to support his temples and priests. Some of it, however, was given to privileged persons, and other parts were rented.

Food production was ample enough to allow many people to work in trade and industry. Sumerians were trading with other peoples of the ancient Near East before 3000 B.C. Merchants had agents in far places and salesmen who traveled from city to city.

Architecture, engineering, and science

For building materials, the Sumerians used sun-dried clay bricks. Their brick structures did not last as long as the stone buildings of the Egyptians, but their architecture was well planned and executed. The Sumerians seem to have invented several important architectural elements. One was the arch, a curved structure over an opening and one of the strongest forms in building. By combining several arches, they could also build rounded roofs in the shape of domes or vaults. They knew and used the ramp. They even built sewers beneath their buildings and roofed them with arches of brick.

The most striking Sumerian buildings were the temples, built on man-made hills that rose above the flat valley floor. A Sumerian temple, or ziggurat, was built in layers, each one smaller than the one below, so that it looked somewhat like a "stepped-back" skyscraper. On some ziggurats each story was painted a different color, and each was dedicated to a different star or planet. Usually there were seven stories. The top story was the shrine of the god.

Sumerian engineers and scientists made many important discoveries. Some scholars think that the first Neolithic men to develop and use the wheel were Sumerians. Later the Sumerians developed some of the principles of algebra. In mathematics they used a system of numbers based on 60. Large numbers were stated in 60's—for example, 120 was expressed as two 60's and 180 as three 60's. They divided a circle into 360 degrees (six 60's), each degree with 60 minutes, each minute with 60 seconds. When you look at the face of a compass or a watch, you are seeing a principle developed by the Sumerians thousands of years ago.

The Sumerians developed a lunar calendar with twelve months. When the passage of years made their calendar inaccurate, they added a thirteenth month to bring it back into line with the seasons.

Education

The Sumerians considered education very important, although it was reserved for boys of the upper class. Schools were usually held in the temples and conducted by priests.

Writing and spelling were important subjects. Students learned to write by copying religious books and songs. They also studied reading, history, mathematics, foreign languages, and map-making. There was advanced education in law, medicine, and surgery. Much time was spent learning divination, or foretelling the future from various signs and omens.

Religion

The Sumerians were polytheistic, believing in many gods. These gods were identified with the forces of nature, like the sun and moon. The people thought of these forces as supermen, with the same habits and passions as men but much more powerful. The important Sumerian gods included Anu, lord of heaven; Enlil, god of air and storms; and Ea, god of the waters.

Sumerian belief about the future life was vague. People did not believe in reward or punishment in heaven or hell, but they did believe that there was some sort of life after death. They were afraid of ghosts. They thought, for instance, that if they did not bury such personal objects as jewelry with a dead person, his spirit would be displeased and would return to haunt his house and family.

1. Where do the Tigris and Euphrates rivers rise? Where do they empty? Why did the inhabitants of the valley regard nature as a hostile force?

2. Why do you think Sumerian civilization was important in the history of mankind's early growth and development?

3. IDENTIFY: city-state, cuneiform, ziggurat, divination.

4. LOCATE: Fertile Crescent, Persian Gulf, Sumer.

2 The Babylonians, Hittites, and Assyrians conquered empires

Although the Sumerians had a high culture, their lack of unity was a fatal weakness. Sometime after 2300 B.C., a new people attacked and conquered them. The invaders built a new capital city and called it Babylon; thus they are called Babylonians.

Hammurabi and Babylonian law

About 1700 B.C., a strong ruler, Hammurabi, came to power in Sumer and conquered the upper Tigris-Euphrates Valley (see map, page 42). Hammurabi was more than a great military leader. He turned out to be an able organizer and a wise and just statesman as well. He is best known for the *code*, or collection of laws, that was drawn up under his direction. In it he speaks of himself as the father of his people, their "pastor, savior, and good protecting shadow."

Hammurabi's code of 282 laws controlled all aspects of Babylonian life. Agriculture was carefully regulated. For example, men who failed to cultivate their fields or to maintain the irrigating canals and ditches were punished. Some laws concerned commerce and industry, and included provisions regarding wages, hours, and conditions of work. There were laws dealing with property rights, contracts, and bankruptcy. Others dealt with marriage and divorce. The laws were enforced by judges, under the supervision of the king's advisers and officials. There were severe penalties for trying to bribe a judge or a witness.

The laws of Hammurabi gave some degree of justice to everyone—a real advance over the political and social customs of the rest of the ancient world. The idea of punishment was basically "an eye for an eye; a tooth for a tooth." If a man caused another to lose an eye, then his own eye was put out. If a son struck his father, his hand was cut off.

Justice was not equal for all people, however. If a wealthy man destroyed the eye of a poor man, he did not lose his eye but merely paid a fine. A thief who could not repay what he had stolen was put to death. If he had money, he had only to repay more than he had stolen.

Babylonian culture

Like the Sumerians, the Babylonians were primarily an agricultural people, raising domesticated animals and large amounts of foodstuffs. They wove textiles which were not quite so fine as those of the Sumerians. However, as traders the Babylonians were even more enterprising than the Sumerians. They carried on trade with other parts of the Fertile Crescent, with Egypt, and even with India and China.

The social organization of the Babylonians was also like that of the Sumerians: there was a nobility made up of priests and government officials, a middle class of artisans and merchants, and peasants and slaves at the bottom. The Babylonians were humane in their treatment of slaves and often set them free.

Babylonian women seem to have been slightly less privileged than Egyptian women, but their position was higher than among most peoples of that day. Other ancient peoples considered women as property to be owned, to be treated as slaves. Babylonian women had legal and economic rights, and their property was protected. However, a man might sell his wife and children to pay his debts.

Babylonian women could enter the trades and professions, and even become priestesses. There is some evidence that they were paid as much as men doing the same work. In this respect women in many places are not so well off even today.

The Babylonians adopted Sumerian cuneiform

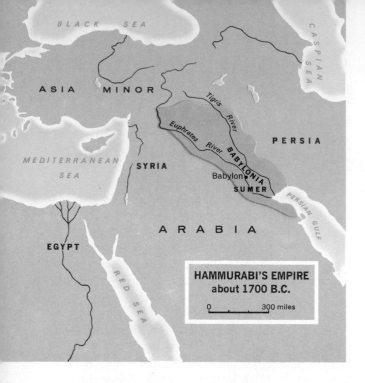

**HAMMURABI'S EMPIRE
about 1700 B.C.**

0 — 300 miles

writing. They also copied Sumerian architecture and science, but seldom equaled the Sumerians in these fields.

Babylonian religion

The Babylonians took over many Sumerian religious ideas. Marduk, god of the city of Babylon,

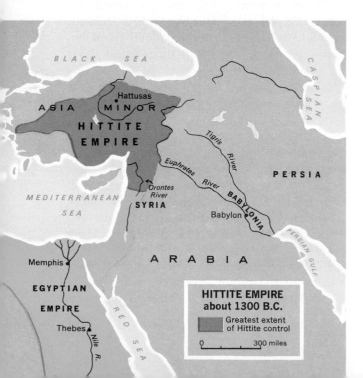

**HITTITE EMPIRE
about 1300 B.C.**

Greatest extent
of Hittite control

0 — 300 miles

became the principal god, but the old gods remained. The Babylonians made many sacrifices to their gods, not in the hope of a better future life but for such things as good harvest and business gains. They believed that life after death was gloomy and hopeless and was spent in a place called the Land of No Return.

Babylonian priests were as powerful as Sumerian priests, gaining much influence from the charms and spells they used against evil spirits. They also claimed the power of divination.

The rise and fall of the Hittites

Many times in history, you will read of conquerors who adopted the culture of the people they conquered. This was certainly true of the Babylonians after they conquered the Sumerians. However, it was definitely not true of the Hittites. This warlike people invaded the Tigris-Euphrates Valley about 1600 B.C.

The Hittites were one of the most powerful peoples of the ancient world. Until recent times they were also one of the most mysterious. Since the 1940's, however, scholars have made great progress in deciphering Hittite writing, and their history is becoming better known.

Hittite culture. Originally, the Hittites were herdsmen of the grasslands north of the Black and Caspian seas. Like other peoples from this region about whom you will read later, they spoke a language of the Indo-European family. About 2000 B.C., they migrated south and west to Asia Minor.

The Hittites were the first people to make extensive use of iron for weapons. They also had copper and silver mines and traded these metals with other peoples for the goods they wanted. The Hittites did not trade their iron, however, nor the knowledge of how they made it. They kept the process secret. Using the advantage of superior iron weapons, they defended themselves against stronger and more numerous peoples, conquered weaker ones, and expanded into territories over most of Asia Minor, establishing their capital at Hattusas (see map, this page).

The supreme achievement of the Hittites was their legal system, which was less brutal than the code of Hammurabi. Capital punishment was reserved for major crimes, such as rebellion, and mutilation was limited. Hittite law emphasized payment of damages rather than retribution. For example, if someone broke the arm of a freeman, he paid twenty pieces of silver rather than have his own arm broken. In assessing punishment, the law also took account of premeditation—that is, whether a person intended beforehand to commit the crime.

The Hittite Empire. When the Hittites invaded the Tigris-Euphrates Valley, they conquered and looted Babylon itself. The Hittites were too far from their homeland to control Babylonia permanently, and soon withdrew. However, they remained powerful in the western part of the Fertile Crescent, where they came into conflict with the Egyptians. When Ikhnaton was making his social and religious reforms in Egypt in the 1300's B.C., he did not pay much attention to the outlying parts of his empire along the eastern Mediterranean. The Hittites were quick to take advantage of that fact and gained control of most of Egypt's northern territory (see map, opposite page).

Then, for unknown reasons, the Hittites fell from power. Possibly, they finally failed to keep their great secret—the process of smelting iron. Possibly a trader was willing to sell that knowledge for gold. At any rate, the Hittite Empire ceased to exist about 1200 B.C.

The conquering Assyrians

In Babylonia, meanwhile, another mountain people, the Kassites, had moved in after the Hittite raid on Babylon. The Kassites controlled the area until about 900 B.C., when they in turn were overwhelmed by the Assyrians—one of the fiercest, cruelest, most aggressive, and most warlike of all ancient peoples.

The Assyrians first settled along the Tigris River, northwest of Babylonia, and built a city-state, Assur, named for their chief god. It was from the word *Assur* that both the region, Assyria, and the people took their name. The Assyrians eventually conquered the entire Fertile Crescent and at one time even ruled Egypt. At their height—in the 700's and 600's• B.C.—they ruled

HISTORY THROUGH ART

Assyrian Winged Bull

The art of the Assyrians was as mighty and as powerful as they were. The colossal winged bull above stood guard at the gate of an imperial palace. Four types of living beings, each a symbol of power, are combined in this gigantic animal—the face and beard of a noble Assyrian; the ears, body, and legs of a bull; the chest of a lion; and the wings of an eagle. This guardian figure seems to be at rest when faced head-on. Viewed from the side, there is the illusion of movement, skillfully achieved through the addition of a fifth leg.

an empire larger than that of any people up to their time (see map, page 45).

Assyrians were specialists in warfare. Instead of chariots they used cavalry, or mounted horsemen. They made extensive use of iron weapons and invented the battering ram to break through the brick walls of cities they besieged.

43

The Babylonians and Assyrians were important peoples of the Fertile Crescent. Hammurabi is shown above left as an old man. At lower left, the great king tells a god about his code of laws. The code itself is engraved below on a seven-foot pillar of stone (only partially shown). Among the peoples who later overran Babylonia were the Assyrians. Above, Assyrian soldiers wreck and burn a city as its inhabitants, in the foreground, are driven into captivity. Below, an Assyrian archer and spearman rout their camel-borne enemy.

And how cruel they were! They put to death the enemies they captured in battle, often by savage methods. They enslaved conquered peoples and deported them to other areas, replacing them with Assyrian colonists. In this way they held conquered lands more easily and gained many slaves. Around 700 B.C., the Assyrians captured Babylon, looted it, and finally destroyed it completely, changing the course of the Euphrates River to flow over the site. It was for such acts of destruction that the people of the ancient world hated and feared them.

Assyrian government

The Assyrian king was a despot, or autocrat, with absolute power. Every priest and government official took orders from him and was responsible to him. He himself was responsible only to the god Assur, whose earthly representative he claimed to be.

The government of the Assyrian Empire was cruel and harsh but highly efficient. Roads were built so that troops could move about quickly. The kings established a postal service to help the army to act quickly against rebellions. Governors ruled conquered lands and collected heavy taxes. They had to make regular and frequent reports, and inspectors checked on their activities. In conquered areas, there was always an army of occupation—that is, an army to keep the conquered people under control. This army usually consisted of paid soldiers, or mercenaries, recruited in part from among other conquered peoples. It was paid for, of course, by the conquered peoples themselves.

The Assyrians were the first people to work out an effective system of imperial administration, or government of an empire. All other empires of the ancient Near East were modeled on it. In other fields, however, the Assyrians contributed little to civilization. Their religion contained no new ideas. In literature, art, and sculpture they were imitators, not creators.

Assyrian greatness and decline

After the Assyrians became powerful, they made the city of Nineveh their capital. Here they

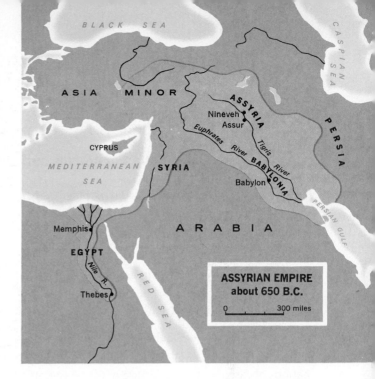

ASSYRIAN EMPIRE
about 650 B.C.

0   300 miles

gathered all their splendor—the wealth from the spoils and taxes of conquered countries and from the labor of slaves. Nineveh was the symbol of the pride and cruelty of this barbarous people. They tried to make it the strongest fortified city in the world. A huge double wall, 50 feet thick and 100 feet high, stretched for 7 miles around the city. There were fifteen gates, each beautifully decorated and strongly defended. Eighteen mountain streams flowed through the city to assure a supply of water. There was a large library in which scholars collected clay tablets from all over Assyria and Babylonia.

But powerful Nineveh was not powerful enough. As so often happens with a bully, other people "ganged up" on the Assyrians. There were plenty of enemies. Finally, in 612 B.C., the Chaldeans (kal·DEE·unz), Medes, and Persians—about whom you will read in the next section—joined forces. Together they captured and destroyed Nineveh and later conquered the entire Assyrian Empire. All of the Near East could breathe a sigh of relief. Three hundred years later another conqueror, Alexander the Great, led an army from Greece to the site of Nineveh. There was almost nothing left of the once great city by that time.

1. Name four subjects dealt with in the code of Hammurabi. From the modern viewpoint, what were the weaknesses of the code?

2. What do you consider the greatest achievement of the three peoples described in this section? Explain your answer.

3. IDENTIFY: Marduk, Land of No Return, mercenaries.

4. LOCATE: Babylon, Hattusas, Assur, Nineveh.

The Chaldeans and Persians ruled large areas

The story of the Fertile Crescent is chiefly one of empires that became ever larger until they collapsed or were overthrown. The Sumerians and Babylonians occupied and ruled only the southern part of the Tigris-Euphrates Valley. The warlike Assyrians ruled the entire Fertile Crescent. Now you will read about two other empire-building peoples—the Chaldeans and the Persians.

The Chaldeans

The people who organized and led the combination of armies that overthrew the Assyrians were the Chaldeans. They took the largest share of the Assyrian Empire and rebuilt the old city of Babylon as their capital. Under an able ruler named Nebuchadnezzar (neb·yoo·kud·NEZ·ur), who ruled from 605 to 562 B.C., they conquered most of the Fertile Crescent (see map, opposite).

The rebuilt city of Babylon was a thing of wonder. Its thick outer wall was 13 miles long. Part of the land enclosed within the wall was used for farming so that the city had a food supply in case of siege. Outside this vast wall was a moat, a deep ditch filled with water.

The Chaldeans of Babylon enjoyed a high standard of living and surrounded themselves with richly beautiful buildings. Perhaps the most striking building of all was the palace of Nebuchadnezzar, which was faced with glazed brick. It had an enormous courtyard and huge rooms. Its most unusual feature was the Hanging Gardens. There is a legend that Nebuchadnezzar's wife had lived in the mountains and was homesick on the flat plains of Babylonia. To please her, the king planted tropical plants and flowers on the roof of the palace. The Greeks regarded these "Hanging Gardens of Babylon" as one of the Seven Wonders of the World. Near Nebuchadnezzar's palace stood a great ziggurat, which may have been the Tower of Babel that the Bible describes.

All the strength of the Chaldeans seemed to lie in the ability of Nebuchadnezzar. Within thirty years after his death, Babylon was captured by the Persians, and the Chaldean Empire ended.

Like the Assyrians, the Chaldeans contributed little to civilization. They were deeply interested in astronomy, however, and correctly calculated the length of the year within 26 minutes. The Chaldeans also practiced astrology, the prediction of the future by the stars. They believed that comets, eclipses, and other phenomena in the sky influenced the lives of people on earth.

The mighty Persians

You have read of herdsmen in the great grasslands north of the Caucasus Mountains, between the Black Sea and the Caspian Sea. The Hittites were one of the Indo-European tribes that migrated from this region. About 1800 B.C., two other such tribes, the Medes and the Persians, moved southeast from the grasslands to the high plateau of Iran (often called Persia °), east of the Tigris River. For several centuries they lived in tribal groups and herded their sheep. In time, both tribes became united under the Medes and joined the alliance that overthrew the cruel Assyrian Empire. After the downfall of the Assyrians in 612 B.C., the Medes and Persians held all of Iran as well as part of the northern Tigris-Euphrates Valley.

° **Persia:** This name in its strict sense refers to the southern homeland of the Persians along the eastern shore of the Persian Gulf—a region known in ancient times as Persis (see map, page 48). In common usage, however, the name refers to the whole Iranian plateau and to the country of Iran, which occupies most of that plateau.

Cyrus, Darius, and Xerxes

About 550 B.C., Cyrus, a Persian and one of the ablest leaders in all history, led a revolt against the Medes, defeated their king, and became ruler of the two tribes. The Persians were fierce fighters who made extensive use of horsemen and archers. Herodotus, the Greek historian, wrote that Persian education emphasized three things above all others: to ride, to draw the bow, and to speak the truth.

After defeating the Median king, Cyrus began a career of conquest that was continued by his successors. Cyrus defeated the Chaldeans, captured Babylon, and gained the rest of the Tigris-Euphrates Valley. He then took the rest of the Fertile Crescent—the part along the eastern end of the Mediterranean Sea—and Asia Minor. Cyrus' son Cambyses conquered Egypt.

A later ruler, Darius the Great, added regions south and east of Iran as far as the Indus River in India, as well as parts of southeastern Europe. Both Darius and his son Xerxes (ZURK·seez) invaded Greece in the 400's B.C., but, as you will read in Chapter 5, they were unable to conquer it. Although they failed to conquer Greece, the Persians ruled the mightiest empire known up to that time. At its peak, under Darius, it stretched from the Indus River to the Nile and beyond, and north to the Black and Caspian seas (see map, page 48).

Persian government

The early Persian kings were not only great generals but were also wise rulers. They were all-powerful in government, but they showed great concern for justice and fair dealing. Tax collection and the administration of justice were fair. Cyrus was especially concerned that the laws should be applied equally, without favor to anyone. He was a kind man. He allowed the Hebrews who had been carried into slavery by the Chaldeans to return to Palestine and rebuild their temple in Jerusalem.

In governing their large empire, Persian rulers chose the ablest officials they could find—often men from the conquered peoples. They paid close attention to local customs and allowed people

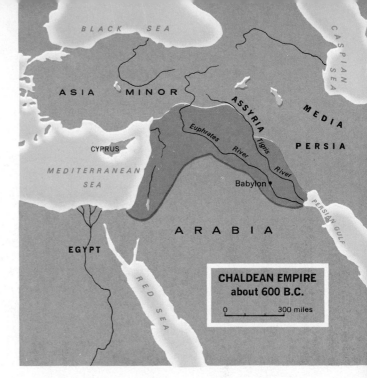

they conquered to keep their own religion and laws. This tolerant practice won the favor of the priests and the loyalty of the people.

The Persians copied many features of Assyrian imperial administration, especially the kinds of officials that were used to govern the empire. There were three sets: (1) a governor and his officials; (2) a general and his troops; and (3) inspectors, called by the Persians "the King's Eyes and Ears." The inspectors checked on the governors and generals to see that they used their power wisely.

The Persians maintained and extended the Assyrian road system and continued the postal service so that governors could make regular reports. The most famous road, the Royal Highway, extended all the way from Sardis in Asia Minor to Susa, one of the capitals of the empire (see map, page 48). The roads were built primarily for the army and post riders, of course, but they were used by merchants, too. There was a lively interchange of customs and ideas in the empire.

Persian religion

The greatest cultural contribution of the Persians was in religion. At first, like other early

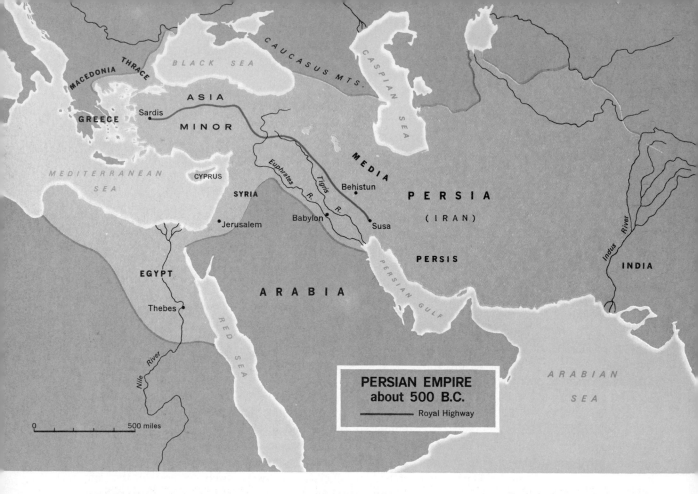

**PERSIAN EMPIRE
about 500 B.C.**
————— Royal Highway

0   500 miles

peoples, they worshiped many gods. Then, about 600 B.C., a great prophet and religious reformer completely changed their religious ideas. His name was Zoroaster (zoh·roh·AS·tur).

Zoroaster taught that the world was a place where human beings were trained for a future life. There was a great struggle between the forces of good and evil. The forces of good, symbolized by light, were led by Ahura Mazda (AH·hoo·rah MAHZ·dah), the source of truth and purity, the creator and upholder of the universe. The forces of evil or darkness were symbolized by the spirit Ahriman.

Human beings could choose sides and help in this struggle. Those who chose the good would be rewarded with eternal life. Those who chose evil would have darkness and misery after death. In the far, far distant future, the forces of good would finally triumph. Then the earth would dis-

appear, for it would have served its purpose as the stage on which the great conflict took place.

Zoroaster's ideas strongly influenced the lives of the Persians. According to him, nothing was so shameful as lying. Persian children were taught that they must always tell the truth. Getting into debt was considered a form of lying and therefore debt was disgraceful.

Early Persian rulers were influenced by Zoroaster's teachings. Darius, you will recall, had carvings made on the Behistun Rock (see page 39). Among them were these words: "On this account [suppressing the rebellion] Ahura Mazda brought me help. . . . because I was not wicked, nor was I a liar, nor was I a tyrant, neither I nor any of my line. I have ruled according to righteousness."

The thinking of the Hebrews and, later, of the Christians seems to have been affected by Zoroaster's idea of a struggle here on earth between

Chaldeans and Persians

When the Chaldeans rebuilt Babylon as their capital, they included a magnificent ziggurat, splendid palaces, and the famous Hanging Gardens. Nebuchadnezzar erected the beautiful Ishtar Gate, at left, as an entrance to a sacred shrine. This is a reconstruction of the gate, made with thousands of glazed bricks found at the site. The animals on either side of the portal—bulls and dragons—were made of special tiles, each with its surface raised to create a three-dimensional effect.

Near his palace at Persepolis, Darius the Great of Persia built a huge audience hall, above, where he sat in judgment over his subjects. The 40-foot columns still standing are all that remain of the thirty-six that originally supported the roof. This building and others at Persepolis were decorated with fine carvings, including the one of Darius himself, at upper left. The precise details of his ceremonial costume and throne reveal the technical skill of Persian craftsmen.

good and evil, and a final judgment in which reward or punishment depended on man's choice.

The decline of the Persians

The Persian kings who followed Darius and Xerxes were neither so strong nor so wise. As time went on, both the government and the army grew weak, partly because the empire contained so many different peoples who quarreled among themselves. In 331 B.C., as you will see, Alexander the Great became ruler of the Persian Empire.

CHECKUP

1. According to legend, why were the Hanging Gardens of Babylon built?
2. What areas were conquered by Cyrus? Cambyses? Darius the Great?
3. State briefly some of the main ideas of the Zoroastrian religion and compare it with the religion of the Egyptians.
4. IDENTIFY: Nebuchadnezzar, astrology, "King's Eyes and Ears."
5. LOCATE: Royal Highway, Sardis, Susa.

4   The seagoing Phoenicians traded and established colonies

The western end of the Fertile Crescent is a narrow strip of land along the eastern end of the Mediterranean Sea. Within this strip are two regions which in ancient times were inhabited by peoples who had a great influence on the modern world—the Phoenicians (fuh·NEE·shunz) and the Hebrews. These peoples differed from the peoples of the Tigris-Euphrates Valley that you have been reading about so far in this chapter. Their influence came not from wars and empire-building but from the arts of peace and from the world of ideas.

On the map on page 54, examine the physical features of this western end of the Fertile Crescent. The entire region is about 350 miles long. At its widest point, it is about 100 miles across. The southern portion, now in the countries of Israel and Jordan, was formerly known as Palestine. The northern portion, today included in Lebanon and modern Syria, was called Phoenicia.

A seafaring people

Phoenicia was a loose union of city-states, each with a king. On the map on page 54, notice the cities, Tyre and Sidon, two seaports that became world famous. Seldom in their history were the Phoenician city-states independent. They were conquered by, or paid tribute to, the Egyptians, Hittites, Assyrians, Chaldeans, Persians, and Greeks.

Phoenicia was less than 200 miles long and averaged 12 miles in width. It was hilly, even mountainous, and there was little fertile land. No large-scale farming was possible, and the Lebanon Mountains prevented the people from expanding eastward. From very early times the people of Phoenicia turned to the sea and to commerce for their living. They became the greatest traders of the ancient world.

The Phoenicians built seagoing ships very early in their history. To us these ships seem small and frail, but the Phoenicians were skillful and fearless sailors. Propelled by sails and oars, Phoenician ships traveled all over the Mediterranean Sea (see map, opposite). Some historians believe that the Phoenicians sailed to Britain for tin. They may also have sailed around Africa. In those days, it took great courage to make such long voyages.

Articles of trade

Phoenicia lacked minerals. The only important natural resource was lumber—the beautiful, straight-grained cedar trees of the Lebanon Mountains that many ancient peoples used in their building. Despite their lack of minerals, the Phoenicians became skilled artisans. They bought the metals of other lands and created beautiful objects of gold, silver, copper, and bronze. From the Egyptians they learned how to make exquisite glass.

Along their seacoast the Phoenicians found a shellfish called murex, which they used to make

50

PHOENICIAN COLONIES
about 700 B.C.

- - - - - Phoenician trade routes

0   500 miles

purple dye. Phoenician woolen cloth, dyed purple, was a prized possession of the ancient world. It was so expensive that only the wealthy could afford it. That is why purple became the color worn by kings—the royal purple.

Although the Phoenicians sold their own fabrics, metal goods, and glassware, most of their trading involved goods manufactured by other peoples. Thus they were what we call middlemen. These Phoenician traders were shrewd businessmen who carefully guarded information about their trade.

Phoenician colonies

From about 1000 to 700 B.C., conditions in the ancient Near East favored the Phoenicians. The Hittite Empire had disintegrated and the Egyptian Empire was declining. The Phoenician city-states were united under Tyre, the center for trade, and established colonies throughout the Mediterranean region (see map, this page).

The Phoenicians set up colonies as centers for trade on the islands of Sicily, Sardinia, and Malta. Farther west, beyond the Strait of Gibraltar, they established a colony on the site of the modern city of Cadiz, Spain.

The Phoenicians boasted that they had founded almost 300 cities on the northern coast of Africa. The greatest of these was Carthage. You will read more about it in Chapter 7; it became greater than either Tyre or Sidon.

Phoenician culture

Culturally the Phoenicians were imitators and improvers rather than creators. They copied their government and most of their culture from the Egyptians and Babylonians and, through trading, indirectly spread the knowledge of what they had learned throughout the Mediterranean area.

The religion of the Phoenicians was harsh. They worshiped many gods, or Baals (BAY·ulz). These were angry gods, and the Phoenicians sometimes sacrificed their own children to them to win their favor. The Phoenicians had no belief in an afterlife.

Although the Phoenicians created little that was original, one of their improvements had far-reaching effects. It was they who transmitted what became our alphabet.

You will remember that both the Egyptians and Sumerians progressed in the art of writing to

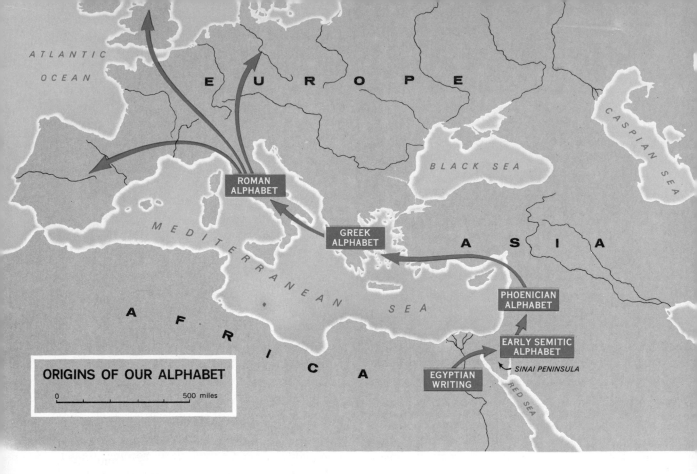

ORIGINS OF OUR ALPHABET

0 — 500 miles

the point of phonograms—signs for syllables—but that neither people produced a true alphabet. This invention came about when a people of the Sinai Peninsula, north of the Red Sea, took the idea of phonograms from the Egyptians and developed signs to represent consonants only. (The language of this region belonged to the Semitic family. Hebrew and Arabic, also Semitic languages, are still written without vowels.) The Phoenicians adopted this system and developed an alphabet of twenty-two consonants.

The spread of the alphabet is a good example of the civilizing influence of commerce. To the practical Phoenicians, writing was useful in their business for recording contracts and drawing up bills of lading and bills of sale. Phoenician commerce spread the knowledge of alphabetical writing throughout the Mediterranean world. It is said that the Greeks, when they first saw the Phoenician signs, feared them as magic. They

overcame their fear and improved the alphabet greatly by adding symbols for the vowel sounds. Later, the Romans copied this alphabet from the Greeks, altering the forms of some of the letters. For example, the Greek letter Σ—sigma—became S, and the Greek Δ—delta—became D. It is the Roman alphabet that is in use today in the Western world (see map, this page).

Thus the letter symbols you are now reading trace back through the Romans and Greeks to the improvements made by the Phoenicians and others on the system of writing created by the Egyptians. Even the word *alphabet* can be traced back. The Phoenician first letter was called *aleph,* and the second, *beth.* The Greeks changed them to *alpha* and *beta.* These first two letters are combined in our word *alphabet.*

The Arameans, another people of the western Fertile Crescent, also developed an alphabet, using cuneiform characters. They were famous overland traders, and spread their alphabet eastward, where it influenced Persian and Indian writing.

CHECKUP

1. What were some items traded by the Phoenicians?

2. Trace the development of our alphabet, with reference to (a) the Egyptians; (b) the Phoenicians; (c) the Greeks; (d) the Romans.

3. Explain, with examples, what is meant by the "civilizing influence of commerce."

4. LOCATE: Phoenicia, Tyre, Sidon, Sicily, Sardinia, Malta, Carthage, Sinai Peninsula.

5   The Hebrews contributed basic ideas to Western civilization

South of Phoenicia, also in the western end of the Fertile Crescent, lay the region formerly called Palestine, now in Israel and Jordan.

Resources and location

Palestine was a small strip of land, no more than 150 miles long. It had few natural resources. There were no forests and not many minerals. As for the land itself, as you can see on the map on page 54, it really consists of two regions. The northern part is watered by the Jordan River. There the soil is fertile enough to grow grain, olives, figs, and grapes. The southern region, around and south of the Dead Sea, is mostly desert. The soil is poor and rocky.

Because of its location, Palestine was involved in the history of all the ancient Near Eastern civilizations. In one way, its location was an advantage, because it lay along the great land bridge between Asia and Africa. Through Palestine ran the route from Egypt to the Tigris-Euphrates Valley. The merchants who carried the goods, and also the ideas, of these two great civilized regions traveled this route.

In another way, however, the location was not an advantage, for armies also passed along the route. The peoples of Palestine had to fight for their freedom against Egyptians, Hittites, Assyrians, Chaldeans, and Persians. They were conquered often, for they were not powerful.

The early Hebrews

Like the eastern part of the Fertile Crescent, Palestine was inhabited by a series of peoples. The people who had the greatest influence on their own times and on all later history were the He-brews, or Jews. They did not always live in Palestine. Abraham, the traditional founder of the Jewish people, once lived in Sumer. He left there and led his people across the Syrian Desert to the borders of northern Palestine. Some Jews stayed near there in the bordering deserts. Others went farther south and crossed the Isthmus of Suez into Egypt. They settled in the "Land of Goshen"—east of the delta region where the Nile spreads out as it flows into the Mediterranean Sea. It was swampy country and not very desirable. The Jews, however, improved the land and began to prosper.

These Hebrews lived peacefully in Egypt for some time, but eventually they fell from favor. Some scholars believe that one group of Hebrews entered Egypt along with the Hyksos in the 1700's B.C.; when the Hyksos were expelled in the 1500's, all the Hebrews incurred disfavor. For many years, they were forced to work as slaves.

Then a great leader, Moses, arose among the

PEOPLES OF THE FERTILE CRESCENT	
3000-2300 B.C.	Sumerians
2300-1600 B.C.	Babylonians
2000-1200 B.C.	Hittites
1275- 586 B.C.	Hebrews
1000- 700 B.C.	Phoenicians
900- 612 B.C.	Assyrians
612- 539 B.C.	Chaldeans
550- 331 B.C.	Persians

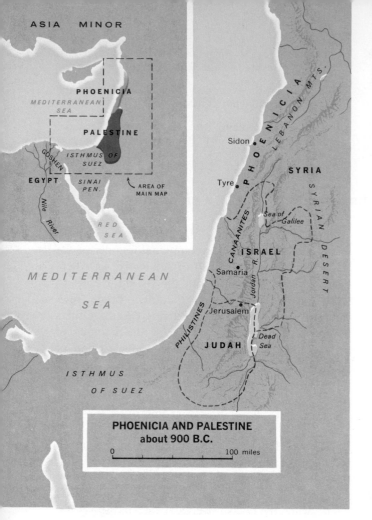

pharaoh changed his mind and sent an army to bring the Hebrews back, the waters of the sea closed on the Egyptians and drowned them.

Settling in Palestine

Many of the Hebrews were unhappy in the deserts of the Sinai Peninsula. They and their ancestors had lived in Egypt for centuries. They had accepted Egyptian customs and worshiped Egyptian gods. They thought that life in Egypt, even in slavery, was better than life in the harsh desert. It was then, according to tradition, that Moses went up Mount Sinai and came back to the Jews with the Ten Commandments, moral laws revealed to him by the Hebrew God Yahweh, or Jehovah. With the Commandments as a guide, and inspired by Moses, who began to tell them of Palestine as the Promised Land, the Hebrews went onward, not back.

The Jews who had come from Egypt joined with those who had lived for so long on the borders of northern Palestine. By this time they were all desert tribes again, hardened by the harsh life of desert herdsmen. But winning a homeland in Palestine was not easy. The good land was held by the Canaanites, a people of northern Palestine, and by the Philistines, a tribe that had settled along the coast. Both groups fought hard to hold on to their land. The struggle lasted for more than a century. The Canaanites were the first to be conquered, so that some of the Hebrews were able to settle down in the Jordan Valley. The Philistines were fiercer. The Hebrews drove them closer to the seacoast, but never conquered them completely.

A new government and new customs

As nomads, the Hebrews had been divided into twelve tribes. Each was headed by a religious leader called a Judge. But the long years of fighting for Palestine united the tribes under the rule of kings—first Saul, then David, then Solomon.

The Hebrews, however, did not remain united very long. Those in the north settled down in towns, making their living by farming. They adopted the customs of the conquered Canaanites, and many worshiped the Canaanite gods instead

Hebrews. In time he came to believe that it was his destiny to lead his people out of slavery. You may remember the Bible story of how Moses tried to persuade the pharaoh to set the Hebrews free. When the pharaoh refused, ten great plagues came to punish the Egyptians. In the tenth plague, the angel of death came to every Egyptian household and took the oldest child, but he passed over the houses of the Hebrews. (This event is the origin of the great Jewish festival of the Passover.)

The pharaoh at last consented to free the Hebrews. Around the year 1275 B.C., Moses led them out of Egypt in a great movement called the Exodus. According to the Bible, the waters of the Red Sea parted so that the Hebrews could walk safely across to the Sinai Peninsula. When the of Yahweh. Southern Palestine remained a rural, herdsman's region, where people clung to their old ideas, ways of living, and religion.

The reign of Solomon led to a definite split. He was famous for wisdom, but also for love of luxury and good living. To beautify the capital city of Jerusalem, he built a great temple and a palace for himself. He brought in architects, artisans, and building materials from Egypt and Phoenicia. The cost was great for a poor country. Taxes were heavy, and many men were forced to work on the great buildings without pay.

At the end of Solomon's reign, in 933 B.C., there was a revolution and the kingdom split in two. The northern area became the kingdom of Israel, with its capital at Samaria. The southern part, around the Dead Sea, became the kingdom of Judah, with Jerusalem as the capital (see map, opposite page).

The Hebrew kingdoms were not strong enough to withstand invasions from the east. The Assyrians captured Samaria, conquered Israel about 722 B.C., and carried many Jews into captivity and slavery. Later, in 586 B.C., the Chaldeans captured Judah and its capital, Jerusalem. They destroyed Solomon's temple and took the southern Hebrews into captivity. But after Cyrus, the Persian king, conquered the Chaldeans, he allowed the Hebrews to return to Palestine and to rebuild the temple at Jerusalem.

Thereafter the history of the Jews is a long story of conquest by one people after another and of wanderings over the earth. The Jews, however, never lost their identity as a people. Three great achievements not only gave them a unifying heritage but also were a supreme gift to the rest of the world: a code of laws, a great work of literature, and a truly noble religion.

Jewish law

The Jewish code of laws included the Ten Commandments and a body of law developed during the period of the Judges. It is called Mosaic law, after Moses. This code is often compared with the code of Hammurabi. Mosaic law, like the code of Hammurabi, demanded "an eye for an eye," but it set a much higher value on human

The Hebrews

Biblical accounts provide most of our information about the early Hebrew kingdoms. According to one tradition, the prophet Samuel was sent by God to find a successor to Saul among the sons of Jesse. He chose David, the youngest, and is shown above anointing him with a horn of oil. In the scene below, a later prophet, Elijah, sacrifices a bull. Because God sent flames to the altar, Elijah was able to triumph over the priests of Baal, whose sacrifice would not burn. Both of these paintings are from a group found in a Syrian synagogue of the 200's A.D. They are the earliest-known illustrations of the Bible.

life. Jewish law also accepted slavery, for it was the custom of the ancient world. However, Jewish law demanded kindness for slaves, while Hammurabi's code punished a slave more severely than a freeman for the same crime. Jewish laws required, as Babylonian laws did not, kindness to the poor and to strangers. Mosaic law was most severe against witchcraft and sacrifices to idols. These were crimes carrying the death penalty. In Hebrew thinking, man need only trust in Yahweh and the religious leaders, and he would learn all he needed to know.

The Old Testament

The great Hebrew work of literature is the Old Testament of the Bible. This rich and varied collection of writings contains thirty-nine books, or parts. The first five books contain the story of creation, the early history of man, and the laws. Next come the sermons and poetry of the great Jewish prophets. (Among the Jews, a prophet was a great religious thinker and teacher, not necessarily a man who could foretell the future.) Other writings include hymns, poems, proverbs, stories, and prophecies. These writings, together with the later writings of the New Testament, have influenced Western civilization more than any other single work.

Judaism

The religion of the Hebrews, called Judaism (JOO·dee·iz·um), was great partly because it developed rather than stood still. The early Hebrews worshiped Yahweh as a God who belonged to them alone. He was what might be called a tribal war god. According to the description of Him in the Ten Commandments, He was a jealous God. If a man sinned against Him, not only would he be punished, but also his children, and their children, and their children. This was a God to fear, not to love.

The Hebrews changed their idea of Yahweh partly because of their many sufferings and partly because of the teachings and writings of their prophets. Amos taught that Yahweh wanted justice for all men. Hosea wrote that Yahweh loved and forgave men. When Jews of the northern region adopted the Canaanite practice of worshiping idols and making sacrifices to them, Micah rebuked them sternly. He then described one of the noblest standards of conduct man has ever known—one that anyone could learn and try to follow: "He hath showed thee, O man, what is good; and what doth the Lord require of thee, but to do justly, and to love mercy, and to walk humbly with thy God?"

The Jews came to think of Yahweh as a loving father, a universal power living in the hearts of his worshipers. They began to think of Him as the God of all peoples. Other ancient peoples thought of their gods as having human qualities, but as more powerful. To the Jews, Yahweh was not like a human being. He was a spiritual force. The kings of other ancient peoples claimed to be gods or the representatives of gods in order to gain power. Jewish kings were mortal beings; only Yahweh was divine.

Belief in one God, as you have read earlier, is called monotheism. The Jews believed not only that there was a single, universal God, who belonged to everyone, but also that He was just, kind, merciful, loving, and forgiving. He was righteous, and He demanded righteous conduct of man.

Because of its emphasis on ethics (proper conduct), the Jewish form of monotheism is often called ethical monotheism. It is the supreme gift of the Hebrews to Western civilization. It is not an invention or a discovery to make life easier. It is a great and noble idea; and ideas, as you know, are powerful. No other single idea has so profoundly influenced Western civilization.

CHECKUP

1. When did the Hebrews leave Egypt? Why did they continue to Palestine instead of turning back?

2. What were the three most important contributions of the Hebrews to our civilization?

3. Why do you think the religion of the Jews is considered one of the world's great religions?

4. IDENTIFY: Abraham, Moses, Passover, Canaanites, Philistines, Solomon, prophet.

5. LOCATE: Palestine, Jordan River, Dead Sea, Syrian Desert, Goshen, Israel, Samaria, Judah, Jerusalem.

CHAPTER REVIEW

Chapter 3 | Many Different Peoples Ruled the Fertile Crescent (3000 B.C.—331 B.C.)

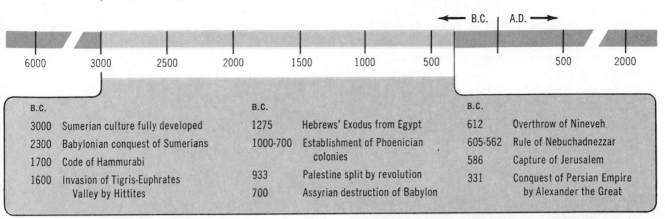

B.C.		B.C.		B.C.	
3000	Sumerian culture fully developed	1275	Hebrews' Exodus from Egypt	612	Overthrow of Nineveh
2300	Babylonian conquest of Sumerians	1000-700	Establishment of Phoenician colonies	605-562	Rule of Nebuchadnezzar
1700	Code of Hammurabi			586	Capture of Jerusalem
1600	Invasion of Tigris-Euphrates Valley by Hittites	933	Palestine split by revolution	331	Conquest of Persian Empire by Alexander the Great
		700	Assyrian destruction of Babylon		

CHAPTER SUMMARY

The Fertile Crescent was controlled by many different peoples. The Sumerians developed the earliest civilization there. By 3000 B.C., they were using metals. Early in their history, they developed the city-state and cuneiform writing. The arch, the dome, the ziggurat, and a mathematics system based on 60 were other Sumerian achievements.

The Sumerians were conquered by the Babylonians, most famous for Hammurabi's code. The Babylonians in turn were conquered by the Hittites, a warlike people who invaded the Tigris-Euphrates Valley about 1600 B.C. The Hittites, whose home was in Asia Minor, were the first people to make extensive use of iron for weapons; they are also known for their excellent legal system.

Among the strongest rulers of the Fertile Crescent were the Assyrians, a cruel, despotic people, who were the first to work out an efficient system of imperial government. The Chaldeans overthrew the Assyrians and rebuilt the city of Babylon. After the death of Nebuchadnezzar, they were overrun by the Persians.

At its peak, under Darius the Great, the Persian Empire stretched thousands of miles in extent. The Persians were wise and able rulers. Their great religious leader, Zoroaster, was a prophet who lived around 600 B.C., and preached that man must choose between good and evil in order to attain eternal bliss.

In the western end of the Fertile Crescent lived the Phoenicians, a seafaring people. Their most significant achievement was the development and transmission of an alphabet that was the basis for ours.

The Hebrews, after living in Egypt and spending many years in the deserts of the Sinai Peninsula, settled in Palestine. Although they were not strong enough to withstand invasion and conquest, they left an enormous heritage—a code of laws, which included the Ten Commandments; the Old Testament of the Bible; and the religion of Judaism.

QUESTIONS FOR DISCUSSION

1. What are some of the reasons why people move to cities today? Are there any parallels between this movement and the movement of peoples in the Fertile Crescent? Explain.

2. Present-day statesmen in a number of countries in Western Europe are trying to form one united government. What lessons might they learn from the history of the Sumerians?

3. For a time the Hittites ruled part of the Fertile Crescent through their monopoly of iron weapons. Discuss whether you think power in the world is still based on superior weapons.

4. Phoenician traders were responsible for the spread of culture in the Mediterranean world. Does international trade in the contemporary world aid the spread of culture? Explain.

5. How is it that the Babylonians could live according to the relatively short code of Hammurabi, while nations today have much more complicated legal systems?

6. Which area offered greater advantages to its people, ancient Egypt or the Tigris-Euphrates Valley?

PROJECTS

1. As an inspector, one of "the King's Eyes and Ears," write a report to the Persian government.

2. Make a list of the people of the Fertile Crescent, and next to each group write down some of their achievements.

3. Draw a map showing Phoenician trade routes.

Early Peoples of India and China Created Civilizations

From your earlier reading, you know that civilizations developed in the valleys of the Indus River in India and the Yellow River in China. This chapter will discuss these civilizations in the period from about 2500 B.C. to 1000 B.C.

Thinking back, you will remember that in Egypt during this time hieroglyphic writing was developed, the pyramids were built, and a remarkably stable society developed along the banks of the Nile. In the Fertile Crescent, city-states and empires rose and fell as one people conquered another. By the year 1000 B.C., adventurous Phoenician seamen were starting to build their far-flung commercial empire. And in Palestine, David, the successor of Saul and father of Solomon, was reigning over the twelve tribes of the Hebrews from the beautiful capital city of Jerusalem.

The civilizations of China and India were similar in some ways to the early civilizations of the Nile and Tigris-Euphrates valleys. In this chapter, for example, you will see the early peoples of India and China learning to farm, discovering writing and calendars, and creating governments. Through philosophy and religion they tried to understand the mysterious forces of nature, the mind, and the soul.

There were, however, important differences between Eastern, or Oriental, civilizations and those of the West, or Occident. Unlike Western civili-

A priest-king or god from Mohenjo-Daro

zations, those of India and China have been nearly continuous from earliest times to the present day. Here, truly, the roots of the present lie deep in the past. Such long and continuous history gives rise to deep-seated customs and traditions. Jawaharlal Nehru (juh·WAH·hur·lahl NAY·roo), a famous Indian statesman, once wrote: "The burden of the past, the burden of both good and ill, is overpowering, and sometimes suffocating, more especially for those of us who belong to very ancient civilizations like those of India and China." Thus, it could be said that, while the problems of East and West have often been the same, the solutions reached by the people of the two regions have frequently been different.

THE CHAPTER SECTIONS:

1. The first Indian civilization arose in the Indus Valley (2500–1500 B.C.)

2. Aryan invaders ruled India's northern plain during the Vedic Age (1500–1000 B.C.)

3. Geographic and cultural features helped shape Chinese history (2000–1500 B.C.)

4. The first Chinese civilization flourished under the Shang dynasty (1500–1028 B.C.)

1   The first Indian civilization arose in the Indus Valley

The earliest civilization of India arose in the Indus Valley in the northwest. In time, people settled all over India until now there are nearly 700 million people living there.

The four regions of Indian geography

India is shaped like two triangles joined base to base. The point of the smaller triangle lies in the mountains to the north. The point of the larger triangle lies nearly 2,000 miles to the south, in the Indian Ocean. At its widest point, where the bases of the triangles join, India stretches nearly 1,400 miles from the Arabian Sea to the Bay of Bengal.

India, jutting southward from central Asia, is often called a subcontinent of Asia. It is nearly half as large as the continental United States. However, the contrasts of India's geography and climate are greater than those of the United States. There are dense jungles, great fertile plains, high plateaus, dry deserts, low coastal plains, vast rivers, and the highest, most rugged mountains in the world. Because of the variety of Indian geography, languages, races, and people, it will be easier to understand Indian history if you do not think of India as a country like Egypt or Greece, but as a continent like Europe.

Geographically, India can be divided roughly into four main regions, each with its own surface features, climate, and resources. As you read about each region, look carefully at the map of India on page 60.

(1) *The northern mountains*. Two mighty mountain ranges, the Himalayas (hih·MAHL·yuz) and the Hindu Kush, meet in the north to form the point of the smaller triangle, a sort of peaked roof over the Indian subcontinent. The Himalayas, a series of parallel mountain ranges, stretch east and southeast for more than 1,500 miles. In all this distance there are few usable passes, and even these are higher than the highest peak in the continental United States.

The Hindu Kush stretch southwest from the point of the triangle and are not quite so forbidding as the Himalayas. There are some usable passes—the Khyber Pass is the most famous—through which migrating and invading tribes have been able to enter India. These passes were not low enough to attract large numbers of invaders. When invaders did come, however, they came in groups large enough to leave their mark, but small enough to be absorbed eventually into the population. Through immigration and invasion, the population of India became as varied as the geography and climate.

(2) *The Indus-Ganges plain*. Two great rivers lie south of the mountains. The Ganges (GAN-jeez), the more important, flows to the southeast, parallel to the Himalayas, through an immensely fertile valley. The Indus flows southwest through

drier lands. The northern ends of their two valleys are separated only by a low divide. It is helpful to think of the two valleys as one broad plain stretching more than 1,500 miles from west to east. After immigrants and invaders made their way through the narrow mountain passes, they spread out along the plain and made contact with the people already there.

(3) *The Deccan.* South of the Indus-Ganges plain, the interior of the Indian peninsula is a high plateau called the Deccan, meaning "south-

land." A range of hills, which reach an elevation of 4,000 feet, separates the Deccan from the Indus-Ganges plain. At the western edge of the Deccan, a mountain range, the Western Ghats, slopes gradually eastward to the inland plateau. The eastern edge of the Deccan is marked by a lower mountain range called the Eastern Ghats.

The Deccan is cut by rivers that flow eastward. Unlike the Ganges and the Indus, these rivers are of little use. During the rainy season they rise in destructive floods. At other times they dry up

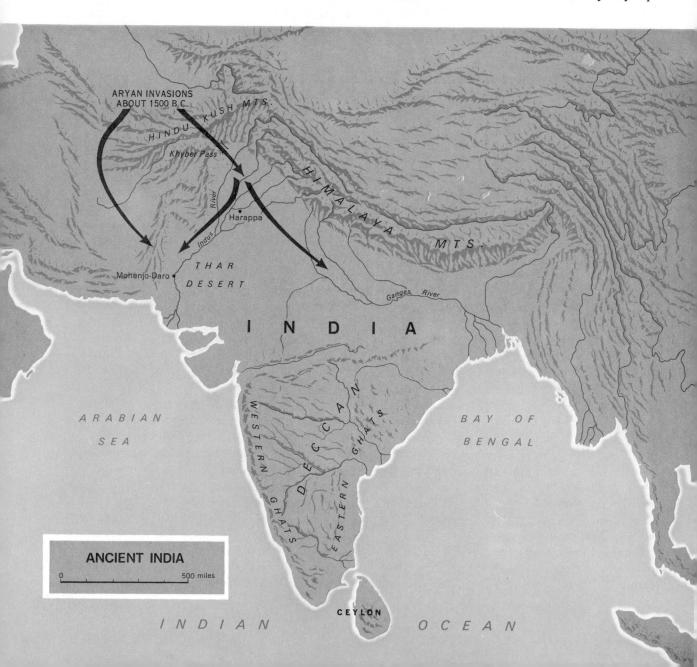

ANCIENT INDIA

0   500 miles

almost completely. The Deccan is a varied region, with agricultural, grazing, forest, and mining lands.

(4) *The coastal rim.* The coastal rim of flatlands extends around the lower triangle of India, facing the Arabian Sea on the west and the Bay of Bengal on the east. The western rim is narrow, hemmed in not far from the sea by the abrupt rise of the Western Ghats. The eastern rim is broader, sloping gradually upward toward the Eastern Ghats.

The people of the coastal rim turned to the sea very early. Those in the west traded with the Fertile Crescent, Egypt, and the Mediterranean region; those in the east traded with Ceylon and Southeast Asia, including the islands now called Indonesia. The coastal people had more contacts with people overseas than with the people of the Indus-Ganges plain.

The climate of India

Two features dominate the climate of India: the monsoon and the heat.

The monsoon is a seasonal wind. From late September until the end of the following March, the monsoon blows from the north and northeast. Any moisture it carries falls on the northern slopes of the Himalayas before reaching the rest of India. Then the monsoon swings around and, beginning in late May or early June, comes out of the southwest. As it crosses the Indian Ocean, it picks up moisture, which falls unevenly throughout India. Rainfall is heavy along the coastal rim, light behind the coastal mountains and hills, heavy in the lower Ganges Valley and heaviest of all in the eastern Himalayas.

Thus, in most of India, the rainfall for the entire year comes during the four months of the southwest monsoon. This is the critical time. If the monsoon is late or if the rainfall is light, crops are lost and there is famine. If there is too much rain, destructive floods result. There is some compensation in the fact that except in the northern mountains, temperatures rarely drop below freezing. Two or more crops can be grown in a year if enough moisture is available.

The second climatic feature of India is the heat. While the entire coastal rim is tropical, the heat there and on the Deccan is not excessive. But heat as a cruel force of nature—oppressive, crushing, furnacelike heat—is common on the Indus-Ganges plain. The winter months of December, January, and February are cool and bracing, but most of the rest of the year is hot. There may be many days in a row in May and early June with temperatures of 120° F.

Early civilization in the Indus Valley

Around 2500 B.C., not long after Egypt and Sumer developed civilizations, an impressive civilization appeared in India. Like the others, it came in a river valley—the valley of the Indus River in northwestern India.

Our knowledge of this early civilization is full of gaps. We believe that many of its people came from the Mediterranean area sometime before 2500 B.C. They already knew how to work copper and bronze. Some of their remains, and some features of the civilization they brought, are like those of Sumer. There may have been a link between the two peoples.

Harappa and Mohenjo-Daro. This early Indus Valley civilization is best seen in the excavated remains of two cities, Harappa and Mohenjo-Daro (see map, opposite). Neither city represented a natural growth—village to town to city. Both were built on the remains of earlier villages, carefully laid out according to the same systematic plan. Archeologists think that this Indus Valley civilization was not developed by the people of the region but was brought in by invaders.

For their day, Harappa and Mohenjo-Daro were miracles of city planning and convenience. Streets were laid out in a regular pattern, intersecting at right angles. Main streets were wide. Each city had a water system, with public baths, and a sewer system.

The two cities were built of bricks superior to those used in Sumer. The bricks were baked in kilns, or ovens, instead of being sun-dried. They have not crumbled over the centuries. They were standard in size, and skillfully joined by a mortar of pitch or asphalt. Although the Harappa and Mohenjo-Daro people could make better bricks

61

Seals from the Indus Valley

Our knowledge of the Indus Valley civilization consists of tantalizing bits and pieces from which archeologists weave various theories. The seals at left are the most puzzling and intriguing of the Indus remains so far unearthed. Objects of this sort bear the only known examples of the pictographic writing of the Indus Valley people. Since the writing has not yet been deciphered, the exact purpose of the seals is unknown. It seems likely, however, that they were used to stamp property or otherwise identify their owners.

Many of the seals undoubtedly had religious significance; the most common carving is that of a bull, a familiar figure of worship throughout the ancient world. The seated human figures may have been gods or idols. Some Indus Valley seals have been discovered in the Tigris-Euphrates region—evidence that people from India traded with those from the Near East.

than the Sumerians, their architecture was neither as skillful nor as interesting. They did not use the arch, vault, or dome. Their buildings were undecorated and were designed for use, not beauty.

The two cities, alike in plan, seem to have been twin capitals, not rivals. Each had a strong central fortress built on a platform of bricks. There were large storehouses for grain, possibly food for the defenders in case of attack. Homes of the wealthy, many of which were two stories high, were well built of bricks, each with a bathroom and a rubbish chute. There were also rows of identical huts in the cities, probably workmen's quarters.

Indus Valley culture. The areas surrounding Harappa and Mohenjo-Daro were agricultural regions, worked by farmers. Because the Indus River, like the Euphrates, has a swift current with heavy silt, irrigation problems must have been difficult. Archeologists do not know how the Indus Valley people solved them because the level of the plain around the two cities has been raised by up to 12 feet of silt deposits since their time.

City dwellers lived by industry and trade. There is evidence that they traded with people of the Tigris-Euphrates Valley as early as 2300 B.C. Their industries produced fine articles for trade. They made excellent cloth and painted pottery. They worked copper and bronze by both casting and forging. Their bronze sculpture showed artistic ability that was lacking in their architecture. Excavated articles include weapons and implements of copper and bronze, and a copper model of a two-wheeled cart. Jewelry, including gold and silver bangles, ear ornaments, rings, and necklaces, was of fine quality.

These early Indus Valley people had a written language. Examples have been found dating back to about 2300 B.C. The system was then fully developed, with uniform characters, mainly pictograms. We cannot yet read the language, partly because most of the examples found are short

Indus Valley Civilization

Archeologists have learned most of what is known about the civilization that existed in the Indus Valley from such excavated sites as Mohenjo-Daro, below. The ruins reveal the remains of straight streets, large buildings, water and sewage systems, and other conveniences associated with city life. Many articles of daily use have also been found, among them clay figures like those shown here. The seated monkey at left may have been a religious idol of some sort. The figures above—a small dog and a cart with driver and oxen—were probably toys. In India today, pottery makers stop their regular work to make toys and masks for certain festivals. They may be carrying on a tradition started many centuries ago by the people of the Indus Valley.

inscriptions on personal seals, probably the names of individuals. No connection with any other language has been established. One theory is that the people of Harappa and Mohenjo-Daro took the idea of writing, though not the actual characters, from the Sumerians.

The little we know of Indus Valley religion indicates that it was a form of animism. This means that the people believed that spirits inhabited everything—animals, trees, and other natural objects as well as people. No temples, shrines, or inscriptions have been found. The people seem to have worshiped certain animals such as snakes, monkeys, and bulls. They believed that certain trees were sacred, and they worshiped the fertility of nature. These customs did not die out with the early Indus Valley civilization, but were handed down through generations of peasants to become part of Indian religious tradition. You can see that our knowledge of this early civilization consists of tantalizing bits and pieces.

The people of Harappa and Mohenjo-Daro ruled the valley for about a thousand years. Strangely enough, the culture did not improve with time. In fact, artifacts found in the most recent levels of remains are actually poorer in quality than older objects. According to one theory, an upwelling of mud dammed the Indus River, causing the valley to flood and destroying cities and farms. In any case, it seems likely that the civilization was declining when, about 1500 B.C., invaders appeared and destroyed it.

CHECKUP

1. Name and briefly describe the four main geographical regions of India.
2. Based on archeological findings in the Indus Valley, what are some conclusions that can be drawn about the early civilization there?
3. IDENTIFY: Oriental, Occident, monsoon, animism.
4. LOCATE: Arabian Sea, Bay of Bengal, Himalayas, Hindu Kush, Indus-Ganges plain, Deccan, Western Ghats, Eastern Ghats, Harappa, Mohenjo-Daro.

2   Aryan invaders ruled India's northern plain during the Vedic Age

About 1500 B.C., a new group of people began working their way through the northwestern mountain passes into the Indus Valley. Like the Hittites, Medes, and Persians, they came from the grasslands north of the Black and Caspian seas and spoke an Indo-European language.

The conquering Aryans

The Indo-European tribes that forced their way into northwestern India, one after another, are called Indo-Aryans, or Aryans (see map, page 60). They spoke a language known as Sanskrit. They were a simple people who herded sheep and cows. (Their word for "war" meant "a desire for more cows.") They were strong, brave, and skillful fighters. In battle, bowmen were led by men in horse-drawn chariots. They conquered the Indus Valley, then spread eastward along the Ganges until they controlled the entire northern plain.

The Aryans were contemptuous of cities and trading. They destroyed Harappa and Mohenjo-Daro and the urban civilization that the twin cities supported. Many of the city dwellers were massacred. Survivors either fled to the south or became slaves.

The conquerors were not builders; they had no word for "brick" in their language. They left the ruins of the cities to decay. They had no written language. Their history for several centuries after their arrival is only vaguely known. What we do know comes from the Vedas, the great literature of the Aryan religion. The period from 1500 to 1000 B.C. is known as the Vedic Age in Indian history.

The Vedas

The word *veda* means "knowledge." The Vedas are books of sacred knowledge—collections of religious rituals and hymns to the gods. Only four major ones have survived: (1) the *Rig-Veda,* hymns of praise; (2) the *Sama-Veda,* melodies or chants; (3) the *Yajur-Veda,* sacrificial formulas; and (4) the *Atharva-Veda,* charms and magic spells.

Since the Aryans had no system of writing, the Vedas were memorized in the unchanging Sanskrit of their original composition and handed down by word of mouth. The Vedas were not written down until long after the Vedic Age.

The Vedas contain an amazing variety of subjects. The *Atharva-Veda* has spells and incantations for many purposes: to obtain children, to ward off evil, to prolong life, or to destroy enemies. The *Rig-Veda,* the greatest of the Vedas as literature, has more than a thousand hymns of praise to all the objects of Aryan worship. Some are straightforward prayers for good crops or long life. Some show a simple, childlike wonder: why doesn't the sun fall very rapidly, once it begins to slip downward? Still others are as eloquent and beautiful as the Psalms of the Bible.

Aryan religion

The earliest gods mentioned in the Vedas were forces of nature such as the sky, sun, earth, light, fire, wind, storm, water, and rain. These natural objects and forces were personified—that is, they were regarded or represented as persons. Thus the sky became a father, the earth a mother.

The Vedic religion of the Aryan people, like that of the Hebrews, was not fixed, but changing and developing. For a time Agni—fire—was the most important god, because sacred flames carried sacrifices to heaven. Indra, god of thunder and storm, was always popular. It was he who brought the life-giving rain. Prajapati (prah-JAH-put-ih), the sun as the generator of life, the lord of all living things, received profound devotion.

The development of the god Varuna best shows how Aryan religion changed. He began as the heaven; his garment was the sky, his breath the storm. As the spiritual understanding of his worshipers matured, so did he. He became the guardian of ideas of right and wrong. He watched over the world through his eye, the sun, rewarding good and punishing evil. Thus he became the enforcer of an eternal law of morality—of right and wrong.

Like the Persians, the early Aryans believed in personal immortality. After death the soul was either thrust by Varuna into a dark pit of eternal punishment or raised into a heaven where every earthly joy was endless. Later in Indian history (as you will read in Chapter 9), these rather simple ideas of a future life became vastly more complex.

There were apparently no temples or images in the early Vedic religion. Rituals consisted of burnt offerings; new altars were built after each sacrifice. The usual offering was a libation, or pouring out, of the juice of the sacred soma plant, along with the pouring of liquid butter into the fire. The important point was to perform the ceremony properly; the merits of the person performing it did not matter.

As time passed, the rituals of sacrifice became more complicated. The spoken language of the Indian people also changed, until it became quite different from the Sanskrit of the first Aryan invaders. Since proper observance was so important, priests called Brahmans, who knew the proper forms and were learned in Sanskrit, also became more important. They fixed the proper ceremony for almost every occasion of life, and charged heavily for their services.

Early Aryan society

The Aryans had been nomads, with the habits and customs of wanderers. In the Indus-Ganges plain, however, they gained one of the richest and most fertile areas in the world. Here they settled down. When conquest was replaced by farming and settled living, they developed simple forms of government.

Aryan tribes joined to form small states. Each tribe was led by a chief and a tribal council. Each state was ruled by a king and a council of warriors. But each state was made up of nearly independent villages. Each village was governed by an assembly of heads of families.

There were physical and social differences between conquerors and conquered. Aryans were light-skinned; the original Indus Valley people were dark-skinned. Aryans had been nomads; the Indus Valley dwellers had been city-dwellers.

The conquerors looked down on the conquered. The Aryans, however, were outnumbered by the conquered, their supposed inferiors. They believed that they had to prevent intermarriage in order to maintain their identity. Therefore they passed laws prohibiting mixed marriages. At first these restrictions were simple, but later they became much more complicated.

Class divisions began to form during the Vedic Age, but it was not until later that fixed hereditary classes appeared. The early Aryans considered the warrior to be the most admirable member of society. When war gave way to peace, and farmers needed the help of religion against the forces of nature, the Brahman priests gained importance. However, many centuries passed before the Brahmans were considered to be as important as warriors.

The Vedas provide a great deal of information about family life in the Vedic Age. Marriages took place by kidnaping, by purchase, or by mutual consent. Women seem to have valued the methods in about that order. It was a great compliment to be stolen. To be bought and paid for was more flattering than to marry by mutual consent. Men were permitted to have more than one wife. They held the right of ownership over wives and children. In certain circumstances, a man might sell his wives and children.

The Aryan economy

When the Aryans took up farming in the Indus-Ganges plain, they raised barley as the principal crop. Rice was apparently unknown in Vedic times. Each village divided its land among its families, but irrigation was a common project. Land could not be sold to outsiders; it could be willed only to male heirs. Most Aryans owned their land. To work for someone else was considered a disgrace.

Handicrafts gradually appeared in the villages. There was some trade, but it was hampered by poor transportation and poor trading methods. This early trade was by barter, but later, cattle were used as a medium of exchange. As in parts of present-day Africa, wives were bought with cows.

Thus the picture we get of the Aryan invasions of India is one of the destruction of a high civilization by an invading people at a much lower level of culture. Only in the field of religious thought and in the religious literature of the Vedas did the Aryans give promise of the greatness that lay ahead.

CHECKUP

1. Who were the Aryans? What did they do to the civilization of the Indus Valley?
2. What are the Vedas? What period in Indian history is known as the Vedic Age?
3. Summarize the most important features of the Aryan religion.
4. Who were the Brahmans? Why did they gain importance in Aryan society?
5. IDENTIFY: Sanskrit, Agni, Prajapati, libation.

3   Geographic and cultural features helped shape Chinese history

China's story begins, as you read in Chapter 1, with the Paleolithic settlements of Peking man. Later Neolithic developments along the Yellow River were similar to those in Europe. The people domesticated animals, improved their tools and weapons, and developed permanent communities as agriculture became the dominant way of life.

Before picking up the story of China at this point, however, it is helpful to do two things: first, to examine the geography of China, and second, to learn of the patterns of recurring events associated with the dynasties of China's rulers.

The geography of China

On the map of China, opposite, notice the great mountain ranges of the west, northwest, and southwest. These mountains slope down to high plateaus, which are either deserts or semi-deserts. In the north the plateaus slope gradually down to a coastal plain along the Pacific Ocean.

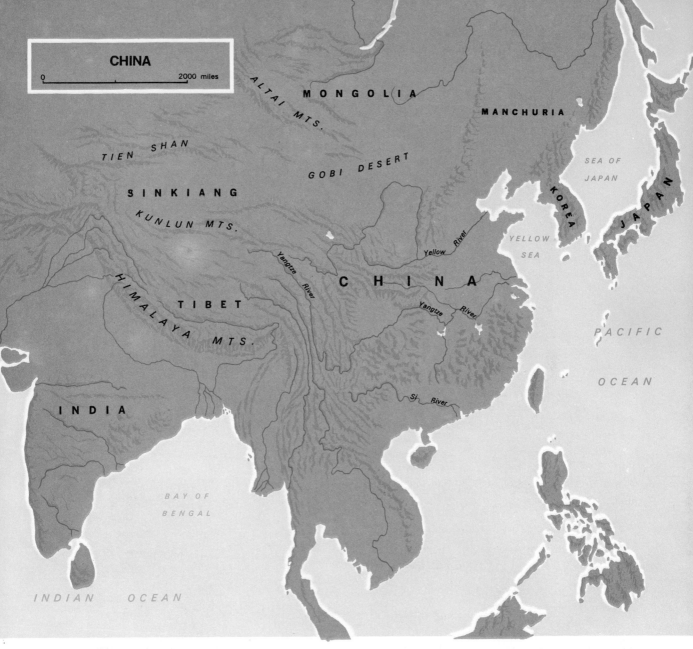

In the south the plateaus give way to a region of many low hills and valleys.

Another range of mountains cuts from west to east across the center of China, separating the valleys of the two greatest rivers, the Yellow and the Yangtze. These mountains divide the land into two major agricultural areas. In the north, where relatively little rain falls, wheat is the principal crop. In the center and south, where there is more rainfall, rice is the leading farm product.

Throughout its history, China has also been divided politically into two main parts. The smaller and more important part lies along the seacoast and stretches inland up the valleys of the Yellow and Yangtze rivers. This is the heart of China, which may be called China Proper or often just China. For many centuries the Chinese called this land the Middle Kingdom.

The second part surrounds China Proper with

(continued on page 70)

67

The Geography of China

Like most large countries, China has varied physical features. The Gobi Desert, left, is a wasteland traversed only occasionally by nomadic tribes or travelers; the caravan here is en route from India to China. By contrast, some Chinese mountain lands are among the richest in the world. Those shown below left have been terraced, a technique used by Chinese peasants to make their land as productive as possible. Since several million more Chinese people must be fed every year, the need for arable land is a constantly pressing one. Flat and fertile lowlands are used for rice, which has for centuries been a staple of the Chinese diet. Below, center, is a recently planted rice crop; behind the paddy a boy is grazing water buffalo. China's longest river, the deep and navigable Yangtze, is shown below right. On the banks of the muddy-looking river are houses bearing traditional Chinese roofs.

69

a great semicircle of regions, including Tibet, Sinkiang, Mongolia, Manchuria, and Korea. At various times throughout its history, China Proper has conquered and ruled these regions, usually to protect itself from attack by their nomad populations.

China Proper. China Proper is naturally suited to have become the birthplace of a great civilization. Its soil is wonderfully fertile. On the northern plains, a yellow, finely powdered soil called loess (LOHS) is hundreds of feet deep in places. Farther south, toward the seacoast, is a great plain formed by deposits of silt from the Yellow and Yangtze rivers. Elsewhere there are many smaller fertile plains and valleys. The climate is generally good for farming, and rain usually falls when it will do the most good.

China Proper has many rivers, but the Yellow, the Yangtze, and the Si (SHEE) have played especially important parts in its history. The Yellow River—often called by its Chinese name, the Hwang Ho—is 2,900 miles long, but it is so shallow that most of it is useless for navigation except by small boats. Its water is vital for irrigation, but controlling it has always been a problem. It carries a heavy burden of silt; the silt is yellowish in color, which accounts for the name of the river. The silt settles rapidly to the bottom, raising the water level of the river higher than the surrounding land.

The Chinese have built dikes to keep the Yellow River within its banks, but if the dikes break in flood time, the river runs wild. Sometimes it cuts a completely new channel to the sea. The river has changed its course often during China's long history. In ancient times it emptied into the sea far to the north of its present mouth. Because of its destructiveness and the toil of trying to control it, the Chinese called the Yellow River "China's Sorrow."

The Yangtze River in central China is 3,400 miles long and quite deep most of the way. In modern times, large ocean-going ships are able to go 600 miles upstream to the great city of Wuhan. Smaller ships can go to Chungking, about 1,300 miles from the sea.

The Si River in southern China is more than 1,200 miles long. Like the Yangtze, it is important as a commercial waterway. Large ships can navigate it as far as Tsangwu, 220 miles inland.

China's isolation. China has made many contributions to other civilizations, but the Chinese have always been suspicious of foreigners and of foreign influence. There are excellent seaports, but in ancient times they were little used for overseas commerce.

China was shielded to some extent from outside influence by the Pacific Ocean, by a semicircle of high mountains, and by formidable deserts, such as the Gobi. To the north and south, however, these barriers were not wholly effective. Especially in the north, nomads of central and northeastern Asia pressed steadily toward the fertile valleys of China, as hill and desert tribes had moved into the fertile Tigris-Euphrates Valley.

There was some Chinese trade over the mountains with India. There was also a long overland caravan route from northwestern China over deserts and through mountains to the Black Sea and the Near East. Some ideas and merchandise passed back and forth over this route, but it was a rigorous trip, and the commerce was scanty and irregular.

Although the Chinese adopted both ideas and skills from other peoples, they probably owed less to outside influence than any people you have yet read about. Lack of contact with other peoples of equal culture gave the Chinese contempt for foreigners, all of whom they regarded as barbarians. Even when outsiders overran the Middle Kingdom, as sometimes happened, the Chinese knew that the strangers would in time lose their identity and be absorbed into China's vast population. "China," they said, "is a sea which salts all rivers that run into it."

Chinese dynasties

As you take up the story of China's past, your reading will be clearer if you understand that Chinese history does not tell of an even, gradual rise of civilization over the centuries. It is a story of dynasties whose fortunes were spun out in patterns of events that often repeated themselves.

During a time of orderly government under a given dynasty, civilization would gradually rise to a peak. Then it would decline as government under that dynasty became weaker. When the decline reached a low point, with disorder and rebellion, the dynasty would be overthrown.

The end of a dynasty was usually a time of wars, revolts, invasions by nomads from surrounding regions, and famines—a period of chaos that sometimes lasted several centuries. Many people died from starvation or in war. Then land would be redistributed and there would be enough to go around. When, after a considerable period of time, a new dynasty was able to establish itself, most families had enough land to support themselves and to pay taxes in support of a government. Thus, a new dynasty could start under favorable circumstances.

Family landholdings. Chinese dynastic history was affected by traditional methods of land ownership. Landlords rented their land to farmer-tenants at high rentals, usually from 50 to 60 percent of the crop. They also had charge of tax collecting. They used agents as tax collectors, who paid themselves well by "squeezing" the tenants for everything they could get. Large and powerful landowners usually managed to pay little in taxes, so that the brunt of the tax burden fell on the tenants. Landlords were also money-lenders, making loans at high interest rates when tenants needed funds between planting time and harvest.

The Chinese family also played an important part in dynastic history. It was composed of the father, his wife, the sons with their wives and children, and the unmarried daughters. The father had complete control. If he was a landowner, the family worked for him. When he died, the land was divided equally among his sons.

As time passed, individual landholdings became smaller and smaller as they were divided up among sons and grandsons. Taxes had to be paid. If the government were in financial trouble, taxes might be collected years in advance. Eventually the landholding became too small to support a family and pay the taxes, no matter how hard the landlord's agents oppressed the tenants. Money

had to be borrowed. When it could not be repaid, the owner lost his land and became a tenant himself. Sometimes he was forced to leave the land altogether.

Bandits and warlords. In a farming country, there were few things that a landless man could do. He could become a beggar, and many did. He could try to find work as a laborer, but such jobs were scarce. Many proud men became bandits. Their number increased as high rentals, high taxes, high interest rates, and constant subdivision of land among sons drove men off their land. Groups of bandits joined together under leaders. As conditions became worse, a bandit leader might gain control of a large area of land. He was then called a warlord.

The rulers of a dynasty, faced with a growing number of rebellions by warlords, would spend an increasing amount of government time and money on fighting. Dikes and irrigation systems would be neglected.

In the anarchy and confusion that followed the overthrow of a dynasty, warlords would struggle for power. Eventually a warlord might gain control of several large areas. If his sons and grandsons could extend their power and make it hereditary, a new dynasty would be born.

If you keep in mind the facts about Chinese geography, as well as the Chinese attitude toward the family and their rulers, you will be able to understand many things about China that might otherwise be puzzling.

Legendary China under the Hsia dynasty

To the Chinese, it was important that the distant past be explained and connected with historic times. The Chinese have many legends about the beginnings of the world and about early China and its people. They tell of P'an Ku, the first man, who worked for 18,000 years to create the universe. They tell of hero-kings who ruled for more than a century each and personally created such institutions and inventions as marriage, music, painting, and the wheel. The legends also tell of the Hsia (SHYAH) dynasty, which ruled the Yellow River country from about 2000 B.C. to about 1500 B.C.

71

Unfortunately, the Chinese legends reveal more charm than they do proved facts. Whether or not the Hsia dynasty existed, there is no doubt that the people of the Yellow River Valley made great advances during these five centuries. They improved their agriculture. There is some evidence that they began to use written symbols. With the appearance of writing, China was prepared for its first historic dynasty, the Shang.

CHECKUP

1. What are the two major agricultural areas of China? the two main political divisions?
2. How was Chinese history affected by the system of landholding?
3. What gains were made in China from about 2000 B.C. to about 1500 B.C.?
4. LOCATE: Yangtze River, Tibet, Sinkiang, Manchuria, Korea, Si River, Gobi Desert.

4   The first Chinese civilization flourished under the Shang dynasty

We know that the Shang dynasty began about 1500 B.C. along the Yellow River, but we do not know how the Shang rulers established themselves there. We can make some informed guesses, however, based on the geography of the region.

Irrigation systems

Prosperity in the valley of the Yellow River depends upon irrigation and flood control, and must have done so from earliest times. Dikes along the banks of the river must be kept in repair because of the high level of the water, especially at flood time. Irrigation is easy because of the high water level, but excess water must be carried away in long drainage canals to a point far downstream where it can flow back into the river.

Throughout China's history, any break in the dikes along the river has brought disaster to crops, animals, and people. Also, as you have read, the Yellow River in flood may cut a new channel, leaving irrigation and drainage systems useless. Organized, centralized government is needed to build and maintain such systems and to guard against floods. Prior to the coming of the Shang, the people of the valley did not have a government to provide for irrigation, drainage, or flood control. They lived from hand to mouth—well in good years, starving when the area was stricken by drought or flood.

Beginning with the Shang dynasty, this situation changed. Legend tells us that the Shang were immigrants, not natives. It seems likely that they introduced simple irrigation and flood control systems. Control of these systems meant control of the country.

Government under the Shang

The first Shang rulers are said to have conquered 1,800 city-states. Apparently the Shang moved their capital city a number of times, either because it was hard to defend or because of floods. During the last centuries of Shang rule, the capital of the dynasty was situated near the modern city of Anyang.

Shang government was relatively simple. There was a hereditary king, who granted land to his principal followers in return for a pledge of loyalty, the performance of services, and the payment of dues. The valley of the kingdom was surrounded by barbarian peoples, against whom the Shang maintained their power by using war chariots and superior weapons of bronze. Their military force enabled them to gain territory and to spread the knowledge of their superior civilization. At one time or another, they ruled most of northern and central China (see map, opposite page).

The position of king was a demanding one. He led in battle, in the hunt, and in certain sacrifices and religious ceremonies. People believed that the spirits helped him in war and in planning for good crops. However, the king had to produce results. Poor crops or defeat in battle meant that he had lost favor with the spirits and he was likely to lose favor with the people.

Civilization under the Shang

The years of the Shang dynasty, from about 1500 to 1028 B.C., were a formative period for Chinese culture and civilization. Under the Shang, Chinese people improved upon the discoveries and skills of earlier periods and developed new ones. Later dynasties added further improvements, but the basic advances were made during the time of the Shang.

Economy and handicrafts. The Shang economy was mainly agricultural. Farmers grew millet as their main crop, along with some barley. They also grew some rice, but more was imported from the south. Compared with millet, rice was counted a luxury. Wheat growing did not begin until late in the dynasty.

Domesticated animals included cattle, horses, sheep, pigs, chickens, and dogs. The Shang used elephants from southern Asia in war and for some other kinds of work. Sometime during the Shang dynasty, the Chinese learned to raise silkworms, to spin thread from their cocoons, and to weave silk cloth from the thread.

Not all the Chinese were farmers, however. In the cities lived merchants and craftsmen. Some made clothing from silk, and others made cord from hemp. Artisans carved jade to make jewelry. They also carved ivory and bone to make various objects inlaid with turquoise.

Shang artisans of the cities laid the foundations for all later Chinese ceramic art. They learned to use kaolin (KAY·uh·lin), a fine white clay, and to shape vessels on the potter's wheel. They glazed some of their pottery. Shang potters developed every form and shape that was used later in Chinese ceremonial vases.

The bronze castings of Shang artisans have been a marvel of later times. The Chinese may have learned the technique of casting from the Near East, possibly Sumer. But the artistry and craftsmanship—the forms of the vessels and the designs of the decorations—were essentially Chinese. Chinese artisans probably imported copper and tin ores and mixed the bronze themselves. They cast small figures as well as large ceremonial vessels whose surfaces were covered with delicate relief work.

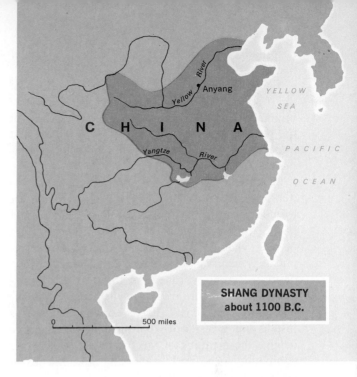

SHANG DYNASTY
about 1100 B.C.

Astronomy and the calendar. A calendar was as important to Shang farmers and their rulers as it was to the peoples of Egypt and the Fertile Crescent.

The Chinese had a kind of lunar calendar. The shortest period of the calendar was ten days. Three such periods, sometimes shortened by a day, made a month. Six ten-day periods made a "cycle"; six cycles made a year of 360 days or less. To make up the extra days for a 365-day year, those in charge of the calendar added days as needed.

Adjustment of the calendar was the work of priest-astronomers employed by the government. They had to be responsible and skillful. The king's popularity depended upon the success of the harvest, which in part depended upon the time of planting as determined by the calendar.

The Shang calendar seems clumsy and confusing to us, but apparently the astronomers were skillful enough to make it work. We know that they could calculate eclipses of the moon in advance so accurately that an error of twenty-four hours alarmed the authorities. Because of their skill with the calendar, the astronomers were given the duty of keeping other records. Thus, the Chi-

73

nese had very early what might be called official historians.

Language and writing. The Chinese are one of the few peoples known to have developed an original written language. To understand some of the peculiarities of Chinese writing, one must first understand some characteristics of spoken Chinese.

Scientists call Chinese an agglutinative (uh-GLOO·tuh·nay·tiv) language; that is, words are formed by the "clinging together" of distinct parts. Almost all of the basic Chinese words are of one syllable. To express a new or more complicated meaning, the Chinese put together two or more simple words. Thus the word for "magnet" is made up of three one-syllable words meaning "pull-iron-stone." Each word-syllable keeps just as much of its original meaning as is needed to give the meaning of the compound word. This compound meaning is something new, not just a collection of the three things named.

When written symbols are developed to express such a language, they are more likely to represent syllables than single alphabetic letters. Chinese writing began with pictograms, but went on to develop ideograms and phonograms. Written characters came to be formed of two parts. One was a "sound sign," giving a clue to pronunciation. The other was an "idea sign," giving a clue to meaning.

The Chinese developed their system of writing in an effective way. By combining signs, they were able to invent new characters freely. The system spread throughout most of eastern Asia. The traditional, written language is difficult to learn. Each character must be memorized. For centuries, a well-educated Chinese had to know more than 10,000 characters. Thus, until a simplified version of the language was developed in recent times, the ability to read and write was limited to a fairly small percentage of the Chinese people.

Unlike the Aryans of India, the Chinese from early days used writing to compose and preserve literary works. Writing itself became an art, called calligraphy (kuh·LIG·ruh·fee). It became a challenge to form the characters beautifully. The Chinese admire beautiful calligraphy as much as they admire beautiful painting.

The script of the characters was usually written with a brush on silk or bamboo. The lines ran from top to bottom, beginning on the right side. In time, the pictograms of early writing became more and more formalized and abstract so that an uninformed reader could hardly recognize the pictorial origin.

Religion in the Shang period. The religion which developed during the Shang dynasty was a combination of animism and ancestor worship. Animism you know about. Ancestor worship includes reverence for older people in the family as well as for the family's forebears.

Many things in nature were personified. People believed in a dragon which lived in the seas and rivers and was all-powerful and kindly. He could rise into the clouds. Summer thunderstorms that brought longed-for rain were caused by dragons fighting in the heavens. In time the good dragon became the symbol of Chinese rulers.

The Chinese held great religious festivals in spring and autumn. In spring, the planting time, there were ceremonies to bring fertility, when the ruler plowed the first furrow. In autumn, there were rites of thanksgiving for the harvest.

Along with these animistic beliefs, there developed the idea of reverence toward the elders and ancestors of the family. The family was regarded as both earth-dwelling and spirit-dwelling; all members of the family were united forever through their religion. The duty of the child toward the parent was most important. The ideogram in Chinese writing for "filial piety"—that is, for the honor and reverence that was owed to parents—shows a son supporting his aged father as he walks.

There were priests in Chinese religion. Some, as you know, were priest-astronomers. Others used divination to tell the wishes of the spirits, especially of the spirits of ancestors. The priests wrote questions on bone or tortoise shell, into which they thrust a heated metal rod. They interpreted the answers of the spirits from the pattern of cracks that appeared, and wrote the answers on the bone or shell. Scholars have

The Shang dynasty is noted for its fine bronze. Although the ceremonial mask above is more than 3,000 years old, its facial features resemble those of northern Chinese today. The urn with tripod legs, right, has delicately engraved patterns on its sides and a lid in the shape of a bird. The ladle below is about a foot long. It, too, is carefully decorated, with a handle ending in a snake's head.

The Shang are famous, too, for their practice of divination. The piece of bone at left, inscribed with an early form of Chinese writing, bears cracks caused by a hot metal rod.

Ancient Chinese Owl

Ancestors have traditionally been revered, respected, and honored in China. Older people were consulted about every important matter during their lifetime. After death their memories and achievements were perpetuated by constant ritual observance. This proud owl, cast in bronze about 1000 B.C., was used as a jar for wine offerings at ancestral sacrifices. The owl is decorated with spiral designs that are thought to symbolize clouds, rain, and water. Vessels of this sort thus give us some idea of the importance of nature among the early Chinese. This piece of bronze, an excellent example of casting, is an extraordinary achievement in view of the few crude instruments possessed by the Chinese of that period.

learned much about Shang culture from these questions and answers.

Unlike the Aryans of India, the Chinese were not greatly interested in religious problems, such as the existence of a life after death. Thus, Chinese priests never became as important as the Indian Brahmans; indeed, their power declined as time passed. The Chinese were more concerned with ethical problems—with proper behavior in this life. They believed that their ruler received his power through communication with the spirits and orders from them. Such orders were called the Mandate of Heaven. There could be rebellion against the ruler, however. If it succeeded, it proved that he had lost divine favor. It is significant that the legendary P'an Ku was a man, not a god.

Fall of the Shang dynasty

Documents of a later period tell of the overthrow of the last Shang king, the thirty-first ruler of the dynasty, in 1028 B.C. Probably the Shang rulers lost vigor, becoming less able to carry on the necessary hard fighting. Legends say that the last king and his wife were monsters of corrupt wickedness and cruelty. We must remember, however, that these are legends about a loser, possibly invented by his successors.

Earlier, the Shang had conquered a western people, the Chou (JOH). The Chou were barbarous, but their leaders learned to appreciate Shang culture. As the Shang became weaker, the Chou joined with other western tribes to overthrow them, much as hill and desert people overthrew weakening valley peoples in the region of the Fertile Crescent.

CHECKUP

1. How is it thought that Shang rulers were able to establish themselves? What kind of government did they have?

2. What were the principal occupations of Shang China? What were the chief products?

3. Chinese priests had two important duties. Explain them.

4. Why is written Chinese such a difficult language?

5. IDENTIFY: kaolin, agglutinative language, calligraphy, ancestor worship, Mandate of Heaven.

CHAPTER REVIEW

Chapter 4   Early Peoples of India and China Created Civilizations   (2500 B.C.—1000 B.C.)

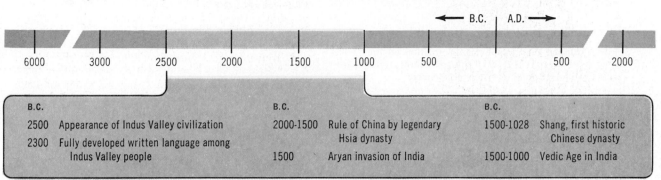

B.C.		B.C.		B.C.	
2500	Appearance of Indus Valley civilization	2000-1500	Rule of China by legendary Hsia dynasty	1500-1028	Shang, first historic Chinese dynasty
2300	Fully developed written language among Indus Valley people	1500	Aryan invasion of India	1500-1000	Vedic Age in India

CHAPTER SUMMARY

The subcontinent of India is divided roughly into four geographical regions: the northern mountains, the Indus-Ganges plain, the Deccan, and a coastal rim of flatlands. Monsoons and oppressive heat are dominant climatic features of India.

About 2500 B.C. an impressive civilization appeared in the Indus Valley. Industry and trade centered on such cities as Harappa and Mohenjo-Daro. Indus Valley people had a written language and a form of animistic religion.

About 1500 B.C. the barbarian Aryans overthrew the Indus Valley civilization. Because the Aryans lacked a written language, knowledge of their early history comes mainly from the Vedas. Originally herdsmen and nomads, the Aryans became farmers and founded small tribal states. Intermarriage with the original Indus Valley people was prohibited, and class divisions began to form during the Vedic Age. At first warriors were the most admirable members of Aryan society, but gradually Brahman priests became more important.

Like India, China was influenced by its geography. China is divided into two main parts, China Proper and the vast semicircle of regions that surrounds it.

Chinese political history is the story of many ruling dynasties. They rose and fell in a recognizable pattern, which was influenced by systems of land ownership and tax collecting and by the rule of warlords.

According to legend, the Hsia dynasty ruled China in ancient times. The first historic dynasty was the Shang, which began along the Yellow River. The Shang introduced simple irrigation and flood control systems that were essential to the prosperity of the valley. Shang craftsmen produced excellent work. A lunar calendar was developed, as was an original written language. Shang religion was a combination of animism and ancestor worship.

QUESTIONS FOR DISCUSSION

1. What problems of city planning did the people of Harappa and Mohenjo-Daro solve? What are some city-planning problems today that were unknown to the inhabitants of these ancient Indian cities?

2. Why did class divisions emerge during the Vedic Age in India? Did class systems arise for similar reasons in other societies? Explain.

3. How was the Chinese attitude toward foreigners, whom they regarded as barbarians, related to Chinese geography? Are the Chinese the only people that have developed such an attitude, or can we find the same thing in the United States and in other countries?

4. Why would a religion based on ancestor worship, emphasizing reverence for older people—such as that of the Chinese during the Shang dynasty—help to create a conservative society?

5. What factors suggest that India must be considered as a continent like Europe rather than as a country like Egypt or Greece? Why is the United States, which is more than double the size of India, not considered to be a continent?

6. Compare and contrast the geography of India with that of China in its effect on the development of civilization.

7. Why do you think the early religion of so many peoples was animistic?

8. Why was it important for kings of the Shang dynasty to have the power to grant land?

PROJECTS

1. Draw a cross section of the Yellow River showing how dikes hold back the river water.

2. Draw a topographical map of India showing plains, plateaus, rivers, and mountains.

3. Make a chart listing the accomplishments of the Indus Valley civilization, the Aryans, and the Shang dynasty.

STUDY IN DEPTH

UNIT ONE

For additional bibliographical information on the books cited in these projects, see the Basic Library (page xviii) and Further Reading on the opposite page.

INDIVIDUAL PROJECTS

1. For thousands of years the Nile River has been vitally important to the people living near it. In recent years the Egyptian government has built the Aswan High Dam to make added use of the Nile. Report on the construction of the Aswan High Dam. Use *Readers' Guide to Periodical Literature* to locate the many magazine articles available on this topic. From the information gathered put a five- to ten-minute newscast on tape to play back to the entire class. This newscast could come directly from the site of construction in Egypt, and sound effects could be added. The main theme should be the great importance of the Nile River, in ancient and modern times.

2. Excavations leading to the exciting discovery of East Africa man have been made by the Leakeys, archeologists in Africa. Both the story of the discovery and the methods of archeologists are vividly portrayed in three articles by L. S. B. Leakey in *National Geographic:* "Finding the World's Earliest Man," September 1960; "Exploring 1,750,000 Years into Man's Past," October 1961; and "Adventures in the Search for Man," January 1963. Give an oral report to the class based on these articles.

3. The life of the Egyptian peasant has remained much the same over the centuries. Prepare an oral or written report on this topic. You can find a description of Egyptian peasant life in Stewart, *The Arab World,* "The Immemorial Village."

4. Study photographs of Egyptian gods and pharaohs and of murals depicting daily life in Egypt. Draw similar pictures for the bulletin board.

5. Write a newspaper story dated February 1923, the official opening of King Tutankhamen's tomb. The article should give the background of the discovery of the tomb and a description of the interior of the burial chamber. The significance of some of the articles found with Tutankhamen should also be discussed. A good source is Desroches-Noblecourt, *National Geographic,* "Tutankhamen's Golden Trove," October 1963. A more detailed account by the same author is the book *Tutankhamen.*

6. Prepare a report on Sumerian culture. Some excellent readings summarizing the achievements of the Sumerians are: Eisen and Filler, *The Human Adventure,* Vol. 1, "The First Case of Juvenile Delinquency" and "Gilgamesh Seeks to Conquer Death." Pictorial accounts can be found in *Life* eds., *The Epic of Man,* "The Beginnings in Sumer"; Cottrell, *The Horizon Book of Lost Worlds,* "Sumer: The Dawn of Civilization."

7. Referring to Landström, *The Ship: An Illustrated History,* give a report on the development and variety of Phoenician ships. Using the same source, draw to scale a number of ship silhouettes of both Phoenician ships and modern ocean-going freighters.

8. Give a report to the class on Jewish beliefs and religious practices. Consult the following readings: Smith, *The Religions of Man,* "Judaism"; Gaer, *How the Great Religions Began,* "Judaism, Religion of Many Prophets"; Champion and Short, *Readings from World Religions,* "Judaism"; *Life* eds., *The World's Great Religions,* "The Law of Judaism"; Bach, *Major Religions of the World,* "Judaism—Religion of a Divine Destiny."

9. Write a report on the origin and effects of monsoons, and draw atmospheric pressure maps of India for the months of October and June. The following questions should be answered in the report: (1) How are the low and high pressure areas created? (2) Why is there a shift in the direction of monsoons? (3) What is the pattern of the monsoon winds in India? (4) How do monsoons affect Indian life? (5) What other areas are influenced by monsoons?

GROUP PROJECTS

1. Working together, three students should give a series of oral reports on the subject of Egyptian hieroglyphics. The first report should explain, generally, what hieroglyphics are. The second should demonstrate how hieroglyphics are read. For this, illustrations can be drawn on the blackboard or on large posters. The final report should relate how Champollion deciphered hieroglyphics from the Rosetta Stone. Read the following: Casson, *Ancient Egypt,* "Works of the Mind," and *Life* eds., *The Epic of Man,* "The 'Divine Words' of Egypt."

2. Organize a panel discussion on the following topic: It is important that young Americans learn about such non-Western countries as India and China. To prepare for the discussion, students should read Isaacs, *Images of Asia: American Views of China and India* (Part Four: "Some Reflections") and newspaper and magazine articles.

3. The Chinese have traditionally revered and respected their elders. Hold a panel discussion on the American reversal of the ancient Chinese tradition— that is, American society's neglect of older people and its glorification of youth.

Further Reading

BIOGRAPHY

Bothwell, Jean, *Flame in the Sky: The Story of the Prophet Elijah*. Vanguard.

Hill, Dorothy B., *Abraham: His Heritage and Ours*. Beacon.

Johnson, E. H., *Piankhy the Great*. Nelson. African king who conquered ancient Egypt.

Lamb, Harold, *Cyrus the Great*. Doubleday.

McGraw, Eloise J., *Pharaoh*. Coward-McCann. Story of Queen Hatshepsut.

Malvern, Gladys, *Behold Your Queen*. McKay. Story of Esther, Persian queen.

———, *The Foreigner*. McKay. Biblical story of Ruth and Naomi.

Shippen, Katherine B., *Moses*. Harper & Row.

NONFICTION

Breasted, James, *History of Egypt*. Scribner.

Casson, Lionel, *Ancient Egypt*. Time-Life.

———, *The Ancient Mariners: Seafarers and Sea Fighters of the Mediterranean in Ancient Times*. Macmillan.

Ceram, C. W., *Gods, Graves, and Scholars*. Knopf.

———, *The Secret of the Hittites*. Knopf.

Chiera, Edward, *They Wrote on Clay: The Babylonian Tablets Speak Today*. Univ. of Chicago.*

Contenau, Georges, *Everyday Life in Babylon and Assyria*. St. Martin's.

Cottrell, Leonard, *The Anvil of Civilization*. New American Library.* History of the early Egyptians, Sumerians, Assyrians, Babylonians, Greeks, and Jews.

———, *Land of the Two Rivers*. World. Ancient Tigris-Euphrates Valley.

———, *Life Under the Pharaohs*. Holt, Rinehart and Winston.

Desroches-Noblecourt, Christiane, *Tutankamen*. New York Graphic Society.

Edwards, I. E., *The Pyramids of Egypt*. Penguin.*

Fairservis, Walter A., Jr., *India*. World.

———, *The Origins of Oriental Civilization*. New American Library.*

Falls, C. B., *The First 3000 Years: Ancient Civilizations of the Tigris, Euphrates and Nile River Valleys, and the Mediterranean Sea*. Viking.

Hawkes, Jacquetta, *Pharaohs of the New Kingdom*. American Heritage.

Honour, Alan, *The Man Who Could Read Stones*. Hawthorn. The story of Champollion.

* Paperback.

Hume, I. N., *Great Moments in Archaeology*. Roy.

Isaacs, Harold R., *Images of Asia: American Views of China and India*. Putnam.*

Jessup, R., *Wonderful World of Archaeology*. Doubleday.

Keating, Rex, *Nubian Twilight*. Harcourt Brace Jovanovich. An account of Upper Egypt and the monuments flooded by the Aswan Dam.

Kramer, Samuel, *History Begins at Sumer*. Doubleday.*

Lauber, Patricia, *All About the Ice Age*. Random House.

Mayer, Josephine, and Tom Prideaux, *Never to Die*. Viking. Ancient Egypt revealed through its art and literature.

Miller, S., *Desert Fighter: The Story of General Yigael Yadin and the Dead Sea Scrolls*. Hawthorn.

Mills, Dorothy, *The Book of the Ancient World*. Putnam.

National Geographic Society, *Everyday Life in Ancient Times*. National Geographic Society.

Ogg, Oscar, *The 26 Letters*. Crowell-Collier. The origin and development of our alphabet.

Orlinsky, Harry M., *Ancient Israel*. Cornell Univ. Press.*

Pfeiffer, John E., and C. S. Coon, *The Search for Early Man*. Harper & Row.

Quennell, Marjorie, and C. H. B. Quennell, *Everyday Life in Prehistoric Times*. Putnam.

Spencer, Cornelia, *Land of the Chinese People*, Lippincott.

Steindorff, George, and K. C. Seele, *When Egypt Ruled the East*. Univ. of Chicago.

Stewart, Desmond, *The Arab World*. Time-Life.

HISTORICAL FICTION

Barringer, D. Moreau, *And the Waters Prevailed*. Dutton. Stone Age Mediterranean setting.

Baumann, Hans, *The Caves of the Great Hunters*. Pantheon. Describes the discovery of Cro-Magnon caves in France.

Coolidge, Olivia E., *Egyptian Adventures*. Houghton Mifflin. Short stories.

Sutcliff, Rosemary, *Warrior Scarlet*. Walck. Prehistoric England.

Treece, Henry, *The Golden Strangers*. Random House. Prehistoric England.

Waltari, Mika T., *The Egyptian*. Putnam. Social life and customs.

White, A. T., *The First Men in the World*. Random House.

Yefremov, Ivan, *Land of Foam*. Houghton Mifflin. Young man's story in ancient Egypt.

THE DEVELOPMENT

Alexander the Great, left, battles the Persians. This damaged mosaic is one of the few classical views of the great conqueror.

OF EAST AND WEST

Greek City-States Once Dominated the Mediterranean

When historians write about world history, they sometimes wish that their readers could read several passages at once so that they might be more aware of events that were happening in different parts of the world at the same time. Since this is not possible, the historian keeps shifting a spotlight from one civilization to another, hoping that the reader, before he is through, will fit the pieces together in his mind.

So far in this book, the spotlight has shifted from Egypt to the Fertile Crescent to India and China. Now it swings back from China to the eastern end of the Mediterranean Sea, not far from the peoples of Egypt, Phoenicia, and Palestine that you have read about. In Greece and Asia Minor and on the nearby islands developed the Greek civilization—one of the greatest the world has ever known.

When the spotlight of history reaches Greece, it lingers there longer than it has on any area so far. At first it is difficult to see why. The Greeks were a quarrelsome people who could never agree among themselves for very long a time. And the Assyrians and Persians were much more efficient empire builders. We take a special interest in the Greeks, however, not because they built great empires, but because they were the first people in history to think and act in ways clearly similar to our own. All the people who share what we call Western civilization owe a great debt

Greek coast along the Aegean Sea

to the Greeks. To the extent that people in other parts of the world have adopted Western civilization, Greek ways of thinking and acting are important to them, too.

Government? The Greeks were the first people to experiment successfully with the idea that citizens might govern themselves. Science? The Greeks were curious about everything; what they observed and wrote down may be regarded as the beginning of scientific thought. Architecture, sculpture, poetry, drama, philosophy, history? Our traditions in these and many other fields have their roots in the rocky soil of ancient Greece.

Greek civilization, like the others you have read about, developed gradually. Distinctive cultures were flourishing on the islands and the mainland about 1500 B.C., the time of the Empire in Egypt and the Indo-Aryan invasions in India. Greece, too, had its invasions. As elsewhere, the invaders absorbed the cultures of the people they conquered and then developed new cultures. By the 500's B.C., they stood on the threshold of that incomparable period of Greek civilization known as the Golden Age. Greek culture, absorbed by the Macedonians and spread by Alexander the Great, had a remarkably profound and long-lasting effect on the rest of the world.

THE CHAPTER SECTIONS:

1. Greek civilization began among island dwellers and invaders (3000–1000 B.C.)

2. Self-government gradually developed in the Greek city-states (1000–500 B.C.)

3. Sparta and Athens created strikingly different ways of life (1000–500 B.C.)

4. Wars with Persia led to Athenian domination of Greece (500–431 B.C.)

5. Alexander the Great spread Greek ideas throughout a vast empire (431–133 B.C.)

1   Greek civilization began among island dwellers and invaders

History is always influenced by geography. In Greece, for instance, the location of cities and areas around them influenced the way they grew and what happened to them. But the history of Greece as a whole was affected by a special and powerful geographic influence: the Mediterranean Sea (see map, page 84).

The sea

The word *mediterranean* means "in the midst of land." The Mediterranean is the world's largest inland sea. It borders the shores of three continents—Europe, Asia, and Africa—and has many good harbors. Islands are numerous and close together, especially at the eastern end. Early in history the Mediterranean Sea became a busy pathway for trade and ideas. As a result, the Mediterranean area was the center of Western civilization for many centuries.

On the European side of the Mediterranean Sea, there are three great peninsulas jutting southward: the Iberian, the Italian, and the Balkan. Notice on the map that each peninsula is cut off from the rest of Europe by a range of mountains: the Pyrenees, the Alps, and the Balkans. Notice also that each of the three peninsulas is separated from the next by a large branch of the Mediterranean Sea.

The Balkan Peninsula is separated from the Italian Peninsula by the Adriatic Sea. On the east it is separated from Asia Minor by the Aegean (ih·JEE·un) Sea. At the southern tip of the Balkan Peninsula lie the smaller peninsulas that form the mainland of Greece.

Look at the many islands of the Aegean Sea, and note how close together they are. Early men could sail from one to another, even in small boats. From Egypt and the Fertile Crescent, people brought knowledge and ideas to these islands, to the mainland of Greece, and to the Aegean shores of Asia Minor.

The land

It may seem surprising that Greece became the home of such an important civilization. Nature was unkind in some ways. Look at the map of

Greece on page 97. Notice how the mainland is cut up and divided by short mountain ranges. These mountains are not as high as many others in the world, but they tended to separate the communities of the mainland and prevent them from developing a sense of unity.

Greek civilization was not a river-valley civilization, for Greece has no rivers worth mentioning. But there was enough good soil, a mild climate, and sufficient rain to grow grain, grapes, and olives in the small valleys and on the lower slopes of the mountains. The foothills of the mountains also provided pasture land for sheep and goats. Greece itself, however, could never produce enough food for its population. The Greeks had to become traders to live. For this purpose, Greek geography was ideal. There were many good harbors on both the mainland and the islands. The long, irregular coastline of the mainland brought every part of it close to the sea. Thus the Greeks became fishermen, sailors, traders, and colonizers.

Cretan civilization

Look once again at the islands of the Aegean and at the long island of Crete to the south. The earliest civilization of the region began on these islands.

People on Crete and the Aegean Islands developed a Neolithic culture before 3000 B.C. In time, they learned to use copper and bronze and to make beautiful pottery. Distinctive ways of life grew up. The culture of the Aegean Islands is usually called Aegean civilization. Traces of this civilization have also been found in Asia Minor, particularly at the city of Troy.

The culture of Crete—related to the Aegean but more highly developed—is called Cretan civilization. According to legend, an early king of Crete was named Minos (MY·nus), so Cretan civilization is sometimes called Minoan. Cretan civilization flourished between 1600 and 1400 B.C. The Cretans were influenced by the great civilizations of nearby Egypt and the Fertile Crescent, but they added ideas of their own.

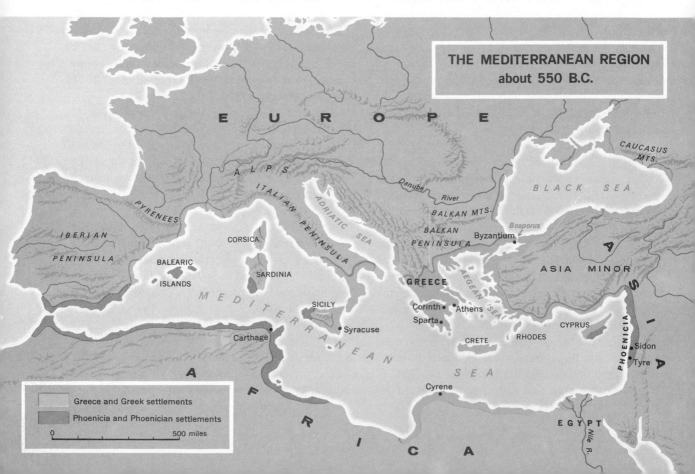

THE MEDITERRANEAN REGION about 550 B.C.

Greece and Greek settlements

Phoenicia and Phoenician settlements

0   500 miles

A large and important city was Knossos (NAHS-us). Remains found there give some indication of the high culture of the Cretans. The royal palace and the homes of the nobles were decorated with colorful frescoes—paintings made on wet plaster walls—and were equipped with running water. Artisans made beautiful carved figures of ivory, stone, gold, silver, and bronze.

The Cretans controlled the Aegean Islands and probably planted some colonies there and in Asia Minor. They were excellent seamen and built ships that were powered by both oars and sails. They traded widely, bringing much of the art and civilization of Egypt and the Fertile Crescent to Crete. The kings of Crete were so confident of their navy that they did not fortify their cities.

Archeologists are not sure what happened to Cretan civilization. Knossos was destroyed sometime around 1400 B.C. The Cretans may have been conquered by people from the Greek mainland. According to another theory, volcanic eruptions on a nearby island caused earthquakes and tidal waves that destroyed the Cretan civilization.

Cretan influence, however, remained strong on the mainland of Greece (indicated by the great number of Cretan art objects found there); its civilization helped lay the foundations for that of classical Greece, about which you will read in this and the following chapter.

Early migrations into Greece

During the period when Aegean and Cretan civilizations were developing, important changes were taking place on the Greek mainland. Beginning about 2500 B.C., two groups of people came into Greece from the north. Like the Hittites, Medes, Persians, and Aryans, these invaders were herdsmen from the grasslands north of the Caucasus Mountains. It is believed that they spoke an Indo-European language that was an early form of Greek.

The Indo-European invaders were organized into clans and tribes. Several related families formed a clan, headed by a chief. A number of clans made up a tribe, with a tribal chief. The clan chiefs formed a council to help in governing. In Greece these wandering herdsmen learned

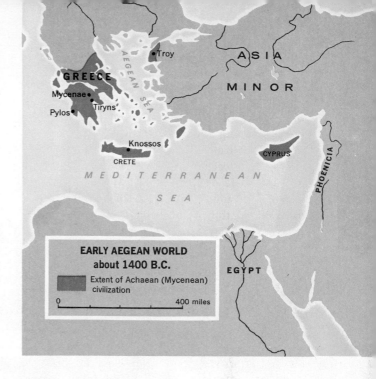

**EARLY AEGEAN WORLD
about 1400 B.C.**

Extent of Achaean (Mycenean) civilization

0 ————————————— 400 miles

how to grow grain, grapes, and olives. They also learned seamanship. We first hear of them in Mediterranean history as skillful and much-feared pirates.

One group, the Ionians, settled in central Greece and on the islands of the Aegean. Later, as you will read, they created the famous city of Athens. The other group, the Achaeans (uh·KEE·unz), swept through the entire Greek mainland.

The Achaeans were the dominant power on the Greek mainland from about 1600 to 1100 B.C. They built fortified cities in the Peloponnesus (pel·uh·puh·NEE·sus), the southern part of Greece. These included Mycenae (my·SEE·nee), Tiryns, and Pylos (see map, this page). Because Mycenae was the first of these settlements to be excavated in modern times, Achaean culture is often called Mycenaean. The Achaeans were a warlike people who carried on raids throughout the eastern Mediterranean area. They may have been the destroyers of Knossos, and were certainly influenced by Cretan civilization. The Achaeans' most famous military exploit was their ten-year siege of Troy—the background of the *Iliad,* about which you will read shortly.

Crete and Mycenae

The islanders of Crete and the Achaeans of the Greek mainland developed different but related cultures. Cretans regarded the bull as sacred, and erected a pair of giant bull's horns, left, at Knossos. Below, Cretan mourners bear offerings of wine, calves, and a funeral boat to the dead. Far right, lions guard the thick-walled Achaean citadel of Mycenae. In the round grave pit were found gold treasures, including the handsome mask at right.

A scientific "detective story." Modern scholars have learned much about the early centuries of Greek history because they were able to decipher the writing used then. The story of how they did so is an example of the detective-story fascination of archeology.

The Cretans developed three kinds of writing: (1) one using pictographs only; (2) "Linear A," in which pictographs were combined with additional characters; and (3) "Linear B," which combined signs from Linear A with still other new characters. Neither the pictographic writing nor Linear A can be read yet, but Linear B has been deciphered. To translate this ancient writing, scholars used cryptography, the art of solving (and creating) codes. The "decoding" of Linear B also shows the cumulative nature of science—how the work of one person furnishes the starting point for the next, and how the final result depends on the contributions of many.

The story begins in 1900, when Sir Arthur Evans, an English archeologist, uncovered the royal palace at Knossos, with a rich store of remains of Cretan civilization. He found examples of the three scripts and gave them their names.

No examples of Linear B were found on the Greek mainland until 1939. Then Carl Blegen, an American, located what seemed to be a palace at the Achaean city of Pylos. By an amazing stroke of luck, his first excavation uncovered the office of the king's tax collector, with 600 clay tablets in Linear B containing (it was later learned) records of taxes.

One of Blegen's students, Emmett L. Bennett, Jr., published the Pylos tablets. Now there were enough examples of Linear B available to allow the use of cryptography. The way was prepared for the genius of Michael Ventris. Ventris was an English architect with a remarkable gift for languages. Archeology, especially the study of Cre-

tan writing, had been his lifetime hobby, begun when he was a very young man. Making brilliant deductions and amassing airtight evidence, Ventris proved that Linear B was a system of phonograms used to write an ancient form of Greek. He announced his discovery in 1952, when he was only thirty years old. (Four years later he was killed in an automobile accident, but his work will long be remembered.)

Archeologists now believe that the Achaeans controlled Crete during the latter years of its flowering. During this period the Cretans may have learned Greek and adapted their Linear A script —used to write their own language—to create Linear B, used for writing the new language.

The Dorians

Sometime around 1100 B.C., a third group of Indo-European invaders, the Dorians, came into Greece from the north. They moved south to the Peloponnesus, where they destroyed Mycenae and other Achaean cities. The Dorian invasions brought to an end the early period of Greek history. During the centuries that followed, the Dorians—like the Achaeans and Ionians before them—gradually settled down in their new home and learned the arts of peace.

CHECKUP

1. Why did the Greeks have to be traders to live?

2. When did Cretan civilization flourish? What were the outstanding characteristics of Cretan civilization?

3. Into what areas of Greece did the Ionians move and settle? the Achaeans? the Dorians?

4. IDENTIFY: Minos, frescoes, clan, tribe, cryptography, Ventris.

5. LOCATE: Balkan Peninsula, Adriatic Sea, Aegean Sea, Crete, Troy, Knossos, Peloponnesus, Mycenae, Tiryns, Pylos.

Cretan Octopus Jar

Crete was the home of one of the earliest island civilizations. Its people traded widely with Egypt and the Fertile Crescent. Among their wares was pottery like the container shown at left. Such jars were light enough to be transported in the small ships of the period. They were also well suited for carrying the olive oil and wine that were so much in demand throughout the Mediterranean world.

Minoan artists created pleasing designs based on objects from their everyday surroundings. Since the sea was important to them, they naturally turned to it for motifs. Here the octopus—which we normally think of as an unattractive fish—has been transformed into a thing of beauty, its eight tentacles curling outward in graceful patterns. In between are small designs that represent seaweed and shells.

② Self-government gradually developed in the Greek city-states

In the years between 2500 and 1100 B.C., as you have read, invaders gained control of the Greek mainland and the islands of the Aegean Sea. They destroyed Aegean and Cretan settlements, but they absorbed much of Aegean and Cretan culture. In the centuries that followed, many changes occurred in Greek society. Gradually, out of the intermingling of peoples and cultures, a new way of life began to emerge.

The city-state

Because of the geography of Greece and their own tribal organization, the early Greeks settled down in city-states. The Greek word for city-state

was *polis*. Originally the word meant a fort, a refuge in time of danger. As a village or city grew up around the fort, *polis* came to mean not only the fort, but also the city and the surrounding region, and the government as well. Our words *police, politics,* and *policy* are all derived from the Greek word *polis*.

Greek city-states differed in many ways, but they all had certain physical features in common: (1) *Small size.* Athens at its greatest extent was smaller than Rhode Island. Sparta, the largest city-state, was only three-fourths the size of Connecticut. (2) *Small population.* The Greeks considered the ideal city-state population to be 5,000 to 10,000 citizens (plus slaves and other non-citizens). Some city-states had more than that, but most of them had fewer. Athens at its peak had about 40,000 citizens. Only two other city-states had even half that many. (3) *The original polis, or fort*. In most city-states the fort stood on an *acropolis,* a hill or mountain, together with temples and other public buildings. (4) *A public meeting place,* where all citizens could gather; sometimes it was the city marketplace.

The Age of Kings

Greek city-states in the period from about 1000 to 800 B.C.—the so-called Age of Kings—had similar forms of government. During these centuries, tribal chiefs became kings and clan chiefs became nobles. The tribe owned the land in common. Local warfare among these small kingdoms, or *monarchies,* was constant. There were few skilled workmen and little commerce.

Regardless of tribe or clan, all the Greeks of the Age of Kings had similar, rather primitive cultures. The knowledge of writing was not widespread, and literary works were sung or recited by poets who wandered from one village to another. This early literature consisted of folk songs, ballads, and epics (long poems describing heroes and great events).

Sometime during the 800's B.C., much of this oral poetry was gathered together and woven into two great epics. According to tradition, they were composed by the blind poet Homer. If it was he, Homer was one of the great poets of all time, for he produced two masterpieces—the *Iliad* and the *Odyssey.*

The Homeric epics were composed against the background of the Trojan war. Legends told how a Trojan prince, Paris, stole Helen, the beautiful wife of a Greek king. The Greeks then sent a great sea expedition against Troy. After years of fighting, Troy was captured by a trick and looted. The *Iliad* describes incidents in the tenth year of the war centering on the Greek hero Achilles and the death of the Trojan prince Hector. The *Odyssey* tells the story of the many adventures of the Greek hero Odysseus on his long journey home from the Trojan war.

Although the *Iliad* and the *Odyssey* supposedly describe the Achaeans of the 1100's B.C., they actually provide the best and richest source of information about the life, customs, and ideals of the Greeks during the period from 1000 to 800 B.C. In fact, the Age of Kings is often referred to as the Homeric Age because of Homer's magnificent descriptions of it. Homer's works also tell us much about Greek religious beliefs of this period.

Religious beliefs. The religion which developed among the Greeks during the Homeric Age was quite different from the religions of the Egyptians, Persians, and Hebrews. The Greeks asked three things of their religion: (1) an explanation for the mysteries of the physical world such as thunder, lightning, and the change of seasons; (2) an explanation of the passions which make a man lose that self-control which the Greeks considered necessary; and (3) a way to gain such benefits as long life, good fortune, and abundant harvests.

The Greeks' ideas of morality were only vaguely connected with their ideas about religion. They did not expect their religion to save them from sin, to bring them spiritual blessings, or to ensure a life after death. There were no commandments. A temple was no more than a shrine which a god might visit occasionally.

Greeks of the Homeric Age were not as concerned as some other peoples about what happened to them after death. Often they cremated, or burned, the dead with only a simple ritual. They thought that with a few exceptions the shades, or spirits, of all men went to a gray and gloomy place called Hades (HAY-deez). It was not a place of reward or punishment. Each shade seemed to continue the same kind of life he had lived on earth.

The Greek gods. In his beliefs about the gods, the Greek was a practical man. He did not want to worship a faraway, all-powerful being, like the Yahweh of the Hebrews or the Ahura-Mazda of the Persians. The Greek wanted gods he could bargain with on almost equal terms. Therefore he thought of his gods as having human weaknesses and wants much like his own, only on a larger

(*continued on page 92*)

Greek Gods and Heroes

Light streaming through the clouds illuminates Mount Olympus, above, which early Greeks believed to be the home of the gods. Three of the most important deities are represented by small bronze figures, above right. Helmeted Athena stands poised; it is likely that she originally held a spear in her right hand. Zeus, seated stiffly, grasps a scepter in his left hand, a thunderbolt in his right. The messenger Hermes is wearing his traditional cloak and winged boots. These gods and others played important roles in Homer's *Iliad* and *Odyssey*. A scene from the latter is shown at right. Odysseus, lashed to the mast of his ship, listens to the song of the sirens (three birds with women's heads). Because their singing lured men to destruction, Odysseus ordered his companions to stop their ears with wax and forcibly restrain him so that they could steer a safe course. The coin at left depicts Homer himself.

90

scale. Greek gods lived not in some remote heaven but on the top of Mount Olympus, a peak in northern Greece (see map, page 97).

To explain their world, the Greeks developed myths—traditional stories about the deeds and misdeeds of gods, goddesses, and heroes. There were many gods, and no one of them was considered much higher than the others. However, Zeus (ZOOS), god of the sky, was sometimes spoken of as the king of the gods or the father of gods and men. Hera was his sister and wife, the protectress of women and marriage. Poseidon (poh·SY·dun), brother of Zeus, was god of the sea—a very important god to the seafaring Greeks. Pluto, another brother, was lord of Hades, the underworld.

Athena, daughter of Zeus, was the goddess of wisdom and womanly virtue, the special protectress of the great city-state of Athens, which was named for her. Aphrodite (af·ruh·DY·tee), another daughter, was goddess of love and beauty. Apollo was god of light, music, and poetry, as well as the symbol of manly beauty. Hermes (HUR·meez), with his winged feet, was the swift messenger of the gods. Eros was the son of Aphrodite. As the god of love, he shot the arrows which brought love to those they pierced. Dionysus (dy·uh·NY·sus) was the god of fertility and wine.

Religious practices. The Greeks believed that if the gods were kept friendly by ceremonies and sacrifices, they would give aid and guidance. At certain sanctuaries called oracles, the gods were believed to speak through priests or priestesses, usually in answer to questions about the future. The most famous oracle was that of Apollo at Delphi.

Because the gods were thought to be pleased by displays of manly strength and courage, the Greeks held athletic contests in their honor. Most famous were the games at Olympia, held every fourth year in honor of Zeus. Olympia was a district in the Peloponnesus where a league of city-states maintained a center at which all Greeks could worship Zeus.

At first the Olympic games consisted only of foot races. Later, jumping, javelin and discus throwing, boxing, wrestling, and horse and chariot racing were added. At the games, winners received only wreaths of wild olive branches, but when they returned home they received many honors and rich gifts. The games were so important that the Greeks used them for dating events; beginning in 776 B.C., they reckoned time in four-year periods called Olympiads.

Rise of the nobles

Toward the end of the Age of Kings, around 800 B.C., nobles (the chief landowners) began taking power from the kings. One reason for the nobles' importance was the fact that they supplied cavalry to the military forces. Another reason was that many farmers lost their land. At this time, population was increasing, although the amount of usable land was not. Small farmers had trouble providing for their families. When a crop failed, the small farmer frequently had to mortgage his land to a noble.

Another development affecting farmers was the increasing number of slaves. Some were imported from Asia Minor. Men who could not pay their debts were sold into slavery. Prisoners of war were enslaved, and the children of slaves were slaves from birth. Free workers found it increasingly difficult to compete with slave labor.

Many unemployed peasants and workers moved to the cities. The nobles encouraged industry and trade to provide jobs for them. A commercial class of merchants grew up, often wealthy but beneath the nobles in social position.

The nobles also encouraged discontented peasants and laborers to leave Greece and go out to establish colonies. Colonization was often well planned, with leaders, laws, and forms of government chosen in advance. Greek settlements, established as city-states like those on the mainland, were planted on islands and shorelines throughout the Black, Aegean, and Mediterranean seas. Among the most important were Byzantium (bih·ZAN·shih·um), on the Bosporus (the narrow strait at the entrance to the Black Sea); Syracuse, on the island of Sicily; and Cyrene, in North Africa (see map, page 84).

The nobles controlled many Greek city-states for roughly 150 years, from about 800 to 650 B.C.

The Gorgon Medusa

The world of the early Greeks was often violent and dangerous, qualities reflected in Greek mythology and art. Among their mythical figures were the Gorgons, three winged sisters with serpent hair, whose glance turned men to stone. The early Greeks believed that the Gorgons could paralyze an enemy and provide protection against magic spells. Thus they placed images of these creatures on armor of all sorts, and on walls, gates, furniture, and costly ornaments.

The Gorgon at right, Medusa, holds her child, the winged horse Pegasus, under her arm. The figure is a painted clay relief that may have decorated an altar. It was discovered at Syracuse, in Sicily, which was founded by Greek colonists from Corinth, a leading commercial city of ancient Greece. The relief dates from the late 700's B.C.; its kneeling position is the conventional way artists then showed running or flying.

The city-states governed by nobles were called *aristocracies*. During this time, however, there were many changes that eventually weakened the nobles' power. Foot soldiers became more important in war so that the nobles' cavalry was not needed. Nobles fought among themselves. Merchants accumulated enough money to hire armies of their own and to fight for power. Great numbers of people became discontented with the rule of the nobles and looked for leaders who could promise better things.

The Age of Tyrants

The men who appeared with the promises were called *tyrants*. To the Greeks, a tyrant was a man who seized power by force rather than inheriting it. Tyrants often came from the merchant class. They always promised to bring peace and prosperity and to defend the poor against the nobles and officials. Many of the tyrants were excellent rulers. Their interest in commerce made them want peace. Hence they put an end to the nobles' struggles for political power, encouraged trade, and passed just laws.

Tyrants ruled many Greek city-states during the period from 650 to 500 B.C. As time went on, some of them became harsh and unjust, giving the word *tyrant* its present meaning of a ruler who exercises absolute power brutally and oppressively.

Self-government and independence

During the period from 1000 to 500 B.C., Greek ideas about government changed. At various times the major power might be held by kings, nobles, or tyrants. But there was constantly developing the idea of *self-government*—the idea that men could and should rule themselves. By the time the Age of Tyrants was ending, this idea had taken root in many city-states.

When cities ousted their tyrants, some restored the old monarchies or aristocracies. Others developed the form of government called a *democracy,* in which all citizens took part. Even in

93

monarchies and aristocracies, a council of citizens checked the power of the rulers.

At this time, there were many influences that might have led the Greeks to unite. All spoke the same language, which they regarded as a common tie; they referred to peoples who did not speak Greek as "barbarians." The ancient Greeks also believed that they were descended from the same ancestor, the hero Hellen, and thus they called themselves Hellenes and their country Hellas. They had a common religion, and great festivals such as the Olympic games brought them together. They joined in common management of certain temples, such as those of Zeus at Olympia and Apollo at Delphi.

However, factors stronger than all the forces of unity kept the Greeks apart. One was geographic—the rugged mountains that separated the small valleys from each other. Another was the fierce spirit of independence that made each Greek proud of his own city-state and distrustful of others. Each city-state had its own laws, calendar, coinage, and system of weights and measures. Citizens loved their city and were willing to give their lives for it.

CHECKUP

1. What things did all Greek city-states have in common?

2. Give a brief description of each of the Greek gods and goddesses discussed in this section.

3. How did the nobles win power in Greece? Why did they lose it? What part did tyrants play in the process?

4. There were many factors which might have led the Greeks to unite. Name them and discuss why the Greek city-states did not unite.

5. IDENTIFY: polis, acropolis, Age of Kings, epics, *Iliad, Odyssey*, aristocracies, tyrant, self-government, democracy.

6. LOCATE: Mount Olympus, Delphi, Olympia, Byzantium, Bosporus, Syracuse, Cyrene.

3   Sparta and Athens created strikingly different ways of life

There were, as you have seen, both similarities and differences among Greek city-states. The wide range of differences that might exist is clearly shown by comparing the two city-states that became the most important, Sparta and Athens.

Totalitarian Sparta

The Dorians, the last and least civilized of the groups that invaded Greece from the north, moved south to the Peloponnesus about 1100 B.C. They conquered and settled the region of Laconia and made the city of Sparta their capital (see map, page 97). The enslaved natives numbered twenty times as many as the Spartans, but the Spartans controlled them by force. The natives and their descendants were always hostile.

In spite of this danger, Sparta seemed almost undefended as compared with most Greek cities. It was built in a valley, not on a hill, and no wall surrounded it. Spartans were boastful people, and one of their leaders said, "A city is well fortified which has a wall of men instead of brick." Nearly everything in Spartan culture was devoted to this militaristic idea—this "wall of men."

Social groups. The population of Sparta was divided into three groups. Most important were the citizens—the descendants of the Dorian invaders—who controlled the government. To support the citizens and their families, the government divided all its land equally among citizens. With each allotment went slaves to work it.

The Spartans called the second group of people by the Greek word that meant "neighbors." They were free, but were not citizens. They lived in the towns and cities, and most of them engaged in commerce and industry. Some "neighbors" became rich, but they could never be citizens.

The lowest group were the conquered people of Laconia who had been enslaved; they were called helots (HEL-uts). Because the Spartans lived in constant fear of a slave revolt, they tried to prevent the helots from developing any leaders. At regular intervals the Spartans killed all helots who were either mentally or physically outstanding. There never was a successful helot rebellion. The brutal system worked, but as you will see, it had its price.

Government. An Assembly of all citizens over thirty years of age elected the officials and voted on major policies. A Council of Elders consisting of two kings and twenty-eight members, all over sixty years of age, proposed the laws and policies on which the Assembly voted. The two kings, elected by the Assembly from two royal families, served as high priests, judges, and army commanders.

Neither the Assembly nor the Council of Elders had much authority. The real rulers of Sparta were five ephors (meaning "overseers") elected by the Assembly. These five men had unlimited power to act as guardians of the state.

Sparta's rulers used their unlimited powers harshly. For example, because the ephors feared that the people would come to love money and luxuries, they prohibited the use of gold and silver. Money was made of iron bars, which were too heavy to carry around and would not buy much. The ephors also feared that contact with outside peoples and ideas would weaken discipline and obedience. Therefore, they did not permit citizens to travel, and foreign visitors were made to feel unwelcome.

The military machine. It has been said that, in enslaving the local population, the Spartans also enslaved themselves. Indeed, citizens did live in a sort of slavery, for their lives were regulated from birth to death. All the rules had a single basic aim: to make every adult male citizen part of an efficient military machine. This army was needed to control the conquered people and to extend Spartan power.

The development of Spartan fighting men, and of women fit to marry them, began at birth. Newborn babies were examined by a group of officials. Any child who seemed weak, unhealthy, or deformed in any way was taken up a mountainside and left to die. At the age of seven, boys were taken to live in barracks, in military groups. They were taught to read and write, but the greater part of their education was military. They were trained in the use of weapons and in the

"Spartan virtues"—courage, strength, endurance, cunning, and devotion to Sparta.

It was a harsh education. To learn endurance, boys wore only a single garment, summer and winter. They never wore shoes. Often they were beaten publicly so that they would learn to bear pain without crying out. To teach them to forage for themselves in wartime, the authorities provided food so coarse and scanty that the boys had to steal food to keep from starving.

Spartan boys were taught to walk in silence with their eyes downcast, and to use the fewest possible words in speaking. (Even today, short, abrupt speech is called laconic speech, from Laconia, the location of Sparta.) Spartans were always taught the glories of Sparta, and how noble it was to die in battle for the fatherland.

The citizen began his military service at the age of twenty, and remained in the army until he was sixty. At thirty, a Spartan was compelled to marry, but he had little family life. He spent most of his time in military training. He ate his meals and spent his leisure time in a military club, which he had to join. He was not allowed to engage in any trade or business, because business activities and love of money were considered bad for military discipline.

Spartan girls, as the future mothers of soldiers, had to be healthy, too. They received strict physical training for strength and endurance. They were also trained in patriotic devotion.

Today there is a name for the Spartan kind of civilization. A system in which the government controls every aspect of the individual's life is called a *totalitarian* system. Totalitarian societies often glorify war, as did Sparta. The regimentation, or strict discipline, of Sparta did lead to efficient government and an almost unconquerable army. But the Spartans produced little in the fields of art, literature, philosophy, science, and inventions.

Democratic Athens

The early history of Athens was quite different from that of Sparta. The peninsula of Attica, on which Athens lies, was settled by the Ionians. Unlike the Dorians, who had to conquer Laconia,

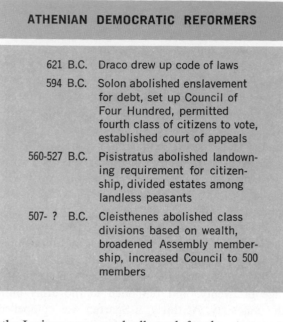

ATHENIAN DEMOCRATIC REFORMERS

621 B.C.	Draco drew up code of laws
594 B.C.	Solon abolished enslavement for debt, set up Council of Four Hundred, permitted fourth class of citizens to vote, established court of appeals
560-527 B.C.	Pisistratus abolished landowning requirement for citizenship, divided estates among landless peasants
507- ? B.C.	Cleisthenes abolished class divisions based on wealth, broadened Assembly membership, increased Council to 500 members

the Ionians came gradually and, for the most part, peacefully. In Athens, then, there was not a military class of conquering invaders imposing its rule upon a conquered people, as in Sparta.

Much of the soil of Attica was rocky and unproductive. The Athenians were compelled to become sea traders to make a living. They built Athens some 6 miles inland to protect it against pirates and constructed Piraeus (py·REE·us) as a special port city for Athens (see map, opposite). Athens itself was a typical polis. The city was built around the rocky, fortified hill of the Acropolis. The entire city was surrounded by a strong wall. It was a place of defense for all of Attica in time of war.

Social groups. As in Sparta, the population of Athens was divided into three groups. First were the citizens. In Athens, as a rule, no one could be a citizen unless both his father and mother were citizens. (Although women were citizens, they could not vote and were regarded legally as minors.) But if only one parent had been a citizen, a person might become one by decree.

Next came the aliens, the non-Athenians, who were called metics. Most metics were merchants or skilled workmen. They were free men but could not own land, take part in government, or

become citizens. Metics, however, paid the same taxes as citizens and moved about freely.

Lowest of all were the slaves. At the time of Athens' greatest glory, more than half the population consisted of metics and slaves. In Athens, as in all of Greece, slaves were considered property, dependent on their master's will. However, an Athenian slave had some legal safeguards. A master could not treat his slaves brutally, nor did he have the power of life and death over them. If the master permitted it, the slave might acquire property and even become wealthy. A slave who was freed—as many were—became a metic.

To the Greeks, slavery was part of the natural order of things, a necessary institution. The philosopher Aristotle believed that there were some people so poor in natural ability that they could be nothing else but slaves.

Early government. The original Ionian invaders of Greece set up an aristocratic form of government in Athens, with the citizens divided into four classes according to the amount of land they owned. Only the three highest classes could vote.

The voters met in an Assembly and elected nine archons from the two highest classes. The archons served terms of one year each. They appointed all officials and made all the laws, but these laws were not written down. The judges, who were always nobles (the first of the four classes), interpreted the law and applied it in each case. Needless to say, the laws always seemed to favor the noble class.

Four reformers. Four men—Draco, Solon, Pisistratus (py·SIS·truh·tus), and Cleisthenes (KLYS·thuh·neez)—transformed Athens into the greatest democracy of the ancient world.

Draco, archon in 621 B.C., is known for the code of laws he drew up. He did not make much change in the existing laws, but had them written down so that everyone could know them. We do not know what the laws were, but we do know that they were harsh and severe. Almost every offense was punished by death. (Today we call a harsh law a Draconian law.)

Conditions in Athens remained unsatisfactory. Nobles and metics became wealthy from trade, but small farmers grew poorer. More and more citizens were being sold into slavery for debt. The poor began to demand that their debts be canceled and that the land be divided equally. Creditors and landowners opposed both of these demands.

In this emergency, Athens came under the control of Solon, a well-known and trusted businessman, who served as archon about 594 B.C. He took a moderate position between debtors and creditors. He canceled the debts of the poor and made laws providing that there should be no more enslavement for debt. He freed those who had been enslaved for nonpayment. Although he refused to divide the land equally, he did set a limit on the amount of land that a noble was permitted to own.

To check the power of the archons, Solon set up a Council of Four Hundred, with members chosen by lot from the three upper classes. The Council proposed the laws voted on by the Assembly. Solon also permitted the fourth class of citizens to vote. To check the power of the judges, he set up a court, composed of large numbers of citizens, to which a citizen could appeal. Because of the wisdom of Solon's reforms, a wise lawmaker today is called a Solon.

Athens still suffered much unrest. The nobles formed political parties, struggled for control of the government, and plotted to take away the political rights of the lower classes.

Then Pisistratus, a wealthy aristocrat and a relative of Solon, created a following among the lower classes. About 560 B.C. he became a tyrant, and remained one off and on until 527 B.C. He aided the growth of democracy by abolishing the requirement that only landowners could be citizens. He lessened opposition by exiling nobles who disagreed with his policies; their estates were seized and divided among landless peasants. Pisistratus also encouraged farmers to grow grapes for wine—a crop more suitable than wheat for Attica's rocky soil—and imported grain from abroad.

About 507 B.C., Cleisthenes came to power in Athens. (Historians have no record of how long he remained in authority.) Although a man of wealth and high social position, he was deeply

ANCIENT GREECE
Major Greek settlements in Asia Minor underlined

interested in the welfare of the common people. He opposed class divisions based on wealth and instead divided citizens into ten tribes based on geographic location. All male citizens over twenty years of age became members of the Assembly. The Council was increased to 500 members, fifty from each tribe, who were drawn by lot from all male citizens over thirty years of age. The Council took over most of the powers and duties formerly held by the archons.

A democratic state. Cleisthenes' reforms made Athens an almost complete democracy. The Assembly of all citizens had full and final power. It chose archons and generals, and could punish them for wrongdoing. Jurors and officeholders were chosen by lot, in keeping with the Athenian belief in the equality and fitness of all citizens for government service. The Council of Five Hundred proposed laws to the Assembly. Even the courts were completely democratic. Each man could plead his own case. There was no judge; the jury of citizens was the entire court. Juries were very large; 501 was a common number. Each juror voted by secret ballot.

For the citizens it was probably the most completely democratic government in history. How-

97

ever, more than half of the residents were not citizens. Many an Athenian was able to give so much of his time and service to his government because he was supported by slaves.

CHECKUP

1. How did Spartans try to prevent slave revolts? How did they discourage love of luxury?

2. What was the aim of the regulations under which Spartans lived? How were Spartans educated to fulfill this aim?

3. Give three examples of the contrast between Spartan and Athenian life. Why do you think these differences came to exist?

4. IDENTIFY: Council of Elders, ephors, totalitarian, metics, archons, Draconian law.

5. LOCATE: Sparta, Laconia, Athens, Attica, Piraeus.

94-102 **4** Wars with Persia led to Athenian domination of Greece

Sparta, Athens, and other Greek city-states established many colonies around the shores of the Aegean, Black, and Mediterranean seas. These colonies, and Greece itself, developed for a long time without interference from the powerful empires of the Near East. But this freedom from interference finally came to an end.

Conflict with Persia

In 546 B.C., Cyrus, the great Persian ruler, conquered Asia Minor and with it the Greek city-states along its shores. He gave these cities the same tolerant rule that the rest of his empire enjoyed. The cities had to pay tribute to Persia, but they were allowed to keep their own local governments, laws, and religion. However, the Greeks in Asia Minor loved independence as much as did their brothers on the mainland. Some of their leaders in Asia Minor denounced the "tyranny" of the Persians and stirred up revolts. The Persians easily put down the uprisings and did not punish the cities severely.

Darius came to the Persian throne in 521 B.C. Not long afterward, he launched an unsuccessful campaign against a fierce tribe from the Danube River region. The failure of this campaign encouraged the Greeks, who realized that the Persians were not invincible. In 499 B.C., revolts occurred in several Greek city-states in Asia Minor, led by the city-state of Miletus and encouraged by aid from Athens. These revolts began the Persian Wars, which were to last until 479 B.C.°

Once again, the Persians were able to put down the Greek revolt easily. Again the penalty was not as severe as might have been expected. However, the incident made Darius determined to control the city-states of the Greek mainland as well as those in Asia Minor.

The first campaign. In 492 B.C., Darius sent a Persian army marching northward up the coast of Asia Minor to cross the Hellespont, one of the two narrow straits separating Asia from Europe. The troops then marched through Thrace (a region between the Aegean and Black seas) and neighboring Macedonia into Greece. A great Persian fleet followed them all the way along the coast (see map, opposite). Although the long march cost the army many men and the fleet was wrecked in a storm off Macedonia, Darius considered the campaign a success.

The second campaign. The next year, 491 B.C., Darius sent ambassadors to several of the Greek city-states, asking the Greeks to accept him as their king. If they would do so and pay tribute, he would allow them to keep their governments, laws, and religion. They were told to send Darius some earth and water as a sign that they acknowledged him as ruler of land and sea.

Although some city-states submitted, others remained neutral. Both Athens and Sparta refused Darius' terms. He then gathered a great army and fleet. In 490 B.C., the Persians sailed directly across the Aegean to Greece. They landed on the

° Some authorities consider the Persian Wars to have lasted until 449 B.C., when an agreement was reached

between the Greeks and the Persians. However, although fighting did take place after 479 B.C., Greece was never again invaded by Persian armies.

98

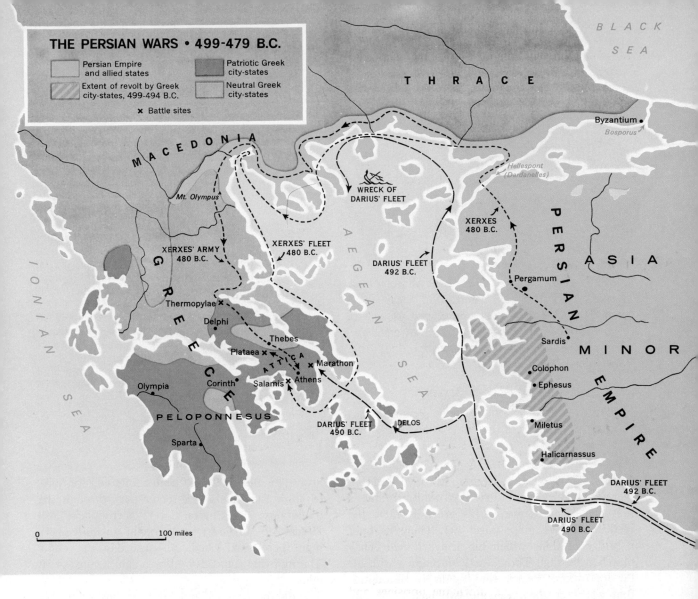

THE PERSIAN WARS • 499-479 B.C.

Persian Empire and allied states

Extent of revolt by Greek city-states, 499-494 B.C.

Patriotic Greek city-states

Neutral Greek city-states

× Battle sites

BLACK SEA

THRACE

Byzantium

Bosporus

MACEDONIA

Mt. Olympus

Hellespont (Dardanelles)

WRECK OF DARIUS' FLEET

XERXES 480 B.C.

PERSIAN

ASIA

XERXES' ARMY 480 B.C.

XERXES' FLEET 480 B.C.

DARIUS' FLEET 492 B.C.

Pergamum

G R E E C E

Thermopylae ×

Delphi

AEGEAN SEA

Sardis

MINOR

IONIAN SEA

Thebes

Plataea ×

Marathon ×

ATTICA

Corinth

Salamis × × Athens

Olympia

PELOPONNESUS

Sparta

EMPIRE

Colophon

Ephesus

Miletus

Halicarnassus

DELOS

DARIUS' FLEET 490 B.C.

DARIUS' FLEET 492 B.C.

DARIUS' FLEET 490 B.C.

0   100 miles

coast of Attica and advanced to the plain of Marathon, not far from Athens.

At Marathon the Persians were met by the Athenian army. Herodotus, the Greek historian, writes that the Athenians had 10,000 troops, but that the Persians outnumbered them ten to one. It is possible that he exaggerated the odds to make the story better. It is certain, however, that the smaller Athenian army attacked bravely, routing the Persians. One report says that the Persians lost 6,000 men and the Athenians 192. The Athenians immediately marched to Athens and prevented the Persian fleet from landing. This

was the end of the second campaign of the Persian Wars.

The third campaign. After being defeated at Marathon, the Persians went home, threatening to come back with a larger army and to conquer all Greece. Soon afterward Darius died, but his son Xerxes began to gather another large army and fleet for still another invasion of the mainland of Greece.

In 480 B.C. came the dreaded news that Xerxes had raised a great army made up of troops from every part of the vast Persian Empire. Herodotus, who loved a good story, wrote that the

99

Greek Water Jug

Beautiful everyday objects were important to the Greeks. The handsome vase pictured here was a common jug used to bring water home from the spring. It is decorated with a lively and amusing scene from the rich Greek mythology that played so vital a part in the daily lives of the ancient Greeks.

The hero Hercules was forced by the king of Mycenae to perform twelve difficult and humiliating tasks. One of them was to bring Cerberus, the many-headed dog who guarded the entrance to Hades, back to earth. Hercules mastered the beast with his bare hands. Here he is shown, at right, holding Cerberus, who bristles with snakes. The terrified king has jumped into a storage vat, left. Hercules is usually shown like this, wearing a lion's skin and carrying a club. He was regarded as the ideal of manly strength. He was also considered the founder of the Olympic games and the first competitor and victor in the contests.

Persian army was so large that when it drank water, whole rivers ran dry. Following his father's first plan, Xerxes moved his army north to the Hellespont (see map, page 99). There he built a bridge of ships which his army crossed. They marched through Thrace and Macedonia with little opposition. We are told, again by Herodotus, that wherever the army ate two meals, the city that had to feed it was utterly ruined.

To advance from northern Greece into central Greece, the Persians had to march through the narrow mountain pass of Thermopylae (thur-MAHP·uh·lee). There they were met by King Leonidas of Sparta and a force of 300 men. Leonidas appealed for reinforcements, but none of the other Greek city-states was ready to send more troops.

Now the Spartan training proved its worth. Leonidas and his men scorned retreat; to surrender would be a disgrace. For three days they held the narrow pass against the entire Persian army. Finally a Greek traitor offered, for pay, to show the Persians a secret pass through the mountains. The Spartans were surrounded. Still refusing to surrender, they fought on until every man there was killed. To this day the name Thermopylae stands for a brave fight against great odds.

With the pass cleared, the Persians were able to move southward. Every city-state was in danger, and there was no army in the field. Athens was in a turmoil. Should its people try to defend the city or abandon it by sailing away in their fleet? The able Greek general Themistocles persuaded the Athenians to abandon their city and sail to the island of Salamis. The Persians captured Athens and destroyed the walls and most of the city.

Now Themistocles used wily strategy. Pretending to be a traitor, he sent word to Xerxes, advising him to attack the Athenians with his fleet in the narrow waters between Salamis and the coast. Xerxes ordered the attack and set up his throne on a high coastal point to watch the defeat of the Athenian fleet. To his horror he saw the small Greek ships outmaneuver the larger Persian ships, ramming and sinking many of them.

Xerxes ordered his fleet to abandon the attack. Just then he received news of revolts in the Persian Empire. Fearing that the Athenian fleet would sail to the Hellespont and destroy his bridge of ships, he ordered most of his army to withdraw, leaving only part of it behind with orders to conquer Greece. In the following year, 479 B.C., this army was defeated by a combined Greek army at Plataea, northwest of Athens.

Importance of the Greek victories

The immediate results of the Persian Wars do not seem like a great victory for Greece. Athens and much of the rest of Greece were ruined. The Greek cities of Asia Minor were free for a short time, but soon fell under Persian rule again. The Persian Empire remained powerful, and its rulers continued to meddle in Greek affairs. It became a fixed Persian policy to try to prevent any unity in Greece. The Greek city-states regarded the Persians as their traditional enemies.

From a long-range viewpoint, however, the battles of Marathon, Salamis, and Plataea are considered important and decisive in world history. The wars were a struggle between autocratic civilization, headed by a king-god with absolute powers, and Greek city-state civilization, with governments of free citizens. Persian defeat meant that the Greeks could continue to develop their culture and pass it on to Western civilization.

Athens as leader

Although badly damaged, Athens was still the leading city of Greece. The city was rebuilt, with temples and public buildings even more magnificent than before. The Athenians also rebuilt the city walls and constructed the so-called Long Walls to protect the route to Piraeus.

Claiming to be the saviors of Greek civilization, the Athenians undertook to unite all Greece. Fear of further Persian attempts at conquest made unity seem necessary. Sparta, however, wanted unity under its own leadership. Too proud to use diplomacy, the Spartans tried conquest. Now the weakness of their slave system showed up. Fear of helot revolts kept them from sending expeditions far from home. Even their strong army could not extend Spartan power much beyond the Peloponnesus.

Still determined to unify Greece, the Athenians used diplomacy. In this way they were able to persuade some 200 city-states to form a system of alliances called the Delian League. The agreement gave each city-state one vote. Each contributed either ships or money. Funds were deposited on the island of Delos (hence the name Delian). No city-state could withdraw from the league without unanimous consent. Athens was given power to decide how many ships or how much money each should contribute. In time, Athens gained complete control of the Delian League, which became an Athenian Empire.

Pericles, Athenian statesman

It was at this time that Pericles (PER·uh·kleez), the greatest of all Athenian leaders, rose to prominence in the city. Pericles was a dignified, reserved aristocrat, and one on the best orators in a land of good orators. His ability and reputation for honesty were so great that he was chosen general for sixteen successive years. Even when he did not hold this official position, he was the most influential speaker in the Assembly.

Pericles was the real leader of Athens for over thirty years, from 461 to 429 B.C., the time of its greatest power and prosperity. This period of Athenian history is called the Age of Pericles. Because the cultural achievements of this era are of great importance, they are treated separately in the next chapter. The rest of this chapter deals with political events of the Age of Pericles and the years that followed.

Pericles continued Athenian control of the Delian League and increased the empire by forcing more city-states to join. He moved the league treasury from Delos to Athens, using the money openly for Athenian purposes. Revolts against these policies were crushed; land was taken from the rebels and given to Athenians, who were established on it as colonists.

Athens wanted to weaken its commercial rival, Corinth, and so made alliances with several nearby city-states. To defend itself against Athenian ambition, Corinth became an ally of Sparta, which feared that Athens planned to take the northern Peloponnesus. The long rivalry between Athens and Sparta increased. You can see that Athens' policies could end in only one of two ways: either Athens would control all of Greece, or there would be a great war.

CHECKUP

1. Why are the battles of Marathon, Salamis, and Plataea considered decisive in the history of the world?

2. What was the Delian League? How did Athens use it?

3. What qualities gave Pericles his great hold over the Athenians?

4. How did the Persian Wars show both the strength and the weakness of Greece?

5. LOCATE: Hellespont, Thrace, Macedonia, Thermopylae, Delos, Corinth.

5 Alexander the Great spread Greek ideas throughout a vast empire

Athens and all of Greece were politically unsettled during the Age of Pericles. Athens had turned the Delian League into an Athenian Empire, and had then come into conflict with Corinth and Sparta. City-state rivalries led to a devastating war, which lasted from 431 to 404 B.C. It involved the whole Greek world (and Persia as well) and left Greece in ruins. This war is called the Peloponnesian War because most of the fighting took place in the Peloponnesus.

The Peloponnesian War

The responsibility for the Peloponnesian War was shared mainly by Athens and Sparta. There was, of course, economic and commercial rivalry among a number of city-states. But there was also a long-standing social and cultural rivalry between Athens and Sparta. Athens was progressive, commercial, and culturally advanced. Sparta was conservative, agricultural, and culturally backward. Athenians regarded Spartans as boors; Spartans looked upon Athenians as money-mad.

Actual hostilities were started by the Spartans, but they had been provoked into action by the Athenians. Neither side made much effort to avoid war. Thucydides (thoo·SID·uh·deez), the great Greek historian of the Peloponnesian War, wrote: "The Peloponnesus and Athens were both full of young men whose inexperience made them eager to take up arms."

The Spartans invaded Attica, destroying fields and villages. The Athenian army and the entire population withdrew behind the Long Walls and the fortifications of Athens. The Spartans and their allies could not starve them out because Athens controlled the sea. However, a great plague broke out among the Athenians. Many people died, including Pericles himself.

After that, nothing went well for the Athenians. The Spartans got help from Persia. Several Athenian fleets were lost and several armies defeated. Finally Athens surrendered in 404 B.C.

Greek disunity

All Greece lived under Spartan rule between 404 and 371 B.C. The Spartans proved even more harsh and selfish than the Athenians had been with the Delian League. Furthermore, Sparta lacked the men, money, and sea power to be an effective ruler. Conditions were ripe for another civil war. The city-state of Thebes formed a league against Sparta. Aided by Athens and other city-states, and by Persia, Thebes defeated Sparta and controlled Greece from 371 to 362 B.C. But Theban rule was not successful, and the ruinous wars continued.

All the city-states realized that unity was necessary, but each of the leaders wanted to dominate any union that was formed. Each promised democratic rule, but practiced tyranny. Some Greeks believed that union could come only under a foreign power, and Persia seemed the logical choice.

102

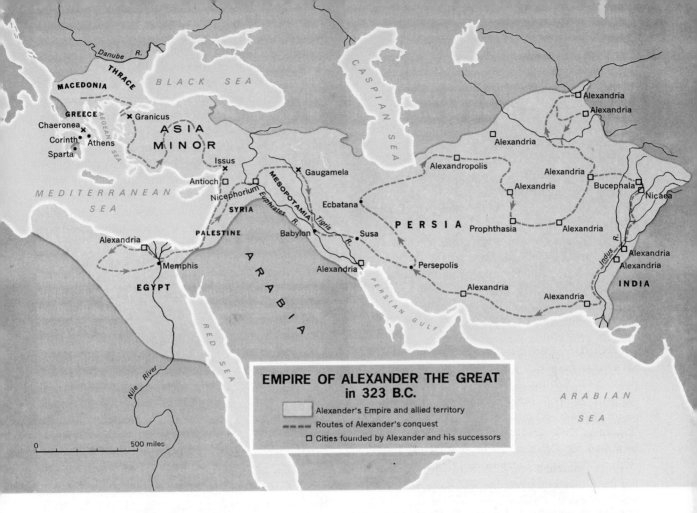

EMPIRE OF ALEXANDER THE GREAT in 323 B.C.

Alexander's Empire and allied territory

--- Routes of Alexander's conquest

□ Cities founded by Alexander and his successors

0   500 miles

However, the Persians had interfered in Greek affairs again and again to prevent unity, and most Greeks still distrusted them.

Philip of Macedon

The power that unified Greece came from an unexpected direction. Look again at the map on page 97. North of Greece is a mountainous land called Macedonia. In the 300's B.C., it was inhabited by a hardy, warlike people, closely related to the Greeks but less civilized. The Macedonians lived in small villages, each ruled by a powerful noble. Macedonia had a king, but his power depended on his own ability and the help of the nobles.

In 359 B.C., a remarkable young man known as Philip of Macedon came to the Macedonian throne. In his youth he had been taken as a captive hostage to Thebes, where he spent three years. During that time, Philip came to admire Greek ways of living and learned the art of war from the great Theban general, Epaminondas.

Philip was determined to be a strong king and to control the unruly Macedonian nobles and people. Instead of depending on the nobles to supply men for an army, he built up the first regular army in Macedonian history. The Macedonian phalanx (FAY-langks)—a body of troops moving in close, deep ranks—became the finest fighting unit in the world of Philip's time.

The conquest of Greece

After unifying his own kingdom, Philip extended his power by conquering surrounding peoples. He increased his control of the northern Aegean coast by taking some Greek towns which Athens claimed as colonies. Then he turned south and began the task of unifying the Greek city-states under his rule.

Opinion about Philip was divided in Greece. In every city-state, some men looked upon him as a savior who could bring unity to Greece. Others opposed him as a menace to liberty. In Athens the opposition was led by Demosthenes (dih·MAHS·thuh·neez), one of the greatest orators of all Athenian history.

Demosthenes used all his great powers of oratory to arouse the Athenians to the danger from Philip of Macedon. He attacked Philip bitterly in a series of speeches to the Assembly and tried to get Athens to lead the Greeks once more in a fight for liberty. (Today a speech which is a violent attack is called a philippic, from these speeches of Demosthenes.) But times had changed in Athens since the Age of Pericles. Citizens had become more interested in money-making and pleasure than in serving the city. In spite of his great oratory, Demosthenes failed to arouse the Athenians. There was no united opposition to Philip of Macedon.

Philip marched south with his army, conquering the Greek cities one by one. Some resisted and were defeated. Others were turned over to him by traitors. As he said: "No fortress is inaccessible if one can only introduce within it a mule laden with gold." When the Athenians did decide to fight, it was too late. Philip defeated them at the battle of Chaeronea in 338 B.C. (see map, page 103) and became master of Greece.

Greek unity was still not complete. Philip planned to make himself king of Greece, allowing some local self-government. He wanted Greek soldiers to join Macedonian troops in an invasion of Persia. In 336 B.C., however, before Philip could carry out his ideas, he was assassinated. His son and successor, Alexander, was only twenty.

Alexander the Great

It did not seem likely that young Alexander would be able to carry out Philip's plans. But those who thought so were wrong. The son proved to be even more remarkable than the father. History knows him as Alexander the Great.

Alexander was very much like his father, but the two could never agree, and quarreled bitterly. However, Philip did everything to give his son the best training and education possible. Alexander received his military training in the Macedonian army. Like Greek boys, he was drilled in gymnastics until he was a splendid athlete. To train Alexander's mind, Philip sent for Aristotle, the greatest living Greek philosopher, to be his tutor. Alexander's fine education made him a lifelong admirer of Greek culture.

When the time came for Alexander to command the army, he proved to be an even better general than his father. His campaigns are considered among the greatest in history. Some of his battles were such masterpieces of tactics that they are still studied as models by army officers. He was strong and brave to the point of rashness. His dramatic acts in battle so captured the imagination of his troops that they were willing to follow him anywhere.

Alexander began his military career by putting down rebellions in the Greek city-states and making himself master of Greece. Then he marched into Asia Minor and defeated the Persians, first at the battle of Granicus and a year later at Issus. Having conquered all of Asia Minor, he then marched on to take Syria. Next he invaded Egypt, meeting almost no resistance. From Egypt he moved into Mesopotamia, defeating another Persian army at Gaugamela, and in 331 B.C. captured Babylon. He then marched eastward and took control of the entire Persian Empire (see map, page 103).

Alexander now ruled a huge territory, but he was still not satisfied. Beyond Persia lay India, the end of the world as it was then known to the peoples around the Mediterranean Sea. For four years he led his army eastward. He met little resistance in going as far as the Indus River. From there he wanted to march on to the Ganges River, and so control the whole of the vast plain of northern India. But his long-suffering army had finally had enough fighting and forced him to turn around and go back.

Alexander the Great lived on as a legendary hero for centuries, becoming absorbed into the cultures of many different periods and places. In the Persian painting above, he appears as a Mongol horseman. An early Russian manuscript, right, pictured him on a throne before a windowed turret. The Indian work below was painted in the 1500's. Here Alexander, turbaned and bearded, is being lowered into the sea in a glass barrel; according to legend, he asked to have the barrel made so he could observe underwater life.

At Babylon, in the midst of a great victory celebration in 323 B.C., Alexander became ill. In a few days he was dead of a fever. In thirteen years he had conquered almost all of the world known to him.

Alexander's plan. Alexander the Great is famous as a general and conqueror, but he was even greater as a statesman. His plan was nothing less than a world empire, with himself at the head. He wanted to unite all peoples into one, combining the best of the cultures of Greece, Egypt, the Fertile Crescent, and India. Even in his short lifetime he was able to change the world. It is difficult to imagine what he might have done had he lived to old age.

Alexander planned to create his united world empire in two ways. First, he wanted to found new cities and rebuild old ones as cultural centers of his empire. He actually established more than seventy such cities, many of them named Alexandria in his honor. Groups of Greeks and Macedonians settled in each one. Alexandria, in Egypt, was founded by Alexander nearly 2,300 years ago.

Alexander's second aim was to create a united people. He did everything he could to encourage intermarriages among Macedonians, Greeks, and Egyptians and other peoples of the Near East. He himself married Roxana, the daughter of the Persian king, and at times wore the robes of a Persian ruler. He took men of all religions into his army or used them as officials in his government. He established a uniform money system for the whole empire to promote prosperity and expand trade.

When Alexander died, his plans for a world empire had not been completed. He left no successor, and the empire soon broke apart.

Greece after Alexander's death

After Alexander's death, generals of his armies seized power and ruled as kings. His empire was divided into three parts: (1) Macedonia, ruled by Antigonus (an·TIG·uh·nus); (2) Egypt and Palestine, ruled by Ptolemy (TAHL·uh·mee); and (3) the Asiatic possessions—except for Palestine—ruled by Seleucus (sih·LOO·kus). Each general established a dynasty. In Greece, however, attempts to form a dynasty failed.

Some Greek city-states tried an interesting experiment during this period. Attempting to solve the problem of union without giving up their independence completely, they formed two leagues of city-states, the Achaean League and the Aetolian League. Each league had a central government, including a congress in which each member state was represented. The congress was given power to tax each state and to raise an army. The individual states kept all other powers. Thus there was much local self-government, but there was also a common government for common problems. This system—with authority shared by a central government and individual states—has become known as the *federal* principle of government.

The two Greek leagues did not last long. It was impossible to unite Greece without the two most powerful city-states, and neither Athens nor Sparta would join. However, the federal principle of these two leagues was studied in later centuries and provided an example for other federal systems of government.

Although Alexander's work was unfinished when he died, and his empire fell apart soon afterward, his influence was enormous. His new cities preserved and spread Greek civilization long after his death. The peoples of the Mediterranean world were more unified than ever before. So great was his influence that the period for two centuries after his death is often called the Age of Alexander.

CHECKUP

1. What kinds of rivalry led to the Peloponnesian War?
2. What was Alexander's plan of empire? How did he intend to create it?
3. Describe the federal system of government. Why did it fail in Greece?
4. IDENTIFY: Philip of Macedon, Epaminondas, phalanx, Demosthenes, philippic, Antigonus, Ptolemy, Seleucus.
5. LOCATE: Thebes, Chaeronea, Granicus, Issus, Gaugamela, Alexandria (Egypt).

CHAPTER REVIEW

Chapter 5   Greek City-States Once Dominated the Mediterranean   (3000 B.C.—133 B.C.)

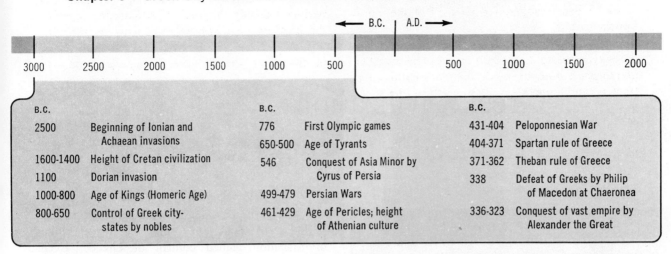

B.C.		B.C.		B.C.	
2500	Beginning of Ionian and Achaean invasions	776	First Olympic games	431-404	Peloponnesian War
1600-1400	Height of Cretan civilization	650-500	Age of Tyrants	404-371	Spartan rule of Greece
1100	Dorian invasion	546	Conquest of Asia Minor by Cyrus of Persia	371-362	Theban rule of Greece
1000-800	Age of Kings (Homeric Age)	499-479	Persian Wars	338	Defeat of Greeks by Philip of Macedon at Chaeronea
800-650	Control of Greek city-states by nobles	461-429	Age of Pericles; height of Athenian culture	336-323	Conquest of vast empire by Alexander the Great

CHAPTER SUMMARY

The earliest civilization of the Greek islands developed on Crete. Cretans controlled a large empire in which ships and overseas trade played an important role. They were excellent seamen and traded widely.

Meanwhile, Indo-European invaders had come into the Greek mainland from the north. The Ionians settled in central Greece and on the Aegean Islands, the Achaeans in the Peloponnesus. Later the Dorians moved south and destroyed the Achaean cities.

The Greeks settled in city-states. During the Age of Kings, most of the city-states had some form of monarchy. We have learned much about this period from the *Iliad* and the *Odyssey*, which were composed then. Later, nobles seized power from the kings and city-states were organized as aristocracies. The nobles encouraged industry and trade and stimulated Greek colonization. They, too, however, gradually lost power, and for several decades Greek city-states were ruled by usurpers known as tyrants.

At the same time the idea of self-government was becoming firmly established. Although the Greeks had much in common, geographic factors and a fierce spirit of independence prevented them from uniting.

Sparta and Athens illustrate the extremes of city-state culture. Sparta developed a totalitarian government and created an efficient military machine, but little else. Athens, under four great reformers, became probably the most complete democracy in history for those who were citizens.

Greek independence was threatened by Persian invasions, but Greek forces were finally victorious in the Persian Wars. Fear of further Persian attacks made unity seem necessary. Athens established the Delian League, which became an Athenian Empire.

Intense city-state rivalries disturbed Greece for many years. After the Peloponnesian War, Sparta and then Thebes controlled Greece. The country was not united, however, until Philip of Macedon defeated the Greeks. His son, Alexander the Great, went on to conquer a vast empire. Although he wanted to unite all its peoples, he died before he could carry out his plan.

QUESTIONS FOR DISCUSSION

1. What advantages might the Greeks have enjoyed if they had succeeded in uniting?

2. In Sparta, military training was of supreme importance. Do you think it helps a young man's character development today for him to serve in the armed forces? Justify your answer.

3. Modern Olympic games have become occasions for intense international competition. Explain whether you think this is beneficial.

4. A feature of Athenian democracy was the practice of choosing government officials by lot from all the citizens. Would you advocate this system today?

PROJECTS

1. Write four short paragraphs describing Athenian government from the viewpoint of (1) a citizen, (2) a metic, (3) a slave, and (4) a Spartan.

2. Write an imaginary diary of a day in the life of a youth in Sparta.

3. Draw a map of Greece and Asia Minor during the Persian Wars showing the routes of the Persians.

4. Draw a map of the empire of Alexander the Great showing the routes of his conquests.

Greek Civilization
Produced a Lasting Heritage

Greek civilization was at its height during the period from about 500 to 338 B.C., when Philip of Macedon gained control of Greece. Even though the Greeks made important contributions to democratic thought during this period, called the Golden Age, their political history was not otherwise impressive. It was a record of wars against the Persians, of wranglings among the city-states under the Delian League, and of actual fighting among them in the Peloponnesian War. Although Alexander later made great conquests and had a noble idea of world unity, his empire fell apart into many different political divisions after his death.

The greatness of Greek civilization during this time is to be found in its love of beauty and its enthusiasm for ideas; that is, in its art, architecture, literature, and thought. You may remember a parallel from your reading. It was not the political history of the Hebrews that placed them among the great peoples of history. They were great because of their religious thought.

One often hears of the "lasting heritage" of the Greeks. The word *heritage* means "that which we inherit," or that which is handed down from preceding generations. Our heritage from the Golden Age of Greece is artistic and intellectual, not material. Like that from the Hebrews, it is a heritage of ideas, not of things.

How was it possible for the Greeks, living on a

Bronze head of the goddess Athena

rocky peninsula, isolated both from each other and from the rest of the world, to develop the remarkable works that have come down to us?

Many city-states contributed to Greek art, architecture, literature, and thought, although some, such as Sparta, cared little for the fine arts or learning. But the greatest achievements were made in Athens during the Age of Pericles—the peak of the Golden Age.

1 In their daily lives, Athenians gave time to public affairs

Under the four reformers of the 600's and 500's B.C., as you have read, Athens adopted a number of democratic political reforms. Further progress toward political democracy was made under Pericles. You will recall that it was he who led Athens at the time of the Delian League.

Reforms under Pericles

During the Age of Pericles, from 461 to 429 B.C., Athens began for the first time to pay public officials, including jury members, for their services. Now all citizens could afford to take part in the government. The Assembly met frequently, forty times a year, and gained the right to check the accounts of outgoing officials. Generals were the only elected officials; all others, including jury members, were chosen by lot. In this way, every citizen had the right to help determine policies and had an equal chance to be chosen to help administer the government.

When thinking of Athenian democracy, however, it is important to remember its limitations. Democracy was only for the citizens. The metics, you recall, were free men but not citizens, and there were many slaves.

Farming

Farming was the most honored occupation for an Athenian citizen. More than half of all citizens were farmers, including many small farmers who usually owned the land they worked. Unlike small farmers and peasants in most other societies, they could vote and hold public office.

The soil of Attica was poor, and fields had to lie fallow, or unplanted, every second year to regain fertility. To make matters worse, there was little level land for raising grain. Thus farmers concentrated instead on cultivating olives, grapes, and figs on terraced hillsides. Terracing means that they created small flat plots of land by building low walls around the hillsides and filling the space behind them with soil. A terraced hill seems to go up in a series of steps. Athens exported olive oil and wine, and imported from two thirds to three fourths of the grain that was necessary to feed its people.

The principal domestic animals were sheep and goats. Both furnished milk for making cheese. In addition, sheep were valued for their wool and meat. However, Athenians did not eat much meat. Fish and cheese were more common in their diet.

Manufacturing and trade

Athenian manufacturing was carried on in small shops. The largest business establishment was a shield factory, owned by a metic, which employed 120 men. There was no other shop more than half as big; a shop with twenty workers was considered a large one. Many craftsmen worked in their own homes; members of the family labored side by side with slaves and free employees. They worked only to fill actual orders, and usually the customer supplied the raw materials. The quality of the work was extraordinarily high. Today, Athenian vases and household utensils are highly valued for their simple grace and beauty. Yet most of them were made not by famous artists but by ordinary artisans.

Foreign trade formed an extremely important part of the Athenian economy. The need to increase the food supply influenced all government policy. It made foreign trade a necessity and led to the building of the Athenian fleet and the establishment of colonies. Athenian ships went everywhere in the Mediterranean world, from the Black Sea in the east to Spain in the west. The ships sailed out with olive oil, wine, and Athenian manufactured goods, and brought back the all-important grain and raw materials that could not be provided at home.

Homes and streets

As you will read later, the Athenians built beautiful temples and other public buildings. There was a remarkable contrast between these structures and Athenian homes. The Athenian ideal was to spend money on buildings to beautify and benefit the whole community, not on private homes. Then, too, life in Athens was a man's life, and men spent little time in their homes.

Houses were simple and plain, built close to the street, and usually one story high. The walls were made of sun-dried brick. The street wall was unbroken except for a door which led into an open court. From the court, doors opened into the living room, dining room, bedrooms, storerooms, and kitchen. Little care was given to the appearance of the house itself, although its contents were usually beautiful.

Athenian homes were not luxurious. The only heat came from braziers, or open pans that held burning coals. Light was furnished by dim lamps that burned olive oil. There was no plumbing and no running water. Water was carried from wells or springs in large jars.

The streets showed another contrast in Athenian life. Most streets were narrow and crooked. They were usually dirty, too, because people threw rubbish and garbage into them. There were no sidewalks, no sewage system, no garbage collection, no street cleaning, and no paving.

Family life

Athenians considered marriage a necessary institution, but there was little sentiment or romance

connected with it. Its main purpose was the bearing and rearing of children. Marriages were always arranged by the parents. Often the bride and groom did not see each other until the day of the wedding. A girl married early, at thirteen or fourteen. Usually her husband was at least twice her age.

A married woman had few legal rights. She could not make a contract or bring a suit in court. When a man died, his wife did not inherit his property. Solon's laws included one which said that nothing done under the influence of a woman had any standing in a court.

In social life, too, women were considered inferior to men. Their duty was to manage the household and the slaves and see to the upbringing of the children. They rarely appeared in public, and then only by permission of their husbands. If there was a banquet or entertainment in the home, the wife withdrew to another part of the house.

In a well-to-do household, the Athenian mother, aided by a woman slave, took care of both boys and girls until they were six. At the age of six a boy was placed in the care of a male slave called a pedagogue (PED·uh·gahg), who taught him manners and went everywhere with him, including school. Girls stayed in the home, rarely going outside, and then only when accompanied by their parents. They were trained at home in household management, but received no other schooling.

Social life and recreation

The Greeks had an almost indifferent attitude toward making a living. Wealth was not considered to be a source of power or prestige, and Athenians did not labor to accumulate great sums of money. They worked hard enough to enjoy a reasonable income, but intellectual and physical excellence were more important to them than material comfort. They spent most of their time engaging in politics, gossip in the marketplace, conversations with friends, and intellectual and artistic activities.

Wealthy men led the most interesting lives, but others also lived well. Skilled workers had a good deal of leisure time. There was little unemployment and workers could be quite independent, taking time off for public business or athletic events. Unskilled workers, however, toiled long hours at monotonous work, with little time off.

Education

The Athenians realized that if their democracy was to be successful, every citizen had to be educated. There were many schools that charged only small fees. Almost all boys between the ages of six and fourteen attended elementary schools.

Three main subjects were taught in these elementary schools: grammar, music, and gymnastics. Grammar included reading, writing, and arithmetic. Boys learned to write with a stylus on a wooden tablet covered with wax. Much of their reading consisted of traditional Greek literature such as Homer's *Iliad* and *Odyssey*. Boys were taught to sing and to play musical instruments.

The Athenian ideal was a sound mind in a healthy body. While grammar and music developed the mind and the emotions, gymnastics developed the body. In open fields at the edge of the city, boys practiced running, jumping, boxing, and throwing the discus and the javelin.

At fourteen, when they had finished elementary education, boys of poor families were apprenticed to learn a trade. Parents who could afford to do so sent their sons to higher schools, which were more expensive than elementary schools. These schools were conducted by men who called themselves Sophists, from the Greek word *sophos,* meaning "wise." Here the boys studied poetry, government, ethics, geometry, astronomy, and rhetoric (RET-uh·rik). Rhetoric was the study of oratory and debating, so important in Greek life.

Many of the Sophists were excellent teachers and truly wise men. However, they were disliked by some Greeks, who considered it deceitful to argue about fundamental issues. To them, truth was not something to be reached by debate, but was the result of calm reasoning. Our word *sophistry* is derived from the Sophists' reputation for tricky argumentation, and means reasoning that sounds good but is basically deceptive.

When a boy was eighteen, he received a year of military training. At nineteen, in an impressive public ceremony, he became a full citizen. The highest public officials of the city presented him with his shield and spear, the symbols of citizenship. He took a solemn oath, swearing, among other things, to obey the laws and magistrates and defend them from attack, not to disgrace his arms or to forsake his comrades, and to leave his country better than he found it. After becoming a citizen, a young man served in the army or navy for a year.

CHECKUP

1. What did Athenian homes look like? Why were they not more elaborate?
2. Explain the Greek attitude toward women as it was shown in (a) marriage customs; (b) law; (c) social life; (d) education.
3. Compare your education with that of an Athenian boy. In what respects do you consider your education better? In what ways do you think his was better?
4. IDENTIFY: pedagogue, grammar, Sophists, rhetoric, sophistry.

2 The art of Greece represented the ideals of Greek civilization

The daily lives of Athenian citizens, as you have seen, combined work, public duties, and recreation. Citizens in other Greek city-states lived in much the same way. These ways of life were those of thousands of men, living from generation to generation. As in all times and places, however, certain men stood out from their fellows; in Athens they were almost without exception leaders in art, writing, and thought. These men, and others like

them elsewhere in Greece, helped create the Golden Age of Greek civilization—a shining light in all history.

Architecture

The city of Athens, you will remember, was destroyed in 480 B.C. by the Persian army of Xerxes. When the Persians were driven off by Themistocles, Athenians began rebuilding their

111

city, completing it during the thirty-two years of Pericles' leadership. They showed their love of Athens, and their pride in it, by erecting many beautiful public buildings: temples, gymnasiums, and theaters. They decorated buildings and all public places with their finest works of art, especially sculpture. The Athenians made beautiful art a part of their daily life.

The Acropolis, the hill where the original polis was located, was the scene of special artistic creations. A magnificent gate stood at the entrance to the path up the hill. Inside the gate towered a huge bronze statue of the goddess Athena, 70 feet high. As the special protectress of Athens, she was armed with shield and spear.

On top of the Acropolis stood the Parthenon, a temple in honor of Athena. Begun in 447 B.C., it is considered the finest example of Greek architecture. The beauty of the Parthenon lay not in its great size but in its pleasing proportions—the relation of length to width, and of both to height. A Greek ideal was the Golden Mean: "Nothing in excess, and everything in proportion."

At each end of the Parthenon was a pediment, or gable, adorned with sculptured figures. Like much Greek sculpture, these figures were painted in various bright colors. A series of columns, the colonnade, encircled the building. Many works of sculpture stood outside the columns. The temple itself had doors but no windows. Greek temples were shrines rather than meeting places for worshipers. The inside was seldom decorated as much as the outside. Within the Parthenon, though, stood another large statue of Athena; its surface was of carved ivory, and there were draperies of gold decorated with jewels.

Painting

The best-preserved Greek paintings are those used to decorate vases. Vase painters illustrated everyday life as well as myths. They delighted in showing graceful and natural movements. The best of them could depict light and shade on the pottery, and could show contours and depth in figures and draperies.

Other Greek painters decorated public buildings with murals, or wall paintings, noted for their skillful execution. Few of these have survived. Our knowledge of Greek painting comes mainly from literary descriptions and from Roman copies. The mural painters often chose to illustrate scenes from the *Iliad* or *Odyssey*. On one of the public buildings of Athens, for example, an artist painted "The Sack of Troy." With a true sense of tragedy, he did not depict the massacre at the moment of victory, but the silence of the following day, with the defeated lying in death amid the ruins of the city.

Sculpture

In spite of the tributes to the greatness of Greek painting, it is generally held that the greatest Greek art was sculpture. Not many original works of Greek sculpture are still in existence. What we know about Greek sculpture has also come to us chiefly through copies made during Roman times. Two of the greatest sculptors of all time lived during the Golden Age. The first was Myron, whose figure of the Discus Thrower is very familiar. The second, Phidias, was artistic adviser to Pericles during the rebuilding of Athens. He was the creator of the two wonderful statues of Athena—one at the entrance to the Acropolis and one in the Parthenon. His greatest work was the statue of Zeus at the Temple of Olympia. Greeks who attended the Olympic games looked at it with awe. A man who had not seen it considered himself unfortunate.

Praxiteles (prak·SIT·uh·leez), who lived about a hundred years after Phidias, made quite different sculpture. Phidias' works were large, formal, and dignified, as was fitting for the gods. Praxiteles made his figures more human and lifelike. Often they were life-sized. They were more graceful than those of Phidias, but did not inspire awe and reverence as had the works of the earlier master. Above all, Praxiteles expressed the Greek admiration for the beauty of the human body.

The nature of Greek art

All that you have learned about Greek architecture, painting, and sculpture will help you to understand the Golden Age, for the art of the Greeks reflected their culture.

The Art of Greece

In its many forms, Greek art has had a timeless appeal. Vase paintings are admired for their economy of line and decorative qualities. They are also invaluable records of Greek life; above are a woman washing clothes and a man on horseback. Sculpture expressed in three-dimensional form Greek ideals of human beauty. The marble head at right, from a statue of Hermes by Praxiteles, is the only surviving original work by this master sculptor of Greece's Golden Age. In the Parthenon and the other buildings of the Acropolis, below, Greek architecture reached classical perfection.

What were the most important characteristics of this great art? First and foremost, it glorified man as the most important creature in the universe. It is true that much of the painting and sculpture portrayed gods and goddesses, but you will recall that to the Greek, the deities existed for the benefit of man. When he glorified them he glorified himself. To gain this effect, the Greek painter or sculptor idealized his subject, omitting any blemishes. The faces and figures of women represented the Greek ideal of female beauty; images of men suggested ideal traits admired by the Greeks—strength, intelligence, pride, grace, and courage.

Second, Greek art symbolized the pride of the people in their city-states. At the same time, it honored the gods, thanked them for life and fortune, and tried to win their favor. Thus, in giving Athena a beautiful shrine in the Parthenon, the Athenians showed their love for their city and their hope for its continuing good fortune.

Third, Greek art, whether architecture, painting, or sculpture, expressed Greek ideals of harmony, balance, order, and moderation—the qualities of simplicity and restraint. Pericles was quoted as saying, "We love beauty without extravagance."

Finally, the Greek believed in combining beauty and usefulness. To him, the useful, the beautiful, and the good were closely bound together. He wanted his furniture, and even his kitchen utensils, to be both serviceable and beautiful.

This feeling for balance, harmony, and proportion was well expressed in a rather unlikely place and way. The Greek historian and essayist Xenophon (ZEN·uh·fun) wrote a book called *Economics,* dealing with the management of house and farm, which tells us much about Greek daily life. In it he says:

> How beautiful when shoes, of whatever kind, are arranged in order; how beautiful it is to see garments deposited in their several places; how beautiful it is to see bedclothes, brass vessels, and tableware so arranged; and (though some might laugh) even pots have a graceful appearance when they are placed in regular order. Other articles, too, somehow appear more beautiful when they are arranged symmetrically.

CHECKUP

1. What was the difference between the sculpture of Phidias and that of Praxiteles?

2. What were four main characteristics of Greek art?

3. Briefly explain the meaning of the following two quotations: "Nothing in excess, and everything in proportion." "We love beauty without extravagance."

4. IDENTIFY: Parthenon, colonnade, murals, Myron.

3 Philosophers and writers added to the heritage of Greece

The Greeks have been honored through the ages for their artistic and intellectual achievements. No people before them—and few since—demonstrated so clearly the greatness of which the human hand and mind are capable. The Greeks were eager to learn all they could and to think through everything that the human mind is capable of understanding. These traits are clearly shown in the record of their thinkers and writers.

Socrates

One of the greatest thinkers and teachers of all time was a short, bald, snub-nosed little man named Socrates (SAHK·ruh·teez), who lived in Athens from 469 to 399 B.C. Trained as a sculptor, he gave up that work to be a teacher. He would not take pay for teaching, and lived in poverty. Homely as he was, most people loved him because he was wise, honest, and kindly.

Socrates was a critic of Athenian education, especially of the Sophists. He said they boasted too much of their wisdom and made their pupils conceited. He would not allow himself to be called a Sophist, preferring the term *philosopher*—a word which in Greek means "lover of wisdom." From this term comes our word *philosophy,* which may be defined as inquiry into the most fundamental questions of reality and human existence. The Greeks were the first people to reason about the entire range of human experience systematically.

Socrates criticized the Sophists for teaching boys to live by memorizing proverbs and imitating their elders instead of thinking for themselves. By learning to think for himself, he said, man could learn wisdom, which would lead him to right living. Only evil could result from ignorance. Man must depend on his reason to guide his life, to show him what was truly important.

Socrates himself did not teach as the Sophists did, but instead asked questions of anyone he met, anywhere. The purpose of his questions was not to get information, but to make men think in order to answer the questions themselves. "Know thyself" was his motto. He wanted men to understand what such ideas as love, friendship, duty, patriotism, honor, and justice really meant to them. Each man must find his own answers to these problems. This way of teaching is known as the "Socratic method."

Socrates inspired great love among his followers, but he also made enemies. He had come to believe that there was only one God, and that the soul was immortal. His enemies accused him of denying the existence of the many Greek gods, and he was brought to trial on charges of teaching false religion and corrupting the minds of Athenian youth. At the trial he said that his conscience, which he considered the voice of God, made him teach. If he were allowed to live, he would continue to teach, because his conscience would compel him to. He was found guilty and condemned to die by drinking a poison made from the hemlock plant.

Plato

Socrates had always been too busy teaching to write down his ideas. Later generations learned about them from the writings of Plato, the greatest of his students. Plato was a wealthy young aristocrat. After Socrates' death, he began to teach in the grounds of the Academy, a public park and athletic field.

Plato used a dramatic form, the dialogue, for his philosophical writings. There are dialogues on government, education, justice, virtue, and religion. Each dialogue is in the form of an imagined conversation among several people, with Socrates usually asking questions of the others. The dialogues include many of Plato's own theories. Scholars cannot be sure which ideas presented as those of Socrates are his, and which are those of Plato.

To answer the question "What is justice?" Plato wrote a long dialogue called the *Republic*. This dialogue described Plato's idea of the ideal form of government. Everyone, he said, should do the work for which he is best fitted. Men noted for bravery should be in the army. People interested in material things like food, clothing, and luxuries should conduct the business and do the labor. All workers should be free, though not all should be citizens, for Plato's ideal government was to be operated and controlled by a few men only. They were the philosophers, to be chosen for their wisdom, ability, and correct ideas of justice. Everything was to be owned in common.

You will recognize that Plato's ideal government was an aristocracy—a government by an upper ruling class. However, it was not an aristocracy of birth or of wealth but one of intelligence, ability, and high ideals.

Aristotle

Among Plato's students in the Academy was a young man named Aristotle, whom Plato called "the mind of the school." You will remember that he was the teacher of Alexander the Great. Aristotle founded his own school at Athens in 335 B.C.

Aristotle was an accomplished scientist as well as a great philosopher. He set himself the task of investigating every kind of knowledge. He collected as many facts as possible. Then he arranged and organized them into systems, comparing one fact with another to try to find out what they meant or showed. He was especially skillful at definitions and grouping similar or related facts. This process is an important part of modern scientific thinking.

Aristotle almost accomplished his purpose of searching out every field of knowledge in his time. He collected, described, and classified plants and animals. In order to describe the principles of government, Aristotle studied the political organization of 150 city-states and put down his con-

The Greek mind was inquisitive and eager to investigate the unknown. At its best, it was typified by Socrates, one of the greatest Greek philosophers. He thought of himself as a gadfly who went about stinging the Athenians out of their lethargy and ignorance. He is shown at left.

The legends of the Greeks also reflected their concern with man's fate. One such legend is illustrated in the vase painting below left, which shows Oedipus and the Greek form of sphinx, a devouring monster that threatened the city of Thebes. Oedipus here ponders the riddle of the sphinx: "What walks on four legs in the morning, two at noon, and three in the evening?" Thebes was saved when Oedipus answered the riddle correctly: "Man, who crawls on all fours as a baby, walks on two legs during his prime, and needs a cane in old age."

Hellenistic Greeks excelled in scientific learning. Below is a section of an Alexandrian treatise on astronomy. Illustrated with drawings, it describes the movements of the planets. Astronomy was only one of several sciences in which the Alexandrians excelled; they were equally skilled and famous as geographers, mathematicians, and physicians.

clusions in a book called *Politics*. For his book *Ethics,* he studied the acts and beliefs of men to learn what brought the greatest virtue and happiness. In his *Poetics,* he made a study of Greek drama to show the differences between a good and a bad play. His *Logic* is an attempt to show the principles of correct reasoning.

Mathematics and science

In the 500's B.C., before the Golden Age, Pythagoras (pih·THAG·ur·us), a philosopher and mathematician born on the island of Samos, wrote that everything could be explained or expressed with numbers. Pythagoras also established some of the principles of geometry in order to define and measure the surface of the earth. He is probably best known for the Pythagorean theorem, which states that the square of the hypotenuse of a right triangle is equal to the sum of the squares of the other two sides.

The Greeks of the Golden Age made some advances in science, although Greek scientific achievements did not reach their fullest development until a later period. Aristotle laid the foundations of botany, zoology, and anatomy (how the bodies of living things are constructed). The Greek philosopher Democritus (dih·MAHK·ruh·tus) believed that all matter is composed of moving atoms—small particles which he thought could not be divided. Science has proved that the atom can be divided, but still holds to the theory that all matter is made of atoms.

One of the greatest scientists of the Golden Age was Hippocrates (hih·PAHK·ruh·teez), who has come to be known as the Father of Medicine. He taught that all disease comes from natural causes, not as punishment from the gods. The best cures, he said, were rest, fresh air, and a proper diet. Hippocrates had high ideals for physicians. A pledge based on his teachings, the Hippocratic Oath, is still used and may be seen in many physicians' offices.

Greek drama

A surprising proportion of the world's greatest literature was written by Greeks who lived in Athens during the Golden Age. That brief period saw a tremendous flood of creative writing. Greek literature was great because of its simple expression, its beauty and grace both of style and ideas, and its realism—that is, truthfulness in portraying how people live and act.

The Greeks were the first people to write dramas, and it is this form of literature in which they excelled. Greek plays were almost always written in poetic form. They were spoken or sung by two or three actors and a chorus. Plays were performed in outdoor theaters, constructed where there was a natural bowl—often on the slopes of hills. The audience sat in seats built into the hillside. The actors performed on a stage at the bottom of the bowl. There was almost no scenery; instead, the chorus—a group of singers and dancers—described the scene.

The actors were always men, each with a voice trained to play several parts, including women's parts. They wore elaborate padded costumes and thick-soled boots to make them look larger than human beings. Actors used masks to indicate the characters and emotions they were portraying.

The plays often had a religious theme and were almost always given in connection with religious festivals. For three successive days at the Festival of Dionysus, three tragedies were given each day. Each day the audience selected the best one, judging it by the beauty of the language and the wisdom of its ideas. The winning author was awarded a crown of ivy. Pericles considered these plays so important in educating citizens that he provided for free admission to the great festivals for all citizens who could not afford to pay for admission.

Tragedies. A Greek tragedy showed the protagonist, or central character, struggling against fate. Usually he was overcome by outside forces that were too strong for him, together with some weakness in his own character. This weakness was often what the Greeks called hubris (HYOO·bris), an arrogant recklessness or an insolent disregard of moral laws or restraints. The end was always inevitable and could not be escaped.

Three great writers of tragedy lived during the 400's B.C. Aeschylus (ES·kuh·lus) was called the Father of Greek Tragedy. Thirteen times he won the ivy crown as writer of the best play. He wrote of the old religious beliefs about the relationship between gods and men. Most famous of his plays to survive today are three which center on the murder of Agamemnon, the king who led the Greeks against Troy, and the revenge that followed it.

Another tragedian, Sophocles (SAHF·uh·kleez), defended the traditional values. His most famous play was *Oedipus Rex,* which Aristotle called a perfect example of tragedy.

Euripides (yoo·RIP·uh·deez), the third tragedian, was more of a realist than Aeschylus or Sophocles. Like Socrates, he questioned many old beliefs and ideas. Earlier writers often glorified war for its deeds of courage and heroism. In *The Trojan Women,* Euripides showed war as it was, with all its miseries.

Comedies. Greek comedies were what we would call satires, because they made fun of ideas and people. The Athenians were accustomed to criticism of government leaders. Their satires often ridiculed politicians who tried to fool the people. Sometimes they praised leaders or their ideas by making fun of people who opposed them.

Aristophanes (ar·iss·TAHF·uh·neez) was the greatest writer of comedies. No person or institution was safe from his wit. In *The Clouds* he poked fun at Socrates for his theories about education. (It was said that Socrates went to the play and laughed harder than anyone else.) Several plays showed women taking over the government, which amused the Athenians greatly because of their low opinion of women. Aristophanes also used satire to make Athenians think about the folly of war and its causes.

History

The Greeks were the first people to take the writing of history seriously. Herodotus, whose name you have seen several times in this book, was the first great historian of the Western world. A great traveler, he visited Babylonia, Phoenicia, and Egypt, and included his impressions of these countries and their people in his history of the Persian Wars.

Herodotus was an engaging writer and a wonderful storyteller. Sometimes he exaggerated, but he was always careful to distinguish between the things he had personally seen or investigated and those which he had been told. He often expressed doubt about legends, but reported them for whatever they were worth. He is called the Father of History, and historians still consult his writings for information about the world of his time.

Another Greek historian was Thucydides (thoo·SID·uh·deez), famous for his *History of the Peloponnesian War.* He wanted his history to be a guide to future statesmen, so he took care to make it accurate. His work, also, is still read today.

CHECKUP

1. Why did Socrates criticize the Sophists? What method of teaching did he use?

2. What were the chief characteristics described in Plato's *Republic?*

3. What were some of Aristotle's contributions to knowledge?

4. Describe at least three basic features of Greek drama.

5. IDENTIFY: philosophy, Pythagoras, Democritus, Hippocrates, hubris, Aeschylus, Sophocles, Euripides, satires, Aristophanes.

4 Greek culture changed and spread in the Hellenistic Age

You have been reading about the culture of the Greeks—how they lived—during the Golden Age, from about 500 to 338 B.C. After 338 B.C., when Philip of Macedon conquered and united the Greek city-states, Greek culture began to change and to spread.

The conquests of Alexander the Great carried Greek culture to Egypt and other lands of the Near East, right up to the border of India. Greek ideas continued to influence these areas long after Alexander's death in 323 B.C. At the same time, Greek culture at home was modified by ideas brought from the other lands by Alexander's followers.

This period of the intermingling of cultures, and especially of the spread of Greek culture, is called the Hellenistic Age, or the Age of Alexander. It lasted from 323 B.C. until 133 B.C. when, as you will read in Chapter 7, Roman influence became predominant throughout the eastern Mediterranean area.

Government and society

Greek ideas about self-government did not spread into other parts of the Hellenistic world—that is, the area ruled by Alexander and his successors. In Egypt and other parts of the Near East, the absolute governments of the king-gods continued. Even in Greece itself, there was less democracy and a lower ideal of citizenship.

Greece was not prosperous, and many ambitious Greeks left the country to make their fortunes elsewhere, in cities far from their homeland. There they became the ruling class. Most of the wealthy city-dwellers in the Hellenistic world adopted Greek ways and spoke Greek. The rest of the people, however, usually continued to speak their own languages and maintain their own customs.

The economy

Throughout the Hellenistic world both industry and land were owned largely by the ruler or the government. The land that was owned privately was usually held in large estates by wealthy aristocrats. Slaves or poorly paid free laborers did the work. There was a small class of very wealthy people and a large class of miserably poor people.

Trade was the most profitable activity. The main trading centers were the cities of Alexandria, in Egypt; Rhodes, on the island of Rhodes off the coast of Asia Minor; and Antioch, in Syria. Trade routes now connected the whole Mediterranean world, and even reached far-off India. Ships were bigger and better than they had been in earlier times.

The new cities built or rebuilt by Alexander were the wonders of the Hellenistic world. They were carefully planned and laid out with straight streets. They had market squares and large public buildings, including indoor theaters, schools, and public baths. Homes of the wealthy were improved to include elaborate furniture, running water, and drain pipes. Alexandria, in Egypt, was the greatest city, with a population estimated as high as one million. Its museum and library made it a great center of learning as well as of commerce. The library contained 750,000 papyrus rolls.

Education

Children of free parents, even some girls, received free elementary education in reading, writing, music, and literature. Higher education was still private, for fees. The principal type of secondary school was called the gymnasium, a school for children of purely Greek descent. There they studied reading, writing, literature, music, rhetoric, philosophy, and physical training. Academies and libraries were centers of higher learning.

Education was an important factor in spreading the Greek language—and Greek civilization as well—throughout the Mediterranean world. Greek was commonly used by traders and was a second language for educated non-Greeks everywhere. It was the language of the early Christians. Almost all the books of the New Testament were first written in Greek.

Originally, as you read in Chapter 3, the Greeks adopted the Phoenician alphabet and improved on it by adding letters for vowel sounds. They continued to improve the language until, by Hellenistic times, it was capable of expressing a wide variety of meanings and feelings.

We use many words derived from Greek. We can hardly write or talk about government, for example, without using Greek terms: *politics, democracy, aristocracy, monarchy, tyranny.* Almost every term used in medicine comes from the Greek. For example, the Greek ending *–itis* meant "an inflammation." Thus we have the words *appendicitis, bronchitis,* and *meningitis,* among many others.

Philosophy

The philosophers of the Hellenistic Age were more concerned with ethics than with fundamental questions of reality and human existence. There

Hellenistic Dancer

Hellenistic artists are noted for their intensely realistic work. Whereas Greeks of the classical period portrayed the ideal beauty of gods and heroes, later sculptors tried to capture fleeting moments and show human emotions. The bronze veiled dancer above, twisting gracefully and pointing her foot, conveys a feeling of motion, as do the folds of her clinging drapery. During the Hellenistic Age, when monarchs subsidized artists at court, Alexandria rivaled Athens as an artistic and intellectual center. This figure was made there during the 100's B.C.

were three chief schools, or groups, of Hellenistic philosophers—the Cynics, the Stoics, and the Epicureans.

The Cynics taught that men should seek virtue only. They scorned pleasure, wealth, and social position. The most famous Cynic was Diogenes (dy·AHJ·uh·neez), about whom there are many stories. One concerns the meeting of Diogenes and Alexander the Great. "If I were not Alexander, I would prefer to be Diogenes," the conqueror said. But Diogenes growled in reply, "If I were not Diogenes, I would prefer to be any man except Alexander." (The present meaning of the word *cynic* has been degraded. It usually means a person who is sarcastic but not necessarily thoughtful, one who believes that the motives for people's actions are always selfish and insincere.)

The philosopher Zeno, born on the island of Cyprus, established the Stoic school in Athens in the late 300's B.C. He and his followers believed that the world was full of divine spirit, and that there was some of it in the soul of every man. At death the individual soul rejoined this universal spirit. All men were therefore brothers. (It was the Stoics who popularized the phrase "the fatherhood of God and the brotherhood of man.") The best life was one spent in working for the welfare of others. Reason, not emotions, should be the guide to conduct. Man had to learn to accept whatever the laws of nature might bring, and to be indifferent—as much as possible—to grief, fear, pain, and pleasure.

The Stoic philosophy had great influence later on the thinking of the Romans and the Christians. (The word *stoic* means much the same now as it did in Hellenistic times—a person who remains outwardly unaffected by either pain or pleasure.)

Epicurus, founder of the Epicurean school of philosophy, taught that the aim of life was to seek pleasure and avoid pain. Pleasure to him was intellectual, not physical. After his death, however, his followers came to seek the pleasures of the senses and appetites. Their motto was "Eat, drink, and be merry, for tomorrow we die." (Today the word *epicure* means a person who indulges his senses, particularly someone who enjoys fine food.)

Mathematics and physics

Greeks of the Hellenistic Age were outstanding scientists. Extremely important work in mathematics was done by Euclid. He developed geometry into a system by showing how geometric statements of truth, or theorems, develop logically from one another. His textbook, *Elements,* was used for over a thousand years and is the basis for many of today's geometry books.

Archimedes (ar·kuh·MEE·deez) was the greatest all-round scientist of the Hellenistic period. He used geometry to measure spheres, cones, and cylinders. He calculated the value of π (pi), the relation between the diameter and circumference of a circle. He also used mathematics to explain the principle of the lever and built many machines in which levers were used. His inventions included the compound pulley (or block and tackle) and cogged wheels used as gears.

Medicine

Hellenistic scientists added greatly to the medical knowledge of the Greeks. Alexandria became the center for the study of medicine and surgery. The knowledge of human anatomy was greatly advanced by dissection of the bodies of executed criminals. Alexandrian physicians discovered the nervous system and learned that the brain is its center. They performed delicate surgery, using anesthetics to deaden pain. Much of their knowledge was later lost, or was ignored for many centuries.

Astronomy and geography

In astronomy, Hellenistic scientists combined all the knowledge of the Near East and the Golden Age of Greece, and added to it. They used mathematics to calculate the position of stars and planets from day to day. Aristarchus of Samos believed that the earth and other planets move around the sun, but was unable to convince other scientists of his day. Hipparchus of Rhodes calculated the times of eclipses of sun and moon, and the length of the year according to both the sun and the moon. He was the first scientist to make systematic use of trigonometry.

Hellenistic geographers knew that the earth was round. At Alexandria, Eratosthenes (er·uh·TAHS·thuh·neez) calculated the diameter of the earth with an error of less than 1 percent. He also claimed that men could reach India by sailing westward around the world—an idea that may have influenced Columbus sixteen centuries later.

Characteristics of Hellenistic science

Two features of Hellenistic science are remarkable. One is that scientists learned so much without instruments for observing and measuring. They had no microscopes or telescopes. They did not know of the compass, nor had they any mechanical means of measuring time accurately. They lacked delicate balances for weighing small quantities. It may be said that modern scientists are not necessarily better thinkers than the Hellenistic Greeks, but just have better instruments.

A second striking fact is that the Hellenistic Greeks made little effort to apply their scientific knowledge in practical ways, except perhaps in the field of geography. They valued knowledge for its own sake and were not interested in inventions or mechanical progress. For example, an Alexandrian scientist named Hero invented a steam engine, but it was regarded only as an interesting toy. One explanation for this attitude was the fact that Hellenistic civilization was based on slavery. These laborsaving inventions would have aided only the slaves, and it was not deemed necessary or fitting to improve their lot.

CHECKUP

1. When and what was the Hellenistic Age? What were the wonders of the period?

2. Which of the three chief Hellenistic philosophies do you like best? Why?

3. Name some of the most important contributions of Hellenistic scientists.

4. What were the two most striking characteristics of Hellenistic science?

5. LOCATE: Rhodes, Antioch, Samos.

CHAPTER REVIEW

Chapter 6 Greek Civilization Produced a Lasting Heritage (500 B.C.—133 B.C.)

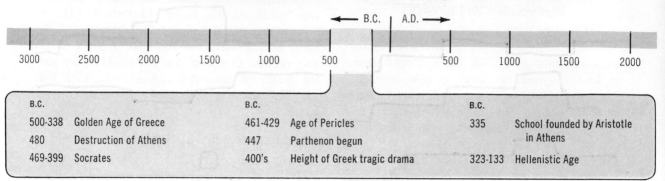

B.C.		B.C.		B.C.	
500-338	Golden Age of Greece	461-429	Age of Pericles	335	School founded by Aristotle in Athens
480	Destruction of Athens	447	Parthenon begun		
469-399	Socrates	400's	Height of Greek tragic drama	323-133	Hellenistic Age

CHAPTER SUMMARY

Greek civilization reached its height during the Golden Age. Many city-states helped form the Greek heritage, but the greatest achievements were made in Athens during the Age of Pericles. In this society, farming was the most honored profession, but manufacturing and trade were also important. Athenians valued simplicity in their homes, intellect more than wealth, and education that would produce a sound mind in a sound body.

Greek artists produced masterpieces in several fields. In architecture, the finest example is the Parthenon, built on the Athenian Acropolis. Greek painting survives only on vases, although we know that many public buildings were decorated with murals. Sculpture, the greatest Greek art, reached its peak with the work of Myron, Phidias, and Praxiteles. Greek art glorified man, symbolized pride in the city-state, expressed the Greek ideals of harmony and moderation, and combined beauty with utility.

The Greeks were the first philosophers. Socrates taught by asking questions in order to make men think for themselves. Plato used dialogues of imagined conversations for his philosophical writings, such as the *Republic*. Aristotle was outstanding not only as a philosopher but also as a scientist. Other important Greek scientists were Pythagoras, Democritus, and Hippocrates.

Greek literature reached its greatest expression in the drama. Three great writers of tragedy were Aeschylus, Sophocles, and Euripides. Greek comedies, such as those by Aristophanes, satirized ideas and people. The Greeks were also the first serious historians: Herodotus wrote about the Persian Wars and Thucydides wrote a *History of the Peloponnesian War*.

During the Hellenistic Age, Greek culture spread throughout the Mediterranean world. Although democracy declined, trade and cities flourished. The philosophers of this period—Cynics, Stoics, and Epicureans—were particularly concerned with ethics. The Hellenistic Age produced outstanding scientists, including Euclid, Archimedes, Aristarchus of Samos, Hipparchus of Rhodes, and Eratosthenes.

QUESTIONS FOR DISCUSSION

1. Aristocrats with leisure time played a major role in Athenian government. Is leisure time necessary for a present-day American who wants to become an active politician? Justify your answer.

2. In order to have a working democracy, Athens provided education for all its citizens. Why do you think this was considered necessary? The United States is pursuing the same goal. Do you think it is successful in educating its citizens to live in a democracy? Explain.

3. Socrates taught that a person is wise if he knows that he does not know everything. Do you agree or disagree with this definition of wisdom?

4. Who was to control Plato's ideal government? Do you think such a government is possible, and if so, would you like to live under it?

5. Hellenistic Greeks valued knowledge for its own sake and had little interest in its application. Do you think knowledge in the United States is pursued for its own sake or only for its practical application?

6. What were the teachings of the Stoic and Epicurean philosophers? Which one of these philosophies do you prefer? Justify your choice.

PROJECTS

1. Write a short defense of Socrates, to be used at his trial.

2. Make a list of some of the great Greek philosophers, writers, and scientists, together with their accomplishments.

3. Draw a sketch of a Greek temple—for example, the Parthenon.

Rome Ruled the Western World for Centuries

The date 133 B.C. is often given as the end of the Hellenistic Age because by that year Romans from Italy had extended their power over large parts of the eastern Mediterranean. Who were the Romans? How did they become powerful enough to gain control of the Mediterranean area and, eventually, of much of Europe as well? The geography of Italy and the location of the city of Rome itself had a great deal to do with this rise to power.

Italy is the central peninsula of the three great peninsulas in the Mediterranean region. The Iberian Peninsula is to the west of it and the Balkan Peninsula to the east. On the map on page 125, note that Italy resembles a boot, with its top in the Alps to the north and its toe and heel in the Mediterranean Sea to the south. Italy juts into the Mediterranean so far that it cuts the sea nearly in half. The toe of Italy is only 2 miles from the large island of Sicily, which is only 80 miles from the African coast. Italy is the heart and center of the Mediterranean region.

The people of Italy have often had to fight to protect their territory. The high Alps which separate Italy from the rest of Europe may seem to be good protection against land invasion, but the protection is not perfect. There are several passes in the Alps through which invaders can enter the peninsula. Italy has often been overrun by hostile peoples.

Geographical factors favored unity in Italy as

Roman road and triumphal arch in North Africa

much as they prevented it in Greece. Notice on the map that the peninsula is divided by the Apennine Mountains, which run the full length of the "boot." The Apennines of Italy are less rugged than the mountains of Greece, and they did not hinder trade and travel. For this reason, and also because there were fewer harbors in Italy, the people living in the early coastal settlements turned inland for trade and growth rather than toward the sea, as the Greeks had done.

Except for the long coastal plain to the west and the great valley of the Po River to the north, where grain is grown, most of Italy is foothill and mountain country. The soil is sandy and easily eroded, or washed away, and is useful mainly for pasture. Nevertheless, Italy's temperate climate and plentiful winter rains enable farmers to raise vegetables, olives, grapes, and citrus fruits.

Italy's rivers are short and shallow. Most of them are partially blocked at their mouths by soil washed down from the higher land, making the surrounding region swampy. Throughout history the peninsula has had epidemics of malaria and other fevers caused by mosquitoes which thrive in these marshes.

The Italian Peninsula, well situated at the center of the Mediterranean area, became in time the heart of a vast empire. Like most empires, it took shape gradually.

THE CHAPTER SECTIONS:

1. The Romans founded a republic and gained control of Italy (1000–250 B.C.)
2. The Roman Republic expanded into the entire Mediterranean region (250–133 B.C.)
3. A century of civil war ended in the founding of the Roman Empire (133 B.C.–180 A.D.)
4. The Romans maintained peace for over two centuries (27 B.C.–180 A.D.)
5. By preserving Greek culture, Romans passed it on to later times (27 B.C.–180 A.D.)

1   The Romans founded a republic and gained control of Italy

There were people living in Italy as early as the Old Stone Age. They had developed a Neolithic culture there before 3000 B.C. After 2000 B.C. the peninsula was invaded from the north many times. As in Greece, these invaders were Indo-European peoples from the grasslands north of the Black and Caspian seas.

Early peoples in Italy

About 1000 B.C. the invasions increased in number. Many peoples entered and settled in various parts of the peninsula. The most important were the Latins, who settled in the west-central plains region called Latium (LAY-shee-um). Some of the Latin settlers built villages along the Tiber River. In time these villages were united into the city of Rome (see map, opposite), one of many cities on the plains of Latium.

The Etruscans, a people who came either from the Aegean Islands or from Asia Minor, entered Italy sometime after 900 B.C. They first conquered and held the coastal plains of Etruria to the north of the Tiber. In the late 600's B.C., they captured the plains of Latium, including the city of Rome, and held the area for about a century. In Rome an Etruscan family called the Tarquins ruled as kings for a time. Then fortune turned against the Etruscans. The Latins conquered them in 509 B.C., and they eventually disappeared into the mixed population of the region.

Although the Etruscans as a people disappeared, their culture lived on through its influence on the Latins. Etruscan culture was more highly developed than that of the Latins. The Etruscans had a written language with an alphabet based on Greek characters; scholars have had difficulty translating it, however. They made fine clothing and jewelry, and were skilled workers in metal, pottery, and wood. From the Etruscans the early farmers of Latium learned how to pave roads, drain unhealthy marshes, and build sewers.

There were also Greeks in early Italy. Greek colonies in Sicily and southern Italy became city-states, as disunited and quarrelsome as those of the homeland. The Greek culture of these colonies was to have a strong influence on the Romans.

Rome and the Romans

Latins, Etruscans, and other peoples living in Rome gradually began to think of themselves as Romans. Rome, at first only one of many city-states on the plains of Latium, became the most powerful city-state for several reasons.

Look again at the map of Italy and find the city of Rome in the west-central part. It is built on hills along the Tiber River—the famous Seven Hills. Rome is not at the mouth of the Tiber, but some 15 miles inland. The city was built where the waters of the Tiber are especially shallow and where there is a small island in the river; thus it was located at the easiest crossing for many miles.

Rome was the center of land trade routes which fanned out in all directions. Early Romans were not much interested in shipping. Later, when foreign commerce became important, a port city named Ostia was built on the coast.

Roman expansion

For more than two centuries after the expulsion of the last Etruscan king in 509 B.C., the Romans fought many wars against neighboring peoples in Italy, usually to remove some threat to their frontiers.

In the south, for example, the Greek city-states began quarreling among themselves. One side in the dispute begged help from Rome; the other side looked to the Greek city-state of Epirus for aid. Rome, entering the dispute, conquered and then annexed the Greek colonies. When the Romans defeated a neighbor, they retained control of its territory so that they would not be disturbed again.

By 265 B.C., Roman territory included all of Italy south of the Rubicon River on the northeast coast. The Po Valley and all Italy north of the Rubicon was held by the Gauls.° This region was

---

° **Gauls:** the people of Gaul, a region corresponding roughly to present-day France, northern Italy, Belgium, and parts of the Netherlands, Germany, and Switzerland. The Gauls, like the early inhabitants of the British Isles, belonged to the Celtic branch of Indo-European peoples.

ANCIENT ITALY
about 325 B.C.

0 ____ 200 miles

CISALPINE GAUL
Po R.
GAULS
Rubicon R.
ETRURIA ETRUSCANS
Tiber R.
CORSICA
Rome
Ostia
LATIUM LATINS
ADRIATIC SEA
ILLYRIA
APENNINES
Mt. Vesuvius
GREEKS
SARDINIA
MEDITERRANEAN SEA
SICILY GREEKS
Strait of Messina
Carthage
AFRICA

called Cisalpine Gaul, meaning "Gaul on this side (the Roman side) of the Alps" (see map, page 128). The rest of Gaul was called Transalpine Gaul—"Gaul on the far side of the Alps"—or simply Gaul.

The early Roman Republic

When the Romans drove out the last Etruscan king, they set up a *republic*. In this form of government, power rests with all the citizens who are entitled to vote. A republic is more or less democratic, depending on how many people have this right. The early Romans were democratic, with little class distinction. Most of them were farmers, and even the wealthiest men worked in the fields. No one was very rich and no one was miserably poor.

As time went by, distinctions among classes became greater. A powerful aristocratic class, the patricians, gained control of the government. All other citizens were called plebeians.

Plebeians were at a great disadvantage for

125

Etruscan Archers and Discus Thrower

The Etruscans were a powerful and wealthy people in Italy before the days of the Romans. They were skilled fighters and shrewd merchants. Etruscan wealth, which encouraged a taste for luxury, came mostly from their control of Mediterranean shipping. The Etruscans traded widely with the Egyptians and with people of the Fertile Crescent.

As is the case with many ancient peoples, objects found in tombs have provided much of our knowledge of Etruscan customs and daily life. We know that they enjoyed games and amusements, including wrestling, boxing, horseback riding, chariot races. And there was music on almost every occasion.

The bronze funeral urn at left, used to hold ashes, illustrates the Etruscan artists' preference for subjects taken from real life. The discus thrower and four mounted archers may have been placed on the lid to remind the deceased of pleasures he enjoyed when he was alive. A very practical people, the Etruscans sometimes used such urns for other purposes in their daily lives before burying ashes in them.

many years. They could not hold public office and were forbidden to marry patricians. They could not even know what the laws were because the laws were not written down. In court, the laws were stated and applied by a judge—and all the judges were patricians.

Gradually the plebeians increased their power by making demands at strategic moments and by revolts. They gained the right to marry patricians and to hold office in the government. One of the greatest victories of the plebeians was to have the laws written down. They were engraved on tablets known as the Twelve Tables and were placed in the Forum—the chief public square—for all to see. By 265 B.C. the Roman Republic had become fairly democratic.

Government. Three bodies of citizens helped govern Rome:

(1) The Senate was composed of 300 patricians, chosen for life. The Senate elected some officials, passed laws, often determined foreign policy, and sometimes acted as a court. It was the most important and powerful of the three governing bodies.

(2) The Assembly of Centuries took its name from the *century,* a military formation of 100 men. There were 193 of these voting units: 170 centuries of foot soldiers, 18 centuries of horsemen, and 5 centuries of noncombatants. The equipping of a century was expensive. Patricians paid most of this expense, so they controlled the voting in this assembly. And elect magistrates.

(3) The Assembly of Tribes was made up of citizens grouped into thirty-five tribes according to residence. Plebeians controlled this assembly. It elected officials called tribunes (see below), and gradually gained power to make some laws.

The officials who ran the government were called magistrates. Four kinds of magistrates, all elected by the Assembly of Centuries, had supreme administrative authority, including the right to interpret and execute laws. At first only patricians could hold these posts, but by 339 B.C. they were all open to plebeians.

(1) Consuls were two officials elected for one-year terms. They were the chief executives and army commanders. Each could veto, or refuse to approve, acts of the other. (The Latin word *veto* means "I forbid.")

(2) Praetors (PREE-turs) were judges. They were very important because they actually created much of the law by their decisions in court cases.

(3) Censors registered people according to their wealth for taxes and membership in the Assembly of Centuries. After 318 B.C. they chose the senators.

(4) A dictator had absolute power for a term limited to six months. He was nominated by the consuls and elected by the Senate, but only when Rome was in great danger.

The tribunes were the most important officials without supreme administrative authority. There were ten tribunes, elected annually by the Assembly of Tribes, over which they presided. They could not be elected twice in succession. They had to be plebeians, and represented only the plebeians. They could veto any act of any magistrate. This veto power protected the interests of the plebeians somewhat against abuse of power by patricians.

The army. Every adult male citizen was obliged to serve in the army when needed. In the early days, men fought without pay and furnished their own weapons. The most important military unit was the legion, consisting of 4,500 to 6,000 men, called legionaries. Because of excellent organization and training and the high morale of individual soldiers, the Roman legions were able in time to defeat even the great Macedonian army.

The Roman army was a citizen army. No man could be a candidate for high office until he had served at least ten years in the army, and for many centuries only citizens could serve in the legions. Discipline was strict and was enforced by the soldiers themselves.

The people of some conquered areas were given Roman citizenship. However, citizens had to come to Rome to vote; great numbers of them could not make this trip and therefore were not represented in the government. Other conquered peoples became allies. Allies kept much self-government, but Rome required them to furnish troops for war and controlled their relations with other cities and countries.

The family. The family was the most important unit in Roman society during the days of the republic. It was the center of religion, morals, and education. A Roman family, like the Chinese family, included all unmarried children, married sons and their families, all dependent relatives, and the family slaves.

The father had absolute authority. He conducted religious ceremonies, made all important decisions, and looked after the education of his sons. Roman women were more honored than Greek women. The mother managed the household, did the buying, and shared with her husband the entertainment of guests.

Education. Roman education aimed more at good habits than at knowledge. Children were trained to be loyal, brave, and patriotic citizens, and to be modest, sober, and above all obedient to their elders and superiors. They received their early education at home. The Roman father taught his sons farming and the duties of citizenship. The mother instructed her children in reading, writing, and arithmetic. They also memorized the Twelve Tables.

Religion. The religion of the early Romans, like many ancient religions, was a form of animism. The Romans believed that the spirits inhabiting everything had neither form nor sex. They had to be made friendly by rituals and sacrifices because man depended on them.

**GROWTH OF ROMAN POWER
to 265 B.C.**

- Roman territory in 509 B.C.
- Roman territory in 265 B.C.
- Carthaginian territory in 265 B.C.

0 ————————— 500 miles

To the Romans the spirits of the home were the most important. These included the lares (LAIR·eez), who were ancestral spirits, and penates (puh·NAY·teez), guardians of the storeroom. Janus guarded the doorway and kept out evil spirits. Family worship centered on Vesta, guardian of fire and hearth. Other spirits governed every aspect of farm life.

Contacts with other peoples changed Roman beliefs. Under Etruscan influence, Romans came to think of their spirits as having human forms and qualities. Thus Jupiter was thought of as the father of the gods and Juno as his wife. From the Etruscans the Romans also adopted the practice of trying to learn a god's will by observing the entrails of animals or the flight of birds. The Romans also adopted much of Greek religion and mythology. For example, the Greek supreme god, Zeus, became identified with Jupiter, and Zeus's wife Hera with Juno.

Rome's many wars brought another change.

Romans had to be concerned with success in war as well as in farming. In March, the month of Mars, god of war, they held special rites to prepare for the opening of military campaigns. In October, when campaigns ended because of cold weather, there were ceremonies to purify soldiers from the taint of blood and contact with strange spirits.

Thus, in time, the old family religion became a state religion with temples, priests, ceremonies, and processions. The high priest, elected for life by fellow priests, was called the Pontifex Maximus.

CHECKUP

1. Name at least three important geographic features of Italy.
2. What did the Latins learn from the Etruscans?
3. Name the three bodies of citizens that helped govern the Roman Republic. Which group was the most powerful? Why?

128

4. Why is it said that the family was the most important unit in Roman society during the days of the republic?
5. IDENTIFY: Gauls, patricians, plebeians, Twelve Tables, Forum, consuls, praetors, censors, tribunes, legion, lares, penates, Janus, Vesta, Mars, Pontifex Maximus.
6. LOCATE: Alps, Apennine Mountains, Po River, Latium, Tiber River, Etruria, Rome, Ostia, Rubicon River, Cisalpine Gaul.

2   The Roman Republic expanded into the entire Mediterranean region

By the middle 200's B.C., the Roman Republic was well established and had extended its power over all of the Italian Peninsula south of the Rubicon River. The addition of so much territory and so many new people to the republic increased its power and strength, but the burden of defending the republic was also increased. Rome had to protect the entire Italian coast against invaders, and also had to safeguard its growing overseas commerce.

Rome versus Carthage

Fear of invasion and protection of Italian commerce brought Rome into contact with Carthage, a large and powerful city on the coast of North Africa, directly across the Mediterranean Sea from the tip of Sicily. Carthage, as you recall, had been founded as a colony by the Phoenicians, those great traders of the Near East. Like its mother country, Carthage became a great commercial power, with territory in North Africa and Spain, and colonies scattered about the central and western Mediterranean areas (see map, opposite page).

Carthage had no colonies on the Italian Peninsula, but there were Carthaginian settlements on the nearby islands of Sicily, Sardinia, and Corsica. By 265 B.C., Carthage was the world's greatest sea power, with many merchant ships and a large navy to protect them. Its people boasted that the Mediterranean was a "Carthaginian lake," in which no one could so much as wash his hands without their permission.

After the Romans took southern Italy, Carthage feared that they would also try to take Sicily, with its Carthaginian colonies and markets. The Romans in turn were afraid that the Carthaginian navy would close the Adriatic Sea and the narrow Strait of Messina between Italy and Sicily. War could probably have been avoided, but neither side tried very hard to do so. Rome and Carthage fought three wars which, with intervals of peace, lasted from 264 to 146 B.C. These are called the Punic Wars, because the Latin adjective for "Phoenician" was *punicus.*

The opponents were well matched. Rome had the better army, Carthage the better navy. Carthage had more territory, but Roman lands were more compact and more easily defended. Carthage had the larger population; Romans were more fiercely loyal to their nation. At first, Carthaginian military commanders were more skillful, but Rome finally found generals who could win.

The first Punic War. The first war began in 264 B.C. and at first went against the Romans, who had no ships. According to tradition, the Romans soon built a navy, using a captured Carthaginian vessel as a model. The Romans used land tactics at sea. They equipped their ships with "boarding bridges." The Romans would ram their ship into a Carthaginian ship and then let down the bridge so that heavily armed soldiers could cross and take the enemy. This tactic was quite successful.

By 241 B.C., Rome ruled the western Mediterranean; Carthage asked for peace. It had to pay a large indemnity and give up its control of Sicily. In 238 B.C. the Romans threatened Carthage with war and secured Sardinia and Corsica as well. Not long afterward, Rome pushed north in Italy, defeated the Gauls in Cisalpine Gaul, and annexed this region. To free itself from pirates it also fought and won a war against the pirate kingdom of Illyria, on the eastern Adriatic coast (see map, page 131). Thus Rome now controlled all of Italy, the islands of Sicily, Sardinia, and

129

Corsica, and the eastern coast of the Adriatic.

The second Punic War. The second Punic War was launched in 218 B.C. The Carthaginian general Hannibal, one of the great generals of all time, planned to take Rome by surprise, invading from the north. He hoped that Rome's allies would revolt and join him.

Hannibal assembled a great army of infantry, cavalry, and armored elephants in Spain, which Carthage controlled. They marched across what is now southern France and began the difficult job of crossing the Alps into Italy in August. It was truly a dreadful crossing, made doubly difficult by early snows and landslides, and Hannibal lost nearly half his army there. At the end of September, he led his remaining men, half-starved and half-frozen, into the Po Valley (see map, opposite page).

It was a strange war. The Roman armies were no match for Hannibal. He defeated several of them, after which they shut themselves up in their fortified cities. Only a few of the Roman allies revolted and joined him. Hannibal had no siege equipment, so he could not capture the fortified Roman cities. For fifteen years he ranged up and down Italy, rarely provoking the Romans into pitched battle.

Then Rome turned the tables. A Roman army invaded Africa and threatened Carthage. Hannibal's government ordered him home to defend the city. In Africa he finally met his match, the Roman general Scipio. Hannibal and his army were defeated in 202 B.C. at the battle of Zama, near Carthage (see map, opposite). Once more Carthage asked for peace and had to pay a huge indemnity in money. It gave up its Spanish colonies. The city of Carthage remained independent, but Carthaginian power was broken.

The third Punic War. The third Punic War was fought to satisfy the greed of a small group of wealthy Roman landowners who wanted Rome to annex all Carthaginian territory. Their spokesman in the Senate was Cato the Elder. No matter what subject he spoke on, he always ended his speech by saying *"Carthago delenda est"*—"Carthage must be destroyed."

Finally, those senators in favor of war were successful. On a slight pretext, Rome declared war in 149 B.C., sent an army to Carthage, and captured it. In 146 B.C., Cato's wish was granted. The city of Carthage was entirely destroyed. It is said that the ground was plowed up and sown with salt so that nothing would grow, and that a curse was placed upon the site. The Romans were now undisputed rulers of the central and western Mediterranean.

Conquest of the Hellenistic east

In the eastern Mediterranean the former empire of Alexander was divided into several kingdoms. One of these, Macedonia, had joined in an alliance with Carthage during the second Punic War. Although the Romans defeated the Macedonians then, they did not take territory. Shortly after the war, Macedonia attacked Rome. The Romans won a decisive victory in 197 B.C. but again took no Macedonian territory. A renewed threat in the 160's resulted in further warfare and the reduction of Macedonia to a Roman province in 148 B.C. Its governor was put in charge of all Greece two years later.

In 133 B.C., Rome acquired western Asia Minor when its ruler died and left his kingdom to Rome in his will. By this date Rome had also gained control of most of Spain.

Problems of Roman expansion

By 133 B.C., the Roman state had grown from a federation of Italian cities into a great Mediterranean power. Look at the maps on pages 128 and 131, and compare the extent of the Roman state in 265 B.C. with the vast territory ruled by Rome in 133 B.C.

Government. Rome itself retained a republican form of government, but the machinery of government changed in certain ways to meet the problems of ruling the greatly increased territory. During a period of more than a hundred years, the influence and power of the Senate increased. The large, unwieldy Assembly of Tribes could not meet on short notice, as was often necessary during the Punic Wars. The smaller Senate could and did. It consequently gained control of the army, finances, and foreign affairs, and of the

GROWTH OF ROMAN POWER
to 133 B.C.

- - - - Hannibal's route, 218-203 B.C.
Roman territory in 133 B.C.

0   500 miles

new territories as well. Rome was still a republic, but it was ruled by an aristocracy.

The provinces. Government in the recently organized territories, called provinces, was poor. The people were not given citizenship, nor were they made allies like the people of conquered Italian cities. Instead, the provinces were treated like colonies belonging to the city of Rome.

Provincial cities became centers of local government under local magistrates chosen from the upper classes. New cities were built in backward regions, each controlling the surrounding countryside. In effect, the provinces became a collection of city-states, each one subject to Rome.

Each province had a Roman governor called a proconsul. He was appointed by the Senate, given absolute financial, legal, and civil power, and backed by a Roman army of occupation. Because his term was for one year only and he received no salary, he was under strong temptation to take graft from the province and to neglect the gov-

ernment. The proconsul's great power made it easy for him to become wealthy during his year in office, for the opportunities to take money for himself were enormous.

The proconsuls were not the only Romans who became wealthy by preying on the provinces. The system of collecting taxes, for example, increased the prevailing corruption. This system was called tax farming. In Rome the censors made contracts with men called publicans, who agreed to collect the taxes and pay a fixed sum to the Roman treasury. Publicans were allowed to keep whatever they collected in excess of this fixed sum.

Changes in agriculture and manufacturing. Rome's annexation of distant territories diminished the role of the small citizen-farmer in Roman life. The Roman government owned much land in the new provinces and leased it in large estates to anyone who could pay the price. Only wealthy people could afford to rent the land and buy the slaves who did the work. Since the prov-

131

The Roman army was a powerful force in Rome's expansion. The reconstruction at left of a battle between the Romans and the Macedonians in 197 B.C. shows a massive Macedonian phalanx surrounded by Roman soldiers, some on war elephants. Holding 21-foot spears and heavy shields, the Macedonians could not wheel about to face the flexible and highly trained Romans. Julius Caesar, above, was one of Rome's most brilliant generals. He used his army to gain control of the government and to maintain order in the provinces. Some conquered peoples were treated like the barbarians in Gaul shown below. They are bound with chains to a victory monument.

inces produced grain more cheaply than Italy could, they paid some of their tribute to Rome in this form. As time passed, Italy came to depend on the provinces for most of its grain, which was the chief article of food.

Small farmers in Italy could not compete with the cheaper grain from the provinces, nor could they compete with the cheap slave labor increasingly used by owners of large estates. Much Italian land was turned into pasture for cattle or used to grow grapes and olives. Raising cattle and growing fruit take more money and larger acreages than growing grain does. Many small farmers gave up their land and moved to the cities. Not all of them could find jobs there, and they came to depend upon the government for food.

The movement of small farmers to the cities was only one trend that made wealthy Romans wealthier and poor ones poorer. Manufacturing was carried on in small establishments. Since most of the work was done by slaves or poorly paid freedmen (freed slaves), the Romans saw little reason to invent laborsaving devices or to increase production. The constant opening of new lands for farming shifted money and energy away from industry.

Finally, Italy was importing more grain and manufactured goods than it exported, paying its bills with wealth gained from its wars. But what war brought in was quickly spent; there was a steady movement of gold and silver out of Italy to pay for imported luxuries.

Growth of commerce. While farming and manufacturing declined in Italy, commerce with Rome's vast empire increased. Businessmen engaged in commerce were not patricians, for patricians were prohibited from entering commerce. The businessmen formed a new class, the equites (EK·wih·teez), or knights. They had great wealth but little political power. In addition to wealth from trade, they made money from contracts for public works, tax farming, and the loot of war.

Decline of morals. The wars with Carthage and the changes brought about by the expansion of the Roman Republic were accompanied by a change in the attitude of many Romans. The increase of slavery, the decline of the small inde-

HISTORY THROUGH ART

Engraved Glass Bottle

Animas Felix Vivas—"May you live a happy life"—is engraved around the top of this Roman glass bottle. The beautifully shaped decanter was made by the then revolutionary technique of glassblowing. Since the invention of the blowpipe in Roman times, there has been no change in the basic technique of glassmaking—an indication of the modernity of Roman industrial processes. The bottle pictured here depicts various waterfront structures of an ancient harbor near Naples. Two pillars (*pilae*) are flanked by triumphal arches, one surmounted by four horses. The nets of oyster beds are engraved around the bottom of the bottle.

pendent farmer, and the growth of jobless masses in the cities weakened the old-fashioned ideals of discipline and devotion to the state. Men were judged by their wealth, regardless of how it had been gained, rather than by their character. One historian has written that in all of ancient times there was not a government that was so rich, so powerful, and so corrupt as that of Rome during this period.

133

1. In general, what were the causes of the Punic Wars? Who were the great leaders on each side during the second Punic War?

2. By 133 B.C., Rome ruled a large territory. What changes followed in (a) government; (b) agriculture and manufacturing; (c) commerce; (d) morals?

3. IDENTIFY: proconsul, publicans, equites.

4. LOCATE: Corsica, Strait of Messina, Illyria, Zama.

3 A century of civil war ended in the founding of the Roman Empire

By 133 B.C., when Rome extended its power into the eastern Mediterranean area, many problems had arisen. The increasing number of slaves made life difficult for free farmers and workers. The provinces were badly governed. Equites and plebeians had no political power, yet both groups had aims and needs for which government action was required.

Democratic reformers

Two brothers, Tiberius and Gaius Gracchus (GRAK-us), were among the first to attempt reforms. They came from a wealthy plebeian family. They had been trained by their mother to believe that service to the state was the most important aim of life.

Tiberius was elected tribune in 133 B.C. He gained passage of a law limiting the amount of land a man could own, and dividing up parts of large estates among those who had no land. This measure earned him many enemies, however, and he was assassinated. Gaius, elected tribune in 123 B.C., tried to restore power to the Assembly of Tribes. Under him, the tribunes gained the power to use public funds for the purchase of grain to be sold to the poor below cost. Other measures improved the political status of the equites. Gaius too lost favor and, at his own command, was killed by his slave in 121 B.C. in order to escape death at the hands of his opponents.

Any gains brought about by the brothers Gracchus were small and had little effect. The land reforms were not enforced. The sale of grain below cost set the example that private citizens should be supported at public expense. This practice eventually was a great drain on the treasury.

The next man to appear as a leader of the democratic forces was Gaius Marius, a plebeian and a military hero. In 105 B.C., Germanic tribes ° invaded Cisalpine Gaul. To head the nation in this time of danger, Marius, with the backing of equites and plebeians, was elected consul seven times.

Marius defeated the Germans and also tried to bring about reforms. He made one change that proved dangerous. Instead of having armies of citizens serving short terms without pay, Marius created a long-term volunteer army that included noncitizens. The rewards for enlistment were citizenship, land, and a share of the booty. The result was that armies became loyal to their leaders instead of to the Roman government.

Military rule

In 88 B.C., Lucius Cornelius Sulla, a senator, was elected consul to repel an invasion in Asia Minor. In his absence, civil war broke out in Rome. To put down the outbreak, Marius seized control and executed many patricians. Seven years later, Sulla returned to Rome with his army and defeated the followers of Marius. With terrible brutality and complete disregard for the law, Sulla executed thousands of citizens.

Sulla ruled as a military dictator for three years. He placed all the powers of government in the hands of the Senate, which he enlarged by 300 members. Increasingly, however, army commanders who had the loyalty of their troops could force the Senate to do what they wanted.

When Sulla retired in 79 B.C., there was a great struggle for power among a new group of leaders. Two generals, Gnaeus Pompey and Marcus Licinius Crassus, had become famous. When the Sen-

° **Germanic tribes:** groups of related peoples living in what are now Germany and Scandinavia. You will read more about them in Chapter 8.

ate refused to elect them consuls they threatened to use force, and the Senate gave in.

The First Triumvirate

A rising politician of this time was Gaius Julius Caesar, a nephew of Marius. He had been a leader of his uncle's reform movement, although he was a member of a wealthy patrician family. In his younger days he led an idle life, but when he became interested in politics, he soon proved to be a master politician. Caesar was a spellbinding orator and a liberal spender. With fine speeches and gifts of grain, he built up a great following among the poor citizens of Rome.

Caesar, Pompey, and Crassus each wanted to be sole ruler, but none of them was strong enough. Hence, in 60 B.C. they formed an alliance which became known as the First Triumvirate. The word *triumvirate* means "rule of three men."

Caesar's road to power

Caesar realized that he could not win power without an army loyal to him, so he made himself proconsul of Gaul for two terms of five years each. By this time Rome controlled both Cisalpine Gaul and the southernmost part of Transalpine Gaul, but Gauls and Germans held the rest. In his ten years as proconsul, Caesar brought all Gaul under Roman rule. He proved to be a superb military leader and organizer.

Caesar carefully kept the Roman people well informed about his campaigns and victories by sending home written reports of his progress. These reports are known as *Commentaries on the Gallic Wars*. Written in clear and simple style, they are still read by students of Latin.

Crassus was killed in battle in 53 B.C. Pompey meanwhile was growing jealous of Caesar's rising fame. To head off his rival, Pompey had himself made sole consul. Then he persuaded the Senate to order Caesar to resign as proconsul and return home without his army. Caesar refused, because to obey meant death at the hands of Pompey's troops. Instead, he led his army toward Rome in 49 B.C.

When Caesar reached the Rubicon River (the border between Cisalpine Gaul and Italy), he was met by a messenger from the Senate, who told him that if he crossed the river with his army, he would be declared a rebel. Caesar hesitated a short time, then made his decision. He ordered his army to march on to Rome. Since then it is said of a person who has made a decision from which he cannot turn back that he has "crossed the Rubicon."

Caesar the dictator

Pompey and his followers fled to Greece, and the way was open for Caesar to assume sole power. He first made himself secure in Italy and Spain, then defeated Pompey in Greece. He moved over into Africa, where the kingdom of Egypt, independent since the breakup of Alexander the Great's empire, had come increasingly under Roman domination. Caesar put Cleopatra, a daughter of the ruling Ptolemy family, on the throne and made Egypt an ally of Rome.

In 46 B.C., Caesar returned to Rome and took control of the government. He had become so powerful that in 45 B.C. he was appointed dictator for life. He was called *Pater Patriae*—the father of his country. The form of the republican government was kept, but Caesar was king in everything but name. The title of king was offered to him by the Senate, but he refused it.

Caesar's programs of reform. Once in power, Caesar showed himself to be a statesman as well as a politician and general. He first turned attention to the provinces. Citizenship was granted to many provincials (people who lived in the provinces). Caesar chose men with proved ability to be proconsuls and paid them a fixed salary. Other officials were sent to check on the proconsuls, removing those who did not rule well. The government took back land which had been seized by rich men and divided it among the landless.

Caesar reduced the Senate to the position of an advisory council and brought its membership to 900 by appointing 300 new members. Among them were Roman equites, leading citizens of Italian and provincial cities, chieftains of conquered Gaul, and even sons of slaves.

To make the calendar more nearly correct, Caesar ordered a reform. The Romans had been

Mark Antony and Caesar's second-in-command, Lepidus (LEP·uh·dus), drove out the conspirators and took control.

Octavian hurried home from Greece to claim his inheritance. He, Mark Antony, and Lepidus formed the Second Triumvirate in 43 B.C. They divided the Roman world among themselves. Antony took an army east and reconquered Syria and Asia Minor from the armies of Brutus and Cassius. Then he fell in love with Cleopatra and joined her in Egypt. Octavian forced Lepidus to retire from political life but allowed him to hold the office of Pontifex Maximus.

Octavian, the Emperor Augustus

After Lepidus was forced out of the Second Triumvirate, Antony and Octavian divided Roman possessions between them. Antony took the east and Octavian the west. Octavian, however, was still not satisfied. Within a few years, he persuaded the Senate to declare war on Antony and Cleopatra. In 31 B.C., in a great naval battle at Actium, on the west coast of Greece, Octavian defeated their fleet. Both of them committed suicide a year later. Octavian then took Egypt as his own personal province. Returning to Rome in 29 B.C., he declared that the wars were finished. They were indeed, but the republic was also finished, for Octavian established one-man rule.

Although there was no opposition to Octavian, he proceeded cautiously. Julius Caesar had been assassinated because many people feared his power. Octavian was determined to avoid his granduncle's fate.

In 27 B.C., he resigned his offices, including the consulship, announcing that the republic was restored. But this was only a political maneuver; the Senate thanked him and then granted him a number of new offices and titles. They really made him sole ruler, but he was careful to preserve the outward form of the republic.

The first title granted to Octavian was *princeps* —the "first man" of all the citizens. (From this word comes our modern word *prince*.) The Senate also gave Octavian the title *Augustus,* which means "exalted" or "majestic." He has been known ever since as Augustus Caesar, or simply

using a lunar calendar of 354 days. The so-called Julian calendar of Caesar had 365¼ days and was used in Europe until relatively modern times.

The conservative patrician families of Rome did not welcome all of Caesar's reforms. Some sixty men, who feared his great power, formed a conspiracy against him. Two of these were men Caesar considered his friends: Gaius Cassius and Marcus Brutus. On the Ides of March (the fifteenth day of the month), 44 B.C., the conspirators stabbed Caesar to death.

The Second Triumvirate

A weakness of all dictatorial government—in Caesar's time as well as our own—is the uncertainty of who is to succeed to power and how he is to be chosen. There is generally a struggle that often leads to basic changes in the government. Although Caesar had named his grandnephew Octavian as his political heir, there was a scramble for power after Caesar's death.

Octavian was only eighteen when Caesar was murdered. He had no political experience and was studying at a school in Greece. In Rome,

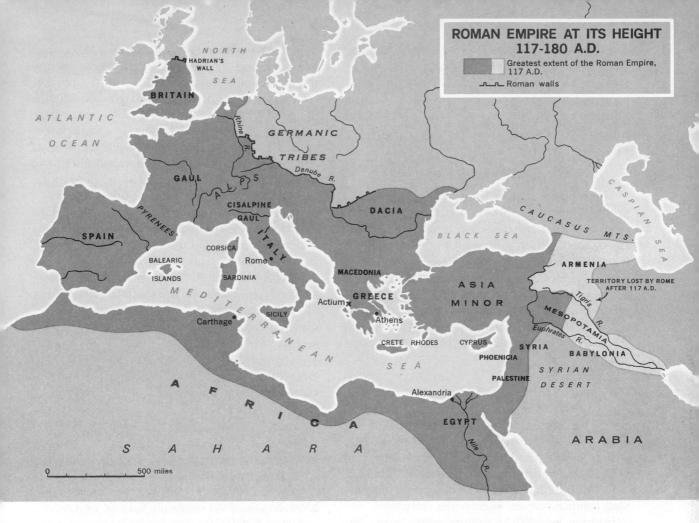

Augustus. (Many later Roman rulers used the word *Caesar* as part of their title. From it came the Russian word *czar* and the German word *Kaiser*.) At the death of Lepidus, Augustus also became Pontifex Maximus.

Augustus was made proconsul of all provinces. He administered them through aides called procurators (PRAHK·yuh·ray·turz), whom he appointed and removed. He commanded all the armies and had power to declare war and make peace. He was given the power of a tribune; that is, the right to propose or veto laws.

Although Augustus himself did not use the title, he is generally called the first Roman emperor, and the Roman state beginning with his rule is called the Roman Empire. Rome had truly become an imperial power. Its territory stretched from Spain in the west to Syria in the east, from the Rhine and Danube rivers in the north to Egypt and the Sahara in the south (see map, this page).

The Julian Emperors

Augustus died in 14 A.D. For the next fifty-four years, the Roman Empire was ruled by men related in some way to Julius Caesar, and thus they are called the Julian Emperors. Tiberius (14–37 A.D.), the adopted son of Augustus, was an adequate ruler. But his successor Caius, called Caligula, was insane and was murdered after four years on the throne.

Caligula was followed by Claudius, an intelligent and scholarly man who administered the empire wisely. It was during his rule that Britain

137

was conquered and added to the Roman Empire. During the reign of Nero, which began in 54 A.D., Rome was swept by a disastrous fire, which many people believed Nero started while insane. Whether or not the emperor was to blame, he was widely hated and was forced to commit suicide in 68 A.D.

The Good Emperors

There followed an interval of rule by a succession of emperors supported by the army. Then, in 96 A.D., the Emperor Nerva came to the throne. He was the first of a group of five, known as the Good Emperors, who ruled Rome for almost a hundred years. Trajan, who ruled from 98 to 117 A.D., was a great general and conqueror. He added Dacia (part of present-day Rumania), Armenia, and portions of Arabia and Babylonia to the empire, bringing it to its greatest size (see map, page 137).

Hadrian. Hadrian, Trajan's successor, was a Stoic, with a high sense of duty to the state. He was a patron of art, an able diplomat, and a tolerant ruler. Born in the provinces himself (in Spain), he understood their needs and spent much time organizing and Romanizing them. To help protect the boundaries of the empire, Hadrian built fortifications along the frontiers and encouraged frontier peoples to enter the army.

Hadrian established definite ranks in the bureaucracy, the civil servants of the government. Each office had fixed requirements, duties, rank, and salary.

Marcus Aurelius. Hadrian died in 138 A.D. and was succeeded by Antoninus Pius, whose twenty-three-year reign was uneventful. In 161, just before he died, he designated Marcus Aurelius as the next emperor. Marcus Aurelius, the last of the Good Emperors, was famous as a Stoic philosopher. His book, *The Meditations of Marcus Aurelius,* is considered a superb statement of Stoic ideas of the brotherhood of man, the need to accept whatever the laws of nature bring.

Marcus Aurelius had to give much attention to the defense of the empire. Barbarian tribes crossed the Danube River and reached northeastern Italy. It took thirteen years to drive them out. Barbarians threatened Rome's eastern borders, too, and were also defeated. The troops returning from this campaign brought with them a great plague, which lasted several years and caused a serious decline in population.

After the death of Marcus Aurelius in 180 A.D., there came a long period of confusion and decline, which you will read about in Chapter 8.

CHECKUP

1. Who was the first man to become dictator for life in Rome? List the steps by which he rose to power.
2. What powers did Augustus hold as ruler of the Roman Empire?
3. IDENTIFY: Tiberius and Gaius Gracchus, Marius, Sulla, Pompey, Cassius, Antony, Lepidus.
4. LOCATE: Actium, Danube River, Dacia.

4 The Romans maintained peace for over two centuries

You have read how Rome grew to be an empire, and about the kinds of men who ruled it in the period up to 180 A.D. Now it is necessary to study the essential features that helped the Romans build their empire and maintain it in peace.

Augustus, the first Roman emperor, had opposed taking any more territory. He thought the real problem was to rule well what Rome already had. So he began, and his successors followed, a policy of avoiding wars whenever possible. As you

have read, this wise policy was not followed with complete success. Some of Augustus' successors did take more territory, and there were frontier wars against barbarian tribes. However, inside the Roman Empire there was peace for over 200 years. The period from 27 B.C. to 180 A.D.—from the beginning of Augustus' reign until the death of Marcus Aurelius—is known as the time of the Pax Romana, the "Roman Peace." The world has rarely known such unity, peace, and stability.

AUGUSTUS

CLAUDIUS

HADRIAN

MARCUS AURELIUS

Rome and the Emperors

Four of Rome's greatest emperors during the Pax Romana are shown at left. To help establish his authority, Augustus had his own image stamped on coins, like the one shown here. Claudius gave extended powers to imperial governors. Traveling constantly through a prosperous empire, Hadrian founded cities and encouraged the arts. Marcus Aurelius had to wage incessant warfare, and wrote his *Meditations* while camping with his armies.

Just as Rome was the center of the empire, the Roman Forum, whose ruins are shown below, was the center of Rome. Originally a simple gathering place, the Forum gradually grew into a complex of open plazas, government buildings, temples, and shops. The columns at left and right are all that remain of Roman temples. In the background at left is the Colosseum.

The Romans had a talent for ruling others and maintained their authority through an efficient government both at home and abroad. Law, military organization, and widespread trade and transportation also knit the empire together.

Government

The imperial government was the strongest tie uniting the empire. It maintained order, established justice, defended the frontiers, and provided food for the poor.

The position of the emperor was a demanding one. He had to make all policy decisions. He appointed the officials who controlled the provinces and ran the entire government. The responsibilities of the emperor's job were too much for one man, however, even a wise, intelligent, able man like the best of the Good Emperors. When the emperor was weak, incompetent, and selfish, good government depended entirely on the officials of the bureaucracy.

From the time of Augustus on, bureaucrats were trained men, appointed and promoted on the basis of ability alone. The positions were highly prized and much sought after not only for the salary but also for the honor.

The provinces

The provinces were much better governed during the time of the Pax Romana than they had been under the late republic. A closer check was kept on provincial governors through the procurators, who administered revenues. Any provincial citizen could appeal directly to the emperor over a governor's decision.

The western provinces, especially Gaul and Spain, benefited greatly from their closeness to Roman civilization. Each of the new cities was a small copy of Rome, with a senate building, theaters, and public baths. Most of the cities brought in water by aqueducts, and most had paved streets and sewer systems. Usually there were no direct taxes because of income received from publicly owned land, mines, and quarries. Wealthy provincials took great pride in their cities. They gave large gifts of money to be used for public buildings, streets, schools, and entertainment.

Law

Roman law was another important tie binding the empire together. The code of the Twelve Tables had grown out of a small agricultural society. These laws had to be developed to fit a huge empire with its varied conditions.

The Twelve Tables were modified and expanded in two ways. First, new laws were passed as they were needed. Second, the trained judges, or praetors, interpreted the old laws to fit new circumstances. As Rome gained more territory, the praetors often adopted the best legal practices of the non-Romans they governed. At the same time, they adapted Roman law to fit the customs of provincial peoples as varied as the barbaric Germans and the civilized Egyptians.

The praetors helped develop the belief that certain basic legal principles are common to all mankind. For example, we are indebted to the Romans for the idea that an accused person is considered innocent unless and until he is proved guilty.

During the Middle Ages, the Roman system of law became the foundation of legal codes in all the European countries that had been part of the Roman Empire. Roman law also had a strong influence on the laws of the Christian Church.

The army

The territory of the empire was held together, as it had been gained, mainly by military force. Augustus had reorganized the army into three units. The Praetorian Guard—first organized by Augustus to guard the *praetorium,* or headquarters of the commander in chief—was stationed near Rome to protect the city if necessary. Its soldiers, who were all citizens, served sixteen years. The second unit, the Roman legions, consisted of citizens who served twenty years. The legions were stationed in great fortified camps along the frontiers. People often settled around these camps, so that they grew into towns and cities.

The third army unit, the auxiliaries, contained natives of the provinces or the border tribes. They enlisted for twenty-five years, with the promise of Roman citizenship when they completed their service. Soldiers of all three units were given bonuses of land along the frontiers when they had completed their army service. Thus there was a population of trained veterans to help guard the frontiers. It has been estimated that there were between 250,000 and 300,000 men under arms at the time of Augustus' death. Although this number increased under later emperors, there were probably never more than 500,000 men in the army at a given time.

The Romans tried to maintain natural frontiers as the boundaries of the empire wherever possible. In the west, there was the Atlantic Ocean; in the north, the Rhine and Danube rivers; in the east, the Black Sea and the Syrian Desert; in the south, the Sahara in Africa.

In regions where neither oceans, rivers, nor deserts gave protection, the Romans built great lines of fortifications. In Britain, Hadrian's Wall stretched entirely across the island in the north. There was a line of forts between the Rhine and Danube rivers. Between the great camps of the legions were protective ditches, fortresses, and walls. At first the walls were made of earth and timber, but later they were built of stone and were so substantial that many portions still stand. Paved highways joined these military outposts with cities in the interior, and all provincial cities were linked to Rome by highways—the origin of the saying that "All roads lead to Rome."

Trade and transportation

Throughout the time of the Pax Romana, agriculture remained the basic occupation of most people in the empire. In Italy itself most farming was done on large estates devoted to vineyards or livestock. In the provinces there were more small holdings. Much grain land became worn out, however, and farming districts in Greece and southern Italy were abandoned. Even though new ones were established in Gaul and North Africa, the grain supply was always uncertain. Crop failure anywhere meant scarcity.

A new type of agricultural worker, the colonus, began to replace slaves on the large estates. The coloni (plural of colonus) were neither slave nor free, but were bound to the land. Each colonus received a small plot of land from the owner. It was his to work, but he had to remain on it for a certain period, which at first was five years. He paid the owner part of the crops he raised. The coloni worked long and hard, with little return.

Such a vast empire, with so many different lands and peoples, provided great opportunities for commerce. Taxes on trade were low, and the same system of currency was used everywhere so that the exchange of goods was easy. Rome and Alexandria, in Egypt, were great commercial centers; goods came to them from all over the known world.

From the provinces, Italy imported grain and raw materials such as meat, wool, and hides. From the East came silks, linens, glassware, jewelry, and furniture to satisfy the tastes of the wealthy. During Roman times and on through later centuries, India was the source of many products that Europe had never known before. Demand for Indian spices, cotton, and other luxury products was great.

Manufacturing also increased throughout the empire. Italy, Gaul, and Spain made cheap pottery and textiles for domestic use. As in Greece, shops were small and most work was done by hand.

Transportation was greatly improved during the period of the early empire. Travel by sea was reliable and faster than that by land. Roads and bridges for land travel were well built, and there was postal service from all parts of the empire to Rome. However, even with improved transportation and communications, it took a Roman messenger at least ten weeks to cross the entire empire, traveling at top speed and using every known means of transportation. You can see what this might mean if a crisis occurred.

CHECKUP

1. What was the Pax Romana? When did it exist?
2. What were the most important ties unifying the Roman Empire?
3. How was Roman law adapted to fit changing conditions?
4. IDENTIFY: Praetorian Guard, Hadrian's Wall, colonus.

Daily life among the Romans was full and exciting. The streets of Rome were noisy with the sounds of people, chariots, and animals being herded to market. After a busy morning at the Forum, a Roman man might do the shopping for the family. A baker's stall on the street, left, offers fresh bread and cakes. During festivals huge crowds converged on the Colosseum for a day of games. A combat between gladiators, below, is accompanied by musicians playing bronze horns and an early form of the organ. Fishing was popular. At bottom, Romans bait lines and spread nets in water that is teeming with fish.

5 By preserving Greek culture, Romans passed it on to later times

Roman culture borrowed heavily but wisely from the Greeks. Roman philosophy, literature, art, and science were based on Greek learning. But the Romans often excelled the Greeks in making practical use of what they knew.

For example, the Greeks devoted much thought to the problem of what justice really is, but the Roman system of law brought practical justice to far more people. Romans thought less about the problem of ideal government than the Greeks did, and wrote about it less brilliantly. But the Romans created a stable and peaceful empire in which Greek culture could spread and take root. Thus many of its features were preserved for people of later eras.

Living conditions

The time of the Pax Romana was prosperous for many people, but wealth was unevenly distributed. The rich citizen usually had both a city home and a country villa. Each was elaborately built and furnished with many conveniences, such as running water and baths.

The life of the wealthy included some time for business, both private and public. But there was much time for leisure—siestas, exercise, public baths, and banquets. Many wealthy Romans ate and drank enormous quantities at banquets, and drunkenness was common.

The contrast between the lives of the wealthy and the poor was extreme. In Rome the poor lived in three- or four-story wooden tenements. There was always danger from fire or from the collapse of these cheaply constructed buildings.

Poor men found their best chance for employment in the army. Some were craftsmen or agricultural workers, but they had little security because of frequent unemployment and low wages. However, rent was low, and the government provided grain free or below cost. Political candidates often gave gifts of grain to the people. Both the government and candidates for public office furnished amusements and public baths either free or quite cheaply. Small farmers who lost their

land drifted to the towns to form an unruly mob that existed off the government dole.

Many slaves, especially agricultural slaves, led miserable and hopeless lives. Rarely in history has such a large group of fairly civilized human beings lived under such bad conditions. However, the number of slaves declined greatly during the early days of the empire. The long period of peace meant fewer war prisoners so that slaves became expensive to buy. A slave was also expensive to feed, clothe, and care for. Owners of large estates found it more profitable to free their slaves and make them coloni, bound to the land. The colonus worked better and had to support himself.

Amusements

Romans enjoyed the theater, especially light comedies and satires. Pantomimes and vaudeville performers such as jugglers, dancers, acrobats, and clowns were quite popular. Romans also enjoyed savage and brutal sports. Greek games like boxing were made more bloody with the use of brass knuckles. Large crowds watched chariot racing in the huge Circus Maximus of Rome, a kind of racetrack. At first, chariot racing was a fairly civilized sport, but later foul play was permitted and almost expected. There were many accidents in which horses and drivers were injured or killed.

Spectacles in the Colosseum, the great amphitheater in Rome, were the favorite pastime. Wild beasts, made more savage by hunger, were let into the arena to fight one another. Men sometimes fought against animals. Often condemned criminals or slaves were thrown into the arena to be killed by the beasts.

Most popular were combats between gladiators, trained fighters who were occasionally freedmen but usually slaves. They sometimes fought animals, but often fought one another, either singly or in groups. The fights usually ended in death for one or both fighters. Even Roman women screamed with delight at a death blow. When a gladiator was wounded, he appealed for mercy to the crowd, which signaled whether he should be killed or spared. By the 300's A.D., there were 175 public holidays a year.

Science, engineering, and architecture

The Romans were less interested in scientific research to increase knowledge than in collecting and organizing information. Galen, a physician from Asia Minor who lived in Rome during the 100's A.D., wrote several volumes, summing up all the medical knowledge of his day. He was long regarded as the greatest authority on medicine. The astronomical summaries of Ptolemy also won wide acceptance. Ptolemy, a scientist from Alexandria, believed that the earth was the center of the universe; most men accepted the Ptolemaic theory until the 1600's.

The practical Romans applied the scientific knowledge they gained from the Greeks in planning cities, building water and sewage systems, and improving farming and livestock breeding. Roman engineers surpassed all ancient peoples in constructing roads, bridges, aqueducts, amphitheaters, and public buildings. They were probably the first to use cement.

Architecture was the greatest contribution of the Romans in the field of art. Great public buildings—law courts, palaces, temples, amphitheaters, and triumphal arches—were erected for the emperor and the government. Roman buildings were based on Greek models to some extent. But the Romans used the arch and vaulted dome, which the Greeks had not known how to build, and emphasized size rather than proportion.

Education

Every important town or city throughout the Roman Empire had elementary, secondary, and higher schools. A boy or girl of the free classes entered elementary school at the age of seven, to be taught reading, writing, arithmetic, and music, usually by Greek slaves or freedmen. At about the age of thirteen, students entered a secondary school, where they studied grammar, Greek, literature, good writing, and expressive speech. The teachers were almost always Greek freedmen.

The equivalent of our college education was given in rhetoric schools, where the chief subjects were oratory, geometry, astronomy, and philosophy. A student entered a school of rhetoric in his sixteenth year and stayed as long as he liked. There were no degrees. For further education there were schools at Athens for philosophy, at Alexandria for medicine, at Rhodes for rhetoric, and a school called the Athenaeum at Rome for law, mathematics, and engineering. Students in all these schools paid fees for their education.

Literature

Augustus and several of the Good Emperors encouraged art and literature, often supporting artists and writers. Greek influence was strong, but a number of Romans produced works of distinction, particularly in the field of literature.

You have already read about the *Commentaries* of Caesar. Another important writer of the late Republic was Cicero, a great orator noted for his works on politics.

The greatest Roman poet was Vergil, who lived during the reign of Augustus. His *Aeneid* is an epic, a sort of sequel to Homer's *Iliad*. It tells the story of Aeneas, prince of Troy and supposed ancestor of the Latins. When the Greeks captured Troy, Aeneas fled and, after many adventures, came to Italy; his descendants, Romulus and Remus, founded Rome. Another Roman poet, Horace, wrote odes, satires, and epistles (letters), all in poetry. He had great knowledge of human emotions. Ovid wrote love lyrics and the *Metamorphoses,* a collection of legends written in verse.

Tacitus was one of the greatest Roman historians. His *Annals* is a history of Rome under the Julian emperors. He was pessimistic about the luxurious living of the wealthy and the lack of public virtue. More important to us is his *Germania,* an account of the Germanic tribes along the borders. He may have exaggerated the virtues of the Germans because he wrote the book to shame the Romans for their decadence. But it is almost the only, and certainly the best, account of the early Germans.

Plutarch, a Greek who lived in Rome, wrote *Parallel Lives*. These are a series of biographical

Two Roman Women

In the summer of 79 A.D., burning lava burst forth from the crater of Mt. Vesuvius, near Naples, and buried cities, villages, farms, and the villa that housed the fresco at right. Archeologists know that the villa was set among vineyards and that its owner prospered enough from the sale of his wine to pay for the magnificent frescoes that decorated his home. The one shown here is part of a series depicting the celebration of the annual cycle of planting and harvesting.

Women were the most ardent worshipers in these rites, which included the playing of music. We know that the woman holding the stringed instrument was a member of the nobility, for she is dressed in the purple and white worn by aristocratic families and is sitting in a high-backed chair—a Roman symbol of dignity reserved for high officials or women of rank. (The modern throne is derived from this Roman custom.) The young woman standing behind the chair is probably learning to take part in the rites.

sketches, one of a famous Greek followed by one of a Roman whose life in some way resembled that of the Greek.

Language

The Romans learned the Greek alphabet from the Etruscans and changed some of the letters. The Roman, or Latin, alphabet of twenty-three letters—plus the J, U, and W, which were added after Roman times—is the alphabet we use today.

Long after the end of the Roman Empire, the Latin language continued to be used, with some changes, in most of Europe. It was the language of most medieval European universities. It became the official language of the Christian Church, and is still used today by the Roman Catholic Church. For centuries, all government laws and decrees in Western Europe were written in Latin. Latin was

the parent of the modern Romance languages (a word derived from *Roman*): Italian, French, Spanish, Portuguese, and Rumanian.

Today, many scientific terms have either Latin or Greek origins. Although the English language developed mainly from the language of the early Germans, more than one third of all English words are of Latin origin.

CHECKUP

1. Briefly describe some Roman amusements.

2. Name three important Roman writers, and describe the writings of each.

3. In what ways did the Latin language last after the fall of the Roman Empire?

4. IDENTIFY: Circus Maximus, Colosseum, Galen, Ptolemy, Athenaeum.

CHAPTER REVIEW

Chapter 7   Rome Ruled the Western World for Centuries   (1000 B.C.—180 A.D.)

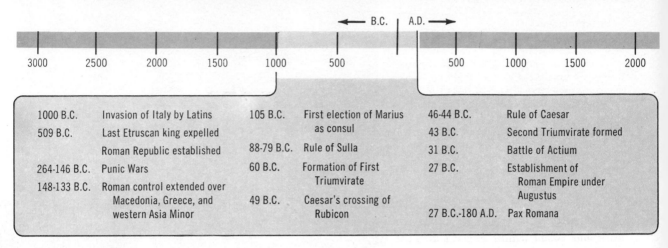

1000 B.C.	Invasion of Italy by Latins
509 B.C.	Last Etruscan king expelled
	Roman Republic established
264-146 B.C.	Punic Wars
148-133 B.C.	Roman control extended over Macedonia, Greece, and western Asia Minor
105 B.C.	First election of Marius as consul
88-79 B.C.	Rule of Sulla
60 B.C.	Formation of First Triumvirate
49 B.C.	Caesar's crossing of Rubicon
46-44 B.C.	Rule of Caesar
43 B.C.	Second Triumvirate formed
31 B.C.	Battle of Actium
27 B.C.	Establishment of Roman Empire under Augustus
27 B.C.-180 A.D.	Pax Romana

CHAPTER SUMMARY

The Latins, who invaded Italy from the north, built villages along the Tiber River that were in time united to form the city of Rome. The Etruscans ruled Rome for some time. Although their king was eventually overthrown, their culture influenced the Latins.

After the Romans expelled the last Etruscan king, they conquered much of Italy. Rome was governed as a republic, but class distinctions developed between patricians and plebeians. The family was the center of religion, morals, and education.

The growth of Rome's power brought it into conflict with Carthage, and the three Punic Wars resulted. When these were over, Rome ruled the central and western Mediterranean region. The Romans then went on to extend their control over the eastern Mediterranean. Roman expansion led to greater control by the Senate, corrupt rule in the provinces, the growth of large estates, and a decline in morals.

Tiberius and Gaius Gracchus unsuccessfully attempted reforms. After a long power struggle, the First Triumvirate was formed by Caesar, Pompey, and Crassus. Eventually, Caesar became dictator, but his reforms made him unpopular, and he was assassinated. A second Triumvirate—made up of Octavian, Mark Antony, and Lepidus—soon gave way to one-man rule under Octavian, the Emperor Augustus. He was followed by the Julian Emperors, a period of army-supported rulers, and the five Good Emperors.

The Pax Romana was a time of peace and stability. Imperial government was an important factor, with a trained bureaucracy and improvements in provincial administration. Roman law, the army, trade, and good transportation helped unite the empire.

The Romans borrowed and passed on Greek culture; their chief original contribution in art was their public architecture. Latin literature included Vergil's *Aeneid*, and works by Horace, Ovid, Tacitus, and Plutarch. The Latin alphabet of the Romans is essentially the one we use today, and their language is the parent of the modern Romance languages.

QUESTIONS FOR DISCUSSION

1. The Roman Empire expanded over a great area. In what ways might control of a large territory be both good and harmful for a nation?

2. Would you have preferred to live in Egypt during the Old Kingdom, in Athens during the Age of Pericles, or in Rome under the Good Emperors?

3. What do you think was the most outstanding achievement of the Romans? Why?

4. The Roman Republic had a citizen army instead of a professional one. What are the advantages of a citizen army?

5. The United States Constitution designates the President as commander in chief of the armed forces. In the light of Roman history, why is it important that the President preserve this power?

PROJECTS

1. Write a one-page comparison between the geography of Greece and Italy.

2. Write a letter to a newspaper, denouncing the brutality of some of the Roman amusements.

3. Make a diagram of the government of the Roman Republic as it had developed by 265 B.C. Show the relationships among the assemblies, the Senate, and the officials.

Christianity Rose as the Roman Empire Declined

For more than two hundred years, during the Pax Romana, there was orderly government in Rome and peace within Rome's massive empire. For many people, this was a time of comfortable living. It was a time when Roman culture, deeply influenced as it was by the Greeks, matured and put a stamp on Western civilization that has endured into our own times. A great historian has said that if he could choose a time and place in which to live, he would choose the Roman Empire during the Pax Romana.

No doubt many Romans at this time, if asked about the future, would have said that Roman civilization would probably go on nearly unchanged for many centuries, if not forever. The strength and stability of Rome would have made them think so. But they would have been wrong. Weaknesses began to appear in the Roman state. Roman power declined and the influence of Rome upon Western Europe decreased greatly.

Even during the Pax Romana, however, an important new force was stirring. No Roman at the time could have recognized it for what it was. For one reason, it began in Palestine, a small and seemingly unimportant part of the Roman Empire whose people were troublesome to Roman rulers only when officials interfered with their religion. For another reason, this new force was not one that could be seen and measured, like military power. It was, rather, a sublime idea.

An early Christian martyr standing beneath a cross

For centuries, the Jews of Palestine had been developing a form of religion that has been called ethical monotheism. They believed that there was a single God who was righteous and who demanded righteous conduct from men. This great concept, as interpreted by a new religious leader, Jesus Christ, was soon to become a basic idea in the Christian Church, which gave a measure of continuity to Western civilization when Roman power declined. The idea itself, which is the heart of what is called the Judeo-Christian tradition, became a vital element in our own civilization.

THE CHAPTER SECTIONS:

1. Christianity was born in Palestine and then spread widely (1–400 A.D.)
2. Roman collapse was postponed by reorganization of the empire (180–375 A.D.)
3. Invasions and internal weakness ended the Roman Empire in the west (375–476 A.D.)

1   Christianity was born in Palestine and then spread widely

Augustus ruled as emperor from 27 B.C. until 14 A.D. During his reign there was born a child destined to become far greater than the mighty emperor. That child was Jesus of Nazareth.

The life and teachings of Jesus

Jesus was born in the town of Bethlehem, near Jerusalem in southern Palestine. Roman histories written during the lifetime of Jesus do not refer to him at all. Our knowledge comes mainly from the Gospels—the first four books of the New Testament of the Bible.

Very little is known about the early life of Jesus. He grew up in the town of Nazareth and was said to have been a carpenter and a student of the writings of the Jewish prophets. In time he began preaching to those who crowded around him. As he traveled through the villages of Palestine, he gathered a small group of disciples, or followers. From these he chose twelve, the Apostles, to help him preach.

Jesus spoke of himself as "the Son" and of "my Father in heaven," and his followers believed that he was the Son of God, the Messiah described by some of the Old Testament prophets. (The word *Messiah* means "anointed" in Hebrew; the Greek form of this word is Christos.) Jesus believed that his mission was to help all mankind attain the Kingdom of God through his life and teachings.

The teachings of Jesus have become one of the greatest influences of the Western world. He accepted the Hebrew Ten Commandments as guides to right living but gave them meaning beyond that of the words themselves, as did many of the Jewish scholars of the time. For example, he taught that the commandment "Thou shalt not kill" prohibited not only killing but hating. He summarized the ten rules in two great commandments: Men must love God above all else, and they must love others as they love themselves. Here are more of his important teachings:

(1) All men are equal in the sight of God; God's love is not affected by wealth, race, or nationality.

(2) Men must serve their fellow men; they must love even their enemies. Men must follow the Golden Rule: "Do unto others as you would have others do unto you."

(3) No man has the right to avenge wrongs done to him. God alone may judge and punish.

(4) Men must respect their government. They must be obedient to its laws, pay taxes, and be good citizens in every way.

(5) All quarreling and war are wrong.

The death of Jesus

Jesus believed that men could gain salvation, not only through his life and teachings, but also through his death—that God would forgive men's sins if Jesus gave up his life for mankind. When he traveled to Jerusalem in about 30 A.D., many Jews there hailed him as the Messiah and as "King of the Jews." Others, however—especially the conservative priestly class of Jews—denied that he was the Messiah and opposed this claim.

148

The Romans feared that Jesus wanted to lead an uprising and regarded him as an enemy of the state. Jesus was tried before a Roman court and executed by crucifixion—a common Roman punishment at that time.

The spread of Christianity

According to the Gospels, Jesus arose from the tomb and remained on earth for forty more days. He commissioned his followers to carry on his work and then ascended into heaven. His resurrection became a central part of the message of his disciples, who, as missionaries, set out to convert all peoples to his teachings. At first they worked mainly in the Jewish communities of the Near East.

Some years after the crucifixion of Jesus, there occurred an event that was to spread the Christian religion far and wide. A Jew named Saul of Tarsus—a town in southern Asia Minor—was suddenly converted to Christianity. He then took the name Paul and became a great Christian missionary, carrying on his work not only among Jews, but among all peoples. Between 45 and 65 A.D., during four long journeys, he spread the teachings of Jesus throughout the eastern Mediterranean (see map, this page).

Paul's inspired missionary work spread the re-

BIRTHPLACE OF CHRISTIANITY

CONSTANTINE'S EDICT OF MILAN, 313 A.D.

SPREAD OF CHRISTIANITY to 400 A.D.

- Christian areas in 200 A.D.
- Christian areas in 400 A.D. (Christianity became the official religion of the Roman Empire in 380 A.D.)
- Limits of the Roman Empire about 400 A.D.
- ◇ Patriarchal cities
- ·········· Journeys of Paul

0   500 miles

According to the Bible, Pontius Pilate — Roman ruler of Jerusalem — asked a crowd to decide whether Jesus or a thief, Barabbas, should be crucified; they condemned Jesus. The painting above, from a Greek manuscript, shows Pilate seated and Jesus standing at left.

ligion rapidly. His Epistles to Christian congregations in Greece and Asia Minor form an important part of the New Testament. Paul visited Rome, where, according to tradition, he was put to death by the Emperor Nero.

In the Roman Empire, the old religious beliefs were dying out. Augustus had tried to revive the old Roman gods, but they were as dead as the old Roman virtues. He and many of his successors were declared to be divine and were worshiped throughout the empire. But neither emperor worship nor Greek philosophy satisfied many persons. People wanted a firm guide to personal conduct and some promise of a future life. Christianity furnished such a guide and such a promise, but so did three other eastern religions: the Persian belief in Mithras; the worship of Cybele, a goddess of Asia Minor; and the Egyptian worship of Isis and Osiris.

Christianity, however, had a special appeal that these other religions lacked. It taught that all souls were equal in the eyes of God. Mithraism excluded women; in the worship of Cybele and Isis, women were more important than men. Christianity was a religion for everyone. Unlike the other religions, Christianity taught respect for human labor. A man could continue his everyday life and still be a good Christian, finding that his religion helped him in his daily life. Moreover, he could look forward to salvation. Christianity taught that there would be not only a changed way of life in the present, but also eternal life in the future for those who accepted God as the only God, and Jesus as His Son, the Saviour.

Persecution of the Christians

The Romans were tolerant of the many religious beliefs within the empire. As long as a person observed the rituals of the state religion, based upon the worship of the emperor, he could also practice any other religion that suited him.

The early Christians were good citizens. As you have seen, their religion taught them to respect the government. But they refused to worship the emperor as a god. To others, the offering of wine and incense to a statue of the emperor was only a gesture. To Christians it was the worship of an idol, and they would not do it, no matter what the penalty. In addition, many of them refused to join the Roman army because Jesus had preached against war.

To the emperors, these actions of Christians were a defiance of Roman religion and law. It became a crime to be a Christian. The property of Christians was seized and many Christians were executed. Even the Good Emperors followed this policy to some extent, although not every emperor tried equally hard to enforce the laws. Some tried to stamp out Christianity entirely. Others thought that the government should act only when Christians were accused and found guilty of breaking the law.

A little persecution often has less effect in accomplishing its purpose than none at all. Execution of Christians and seizure of their property did not stop the spread of the religion. It has been said that "the blood of the martyrs is the seed of the Church."

In the 200's A.D., as you will read later, the Roman Empire was shaken by civil wars. Many people turned to Christianity during these terrible years. City dwellers of the middle and upper classes suffered greatly, and many of them were converted to this new religion which gave them hope. By the end of the 200's A.D., the Christian Church had become too big for the government to try to punish all its members. The laws were changed at that time to prohibit only the making of converts.

The success of Christianity

The position of the Christians was vastly improved early in the 300's A.D. when the Emperor Constantine became a supporter of Christianity. According to one story, in 312, Constantine was leading his army into battle against a rival for his throne when he saw a blazing cross in the sky. Beneath it were the words *In Hoc Signo Vinces*, Latin words meaning "By this sign you will conquer." He is said to have placed himself and his army under the protection of the Christian God. Although this story is probably only a legend, Constantine did win the battle, and the next year he issued the Edict of Milan, which gave Christi-

Jesus as the Good Shepherd

Because we are accustomed to seeing Jesus as a bearded man of middle age, representations like the one above seem unusual and even shocking. Early Christian artists, however, worked within classical traditions, since those were the only ones they knew. To them it was natural to portray Jesus very much like the Roman god Apollo, dressed in a short Roman tunic. But even by the 200's A.D., when this carving was made, certain symbols had come to be associated with Christianity. Thus Christ is shown as a shepherd carrying a lost sheep on his shoulders—symbolic of how he restores the wayward sinner to the flock of God. At his feet are a dog, symbol of fidelity, and a lamb, representing the faithful.

anity legal status and protected it by law on the same basis as other religions.

Finally, in 380, Emperor Theodosius made Christianity the official religion of the Roman Empire. In 392 he forbade the worship of all heathen gods, even in private. In less than 400 years, Christianity had spread from its birthplace in Palestine to become the official religion of a huge empire (see map, page 149).

Organization of the Church

During the first few years after the crucifixion of Jesus, there was little need for Church organization. There were few believers, and they expected his early return. Christians lived together in groups, sharing their possessions and holding all property in common. Members were selected in each group to hold church services, preach, and help the sick and needy.

In time a more definite church organization grew up, based largely on the territorial divisions of the late Roman Empire, which you will read about shortly. In this later Church, a priest served the people within the smallest division, a parish. A number of parishes made up a diocese (DY-uh-seese), administered by a bishop. The cathedral church of the bishop was located in the most important city of the diocese. (*Cathedra* is the Latin word for the bishop's throne, or chair.) Several dioceses were combined into a province, ruled by an archbishop. In time, five cities—Rome, Constantinople, Alexandria, Antioch, and Jerusalem—gained special importance as administrative centers for the Church. The bishops of these cities were called patriarchs.

Bishops were very important officials. According to Church tradition, Jesus gave to the Apostles, the first missionaries, the authority to continue his work. They in turn commissioned others, the bishops, with authority to administer rites and govern the Church. The bishops could then transmit this authority to succeeding bishops and priests.

The services of the new Church centered on rites called sacraments—baptism, Holy Eucharist (or Communion), confirmation, penance, ordination (or holy orders), matrimony, and extreme unction

152

(the anointing of the sick). The parish priest administered all but two of these sacraments. Only bishops could confirm a person in the Christian Church or ordain a member of the clergy. They also supervised the priests, managed Church property, and directed relief for the poor and needy.

CHECKUP

1. What did Jesus believe his mission to be? State three of the teachings of Jesus.

2. Why was the work of Paul important to the spread of Christianity?

3. What conditions in the Roman Empire favored the spread of Christianity?

4. Why were the Christians persecuted by the Romans?

5. IDENTIFY: Gospels, disciples, Apostles, Messiah, Edict of Milan, parish, diocese, bishops, sacraments.

6. LOCATE: Bethlehem, Jerusalem, Nazareth, Tarsus.

2 Roman collapse was postponed by reorganization of the empire

The events about which you have just read occurred during a long period of time, from the birth of Jesus to the late 300's, when Christianity became the official religion of the Roman Empire. During the latter part of that period, the Roman Empire grew constantly weaker, until it broke up in the late 400's. To understand this long decline, it is necessary to turn back to the time of the Good Emperors.

You have read that Marcus Aurelius, the last of the Good Emperors, ruled from 161 to 180 A.D. When it came to his choice of a successor, Marcus Aurelius failed to show his usual wisdom. Instead of choosing an able man, he appointed his son Commodus, who was weak and spoiled. The reign of Commodus ended the days of the Pax Romana and the great period of the empire.

Civil wars and Barrack Emperors

After a reign of thirteen years, during which time the strength of the empire declined, Commodus was assassinated. Three candidates for emperor, each backed by a different force in the empire, struggled for power in a civil war. The winner was Septimius Severus, a general from the African provinces. He was the candidate of the legions. Severus used his power to strengthen the military dictatorship. The next two rulers each gained the throne as a result of an assassination. Neither was a good ruler.

During most of the 200's, the empire experienced dreadful confusion and civil war. There were twenty emperors in the period from 235 to 284 A.D.; all but one died violently. If an emperor tried to enforce discipline, or failed to reward the soldiers of the legions and the Praetorian Guard, they would assassinate him and put someone else on the throne. For this reason the emperors of this period have come to be called the Barrack Emperors. The legions, moreover, did not perform their job of defending the frontiers. Every frontier of the empire was invaded by barbarian tribes.

Problems of the empire

Many aspects of Roman life were affected by the political disorder. Travel became unsafe, and merchants hesitated to send goods by land or sea. The rural population grew even poorer than before. Since farmers had no money to buy goods, city industries suffered and unemployment increased. Population decreased throughout the empire, partly because of a great plague that spread through the provinces and caused several million deaths.

It became very difficult to collect taxes. Money was so scarce that taxes were often paid in grain, and the army was paid in land. In 212 A.D. the government granted citizenship to all the peoples of the empire in order to collect from everyone the 10 percent inheritance tax that citizens had to pay. After 250 A.D. the government was seldom able to pay all its expenses.

A sad fate befell the wealthy businessmen who made up the city councils of the provincial cities. They had always served without pay, taking great

153

pride in their offices and often making rich gifts to their cities. When tax collection in the empire became difficult and uncertain, the imperial government made the city councils responsible for taxes in their districts. If the required amount was not collected, the council members had to make up the difference. As the amount of taxes collected grew smaller, the council members saw their personal fortunes dwindle. When many of them began to resign, the government made their positions compulsory and hereditary.

The only relatively prosperous people in the empire were the large landowners. As small farmers were forced to sell their land, large estates grew even larger. Many landowners left the cities and moved to their country villas. They organized and paid private armies and defied the government officials who came to collect taxes. With the decline in population, there was danger that there might not be enough labor to work the land. A new law forbade coloni to leave the land and made their status in life hereditary.

The people in the cities were no better off. When manufacturing declined and unemployment increased, many artisans tried to leave the cities and find work in the country. To prevent this, the government made use of the workers' trade associations, called collegia (kuh·LEE·jih·uh).

Originally, the collegia were voluntary organizations designed mainly for social relations among members. Now a new law made workers' membership in the collegia compulsory. To maintain what industry there was, and to be sure of the taxes paid by workers and their organizations, the government required members of the collegia to stay at their jobs and to perform certain public services. When men tried to resign from the collegia, another law made membership not only compulsory but also hereditary.

Diocletian

The Roman Empire would undoubtedly have collapsed in the late 200's except for two able emperors, Diocletian (dy·uh·KLEE·shun) and Constantine, whose reforms and reorganizations postponed the collapse for nearly 200 years.

Diocletian was the son of a humble peasant from Illyria. He had risen through the ranks of the army to become a general. The army made him emperor in 284, but he proved to be very different from the Barrack Emperors. He was an able organizer and administrator.

Diocletian's greatest work was the reorganization of imperial administration. The empire was too much for one man to manage, so Diocletian appointed a co-emperor. Each was known as an augustus. Although the empire was not officially divided, each augustus administered approximately half of its territory. Diocletian ruled in the east—roughly the area stretching eastward from the Balkan Peninsula in Europe to Cyrenaica (sihr·uh·NAY·ih·kuh) in North Africa (see map, page 156). He established his headquarters at Nicomedia, a town in northern Asia Minor. His fellow augustus, Maximian, ruled the western half of the empire from his headquarters at Milan in northern Italy. Rome was thus no longer the capital of the empire.

Each augustus chose an assistant, called a caesar, to help him rule and be his successor. The empire was divided into four parts, called prefectures. They were subdivided into dioceses. The dioceses in turn were subdivided into provinces—about a hundred in all. This division reduced the territory and limited the power of provincial governors, thereby lessening the danger that an ambitious governor might threaten an augustus. Each augustus appointed officials, subject to his orders, within his own territory. High officials served one year only; the lower officials held permanent positions.

Although Diocletian shared his power with others, he held supreme authority. From the time of Augustus, most Roman emperors had pretended to keep some of the forms of republican government. Beginning with Diocletian, no one pretended any more. The emperor was an autocrat in theory as well as in fact.

Diocletian ended lawlessness within the empire and drove out the invading barbarian tribes. He tried to improve commerce and manufacturing and to increase the wealth of the empire. Diocletian planned to make the empire so prosperous that taxes alone would produce enough money to

Empire uparts
  Prefectures
DIOCESES - a subdivision of empire
   done by Diocletian
Provinces from Dioceses.

run the government, but this task was too much for any emperor.

Constantine

The system of divided rule set up by Diocletian did not work well after he retired in 305. Rivalry between the co-emperors and their caesars was intense. Constantine, who came to power as a caesar in 306, became sole emperor in 324. His reign is known for two great events. The first was his legal recognition of the Christian religion (see page 151). The second was his creation in 330 of a new capital at Byzantium, which had been founded by the Greeks about a thousand years earlier. It was renamed Constantinople after the emperor. (Today it is the Turkish city of Istanbul.)

Constantinople controlled navigation through the narrow passage from the Black Sea to the Aegean Sea (see map, page 156). The city was difficult to attack from both land and sea and thus had tremendous military and commercial advantages.

After Constantine's death in 337, there was a return to the rule of two co-emperors. The division of the empire became more pronounced. By the year 400, there were in effect two empires, one in the west and one in the east. The one in the west grew constantly weaker, as you will read shortly. Power had shifted to the east, where the wealth was. The fact that both Diocletian and Constantine chose to rule the east tells its own story.

CHECKUP

1. Explain the effects of the period of the Barrack Emperors on (a) defense of the empire; (b) the economy; (c) businessmen of the provinces; (d) city workers.

2. How did Diocletian change the organization of the Roman government?

3. For what two events is the reign of Constantine noted?

4. IDENTIFY: Commodus, Septimius Severus, Maximian.

5. LOCATE: Cyrenaica, Nicomedia, Milan, Constantinople.

This head of the emperor Constantine, eight feet high, is one of the few remaining fragments of a gigantic statue that once stood in Rome. At the time it was made, Roman sculptors no longer tried to convey a ruler's individual appearance or personality. It was an era of complete despotism, when emperors maintained elaborate courts in order to overawe their subjects. Artists served the state by emphasizing imperial pride and the brute force that lay behind it.

155

3 Invasions and internal weakness ended the Roman Empire in the west

It might seem that the western Roman Empire would have fallen apart from inner weaknesses alone. But there were also pressures from the outside. During the 200's, while the government was weakened by civil wars and the Barrack Emperors, enemy peoples attacked every frontier of the empire. The most important of these were the Germans, whose migrations through Europe and into North Africa were to influence history for many centuries.

The Germans

The Germans had begun to move south from their original home in Scandinavia sometime before 1000 B.C. By 200 B.C., some tribes had occupied what is now western Germany. Others moved into the Netherlands and northern France, forcing out the Gauls who lived there. One Germanic tribe, the Ostrogoths, eventually migrated southeastward to settle in the grasslands north of the Black Sea. Another tribe, the Visigoths, occupied land north of the Danube River (see map, this page).

The Germans had no written language, and we know about them mostly through Roman writings. Caesar, for example, described German life and customs in his *Commentaries.* Tacitus, in his *Germania,* gives a fuller picture.

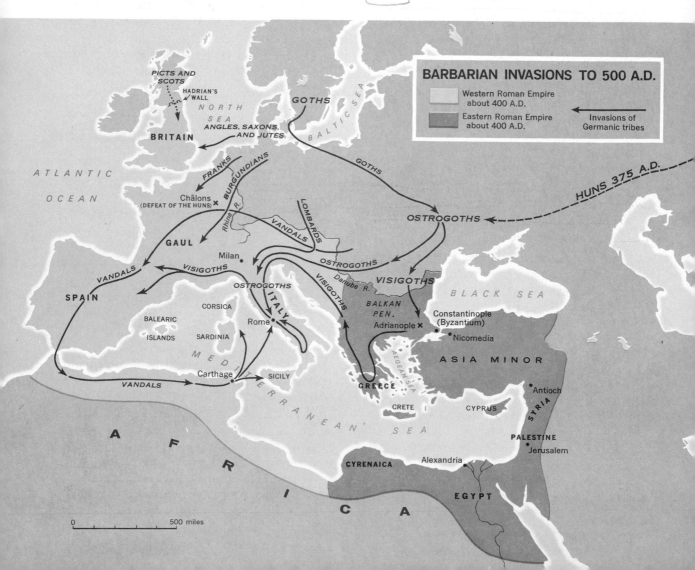

BARBARIAN INVASIONS TO 500 A.D.

Western Roman Empire about 400 A.D.

Eastern Roman Empire about 400 A.D.

Invasions of Germanic tribes

0   500 miles

The Germans of Tacitus' time, about 100 A.D., did some primitive farming, but most of the men were warriors rather than farmers. In times of peace, German men spent much of their time gambling and drinking. They left the work, both at home and in the fields, to women and slaves.

Some Germanic tribes had kings with considerable powers, but most of the important decisions were made by assemblies of all warriors. A proposal would be made by king, chief, priest, or general. The warriors showed approval by clashing their spears on their shields; disapproval, by shouting the proposal down.

German tribesmen often formed voluntary associations for warlike adventure or plunder. A chief with a reputation for bravery usually attracted a following of young warriors who became members of his household. It was an honorable relationship on both sides. The followers received food, shelter, and equipment; the chief acquired a following of good fighters, giving him a chance to perform greater deeds. The chief and his followers fought together, and they either shared the profits of victory or died together.

Germans in the empire

The northern frontier of the Roman Empire along the Rhine and Danube rivers was strongly fortified against the Germans. As early as the reign of Augustus, however, many Germans began crossing the frontier peacefully. Some enlisted in the Roman army. Many veteran Roman soldiers who had received land along the frontiers married German women.

Beginning about 375, the movement of Germans into the Roman Empire increased greatly. At this time, the Huns, an Asiatic tribe, were making one of their periodic invasions of Europe. The Huns were nomads who lived by raiding and plundering. Their belongings were limited to tents and necessary implements which could be moved easily on horseback. Roman writers described them as more like beasts than men, and their ferocity filled the people of Europe with terror.

Among those menaced by the Huns were the Ostrogoths of the Black Sea area. These Ostro-goths, terrified of the Huns, moved westward into land held by the Visigoths, who were still living north of the Danube River (see map, opposite), across from the Roman line of frontier forts.

The Visigoths begged the eastern emperor, Valens, for permission to cross the Danube. They were allowed to cross the river and settle on Roman land in return for patrolling and defending the frontier. However, Roman officials soon began mistreating the new settlers. In 378 the Visigoths revolted. In a battle at Adrianople, they annihilated a Roman army and killed Valens, who led it. Then there was peace for a time.

In the late 300's, an ambitious leader named Alaric became king of the Visigoths. For a while it looked as though he might try to seize the throne of the eastern empire, but the eastern emperor persuaded him to march westward instead. In 401, Alaric led the Visigoths into Italy. The western emperor ordered all the Roman troops from the northern frontiers to return and defend Italy, but they were not numerous enough. Alaric captured Rome in 410 and gave his troops three days to plunder it. After the sack of Rome, he moved his army toward Sicily, planning to take North Africa, too, but he died suddenly. The Visigoths later settled in southwestern Gaul and Spain (see map, opposite page).

Final invasions of the west

The two parts of the empire drifted farther and farther apart. The east revived and gained strength, while the west sank to ruin. In the west, the northern frontiers had been stripped of troops. Barbarians poured in everywhere, doing what they pleased in the provinces (see map, opposite). Britain, from which the Roman legions had been withdrawn in the early 400's, was overrun by Picts and Scots from the north and by the Germanic Angles, Saxons, and Jutes from the continent.

A number of Germanic tribes overran Europe. Northern Gaul was taken by the Franks, eastern Gaul by the Burgundians. Southwestern Gaul and Spain, as you have read, fell to the Visigoths. The Vandals set up a kingdom in North Africa. (They were so destructive that the word *vandal* has come into our language meaning one who causes senseless destruction.) Italy was overrun by the Ostrogoths.

In the mid-400's, a strong leader named Attila came to power among the Huns—a leader so ferocious that he was called the "Scourge of God." Attila led his Huns in an attack on Gaul. The western emperor was powerless, but his general Aetius led an army against the Huns. Aided by the Visigoths, he defeated the Huns in a great battle at Châlons in 451 (see map, page 156). Attila himself died two years later. His army quickly broke up, and the Huns were no longer a threat. Aetius' victory over Attila at Châlons saved Europe from Asiatic invaders, but it was far too late to save the western Roman Empire, which was weakened and shattered beyond repair.

The last Roman emperor in the west, Romulus Augustulus, was overthrown in 476 by a barbarian commander. Because of this event, people sometimes refer to the "fall" of the Roman Empire in 476. Actually, of course, there was no such thing as a single "fall," but instead a gradual disintegration. It is safe to say that Roman imperial authority had ceased to mean anything by the early 400's.

European civilization suffered a grave setback when the western Roman Empire broke up. The Germans that invaded and settled in the west established tribal kingdoms, but they were not capable of ruling an empire. The result was anarchy—the absence of any government at all.

Roads and bridges fell into disrepair, for there was no one to see that they were kept up. Trade and manufacturing almost disappeared, for few people had money to buy goods. It was not even safe to move goods from place to place, for there was no protection against bandits.

Towns and cities were regularly plundered by wandering bands of barbarians. Most people left the cities, both for greater safety and to find food. In the country, however, crops were often destroyed in the fighting, and fields were overgrown with weeds. Learning declined, for there was no government to set up and maintain schools. Libraries, with their great stores of knowledge, were destroyed. Western Europe was to suffer anarchy and disorder for centuries.

Why Rome declined: individual causes

Historians have offered many explanations for the collapse of Rome. Some of their theories hinge on what might be called specific, individual causes. At various times each of these causes has been held responsible for the weakening or fall of the empire.

Slavery has been stressed by some historians as the cause of Roman decline. Slavery undoubtedly weakened Roman life in many ways. It produced a class of people who were always discontented and often in revolt. It tended to make slaveowners brutal, selfish, and lazy. However, the number of slaves decreased greatly during the period of the empire; in fact, the number was lowest when Rome was weakest.

Another weakening element, according to some historians, was the great mixture of peoples in the empire. Actually this mixture was both a strength and a weakness. Compared to the Romans of the period, newcomers like the Germans had greater physical strength and, often, higher moral standards. However, when great numbers came into the empire, Roman culture could not absorb them and the barbarians did not develop loyalty to the Roman government.

Some scholars blame Roman decline on Christianity. It is true that some Christian ideas—refusal to worship the emperor and opposition to war—weakened the government and the army. On the other hand, Christian teachings produced honest, hard-working, obedient citizens. These were not the qualities that brought the final breakup of the Roman Empire.

The army has also been blamed as a weakening factor. After the time of the Good Emperors, leadership was poor and discipline could not be enforced. Military interference in the choice of an emperor made the government unstable. It seems likely, though, that the weakening of the army over the years was as much a result as a cause of Roman decline.

It is undoubtedly true that barbarian invasions played an important role in Roman collapse. However, barbarian tribes lived on the frontiers throughout the time of both the Roman Republic and the Roman Empire. Not until the empire had declined were the barbarians able to break through the frontiers.

Why Rome declined: interacting forces

The important point to remember is that no one cause was responsible for Roman decline. Like many other complex movements and events in history, it resulted from a combination of interacting forces. Between the years 200 and 400, no aspect of Roman life—political, economic, or social—was free from decay. Each aspect influenced and acted upon the others.

Political weakness. Rome tried to control the entire Mediterranean world with a government originally designed for a small city-state. The miracle is that it worked for 600 years. In an age of slow transportation, the empire grew too fast and became too large for the governmental machinery the Romans could build.

Another political weakness was the lack of a fixed succession to the throne. After about 200 A.D., the army made and unmade emperors as it wished. The Praetorian Guard, stationed near Rome, became the greatest single force in deciding who should be emperor. Later the legions competed among themselves in placing their generals on the throne.

Economic decline. Even more important than political breakdown was economic decline. Government expenses were heavy. Taxes had to finance the erection of public buildings, the purchase of grain for the poor, the maintenance of the army, and, in the later empire, the cost of two imperial courts—one in the west and one in the east. Even unbearably heavy taxes could not produce enough revenue to run the government. For centuries the Roman government maintained itself on rich plunder from the eastern part of the empire. By the time of Diocletian, however, this source of revenue was exhausted.

Some emperors tried to fix prices and regulate business activity, but they failed. Decreased revenue for the government resulted in unrepaired roads and bridges and increased banditry. The greater danger in travel, in its turn, led to a decrease in trade. When trade declined, manufacturing suffered. Eventually nearly all trade and manufacturing disappeared, and towns began to empty. Agriculture suffered the same fate as trade and commerce. Small farmers—once the strength of the empire—gradually lost their lands.

Basically, the Roman economy did not produce enough wealth to support a great civilization permanently. What wealth was produced went into too few hands. One historian, writing about Rome in the 400's A.D., has pointed out that, in a world where poverty was a disgrace, poverty steadily increased.

Social decay. A third force of great importance was social decay. There was a marked decline in morality throughout the empire. Early Romans may have been rude and uncultured, but they were stern, virtuous, hard-working, and patriotic. They had a strong sense of duty and believed in serving their government. These qualities were not prominent in the later days of the empire. Romans of the later empire were not patriotic, took little interest in government, and lacked political honesty. For example, at a time when every frontier was threatened, there was wholesale desertion in the army and frontier posts were abandoned.

The breakup of the western empire did not mean the end of Roman civilization. It lived on in Constantinople and the eastern empire for another thousand years, as you will read in Chapter 12. It lived on in the Christian Church, which it greatly influenced. The barbarians whose kingdoms had once been part of the empire were influenced by its customs and civilization. Thus the heritage of the Romans—which in turn contained elements of the culture of the Greeks and other ancient peoples—was passed on to the modern world.

CHECKUP

1. Name the barbarian groups and tell in what ways they came into the Roman Empire.
2. Why is the word *anarchy* appropriate in describing the final period of the Roman Empire?
3. Discuss the interacting forces that contributed to the decline of the Roman Empire.
4. IDENTIFY: Attila, Aetius, Romulus Augustulus.

CHAPTER REVIEW

Chapter 8 Christianity Rose as the Roman Empire Declined (1—476 A.D.)

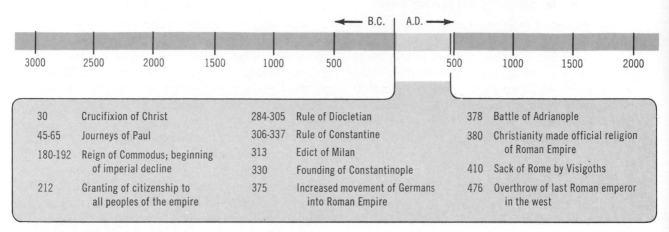

30	Crucifixion of Christ	284-305	Rule of Diocletian			378	Battle of Adrianople
45-65	Journeys of Paul	306-337	Rule of Constantine			380	Christianity made official religion of Roman Empire
180-192	Reign of Commodus; beginning of imperial decline	313	Edict of Milan				
		330	Founding of Constantinople			410	Sack of Rome by Visigoths
212	Granting of citizenship to all peoples of the empire	375	Increased movement of Germans into Roman Empire			476	Overthrow of last Roman emperor in the west

CHAPTER SUMMARY

Jesus was born in Roman Palestine during the reign of Augustus. His followers believed him to be the Messiah (or Christ) described in the Old Testament. He taught that men must love God and each other, and believed that his death would bring them salvation. The Romans regarded Jesus as an enemy of the state and executed him by crucifixion.

The teachings of Jesus, which formed the basis of the new religion of Christianity, were spread by his disciples and by missionaries, such as Paul. Christianity had great appeal for many people in the Roman Empire, but the Roman government regarded Christians as criminals and persecuted them for many years. In the 300's, however, Christianity became the official religion of the Roman Empire.

The Christian Church was organized around the parish, the diocese, and the province. Church services centered on the seven sacraments.

While Christianity was growing in strength, the Roman Empire was weakening. During the 200's there was great confusion and civil war, with growing poverty and a decline in population and tax revenues. Diocletian reorganized the empire but failed to restore prosperity. His successor, Constantine, built a new capital at Constantinople. By the year 400 there were two empires, one in the east and one in the west.

In the late 300's, more and more Germanic tribesmen crossed the Roman frontiers. Visigoths sacked and plundered Rome. Other German tribes overran much of the empire and anarchy resulted. The last Roman emperor in the west was overthrown in 476.

Many factors have been held responsible for the collapse of Rome—slavery, the mixture of peoples, Christianity, the army, and barbarian invasions. Actually, a number of forces interacted. Politically, Roman government was inadequate for its task. Economically, not enough wealth was produced to support a great empire. Socially, there was a decline in patriotism and political honesty.

QUESTIONS FOR DISCUSSION

1. Do you feel that the teachings of Jesus are observed today? Explain.

2. What kind of character must a person have had to become and remain a Christian in the Roman Empire during the time of the persecutions?

3. How do you account for the fact that mild persecution usually helps rather than hinders the spread of ideas and movements?

4. During the time of the Barrack Emperors, there was a lack of authority and power in the Roman Empire. On what was government power based earlier in the Roman Empire?

5. Why did the Germans cross the borders of the Roman Empire? Do you think that, in the modern world, there has been territorial expansion arising from the same motives as those of the barbarians?

PROJECTS

1. Write short sketches summarizing the accomplishments of (1) Diocletian and (2) Constantine.

2. List the chief causes for the decline of the Roman Empire, and explain each of them.

3. Draw a cartoon symbolizing the downfall of the Roman Empire at the hands of the barbarian invaders.

4. Draw a map showing the routes of the barbarian invasions into the Roman Empire.

India and China Developed Lasting Traditions

Our spotlight now turns back from the Occident, where Greece and Rome were playing their great dramas on the stage of history, to the Orient. This chapter tells the stories of India and China from about 1000 B.C. to about 600 A.D.

In the Orient as in the Occident, you will read of wars and rulers and of empires that rose and fell. But, of greater importance, you will read about one of history's most momentous coincidences—the simultaneous lives in India and China of two great leaders whose influence upon Oriental life has remained strong for almost 2,500 years. The Indian was Gautama Buddha, a religious leader who was born about 563 B.C. The Chinese was the philosopher Confucius, born about 551 B.C. When historians say that Indian and Chinese civilizations have been more nearly continuous than Western civilization, they have in mind, among other things, the enduring influence on Oriental life of these great leaders. Both of them shaped the existence of millions of people, not only in India and China, but also in many other regions of the East.

The lives of Buddha and Confucius represent pinnacles of achievement in human history. As you read about them, remember that Zoroaster had only recently presented the ideas about the struggle between good and evil that greatly altered Persian religious thinking. In Palestine, prophets like Ezekiel were refining the ethical

An Indian statue of Buddha enshrined between columns

monotheism that would become the greatest contribution of the Jews to Western civilization.

In Athens, Pisistratus and Cleisthenes were bringing about reforms that paved the way for the Golden Age; even then, indeed, the first great Athenian dramatist, Aeschylus, was writing heroic tragedies about Greek gods and men on earth. And, little noticed by anyone, Romans were establishing a republic in their small city on the banks of the Tiber River.

Thus, across much of the world in the 500's B.C., the foundations of many great civilizations were in the first stages of development. Some would survive and some would not. But in them men were working out ideas and creating traditions that are still shared by most of the people of the world.

THE CHAPTER SECTIONS:

1. Caste and Hinduism became rooted during the Epic Age in India (1000–500 B.C.)
2. Buddhism spread widely as Indian empires rose and fell (563 B.C.–220 A.D.)
3. Indian civilization flourished during the golden age of the Guptas (320–535 A.D.)
4. Chinese civilization endured through changing dynasties (1028 B.C.–589 A.D.)
5. Early China produced great philosophers and classic literature (551 B.C.–589 A.D.)

1 Caste and Hinduism became rooted during the Epic Age in India

The earliest known civilization of India, you recall, developed in the valley of the Indus River. Beginning about 1500 B.C., this civilization was overrun by Indo-European invaders from the north, the Aryans. During the Vedic Age, from about 1500 to 1000 B.C., they pushed eastward until they controlled the valley of the Ganges River as well. In the period from 1000 to 500 B.C., known as the Epic Age, they formed numerous city-states.

The Aryan city-states resembled each other in many ways. A rajah, or petty king, ruled each one, acting as military leader, chief priest, lawmaker, and judge. A royal council of friends and relatives assisted him. For hundreds of years, the city-states enjoyed peace and independence.

The great epics

You will recall that the Vedic Age was named after the Vedas, collections of religious rituals and hymns to the gods. The Epic Age also takes its name from religious literature.

You have read that interpretation of the rituals and hymns of the Vedas was left to priests called Brahmans, who became increasingly important in Aryan society. During the Epic Age, the Brahmans gained even more importance when they composed the *Upanishads* (OO·PAN·uh·shadz),

complex philosophical explanations of the Vedic religion.

Ordinary people were no more able to understand the *Upanishads* than they could the Vedas themselves. But they could understand stories in which many ideas about Vedic religion were made clearer. These stories were told from generation to generation. Finally they were combined by unknown geniuses in two epics, the *Mahabharata* (muh·HAH·BAH·ruh·tuh) and the *Ramayana* (rah-MAH·yuh·nuh).

The *Mahabharata* has been compared with Homer's epic, the *Iliad*. The main story tells of a great war, which it glorifies. The narrative is often interrupted, however, by myths, love stories, family histories, and lives of holy men. The *Ramayana* can be compared with Homer's other epic, the *Odyssey*. Its hero, Rama, wanders about for many years while his wife, Situ, faithfully awaits his return. The chivalry, compassion, gentleness, and generosity depicted in the poem set ideals for Indian manhood and womanhood.

From the *Mahabharata* and the *Ramayana,* and from the *Upanishads* and the Vedas themselves, scholars have been able to piece together the origins of the two most important influences in Indian history: the caste (KAST) system and the religion called Hinduism.

Indian art was profoundly influenced by Buddhism, as discussed on page 173. Of the many pillars of law erected by Asoka, perhaps the most famous was one at the site where Buddha first preached. Around its base were some of the milder laws adopted by Asoka after his conversion to Buddhism. On top of the pillar was the capital, at left, now the Indian national emblem. The lowest portion of the capital represents an inverted lotus blossom. Next comes a flat cylinder of stone on which are carved four animals and four wheels. This stone supports four magnificent lions, which stand back to back. Originally the lions held up a large polished sandstone disk representing the Wheel of Law. A Chinese pilgrim described the whole column as "a stone pillar about seventy feet high . . . as bright as jade. It is glistening and sparkles like light." Below is a large stupa built in central India between 300 B.C. and 100 A.D. The solid dome measures over 100 feet in diameter and 40 feet high.

The God Siva

Siva had many roles in the Hindu religion, and some are depicted in the bronze statue at left. Siva's power as the destroyer is particularly emphasized. Around the edge of the circular frame and in one of the god's hands are flames of destruction. Another hand points down to a dwarf, one of the many enemies overcome by this lord of death. Yet another hand is raised in a gesture indicating "do not fear," representing a kindly aspect of Siva. His fourth hand holds a drum, the instrument that created the first sound in the universe; it symbolizes the god's role as regulator of the rhythms of life. Siva's vast energy is represented by a third eye, vertically engraved on his forehead.

The caste system

No other people in the world have developed anything like the caste system of India. It began in northern India when the invading Aryans laid down rules to prevent intermarriage between themselves and the peoples they had conquered. By the beginning of the Epic Age, four distinct classes had emerged in Indian society: (1) at the top were the rulers and warriors, called Kshatriyas (KSHAHT·rih·yuz). (2) Next came the priests, scholars, and wise men, called Brahmans. During the Epic Age, the Brahmans and the Kshatriyas changed positions, with the Brahmans becoming first. (3) Next came the merchants, traders, and owners of small farms, called Vaisyas (VY·syuz). (4) At the foot of the ladder were the Sudras, who were peasants bound to work the fields of large landowners.

A fifth group of people in Indian society was not even on the ladder. These people were the pariahs (puh·RY·uz). They were also called "untouchables," because it was thought that merely to touch them would defile other people; indeed,

it was believed that even their shadows would defile a Brahman. Many of the conquered peoples were included among the pariahs.

As time passed, the original four groups were subdivided many times into the smaller groups called castes, and the caste system emerged. As society became more complex and new occupations were created, castes themselves were subdivided and new castes appeared.

Eventually there developed some 3,000 hereditary castes, each with its own fixed social position and rules about eating, marriage, labor, and worship. For example, a person could not eat or drink with someone of a lower caste, nor could he render any service to a person of lower caste. He could work only at those occupations recognized for his caste. He could not marry outside his caste. A person who violated any of the rules could become an untouchable, or "outcaste."

Hinduism

The major religion of India, Hinduism, developed through interpretations of the Vedas by

164

Brahman scholars. According to the *Upanishads,* everything in the world is permeated by a basic essence known as Brahma. A universal soul, Atman, is a part of every individual. When a Hindu —a follower of Hinduism—says that Brahma and Atman are one and indivisible, he means that God and man are one.

The world known to our senses is merely an illusion called Maya, which betrays man, giving him sorrow and pain. Man can have deliverance from his suffering if he identifies Maya. To identify Maya, however, requires many lifetimes of experience. This experience, according to a principal belief of Hinduism, is provided by reincarnation, or the transmigration of souls. According to this belief, the soul does not die with the body but enters the body of another being, either human or animal. The progress of the soul toward deliverance from suffering depends upon the life one lives and is regulated by what Hindus call karma, or destiny.

Karma has no favorites. Good persons are rewarded; evil ones are punished. Reward means that the soul enters the body of someone of a higher caste. An evil person is punished when his soul is reborn in the body of a person of lower caste, or in the body of an animal. Some Hindus take this belief so seriously that they will not kill an insect or animal—even a poisonous snake or man-eating tiger—because it may be the bearer of a human soul. They take this belief seriously because of the Hindu conviction that life is sacred and that the body has a direct relation to the spirit. For the same reason it is important that no forbidden foods or practices make the soul impure. One outgrowth of this attitude has been yoga, a physical and mental discipline harmonizing body with soul. A Hindu practicing yoga might, for example, sit for many hours in a certain position in order to free his mind of all things except the one upon which he wishes to concentrate.

The caste system is closely woven into Hindu religion. Hindus believe that men were divided into castes at the time of creation. The soul moves upward or downward on the ladder of castes according to the sort of life its bearer lives. The good life, in turn, means acceptance of caste and observance of all caste rules. By constantly identifying Maya, or illusion, through many lifetimes, the soul reaches nirvana and becomes associated with the soul of Brahma, when personal existence ceases altogether.

Religious practices. These principles of Hinduism, stated in the *Upanishads,* were simplified in the epics and in the teachings of the Brahmans. The Brahmans taught that salvation was achieved by the love and worship of savior gods. These gods included a basic trinity composed of (1) Brahma the Creator, (2) Vishnu the Preserver, and (3) Siva the Destroyer. Below these gods came many other gods, represented in the spirits of trees, animals, and persons. Some Hindus pay special reverence to certain animals, such as monkeys, snakes, and dogs. Cows are especially sacred. No Hindu will eat the meat of a cow, although he will eat cheese and butter and drink milk.

To us, this religion of many gods sounds polytheistic, but educated Hindus insist that it is monotheistic—that the basic trinity and all of the other gods are merely different representations of one supreme being.

Establishment of the caste system and of Hinduism were the most important developments of Indian history in the Epic Age—or, indeed, of any other age in Indian history. These two ideas became interwoven in the whole fabric of Indian society.

CHECKUP

1. With what two epics have the *Mahabharata* and the *Ramayana* been compared? Why? Why have all four epics been important in the study of history?

2. Explain briefly the chief features of the caste system.

3. Explain these main ideas of Hinduism: Atman, Maya, reincarnation, karma, nirvana.

4. "...this religion of many gods sounds polytheistic, but educated Hindus insist that it is monotheistic...." What does this statement mean?

5. IDENTIFY: Epic Age, rajah, *Upanishads,* Brahma, Vishnu, Siva.

2   Buddhism spread widely as Indian empires rose and fell

Toward the end of the Epic Age, about 540 B.C., the city-state of Magadha (MUH·guh·duh), in the Ganges Valley, gained control over many city-states in northeastern India and created a kingdom. Shortly afterward, Darius the Great of Persia invaded the Indus Valley and organized that area as part of the Persian Empire.

Like other periods before and since, however, the period following the Epic Age is best remembered, not for political and military reasons, but because it saw the emergence of a great religious leader—Gautama Buddha. His family name was actually Gautama. The word *Buddha* was given to him later as a title meaning "The Enlightened One," just as *Christ* is a title meaning "The Anointed One."

Gautama Buddha

Gautama was born about 563 B.C. and died about 483 B.C. The son of an Indian prince, he was himself a prince. He lived in luxury, shielded from the ordinary people of his native city. At the age of twenty-nine, he ventured into the city streets, where he became troubled by age-old problems. Why, he asked himself, should life bring joy and comfort to a few and only poverty and suffering to so many? Why must there be misery and death?

When Gautama returned to the palace of his father, these questions continued to trouble him. He then decided to spend the rest of his life seeking answers. In what is called the Great Renunciation, he put aside all his possessions, left his wife and infant son, and set out to search diligently for the truth.

Gautama followed all the practices that were recommended as leading to wisdom. He lived as a hermit and a scholar. He practiced the mental and physical discipline of yoga so diligently that he almost died. He tried fasting and self-torture. None of these things gave him the answers he wanted so much to find.

Then one day, after six years of searching, as Gautama sat meditating under a fig tree, he felt that he understood the truth on which life is based.

In that moment, according to his followers, he became Buddha, the Enlightened One. He spent the remainder of his life teaching the Enlightenment, the Way of Life.

Buddha's teachings. Buddha accepted the Hindu doctrine of karma, that the progress of the soul depends on the life a person leads, and that good is rewarded and evil punished. Men must seek the good and avoid the evil. However, Buddha said that since only deeds, good or bad, are important, salvation cannot come through self-torture or from the sacrifice of animals. This belief was a departure from Hindu doctrine. Salvation, according to Buddha, comes from knowing the Four Noble Truths and following the Middle Way.

The Four Noble Truths are these: (1) All human life is full of suffering and sorrow. (2) Suffering and sorrow are caused by man's greedy desire for pleasure and material things. (3) By renouncing desire, a person is freed from suffering and his soul attains nirvana. Nirvana is the perfect peace, in which the soul is freed from having to be born again. (4) Renunciation of desire and attainment of nirvana may be gained by following the Middle Way.

The Middle Way may be pursued by following the Eightfold Path, eight guides to thought and conduct: right views, right intentions, right speech, right action, right living, right effort, right mindfulness, and right concentration.

Buddha stressed ethics rather than ceremonies. Unselfishness was the key to his ethics, and he gave definite rules for unselfish behavior: not to kill or steal; not to lie, gossip, indulge in faultfinding, or use profanity; and to abstain from greed.

As you have seen, Buddha accepted the Hindu ideas of karma and nirvana, but he did not accept the Hindu gods as sacred. According to Buddha, man alone could do the supreme thing—change good to evil and evil to good. He did not need the help of gods or priests or temples or idols. Buddha taught that there are only two kinds of people, the good and the bad. Thus, although he did not attack the Hindu caste system openly, he did not accept it.

BUDDHISM AND HINDUISM IN 1200 A.D.

Extent of Hindu civilization

Extent of Buddhism

Mixed areas (Buddhism and Hinduism)

Spread of Buddhism

The spread of Buddhism. Buddha gained some followers in his lifetime, but not many. Over several centuries, however, his teachings—called Buddhism—won wide acceptance (see map, this page). By the 100's B.C., Buddhism had split into two branches: Hinayana, or the Lesser Vehicle; and Mahayana, or the Greater Vehicle. Hinayana kept the traditional beliefs of Buddhism, regarding Buddha as a teacher. This form of Buddhism in time spread to countries other than India, among

167

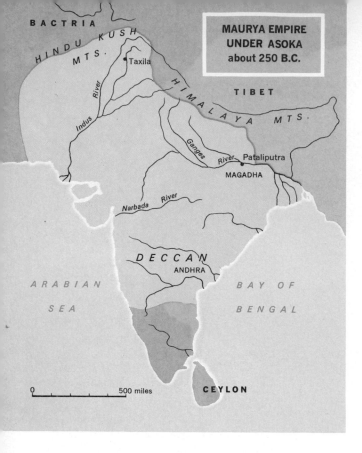

MAURYA EMPIRE UNDER ASOKA about 250 B.C.

BACTRIA

HINDU KUSH MTS.

Taxila

Indus River

HIMALAYA MTS.

TIBET

Ganges River Pataliputra

MAGADHA

Narbada River

DECCAN
ANDHRA

ARABIAN SEA

BAY OF BENGAL

0   500 miles

CEYLON

them Burma, Thailand, Cambodia, and Malaya.

Believers in the Mahayana form of Buddhism regarded Buddha as a god and the savior of mankind. They made Buddhism into a religion with priests, temples, creeds, and rituals. Mahayana Buddhism spread over a wide area, including Afghanistan, central Asia, China, Korea, and Japan.

In India itself, Buddhism was opposed by the priestly Brahmans. Their high position depended on acceptance by the people of the idea of reincarnation—rebirth into a higher or lower caste according to how a person had lived. The Brahmans were bound to oppose any religion which taught that anyone, regardless of caste, could reach nirvana without help if only he were good.

Despite the opposition of the Brahmans, Buddhism gained many followers in India over several centuries, then declined, as you will see. Today, about 3 million Indians are Buddhists. Buddhism had greater success in the areas to which it spread. In all, there are over 160 million Buddhists.

Rule of the Nine Nandas

Darius, as you have read, sent a Persian army to invade the Indus Valley and organized the area as a part of the Persian Empire. Herodotus, the Greek historian, says that the area was prosperous, for it was rich in gold and supplied numerous well-trained archers to the Persians in their attacks upon Greece. Some of these archers were among the Persian forces that were defeated by the Greeks at the battle of Plataea in 479 B.C.

Native Indians slowly reduced Persian control of northwestern India. This region was finally absorbed by Magadha, in northeastern India. From 413 to 322 B.C., Magadha was ruled by a dynasty called the Nine Nandas. It was a Nanda ruler and his army that were defeated by Alexander the Great at the Indus River in 326 B.C. Alexander wanted to go on but, as you recall, his army mutinied and he was forced to turn back. He stayed long enough, however, to see the great Indian city of Taxila, a bustling center of learning.

The Maurya Empire

The last of the nine Nanda rulers, an unpopular king, was overthrown in 322 B.C. by a young Indian adventurer named Chandragupta. He became the first of the Maurya (MOWR·yuh) line of Indian rulers, and is usually known as Chandragupta Maurya.

Chandragupta Maurya. We know a good deal about Chandragupta because a Greek ambassador to his court wrote a fascinating book about him. According to the account, Chandragupta was an able general and administrator. He took over the Magadha capital at Pataliputra—now Patna—on the Ganges and made it a magnificent city. He learned both the science of government and methods of warfare from the Macedonians. His army of 700,000 men was equipped with 10,000 chariots and 9,000 elephants. He maintained an efficient postal service that moved swiftly over excellent roads. He united northern India from the delta of the Ganges River to the region west of the Indus. Eventually he took over all of northwestern India up to the Hindu Kush mountains.

Chandragupta was an able ruler but he was also highly autocratic. He learned the hard way that

168

"uneasy lies the head that wears a crown." Conspirators dug tunnels under the palace in attempts to destroy him. He lived in such fear that sleep came only with lulling music. To avoid assassination, he changed his bedroom nightly and employed food tasters as protection against being poisoned at meals. Finally, according to tradition, he abdicated the throne in favor of his son.

Bindusara. Chandragupta's son, Bindusara, was also an able administrator and military leader who pushed the Maurya Empire farther southward. In addition, he was interested in philosophy and enjoyed good living. He once wrote to a successor of Alexander the Great named Antiochus, asking for samples of Greek wine, raisins, and a Sophist philosopher. Antiochus replied that he was sending wine and raisins, but that the Greeks did not consider it good form to trade in philosophers.

Asoka. One of India's greatest rulers was Asoka, Chandragupta's grandson, who gained the throne about 270 B.C. By this time the Maurya Empire had been extended far to the south. Asoka enlarged the empire by conquest until it included all of India except the southern tip (see map, opposite). Asoka's campaign became a war of annihilation in which 100,000 people were killed, and 150,000 taken captive. Many more people died in the aftermath of the war.

Asoka became so sickened by this slaughter that he renounced war and became a devout Buddhist. He did not force the Indian people to accept Buddhism, but during his rule many did. He sent his brother as a missionary to Ceylon, and sent other missionaries to Tibet, China, Burma, Java, and even to Egypt, Syria, and Macedonia.

After his conversion to Buddhism, Asoka thought constantly of piety and duty. He urged religious toleration and relaxed the harsh laws that had supported the autocratic rule of his father and grandfather. He pardoned prisoners and forbade animal sacrifices. Asoka is unique among the rulers of history. Others have ruled well over larger territories. Only Asoka, after his conversion to Buddhism, was able to gain and hold followers by humility and compassion, by love rather than force.

HISTORY THROUGH ART

Relief Sculpture from Gandhara

One of the earliest meetings between East and West took place in Gandhara, a region in eastern Bactria. First conquered by Alexander the Great, it then became part of the Greco-Bactrian Empire, and still later was ruled by the Kushans. The sculptured relief above, which dates from the 100's or 200's A.D., shows how the people of Gandhara combined the elements of several cultures.

Dancers, a musician, and offering-bearers pay tribute to Buddha. (The offerings are probably fruit, a bowl of rice, and flowers—objects commonly presented to Buddha.) The necklaces and ankle bracelets they wear are Indian, as is the stringed instrument. The costume of the dancer in the center, with its trousers and tunic, is Persian, and the musician at right wears a Roman toga. The modeling of the figures shows Hellenistic influences. The relief is a remarkable blending of elements from several great and productive civilizations.

When Asoka died about 230 B.C., the Maurya Empire began to fall apart. The last Maurya ruler was assassinated in 184 B.C.

The Greco-Bactrian Empire

The Greeks had never forgotten the splendors of India. The eastern portion of Alexander's empire, bordering northern India, had become the Greek kingdom of Bactria (see map, page 168). At about the time the last Maurya ruler was assassinated, Demetrius, king of Bactria, moved into northwestern India and put a native ruler on the throne as a figurehead.

In imitation of Alexander's policies favoring the unification of various peoples, Demetrius tried to establish a combined Greek and Indian civilization in the Greco-Bactrian Empire. For example, he had coins made with lettering in both Greek and Brahmi, one of the languages of India. But many Greeks disliked Demetrius' policy and brought on a revolt in which Demetrius was killed.

Menander, a Greek general and son-in-law of Demetrius, restored order in northwestern India. Like Alexander, Menander became a legend in India. After he was converted to Buddhism, he was made the subject of an Indian dialogue entitled *The Questions of Milinda* (that is, Menander). Remnants of Menander's kingdom lasted until about 30 B.C. At that time a nomadic tribe, the Kushans, driven by the Huns from their home in central Asia, took Bactria. By 48 A.D., they were masters of northwestern India as well.

The Kushan Empire

The Kushans were described as "big pink-faced men . . . dressed in long-skirted coats," who wore "soft-leather boots" and "sat on chairs." They gave northern India one of the richest periods in its history.

The greatest Kushan king was Kanishka, who ruled from 120 to 162 A.D. His empire included northwestern India and extended as far south as the Narbada River in central India. Like Asoka and Menander, Kanishka became a Buddhist. Although he fostered the spread of Buddhism outside of India, the religion lost Indian followers under the Kushans because it was associated with rule by foreigners.

When the last known Kushan king died in 220 A.D., the empire had already broken up. There followed a period of 100 years in which Indian civilization was chaotic and about which little is known.

CHECKUP

1. What ideas did Buddha accept from Hinduism? What Hindu ideas did he reject?

2. State the Four Noble Truths and the principles of the Eightfold Path.

3. Find evidence in this section to prove the statement, made in Chapter 4, that India was often invaded from the outside.

4. Indians often say that they are more interested in spiritual things and less interested in material possessions than are Westerners. Can you find evidence in this section to support their statement? Can you find evidence to the contrary?

5. IDENTIFY: Great Renunciation, Hinayana, Mahayana, Nine Nandas, Chandragupta Maurya, Bindusara, Asoka, Menander, Kanishka.

6. LOCATE: Magadha, Burma, Thailand, Cambodia, Afghanistan, Taxila, Bactria.

3 Indian civilization flourished during the golden age of the Guptas

The period of disorder after the break-up of the Kushan Empire ended when the first of a new line of kings, the Guptas, began ruling in 320 A.D.

The Gupta rulers

The Guptas first came to power in the Ganges Valley. By intermarriage and conquest, they extended their power from the Himalayas in the north to the Narbada River in the south, and from the tributaries of the Indus River in the west through most of the Ganges Valley in the east (see map, opposite page).

The Gupta rulers were autocratic, holding "all the levers and handles which worked the governmental machinery." But the best of them—the first three, who ruled from 320 to about 412 A.D.—used their great powers benevolently. These three were Chandragupta I, the warrior king (who was not related to the earlier Chandragupta of the Maurya line of rulers); Samudragupta, known as the poet king; and Chandragupta II, under whom the Gupta Empire reached its greatest extent. He established the Gupta capital at Ayodhya, in the northeast.

The Guptas claimed that they had been appointed to rule by the gods. They favored Hinduism over Buddhism, since Hinduism stressed the gods and Buddhism did not. The Guptas were tolerant of Buddhism, but they favored the Brahmans, who wanted to restore Hinduism to its former strength. By the end of the Gupta period, Buddhism had dwindled in India itself, while gaining strength in other parts of Asia. Hinduism, somewhat influenced by Buddhism, became again the dominant religion of India.

Economy and social life

From ancient times, the land had provided a living for nearly all northern Indians. For a limited few at the top of the caste system, the land provided great luxury, but most people were poor. During the Epic Age, the rajahs in theory owned all the land and took what they wanted from those who tilled it. By the time of the Guptas, the rulers were taking one sixth of the agricultural produce as their share.

In Gupta India, a woman's status was lower than a man's. The *Mahabharata* called a man's wife his "truest friend," but the *Code of Manu,* a legal treatise, recommended that the wife worship her husband as a god. Polygamy, or marriage to more than one wife, was common in the Epic Age and became widespread under the Guptas. Another practice that became common during the Gupta period, especially among the upper castes, was suttee, the suicide of a widow on her husband's flaming funeral pyre.

Literature

Throughout Indian history, including the Gupta period, the most popular writings were the two

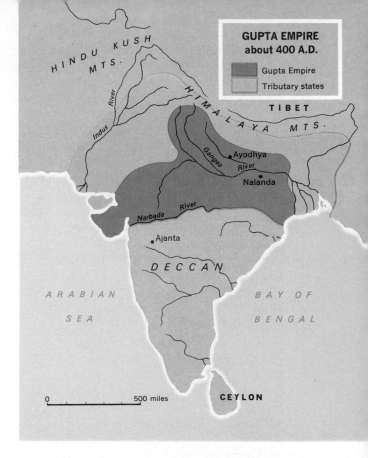

great epics, the *Mahabharata* and *Ramayana.* People also enjoyed the stories in the *Panchatantra,* a series of tales woven into a single narrative. Among its stories were those about Sinbad the Sailor, Jack the Giant Killer, the Magic Mirror, and the Seven League Boots—stories that are known all over the world. Next to the Bible, the *Panchatantra* is the most widely translated book in the world today.

Indian drama developed greatly under the Guptas. Unlike Greek plays, those of India always had a happy ending. They offered little action and used different dialects for different characters. Like early English drama, Indian plays were performed in a courtyard, using simple scenery. Actors formed a distinct caste.

Kalidasa, who lived in the 400's A.D., has been called the Indian Shakespeare. He wrote three plays, the most famous of which is *Sakuntala.* The story, a romantic one, concerns a king and the daughter of a sage, who fall in love and marry.

171

In a painting from the Ajanta caves, Buddha sits placidly at left, a halo around his head, and a monk stands before him. The painting dates from the 400's A.D.

A curse causes the king to lose his memory of the marriage, and the pair are separated. A boy child is born. The king, returning from battle, recognizes his son and the lovers are reunited.

King Sudraka, who lived about the same time as Kalidasa, wrote *The Little Clay Cart*. The play tells how a rich merchant falls in love with and eventually marries an entertainer. A hilarious incident in the play concerns a gambler who evades paying a debt and has to flee. To escape his pursuers, he enters a ruined temple and pretends to be the statue of a god.

Art

Not much is known about Indian art before the reign of Asoka in the 200's B.C. because earlier Indian artists used wood and other perishable materials. Throughout his empire, Asoka set up pillars with his laws carved on them. (The capital, or upper part, of one of these pillars, showing four lions, was chosen by India as its national emblem.) A common building during Asoka's time was the stupa, in the shape of a hemisphere, where relics of Buddha were kept. Asoka is said to have built 84,000 stupas.

By the time of the Kushan Empire, images of Buddha showed Greek influence; many resembled Greek statues of the god Apollo. During the rule of the Guptas, however, Indian sculptors developed their own style, more formal and less realistic; it has been followed down to the present day. It was also in this period, as Hinduism increased in importance, that Indians created a style of Hindu temple. This distinctive style—a square building with heavy walls that enclosed a god's statue—remained basically the same for centuries.

Mural paintings in caves tell us something about the artistic style of early Indian painters, but we know most about mural painting in the time of the Guptas. Today thousands of people visit the caves at Ajanta in central India every year to admire paintings of Buddha and his followers—beggars, women and children, farmers and rulers—all crowded together with pictures of animals, birds, and flowers. These paintings are a source of information about the daily life of Indian people under the Guptas.

Education

Although the children of the poor learned only crafts or trades, upper-class Indian children had formal lessons. Just as Greek children learned to read Homer's *Iliad* and *Odyssey,* Indian children learned to read the *Upanishads* and the great Indian epics, the *Mahabharata* and the *Ramayana*. Formal schooling began at the age of nine.

By the time of the Guptas, Nalanda had replaced Taxila as the chief center of Indian scholarship. This center, located in the lower Ganges Valley, attracted students from as far away as Tibet, China, and Korea. Nalanda had more than a hundred lecture halls, three large library buildings, an observatory to study the skies, dormitories, and a model dairy. The curriculum included religion, philosophy, medicine, art, architecture, and agriculture.

One Gupta ruler supported Nalanda with the income from 100 large villages. Between 20 and 30 percent of the students received financial help from the government. Student life was described in this way in one account of Nalanda: "Learning and discussing they found the day too short, day and night they admonished each other, juniors and seniors mutually helping to perfection."

Mathematics and astronomy

Indian mathematicians had greater ability at dealing with abstract numbers than did the mathematicians of Greece and Rome. Indians actually invented the numeral system that we call Arabic— 1 through 9 and the zero. The zero was an especially important contribution, since it allowed the position of a number to indicate its value; this concept is basic to our modern decimal system. These so-called Arabic numerals are known to have been in use in India by 595 A.D., and were probably used before the end of Gupta rule in 535 A.D.

Indians also had a concept of negative numbers (numbers preceded by a minus), without which algebra could not exist. They calculated the square root of 2 and prepared a table of sines, used extensively in trigonometry. Aryabhata (AHR·yuh·BUT·uh), who lived in the 400's A.D., computed the value of π (pi) more exactly than

Archimedes had. He also solved algebraic equations.

Indian astronomers identified the seven planets which can be seen with the naked eye. They knew that the planets and the moon shone by reflected light. They understood solstices, equinoxes, and the daily rotation of the earth on its axis. They also predicted eclipses, calculated the diameter of the earth, and developed a theory of gravitation.

Medicine

The earliest Indian medical writings, written soon after the birth of Christ, resemble the studies of the Greek physicians Hippocrates and Galen. Indian physicians understood the importance of the spinal cord. Their surgery included bone setting and plastic surgery on ears, noses, and lips. They perfected the technique of inoculation— communicating a mild form of a disease to a person so that he will not fall ill with the more serious form. They used the less harmful cowpox to inoculate against smallpox, a method unknown in the countries of the Western world until the end of the 1700's.

Free hospitals were built in India in the early 400's. Susruta, a great Indian doctor, practiced strict cleanliness before an operation and sterilized wounds—another procedure which Western surgeons did not use until modern times. Susruta urged that dissection be permitted as an aid to medical education. Like Hippocrates, he insisted upon the highest moral standards among physicians.

The end of the Guptas

Civilization in India reached a high peak during the rule of the Guptas, as you have seen. Their rule has been called a golden age because of the brilliant civilization that flourished then. Gupta rule ended in 535 A.D., when Hun invaders pushed into northwestern India. These Huns were related to those that invaded Europe under Attila in the 400's A.D. Although a league of Indian princes succeeded in holding the Huns back from expanding into the Deccan, they ravaged northern India and destroyed Taxila.

174

Southern India

Few of the Indian empires you have read about controlled southern India. That of Asoka extended farthest south, but it did not last long. Neither the Kushans nor the Guptas ruled south of the Narbada River.

As you read in Chapter 4, a range of hills separates the Indus-Ganges plain from the southern plateau known as the Deccan. Because of these hills, southern India was isolated from the north and thus developed differently.

Two influences played a major role in the history of southern India: (1) location and (2) natural resources. The peninsula of India is located midway between Africa and Southeast Asia, with the Arabian Sea on the west and the Bay of Bengal on the east. The land produced cotton, pepper and other spices, and many drugs, and also had plentiful amounts of ivory and gold. Thus southern Indians, particularly those along the coast, turned to the seas and to commerce both because of their geographical location and because of products which other peoples were eager to obtain.

Southern Indians became successful merchants and businessmen. Special organizations regulated crafts and trade. Commercial ties, especially with Arabia and the Roman Empire, made the land wealthy. Indian poets wrote of the magic of this foreign commerce, and the Roman writer Pliny the Elder described trade with India in the 70's A.D.

Although southern India was isolated from the north, Hinduism penetrated the region sometime after the 600's B.C. The first recorded date in the history of southern India is 256 B.C., when Asoka sent Buddhist missionaries to the Deccan. During the period of Maurya decline, beginning around 230 B.C., the Andhra dynasty arose in the south. The Andhras created an empire that eventually included a large part of southern India. When the empire declined, about 225 A.D., the south broke up into a number of small, warring states.

CHECKUP

1. Why did the Guptas favor the religion of Hinduism over that of Buddhism?

2. From what books did Indian children learn to read? What subjects were studied at Nalanda?

3. What contributions did Indians make in the fields of mathematics? astronomy? medicine?

4. What two factors played a major role in the history of southern India?

5. IDENTIFY: Guptas, suttee, *Panchatantra*, Kalidasa, *Sakuntala*, stupa, Andhra.

4   Chinese civilization endured through changing dynasties

Around 1000 B.C., important changes were taking place in the Western world. It was at this time that the Dorians were settling down in Greece and the Latins were moving into Italy. In China, too, a new people, the Chou, appeared on the scene. As you read in Chapter 4, the Shang dynasty, the first of many dynasties in the recorded history of China, began about 1500 B.C. and was overthrown by the Chou in 1028 B.C.

The Chou dynasty

The dynasty established by the Chou was the longest in China's history. It lasted from 1028 to 256 B.C., nearly 800 years. During this time, certain ideas about living and thinking became so firmly rooted in Chinese society that they endured into modern times.

The Chou were a people from the Wei River Valley in north-central China. Their culture was primitive, but they were better warriors than the Shang. Among other things, they used chariots in warfare. With these, and a number of allies, they toppled the Shang forces. Soon they created an empire stretching from the north side of the Yellow River southward to the Yangtze River, and a bit inland from the Yellow Sea westward to modern Kansu province in north-central China (see map, this page).

The Chou rulers called themselves Sons of Heaven and claimed to rule by the Mandate of Heaven—that is, by order of the gods. Like earlier Chinese rulers, they were obliged by this claim to keep the gods contented, perform rites to insure the fertility of the soil, and control the rivers.

The Chou government was decentralized. There was a central government, run by a chief minister and officials in charge of agriculture, public works, the army, and other royal affairs. But local gov-

ernments were numerous and independent. The Chou had conquered the Shang with the help of allies. These allies were paid off in land, and hundreds of small states resulted. Although these states owed certain obligations to the Chou, they were also capable of acting independently. There was, however, a strong enough political organization under the Chou rulers to keep China from falling apart for a long time.

By the 700's B.C., however, the small states were acting with increasing independence. The Chou then did not so much govern as perform religious duties and settle quarrels between states. By the 400's B.C., the Chou rulers were no longer able even to settle quarrels. Finally, a people called the Ch'u, living around the Yangtze River, and a people called the Ch'in, in the Wei Valley, struggled to replace the Chou.

The last Chou ruler resigned in favor of the

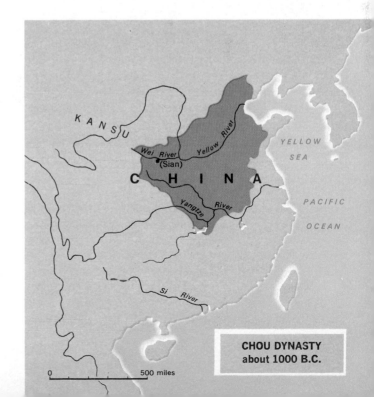

CHOU DYNASTY
about 1000 B.C.

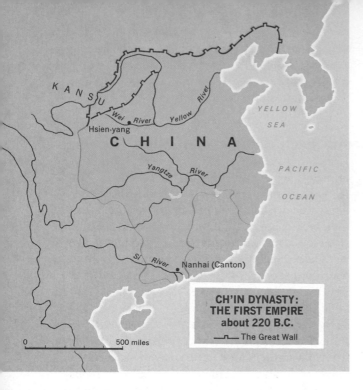

CH'IN DYNASTY: THE FIRST EMPIRE about 220 B.C.
— The Great Wall

0   500 miles

northern China and the Ch'u lands in the Yangtze Valley, Shih Huang Ti sent his armies far to the south. In a brilliant campaign, he conquered the central part of southern China as far as the delta of the Si River (see map, this page).

Before Shih Huang Ti's rise to power, when the Chou dynasty was weakening, a group of Chinese scholars called Legalists had given thought to the problem of ruling a land of many unruly, semi-independent states. They concluded that society could be kept in order only by ruthless application of the law. Shih Huang Ti adopted the political thinking of the Legalists and put it into practice with great speed. He tore down the walls of unruly city-states and divided China into military districts under governors who used stern military and civilian authority. To help keep order, he put a uniform tax system into effect. Conflicting local laws were also made uniform in the code of Ch'in.

The Ch'in as builders. To guard against invasion, particularly invasion from the north and west, the Chinese over the years had built several walls. The Ch'in completed and connected these walls to form the Great Wall of China. This massive structure, 25 feet high, ran 1,400 miles from Kansu province to the sea (see map, this page). It was 15 feet wide, and a road along the top enabled soldiers to travel quickly to any area of the frontier that was threatened. Men were brutally driven to build the wall; it is said that each of its stones cost a life.°

Understanding the importance of transportation and communication in an orderly society, Shih Huang Ti built broad, tree-lined highways. He set a standard width for the axles of carts and other vehicles so that they could pass each other on roads and bridges. The Chinese also built canals during this period.

Harshness of the Ch'in. Ch'in rule was orderly, but it was also autocratic. Like autocrats ever since, Shih Huang Ti saw the danger of allowing scholars to investigate and discuss problems freely.

Ch'in in 256 B.C., but the struggle for the throne continued for thirty-five years, until the last rival to the Ch'in gave up. The Chou dynasty is memorable not for its political achievements but, as you will see later, for the brilliant civilization that flourished under it.

The Ch'in dynasty

The Ch'in dynasty was founded by a young man, Cheng. He came to power in 221 B.C. by using cavalry armed with bows and arrows, a military technique new to the Chinese. Once in power, he was called Shih Huang Ti (SHIR HWAHNG tee), which means "first emperor"—the first, that is, of many Chinese emperors. The Ch'in dynasty, which he founded, gave China its name, even though it lasted only until 207 B.C. (Cheng ruled until 210 B.C., when his son succeeded him.) From its capital at Hsien-Yang, the Ch'in dynasty ruled a larger area than either of the preceding dynasties and controlled it more firmly.

Shih Huang Ti is sometimes called the Chinese Caesar, partly because of his conquests and partly because of far-reaching changes he made in China's government. Not satisfied with ruling

° Since that time the wall has been extended, destroyed in part, allowed to fall into disuse, and rebuilt many times—often in new sites. Today much of it still remains standing.

176

He began by burning the important books called *Classic of Songs* and *Classic of Documents*. When scholars did not heed this warning, Shih Huang Ti had 460 of them executed.

Discontent became widespread under the Ch'in. There was a wide gap between the ruler, supported by his warriors, and the mass of people. Workers and peasants were downtrodden. In 207 B.C. a general of peasant background, Liu Pang, led a revolt against the Ch'in. He overthrew them and in 202 B.C. founded the Han dynasty.

The Han dynasty

The new dynasty took its name from the Han River, where Liu Pang had been stationed as a general for several years. The dynasty became so popular that to this day some Chinese call themselves "Sons of Han."

The most famous Han emperor was Wu Ti, who ruled from 140 to 87 B.C. He established his capital at Changan (now Sian) and extended Chinese territory northward into Manchuria and Korea, southward to Indo-China, and westward to central Asia (see map, this page). Wu Ti's government was strong, but he was less autocratic than the Ch'in rulers had been. It was during the Han dynasty that the Chinese civil service system was established. Candidates were examined on the great classics of Chinese literature and law, so that they had to be scholars as well as administrators. In 124 B.C., Wu Ti established a national school to help prepare candidates for the examinations. This use of examinations for choosing government officials continued in China until as recently as 1905.

For a long time the Chinese people had suffered hardships because of the rise and fall of prices for farm products. To prevent this, Wu Ti instituted an economic policy called "leveling."

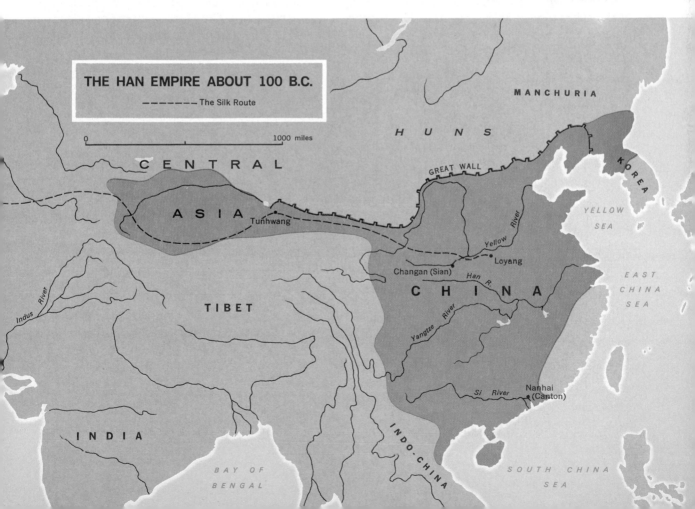

THE HAN EMPIRE ABOUT 100 B.C.
- - - - - - - The Silk Route

0   1000 miles

In years of good crops, government agents bought and stored surpluses to keep prices from falling. In lean years the agents sold the surpluses to prevent food scarcity and high prices.

To keep the peace at home, Wu Ti had to find a way to curb the power of the warrior-landowners, who had caused the downfall of the Chou dynasty. During the Ch'in and early Han periods, many of them had formed the custom of leaving their estates to their eldest sons only. This practice created a strong class of large landowners, difficult for the emperors to control. In 127 B.C., Wu Ti issued a decree requiring that one half of an estate must go the the eldest son upon the death of his father. The other sons divided the remaining half of the estate among themselves. This decree led to smaller estates and thus to a reduction in the power of the landowners.

The Pax Sinica. Wu Ti waged vigorous military campaigns against nomadic people of central and eastern Asia who might have threatened the frontiers of his empire. About a hundred years before the Pax Romana began in the West, Wu Ti established what historians call the Pax Sinica, or Chinese Peace, throughout much of the continent of Asia.

During this period of peace, merchants were able to open the famous Silk Route from China across central Asia—"the roof of the world"—to the Mediterranean area (see map, page 177). Long camel caravans carried silk, jade, and other valuable Chinese goods to be sold to the wealthy people of Greece and Rome. They returned with glass, amber, asbestos, and wool and linen textiles, which were purchased by the Chinese.

Wu Ti's successors were not so capable as he, and there was an interruption in the Han dynasty when a usurper took over in 9 A.D. He was ousted in 25 A.D., however, and the Han dynasty then endured until 220 A.D., when a revolt overthrew the last of the Han emperors.

The Six Dynasties

For more than 350 years after the end of the Han dynasty, China was plagued by wars from within and without. A succession of six different dynasties tried to restore order, but none was successful in setting up a strong central government. The most important event of this period occurred in 317 A.D., when Huns from central Asia successfully invaded northern China but were prevented from taking southern China. These invaders were related to the people who invaded the Roman Empire in the 400's and India in the 500's.

The Hun invasions had important consequences for China: (1) The Huns had little experience in government, so that they relied heavily upon the Chinese civil service system. As a result, this system became deeply entrenched in Chinese life. (2) Refugees from northern China fled before the Huns into southern China, where they helped tremendously in the development of that region. (3) The Huns encouraged Buddhist missionaries from India to move into China and gain converts.

The troubled period of the Six Dynasties came to an end in 589 A.D., when Yang Chien, a Chinese official of the Hun government in northern China, overthrew the Huns and went on to conquer southern China as well. He established the Sui dynasty, which you will read about in Chapter 13.

CHECKUP

1. How did government under Chou rulers differ from other imperial governments you have studied —the Guptas in India, or the Roman Empire, for example?

2. How were Chinese government officials chosen?

3. Two emperors, Shih Huang Ti and Wu Ti, are considered among China's greatest. What did each

4. What were the important consequences of the Hun invasion of China in the 300's A.D.?

5. IDENTIFY: Legalists, Liu Pang, Han, "leveling," Pax Sinica, Silk Route.

6. LOCATE: Wei River, Yellow Sea, Kansu, Hsien-Yang, Great Wall, Changan.

5 Early China produced great philosophers and classic literature

During the long period of Chinese history from the beginning of Chou rule in 1028 B.C. to the end of the Six Dynasties in 589 A.D., important developments took place in Chinese ways of thinking and living. These developments put Chinese civilization on paths that it followed steadfastly for many centuries.

Chinese ideas about life and government were strongly influenced by three great philosophers. Two of them were Chinese; the third was Gautama Buddha of India.

Confucius

The most influential Chinese philosopher was K'ung Fu-tse (meaning Kung the Philosopher, or Reverend Master), known to Westerners as Confucius. He lived from about 551 to about 478 B.C., a time of great disorder and confusion in China. The central government of the Chou dynasty was breaking down, and warlords were everywhere.

Confucius had little to say about the idea of god, the meaning of death, or the idea of life after death. He was not a religious prophet, nor especially a religious man, as we use the term. Essentially, he was interested in what made the good life. Because of the times in which he lived, he believed that the good life depended on order, and that order depended on good government.

Confucius' father died when the boy was only three years old, and the family was left in poverty. In spite of this, Confucius managed to get a good education. At the age of twenty-two, he set himself up as a teacher and soon gained a great following.

Confucius taught that government depends on good example. If a ruler lives and governs virtuously, he will be obeyed by a virtuous people. Virtue, in Confucian teaching, consists of correct behavior toward others. A basic principle resembled the Christian Golden Rule, although stated negatively: "What you do not like when done unto yourself, do not do unto others."

Confucius hoped to put his ideas into practice by becoming minister to a local ruler. The story is that he was given a high post, minister of crime, in his native province of Shantung. Within a year, according to the story, crime had almost disappeared. Neighboring rulers, however, became jealous and in time Confucius had to retire. He spent the rest of his life teaching.

But the teachings of Confucius lived on. They taught right living and were based on the deep Chinese feeling of reverence for ancestors and traditional wisdom. His teachings had a powerful influence on Chinese life and thought down through the centuries. They eventually took on religious significance. In 195 B.C., for example, Liu Pang (founder of the Han dynasty) visited the tomb of Confucius and offered a sacrifice to his spirit. In 58 A.D. the emperor decreed that schools were to make sacrifices to Confucius.

Lao-tzu

Lao-tzu (LOW-DZU), who is thought to have lived in the 500's B.C., during the long Chou dynasty, was the founder of a philosophy called Taoism (DOW-iz-um). Taoism got its name from its central idea, Tao, which can be defined as the Way of Nature. In nature, according to Lao-tzu, man finds a vital impulse directing life. He reaches understanding by withdrawing from the world and contemplating nature.

Lao-tzu said that Tao is an indescribable force that governs the universe and all nature. Man may bring himself into harmony with Tao by practicing three great virtues: humility, frugality, and contentment. Men should not strive for learning,

179

riches, or power. They should try, rather, to bring themselves into harmony with Tao by being quiet, thoughtful, and humble. As Lao-tzu said, "He who overcomes others is strong; he who overcomes himself is mighty." Unlike Confucius, Lao-tzu believed that the less government the better. He advised men to withdraw from public affairs and not to participate in them.

Lao-tzu himself did not believe in temples or a formal religion. After his death, however, his teachings were organized into a religion. He had laughed at the idea of gods, yet he came to be worshiped as a god.

Taoism had a strong appeal for the masses of peasants. Its teachings implied that wealth and power were meaningless, and peasants were surely poor and weak.

Buddhism in China

The third great influence on Chinese thought and religious belief came not from China but from India—from the teachings of Buddha. From 202 B.C. to 220 A.D., as you have read, the Han dynasty ruled in China. During this time, missionaries from India brought Buddhism to China.

When the Han dynasty was breaking up and Huns from the north were raiding China, Buddhism found many converts, especially among the peasants. People were looking for consolation in this time of crisis. Mahayana Buddhism, with its worship of Buddha as a savior, offered an escape from the miseries of the present. Its temples and ceremonies also appealed to the Chinese.

The ideas of Confucius, Lao-tzu, and Buddha influenced the attitude of the Chinese toward life itself and toward government. Confucianism, with its reverence for the past and emphasis on the family, won the most followers. The Chinese had always revered their ancestors and worshiped the emperor as almost a divine being. These things continued. The other ideas—humility, contentment, loyalty, justice, wisdom, and obedience—made the Chinese patient and enduring.

Government

In Chinese society it was the family, not the government, that was the center of national life

and to which every citizen owed his basic loyalty. If the family units were properly administered, political affairs were bound to be healthy. The government was a sort of overseer of the relationships among families.

This basic idea of family responsibility meant that the central government did not need to be all-powerful, and that local governments could be given a great deal of freedom and responsibility. As long as local authorities met their tax collecting responsibilities, they could carry on their administrative duties in any way that they saw fit.

The system of appointing local officials was important. Confucius considered politics and government an honorable profession, but he believed that a person should enter government service only after rigid training. These ideas of Confucius became the basis for China's system of civil service examinations. As a result, government officials shared with scholars the highest social rank; in fact, scholars and officials were really the same.

Family and social life

The family, as has been said, formed the foundation of Chinese society. A man rose or fell in the social system, not by wealth or personal accomplishment, but according to his family position. Each family had its great ancestor, its hero-god. It maintained a careful genealogy, or record of the family tree, even including third cousins. The Chinese father, like the Roman father, was the source of all family authority.

Women were subordinate to men and had no property rights of their own. Marriages were arranged by the parents, and a young wife became almost a servant in the household of her husband's family. Before marriage she often cried, not because she did not yet know her husband, but because she might not like her mother-in-law. But with motherhood and age, the wife became an important figure in the family.

The economy

Farming was basic to the Chinese way of life. There were two kinds of agricultural economy, a millet and wheat economy in the north and a rice economy in the south. In both northern and south-

Early Chinese dynasties left their mark on Chinese life. The amusing wrestlers above were made of bronze during the Chou dynasty. Below is the Great Wall of China, an achievement of the Ch'in dynasty. The bounties of nature appear, above left, in a rubbing of a pottery tile made by Han craftsmen. In the upper panel, two spirited bowmen are shooting at flying birds. The lower panel shows a harvesting scene. The clay figure of a woman, lower left, also dates from the Han dynasty. It displays the good-natured serenity and poise expected of Chinese women.

ern China, fields were worked in common by about eight families. The farmers went to the fields each day from the village where they lived. They began using ox-drawn plows about 300 B.C. Complex systems of irrigation and flood control were constructed in northern China beginning with the Chou dynasty. These systems were so well constructed that some of them that were built in the 200's B.C. are still in use today.

Trade was never of great importance to the Chinese economy, but it increased early in the Chou dynasty, when the northern Chinese began immigrating into southern China. Leather goods, silk, jade jewelry, screens, and couches were common items of trade between northern and southern China. Trade was improved when the brief but efficient Ch'in dynasty standardized the currency system and weights and measures. Trade increased further when Wu Ti of the Han dynasty opened the famous Silk Route westward to the Mediterranean area.

Education and literature

Education in China was not a responsibility of government, either national or local. It was the responsibility of the family to hire a tutor. In those families that could not afford to do so, children went uneducated. Even as late as the year 1900, it was estimated that not more than 5 percent of the Chinese people could read or write. This low rate of literacy was caused in part by the expense of paying a tutor, in part by the difficulty of learning Chinese reading and writing.

The most important works of Chinese literature and the basis for all Chinese education were the Five Classics. We do not know who wrote them, or when, although they were already important by the time of the Chou. Two of the Five Classics were used in civil service examinations. They were (1) the *Classic of Songs,* more than 300 songs about love, joy, politics, and domestic life; and (2) the *Classic of Documents,* which contains semihistorical speeches and documents about government. The other three Classics were (3) the *Classic of Changes,* about the art of foretelling the future; (4) *Spring and Autumn Annals,* a record of events in the important city-state of Lu

from 722 to 481 B.C.; and (5) *Ceremonies and Rituals,* about etiquette and ceremonies.

Shih Huang Ti, as you recall, ordered the destruction of all copies of the *Classic of Songs* and the *Classic of Documents,* and tried to ban the reading of the other three. Toward the end of the Ch'in dynasty, the ban was lifted and the texts were restored in the form in which they have been used ever since. In 175 A.D. the Five Classics were carved in stone so that none of them could ever be lost again.

The Five Classics became what every well-brought-up young man of China should know. He was also expected to know many of the *Analects* of Confucius. These were the sayings of Confucius collected by his disciples.

Science

Chinese astronomers computed the year at $365\frac{1}{4}$ days as early as 444 B.C., and refined their calculations even further during the Han dynasty. By 350 B.C., Chinese astronomers had collected information on the movements of the planets Jupiter and Saturn. They sighted Halley's comet as early as 240 B.C., and recorded thirty more sightings through the last one in 1910 A.D. In 28 B.C. they observed sunspots, which were not known about in Europe until the 1600's A.D.

Sometime before 100 A.D., Chinese astronomers built special instruments with which they observed the ecliptic, the orbit which the sun apparently follows. Using these instruments, an early astronomer estimated the number of stars at 11,520. Other scientists invented a primitive seismograph which registered earthquakes so faint that they were unnoticed by the royal court.

CHECKUP

1. Confucius' ideas about the good life are said to have been influenced by the times in which he lived. Explain. What success did he have in putting his ideas into practice?

2. What are the basic teachings of Taoism? How does Taoism differ from Confucianism?

3. Explain the importance of the family in Chinese government and social life.

4. What were the Five Classics? the *Analects?*

CHAPTER REVIEW

Chapter 9   India and China Developed Lasting Traditions   (1000 B.C.—589 A.D.)

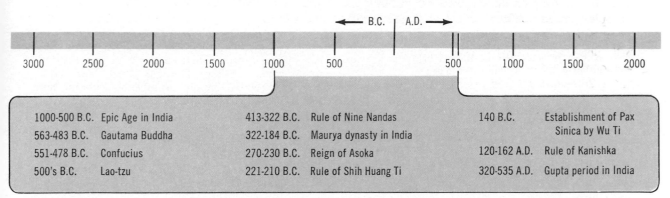

1000-500 B.C. Epic Age in India	413-322 B.C. Rule of Nine Nandas	140 B.C. Establishment of Pax Sinica by Wu Ti
563-483 B.C. Gautama Buddha	322-184 B.C. Maurya dynasty in India	
551-478 B.C. Confucius	270-230 B.C. Reign of Asoka	120-162 A.D. Rule of Kanishka
500's B.C. Lao-tzu	221-210 B.C. Rule of Shih Huang Ti	320-535 A.D. Gupta period in India

CHAPTER SUMMARY

The Epic Age in India took its name from two great works, the *Mahabharata* and *Ramayana*. From them and from the *Upanishads*, we have learned much about the origins of caste and Hinduism. The early Aryans developed a class system out of which eventually grew some 3,000 hereditary castes. Hinduism teaches that the world of the senses is an illusion. A man must escape from it through many lifetimes by being constantly reincarnated. Eventually his soul will attain nirvana.

As important as caste and Hinduism in the Eastern world is Buddhism. It began with Gautama, an Indian prince who became known as Buddha. He taught that man could attain nirvana by accepting the Four Noble Truths and following the Middle Way.

After the Epic Age, northern India was ruled by the Persians and then by the Nine Nandas, who were in turn overthrown by Chandragupta Maurya. The Maurya Empire he founded was extended by his son, Bindusara. His grandson, Asoka, one of India's greatest rulers, renounced war and became a Buddhist. The Mauryas were followed by a Greco-Bactrian Empire and, later, by the Kushans.

India enjoyed a golden age under the Guptas. Literature and fine arts flourished; mathematicians developed the numeral system we use; astronomers and physicians made notable progress.

In China the Chou ruled for centuries. Their government became increasingly decentralized, however, and they were finally overthrown by Shih Huang Ti of the Ch'in dynasty. He centralized the government and built the Great Wall. Under a new dynasty, the Han, the civil service was created, land reforms were instituted, and trade flourished. The period of the Six Dynasties that followed was one of confusion.

China's most influential philosopher was Confucius. His teachings were based on reverence for ancestors and traditional wisdom. Lao-tzu, the founder of Taoism, taught that men should withdraw from the world and try to achieve harmony with nature.

Throughout this period the family was the center of Chinese society, as farming was basic to its economy. Education was based on the Five Classics and on the *Analects* of Confucius.

QUESTIONS FOR DISCUSSION

1. It is sometimes said that a religion and a culture can be judged by the class of people to whom the greatest honor is paid. What people were most honored in India? in China? Do you agree that this is a good standard for judging?

2. Both Indian and Chinese society have been greatly determined by tradition. Why is it true that this can be both a strength and a weakness?

3. What are the characteristics of a caste system?

4. How do you explain that Buddha, Confucius, and Lao-tzu, none of them claiming to be gods, were eventually worshiped?

5. While Confucius taught that order depended on good government, Lao-tzu taught that the less government the better. With whom do you agree?

PROJECTS

1. Write a letter to Shih Huang Ti protesting the burning of books by the government.

2. Write a one-page paper on Confucius' basic principle, "What you do not like when done unto yourself, do not do unto others."

3. Draw up a chart summarizing the teachings of Hinduism, Buddhism, Confucianism, and Taoism.

4. Make a sketch of a Hindu or Buddhist temple.

For additional bibliographical information on the books cited in these projects, see the Basic Library (page xviii) and Further Reading on the opposite page.

INDIVIDUAL PROJECTS

1. Two oral reports can be given to the class on Crete and Mycenae. Excellent accounts of these civilizations are in Cottrell, *The Horizon Book of Lost Worlds,* "Crete: The Island of Minos" and "Mycenae: Home of Heroes"; *Life* eds., *The Epic of Man,* "Crete and Mycenae: The Shaping of the West."

2. Write or present orally a comparison of the Olympic games of the ancient Greeks and today's Olympics. For an explanation of the Greek games see Bowra, *Classical Greece,* "The Panhellenic Games." You can find descriptions of modern Olympics in magazine articles.

3. Report to the class on the speeches of Demosthenes and discuss the arguments that he advanced against Philip of Macedon. You can locate the appropriate speeches in Copeland and Lamm, *The World's Great Speeches,* "The Second Oration Against Philip," and in Peterson, *Treasury of the World's Great Speeches,* "Demosthenes Denounces the Imperialistic Ambitions of Philip of Macedon."

4. Draw a poster for the classroom bulletin board using as a theme Cato's often repeated phrase *"Carthago delenda est"* ("Carthage must be destroyed").

5. Read a biography from the list given on the opposite page and report on it to your class, concentrating on one or two incidents in the person's life that might be of interest to your classmates.

6. Report on the destruction of Pompeii in 79 A.D. Two useful sources are *National Geographic,* "Last Moments of the Pompeians," November 1961, and Hadas, *Imperial Rome,* "Pompeii: A Self-Portrait."

7. Prepare an oral report for class presentation on the Hindu religion. For such a report consult the following reading selections: Brown, *India,* "A Preoccupation with the Spirit"; Eisen and Filler, *The Human Adventure,* Vol. 1, "The Meaning and Practice of Yoga"; Bach, *Major Religions of the World,* "Hinduism—Religion of the One God Who Is Many"; Gaer, *How the Great Religions Began,* "Hindustan, Land of Many Deities"; Champion and Short, *Readings from World Religions,* "Hinduism"; *Life* eds., *The World's Great Religions,* "The Spirit of Hinduism."

8. Write a paper on Zen Buddhism, which has its home in Japan and followers around the world. You can obtain information from the First Zen Institute of America, 113 East Thirtieth Street, New York, New York 10016. An authoritative book on the subject is Suzuki, *Zen Buddhism.*

9. Much of our knowledge of daily life in the Gupta Empire is based on the mural paintings in the Ajanta caves. Prepare an oral report on the Ajanta caves. An illustrated book with a brief introductory essay is Rowland, *The Ajanta Caves: Early Buddhist Painting from India.*

GROUP PROJECTS

1. Organize a debate on the following topic: The Spartan way of life was both socially and politically superior to that of the Athenians. Students participating in the debate should read Hale, *The Horizon Book of Ancient Greece,* "The Rival Cities"; Eisen and Filler, *The Human Adventure,* Vol. 1, "The Severity of Spartan Life and Training."

2. Two groups of students might illustrate a time line of the Golden Age in Greece for display on the classroom bulletin board. One group should make a time line that will cover a long area on the bulletin board. The other group should provide illustrations of Greek art and architecture, either by securing photographs or by making their own drawings. The illustrations should then be grouped along the time line on the bulletin board. Students participating in this exercise should be prepared to discuss the illustrations and to answer any questions on them from the class.

3. With another student prepare an interview between Julius Caesar and a reporter from the city of Rome just before Caesar made his decision to cross the Rubicon River.

4. Organize a panel discussion on the reasons for the decline of the Roman Empire. Each student should read a different essay and present to the class the point of view found in the reading. The collection of writings edited by Chambers, *The Fall of Rome,* will be very useful.

5. For the classroom bulletin board, a group of students can draw large maps of the Magadha, Maurya, Bactria, Kushan, and Gupta states. For information consult a historical atlas, such as Palmer, *Historical Atlas of the World,* or Shepherd, *Shepherd's Historical Atlas.*

Further Reading

BIOGRAPHY

Braymer, Marjorie, *The Walls of Windy Troy: A Biography of Heinrich Schliemann.* Harcourt Brace Jovanovich.

Brun, Jean, *Socrates.* Walker.*

Burn, Andrew R., *Alexander the Great and the Hellenistic World.* Macmillan.*

_____, *Pericles and Athens.* Macmillan.

Clausen, Wendell, ed., *Plutarch's Lives of Nine Illustrious Greeks and Romans.* Washington Square.*

Coolidge, Olivia, *Lives of Famous Romans.* Houghton Mifflin.

Duggan, Alfred, *Julius Caesar.* Knopf.

Ferrero, G., *The Life of Caesar.* Norton.*

Isenberg, Irwin, and Richard M. Haywood, *Caesar.* Harper & Row.

Lamb, Harold, *Alexander of Macedon.* Doubleday.

_____, *Hannibal: One Man Against Rome.* Bantam.*

Mason, Cora, *Socrates: The Man Who Dared to Ask.* Beacon.

Mercer, Charles, *Alexander the Great.* Harper & Row.

Oman, Charles, *Seven Roman Statesmen of the Later Republic.* St. Martin's.

Percheron, Maurice, *Marvelous Life of Buddha.* St. Martin's.

NONFICTION

Abbott, F. F., *History and Description of Roman Political Institutions.* Biblo & Tannen.

Bowra, C. M., *Classical Greece.* Time-Life.

Brown, J. D., *India.* Time-Life.

Burtt, Edwin, *The Teachings of the Compassionate Buddha.* New American Library.*

Chambers, Mortimer, ed., *The Fall of Rome: Can It Be Explained?* Holt, Rinehart and Winston.*

Cottrell, Leonard, *The Bull of Minos.* Grosset & Dunlap.*

_____, *Tiger of Ch'in: The Dramatic Emergence of China as a Nation.* Holt, Rinehart and Winston.

Creel, H. G., *The Birth of China: A Study of the Formative Period of Chinese Civilization.* Ungar.*

Dickinson, G. L., *Greek View of Life.* Univ. of Michigan.*

Hadas, Moses, *Imperial Rome.* Time-Life.

Hale, William Harlan, ed., *The Horizon Book of Ancient Greece.* American Heritage.

Hall, Jennie, *Buried Cities.* Macmillan. Mycenae, Olympia, Pompeii.

Herodotus, *Persian Wars.* Modern Library.

Hignett, Charles, *Xerxes' Invasion of Greece.* Oxford Univ. Press.

Johnston, Mary, *Roman Life.* Scott, Foresman.

Laffont, Robert, *A History of Rome and the Romans: From Romulus to John XXIII.* Crown.

Mills, Dorothy, *The Book of the Ancient Greeks.* Putnam.

_____, *The Book of the Ancient Romans.* Putnam.

Quennell, Marjorie, and C. H. B. Quennell, *Everyday Things in Ancient Greece.* Putnam.

Robinson, Cyril E., *Everyday Life in Ancient Greece.* Oxford Univ. Press.

Rowland, B., ed., *The Ajanta Caves: Early Buddhist Painting from India.* New American Library.

Sen, K. M., *Hinduism.* Penguin.*

Suzuki, D. T., *Zen Buddhism.* Doubleday.*

HISTORICAL FICTION

Anderson, P. L., *Slave of Catiline.* Biblo & Tannen. Story of a conspiracy.

_____, *Swords in the North.* Biblo & Tannen. Caesar's legions in Britain.

Bothwell, Jean, *Dancing Princess.* Harcourt Brace Jovanovich. Set in ancient India.

Bryher, *Roman Wall.* Pantheon.* Life on a Roman frontier.

_____, *The Coin of Carthage.* Harcourt Brace Jovanovich. Second Punic War.

Bulwer-Lytton, Edward R., *The Last Days of Pompeii.* Doubleday.*

Coolidge, Olivia, *Caesar's Gallic War.* Houghton Mifflin.

_____, *Greek Myths.* Houghton Mifflin.

_____, *Men of Athens.* Houghton Mifflin.

Costain, Thomas B., *The Silver Chalice.* Pocket Books.* A novel based on the legends of the years following Christ's crucifixion.

DeWohl, Louis, *The Spear.* Lippincott. Story of a young Roman soldier.

Douglas, Lloyd C., *The Robe.* Pocket Books.* Story of a soldier who possessed Christ's robe.

_____, *The Big Fisherman.* Pocket Books.* Story of the Apostle Simon Peter.

Duggan, Alfred, *Three's Company.* Ace Books.* Second Triumvirate.

Ingles, J. W., *Test of Valor: A Story of the Ancient Olympic Games.* Grossett & Dunlap.*

Sienkiewicz, Henryk, *Quo Vadis.* Bantam.* Christian martyrs in Nero's Rome.

Wallace, Lew, *Ben Hur.* Bantam.*

Warner, Rex, *The Young Caesar.* New American Library.*

* Paperback.

185

UNIT
THREE

THE WORLD

Armored knights prepare to leave Europe on a crusade

OF THE MIDDLE AGES

Feudal Lords and Churchmen Dominated Medieval Europe

As we look back from the present day to the collapse of the Roman Empire in the west, we can view it as a continuous process. With the knowledge of history that many scholars have gained and passed on to us, we can see the various elements of that collapse and how each one affected the others.

The Roman Empire did not end with a sudden crash. Rather, it fell apart a little at a time so that few people realized what was happening. A border fort would be abandoned; a legion would be withdrawn; mail and news no longer came to a city; the aqueducts were not kept in repair and water was hard to get. And slowly, ever so slowly, what had been an empire lay in splintered ruins. Each fragment retained something of the original, but the empire as a whole was unable to return ever again to its former grandeur.

Gradually Roman culture died out. For example, people forgot how to construct buildings as the Romans had done. For those people who remained in the cities, temples and stadiums were often nothing more than a source of stones to patch up a house when it was near collapse. In Rome itself, the beautiful buildings of the Forum and even the Colosseum were partly wrecked; portions of them have been found in all parts of the city, where they were used to make repairs for a thousand years after the last emperor died.

The period following the collapse of the Roman

The king of England with his nobles and clergymen

Empire—between classical times and the modern era—is called the Middle Ages, or the medieval period. (The word *medieval* comes from the Latin word *medius,* meaning "middle," and *aevum,* meaning "age.") This period is generally considered to have lasted from about the year 500 to about 1500.

The idea of calling this period the Middle Ages is a fairly recent one. The people of that time never thought of themselves as living in a "middle age," or indeed in any kind of age at all. They thought of human history as a simple chain of events from the Biblical era to their own time. In general, they did not feel that they were very different from their ancestors. They might wonder about some of the remnants of past glory which they saw here and there, but they had little understanding of the past.

For a long time, historians applied the term "Dark Ages" to the medieval period. They regarded it as a time when there was little culture and few achievements worth noting. As you will see, applying this term to almost a thousand years

of European history is not correct. There were many light spots in the "Dark Ages," and many individuals who made important achievements. It was not a time like the Pax Romana, with widespread peace and security. But it was a time during which men developed their own customs and distinctive institutions to suit the particular conditions that prevailed.

THE CHAPTER SECTIONS:

1. Frankish rulers governed much of Western Europe for centuries (481–900)

2. Germanic peoples from northern Europe conquered Britain (432–1066)

3. Medieval life was organized around feudalism and the manor (900–1200)

4. The Church performed many functions in the Middle Ages (590–1250)

5. Kings and nobles struggled for power in France and England (987–1328)

6. Popes and emperors clashed over Germany and Italy (936–1250)

1 Frankish rulers governed much of Western Europe for centuries

When the Roman Empire fell apart in the 400's, Western Europe descended into anarchy and confusion. Government nearly ceased to exist, and invaders roamed about almost at will.

You have read how Germanic tribes, including Visigoths, Vandals, Burgundians, and Ostrogoths, overran Europe. These tribes set up kingdoms, but they did not create strong governments. The invaders were usually a small group ruling a much larger population by military force. Many groups were defeated, and others were absorbed into the native population without leaving much trace.

Some Germanic tribes, however, were destined to play greater roles in history. Of all these, the Franks were the most important. They first entered the Roman Empire in the 300's, near the mouth of the Rhine River. One source of their strength was that they spread slowly and permanently, never losing touch with their homeland in the Rhine Valley. They settled in the area of

northern Gaul corresponding roughly to present-day Belgium and the Netherlands.

Clovis and the Merovingians

In 481, a ruler of great ability, Clovis, became king of one of the Frankish tribes. He and his successors were called Merovingians because Clovis traced his family back to an ancestor named Meroveg. Clovis was brutal, cruel, and conscienceless, but an excellent military leader. Under his command his people conquered the other Frankish tribes and soon controlled all northern Gaul.

A few years after Clovis became king, an important event took place. Influenced by his Christian wife, he made a vow to accept her religion if he won a certain battle. He did win, and not only kept his vow but forced 3,000 of his warriors to be baptized. Clovis became a champion of Christianity, and he and his Franks gained the support of the Church.

Merovingian Manuscript

During the early Middle Ages in Europe, monks were among the few people who could read and write. Almost all the books dating from this period were produced by hand in monastery workshops. The monks were painstakingly careful when they worked on religious books, for a manuscript containing the word of God was considered to be a sacred object whose visual beauty should reflect the importance of its contents.

The page pictured above opens a book of meditations and prayers. "In the name of our Lord Jesus Christ, we salute you" is the introductory greeting, written in a combination of Greek and Latin. The cross and the initial letter "I" have been decorated with fanciful birds, fish, and geometric designs. Historians think that this manuscript was produced near Paris, perhaps at a monastery supported by Charles Martel and Pepin the Short.

Later, Clovis conquered southwestern Gaul from the Visigoths. He thus ruled most of present-day France (which took its name from the Franks). Unfortunately for the Franks, however, Clovis was unable to pass on to his successors either his rugged qualities or his united kingdom. In accordance with Frankish custom, the kingdom was divided among Clovis' sons.

The later Merovingian kings thought only of the pleasures and luxuries of court life. One writer of the period tells of a Merovingian king who spent his time combing his long yellow curls with a jeweled comb. These "Do-Nothing Kings" left the business of governing to palace officials.

Although in theory there was only one Frankish kingdom, there were actually several because of the custom of dividing the kingdom among a monarch's heirs. In these Merovingian kingdoms, the chief of the royal household was called the Mayor of the Palace. Under the Do-Nothing Kings, the Mayors of the Palace became the real rulers of the various Frankish kingdoms. In about the year 700, Pepin II, the Mayor of the Palace of one kingdom, succeeded in making the office hereditary. His successors were Frankish kings in everything but name.

Charles Martel and Pepin the Short

The able son of Pepin, Charles Martel (meaning "Charles the Hammer"), succeeded his father as Mayor of the Palace. In 732, Moslems invaded France from Spain, as you will read in Chapter 12. Charles Martel met them with his cavalry between Tours and Poitiers, in central France. He defeated them and drove them southward, back toward Spain. The Frankish victory checked the Moslem advance in Western Europe, removing an immediate danger and a constant menace.

When Charles Martel died in 741, he left his son Pepin III, or Pepin the Short, a large and strong kingdom to rule. Pepin's title, however, was still only Mayor of the Palace. He wished to be king in name as well as in fact. He wrote to the pope (the head of the Church in the west), asking his opinion. The pope replied that the man who wielded the power should also have the title. In 751 an assembly of Franks took the throne from the Merovingian king and elected Pepin king of the Franks.

Three years later, in 754, the pope traveled to France and personally crowned Pepin "king by the grace of God." His action was regarded as a precedent (a standard for future actions) by later popes who claimed that they had the authority to install and depose kings.

The pope also asked for Pepin's help against the Lombards. They were a Germanic tribe who had conquered and settled in the valley of the Po River—a region in northern Italy that is still called Lombardy. In the 740's they had begun to raid and conquer central Italy and to threaten the city of Rome.

After the pope's visit, Pepin led an army of Franks into Italy and defeated the Lombards. He took territory around Rome from the Lombard king and gave it to the pope. This gift of land, called the Donation of Pepin, created the Papal States, a region ruled by the pope for centuries afterward, and in time greatly expanded.

It is not known whether the pope and Pepin actually made an agreement—Pepin's defense of Rome in exchange for his coronation by the pope. It is certain, however, that these events began an alliance between the Franks and the papacy that greatly strengthened both sides. The way was prepared for the greatest of all Frankish kings, Charlemagne.

The empire of Charlemagne

The son of Pepin is claimed as a national hero by both the French and the Germans. The French call him Charlemagne; the Germans, Karl der Grosse. His Latin name was Carolus Magnus (from which comes the name of his dynasty, Carolingian). All of his names translate into English as Charles the Great.

Charlemagne, who ruled the Franks for forty-six years, from 768 until 814, is one of the outstanding men of history. He was tall, strong, handsome, and dignified. He was deeply religious. Although he had little formal education, he was highly intelligent.

Charlemagne spent much of his life at war. He defeated the Lombards in Italy and the Saxons in

CHARLEMAGNE'S EMPIRE IN 814 A.D.
Frankish territory before Charlemagne
Charlemagne's conquests, 768-814 A.D.

northern Germany. He defeated the invading Avars, a nomad people much like the Huns, in a single campaign in the central Danube region. He drove Moslem invaders back across the Pyrenees and was thus able to gain a small strip of Spanish territory, though he failed in his attempt to conquer all of Moslem Spain. By the end of his reign, he controlled Western Europe from just south of the Pyrenees to the North Sea and from the Atlantic Ocean to the Elbe and Danube rivers and south beyond the city of Rome (see map, this page).

On Christmas Day in the year 800, Charlemagne knelt at worship in St. Peter's Church in Rome. The pope placed a crown on Charlemagne's head and declared him "Emperor of the Romans." The title had almost nothing to do with the Frankish Empire. The peoples that Charlemagne ruled represented a mixture of Roman, Celtic, and Germanic cultures. Charlemagne himself was a war-

191

TREATY OF VERDUN · 843 A.D.

0 _____ 500 miles

were met by the wealth produced on the vast estates owned by the emperor. Each subject contributed in some way to the army. Wealthy lords furnished cavalry. Freemen usually served three months of each year. Thus the emperor had an army at no expense to himself or the government.

Education and learning. Charlemagne was greatly interested in education. To teach his own children and the other young nobles, he established a school called the Palace School at his court. Learned men from England, Ireland, Germany, and Italy were invited to teach there along with Frankish scholars.

Bishops were ordered to collect libraries by copying ancient Latin manuscripts and to organize schools. Children of ability from the lower classes were admitted to these schools along with the children of nobles.

Division and fall of the Frankish Empire

Charlemagne's empire was never strongly united except through the power of his own energy, ability, and personality. The local counts had to be watched constantly to see that they served the emperor, not themselves.

The empire went into decline during the lifetime of Charlemagne's only surviving son, Louis the Pious. At Louis' death the Frankish lands were divided among his three sons. After some quarreling they agreed, in 843, to a settlement called the Treaty of Verdun. The treaty divided the empire into three parts, each brother taking a part as his own kingdom. Charles the Bald took the western part of the empire, roughly the area of present-day France; Louis the German received the eastern region, which included present-day Germany. In between was a long narrow strip of territory extending from the North Sea through northern Italy. Lothair received this kingdom and the title of emperor (see map, this page).

Charlemagne's descendants were incompetent rulers. They fought among themselves instead of uniting against powerful and ambitious local rulers. By 870, Lothair's middle kingdom was broken up and divided between Charles and Louis. Fifty years after the Treaty of Verdun, the great lords of both the east and west Frankish kingdoms

rior Frank, speaking the language and maintaining the customs of his people.

The new title was important, however. It showed that Charlemagne, who had united much of Europe for the first time in 400 years, was regarded as a successor to the emperors of Rome. His coronation by the pope also dramatized the close ties between the Franks and the Church.

Government. Charlemagne's empire was divided into several hundred regions, each ruled by one of his representatives called a count. Each count raised armies and administered laws within his own lands. Charlemagne established his capital at Aix-la-Chapelle (now Aachen), but traveled through his empire a great deal. He also sent out agents, called *missi dominici* (king's messengers), to check on government officials and hear complaints.

There were no direct taxes on land or people. Government expenses were not great, and they

Charlemagne sits proudly astride a horse in this bronze statuette made in the 800's. He wears a crown and carries an orb, traditionally a symbol of royal power.

had cast off their Carolingian monarchs and were electing kings of their own choice.

The empire of Charlemagne was torn apart not only by internal feuds, but also by invaders who drove into it from every direction. During this period, Europe suffered from invasions more terrible than those of the 400's (see map, this page).

From North Africa came Moslems, who conquered and occupied Sicily, Sardinia, and Corsica, and terrorized the whole Mediterranean coast. From the east came the Slavs, pressing from eastern into central Europe. From Asia came a new group of nomads, the Magyars. They were so much like the earlier Huns that Europeans called them Hungarians. After a century of terrifying raids, the Magyars settled down and established a kingdom in what is now Hungary.

The Vikings

The most feared of all invaders were those from Scandinavia, in the north. The Germanic peoples of what are now the countries of Norway, Sweden, and Denmark called themselves Vikings; the English called them Danes; other Europeans called them Northmen, or Norsemen. Although there were kings and nobles among the Vikings, their government was surprisingly democratic. The Vikings honored work, and all classes worked. Land was widely distributed, and there were few large estates. Assemblies of landowners made the laws.

Vikings were men of supreme courage, hardened by a bitter struggle for existence. They enjoyed battle. A Viking once complained that "peace lasted so long that I was afraid I might come to die of old age, within doors, on a bed."

VIKINGS — A.K.A. = DANES, NORTHMEN NORSEMEN

INVASIONS OF EUROPE
800 to 1000 A.D.

← Vikings   ← Slavs
←-- Moslems   ←···· Magyars

0   500 miles

During the 800's, many Vikings sailed from their homeland in search of food, treasure, wives, and slaves. Viking ships were sturdy. They were 4 to 6 feet deep, 60 to nearly 200 feet long, and were propelled partly by sail but mostly by oars. The Vikings sailed along the coasts of Europe and up the rivers of Russia, Germany, and France. They also reached Iceland, then pushed on to Greenland and the northeast coast of North America.

The Vikings were skilled in siege operations, and sometimes captured strongly fortified towns. Their savage fighting and pitiless cruelty struck terror everywhere. They settled in England, Ireland, Russia, and France. A large settlement of Vikings in northwestern France gave the region its name. The French word for "Northmen" was *Normans;* thus this area became known as Nor-

mandy. Later the Normans, as you will read, raided and settled elsewhere in Europe.

CHECKUP

1. What were the accomplishments of Clovis? of Charles Martel?

2. How did Pepin the Short become king of the Franks? What precedent was established with the crowning of Pepin?

3. Discuss the importance of the reign of Charlemagne in terms of territory, government, and education.

4. IDENTIFY: Franks, Mayor of the Palace, Donation of Pepin, Louis the Pious, Treaty of Verdun, Magyars, Vikings.

5. LOCATE: Tours, Poitiers, Lombardy, Papal States, Normandy.

2 Germanic peoples from northern Europe conquered Britain

The early inhabitants of Britain, like the Gauls of continental Europe, were Celts. The Celts had a fairly high culture and were brave, but they were no match for the Romans. Most of Britain fell to the Romans in the 40's A.D. and remained a Roman province for nearly 400 years.

Roman legions controlled the province from their fortified camps. Latin and some Roman customs were introduced. Britain, however, did not adopt Roman culture as completely as did many other regions of the empire. Neither the Latin language nor Roman traditions became thoroughly rooted there.

Saxon invasions

Roman legions remained in Britain until about 410, when they were called back to guard frontiers in central Europe. Around 450 the island was raided by Germanic tribes who came from northern Europe. They came first as raiders but many of them stayed as settlers. Although there were three different Germanic tribes—Angles, Saxons, and Jutes—the Saxons eventually dominated the others and the term *Saxons* is often applied to the descendants of all three groups. The Angles, however, gave their name to the new

land; the word *England* comes from *Engla-land,* meaning "land of the Angles." °

Some native Celts were killed and some were enslaved; others retreated to Ireland and into the highlands of Wales and Scotland. Roman culture, Latin, and Christianity disappeared. They were replaced by Germanic customs, the Anglo-Saxon language, and the animistic religion of the Saxons.

The Saxons in England formed several small independent kingdoms. Later these kingdoms combined into three important ones: (1) Northumbria, in what is now southern Scotland and northern England; (2) Mercia, in central England; and (3) Wessex, in southern England (see map, page 197). In time each kingdom was divided into districts called shires. These were governed by officials known as shire-reeves (which became the word *sheriffs*).

The government of each kingdom was simple. The king had a great deal of power. A council of

° **England:** Historians use the name *Britain* to refer to the eastern island of the British Isles during pre-Roman and Roman times. The word comes from the Latin *Britannia,* meaning "land of the Britons." The name *England* refers to the island—except for Scotland in the north and Wales in the west—after the Anglo-Saxon invasions.

Early England underwent a series of invasions. Among the earliest were those of the Saxons. The English countryside is still dotted with reminders of their presence—huge stone crosses where they conducted religious services if there was no church. The one at right, dating from the 700's, stands 18 feet high and has a carved image of Christ at the bottom. Danish invasions made serious inroads on Saxon settlements until the time of Alfred the Great, left, the first ruler to be victorious over the Danes. The most important invasion of England was that of the Normans. England's last Saxon king, Harold, is shown above on his throne in a contemporary tapestry. He "met little quiet . . . as long as he ruled the realm," according to the *Anglo-Saxon Chronicle*. Although shrewd and wily, he was unable to outwit William the Conqueror. The Norman duke, on horseback second from left below, had the best army in Europe and planned his invasion carefully. The man riding ahead of William carries the papal banner.

nobles, called the Witan, advised him. Together, the king and the Witan made laws and levied taxes. Below the king and the nobility were the freemen, who were nearly all warriors. There were many slaves.

Christianity in Ireland and England

Christian missionaries first arrived in Ireland in the 400's. St. Patrick, the best known, began his work there in 432. Several monastic schools were founded. These were the basis of a high culture which lasted from about 500 to about 800. Missionaries and teachers from Irish schools went out to all parts of the British Isles and to the courts of continental Europe.

About the year 600, missionaries were sent to England by Pope Gregory I (Gregory the Great). According to legend, Pope Gregory had seen a group of English captives in Rome. Told that the golden-haired prisoners were Angles, the pope exclaimed, "not Angles, but angels."

Pope Gregory's missionaries, led by St. Augustine, were successful in England. The wife of the king of Kent, in southern England, was already a Christian. She persuaded her husband to allow Augustine and the other missionaries to preach. Eventually, all England accepted Christianity. St. Augustine was made the first archbishop of Canterbury, and was thereafter called St. Augustine of Canterbury. Canterbury became the center of the Christian Church in England.

The Danes and Alfred the Great

By the year 800 the kingdom of Wessex controlled almost all of England. Then came new Germanic invasions, by the Vikings from Scandinavia.

The Vikings—known to the English as Danes —attacked England in the early 800's. At first, like the Saxons before them, they came as raiders for plunder. Then they began to take over land and settle permanently. Saxon resistance was ineffective until the time of Alfred, who became king of Wessex in 871.

Alfred, known as Alfred the Great, led Saxon armies to their first real victory over the Danes. Although he was unable to drive them out of the

ANGLO-SAXON KINGDOMS OF ENGLAND about 800 A.D.

island entirely, he forced them to remain in northeastern England, in a region known as the Danelaw. There they lived under their own laws and governed themselves.

Alfred the Great is best known for his peaceful accomplishments. He was an educated and scholarly man who wanted his people to be educated, too. He established schools and invited scholars from Ireland and the Continent to teach. He himself translated books from Latin into Anglo-Saxon. At his command, scholars began a history of England from the earliest times. This *Anglo-Saxon Chronicle,* written in Anglo-Saxon, was continued for 250 years after Alfred's death.

Alfred and his successors won back much Danish-held land. England was united for the first time, the government was strengthened, and the Christian Church was firmly established. Then in

197

the late 900's came a series of weak rulers. The Danes again attacked from Scandinavia and marched through the Danelaw to conquer the whole country by 1013.

In 1019, under the Danish ruler Canute, England became part of a large kingdom that included most of Scandinavia as well as England. Canute lived in England most of the time and ruled wisely. His sons and successors, however, were weak rulers. By 1042 the Danes were driven out of England, and a Saxon ruled again.

The Norman Conquest

Edward the Confessor, who became king of England in 1042, was Saxon only on his father's side. He had been brought up in Normandy by his Norman mother. One of his kinsmen was William, Duke of Normandy. When Edward died in 1066, William of Normandy claimed that the childless Saxon king had promised him the throne of England. The Saxon nobles refused to give the throne to William and elected Harold of Wessex. The Norman duke then appealed to the pope, who upheld his claim. William gathered a fleet and an army of nobles, promising them plunder if his invasion succeeded.

William and his invading Normans landed at Hastings, on the southeastern coast of England, in 1066. They defeated the Saxon forces and killed Harold. William was crowned in London as King William I of England. He is usually called William the Conqueror.

It took William several years to overcome Saxon resistance in other parts of the island. It took many more years for the Norman conquerors to overcome the hatred of the defeated Saxons. The Saxons did not adopt Norman ideas, customs, or language willingly or quickly. Like any conquered people, they disliked their new masters. Anglo-Saxon, a Germanic language, remained the language of the people; Norman French, a Romance language based on Latin, was the language of the nobles.

As time went on, however, the culture of England became as much Norman as Saxon. Even the language became a mixture. Eventually, Anglo-Saxon and Norman French blended to form the English language of today. About half of the words in English are of Anglo-Saxon, Germanic origin; 30 to 40 percent are of Latin origin through both Roman and Norman-French influence; the remainder come from Greek, Arabic, and other sources.

CHECKUP

1. What three waves of invasion did England undergo between 400 and 1066?
2. What did Alfred of Wessex do to earn his title "the Great"?
3. IDENTIFY: shire-reeves, Witan, St. Augustine of Canterbury, Danelaw, *Anglo-Saxon Chronicle,* Canute.
4. LOCATE: Northumbria, Mercia, Wessex, Kent, Canterbury, Hastings.

---

③ Medieval life was organized around feudalism and the manor

In continental Europe, organized government again disappeared within a century after Charlemagne's death in 814. Local lords had to protect and govern their own territories because weak kings were unable to do so. Europe entered upon a time of small, independent local governments. The political system that grew up is called *feudalism,* and the time during which it flourished is known as the *feudal* period. By the end of the 900's, feudalism was firmly established in north-

ern France. By the middle 1000's, it was the way of life throughout most of Western Europe.

Feudalism

Feudalism arose when local lords began to govern their own lands in the absence of a strong central government. To get needed military help, weak kings granted powerful lords the use of land from the royal estates. The strong lords, with more land than they needed, granted the use of part of it to lesser lords in return for military aid and other services. Many small landholders who needed protection gave their land to more powerful lords and were granted the right to occupy and use the lands in return for military service to the lord.

Each man who granted land was a lord; each man who held land in return for services was a vassal. The grant of land was called a fief. (The Latin word for fief is *feudum,* from which comes the word *feudal.*) In time the fief became hereditary. Legal ownership passed from the lord to his son, while legal possession and use passed from the vassal to his son. Only the oldest son inherited, for a fief was never divided. Many lords held more than one fief, often in widely scattered locations.

Many of the powers of government were held by local noble landholders. The king himself had become a feudal lord. In theory every holder of land was a vassal to the king, but in practice the king had power only over those who lived on his own feudal lands.

The Church, too, was drawn into the feudal system. By the 900's, it owned vast amounts of land. Some of this land was granted as fiefs to laymen in return for military protection.

The feudal relationship. In order to understand the relationship between lord and vassal, it is helpful to remember three things: *memorize*

(1) It was an honorable relationship between legal equals. Only nobles could be vassals. The greater lords were vassals and tenants of the king; the lesser lords were vassals and tenants of the greater lords, and so on down.

(2) The same man might be both vassal and lord—vassal to a more powerful lord above him and lord to a less powerful vassal below him.

(3) It was a very personal relationship. Each man's loyalties and obligations were owed only to the lord immediately above him or to the vassal below him. Each owed certain obligations to the other, and to the other only. The feudal relationship had much in common with the bond between the early Germanic chieftains and the young warriors who gathered around them.

The obligations of feudalism. The granting and holding of a fief was really a contract between lord

and vassal. The lord granted the fief—that is, use of the land. He also guaranteed the vassal protection and justice.

The obligations of the vassal were more numerous. He promised the lord a certain number of fully equipped horsemen and foot soldiers and agreed to pay their expenses while at war. Military service was usually limited to forty days a year.

Another obligation of a vassal consisted of feudal aids—special payments to help bear extraordinary expenses of the lord, such as ransom if the lord were captured in war. The vassal was also expected to house and feed the lord and his companions for a certain number of days a year, to attend such ceremonies as the marriage of the lord's daughter, and to serve on the lord's court to administer justice.

Feudal justice and warfare

Feudal justice was quite different from Roman ideas of law. Trial decisions were made in any one of three ways: *memorize*

(1) *Trial by battle.* The accused and the accuser, or men representing them, fought a duel. The outcome determined guilt or innocence.

(2) *Compurgation,* or oath-taking. The accused and the accuser each gathered a group of people who swore that "their" man was telling the truth. Compurgators, the oath-takers, were similar to the character witnesses in today's trials.

(3) *Ordeal.* The accused carried a piece of hot iron in his hand, or walked through fire, or plunged his arm into a pot of boiling water to pick up a hot stone. If his wounds healed rapidly, he was judged innocent; if not, he was found guilty.

War was the usual rather than the unusual state of the feudal world. Sometimes two kingdoms fought, or a king tried to subdue a powerful, rebellious vassal. Most wars, however, were private fights between feudal lords or between lords and vassals.

In the early Middle Ages, the armor of the fighting man was simple. He wore an iron helmet and a shirt of chain mail—small metal links hooked together to form a flexible protection. He carried a sword, a large shield, and a lance. Armor

199

became complicated in later medieval times, with metal plates replacing chain mail. Because this armor was so heavy, a knight often had to be hauled or boosted onto his horse.

For nobles, wars were fascinating affairs, but they brought suffering and famine to the peasants. The Church tried to improve conditions by limiting private wars. It issued decrees, known together as the Peace of God, which set aside certain places, such as churches, where fighting was not permitted. The Church tried to get all lords to accept another decree, known as the Truce of God, which forbade fighting on weekends and holy days. Gradually more days were added to the Truce of God, until there were only eighty days a year during which fighting was legal. These prohibitions, however, could not be strictly enforced. Private wars continued until kings were strong enough to enforce peace.

The manor

Feudalism, as you have read, was essentially a governmental and military system. The economic basis of early medieval life was a large estate that included a village. For convenience, the word *manor*—actually used only in England—can be applied to all such estates. The manor was the economic unit of the early Middle Ages, just as the fief was the governmental unit. While a small fief had only one manor, large fiefs had several.

Because of the breakdown of central authority and trade, each manor tried to be self-sufficient— that is, to produce everything it needed. Most manors produced their own food, clothing, and leather goods. Only a few items, such as iron, salt, and tar, were imported.

The land of a manor (see below) was divided among the lord and a number of peasants. The lord kept about a third of the manor land, called the domain, for himself. (It was often divided into several plots, although it might form one large block near the lord's house.) The peasants paid for the use of the remaining land by giving the lord part of their crops and by working on his land. They also performed other services on the manor and paid taxes and tolls of many kinds.

A typical manor village had houses along a single street. The manor house or castle of the lord stood a little distance away. The village was usually located on a stream which furnished water-power for its mill. The land of the manor extended out from the village. This land included vegetable plots, cultivated fields, pastures, and forests.

The cultivated land of the manor was often divided into three large fields for growing grain. Only two fields were planted each year. Each field had to lie fallow every third year to regain its fertility. The large fields in turn were divided into small strips. Peasants held strips in each field; if the lord's domain was divided (as in the plan below), he too had strips in each field.

Peasant life

Most of the peasants on a manor were serfs, whose legal status was less than free but higher than slave. Like the coloni of Roman times, they

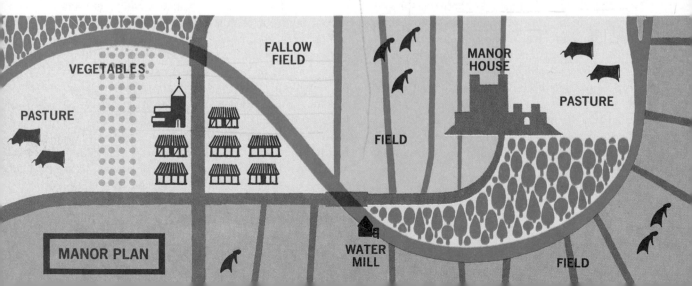

PASTURE

VEGETABLES

FALLOW FIELD

MANOR HOUSE

PASTURE

FIELD

MANOR PLAN

WATER MILL

FIELD

Life on a Medieval Manor

Menial work of all kinds fell to the serfs who lived on a manor. The most basic task, of course, was farming. At right, women use sickles to harvest grain, while a man follows behind them tying it into sheaves. This scene is from an English manuscript of about 1300. Below it are three other manor activities, as depicted in a French religious book of the 1400's. Bread was usually baked once a week. Slaughtering—in this case a pig—was done in the fall, since medieval farming did not produce enough grain to feed livestock through the winter. The woman holds a pan to catch the blood, which was used to make sausage. In a typical winter scene, a man toasts his feet before a fire and a woman spins wool. The lord and lady of the manor had a more leisurely existence than their serfs. They are shown below playing chess, while musicians entertain them.

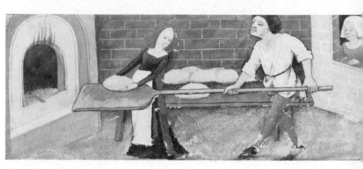

Medieval Tapestry

The dark, damp castles of medieval nobles were made somewhat cozier and warmer when tapestries were hung on the walls. These skillfully woven fabrics were both decorative and practical. They not only gave protection against the cold but also could easily be packed up and moved. Tapestries could be cut apart into small pieces and resewn to fit rooms of various sizes, so that people who found themselves in foreign lands or new and strange surroundings could still have familiar belongings with them.

The tapestry at left shows the archangel Michael slaying the dragon, symbol of the enemy of God and a devouring monster who angrily destroys his victims. It was woven of wool, silk, and gilt thread in Germany.

were bound to the land. They could not leave it without the lord's permission, and the price of his permission was usually a large sum of money. Serfs were not slaves, for they could not be sold away from the land. If the land were granted to a new lord, the serfs became his tenants.

There were some freemen on the manor who rented land from the lord. This group included the skilled workers necessary to the village economy, such as millers, blacksmiths, and carpenters. Most villages also had a priest to provide for the spiritual needs of the villagers.

Daily life was hard, with long hours spent working the fields. Food was poor, consisting mainly of coarse black bread, cabbage and a few other vegetables, cheese, and eggs. Beer was plentiful in northern Europe, and wine in the grape-growing regions farther south. Meat was rarely eaten.

The life of the nobility

Almost everyone has a mental picture, usually romantic and somewhat hazy, of the Middle Ages. The picture often includes luxurious castles and knights in shining armor. Like most romantic pictures, this one has some truth but much that is out of focus.

A castle was a fortified home for a lord, serving as a base for protecting the surrounding country and enforcing his authority. Most people today picture a castle as a great stone structure with elaborate turrets and battlements. Actually castles of this type were not built until the later Middle Ages. Throughout the early medieval period, castles were relatively simple structures built of earth and wood.

Castles were built for defense, not for pleasant living. They were located on hills or in other places that were easy to defend. If a castle had to be built in flat country, a moat surrounded the outer walls. The gate to the courtyard inside the walls was reached by a drawbridge across the moat. In case of an attack the drawbridge was raised.

The main part of the castle was the keep, a strong tower that contained storerooms, barracks, and workshops, as well as the lord's living quarters. In the great hall the lord held court and received visitors, and here the family lived during the day. The lord and his family usually had a separate bedroom, but everyone else slept in the great hall with screens for privacy. There was not much furniture. The thick walls with their small, usually uncovered windows made the rooms dark, damp, and chilly. Fowl, dogs, and other small animals ran everywhere. The floors were covered with straw in which filth and vermin abounded.

The greatest sport of the feudal lord was the tournament, a mock battle. A joust was a fight between two men in armor; a tourney was a battle between two groups of armored men. In early times these were real fights, but later they were more like pageants.

Chivalry

During the 1100's, feudal society was changed by the development of chivalry, a code of conduct for knights. The word comes from the French word *cheval,* meaning "horse." A knight was almost always mounted on horseback when performing the deeds demanded by the code of chivalry.

In the early days, becoming a knight was quite simple. Any noble, by proving himself in battle, could be knighted by any other knight. As time passed, chivalry became much more complex.

To become a knight, a boy had to pass through two preliminary stages of training supervised by a knight. At the age of seven, a boy became a page, learning knightly manners and beginning his training in the use of weapons. In his early teens, he became a squire, a knight's assistant. He continued his training in both manners and weapons. He took care of the knight's horses, armor, weapons, and clothing. When he was considered ready, he accompanied the knight in battle to prove himself worthy to be a knight. After proving himself, he was initiated into knighthood in an elaborate religious ceremony.

Chivalry required a knight to be brave—even foolishly brave. He had to fight fairly, according to the rules. Tricks and strategy were considered cowardly. He had to be loyal to his friends, keep his word, and treat conquered foes gallantly. Chivalry made a great improvement in the rough and crude manners of early feudal lords. Behavior, however, did not become perfect by any standards. The courtesy of the knight was extended only to people of his own class. Toward all others his attitude and actions were likely to be extremely coarse.

CHECKUP

1. What was feudalism? Why did it develop?
2. How were decisions made in feudal courts?
3. Name and describe the economic basis of early medieval life.
4. Under the rules of chivalry, what were the steps leading to knighthood?
5. IDENTIFY: vassal, fief, Peace of God, Truce of God, serfs, joust, tourney.

4 The Church performed many functions in the Middle Ages

You have seen that central government in medieval Europe was weak and often nonexistent. Many of the functions carried on by modern governments were performed by the Church. In one way or another, it touched the lives of medieval people at almost every point.

The Church hierarchy

All members of the clergy occupied a place in the hierarchy (HY·uh·rahr·kee)—that is, they were organized in ranks according to their powers and responsibilities. The levels of the hierarchy, starting at the bottom, were as follows:

(1) *The parish priest.* The parish priest was usually of peasant origin, with little formal education. He was the hardest working and poorest member of the clergy.

Though he was at the bottom of the hierarchy, the priest was, in one sense, the Church's most important officer. He conducted the church services in his parish and administered all the sacraments except confirmation and ordination. He supervised the moral and religious instruction of his people and the moral life of the community.

(2) *The bishop.* The bishop managed a diocese consisting of several parishes. He administered the sacraments of confirmation and ordination. He presided from the cathedral in his diocese, appointed and removed parish priests, and managed Church property in his diocese.

The choice of a bishop was usually controlled by the king or great nobles. Bishops were often feudal lords or vassals and had vassals themselves. They were frequently chosen for their family connections and political power.

(3) *The archbishop.* The archbishop had a diocese himself and all the powers of a bishop. In addition, he exercised some authority over the other dioceses and bishops in his province. He could summon provincial councils of the clergy to decide questions of Church belief and policy.

(4) *The pope and his curia.* As you read in Chapter 8, the organization of the early Church included patriarchs in various cities. The bishop of Rome was the only patriarch in Western Europe. According to Church doctrine, Jesus had appointed as head of the Church the Apostle Peter, who was believed to have traveled to Rome and served as its first bishop. Because of this tradition, and because Rome had been the capital of the Roman imperial government, the bishop of Rome gradually gained recognition as the head of all the bishops in Western Europe. He came to be called *pope,* from the Latin word *papa,* meaning "father." By the year 400, the pope was considered to be the spiritual head of the Church in Western Europe.

Gregory I, called Gregory the Great, was the first pope to hold great earthly power. He became pope in 590, during the Lombard occupation of northern and central Italy. Gregory became the real ruler of Rome, and successfully led its defense against Lombard attack. It was Gregory the Great who sent out the missionaries that converted Anglo-Saxon England, Lombard Italy, and Visigothic Spain to the Christian faith (see map, opposite). At the end of his reign, papal authority was recognized throughout Italy, Spain, France, North Africa, and most of England.

To advise them, the popes had a court, the curia, made up of officials whom they appointed. The most important members of the curia were the cardinals, papal advisers on legal and spiritual matters. After 1059, the cardinals had the duty of electing the new pope.

Only in the Church hierarchy could the son of a commoner rise in the world. It did not happen often, but a man of great ability, regardless of birth, might rise to great heights in the Church.

The Church as a state

The medieval Church was much like a present-day government. Everyone became a member at birth, just as we become citizens. The Church had its own laws and courts. It could enforce these laws, even upon kings and emperors, by such means as excommunication and interdict.

Excommunication meant that an individual was cut off completely from the Church. He could not receive the sacraments or be buried in sacred ground. All Christians were obliged to avoid the excommunicated person, and the state treated him like an outlaw. After his death, he was thought to be surely damned.

Interdict was the punishment of an entire region. No religious services could be held, no sacraments administered except baptism and extreme unction. Everyone who lived in the region was in danger of eternal damnation.

Like a national government, the Church had the power of taxation. Through the parish priest it collected the tithe from all Christians—a tenth of their income. In England and Scandinavia there was also "Peter's Pence," a tax of one penny per year on every household. The Church received fines from its courts and fees for the performance of ceremonies such as baptism and marriage. Finally there was also vast income from Church-owned lands. In the early 1200's, when the Church was at the peak of its power, its income was greater than that of all the kings of Europe combined.

Monasticism

Priests, bishops, and the pope belonged to what was called the secular clergy. They lived, according to the Latin phrase, *in saeculo,* meaning "in the world," or among mankind. They administered the sacraments and preached the gospel. A second group of churchmen were called regular clergy because they lived according to a strict rule, or *regula.* These were the monastics—monks and nuns.

Monks and nuns believed that one of the best ways to live a perfect Christian life was to withdraw from the world and its temptations and to serve God by prayer, fasting, and self-denial. At first each monk lived alone; later monks gathered

in religious communities and lived in monasteries. Nuns lived in nunneries or convents.

Monasticism in Western Europe lacked organization and direction until the early 500's. At about that time, Benedict, a young Roman noble, became disgusted with worldly corruption and left Rome to become a hermit. In time his reputation for holiness attracted so many followers that he established a monastery at Monte Cassino in central Italy.

St. Benedict drew up a set of standards, the Benedictine Rule, to regulate the lives of the

SPREAD OF CHRISTIANITY
600 to 1300 A.D.

Christian areas in 600 A.D.
Areas Christianized 600-800 A.D.
Areas Christianized 800-1100 A.D.
Areas Christianized 1100-1300 A.D.

Reliquary of St. Faith

This golden image of St. Faith illustrates a characteristic feature of medieval religion—the devotion given to the relics, or remains, of saints. St. Faith was martyred as a young girl during the last Roman persecution of Christians, in the early 300's. In the 800's, tales of miracles performed by the young saint began circulating. People flocked to the church in France where some of her remains had been taken, hoping for further miracles. As time passed, the church accumulated a collection of valuables that pilgrims had donated as offerings. In about 985 they were used in making this reliquary (a container for relics). The little saint's skull is in a cavity in the back, wrapped in a covering of silver.

206

monks. It was adopted by monasteries throughout Europe.

A monk could own absolutely nothing. Everything he used or wore belonged to the community of monks. All property was controlled and distributed by the abbot, the elected head of the community. The monk swore to obey the abbot in all things.

Monks spent several hours every day in prayer. Work was a second obligation. All the necessary tasks in and about the monastery were assigned by the abbot to groups of monks.

Some monks, at the command of their superiors, left the monasteries to become missionaries. St. Patrick in Ireland, St. Augustine in England, and St. Boniface in Germany were among those who did important missionary work.

The Church and medieval life

Both the secular and the regular clergy played a leading part in medieval institutions and medieval life. The Church sought out the best minds among all classes to become members of the clergy. During the early Middle Ages, churchmen were almost the only educated people in Europe.

Since printing was unknown in the early Middle Ages, all books had to be copied by hand. Monks did most of this work. To relieve the tedious work of straight copying and to beautify the texts, the monks often added small paintings at the beginning of a page or along the side margins. The gold leaf and brilliant colors they used brightened the pages so much that such works are called illuminated manuscripts. They were the finest artistic works of the early Middle Ages.

Political role. The Church entered into the political life of the Middle Ages in many ways. In the Papal States, the pope was the political as well as the spiritual ruler. In addition, many popes claimed that the Church was politically supreme and that all monarchs had to obey them. Churchmen also held positions of power as feudal lords and as advisers to emperors, kings, and nobles.

The Church preached that men should obey the laws of kings unless they were contrary to Church laws. It had its own code of law, called canon law, and courts where members of the clergy

were tried. The right of the clergy to be tried in Church courts was called benefit of clergy, valued because sentences were lighter than in other courts. Church courts also heard cases involving Church property, marriage, wills, and witchcraft.

Economic life. The moral ideas of the Church affected all economic life. The Church opposed the gaining of wealth at the expense or disadvantage of others. It insisted that labor was in keeping with the dignity of free men.

Monks were leaders in agriculture. They developed new ways of raising crops, breeding cattle, and cultivating fruit, especially grapes. Monks greatly increased the amount of land which could be farmed by clearing forests, draining swamps, and building dikes and roads.

Monasteries carried on widespread trading activities. They owned their own pack animals, ships, markets, and warehouses. Their routes were carefully mapped; often, monks built roads themselves.

Social work. Of great social importance to the Church was the maintenance of the family as a sacred institution. Divorce was forbidden. The Church took responsibility for all widows and orphans. It also took complete charge of all social work, such as relief for the poor.

To relieve the sick and distressed, it established hospitals, orphanages, and poorhouses. Special religious orders provided hospital care, care of lepers, burial of the poor, and general charity. Monasteries made gifts of food and clothing to the neighboring poor. Monasteries also provided the best inns for travelers.

Problems of the Church

At the very peak of its power, the Church faced certain difficulties and problems.

(1) *Lay investiture.* The tremendous wealth of the Church created problems, especially after churchmen became feudal lords and vassals. Appointments to high Church offices became the spoils of politics.

The appointment of Church officials led to the problem of lay investiture—the investing of, or granting authority to, a clergyman by a layman. The Church maintained that only a churchman could pass on spiritual authority to another churchman. In the case of a bishop, this authority was symbolized by a ring and crosier, or staff. A king or lord who granted a new bishop his fiefs often insisted on giving him his ring and crosier as well.

(2) *Worldly lives of the clergy.* Some members of the clergy brought criticism upon the entire Church because of their worldliness. Some lived in luxury; some seemed to be more interested in wealth than in holy living. As you will read later, the immorality of the clergy became a favorite subject for critics of society.

(3) *Simony.* Simony (SY·muh·nee) meant the buying and selling of Church positions, a widespread practice in feudal times. The purchaser expected to get his money back from Church income or by charging high fees for the religious services he performed.

(4) *Heresy.* The Church permitted some criticism of its practices. But it forbade questioning of its doctrines (Church teachings as revealed in the Bible) or dogmas (truths of the faith as revealed by God). People who denied the truth of dogmas or preached unauthorized doctrines were heretics, guilty of the unpardonable sin of heresy, which brought eternal damnation. Heresy threatened the Church itself, as treason does a modern government.

Attempts at Church reform. Many churchmen and lay rulers tried to solve Church problems by various reforms. Two religious orders, established in the 1200's, were dedicated to reform. The Franciscans, founded by St. Francis of Assisi, and the Dominicans, founded by St. Dominic, lived and preached among the people instead of secluding themselves in monasteries.

In the mid-1200's, the pope ordered the Dominicans to seek out heretics and eliminate heresy. This search was known as the Inquisition. Suspected heretics were tried in secret and tortures were sometimes used to force confessions. Heretics who recanted, or confessed that they had been wrong, had to perform heavy penance. Heretics who did not recant were condemned and turned over to the civil government to be punished, usually by burning at the stake. These severe penalties were thought necessary to save the souls of heretics and to prevent heresy from spreading.

CHECKUP

1. Name the members of the Church hierarchy and describe briefly the duties of each.

2. What were three ways in which the medieval Church resembled a state?

3. State some great contributions made to medieval life by the Church.

4. IDENTIFY: secular clergy, regular clergy, Benedictine Rule, abbot, canon law, benefit of clergy, lay investiture, simony, heresy, St. Francis of Assisi, Inquisition.

5   Kings and nobles struggled for power in France and England

Kings had little power during the 800's and 900's. Some great lords were as powerful as the kings themselves, and served them only when it was convenient. Kings and lords struggled for power in what might be called a feudal tug of war. From this struggle gradually emerged such kingdoms as France and England, where the king's authority actually meant something.

Rise of the Capetian kings in France

In 987 the last Carolingian king of France died without heirs. An assembly of nobles chose Hugh Capet, a French noble, as king. The line of kings he founded, called the Capetians, ruled France for over 300 years.

As king, Hugh Capet ruled only a small region around the city of Paris called the Île-de-France. *Île* is the French word for "island," and this region was indeed a small island of royal authority in the midst of feudal lands. Even there the king's vassals resisted him.

The rest of what we know as France was divided into provinces ruled by powerful feudal lords. Among the most important provinces were Champagne and Burgundy to the east; Flanders to the north; Normandy, Brittany, Maine, and Anjou to the west; and Aquitaine, Toulouse, and Gascony to the south (see map, opposite).° The Capetian kings set out to unite these provinces and to develop a strong central government.

The Capetians had one strong advantage. They

° The areas, and even the names, of the French provinces changed over the years. For example, during some periods, Gascony was considered to be a part of Aquitaine, and the latter name referred to both provinces.

did not divide the kingdom among their sons. Only the eldest son could inherit. For over 300 years there was always a son to inherit the throne. Thus the Capetians were able to outlast many other noble families.

The history of the Capetian kings is a good example of the feudal struggle for power. Strong kings increased royal lands and authority. Weak kings allowed nobles to regain power and privileges. Fortunately for the Capetians, able kings came often enough to make up for the losses. The strong Capetian kings added to their power in three ways: (1) by adding to the royal lands; (2) by developing a strong central government; and (3) by increasing the revenue from taxes.

The growth of royal territory. Kings added to the royal domain by various means. They married the daughters of great feudal lords and thus gained fiefs that were often included in dowries. Some noble families died out and the kings took over the nobles' lands.

After 1066, when William of Normandy conquered England and became its king, the territorial problems of the Capetians became even more complicated. For centuries the English kings held vast territories in France. Strong Capetians were always alert to regain these lands. The shrewd Philip Augustus, king of France from 1180 to 1223, seized much English-held land in France. He took advantage of the absence of King Richard from England on a crusade, and of the weakness of Richard's successor, John. By 1328, when the last Capetian king died, the only large land areas held by the English in France were parts of Aquitaine and Gascony (see map, opposite page).

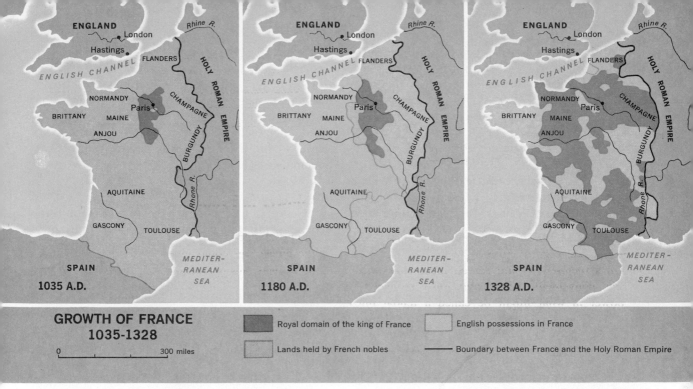

ENGLAND	ENGLAND	ENGLAND
1035 A.D.	1180 A.D.	1328 A.D.

**GROWTH OF FRANCE
1035-1328**

0 ____ 300 miles

■ Royal domain of the king of France
□ Lands held by French nobles
□ English possessions in France
— Boundary between France and the Holy Roman Empire

Central government. For a strong central government, the Capetians needed loyal, trained officials, not undependable feudal lords. Philip Augustus sent out inspectors, recruited from the relatively new middle class, to make investigations, hear complaints, and report to the King's Council. It was this body that conducted government affairs.

During the 1200's and early 1300's, two new government departments were set up. A Chamber of Accounts collected and looked after the taxes, and a supreme court, called the Parlement of Paris, heard appeals from all parts of the kingdom. These bodies, and the King's Council as well, were staffed and run by professional officials.

Revenues. Strong central government needed money for a paid army because feudal armies were unreliable. Money was also needed to pay officials and for other expenses. The increasing royal domain produced more wealth, as did fees and fines from royal courts. Because a wealthier country would produce more revenue from taxes, the Capetians encouraged the growth of towns, trade, and manufacturing. This policy also gained

kings the support of townsmen against the feudal lords. By the early 1300's, France was a strong, well-organized country, and the power of the king was supreme. The three sons of Philip IV, however, each died without a male heir, and in 1328 the long line of the Capetians came to an end.

Feudalism in England

William the Conqueror, who reigned from 1066 to 1087, imported feudalism from France to England. But he was careful to alter it so that the king, rather than the nobles, held the authority. He kept much English land as his own. The fiefs he gave his followers were scattered throughout England, to weaken the lords and prevent them from uniting.

Each feudal lord had to swear allegiance directly to William rather than to the lord immediately above him. Thus all the feudal lords became vassals of the king. In this way, William laid the foundation for a centralized government. Nevertheless, England, like France, underwent a feudal struggle for power.

In order to determine the population and wealth of England, William sent out commissions to gather information on everyone in the country. This information was then used to set taxes. Since it was said that it would be easier to escape doomsday than to avoid the royal commissioners, the survey became known as the *Domesday (Doomsday) Book.*

Reforms under William's successors

William was succeeded by his sons William Rufus and, later, Henry I. Henry I, who ruled from 1100 to 1135, made the central government more efficient. He set up a new department, the Exchequer (eks·CHEK·ur), to handle finances. His other innovation was in the legal system. He wanted to weaken the feudal lords by having as many cases as possible tried in the king's courts rather than in feudal courts. He sent judges out to travel through the country and hold court at many different places.

Under Henry II, who reigned from 1154 to 1189, royal authority increased greatly. To get a dependable army, he required every freeman to obtain arms appropriate to his position and to serve in the king's army. He allowed nobles to pay him instead of rendering military service and used the money to hire a professional army.

Henry II made greater use of the traveling judges than had earlier rulers. He also established definite circuits, or routes, on which they were to travel. Thus they became known as circuit judges.

To let the judge know what cases should be tried, the king appointed groups of men called juries in each district. A grand jury of twenty-five or more submitted the names of suspected criminals. Later, in the 1200's, there developed the petit (PET·ee) jury of twelve. (*Grand* is the French word for "large," and *petit* the French word for "small.") At first petit juries decided only civil cases, such as disputes over land, while criminal cases were still tried by the feudal procedures of ordeal or combat. In time, however, petit juries came to decide criminal cases too. Thus the king's law replaced feudal law.

In his efforts to increase his authority, Henry II tried to transfer trials of certain members of the clergy from Church to royal courts. The Archbishop of Canterbury, Thomas à Becket, refused to allow this, and the two men became bitter enemies. The quarrel was finally settled when a group of the king's knights, thinking they would be doing the king a great favor, murdered the archbishop in his cathedral. Henry II, probably truthfully, denied any part in the assassination; in any case, it forced him to abandon further attempts at legal reform.

Political problems

Henry II had inherited the provinces of Normandy, Maine, and Anjou in northwestern France. To these lands he added Gascony and Aquitaine by marrying Eleanor, daughter of the Duke of Aquitaine. Before the end of his reign, he also acquired Brittany. These English holdings on the continent (see map, page 209) influenced both English and French history. For centuries, English kings divided their interests instead of concentrating on England.

The last years of Henry II were troubled. His sons often plotted against each other because of their jealousy and hatred. When they did unite, it was to plot against their own father. Just before his death, Henry learned that Philip Augustus of France had gained the support of two of his sons in a rebellion against him.

At Henry II's death in 1189, his son Richard (known as the Lion-Hearted) became King Richard I of England. He is famous for deeds during the Crusades against the Moslems, but he was a poor king. He disliked England and was bored by the problems of governing the country. During his ten-year reign, he spent only six months in England. The English were cruelly taxed to pay for Richard's heroic adventures in the Holy Land and for his ransom when he was captured. Many Englishmen were relieved when Richard was killed in 1199 while fighting in France.

King John and Magna Carta

Another son of Henry II, John, succeeded Richard as king. He lost much of the land and power his father had gained. Philip Augustus defeated him in France and took Normandy, Brittany, Maine, and Anjou. In England, John brought on a revolt among the nobles by forcing them to pay taxes they considered unjust.

In 1215, English nobles forced John to accept a document known as Magna Carta (Latin for "great charter"). It was intended mainly to protect the lords' liberties. Some provisions, however, dealt with rights of commoners, and it is these parts that have come to be considered the most important provisions in the document.

The king made the following promises: not to collect any new or special tax without the consent of the Great Council (a body of important nobles and churchmen who advised the king); not to take property without paying for it; and not to sell, refuse, or delay justice. He agreed not to hold a freeman in prison "except by the lawful judgment of his peers and . . . by the law of the land." That is, he promised to grant any accused person a trial by a jury of his peers, or equals. Basically, Magna Carta meant that the king was not above the law, but had to obey it, just as his subjects did.

Although the charter was not considered unusually significant at the time, later political thinkers regarded many of its clauses as important precedents.

Parliament and the common law

In the century that followed Magna Carta, the two most important trends in English history were the development of Parliament and the growth of the common law.

Parliament grew out of the Great Council. In the 1260's there was a nobles' revolt against King Henry III. The leader of the nobles, Simon de Montfort, virtually ruled England for several months. He hoped to get greater support for the nobles' cause by broadening representation in the Great Council. In 1265 he summoned representatives of the middle class to meet with the higher nobles and clergy in the Great Council. There were two knights from each shire and two burgesses (citizens) from each of several towns.

De Montfort's revolt was crushed, but a precedent had been set—that of including knights and burgesses in the Council. At first, all groups met together. In time, Parliament, as this representative body came to be called, was divided into two houses. Nobles and clergy sat as an upper house, the House of Lords. Knights and burgesses met as the lower house, the House of Commons.

The early Parliament did not have the power to pass laws, but did have the important right of refusing to consent to new and special taxes. As the cost of running the central government increased, new taxes were necessary, and Parliament's consent became vital. Over the years, Parliament used this power to its advantage.

You have read about developments in English law courts under Henry I and his successors. Edward I, who ruled from 1272 to 1307, divided the king's court into three branches. The Court of the Exchequer kept financial accounts and tried tax cases. The Court of Common Pleas tried cases between private citizens. The Court of the King's Bench heard cases that concerned the king or the government.

Each of the three royal courts handed down many verdicts, or decisions. Each year the most important of them were collected and written down. These written decisions became the basis for future decisions made in the king's courts and in the circuit courts. This type of law, based on judges' decisions rather than on a code of statutes like that of the Romans, is known as common law. (It received this name because it was common to all of England.) It is the basis for the legal system of the United States as well as of England.

CHECKUP

1. What problems did the Capetian kings of France face? What advantage did they have? How did the strong Capetian kings add to their power?

2. What were some of the main provisions of Magna Carta? What was its basic importance?

3. How did each of the following develop in England: Parliament? common law?

4. IDENTIFY: Philip Augustus, Parlement of Paris, *Domesday Book,* Henry I, grand jury, petit jury, Becket.

5. LOCATE: Champagne, Burgundy, Flanders, Brittany, Maine, Anjou, Aquitaine, Toulouse, Gascony.

You have read how important the Church was in the medieval period. Although its spiritual authority was recognized throughout Europe, many conflicts arose over its temporal authority—that is, its role in affairs of the world.

After the time of Pope Gregory the Great, in the late 500's and early 600's, the papacy declined. Charlemagne used the Church almost as a branch of his government. Later, as you have read, the Church became feudalized. Bishops and abbots became feudal lords or vassals. The pope himself was a feudal lord. For a time the nobles of Rome controlled the papacy and it lost much of its spiritual influence. The greatest threat to the power of the medieval popes came from the rulers of Germany.

The Holy Roman Empire

After the breakup of Charlemagne's empire in the late 800's, Germany was little more than a group of practically independent states. There was an elected king, but he was merely a feudal lord among other feudal lords.

Italy, part of which had belonged to Charlemagne's empire, was in a state of feudal anarchy. Several of Charlemagne's descendants held the title of Emperor of the Romans without really ruling. Later, no one had even the title. The pope ruled in the Papal States. Some parts of Italy were held by the eastern Roman Empire. Moslems held the island of Sicily and often invaded the Italian mainland.

In 936, Otto I, known as Otto the Great, was elected king of Germany by the great feudal lords. He was a powerful ruler and might have developed a strong kingdom in Germany, like that of the Capetians in France, but Italy tempted him. He took territory in northern Italy. Then Pope John XII begged Otto's help in his struggle with the Roman nobles. Otto supported the pope, who crowned him Emperor of the Romans in 962. Otto later installed his own secretary as pope, and for the next forty years, German kings chose the popes.

Although Otto's title was the same as that given Charlemagne 162 years earlier, he ruled a different territory—Germany and northern Italy. This territory was called the Holy Roman Empire (see map, page 238). It was a shadowy sort of empire, but it lasted, in name at least, for centuries. It established a relationship between Germany and Italy that continued for more than 800 years, to the great harm of both.

The power of the Holy Roman Emperors reached a high point under Henry III, who reigned from 1039 to 1056. Like Charlemagne, Henry regarded the Church as a branch of the royal government. At one time during Henry's reign, three different men claimed to be pope. Henry III deposed all three claimants and had a German elected. He also dictated the choice of the next three popes.

Struggle with the papacy

Henry III's son, Emperor Henry IV, was only a child when his father died. For this reason and because there was civil war in Germany, the Church had a chance to increase its powers. It was then that Gregory VII became pope.

The new pope was determined to restore the papacy to power. He believed that as representative of God he had supreme power not only over the Church but also over all worldly rulers and their subjects. As pope he controlled the most terrible punishments of the Church—excommunication and interdict. Gregory used these weapons in his conflicts with emperors, kings, and nobles. His greatest struggle was with Henry IV.

The struggle between Gregory VII and Henry IV was long and complex. It concerned chiefly the issue of lay investiture. Henry IV insisted that he had the right to appoint bishops within the Holy Roman Empire. Gregory disagreed and finally excommunicated the emperor, releasing all his subjects from their oaths of allegiance and urging them to elect another emperor. Soon afterward, Henry gave in to the pope. He journeyed to Italy, to the castle at Canossa where Gregory was staying. Barefoot and dressed as a pilgrim, he begged and received the pope's forgiveness.

The struggle over lay investiture continued during the reign of Henry's son. Finally, in 1122 at the German city of Worms (VORMS), there was a great Diet, or assembly. Churchmen, nobles, and representatives of the Holy Roman Emperor reached an agreement known as the Concordat of Worms. The emperor agreed that Church officials should elect bishops and grant them their spiritual powers. The emperor promised not to try to influence the elections. He was allowed to grant only lands and secular powers to elected Church officials.

The struggle between popes and emperors was by no means ended, however. Later conflicts involved not only the powers of the Church and temporal rulers, but also the territories each claimed to rule. German rule in Italy continued to threaten papal rule in the Papal States. The papacy therefore opposed all attempts of the Holy Roman Emperors to rule any part of Italy.

Frederick Barbarossa

The greatest medieval German ruler was Frederick I, called Frederick Barbarossa (meaning "Frederick of the Red Beard"). He ruled from 1152 to 1190. Like the emperors who preceded him, Frederick could have been a real ruler in Germany, but he, too, was lured by Italy.

The rich city-states of Lombardy in northern Italy—Milan, Parma, Padua, Verona, and Bologna—had prospered in trade and had become increasingly independent. There was a wealthy merchant class, and the government was partly democratic. Frederick sent representatives to take

Otto the Great, Holy Roman Emperor, receives homage from German and Italian states. Like Charlemagne, he encouraged learning, although he himself could not read.

over the government in the cities. When Milan refused to receive his representative, Frederick captured the city, destroyed it, and scattered its population.

The other Lombard cities, aided by the pope, united to form the Lombard League. They raised an army and defeated Frederick in 1176. The peace settlement was a victory for the league and the pope. The cities recognized Frederick as overlord, but he had to agree that they could govern themselves.

Papal power under Innocent III

Innocent III, pope from 1198 to 1216, led the papacy to the height of its prestige and power. A learned and intelligent man, Innocent wrote books on law, theology, and Christian discipline. He was also a skillful diplomat and one of the greatest statesmen in all history.

Innocent III made even more sweeping claims to power than had Gregory VII, and was even more successful in enforcing them. He believed himself supreme over both the clergy and all temporal rulers. He believed, in fact, that emperors and kings were merely servants of the Church. Thus Pope Innocent III claimed the right to settle all problems, political or religious. No person or group could do more than advise him; the final decision was his.

Innocent took part in disputes throughout Europe and made free use of his powers of excommunication and interdict. In a quarrel with King John, he placed England under interdict. To have the interdict lifted, John had to become the pope's vassal and pay an annual tribute to Rome.

Innocent dominated Italy as ruler of the Papal States, protector of the Lombard League, and feudal overlord of Sicily (which the Normans had seized from the Moslems in the 1000's). In Germany he deposed two kings and installed others.

Under Innocent III, Europe became practically an absolute monarchy ruled by the pope, but it did not remain so. Such a government needed a pope of almost superhuman ability and energy. Innocent III was such a man; but even so, his success came partly because conditions in Europe were favorable to his claims and activities. Later popes were less skillful, and circumstances were less favorable.

Frederick II

The last German ruler to try to rule Italy was Frederick II, who reigned from 1215 to 1250. In many ways he was the most interesting of all the Holy Roman Emperors. Besides Germany, he was heir to the Kingdom of the Two Sicilies, which the invading Normans had established in the late 1000's. This kingdom included southern Italy as well as Sicily, and was very powerful.

Frederick II was more interested in Sicily than he was in Germany. In Germany he kept the rivalries of the great families stirred up so that powerful lords would not unite against him. On the other hand, he granted various privileges to the German nobles in order to have his infant son accepted as his heir. Frederick tried, but failed, to unite Italy into a single kingdom. At his death, his son ruled briefly as emperor. There followed a long period of civil war in Germany. Later German rulers kept the title of Holy Roman Emperor, but they did not try to impose their rule in Italy.

You can see that the attempts to unite Germany and Italy not only failed, but also prevented either one from being united. One writer has said that the German rulers tried to get an empire and did not even get a duchy. Germany remained a jumble of independent cities and feudal states, over which the emperor had little authority. Italy was disunited, too, with the Lombard cities in the north, the Papal States in the central region, and the Kingdom of the Two Sicilies to the south. Neither Germany nor Italy became a unified nation until the 1800's.

CHECKUP

1. What major problem was involved in the conflict between Gregory VII and Henry IV? How was the issue resolved?

2. Who was Innocent III? Why was he important?

3. IDENTIFY: Otto I, Holy Roman Empire, Henry III, Frederick Barbarossa, Lombard League, Frederick II.

Chapter 10   Feudal Lords and Churchmen Dominated Medieval Europe   (432—1328)

⟵ B.C. | A.D. ⟶

| 750 | 500 | 250 | 250 | 500 | 750 | 1000 | 1250 | 1500 | 1750 | 2000 |

432	St. Patrick in Ireland	871	Beginning of rule by Alfred the Great	1152-1190	Reign of Frederick Barbarossa
450	Britain raided by Angles, Saxons, and Jutes	962	Otto the Great crowned emperor	1154-1189	Royal authority increased by Henry II of England
590	Gregory I chosen pope	987-1328	Capetian rule of France	1180-1223	Philip Augustus king of France
754	Crowning of Pepin by pope	1066	Norman conquest of England	1198-1216	Height of papal authority under Innocent III
768-814	Rule of Charlemagne	1100-1135	Rule of Henry I in England		
843	Treaty of Verdun	1122	Concordat of Worms	1215	Magna Carta

476-Roman Empire

CHAPTER SUMMARY

After the Roman Empire declined, Germanic tribes overran Europe. Clovis, king of one of the Frankish tribes, and succeeding Merovingians created a large kingdom in France. It was later controlled by Charles Martel and Pepin the Short. The greatest Frankish king, Charlemagne, created an empire that included much of Western Europe.   *Clovis*

Britain, too, was ruled by Germanic tribes, the Saxons. During their rule the people were converted to Christianity, and England was invaded by the Danes. Although they were driven out of England, the country was soon overwhelmed by the Normans.

Two important medieval institutions were feudalism and the manorial system. Feudalism was basically a political system, with lords granting fiefs to vassals in return for military service and other aids. The manorial system was an economic system based on the self-sufficient manor worked by serfs.

During the Middle Ages the Church performed many functions. All the clergy occupied a place in the hierarchy, with parish priests at the bottom and the pope at the top. The Church had its own laws and the power of taxation. Monasticism attracted many people. Both secular and regular clergy played important roles in education and in political, economic, and social life. However, the Church was troubled by lay investiture, the worldly lives of the clergy, simony, and heresy. Attempts at reform included the founding of the Franciscan and Dominican orders and the establishment of the Inquisition.

Kings gradually extended their authority. The Capetians in France added territory, developed a strong central government, and increased tax reve-

nues. In England the Exchequer was set up, royal courts were strengthened, and the jury system was developed. The ruler himself was made subject to the law when King John was forced to accept Magna Carta. The 1200's also witnessed the development of Parliament and the common law.

Germany and northern Italy were ruled by the Holy Roman Emperors, who struggled for power with the papacy. Popes such as Gregory VII and Innocent III made sweeping claims to power. Strong emperors, including Henry IV, Frederick Barbarossa, and Frederick II tried but failed to make the Holy Roman Empire a meaningful political force.

QUESTIONS FOR DISCUSSION

1. Do you feel that men during the Middle Ages had much more security, living a relatively communal life, than do men in today's individualistic society?

2. Why was it significant that the English king, in accepting Magna Carta, agreed not to be above the law?

3. It has been said that the Holy Roman Empire was neither holy, nor Roman, nor an empire. Would you agree?

4. Why do you think the Church has failed to abolish war, in both medieval and modern times?

PROJECTS

1. In a short essay describe a typical day on a manor.

2. List the powers and functions of the medieval Church that now belong to the civil government.

3. Draw pictures to illustrate the differences in the daily activities of medieval clergy, nobles, and serfs.

(Pepin the Short III) king
Pepin II hereditary Mayor of Palace   Very important STUDY

215

Trade Revived and European Nations Slowly Emerged

TEST THURSDAY

Medieval merchants loading a ship

If you had lived during the Middle Ages, you would probably have grown old without being aware of any changes in the world around you. Few people journeyed very far. There were no newspapers; news traveled by word of mouth, carried from place to place by wandering peddlers, monks, and musicians. Books were few, and most people could not read, anyway. The average person, and indeed many a noble and clergyman, knew almost nothing about the world beyond his own small village.

During the Middle Ages there was no universal state like the Roman Empire to give a sense of political unity to the people of Europe. But there was unity of a different kind under the Church, which influenced almost every aspect of men's lives. The Catholic Church was the only church of Western Europe. (The term *catholic* comes from the Latin word *catholicus,* meaning "universal.") The Church taught all men the same traditional beliefs and the same basic truths.

The period of the Middle Ages in Europe has been described as the Age of Faith. With few exceptions, the salvation of a man's soul was more important to him than earthly concerns. Most literature, learning, and art of the period existed for the glory of God and His Church.

In spite of the isolation of medieval Europeans and the unity provided by the Church, Europe in the Middle Ages was not a land of static sameness. There were great contrasts—on the one hand, faith and chivalry; on the other hand, drudgery, violence, and superstition. A majestic cathedral might be surrounded by dark, filthy streets where no one dared walk after nightfall. Beneath the castle on the hill huddled the miserable huts of the serfs.

Changes were occurring, too. After centuries during which European life was based almost entirely on farming, cities and trade began to grow. People wanted more and better goods. Merchants began to look outward, away from Europe, seeking new products and new ways of making money.

Another influence was also at work. For years the Christian world had maintained an armed truce with the Moslems, who followed the religion of Islam. In the later Middle Ages the two groups came into conflict. Christian armies went to foreign lands to conquer the Moslems by force of arms. They returned, little realizing that they themselves had been conquered—by new and remarkable ideas.

THE CHAPTER SECTIONS:

1. The Crusades had important effects on the people of Europe (1095–1291)
2. After a period of stagnation, trade began to increase (1000–1300)
3. The growth of towns brought great social and political change (1000–1300)
4. The culture of the Middle Ages flourished in the cities (1000–1350)
5. A spirit of nationalism spread throughout Western Europe (1300–1500)
6. Problems beset the Church, and its temporal power declined (1300–1418)

1 The Crusades had important effects on the people of Europe

The Arabs, as you will read in Chapter 12, conquered Palestine, the Holy Land of Jesus' birth, in the 600's. Although the Arabs were Moslems, they were usually tolerant of other religions. If Christians or Jews paid their taxes and observed other regulations, they could live in Palestine and practice their religion. For centuries, Christian pilgrims visiting Palestine met with little interference. European traders generally were able to do business there.

During the 1000's, however, the Arabs lost Moslem leadership to the Seljuk Turks, a warlike people, originally from central Asia, who had adopted the Moslem faith. They won control of Palestine. They also attacked Asia Minor, which was part of the Byzantine Empire (the successor to the Roman Empire in the east). When they threatened the city of Constantinople, the Byzantine emperor appealed to the popes at Rome several times. He asked for mercenary soldiers to help defend his city and regain the territories he had lost to the Turks.

In Palestine, the Turks proved much less tolerant than the Arabs had been. Reports of persecutions of Christian pilgrims began to come back to Europe. The Byzantine emperor's appeal for help now found a warm reception.

The pope's call for a crusade

Pope Urban II was eager to promote the idea of a Christian offensive to regain the Holy Land from the Moslems. In 1095 he called a great meeting of churchmen and French nobles at Clermont, France. He urged the powerful feudal nobles to stop warring among themselves and join in one great war against the unbelievers.

Urban's plea fired his listeners with enthusiasm, and they joined in one mighty cry, "God wills it!" From Clermont, men traveled through France preaching the cause. Those who joined the expeditions sewed a cross of cloth on their garments. They were called crusaders, from the Latin word *cruciata,* meaning "marked with a cross."

Men joined the Crusades for many different reasons. The pope promised both heavenly and earthly rewards. All the sins of a crusader were forgiven. His property and family were guaranteed protection by the Church during his absence. A debtor who took the cross had his debts canceled; a criminal was relieved of punishment.

Knights were dazzled by the lure of lands and plunder in the rich Near East. Merchants saw a chance for commercial gain. The Crusades were partly religious expeditions, but they also appealed to men's love of adventure, hope of gain, and desire to escape debts, punishment, or boredom.

The First Crusade

The First Crusade, which lasted from 1096 to 1099, was led by French and Norman nobles. In three organized armies, they moved across Europe to Constantinople (see map, this page).

It is not surprising that the crusaders were coolly received at Constantinople. The Byzantine emperor had asked for some mercenary fighters, but now he saw three armies approaching the city. He was afraid that they might capture and plunder Constantinople. After much discussion, the Byzantines ferried the crusaders across the narrow strait of the Bosporus to begin their long hot march across Asia Minor toward Palestine.

With their garments of wool and leather and their heavy armor, the crusaders suffered severely from the heat. Because of a shortage of pack animals, supplies of food and water were inadequate. The leaders quarreled over fiefs in the lands they took. If the Turks had not also been quarreling and disunited, the expedition would have failed. The crusaders captured the city of Antioch and marched on toward Jerusalem.

Conditions improved as the crusaders marched down the seacoast toward Palestine. Fleets of ships from the Italian cities of Genoa and Pisa brought them reinforcements and supplies. The crusaders captured Jerusalem after a short siege and slaughtered the Moslem inhabitants in a terrible massacre. One leader wrote to the pope that his horse's legs had been bloodstained to the knees from riding among the bodies of the dead.

The crusaders set up four small states: the County of Edessa, the Principality of Antioch, the County of Tripoli, and the Kingdom of Jerusalem

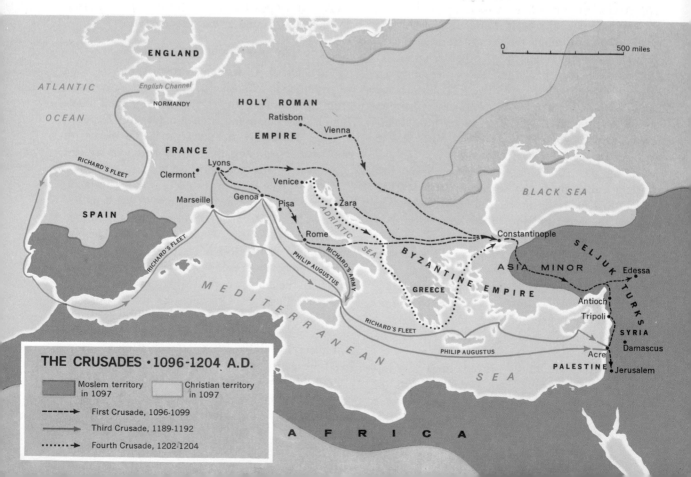

THE CRUSADES · 1096-1204 A.D.

Moslem territory in 1097
Christian territory in 1097

- - - → First Crusade, 1096-1099
——→ Third Crusade, 1189-1192
······→ Fourth Crusade, 1202-1204

(see map, this page). European feudalism was introduced; the land was subdivided into fiefs, with vassals and lords. For almost a century the Europeans held these lands. There was brisk trade with Europe, carried on mostly in Italian ships. Christians and Moslems lived in close relations and grew to respect each other. Many Christians adopted eastern customs and came to prefer eastern food and clothing.

The Second Crusade

The Second Crusade began in 1147, after the Turks recaptured the important city of Edessa and threatened the Kingdom of Jerusalem. In this crusade, Louis VII of France and the Holy Roman Emperor Conrad III led armies to the Holy Land.

The Second Crusade was a failure. The armies of the two monarchs met many misfortunes on the march to the Holy Land. They fought separately instead of joining forces until they reached Damascus, which was held by the Turks. Then even the large combined forces of Louis and Conrad failed to capture the city. After only two years, the defeated armies returned home.

The Third Crusade

In 1187 the news reached Europe that Jerusalem had been recaptured by the Moslem leader Saladin. Europe's response was the Third Crusade, from 1189 to 1192, called the "Crusade of the Three Kings." King Richard the Lion-Hearted of England, King Philip Augustus of France, and Emperor Frederick Barbarossa of the Holy Roman Empire each started out at the head of a great army to regain the Holy Land.

Again there was failure. Frederick Barbarossa drowned on the way to the Holy Land, and most of his army turned back. Philip and Richard quarreled, and Philip took his army home to seize English lands in France. Several times, Richard might have gained the whole Kingdom of Jerusalem by diplomacy, but he preferred knightly adventure. In the end he made no gains worth mentioning.

The Third Crusade is famous in romantic literature, but the actual events were less romantic

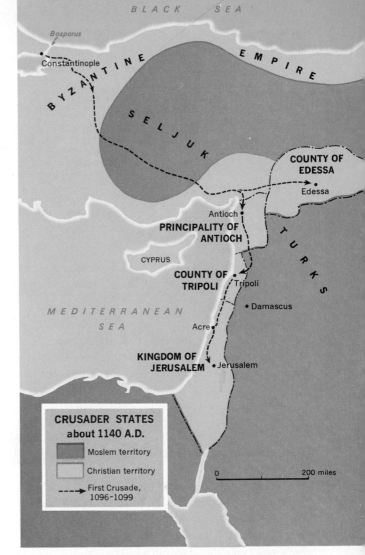

CRUSADER STATES
about 1140 A.D.
- Moslem territory
- Christian territory
----> First Crusade, 1096-1099

0   200 miles

than the stories. The dashing Richard was captured while on his way home and held for ransom. One writer has said dryly that "he was not worth the ransom." It is estimated that, in this crusade which accomplished so little, 300,000 Christians and Moslems lost their lives.

Later crusades

Pope Innocent III persuaded a group of French knights to make the Fourth Crusade in 1202. Venice agreed to furnish transportation, but at a fee too high for the crusaders to pay. Venice then offered to lower the cost of transporting the crusaders if they would capture Zara, a city on

219

though historians differ on the correct numbering of them. Crusading was, in fact, a continuous process that lasted from 1096 to 1291, when the last Christian stronghold, Acre in Syria, was captured by the Moslems. For two centuries scarcely a year went by in which new groups did not go to the Holy Land; there was a constant flow of men from west to east and back again. The religious zeal of the crusaders, however, steadily dwindled and none of the later crusades was on a scale that compared in scope with the Third Crusade.

Not all of the crusades were directed against the Moslems in the Near East. Some crusaders, such as the Teutonic Knights, fought other non-Christians in northern and eastern Europe.

Results of the Crusades

From a military standpoint, all the Crusades except the first were failures. Jerusalem and the rest of Palestine were taken from the Turks by the Christians in the First Crusade and held for nearly a century, but the Moslems eventually recaptured them.

However, Europeans learned about many things of military importance, including the crossbow and use of carrier pigeons to transmit messages. From the Byzantines they learned such new siege tactics as the mining of walls and use of catapults to hurl stones. In addition, they may have learned about gunpowder from the Moslems (who probably acquired knowledge of this explosive from the Chinese).

Politically the Crusades increased the power of kings and decreased the power of feudal lords. Some nobles died in the Crusades. Others, as you will read later, sold political privileges to towns in order to raise money for their crusading ventures. The political role of the Church was strengthened in Europe.

There were other important results of the Crusades. The status of women improved; with their husbands absent on the Crusades, many wives took over the management of feudal estates. Europe was stimulated intellectually by the exchange of ideas, both among the crusaders and between the crusaders and the other peoples they encoun-

the Adriatic coast. Zara was a Christian city, but it was also a commercial rival of Venice. The crusaders took Zara, and Pope Innocent excommunicated the entire army of crusaders for attacking a Christian city.

Soon after the capture of Zara, Venetian leaders and crusaders planned an attack on Constantinople. It, too, was a Christian city, but its capture offered loot to the crusaders and commercial advantages to Venice.

In 1204, without striking a blow at the Moslems, the crusaders took Constantinople and set up a feudal kingdom there, with feudal states scattered through Greece. After some fifty years of Western rule, the Byzantines regained Constantinople and a part of their lands, but the great city and the Byzantine Empire were both permanently weakened by this incident.

A tragic episode in the story of the Crusades came in 1212, when a group of young children undertook a march to the Holy Land, believing that in their innocence they could triumph where their elders had failed. This Children's Crusade had untrained leaders and no equipment. Some children were turned back by the pope. Others reached Marseille, only to be tricked into boarding ships which carried them off to be sold to Moslem traders as slaves.

There were additional crusades after 1212, al-

The Crusades

Crusader knights, such as those at right, dressed in chain mail and helmets and carrying spears, swords, and shields, embarked on crusades with fanciful illusions about themselves. They would visit Jerusalem, sweep away the infidels, and free the Holy Land, that region which the pope called "a second Paradise of delights."

Ready to meet the Christian challenge were Arabs much like those at right, below. Their swift horses were capable of greater speed than those of the crusaders. Since the Arabs wore only light armor, they could descend quickly on their enemies, attack them, and gallop away before the crusaders could launch a counterassault.

Many knights soon wearied of fighting the skillful Arabs, but could not face the long and perilous journey home. Some settled in the Holy Land, where they built mighty castles. The Krak des Chevaliers (Knights' Castle), below, is located in Syria and guarded the northern approaches to Palestine. The castle was built in the early 1100's and was held by Europeans, amidst continuous battle and bloodshed, for 150 years. It was never captured, but had to be abandoned in 1271.

tered. Commercial changes also occurred. Italian cities benefited from their role in transporting crusading armies. Europeans learned about products from the Near East—rice, sugar, lemons, apricots, and melons, among other things—which stimulated trade in such goods. Cotton was also introduced into Europe in the form of muslin (cloth of Mosul, a city in Persia) and damask (cloth of Damascus).

2 After a period of stagnation, trade began to increase

Trade nearly died out in Western Europe after the 400's. Manors became almost entirely self-sufficient, growing or making nearly everything they used. There was some exchange of goods, but trade was not important. Towns and cities, which depended on trade and manufacturing, decreased in population and size. Some towns disappeared completely during this period of commercial stagnation.

Commerce was hindered by many obstacles. There was a shortage of money. Roads were poor and bridges were few. Robbers on land and pirates at sea made travel dangerous. Tolls were a great hindrance; each feudal lord charged tolls for the use of roads, bridges, and fords in his territory.

Church laws also made trade difficult. The Church insisted on a "just price." This price covered only the cost of labor and materials, with no profit. The Church prohibited the purchase of articles for resale at a higher price. It also prohibited usury, which at that time meant the charging of interest for the loan of money.

Trade routes

Trade first began to revive in Italy. Neither trade nor towns had declined as much there as elsewhere. Also, the Italian Peninsula was in a favorable geographic location. It lay between northern Europe, where people were becoming interested in goods from the Far East, and the Near East, where such goods could be bought.

Goods from the Far East were brought westward by Chinese and Moslem traders along three main routes: (1) overland to ports on the Black Sea and then by ship to Constantinople; (2) by water through the Indian Ocean and the Red Sea and then by land to ports in Egypt; and (3) by water through the Indian Ocean and the Persian Gulf and then by land to ports on the eastern Mediterranean (see map, pages 224–25). The Italians became the great European middlemen in this trade—middlemen between traders from Asia, on the one hand, and traders from central and northern Europe, on the other.

During the late 900's and early 1000's, Italian traders began to make contacts with the Near East. By a combination of force and negotiation, the Italian city-states of Venice, Genoa, and Pisa won trading rights in Constantinople, Syria and Palestine, and North Africa. (Trade did not flow freely in every nation or region; trading rights were a privilege to be bought or won.)

By the time of the Crusades, Italian city-states were eager to carry crusaders to the Holy Land and bring back rich cargoes of eastern goods. From Italian seaports, these goods were carried by pack train through northern Italy and across the Alps into central and northern Europe. This overland trade route stimulated the fortunes and growth of cities in Lombardy, southern France, and Germany.

The revival of trade also stimulated northern Europe. Before the year 1000, Viking traders from Kiev, in what is now Russia, traveled regularly to the Black Sea and on to Constantinople to collect wares from the East. They brought these goods northward and then traded them in the cities of northern Europe.

Old Viking routes also linked the Baltic Sea and the North Sea with England, the Atlantic coast of Europe, and the Mediterranean Sea. By the 1100's, German merchants carried on a busy trade along the Baltic and Atlantic coasts. Beginning in the 1200's, Italian merchants, too, engaged in trade in the Atlantic. Ships from Genoa and Venice made regular voyages through the Strait of Gibraltar and northward to England and Flanders.

The region of Flanders, which is now part of Belgium and northern France, gained importance. It was the meeting point of trade routes that led across France, down the Rhine River from Germany, across the English Channel from England, and down from the coasts of the Baltic Sea. Moreover, the chief product of Flanders, fine woolen cloth, was eagerly sought by people throughout Europe. During the 1200's, Flanders became the textile headquarters of Europe. Such Flemish cities as Ghent and Bruges became thriving centers of population and wealth.

The Hanseatic League. Hamburg, Lübeck, and Bremen were the most important commercial cities on the coasts of the North and Baltic seas. Because there was no strong central government in Germany, the trading cities formed a league called the Hanse for protection (see inset map, page 225). The Hanseatic League, as it is usually called, had over seventy member cities, and became a powerful influence upon the commerce of northwestern Europe during the 1300's and 1400's. It was not a political organization, but existed only to promote and protect trade.

The Hanseatic cities had permanent trading posts in Flanders, Scandinavia, England, and Russia. If a member failed to abide by League agreements, he lost his trading privileges. If the privileges of Hanseatic traders were taken away by a nation, the League stopped all shipments of goods to that country. Sometimes League members even carried on a small-scale war in order to regain trading rights.

Articles of trade

By far the most profitable trade for medieval merchants involved luxury products and goods from the East. These were articles of high value in small bulk, and the profits were enormous. There was a great demand, stimulated by the Crusades, for Oriental spices, drugs, perfumes, dyes, and precious gems. Manufactured goods included silks, cotton and linen cloth, and art products in gold, silver, and ivory. The Near East supplied textiles, rugs, grain, and fruit.

Europe offered various products in exchange for Oriental goods. The Baltic region supplied fur, timber, fish, and grain. From Spain came wine, oil, leather, and inlaid arms and armor. Other European products included Venetian metal goods and glassware, fine English and Flemish woolen cloth, and French wine.

Markets and fairs

As trade grew, merchants needed places where they could exchange goods. Many villages had weekly market days, but such markets did not attract large crowds. Enterprising merchants began to sell goods during religious festivals. Then some feudal lords established fairs for the sale of imported goods. They realized that they could make themselves wealthy by charging fees on the merchandise sold. They guaranteed special protection to merchants for the holding of a fair. Fairs were held for several days or weeks yearly.

The most important and best-known fairs were those of Champagne, a region in northeastern France (see inset map, page 224). Champagne was ideally situated for trade. It lay directly along the route used by traders traveling between Italy and northern Europe. In Champagne the textiles, wool, and wines of Europe were exchanged for Oriental luxury goods brought overland from the south. Six fairs, each lasting four to seven weeks, were held at four towns in Champagne. The fairs were scheduled to come in sequence, and provided a central marketplace for all of Europe during most of the year.

A simple barter economy, in which goods are exchanged for goods, could not meet the needs of fairs as large and elaborate as those of Champagne. Even though little money might actually change hands at a fair, the value of goods had to

(*continued on page 226*)

CHIEF TRADE ROUTES OF THE LATER MIDDLE AGES

Routes of Italian traders
Routes of German and Flemish traders
Routes of Chinese and Moslem traders
Old Viking trade route

ATLANTIC OCEAN

NORWAY

SWEDEN

Stockholm

Novgorod

NORTH SEA

RUSSIAN

BALTIC SEA

LITHUANIA

STATES

ENGLAND

Danzig

London

Hamburg

HOLY

POLAND

Bruges

ROMAN

Kiev

Ghent

Rhine R.

Nuremberg

Dnieper River

Paris

EMPIRE

EUROPE

FRANCE

HUNGARY

Lyons

ALPS

Venice

Danube River

Azov

Genoa

Pisa

CASPIAN SEA

Marseille

ITALY

Rome

BLACK SEA

A

SPAIN

Constantinople

Trebizond

Lisbon

PORTUGAL

Toledo

BYZANTINE

ASIA

Cordova

EMPIRE

MINOR

Mosul

Strait of Gibraltar

Seville

Tunis

Antioch

SI

MEDITERRANEAN SEA

SYRIA

Baghdad

Tangier

Tyre

Damascus

PERSIA

ATLAS MTS.

PALESTINE

Tripoli

Alexandria

Cairo

AFRICA

EGYPT

Nile River

ARABIA

RED SEA

PERSIAN GULF

Jidda

Mecca

NORTH SEA

ENGLAND

Hamburg

Danzig

Stourbridge

Magdeburg

London

HOLY

Antwerp

Leipzig

Cologne

ROMAN

Ypres

Bruges

Aachen

Frankfort

Paris

EMPIRE

Nuremberg

Lagny ∧ ∧ Provins

Troyes ∧ ∧ Bar

Augsburg

FRANCE

ATLANTIC OCEAN

Venice

Genoa

Florence

Marseille

Pisa

ITALY

PORTUGAL

Medina del Campo

SPAIN

Seville

PRINCIPAL MARKET TOWNS AND FAIRS

∧ Fairs of Champagne

INDI

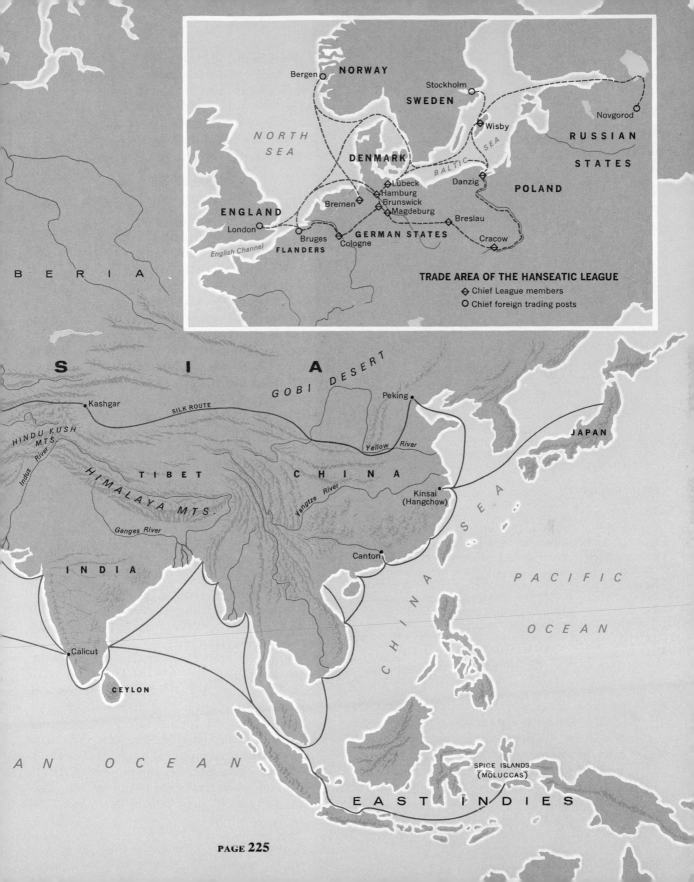

TRADE AREA OF THE HANSEATIC LEAGUE
◆ Chief League members
○ Chief foreign trading posts

Moorish Dancer

Enthusiasm for the exotic was common in Western Europe during the late Middle Ages. The Crusades, the revival of trade, and markets and fairs made Europeans keenly interested in foreign peoples and customs. Moorish dancers from Spain, such as the one pictured above, traveled throughout Europe, captivating audiences when they performed during the intermissions of comedies and dramas. A German sculptor carved this little figure so skillfully that we can almost hear the dancer's jingling bells and see him move.

Fairs helped to break down the separateness of each region and the narrow outlook of the people. Travelers came from great distances to attend large fairs, which offered more than just buying and selling. They were festive occasions. Jugglers, clowns, and musicians entertained crowds, as at county fairs today.

Capitalism and banking

Two important aspects of the revival of European trade were capitalism and banking.

Capital is wealth earned, saved, and invested in order to produce profits. *Capitalism* is the economic system in which private individuals use wealth in this way. Capitalism did not suddenly appear during the Middle Ages. It dates back to man's earliest business activities, and certainly existed during Greek and Roman times. But it became more important in the later Middle Ages than it had been before.

With increased trade, a good investment was shipbuilding and financing voyages. Men with capital formed shipping companies. Each contributed part of the cost and received a share of the profits.

Another capitalist activity was manufacturing. A new method of production, used in many industries but seen best in the woolen industry, was the domestic system. (The system was so named because work was done in laborers' homes rather than in a shop or factory.) The capitalist bought wool and distributed it to different workers. For an agreed price, each of them did a particular job, such as spinning, weaving, or dyeing. The capitalist then collected the finished cloth and sold it for the highest price he could get, certainly for more than his expenses.

Town real estate was another capitalistic investment during the late Middle Ages. The cramped size of medieval cities meant that city land always brought a good price.

Banking was still another capitalist activity that developed in the later Middle Ages. You have read how moneychangers at medieval fairs evaluated and exchanged the various currencies. In time, moneychangers began to provide other services, and thus by steps banking developed. (The

be fixed in terms of a definite medium of exchange. Since there were many different systems of coinage, a special class of moneychangers became important at the fairs. They estimated the value of the currency of one region in terms of the currency of another, thus helping the exchange of goods.

word *bank* comes from the Italian word *banca*, meaning the moneychanger's table.)

The most important service performed by early bankers was lending money. Rulers, nobles, and merchants often needed to borrow funds to finance their activities. During the early Middle Ages, Jews had done most of the moneylending because the Christian Church forbade charging interest on loans. By the 1200's, however, Christians had become involved in this business. Merchants in the Lombard cities of northern Italy were leaders in banking, and employed regular agents in all important cities. Officially they did not charge in-

terest, but paid themselves by rents and charges for services and damages.

CHECKUP

1. Why did trade decline during the early Middle Ages?

2. What were some of the articles of trade imported into Europe? exported from Europe?

3. What is capitalism? In what capitalist activities did medieval businessmen engage?

4. IDENTIFY: just price, usury, Hanseatic League.

5. LOCATE: Baltic Sea, North Sea, English Channel, Ghent, Bruges.

3 The growth of towns brought great social and political change

The revival of trade in the Middle Ages was accompanied by the growth of towns and cities. In fact, trade and cities always grow together. The two kinds of growth are related to each other, and there is an interaction between them.

Trade is essentially an exchange of goods. The goods must, of course, be produced by someone. To carry on trade, the producer must have a surplus—more than the amount he needs for himself. He exchanges this surplus for the surplus merchandise of some other producer so that each receives something he wants. In a town or city, we find all the conditions needed for exchanging surpluses of goods.

Towns did not disappear completely during the period from 400 to 1000, although they dwindled in population and size. Many Roman towns survived, especially those that were easy to defend. During those years some new towns even grew up around castles, shrines, cathedrals, or mines.

Beginning in the late 900's, however, old towns began to grow larger and new ones came into being. These new towns grew up at locations important for trade—natural harbors, river mouths, and transfer points where goods were shifted from ocean-going ships to river barges.

The liberties of townsmen

As towns increased and their populations grew, it became clear that the town dweller did not fit into the feudal system. The townsman was neither lord nor vassal nor serf. Manufacturing and trade, at which he made his living, played little part in the village agricultural economy.

Townsmen wanted to control their own governments. Under feudalism, however, each town was subject to some lord. Naturally, the lords were unwilling to give up their control without receiving something in return. Sometimes townsmen won rights of self-government by peaceful means; in some cases, however, they resorted to violence and even war.

Some lords granted political liberties to towns in order to encourage their development, for a lord could get a rich income from a town on his lands. Sometimes towns bought charters of liberties (written statements of their rights) from their lords.

Town and city charters differed widely from place to place. In time, though, every townsman in Europe was assured of at least four principal liberties:

(1) *Freedom.* No matter what his birth or origin, a man who lived in a town unchallenged for a year and a day was a free man. All ties to a manor or manor lord were broken. The Germans said: *"Stadtluft macht frei"*—"City air makes [a person] free." A serf who escaped to a town could thus become a free townsman.

(2) *Exempt status.* A townsman was exempt

church insists on just price— can't get a profit on lending money.

227

from all manorial services and obligations. Services owed to the lord were owed by the entire community, not by an individual. The services were always carefully defined and written down.

(3) *Town justice.* Towns had their own courts, made up of prominent citizens familiar with local customs. Townsmen and their cases were tried in town courts, not in feudal courts.

(4) *Commercial privileges.* Townsmen had the right to sell freely in the town market and to charge tolls to all outsiders trading there. Some towns, especially the Lombard cities in northern Italy, gained the right of complete self-government. Their officials were elected by the leading citizens.

Guilds

As trade increased and towns grew larger and wealthier, medieval merchants began to unite in associations. The dangers of travel were great, and it was safer to travel in groups with armed escorts. Arranging such convoys took much planning and money. Gradually, merchants founded associations called guilds.

Merchant guilds became powerful and exclusive. In each town a merchant guild gained a monopoly, or the sole right to trade there. Merchants from other towns or foreign nations could not trade in that town unless they paid a fee. The guilds also fixed standards of quality for manufactured goods. In addition, guilds acted as welfare and charitable organizations. They made loans to members and looked after those who were in any kind of trouble. They supported the widows and children of former members.

In time the skilled workers who were engaged in manufacturing also formed guilds. Each of these guilds included all the men engaged in one particular craft, such as shoemaking or weaving; thus they were called craft guilds. A craft guild regulated wages and fixed hours and conditions of labor in the industry. It also fixed the prices and conditions for selling the goods. It disciplined workers and looked after those who were ill or disabled.

Craft guilds supervised the training of skilled workers through the apprentice system. To become a master workman—that is, a fully accepted member of the guild—a candidate went through two preliminary stages of training.

In the first stage, he served as an apprentice. When he was still a boy, his parents apprenticed him—bound him by legal agreement—to a master workman to learn a trade. He lived at the home of the master. The master furnished food, clothing, training, and moral guidance. The apprentice promised to obey his master, to keep the secrets of workmanship, and to behave himself properly. The period of apprenticeship varied from three to twelve years.

When he completed his apprenticeship, a young man went on to the second stage, that of journeyman. A journeyman was a skilled worker who worked for a master for daily wages. After working for wages for some time, he could become a master by submitting proof of his skill—a "masterpiece," or piece of work judged worthy of a master craftsman. If this were approved by the guild masters, he could open a shop of his own.

Toward the end of the Middle Ages, the line between masters and journeymen became much more distinct and much harder to cross. The journeyman usually remained a wage earner all his life. Increased prosperity turned masters into a sort of industrial aristocracy. Often the master's son inherited the business and position without the required apprenticeship.

The rise of the middle class

You can see that medieval society was changing. Between nobles at the top and peasants at the bottom, there was now a new class of merchants, master craftsmen, and skilled workers. The members of this middle class were called burgesses in England, *bourgeois* (BOOR·zhwah) in France, and *Bürger* in Germany.

The rise of the middle class was one of the most important developments in European society during the later Middle Ages. Members of the middle class wanted stable and uniform governments to protect trade and property, so they usually favored kings against nobles. To gain the support of the middle class, kings began to consult its members and to employ them in government positions.

Along with the rise of the middle class went a decline of serfdom. The growing towns offered the serf a chance to improve his hard life. He might escape to the city and become a free man. Even if he did not, the city changed his way of living. Because the city needed food, the serf could sell his produce for money. Thus he could pay for the use of his land in money rather than in work.

The disappearance of serfdom was also hastened by changes in agricultural methods and production. In England, for example, landowners fenced off much of the farm land for use as sheep pastures; this trend left many serfs without work. Another reason for the decline of serfdom was a devastating epidemic that began in 1348. In that year the bubonic plague, which Europeans called the Black Death, swept out of Asia into Europe. In England alone, a third of all the people died. Farm labor became scarce and, as a result, could command high wages.

Life in medieval towns

Medieval towns were small by modern standards. According to some estimates, Paris in the 1300's had a population of about 60,000. Ghent and Bruges with about 50,000 inhabitants each were considered huge. London with about 35,000 was far above average. The usual city had from 5,000 to 10,000 people.

Physically, the medieval city was compact. It was often built on top of a hill or at the bend of a river so that it could easily be defended. Because city land was scarce and valuable, houses were built five or six stories high. To gain interior space, each story projected out a little farther than the one below. Thus, at the top the houses almost met in the middle of the street. Each city had some outstandingly fine buildings such as a cathedral, a town hall, and the guild halls.

A medieval city would have outraged both the eyes and noses of people today. The streets were dark and filthy. The only way of disposing of sewage was in open gutters which ran only when it rained. Epidemics were frequent. There was no street lighting. Honest people who went out at night were accompanied by servants who protected them from robbers, for there were no police.

Suspicious and irreverent townsmen distrusted the nobles and criticized the clergy. The feelings were obviously mutual, for a clergyman of the time described towns sourly as *"Tumor plebis, timor regis"*—Latin, meaning "a cancer of the people, a threat to kings." Despite this ill-feeling and the uncomfortable conditions of the city, medieval town life was not completely disagreeable. The medieval city was a throbbing, busy place, alive with people—townsmen and visitors, merchants and strolling actors, musicians, and jugglers.

CHECKUP

1. Why are cities essential to trade?
2. How did townsmen gain rights of self-government? What were their most important liberties?
3. What were the differences between merchant guilds and craft guilds?
4. Explain why the middle class was so called.
5. IDENTIFY: charters of liberties, monopoly, apprentice, journeyman, bourgeois, Black Death.

4 The culture of the Middle Ages flourished in the cities

You will recall that civilization itself grew up only after early men settled in cities. In a similar way, the culture of the Middle Ages did not flourish until city life had revived.

Language and literature

Latin was the written language of Western Europe for centuries after the Roman Empire ceased to exist. In a form called Medieval Latin, it was spoken by most educated people. During the Middle Ages, however, the common people began to speak vernacular languages—"everyday" speech that varied in different localities. These languages included English, Italian, French, German, and Spanish.

In time, writers also began to use vernacular languages. The first vernacular literature con-

(continued on page 232)

Medieval Art and Learning

The cultural life of the Middle Ages centered in cities much like the one below, protected from attack by a river and by sturdy fortifications. It was in cities that people built the great churches which were the glory of medieval times. The simple Romanesque structure at left, begun in the 800's, has gently rounded arches and small windows. In striking contrast is the soaring cathedral of Reims, far right, built in the 1200's.

230

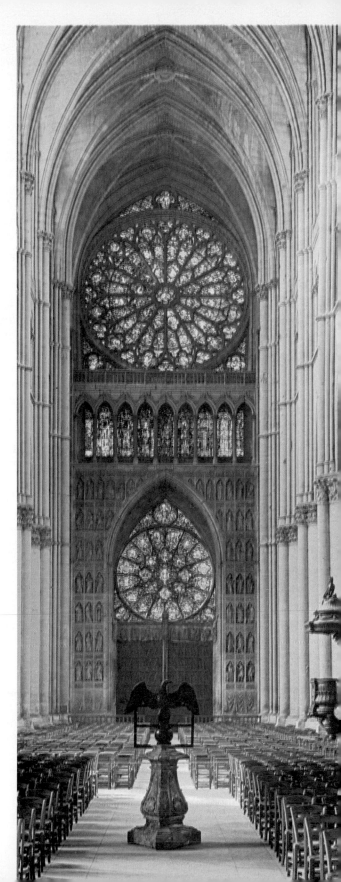

Its jewel-like stained glass and intricate carvings typify the Gothic style. Much medieval learning was based on Latin translations of Aristotle's work. In the stone carving above left, from the cathedral of Chartres, he looks like a monkish scribe. Vernacular languages, however, became more and more widespread. Dante, the father of modern Italian, is shown above.

sisted of troubadour songs. Troubadours were minstrels, or traveling singers, who wrote lyrical poems of love and chivalry and sang them in the castles and courts of feudal lords.

Another form of vernacular literature was the national epic. In England there were stories about King Arthur and his knights of the Round Table, which became popular all over Europe. France had its *Song of Roland*. Roland was a brave knight who lost his life in Spain while guarding the retreat of Charlemagne's army northward after an unsuccessful campaign against the Moslems. Germans had the *Nibelungenlied,* a legend of how the hero Siegfried gained a magic treasure guarded by a dragon.

The rise of the middle class brought a new kind of literature which the French called *fabliaux* (FAB·lee·oh). The *fabliaux* were short comic stories in rhymed verse. They made fun of chivalry and ridiculed the foolishness of all human beings. They were especially critical of greedy, proud, lazy, and immoral clergy. Similar to the *fabliaux* were animal stories. Those about Reynard the Fox were especially popular.

Another form of vernacular literature that developed during the Middle Ages was the mystery play, or miracle play. Originally these plays were short religious dramas on Biblical subjects. They were written in Latin and were added to the church services at Easter and Christmas. Later, as towns grew, miracle plays were written in vernacular languages, lengthened, and presented in town marketplaces to large audiences. One very popular miracle play was *Noye's Fludde* (*Noah's Flood*). It told how Noah built his ark, collected pairs of all creatures, and kept them and his family safe during the flood.

Dante and Chaucer. Two great writers, Dante and Chaucer, represented the flowering of medieval vernacular literature. Dante Alighieri (DAHN-tay ah·lee·GYAI·ree) was born in Florence, Italy, in 1265. He used Latin for his scholarly works. When writing poetry, however, he preferred the Italian dialect of his native Tuscany. Because Dante used the Tuscan dialect in his most famous works, which were widely read throughout Italy, it became the written language of all Italy. Thus

Dante is considered the father of modern Italian.

Dante's greatest work is *The Divine Comedy*. It tells of a pilgrimage in which Dante is guided by the Roman poet Vergil. Together, the two men pass through hell, purgatory, and heaven. They meet the souls of famous people, good and evil. A work of this sort gave Dante the opportunity to criticize the society of his own time, and he used it fully. *The Divine Comedy* is like a mirror that reflects the period in which Dante lived.

Geoffrey Chaucer was born in England in 1340. His *Canterbury Tales* is a series of stories told by a group of pilgrims on their way to Canterbury. Chaucer poked good-natured fun at his fellow Englishmen and, like many other writers of the time, satirized the clergy. Chaucer used the Midland dialect of English. Because of the popularity of his writings, this dialect became the forerunner of modern English.

Universities

During the early Middle Ages, only nobles and clergy were educated. Gradually, however, schools grew up in which anyone could study. These new schools were located in the thriving towns. They had simple beginnings. Any man who thought he had something to teach could set himself up in a town where he might attract students. Anyone who wanted to study with him could do so by paying a fee. This educational system was very much like that of Athens when Plato and Aristotle taught there.

As the number of teachers and students increased, they united to form guilds for protection and privileges. Such a guild was called a *universitas,* a Latin word which meant any association of people. Gradually the word *university* came to mean an association of people for the purpose of teaching and learning.

Four great universities developed between 1000 and 1200. Those at Paris and Oxford specialized in theology and the liberal arts. (In the Middle Ages, the liberal arts was a definite course of study including Latin grammar, logic, rhetoric, arithmetic, geometry, astronomy, and music.) The University of Bologna, in Italy, taught Roman and canon law. The University at Salerno, also in Italy, specialized in medicine. During the 1200's and 1300's, universities were founded throughout Western Europe.

In time, medieval universities established standard courses of study, with uniform requirements for the various stages of progress. These stages were shown by academic degrees. The degree of Bachelor of Arts showed that a student had finished his apprenticeship.

After further study and examination, the student qualified for the degree of Master of Arts; he was then ready to teach the liberal arts. He was admitted to the guild of teachers at a ceremony called a commencement because it signified the beginning of his work as a teacher. Indeed, the holder of a Master of Arts degree had just begun his studies, too. Before him lay the three great fields of professional study: theology, law, and medicine. At the University of Paris, the degree of Master of Theology could be gained only after ten more years of study.

Philosophy

During the Middle Ages, scholars spent much time trying to reconcile the ideas of Aristotle, whom they revered, and those of the early Church writers. Aristotle emphasized man's reason, while the early Church writers emphasized faith. The attempt of medieval philosophers to reconcile faith and reason is often called scholasticism. The aim of the scholastic philosophers was to discover how man could improve himself in this life by reason and insure salvation in the life to come.

Peter Abelard, who taught at the University of Paris in the 1100's, was an important scholastic philosopher. In his book *Sic et Non* (*Yes and No*), he raised many questions about Church doctrine. After each question he placed opinions gathered from the Bible, papal decrees, and the writings of Church philosophers. Many of these opinions were contradictory. Abelard made his students work out the problems for themselves; he wanted them to think and to inquire. His motto was: "By doubting we come to inquiry, and by inquiring we perceive the truth."

Probably the greatest of all medieval philosophers was Thomas Aquinas, a Dominican monk.

His principal work, written in the late 1200's, is a summary of Christian thought called *Summa Theologica*. In it Aquinas took up each point of Church doctrine, examined it, and tried to show that it could be arrived at by logic or reason. Today the *Summa* is the basis for all teaching of theology in Roman Catholic schools.

Science

There was little scientific progress during the Middle Ages. Medieval thinking was deductive; that is, an idea was taken from an authority, usually the Bible, accepted as true, and used as a basis for reasoning. Classical writings, like those of Galen and Ptolemy, formed the basis of much medieval science.

Many medieval "scientists" practiced a strange craft called alchemy (AL·kuh·mee), which the Europeans learned from the Moslems. One of the basic aims of alchemy was to change other metals into gold. Medieval scientists believed that all metals were ultimately the same and could therefore be changed into one another. They sought the "philosopher's stone," a substance that could perform this change and could also prolong life. The search for the philosopher's stone was widespread during the later Middle Ages. Several kings employed alchemists in the hope of solving their financial problems.

Although alchemy may bring an amused smile today, it did have some positive results. In their search for the philosopher's stone, Moslem alchemists discovered some important drugs and chemicals, and Europeans added to the list. In the 1300's the Church condemned alchemy as a kind of devil's magic, but its practice continued in secret. It was important because it gave rise to the modern science of chemistry.

Art and architecture

During the Middle Ages, architecture, painting, and sculpture were used almost entirely in the service of the Church. Church architecture was the central art of the period, and the other arts were used to embellish, or beautify, it. The building and beautifying of a church was considered a community project during the Middle Ages. In their churches, medieval people expressed both religious feeling and local pride.

During the period from 1000 to 1200, most medieval church builders used the round arches, domes, and low horizontal lines of Roman architecture. This style later came to be called Romanesque (meaning "similar to the Roman"). The enormous weight of the domed stone roof of a Romanesque church made it necessary to have thick walls and only a few small windows. For this reason the interior was dark, but the simple style of the columns and arches lent dignity and serenity. There was little sculpture inside Romanesque churches, but many were adorned with frescoes.

During the mid-1100's, master builders in Western Europe began to develop a new style of church architecture. This style was so different from the Romanesque that critics in the 1500's ridiculed it because it did not conform to the standards of classical architecture. They called it Gothic, after the barbarian Goths. The name stuck, but Gothic has come to be considered one of the most beautiful styles of architecture ever developed. France has many of the finest examples of Gothic architecture, among them the cathedral of Notre Dame in Paris and the cathedrals at Chartres (SHAR·tr') and Reims (REEMZ).

Gothic churches, in contrast to the low, heavy Romanesque churches, were tall and delicate in appearance. Builders used rows of supporting ribs, called flying buttresses, outside the walls, connecting them to the church with arches. Thus part of the outward push of the roof was carried away from the walls and onto the buttresses. The walls could be high and thin, with large windows. Arches became pointed. High-pointed spires replaced low, flat towers. It has been said that everything in Gothic churches pointed up toward heaven.

The inside of the Gothic church was also very different from that of the Romanesque church. Statues of saints and rulers lined the interiors, reliefs adorned the walls, and stained glass windows let in shafts of sunlight in many colors.

In many ways the Gothic church exemplified the changing world of the late Middle Ages. The tall structure rose above the growing town around and under it. Traders with goods from the Near East and the Orient were active in marketplaces in the shadows of its spires. Religious pageants and miracle plays were given within the church and outside its carved doors. All the skills of the medieval world went into the building of these monuments to God in the Age of Faith.

CHECKUP

1. Name some medieval epics. How did the *fabliaux* differ from the epics?

2. How did medieval universities originate? Why do you think the Church might have preferred the writings of Thomas Aquinas to those of Peter Abelard?

3. What were some characteristics of Gothic churches?

4. IDENTIFY: vernacular language, troubadours, miracle play, liberal arts, scholasticism, alchemy, Romanesque.

5 A spirit of nationalism spread throughout Western Europe

During the 1100's, many of the nations of Western Europe—nations that are still in existence today—developed out of the petty fiefs and states of feudal days.

Under feudalism in the early Middle Ages, the power to rule was divided among feudal lords. The king himself was little more than a feudal lord. The people of a country did not look to a central government for defense or help, nor did they feel any loyalty toward the country as a whole. Instead, they were loyal to a local feudal lord, or to a manor village, or to a town.

The development of a nation was usually accompanied by the growth of *nationalism* among its people. Nationalism is a feeling of loyalty or patriotism for the country as a whole. It is the feeling of belonging to a large society rather than to only a small locality. Nationalism, which was almost entirely lacking during the early Middle Ages, began to appear, very slowly, after 1100.

234

England

The authority of the English king, although partially checked by Parliament, was strengthened by various means. These included the development of a single system of law and courts, increased revenue as the country grew more prosperous, the military might of a standing army of professional soldiers, and the support of the rising middle class, which sided with the king against the feudal lords.

The power of feudal lords decreased as that of the English king increased. Manors began to disappear as serfdom declined. By the end of the 1500's, serfdom had disappeared completely in England. The villages and farms of free peasants dotted the English countryside.

The Hundred Years' War. English prosperity and the development of a strong national government received a setback during a long war with France. The Hundred Years' War, which began in 1337, had three basic causes: rivalry over the provinces of Aquitaine and Gascony in France, which were claimed by the English king; the English king's attempt to take the French throne when the male Capetian line died out; and rivalry over the commercially rich territory of Flanders. The war brought two important developments.

(1) Feudalism was weakened by the use of two new weapons, the longbow and the cannon. Important battles took place in France, at Crécy (1346), Poitiers (1356), and Agincourt (1415). There the French feudal cavalry was completely routed by English foot soldiers armed with longbows. The English longbow was 5 or 6 feet long, with a range up to 400 yards. Archers using it could shoot so fast and accurately that mounted opponents could not get near them. Longbows helped put an end to knights on horseback as the dominant element of warfare.

Cannons were used at the siege of Calais, France, in 1346. Europeans may have learned the use of gunpowder from the Moslems during the Crusades. To this knowledge they added the use of the gun. At first the gun was only a crude tube of wood and metal from which the explosion of gunpowder hurled stones or chunks of metal. Cannons were developed from these rather simple weapons.

The powerful blast of a cannon could break through the thick walls of castles. Castles, which had been very important as protection for the feudal lord and his men, were no longer such a strong defense. National armies made up of commoners, armed with longbows and cannons, could defeat powerful lords. These two weapons helped to weaken feudalism and thereby increase the power of national monarchs.

(2) The English Parliament temporarily gained power at the expense of the king. Through its right to grant or withhold taxes, Parliament forced some weak English kings during the course of the war to recognize a number of important principles: (a) Parliament, as well as the king, had to approve any restatement or change of a law; (b) Parliament gained the right to levy all taxes, and any new tax had to be proposed first by the House of Commons rather than by the House of Lords; (c) The king could spend money only for the purpose for which Parliament had appropriated it.

Despite the English victories mentioned above, when the Hundred Years' War ended in 1453, England had lost all its lands in France except Calais (see map, page 236). Actually, these losses were a disguised gain. Now the English king could pay attention to his real job of governing the nation.

The Wars of the Roses. The further establishment of strong centralized government in England was delayed for thirty more years by civil war, the Wars of the Roses. This conflict, which began in 1455, was a struggle for the throne between the York and Lancaster families. It was fought mostly by small bands of nobles and their vassals. The monarchy profited because many of the great nobles of England were killed.

In 1485, Henry Tudor, a member of the House of Lancaster, ended the wars by defeating the Yorkist king. He seized the throne of England and by marrying the daughter of one of the Yorkist claimants gained the support of both families. He became Henry VII, founder of the Tudor dynasty. The English people, tired of war and disorder, were willing to accept the strong government that Henry VII established.

235

France

The history of France during the 1300's and 1400's resembled that of England. Capetian kings had developed a strong monarchy, although the Hundred Years' War with England caused French kings to lose some of their power.

France suffered much more than England during the Hundred Years' War because the war was fought on French soil. Even during the periods of relative peace, the countryside was ravaged by bands of robbers. Rivalry broke out between two branches of the royal family—Burgundy and Orléans—when one king became insane. This rivalry made it difficult for the French to unite in fighting England. Defeat followed defeat.

Joan of Arc. French fortunes in the war were revived by Joan of Arc. An uneducated peasant girl in her teens, Joan heard "voices" telling her to leave her small village and help the French defend the city of Orléans, which the English were besieging. She persuaded the French authorities of her sincerity and made her way to the city. In 1429, inspired to greater efforts by Joan's presence, the weary French troops ended the siege and saved the city. That same year, Joan helped the heir to the French throne take the crown as Charles VII.

Eventually Joan was captured by enemy forces and turned over to English authorities. A Church council tried her for witchcraft and convicted her; she was burned at the stake by the English in 1431. As the sentence was being carried out, an English leader cried, "We are lost! We have burned a saint!" °

Joan's fate created a strong feeling of nationalism among the French. Her example helped to bring about the successful conclusion of the war in 1453. The English were driven out and a national monarchy was re-established.

Louis XI. For a time during the Hundred Years' War, it looked as if the Estates-General of France might become the real ruler of the nation. The Estates-General, a representative assembly resembling the English Parliament, was established by Philip IV. It took its name from the groups that attended the meetings—members of the clergy (First Estate, or class); nobles (Second Estate); and bourgeois from the towns (Third Estate). During the war, when no strong king was on the French throne, the Estates-General exercised control of finances and lawmaking. When the war ended, however, Charles VII was strong enough to rule without the Estates-General, which seldom met thereafter.

The French monarchy was further strengthened by Louis XI, one of the most remarkable men ever to hold the French throne. He became king in 1461 and ruled until 1483.

Louis avoided war except as a last resort. He preferred to use diplomacy, at which he was a master. His opponents called him "The Spider." He used any methods to get what he wanted. His administration was harsh and taxes were heavy,

FRANCE AFTER 1453
- ▦ English possessions in France
- ☐ Burgundian possessions until 1477
- ▬ Boundary between France and the Holy Roman Empire
- ✕ Battle sites (Hundred Years' War)

NORTH SEA

London
ENGLAND
Calais
FLANDERS
ENGLISH CHANNEL
Agincourt ✕
✕ Crécy
NETHERLANDS
HOLY ROMAN EMPIRE
Paris
BRITTANY
MAINE
ANJOU
✕ Orléans
BURGUNDY
SWISS CONFED.
Poitiers ✕
FRANCE
AQUITAINE
GASCONY
PROVENCE
MEDITERRANEAN SEA
SPAIN
0   200 miles

° In 1456 the case of Joan of Arc was retried by another Church court and she was found innocent. Several centuries later, in 1920, she was proclaimed a saint by the Roman Catholic Church.

but he used the money to strengthen the kingdom.

Louis' great problem was the increasing power of the House of Burgundy. Charles the Bold, duke of Burgundy, ruled over a large area along France's eastern borders (see map, opposite), including the prosperous region of the Netherlands.° He was fearless and eager for war. His great ambition was to revive the middle kingdom of Charlemagne's successor Lothair (see page 192) as an independent state.

Louis XI used diplomacy to build an alliance against the duke. Louis frightened the Holy Roman Emperor into opposing the idea of a kingdom of Burgundy and persuaded the independent Swiss that such a kingdom would threaten their freedom.

The Swiss did Louis' fighting for him. They were free commoners armed with pikes—long poles with metal spearheads. These Swiss pikes were so effective against cavalry charges that, like the English longbows, they helped end the military supremacy of feudal knights. Twice in 1476 the Swiss infantry defeated the knightly cavalry of the Burgundians. In another battle in the following year, the duke of Burgundy was killed. Since the duke had no son, Louis XI seized much Burgundian territory.

The French king soon met with more good fortune. Various provinces that had once been part of the royal domain were now held by French nobles. In 1480 the House of Anjou, one of the great French families, died out and Louis regained that province for the crown. At the death of the count of Maine, Louis also gained Maine and Provence. The only great province outside royal control was Brittany, and Louis' son gained it by marriage. Thus France became a unified absolute monarchy.

Feudalism and serfdom. Because of the increased authority of the French kings, the power of French feudal lords declined, but not as much as that of the English nobility. French nobles remained rich and influential until the middle of the

° **Netherlands:** Until the late 1500's the term Netherlands referred to seventeen provinces along the North Sea. They included Flanders (now part of Belgium and northern France), the present-day Netherlands (often called Holland), and Luxembourg.

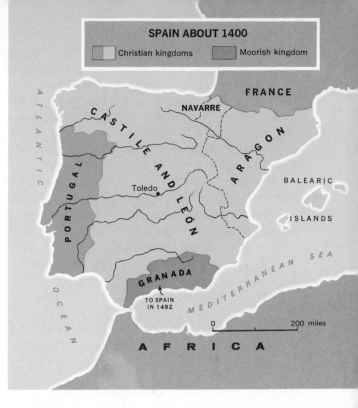

SPAIN ABOUT 1400
☐ Christian kingdoms   ■ Moorish kingdom

1700's. They had many special privileges, including exemption from taxes.

French serfs did not gain as much personal freedom as English serfs. Unlike the English, they still had to pay many dues and give services to the manor and its lord.

Spain

By 1400 there were four chief Christian kingdoms on the Iberian Peninsula—Portugal, Castile-León, Navarre, and Aragon (see map, this page). They shared the peninsula with the Moorish kingdom of Granada. (Moslems in Spain were called Moors.) Over the years, the Christians had reduced Moorish territory in Spain until Granada was the only stronghold left.

The first real step toward unification of the peninsula came in 1469. In that year, Isabella of Castile-León married Ferdinand of Aragon. The two kingdoms remained separate, but the rulers joined forces in a war against the Moors. In 1492 the state of Granada was captured. In the 1500's, Castile-León and Aragon were united to form the new nation of Spain, and the kingdom of Navarre was added to its territories.

237

Ferdinand and Isabella made Spain an absolute monarchy. They took powers away from the Church courts and weakened the nobles. Ardent Catholics, they looked with displeasure at the many Moors and Jews in Spain. Even after the fall of Granada, Moors had continued to live peacefully in Spain. Jews had been in Spain since the time it was a part of the Roman Empire.

In 1492, Ferdinand and Isabella ordered that all Jews within their two kingdoms must either become Christians or leave Spain. Several years later they offered the Moors the same choice.

Most people of both groups chose to leave rather than accept Christianity. In the long run this policy weakened Spain because Moors and Jews made up the industrial and commercial middle class.

The Holy Roman Empire

While strong nations were formed in England, France, and Spain after 1100, neither Germany nor Italy—the regions that made up the Holy Roman Empire—became nations until the 1800's. In theory the empire was ruled by the Holy Roman

EUROPE ABOUT 1500

— Boundary of the Holy Roman Empire

Emperor; however, few of the emperors were powerful enough to make their rule supreme.

In the early days of the Holy Roman Empire, the emperor was elected by the rulers of many German states. Gradually the number who could vote for emperor was reduced. Finally, by an imperial decree in 1356, Charles IV ruled that there were to be seven electors. These electors were the archbishops of Cologne, Mainz, and Trier, and the rulers of Bohemia, Saxony, Brandenburg, and the Palatinate, a region along the Rhine (see map, opposite page).

The electors were afraid to give too much power to one of their own group or to any other powerful prince. For many years they elected as emperors only petty princes who had little land or power. The title of Holy Roman Emperor conferred no real authority, but it did have prestige. For this reason the election was always an occasion for bribery and the demanding of political favors. Many powerful princes promised to give up certain of their powers if they were chosen emperor. This situation prevented the emperors from increasing their power or building a strong central government for the empire.

Around 1300 a member of the Hapsburg family, which ruled a small state in western Germany, was elected emperor. The first Hapsburg emperors were only weak princes with little land, but the family used the prestige of the title to arrange marriages with powerful families. By mar-riage the Hapsburg family gained control of the duchy of Austria and nearby lands. Through many such well-planned marriages, they eventually controlled vast amounts of territory throughout Germany.

After 1437 the election always went to a Hapsburg. However, even the most powerful Hapsburg emperor did not rule Germany, but only the family lands. Germany remained a nation in name only, made up of more than 300 separate and independent governments.

Italy, too, suffered from being a part of the Holy Roman Empire. Another problem that delayed the unification of Italy was that it was divided, as by a belt across the middle, by the Papal States, ruled by the pope.

CHECKUP

1. What were two important results of the Hundred Years' War in England? What ruler ended the Wars of the Roses and established a strong monarchy in England?

2. Why was the reign of Louis XI important to France? What territory did he gain?

3. Explain why Italy and Germany failed to become nations during the later Middle Ages.

4. IDENTIFY: Joan of Arc, Charles VII, Estates-General, Charles the Bold, Ferdinand and Isabella.

5. LOCATE: Crécy, Agincourt, Calais, Orléans, Portugal, Castile-León, Navarre, Aragon, Granada.

6   Problems beset the Church, and its temporal power declined

As you read in Chapter 10, Innocent III, most powerful of all the popes, made himself both the supreme ruler of the Church and the judge of political questions throughout Europe. After his time, however, the temporal, or worldly, power of the Church began to weaken. There were several reasons for this weakening.

Europe was changing. Kings were developing strong national governments with rich revenues from the commerce and industry of the growing cities. Their officials were men trained for professional service, often students of Roman law.

The middle class was growing in importance, and the members of that class often felt that trade and industry were hampered by the restrictions of Church laws.

A new learning began to appear—the wisdom of the Moslems and the pagan Greeks. Much of it did not agree with the teachings of the Church, and a spirit of skepticism, or questioning, began to develop. The Church received increasingly widespread criticism because of its great wealth, its methods of raising money, and the worldly lives of some members of the clergy.

Europe in the later Middle Ages was beset by serious difficulties. The Hundred Years' War pitted the English against the French; soldiers battle with longbows and pikes at Agincourt, below. Rome during the Babylonian Captivity is personified above left as a widow dressed in rags, forsaken by the popes in Avignon. Emperor Charles IV tried to bring some order to the confusing conglomeration of states that formed the Holy Roman Empire. He sits enthroned, above right, with two of his seven electors.

Boniface VIII versus Philip IV

As nationalism increased, papal claims to authority met with opposition. The popes claimed the exclusive right to make all appointments to Church offices. They also demanded that the clergy be exempt from national laws and taxes. This question led to a serious clash between Church and lay authority.

In 1294, Philip IV of France (called Philip the Fair) demanded that the clergy pay taxes to the national treasury. His demand aroused Pope Boniface VIII, a man of learning and culture, but proud, tactless, and eager for power. The pope created much antagonism in Italy by interfering in the affairs of Italian city-states, and by wars to extend the territory of the Papal States. Boniface hesitated to antagonize France, which had long supported the popes against the German emperors. Still, he feared that taxation of the clergy by national governments would weaken the independence and the great economic power of the Church.

In 1296, Boniface moved against royal taxation of the clergy by issuing a papal bull ° called *Clericis Laicos.* In it he ordered the clergy not to pay taxes without the consent of the pope. Philip struck back by forbidding the export of gold and silver from France, thus cutting off payments to the pope. Boniface had to modify his pronouncement slightly and permitted the clergy to make voluntary contributions for the necessary defense of a kingdom, the necessity to be determined by the king.

Boniface resumed his struggle with the French king later. In the bull *Unam Sanctam,* issued in 1302, he stated that the pope was supreme on earth in both spiritual and temporal matters. He was judge of all others, but he himself was responsible only to God.

To block the pope, Philip the Fair summoned a meeting of the Estates-General in 1302. (This was actually the first meeting of the Estates-General.) On this occasion, Philip protested against

° **papal bull:** a formal announcement or official order issued by the pope. The word *bull* comes from the Latin word *bulla,* meaning "seal," because a seal is attached to the papal order. A bull is always in Latin and is given a title from its first two or three words.

Boniface's demands, accused Boniface of simony and heresy, and demanded that a general council of the Church bring him to trial. The French king then had his envoy in Italy seize the pope and hold him prisoner. Although he was quickly released, Boniface died soon afterward. After his death the political power of the medieval papacy outside the Papal States was greatly lessened.

The Babylonian Captivity

Shortly after Boniface's death, Philip IV managed to have one of his French councilors elected pope. The new pope moved the seat of the papacy from Rome to Avignon (ah·vee·NYAWN), in southern France. The next six popes were also Frenchmen, and Avignon was the papal capital for nearly seventy years.

The period of papal history from 1309 to 1377 is called the Babylonian Captivity, from the time when the Hebrews were prisoners in Babylonia. It was an unfortunate time for the papacy. For a thousand years, Rome had been the center of the western Church. Papal residence in France aroused suspicion among other peoples. Moreover, the French popes seemed more interested in maintaining a luxurious court than in the spiritual welfare of Christians. Rome, always a difficult city to govern, fell into lawlessness in the absence of papal rule.

The Great Schism

In the 1370's the papacy fell on especially evil days. A French pope was persuaded to leave Avignon and return to Rome, where he died. The threats of a Roman mob forced the College of Cardinals to elect an Italian pope. The French cardinals then left Rome, declared the election void, and in 1378 elected a French pope, who remained at Avignon. The Italian pope excommunicated the French pope and cardinals, replacing the French cardinals with Italians. The French pope in turn excommunicated the Italian pope and cardinals.

The period from 1378 to 1417 is known as the Great Schism (SIZ·um), meaning a division into hostile groups. For political reasons, each of the two popes was supported by certain national rulers. Generally the people and clergy of a country followed the choice of the ruler of their country.

In 1414 a Church council met at Constance in Germany. It remained in session for four years. Among its tasks were to heal the schism and to consider reforms of all the weaknesses of the Church. The schism was quickly dealt with. The council deposed both the Italian and French popes. It agreed that a new pope should be elected, but not until a program of reforms had been adopted.

The Council of Constance had more difficulty agreeing on a program of reforms. Everyone agreed that corruption in the Church and immorality among the clergy must be ended. However, when a definite plan was proposed to deal with a problem, there was such great disagreement about the details that no conclusion could be reached.

After long and bitter debate, the council compromised. It decided that a Church council should be called at regular intervals to deal with problems, including needed reforms. The cardinals were then allowed to elect a new pope. The council drew up a statement of reforms to be made, then wearily adjourned.

Continued criticism of the Church

The Babylonian Captivity and the Great Schism weakened the authority and prestige of the papacy and increased criticism of the Church. Some of this criticism came from inside the Church itself.

In 1324, two members of the Franciscan order, Marsilius of Padua and John of Jandun, wrote an influential work called *Defender of the Peace*. It criticized both kings and popes. The authors stated the democratic idea that powers of government really belong to the people, who only delegate them to the rulers.

Defender of the Peace also expressed original ideas about the Church. The Church, it said, was made up of the entire body of believers. The only duty of the clergy was to save souls by preaching and administering the sacraments. The clergy could decide purely religious questions, but they could not fix worldly penalties for sins because God alone could punish.

According to the writers, the pope was only the elected head of the Church and had no other power. All power belonged to the members of the Church. They could delegate power only to a general Church council. A council had authority to make sweeping reforms in the entire Church, including the papacy.

John Wycliffe. In England these beliefs were adopted and spread in the late 1300's by John Wycliffe, a member of the clergy and teacher at Oxford University. He attacked the wealth of the Church and immorality among the clergy. Wycliffe wrote that the pope's claim to absolute authority in the Church was unjustified. He also said that Jesus could save one's soul without the aid of a priest; the authority of salvation was in the Bible, not in the clergy. About 1382, Wycliffe translated the Bible from Latin into English so that people could read it and learn what to believe and how to act.

John Huss. Wycliffe's books were widely read both in England and on the continent. John Huss of Bohemia, a teacher at the University of Prague, was influenced by Wycliffe's writings. Huss became popular with the people of Bohemia by denouncing abuses in the Church, but he angered the clergy and was excommunicated in 1410. He was told to appear before the Council of Constance to answer charges of heresy. The emperor ordered him to go, but guaranteed his safe return. When the emperor later withdrew the safe conduct, Huss was tried by the council and condemned as a heretic. In 1415 he was burned at the stake.

By the end of the 1400's the Church was subject to widespread criticism throughout Europe.

CHECKUP

1. Why did the temporal power of the Church decline after the reign of Innocent III?

2. What quarrel ended the temporal power of the medieval papacy? What was the cause of the quarrel and what were some of the incidents?

3. Explain the importance of the ideas of *Defender of the Peace;* John Wycliffe.

4. What were the Babylonian Captivity and the Great Schism? Why did they weaken the Church?

5. LOCATE: Avignon, Constance, Prague.

CHAPTER REVIEW

Chapter 11   Trade Revived and European Nations Slowly Emerged   (1000—1500)

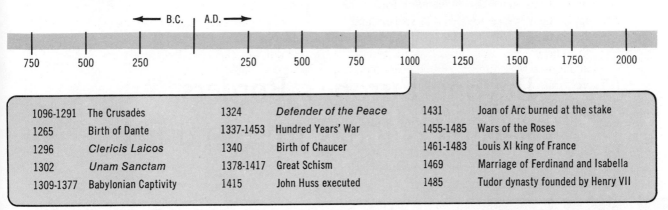

1096-1291	The Crusades	1324	*Defender of the Peace*	1431	Joan of Arc burned at the stake
1265	Birth of Dante	1337-1453	Hundred Years' War	1455-1485	Wars of the Roses
1296	*Clericis Laicos*	1340	Birth of Chaucer	1461-1483	Louis XI king of France
1302	*Unam Sanctam*	1378-1417	Great Schism	1469	Marriage of Ferdinand and Isabella
1309-1377	Babylonian Captivity	1415	John Huss executed	1485	Tudor dynasty founded by Henry VII

CHAPTER SUMMARY

The Crusades were organized chiefly to regain the Holy Land from the Moslems. Although they were military failures, these expeditions had important effects on Europe: the introduction of new weapons, increased royal power, the weakening of feudal lords, and intellectual and commercial stimulation.

Even before the Crusades, trade had begun to revive in Europe. Italians acted as middlemen between traders from Asia and those from central and northern Europe, where the Vikings and German merchants played vital roles. Flanders had great commercial importance, as did the Hanseatic League. Trade was aided by fairs and led to the development of capitalism and banking.

Towns grew as trade revived. Townsmen gained important liberties: freedom, exemption from manorial services and obligations, town justice, and commercial rights. Merchants and craftsmen organized guilds. As time went on, the middle class became increasingly prominent.

Medieval culture flourished with the revival of cities. Vernacular languages developed and were used by such writers as Dante and Chaucer. At great universities, scholastic philosophers, including Abelard and Aquinas, sought to reconcile faith and reason. Outstanding medieval monuments were the Romanesque and Gothic churches.

National governments continued to grow stronger. Although the Hundred Years' War and the Wars of the Roses hindered centralization in England, the process was greatly aided by Henry VII, founder of the Tudor dynasty. In France, nationalism was stimulated by Joan of Arc and French victory over the English in the Hundred Years' War. Louis XI added much land to the royal domain and helped France become unified. In Spain, Ferdinand and Isabella created a strong absolute monarchy, but weakened the country by driving out Moors and Jews. Germany and Italy remained disunited.

The papacy's temporal power declined as nationalism increased. A quarrel between Philip IV of France and Pope Boniface VIII weakened papal authority, which was further diminished by the Babylonian Captivity and the Great Schism. The Church was criticized by such reformers as Wycliffe and Huss.

QUESTIONS FOR DISCUSSION

1. During the Middle Ages, markets and fairs helped break down the separateness of various regions. Do you think international fairs and trade serve the same purpose today?

2. Is it still true today, as it was during the Middle Ages, that "City air makes free"? For instance, is a man living in a city freer in his personal actions than a man in a small village?

3. Looking at Europe as a whole, do you think feudalism died out first in the western or in the eastern part of Europe? Justify your answer.

4. Medieval thinking was deductive; reasoning was developed from accepted ideas. What are the shortcomings of such a system of thinking?

5. Why did the Crusades not begin in the 600's, when the Moslems first conquered Palestine?

PROJECTS

1. As a feudal lord, write a letter to another lord criticizing the king's attempt to establish a strong central government.

2. Write a short essay in support of usury during the Middle Ages.

3. Make a pencil sketch of a Gothic cathedral.

243

Beyond Europe's Borders, Several Nations Rose and Fell

The last two chapters of this book have dealt chiefly with Western Europe during the Middle Ages. Now we turn to a number of peoples and cultures that existed in nearby areas during the same period.

In studying them, you will first return, so to speak, to the Near East and Africa. The stage of history there now has a group of players entirely different from those who occupied it earlier. You will find, if you think about it for a moment, that you have read almost nothing about Egypt for many chapters. The Persians have vanished from the scene as a great power. The Hebrew nation exists no longer. Even the mighty Roman Empire has been discussed only as its collapse produced many changes in the vast territory it once controlled.

Because of the appearance and disappearance of nations in the past, some historians have suggested what they call the cyclic (SY·klik) theory of history. According to this theory, nations, like people, go through a cycle of birth, growth, maturity, decline, and death. Even though a nation may exist for a long time, it will eventually vanish and be replaced by another.

Other historians disagree with this idea. They say it means that a nation has no control over its affairs, but grows because it is destined to grow and falls because it *must* fall, no matter what other influences are at work to keep it alive.

An old map, showing parts of Asia and Africa

This argument has not been settled, nor is it likely to be. It is a fact that very few nations have existed for even a thousand years. Pressures from outside their borders and decay and corruption within have worked separately or together to cause their downfall and disappearance from the scene of history.

It is also a fact, however, that while nations have declined or vanished, they have not been forgotten. Even in the case of peoples who left few or no written records, their learning, art, literature, and codes of government have usually been absorbed by later peoples. Often the best parts of a vanishing culture are preserved, like a torch passed from the hand of a faltering runner to a newcomer who will carry it forward.

THE CHAPTER SECTIONS:

1. The Byzantine Empire helped preserve Western civilization (500–1453)
2. Islam and the Moslem Empire spread outward from Arabia (570–1400)
3. Several different cultures arose in Africa south of the Sahara (700 B.C.–1600 A.D.)
4. Russia, long part of the Mongol Empire, finally became independent (800–1478)

1 The Byzantine Empire helped preserve Western civilization

While barbarians overran the western part of the Roman Empire in the 400's and 500's, the eastern part lived on. This eastern part in time became known as the Byzantine Empire. The name comes from the capital city, Constantinople, which was built on the site of the ancient city of Byzantium. Throughout its long history the Byzantine Empire was surrounded by enemies. Nevertheless, it maintained itself for a thousand years.

Territory of the empire

In the year 500 the Roman Empire in the east included Greece and the northern Balkan Peninsula, Asia Minor, Syria, Palestine, Egypt, and Cyrenaica. Although the eastern empire was invaded by Germanic tribes earlier than the western empire, it had internal strengths that enabled it to survive the attacks. By the early 500's, the empire in the west had broken down into a group of Germanic tribal kingdoms (see map, this page). The eastern empire, on the other hand, had rid itself of barbarians and was ready for a great political, economic, intellectual, and artistic revival.

The leader of this revival was the Emperor Justinian, who ruled from 527 to 565. While the new Germanic kingdoms in the west quarreled among themselves, Justinian's armies regained most of North Africa, Corsica, and Sardinia from the Vandals; Italy, Sicily, and the eastern Adriatic

coast from the Ostrogoths; and a strip of southern Spain from the Visigoths. With these conquests, the territory of the eastern empire reached its greatest extent (see map, page 246). The eastern empire was unable to hold the regained territory for long, however, and Germanic tribes won most of it back by the early 600's.

After Justinian's death, the weakened eastern empire suffered half a century of civil wars, made worse by attacks from the outside. From the east came the Persians. The Balkan Peninsula was invaded by an Asiatic group, the Avars, and by a European people called the Slavs. Italy was overrun by the Lombards.

GERMANIC KINGDOMS in 526 A.D.

245

Justinian's successors defeated the Persians in the late 500's, but during the 600's they faced a new and highly energetic force—the armies of the Moslem Empire, which you will read about shortly. The Moslem drive for conquest soon gained Armenia, Syria, Palestine, and much of North Africa, including Egypt. After 650 the eastern empire ° consisted of little more than Asia Minor, the southern Balkan Peninsula, parts of Italy, and the nearby islands (see map, page 251). However, the empire existed 800 more years.

Strengths of the empire

The Byzantine Empire survived for a long time because its people were skilled at adapting themselves to change. It also had other strengths.

° **eastern empire:** Since the territory of the eastern empire after 650 was concentrated around Constantinople (former Byzantium), many historians apply the term Byzantine Empire only after that date. Actually, its people never called themselves Byzantines, but rather Romanoi (Romans).

(1) *Political strength.* The government of the Byzantine Empire was highly centralized and autocratic. The emperor was all-powerful. His commands and policies were carried out by a well-paid bureaucracy of trained officials who were efficient, skillful, and usually loyal. The bureaucracy was strong enough to bridge over the bad times of weak emperors or civil war.

The Byzantines were especially skillful diplomats. They used gifts and bribes liberally, and their excellent intelligence service kept the emperor well informed of important foreign developments. Byzantine princesses were often married to foreign princes to help prevent attacks on the empire. It was also Byzantine practice to provoke one neighbor to attack another in order to prevent either one from attacking the empire.

(2) *Military strength.* Part of the military strength of the Byzantine Empire lay in its good

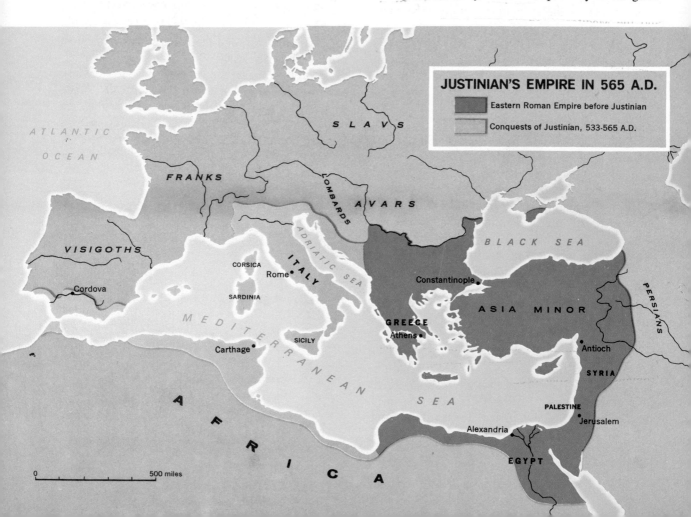

JUSTINIAN'S EMPIRE IN 565 A.D.

Eastern Roman Empire before Justinian

Conquests of Justinian, 533-565 A.D.

defenses. Considering the large size of the empire, it could be defended with a fairly small army. Regiments were assigned to the various districts of the empire, where they kept watch to defend the frontiers. Leadership was excellent and there was a good intelligence system.

After the Moslems became a threat in the 600's, the Byzantines developed a good navy. Byzantine ships used battering rams, but the sailors' chief weapon—a "secret weapon"—was an inflammable liquid called Greek fire which they hurled at enemy ships to set them on fire.

(3) *Economic strength.* The east had always been the wealthy part of the Roman Empire. The wealth of the region was based on a sound mixture of agriculture, manufacturing, and trade. Constantinople was the heart of the empire. Its advantage lay in its location. Situated on the border of two continents, Asia and Europe, it commanded the entrance to two seas, the Black and the Mediterranean.

Merchandise from all the civilized world poured into the markets of Constantinople. There and throughout the empire, the government regulated trade and manufacturing to produce large tax revenues, used to pay the bureaucracy and the army and to build great public buildings.

Religion

As you have read, the patriarchs of Rome, Constantinople, Alexandria, Antioch, and Jerusalem were important figures in the early Christian Church. In time, Rome and the pope came to have supreme authority in the west. This authority was not recognized in the Byzantine Empire, however. There the patriarch of Constantinople came to be the most important churchman.

As time went by, two branches of the Church developed. They drifted apart partly because of doctrine and partly for political reasons. (For one thing, the Byzantines resented the pope's coronation of Charlemagne, a Frank, as Emperor of the Romans.) The split became final in 1054, when the pope and the patriarch at Constantinople excommunicated each other. The Church in the west became known as the Roman Catholic Church. The Church in the east is generally called the Eastern Orthodox Church, or Greek Orthodox Church.

The Christian faith was of overwhelming importance to the Byzantines. They were keenly interested in matters of dogma. One writer has said that Byzantines would fight for a religious dogma when they would fight for nothing else.

The Orthodox faith was a source of both weakness and strength for the Byzantine Empire. Conflicts over dogma tended to divide and weaken the empire. One such conflict helped to make possible the easy Moslem conquest of Egypt and Syria. But in the heart of the empire—the region around Constantinople—the Church provided the basis for a kind of patriotism that strengthened the government. The emperor was accepted as head of the Church with little question.

Byzantine culture

The Byzantine Empire performed a great service for civilization. Its scholars did not produce much that was original, but they did preserve and pass on classical learning—the learning of ancient Greece and Rome. For a thousand years, while the states of Western Europe were struggling to develop a new way of life, Constantinople was the center of a brilliant civilization.

The Byzantines not only preserved the culture of the Mediterranean world but also carried it beyond the borders of their empire. An example of Byzantine cultural influence was the work of two brothers, St. Cyril and St. Methodius, who lived in the 800's. As missionaries they worked to convert the Slavs of central Europe, the Balkan region, and southern Russia to Christianity. The Slavs had no written language, and Cyril wanted them to be able to read the Bible. He created a modified Greek alphabet which, after further changes, became the so-called Cyrillic (sih·RIL·ik) alphabet. Such Slavic peoples as the Serbs, Bulgarians, and Russians still use the Cyrillic alphabet or one derived from it.

The missionary work begun by Cyril and Methodius was successful. Serbs and Bulgarians were converted to Christianity beginning in the 800's, the Russians beginning in the 900's. Great numbers of these people still follow the Orthodox faith.

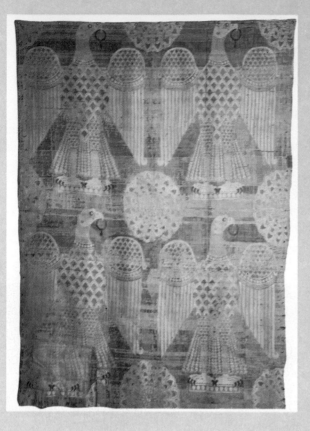

Byzantine Cloth of Purple Silk

For hundreds of years all silk came from China. Europeans, who did not know how to make it, paid huge sums for the precious material. When Justinian was emperor, he learned the secret of silk-making from two Persian monks who had lived in China. Because he wanted his own artisans to be able to make the elegant fabric, he sent the monks back to China with instructions to return with some silkworm eggs. The monks smuggled the eggs in hollow bamboo staffs they carried, thus enabling the Byzantines to establish their own silk industry.

The textile at left was made for the emperor. We know this because of the eagle, which symbolized the authority of the state, and because only the emperor was allowed to wear purple. Even though this fragile silk was woven almost a thousand years ago, the great care and attention lavished on it have kept it in a remarkable state of preservation down through the centuries.

Art. Byzantine art is noted for its use of color and ornamentation. In the markets of Constantinople, artists and traders sold tapestries luxuriously embroidered in gold. There were also enamels framed in gold, delicately carved ivory, and jewelry made of bronze inlaid with silver. These were all luxuries hardly known in early medieval Europe.

At its best, Byzantine art glorified religion. The walls and ceilings of churches were covered with murals. Floors, walls, and arches were bright with colored mosaics (pictures or designs formed by inlaid pieces of stone, glass, or enamel). Both painting and mosaics were used in icons—small religious pictures set up in churches or homes, or carried on journeys as aids to devotion.

The subjects of this art, whether angels, saints, or martyrs, were stiff and artificial. They could not be mistaken for ordinary human beings, but were clearly inhabitants of another world. Art served the emperor as well as the Church.

Architecture. Architecture, especially religious architecture, was the greatest of Byzantine arts. The finest Byzantine building—indeed, one of the architectural masterpieces of the world—is the church of Santa Sophia (Greek words meaning "holy wisdom") in Constantinople.

Santa Sophia, begun in 532, was built by order of Justinian. It is a huge building. The ground plan, in the form of a cross, measures 240 by 270 feet. The interior, lighted by windows in domes and side walls, was marvelously decorated. Every available surface was covered with murals, mosaics, stone carvings, and metal work. The pulpit was inset with ivory, silver, and jewels. The patriarch's throne was solid silver.

The central feature of Santa Sophia is a huge dome, 165 feet high. It rests on massive columns instead of walls and has a half-dome at either end. Byzantine architects were the first to solve the difficult problem of placing a round dome over a rectangular building.

The Byzantine Empire

Under Justinian, the Byzantines reached their greatest glory. Santa Sophia, at right, is now over 1,400 years old. Yet its beauty, especially when illuminated with shafts of sunlight, is still as awesome as it must have been the day Justinian first stepped inside. He had the mosaic at top right placed above the entrance. Before the central figures of the Virgin and Child stand two men. At right Constantine presents a building symbolizing his city, Constantinople. At left is Justinian himself with a model of Santa Sophia. The silver book cover directly above was made to enclose the *Digest* portion of Justinian's Code.

When Santa Sophia was completed in 537, one Byzantine writer said that it was a church "the like of which had never been since Adam, nor ever will be." The church was solemnly consecrated by Justinian himself. As he first entered Santa Sophia, he exclaimed, "O Solomon, I have outdone thee!" (He was referring, of course, to the famous temple of King Solomon as described in the Bible.)

Law

Of all the Byzantine contributions to civilization, the greatest was probably the preservation of Roman law. Early in his reign, the Emperor Justinian ordered his scholars to collect and organize all Roman law. The entire collection is known as the *Corpus Juris Civilis* (Latin for "Body of Civil Law"), or Justinian's Code. It is in four parts called the *Code,* the *Digest,* the *Institutes,* and the *Novels.*

The *Code* was a collection of Roman laws, omitting repetitions, inconsistencies, and statutes dealing with Roman religion. The *Digest* was a summary of the writings of the great Roman legal experts, organized alphabetically by ideas. The *Institutes* was a textbook on the basic principles of Roman law. Justinian's own laws were published in the *Novels.* In Western Europe, Roman law was studied principally from the *Digest* and *Institutes.* Justinian's Code forms the basis of many modern European legal systems.

Decline of the empire

In the 1000's, the Seljuk Turks, originally a nomadic people from central Asia, captured most of Asia Minor, a vital part of the Byzantine Empire. When the Turks prepared to attack Constantinople, the Byzantine emperor appealed to the west for help. As you have read, help came in 1096 and 1097 with the First Crusade. Europeans rewon western Asia for the Byzantines. The Fourth Crusade, however, became an attack on the Byzantine Empire instead of the Moslems, and Constantinople fell to the invading crusaders in 1204.

After half a century of Western rule, the Byzantines recaptured the city. The empire was reorganized and continued to exist for nearly two centuries, but it was never able to regain its strength. A new Asiatic people, the Ottoman Turks, rose to power. In 1453 they captured Constantinople, and the Byzantine Empire at last came to an end.

CHECKUP

1. What sources of strength enabled the Byzantine Empire to survive as long as it did?
2. What did Cyril and Methodius contribute to the civilization of central and eastern Europe?
3. Name and identify the four parts of Justinian's Code.
4. IDENTIFY: Greek fire, mosaics, icons, Santa Sophia.

2   Islam and the Moslem Empire spread outward from Arabia

While the Byzantines were maintaining their rule in Asia Minor and the Balkan region, a new empire was taking shape to the south and east. This empire, like that of the Byzantines, developed a civilization that far surpassed that of Western Europe for centuries. It began in Arabia.

Arabia and the Arabs

South of the Fertile Crescent lay the great peninsula of Arabia (see map, opposite). Most of it was a desert plateau whose scanty vegetation could support only nomadic herdsmen and their flocks of sheep. These Arabs who lived as nomads were called Bedouins (BED-oo-inz). They were organized into tribes, each under the absolute rule of a sheik, or chief.

Some coastal regions of Arabia, with greater rainfall, could support more people. Here towns grew up. The Arabs who lived in these centers were traders. Goods from Asia and Africa were brought to the port of Jidda, then taken overland to Mecca, the starting point of a caravan route running north to Syria. The town-dwelling Arabs had a higher level of culture than the Bedouins.

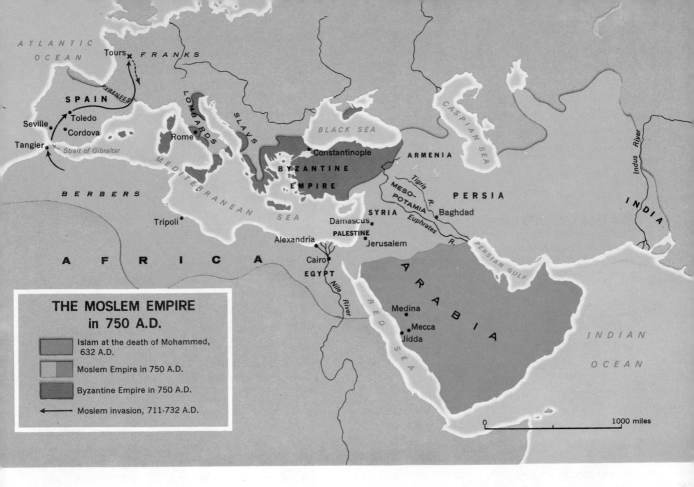

THE MOSLEM EMPIRE
in 750 A.D.

Islam at the death of Mohammed, 632 A.D.

Moslem Empire in 750 A.D.

Byzantine Empire in 750 A.D.

Moslem invasion, 711-732 A.D.

0   1000 miles

Mohammed

A child was born in Mecca about 570 and given the name Mohammed. He was orphaned at an early age and spent his youth in poverty. Having little formal education, he probably never learned to write. He became a camel driver and caravan trader.

While still a young man, Mohammed began to think seriously about problems of religion and conduct. At that time the Arabs worshiped many gods. Through meditation and prayer, Mohammed became convinced that there was but one Supreme Being, one God, whom he called Allah.

When he was about forty years old, Mohammed had a great religious experience. He believed that the archangel Gabriel ordered him to preach to the Arabs to bring them religious purity. Mohammed did not claim to have any supernatural powers. He considered himself a prophet and teacher, like Moses.

Mohammed's preaching met bitter opposition and threats from the rulers of Mecca. Fearing for his life, he took his little band of followers to a nearby town, Medina, where he had promise of better support. The event is known as the Hegira (hih·JY·ruh), meaning "flight." It was such an important event in Mohammed's life that the date, 622, became the first year of the Moslem calendar.

In Medina, Mohammed made many converts and became the leader of the community. In a few years he returned to Mecca at the head of an army and captured it. By a combination of wise policies, toleration, and force he converted many of the Bedouin tribes to his new religion. By 632, when Mohammed died, almost all Arabia had accepted Allah (see map, this page).

The faith of Islam

The formal name of the religion that Mohammed established is Islam, which means "sub-

The Moslem world was founded on the faith of Islam. Above, a manuscript of the Koran lies open to show its handsome calligraphy and colored borders. Wherever they settled, the Moslems built mosques. The one at right, called the Dome of the Rock, is a shrine in Jerusalem. From this site, according to tradition, Mohammed ascended into heaven. Skillful craftsmen, the Moslems invented several clever devices. The drawing below diagrams a mechanical hand-washing apparatus in the form of a woman holding a pitcher.

mission to God." A member of this faith is called a Moslem. The central belief is simple: "There is no God but Allah, and Mohammed is his Prophet." Like most religions, Islam has a holy book and definite rules for its believers, and emphasizes certain moral teachings.

The holy book of Islam is the Koran (meaning "recital"). It is a presentation of Mohammed's most important teachings written down by scribes and assembled in book form. It contains much that is also found in the Bible. All Moslems recognize the Koran as their sacred book. Because it was written in Arabic, and because its translation into other languages was discouraged, Arabic became a common language among Moslems.

A Moslem must meet four chief obligations. (1) He must pray at certain fixed hours of the day, facing Mecca, the holy city of Islam. (2) He must, if possible, make a pilgrimage to Mecca once in his lifetime. (3) He must give alms to the needy. (4) He must fast from sunrise to sunset during the month of Ramadan—the ninth month of the Moslem year. This month is considered sacred because it was the month in which Mohammed had his vision of the archangel Gabriel.

Mohammed required and emphasized the virtues of temperance, humility, justice, generosity, tolerance, obedience to authority, and courage. A Moslem was allowed to have as many as four wives, but only if he treated them all with equal kindness. Slavery was permitted, but slaves had to be treated humanely. Moslems were forbidden to drink alcoholic beverages or to eat pork.

In contrast to the teachings of Jesus, Mohammed praised what he called the Holy War. He said: "The sword is the key of heaven and hell; whosoever falls in battle, his sins are forgiven." The fallen warrior was promised enticing heavenly rewards.

Islam has no religious images because Mohammed forbade his followers to make representations of human or animal forms. There are no elaborate ceremonies. There are men called mullahs, learned in Islamic faith and law, but there is no formal priesthood. At a service in a Moslem temple, or mosque, the people pray together under the guidance of a leader.

The spread of Islam

When Mohammed died in 632, an informal assembly of Moslems chose as his successor Abu-Bekr (uh·boo-BEK·ur), an early convert and an able man. He was called caliph, a word meaning "successor to the prophet." When Abu-Bekr died, an assembly chose his friend and counselor Omar as caliph. To avoid civil wars over the succession, both Abu-Bekr and Omar followed a policy aimed at conquering neighboring territory of non-Moslems. This policy diverted attention from the selection of the new caliph.

Fortunately for the caliphs, the Arabs had many opportunities for conquest in the 600's. Both the Byzantine and Persian empires were weak and unstable, partly because they had been fighting each other for years.

Arab conquests were made easier by the Arab policy toward conquered peoples. The Arabs were fierce and fearless in battle but generous in victory. Non-Moslems who surrendered were given three choices: to accept Islam, to pay an annual tribute, or to be put to death. Those who paid the tribute could keep their religion and customs. Few of the conquered chose to die; they either paid or were converted.

In less than a century after the death of Mohammed, his followers had overrun Arabia, Palestine, Syria, Armenia, Mesopotamia, Persia, part of India, Egypt, and the rest of North Africa (see map, page 251). Then they took to the sea and eventually conquered the islands of the Mediterranean. They controlled the southern part of that sea for trade. They besieged Constantinople, but were turned back.

At the other end of the Mediterranean Sea, Moslems had more success in entering Europe. A people of North Africa called the Berbers were recent converts to Islam and eager for conquest. In 711, a general named Tarik led an expedition against the Visigoths in Spain, past the great rock that guards the strait between Africa and Spain. (The rock was named Jebel Tarik, the "Mountain of Tarik"; Europeans have altered the name into Gibraltar.)

Spain was an easy conquest. In seven years the Moors (the Moslems of Spain) had passed beyond the Pyrenees to raid the plains of what is now central France. In 732, near Tours, as you have read, they were defeated by the Franks and driven back into Spain (see map, page 251). They ruled there for over 700 years.

Government and economy

At the head of the government was the caliph. He was the supreme civil, military, and religious leader of the whole vast empire. Although at first the caliph was elected, the position later became hereditary. The territory of the empire was organized into provinces, with Arabs in all the high positions.

Later the empire was divided into three parts (called caliphates, since each was ruled by a caliph). Headquarters for these were at Baghdad, in Persia; Cairo, in Egypt; and Cordova, in Spain.

The Arabs had long been traders, and Mohammed had praised and encouraged commerce. Goods from India and China were brought across the Indian Ocean to the Persian Gulf and the Red Sea, then overland to the ports of Syria and to Cairo and Alexandria in Egypt (see map, pages 224–25).

Manufacturing was stimulated by the demands of trade. The empire produced silk, cotton, and linen textiles, as well as tapestries and carpets. There were luxuries such as jewelry, perfumes, and spices. Metal products included objects made of gold, silver, steel, brass, and copper. Steel swords from Damascus in Syria and Toledo in Spain became world-famous. There was a great variety of pottery and glassware. Tangier in North Africa and Cordova in Spain made fine leather goods.

The Arabs promoted the development of agriculture everywhere. Fruits, vegetables, and other products native to any part of the empire were introduced in other areas where they might grow.

Culture and scholarship

Though divided politically, the Moslem world remained united in one great civilization. In the beginning the Arabs were a backward but intelligent people. They were willing to adopt the best ideas, customs, and institutions they found. They took the science and philosophy of Greece, Rome, and the Orient and tried to combine them.

Moslem scientists wrote handbooks and encyclopedias on many subjects. Their geographers and navigators were the finest in the world. They perfected the astrolabe, an instrument used in navigation to determine the altitudes of planets and stars. From the Chinese, Moslems learned paper-making.

Moslems added much medical knowledge to that of Hippocrates and Galen. At Baghdad in the early 900's, the Moslem physician Rhazes (RAY-zeez) wrote about surgery, diseases of the eye, smallpox, and measles. He compiled a huge medical encyclopedia which, translated into Latin, was used in Europe for centuries. About a century after the time of Rhazes, Avicenna wrote *The Canon of Medicine,* used as a textbook by Moslems and Christians alike as late as the 1600's.

The Moslems were excellent mathematicians. They perfected algebra as a science. (Our word *algebra* comes from the Arabic words *al-jebr,* meaning "the reunion of broken parts.") Another Moslem contribution to mathematics was the introduction to the Western world of Arabic numerals. As you have read, mathematicians of India developed this system, but the Arabs learned it from them and transmitted it to the West.

Europeans came into contact with Moslem culture in two ways. One was through Spain. Cordova and Toledo were famous for learning, and Seville was a center of art and luxury. Christian and Jewish scholars brought Moslem learning from Spain into Western Europe. The other point of contact was the Crusades. In Palestine and other Moslem regions, the crusaders learned of the achievements of Moslem civilization. They took back ideas that improved European culture.

The great era of Moslem culture lasted from about 700 to 1000. After that, men who believed in "following the letter of the Koran" became powerful in the Moslem world. These men opposed free thought and foreign ideas. Invasions by Turks and Mongols also lowered the cultural level by disrupting trade and destroying cities. However, Moslem culture flourished longer in Spain because this region was more independent.

The Turks

The Seljuk Turks, as you have read, seized much of Asia Minor from the Byzantines during the 1000's. They also extended their rule into the Moslem territories of Syria and Mesopotamia. The next two centuries witnessed a great deal of confusion in the eastern Mediterranean area. There were conflicts not only among Arabs, Turks, and Byzantines, but also between these peoples and Europeans in the Crusades.

Then, at the beginning of the 1300's, a new group of Turks appeared. They were called Ottomans after their first ruler, Osman. The Ottomans fought as well as the Seljuks and were much better at administering a government.

Ottoman success in battle and in government was due, in part, to a group of slaves called janizaries. Most of the janizaries were taken as children from conquered Christians. All of them were carefully instructed in Islamic beliefs and laws.

The janizaries were a standing army of disciplined, trained infantry. As bodyguards to the Turkish rulers, or sultans, they became influential in the government. Encouraged by promotions for merit and by a system of rewards and punishments, they were at first a source of great strength. Later they became a danger to the government, somewhat like the Praetorian Guard of the late Roman Empire.

During the first half of the 1300's, the Ottomans conquered most of northwestern Asia Minor. Then they invaded Europe and established their capital at Adrianople, northwest of Constantinople. By the late 1300's, the way was open for them to move against Constantinople itself. Although they were halted temporarily by a new force, the Mongols, they eventually captured the city in 1453 and made it the capital of a new empire, the Ottoman Empire. You will read more about this empire in later chapters.

CHECKUP

1. What are the holy book and the four chief obligations of Islam? What are some other teachings?

2. Give two reasons why the Arabs had little difficulty in conquering an empire. How were the Moslems prevented from gaining more of Western Europe?

3. Why was the Moslem economy strong?

4. What were the greatest contributions of Moslem scholarship? How did Moslem learning come into Western Europe?

5. IDENTIFY: Bedouins, Allah, Hegira, mullahs, Abu-Bekr, Berbers, Moors, Rhazes, Avicenna, Osman, janizaries.

6. LOCATE: Arabia, Jidda, Mecca, Medina, Gibraltar, Baghdad, Cairo, Cordova, Toledo, Tangier, Seville.

3 Several different cultures arose in Africa south of the Sahara

At several points in this book, you have read about North Africa—the northern strip of the continent along the Mediterranean, stretching from the Red Sea to the Atlantic Ocean. It was here that the great Egyptian civilization flourished. Later, parts of the area belonged to the Roman Empire, to the Byzantine Empire, to the Vandals, and to the Moslem Empire.

What of the rest of the continent, the vast region that lay to the south? Its background and history differed from those of North Africa. For one thing, its people were different. Most North Africans were of the Caucasoid, or white, racial stock; most other Africans were Negroid. More important than racial differences, however, was the geographic isolation of most of Africa.

The land

On the inset map on page 256, you can see that Africa consists of several different regions that run like irregular bands across the continent. Except for fertile land in a thin strip near the coast and along the Nile River, most of North Africa is part of the vast desert of the Sahara. South of the Sahara lies a region called the Sudan. Much larger than the present-day country of Sudan, it stretches 4,000 miles from the Atlantic eastward to the Nile Valley and beyond and consists mainly of desert and dry grasslands called savannas. To the south are the dense tropical rain forests of West Africa and the Congo River basin; then another region of savannas; then the Kalahari Desert; and finally a temperate region consisting of high plateaus and mountains.

As you can see on the map, the Sahara is a formidable barrier, separating North Africa from the rest of the continent (often called sub-Saharan Africa). Not only did the Sahara isolate this region from the north, but other geographic features made much of it inaccessible from east and west. For one thing, sub-Saharan Africa has few natural harbors. For another, most of the region is a plateau, rising fairly sharply from the seacoast. Thus, although there are many large rivers—including the Congo, the Niger, and the Zambezi—most of them have rapids a short distance inland and cannot be navigated far into the interior.

Prehistoric Africa

Archeologists have only recently begun to piece together the story of early Africa south of the Sahara. Excavations in eastern Africa, southeast of Lake Victoria, have revealed remains of an early manlike creature that may date back a million years or more. An Old Stone Age culture existed for thousands of years. Evidence shows

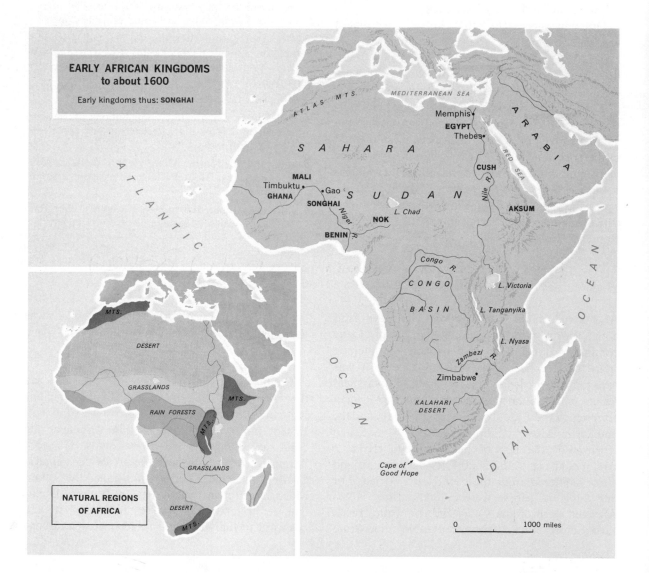

EARLY AFRICAN KINGDOMS
to about 1600

Early kingdoms thus: SONGHAI

NATURAL REGIONS OF AFRICA

that many African peoples emerged from this hunting and gathering stage into a Neolithic life between 6,000 and 7,000 years ago.

Our knowledge of these peoples is scanty, since most of them did not have writing. We do know, however, that many of them believed in what is called divine kingship. According to this belief, the king had divine powers and had to be revered like a god. The well-being of the tribe depended on his health; the rain fell and the crops grew because of his power. He was an absolute monarch who wielded enormous power.

Such divine kings might rule as many as a million subjects through an extremely complex governmental administration—all of it conducted without the aid of writing.

Although the prehistory of much of sub-Saharan Africa is not known to us, archeologists and scholars have learned about several early peoples and kingdoms. Some of these had contacts with each other. Others seem to have grown up in isolation.

Kingdoms in eastern and southern Africa

Two early African kingdoms developed in eastern Africa (see map, opposite). One, the kingdom of Cush, grew out of early Egyptian settlements along the upper Nile Valley. By 700 B.C., it was strong enough to declare its independence from Egypt. For more than a thousand years, Cush dominated a large region of the eastern Sudan and traded with Greece and Rome.

The kingdom of Aksum had its beginnings in the highlands of what is now Ethiopia early in the Christian era. By the 300's A.D., it was powerful enough to make war on Cush and completely destroy it. The people of Aksum were converted to Christianity at about the same time and were a power in eastern Africa until around 600.

Europeans must have traded with these kingdoms, as is shown by a Greek book of directions for sailors. It describes the goods which could be obtained at African ports on the Red Sea and the Indian Ocean, including ivory, cinnamon, spices, and slaves.

Much farther south and inland, south of the Zambezi River, there existed a culture about which

HISTORY THROUGH ART

Royal Figure from West Africa

Although much is known about early sub-Saharan Africa, many puzzles remain. The bronze head above is one of them. It was made in what is now Nigeria over 600 years ago. The beaded crown indicates that the person is of royal blood, but scholars do not know whether it is a man or a woman. The vertical lines on the face probably represent ritual scarring—a practice still followed by some Africans—but scholars are uncertain about the purpose of the holes around the mouth. It is clear, however, that the head was made by a skilled and sensitive craftsman. for it is a magnificent example of bronze casting.

little is known, but which has led to a great deal of speculation. It centered on Zimbabwe, which is now a huge ruin of several buildings, massive walls, and a tower constructed of stone blocks many feet thick. Archeologists believe that the main wall was built in the 500's, and that the culture may have lasted about a thousand years.

257

Gold has been found in the ruins of Zimbabwe, along with tools and ornaments of iron and copper. The people must have had a highly organized government in order to build such a settlement.

West Africa

Northwest Africa, between Lake Chad and the Atlantic Ocean, was the home of several important societies. The Nok culture occupied what is now northern Nigeria for about a thousand years, from before 700 B.C. to 200 A.D. Its people lived in villages and knew how to work iron. They produced jewelry, tools, and a distinctive sculpture of terra-cotta, a durable reddish clay.

Farther north along the Niger River grew up a succession of kingdoms—Ghana, Mali, and Songhai (see map, page 256). They traded with Moslem caravans that traveled across the Sahara, bringing salt and manufactured goods in exchange for gold and slaves. Busy commercial cities grew up and flourished in this area.

The kingdom of Ghana, the earliest kingdom of the western Sudan, developed in the 700's. (The present-day nation of Ghana, to the south, took its name from this early state.) In the mid-1000's, however, Ghana was attacked and destroyed by Berber Moslems from North Africa. Islam was imposed on the whole western Sudan.

Beginning in the 1200's, the kingdom of Mali came to power over what had been Ghana, as well as vast areas to the north and west and along the upper Niger River. (Modern Mali includes much of the ancient kingdom.) Its greatest ruler was Mansa Musa, who ruled from 1307 to 1332. The city of Timbuktu became a center of Moslem learning, visited by scholars from Egypt and Arabia. Mali controlled the desert trade until about 1500, when it was overthrown and replaced by the kingdom of Songhai. Songhai revived learning and scholarship in Timbuktu, and built another prosperous city, Gao. However, this empire was in turn overthrown by Moroccan armies in 1591.

Another prominent kingdom in West Africa was Benin, located in what is now southern Nigeria. It grew up in the 1200's and was a flourishing center when the Portuguese arrived in 1483. Artisans of Benin excelled in carved ivory, iron work, and bronze portrait busts.

CHECKUP

1. What geographic features isolated sub-Saharan Africa?

2. What do we know of the cultural accomplishments of Zimbabwe? Nok? Mali? Benin?

3. IDENTIFY: Caucasoid, savannas, Mansa Musa.

4. LOCATE: Sahara, Sudan region, Congo River, Kalahari Desert, Niger River, Zambezi River, Cush, Aksum, Lake Chad, Timbuktu, Gao.

4 Russia, long part of the Mongol Empire, finally became independent

In a sense, one purpose of this chapter has been to fill in some of the "missing blanks" in your study of world history. You have just read about sub-Saharan Africa, a region which had not been previously discussed in this book. Another such area is the vast plains region that stretches across eastern Europe and central Asia.

This region extends southward from the Arctic Ocean and the Baltic Sea to the Black and Caspian seas, and eastward from the Carpathian Mountains in Europe to Manchuria in eastern Asia. It is divided north to south by the long range of the Ural Mountains. These mountains separate the continents of Europe and Asia. Because the two continents actually form one great land mass, they are sometimes referred to as Eurasia.

The European part of the vast plains region is generally known as eastern Europe. It is isolated by three mountain ranges—the Urals in the east, the Carpathians in the west, and the Caucasus in the south (see map, opposite). Much of eastern Europe consists of grassy plains called steppes, which roll on endlessly without trees as far as the eye can see. They are crisscrossed by a number of rivers which provide good transportation within the region. The Dvina and Vistula rivers flow into the Baltic Sea; the Dniester (DNYES·tur), the

Dnieper (DNYEH·pur), and the Don flow into the Black Sea; the Volga and Ural rivers flow into the Caspian Sea.

Early Russia

The southern part of eastern Europe has been inhabited since Neolithic times. Greek merchants traded with the peoples north of the Black Sea. Later the area was the scene of many migrations, often caused by barbarian invasions from Asia.

Beginning in the 200's, much of eastern Europe was settled by Slavs. Because they were peaceful and had only a loose political organization, they were often ruled by invaders, including the Huns, the Avars, and the Magyars.

During the 800's, new invaders came into eastern Europe. They were Vikings from Scandinavia, and they came more as traders than as conquerors. In the fall of the year they would sail up the rivers from the Baltic Sea and from Lake Ladoga

EARLY RUSSIA TO ABOUT 1200

Kievan Russia about 1000

→ Viking trade routes

0   500 miles

(see map, page 259). When winter came, they would put their ships on large sleds and haul them overland to one of the rivers that flowed into the Black Sea. In the spring, when the ice melted, they would sail southward to trade in the Black Sea region. They would return to their homeland by retracing their route. One tribe of Vikings that regularly traveled this route were called the Rus. It is probably from their name that the word *Russia* is derived.

The Kievan state. Several cities grew up along the Viking trade routes. One of them was Novgorod (Russian for "new city"), south of Lake Ladoga. Another was Kiev (kee·EV), on the Dnieper River. Kiev prospered because it was strategically located to control the rich trade route that extended from Constantinople and the Black Sea to the Baltic Sea and northern Europe.

In the 860's the Slavs of Novgorod were threatened by enemies and asked Rurik, a Viking, to help them. Soon he and his successors became rulers not only of Novgorod but also of a large region around it. Rurik founded a dynasty of princes who ruled several city-states. Since Kiev grew to be the most important of these, historians group them together under the name of Kievan Russia.

Kievan Russia developed links with Constantinople and the Byzantine Empire that greatly enriched Russian culture. As you have read, the Russians were converted to Orthodox Christianity beginning in the 900's by missionaries from Constantinople. Russian churches show the influence of Byzantine architecture.

In the early 1000's, Kiev was as strong and as wealthy as any Western European capital of the time. Its highest point came under Yaroslav I, called Yaroslav the Wise, who ruled from 1019 to 1054. During his reign the first Russian law code was compiled.

Over the next 250 years, Kiev declined in power and wealth. The rulers of Kiev gave their younger sons outlying towns to rule independently. These princes and their descendants fought among themselves and with the ruler of Kiev itself. Kiev's trade declined because of raids on southern Russia by the Pechenegs, an Asiatic tribe, and also

because Italians were developing new trade routes in the Mediterranean Sea.

A group of Russian princes eventually united in 1169 to capture and loot Kiev, ending its prosperity. As these princes fought among themselves, new invaders appeared to threaten Russia again. These were the Mongols from Asia.

The Mongol Empire

The Mongols came from the Asiatic part of the vast plains region that also included Russia. You have already read of other peoples who came from this region—the Huns, the Seljuk Turks, and the Ottoman Turks. But it was the Mongols (also known as Tartars or Tatars), who created one of the largest empires the world has ever known.

Nomads in Asia. The central Asian plain, as you recall, lies east of the Ural Mountains. Within this vast expanse are a few sharply defined mountain ranges and some rivers that provide good inland transportation—among them the Ob, the Yenisei, and the Irtysh. Most of the land, however, consists of deserts, semi-arid plateaus, and steppes.

The many peoples of this vast Asiatic region were nomads who lived by and for their animals—enormous flocks of sheep and goats, along with such work animals as camels, yaks, and horses. Each group guided and followed its animals back and forth in search of pasturage.

It was a difficult way of life, affording only a low standard of living. Occasionally a group of nomads would become envious of the great civilizations surrounding them and would set out to plunder. This might happen when a strong leader organized his own group into a fighting force and conquered neighboring tribes of the same racial group. With this start, the leader would then force every group for hundreds of miles around either to join him or move on. Usually they joined, and a large fighting force would then sweep forth to attack China, India, western Asia, or Europe.

These fighting forces were cavalry forces. The nomads' lives had made them magnificent horsemen. They invented such devices as horseshoes and stirrups. Traveling light and living off the land, they could move swiftly and defeat much larger forces by surprise. One group rode 270 miles through eastern Europe in three days. Their endurance and character had been formed during the burning summers and freezing winters of their homelands. They were strong, hardy, unafraid of death, pitiless in victory, and greedy for plunder.

Mongol conquests and Genghis Khan. One such group of nomads was the Mongols. Like other Asiatic nomads, they were hardy and excellent horsemen. In addition, they developed a corps of officers, drawn from the leader's personal bodyguard, who were trained to carry out orders intelligently and without hesitation. The Mongols also worked out an effective system of battle communication, using colored flags and lanterns, smoke signals, and fast-riding messengers. They sent master spies ahead of their armies to spread terror among their enemies with stories of their strength and ferocity. Finally, they learned how to organize, govern, and hold the lands they conquered.

From their homeland in what is now Mongolia, Mongols began raiding northern China in the 900's. Early in the 1200's, from their capital at Karakorum, they began their conquest first of northern and then of southern China, as you will read in the next chapter. Beginning in 1215, they launched an extraordinary career of conquest under Genghis Khan (JEN·giz KAHN), their greatest leader. (*Khan* means "ruler" or "emperor.") From China, Genghis Khan and his forces pushed thousands of miles westward across Asia, conquering everything in their path and raiding in India, western Asia, and eastern Europe.

Genghis Khan was illiterate but an able statesman, a brilliant organizer, and a great general. He planned well and on a large scale. He was merciless in victory as well as in battle. Believing he could never win loyalty from the peoples he conquered, he slaughtered many of them for the safety of his own rule.

When Genghis Khan died in 1227, his successors struck out in many directions. The empire they won (see map, page 274) was the largest the world had ever seen—larger even than the Roman Empire. As you will see, the Mongols es-

Genghis Khan and Ivan III

Genghis Khan, above, was originally called Temuchin. He took the name Genghis (meaning "perfect warrior") after several early conquests. He is said to have remained essentially a fierce, crude bandit chieftain all his life. Much more cautious in temperament was Ivan III of Russia, below. After he married the niece of the last Byzantine emperor, many Byzantine customs were introduced at the Russian court.

tablished strong rulers in China. One of their armies overran Persia and drove toward the Mediterranean Sea, where it was halted by Moslem troops from Egypt. Still another army conquered Russia and ruled it for centuries.

The Mongols in Russia

The Mongols first attacked Russia in force in 1237. Russian resistance was not strong enough to hold back the fierce onslaught, and all of Russia had fallen by 1240.

The Mongols who overran Russia belonged to a group known as the Golden Horde (so called because of the magnificence of their leader's camp). They pushed on across the Carpathian Mountains into Hungary and across the plains into Poland, defeating the Hungarian and Polish armies. Then the Mongol leader learned of the death of the khan who had succeeded Genghis. He rushed back to the Mongol capital in central Asia to use his influence in the choice of a successor. Although terribly damaged by war and savage plundering, Hungary and Poland were spared continuing Mongol rule. Russia, however, remained under the Mongols until the late 1400's.

The Mongols who ruled Russia were lenient. They were interested only in collecting tribute from the conquered people. As long as it was paid, they allowed the Russians to live under their own princes and keep their own religion and customs. The Mongols themselves grazed their flocks on the steppes north of the Caspian Sea and the Sea of Azov, where they had little contact with the great mass of the Russians. They established their capital at Sarai, on the lower Volga River, far from Kiev and Russia's other cities.

During the time of Mongol rule, the Russians were out of touch with Western Europe. Russian territory to the west was taken by Lithuania and Poland. In the late 1300's, these two nations united to form a kingdom that was usually unfriendly toward Russia. In addition to territorial rivalry, there was a religious conflict. The Poles had been converted to Roman Catholicism; the Russians clung to their Orthodox faith, which set them apart from both the Poles and the Mongols. The Russians grew more and more suspicious of Western Europeans and of Western influences.

While the Mongol Empire remained united, Russia did make contact with the civilizations of the Orient, however. Russians traveled the long overland trade route to China and brought back goods and ideas. Later, when the empire broke up into independent parts, trade with the Orient declined.

The rise of Moscow. Mongol rule grew weaker in time and Russian princes became more independent. They made themselves absolute rulers in their own regions. As trade declined, farmers and peasants became the only productive group in the country, supporting everyone else. The new rulers of Russia bound these workers to the land as serfs.

During the 1300's the city-state of Moscow became the strongest in Russia, partly because of its cooperation with the Mongols. They rewarded Prince Ivan I, who ruled from 1325 to 1341, with the title of Grand Prince of all Russia. His power was increased further when the chief patriarch of the Orthodox Church in Russia moved from Kiev to Moscow. By the time of Ivan III, Grand Prince from 1462 to 1505, Moscow was powerful enough to refuse to pay tribute to the Mongols. The Mongol yoke was thrown off in 1480. Ivan III united many other Russian territories and emerged as an autocratic ruler—the first ruler of an independent Russia.

CHECKUP

1. Where did the first strong government rise in Russia? What were its strengths? Why did it decline?

2. What was the usual pattern by which an Asiatic tribe became a great conquering force? Why were these peoples so feared as fighters?

3. How was Russia affected by the Byzantine Empire? by Mongol rule?

4. IDENTIFY: steppes, Rus, Yaroslav I, Pechenegs, Genghis Khan, Golden Horde, Ivan III.

5. LOCATE: Carpathian Mountains, Ural Mountains, Dvina River, Vistula River, Dniester River, Dnieper River, Don River, Volga River, Ural River, Lake Ladoga, Novgorod, Kiev, Sea of Azov, Sarai, Moscow.

CHAPTER REVIEW

Chapter 12   Beyond Europe's Borders, Several Nations Rose and Fell   (700 B.C.—1600 A.D.)

← B.C. | A.D. →

| 750 | 500 | 250 | | 250 | 500 | 750 | 1000 | 1250 | 1500 | 1750 | 2000 |

300's	Cush destroyed by Aksum	711	Moslem invasion of Spain	1237-1240	Mongol conquest of Russia
527-565	Rule of Emperor Justinian	800's	Sts. Cyril and Methodius	1307-1332	Rule of Mali by Mansa Musa
532-537	Building of Santa Sophia	1019-1054	Reign of Yaroslav I	1453	Fall of Byzantine Empire
570-632	Mohammed	1054	Final split between Roman and Orthodox Churches	1462-1505	Rule of Ivan III
622	The Hegira			1480	End of Mongol rule in Russia

CHAPTER SUMMARY

The Byzantine Empire, which grew out of the eastern Roman Empire, lasted for centuries because of its political strength, good military defenses, and a prosperous economy. The Eastern Orthodox Church was a source of both strength and weakness.

The Byzantines passed on classical learning and created original masterpieces, such as the church of Santa Sophia. Justinian's Code was probably the greatest Byzantine contribution. The Fourth Crusade and Turkish attacks weakened the empire, which came to an end when the Ottoman Turks captured Constantinople.

Another empire took shape in Arabia, where Mohammed united the Arabs around the new religion of Islam. Its followers, called Moslems, revere the Koran as their holy book.

The empire begun by Mohammed spread outward to include most of the Near East, North Africa, and Spain. Moslems were united economically and culturally. They excelled in science, medicine, and mathematics. However, Moslem culture declined after 1000; leadership of the empire passed from the Arabs to the Turks.

Africa below the Sahara was geographically isolated, and archeologists have only recently begun to piece together the story of its people. Early cultures in eastern Africa included Cush and Aksum, whose people probably traded with the Greeks. Remains at Zimbabwe, in the south, show that a highly organized government must have existed there. West African societies included the Nok culture and the kingdoms of Ghana, Mali, and Songhai.

Eastern Europe, settled by Slavs, was invaded by Vikings in the 800's. They dominated trade routes and built a strong state known as Kievan Russia. Kiev and the rest of Russia, however, fell to the Mongols in the 1200's. Unfriendly neighbors and religious conflicts isolated the Russians from Western Europe. In time, Mongol rule weakened, and independent Russia emerged in 1480.

QUESTIONS FOR DISCUSSION

1. What is the cyclic theory of history? Do you agree or disagree with it?

2. What did Jesus teach about war, and what did Mohammed teach about it? How is it that, although Jesus and Mohammed differed in their views, their followers in the Christian Crusades and in the Islamic wars of expansion engaged in essentially the same methods to spread their faith?

3. Do you think the Arabs were fair to the people they conquered by giving them three choices?

4. After about the year 1000, men who believed in "following the letter of the Koran"—who opposed free thought and shunned foreign ideas—came to power in the Moslem world. Why should this have been a factor in the decline of Moslem culture?

5. Kiev's trade declined when Italian ports developed new trade routes in the Mediterranean Sea. Since Kiev was hundreds of miles away from these ports, why should it have been affected by them?

PROJECTS

1. Write a short travel brochure for people living in medieval Europe advertising a journey to the Byzantine Empire.

2. Write an editorial for an American newspaper illustrating the abilities of Negroes by describing the accomplishments of early African cultures.

3. Make a chart showing the contributions and activities of the Byzantines, Moslems, and Mongols.

Civilizations in Asia and America Reached High Levels

A Mogul emperor, right, seated talking to a sage

If you had studied a course like the one you are now taking about thirty years ago, it would have been very different. One of the most important differences is that you would not have been studying "world" history.

Although the course might have been called "world history," it would have been chiefly a history of Western civilization. Your textbook would have begun with prehistoric times, dealt next with Egypt and the Fertile Crescent, gone then to Greece and Rome, and after that moved to the Middle Ages in Europe.

As the book continued down to the present day, it would have given much information about Europe and some about America, but hardly anything about the rest of the world. It would have slighted the Byzantines and Moslems. It would have almost ignored the nations of the Orient.

As you have learned, however, the Mediterranean area and Europe did not have a monopoly on culture. Civilization in India and China was developing at about the same time as it did in Egypt and the Fertile Crescent. And during the Middle Ages, people in Asia, Africa, and America developed ways of life which in many respects were more complex and more sophisticated than those of Europe.

If we are to understand what the world is like today, and why certain nations have taken certain positions in world affairs, we must always look at their past. Migrations, conquests, religious wars, times of peace and plenty, great men and women—all have shaped nations through the centuries. We cannot look at the events of the past few years and expect to understand them if we do not know what preceded them.

That is why world history today tries to tell much more than older histories did, discussing many nations and periods that they left untouched. Events in every part of the world are important. John Donne, an English poet, wrote: "No man is an island." That is, no one is separate from the world, or is unaffected by it. The more we know about why events take place, the more we will understand about their daily effect on us. These reasons are often to be found far back in a nation's history.

THE CHAPTER SECTIONS:

1. Moslem and Mogul rulers brought important changes to India (606–1658)
2. China maintained its age-old traditions and resisted innovation (589–1644)
3. Japan, influenced by China, gradually developed its own culture (100–1600)
4. In the Americas, Indians developed distinctive ways of life (500 B.C.–1550 A.D.)

1　Moslem and Mogul rulers brought important changes to India

Gupta rule in India came to an end in the 500's A.D., as you read in Chapter 9. At that time the Huns invaded through the northwestern mountain passes and conquered all of northern India. Disorder and confusion followed, until the reign of a ruler named Harsha.

Harsha's rule

By the early 600's, when the Huns had been overcome, three warring states controlled the Ganges Valley. In one of them, a leader named Harsha rose to power and built an effective army. When it was on the move, cavalry rode ahead of the infantry, which advanced with spears and large shields. Elephants wore armor plates.

Harsha came to power in 606, and in six years conquered what had been the Gupta Empire (see map, page 171). He failed when he tried to push through the hill country south of the Narbada River to conquer the Deccan. He then settled down to govern his empire in northern India, which for a long time he did wisely and well.

A Chinese Buddhist pilgrim to India, Hsuan Tsang (shu·AHN DZAHNG), wrote of the excellence of Harsha's early reign. The people were law-abiding, taxes were light, and living standards were high. Thousands of students studied grammar, philosophy, and science.

In the later years of his reign, Harsha listened to evil advisers and became cruel and suspicious. By 647 his rule had become so oppressive that his army assassinated him.

The Rajputs

After Harsha's death, northern India split up into numerous small states, ruled over by the Rajputs. (*Rajput* means "son of a king.") The Rajputs were descended from tribes that had migrated from central Asia into northern India during the 400's and 500's. Claiming divine origins, the Rajputs intermarried with Hindus, adopted the Hindu religion with its caste system, and took control of the small states.

Rajput rule was generally good. Literature of the time included codes of chivalry stressing respect for women, fair play in combat, and mercy for the fallen warrior. There were also well-developed law codes. Civil cases were decided on the evidence of sworn witnesses or written statements. A man's children inherited his property. His widow was entitled to support by her husband's family and was further protected by a dowry from her husband.

Northern Indians under the Rajputs took great pride in their land. One visitor wrote that Indians "believe that there is no country but theirs, no nation like theirs, no kings like theirs, no religions like theirs, no science like theirs."

265

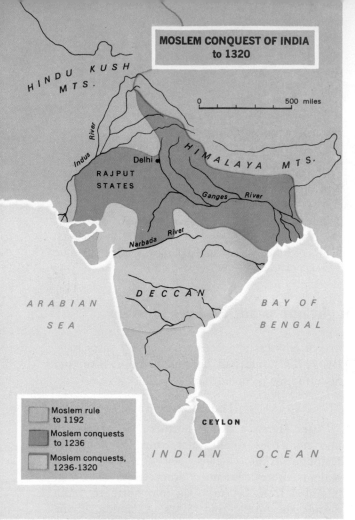

MOSLEM CONQUEST OF INDIA
to 1320

HINDU KUSH MTS.

Indus River

Delhi

RAJPUT STATES

HIMALAYA MTS.

Ganges River

Narbada River

ARABIAN SEA

DECCAN

BAY OF BENGAL

CEYLON

INDIAN OCEAN

0   500 miles

Moslem rule to 1192

Moslem conquests to 1236

Moslem conquests, 1236-1320

The economy of northern India was based, as it had long been and would long remain, on the small, self-sufficient, agricultural village. But overseas trade also flourished, especially among local nobles who set up trade monopolies that returned large profits. So things remained in northern India until about the year 1000.

Southern India

Southern India, as you have read, developed independently of northern India except for a short period in the 200's B.C., when most of it was part of Asoka's empire.

In the 600's A.D., a dynasty called the Chalukya held power in the Deccan. It was a Chalukya ruler, Pulakesin II, whose army bravely defeated

Harsha in 620 when Harsha tried to invade the Deccan. It is reported that Pulakesin gave wine to both troops and elephants on the eve of battle to make them warlike and ready for combat. Hsuan Tsang, the same Chinese pilgrim who visited Harsha, described Pulakesin II as a man of large and profound ideas, full of sympathy for his subjects.

Other dynasties ruled elsewhere in southern India along the east coast and in the southernmost region. All of these states of southern India were important and wealthy, mainly from trade. An Arab traveler of the 800's ranked a Deccan king with the caliph of Baghdad, the Byzantine emperor, and the emperor of China.

Moslems in India

Beginning in the 600's, you will recall, the Moslem followers of Mohammed began spreading out in several directions, inspired by zeal for the Islamic Holy War. In the early 700's, Indian pirates from the Indus Valley began attacking Moslem ships. About 712 the Moslems struck back by conquering the Indus Valley (see map, this page). They organized the valley as a Moslem province but gave the Indians considerable freedom. Moslem criminal law applied to everyone, but Indian civil cases were tried according to Indian law.

The Moslems made no further conquests in India for about 300 years. Meanwhile Turkish Moslems had occupied the area now called Afghanistan, northwest of the Indus River. About the year 1000, they began invading India through the northwest mountain passes. One by one they conquered the small states of the Rajput princes. In battle the Indians always outnumbered the Moslems, and made use of war elephants. However, the Moslems, adopting tactics originally worked out by Alexander the Great, used horsemen to turn the elephants back upon their own troops. In 1193 the Moslems occupied Delhi, and by 1236 they controlled all of northern India (see map, this page).

The Delhi sultans. One Moslem leader, Mohammed Ghori, conquered a large area of northern India. When he died in 1206, one of his lieutenants, formerly a slave, took over and founded a new line of rulers. Because they used Delhi as their capital, they are called the Delhi sultans. This dynasty lasted about 300 years. Many of its rulers were fanatical and cruel, but they did provide unity for northern India. Early in the 1300's, one of the Delhi sultans conquered the Deccan. By 1320, Indian resistance to the Moslems had collapsed throughout most of the subcontinent of India.

Two Delhi sultans represent the worst and the best of Moslem rule in India. Probably the worst was Mohammed Tughlak (tug·LAK), who ruled from 1325 to 1351. He murdered his father, and on one occasion fed the flesh of a rebel nephew to the rebel's wife and children. He once ordered the evacuation of Delhi in three days and a forced march of its inhabitants to a new capital 600 miles to the south.

Perhaps the best of the Delhi sultans was Firuz Shah, a social reformer and cultivated man, who reigned from 1351 to 1388. He laid out more than 2,000 gardens and built five large canals. He also set up an employment agency for young men and a marriage bureau for young women. The bureau not only found husbands for the young women, but also provided them with dowries for their marriages.

Tamerlane. When Firuz Shah died, the rule of the Delhi sultans was interrupted, first by civil wars and then by the devastating onslaught of the Mongol leader Tamerlane.

Tamerlane (Timur the Lame) claimed to be descended from Genghis Khan, and was as ferocious as his supposed ancestor. Following the usual pattern of Asiatic nomad fighters, he created an army and established his power in central Asia, with his capital at Samarkand. Then, about 1380, he began a career of conquest. After defeating the Golden Horde north of the Caspian Sea, he led his army southeastward into India (see map, this page).

Tamerlane captured Delhi in 1398 and slaughtered 100,000 of its inhabitants. When his campaign was over, he returned to Samarkand with all of the surviving artisans of Delhi. The city was left to die. Tamerlane reportedly said of the de-

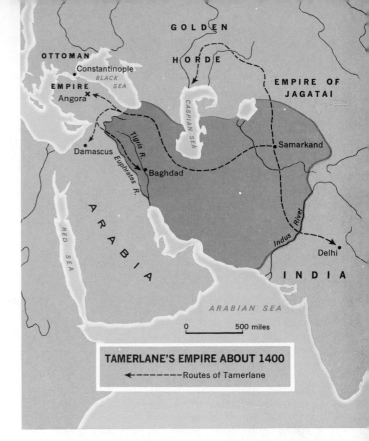

TAMERLANE'S EMPIRE ABOUT 1400
←-------Routes of Tamerlane

serted capital, "For two whole months, not a bird moved in the city." °

Tamerlane's successors in India ruled until 1450. At that time the Delhi sultans again gained power and maintained their Moslem rule until 1526.

Results of Moslem rule. The long period of Moslem rule in India, despite the interruption of Tamerlane and his Mongol successors, had important and lasting consequences in India. Most northern Indians and nearly all southern Indians were Hindus. At first the Moslems carried out ruthless, wholesale slaughter of Hindus. Later they were content to confiscate land, leaving vil-

° After returning to Samarkand, Tamerlane moved westward again. He captured and looted Baghdad and Damascus and massacred their inhabitants. His forces defeated the Ottoman Turks in a great battle at Angora (modern Ankara) in Asia Minor, capturing the sultan. The Turks at the time were menacing what was left of the Byzantine Empire, and their defeat at the hands of the Mongols saved Constantinople for another fifty years. Tamerlane was planning a campaign against China when he died in 1405.

267

Moslems in India had a lasting influence on the country. Their most violent impact came with the invasion of Tamerlane, above. The ferocious Mongol leader marched into India on the pretext that the Delhi sultans—fellow Moslems—were showing too much toleration toward their Hindu subjects. Over a hundred years passed before the city of Delhi had recovered from Tamerlane's onslaught. Far more peaceful and beneficial were the Moguls, whose empire began with Baber, shown at right as a young man. Under Mogul rule, so-called Koran schools flourished. In the one shown below, a bearded mullah, seated at left, instructs his pupils in the principles of Islam.

lage life to go on about as it had for so long. Even so, many Hindus were converted to Islam, either to gain favor with the conquerors or to escape from the Hindu caste system.

Moslem and Hindu religious differences were profound. Hindu worship of many gods and of idols repelled the Moslems, and the Hindu caste system contradicted Moslem belief in the equality of all men. Moslems introduced the seclusion of women, called *purdah,* into India. They also introduced the harem of several wives, which Hindus disliked. The cows so sacred to the Hindus were eaten by the Moslems, while Hindu fermented beverages were rejected by Moslems. Hindus used music in their religious ceremonies; Moslems did not.

The Moslems made several positive contributions to Indian life. They introduced a new and important language, Urdu, which combines Persian and Arabic words with Hindu grammar. Indian architects learned from the Moslems how to build the dome and the arch. From China the Moslems imported paper, gunpowder, and the art of making porcelain. Perhaps most important, Moslem influence made Hinduism more democratic and more open to reform.

The Mogul Empire

As the Delhi sultanate drew to a close, Rajput princes began struggling for control of India. Thus, as in the time of Tamerlane, India lay open to Mongol attack. It came under the leadership of the youthful and talented "Baber the Tiger," a descendant of Tamerlane. He captured Delhi with a small force in 1526 and brought the Rajput princes under his control. He then set up the Mogul Empire (see map, this page), which he and his successors held until 1761. ("Mogul" is a form of the word *Mongol*.)

Baber died in 1530 but was succeeded by a series of energetic and talented rulers. They finally brought most of southern India, as well as northern India, under their control. After Tamerlane, Indians had reason to fear Mongol rulers, but instead the Moguls fostered unity, orderly government, and culture.

The rule of the Mogul emperor Shah Jehan,

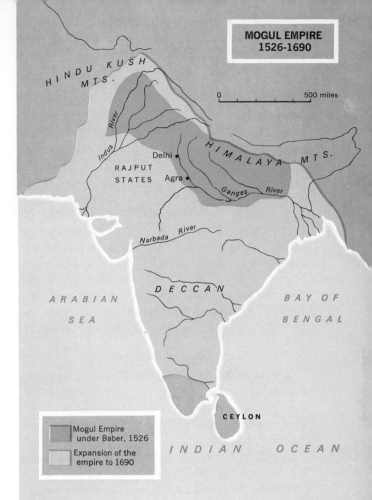

MOGUL EMPIRE 1526-1690

Mogul Empire under Baber, 1526

Expansion of the empire to 1690

from 1628 to 1658, was outstanding. He is best remembered for two famous buildings that he ordered built, the magnificent Taj Mahal at Agra and the Hall of Private Audience in the Red Fort at Delhi. The Taj Mahal was a tomb for the ruler and his wife. In the cornices of the Hall of Private Audience are carved these famous lines:

If on earth be an Eden of Bliss,
It is this, it is this, it is this.

These great buildings of marble, studded with semiprecious stones, were enormously expensive. Their cost was a grinding tax burden on Shah Jehan's subjects. It took 22,000 workmen twenty-two years to finish the Taj Mahal.

For all its brilliance, Indian civilization under the Mogul emperors was largely a copy of Moslem culture in the Near East. The Moguls, as aliens in a strange land, were never confident enough to create an original culture of their own.

CHECKUP

1. Name some good features of Rajput rule.

2. How were both Turkish Moslems and Mongols able to conquer India?

3. Contrast the reigns of Mohammed Tughlak and Firuz Shah.

4. What religious differences between Moslems and Hindus led to antagonism? What positive contributions did the Moslems make to Indian life?

5. IDENTIFY: Harsha, Hsuan Tsang, Chalukya, Pulakesin II, Tamerlane, Baber, Shah Jehan.

6. LOCATE: Delhi, Samarkand, Angora, Agra.

 ## 2 China maintained its age-old traditions and resisted innovation

When you last read about China, it was undergoing the troubled period of the Six Dynasties, beginning in the 300's A.D., when Huns controlled northern China. Although the country was divided for over 250 years, it was able to survive as a nation and eventually surpass its earlier greatness.

The Sui dynasty

The work of driving out the Huns and reuniting China was accomplished by the short-lived Sui dynasty. Yang Chien, a Chinese official of the Hun government in northern China, despised his masters and succeeded in overthrowing them. He then reunited northern and southern China under the Sui dynasty, which he founded in 589.

During this period the Grand Canal was formed from existing waterways between the Yellow and Yangtze rivers and was extended to link northern and southern China.° But the Sui dynasty was overambitious and unskilled in administration. The rulers tried unsuccessfully to conquer southern Manchuria and northern Korea. Yang Chien's successor wasted government money and suffered a defeat from invading Turks. He then fled to southern China, where he was assassinated.

The Tang dynasty

The uprising against the Sui dynasty was led by Li Yüan, who established the Tang dynasty in 618. The early Tang rulers defeated the invading Turks to the north and west and extended

---

° The Grand Canal, like the Great Wall, suffered from lack of repair over the centuries and much of it fell into disuse. During the Ming dynasty the canal underwent improvements and was repaired.

the frontiers of China farther west than ever before (see map, opposite). Tang rulers made contact with India and the Moslem Empire, and Chinese ideas greatly influenced China's eastern neighbors, Korea and Japan. The Tang capital, Changan, became a center of culture where people from many parts of the world lived side by side.

Like the Han dynasty centuries earlier, the Tang gave China a golden age. Although the Tang dynasty itself lasted only until 906, it began a thousand-year period during which China was the most powerful, most sophisticated, and wealthiest country in the world.

Under the Tang rule the Chinese perfected their civil service system. Examinations covering current politics, classical literature, calligraphy, and mathematics were conducted by the Ministry of Rites in an elaborate series of rituals.

The Tang dynasty was known for its poetry. Later Chinese anthologies itemize more than 2,300 Tang poets and 48,900 poems. Two men of the 700's, although opposites in personality, symbolize the best of Tang poetry. Li Po, at one time a Taoist priest, was a pleasure lover and a favorite of the court. His writings happily, lightly, and often elegantly described the delights of wine and poetry. According to legend, Li Po became tipsy and drowned while reaching from a boat for his reflection in the moonlit waters.

Tu Fu, on the other hand, was a serious, even solemn, man and a devout follower of Confucius. His carefully written lyrics showed his deep interest in the suffering and tragedy of man's lot.

In China, you will recall, there were three religious traditions: Confucianism, Taoism, and

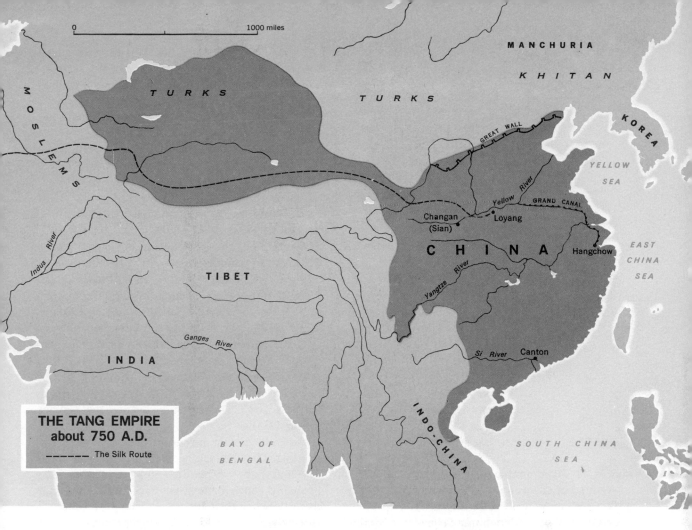

THE TANG EMPIRE
about 750 A.D.

-------- The Silk Route

Buddhism. Buddhism reached its highest point in China about 700. The most famous Chinese version of Buddhism is known by its Japanese name, Zen. Zen Buddhism stressed meditation and enlightenment and was similar to Taoism.

In the middle 800's, a half-mad Tang emperor began to persecute Buddhists. He destroyed 40,-000 shrines and 4,600 monasteries, and returned 260,000 monks and nuns to ordinary life. Buddhism in China never recovered from this blow.

The Tang dynasty reached its height about 750 and then gradually declined under weak emperors. By 900, Tang rulers had lost their power. Tax revenues had diminished, barbarians were invading, and provincial governors were challenging the royal power. Finally, in 906, the last Tang emperor, a child, was deposed and murdered.

The Sung dynasty

Tang rule was followed by over fifty years of disunity and civil war. Order was finally restored in 960, when Chao K'uang-yin established the Sung dynasty. It inherited the same difficulties that had beset the Tang, among them barbarian invasion and civil wars. It also faced a new economic problem.

By the mid-900's, the principal barbarian pressure came from the north, from a Mongolian people called the Khitan. They had occupied Chinese territory in southern Manchuria and in time invaded as far south as the Yellow River. When they threatened the Sung capital at Kaifeng, the Sung emperors decided to buy peace with the Khitan by paying them annual tributes. By 1042, these tributes cost the Sung more than 200,000

271

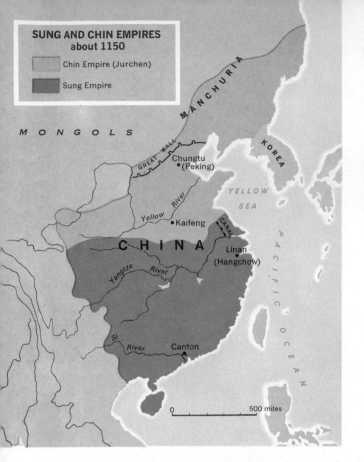

SUNG AND CHIN EMPIRES
about 1150

Chin Empire (Jurchen)

Sung Empire

ton. A thriving caravan trade also brought goods in from central Asia and India, including incense, rhinoceros horn, ivory, coral, amber, rock crystal, pearls, tortoise shell, ebony, and steel.

A Chinese customs list of the year 999 shows exports of gold, silver, and copper "cash" (a small coin). It also lists porcelain, which, from this period on, was one of China's most valued manufactures. Porcelain, a fine, translucent pottery, was probably first made during the Tang dynasty. Sung craftsmen perfected the art, creating eggshell-thin vases of incredible delicacy.

Another art perfected during the Sung dynasty was that of landscape painting. Inspired partly by the Taoist love of nature, Sung artists painted scenes of majestic grandeur, with jagged mountain peaks rising over misty hills and rushing torrents. Many of these landscapes were painted on silk.

Great inventions. The Chinese invented gunpowder during the Tang dynasty but used it at that time only for firecrackers. They first used it in warfare during the Sung dynasty—perhaps as early as 1043, and certainly against the Jurchen in the 1100's.

An even greater invention of the Chinese was printing. They had learned very early how to make ink and paper. The first step toward printing probably came in the year 175, during the Han dynasty, when the Chinese classics were carved in stone. Artisans could copy these writings by carefully fitting damp paper over the stone inscription and patting the flat surface with soot. The result was a white-on-black picture of the original.

The next step probably came with seals of metal or wood on which an inscription was carved in reverse. Imprints from these seals could be read in correct order. By the 600's, such seals had become quite large and were similar to today's block prints.

The oldest printed book is the *Diamond Sutra,* a Buddhist religious text. It was printed in China in 868, during the Tang dynasty. It was made in the form of a roll of six sheets of paper pasted together. Carved blocks were used to print the words on the roll. The same method was used to print the Chinese classics.

Movable type, by which separate characters

ounces of silver annually, a tremendous burden.

Another menace to the Sung appeared in the 1100's, when a new barbarian people, the Jurchen, moved into Manchuria behind the Khitan. The Sung then devised what they thought was a good plan for the destruction of the Khitan. They would enter into an alliance with the Jurchen and together defeat the Khitan. The plan worked but it had a flaw. After the Khitan were defeated, the Jurchen moved in and took over northern China. China was again divided. The Jurchen established the Chin dynasty in the north, with its capital at Peking, while the Sung dynasty ruled in the south from Hangchow (see map, this page). So matters stood from 1127 until the mid-1200's.

Sung civilization. Despite the problems of the Sung emperors, Chinese civilization remained at a high level under the Sung. Foreign trade expanded, aiding the hard-pressed economy. Overseas commerce centered on Hangchow and Can-

The Achievements of China

The inventiveness and creativity of the Chinese have been evidenced in many fields. For centuries they were unsurpassed in the making of silk. The painting above (a Sung copy of a Tang work) shows women preparing the fabric. Both paper and printing originated with the Chinese. A portion of the oldest printed book, the *Diamond Sutra*, is unrolled below.

Painting was among the most outstanding of all Chinese arts. The Ming scroll at left, "The Poet Lin P'u Wandering in the Moonlight," continues the great tradition of landscape painting established in the Sung dynasty. To the Chinese, natural settings had moral and philosophical meanings that were often related to the teachings of Confucius or Lao-tzu. "Indeed," one painter wrote, "the pine trees of the forest are like the moral character of virtuous men."

273

can be rearranged to make different words, apparently came into China from Korea about 1030. The characters were made of wood, porcelain, or copper. This technique did not become common in China, however. Since there are so many characters in the Chinese language, printers would have had to make about 40,000 separate movable blocks to represent every character. For this reason the Chinese preferred blocks carved with a page of text.

China under the Mongols

In the 1100's, you will recall, the Sung emperors lost northern China to the Jurchen, who established the Chin dynasty there. In the early 1200's, Mongols under Genghis Khan swept westward from Karakorum to conquer much of the known world. Genghis Khan returned to the east, but died in 1227 before he could continue his conquests. His successors pushed southward into China, defeating the Chin in 1234. In 1260, Kublai Khan, grandson of Genghis Khan, established the Yüan dynasty and set up his capital at Peking. In 1279 the last Sung ruler in southern China was killed, and the Mongols became rulers of all China.

It was about Kublai Khan and his summer palace at Shangtu, north of Peking, that the English poet Samuel Taylor Coleridge wrote a famous poem which begins with these lines:

THE MONGOL EMPIRE IN 1294

—————▶ Routes of Marco Polo, 1271-1295

0   1000 miles

In Xanadu did Kubla Khan
A stately pleasure-dome decree,
Where Alph, the sacred river, ran
Through caverns measureless to man
Down to a sunless sea.

At the height of his power, Kublai Khan ruled an empire that included not only China but also central Asia, Persia, and Russia—the largest empire the world had ever known (see map, opposite). Although he was recognized as the head of the whole Mongol Empire, it was actually divided into four parts: the Empire of the Great Khan, which included China; the Empire of Jagatai; the Ilkhan Empire; and the Empire of Kipchak, or the Golden Horde.

Under Mongol rule, China made notable progress. To help bind his great empire together, Genghis Khan linked China to Persia and India by post roads. In China itself he built the first imperial highway in 1219. One stone-surfaced road ran parallel with the Grand Canal for 1,100 miles between Hangchow and Peking. A messenger could cover this distance in forty days. At intervals along the road were post houses offering shelter, supplies, and protection.

Contacts with foreigners. During Mongol rule, Europeans and Chinese came to know one another better than ever before. Among Europeans living in China were Russian artisans and soldiers captured by the Golden Horde, a Parisian goldsmith kidnaped in what is now Yugoslavia, and the nephew of a Norman bishop.

King Louis IX of France and the pope in Rome sent ambassadors to China during the 1200's. Christian missionaries also made the trip. One built a chapel and trained 150 Chinese choir boys to sing the Gregorian chant, a form of Western church music pleasing to the Chinese ear. Another missionary gave Europe its first report of the bound feet of Chinese women, the long fingernails of Chinese gentlemen, and fishing by means of tethered birds.

Marco Polo, of whom you will read later, was the most famous of all European travelers in China. He had a counterpart in Rabban Sauma of Peking. In the 1280's, Rabban Sauma traveled

CHINESE DYNASTIES 589 — 1644	
589-618	Sui dynasty
618-906	Tang dynasty
906-960	Disunity and civil war
960-1279	Sung dynasty (after 1127, in southern China only)
1127-1234	Chin dynasty (northern China)
1260-1368	Yüan dynasty
1368-1644	Ming dynasty

across Asia to Persia, then to Constantinople, and eventually to Italy, where he talked with the pope. He also went to France, where he met Philip IV and visited the University of Paris.

Chinese-Mongol differences. Despite the benefits that the Yüan dynasty brought to China, the natural antagonism between the conquerors and the conquered was increased by striking differences between Mongol and Chinese ways of living. Their languages differed. The Chinese disliked the unsavory smell of the invaders, who did not often wash, and objected to the freedom Mongol women were allowed. They disagreed about foods, too, but the Chinese did welcome the art of distilling liquors, an art which they learned from the Mongols.

When Kublai Khan died in 1294, he left China to weak and unworthy successors. Seven Mongol emperors ruled China in the next twenty-six years. The country's finances were undermined. Famine, which depleted government granaries, resulted from floods along the Yellow River.° Numerous secret societies promoted revolt, among them the White Lotus Society, which later became notorious in China's history. Finally, in 1368, the last Mongol emperor was overthrown and the Yüan dynasty came to an end.

The Ming dynasty

The rebellion against the Yüan dynasty was led by Chu Yüan-chang, a former Buddhist monk, who

° **Yellow River:** The lower course of the Yellow River, as you have read, changed many times over the centuries. Beginning about 1200, the river flowed into the Yellow Sea about 250 miles south of its former mouth.

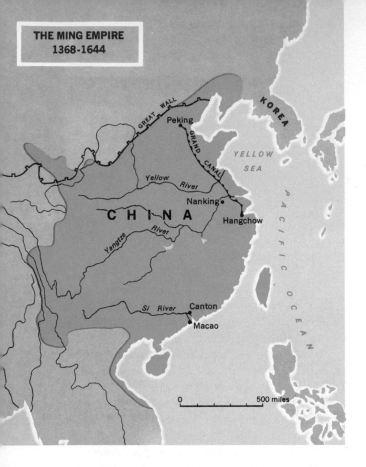

THE MING EMPIRE
1368-1644

The Ming dynasty lasted for almost 300 years, until 1644. During the early Ming period, China exerted influence abroad. You will recall that Indian traders had been traveling to Southeast Asia and to islands in the Pacific Ocean for a long time. Now China sent naval expeditions to some of these same places, including what are now South Vietnam, Cambodia, Thailand, and Indonesia. In these areas, China's influence was secondary to India's. In Japan, as you will see, China's influence was primary and overwhelming.

In the mid-1400's, these foreign expeditions ended as suddenly as they had begun. China withdrew from the world and came to hate foreigners. The Chinese felt that they had achieved the good life and did not need to seek elsewhere for it. China thus achieved a stable society, but at the cost of what we might call "backwardness."

CHECKUP

1. What dynasty was established by each of the following, and when: Yang Chien? Li Yüan? Chao K'uang-yin? Chu Yüan-chang?

2. What were some of the good features of Mongol rule in China? What were some customs of the Mongols that made them unpopular with the Chinese?

3. What were the most outstanding features of the Tang, the Sung, and the Ming dynasties?

4. IDENTIFY: Li Po, Tu Fu, Zen, Khitan, Jurchen, *Diamond Sutra*, Rabban Sauma, White Lotus Society.

5. LOCATE: Grand Canal, Peking, Hangchow, Karakorum, Shangtu, Nanking.

founded the Ming dynasty (see map, this page). From his capital at Nanking, the new emperor re-established order in China and suppressed all secret societies. He restored scholar-administrators—whom the Mongols had not used—to the civil service and issued a new code of law called the Code of Great Ming. All power was concentrated in the hands of the emperor.

3 Japan, influenced by China, gradually developed its own culture

Japan is an archipelago, or island chain, in the Pacific Ocean off the northeast coast of Asia. Although there are numerous small islands, most of Japan's large population lives on the four main islands of Honshu, Kyushu, Shikoku, and Hokkaido (see map, opposite page).

All of Japan is mountainous and only about one sixth of the land can be cultivated. The cultivated land, however, is among the most productive in the world, thanks to abundant rainfall, plentiful sunlight, long growing seasons, and the diligence of Japanese farmers. The plentiful water supply provides easy irrigation and, in modern times, a source of electric power. The rains also encourage a large timber supply. But nature is not wholly kind to Japan. Earthquakes, tidal waves, and typhoons often strike the islands, causing extensive damage.

Japan's beginnings

The people of Japan migrated to the islands from the Asian mainland. The two oldest and most fundamental characteristics of their society have been the Shinto religion and a deep reverence for their emperor.

Shinto, an ancient religion, is similar to the religion practiced by certain nomadic tribes in eastern Russia today. Shinto means "the way of the gods." It is animistic, teaching that spirits inhabit such inanimate objects as sand, waterfalls, great trees, and irregular stones. It is also polytheistic, recognizing a number of gods called Kami, which means "superior." The Kami are generally helpful, especially in promoting fertility in families and crops. From one viewpoint, Shinto is not so much a religion as a set of prayers and rituals to satisfy the Kami. The chief Shinto virtue is ceremonial cleanliness, rather than ethical good, which is valued by many other religions.

Reverence and respect for the emperor is even stronger than Shinto as a foundation for Japanese life. According to tradition, Jimmu, the first emperor, was crowned on February 11, 660 B.C. However, this date may have been chosen in 601 A.D. by counting back 1260 years, a period of time that the Japanese borrowed from the Chinese as representing a major historical cycle. Japanese emperors claimed divine descent from the sun goddess, a belief that was not officially denied until after World War II. The Japanese have had only one imperial family in their entire history, making it the longest unbroken dynasty in the history of the world.

Early history of Japan

Early records of Japanese history are scanty. It is known that the Chinese, from an outpost in Korea, knew the Japanese at first hand before 100 A.D. The Chinese described the Japanese at that time as a polygamous people who tattooed their faces, drank heavily, and wore one-piece garments. At that time they did not have oxen or horses.

Chinese writing was introduced into Japan from Korea about 405, and was adopted by the Japanese to write their own language. Another

JAPAN ABOUT 1600
0   300 miles

Chinese influence came in about 550 when a Buddhist monk carried Buddhism to Japan. Up to that time the Japanese had had no experience with a religion that promised future life, and were disturbed by the idea. The first statue of Buddha sent to Japan was tossed into a canal when an epidemic broke out. In time, however, Buddhism was blended into Japanese life.

Japanese adoption of Chinese writing and Buddhism led to the adoption of other Chinese ideas and ways of life. Among these were artistic designs, road engineering, medical knowledge, weights and measures, clothing, and furniture. Chinese ideas about ancestor worship and family feeling came naturally to the Japanese because of their reverence toward the emperor and toward his family.

The Japanese sent their first envoys to China in 607. Japanese students returning from China in the 640's realized that Japan was inferior in various ways and worked to promote further adoption of Chinese culture in Japan.

277

Feudal Japan was dominated by powerful families and by respect for the emperor. An illustration from *The Tale of Genji*, above, depicts the emperor and a companion playing the Japanese board game called *go*. Behind the screen are women of the court. At left, an aristocratic lady holds Buddhist prayer beads while chanting prayers. In his formal robes the first shogun, below, looks every inch the vigorous and power-hungry general he was.

Early Japanese society was based on clans. The heads of the clans formed an aristocracy. In 645, an edict called the Great Reform destroyed this clan system. It proclaimed that the emperor had absolute power and that he owned all Japanese land.

In 702, the Great Treasure, a law code modeled on one from the Tang dynasty in China, was issued by the emperor. The code regulated all aspects of Japanese life: landholding, taxes, defense, religious services, marriage, and funerals. The code stressed the allegiance of all subjects to the emperor and insisted that no sacrifice was too great for a Japanese to make for his emperor. This obligation of the Japanese toward their emperors remained strong.

During this period of strong emperors, the Japanese built two capital cities. The first, at Nara, was an almost exact duplicate of the Tang Chinese capital at Changan. Later, in 794, the Japanese built a new capital at Kyoto.

Feudal Japan

To support the emperor's power, the Japanese tried, but failed, to develop a civil service system similar to that of the Chinese. Instead, beginning in the 800's, the Japanese developed a system that resembled European feudalism in some ways.

This system had two conflicting power structures. One was an indirect form of central government under which an important family exercised power in the name of the emperor. The other Japanese power structure, outside the control of the central government, consisted of military units which exercised authority over the territories they occupied. These units were not unlike the warrior forces maintained by semi-independent nobles in medieval Europe. The two conflicting systems of power prevailed in Japan until 1603.

Central government. The first family to gain control over the emperor and to use his power to their advantage were the Fujiwara. By holding important government offices and by intermarrying with the emperor's family, the Fujiwara held control of the central government from the early 800's to the mid-1100's. After a power struggle, the Minamoto family finally won control in 1185 and held the central power until 1338. The Minamoto, in 1192, introduced a new kind of official, the shogun. He was seemingly the chief officer of the emperor and was always careful to be dutiful to him. In fact, he was the agent of the Minamoto and of the powerful families that succeeded them. From this time, indeed, the major aim of an ambitious family was to gain control of the shogunate (the office of shogun).

The shogun was not only the chief military officer of the central government; he also controlled finance, law, the courts, and appointments to office. He often exercised these powers of government from his military headquarters at Kamakura. In 1338 the Ashikaga family took over the shogunate from the Minamoto. They controlled the office for over 200 years.

Local military rule. The leading families, such as the Minamoto, and their shoguns were strong, but not strong enough to exert their power at local levels. There, military units were led by warrior-landlords called samurai. The power of a samurai rested in part on his control of land, in part on descent from earlier clan chieftains, and in part on his ability with the sword. This relationship of landholding to political power resembled European feudalism. The samurai themselves resembled the knights of medieval Europe, for they had a code of honor called bushido that stressed bravery, loyalty, politeness, and honor.

The samurai developed an order of preference among themselves. At the top were the daimio (Japanese for "great names"), who gained the loyalty of the lesser samurai. As the power of the daimio increased and they became like petty kings, the samurai lost power and prestige.

Independence from China. After the initial impact of Chinese culture, in the 1200's the Japanese began a period of independence from Chinese and other foreign influences. In the first place, the Chinese were so busy fighting off the Mongols that they were unable to follow up their advantage in Japan. In the second place, the seas surrounding Japan shielded the islands from all but the most powerful forces.

Even the Mongols under Kublai Khan were unable to conquer Japan, although they tried several

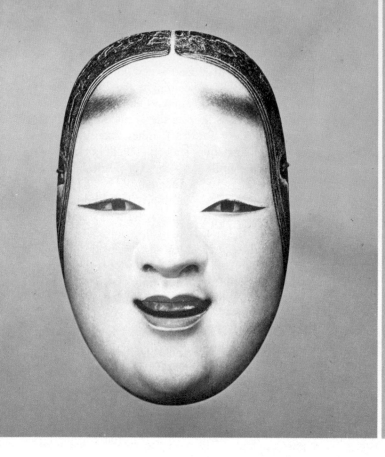

Japanese No Mask

No plays are a kind of Japanese morality drama. Still performed today, they were first introduced during the Ashikaga period as a way of teaching the Zen sect of Buddhism. Zen advocates strict individual discipline, concentration, self-control, and self-reliance. The *no* plays depict these qualities in slow-moving, dignified dramas. A chorus tells much of the story, chanting to music while the actors dance and use pantomime. Every word and gesture must conform to a formal set of rules.

There are very few characters in *no* drama. Masks, like the one at left, are used to represent imaginary animals, supernatural beings, and male and female characters of different ages and conditions. The cheerful, serene mask of a woman pictured here dates from the 1400's. It was carved in wood, painted, and lacquered.

times. Once, in 1281, a Chinese-Mongol fleet of 3,500 ships carrying 100,000 soldiers assembled to invade Japan but was dispersed by the "Great Wind" which the Japanese call the Kamikaze. It was a typhoon of extraordinary power.

The decline of feudalism

While the Ashikaga family held the central power in Japan, Japanese feudalism was weakened by a series of wars among the more influential daimio. These wars reduced the number of the daimio and their followers. During the disorders, robbery became common.

From the struggle among the daimio, Oda Nobunaga emerged victorious. By conquest and intermarriages, he so greatly increased his power that he was able to end the Ashikaga shogunate in 1573 and set up a military dictatorship. Nobunaga put down robbery and piracy and reduced the power of the peasant-soldiers by disarming them.

Nobunaga was ambitious to build an empire. Korea was first on his list of conquests; China was to follow. He died, however, before he could launch his plans. The plan was inherited by his best general, who invaded Korea with 160,000 men in 1592. The Japanese armies landed in Korea, fanned out northward, and were at first successful. However, the Korean navy sank Japanese ships carrying troop reinforcements, and a Chinese army pushed the invaders back to the coast of Korea. Eventually the Japanese withdrew to their homeland.

In the late 1500's and early 1600's, a member of the Tokugawa family introduced significant changes in Japan by uniting the power of the shogunate and the power of the leading daimio. Tokugawa control began in 1603. To control the lesser daimio, tax assessments were levied against them to provide relief after earthquakes and volcanic eruptions, and to build temples and forts. The lesser daimio also had to spend half of their

280

time at the Tokugawa capital at Yedo (later re-named Tokyo) and to leave their families there as hostages when they were away.

Thus the shogun finally gained control over the daimio, and Japan for the first time attained political unity. The Tokugawa family controlled the shogunate until 1867, when the office was abolished.

The Tokugawa family, like the Ming dynasty in China, adopted a policy of isolation after Japan's misadventures in Korea and Manchuria. Thus Japan, like China, stood aside from powerful forces that began to transform the world during the 1500's and 1600's.

A stable society

During its feudal period, Japanese society was organized according to standards that had been adapted from the writings of Confucius. In spite of political changes, Japan maintained a fairly stable society for centuries.

Japanese traditions included what to Western eyes seem to be extremes of barbarism and refinement. At one extreme was the custom of seppuku (commonly called hara-kiri, or "belly-slitting"). This form of ceremonial suicide, practiced mainly by the samurai, was an honorable way to avoid torture, execution, or defeat in battle.

At the other extreme was the sophisticated elegance of the tea ceremony. This ritual grew out of Zen Buddhism during the Ashikaga period. There were fixed rules for every stage of preparing and drinking the tea.

The elegance of imperial society was vividly portrayed by Lady Murasaki Shikibu in one of the greatest works in Japanese literature, *The Tale of Genji*. This long novel, written in the 1000's, tells the story of Prince Genji, the perfect courtier. It is written in a quiet, sensitive style and involves 30 main characters and over 300 minor ones.

Another indication of Japanese sophistication were the *no* plays. These were dance dramas and were first performed in the 1300's. The subjects were usually religious. Like Greek plays, *no* dramas were performed on a bare stage by actors in masks.

The stability of family life and social structures in Japan and China no doubt had much to do with the decision of these great civilizations to retire into isolation in the 1500's and 1600's. Their decision to do so, as you will see, had important consequences not only for them but for most of the world.

CHECKUP

1. What are the favorable and unfavorable features of Japanese geography?
2. Describe the chief characteristics of Shinto. What teaching of Buddhism was disturbing to the Japanese?
3. What were the major contributions and influences of China upon Japan?
4. When did Japanese feudalism develop? What were its chief features? How was it weakened and when did it end?
5. IDENTIFY: Kami, Jimmu, Great Reform, Great Treasure, Fujiwara, shogun, samurai, bushido, seppuku, *no* plays.
6. LOCATE: Honshu, Kyushu, Shikoku, Hokkaido, Nara, Kyoto, Yedo.

4 In the Americas, Indians developed distinctive ways of life

From the beginning of history until about 500 years ago, the two great divisions of the world—the Eastern and Western Hemispheres—knew little of each other. Even during the medieval period in Europe, when there was little trade, knowledge about India and China was not wholly lost. But neither Europe nor Asia knew much about the vast continents of North and South America.

Some Chinese missionaries may have reached Central America in the 400's. Daring Viking explorers landed on the coast of North America at several places around the year 1000. But accounts of their explorations were not generally circulated, so their voyages were not followed up by others. Many old maps showed a vast blank space where the Western Hemisphere lay. Actually that space was occupied by several different cultures, many of which developed to high levels.

The great migrations

While the Ice Age still gripped the earth, people migrated from Asia to the Americas across what is now the Bering Strait, off the coast of Alaska (see map, page 7). This strait is the narrowest point between the continents of Asia and North America, and at several periods in the past, there was a bridge of land there. Even when there was a water barrier, it was only a few miles across and could easily have been crossed by small boats.

There was neither a single large migration nor a continuous flow of people from Asia. Rather, there was a series of waves of different peoples on the march. Changes in the climate in Asia may, from time to time, have forced people northeastward and across the strait. From there they would move southward toward warmer climates. Finding some areas already inhabited by those who had come earlier, they would move on, looking for a favorable place to settle. All the migrants (except for the Eskimos, who came last of all) are called Indians.

This process of migration took thousands of years. The remains of some of the early people have been found and studied. Archeologists have found remains in western North America that may date back to around 30,000 years ago. The people were hunters who lived in caves and hunted the giant bison, or buffalo.

Some Indians moved into the eastern and central areas of North America. Others drifted farther south, through Mexico and Central America and across the narrow land bridge of the Isthmus of Panama. From there all South America was spread out before them.

About 14,000 years ago, some groups moved eastward into what is now Venezuela. However, the rain forests of the Amazon River basin made it difficult for people to penetrate farther into the eastern bulge of South America. Instead, they kept to the western shoreline, pushing ever southward. Some groups settled in the Andes Mountains. Others kept moving until they could go no farther. They settled at Tierra del Fuego on the southern tip of South America. Survival there, in the extremely cold climate, was difficult.

From Alaska to Tierra del Fuego, the Western Hemisphere was peopled by about 500 B.C. The process had taken thousands of years. Although many Indian tribes never progressed beyond a Stone Age culture, some developed civilizations.

The Mayas

One group of Indians settled on the Yucatán peninsula and nearby areas of Central America (see map, opposite). These people, known as the Mayas, arrived in the area considerably before 1000 B.C., but their history for many centuries can only be guessed at. Sometime before 300 B.C., they began to construct groups of buildings which, while often thought of as cities, were actually religious centers. The people lived in agricultural communities outside these centers.

The Maya economy was based on agriculture. As with so many farming peoples, the need for accurate dates for planting seems to have led the Mayas to develop a reliable calendar. Independently of any outside influence, the Mayas also developed a sophisticated system of mathematics which included the concept of zero. They evolved a system of writing which included both ideograms and phonograms. They used these in writing books on bark or cactus fiber and in carving stone pillars commemorating important events in Maya history.

In contrast to some of their neighbors, the Mayas were a peaceful people who worshiped peaceful gods. Sometimes in periods of crisis, such as droughts, they would offer human sacrifices, but this was not an important part of their religion.

About 800 A.D. the outlying regions of the Maya civilization were suddenly stricken by some catastrophe. Intensive agriculture may have exhausted the soil; the climate may have changed and reduced the rainfall; epidemics may have swept through the region. In any case, within fifty years Maya culture remained alive only in the northern part of the Yucatán peninsula. There the Mayas carried on a great program of temple building; they created a stepped-pyramid style similar to the ziggurats of Babylonia. Immigrants from central Mexico brought with them their own god, Quetzalcoatl (ket·sahl·koh·AT'l), whom the Mayas adopted under the name of Kukulcan.

For a time the Mayas dominated the northern Yucatán peninsula. But plagues and hurricanes struck the land, and the last commemorative pillar was erected in 1516. The Mayas left their cities, including their capital of Chichén-Itzá, and took to the jungle-covered countryside, where their descendants still live.

The Toltecs

Another important group of Indians were the Toltecs. Originally from the Pacific coast of North America, the Toltecs had established themselves as rulers of part of central Mexico by about 700 A.D. Their capital was at Tula (see map, this page). They were pyramid builders, too, but their art was inferior to that of the Mayas. They were probably responsible, however, for introducing the use of metals into Central America.

The major deity of the Toltecs was Quetzalcoatl. He was the god of air and water, and of the planet Venus. He was depicted as having a white skin, blue eyes, and a long flowing beard. He was a humane deity. Eventually, surrounding tribes which still believed in human sacrifice asserted their independence of the more peaceful Toltecs. This loss of their allies apparently weakened the Toltecs, so that when the Aztecs invaded the territory around 1200, the Toltecs were defeated.

The Aztecs

Around 1200 there were further invasions of people from the north. A number of groups engaged in intertribal warfare in central Mexico. Out of this warfare emerged the strongest single group, the Aztecs.

The Aztecs had been wandering warriors, fighting for whoever would pay them. But their priests finally instructed them to settle where they should see a sign—an eagle sitting on a cactus and devouring a serpent. They finally saw the sign on one of a pair of islands in Lake Texcoco, in Mexico, and there they built their city of Tenochtitlán (tay·nohk·tee·TLAHN).

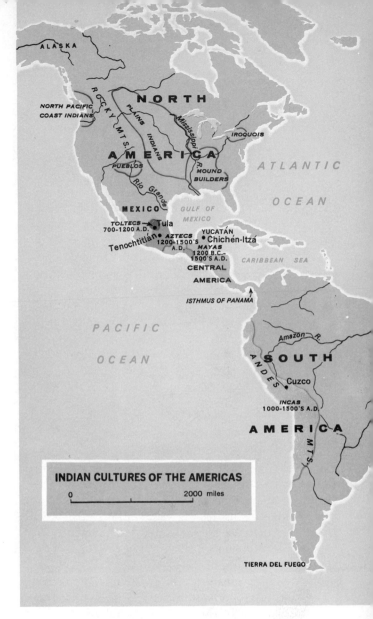

INDIAN CULTURES OF THE AMERICAS

0 — 2000 miles

From about 1325 on, Aztec power grew until the Aztecs were the dominant people in central Mexico. Conquered tribes paid them tribute in the form of gold, turquoise, corn, animals, and slaves. Aztec chieftains became the rulers of a splendid court.

By building causeways and stone foundations, the Aztecs expanded Tenochtitlán to make room for great pyramidal temples, marketplaces, and palaces for the nobles and wealthy families. Food came from the fields surrounding Lake Texcoco. The city of Tenochtitlán may have had as many

Mayan Fat God

This mean-looking little man is known as the Fat God, and occurs often in Mayan art. Here he appears as a clay whistle that was found in a tomb. (Whistles and rattles were often placed as offerings in Mayan tombs; archeologists do not know why.) The Fat God is dressed in a feathered cape and headdress that symbolize a sacred Mayan bird-snake and he carries a shield. On his cheeks are ritual scars and he is squinting. Mayan mothers deliberately induced crossed eyes and squinting in their children by dangling objects in front of their noses. They may have done this to honor the sun god, who is represented in Mayan art as cross-eyed. The figure dates from the 700's or 800's and was found on an island off Yucatán.

as 100,000 inhabitants at its period of greatest power and prestige.

The Aztecs were not inventors. They adopted the inventions of those tribes which they conquered or with which they traded. While they knew the use of metals, weaving, and pottery-making, and had a calendar and a system of mathematics, most of these were borrowed.

There were eighteen annual Aztec ceremonies that honored the deities of the field, the rain, and the sun. During these ceremonies there were dances, combats between Aztec warriors and captives, and colorful processions. In keeping with their war-loving nature, the Aztecs worshiped deities who, they believed, demanded human sacrifice. The victims were captives from defeated tribes, and hundreds might be put to death each year. In 1478, the period when Aztec power was at its height, 20,000 victims were sacrificed.

Just as the great Aztec civilization had grown rapidly, so it was to fall in a very short time. By the end of the 1400's, there were rebellions by surrounding peoples who had been paying tribute to the Aztecs. But the final blow to the Aztec Empire was to come from foreign conquerors—Spanish explorers of the 1500's, about whom you will read in Chapter 15.

The Incas

At about the same period that the Aztecs were building their great civilization in Mexico, another group of Indians was creating a civilization in the Andes Mountains of South America. The religion of these tribes was based on sun worship; their name, Incas, meant "children of the sun."

The Inca state expanded steadily. By the late 1400's, it extended along most of the west coast of South America and far into the Andes, covering much of the present-day nations of Peru and Chile (see map, page 283). Like ancient Egypt, it was a state in which everything belonged to the Inca ruler, and everyone owed absolute obedience to him. Although he was an autocrat, his power was directed toward improving the state.

The Incas built great cities, including their capital, Cuzco, known as the "City of the Sun." They erected fortresses, dug irrigation systems, and laid

American Indian cultures were largely destroyed with the coming of the white man, but archeologists have learned much from the remains. The carved Aztec stone above was found near the main temple at Tenochtitlán. Its symbols represent the extremely complex Aztec calendar, according to which these superstitious people regulated their entire lives. At Tula, the Toltec capital, a large pyramid is still standing. Its summit is crowned with four massive warrior figures, one of which is shown at right. The ceremonial knife below comes from Peru, the land once ruled by the Incas. Both the crowned idol on top and the blade to which it is joined are made of gold. The small green stones are turquoises.

down paved roads from one end of their realm to the other. Since they never discovered the use of the wheeled vehicle, pack animals carried goods and swift runners brought news to the capital.

The Incas did not have a system of writing. Instead they used the *quipu*, a kind of knotted string, to assist the memory. They did have an excellent school system in which the history and customs of the Incas were taught to young Inca children and to children from subject tribes. The Incas kept their history alive in the form of narrative verses which were memorized and recited by minstrels.

As the Inca ruler lay dying in 1529, wise men told him that there was great trouble in store for the Inca empire. Four years later, invading Spanish forces conquered the empire and forced the new ruler into exile, as you will read later.

North American Indians

In North America above Mexico—that is, the United States and Canada—there were no major civilizations like those of the Mayas, Aztecs, or Incas. There were several different Indian cultures, however, and some were highly organized societies (see map, page 283).

A well-developed culture in what is now the United States was that of the Pueblo Indians of the Rio Grande Valley. These Indians were farmers who lived in permanent settlements. Using adobe, a sun-dried brick, they built communal houses for all the members of a community. Some of these houses were several stories high and others were clustered together beneath overhanging cliffs so that they could be better defended.

On the northwest coast of North America lived several tribes whose economies were based largely on fishing. These Indians were also expert woodworkers and weavers. They were famous for their totem poles, great wooden carvings of men and beasts that symbolized tribal history.

An entirely different culture flourished in the vast plains region between the Rocky Mountains and the Mississippi River. Here Indians lived by hunting the huge herds of wild buffalo that roamed over the land. Plains Indians ate the meat of the buffalo, made clothing of its skin, and used its hide to build their cone-shaped tents, called tepees.

They loved fighting and placed a high value on personal deeds of bravery.

One of the highest Indian cultures of North America flourished in the midwestern and southern regions of the United States. Indians who lived there are sometimes called the Mound Builders because of the large number of earthen mounds they constructed throughout the area.

Most of the mounds were built as burial places. The tools, jewelry, and weapons found in them reveal that these Indians had highly developed artistic skill. Some of the mounds are in the shapes of animals. One in Ohio, the Great Serpent Mound, is more than $\frac{1}{4}$ mile long. Building the mounds obviously took cooperative effort. Much mystery still surrounds them; archeologists do not know what happened to the Indians who built them or why such building ceased.

On the eastern seaboard of North America were a number of related Indian tribes. They had a farming and hunting economy, but also showed great skill and organization when they made war. They lived in walled towns and had a high level of political organization. Their common language was Iroquois.

In the 1400's and 1500's, five of these tribes—the Cayugas, Mohawks, Oneidas, Onondagas, and Senecas—formed the League of the Iroquois. The League was established in an attempt to stop intertribal warfare. The Iroquois League lasted for several hundred years. Its influence and benefits were expanded to include several other tribes. Some historians believe that if it had been allowed to develop unhindered, its peaceful influence might eventually have been extended to all of the North American Indian tribes.

CHECKUP

1. Where did the Indians come from? How?

2. What were the chief accomplishments of the Mayas? Toltecs? Aztecs? Incas?

3. IDENTIFY: Quetzalcoatl, quipu, adobe, tepees, League of the Iroquois.

4. LOCATE: Bering Strait, Isthmus of Panama, Amazon River, Andes Mountains, Tierra del Fuego, Yucatán, Chichén-Itzá, Tula, Tenochtitlán, Cuzco.

CHAPTER REVIEW

Chapter 13 Civilizations in Asia and America Reached High Levels (500 B.C.—1658 A.D.)

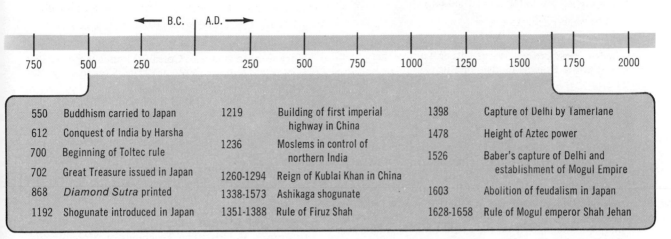

550	Buddhism carried to Japan
612	Conquest of India by Harsha
700	Beginning of Toltec rule
702	Great Treasure issued in Japan
868	*Diamond Sutra* printed
1192	Shogunate introduced in Japan
1219	Building of first imperial highway in China
1236	Moslems in control of northern India
1260-1294	Reign of Kublai Khan in China
1338-1573	Ashikaga shogunate
1351-1388	Rule of Firuz Shah
1398	Capture of Delhi by Tamerlane
1478	Height of Aztec power
1526	Baber's capture of Delhi and establishment of Mogul Empire
1603	Abolition of feudalism in Japan
1628-1658	Rule of Mogul emperor Shah Jehan

CHAPTER SUMMARY

Harsha conquered the former Gupta Empire and ruled northern India for forty years. Then the region split into small states controlled by the Rajputs. Independent southern India grew wealthy from trade.

Between 712 and 1236, Moslems took control of all northern India. Further Moslem conquests were made by the Delhi sultans. Moslem contributions to Indian life included Urdu, architectural innovations, and a democratizing influence on Hinduism.

During the 1500's, Baber brought the Indian princes under his control and set up the Mogul Empire. The Moguls fostered unity and orderly government.

In China the Sui dynasty overcame the Huns and reunited the country. Its rulers were overambitious, however, and were soon replaced by the Tang. Under the Tang, the civil service system was perfected and there was a flowering of poetry. China next came under the control of the Sung. Although the country was divided in the 1100's—with the Sung in the south and the Jurchen in the north—culture continued to flourish.

China came under Mongol control in the 1200's. Roads were built and contacts were made with Europe. However, weak rulers, natural disasters, and Chinese antagonism enabled the Ming to overthrow the Mongols in 1368. After about a century, Ming China adopted a policy of complete isolation.

Nearby Japan was profoundly influenced by Shintoism and emperor worship. Other strong influences came from China. Although the early Japanese emperors were strong, they later lost authority. Two power structures developed; central authority was wielded by the shoguns, local power by the daimio.

North and South America were settled over many centuries by migrating Asians, later named Indians. The Mayas developed a reliable calendar, a sophisticated system of mathematics, and a written language. The Toltecs introduced the use of metals to Central America. The Aztecs, a dominant and cruel people, built a great city, Tenochtitlán. Sun-worshiping Incas created an advanced civilization in western South America, with complex irrigation and road systems. In America above Mexico, Indian cultures included those of the Pueblos, Plains Indians, and Iroquois.

QUESTIONS FOR DISCUSSION

1. Under the Rajputs, northern Indians took great pride in their country, believing it to be superior to all others. Was this true? Would it be right for Americans to say that their country is presently the best in the world?

2. What advice would you have given the Chinese or Japanese when they decided to isolate themselves?

3. What were the differences and similarities between feudalism in Europe, Rajput rule in India, and Japanese feudalism?

4. Different peoples have made similar discoveries independently—for example, the concept of zero developed both in India and among the Mayas. How would you explain this phenomenon?

PROJECTS

1. Make a chart to show the accomplishments and weaknesses of the four American Indian civilizations discussed in the chapter.

2. List invasions by central Asian nomads into surrounding regions that have influenced history.

287

For additional bibliographical information on the books cited in these projects, see the Basic Library (page xviii) and Further Reading on the opposite page.

INDIVIDUAL PROJECTS

1. Why was Charlemagne the central figure in the early Middle Ages? Read one of the biographies of Charlemagne listed on the opposite page. Refer also to the following selections: Eisen and Filler *The Human Adventure,* Vol. 1, "The Reign of Charlemagne" and "The Disintegration of Charlemagne's Empire"; Hughes and Fries, *European Civilization,* "Charlemagne Commands That the Local Church Authorities Establish Schools" and "Charlemagne Establishes the Missi Dominici."

2. Report on the Vikings' contact with North America. For this report read: *American Heritage,* "Was America Discovered Before Columbus?" April 1955; Bakeless, *They Saw America First: Our First Explorers and What They Saw.* Information on the Vikings' key to success, boats, can be found in Landström, *The Ship: An Illustrated History.* Consult *Readers' Guide to Periodical Literature* for current magazine articles on the Vikings.

3. *National Geographic* has published a number of articles focusing on the Middle Ages. Prepare a report for class presentation on one of the following articles: "A New Look at Medieval Europe," December 1962; "Triumph of the First Crusade to the Holy Land," December 1963; "900 Years Ago: The Norman Conquest," August 1966.

4. Discuss in an essay life in the Middle Ages, showing the role of the various classes and relationships among them. Read the following selections: Eisen and Filler, *The Human Adventure,* Vol. 1, "Feudal Society"; Fremantle, *Age of Faith,* "The Rise of Feudalism."

5. Prepare an oral report on the revival of trade in medieval times. Explain to the class how the growth of cities influenced the increase in trade. Consult Eisen and Filler. *The Human Adventure,* Vol. 1, "The Revival of Commerce" and "The Regulation of a Craft Guild"; Fremantle, *Age of Faith,* "A New Urban Class"; Power, *Medieval People,* "Thomas Betson, a Merchant of the Staple in the Fifteenth Century" and "Thomas Paycocke of Coggeshall, an Essex Clothier in the Days of Henry VII."

6. Write a newspaper article analyzing the dispute between Henry IV and Pope Gregory VII before Henry went to Canossa. Consult Eisen and Filler, *The Human Adventure,* Vol. 1, "The Controversy Between the Empire and the Papacy."

7. Mohammed, as the founder of Islam, has been one of the most influential men the world has known. Prepare an oral report on Mohammed's life and the teachings of Islam. Some of the sources that you should consult are: Smith, *The Religions of Man,* "Islam"; Bach, *Major Religions of the World,* "Islam—Religion of the Book"; Gaer, *How the Great Religions Began,* "Mohammedanism, Flaming Sword of the Desert"; *Life* eds., *The World's Great Religions,* "The World of Islam"; Eisen and Filler, *The Human Adventure,* Vol. 1, "The Teachings of Mohammed."

8. Choose one of the early civilizations that flourished in Africa, and give a report on it to the class. You can find material for your report in selected chapters of the following books: Bacon, *Vanished Civilizations of the Ancient World;* Chu and Skinner, *A Glorious Age in Africa;* Cottrell, *African Kingdoms* and *The Lost Cities of Africa.*

GROUP PROJECTS

1. On tape, record the speech made by Pope Urban II calling for the first crusade. Lead a class discussion on his reasons for calling the crusade. For this project see Peterson, *Treasury of the World's Great Speeches,* "Pope Urban II Calls for the First Crusade."

2. Three students might work together to prepare reports on the Indian civilizations of the Mayas, Aztecs, and Incas. Special attention should be given to the religions, social systems, and material accomplishments of these civilizations. Information can be found in Bacon, *Vanished Civilizations of the Ancient World,* "The Gods That Failed: The Glory and Decay of Maya Culture"; Cottrell, *The Horizon Book of Lost Worlds,* "The Riddle of the Maya"; *Life* eds., *The Epic of Man,* "The Maya, Priestly Peoples of the New World" and "The Imperial Inca of the Andes."

3. A number of students might cooperate on reports about the Byzantine Empire and hold a panel discussion. Topics for the reports might be the political, cultural, and religious development of the Byzantine Empire. Refer to Eisen and Filler, *The Human Adventure.* Vol. 1, "The Byzantine Empire," and Sherrard, *Byzantium.*

Further Reading

BIOGRAPHY

Andrae, Tor, *Mohammed: The Man and His Faith*. Harper & Row.

Appleby, J. T., *John, King of England*. Knopf.

Chute, Marchette, *Geoffrey Chaucer of England*. Dutton.*

Costain, Thomas B., *William the Conqueror*. Random House.

Duckett, Eleanor Shipley, *Alfred the Great: The King and His England*. Univ. of Chicago.*

——, *Alcuin, Friend of Charlemagne: His World and His Work*. Shoe String Press.

Einhard, *Life of Charlemagne*. Univ. of Michigan.

Fennell, J., *Ivan the Great of Moscow*. St. Martin's.

Kantorowicz, E., *Frederick the Second*. Ungar.

Kendall, Paul M., *Richard the Third*. Norton.

Lamb, Harold, *Charlemagne*. Bantam.*

——, *Genghis Khan: Emperor of All Men*. Bantam.*

McFarlane, Kenneth B., *John Wycliffe and the Beginning of English Nonconformity*. Verry.

Power, Eileen, *Medieval People*. Barnes & Noble.*

Steele, William O., *The Story of Leif Ericson*. Grosset & Dunlap.

Williams, Jay, *Joan of Arc*. Harper & Row.

Winston, Richard, *Charlemagne: From the Hammer to the Cross*. Random House.*

NONFICTION

Bacon, Edward, ed., *Vanished Civilizations of the Ancient World*. McGraw-Hill.

Baity, E., *Americans Before Columbus*. Viking.

Bakeless, Katherine and John, *The Saw America First: Our First Explorers and What They Saw*. Lippincott.

Bennett, H. S., *Life on the English Manor*. Cambridge Univ. Press.*

Bernal, Ignacio, *Mexico Before Cortez: Art, History, and Legend*. Doubleday.*

Chu, Daniel, and Elliott Skinner, *A Glorious Age in Africa*. Doubleday.

Chubb, Thomas C., *The Byzantines*. World.

Daugherty, James, *The Magna Charta*. Random House.

Davidson, Basil, *African Kingdoms*. Time-Life.

——, *The Lost Cities of Africa*. Little, Brown.*

Davis, William S., *Life on a Medieval Barony*. Harper & Row.

Dilts, Marion M., *The Pageant of Japanese History*. McKay.

* Paperback.

Duggan, Alfred, *Growing Up with the Norman Conquest*. Pantheon.

Fitch, Florence M., *Allah: The God of Islam—Moslem Life and Worship*. Lothrop, Lee & Shepard.

Fremantle, Anne, *Age of Faith*. Time-Life.

Gibb, H. A. R., *Mohammedanism*. Oxford Univ. Press.*

Hagen, Victor W. von, *The Incas, People of the Sun*. World.

——, *Maya: Land of the Turkey and the Deer*. World.

Hamilton, Franklin, *The Crusades*. Dial.

Hitti, Philip K., *Arabs—A Short History*. Regnery.*

Mills, Dorothy, *The Middle Ages*. Putnam.

Newhall, Richard A., *The Crusades*. Holt, Rinehart and Winston.*

Oliver, Roland, and J. D. Fage, *A Short History of Africa*. Penguin.*

Price, Christine, *Made in the Middle Ages*. Dutton.

Sellman, R. R., *Crusades*. Roy.

Sherrard, Philip, *Byzantium*. Time-Life.

Williams, Jay, *Knights of the Crusades*. Harper & Row.

HISTORICAL FICTION

Bengtsson, Frans G., *The Long Ships*. New American Library.* The Vikings.

Bryher, *The Fourteenth of October*. Pantheon. Background of the battle of Hastings.

——, *Ruan*. Pantheon. Celtic Britain.

Charques, Dorothy, *Men Like Shadows*. Ballantine.* Third Crusade.

Costain, Thomas B., *The Conquering Family*. Pocket Books.* Fusing of Normans and Anglo-Saxons.

——, *Magnificent Century*. Popular Library.* Struggle to limit the power of the English king in the 1200's.

Doyle, Arthur Conan, *The White Company*. Dodd, Mead. English bowmen on the continent.

Eyre, Katherine W., *The Song of a Thrush*. Walck. Wars of the Roses.

Gray, Elizabeth J., *Adam of the Road*. Viking. Minstrels in the 1200's.

Israel, Charles, *Who Was Then the Gentleman?* Simon & Schuster. England of Richard II.

Ritchie, Rita, *The Year of the Horse*. Dutton. Set in Genghis Khan's empire.

Scott, Sir Walter, *Ivanhoe*. Pocket Books.*

Shellabarger, Samuel, *The Token*. Little, Brown.

Sutcliff, Rosemary, *Knight's Fee*. Dell.*

——, *The Shield Ring*. Walck. Vikings resist Normans.

Whitman, Edmund, *Revolt Against the Rain God*. McGraw-Hill. Set in a Mayan city.

UNIT

FOUR

THE EMERGENCE

The Dutch port of Amsterdam bustled with activity in the 1600's. In the print at right, cargo ships lie at anchor outside a breakwater, their sails furled. Small boats busily ply the harbor waters nearer the shore. In the prosperous city itself rise several church towers and, at far right, the domed cupola of the city hall. Along the tree-lined quays are rows of buildings with the stepped gables characteristic of northern Europe.

OF MODERN EUROPE

CHAPTER 14

The Renaissance and the Reformation Changed Europe

When you think of the differences between medieval and modern times, you probably think first of the great difference in material objects. Modern men have machines, tools, and weapons that medieval men never dreamed of. There is, however, another and perhaps even greater difference: a difference in attitude of mind in thinking about life.

In general, medieval men were more preoccupied with religious matters, with the salvation of their souls, than are modern men. Most medieval men considered themselves as part of a group, the Christian community; most modern men think of themselves first as individuals, as unique persons of dignity and worth. Most men today believe that they can solve the problems of life through their own efforts, by applying knowledge gained from experience. People of the Middle Ages accepted many ideas on authority. Men today are more skeptical and more apt to question traditional attitudes.

Of course these changes in attitude did not occur overnight, nor did they affect all of Europe. Like many other changes, they cannot be traced to exact periods of time or definite places. Many historians believe that they grew out of a literary and artistic movement that began in Italy around 1350, spread into northern Europe, and ended about 1600. Because this movement centered on a revival of the classical learning of Greece and

A painting by Holbein of the Dutch scholar Erasmus

Rome, it is known as the *Renaissance* (REN·uh-sahns), a French word meaning "rebirth."

Some scholars think of the Renaissance as merely a continuation and development of the Middle Ages. Others think of it as a break with medieval life and thought, the beginning of modern times. One reason for thinking of the Renaissance as the beginning of modern times is that Renaissance thinkers and writers themselves thought of it in that way.

As you have read, medieval men were not conscious of historical periods or of the past as being much different from the time in which they lived. But men of the Renaissance saw themselves as people of a new age. It was they, in fact, who coined the term "Dark Ages" for the period that had preceded theirs, and gave their own era the proud title of Renaissance. Actually, the term is not accurate. The things that made the period outstanding were not those of a past somehow "reborn," but fresh and new creations of genius.

The name *Renaissance* is applied not only to a literary and artistic movement but also to the period during which it flourished—that is, the years from about 1350 to 1600. This period saw many important developments. You have already read about some of them, including the decay of feudalism and the rise of national states. You will now read about others—the invention of the printing press, a revolution in science, and a movement in Christianity known as the Reformation. Scholars disagree as to how much these various developments were influenced by the Renaissance itself. But it is safe to say that the period was one of great vitality, when men were blazing new pathways in almost every field of human effort.

THE CHAPTER SECTIONS:

1. Renaissance writers and artists created outstanding works (1350–1600)

2. Technology and science progressed during the Renaissance (1450–1632)

3. The Protestant Reformation began in Germany (1517–1555)

4. Protestantism spread and the Counter-Reformation was launched (1536–1600)

 1   Renaissance writers and artists created outstanding works

The Renaissance began in Italy. Since one of its characteristics was a renewed interest in Roman literature and life, it was natural that this interest would be reawakened in Italy, which abounded in remains of Roman antiquity. Also, trade with the Near East had brought Italians into contact with Byzantine civilization, whose scholars had preserved much of classical learning.

The most important cities of the Renaissance were Florence, Rome, Venice, Genoa, and Milan. In these cities there developed an intellectual movement called Humanism, which was the basis of the Renaissance.

Humanism

Beginning about the middle 1300's, many Italian scholars developed a lively interest in classical literature, particularly that of the Romans. Medieval scholars had studied ancient times, too, but they did so within the framework of scholas-

ticism. They tried to make everything they learned harmonize with Christian doctrine. The Italian scholars of the 1300's studied the ancient world as a whole to try to understand it so they could imitate its greatness. They believed, for example, that men of their age could learn from the Romans much of value about manly virtues and moral conduct.

These Italian scholars stressed the study of grammar, rhetoric, history, and poetry, using classical texts. These studies were called the humanities, and the men who advocated them were called Humanists. Humanists searched out Greek and Roman manuscripts that had been neglected during many centuries of the Middle Ages. Often they might find more than one copy of a work. If the copies were not exactly the same, Humanists compared the different versions to discover which was correct. In doing so, they developed a critical attitude that had been lacking in much medieval scholarship. The revived interest in classical texts and critical study of them formed the basis of Humanism.

As time went on, Humanism became more than a certain type of scholarship; it also came to mean a new outlook on life. One characteristic of this outlook was a critical spirit. Some Humanists, for example, criticized the Church, protesting against what they regarded as defects in its organization and administration. Men like these remained religious, but they were less inclined than earlier thinkers to accept Church authority without question.

Another characteristic related to Humanism was enthusiasm for life in this world. Humanists looked on existence not only as a preparation for the life to come but also as a joy in itself. Man, with all his faults, was an intelligent being who could make his own decisions. Along with this belief in individual dignity went an admiration for individual achievement. Many men of this period were remarkable for the variety of their talents. One man might be not only a poet and musician but also a scientist and painter.

Italian Renaissance writers

Many of the early Italian Humanists are known more for their scholarship and teaching than for writings of their own. Some, however, created original works of importance. It was these men who actually began the Renaissance as a literary movement.

Francesco Petrarch (PE·trark) is often called the father of Humanism. He was born in 1304, studied law, and then became a member of the clergy. Petrarch was a master of lyric poetry, which he wrote in beautiful and expressive Italian. He was an enthusiastic student of Latin writings, particularly those of Cicero. He traveled widely and, through his extensive correspondence, had a considerable influence on other Humanists.

Another great figure of the Italian literary Renaissance was Giovanni Boccaccio (boh·KAH·chee·oh). He was born in Paris, but spent much of his life in and around Florence. In his youth he studied banking, but he soon found that he preferred writing.

Boccaccio wrote many poems and stories, but his fame today rests on his *Decameron,* written about 1350. The *Decameron* is a collection of a hundred stories told by a group of people who are staying at a country estate outside Florence to escape the Black Death. Many of Boccaccio's tales were taken from the *fabliaux* of the Middle Ages. The tales are severely critical of the practices of the clergy of the period.

The ideal Renaissance man was the subject of *The Courtier,* by Baldassare Castiglione (kahs-teh·LYOH·nay). This handbook described the well-rounded gentleman, and was widely read as a model for behavior.

Probably the most influential of all Italian Renaissance writers was Niccoló Machiavelli (mahk·ee·uh·VEL·ee), a Florentine diplomat and historian. He wrote a famous essay, *The Prince* (published in 1532), which described government, not in terms of lofty ideals, but as it existed in his day. Machiavelli wrote that a state could not stand still, but must either expand or decay. In the real world, he said, power counts more than ideals.

The Prince expressed contempt for the medieval idea that a ruler's authority was limited by moral law. It advised rulers to maintain the safety of their states by whatever means they thought necessary, and not to be hampered by considerations of honesty, justice, or honor.

Machiavelli's theories had great influence on the people of his own and later centuries. Today we use the adjective *Machiavellian* to describe people who use deceit and are unconcerned with morality in getting what they want.

Writers of the Northern Renaissance

Humanist thought was not confined to Italy. The new ideas soon traveled northward to Germany, the Netherlands, France, and England. They were transmitted primarily by students from northern Europe who studied at Italian universities and took the new ideas back with them.

One of the most influential men of the Northern Renaissance was Desiderius Erasmus. Born in the Netherlands in 1466, Erasmus studied in France and England. In Paris he encountered Italian Humanist ideas, which he accepted eagerly.

Erasmus' most famous book, *In Praise of Folly,* is a satire ridiculing ignorance, superstition, and vice among the clergy. Erasmus criticized fasting, pilgrimages to religious shrines, and even the Church's interpretation of some parts of the Bible. Erasmus felt, however, that the Church could be reformed from within.

Another great writer of the Northern Renaissance was a Frenchman, François Rabelais (RAB-uh·lay). He had two great loves: classical learning and the people of France.

Rabelais' famous book, *Gargantua and Pantagruel,* was written in the language of the French people he loved so well. Like *In Praise of Folly,* it is a satire. Gargantua is a giant king who enjoys life on a grand scale. (The word *gargantuan* has since come to mean "huge.") With great wit and cleverness, Rabelais ridiculed fakes and quacks, outmoded ideas, and hypocrisy. He believed that man could perfect himself by using his own mind and through natural, joyous living.

In 1516 a great English Humanist, Thomas More, published *Utopia,* a book that was as popular as *In Praise of Folly.* In *Utopia,* More criticized the society of his day by describing an imaginary, ideal society. (The word *utopia* comes from the Greek words *ou* and *topos,* meaning "not" and "place"—that is, "nowhere.") According to More the good society was to be made up entirely of free citizens who would elect their own governing officials. Laws would be enforced not by police but by conscientious citizens themselves. There would be complete freedom of religion. More's *Utopia* became so popular that today the word *utopia* means an ideal place or society.

Renaissance literature in England reached its peak in the late 1500's and early 1600's in the plays of William Shakespeare. Although, like other playwrights, he often used familiar plots, Shakespeare built around them masterpieces of poetic drama that have few equals in any language.

Shakespeare was a Humanist in his deep concern for mankind. Few writers have been so skilled at showing human emotions. The jovial Falstaff, the moody Hamlet, the young lovers Romeo and Juliet, and the tragic Macbeth seem as real today as when they were first created.

HISTORY THROUGH ART

The Duke of Urbino

Federigo da Montefeltro, the Duke of Urbino, was described by a contemporary as "the light of Italy." He was a prime example of an important Renaissance type—the intelligent and wealthy patron who supported Humanist scholars and artists. Federigo commissioned Piero della Francesca to paint his portrait about 1465. The work of an artistic genius, the portrait displays the interest in realism so prominent during the Renaissance. The duke himself is shown realistically, his battered profile the result of a jousting accident in which he lost an eye and broke his nose. And the background is a landscape from his own duchy of Urbino, on the east coast of Italy.

295

The Fascination of Perspective

Renaissance artists discovered perspective. To many of them it was a fascinating technique with which they worked endlessly. One Florentine painter, in fact, was said to have loved perspective more than he loved his wife. Artists who experimented with perspective found the perfect medium for their technique in marquetry—inlaid designs made with different kinds, tints, and shapes of wood. Combinations of simple geometrical shapes could produce dazzling displays of perspective skill.

"The Ideal City," above, is an excellent example of Italian Renaissance marquetry. Its subject, architecture, was a favorite with Renaissance artists because it gave them a chance to show off their mastery of perspective. By attempting to duplicate reality, in which things at a distance seem smaller than those close by, artists gave depth to the flat surfaces with which they worked. For example, the church steeple in the background of "The Ideal City" appears smaller than the arch, which is part of the frame, in the foreground. This scene decorates a church and has been well preserved, except for the vertical crack in the steeple, for almost five hundred years.

The Italian Renaissance in art

Great literature was only one aspect of the Renaissance; another was art. The Renaissance in art was one of the greatest creative outbursts the world has ever known.

Innovations in painting and sculpture, like Humanism, began in Italy. The most noticeable characteristic of Renaissance painting is its realism in representing natural life and forms. Like the Humanists, Renaissance painters admired Roman culture, and Roman art had been intensely realistic. In the paintings of the Renaissance, the human figure became ever more lifelike, and landscapes in the background showed the countryside that the artist knew.

Renaissance painters could make their works lifelike because they had learned a most important technique of painting called perspective. By making distant objects smaller than those in the foreground, and by arranging them in certain ways, they could create the illusion of depth on a flat canvas.

Early realists. Giotto (JAH·toh), who lived in the late 1200's and early 1300's in Florence, is often considered the first Renaissance painter. The figures in his frescoes had a solidity that medieval art lacked. It is said that in one of his paintings a fly looked so lifelike that an observer tried to brush it off. Masaccio (mah·SAHT·choh), also a Florentine, used light and shade to give the effect of thickness to objects. He was also a pioneer in the technique of perspective.

Like Masaccio, Fra Angelico was interested in perspective. A Dominican friar, he had begun his career by illuminating manuscripts. The influence of this training can be seen in his use of gold leaf and rich colors. The paintings of Piero della Francesca, who lived in the 1400's, also reflected the aims of Masaccio. Piero believed in scientific perspective as the basis of painting. His skillful use of light and color gave solidity and grandeur to his figures. Sandro Botticelli (baht·uh·CHEL·ee) was known for his mythological subject matter. He used it in his most famous paintings, "Allegory of Spring" and "Birth of Venus."

The High Renaissance. Italian painters of the late 1400's and early 1500's displayed such genius that this period is often called the High Renaissance. Four men were outstanding: Leonardo da Vinci, Michelangelo, Raphael, and Titian.

Leonardo da Vinci was a versatile man—artist, musician, architect, mathematician, and scientist. As a painter, he made use of his experiments in science (see page 301); studies of anatomy helped him in drawing the human figure, and he used mathematics to organize the space in his paintings. His mural of "The Last Supper" is universally known. Probably his most famous painting is the portrait called "Mona Lisa."

Another master of Renaissance art was Michelangelo Buonarroti (my·kul·AN·juh·loh bwaw·nar·RAW·tee). He preferred sculpture to painting, and his stone carvings of such Old Testament figures as David and Moses have a massive dignity. His paintings reflect this quality, too. Thousands of persons have visited the Sistine Chapel of the Vatican (the papal palace) in Rome and looked with wonder at the murals he painted on the ceiling. Imagine an area of some 6,000 square feet on which are painted hundreds of human figures. Think of this being done by a single man in only four years (1508 to 1512).

Michelangelo, almost as versatile as Leonardo, was a poet and an outstanding architect. He was one of the men who designed St. Peter's Church in Rome.

Raphael did much of his work in Rome. Like Michelangelo, he was commissioned by the pope to beautify the Vatican. His frescoes in the papal library include "School of Athens," which depicts the great philosophers of classical Greece. Raphael was also noted for his madonnas (representations of the Virgin Mary), such as the "Sistine Madonna."

Titian (TISH·un) spent most of his life in Venice. His works are noted for their rich colors. A vivid sense of drama characterized his paintings of religious subjects, such as his "Assumption of the Virgin." He was supported by the Holy Roman Emperor and the king of France, and was one of the few painters of the period to acquire a fortune through his work.

Artists of the Northern Renaissance. The new ways of painting were too forceful and their appeal too universal to remain in Italy. Countries engaged in trade with Italian cities were the first to be influenced. Merchants carried Italian paintings home with them, and painters from northern Europe traveled south to study with Italian masters.

The artists of Flanders were outstanding. It was they who perfected the technique of painting in oils on canvas. Among the first Flemish painters were the brothers Hubert and Jan van Eyck, who lived in the 1400's. Their interest in exact detail is evident in such masterworks as the altarpiece at Ghent, called "Adoration of the Lamb."

The greatest Flemish painter was Peter Brueghel (BROY·gul), who worked in the mid-1500's. Brueghel loved the countryside and peasantry of his native land and painted lively scenes of village dances, wedding feasts, and skating parties.

The German artist Albrecht Dürer was most famous for his copper engravings and woodcuts. During his lifetime, in the late 1400's and early 1500's, the printing press was beginning to make books available, as you will read shortly. Dürer was one of the first to recognize the possibilities of printed illustrations for these new books, and created many works for this purpose.

Hans Holbein the Younger was a German, too, but he did most of his work in other countries. During the 1500's, Holbein traveled throughout Europe to paint the portraits of famous men—Erasmus, Thomas More, and King Henry VIII, among others. This emphasis on portraiture shows the Renaissance interest in the individual.

CHECKUP

1. Explain the meaning of the term *Renaissance*. Why did the movement begin in Italy?

2. Define Humanism, giving both its early and later meanings.

3. Explain how Humanism moved northward. How did Erasmus, Rabelais, and More reflect its spirit?

4. What was the most noticeable characteristic of Renaissance painting? How is it achieved? Name at least three early Italian Renaissance painters.

5. IDENTIFY: Petrarch, Boccaccio, Castiglione, Machiavelli, Leonardo da Vinci, Michelangelo, Brueghel, Dürer.

(continued on page 300)

Renaissance art reflected the Humanism of the period and the versatility of the men who created it. Michelangelo—painter, architect, and sculptor—carved the imposing figure of Moses at left as part of a vast sculptural program, never completed, for the tomb of Pope Julius II in Rome. Michelangelo's Moses is both meditative and alert and suggests a man capable of wise leadership as well as fierce anger. Raphael, who viewed mankind as peaceful and beautiful, painted the panel at right. It is part of an altarpiece and shows God the Father surrounded by angels.

Several artists of northern Europe, including Albrecht Dürer and Peter Brueghel, visited Italy. When they returned home, they combined their new discoveries with the traditions of their homelands. Dürer's "Lady from Nuremberg," below right—a pen-and-ink drawing tinted with water color—has the precision of detail often found in northern European art. The snow scene below, painted by Brueghel, shows a typically northern winter, with peasants trudging home from the hunt.

2 Technology and science progressed during the Renaissance

So far in this chapter you have read about the creative flowering of literature and art that made up the Renaissance itself. The rest of the chapter deals with movements and events that occurred during the general period of the Renaissance. Important developments took place in technology and science.

Printing

During the Middle Ages, as you have read, books were laboriously copied out by hand, usually by monks. They were written on costly parchment (treated sheepskin or goatskin). Early in the 1100's, however, Europeans learned how to make paper from the Moslems, who in turn had learned about it from the Chinese.

Sometime in the early 1400's, Europeans also began to print from movable type. Scholars do not know whether Europeans learned this technique from the Chinese, directly or indirectly, or whether they invented it independently. At any rate, credit for the first European books to be printed from movable type is usually given to Johann Gutenberg of Mainz, Germany. The oldest complete surviving book, printed by Gutenberg in 1450, is the Constance Missal—a book of Masses for the German diocese of Constance.

Printing had a revolutionary effect on European civilization. By speeding up the reproduction of books, it simplified the transmission of knowledge. It made the collection of a library of books easy and relatively inexpensive. It popularized the ideas of the Renaissance.

The craft of printing with movable type spread rapidly. In the 1470's, William Caxton began to print books in London. He published the writings of Chaucer and other English authors. It is estimated that 9 million books had been printed throughout Europe by 1500.

Printing became especially common in Italy. The most famous Italian printer was Aldus Manutius of Venice. Aldus resolved to publish all the Greek and Latin classics at a price that middle-class people could afford to pay. He printed books of convenient size on inexpensive paper. They are known as the Aldine editions.

Printed books helped to spread both the rediscovered classics of the ancient world and the writing of the Renaissance. Books also spread the new scientific knowledge of the period.

The birth of modern science

During ancient times, some men were concerned with problems that we call scientific. Astronomy was studied by the Sumerians, Babylonians, and Greeks; physics began with the work of Archimedes; the Roman physician Galen advanced the knowledge of human anatomy.

These early thinkers, however, were not true scientists, but philosophers who were interested in scientific matters. They had theories about the natural world, but they did not systematically test them by conducting experiments or by carefully observing the world around them. Nor did they use mathematics to help unlock nature's secrets. Medieval scientists, as you have read, accepted traditional theories without testing them.

Experimentation, observation, and the use of mathematics are fundamental to modern science. These techniques were first widely used late in the period of the Renaissance. Thus it can be said that modern science was born then.

Scientists during the Renaissance were aware that they were developing a new way of investigating nature; they called it "the new philosophy." They built new instruments in order to make better measurements and observations. They conducted experiments with light, air, water, and magnetism, and they gathered information about the plant and animal world.

Renaissance scientists formed scientific societies to discuss mutual problems and publish books containing the results of their experiments. So much progress was made, and it influenced so many men, that the scientific advances of the time have come to be called the Scientific Revolution.

The men who began the Scientific Revolution soon went far beyond the scientific knowledge of

A Flying Machine by Leonardo

"A bird is an instrument working according to mathematical law," Leonardo da Vinci wrote, "which . . . is within the capacity of man to reproduce." Leonardo's identification with nature was so complete that he believed sufficient study and understanding of birds would provide a way for man to fly. It was his belief that, just as man could swim in the sea, he could conquer the air in silent flight as natural as a bird's. Leonardo spent years studying the flight of birds, dissecting and drawing wings, and making tests to determine the force needed to move wings large enough to support a man.

The drawing of a flying machine at right was made by Leonardo about 1500. The man who is to operate it stands inside, working the machine with his head, hands, and feet. There are two ladders for ascending and descending. Above and below are the artist's notes on the proper measurements and correct operation of the machine. They are written in the mirror-image script that was easiest and most natural for Leonardo, who was left-handed. As far as is known, he never tried to build an airplane, and Leonardo's dream of flight had to wait over four hundred years for realization.

the past. As you will see, the work of one great man was often the starting point for the next.

Leonardo da Vinci. In addition to being a great artist, Leonardo was an outstanding scientist. A man of tremendous curiosity, he experimented in many fields. Leonardo dissected the bodies of executed criminals in order to make his paintings of the human body more accurate. Thus he learned much about anatomy.

Fascinated by water, Leonardo not only devised pumps and canals, but also tried to discover the scientific principles behind waves and eddies. As a military engineer, he designed cannons, movable bridges, and armored vehicles. He also sketched flying machines and parachutes.

Leonardo was extremely interested in mathematics and wrote a treatise on geometry. He believed thoroughly in the value of the experimental method. In his notebook he wrote: "Those sciences are vain and full of errors which are not

born of experiment, the mother of all certainty." He kept notes and sketches to record the objects and events he had observed and the knowledge he had gathered. He did not publish his material, which was a great loss to the world. A modern scientist has said that if Leonardo da Vinci had published his work, science might have advanced in one step to a place not reached until a hundred years after his death.

Copernicus. The Renaissance saw a greatly revived interest in astronomy. Among the Greek writings recovered in the 1500's were those of Aristarchus of Samos. Aristarchus had written in the 200's B.C. that the sun was the center of the universe and that the earth and other planets revolved around it. This theory is called the heliocentric ("sun-centered") theory, from the Greek word *helios,* meaning "sun," and *kentron,* meaning "center."

The ideas of Aristarchus were not accepted. Instead, astronomers for centuries believed in the theory stated by Ptolemy in the 100's A.D., which held that the earth was the center of the universe, and that the other planets and the sun moved around it. This theory is called the geocentric ("earth-centered") theory, from the Greek words *ge,* meaning "earth," and *kentron.*

Then in the 1500's a Pole named Nicholas Copernicus came across the writings of Aristarchus. The ancient theory interested and excited Copernicus, and he began a long period of study and observation. He became convinced that all the known facts of astronomy of his time were best explained by the heliocentric theory. His conclusions were published in 1543 in a book entitled *On the Revolutions of the Heavenly Spheres.*

Copernicus' book caused little stir at the time. Few people believed in the heliocentric theory, for it seemed to contradict the evidence of the senses. Anyone could "see" that the sun and planets move around the earth; anyone could "feel" that the earth under him was solid and stationary, not moving.

Besides, the new idea seemed to contradict the Bible. (For example, according to the Old Testament, the prophet Joshua once commanded the sun to stand still; this passage implied that the sun normally moved around the earth.) Teachers of theology rejected it. It is interesting that the man who published Copernicus' book stressed, in an introduction, that Copernicus was merely suggesting an alternative to the Ptolemaic theory.

Copernicus' idea really was only a theory, for he could not test and prove it with the instruments or the mathematics available to him. Proof of his theory had to wait for the work of two later scientists, a German and an Italian, Kepler and Galileo.

Kepler and Galileo. Johann Kepler, who did his great work in astronomy in the early 1600's, was a brilliant mathematician. Using mathematics as a tool, he tried to test Copernicus' heliocentric theory. At first Kepler could not make it fit the observed facts. It is said that he calculated the problem seventy times before he discovered the error. Copernicus had written that the earth and

other planets went around the sun in orbits, or paths in space, which are exact circles. Kepler found that the orbits are not exact circles, but ovals called ellipses. Now everything fitted together; the theory could be proved mathematically.

Kepler's proof, however, could be understood only by mathematicians. It could not be seen or observed. This additional kind of proof was given by an Italian professor of mathematics, Galileo Galilei.

Galileo had read of a Dutch spectacle-maker who put two glass lenses together in a tube to make a telescope. With this instrument he could see distant objects more clearly. Galileo made such a telescope for himself. By modern standards it was only a small one, but it allowed him to see more of the heavens than any man had ever seen before. He could see the mountains and valleys of the moon, and the rings of Saturn. He observed sunspots, and proved the rotation of the sun on its axis. His discovery that the moons of Jupiter revolve around the planet helped disprove the geocentric theory of Ptolemy because it showed that not every heavenly body revolves around the earth.

Galileo published his findings in 1632 in a work called *Dialogue on the Two Great Systems of the World.* His work caused much more stir than Copernicus' had. Many people now wanted telescopes; many others believed them to be magic and refused to have anything to do with them. Scholars who accepted the authority of Ptolemy scoffed at this new theory. The Church also disapproved. Galileo was summoned to appear before the Inquisition at Rome. He was ordered to recant, which he did, but still the new ideas continued to advance.

Galileo was interested in physics as well as astronomy. Perhaps the most remarkable of his discoveries was the principle of the pendulum. The story is that one day in a cathedral, he watched the swinging of a great chandelier. He observed that, as it swung back and forth, each swing took the same length of time. After experimenting he was able to state the law mathematically. Later this principle was used in the

Renaissance science and technology

The science of astronomy was greatly advanced when Galileo, left, began making telescopes. Two of them are shown at right mounted on a stand for display. Andreas Vesalius aided the study of medicine with his book describing and illustrating the human body. The work of Vesalius influenced not only physicians but also painters and sculptors, who gained invaluable knowledge of anatomy from the detailed drawings. Some of the illustrations, like the one below left, showed skeletons in lifelike poses. Accounts of these and other findings were given wide circulation in printed books. At lower right is a printing shop of the 1600's at Nuremberg.

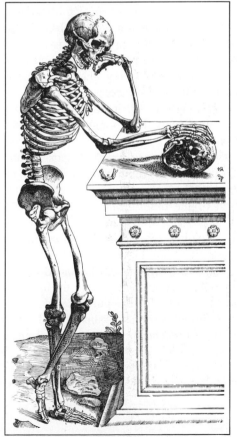

development of the pendulum clock and the accurate measurement of time.

Galileo also exploded a belief common in his time—that heavier bodies fall faster than lighter ones. He was able to prove mathematically that all objects, regardless of their weight, fall at the same speed in the absence of air friction. This discovery laid the foundation for the modern science of mechanics (the study of matter in motion).

Vesalius and Harvey. Progress was also made in the field of biology. Andreas Vesalius, born in Brussels, was a pioneer in the study of anatomy. Instead of accepting without question what Galen had written hundreds of years earlier, he conducted investigations of his own to see how the human body was constructed. In 1543—the same year that Copernicus' book was published—Vesalius published a work called *On the Fabric of the Human Body*. This beautifully illustrated book is a landmark in the history of medicine.

Equally important was the work of William Harvey, an English physician. He was the first man to understand and describe the circulation of the blood, the working of the heart, and the function of the blood vessels.

CHECKUP

1. What effect did printing have on European civilization? Why?

2. What theory was put forth by Copernicus? How did the work of Kepler and Galileo help to prove it?

3. Name two important contributions made by Galileo to the science of physics.

4. IDENTIFY: parchment, Gutenberg, Caxton, Aldus Manutius, orbits, Vesalius, Harvey.

3   The Protestant Reformation began in Germany

At the beginning of the Renaissance, the Church was under attack from two main sources—private individuals and national rulers. As you have read, some people criticized abuses in the organization and practices of the Church; others went further and even questioned basic dogmas. Rulers of growing nations in Europe opposed the Church for what they considered its interference in the affairs of their nations. They also resented the fact that much of the money collected in churches in their nations was sent to the pope in Rome. Often monarchs coveted the great wealth of the Church within their borders.

The sale of indulgences

The first outright break with the Church came in Germany. It began over the question of indulgences, although the controversy soon involved other subjects as well. An indulgence was a kind of pardon for earthly punishment of a sin, and was granted only if the sinner confessed and was truly repentant.

Originally, an indulgence was given only to a person who had performed some good work of special merit, such as an act of charity, fasting, or fighting in a crusade. Some Renaissance popes, however, began the practice of issuing indulgences in return for the payment of money to be used for papal needs. Many uneducated people failed to understand the necessity for true repentance. They thought of the indulgence as a cash transaction by which they bought forgiveness for their sins.

In 1514, Pope Leo X began a campaign to raise funds for rebuilding St. Peter's Church in Rome. The sale of indulgences was to provide most of the funds. In northern Germany, an enthusiastic Dominican monk, Johann Tetzel, was employed to travel about persuading people to give generously.

Tetzel was what might be called today a "high-pressure" salesman. To build up his sales, he began to claim that the purchase of an indulgence could bring pardon for sins. Tetzel was reported to have preached: "So soon as coin in coffer rings, the soul from purgatory springs." Then he went further, claiming that buying an indulgence could bring pardon for sins not yet committed!

Martin Luther's protest

Tetzel's claims were entirely contrary to Church doctrine. They shocked and scandalized many intelligent and devout Germans. One of the men who protested against Tetzel's tactics was Martin Luther, a teacher of theology at the University of Wittenberg. Luther had received a university education and then became a monk and, later, a priest and lecturer in theology. As a devout Christian, he was shocked by Tetzel's irresponsible campaign. When people came to him to confess their sins, he refused to accept the indulgences as valid.

Luther studied the question of indulgences and took action in 1517. On the door of the church at Wittenberg he posted a list of theses, or formal statements, written in Latin. The Ninety-five Theses, as the list is called, forcefully proclaimed Luther's position on the question of indulgences and constituted an invitation for scholars to debate with him on the matter. Luther's action marked the beginning of the movement known as the Protestant Reformation, or Protestant Revolt.

Luther's theses were not meant for the general public. The new printing press, however, now became a factor in the situation. The theses were translated into German, printed, and widely read. Even before a debate took place, the question of indulgences had stirred up a great deal of popular interest.

Luther was challenged in debate by Johann Eck, one of the ablest speakers in the Church. Instead of discussing the question of indulgences, Eck forced Luther to debate whether he was a rebellious clergyman. He asked Luther whether he would submit to the decision of a Church council on indulgences against his own conscience. In such a case, said Luther, he would appeal to the teachings of the Bible itself.

Luther's break with the Church

Luther now found himself taking the same position for which John Huss, the Bohemian priest, had been burned as a heretic. He could do one of only two things: recant or break with the Church. Luther chose to break with the Church. He wrote an open declaration of his position and addressed it to the rulers of Germany's many states. Luther attacked the Church both as a religious and as a political institution. He called on the German rulers to reform the Church within their own borders and to forbid the pope to interfere in the affairs of their states. The pope excommunicated Luther as a heretic in 1520.

Luther continued to write pamphlets. He was an extremely able writer, and he generally wrote in German, not Latin, so that his writings had wide circulation among ordinary people. One of his greatest works was a translation of the New Testament into German. This translation was so widely read that it helped create a single national language for all Germans, as Dante had done for Italian and Chaucer for English. Later, Luther also translated the Old Testament into German.

In his pamphlets, Luther criticized every sort of abuse in the Church. He even attacked the papacy as a foreign power, thus appealing to German national spirit. The taxes Germans paid to Rome, he said, were an unjustified burden that helped to keep Germany poor, weak, and disunited. He appealed to the German rulers to unite and destroy the power of the pope over their states.

Lutheran doctrine. Luther now began to develop doctrines that were the basis for a reorganized church in Germany. It came to be called the Lutheran Church. The greatest difference from Roman Catholic doctrine was over the question of how man might gain salvation. The Catholic Church taught that salvation was possible only through good works and through the sacraments administered by the clergy. Luther taught a doctrine called "justification by faith." According to this doctrine, people would be granted salvation by faith alone. The clergy's role was to preach the Christian message and minister to people's spiritual needs.

Luther rejected several of the sacraments of the Catholic Church on the grounds that they were not authorized by the Bible. He retained only two: baptism and communion. Although Luther was much influenced by earlier theological writers, he claimed that he based his entire faith on the Bible. He believed that a person could find

Religious controversy characterized early modern times. The Protestant Reformation was touched off when Martin Luther, upper right, posted his Ninety-five Theses. Luther was prompted to this bold action by Johann Tetzel's selling of indulgences. In the caricature above left, Tetzel exhorts sinners to buy from him. The movement begun by Luther gained momentum when the teachings of John Calvin, lower right, spread throughout Europe. The Roman Catholic Church reacted to Protestantism with the Counter-Reformation. The Council of Trent, below left, changed some Church practices and reaffirmed basic Catholic doctrines.

in the Bible those things which he had to believe, and that he could be saved through his faith in them.

Lutheranism in Germany

Many German rulers accepted Luther's beliefs and adopted Lutheranism. Some of these rulers were quite sincere and followed Luther because they felt his beliefs were correct. Others, however, adopted Lutheranism because it offered them an opportunity to seize Church lands and other property in their states. Some of these rulers coveted the Church's wealth and desired to avoid paying taxes to Rome. They also wished to become independent of the Holy Roman Emperor (who was closely allied with the papacy).

The Holy Roman Emperor, Charles V, summoned the Diet to meet at Worms in 1521. It issued the Edict of Worms, prohibiting the printing or sale of Luther's works and forbidding anyone to give him shelter. The edict was defied by those who sympathized with Luther's cause. Another Diet, in 1529, ended toleration of the followers of Luther in Roman Catholic states. Many of the German rulers who had adopted the new faith protested this decision and would not accept it. Because of this protest, the members of the new church were called Protestants from that time on.

Shortly after Luther's death in 1546, a war broke out between the forces of the Protestant rulers and those of the emperor and the Catholic nobles. It lasted for several years without a real victory for either side. A compromise was finally reached through the Peace of Augsburg, which was signed in 1555. It had four important provisions:

(1) Each German ruler could decide for himself and for his subjects which religion would be followed in his state.

(2) Protestant rulers had the right to keep all Catholic Church property seized before 1552.

(3) Lutheranism was the only recognized Protestant creed.

(4) Any Catholic bishop or abbot who became a Protestant had to resign his title and lose his lands (which remained in the possession of the Catholic Church).

Most of the rulers of northern Germany chose Lutheranism, while most of the southern German rulers remained Catholic (see map, page 309). The wishes of the people played no part in these decisions. The religion chosen by each ruler became the state religion in his domain. The people there had to accept his decision or move away.

CHECKUP

1. Over what specific issue did the Reformation begin? What action did Martin Luther take?

2. What were the main differences between Luther's ideas and those of the Roman Catholic Church?

3. List the provisions of the Peace of Augsburg. To what extent did it provide for religious toleration?

4. IDENTIFY: indulgences, Tetzel, Eck, Edict of Worms, Protestants.

4 Protestantism spread and the Counter-Reformation was launched

Protestant movements soon began to take shape elsewhere. Some countries adopted Luther's ideas. In others, Protestantism took different forms.

The spread of Lutheranism

Lutheranism had strong appeal, particularly because of its doctrine that man would be granted salvation through faith alone. Lutheran ideas spread rapidly to the Scandinavian countries of Norway, Denmark, and Sweden.

Within ten years after Luther nailed his Ninety-five Theses to the church door at Wittenberg, the ruler of the united kingdom of Norway and Denmark recognized Lutheranism on an equal basis with Roman Catholicism. A few years later the Catholics rebelled, unsuccessfully, against the new order. The ruler then declared the Lutheran Church to be the *established church* of Norway and Denmark. An established church is an official state church, and is supported by taxes paid by everyone, no matter what their religion; its clergy are paid by the government. A little later, Sweden followed the same path when the ruler recognized Lutheranism as the state religion.

John Calvin

A Protestant leader second only in importance to Luther was John Calvin. He was born in France in 1509. Calvin saw little chance of bringing about reforms of any kind in the Roman Catholic Church in France, so he went to the city of Geneva, in Switzerland, where Protestantism had gained a firm foothold. He soon became the leader of the Protestant movement in Switzerland.

Most of Calvin's beliefs are set forth in a book he published in 1536, *Institutes of the Christian Religion*. The most important of Calvin's teachings was the doctrine of predestination. Since God is able to foresee all the future, said Calvin, He must know that many men will be sinful and that by no means all of them can be saved. Calvin believed that God had chosen, long in advance, those who would be saved. Calvin called these people the "elect." The only way a person could be at all sure that he was one of the elect was by living a righteous life.

Calvin became almost all-powerful in Geneva. He made the city a *theocracy*—that is, a government ruled by a clergy claiming God's authority. Because of the great importance he attached to the righteous life, he regulated the lives and conduct of the citizens down to the smallest details. There were laws prohibiting dancing, card playing, showy dress, and profane language. Violation of these laws brought extremely severe punishment. Calvinist Geneva was not a jolly place.

The spread of Calvinist ideas. For two reasons, Calvinism soon spread beyond the borders of Switzerland. First, the new creed had an organized system of beliefs, as stated in Calvin's *Institutes*. Second, it offered a church government which maintained strict discipline, resisted control by the state, and gained from its members a loyalty even stronger than the one they felt for nations or political rulers. There was no central authority like the papacy. Each local congregation had a ruling body of men called a consistory, which included laymen (called presbyters) and clergymen.

By 1550, Calvinism was spreading widely. In most cases it did not become the majority religion in the country. The northern part of the Netherlands adopted Calvinism and organized what was called the Reformed Church; the southern Netherlands, including what is now Belgium, remained Catholic. Other Calvinist minorities were found in Poland, Bohemia, Bavaria, and Hungary (see map, opposite page).

Outside of Switzerland, Calvinism was most successful in Scotland. John Knox, a great admirer of Calvin, spent several years with him in Switzerland. Returning to Scotland, Knox succeeded in overthrowing Roman Catholic authority and setting up a Calvinist church called the Presbyterian Church.

In France many of the bourgeois became Huguenots (HYOO·guh·nahtz), as French Calvinists were called, but the great mass of the French people remained Catholic. Huguenots were considered a threat by the French monarchs, who wanted a strongly united kingdom. To the kings of France, as to most European rulers of the time, a subject who differed with his king in matters of religion committed treason.

Outright civil wars over religion in France began in 1562, accompanied by plots, counterplots, assassinations, and massacres. The wars were as much political as religious. They lasted until the leader of the Huguenots, Henry of Navarre, became king of France as Henry IV. Henry then became a Catholic for political reasons, but in 1598 he issued a decree called the Edict of Nantes which granted Huguenots freedom of worship and political rights.

The Reformation in England

When Lutheran and Calvinist ideas appeared in England, they stimulated some criticism of Catholic Church doctrines and clergy. The greatest challenge to the Catholic Church in England, however, arose from the growth of national government. The Tudor kings did not want interference from any outside power and resented the influence of the Catholic Church in England.

SPREAD OF PROTESTANTISM
in the 1500's

ESTABLISHED CHURCHES IN 1600:

Protestant:
Lutheran
Calvinist
Anglican

Roman Catholic

C Calvinist minorities

—— Boundary of the Holy Roman Empire in 1560

Henry VIII, the second Tudor king, came to the throne in 1509. He was a devout Catholic and persecuted Protestants who tried to spread their ideas to England. However, he had family problems that troubled him greatly. He had married his brother's widow, Catherine of Aragon, a daughter of Ferdinand and Isabella of Spain. The only child of Henry and Catherine to survive was a daughter, Mary Tudor. Henry wanted a son to carry on the Tudor line. In 1527 he asked the pope to annul, or set aside, his marriage to Catherine so that he could marry a younger woman named Anne Boleyn (BOOL·in).

The pope had a difficult decision to make. Marriages were sometimes annulled, but this one had been legalized by a special papal dispensation, necessary because Catherine had been Henry's sister-in-law. Then, too, Catherine was the aunt of Charles V, Holy Roman Emperor, king of Spain, and the most powerful Catholic ruler in Europe. The pope delayed his decision.

But Henry VIII would not be denied. The archbishop of Canterbury had just died. Henry himself appointed the successor, Thomas Cranmer. The newly appointed archbishop summoned a Church court which declared the king's marriage to Catherine dissolved and permitted his marriage to Anne Boleyn.°

The pope immediately excommunicated both Henry VIII and Cranmer, but Henry refused to be frightened. In 1534 he persuaded Parliament to pass the Act of Supremacy. This act declared that the king, not the pope, was head of the Church in England. Parliament also passed a law abolishing monasteries in England, and the king seized their property. He gave much of this land to his supporters, creating a so-called "new nobility" that could be relied on to uphold his policies.

Henry VIII's break with the Roman Catholic Church was more political than religious. Henry himself made this fact clear by stating that the Church in England would continue to be Catholic in doctrine and ritual. The organization remained the same except that the king was at the head.

Persecutions under Henry's successors. England went through troubled times after the death of Henry VIII in 1547. Edward VI was sickly and only ten years old when he became king. The advisers who ruled for him were influenced by Lutheran and Calvinist ideas and made the Church in England more Protestant.

When Edward died after a reign of only six years, Mary succeeded him. She was a devout Roman Catholic and was determined that England should be restored to the Catholic Church and the authority of the pope. Under her influence, Parliament abolished the Act of Supremacy and all the changes made during the reign of Edward VI. Archbishop Cranmer and two bishops were burned at the stake as heretics. Protestants were severely persecuted.

After reigning five years, Queen Mary died childless in 1558. Her half sister Elizabeth succeeded to the throne as Elizabeth I. In a reign

lasting forty-five years, Elizabeth proved to be one of the greatest of English rulers. In religion she was not as strongly Protestant as the advisers of Edward VI had been. On the other hand, she insisted upon a strongly national church—a church that would unite all Englishmen, end the religious troubles, and be independent of the pope.

The Church of England. Thus there came into being the Church of England, or Anglican Church. The monarch was head of the church, which was an established church. Not everyone was required to belong to the Church of England, but nonmembers were under some handicaps.

In matters of belief, the Church of England shared many doctrines with the Roman Catholics, but was also influenced by Protestant teachings. The Anglicans kept many of the ceremonies of the Roman Catholic Church, as well as a church organization under bishops and archbishops. However, church services were in English instead of Latin, rituals were simplified, and priests could marry.°

The Counter-Reformation

The Protestant Reformation was a blow to the Roman Catholic Church. Among other things it showed that the abuses against which men had protested for so long would have to be corrected. The movement of reform that followed the Protestant Reformation is usually known as the Counter-Reformation.

An important factor in the Counter-Reformation was a new organization founded by an extraordinary man. Ignatius Loyola was a young Spanish soldier who had been wounded in battle. His recovery was slow, and he devoted his time to reading and thinking about the lives of Christ and the saints. He became convinced that he should become a soldier of Christ, spreading the teachings of Christianity.

Loyola spent eleven years in studying and preparation for his new work. He gathered about him a group of followers. In 1540 the pope gave

---

° **Anne Boleyn:** Anne Boleyn bore Henry a daughter, Elizabeth, but no son. Henry later had her tried, condemned, and beheaded for misconduct. A third wife pleased him by giving birth to a son, Edward, but she died in childbirth. In all, Henry was married six times; however, only his son Edward and his two daughters, Mary Tudor and Elizabeth, survived him. In his will he provided that his son was to succeed him as Edward VI. If Edward died without an heir, Mary was to succeed to the throne. If she too died without an heir, Elizabeth was to become queen.

° Churches in other countries related to the Church of England make up the Anglican Communion. In the United States this church is known as the Protestant Episcopal Church of America.

them permission to establish a new religious order called the Society of Jesus. Its members, known as Jesuits, took the usual monastic vows. Some took an additional vow which required them to promise to obey the pope and to do any missionary work he might ask of them.

The first aim of the Jesuit order was to check the spread of Protestantism and to regain for the Church those areas that had broken away. The Jesuits were a strong force: well trained, strictly disciplined, and ardently devoted to their work. They traveled throughout Europe preaching, founding schools, and advising Catholic monarchs. Their efforts restored Poland, Bavaria, and Hungary to the Roman Catholic Church. They also checked the spread of Calvinism in France.

The Counter-Reformation also involved other measures that strengthened the Catholic Church. Pope Paul III summoned a council of Church leaders to meet in Trent, Italy, in 1545. They were to consider Protestant criticisms of Church doctrines and to make needed reforms in Church customs and practices. The Council remained in session for eighteen years.

After careful consideration, the Council of Trent restated all the doctrines of the Catholic Church and refused to accept any of the Protestant interpretations and doctrines. It reaffirmed its belief in the seven sacraments and in the pope as the supreme head of the Church.

The Council, however, did condemn and end some of the abuses that had grown up within the Church. Simony was strictly prohibited. The sale of indulgences was banned. Bishops were instructed to see that members of the clergy were better educated and that they lived blameless lives.

To help guard the morals of Church members, the Council prepared an *Index of Prohibited Books*. The Index listed all books which the Church considered immoral and dangerous to the soul. All Catholics were forbidden to read them. The Council also strengthened the Inquisition.

Results of the religious upheaval

The most striking result of the great religious struggles of the 1500's was that the single western Christian Church of the Middle Ages no longer existed. Religion divided Europe. While southern and eastern Europe and the population of Ireland remained firmly Catholic, France and the Netherlands were split. Switzerland, northern Germany, Scandinavia, England, and Scotland became Protestant (see map, page 309).

Another far-reaching result of the Reformation was a new interest in education in Protestant nations. Protestants believed that man could find his way to Christian faith by studying the Bible. As a result, training in reading became important. Education did not mean tolerance of new ideas, however. Luther, Calvin, and their followers felt obliged to set up standards of faith and practice. They did not permit views that differed from their own.

In Catholic countries there was even less toleration of new ideas. Writing and speaking were closely supervised. There was little room for questioning and difference of opinion. Those who did differ with Church authorities found themselves called before the Inquisition. Their writings were placed on the *Index.*°

The Reformation led to an increase in the power of national governments and a decrease in papal power. In Protestant regions, each government took responsibility for the leadership of the established church. Each time a national government did this, the papacy suffered a loss of political power.

CHECKUP

1. What part in the Protestant Reformation was played by John Calvin? John Knox?

2. Why and how did Henry VIII break with the Roman Catholic Church? Was this a political or religious move? Why?

3. Why was the Council of Trent summoned? What actions did it take?

4. IDENTIFY: established church, theocracy, Huguenots, Edict of Nantes, Mary Tudor, Church of England, Ignatius Loyola.

° *Index:* Galileo's *Dialogue* was placed on the *Index* and was not removed from it until 1822. In 1965, Pope Paul VI formally praised Galileo, Dante, and Michelangelo as "great spirits of immortal memory."

CHAPTER REVIEW

Chapter 14   The Renaissance and the Reformation Changed Europe   (1350—1632)

B.C. | A.D. →

| 1300 | 1400 | 1500 | 1600 | 1700 | 1800 | 1900 | 2000 |

1350	Boccaccio's *Decameron*	
1450	Constance Missal printed by Gutenberg	
1508-1512	Painting of Sistine Chapel ceiling by Michelangelo	
1516	Publication of More's *Utopia*	

1517	Luther's Ninety-five Theses
1521	Edict of Worms
1534	Act of Supremacy in England
1536	Calvin's *Institutes*
1540	Founding of Jesuit order

1543	Copernicus' *On the Revolution of the Heavenly Spheres*
1545-1563	Council of Trent
1598	Edict of Nantes
1632	Galileo's *Dialogue*

CHAPTER SUMMARY

The Renaissance, a great literary and artistic flowering, began in Italy. It grew out of Humanism, an intellectual movement characterized by a renewed interest in classical learning, a critical spirit, and enthusiasm for life in this world. Important Italian writers included Petrarch, Boccaccio, Castiglione, and Machiavelli. In northern Europe, Humanism was reflected in the works of Erasmus and More, among others.

Among the best early Renaissance painters were Giotto, Masaccio, Fra Angelico, and Piero della Francesca. The High Renaissance produced four supreme artists: Leonardo da Vinci, Michelangelo, Raphael, and Titian. In the north, the artists of Flanders were outstanding.

Important technological and scientific achievements were made during the Renaissance. One was the development of printing with movable type. Another was the birth of modern science. Copernicus, Kepler, and Galileo proved that the earth and other planets move around the sun, and Galileo made several discoveries in physics. Vesalius and Harvey were pioneers in the field of biology.

The critical spirit of the Renaissance also affected religion. In Germany, Martin Luther broke away from the Roman Catholic Church and began the Protestant Reformation. The doctrines he developed formed the basis for the Lutheran Church. Lutheranism was adopted in many German states and became the established church in Norway and Denmark.

From Switzerland, John Calvin's teachings spread to Scotland, the northern Netherlands, and central Europe. In France, Huguenots were granted freedom of worship by the Edict of Nantes.

England, too, experienced religious conflict. Henry VIII persuaded Parliament to pass the Act of Supremacy, making the king head of the Church in England. There was religious strife under Henry's successors, Edward and Mary. Finally, under Elizabeth I, the Church of England was established.

The reform movement within the Roman Catholic Church is known as the Counter-Reformation. The Jesuit order was founded to check the spread of Protestantism. The Council of Trent reaffirmed all Church doctrines and condemned abuses.

QUESTIONS FOR DISCUSSION

1. For a long time after the Renaissance, the humanities were the most important subjects taught in schools and universities. What do we mean today by the humanities? How do you account for the fact that these studies are no longer given primary emphasis?

2. Gutenberg's invention of movable type revolutionized the transmission of knowledge in Europe. Have radio and television caused a similar revolution in today's world? Explain.

3. Do you agree that, after the Reformation, the growth of religious freedom and toleration was inevitable? Justify your answer.

4. Machiavelli wrote that the ideas of morality which are supposed to govern individual conduct cannot be applied to governments. What is your opinion?

PROJECTS

1. Write a dialogue between Tetzel and Luther about indulgences.

2. Write a letter to a friend in which you express regret that your prince has chosen Lutheranism as the religion for his state.

3. Make a list of the chief writers, artists, and scientists of the Renaissance and name their important achievements.

Europeans Explored, Traded, and Settled in Distant Lands

The first traveler into an unknown region usually has no definite information to guide him. But if he makes careful notes and observations, either he or someone else can later make a map of the new area, which will be valuable to those who wish to visit it.

Maps were in general use among the early Egyptians and the Hellenistic Greeks. Some of these maps were remarkably accurate, particularly in the way they showed the Mediterranean Sea and the surrounding regions.

During the Middle Ages in Europe, map-making was practically a lost art. Some medieval maps were nothing but designs or diagrams. One such map was simply a circle surrounded by water. The circle was divided into three parts, one each for Asia, Europe, and Africa.

The travel of the crusaders and Italian merchants added to Europeans' knowledge of geography. By the 1300's, maps were beginning to show areas and coastlines that we would recognize today. But there was no standard system of making maps. Many cartographers, or map-makers, placed Asia at the top. They did this because the Garden of Eden was supposed to have been located in Asia, thus making that continent the most important. Others placed Jerusalem at the center because of a verse in the Bible stating that "God had set Jerusalem in the midst of the nations and countries."

French explorers landing in North America

As trade increased, maps grew more accurate. A famous map of 1375 included some of the islands in the Atlantic, Negro kingdoms south of the Sahara, and the nations of the Far East. But cartographers of this period still found room to sketch in the kingdom of Prester John, a mythical Christian monarch who was believed to rule in the heart of Asia or Africa.

By 1400, sailors were making wide use of portolanos (Italian for "navigation manuals"). These were charts of coastlines based on actual sailing experience. Early in the 1400's, Europeans rediscovered the *Geography* of the Alexandrian scientist Ptolemy. The original maps accompanying this book had been lost. But Ptolemy's descriptions, based on latitude (the distance north or south of the equator) and longitude (the distance east or west of a given point), were accurate enough so that later cartographers could re-create the maps.

Ptolemy's maps showed that the world was round. Actually, most educated people of the Renaissance knew this to be true, but cartographers did not indicate it on their maps, and un-educated people thought of the world as flat. Late in the 1400's, cartographers made globes that incorporated the geographical descriptions of Ptolemy. One of the best-known early globes showed Madagascar, Java, and Japan. It did not, of course, show North or South America.

A person looking at such a globe would undoubtedly have made this observation: the distance from Europe to the Orient was shorter to the west—that is, across the Atlantic Ocean—than to the east. Daring sea captains of the late 1400's and the 1500's studied the maps and globes of their time, set out on their travels, and opened up new worlds scarcely dreamed of before.

THE CHAPTER SECTIONS:

1. European explorers opened up both east and west (1271–1522)

2. Portugal and Spain acquired many foreign colonies (1500–1650)

3. England, the Netherlands, France, and Russia expanded (1500–1700)

4. Exploration and colonization changed Europe in many ways (1500–1750)

1　European explorers opened up both east and west

The search to learn more about what lay beyond Europe's horizons began during the Middle Ages, when travelers explored distant lands. The crusaders, for example, brought back knowledge of the Near East. Several missionaries made the long journey to China. This trip was undertaken often enough for a Florentine to write a guidebook for travelers to Peking.

News of these travels spread slowly, but it did spread. Accounts of faraway lands influenced men's minds even though they did not produce immediate results.

The travels of Marco Polo

The most famous of European medieval travelers was Marco Polo of Venice, who was born in the 1200's. In the company of his father and uncle, who were merchants, Marco Polo made the long, hard, overland journey across Asia to China. The trip took them four years, from 1271 to 1275. Marco had an easy manner and a talent for languages so that he made friends wherever he went. His reception was especially warm at the court of Kublai Khan, the great Mongol emperor of China. Marco quickly learned Chinese and served for many years as an official of the Chinese government, traveling throughout Asia on official missions. He visited the East Indies, Burma, Tibet, and India.

The Polos returned to Venice in 1295, after twenty years in the Orient. They brought with them rich jewels, rare spices, and beautiful textiles. When Marco told of the millions of people in China and the millions in wealth held by Kublai Khan, his disbelieving fellow townsmen nicknamed him "Marco Millions."

Later, Marco Polo was taken prisoner in a war between Venice and Genoa. While in prison he dictated an account of his experiences to a fellow prisoner who happened to be a professional scribe. His stories, called *The Book of Marco Polo,* became famous throughout Europe, first in handwritten form and later as a printed book.

Among many other things, Marco Polo told of great cities such as Kinsai (now Hangchow), which was divided into twelve sections, each of them larger than Venice. He told of Kublai Khan's summer palace of marble at Shangtu and of lavish ceremonies the Khan held there. He told also of simpler things: of coal, the black rock that gave off heat when burned; of the great horned sheep (later named the Marco Polo sheep); and of the tiny musk deer. But mostly he told of the huge, rich, and peaceful Chinese Empire.

From the start, Marco Polo's book stirred the imagination of its readers and aroused speculation about the lands of the Far East. In the long run, however, the book had even more practical effects. Marco Polo carefully described his outbound route overland across central Asia, and his return by sea around Southeast Asia and across the Indian Ocean to Persia and home to Venice (see map, page 274). Renaissance map-makers used this information to draw maps of great value to explorers.

The search for new trade routes

As you read in Chapter 11, northern Italian cities such as Venice and Genoa dominated the Mediterranean end of the trade that linked the Far East and Europe. This situation was unsatisfactory to the emerging nations of Western Europe. Portugal, Spain, England, and France were interested in this commerce, too. They had to feed from the crumbs of the Italian table, and they did not like it.

There were two courses open to the nations of Western Europe. They could try to break the Italian monopoly of Mediterranean trade so that their own merchants could trade at such ports as Constantinople, Alexandria, and Antioch. Or they could find a new route to the East.

The second alternative was better. The Mediterranean route was only one stage in a long journey that relied heavily on Arab traders and other middlemen. A product from the East that entered Europe in this way went through many lands and many hands before it reached its final user. At each exchange, someone added his costs as well as a profit for himself so that the price increased.

The nations facing the Atlantic wanted to find an all-water route to the Orient, one that would bypass costly overland caravans. Such a route would have the effect of cutting out the Arabs and Italians alike. More important, it would enable its discoverer to undersell the Italians in Western European markets and still make rich profits. This could be done because the price would not have to include so many middlemen's costs and profits.

Improvements in sailing

The search for new sea routes to the Orient was aided by improvements in ships and sailing. You have already read about some of the developments in map-making during the Renaissance. Technical developments also occurred in two other fields: (1) navigation and (2) shipbuilding.

New navigation instruments helped make it possible for ships to venture out to sea instead of hugging coastlines for fear of losing their bearings. One instrument was the compass. As early as the 1100's, Europeans knew that an iron needle rubbed against a piece of lodestone (a kind of magnetic rock) would be magnetized and turn toward the north. They may have learned this from the Chinese by way of the Arabs. At first the magnetized needle was floated on a piece of cork in water; in the 1300's it was fixed to a card marked with directions to create a true compass.

Another instrument applied astronomy and geometry to navigation. This was the astrolabe, which had been perfected by the Moslems. Sailors used it to determine the relative height of stars and planets and thus determine a ship's latitude.

Ships. In 1400, European ships were inferior to those of the Arabs, Indians, and Chinese; by 1600, they were the best in the world.

Before and even during the 1400's, most European coastal trade was carried on by long ships called galleys. They were propelled by oars—twenty-five or thirty on each side—manned by slaves or prisoners of war.

In deeper waters, traders used sailing ships. In the Baltic and North Atlantic, most of these were square-rigged—that is, they had a square sail, supported by a yard, or pole, fastened horizontally to the mast. Square-riggers were clumsy, especially close to shore, and could sail only with the wind. In the Mediterranean, most sailing ships carried a lateen sail. This was a triangular sail, suspended from a short mast by a long, tilted yard. Lateen-rigged ships could sail into the wind, but they were limited in size because of the weight of the yard.

In the late 1400's, ship designers of Portugal and Spain made an important improvement when they developed the full-rigged ship—one that combined square and lateen sails. The most common type was the carrack (KAR·uk), which had three masts: two with square sails; and one, at the stern, with a lateen sail.

Shipbuilders made another improvement by placing the steering rudder at the stern instead of on the side as in earlier ships. A full-rigged ship with a rear rudder could sail fairly fast with or against the wind, and could be steered with reasonable accuracy.

Portugal and Prince Henry

The small nation of Portugal was one of the first to become seriously interested in exploration. This interest was due largely to a member of the royal family, Prince Henry, often called Henry the Navigator. He had four main aims for Portugal: (1) to win new lands and peoples for Christianity by a crusade in Africa; (2) to encircle and outflank the Moslems by finding and joining forces with Prester John, who Prince Henry thought lived somewhere in Africa; (3) to acquire a share of the African slave trade which the Moslems then controlled; and (4) to gain trade with the Orient.

Early in the 1400's, Prince Henry established a school in Portugal in which navigators were trained. Soon his sea captains began a series of explorations westward into the Atlantic and south-

ward along the western coast of Africa. They slowly worked their way south, each captain going a little farther than the one before him. As they explored, they took possession of a number of islands, such as the Azores. Far to the south, below the region of the Sahara, the Portuguese began to develop a trade in Negro slaves, gold, and ivory.

Further explorations brought even greater gains to the Portuguese. In 1487, Bartholomeu Dias sailed around the Cape of Good Hope, at the southern tip of Africa. Finally, in 1498, Vasco da Gama sailed around Africa and across the Indian Ocean to India (see map, pages 318–19). He came home with a cargo of spices and jewels that paid for his trip sixty times over.

The voyage of Da Gama was a tremendous stroke of good fortune for Portugal. Portuguese ships could sail to India and the East Indies and bring back rich cargoes of Oriental goods. Venetians, Arabs, and others could not block Portugal from the wealth of the eastern trade. From this time on, the commercial importance of the eastern Mediterranean region declined.

Christopher Columbus

Even before Vasco da Gama brought wealth to Portugal, Spain also had become interested in the search for new trade routes. Its rulers, Ferdinand and Isabella, decided to finance a voyage by Christopher Columbus, an Italian navigator from Genoa. Influenced by Ptolemy's descriptions, Columbus thought that the world was much smaller than it actually is, so that he could reach India quickly and easily by sailing westward.

In August 1492, with three small ships, Columbus set sail from Spain and crossed the Atlantic. His small fleet landed in October on a small island in the Caribbean Sea, which he called San Salvador (probably Watling Island in the Bahamas). After visiting several other islands, Columbus returned triumphantly to Spain in the spring of 1493 to report on his discoveries. He believed the islands to be off the coast of India and therefore called their inhabitants Indians. Actually he had discovered the islands later known

(*continued on page 320*)

Early Exploration

Marco Polo's adventures in Asia followed those of his father and uncle, who had returned to Italy in 1269 on an errand for Kublai Khan. Two years later the elder Polos set out once again for the East, accompanied by 17-year-old Marco. Above, the Polos leave Venice. They are stepping into the rowboat that will take them to the sailing ship for the first stage of their journey.

Lisbon, which has one of the finest harbors in Europe, was the starting point for many Portuguese voyages of discovery. It was from this bustling harbor, right, that Vasco da Gama set out on his voyage. The portrait above right shows Da Gama after he had been rewarded by the king for his discoveries.

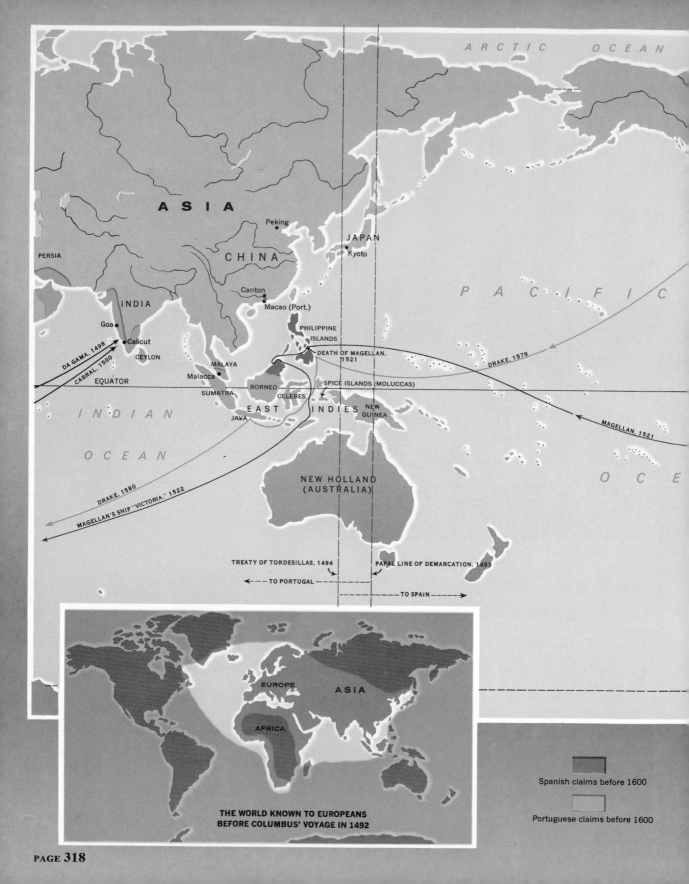

ARCTIC OCEAN

ASIA

PERSIA

INDIA

Goa

Calicut

DA GAMA, 1498

CABRAL, 1500

EQUATOR

Peking

CHINA

JAPAN

Kyoto

Canton

Macao (Port.)

PHILIPPINE
ISLANDS

DEATH OF MAGELLAN,
1521

MALAYA

Malacca

SUMATRA

BORNEO

SPICE ISLANDS (MOLUCCAS)

CELEBES

EAST

INDIES

NEW
GUINEA

PACIFIC

DRAKE, 1579

MAGELLAN, 1521

OCE

JAVA

INDIAN

OCEAN

DRAKE, 1580

MAGELLAN'S SHIP "VICTORIA," 1522

NEW HOLLAND
(AUSTRALIA)

TREATY OF TORDESILLAS, 1494

← TO PORTUGAL →

PAPAL LINE OF DEMARCATION, 1493

← TO SPAIN →

EUROPE

ASIA

AFRICA

**THE WORLD KNOWN TO EUROPEANS
BEFORE COLUMBUS' VOYAGE IN 1492**

Spanish claims before 1600

Portuguese claims before 1600

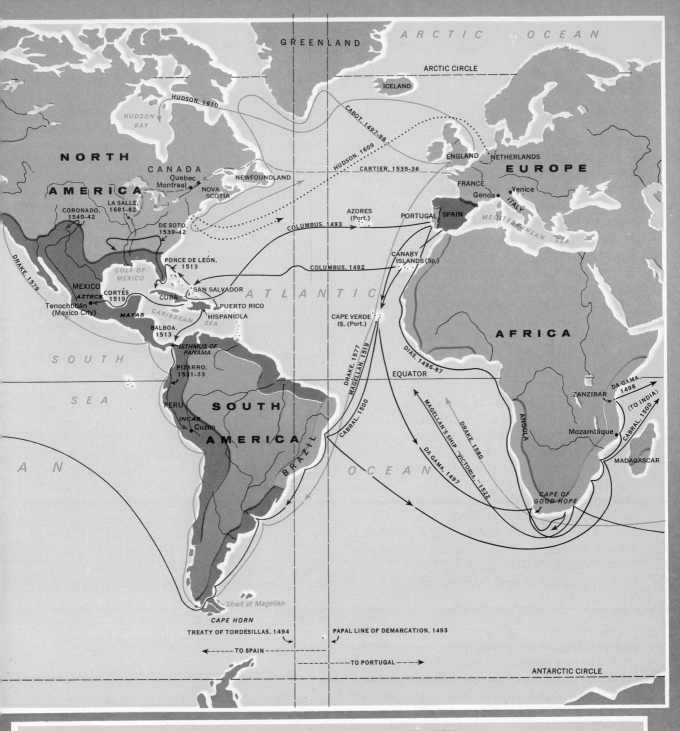

THE AGE OF EXPLORATION AND DISCOVERY

EXPLORERS FOR PORTUGAL →
Dias, 1486-1487
da Gama, 1497-1498
Cabral, 1500

EXPLORERS FOR SPAIN →
Columbus, 1492-1493
Balboa, 1513
Ponce de León, 1513
Cortés, 1519
Magellan, 1519-1522
Pizarro, 1531-1533
De Soto, 1539-1542
Coronado, 1540-1542

EXPLORERS FOR FRANCE ----→
Cartier, 1535-1536
La Salle, 1681-1682

EXPLORER FOR THE NETHERLANDS ·······→
Hudson, 1609

EXPLORERS FOR ENGLAND →
Cabot, 1497-1498
Drake, 1577-1580
Hudson, 1610

as the West Indies. Although Columbus made three more voyages between 1493 and 1504, he believed until his death that the lands he had found were part of Asia.°

Dividing the new lands

Spain and Portugal made sweeping and conflicting claims as a result of their discoveries. Their dispute was referred to the pope for arbitration. In 1493 he laid down the so-called papal line of demarcation—an imaginary line from the North Pole to the South Pole, about 300 miles west of the Azores and Cape Verde Islands. Spain was granted rights to all newly discovered lands west of the line; Portugal could claim all those to the east. A year later, the Treaty of Tordesillas between Spain and Portugal moved the line farther west (see map, pages 318–19).

As you can see by looking at a globe, if either of these nations kept on exploring in the direction allotted, their claims would eventually conflict on the other side of the world. But for practical purposes, the line worked. A Portuguese captain, Pedro Alvarez Cabral, reached the east coast of South America by accident in 1500. He was sailing for India along Da Gama's route, but strong winds blew him off course and forced him westward. When he claimed what is now Brazil for Portugal, his claim was honored because he had landed east of the line of demarcation.

In 1529 the line was extended completely around the globe. Thus, most of Central and South America was claimed by Spain. Portugal exploited chiefly its territories in Asia.

Other explorers

Columbus was followed westward by other explorers. Between 1497 and 1503, Amerigo Vespucci (ves·POO·chee) took part in several Portuguese expeditions across the Atlantic. Vespucci became convinced that the land he saw was not

° In 1965 scholars published a map, thought to have been drawn in 1440, that showed early Viking discoveries in North America. Although the map was later designated a fraud, Vikings are believed to have reached North America long before Columbus' voyages. His discoveries, however, were the major stimulus for the exploration of America.

part of Asia. When he returned to Europe, he described what he had seen as a New World. After reading his writings, a German geographer named the new land America after Vespucci's first name ("Americus" in Latin).

In 1513 a Spaniard named Vasco Núñez de Balboa crossed the Isthmus of Panama and looked out on a great ocean. He called it the South Sea and took possession of it for Spain. Now it seemed clear that the New World was really a great land mass. It was Ferdinand Magellan, a Portuguese navigator sailing for Spain, who proved it to be so.

Magellan and his men succeeded in doing what in that day seemed nearly impossible: they sailed westward and ever westward until they reached home again. In 1519, with five ships, Magellan set forth from Spain, crossed the Atlantic to South America, and sailed along its eastern shore until he reached the southernmost tip. After passing through the strait that now bears his name, he found himself in a great ocean. Magellan struck it at a fortunate time; the sea was so placid that he named it the Pacific Ocean, from the Latin word *pacificus,* meaning "peaceful." This was, of course, Balboa's South Sea.

Magellan sailed westward across the Pacific and reached the Philippine Islands, which he claimed for Spain. There, in 1521, he was killed in a fight with the natives. The surviving members of the crew sailed on to the west. Only one ship, the *Victoria,* and eighteen men survived to finish the voyage and return to Spain in 1522. For the first time, men had circumnavigated the earth—that is, they had sailed completely around it.

CHECKUP

1. Name and discuss the importance of Marco Polo's account of his travels.

2. What factors aided the search for new sea routes to the Orient?

3. What were the four main aims of Prince Henry the Navigator?

4. IDENTIFY: Dias, Da Gama, Columbus, papal line of demarcation, Vespucci, Balboa, Magellan.

5. LOCATE: Azores, Cape of Good Hope, Caribbean Sea, San Salvador, Cape Verde Islands, Strait of Magellan, Philippine Islands.

2 Portugal and Spain acquired many foreign colonies

With the great geographical discoveries of the 1400's and early 1500's, the small world of medieval Europe suddenly expanded. New lands were waiting to be settled, new peoples were found who had never heard of Christianity, and new possibilities for trade opened up. Almost any man willing to cross the sea could own land—a dream come true, because in medieval Europe owning land was the mark of social position and wealth.

Two powerful motives lay behind most European exploration and colonization: the desire to gain wealth and the wish to spread Christianity. Gradually, however, the profit motive drove the missionary purpose into the background.

Portuguese expansion

The Portuguese were the first Europeans to establish an overseas empire (see map, pages 318–19). First, as you have read, they acquired the Azores. Next they took parts of the western coast of Africa, setting up the colony of Angola. Portuguese trading posts on the eastern coast of Africa included Mozambique and Zanzibar.

About the year 1510, the Portuguese conquered part of the southwest coast of India and began to use its port of Goa as a trading and administrative center. Next they attacked and conquered Malacca on the southwest coast of Malaya. From Malacca they moved eastward to take the fabled Moluccas, a group of islands between Celebes and New Guinea. Europeans called them the Spice Islands because they were rich in cloves, nutmeg, and other spices.

Trade with China. Malacca gave the Portuguese a base from which to push on to China. The first Portuguese seamen and traders landed in China in 1514. They quickly aroused the antagonism of the Chinese, who called them "ocean devils." The Ming dynasty, then ruling in China, was following a policy of isolation. The Chinese expelled the Portuguese several times, but each time they returned. Finally, under a special treaty, a Ming emperor allowed the Portuguese to establish a trading post on an island in the Si River delta, but forbade them to move inland from it. Here the Portuguese built the city of Macao (muh·KOW) as a center for their dealings with Chinese traders.

The Chinese did allow Christian missionaries into the country. Such men often did more than seek converts to Christianity. They transmitted some of the best thinking of Renaissance Europe, including the idea of scientific inquiry and a first-rate knowledge of mathematics, astronomy, physics, and geography.

The Portuguese in Japan. The Portuguese may have discovered Japan as early as 1543. According to tradition, some Portuguese sailors, lost at sea, landed in that year at a small island off the southern tip of Kyushu. The Portuguese from that time on came regularly to Kyushu and eventually to the city of Kyoto. Although they barely tolerated most Asians, Portuguese merchants got along well with the Japanese. The Portuguese respected the Japanese, perhaps for their fighting abilities, their sense of humor, or even their touch of haughtiness.

Portuguese merchants brought raw silk and silk textiles to Japan, and traded them for Japanese silver. This silver was then re-invested in Portugal's Asian trade and brought in good profits. The merchants also traded goods for copper mined in Japan.

Christian missionaries followed the Portuguese merchant seamen. A Jesuit, Francis Xavier (ZAY-vee·ur), arrived in Japan in 1549, after preaching in Goa and the Spice Islands. He preached in Japan for three years, converting about 2,000 Japanese to Christianity.

The missionaries in Japan concentrated their efforts on the daimio, the powerful local rulers. When they were converted, their followers would then adopt Christianity. The number of converts increased to 150,000 by 1582, to 300,000 by 1600, and to 500,000 by 1615. Despite their success, Christian missionaries irritated the Japanese with their rigid and intolerant views, which were contrary to Buddhist religious ideas.

During this time, Japan was undergoing important changes: it suffered military setbacks in Korea and Manchuria; the Tokugawa family was gaining power while the daimio were losing theirs; and the idea of isolation was gaining ground. In 1614, all missionaries were deported and Japanese converts were ordered to renounce Christianity or suffer severe penalties.

Although trade and missionary activity declined, some remnants of Portuguese influence remained in Japan. Portuguese words entered the Japanese language—for example *kappa* (from the Portuguese word *capa,* meaning "cape") and *vitro* (from *vidro,* meaning "glass"). European castle architecture, with its moats and stone walls, influenced Japanese building.

The Portuguese in Ceylon. When the Portuguese had gained footholds in China and Japan, they turned back to add another link to their chain of bases for trade and empire. This new link was the island of Ceylon, off the southeast coast of India. Ceylon was important as a stopping point between Goa and Malacca and as a source of tea and spices. With Ceylon and Malacca as bases, the Portuguese for a time dominated the entire East Indies trade.

Weakness of the Portuguese Empire

Portugal's rise to wealth and empire was rapid. Its decline was almost as fast for a number of reasons. First, the Portuguese government was neither strong nor well organized. It had difficulties controlling its officials at home, and found it impossible to control them in its colonies.

Second, the empire was a drain on Portugal's small population. Portuguese ships paid enormous profits, but they were death traps. They were built to carry so much cargo that they were top-heavy and thus dangerous to sail. The voyage from Portugal to Goa took six to eight months. It was a miserable journey. The ships, often manned by inexperienced sailors and usually in bad repair, were almost helpless in storms. Diseases raged unchecked. Each year Portugal sent out its strongest, most daring young men as sailors or traders. Only half, and sometimes fewer, returned. In time the situation in Portugal became so desperate that

criminals and other unwanted persons were sent to the Orient, with ill effects on the colonial settlements.

A third weakness of Portugal as a colonizing nation was the attitude of some of its people toward native populations. Long wars against the Moslems on the Iberian Peninsula had given the Portuguese, as well as the Spaniards, narrow and intolerant views toward non-Christians. The heathen, the unbeliever, was a man to be either converted or destroyed. Such views were bound to create hatred that would play into the hands of Portugal's rivals.

A fourth reason for the decline of Portugal was its annexation by Spain in 1580. The Spanish limited Portuguese trade and neglected its colonies.

The Spanish Empire

As you have seen, the main interests of the Portuguese, with the exception of Brazil, lay in Africa and the rich East. The Spanish, on the other hand, turned most of their energies to the New World; the Philippines formed their chief colony in the East.

After the time of Columbus and Balboa, the Spanish explored the West Indies, Central America, and parts of the mainland of North and South America (see map, pages 318–19). They found out, as you know, that America was not Asia, and that the lands they explored were not the East Indies. They did not find the spices they wanted. However, the soil was fertile, minerals were plentiful, the climate was temperate, and the natives were few enough to be controlled.

Spanish colonization began in the West Indies. From the island of Puerto Rico, Juan Ponce de León sailed northward in 1513 and discovered and explored Florida. Other explorers went to Yucatán and learned of the great Maya civilization that had flourished there. With 10 ships and 600 men, Hernando Cortés invaded Mexico in 1519. He defeated the Aztec ruler Montezuma, captured Tenochtitlán with its vast wealth in gold, and eventually conquered the entire Aztec Empire. Horses and guns, unknown to the American Indians, helped the small Spanish force overcome the much larger Aztec armies.

A Mariner's Astrolabe

To make his way about the oceans of the world, the explorer of the 1500's was at the mercy of a few relatively crude instruments. They helped him plot a course and hold it, keep track of his progress, and estimate his position. An example of one of these instruments, the astrolabe, is shown at left. It has an outer edge divided into degrees and a movable center bar with pointers on each end. Holding the instrument by the ring at the top, the sailor sighted along the bar, rotating it until one of the pointers aimed at the sun. The figure at the other end indicated latitude. Although inaccurate by today's standards this magnificently simple "mathematical jewel," beautifully crafted out of bronze, was one of the most sophisticated instruments of the period.

The Spanish also heard of a great and rich civilization in South America. Francisco Pizarro led an expedition of 180 men and 27 horses from the Isthmus of Panama to the Inca Empire in Peru and seized it for Spain.

Other explorers were less successful in their feverish quest for wealth. Hernando De Soto, exploring westward from Florida, discovered the Mississippi River, but no gold. Francisco Vásquez de Coronado led an army thousands of miles from Mexico into central North America in search of the fabled "Seven Cities of Cíbola." He saw many crude Indian villages, and one of his lieutenants discovered the Grand Canyon of the Colorado River, but again there was no gold.

In time, Spain controlled a vast empire in the New World, consisting of the West Indies, Central America, southern North America, and a large part of South America. The Spanish became colonizers in the true sense of the word.

Unlike the Europeans in Africa and Asia, who were mainly traders, the Spanish in the Americas established settlements. (You will read in Chapter 20 about the kind of society they set up.)

Very early in their settlement of the Americas, the Spanish developed a centralized colonial administration. The colonies were ruled by viceroys, representatives of the king. These officials were responsible to a council in Spain, which in turn was responsible to the king. Thus the development of the Spanish colonies was planned and directed.

Raids on Spain's treasure ships. The Spanish government made every effort to keep the wealth of the Americas for Spain alone. Foreigners were barred from the Spanish colonies. Silver and gold from America could be carried only in Spanish ships and only to the Spanish port of Seville.

It was one thing, though, to make rules, and another to enforce them. Spanish treasure ships became rich prizes. They were attacked by pirates who prowled the seas, and also by the ships of European nations which envied the Spanish wealth. Late in the 1500's the Spanish developed a convoy system, with warships escorting the treasure vessels across the Atlantic. After that, most of the treasure reached Spain safely.

First the Netherlands, and later England and France, used various means to get a share of the wealth from America. They sent ships to American ports, carrying manufactured goods which Spain itself was unable to supply. They made secret deals with individual Spaniards to sail the treasure ships to European ports outside of Spain. Instead of trying to suppress the pirates, they encouraged them to prey on Spanish ships.

Decline of the Spanish Empire

The mighty Spanish Empire declined in the 1600's. The chief reason for this decline was the importation of huge amounts of gold and silver from America, which drove up prices in Spain. As the supply of precious metals increased, they became less precious, and people demanded more of them in exchange for goods and services. High prices hindered the growth of Spanish industry. It already lagged behind that of other European nations for two chief reasons: (1) Spanish nobles thought work was degrading, and (2) the Moors and Jews, who once formed an enterprising middle class, had been expelled in the late 1400's.

Because France, England, and the Netherlands did develop industries, much Spanish wealth simply passed through Spain on its way to buy goods from these other nations. The gold and silver enabled Spain's enemies to develop their industries and grow strong at Spain's expense.

Another reason for the decline of the Spanish colonial empire was the kind of administration Spain provided. Although the government of Spain and its colonies was highly centralized, it was inefficient. At home it did not stimulate the development of industry by private citizens. In the colonies the attempt to maintain a strict monopoly by shutting out all foreign trade brought attacks by England, the Netherlands, and France.

CHECKUP

1. In what regions did Portugal establish its overseas empire? Why did it decline so rapidly?

2. In what ways did Spanish colonization differ from that of the Portuguese?

3. Why did the Spanish Empire decline?

4. IDENTIFY: Ponce de León, Cortés, Montezuma, Pizarro, viceroys.

5. LOCATE: Angola, Mozambique, Zanzibar, Goa, Malacca, Spice Islands, Macao.

3 England, the Netherlands, France, and Russia expanded

The nations of northern Europe were latecomers in the race for empires. England and France were occupied with domestic problems during most of the 1500's. The Netherlands, as you will see, was under Spanish rule until the early 1600's. Russia was just beginning to emerge from Mongol control.

By the late 1500's, when northern European nations were ready to acquire colonies of their own, the Spanish Empire was at its height. The Portuguese Empire, although beginning to decline, was still to be reckoned with. Just as the Spanish and Portuguese had tried to break the monopoly of the Italian cities a century earlier, now the English, Dutch, and French challenged the Spanish and Portuguese monopolies.

English sea power

Because of England's location, its people had always been interested in the sea. Over the centuries they had developed a rich overseas trade. Shortly after Columbus reached America, an Italian captain named John Cabot was commissioned by the king of England to voyage to North America. In 1497 and 1498, he explored the coasts of Newfoundland, Nova Scotia, and New England (see map, pages 318–19). His voyages gave the English a claim in the New World. (Northern European nations did not recognize the papal line of demarcation as applying to them.) But it was almost a century before the English took steps to develop this territory.

In the second half of the 1500's, during the reign of Elizabeth I, there appeared in England a hardy breed of sea captains, half trader and half pirate, whom the English called sea dogs. These men—John Hawkins, Francis Drake, and Walter Raleigh, among others—challenged Portuguese and Spanish trade monopolies.

Hawkins and Drake seized slaves from the Portuguese and sold them in Spanish colonies. Drake, seeking to plunder Spanish ships where they were not defended by convoys, sailed through the Strait of Magellan into the Pacific Ocean, which the Spanish considered to be their private sea. His takings were so rich that the rock ballast of his ship was dumped overboard and replaced with gold and jewels. From the Pacific coast of North America, Drake sailed westward and returned home as the first Englishman to circumnavigate the globe (see map, pages 318–19).

King Philip of Spain protested to Queen Elizabeth about the attacks of the English sea dogs, but she claimed that she was helpless to control them. Secretly she supported the sea dogs and shared in their spoils; for his achievements, she knighted Drake on the quarterdeck of his ship.

Goaded by English attacks and urged on by his desire to wipe out what he considered "Protestant heresy" in England, Philip decided to invade the island. In 1588 he sent a fleet of 130 ships, which he called the "Invincible Armada," northward toward the English Channel.

The English gathered all their ships and received some help from the Dutch. English ships were smaller than those of the Spanish, but easier to handle. Also, their guns fired faster and had a longer range. They damaged and sank a number of the great Spanish vessels. The Spanish ran low on ammunition and tried to escape. A terrible storm added to the destruction caused by the English. Only half of the Spanish ships returned to Spain.

The English in India. The defeat of the Spanish Armada marked the beginning of the decline of Spanish sea power. It also encouraged the English to plant colonies overseas. In 1600, Queen Elizabeth granted a charter to a commercial enterprise called the English East India Company.

The English were interested in the East particularly for the dyes and other Asian products necessary for their woolen cloth industry. They turned their attention to India because the Dutch, as you will read shortly, were firmly established in the East Indies.

The English East India Company set up trading posts at the Indian cities of Madras, Bombay, and Calcutta. The company dealt mainly with local rulers, for India had become divided into many little states as the Mogul Empire declined in power. Where a ruler was weak and submissive, he was given aid. Where force was needed, it was used without hesitation. If bribery was a better means, a generous "gift" was extended. The English established themselves so well in India that they remained there as rulers for 350 years.

The East India Company eventually set up a few trading posts in Malaya and the East Indies, but India remained the main source of English trade and wealth. Within a short time the East India Company became extremely wealthy and powerful, with a vast fleet of merchant ships and warships to protect its interests.

The English in the New World. England was slow to establish colonies in North America because of its great interest in the East. In fact, the first English ventures into North America were made in search of a Northwest Passage to India— that is, a water route around the Americas to the north and west. (The route south and west, around Cape Horn, was dominated by Spain.)

One of those who searched unsuccessfully for such a route was Henry Hudson. In 1609, on a voyage for the Dutch, he explored much of the coast of eastern North America and discovered the river that is named for him. On a voyage for the English in 1610, he discovered Hudson Bay in northern Canada (see map, pages 318–19).

While the search for a Northwest Passage went on, Englishmen became interested in the New World itself and began to establish colonies there. The task was performed by private companies or individuals. During the 1600's, several English colonies were founded along the east coast of North America (see map, pages 326–27). The first permanent settlement was Jamestown, established in 1607 in what is now Virginia. The second, Plymouth, was set up in 1620 in what is now Massachusetts.

These settlements were primarily commercial ventures, undertaken in the hope that the settlers might raise the products England had to import from the East and thus make the mother country

more self-sufficient. Commercially the North American colonies were disappointing; few of the original investors got their money back, to say nothing of making profits. Many individual colonists, however, had other reasons for settling in North America. They succeeded in finding greater political and religious freedom and in making better lives for their families. You will read more about their settlements in Chapter 18.

The English also settled various islands in the Atlantic, including Barbados and the Bahamas. Here their commercial success was greater be-

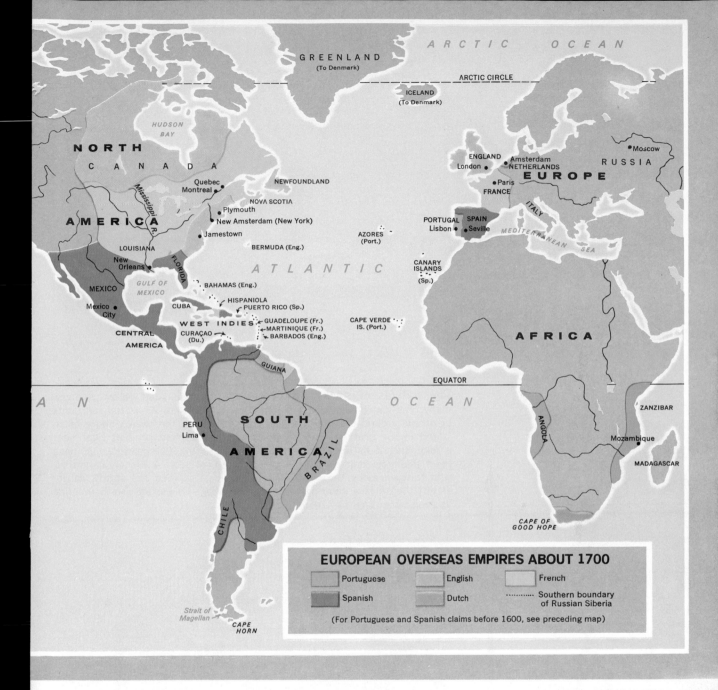

EUROPEAN OVERSEAS EMPIRES ABOUT 1700

- ☐ Portuguese
- ☐ Spanish
- ☐ English
- ☐ Dutch
- ☐ French
- ········· Southern boundary of Russian Siberia

(For Portuguese and Spanish claims before 1600, see preceding map)

cause some of the islands produced sugar, a valuable and important product.

The Dutch colonial empire

The coastal location of the northern Netherlands had turned its people, the Dutch, toward the sea. In the age of exploration, Dutch merchants set up a number of companies to trade in various parts of the world. The Dutch were brave sailors, and they built sturdy ships.

In the 1500's, the northern Netherlands began a long struggle to gain its freedom from

327

The natives of newly discovered lands fascinated early explorers, many of whom brought back pictorial records as well as written accounts of people around the world. A Dutch explorer drew the sketch above at an island in the southern Pacific. His own ships are anchored at right near a long line of native canoes. Most curious to the Europeans would have been the large double canoe, or catamaran, at left. A French naturalist, who traveled along the Niger River in Africa, recorded the sturdy warrior at left. Below is a painting of an Indian village in eastern North America as seen by an English explorer in the 1500's.

the Spanish. (You will read about this struggle for independence in the next chapter.) After Spain's annexation of Portugal in 1580, Portuguese ships and possessions became fair game to the Dutch. They first attacked ships carrying goods from Portugal to northern Europe. Then they preyed upon ships bringing treasure from Asia to Portugal. From these attacks it was only a step to try to take over the Portuguese Empire.

In 1602 the Dutch combined several trading companies into one powerful organization, the Dutch East India Company. The Dutch government gave this company the exclusive right to carry on trade between the northern Netherlands and Africa and the East Indies.

The first Dutch settlement in the East was made at Batavia, on the island of Java, in 1619. From Java the Dutch expanded westward to take the island of Sumatra and eastward to seize the valuable Spice Islands from the Portuguese. Malacca and the island of Ceylon came next, as well as Cochin on the southwest coast of India. In 1652 the Dutch also founded a colony in Africa, at the Cape of Good Hope, in order to secure their trade along the African coast (see map, pages 326–27).

Dutch colonial government was stronger than that of Portugal. The colonies were administered by a governor general, assisted by a council. The governor general had a great deal of authority over local officials, but he was closely controlled by the home government.

The Dutch tried to avoid a mistake the Portuguese had made. The Portuguese had held only strategic points along coasts in order to control the sea lanes. The Dutch realized that a successful empire required much wider control over the land and the people. For example, they did not stop with establishing a trading post at Batavia. Instead, they reached out and gained control of the entire island of Java, with its large population and its sugar, tea, coffee, and spices.

The Dutch gained some commercial influence in Japan. Since they did not come as missionaries, the shogun accepted them, although reluctantly. In 1638 a Dutch ship with its big guns helped overthrow the last Portuguese stronghold in Japan. As a reward for their help, the Dutch were allowed to trade in Japan and to maintain a trading post at Nagasaki.

The Dutch also founded colonies in the New World: in the West Indies, South America, and North America. In 1626 they purchased Manhattan Island from the Indians for about $24. There they founded New Amsterdam, which later became New York City.

The French in America and Asia

Among the first French explorers of North America was Jacques Cartier, who made several voyages between 1534 and 1541. On a voyage in 1535–1536, he sailed up the St. Lawrence River as far as the present city of Montreal and gave the French a claim to much of eastern Canada. However, no French settlements were permanent until the 1600's. In 1608, Samuel de Champlain established the first permanent French settlement at Quebec. France then set up several other settlements in the St. Lawrence Valley and in the Great Lakes region. The French developed a profitable fur trade with the Indians. Fishing off Newfoundland and Nova Scotia also became important.

The French colonies in America developed slowly until the reign of King Louis XIV in the latter half of the 1600's. Then settlement and colonization were encouraged, and the entire Great Lakes region was explored. Robert de La Salle then sailed down the Mississippi River to the Gulf of Mexico and claimed the entire inland region of North America for France. He named the region Louisiana in honor of Louis XIV (see map, pages 326–27).

The French also set up colonies in the West Indies, including the islands of Guadaloupe and Martinique.

In Asia, French efforts were directed by the French East India Company, formed in 1664. The company established a trading post, Pondicherry, on the southeast coast of India. During the 1700's an extremely able colonial administrator, Joseph François Dupleix, set up a smoothly working administration. French trade increased rapidly, and the French expanded into other regions of India. In many places they became rivals of the English.

Russian expansion

During the 1500's, Russia lacked seaports and thus was barred from the kind of overseas expansion carried on by Western European countries.

To the east, however, lay the vast steppes of central Asia, only thinly settled by nomadic tribes. It was in this direction that Russia grew.

Russia's eastward expansion was carried on mostly by a nomadic, freedom-loving people called Cossacks. Like frontiersmen everywhere, they hated the restraints of civilization and loved open spaces. The lure drawing them east was trade, especially the fur trade. Central Asia was a heaven for the trapper and fur trader. Animals were abundant and easy to trap. Most valuable was the sable, whose fur was highly prized. In 1581 a band of Cossacks conquered the remnants of the Mongol Golden Horde and captured the small city of Sibir east of the Ural Mountains that was then the Mongols' capital. With its capture, the way lay open to the entire region east of the Urals, all of which came to be known in English as Siberia (see map, pages 326–27).

Russian pioneers gradually forced their way eastward. To deal with such primitive peoples as the Tungus and the Yakuts, the early Russian settlers built blockhouses like American frontier forts. As centers for trade and defense, these posts became the towns and cities of Siberia: Tobolsk, Tomsk, Yakutsk, Okhotsk, and others. By the 1640's the Russians had reached the Pacific Ocean.

Russian pioneers moved eastward in two streams—one to the north and one to the south. Neither was checked by any strong native people until the southern group reached the Amur River. Here they came in contact with the Chinese. Fifty years of skirmishes and warfare failed to overcome the resistance of the Chinese. In 1689 the Russians and Chinese signed a treaty that fixed a boundary between them north of the Amur River and provided for Chinese-Russian trade. Russia traded furs and raw materials to the Chinese in exchange for such items as silk and tea.

CHECKUP

1. For what reasons was the Spanish Armada sent against England? Why was its defeat important?

2. Where did the English East India Company carry on most of its activities? How successful was it?

3. Summarize the colonial acquisitions of the Dutch and the French during the age of exploration.

4. IDENTIFY: Cabot, sea dogs, Hawkins, Drake, Northwest Passage, Hudson, Cossacks.

5. LOCATE: Nova Scotia, Newfoundland, Madras, Bombay, Calcutta, Batavia, Java, Sumatra, Quebec, Mississippi River, Siberia, Amur River.

4 Exploration and colonization changed Europe in many ways

You have read a great deal about trade in the last several chapters. Its revival during the Middle Ages helped change Europe from a land of manor villages ruled by feudal lords to a region of thriving towns and powerful national states. Trade assisted the exchange of ideas so important to the Renaissance. The great age of exploration that began in the late 1400's grew out of the desire of several European nations to win their share of the trade with the East. The overseas empires in turn affected Europe in several ways.

It could be said that the New World of the Americas made a new world of Europe. For one thing, European commerce, which had formerly centered on Mediterranean ports, now moved to the Atlantic coastal region. Venice and Genoa declined, while London, Amsterdam, and Lisbon bustled and grew.

In some cases the growth of overseas empires simply speeded up developments that had already begun, such as the use of money and the services provided by banks. In other cases, the old methods of doing business became inadequate, and Europeans worked out new ones. The European economy changed so much in the period from about 1500 to about 1750 that some historians refer to the economic developments of this time as the Commercial Revolution.

As Natives Saw the Europeans

After the Spanish arrived in the Aztec kingdom, Montezuma sent artists to record the appearance of the mysterious strangers. Cortés, above, rides a strange animal that resembles a dog (the Indians had never seen a horse before).

Englishmen who settled in India were quick to adopt the delights of the land. In the Indian painting above right, a pompous gentleman smokes a hookah, attended by servants in the manner of a maharajah.

When Portuguese merchants arrived in Japan with Jesuit missionaries, the Japanese were baffled by the strange ship—larger than any ever seen in Japan—the balloonlike trousers and short jackets, and the unintelligible language spoken by the Portuguese. The screen at right represents a Japanese attempt at an accurate portrayal of the foreigners' arrival. It is unlikely, however, that the Portuguese looked so silly or so Japanese.

A Moneychanger and His Wife

The wealth that poured into Europe after the age of exploration brought increased importance to middle-class bankers. Like wealthy men of many ages, these newly rich burghers liked to show off their affluence. Those of Flanders were particularly fortunate; painters there loved to render the trappings and appointments of wealth as much as their patrons enjoyed acquiring them.

In the painting at left by Quentin Massys, a leading Flemish painter of the 1500's, a moneychanger weighs coins. Nearby are pearls and a ring sizer. Massys painstakingly depicted every detail of the comfortable surroundings of the bourgeois banker and his wife, who commissioned the portrait to proclaim their success. The artist may have meant to be slyly satirical, for he shows the moneychanger's work distracting his wife's attention from her Bible.

The increased use of money

Medieval trade relied heavily on barter. This procedure became awkward as trade increased. Large-scale commercial activity is easier if there is a reliable medium of exchange, such as money.

Europeans had had different kinds of money since the early Middle Ages, but several handicaps prevented its wide use. One was the scarcity of precious metals. Europe produced almost no gold and very little silver. A second hindrance was the great variety of money in use. In England and France, the national governments minted, or made, money. Elsewhere individual cities and even nobles and bishops made their own coins. A third difficulty was the lack of a fixed standard for money. The value of certain coins would change according to the amount of precious metal used in them, no matter what the face value of the coins might be. It took an alert expert to tell what a coin was really worth.

This situation gradually changed, however.

Italian cities, deeply involved in trade, led the way in producing coinage of a fixed value; the gold florin of Florence and the gold ducat (DUK·ut) of Venice were very dependable. Then, as the New World colonies of Spain sent home tons of silver and gold, the king of Spain used it to pay the debts he owed to German and Italian bankers. These payments, plus those for goods that the Spanish needed, relieved the shortage of precious metals in Europe and made standard systems of money possible.

The growth of banking

In Chapter 11 you read about the banks that grew up in the later Middle Ages. During the period of the Commercial Revolution, banking systems became more complicated. Among the services they provided were the following:

(1) *Banks of deposit.* Here merchants could deposit money for safekeeping. The banks invested the money in loans that would give them

a good return. Out of the profits they paid interest to their depositors.

(2) *Credit.* Bankers developed letters of credit and bills of exchange. A merchant who deposited money in a bank could have such a paper drawn up and use it to pay bills. Thus merchants did not have to ship coins to distant places, always a dangerous and costly process.

(3) *Loans.* By 1400, most bankers were disregarding the Church's ban on charging interest for loans. Interest rates varied with the risk. A businessman in a safe enterprise might pay interest of only 5 percent on his loan. A man engaged in a risky venture might have to pay 50 percent. English kings were considered especially bad risks because Parliament might refuse to grant them the right to impose new taxes to pay off loans. One English king who borrowed money during the 1300's had to pay interest of 260 percent a year.

In addition to interest, bankers demanded security (something of value pledged as a guarantee that repayment would be made). At first, land was the commonest form of security. After some kings and lords refused either to repay or to give up their land, bankers demanded other security: crown jewels, the right to collect taxes, or monopolies on trade.

The great bankers. Great banking families included the Medici (MED·uh·chee) of Florence and the Fuggers (FOOG·urz) of Augsburg. They were involved in almost every kind of business. The Medici controlled the finances of the papacy for over a century. The Fuggers lent Charles V the money he used to influence his election as Holy Roman Emperor. The Fuggers were shrewd managers, and so relentless in pursuing debtors that at one time they averaged a 54 percent profit for fifteen consecutive years.

Today these interest charges and profits seem enormous. But the risks were great, too. Many bankers failed because a king refused to pay his debts.

The joint-stock company

You have read about the growth of capitalism in the late Middle Ages. Capitalists continued to expand and extend their activities during the period of the Commercial Revolution. They sought profits from the production and sale of goods and from banking. They also created a new kind of business organization.

During the Middle Ages, most business was conducted by individual owners or by partners. However, the large commercial undertakings of the 1500's required large amounts of capital, or invested wealth. Individuals or small groups often had difficulty raising enough capital.

To meet this problem, businessmen developed the joint-stock company. Such a company raised capital by selling stock, or shares in the company, to investors. These shareholders, or stockholders, became joint owners. They might conduct the business themselves, but usually they employed managers to do it. Profits were divided among shareholders according to the number of shares of stock they owned. The part of the profit paid out for each share of stock was called a dividend.

By getting many people to invest their savings in this way, joint-stock companies raised large amounts of capital for all kinds of ventures. Both the English East India Company and the Dutch East India Company were joint-stock companies. Each was amazingly profitable. They frequently paid dividends of 50 percent, and a few times paid as much as 300 percent a year.

However, this form of organization did not guarantee profits. The English joint-stock companies that were formed to establish colonies in America were failures as business undertakings.

Most of the great bankers and stockholding capitalists were members of the middle class. This group was rapidly becoming the most important European class, at least economically.

Mercantilism

During the 1500's and 1600's, European governments developed programs aimed at increasing their wealth and power through the regulation of trade and industry. Behind these programs was a theory of trade called *mercantilism.* According to this theory, the real wealth of a nation consisted of the supply of money and precious metals in the hands of the government or its people. The nation with the greatest supply of gold and silver was the wealthiest, and therefore the strongest.

Balance of trade. Fortunate nations had deposits of gold and silver either in colonies abroad, like Spain, or at home. A nation that lacked precious metals had to obtain them by trade. It had to sell more goods in foreign countries than it bought from them, thus producing what was called a "favorable balance of trade." By bringing money into a country, a favorable balance of trade strengthened the country itself and weakened its foreign rivals, who paid for the goods they bought and thus depleted their supplies of gold and silver. Mercantilism, in fact, was a form of war fought on an economic front instead of on a battlefield.

To gain a favorable balance of trade, a nation could take several measures:

(1) It could reduce the amount of goods imported into the country by setting up tariffs (taxes on imports). The importer paid the tax and added that amount to the selling price of the goods. The higher price discouraged people from buying foreign goods.

(2) It could try to increase the value of its exports. Manufactured goods were the most valuable kind of exports because they sold for more money than raw materials; woolen cloth, for instance, brought more than raw wool. Therefore a mercantilist nation encouraged manufacturers, the exporters of manufactured goods, and shipbuilders. In many cases, governments made grants of money called subsidies to help establish new industries and to build ships.

(3) It could try to make itself self-sufficient by producing everything it needed plus a surplus of goods for export. The self-sufficient nation did not have to depend for its needs on foreign countries, which were always rivals and might at any time become active enemies. The desire for self-sufficiency helped to stimulate the race for colonies.

The role of colonies. Colonies played an important part in mercantilism. Those that produced gold and silver were most desirable. Next best were those which produced raw materials that could not be produced at home. By buying these materials in its colonies, a nation could avoid buying from a foreign rival. Thus money did not go out of the nation or empire.

According to the mercantile idea, such colonies as the West Indies were especially valuable because they produced sugar and molasses which would otherwise have had to be bought elsewhere.

The mainland of North America had other valuable products. For example, pine forests in the southern English colonies were sources of pitch, tar, rosin, and turpentine. These products were called naval stores (supplies) because they were so important to ships. England itself did not produce naval stores and had previously bought them from Sweden or Russia. Therefore the English government encouraged their production in North America by paying bounties (money rewards) to colonists who produced them.

Besides their value as sources of raw materials, colonies were important as markets for the manufactured products of the mother country. Governments passed laws to prevent colonies from developing manufacturing industries of their own. They regulated colonial trade to prevent colonists from buying foreign goods or selling their raw materials to anyone but the mother country.

Financially the relationship between colonies and a mother country was most beneficial to the mother country. A colony was both a producer and seller of raw materials and a buyer of manufactured goods. Some mercantile practices, such as bounties, were helpful to colonial businessmen; but on the whole, mercantilism tended to restrict the economic development of a colony.

CHECKUP

1. What conditions hindered the use of money during the Middle Ages? What changes increased its use?

2. Describe three services provided by bankers during the Commercial Revolution.

3. Explain the ideas of mercantilism concerning (a) the wealth and strength of nations; (b) the favorable balance of trade; (c) the importance of colonies.

4. IDENTIFY: Medici, Fuggers, joint-stock company, dividend, tariffs, subsidies, naval stores, bounties.

CHAPTER REVIEW

Chapter 15   Europeans Explored, Traded, and Settled in Distant Lands   (1271—1750)

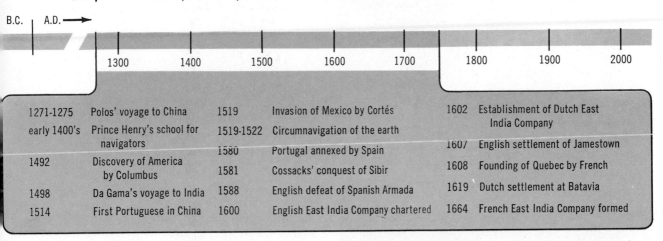

1271-1275	Polos' voyage to China	1519	Invasion of Mexico by Cortés	1602	Establishment of Dutch East India Company
early 1400's	Prince Henry's school for navigators	1519-1522	Circumnavigation of the earth		
		1580	Portugal annexed by Spain	1607	English settlement of Jamestown
1492	Discovery of America by Columbus	1581	Cossacks' conquest of Sibir	1608	Founding of Quebec by French
1498	Da Gama's voyage to India	1588	English defeat of Spanish Armada	1619	Dutch settlement at Batavia
1514	First Portuguese in China	1600	English East India Company chartered	1664	French East India Company formed

CHAPTER SUMMARY

A great era of European exploration and discovery began in the late 1400's. Italian states had long had a monopoly on trade with the east, and other European nations wanted their share. They began searching for new routes to the Orient. Their search was aided by improved maps, navigation instruments, and ships.

Portugal profited from the voyages of Dias and Da Gama. Columbus, sailing for Spain, discovered islands in the Atlantic that he thought were part of Asia. The subsequent voyages of Vespucci, Balboa, and Magellan revealed that Columbus' discovery was a New World.

The desire for wealth and the wish to spread Christianity inspired European colonization. The Portuguese set up trading posts in Africa, India, Malaya, the Spice Islands, and Ceylon, and gained trading rights in China and Japan. The Spanish Empire was concentrated in the New World.

The countries of northern Europe began to acquire colonies in the 1600's. Their defeat of the Spanish Armada encouraged the English to plant overseas colonies—trading posts in India and settlements in North America. The Dutch established themselves in the East, conquering many former Portuguese possessions, and set up colonies in the New World. The French planted colonies in North America and competed with the English in India. Russia gained territory mainly through Cossack expansion eastward.

Europe's great expansion stimulated a Commercial Revolution. Spanish imports of silver and gold relieved the shortage of precious metals in Europe and made possible the standardization of money. Banking expanded, with banks of deposit, credit facilities, and loans. Joint-stock companies were formed to produce capital for expansion. Mercantilism aimed at a favorable balance of trade. It stressed tariffs, exports, and self-sufficiency, with colonies especially valued as sources of raw materials and markets for manufactured goods.

QUESTIONS FOR DISCUSSION

1. In what ways can today's space exploration be compared with the sea exploration that began in the late 1400's?

2. Do you approve of the way European powers obtained colonies and divided the New World? Who do you think should own the moon or planets upon which man may land?

3. In what respects would you agree or disagree with the mercantilistic theory as it applied to a nation's wealth?

4. Why were small numbers of Europeans able to dominate much larger native populations in the East Indies, India, and the Americas?

5. Great bankers and stockholding capitalists had immense economic power during the period of exploration and colonization. Would you expect these people to have become politically powerful also?

PROJECTS

1. Make a chart of European countries and their colonial possessions.

2. Make a sketch of a carrack, the most common type of ship used for exploration.

3. Draw a map showing the routes of ten explorers discussed in this chapter. Use different colors to indicate the routes they traveled.

4. On a map of the Americas, show Portuguese, Spanish, English, and French possessions in 1700.

Strong Monarchs Competed for National Power and Prestige

Louis XIV of France

By the early 1500's, England, France, and Spain had developed strong national governments, under rulers who were almost absolute monarchs.

Strongly centralized governments brought about more tranquil conditions within countries. No longer could feudal lords devastate the countryside with personal wars. Kings had the power to enforce the peaceful settlement of disputes in their courts. The central government was *sovereign* (SAHV·run)—that is, its authority was supreme over the people in its territory.

Although there was less war within countries, destructive wars between them became more frequent. A sovereign nation could settle internal problems by law or by decree of the monarch. But when two sovereign nations clashed, there was no law, no court, and no government to insist on peaceful settlement. Thus, the growth of sovereign nations was accompanied by an increase in international warfare, a prominent feature of modern times.

Many wars in the early modern period were fought over territorial boundaries. Others, involving religion, were the outward signs of the intolerance of the time—a time when members of each church held stubbornly to their own views and regarded nonmembers with suspicion and contempt.

Often, however, political boundaries or religious differences were only part of the picture.

Basically, warfare was regarded as a way of increasing national prestige, and as part of the natural order of things. Machiavelli, the great Italian political philosopher, wrote: "War should be the only study of a prince. He should consider peace only as a breathing-time, which gives him leisure to contrive, and furnishes ability to execute, military plans."

As wars became broader in scope, methods of warfare changed. Feudal skirmishes between small groups of mounted lords were a thing of the past. You have read how the longbow, the cannon, and the Swiss pike played a part in this change. Armies were now made up of full-time professional soldiers, just as they had been in the time of the Roman Empire. These armies developed and used tactics in which infantry, cavalry, and artillery each had specified duties. New types of guns, and improved methods of loading and firing them, turned foot soldiers into skilled fighters. War was no longer a game for the amateur. It had become a serious business.

THE CHAPTER SECTIONS:

1. Spain dominated Europe during most of the 1500's (1516–1600)
2. France emerged from the Thirty Years' War a great power (1589–1648)
3. Louis XIV led France to greatness and ruin (1643–1715)
4. Russia became a major power in the 1700's (1613–1796)
5. Austria and Prussia contended for power in central Europe (1648–1786)

1 Spain dominated Europe during most of the 1500's

At the beginning of the 1500's, Spain was the most powerful nation in Europe. The reigns of two able kings, Charles I (who was also known as Charles V of the Holy Roman Empire) and Philip II, covered almost the entire century.

Charles V

You have read that the Hapsburgs of Austria were highly successful in arranging marriages which increased their lands and power. Through a series of such marriages, a Hapsburg came to the throne of Spain as Charles I in 1516. Three years later he was elected emperor of the Holy Roman Empire, having influenced the election with money borrowed from the Fugger bankers. He received the title of Emperor Charles V.

As king of Spain, Charles ruled that country, its vast possessions in the Americas, the Balearic Islands, Sardinia, the Duchy of Milan, and the kingdoms of Naples and Sicily. Through his Hapsburg relationships, he was also ruler over the Netherlands and Franche-Comté, a province between France and Switzerland. As Holy Roman Emperor, he ruled Austria and had some claims to other German states as well. His brother Ferdinand was king of Hungary and Bohemia. Notice on the map on page 338 the great extent of these territories. Notice also how they almost encircled France.

Charles found that his titles and power brought with them problems and responsibilities. First, there was the problem of his own nationality. He was born in Flanders and spoke French as his native tongue. However, as king of Spain, he had to have a Spanish outlook, and as emperor of the Holy Roman Empire, he had to be sympathetic to German aims.

Shortly after Charles ascended the throne, there was a revolt in Spain because people objected to his being a "foreigner" and appointing men from the Netherlands to Spanish governmental posts. The revolt was unsuccessful, but it added to Charles' many troubles.

As emperor of the Holy Roman Empire, Charles was responsible for defending Europe against the Turks of the Ottoman Empire, who invaded central Europe and also attacked European ships on the Mediterranean. In Germany, Charles was also responsible for upholding the Roman Catholic states against the Protestant princes. As ruler of so many lands, Charles had to contend with the fear and jealousy of other European

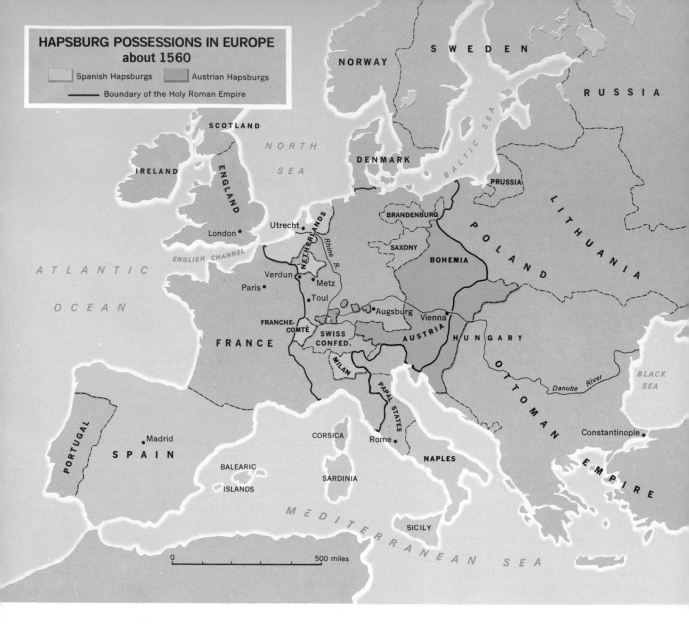

HAPSBURG POSSESSIONS IN EUROPE
about 1560

Spanish Hapsburgs ☐   Austrian Hapsburgs ▨
—— Boundary of the Holy Roman Empire

countries, especially France. All these problems had to be handled at the same time.

The wars of Charles V. Charles had several advantages on his side. The Spanish army at that time was the strongest and best organized in Europe. The Spanish fleet was powerful. Great wealth from the Americas made it possible to buy supplies and weapons and to hire mercenary soldiers. On the other hand, Spain's government was inefficient both at home and in the colonies. Spain lacked industry and had difficulty feeding its people

because so much land was devoted to sheep-raising.

Charles V achieved only partial success in holding his large empire together. In a series of wars with France, he prevented France from seizing the Duchy of Milan, but lost the cities of Metz, Verdun, and Toul, which had been part of the Holy Roman Empire.

In 1529, Charles halted Turkish penetration of central Europe by driving the Turks back from Vienna. However, he had to agree to Turkish rule of the Balkan Peninsula and half of Hungary. In Germany the emperor made strong but unsuccessful efforts to bring Lutherans and Roman Catholics into agreement. As you have read, a religious war broke out there in the 1540's and was settled with the Peace of Augsburg in 1555.

Even before the Peace of Augsburg, Charles V decided to give up his throne. In 1555 he divided his vast territory (see map, opposite). His son Philip received Spain and its possessions and ascended the Spanish throne as Philip II. His branch of the family became known as the Spanish Hapsburgs. Charles' brother Ferdinand became emperor of the Holy Roman Empire; he and his successors are called the Austrian Hapsburgs. Charles retired to a monastery in Spain in 1556. He lived there for two years before his death.

Philip II of Spain

Philip II was born and educated in Spain and proudly considered himself a Spaniard. He wanted Spain to continue as the leading power in Europe and the world, and he worked to make the nation stronger at home so that it might be stronger abroad. Philip concentrated on three domestic issues: the weakness of the central government, religious problems, and financial difficulties caused by wars and rebellions.

Charles V had never found time to unify and centralize the Spanish government. Each of the many provinces of Spain had a separate administration. Philip replaced these separate administrations with a centralized government responsible only to the king, and established a capital at Madrid.

Philip's religious problems involved the Moors and the Jews. After Ferdinand and Isabella set up the Spanish Inquisition, some Moors and Jews were converted to Christianity. Philip, however, suspected them of secretly practicing their former religions. He ordered the Inquisition to redouble its efforts to find and stamp out heresy. Many persons suspected of heresy left the country, but a great number of Moors, who considered themselves Spaniards, revolted against the savage persecution. This revolt, put down in 1571, placed a heavy burden on Philip's government.

Spain's domestic rebellions were a continuous drain on the treasury. The nation also became involved in foreign wars. Even the great treasure from America was not enough to pay the costs. The Spanish government levied heavy taxes, including a 10 percent sales tax, which hurt Spanish trade and industries. The financial problem only grew worse.

Relations with Portugal and England. In 1580 the throne of Portugal became vacant. Philip claimed it, and the Portuguese were too weak to prevent him from taking it. The Portuguese colonies in Asia, Africa, and South America were thus added to the Spanish Empire, while Portugal itself became a province of Spain. But the seizure of Portugal brought Spain more problems and expense than strength. The Portuguese people were never reconciled to the union. More important, Spain now had to defend the Portuguese colonies and their trade. Attacks by English, French, Dutch, and pirate ships made this an extremely difficult task.

After sixty years of Spanish rule, the Portuguese drove the Spanish back across the border, and Portugal again became independent. The Portuguese also regained control of their empire, but it had been so much reduced by conquests and concessions to the Dutch that Portugal never recovered its earlier importance as a leading colonial power.

As you read in Chapter 15, Philip was also involved with England. English sea dogs, such as Sir Francis Drake, attacked Spanish shipping, and Queen Elizabeth made no effective move to stop them. There was also the question of religion. As a staunch Roman Catholic, Philip disliked England's swing toward Protestantism, and hoped to restore the country to the Catholic faith. Still another issue was the fact that England supported the Dutch in their revolt against Spain (see page 340).

Thus Philip's attempt to invade and conquer England with his Invincible Armada stemmed from several causes. The English victory over the Armada in 1588 marked the beginning not only of England as a great sea power but also of the decline of Spain.

Spanish rule in the Netherlands

Philip's position in the Netherlands was a reversal of that of his father. Charles V was considered a foreigner by the Spanish but had always received loyal support from the Netherlands. Philip, Spanish-born and Spanish-speaking, was a foreigner to his subjects in the Netherlands, and they resented him.

The Netherlands was not easy to rule. There were seventeen provinces, each with a long tradition of self-rule. There was no central administration and the country was divided in language. The people of the central and northern provinces spoke Flemish, which resembles modern Dutch. Those in the southern provinces spoke a dialect of French.

The provinces were also divided by religion. The seven northern provinces had adopted Calvinism and set up the Reformed Church. The southern provinces remained Roman Catholic. Thus there was a religious split in the Netherlands and, more important, between the northern provinces and Spain itself. There was also trouble over the heavy taxes and mercantilist restrictions imposed by Spain on Dutch trade and industry.

Philip tried to solve the problems of government and religion at the same time. In order to centralize the administration, he took away the rights of local self-government. He filled the high offices with Spaniards. These officials did not speak the local language, and they neither knew nor cared about local customs. They tried to rule the Netherlands as a Spanish colony, and the people resented them bitterly. Philip tried to stamp out Protestantism among the Dutch by bringing in the Inquisition.

These two Spanish policies served to unite the people of the northern provinces against Spanish rule. Riots broke out throughout the northern region. When the Spanish viceroy there, the Duke of Alva, used harsh measures to try to end the riots, his brutality led to a full-fledged revolt.

Dutch independence

The Dutch revolt was led by a man called William the Silent. In addition to being the largest landholder in the northern Netherlands, William was Prince of Orange, a small state in southern France. Under his leadership the seven Protestant provinces of the northern Netherlands formed a league, called the Union of Utrecht, in 1579. The Union later became the United Provinces, or the Dutch Netherlands (today it is called simply the Netherlands). In 1581 the leaders of the Union declared that they no longer owed allegiance to Spain. The formation of the Union of Utrecht marked the beginning of a truly national struggle—Dutch against Spanish.

The Dutch were weak when they fought on land. Several times they saved themselves from complete defeat only by opening the dikes and letting in the sea to flood parts of their low country. On the sea the story was different. Privately owned ships called privateers, backed by the Dutch government, raided Spanish and Portuguese ships and colonies. They even attacked the coast of Spain itself. And, as you have read, the Dutch took over several Portuguese trading posts in the East Indies.

The war dragged on long after the death of Philip II in 1598. When the Hapsburg emperors of the Holy Roman Empire were faced with the religious revolt that developed into the Thirty Years' War, the Dutch fought on against Spain and the Hapsburgs. At last, in 1648, Spain was forced to yield. The Treaty of Westphalia, which ended the Thirty Years' War, also recognized the independence of the northern Netherlands. The southern provinces remained for a time under the rule of Spain and were known as the Spanish Netherlands (see map, page 346). They later became the Austrian Netherlands and, eventually, the country of Belgium.

CHECKUP

1. What problems faced Charles V? How successful was he in holding his empire together?

2. What caused trouble between Philip II and the Netherlands? What was the result?

3. IDENTIFY: Duke of Alva, William the Silent, Union of Utrecht, privateers.

4. LOCATE: Balearic Islands, Franche-Comté, Vienna, Madrid, Dutch Netherlands, Spanish Netherlands.

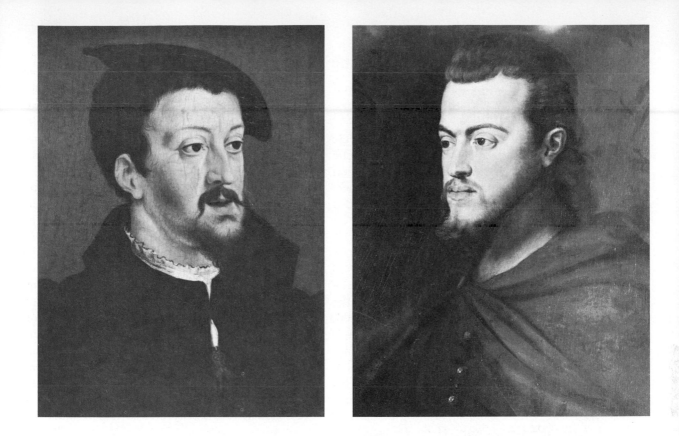

Spanish power and wealth dominated Europe for almost a century under the leadership of the two remarkable rulers shown above. Charles V, left, had strong will power and a stern sense of duty. He needed these qualities as well as steady shipments of treasure from the New World to deal with the problems of his vast domains. Philip II, right, inherited his father's strength of character but was arrogant and proud, and lacked a sense of tact. In his efforts to maintain Spanish authority, he antagonized many people. Below, Dutch Protestants at right fight Spanish forces in the long war that eventually achieved independence from Spain for the northern Netherlands.

Spain dominated Europe during the 1500's, but France became the most powerful nation on the continent during the next century.

France had several advantages in any struggle for European power. Facing both the Atlantic Ocean and the Mediterranean, France's location was strategic. It had good agricultural, commercial, and industrial resources. France also had a number of outstanding leaders.

Henry IV

Henry IV, who ruled France from 1589 to 1610, was the first of the Bourbon family to be king of France. He had been the leader of the Huguenots before he became king. He realized, however, that a Protestant could not unite France. He wanted a strong, united, and peaceful kingdom. Therefore, for political reasons, he adopted Roman Catholicism when he became king. He is said to have remarked, "Paris is well worth a Mass."

To end the religious wars, Henry IV issued the Edict of Nantes in 1598. It was important as a milestone in religious toleration and in the history of France. The Edict of Nantes gave the Huguenots freedom of worship and equal political rights with the Catholics. However, it contained certain provisions that were to cause trouble in the future. Huguenots were permitted to have military fortifications and the privilege of self-government in about a hundred French cities.

At the end of the Hundred Years' War in 1453, the power of the king had been made supreme in France over the nobles, great and small. However, the religious wars that began in the 1500's had plunged France into nearly forty years of anarchy and violence before the Edict of Nantes brought peace. During the reigns of several weak kings, the great nobles had become more powerful and unruly than before. Henry IV began to bring these nobles under royal control. He curbed their powers, reduced their privileges, and forced them to obey his orders.

Prosperity and peace. Henry wanted France to be prosperous. He said he wanted to "put a

chicken in the pot" of every family for Sunday dinner. This goal could be achieved only by drastic reforms. During the religious wars, trade and industry had run down, government administration had become weak and corrupt, and the treasury had been emptied. Henry showed wisdom in choosing the Duke of Sully as his chief minister to carry out the necessary domestic reforms. Sully was a Huguenot and therefore was opposed by the Roman Catholics. However, he was one of the ablest men in France, and Henry supported him and his policies against all objections.

The French system of taxation was inefficient, corrupt, and unjust. As in the Roman Empire, the taxes were farmed—that is, the right to collect them was sold to private individuals who paid the government a fixed sum and then collected all they could. It has been estimated that less than half of the money collected reached the treasury. Nobles and clergy were exempt from taxes, so the tax burden fell heavily on the middle class and peasants.

Sully could not make the system just; nobles and clergy continued to be exempt from taxation for centuries. But he did limit the expenditures of the court, discharge dishonest collectors, and supervise the tax farming more carefully. Finances improved until there was even a sizable surplus in the treasury.

The money coming into the treasury was used to make France more prosperous. Transportation on roads and rivers was improved and canals were built. With peace and order restored, agriculture and commerce revived. The renewed prosperity increased government revenues, especially from the collection of tariffs.

Both Henry IV and Sully were convinced believers in mercantilism. They encouraged manufacturing by granting subsidies and monopolies. The silk industry for which France was to become famous was established at this time. Like all true mercantilists, the king and his minister valued colonies highly. It was under Henry IV that France established a successful and lasting settlement at Quebec in Canada.

The policies and works of Henry IV were popular with most of the French people, but he still had many opponents. In 1610 he was assassinated by an insane monk.

Marie de Medici and Louis XIII

Henry's son and successor, Louis XIII, was only eight years old when his father was killed. The boy's mother, Marie de Medici, became regent—that is, she took over actual rule of the country. She had great ambitions and plans but lacked the ability to carry them out. She did not have her husband's tolerance in matters of religion. An ardent Catholic, she would allow no Huguenots to serve her, and Sully was removed from his position. The administration of the government again became corrupt, and the nobles reasserted their independence and power. Financial troubles again beset the country and the government.

At the age of sixteen, Louis XIII took control of the government. Marie de Medici was forced into the background, and the counselors whose advice she had followed were banished or executed. Louis was not a strong ruler, but, like his father, he selected good men to rule for him and supported them against all opposition. Louis XIII chose as his chief minister Cardinal Richelieu (ree·shuh·LOO), who was the actual ruler of France from 1624 until his death in 1642.

Richelieu as ruler of France

Richelieu had the clearest and most penetrating mind of any statesman of his time. He had a keen understanding of what was possible, politically and diplomatically. His will was like iron, and, in choosing methods to attain his goals, he was untroubled by moral scruples. Richelieu believed in Machiavelli's doctrine that the good of the state was the supreme good, and that any methods should be used to gain it. Although he wore cardinal's robes, he was a shrewd political leader.

The aims of Richelieu's policy are as simple to state as they were difficult to achieve. He wanted to make the king supreme in France, and he wanted to make France supreme in Europe. To accomplish the first aim, Richelieu set out to destroy the political independence of the Huguenots and the power of the nobles. He also wanted to strengthen France economically by reviving Sully's policy of encouraging trade and industry and building a colonial empire. To make France supreme in Europe, Richelieu planned to reduce the power of the Hapsburgs as rulers both of Spain and of the Holy Roman Empire.

Richelieu and the Huguenots. Richelieu believed that the provisions of the Edict of Nantes that allowed the Huguenots to govern fortified cities were politically dangerous. These cities were like states within a state, and made strongly centralized government impossible.

Fearing what might happen to them, the Huguenots sought a promise of help from Protestant England. In 1627, Richelieu moved against them and besieged the strong Huguenot seaport of La Rochelle and other fortified towns. The English were unable to provide enough help to save the Huguenots. After stubborn but futile resistance, the Huguenots asked for peace. Richelieu took away their right to independent towns, but he allowed them to worship freely, hold public office, and attend schools and colleges.

Attacking the nobles. The cardinal next turned to the problem of the nobles. Here he had to finish the work that Henry IV had begun. It was a difficult and dangerous task, but Richelieu was not a man to be discouraged. Moving first to crush the military power of the nobles, he ordered that all fortified castles not necessary for the defense of France be torn down. The nobles rebelled, and he suppressed them without mercy.

Richelieu's next step was to reduce the nobles' political power. With the king's consent, he appointed as governors of provinces men who favored a strong monarchy. He also strengthened the local administrators known as *intendants*. For these positions, he chose men of the middle class. Such men welcomed the chance to reduce the authority of the nobles. The *intendants* were given strong military, political, and administrative powers. They were responsible directly to the king, who appointed them and could remove them. Within a short time the *intendants* completely controlled local government.

The emergence of France as a major European force owed much to King Henry IV, above, and Cardinal Richelieu, right. Henry is even today the most popular king in the minds of many Frenchmen. Richelieu was a wily diplomat who often played one country off against another for the benefit of France. Below, the forces of Sweden, encouraged by Richelieu, battle troops of the Holy Roman Empire in Bavaria during the Thirty Years' War.

The Thirty Years' War

Richelieu's foreign policy was as determined and coldly calculating as his policy at home. He did not allow his position as a Catholic cardinal to interfere with his main aim of strengthening France at the expense of the Hapsburgs. A golden opportunity to achieve this purpose came with the Thirty Years' War.

The Peace of Augsburg of 1555, discussed in Chapter 14, had brought an uneasy peace to Germany, one that lasted some sixty years. It had not, however, created a satisfactory religious settlement. During those sixty years, religious friction continued to plague the German states. In 1618 there began a war that lasted, with intervals of peace, for thirty years.

Most of the immediate causes of the Thirty Years' War grew out of the weaknesses of the Peace of Augsburg. It had provided that the ruler, rather than the people, should choose the religion of each German state. The rulers themselves were limited to choosing between Lutheranism and Catholicism. Calvinism was not recognized, although it was growing continually stronger. The ownership of former Roman Catholic lands in Protestant states also caused trouble. The Peace of Augsburg made provision for Catholic Church property seized by Lutheran rulers before 1552, but not afterward.

Other conditions also led to war. There was constant rivalry among the German princes, rulers of some 300 independent states. Many of them wanted to be independent of the Holy Roman Empire. In addition, France, Denmark, and Sweden looked for opportunities to diminish the power of the Hapsburgs and the Holy Roman Empire.

The Thirty Years' War was really a series of wars. It began as a Protestant revolt in Bohemia, part of the Holy Roman Empire. The emperor was able to suppress this rebellion in 1620, but in doing so he gained the ill will of Protestant German princes and Protestant Denmark and Sweden. Denmark entered the war, but after several defeats its king had to promise not to interfere in German affairs. Sweden then took up arms, leading an alliance against the Hapsburgs.

Richelieu threw the support of France behind the Swedes, rather than helping the Catholic Hapsburg emperor. At first, Richelieu did everything possible to prolong the war without involving France directly; thus the other nations were weakened while France remained strong. In 1635, however, France declared war. Although Richelieu died a few years later, his successor, Cardinal Mazarin, carried on his policies.

In 1645 the French and their allies were victorious after a series of successful military campaigns. Most of the warring nations were exhausted after decades of fighting.

The Treaty of Westphalia

The Treaty of Westphalia, signed in 1648, was a landmark in the history of Western Europe because it made changes that were to affect Europe for centuries. Some of its principal provisions are listed below. (For a map of territorial changes, see page 346.)

(1) Each German ruler was given independence in his own state. He could make war or peace without interference from the emperor.

(2) Sweden received German territory along the Baltic Sea and North Sea, thus becoming the most powerful Lutheran state in northern Europe.

(3) The German state of Brandenburg, ruled by the Hohenzollern family, received lands to the north, along the Baltic Sea, and several bishoprics in Germany.

(4) The Dutch Netherlands and Switzerland were recognized as independent nations.

(5) France received Alsace, an extremely valuable territory along the Rhine River. It also received recognition of its possession of the cities of Metz, Verdun, and Toul.

(6) All former Catholic Church property was to be kept by whoever had held it in 1624.

(7) In Germany, Calvinists were granted the same privileges as Lutherans.

The chief political result of the Thirty Years' War was the rise of France as the leading European power, and the decline of Hapsburg power in both Germany and Spain. When each German prince was recognized as independent, the power of the Hapsburg emperor was weakened. The

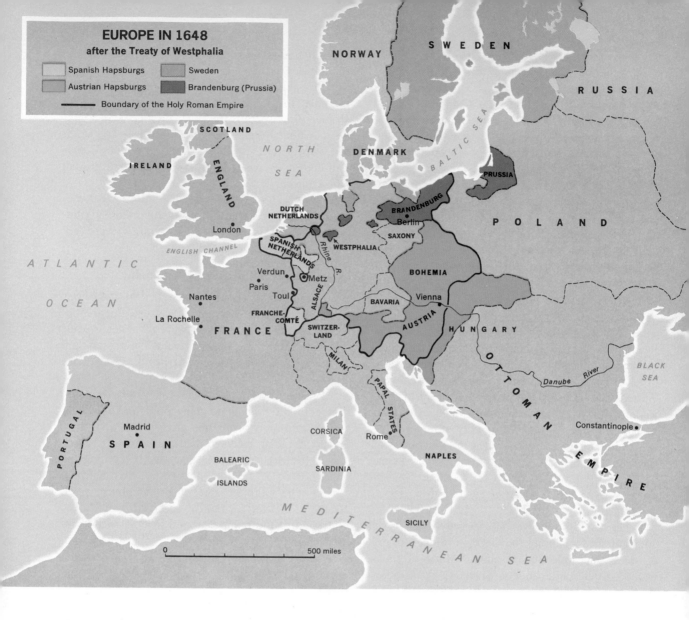

EUROPE IN 1648
after the Treaty of Westphalia

- Spanish Hapsburgs
- Austrian Hapsburgs
- Sweden
- Brandenburg (Prussia)
- ——— Boundary of the Holy Roman Empire

task of uniting the German states, under the Hapsburgs or anyone else, became much more difficult.

The economic and social results of the Thirty Years' War were disastrous for Germany. The war was fought almost entirely on German soil, and armies in those days lived off the land. Thousands of Germans lost their lives to slaughter, disease, or famine. A whole generation grew up to whom violence and brutality were normal conditions of life. Thus were sown the seeds of many hatreds that were to trouble Europe for centuries.

346

CHECKUP

1. What were the chief economic programs of Henry IV?

2. How did Richelieu plan to make the king supreme in France? Show the extent to which he was successful.

3. What were the chief causes of the Thirty Years' War? the chief results?

4. IDENTIFY: Louis XIII, Marie de Medici, Treaty of Westphalia.

5. LOCATE: La Rochelle, Brandenburg, Alsace.

3 Louis XIV led France to greatness and ruin

Cardinal Richelieu did not live to see the outcome of his efforts. He died six years before the end of the Thirty Years' War. Louis XIII died a year later, in 1643. Again France was left with a child as a king, for the new king, Louis XIV, was a mere boy. However, France was again ruled by a great minister, another cardinal of the Church.

Cardinal Mazarin was Italian by birth but French by choice. He had been trained by Richelieu himself in government and diplomacy, and was an able successor. In 1648 he successfully promoted the interests of France in the Treaty of Westphalia. He carried on a war against Spain for another eleven years and made further gains for France. In 1652 he suppressed a rebellion of French nobles, who fought to keep their feudal privileges. When Mazarin died in 1661, the monarchy was supreme in France, and France was the strongest power in Europe.

After the death of Mazarin, Louis XIV began to run the government himself. He proved to be one of the outstanding rulers in history. He believed firmly in the divine right of kings—that he was God's representative on earth and therefore responsible to no one but God. The attitude of Louis XIV toward government is shown by a remark credited to him: *"L'état, c'est moi."* ("I am the state.")

Colbert and mercantilism

Louis XIV took himself and his work as king seriously. To help him, he chose competent men, although he alone made the decisions. One outstanding adviser was Jean Baptiste Colbert (kawl-BAIR), an expert in the field of finance.

Colbert, a member of the middle class, followed the ideas of Sully in promoting the economic development of France. He was a strong believer in mercantilism and tried to build up French industry at home and French trade abroad. Private companies received government subsidies to build new industries or strengthen existing ones. High tariffs were placed on foreign imports, transportation was improved, and forests were replanted.

Like Sully, Colbert tried to improve the tax-collecting system by eliminating corruption and waste. For some years there was enough money to finance all the improvements at home, maintain a large army, and support colonial enterprises. Colbert encouraged French companies to establish colonies and carry on trade in Canada, the West Indies, and the Far East.

Culture and the palace at Versailles

In the fields of art and literature, Louis XIV made outstanding contributions. He was determined to make France the cultural center of Europe, an example to be imitated by all other nations. He gathered about him the finest artists, writers, and musicians of France, and invited outstanding men from other countries. Any man who showed talent was given a government pension so that he could devote all his time to his art. Among these men was the dramatist and comic actor Molière, one of the greatest of French satirists. He and his company of actors received the king's patronage and the title of "King's Comedians."

As a fitting symbol for the greatness of France and the glory of its culture, Louis XIV had a great palace built at Versailles (vur·SY), a few miles outside of Paris. Here were collected the finest works of French architects, painters, and sculptors. The palace was famous for its elaborate gardens and many fountains. Its cost, estimated at $1 billion in today's currency, seriously weakened French finances. On his deathbed, Louis himself admitted that he had spent too much on Versailles.

Louis moved not only the government to Versailles but also the most important nobles of France. They were required to live at the palace, where the king could keep an eye on them and prevent any plots against him from going too far. But in making this move, both the king and the court were removed from any real contact with the people of France.

Versailles became the ideal of European royalty, and its architecture was copied in many countries. French clothing, manners, and cooking were adopted, too. The French language became the court speech of the nobility and the language of diplomacy throughout Europe.

Military policy

Louis chose as his minister of war François Louvois (loo·VWAH), a military genius. Under his direction the army was completely reorganized. Men were promoted on the basis of merit, rather than by buying commissions. Louvois also created a quartermaster's department to furnish supplies to his troops so that they did not always have to live off the land.

No such army had ever been seen in Europe. Officers and men were highly trained and equipped with splendid uniforms and improved weapons. Discipline, which was very harsh, was the responsibility of General Jean Martinet. (Today we call a person who maintains very strict discipline a martinet.)

Having a large and fine army often creates a desire to use it. This was true of Louis XIV. It seemed almost as if his reign was a race between Colbert and Louvois. Could Colbert build prosperity faster than Louis and Louvois could destroy it with wars? During the first half of Louis'

reign, Colbert had more influence, and France grew strong and prosperous. Later the trend was reversed.

Louis XIV seemed to become dizzy with grandeur and power, and with territorial ambitions. He became convinced that the security of France depended on having natural frontiers. The Alps, the Mediterranean Sea, the Pyrenees, the Atlantic Ocean, and the English Channel protected France on the southeast, south, west, and northwest. To make France even safer, Louis wanted to reach the Rhine River in the northeast and east. Here his ambition came into conflict with other powers. The Netherlands barred his way to the northern Rhine, and the Holy Roman Empire barred him from expanding eastward.

Military campaigns

To gain his ends, Louis XIV fought four wars between 1667 and 1713. France could easily have defeated each of its opponents singly. Each single victory would have gained some territory that France wanted, and would have made it that much harder for the next country to resist France.

This prospect alarmed many of the other countries of Europe, even those whose lands were not threatened. To counteract the great power of France, other nations united. At various times the

The palace at Versailles had separate wings for noblemen, elaborate stables, and room for 1,500 servants. This painting, dated 1668, shows Louis XIV arriving in a carriage.

Dutch Netherlands, England, Sweden, Spain, and Denmark, as well as Austria, Brandenburg, and other German states formed alliances to create enough power to equal or surpass that of France. The principle of maintaining a kind of equilibrium in international politics is known as the *balance of power*.

In Louis' first two wars, fought chiefly in the northeast, France gained a few border towns and the province of Franche-Comté. Then Louis made an error that tended to weaken France. He became convinced that the Huguenots were disloyal and a danger to the nation. In 1685, he revoked, or canceled, the Edict of Nantes, which had given the Huguenots religious freedom.

Over 100,000 French Protestants chose to leave France rather than give up their faith. Although they totaled only about a tenth of the French Protestant population, many of them were leaders of industry, tradesmen, and excellent craftsmen. The loss of their skills injured France.

By the end of Louis' third war in 1697, Louvois and other French military leaders were dead. So was Colbert. The treasury was empty. Taxes were heavy, and trade and industry suffered.

The last war of Louis XIV centered on the question of who should succeed to the throne of Spain. The last Spanish Hapsburg king died in 1700 and left the throne to a grandson of Louis XIV, who was indirectly related to the Spanish Hapsburgs. Many European nations feared the prospect of Bourbon rulers in both Spain and France. If Louis had been willing to agree that the two thrones would never be joined under one monarch, he could probably have won recognition for his grandson. But he would not agree to this, so England, the Dutch Netherlands, and the Austrian Hapsburgs allied against him.

The resulting War of the Spanish Succession began in 1701. It was fought throughout Europe, on the seas, and in America. French armies and fleets were defeated everywhere, and Louis was forced to agree to a peace in 1713.

The Treaty of Utrecht. The Treaty of Utrecht (including a number of related treaties), which ended the War of the Spanish Succession, was important in the history of both Europe and America. It recognized Louis' grandson as King Philip V of Spain, but provided that the French and Spanish crowns were never to be united. Great Britain ° had become the chief enemy of France and made the largest gains. From France, Britain obtained several possessions in the New World—the Hudson Bay territory, Newfoundland, and Nova Scotia. From Spain, Britain gained the fortress of Gibraltar at the southern tip of Spain, the island of Minorca in the western Mediterranean, a monopoly on the slave trade to America, and the right to send one shipload of goods annually to the Spanish colonies.

The Austrian Hapsburgs were given the Spanish Netherlands, which then became known as the Austrian Netherlands. The Hapsburgs also received Sardinia, the Kingdom of Naples, and the Duchy of Milan in Italy (see map, page 350).

Two minor provisions of the Treaty of Utrecht had great importance for the future. The ruler of Brandenburg, a member of the Hohenzollern family, was recognized as king of Prussia, a state along the southeastern shore of the Baltic Sea. (You will read more about this state later in the chapter.) The island of Sicily was given to the Italian Duchy of Savoy.° Both Prussia and Savoy were to play vital roles in the coming century.

The decline of French power

The War of the Spanish Succession left France worse off than before. Louis XIV gained the doubtful glory of seeing a Frenchman on the throne of Spain, which he might have had without fighting. France lost important colonial possessions in America. Economically the country was ruined. Trade and industry suffered greatly. In spite of crushing taxes, the royal treasury was empty. France's debt, already enormous, was increased; in less than a century, it would be a

° **Great Britain:** England and Scotland united in 1707 to form the kingdom of Great Britain. Since that time, however, the terms *England* and *English* have continued in use to mean *Great Britain* and *British*.

° **Savoy:** In 1720, Savoy and the Austrian Hapsburgs exchanged Sicily and Sardinia. From then on, the territories of Savoy (including Nice and Piedmont) and Sardinia together were known as the kingdom of Sardinia.

EUROPE IN 1721
after the Treaty of Utrecht and related treaties

- Austrian Hapsburgs
- Prussia
- —— Boundary of the Holy Roman Empire

major factor in bringing about revolution and the end of the monarchy in France.

Louis XIV had lived too long and ventured too rashly. His nation's welfare and all the remarkable progress of his early years had been sacrificed to his boundless ambitions. He outlived his son and his grandson. Louis had centered all powers in the monarchy. Now these powers were to be passed on to a great-grandson, Louis XV, who was young, weak, and incompetent. France had earned the fear and hatred of all Europe. It is small wonder that when Louis XIV died in 1715, the French people rejoiced.

CHECKUP

1. What roles did Colbert and Louvois play during the reign of Louis XIV?

2. Did France gain or lose by the War of the Spanish Succession? Explain.

3. IDENTIFY: Mazarin, Molière, martinet, balance of power, Treaty of Utrecht.

4. LOCATE: Versailles, Prussia, Savoy.

4 Russia became a major power in the 1700's

After more than two centuries of Mongol rule, Russia became independent in 1480, as you read in Chapter 12. By this time the rulers of Moscow had become the most important in Russia, and they continued to expand their territory, like the early Capetians in France, by conquests, marriages, and alliances.

Early Russian isolation

At the time Russia became independent, you may recall, several factors tended to separate it from Western Europe. First, of course, there had been many years of Asian influence under Mongol domination. Second, there was the fact that, even as a Christian nation, Russia was different from the nations of Western Europe. Western civilization had reached Russia, not from the West but from Constantinople and the Byzantine Empire. The Russians had been converted to Christianity by missionaries from Constantinople; Russia's religion was Eastern Orthodox rather than Roman Catholic or Protestant. Russia's use of the Cyrillic alphabet was a bar to communication with the rest of Europe, which used the Roman alphabet.

But it was geography that did most to isolate Russia in the late Middle Ages and early modern times. In a period when men and goods moved mostly by sea, Russia was almost entirely land-locked—that is, without a seacoast. It was blocked from the Baltic Sea by the stronger kingdoms of Sweden and Poland. To the south the Ottoman Turks held the Crimean peninsula, the north shore of the Black Sea, and the city of Constantinople.

The wide plains of Poland and eastern Europe lay to the west of Russia. However, these vast expanses of land gave little opportunity for commercial contacts. Russia had many navigable rivers, but they flowed in the wrong directions. Some ran south into the Caspian Sea, which had no outlet, or into the Black Sea, which was closed to Russia by the Turks. Others ran north into the frozen, ice-choked Arctic Ocean and were no help to overseas trade.

Starting in the late 1400's and continuing through the 1500's, the rulers of Moscow gained power. Serfdom became firmly established. Although there was a kind of feudalism, nobles were completely dominated by the princes of Moscow. The princes constantly added new territories to their realm (see map, page 354). Ivan III, who reigned from 1462 to 1505, had extended his control over most of what is now northwestern Russia. Ivan IV (Ivan the Terrible), who ruled from 1533 to 1584, added much territory to the south and east. He was the first Russian ruler to be known as *czar* (the Russian form of *Caesar*). During his reign the Cossacks began their expansion eastward in Siberia, about which you have already read.

After the death of Ivan IV, there was a period of unrest lasting until 1613. In that year, Michael Romanov became czar. He was the first of the Romanov dynasty that was to rule Russia for 300 years. The first three Romanov rulers accomplished nothing important. Then, in 1682, there came to the throne a man who was to have great influence on both Russia and Europe.

Peter the Great

Czar Peter I, or Peter the Great, was a remarkable man. A seven-foot giant and immensely energetic, he was crude and coarse by nature and mercilessly cruel to opponents. However, he was a born leader and a man of great vision, imagination, and strong convictions. He was sincere, honest, and completely unselfish.

Peter decided that Russia's future lay toward the west, in contacts with European nations. He worked toward a goal that has continued in force in Russia ever since: the acquisition of warm-water seaports that were not dominated by other nations.

To the south of Russia lay the Ottoman Empire, which had been established in 1453, after the Turks had conquered the Byzantine Empire and seized Constantinople. Under a succession of powerful rulers, this Moslem state had expanded into the Balkan and Crimean peninsulas and had taken North Africa and much of the Near East. Suleiman I, sultan from 1520 to 1566, was the greatest Ottoman ruler. During his reign the Turks invaded Hungary and almost captured Vienna. When Peter the Great became czar in the late 1600's, the Ottoman Empire presented a formidable barrier (see map, this page).

The program of expansion to the south, undertaken by Peter the Great, soon ran directly into Ottoman holdings. At first, Peter sought to gain the Sea of Azov. After two wars, his troops took the city of Azov but failed to obtain control of the sea itself. (Before the end of his reign, Peter was also forced to return Azov to the Turks.) Peter then realized that in order to defeat the Turks permanently, he needed two things: help from Western Europe and a stronger, more efficient Russia.

Peter's mission and its results. In 1697 a Russian mission was sent to Western Europe to negotiate an alliance against the Turks. The mission failed in this purpose, but even so it was of great importance.

Peter, who went along with the mission, often disguised himself as a private citizen. He visited England, the Dutch Netherlands, Prussia, and Austria. There he met scientists, artisans, and leaders in many fields. He persuaded many of them to take their skills to Russia. In the Netherlands he worked as a carpenter in a shipyard so that he could learn how ships were made. He visited schools, factories, hospitals, and arsenals to learn Western techniques.

When Peter returned to Russia, he reorganized his army along French lines and equipped it with the best European weapons. He then turned toward the Baltic area, where Sweden blocked Russia from the sea. (At this time Sweden ruled Finland and parts of the Baltic region and northern Germany.) In a war that lasted from 1700 to 1721, Russia gained important territory and ended Sweden's days as one of the great powers of Europe.

Russia's new territory was at the northeastern end of the Baltic Sea, at the Gulf of Finland (see map, page 354). There Peter decided to build a "window to Europe," a completely new city that

THE OTTOMAN EMPIRE · 1453-1683

The Ottoman Empire in 1453

Conquests to 1683

0   1000 miles

would be his capital. The city, built only after many hardships, was named St. Petersburg. On the map on page 354, you can see how Peter's new capital brought the center of Russian government closer to the nations of Western Europe. St. Petersburg was symbolic of the new Russian policy of facing toward Western Europe. With this port, Peter was able to establish a shipbuilding industry and build up a navy.

Domestic policy. Peter's mission to Western Europe had made him determined that Russia should be westernized. He made several minor reforms. He insisted that women should abandon their isolation and take part in the life of the community. He himself taught his courtiers to dance and to smoke tobacco. He forced the nobles to wear European-style clothing. He issued a decree ordering them to cut off their long beards. When the nobles were reluctant, Peter himself cut off some beards.

But these were minor things. Much more important were the changes Peter made in Russian trade, finances, industry, and government. Armies and navies cost money, and to get it, Peter taxed nearly everything—from long beards to the birth of babies. As a mercantilist, he encouraged the development of trade with the West as well as with the Orient, and he made great efforts to promote manufacturing.

In government, Peter followed the absolutist ideas of Louis XIV of France. The Russian czar had complete control of a highly centralized administration. Nobles were entirely subordinated to the monarch. The Church became a branch of the government under control of the czar. As in France, the central government controlled local governments completely.

Peter found the hereditary nobles too set in their ways. He ordered many young nobles to study abroad and then serve the government.

By granting titles, Peter created a new nobility, one of service rather than of hereditary rank and privilege. The title and privileges depended on the amount of service a man gave the state. To this new nobility, Peter granted large estates with thousands of serfs, many of whom had formerly been free farmers.

Peter's changes not only increased the number of serfs but worsened their condition. A Russian serf was almost entirely at the mercy of his master. At a time when serfdom was rapidly declining throughout Western Europe, the serfs of Russia were more completely bound to the land than ever before.

Catherine the Great

After the death of Peter the Great in 1725, a number of relatively weak monarchs ruled Russia. Peter's work was not carried forward until the reign of a remarkable woman, Catherine II, known as Catherine the Great. A princess from a small German state, Catherine had married the heir to the Russian throne. Her husband ruled for only six months in 1762 and then died mysteriously. As czarina, Catherine took over the throne of Russia and ruled until 1796.

Catherine the Great did not earn her title "the Great" from her domestic policy. She extended serfdom and made the lot of the serfs even worse. It is true that she patronized art, science, literature, and the theater. Court life became more Europeanized. The nobility spoke French rather than Russian. However, these changes meant little to most Russians, who lived in deep ignorance and poverty.

Foreign policy. It was in foreign policy, where Catherine continued the policies of Peter the Great, that she earned her fame. Russia still sought to control the Sea of Azov and the Black Sea. Another goal was expansion westward across the Polish plains. In each of these undertakings, Catherine was successful.

Catherine's first move was to fight a successful war in the south against the Turks. Russia gained the Sea of Azov, most of the northern shore of the Black Sea, and won a protectorate over the Crimean peninsula. Russia also became the protector of Eastern Orthodox Christians in the Ottoman Empire and gained the right to send ships from the Black Sea through the Bosporus and the Dardanelles to the Mediterranean.

In the west, Catherine also made great gains. She took advantage of the fact that Poland was declining in strength. Poland was large but had many weaknesses. The kings were elected by the nobles. Until late in the 1500's, the nobles had usually elected the legal heir of the king. After this time, however, they chose anyone they thought they could control. This development brought both domestic and international troubles. Prussia, Austria, France, and Russia each plotted to put its favorite on the Polish throne.

GROWTH OF EUROPEAN RUSSIA
1462-1796

Russia in 1462

Acquisitions to 1682

Acquisitions to 1725 (during the reign of Peter the Great)

Acquisitions to 1796 (at the death of Catherine the Great)

0   500 miles

ARCTIC OCEAN

NORWAY

SWEDEN

FINLAND

Murmansk

Archangel

N. Dvina River

BALTIC SEA

Gulf of Finland

St. Petersburg

Novgorod

Dvina River

Volga River

URAL MTS.

Moscow

PRUSSIA

POLAND

AUSTRIA

HUNGARY

Kiev

Dnieper River

Dniester River

Don River

Ural River

Volga River

CASPIAN SEA

Danube River

Azov

Sea of Azov

CRIMEA

BLACK SEA

Constantinople

Bosporus

Dardanelles

OTTOMAN EMPIRE

MEDITERRANEAN SEA

PERSIA

Poland had a legislature, the Diet, in which only nobles were represented. This body rarely accomplished anything because of a privilege known as the *liberum veto*. Any one member could veto whatever legislation was being considered. What was more, any member could dissolve the Diet and thus veto everything that had been done until then!

Poland contained large minority groups of different nationalities and religions. In western Poland there were large numbers of German Lutherans. Ukrainians of the Orthodox religion lived in the eastern part. The Polish government showed little wisdom in handling these groups. Most Poles were Roman Catholics. They often discriminated against and oppressed the minority groups. From time to time, the ·minorities appealed to Prussia, Austria, or Russia for help.

In 1772, according to a previously made agreement, Russia, Prussia, and Austria each took a slice of Polish territory in what is known as the First Partition of Poland (see map, this page). The seized land amounted to a fourth of all Poland and was occupied by a third of the population.

The Polish government was shocked into trying to reform and strengthen the nation. In 1791, Poland adopted a new constitution and abolished the *liberum veto*. However, in 1793, before reforms could be carried out, Russia and Prussia took a second helping of Polish lands. This Second Partition led to a Polish rebellion that threatened to spread throughout eastern Europe. To prevent the revolt from spreading, Russia, Prussia, and Austria met in 1795 and agreed on a Third Partition. This operation was final and Poland disappeared from the map.

PARTITIONS OF POLAND

1772	Russia, Prussia, and Austria
1793	Russia and Prussia
1795	Russia, Prussia, and Austria

CHECKUP

1. How did its geography isolate Russia in the late Middle Ages and early modern times?

2. What were the most important accomplishments of Peter the Great?

3. How did Catherine the Great continue Peter's policies?

4. What conditions in Poland made it easy for foreign powers to divide the country?

5. What powers took part in the three partitions of Poland?

6. LOCATE: Crimea, Gulf of Finland, St. Petersburg.

---

5   Austria and Prussia contended for power in central Europe

Earlier in this chapter you learned about the effects of the Thirty Years' War on Spain, France, and the Netherlands. It was in Germany, however, where the war was fought, that the effects were most keenly felt. The war affected the development of the small German states in the north; it also influenced Austria, the seat of the Holy Roman Empire, in the south.

Austrian expansion

Austria was weakened by loss of territory in the Thirty Years' War. It also lost authority be-

Early Russia

Moscow, well located near the center of Russia, developed as a strong commercial and political center and eventually became the capital. The cathedral of St. Basil, left, was built there during the reign of Ivan IV. The domes of the richly colored church look like ice-cream cones, giving the building the gay unreality of a fairy tale.

Peter the Great, above left, moved the capital from Moscow to St. Petersburg. To his people the abandonment of Moscow seemed a more drastic defiance of Russia's past than did his reforms in dress and other customs. In the cartoon below left, Peter is snipping off the beard of an unhappy Russian gentleman.

Foreign observers of the rise of Catherine the Great, above, were fearful of her ambitions. In the contemporary British cartoon below, she is shown being tempted by the devil with the cities of Warsaw and Constantinople.

cause of the increased independence granted other German states by the Treaty of Westphalia in 1648. However, Austria remained by far the most powerful and important of the German states in the Holy Roman Empire. Its Hapsburg rulers could almost always be sure of election as emperors, although the elections were still occasions for bargaining and political maneuvering.

Austria's territorial losses through the Thirty Years' War were more than made up during the next century by gains of territory elsewhere. These gains came from two main sources:

(1) *Wars against the Turks in central Europe and the Balkan Peninsula.* From the time of Emperor Charles V in the 1500's, Holy Roman Emperors had fought many wars to drive back the Turks. By 1700 they had completely regained Hungary, and Hapsburg emperors were recognized as kings there.

(2) *The War of the Spanish Succession.* By the Treaty of Utrecht, as you have read, the Hapsburgs received Sardinia (later exchanged for Sicily), the Kingdom of Naples, and the Duchy of Milan, as well as the Spanish Netherlands, which then became the Austrian Netherlands. Notice on the map on page 350 the Hapsburg gains.

Maria Theresa

In 1740, Maria Theresa of the House of Hapsburg became ruler of Austria and the other Hapsburg lands. Her father, who had been Holy Roman Emperor, had tried to make it safe for her to rule. At great expense he had persuaded European rulers to sign an agreement called the Pragmatic Sanction, promising not to take her territory. The laws of the Holy Roman Empire kept her from being elected empress, but in 1745 she gained the title by having her husband elected emperor—the only non-Hapsburg elected in three centuries.

The Austria that Maria Theresa inherited was a strange territory. It was large in area and had tremendous manpower and a strategic location. However, it was a patchwork of territories and peoples. In addition to the ruling group of Germans, there were Hungarians, Italians, Belgians, Rumanians, Poles, and various Slavic peoples

such as Bohemians, Serbs, Croatians, and Slovenes. There were many conflicts of language, religion, and national interest.

Austria was surrounded by envious rulers. Several German states were rivals of Hapsburg power. Bavaria, in southern Germany, jealously guarded its lands and independence, sometimes by forming alliances with France against the Hapsburgs. Saxony and Hanover also preferred to act independently.

But there were strong points in the Hapsburg position. As Holy Roman Emperors, originally deriving their power from the Roman Catholic Church, and as defenders of Western Europe against the Turks, the Hapsburgs could count on the strong support of the papacy. Moreover, they were related to most European royal families.

The Hohenzollerns of Brandenburg

As you read earlier in this chapter, the Treaty of Utrecht in 1713 recognized the Elector of Brandenburg as king of Prussia. The Elector was a member of the Hohenzollern family, and this recognition was an important step in the family's rise to power.

During the Middle Ages, the Hohenzollerns had ruled only a small territory in southern Germany. Hohenzollern rulers were ambitious and eager to get more land. Often they succeeded by arranging marriages for political reasons. They were willing to use any methods as long as they increased the power, influence, and landholdings of the family. Toward the end of the Middle Ages, one branch of the family settled in Brandenburg, a state in northern Germany. The ruler became an elector of the Holy Roman Emperor.

During the Reformation, the Hohenzollern rulers of Brandenburg became Lutherans and seized all the Catholic Church lands in their territories. At the beginning of the Thirty Years' War, they gained control of Prussia, on the Baltic Sea. By the end of the war, they ruled several widely scattered territories in Germany.

In the mid-1600's, Brandenburg was ruled by one of the greatest of the Hohenzollerns, Frederick William, called the Great Elector. He guided Brandenburg through the difficult last years of the Thirty Years' War, and was rewarded with new territories. Then he turned to the rebuilding and further strengthening of Brandenburg.

The Great Elector first reorganized the armies of all his lands into one strong force. Then he improved the system of tax collecting and encouraged agriculture, industry, and transportation.

The Great Elector's successor, Frederick, was ambitious to have the title of king. To gain the necessary consent of the Holy Roman Emperor, Frederick supported the Hapsburgs in the War of the Spanish Succession. It was as a reward for this support that he was granted, by the Treaty of Utrecht, the title Frederick I, king of Prussia. From this time on, all the Hohenzollern possessions in northern Germany were usually referred to as Prussia; the state originally known by that name became known as East Prussia (see map, page 350).

Frederick William I, king of Prussia

Frederick I did not live long to enjoy his title of king of Prussia. His successor, Frederick William I, came to the throne in 1713. He was a man of unusual character. He disliked French ways intensely. His father had tried to copy the Versailles of Louis XIV and had furnished his palace lavishly. Frederick William sold much of the offending furniture.

Frederick William I was also a notorious "penny pincher," but he used the money he saved to strengthen Prussia. He more than doubled the standing army. It was so well organized and drilled that it became the best and most efficient fighting force in Europe. One of his few extravagances was recruiting tall soldiers for his army. He drafted tall Prussians and hired or even kidnaped tall foreigners to form his famous Potsdam Guards.

Frederick William was so strict in his discipline that he was called the Sergeant King. It was said that he ran all of Prussia, including his palace, like a barracks. But for all his quirks, the Sergeant King was a true Hohenzollern.

Frederick William I strengthened his country in many ways. He reorganized the civil service, hiring and promoting efficient men, regardless of birth. A mercantilist, he promoted trade and built up industries, spending government money where necessary. The collection of taxes and the spending of money were carefully planned so that the treasury had a surplus for emergencies. The Sergeant King was convinced that all children should have a primary education. He issued a decree requiring all Prussian parents to send their children to school.

Frederick the Great

Frederick William I had a real worry as he neared the end of his life. His son evidenced little interest in either military life or government service. Instead, he spent his time writing poetry, playing the flute, and reading philosophy. The Sergeant King used the harshest methods, even imprisonment, to force his heir to be more nearly the son he desired.

As it turned out, Frederick William's son proved to be an even stronger ruler than his father. Indeed, the Sergeant King would have been surprised to know that the Prussians would call his despised son "the great Fritz," while the world would know him as Frederick the Great. He turned out to be one of the greatest military leaders and statesmen of the Hohenzollerns.

Frederick William's son took the throne of Prussia as Frederick II in 1740 (the same year in which Maria Theresa became ruler of Austria). He was a skilled administrator, who instituted social reforms and began work on a Prussian law code. Like his grandfather, he admired French culture. He also wrote several books, including a history of Brandenburg and a book on the duties of rulers.

Conflict between Prussia and Austria. The year 1740 was one of decision in Germany and in all of Europe. Each of the two strongest states of the Holy Roman Empire had a new ruler. Prussia was emerging as challenger to the dominance of Austria in the German part of the empire. The clash between the two states came soon.

Austria and Prussia each had strong and weak points. Maria Theresa ruled the vast Hapsburg territories and had some claim on the loyalty of all the German states. Her position was aided by

Rivalry between Austria and Prussia was intensified after 1740, when Maria Theresa came to the throne of Austria and Frederick the Great became king of Prussia. Above, Maria Theresa and her husband pose with eleven of their sixteen children. Frederick the Great is shown in the foreground below, reviewing his troops. Ambitious for territory, Frederick took Silesia from Austria, but the strong-willed empress held her own everywhere else. At her death, Frederick said of his enemy: "She was an honor to her sex and to her throne."

the pledges of European rulers in the Pragmatic Sanction, by her relationship to many rulers, and by the support of the pope.

But Austrian weaknesses were many, including discontented nationalities under Hapsburg rule and inefficient administration of the government. Maria Theresa's father had almost emptied the treasury to get signers for the Pragmatic Sanction. Despite these pledges, Austria could rely on no one for help. However, if France opposed Austria, as it usually did, Austria might get help from Great Britain and the Dutch Netherlands, traditional enemies of France.

Prussia was smaller than Austria in population and territory. Its lands were widely scattered and therefore hard to defend. However, the population was solidly German. Prussia also had a healthy economic system, a well-organized and efficient government, and a formidable army. In a conflict with Austria, Prussia could count on help or at least friendly neutrality from Bavaria, Saxony, and Sardinia.

In 1740, Frederick the Great seized the Austrian province of Silesia, which lay close to his own lands (see map, page 350). He argued that his father's promise in agreeing to the Pragmatic Sanction was not binding on him. Silesia was a valuable region with rich farm lands and iron deposits. Its population was largely German.

Frederick's seizure of Silesia began a series of campaigns, known as the War of the Austrian Succession, which lasted until 1748. Other nations were involved, too. In general, France, Bavaria, and Saxony fought on the side of Prussia, while Great Britain, Russia, and the Dutch Netherlands sided with Austria. Prussia lost almost 10 percent of its population, mostly young men. The Prussian countryside was devastated. The city of Berlin, capital of Prussia, was invaded three times.

After the war there was a diplomatic shift, with both Britain and France changing sides. In 1756 rivalries led to a major conflict, the Seven Years' War, which involved almost every European country. Great Britain and France, rivals for overseas empire, battled for colonies in India and in North America. (In America the war was generally known as the French and Indian War.)

At one time, Prussia was surrounded by enemies in Europe, with only financial help from Great Britain. Fighting against great odds, Frederick dashed from one front to another to hold off his enemies. For all his great skill, he was saved only because Russia switched sides and came to his assistance. Finally, however, his enemies agreed to the Treaty of Hubertusburg in 1763, which allowed Prussia to keep Silesia. (You will read about the Peace of Paris, settling the French and Indian War, in Chapter 18.)

Prussia's peacetime gains. In the years of peace that followed 1763, Frederick the Great showed that he had genius for organization and administration as well as for war. He expanded and further improved public education and the already excellent civil service system. He permitted religious toleration, made legal and court reforms, and fostered trade and manufacturing. Through hard work and wise direction, the expanded state of Prussia recovered its prosperity.

Prussia's territorial gains continued. Frederick the Great helped to engineer the First Partition of Poland in 1772. (His successor shared in the second and third partitions.) By taking Polish territory along the Baltic coast, Frederick was able to join together Prussia and East Prussia. Thus at his death in 1786, Frederick the Great left behind him a solidly formed, greatly enlarged, and prosperous nation. By 1800, Prussia had become a formidable rival of Austria for control of the German states, and a first-class power in Europe.

CHECKUP

1. What were the strengths and weaknesses of Austria during the 1700's?

2. Why was Frederick William I of Prussia called the Sergeant King? What were the results of his reign?

3. What were the chief accomplishments of Frederick the Great?

4. IDENTIFY: Maria Theresa, Pragmatic Sanction, the Great Elector, Seven Years' War, Treaty of Hubertusburg.

5. LOCATE: Bavaria, Saxony, Silesia, Berlin.

CHAPTER REVIEW

Chapter 16   Strong Monarchs Competed for National Power and Prestige   (1516—1796)

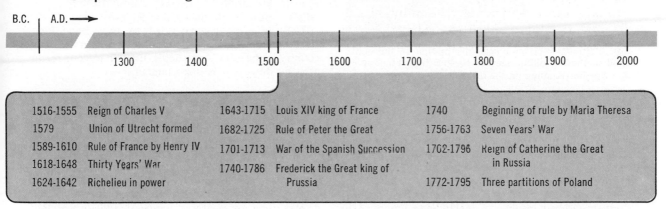

1516-1555	Reign of Charles V	1643-1715	Louis XIV king of France	1740	Beginning of rule by Maria Theresa
1579	Union of Utrecht formed	1682-1725	Rule of Peter the Great	1756-1763	Seven Years' War
1589-1610	Rule of France by Henry IV	1701-1713	War of the Spanish Succession	1762-1796	Reign of Catherine the Great in Russia
1618-1648	Thirty Years' War	1740-1786	Frederick the Great king of Prussia		
1624-1642	Richelieu in power			1772-1795	Three partitions of Poland

CHAPTER SUMMARY

Spain dominated Europe in the 1500's. Charles V ruled a vast empire, but faced several problems: internal revolts, wars against the Ottoman Turks, religious conflicts in Germany, and French territorial demands. His son, Philip II, strengthened the central government, intensified the Inquisition, seized the throne of Portugal, and attempted to conquer England with his Invincible Armada. He tried to rule the Netherlands as a Spanish colony, but the Dutch declared their independence and finally achieved it in 1648.

In the 1600's, France succeeded Spain as the dominant power in Europe. Henry IV improved the country's finances and fostered mercantilism. Richelieu, the real ruler of France during the reign of Louis XIII, destroyed the political independence of the Huguenots and the power of the nobles. He made use of the Thirty Years' War to strengthen France at the expense of the Hapsburgs.

Under Louis XIV, France enjoyed enormous power and prestige. Louis was aided by such great ministers as Colbert and Louvois. Ambitious for power, he fought four wars to gain territory, but ruined France economically.

Russia, landlocked and isolated, grew slowly after it became independent. Peter the Great, however, made far-reaching changes; he built a new capital, stressed westernization, and centralized the government. Catherine the Great carried on Peter's policy of securing warm-water ports, gaining important territory. With Prussia and Austria, Russia divided Poland until it no longer existed.

Among the German states, Austria was the most powerful. Maria Theresa, her throne guaranteed by the Pragmatic Sanction, inherited a large, strategically located realm. It was, however, a patchwork of territories and peoples.

Prussia was strengthened by the Hohenzollern family. Frederick William I doubled the size of the army, reorganized the civil service, promoted trade and industry, and increased tax revenues. His son, Frederick the Great, carried on a series of European wars, gaining Silesia, and made numerous internal reforms.

QUESTIONS FOR DISCUSSION

1. The large empire of Charles V could be regarded as a weakness rather than a strength. Give your reasons for agreeing or disagreeing.

2. Could you respect a leader like Henry IV, who was a Huguenot but became a Roman Catholic in order to gain political advantage? Explain.

3. Why do you think the President of the United States could not say, as Louis XIV did in France, "I am the state"?

4. Under Louis XIV, talented artists, writers, and musicians were given government support. Would you advocate such a policy in the United States?

5. It has been said that Louis XIV's control of a large and fine army gave him the desire to use it. Does the existence of great armies today lead to the same result? Explain.

PROJECTS

1. As a Huguenot living during the reign of Louis XIV, write a letter to the king of Prussia explaining why you want to emigrate to his country.

2. Make a list of the following rulers, identifying them with their realm and summarizing their major accomplishments: Charles V, Philip II, Henry IV, Richelieu, Louis XIV, Peter the Great, Maria Theresa, Frederick William I, Frederick the Great.

3. Draw a map of Europe showing the "natural frontiers" Louis XIV wanted and the actual territorial results of his wars.

361

STUDY IN DEPTH

UNIT FOUR

For additional bibliographical information on the books cited in these projects, see the Basic Library (page xviii) and Further Reading on the opposite page.

INDIVIDUAL PROJECTS

1. Write an essay on the causes of the Reformation. Carl G. Gustavson, a historian, is quoted as saying that, "No single cause ever adequately explains a historical episode." While preparing your essay, keep Gustavson's statement in mind. The following selections should be consulted: Copeland and Lamm, *The World's Great Speeches,* "Before the Diet of Worms"; Eisen and Filler, *The Human Adventure,* Vol. 1, "Luther Refuses to Submit to the Diet of Worms" and "The Doctrines of Calvin"; Simon, *The Reformation,* "The Troubled Time," "The Reformer," "Leaders of the Protest," and "Europe Aroused."

2. Advances in ship design and cartography were largely responsible for the success of the Age of Exploration. One student might draw pictures of carracks and point out to the class some of their distinctive features. A second student can report on cartography and navigation during the Age of Exploration. For illustrations, descriptions, and information see Hale, *The Age of Exploration,* "Ships and Gear," "The Chart-Makers," and "The Art of Navigation"; Landström, *The Ship: An Illustrated History;* Tunis, *Oars, Sails, and Steam.*

3. Write a book report on one of the biographies of Galileo or Copernicus listed on the opposite page. Focus your report on the major achievement of the scientist and comment on the reaction with which it was met.

4. The invention of printing with movable type caused a revolution in learning and communication. A short class report might be based on the operation of an early printing press, with illustrations that can be duplicated and handed to all the students. For this report see Simon, *The Reformation,* "The Birth of Printing."

5. Prepare an oral report on the defeat of the Spanish Armada. Give details on how the Spanish fleet was defeated and discuss the significance of the British victory. You might draw a diagram on the blackboard to illustrate Spain's defeat. Consult Mattingly, *The Armada,* and other books listed opposite.

6. Report to the class on absolutism as it was practiced in France. Read Eisen and Filler, *The Human*

Adventure, Vol. 1, "A Day at the Court of Louis XIV"; Hughes and Fries, *European Civilization,* "Cardinal Richelieu's Program for Strengthening the French Monarchy"; Stearns, *Pageant of Europe,* "Bishop Bossuet on the Divine Right of Kings."

7. Write a news story titled "A New Land Has Been Found" for a newspaper of a European colonial country in the 1500's or 1600's. Explain to your readers why this event is important to them.

GROUP PROJECTS

1. A committee of students should prepare a bulletin-board display on Renaissance art. Organize the display on the theme of the development of Renaissance art or around some major artists of the time. The entire class should be asked to help find material —pictures and illustrations from magazines—for the display. The assigned committee should discuss the characteristics of the art represented on the bulletin board.

2. Divide the class into five groups, each with a chairman. Each group should answer one of the following questions; the chairman reporting the findings to the class. (1) What were the motives for exploration? (2) What did the explorers find in the lands they discovered? (3) How well did Europeans fare in colonizing the lands they discovered? (4) What was a voyage like during the Age of Exploration? (5) How did the Europeans treat the natives of the lands they discovered? Each student should read about the Age of Exploration and find the answers to the question assigned to his, or her, group. The following sources should be consulted: Eisen and Filler, *The Human Adventure,* Vol. 1, "The Brutality of the Conquerors in the New World"; Hale, *The Age of Exploration;* Lucas, *Vast Horizons;* and Saunders, *Crossroads of Conquerors.* Articles of interest in *American Heritage* are: "DeSoto and the Golden Road," August 1955; "The Ordeal of Cabeza de Vaca," December 1960; "Conquest and the Cross," February 1963; "The City of the Living God," April 1964.

3. Mercantilism was designed to make a country self-sufficient; in practice it meant restrictive trade. Organize a debate on the reverse theory: Free international trade is more advantageous for all countries concerned than restrictive trade.

4. Several students might form a committee, each member reading one of the books on the Renaissance cited on the opposite page. The committee should discuss the books that have been read and answer the question: In what ways did Europe change during the Renaissance? The various answers to this question might then become the basis for oral class reports or a panel discussion by committee members.

Further Reading

BIOGRAPHY

Allen, Agnes, *The Story of Michelangelo*. Roy.

Bainton, Roland H., *Here I Stand: A Life of Martin Luther*. New American Library.*

Bixby, William, *The Universe of Galileo and Newton*. Harper & Row.

Carr, Albert, *Men of Power*. Viking. Richelieu and others.

Chidsey, Donald Barr, *Elizabeth I*. Knopf.

Farrow, John, *The Story of Thomas More*. Guild Press.*

Horizon eds., *Shakespeare's England*. Harper & Row.

Irwin, Margaret, *That Great Lucifer: A Portrait of Sir Walter Raleigh*. Harcourt Brace Jovanovich.

Lamb, Harold, *The City and the Tsar: Peter the Great and the Move to the West*. Doubleday.

Levinger, Elma E., *Galileo*. Messner. Sketches of other scientists also.

Ludwig, Emil, *Michelangelo and Rembrandt*. Ace Books.*

Mattingly, Garrett, *Catherine of Aragon*. ·Random House.*

Morison, Samuel Eliot, *Christopher Columbus, Mariner*. New American Library.*

Rugoff, Milton, *Marco Polo's Adventures in China*. Harper & Row.

Scherman, Katherine, *Catherine the Great*. Random House.

Thomas, Henry, *Copernicus*. Messner.

Welch, Ronald, *Ferdinand Magellan*. Phillips.

Wilkinson, Burke, *The Helmet of Navarre: The Story of King Henry IV of France*. Macmillan.

Williams, Jay, *Leonardo da Vinci*. Harper & Row.

Winwar, Frances, *Queen Elizabeth and the Spanish Armada*. Random House.

NONFICTION

Bradford, Ernle, *The Great Siege*. Harcourt Brace Jovanovich. Account of the battle for Malta against the Turks.

Brooks, Polly S., and Nancy Z. Walworth, *The World Awakes*. Lippincott. The Renaissance in Europe.

Burns, Edward M., *The Counter Reformation*. Van Nostrand.*

Byrne, Muriel St. C., *Elizabethan Life in Town and Country*. Barnes & Noble.

Ferguson, Wallace K., *The Renaissance*. Holt, Rinehart and Winston.*

Hale, John, *The Age of Exploration*. Time-Life.

* Paperback.

Horizon eds., *The Horizon Book of the Renaissance*. American Heritage.

Lucas, Mary S., *Vast Horizons*. Viking.

Lucas-Dubreton, J., *Daily Life in Florence at the Time of the Medici*. Macmillan.

Marx, Robert F., *The Battle of the Spanish Armada*. World.

Mattingly, Garrett, *The Armada*. Houghton Mifflin.*

Meredith, Robert, and E. Brooks Smith, eds., *The Quest of Columbus: An Exact Account of the Discovery of America, Being the History Written by Ferdinand Columbus*. Little, Brown.

Price, Christine, *Made in the Renaissance*. Dutton.

Santillana, Giorgio de, *The Crime of Galileo*. Univ. of Chicago.

Saunders, F. W., *Crossroads of Conquerors*. Little, Brown. European conquest of the New World.

Simon, Edith, *The Reformation*. Time-Life.

HISTORICAL FICTION

Bartos-Höppner, B., *The Cossacks*. Walck.

Beers, Lorna, *The Book of Hugh Flower*. Harper & Row. Life in an English town.

Bill, Alfred H., *The Ring of Danger: A Tale of Elizabethan England*. Knopf.

Dumas, Alexandre, *The Black Tulip*. Dutton. William of Orange fights against Louis XIV.

——, *Three Musketeers*. Dodd, Mead. Days of Richelieu.

Finger, Charles J., *Courageous Companions*. Longmans, Green. Magellan's voyage.

Hodges, C. Walter, *Columbus Sailed*. Coward-McCann. How a monk, a sailor, and an American Indian felt toward Columbus.

Irwin, Margaret, *Elizabeth, Captive Princess*. Harcourt Brace Jovanovich.

Kingsley, Charles, *Westward Ho!* Dodd, Mead. Rivalry of England and Spain in discovery and exploration.

Prescott, Hilda F. M., *The Man on a Donkey*. Macmillan.* Attempt to save the English monasteries from suppression by Henry VIII.

Reade, Charles, *The Cloister and the Hearth*. Washington Square.* Panorama of Renaissance Europe.

Schoonover, Lawrence, *The Burnished Blade*. Ballantine.* Later Middle Ages in France and Byzantium.

——, *The Queen's Cross*. Ballantine.* Spanish court intrigue.

Scott, Sir Walter, *Kenilworth*. Dodd, Mead. Set in Elizabethan England.

Shellabarger, Samuel, *Captain from Castile*. Little, Brown. Spain and the conquest of Mexico.

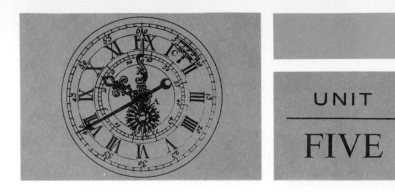

UNIT
___
FIVE

ENLIGHTENMENT,

Parisians storming the Bastille in the first days of the French Revolution

REVOLUTION, AND REACTION

A Century of Change in England Influenced Political Thought

The House of Commons in session

In France the reigns of three kings—Henry IV, Louis XIII, and Louis XIV—spanned the years from 1589 to 1715. During approximately those same years, England was ruled by members of the Scottish family of Stuart. Developments in the two countries, separated only by the narrow English Channel, were quite different.

France's rulers—either the monarch or ministers like Richelieu and Mazarin to whom they gave authority—were able men. They knew the goal they wished to reach: absolute, centralized rule under the king. Under their guidance, France moved from the anarchy of the religious wars to the centralized, divine-right monarchy symbolized by the statement attributed to Louis XIV: "I am the state."

Events in England took a different course. Under the Stuart kings, England moved from the almost absolute rule of the great Tudors, Henry VIII and Elizabeth, to a government in which the monarch had very little power and Parliament was supreme.

There were several reasons for this difference in development. Stuart kings also wanted to be absolute rulers, but they were less able than their French counterparts, and they had a different situation to deal with. The English Parliament had much deeper roots as an effective national body than the French Estates-General. By the 1600's, Parliament could not be completely disregarded by the king. When the Stuarts tried to disregard it, there was a long conflict over *sovereignty*—that is, the supreme authority in the nation—and who should wield it.

Although the rulers on both sides of the English Channel knew clearly what kind of government they wanted, the leaders of the English Parliament did not, at least in the beginning. They knew that they did *not* want a monarch with unlimited powers. Events during the 1600's gave parliamentary leaders a clearer idea of the kind of government they did want. They came to believe that it should be based on laws to which even the king should be subject. They also came to believe that Parliament, representing the ruling group of the people, should have an effective voice in making the laws.

By the end of the 1600's, English ideas about sovereignty could be clearly and definitely stated in the writings of English political philosophers. During the 1700's, these concepts were developed and expanded by other thinkers and writers, especially in France. Their ideas and writings helped to bring about revolutions in both America and Europe. Thus events in England in the 1600's, and the ferment which they produced, marked a real turning point in history and illustrated once again the great power of ideas.

THE CHAPTER SECTIONS:

1. Autocratic kings clashed with Parliament (1603–1640)

2. Opposition to the Stuart kings led to civil war (1688–1760).

3. England established a constitutional monarchy (1688–1760)

4. English political change helped bring about the Enlightenment (1687–1789)

1 Autocratic kings clashed with Parliament

During the 1500's, England was ruled by the Tudor dynasty. Most of the Tudors were autocratic but well liked by the English. The Tudors were succeeded by the Stuarts, who were also autocratic but generally unpopular, and whose reigns were to see much trouble and many changes in England.

The Tudor monarchs

During the 1500's the government of England was similar to governments on the continent of Europe. You have read about the reigns of Henry VIII, who ruled from 1509 until 1547, and of his daughter, Elizabeth I, who was queen from 1558 to 1603. These greatest of the Tudors were almost absolute rulers.

There was a difference, though, between English rulers and monarchs elsewhere in Europe. Continental rulers tried to get along without legislative assemblies. The Tudors allowed the English Parliament to retain its power to make laws and levy taxes. Even Henry VIII and Elizabeth went through the formality of getting the approval of Parliament on most measures, especially those that might prove unpopular. Often the Tudors gained their way with the members by persuasion, flattery, bribery, or bullying.

The House of Lords was made up of nobles and higher clergy. The House of Commons represented two classes, gentry and burgesses. The gentry were landowning people of good family and social position; most of them were the younger sons of nobles, who could not inherit their fathers' titles or positions. Burgesses were merchants and professional people from the towns and cities. Actually, the gentry and burgesses mingled to a surprising extent. Class lines were not so sharply drawn in England as in continental Europe. Rich merchants might buy land and be considered gentry. Younger sons of nobles might go into the professions and come to be regarded as burgesses. It was therefore more difficult for an English king than for a French king to set one class against another.

The long reign of Elizabeth, last of the Tudors, was a period of glory for England. In 1603, when she died, England was well on its way to becoming a great power.

James I

Elizabeth, who had never married, was succeeded by her cousin, King James VI of Scotland. He became King James I of England, and the founder of the Stuart line of English kings. Although England and Scotland had the same ruler, their governments were not united in any other way at this time.

As king of Scotland, James had been successful. Like the Tudors in England and Richelieu in France, he had brought unruly nobles under control and established strong royal authority. James had been carefully educated, especially in languages and theology. He had a taste for learning, but also a tiresome habit of showing off his knowledge. Nor had learning brought him wisdom; he seemed to lack common sense. Henry IV of France called him "the wisest fool in Christendom."

From the very first, James I seemed destined to have a stormy reign. He was a Scot, and many Englishmen considered him a foreigner with no real understanding of their problems. As a man, James was arrogant and tactless. He preferred to ignore or bypass Parliament. If he did consult it, he wanted it to consent slavishly to his proposals. Finally, James was a firm believer in the divine right of kings. He was not willing to have his power checked or his word questioned by anyone. James showed his belief, as well as his learning, by writing a Latin verse: *"A deo rex, a rege lex."* ("The king comes from God, law comes from the king.")

James soon met opposition in Parliament over money matters. He did not have a great personal fortune, and he liked to live in splendor. Unlike the Tudors, the Stuart kings were always short of funds. And they felt that bargaining with Parliament over money was beneath the dignity of their position.

Economic difficulties. Economic conditions in England were poor in the early 1600's. The middle class was prospering from new industries and increased trade; however, other classes were beginning to face hard times. The growth of the woolen industry had increased the demand for raw wool. Many landowners switched from general farming to raising sheep for wool. Some of these landowners seized lands that had formerly belonged to villagers in common. They enclosed, or fenced off, the land so that the sheep could graze there safely. This fencing of common land, which occurred in many regions of England at this time, is called the enclosure movement.

Sheep-raising required fewer workers than farming, and unemployment began to spread among the farm population. At the same time, prices were rising. Gold and silver were coming into England from the sale of goods to Spain and its colonies and from the capture of Spanish treasure ships. The increased supply of money caused inflation—a sharp rise in prices.

Religious problems. The religious situation in England was unsettled. During Elizabeth's reign the Anglican Church, or Church of England, seemed to satisfy most people. The "new nobility" created by Henry VIII supported it staunchly. During the reign of James I, however, there was opposition to the Church of England from two main groups. One group consisted of Roman Catholics. They hoped that the Stuarts, who were known to be sympathetic toward Catholicism, would be more favorable to their cause than the Tudors had been. The second group opposing the Anglican Church were followers of John Calvin. They followed a stern moral code, according to which idleness, the theater, dancing, and many other pleasures were considered sinful. Calvinists were divided into three groups—Puritans, Presbyterians, and Separatists.

The Puritans wanted to stay in the Anglican Church, keeping its organization under bishops but "purifying" its ceremonies and doctrines by removing "popish" elements. Among other things, they opposed making the sign of the cross on a child's head at baptism, kneeling at communion, and the ceremonial robes worn by the clergy during church services.

Presbyterians wanted an established church without bishops. Such a national church had been set up in Scotland by John Knox and his followers in the 1560's. Under the Presbyterian plan, each congregation would elect a ruling body of elders, called presbyters.

Tudors and Stuarts

The rule of the Tudor monarchs was strong and popular. Their ability stands out clearly when contrasted with the blunderings of the Stuarts.

Henry VIII was an agile and athletic youth when he succeeded his father at the age of eighteen. The portrait of Henry by Hans Holbein, above left, shows the monarch in middle age. The accession of Elizabeth was greeted by the English people with great joy. Elizabeth, twenty-five years old when she became queen, is shown above in a coronation portrait. During her reign, England enjoyed internal prosperity, great international prestige, and splendid cultural achievements.

Serving as Elizabeth's successor would have taxed the cleverest and most magnetic person. James I, the first Stuart, left, was an unattractive and pedantic man. The very sight of a sword made him queasy—a sign of cowardice and timidity that hardly inspired respect.

The smallest group, known variously as Separatists, Independents, or Congregationalists, did not want any established church. They believed that each congregation should choose its own minister and make its own rules. Under this plan, each congregation would be completely independent of every other congregation. (One of the first groups of English colonists to come to America—the Pilgrims—were Separatists.)

Calvinism in England was especially widespread in the rising middle class of merchants and businessmen. Such men were strongly represented in the House of Commons. They kept a watchful eye on taxes and on anything that looked like a return to Roman Catholicism. They hoped to use their position in Parliament to accomplish the religious reforms they wanted.

Growing opposition to James I

During his reign of more than twenty years, James I had constant difficulties with Parliament and the English people over money, religion, and foreign policy. When the House of Commons would not grant him money without question, James dismissed Parliament. He then raised funds by selling titles of nobility, granting monopoly rights to private companies, and forcing wealthy men to make "loans" to him that he had no intention of repaying.

When the Puritans came to James with a petition for religious reforms, he raged at them and drove them away. His policy of friendship with Roman Catholic Spain and his refusal to support the German Protestants in the Thirty Years' War caused widespread unrest and made him unpopular. By the end of his reign, James I had aroused opposition on many sides.

The reign of James I was marked by one great accomplishment, however—a new translation of the Bible. At the suggestion of the Puritans, he appointed a group of outstanding scholars to produce a new version of the English Bible. The result of their labors is officially called the Authorized Version of the Bible, and popularly known as the King James Version. As a great work of literature, it has influenced English speech and writing ever since it was published.

370

Charles I

Charles I, son of James I, came to the throne in 1625. He was as firm a believer in autocratic rule as his father, and was even more tactless. He, too, quarreled with Parliament over money and taxes. Before granting him money, Parliament insisted that he sign the Petition of Right. In signing this document, which he did in 1628, the king promised not to levy taxes without the consent of Parliament, not to declare martial law or to quarter soldiers in private homes in peacetime, and not to imprison people without a specific charge.

Later, when the Puritans in Parliament made further demands, the furious king dismissed Parliament. For eleven years he refused to call it into session again. To raise money during this period, he used all the drastic methods of his father and adopted some additional ones by collecting dues and fees that had long been ignored. Charles also required all towns to pay a tax to provide ships for the navy; only certain ports had been required to do so previously. Charles then used the money—called "ship money"—for his own purposes. He used the courts to stifle opposition.

Charles' most hated practice was his reliance on the Court of Star Chamber, which tried people accused of conspiring against the king. This court held its trials in secret, without a jury. A mere rumor was enough to bring a man to trial, and he might be tortured to make him confess. (Today, secret, unfair methods of settling issues are called star-chamber procedures.)

CHECKUP

1. What important rights did the English Parliament have when James I became king? Why did trouble arise between the king and Parliament?

2. What changes in church organization were desired by (a) Puritans, (b) Presbyterians, (c) Separatists?

3. How did the methods of the Court of Star Chamber violate Magna Carta and the Petition of Right?

4. IDENTIFY: sovereignty, gentry, enclosure movement, inflation, King James Version, Charles I.

2   Opposition to the Stuart kings led to civil war

Many Englishmen resented the fact that Charles I ruled alone, without a Parliament. They disliked his methods of raising funds and his use of the courts to silence opposition. However, it was Charles' actions on matters of religion that crystallized all the resentments and brought the opposition to a head.

The Long Parliament

Charles I persecuted the Puritans so severely that many of them went to America. His greatest mistake, however, was to try to establish the Anglican Church in Scotland. The stoutly Presbyterian Scots united to resist the king, and a Scottish army invaded England. In dire need of money for defense, Charles was forced to call Parliament into session.

The Parliament he summoned first met in 1640 and remained in session off and on for twenty years. It is known, therefore, as the Long Parliament. The Puritans who controlled the House of Commons took a number of actions that limited absolute monarchy in England. They abolished the king's power to dissolve Parliament and passed a law requiring a meeting of Parliament at least once every three years. They put an end to ship money and all other forms of illegal taxation. They also abolished the Court of Star Chamber. Two of the king's most hated advisers were sent to the scaffold.

While the Long Parliament was reducing the king's authority, Charles also faced trouble in Ireland. England had ruled Ireland since the late 1100's, but it had never brought the Irish completely under control. Relations between the two countries had grown worse since the time of Henry VIII. The Irish remained Roman Catholic and refused to accept Protestantism. The Tudors followed a policy, which the Stuarts continued, of seizing land from Irish owners and giving it to English and Scottish settlers. In 1641 the Irish rebelled.

Because of the rebellion in Ireland and the need to deal with the Scottish invasion, Charles at first gave in to Parliament and accepted the changes it made. Then, however, the most radical Calvinist group tried to pass an act doing away with bishops in the Anglican Church. At that point, Charles led troops into the House of Commons and tried to arrest the leaders of the opposition. This hostile act led in 1642 to the outbreak of a civil war between supporters of the king and supporters of Parliament.

Civil war and the Rump Parliament

The king's supporters, called royalists or Cavaliers, included Anglicans, Roman Catholics, nobles, and all who disagreed with the Calvinists on political or religious grounds. Supporting Parliament were the middle class and all varieties of Calvinists, for even though Calvinists still disagreed among themselves about church organization, they were united in opposition to the king. The Cavaliers called all Calvinists Puritans. Cavaliers wore their hair long and curled, in the gentlemanly style of the time. Puritans, to show their disdain for their opponents, cropped their hair close and were called Roundheads.

Oliver Cromwell, leader of the Puritans, organized his forces into an army which the Cavaliers could not match. It was a strong army of well-drilled, disciplined, zealous soldiers, who were fined if they swore, and who charged into battle singing hymns. They were pious, prayerful, and highly efficient in the business of killing. Cromwell's Roundhead army outfought the dashing Cavaliers. After two defeats in battle, Charles I surrendered in 1646.

Now began a great maneuvering among the various groups of Calvinists—Puritans, Presbyterians, and Separatists—to see who would control the government. Cromwell's army, made up largely of Separatists, won the struggle. Troops were used to keep all Anglican and Presbyterian members from entering the House of Commons. Because the troops were led by Colonel Thomas Pride, this action was called Pride's Purge. It left only sixty members, all Separatists, sitting in

The English civil war replaced the absolutism of Charles I, upper left, with the dictatorship of Oliver Cromwell, above. The war was reported in such periodicals as *Mercurius Rusticus* ("The Rural Messenger") at left, which devoted its first page to pictures of "the sad Events of the late unparalleld REBELLION." Although Cromwell led Parliamentary forces to success in battle, he ironically could not get along with Parliament itself, though he tried hard to do so. In the contemporary drawing below, he dismisses the body with the words "Be gone you rogues."

Parliament. This remnant became known as the Rump Parliament since it was the only part of the parliamentary body still sitting.

The Rump Parliament abolished both the monarchy and the House of Lords and proclaimed England a Commonwealth, a word used at that time to denote a republic. The Rump Parliament appointed a special court to try Charles I for treason. He was condemned and beheaded early in 1649. Cromwell took over the reins of power and became essentially a military dictator.

Cromwell's Commonwealth

Cromwell and the Separatists faced a threatening situation after the execution of Charles I. The Irish were still in open rebellion. Scottish Presbyterians joined royalist Anglicans in both Scotland and England in support of the exiled son of Charles I, whom they proclaimed Charles II.

The Commonwealth might have been overthrown except for three things: (1) it had enough money from taxes and the sale of confiscated royalist lands to support the government and army; (2) its enemies had no organized army; (3) its own army was disciplined and powerful.

Cromwell and his army were equal to the situation. They suppressed the Irish rebellion so mercilessly that the name of Cromwell is still hated by the Irish. Cromwell defeated the Scots in 1651.

The domestic policy of Cromwell's government was designed to help the middle class by developing manufacturing and trade. Dutch merchants and ships had built up a profitable trade with England and its colonies during the troubled times of the Civil War. Cromwell had Parliament pass the Navigation Act of 1651 to restore this trade to English merchants and shipowners. Thus Cromwell strengthened the policy of mercantilism.

For two years, from 1652 to 1654, the Commonwealth carried on a commercial war with the Dutch Netherlands. The war ended indecisively, but the prestige of the English navy was increased. These victories, added to commercial legislation which favored the middle class, gave the government some popularity.

Oliver Cromwell was an unusual man. A devout Calvinist, he closed all the theaters and limited many other forms of popular entertainment. He was honest and upright, a powerful orator, and a skilled statesman. He was convinced, however, that his ways were the only correct ones, and he suppressed political and religious opposition with great severity.

Despite the power he held, Cromwell was a reluctant dictator. He preferred parliamentary government and made several attempts to create one. He wrote two constitutions,° each providing for a Parliament. One of them, the Instrument of Government, was the first written constitution of a major European nation. It gave Cromwell the title of Lord Protector and provided that Parliament would be elected by the landowners.

Cromwell held the title of Lord Protector from 1653 until 1658. This period of the Commonwealth is often called the Protectorate. Cromwell's experiment was not successful. There was almost as much friction between him and Parliament as there had been between the Stuart kings and Parliament.

Cromwell's difficulty was that he could not get a majority to support him in an elected Parliament. The Separatists, his main support, were in a minority. Roman Catholics and Anglicans opposed him because he would not allow them to practice their own religions. So did Calvinist Puritans and Presbyterians because they wanted an established church and Cromwell did not.

Twice Cromwell and Parliament quarreled and twice he was forced to dissolve it. He ruled alone during most of the Commonwealth period.

The Restoration

As always in a dictatorship, it was difficult to provide for a successor to the dictator. When Cromwell died in 1658, his son Richard tried to rule as Lord Protector but was unable to win the absolutely necessary support of the army.

Then, too, there had been a change in the feelings of the English people. Many had favored

---

° A constitution consists of the fundamental laws and principles that govern a nation. In most countries, these laws are organized in one single document.

the execution of Charles I for his highhanded rule, but the period of the Commonwealth had brought only confusion. People found that they no longer felt a sense of continuity of government which the succession of kings had supplied.

In 1660, after some hesitation, Parliament invited Prince Charles, the son of Charles I, to return to England from his exile on the Continent. He became Charles II. The period of English history during which he ruled is called the Restoration because it restored monarchy in England.

Charles II had learned much from his years in exile. He believed in the divine right of kings, but, as he said, he had no desire "to go on his travels again." When his policies met determined opposition, he gave in, although he often tried to gain his ends by roundabout methods. He loved entertainment and good times and was called the "Merry Monarch." Restrictions on the theater were removed in a reaction against the stern Puritanism of the Commonwealth.

Charles II continued and extended the mercantilist policy favored by Cromwell. His actions brought wars with the Dutch, during which England took the Dutch settlement of New Amsterdam in North America and renamed it New York. Charles II favored Louis XIV of France, and signed several alliances with him. However, English protests forced him to withdraw from these alliances and oppose France. This shift marked the beginning of 150 years of rivalry between England and France for mastery of the sea and for colonial empires.

Parliament and Charles II

Charles II was tolerant of Roman Catholics and hoped to lift some of the legal restrictions on them in England. However, his attempt to do so met with such strong parliamentary opposition that he gave up the effort. Parliament had become overwhelmingly Anglican in its make-up. It was anti-Calvinist as well as anti-Catholic, and dismissed many Anglican ministers who had Calvinist leanings.

An important event of the reign of Charles II was the passage by Parliament of the Habeas Corpus Act in 1679. It provided that anyone who was arrested and imprisoned could obtain a writ, or order, directing authorities to bring him before a judge within a certain period. The judge would decide whether the prisoner should be released or charged and tried for a definite crime. (The writ itself was called *habeas corpus,* Latin for "you shall have the body.")

The Habeas Corpus Act made it difficult for the king to hold his opponents in prison without a trial. Habeas corpus has become one of our most vital *civil liberties*—rights of individuals that are protected by law, especially against unjust acts of the government.

As time went on, it seemed certain that Charles would be succeeded on the throne by his younger brother James, an avowed Roman Catholic. This situation led to the development of England's first political parties.

Parliament was divided into two groups of almost equal strength. One group, the Tories, wanted a strong hereditary king, though not an autocratic one. To keep the monarchy hereditary, they were willing to accept a Roman Catholic as king provided his heirs were Protestant (as were the heirs of Charles' brother James). Opposing the Tories were the Whigs, who favored a weak king and a strong Parliament. They were vigorously opposed to the idea of a Roman Catholic ruler.

In general, Tories were members of the upper classes and supporters of the Anglican Church. Whigs belonged to the middle class, and favored greater political and religious freedom for non-Anglican Protestants. Each of these political parties was given its name by its enemies. In Ireland, Tories were outlaws who preyed on landowners and traveling merchants; Whigs, a Scottish term, described horse and cattle thieves.

James II and the Glorious Revolution

Charles II died in 1685 and his brother came to the throne as James II. James, like his brother, had lived in exile for many years but had profited less from the experience. As a Roman Catholic and an ardent believer in divine right, he antagonized both Whigs and Tories by his arrogant, headstrong speech and acts.

One of the chief problems during the reign of James II involved the succession to the throne. James had two daughters, Mary and Anne. Both were Protestants, married to Protestant princes. Mary was the wife of William of Orange, ruler of the Dutch Netherlands and a staunch opponent of Louis XIV of France. Anne had married a Danish prince. However, James' first wife had died, and he had married again, this time a Roman Catholic princess. In 1688 she gave birth to a son, who would by law succeed his father. Since the boy's father and mother were both Catholics, it was certain that he would be reared in the Catholic faith.

Now all the groups in opposition to James combined to bring about the event known as the Glorious Revolution. Both Whigs and Tories agreed that James must abdicate. They invited William of Orange and his wife Mary to rule England. In 1688 William landed in England with a Dutch army, but armed force was hardly necessary. Unable to rally anyone to his support, James escaped to France. Parliament gave the crown to William and Mary as joint rulers. The following year, James led a rebellion in Catholic Ireland. William suppressed it, however, and James again fled to France.

CHECKUP

1. What actions of the Long Parliament helped end absolute monarchy in England? How did the Civil War begin?

2. Oliver Cromwell is said to have been a reluctant dictator. Explain.

3. How did the issue of Roman Catholicism influence the reign of James II?

4. What were England's first political parties? What did they stand for?

5. IDENTIFY: Cavaliers, Roundheads, Pride's Purge, Rump Parliament, Commonwealth, Lord Protector, Restoration, Habeas Corpus Act, Glorious Revolution.

England established a constitutional monarchy

In the eighty-five years after James I became king in 1603, the English Parliament had engaged in many struggles with Stuart kings. At stake was the question of who should rule the country. At one point the country had been plunged into a civil war. Two kings had been deposed and one executed. For one period of eleven years there had been no king at all.

By 1688, Parliament could feel that it had won the struggle. It had placed on the throne a new king, one of its own choosing. However, it wanted to make sure that there would be no repetition of the disturbances and no return of the problems that had troubled the country for so long.

Safeguards against absolutism

Parliament was careful to set up safeguards even before granting the throne to William and Mary. In a famous document, it fixed conditions to which the new rulers agreed in advance. This document, known as the Bill of Rights, became a law in 1689.

First and foremost, the Bill of Rights declared that the king was merely an official chosen by Parliament and subject to its laws. He could not proclaim or suspend any law, levy any tax, or maintain a standing army in peacetime without the consent of Parliament. Parliament was to meet frequently. Its members were to be elected without interference from the king, and were guaranteed the right to express themselves freely.

The Bill of Rights also protected private citizens. All citizens had the right to petition the government for relief of any injustice. No man could be required to furnish excessive bail or be subjected to cruel and unusual punishment.

In 1689, Parliament also passed the Act of Toleration. This act granted freedom of conscience and the right of public worship to non-Anglican Protestants. It did not, however, bring complete religious freedom. Roman Catholics, for example, still lived under heavy restrictions, and non-Anglican Protestants could not hold public office.

In 1701, Parliament passed the Act of Settlement. It provided that if William should die without children to succeed him (Mary had already died), Mary's sister Anne should inherit the throne. If there were no children to succeed her either, the throne should go to a Protestant granddaughter of James I, the German princess Sophia of Hanover. Thus great care was taken to keep the Roman Catholic descendants of the last Stuart king, James II, from gaining the English throne.

Parliament as the ruler of England

The Bill of Rights and the Act of Settlement ended the long struggle between king and Parliament to see who would rule the country. By 1700 it was clear that, although England remained a monarchy, Parliament was the real ruler. However, it did not by any means represent all the people. The House of Lords, which had been restored, was made up of hereditary nobles and higher clergy. Even the House of Commons, which was gradually becoming the more powerful of the two houses, represented only a small part of the population—the gentry and the middle-class businessmen. The right to elect members to the House of Commons was strictly limited. Workingmen and small farmers could not vote and therefore were not represented at all.

In the fifty years after 1689, Parliament continued to gain importance as the real power in the government of England. The organization and institutions characteristic of English government today gradually emerged.

William of Orange, who became King William III of England, knew little and cared less about the domestic problems of England. His interests lay in checking the vast ambitions of Louis XIV of France on the continent of Europe. As long as he was free to handle foreign affairs, William was quite willing to allow others to deal with domestic issues. He could do so because a new system of governing the nation had developed.

For centuries, a group of advisers had met with the English monarch to discuss government problems and ways of solving them. In time this council became too large to be efficient. Beginning with the reign of Charles II, a smaller group of advisers began to meet separately. Most of them were ministers, or heads of government departments. They were able to make policy and deal with issues effectively because they were leaders in the House of Commons. They became known as the Cabinet.

Although at first the Cabinet included members of both parties, it became clear during William's reign that the government ran more smoothly when all the ministers of the Cabinet belonged to the majority party in the House of Commons. Thus the monarch chose his ministers accordingly.

Several other steps in parliamentary control of the English government came during the reign of William III and shortly thereafter. Parliament gained the right to declare war. The monarch ceased to veto acts of Parliament. Queen Mary's sister Anne, who reigned from 1702 to 1714, was the last ruler to veto an act of Parliament.

In 1707, the Act of Union merged the separate governments of England and Scotland into one kingdom known as Great Britain. The Scottish Parliament was abolished. Scots were given seats in the House of Lords and the House of Commons. There was opposition at first, particularly in Scotland, but the union proved to be beneficial. By removing trade barriers, it stimulated commerce and brought greater prosperity to both England and Scotland.

Parliamentary control increased under the successors to Queen Anne. When Anne died in 1714 without children to succeed her, the throne went to the Elector of Hanover (the son of Sophia of Hanover, who had been designated in the Act of Settlement). He became George I, the first of the Hanoverian dynasty of England. Both he and his son, George II, were German born. George I, who ruled until 1727, spoke no English. George II, king until 1760, spoke English, but is said to have mispronounced both English and German. Although both kings were interested in the details of British government, neither understood the larger issues. As a result, the Cabinet became increasingly important in the English system of government.

The prime minister

For over twenty years, from 1721 to 1742, the Whig party controlled the House of Commons. The recognized leader of the Whigs, Sir Robert Walpole, was always chosen as a minister. He was a strong leader, and came to be recognized as the prime minister—that is, first minister. (Actually, the prime minister was not known officially as such throughout most of the 1700's; instead he usually had the title of First Lord of the Treasury.)

In time the prime minister became the real head of the government of Britain. Today he, rather than the monarch, selects the other members of the Cabinet. Together they plan government policy and propose laws to carry it out. When one party loses its majority control of Commons, the monarch selects a new prime minister, but he has no real choice. He can appoint only the recognized leader of the party that controls Commons.

The British, however, preserved all the forms of royalty. The government has always operated in the name of "His (or Her) Royal Majesty." The monarch opens each session of Parliament with a speech summarizing the laws that are needed. It is the Cabinet, however, that actually determines these. Parliament passes the laws, levies the taxes, maintains the armed forces, declares war, and approves treaties.

HISTORY THROUGH ART

The Successful Fortune Hunter

The first daily newspapers appeared in England during the 1700's. It was an era of outspoken frankness, and artists as well as writers mercilessly lampooned every aspect of public and private life. The satires and caricatures of such skilled practitioners as Thomas Rowlandson were widely circulated in the new dailies. In the caustic drawing above, Rowlandson caricatures a dandified fortune hunter, who seems to have found what he wanted in the form of a short, fat, bleached, and befeathered lady.

Britain as a constitutional monarchy

By the 1700's, Great Britain had become a limited constitutional monarchy. It was a *monarchy*, of course, because there was a king or queen. It was a *limited* monarchy because the powers of the ruler were less than absolute. It was a *constitutional* monarchy because the monarch's powers were limited by a constitution.

The British constitution is not a single written document like that of the United States. It con-

377

sists partly of great documents such as Magna Carta, the Petition of Right, and the Bill of Rights. But it also includes acts of Parliament, which any succeeding Parliament may change. Several features of the system are not written down anywhere—for example, the powers of the prime minister and the functions of the Cabinet.

The British constitution puzzles people who like things organized neatly, carefully, and definitely. But it works. Great Britain is one of the oldest constitutional governments in the world today. Its limited monarchy furnished a model for many other nations. The British experience from 1603 to 1760 became a guide to those who wanted to abolish absolute monarchy elsewhere.

CHECKUP

1. How did the Bill of Rights limit the powers of the king? protect private citizens?
2. Why did the Cabinet gain importance during the reigns of William III, George I, and George II?
3. How did a Dutch ruler and, later, a German prince become kings of England?
4. IDENTIFY: Act of Toleration, Act of Settlement, Act of Union, Walpole, limited constitutional monarchy.

4 English political change helped bring about the Enlightenment

The English Civil War and Glorious Revolution led both to a new kind of government in England and to new ideas about government in general. These new ideas, and others in the fields of science and philosophy, were part of a great intellectual movement known as the Enlightenment. It is often said to have lasted from 1687 to 1789—that is, from the publication of Newton's *Principia* (about which you will read shortly) to the beginning of the French Revolution.

During the Renaissance, Europeans became less concerned with religious matters and more interested in worldly affairs. During the Enlightenment, many thinkers directed their attention toward one specific problem in the world about them: how men should be governed.

The Enlightenment received its name because the intellectuals of the period were awake to, or enlightened about, the problems of their times and made serious proposals for solving them. Revolutionary changes were brought about by scientists, thinkers, and writers. The effects of their thoughts and writings illustrate once again the tremendous power of ideas. It has been said that "there is no force in history more powerful than an idea whose time has come."

Newton and other scientists

One of the first signs of the intellectual explosion of the Enlightenment appeared in a field that seems remote from politics or government— the field of science. In 1687 an Englishman named Isaac Newton, one of the great scientists of all time, published his *Mathematical Principles of Natural Philosophy* (often called the *Principia,* from the chief word of its Latin title). In it he synthesized (combined and related) the contributions of Copernicus, Kepler, and Galileo.

These men had shown that the planets, including the earth, revolve around the sun. Newton explained the laws of force and motion which control planetary motion. His law of universal gravitation stated that the force of gravity not only prevents objects from flying off the earth, but also holds the whole system of sun and planets together by keeping them in their orbits.

Newton's work had an immense influence on the thinking of his own age and on all later scientific thought. The English poet Alexander Pope wrote:

Nature and nature's laws lay hid in night;
God said, "Let Newton be," and all was light.

The *Principia* gave or suggested answers to many questions about nature that had previously gone unanswered. It also stimulated scientific investigation and experimentation.

New discoveries were made elsewhere in Europe. Newton and a German philosopher and mathematician, Gottfried Wilhelm von Leibnitz, worked independently, to develop calculus, a system of calculating that uses algebraic symbols. A Dutch scientist, Anton van Leeuwenhoek (LAY-vun·hook), used the microscope—an invention of the late 1500's—to discover bacteria and a whole new world of life unseen by the naked eye.

Another scientist who worked with the microscope was Robert Hooke of England, the first man to identify cells in living matter. He examined a thin slice of cork and noticed that it was made up of small rectangular "rooms"; he called them cells because they looked like the cells in which bees store honey.

An English scientist of the late 1600's, Robert Boyle, is known as the "father of modern chemistry." Chemistry is the science of the composition of materials, and the changes they undergo. Boyle conducted many experiments with air pressure and worked out a basic principle describing gases that is known as Boyle's Law. Another English chemist, Joseph Priestley, discovered the element later called oxygen. (Elements are the fundamental substances that constitute matter.)

It was a Frenchman, Antoine Lavoisier (lah-vwah·ZYAY), who named oxygen. He showed that fire, previously thought to be an element, was the result of the rapid union of oxygen with another substance. Lavoisier also demonstrated that matter is indestructible and can be neither created nor destroyed, but only changed from one form into another. For example, when water boils down, it does not disappear but forms steam, which combines with the air; its substance has changed but it has not disappeared. Lavoisier's discovery is known as the Law of the Conservation of Matter.

One of the most versatile men of the Enlightenment was the American statesman, writer, and inventor Benjamin Franklin. He studied electricity and in 1752 conducted his famous kite experiment which proved that lightning is an electrical discharge.

Science, rationalism, and natural law

The men of Newton's time greatly admired the scientific attitude of mind. Science does not accept anything as true that cannot be proved by

Wedgwood's Social Revolution

The scientific experimentation and investigation that characterized the Enlightenment touched many aspects of society. The development of sturdy, inexpensive dinnerware is a good example of the practical side of the Enlightenment.

When Josiah Wedgwood of England entered his family's pottery business, only the very rich could afford to eat off plates, since most dishes were made of expensive porcelain. The great majority of people ate out of bowls or wooden plates, making eating unsanitary and clumsy.

Wedgwood did exhaustive research into materials and ceaselessly experimented with new firing techniques, molds, and glazes. He succeeded in developing an earthenware that was hard, resistant to fire, beautiful, and cheap enough for most of the population to afford. Wedgwood, in fact, caused a minor social revolution: table manners became more civilized and eating and drinking more hygienic and refined.

The sauce tureen above, decorated with the popular shell pattern, demonstrates the masterful way in which Wedgwood's skills produced tasteful and artistic earthenware vessels that were also inexpensive.

testing and experiment. It places great importance on cause and effect. Every natural phenomenon has its cause and every cause has its effect; this relationship can always be shown. The writers and thinkers of the Enlightenment attempted to test everything by observation and by determining cause-and-effect relationships.

Another characteristic of the Enlightenment was rationalism—the belief that truth can be arrived at solely by reason, by rational, logical thinking. Because of this characteristic, the period is often called the Age of Reason.

The thinkers of the Enlightenment tried to apply scientific methods to all human ideas and customs. They examined critically the political and social institutions under which they lived. They tried to learn how institutions had developed. They analyzed the power of kings, the special position of churches, the privileges of clergy and nobles. Several men of the Enlightenment attacked the idea of privileged classes. They thought that political and social institutions should be changed so that they would benefit everyone instead of just certain groups.

The Enlightenment was characterized not only by the scientific attitude and by rationalism but also by belief in natural law. The discoveries of Newton and other scientists seemed to point to an orderly universe. Thoughtful men came to feel that there was a natural law which governed the universe and all of its creatures. God, they believed, had created the world and made rules for all living things. Just as the law of gravitation governed the physical movement of planets, so other laws governed human behavior. In order to live in harmony, men had to discover natural law by using their reason. If they lived according to natural law and made their institutions and government conform to it, the world would become a perfect place.

Hobbes and Locke

One of the first modern writers to analyze government was an English philosopher, Thomas Hobbes. Although he lived before the Enlightenment, his work influenced it strongly.

Hobbes lived through the English Civil War and was disturbed by the anarchy of the time. He set forth his political philosophy in a book called *Leviathan,* published in 1651. Hobbes wrote that in the past, men had lived in anarchy, or what he called a "state of nature." Life was almost impossible under these circumstances, so people chose a leader to rule them. In order to maintain a stable society, men had made a sort of unwritten "social contract" with their ruler. Hobbes argued that the monarch had to have absolute power, or anarchy would again result.

John Locke, another English philosopher, adopted many of Hobbes' ideas, but interpreted them differently. He had lived through the Glorious Revolution of 1688, had supported the men who overthrew James II, and wanted to justify them. To do so, he wrote a book called *Two Treatises of Government,* published in 1690.

Like Hobbes, Locke believed that men had first lived in a state of anarchy and then made a social contract with a ruler. However, he believed that people had given up only some of their individual rights and had kept others which no one could take from them. These rights, called natural rights, included the right to live, the right to enjoy liberty, and the right to own property.

According to Locke, a ruler who violated these rights violated natural law and broke the unwritten social contract. The people then had the right to overthrow him and replace him with another ruler who would pledge to observe and protect their rights. Locke thus justified the forced abdication of James II and the offer of the English crown to William of Orange.

The Enlightenment in France

Locke's ideas were enthusiastically adopted by a group of French writers in the 1700's. In a book called *The Spirit of the Laws,* published in 1748, the Baron de Montesquieu (mahn·tus·KYOO) tried to describe a perfect government. After studying all existing governments, Montesquieu concluded that the English form was the one most nearly perfect. He wrote that its greatest strength lay in the fact that power was equally divided among the three branches of government: the *legislative* (which made the laws), the *execu-*

The Enlightenment was characterized by informal gatherings of educated people, who met to discuss new books and ideas. Science, music, philosophy, politics, even interior decorating were examined by the men of the Enlightenment. The scene at right—from a miniature painting on a snuff box of such precision that the paintings on the wall can be identified—was the study in the home of a nobleman.

The gentlemen of the Enlightenment represented a variety of talents. Isaac Newton, below, taught men to "... examine, weigh, calculate, and measure, but never to conjecture." So wrote Voltaire, shown below, center, with Rousseau and Benjamin Franklin. (This triple portrait is a detail from a snuffbox.) Christoph Gluck, below right, was a German composer known for the dramatic elements he introduced into opera. Franz Joseph Haydn of Austria conducts a uniformed orchestra from the keyboard, at bottom. Haydn wrote 104 symphonies, dozens of string quartets, and many other musical compositions. He once said, quite truthfully, "I have had the good fortune to please almost everywhere."

Newton

Voltaire   Rousseau   Franklin

Gluck

tive (which administered them), and the *judicial* (which interpreted and applied them). Each branch balanced and checked the others.

Actually, Montesquieu's praise of the English government was based on a misunderstanding of it. Even when he wrote, the legislative and executive powers were not divided between the two branches of government, but were largely combined in the House of Commons. Nevertheless, his ideas had great influence on the formation of limited monarchies in Europe. And the idea of checks and balances provided by a separation of powers was to be embodied in the Constitution of the United States.

Another influential writer in France was Jean Jacques Rousseau (roo·SOH). His most famous book was *The Social Contract,* published in 1762. In it he wrote that man is born good but becomes bad because of his environment, his education, and his laws. The free and good state to which people are born can be preserved only if men live under a government of their own choice and control. In other words, just laws and wise government must be based upon what Rousseau called *popular sovereignty*—the free choice of the people. The idea had enormous influence.

Voltaire. As famous and influential as Rousseau was the French writer François Marie Arouet, known as Voltaire. In one of his pamphlets he attempted to select the greatest man in history. He considered such men as Alexander the Great and Julius Caesar, but passed them over and named as his choice Isaac Newton.

Voltaire savagely attacked all things he considered sham or superstition. He advocated religious toleration and freedom of speech. He is credited with a famous statement on free speech: "I do not agree with a word you say, but I will defend to the death your right to say it."

Diderot and the *Encyclopedia*. The men of the French Enlightenment left a monumental summary of their views on all subjects in a twenty-eight volume *Encyclopedia* edited by Denis Diderot (dee·DROH). It was compiled between 1751 and 1772 and typifies the age. It was one of the first attempts to encompass all human knowledge, including new ideas in science and government.

The most brilliant writers of the period, including Rousseau and Voltaire, contributed articles to the *Encyclopedia*. They contained much thinly disguised criticism of the Church, the government, and the special privileges of nobles and clergy. For their critical writings, Diderot and several others were imprisoned. But the *Encyclopedia* was widely read, and its ideas were enthusiastically adopted.

Enlightened despotism

The ideas of the Enlightenment influenced not only writers and philosophers but also the rulers of Europe. Those who were interested in the new thought of the period—the so-called enlightened despots—included Catherine the Great of Russia and Frederick the Great of Prussia. Catherine the Great corresponded with Voltaire and invited Diderot to visit her court. Frederick the Great also admired Voltaire. The French philosopher lived at Frederick's court until the two men quarreled over the king's poetry.

The enlightened despotism of monarchs like these, however, was more despotic than enlightened. When they attacked the nobility or limited the power of the clergy, they claimed to be abolishing special privilege, but their actual goal was to increase their own power. They had little interest in political liberty for their people. Serfdom in Russia increased greatly during Catherine's reign, and Frederick issued decrees rigidly fixing social classes in Prussia.

CHECKUP

1. What scientific contributions were made by Newton? Leeuwenhoek? Boyle? Priestley? Lavoisier? Franklin?

2. How did the belief in natural law differ from the medieval attitude toward life?

3. Briefly state the ideas about government expressed in *Leviathan; Two Treatises of Government; The Spirit of the Laws; The Social Contract.*

4. Explain and, if possible, illustrate the quotation: "There is no force in history more powerful than an idea whose time has come."

5. IDENTIFY: Leibnitz, element, rationalism, separation of powers, enlightened despotism.

CHAPTER REVIEW

Chapter 17   A Century of Change in England Influenced Political Thought   (1603—1789)

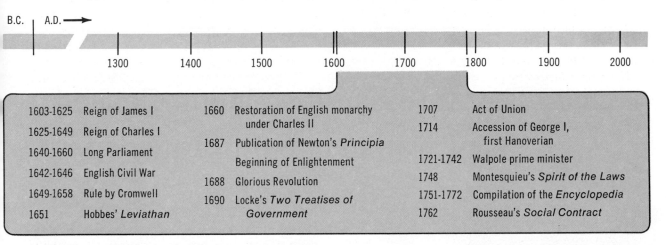

1603-1625	Reign of James I
1625-1649	Reign of Charles I
1640-1660	Long Parliament
1642-1646	English Civil War
1649-1658	Rule by Cromwell
1651	Hobbes' *Leviathan*
1660	Restoration of English monarchy under Charles II
1687	Publication of Newton's *Principia* Beginning of Enlightenment
1688	Glorious Revolution
1690	Locke's *Two Treatises of Government*
1707	Act of Union
1714	Accession of George I, first Hanoverian
1721-1742	Walpole prime minister
1748	Montesquieu's *Spirit of the Laws*
1751-1772	Compilation of the *Encyclopedia*
1762	Rousseau's *Social Contract*

CHAPTER SUMMARY

During the 1600's, England changed from absolutism under the Tudors to parliamentary rule. The first Stuart king, James I, antagonized his subjects by advocating divine right; his problems were intensified by economic difficulties and religious strife.

James' son, Charles I, used unpopular methods of raising funds and autocratic court procedures. When he was forced to call Parliament into session after ruling alone for eleven years, it limited royal powers. Charles' attempt to arrest parliamentary leaders resulted in civil war, in which the Cavaliers were defeated by the Roundheads, led by Cromwell.

After the execution of Charles I, Cromwell ruled England essentially as a dictator. His son was not equal to the task, and the monarchy was restored two years after Cromwell's death.

Under Charles II the Habeas Corpus Act was passed and political parties—the Tories and the Whigs—began to take shape. The birth of a Catholic heir to James II, Charles' successor, united all factions. In the Glorious Revolution, Parliament deposed James and declared William and Mary joint rulers.

The new monarchs accepted the Bill of Rights, which limited royal authority and safeguarded the rights of Parliament. Parliament gained further power as the Cabinet became increasingly important. In time the prime minister became the real ruler.

English political developments helped foster the intellectual movement known as the Enlightenment. Its first landmark was Newton's *Principia*. Other scientific achievements included those of Hooke, Boyle, Priestley, Lavoisier, and Franklin.

Writings of the Enlightenment were characterized by a scientific attitude and belief in rationalism and natural law. Hobbes, Locke, Montesquieu, and Rousseau analyzed government. Voltaire attacked superstition, and the writers who contributed to Diderot's *Encyclopedia* criticized the society of their time. The so-called enlightened despots, although influenced by the Enlightenment, made few basic reforms.

QUESTIONS FOR DISCUSSION

1. England underwent fundamental change between 1603 and 1760—change that is often described as evolutionary rather than revolutionary. What is meant by this distinction? Which kind of change do you think is better? Justify your choice.

2. In a dictatorship, such as that of Oliver Cromwell, it is difficult to find a successor to the dictator. Why? And why should this be a cause of anxiety?

3. The British monarch no longer holds any real power. Would you advise the British to abolish the monarchy completely?

4. What ideas of the Enlightenment are still very much alive in the United States today? Do you disagree with any of these ideas that have been adapted by Americans? Explain.

PROJECTS

1. Write a short essay explaining why the Enlightenment was a truly great period in history.

2. Make a list of the powers Parliament gained at the expense of the king between 1603 and 1714.

3. List the important rights of individual citizens that were protected by the Petition of Right, the Habeas Corpus Act, the Bill of Rights, and the Act of Toleration.

The American Revolution Created a New Nation in North America

If you look at a detailed map of the eastern United States, you will find hundreds of English place names. In a way they represent something most people have experienced at one time or another—homesickness. Englishmen who settled in the New World were often homesick for England, even though thousands had fled from it. They tried in many ways to make America into a rough model of England in customs, appearance, and name.

Many names with "new" in front of them have an English origin, including, of course, New England itself. New Hampshire was named for a county in England, New Jersey for the island of Jersey in the English Channel.

The names which colonists applied to towns and settlements were, in many cases, those of the places from which they had come. Plymouth, Boston, and Worcester in Massachusetts, Hartford in Connecticut, and Dover in Delaware—all had their English counterparts.

Other English settlements honored royalty. The colony of Virginia was named for Queen Elizabeth I, known as the "Virgin Queen." Jamestown, the first English settlement, was named for King James I. The Carolinas were originally the territory of Carolana (a Latin form of Charles), and thus honored Charles I. Settlers in Maryland named their colony after the wife of Charles I, Henrietta Maria. Charleston, South

"The Declaration of Independence," by John Trumbull
(detail) Yale University Art Gallery

Carolina, was named for Charles II, and New York for his brother James, who was Duke of York before becoming king. Georgia, the last of the thirteen original colonies to be established, honored King George II.

The "replanting" of England on American soil could be seen in other ways as well. After the early days of huts and log cabins, the settlers built substantial houses that were copied after English models. Sometimes they even imported English bricks to build them.

In their social life, too, the colonists imitated what they had known in England. They held parties and balls, especially in the southern colonies. There, too, wealthy planters, including George Washington, enjoyed fox hunting in the scarlet coats of English gentlemen.

Thus did Englishmen far from home keep the memory of their native country alive. They kept close to them, even if only in name, something of what Shakespeare called "this blessed plot, this earth, this realm, this England."

THE CHAPTER SECTIONS:

1. European settlers established thirteen colonies in North America (1607–1750)

2. The British colonies declared their independence (1750–1776)

3. Out of the Revolutionary War emerged a new nation (1776–1789)

 1 European settlers established thirteen colonies in North America

You have read about early discoveries and exploration by Europeans in the Americas. In North America, the French established themselves in Canada and claimed the territory of Louisiana. Spain claimed Florida, large parts of what is now the southwestern United States, and Mexico. In the early 1600's there were some small settlements on the Atlantic coast and a scattered few elsewhere. The vast area of North America between Canada and Mexico, however, was largely an unsettled region.

The land

North America between Mexico and Canada includes many different regions. Most of the eastern coast was originally covered with forests. It has many natural harbors, as well as rivers for inland transportation. Much of the northern part of the coast has poor, stony soil and the land is hilly. Farther south a long plain stretches along the Atlantic coast, narrow in the north but broader in the southern sections (see map, page 386). The northern part is characterized by wide, rich river valleys. In the south the coastal plain spreads far inland and the soil is fertile and easy to cultivate.

Beyond the Atlantic coastal plain lie the Appalachian Highlands—often called the Appalachian Mountains—a region of low mountains, gently rolling hills, and valleys. Three good routes led through or around the Appalachians: (1) up the Hudson River and west along the Mohawk River toward Lake Ontario and Lake Erie; (2) up the Potomac River and eventually through the Cumberland Gap, a pass in the southern Appalachians; and (3) around the southern end of the mountains along the coastal plain of the Gulf of Mexico.

Beyond the Appalachians is a region of plains, a flat or gently rolling area stretching far to the west. This vast area is drained by the great Mississippi River and its many tributaries, among them the Ohio and Missouri rivers. The eastern part of the plains region, containing the upper Mississippi Valley, is called the Great Central Lowlands. The western part, called the Great Plains, is a dry, grass-covered region like the steppes of eastern Europe. Important rivers of this area include the Platte and the Arkansas.

Farther west tower the heights of the Rocky Mountains and the Sierra Nevada, with a region of high plateaus, basins, and ranges between them. North of the Sierra Nevada extends the Cascade Range. Finally, there is a narrow region of low mountains and fertile valleys running along the coast of the Pacific Ocean.

Early colonization

The Atlantic coastal area was the scene of the first English attempts at colonization. You have already read about Jamestown, founded in 1607, and Plymouth, founded in 1620. Other settlements followed soon afterward.

Most English colonies were set up in one of two ways: (1) by joint-stock companies, which purchased monopolies for trading and colonizing; and (2) by private individuals called proprietors, to whom the English monarchs gave large tracts of land. In both cases the object was to make a profit. To both joint-stock companies and favored individuals, the kings granted royal charters. These charters gave the companies and individuals the right to establish and govern colonies and to conduct business for profit.

On the whole the American colonies were not profitable as business ventures, but they attracted many settlers from England. Some settlers hoped to find gold; others sought a Northwest Passage to the Far East. Most of them were from the middle and lower classes in England, who found conditions in their homeland intolerable. These included economic hardships, political struggles between the Stuart kings and Parliament, and religious disagreements among Calvinists, Anglicans, and Roman Catholics. Englishmen came to America to seek a better living, peace from political strife, and freedom to worship as they pleased. These were strong and compelling reasons for leaving England, and so they had to be. The life the settlers found in America was filled with great hardships and grave dangers.

Some, in order to pay their way, came as indentured servants. They signed an indenture, or contract, agreeing to serve a master for a certain length of time, sometimes as long as seven years, in exchange for free transportation to America. In the very early years of settlement, Negroes from Africa also came as indentured servants; some were brought to Jamestown as early as 1619.

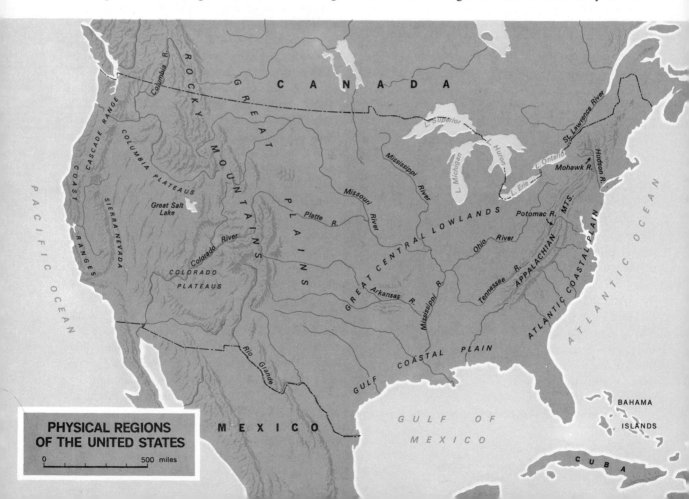

**PHYSICAL REGIONS
OF THE UNITED STATES**

0 ————— 500 miles

Early American Weather Vane

Craftsmen in the English colonies produced many utilitarian objects that are valued today for their naive charm. Such is the weather vane at right. For several years it stood on top of a provincial government building in Boston, turning back and forth to indicate the direction from which the wind was blowing.

This quaint Indian apparently wears only feathers. The figure was welded out of bronze, then gilded and adorned with glass eyes. We know the name of the maker (Shem Drowne). This is unusual, for most work of this sort—known as folk art—is anonymous. However, the piece is typical in its lack of sophistication and in its use of native design elements, in this case those of New England.

However, they soon began coming as slaves. Although slavery existed in all thirteen colonies, it became especially important to the economy of the southern colonies.

In the area between New England and Virginia, some early settlements were established by colonists from the Netherlands and Sweden. There was the Dutch settlement of New Amsterdam at the southern tip of Manhattan Island. This settlement was part of a colony called New Netherland. A Swedish colony, New Sweden, sprang up along the shores of Delaware Bay. But the Dutch seized New Sweden in 1655, and were themselves forced to surrender to the English in 1664. Both the town of New Amsterdam and the colony of New Netherland were renamed New York. From then on, the entire eastern seaboard as far south as Florida was held by England. By 1750 there were thirteen well-established colonies along the Atlantic seacoast (see map, page 388).

Although these colonies were decidedly English in character, they also included settlers from different backgrounds. Scots, Irish, Germans, Swiss, French Huguenots, Jews, and other peoples came to America during the early years of settlement in search of greater personal liberty and better business and social opportunities. Like the English, these settlers selected names that reminded them of their homeland—for example, Germantown, in Pennsylvania, and Geneva, in New York. Although not as numerous as the English, these other early settlers exerted influence that was widely felt.

Colonial government

Although the English government played only a small role in founding or building the American colonies, it did make certain guarantees to them.

387

Each colonial charter promised that every English colonist in America would be considered an Englishman. These colonists were promised the same legal rights and freedoms—the "rights of Englishmen"—as men born and living in England.

Almost from the beginning, both the joint-stock companies and the proprietors found it necessary to give the colonists some voice in their own affairs. By 1750 each colony had a government consisting of a governor, a council, and an assembly. The council advised the governor and also acted as the upper house of the legislature,

somewhat like the English House of Lords. The assembly, the lower house of the legislature, was elected by qualified property owners in the colony.

By 1750 the thirteen British colonies were divided into three main types: royal, proprietary, and self-governing. Royal colonies numbered eight—New Hampshire, New York, Massachusetts, New Jersey, North Carolina, South Carolina, Virginia, and Georgia. In these colonies the king appointed the governor and council, and the colonists elected the assembly.

NORTH AMERICAN COLONIES in 1750

British territory

French territory

□ French forts

Spanish territory

0   500 miles

There were three proprietary colonies—Pennsylvania, Delaware,° and Maryland. Each of these was under a proprietor, who either acted as governor or appointed a governor and council. There was also an elected assembly. In the self-governing colonies—Rhode Island and Connecticut—the voters elected all the officials: governor, council, and assembly.

In the royal and proprietary colonies many conflicts arose between the appointed governors and the elected assemblies. The governors had to act according to the wishes of the king or the proprietor, who had the authority to recommend and veto laws, appoint and remove officials, and summon or dismiss the assemblies.

The assemblies, on the other hand, reflected the viewpoint of the colonial voters—usually the middle-class landowners, merchants, and professional men. Like the English House of Commons, the elected assemblies claimed the right to approve taxes and appropriate money to run the government. There were many disagreements over taxation, defense, the authority of judges, and the enforcement of laws regulating colonial trade.

Colonial products and trade

Almost from the beginning, natural conditions of soil and climate divided the colonies into three main economic groups. New England, where farming was not very productive, developed fishing, lumbering, shipbuilding, trading, and some manufacturing. The so-called Middle Colonies—New York, New Jersey, Pennsylvania, and Delaware—produced enough grain to provide a surplus for export. The southern colonies, from Maryland southward, specialized in growing tobacco, rice, and indigo, a plant from which an important blue dye was made. From their pine forests came the naval stores so important in shipbuilding and shipping.

Every colony had to develop trade because it had to import most of its manufactured goods. To get the money to pay for their imports, the colonists had to find markets in which to sell their

° **Delaware:** Although part of Pennsylvania from 1682 to 1776, Delaware was ruled as a separate colony after 1703.

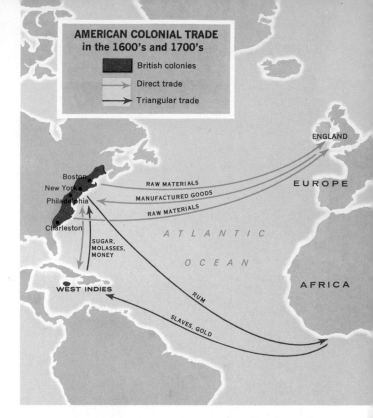

AMERICAN COLONIAL TRADE
in the 1600's and 1700's

- British colonies
- Direct trade
- Triangular trade

own products. The southern colonies found a good market for their tobacco, rice, indigo, and naval stores in England. The Middle Colonies and New England produced grain, fish, and lumber. Since these products were also found in England, the colonists sold most of their surplus in continental Europe, Africa, and the West Indies.

Trade with the West Indian colonies of Spain, England, France, and the Netherlands was especially important to merchants of the Middle Colonies and New England. The islands imported most of their food and therefore were good markets for the mainland colonies. The chief product of the islands was sugar cane, from which refined sugar and molasses were made.

Two trade routes were of special importance to these merchants (see map, this page). One was a direct route back and forth between the islands of the West Indies and such North American ports as Philadelphia, New York, and Boston. West Indian sugar and molasses were exchanged for grain, fish, and lumber. The other route involved the so-called triangular trade. Merchants

389

The American Colonies

The men and women who settled in America pursued the great lure of the New World. Some stayed in the growing cities while others carved farms out of the wilderness.

Baltimore, in the southern colonies, was just a village when the picture above was painted in 1752. Crops like tobacco, growing at right, brought prosperity. By 1776, Baltimore was a busy port and the ninth largest city in the colonies.

During the 1600's, Boston grew to be the largest city in New England. By 1750 it had about 15,000 people and rivaled Philadelphia as the political and cultural center of the American colonies. At left is State Street, the center of Boston's commercial district.

The Middle Colonies were noted for their large farms. A homestead in New York State is depicted in the mural below, painted about 1735. The barn and storage bins at left were probably used for corn, rye, and wheat, products commonly grown in the area.

from the colonies sailed for Africa with casks of rum manufactured from sugar and molasses by the colonists. In Africa the rum was traded for slaves or gold. The slaves were taken to the West Indies and exchanged for sugar, molasses, or money. The sugar and molasses were carried back to North America and used to make more rum. The money from Africa and the West Indies was used to buy needed imports.

Mercantilism and the English colonies

Mercantilism, you will remember, was an economic theory which maintained that colonies existed for the benefit of the mother country. Basically they were to supply needed raw materials and furnish a market for the manufactured products of the mother country.

In line with mercantilistic policies, the English government passed a number of regulations that affected its North American colonies, beginning with the Navigation Act of 1651. One regulation listed, or "enumerated," colonial products to be sold only in England. These "enumerated goods" could not be sold to any other country, where the colonists might have received more money for them. Goods sold to America by continental European countries had to be shipped first to England, where they were taxed and then transported to the colonies in English ships.

Other regulations discouraged Americans from manufacturing. For example, they were forbidden to ship woolen cloth of their own manufacture outside of the colony in which it was made. They could carry on only the first stage of iron manu-facture—the making of pig iron. The pig iron had to be shipped to England, where English manufacturers produced iron tools and utensils from it.

Some features of mercantilism brought benefits to Americans. The British, for example, restricted all trade within the empire to British ships. The American colonists were considered to be British citizens and therefore were allowed to build and operate their own ships. Thus American shipbuilding and shipping grew, making many Americans quite wealthy.

The overall effects of mercantilism, however, were more harmful than good. Trade regulations aroused resentment, and colonists found many ways to evade them. They bought and sold where they could do so most profitably. They avoided paying taxes whenever and however they could. Smuggling became a respectable occupation, difficult to prevent because of the long American coastline with its many harbors and inlets.

CHECKUP

1. What were the three forms of colonial government?

2. Why did conflicts arise between colonial governors and assemblies?

3. How did mercantilism affect Britain's North American colonies?

4. IDENTIFY: indentured servants, "rights of Englishmen," triangular trade.

5. LOCATE: Appalachian Mountains, Hudson River, Mohawk River, Potomac River, Ohio River, Missouri River, Rocky Mountains, Sierra Nevada, Jamestown, Plymouth.

2   The British colonies declared their independence

Although the North American colonists of the 1700's resented British trade regulations, they were far more concerned with the French along their borders. French settlers were not numerous, but they occupied strategic locations.

Rivalry between Britain and France

While the British were establishing colonies along the Atlantic coast, the French had been developing settlements to the north and west, along the shores of the St. Lawrence River, the Great Lakes, and the Mississippi River—a vast region which they called New France. They laid claim to the large territory of Louisiana and, in 1718, established the city of New Orleans near the mouth of the Mississippi River.

In the 1700's, American settlers began to cross the Appalachians in search of new land. As you

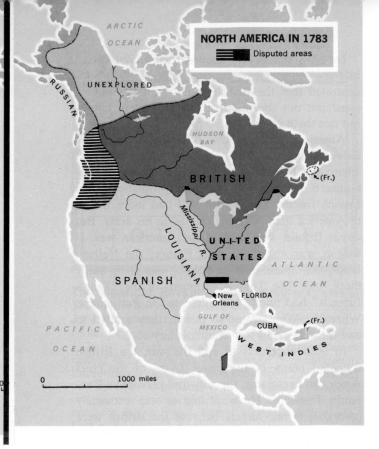

NORTH AMERICA IN 1783
≡ Disputed areas

ARCTIC OCEAN

RUSSIAN

UNEXPLORED

HUDSON BAY

BRITISH

(Fr.)

Mississippi R.

LOUISIANA

UNITED STATES

ATLANTIC OCEAN

SPANISH

New Orleans FLORIDA

GULF OF MEXICO

CUBA (Fr.)

PACIFIC OCEAN

WEST INDIES

0   1000 miles

victory at Yorktown, the American states ratified, or accepted, the Articles of Confederation, a constitution adopted at the Second Continental Congress at Philadelphia in 1777. This constitution provided for a stronger central government, creating a one-house Congress in which each state had a single vote. Congress was given the power to declare war, make peace, conduct foreign relations, and settle disputes between the states.

It did not, however, have the power to tax; to raise money, Congress had to request the states to grant it. Nor could Congress regulate trade with foreign countries or among the states.

The United States was governed under the Articles of Confederation from 1781 to 1789. It was a strange government. There was a legislature with power to pass certain laws. But there was no executive, so the individual states had to enforce and administer these laws. There were also no United States courts, and cases involving the laws of the United States had to be tried in state courts.

398

Although the government created by the Articles of Confederation was weak, it was responsible for one notable achievement—the establishment of a democratic policy for dealing with new American territory.

The land between the Appalachian Mountains, the Ohio and Mississippi rivers, and the Great Lakes was known as the Northwest Territory. This area had been turned over to the United States by those states which had originally claimed it at the time the Articles of Confederation were ratified. Once independence had been gained, hundreds of settlers pushed across the mountains into this land. Congress had to provide some form of government for them. Two basic questions were involved: (1) Were these settlers to be considered citizens of the United States? (2) What kind of government should these settlers have?

The Congress of the Confederation answered these questions in the Northwest Ordinance of 1787, written mainly by Thomas Jefferson. It provided that the United States would have territories but not colonies. The people who lived in the territories would have the same civil rights as citizens of the original thirteen states. They would not receive the full political right of self-government immediately, but were promised it eventually. The Ordinance set up a procedure whereby the people of each territory gained increasing self-government as they grew in numbers. When enough people lived in a territory, it could become a state of the Union, equal in every respect to the original thirteen states.

The American Constitution

The government under the Articles of Confederation succeeded in solving the land problem. However, Americans soon realized that the Articles were inadequate. In 1787, delegates from twelve states (Rhode Island did not take part) met in Philadelphia to draft a new constitution.

The men who attended the Constitutional Convention in 1787 faced several problems. They wanted to create a central government strong enough to act for the states in matters of mutual concern. At the same time they wanted to leave the states free to act for themselves in those matters that were considered to involve them alone.

To solve this problem, the men who wrote the Constitution determined to adopt the federal system, in which powers are divided between a central government and individual states. As a guide, they had the example of Greek leagues of city-states, about which you read in Chapter 5. The central government alone was given power to declare war, make treaties, coin money, raise armies, and regulate trade with foreign countries. All powers not given to the central government or prohibited to the states belonged to the states and the people.

Another problem facing the framers of the Constitution involved the branches of the central government. Their experience under the Articles of Confederation had convinced them that a government could not get along without its own executive to enforce and carry out its laws, and its own courts to interpret the laws and decide when they were violated.

The framers found a solution by making use of ideas stated by the French political writer Montesquieu in *The Spirit of the Laws*. They created three branches: executive (the President), legislative (Congress), and judicial (the federal courts). Each branch was given certain powers, and could act as a check on each of the others.

James Madison, one of the most influential delegates to the Constitutional Convention, described the American system as a republic, where the government "derives all its powers directly from the great body of the people, and is administered by persons holding their offices . . . for a limited period, or during good behavior." It was not a monarchy, of course, since there was no king. Neither was it, at this time, more than a limited democracy; the states restricted voting to adult, free males who, as a rule, owned a certain amount of property.

The new Constitution was ratified in 1788. In the following year, George Washington became the first President under the new government.

Effects of American independence

The American Revolution had immediate and widespread effects. Both during and after the war, many Loyalists, whose property had been confiscated and who were ardently loyal to the British crown, moved to Canada. Many settled in southern Canada, north of Lakes Erie and Ontario. There they insisted on their rights as Englishmen and on a considerable degree of self-government.

The British government, profiting by its bitter experience in the United States, granted some of the demands of English settlers in Canada. Habeas corpus and jury trials were allowed during the 1780's. In 1791, Britain passed the Constitutional Act, dividing the colony into the two provinces of Upper Canada (mostly British) and Lower Canada (mostly French).

In addition to the immediate political effects, events in the United States put into practice ideas of John Locke and the French philosophers that had previously existed only on paper. The idea stated in the Declaration of Independence that all men have certain unalienable rights is the very foundation of the democratic ideal. Another mighty idea behind the Revolution was that all the powers of government belong to the people. The American experience gave encouragement to people in other parts of the world who opposed autocracy and privileged classes.

The federal republic created by the framers of the Constitution showed the world that individual states could be united successfully under a central government but still be free to act for themselves in local problems. In time, many other nations adopted a federal form of government.

CHECKUP

1. What were the strong and weak points of each side in the Revolutionary War?

2. What were the weaknesses of the American government under the Articles of Confederation? What was the chief accomplishment of government under the Articles?

3. American independence put into effect two ideas which have had worldwide influence; what were they? Why was the adoption of the American Constitution important to other peoples?

4. IDENTIFY: Hessians, Cornwallis, Northwest Territory, Constitutional Act.

399

CHAPTER REVIEW

Chapter 18   The American Revolution Created a New Nation in North America   (1607—1789)

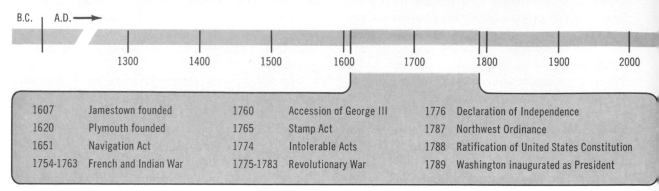

1607	Jamestown founded	1760	Accession of George III	1776	Declaration of Independence
1620	Plymouth founded	1765	Stamp Act	1787	Northwest Ordinance
1651	Navigation Act	1774	Intolerable Acts	1788	Ratification of United States Constitution
1754-1763	French and Indian War	1775-1783	Revolutionary War	1789	Washington inaugurated as President

CHAPTER SUMMARY

North America between Canada and Mexico, a region of varied geography and rich natural resources, was colonized chiefly by the English. Beginning in 1607, joint-stock companies and private individuals established thirteen colonies. Men settled there in hopes of prosperity and political and religious freedom. They had some degree of self-government, whether they lived in royal, proprietary, or self-governing colonies. The three main regions—New England, the Middle Colonies, and the southern colonies—depended heavily on trade and resented English mercantilist restrictions.

After Britain defeated France in the French and Indian War, it tried to enforce trade laws and impose new taxes in order to pay war debts and provide for defense. The British used writs of assistance and trials without jury, which Americans protested as violations of their rights. Colonial resistance increased British determination, and relations deteriorated steadily. The Revolutionary War broke out in 1775. The following year the Second Continental Congress adopted the Declaration of Independence.

American advantages in the war included foreign help, good leadership, and the fact that Britain faced many problems in fighting far from home. However, lack of unity and a shortage of funds hampered the American cause. A decisive victory at Yorktown, plus British war weariness, brought peace in 1783.

The newly independent American states were at first governed by the Articles of Confederation. The central government was weak, but it did establish a democratic policy for territories.

A new Constitution, ratified in 1788, greatly strengthened the United States. Its federal system provided for both an effective central authority and state governments. Power was divided among three branches of the government.

Events in North America had widespread effects. Many Loyalists moved to Canada. The events also influenced many other peoples by providing a living example of democratic ideals.

QUESTIONS FOR DISCUSSION

1. Do you think that the reasons for colonial resentment and eventual revolution were mainly economic rather than political? Can you give examples of present-day situations where economic factors influence the course of events?

2. Prior to the American Revolution, colonists refused to buy British goods. How did the Americans hope that these actions would hurt the British? Should the United States use trade boycotts today against countries that cause it trouble?

3. The Declaration of Independence was adopted on July 4, 1776, but it would have been an almost meaningless document without the American victory at Yorktown in 1781. Explain why you agree or disagree with this statement. What is required of a document or law for it to have any authority?

4. The American Patriots constituted only about a third of the population in the colonies, yet their revolution succeeded. In other countries, even smaller groups have staged successful revolutions. How do you account for such success by small minorities?

PROJECTS

1. Write a short essay in support of the Constitution as against the Articles of Confederation.

2. Write an editorial for an American colonial newspaper stating either a Loyalist or Patriot position.

3. Draw a map of North America in 1763, showing (1) the thirteen original English colonies, indicating which ones were royal, proprietary, and self-governing, and (2) other European possessions after the Treaty of Paris in 1763.

The French Revolution and Napoleon Affected All Europe

In earlier chapters you have read about the growth of France. You will remember that it was a divine-right monarchy, in which the king's will was law. You will remember, too, that society was organized into three classes called Estates. This traditional political and social system of France is known as the Old Regime.

The First Estate consisted of the clergy of the Roman Catholic Church and totaled less than 1 percent of the population. They still retained many of the privileges they had held during the Middle Ages. They were exempted from taxes and could be tried only in Church courts. The Church owned about a tenth of all French land and received enormous revenues from rents, taxes, and fees. Most of this wealth was concentrated in the hands of the higher clergy— archbishops, bishops, and abbots. Some of these men had become lazy, worldly, and neglectful of their spiritual duties. They were the targets of men like Voltaire, who aroused educated people against the Church. The lower clergy, made up of the parish priests, were poorly paid and overworked. The Church, however, in addition to religious guidance, did provide valuable services, including relief for the poor and all education.

The Second Estate in France were the nobles, less than 2 percent of the population. Many of them had special privileges that were carry-overs from medieval times. The nobles, too, were ex-

Napoleon as emperor of France

empted from the heaviest royal taxes, while still collecting feudal dues of various kinds from the peasants. Nobles held the highest positions in the army and government. Some were concerned for the welfare of France, but as a class the nobility were thoughtless, irresponsible, and extravagant.

All the other people of France—approximately 97 percent—belonged to the Third Estate. This Estate itself was subdivided into three groups.

At the top was the bourgeoisie, the city-dwelling middle class, made up of merchants, manufacturers, and professional people such as doctors and lawyers. Many bourgeois were people of wealth and education. Below the bourgeoisie were the manual workers—laborers and artisans—of the cities. Generally they received low wages and lived in poor, crowded quarters. At the bottom of the social scale and poorest of all were the serfs and the peasants. Although most peasants were freemen and there were few serfs, most peasants still owed feudal dues and services. They paid the heaviest taxes and Church tithes, worked long and hard, and lived in ignorance.

In the world of the late 1700's, the three Estates of the Old Regime represented a social structure that was outdated and unrealistic. Those who benefited from it resisted even minor changes in the system. Those who opposed it grew increasingly bitter. Change came suddenly and violently.

 Growing discontent and bankruptcy led to revolution

In the late 1700's, France was probably more prosperous than any other country in Europe. The majority of its population enjoyed a higher standard of living than any people other than the British. However, France suffered from an unjust social system and from poor government.

When the country was ruled by an able king who worked at his job, like Louis XIV, its absolute monarchy could be fairly efficient. Under a lazy ruler like Louis XV, king from 1715 to 1774, the government simply drifted.

France was a crazy quilt of administrative divisions that overlapped in territory and often conflicted in authority. Inefficiency, graft, and waste were everywhere. The system of law was not uniform, and there were hundreds of different courts. Customs duties within the country made it extremely difficult for merchants to carry on business.

Under the Old Regime there were no individual rights or personal liberties such as freedom of speech, or press, or assembly. Judges were appointed and removed by the king. Trials were secret and without a jury. The king could issue a *lettre de cachet* (LEH-truh duh kah-SHAY)—"letter under seal"—ordering the imprisonment, without trial, of anyone who displeased him. Such a person could be sent to a prison, like the Bastille in Paris, for years without knowing why.

Discontent with the Old Regime

Inequality in the social system and inefficiency in government existed in France for a long time. Beginning about the mid-1700's, however, discontent began to grow. There were two chief causes: bourgeois unrest and financial difficulties.

You might expect that opposition to the social system of France would arise first among the oppressed peasants, who bore heavy burdens, but this was not so. Rather, it began among the prosperous bourgeoisie.

The middle class had become the most important economic group in France. Its members owned nearly all of the productive wealth other

Before the revolution, Louis XVI was painted in the ermine robes traditional for a king of France. Posed with his scepter, right, he looks both intelligent and commanding, which he was not. One historian has called him simply "an honest blockhead." His queen, Marie Antoinette, above, had the charm the king lacked, but little common sense. Frenchmen grew increasingly dissatisfied with their royal family and those in authority. The cartoon below, published in 1789, shows a peasant (representing the Third Estate) under the feet of a clergyman and a noble (representing the other two estates). The stone symbolizes the peasant's burden of taxes, import duties, and forced labor.

403

than land and dominated trade, manufacturing, and banking. But the bourgeois did not have political power equal to their economic power; in fact, under the Old Regime they had no political power at all. They resented the fact that the wealthiest bourgeois banker or the most brilliant bourgeois lawyer was the social inferior of the poorest and most ignorant noble or priest.

Another cause of bourgeois discontent was mercantilism. When the Commercial Revolution was beginning, businessmen had welcomed mercantilist ideas and practices. By the mid-1700's, however, these ideas and practices were less popular. The bourgeois now disliked mercantilist regulations governing wages, prices, and foreign trade. They also resented special monopolies granted to favored companies, and government interference with a merchant's freedom to buy in foreign countries.

A middle class such as the French bourgeoisie is not usually revolutionary. But the bourgeoisie were influenced by such thinkers of the Enlightenment as Voltaire, Rousseau, and Montesquieu. The skeptical attitude of these writers toward privileged classes and traditional authority found an especially warm welcome among the French bourgeoisie.

Another strong influence was the American Revolution. Its success had a profound effect on the thinking of the French middle class. The Declaration of Independence, with its ideas about the equality of man and his right to control his own government, became a vivid inspiration.

France found itself in severe economic trouble in the mid-1700's. The wars of Louis XIV had left a huge debt that had been increased by French assistance to the United States during the Revolutionary War. The extravagant French court at Versailles cost vast sums of money.

France's debt was not as large as that of Great Britain. The trouble was that, even with heavy taxes, government revenues were always too low to meet expenses. The basic cause of France's financial problems was the unwillingness of the wealthy to pay taxes.

When taxes did not produce enough revenue to meet expenses, Louis XV borrowed more and more from the bankers. Warned that his actions endangered France, the king remarked cynically, "It will last my time," and "After me, the deluge."

"Reforms" under Louis XVI

In 1774, Louis XVI came to the throne of France. He was weak and rather dull-witted, but might have been an adequate ruler in ordinary times, for he wanted to act wisely and make his country prosperous. These were not ordinary times, however. The royal treasury was not only empty, but in debt; the people were discontented and restless. Louis was encouraged to resist reform by the corrupt and stubborn nobles of his court and by his queen, Marie Antoinette, who was charming, extravagant, and irresponsible.

Louis XVI asked several middle-class financial experts to propose ways of improving French finances. But when they suggested real reforms, such as greater freedom for French industry, the payment of taxes by nobles and clergy, and less extravagant spending by the court, they were dismissed.

France was heading for financial disaster. It was receiving no help from those who should have given leadership—the king, the nobles, and the clergy. In 1787 the country's credit was exhausted; bankers refused to lend the government more money. France was faced with bankruptcy. Reluctantly, Louis XVI sent out a call to the representatives of the Estates-General to meet at Versailles in May 1789. Unable to solve its problems, divine-right monarchy called on the representatives of the people.

The meeting of the Estates-General

The Estates-General met in an atmosphere of confusion and uncertainty. Besides the financial crisis, there were many other problems. France was suffering from a business depression and from unemployment. The harvest of 1788 had been poor and food prices were high.

The Estates-General had not met for almost 200 years. No one knew exactly what its powers and rules were. Many people felt that if it had power only to advise the king, and not to make and carry out laws, its meeting would be useless.

"Spring" by François Boucher

Frivolous elegance characterized the style of art known as rococo, which was popular in the period before the French Revolution. The painting at right, by a master of this style, is typical. One of a series representing the four seasons, it was painted in 1755 for a lady of Louis XV's court.

French aristocrats of the Old Regime were captivated by the rural life of shepherds and other country folk—not, of course, as it really was, but idealized and prettified. They enjoyed poetry, plays, paintings, and music with a pastoral setting. At Versailles, Marie Antoinette had architects build a replica of a rustic village, where she and her favorite courtiers, dressed as peasants, pretended to be milkmaids and shepherds. With the wisdom of hindsight, we can appreciate the irony of the situation: the nobility of France play-acting as common people while those same people daily grew more discontented and dissatisfied.

As for the rules, there was conflict and argument over many questions, particularly over methods of meeting and voting. In the past the three Estates had met separately and each had cast one vote. This procedure had allowed the conservative clergy and nobles of the First and Second Estates to outvote the Third Estate.

The representatives of the Third Estate included many interesting personalities. Most of them were young men and many were lawyers. A few of them, like the Count de Mirabeau, were men of noble birth who had consented to represent the Third Estate. Almost all were acquainted with the ideas of Montesquieu and Voltaire. As the representatives of the majority of Frenchmen, they insisted on having a real voice in decisions, without being automatically outvoted by the other two Estates. Because the Third Estate had as many representatives as the other two Estates combined, they wanted the Estates to meet together, with representatives voting as individuals.

The Estates-General assembled first in a combined meeting on May 5, 1789. The king greeted the delegates and asked their help in solving France's financial problems. Then he instructed them to follow the old custom, each Estate meeting and voting separately as one body. The representatives of the Third Estate refused. They claimed that the Estates-General represented the French people, not the three classes. Therefore, they should meet together and vote as individuals.

When Louis XVI failed to take action, the Third Estate proclaimed itself a National Assembly. This declaration, made on June 17, 1789, has been called the first act of the French Revolution. Then the rebellious representatives invited the members of the other two Estates to join them in working for the welfare of France. When the king had the representatives of the Third Estate locked out of their meeting place, they met at a nearby indoor tennis court. There, on June 20, they made a pledge, called the Tennis-Court Oath, that they would not adjourn until they had written a constitution for France and seen it adopted. Finally the king gave in and ordered the three Estates to meet together.

Riots and violence

Now Louis XVI tried to do secretly what he had feared to do openly. He began to bring large bodies of troops to Paris and to Versailles, where the representatives were meeting. Fearing that he planned to drive out the Estates-General by force, the people of Paris began to riot. On July 14, a Paris mob stormed and captured the Bastille, the hated prison-fortress, in search of weapons. (In France this event is still celebrated as Bastille Day—a national holiday similar to Independence Day in the United States.)

The outbreak of violence in Paris led to the formation of a new government for the city. Under the leadership of General Lafayette, the French hero who had fought for American independence in the Revolutionary War, a people's army, called the National Guard, was formed. The white flag of the Bourbons with its *fleur de lis* (lily) symbols was replaced by the tricolor—a flag of red, white, and blue stripes that has remained the flag of France.

The riots and violence in Paris were echoed throughout France. In July and August, the so-called "Great Fear" swept across the land. The peasants believed rumors that the nobles planned to send bandits into the countryside to round them up and kill them. Eager to avenge old wrongs and be rid of old burdens, the peasants attacked monasteries and the manor houses of the rich. They robbed and destroyed government offices, burning the documents which recorded their rents, feudal dues, and other obligations. They killed some nobles and their agents, and some government officials, especially tax collectors.

CHECKUP

1. Describe the social structure of France during the Old Regime.
2. Why did discontent grow in France beginning about the mid-1700's?
3. For what reason did Louis XVI call a meeting of the Estates-General? Why did representatives of the Third Estate insist that all three groups of the Estates-General meet and vote together?
4. IDENTIFY: Old Regime, *lettre de cachet,* Marie Antoinette, National Assembly, Tennis-Court Oath, Bastille Day.

2 After a period of turmoil, revolutionaries overthrew the monarchy

France was in great disorder after the storming of the Bastille and the outbreaks of violence throughout the country. With the support of the people and the National Guard, the National Assembly assumed power in France.

The end of the Old Regime

Many members of the National Assembly felt that the way to deal with revolutionary violence was to remove the oppression and injustice that produced it. In a little more than a month, they took several important steps in this direction.

Beginning August 4, 1789, the National As-sembly abolished the last remnants of serfdom. Delegates canceled all feudal dues and services of the peasants and repealed the Church tithe. They also did away with the special privileges of French nobles and clergy, including tax exemptions.

All of these reforms were included in a decree known as the Law of the Fourth of August. It was followed on August 27, 1789, by the adoption of the Declaration of the Rights of Man. This document was strongly influenced by the English Bill of Rights, by the writings of Rousseau and others, and by the American Declaration of Independence.

The Declaration of the Rights of Man began by saying that men are born and remain equal before the law and that the law must be the same for all. It went on to proclaim freedom of speech, of the press, and of religion. Men have a right to take part in their government and to resist oppression. All citizens have an equal right to hold public office, with distinction only for virtue and talent. They have a right to personal liberty, which can be taken from them only by fair trial. The Declaration stated and defined the principles that became the slogan of the French Revolution—"liberty, equality, and fraternity."

Although the National Assembly swept away the remains of feudalism in France, the Old Regime died hard. Many nobles were arrogant, unyielding, and thoughtless to the end. Some of them fled from France to neighboring countries such as Great Britain, Italy, and Prussia, where they plotted ceaselessly to return and undo the revolutionary changes. These *émigrés* (EM·uh·grayz) —French for "emigrants"—were a constant source of trouble for France in the years to come.

Nobles who remained at Versailles urged the king to use force to restore order—the old order. Louis XVI again called in troops to Versailles. When news of his action reached the people, a crowd of women marched from Paris to Versailles. They stormed into the palace and forced the king and his family to return to Paris, away from the plotting and scheming royal advisers.

The National Assembly moved to Paris during the fall of 1789. This move placed the entire French government at the mercy of the violent Paris mobs. Meetings were held in a public hall, and spectators often interrupted the debates with shouts, or rose to give their own opinions from the gallery.

Reforms in government

The abolition of feudalism and the issuing of the Declaration of the Rights of Man established the guiding principles of the French Revolution. The National Assembly then began to work out details. Between 1789 and 1791 the Assembly passed more than 2,000 laws aimed at correcting abuses and setting up a new government.

First the Assembly reformed the national administration of France. The provinces, which had possessed many special privileges, were abolished. France was divided instead into eighty-three uniform districts called *départements*. All officials of local governments were to be elected.

The manorial rights of nobles and clergy over the peasants had already been abolished. Now the Assembly confiscated land from the Church and offered it at public sale, with payment to be made in installments. Most of this land was bought by the peasants who had been renting it. Thus the French peasant became the owner of the land he farmed; thereafter he was a man to be reckoned with in French affairs.

In 1790 the Assembly adopted the Civil Constitution of the Clergy. Priests and bishops were to be elected by the voters of their parishes and dioceses. They were subject to the national government and had to swear allegiance to its laws; their salaries were to be paid by the government. The pope forbade the clergy to accept the new arrangement, and the majority refused to do so. Some left the country, while others helped the remaining nobles stir up hatred against the revolution. The Civil Constitution of the Clergy was the greatest mistake of the reformers because it turned many people against the revolution.

The Constitution of 1791. The National Assembly finally completed writing a constitution for France. This Constitution of 1791 provided for a limited monarchy with separate executive, legislative, and judicial branches.

The powers of the king were greatly reduced; he could not proclaim laws, nor could he veto acts of the legislature. The legislature, called the Legislative Assembly, was a one-house body elected by voters who had to be taxpayers. It was to begin meeting in October 1791. No members of the National Assembly were eligible for election to the Legislative Assembly. To hold office a man had to own considerable property. Thus, despite the guarantees of equal rights and powers in the Declaration of the Rights of Man, most of the political power of France was given to the middle class.

Louis XVI reluctantly consented to the limita-

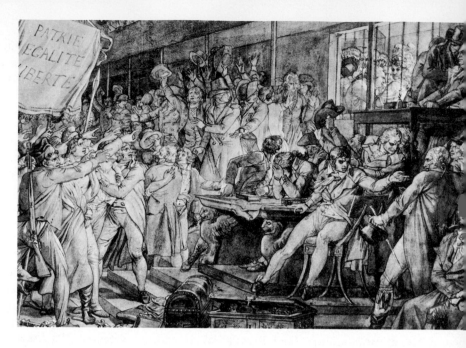

The French Revolution was called by one English historian "a cup of trembling which all nations shall drink." In August 1792 the king and his family were imprisoned in a small barred room that served as a press box for the Assembly, above. Five months and several prisons later, under orders from revolutionaries led by Robespierre, above, the king was beheaded. Below, his head is displayed to the cheering crowd. Marie Antoinette met her death in October 1793. The sketch at right shows her, worn but proud, on her way to the guillotine.

tions that the new constitution imposed on him. At the same time he encouraged the plotting of the *émigrés* with foreign governments, hoping that it would result in the overthrow of the new order and a return to the Old Regime.

Some of the king's advisers urged him to flee and seek help directly from friendly nations. In June 1791, Louis, together with his wife and young son, tried to escape from France to the Austrian Netherlands. He was dressed like an ordinary citizen, but the military escort for his coach aroused suspicion and he was recognized by several people. The coach was stopped at the town of Varennes, near the northern border of France, and its occupants were placed under arrest. As the king was brought back to Paris, some crowds jeered him and others were threateningly silent. Bad feeling was increased by a statement Louis had left behind, calling upon all loyal Frenchmen to restore the Old Regime.

Despite the king's flight to Varennes, the National Assembly determined to retain him as monarch if he would accept the revised constitution. His decision to do so revived his popularity, and he was cheered by the people, who felt that conditions would now be more settled and the revolutionary disturbances would be at an end.

The Legislative Assembly and war

The new government provided for by the Constitution of 1791 went into effect in September 1791, but it lasted less than a year. The revolutionaries had been more skillful in overthrowing the Old Regime than in creating a workable government to replace it. They had set up a weak executive and a powerful but inexperienced legislature elected by only a small minority of the population.

The Legislative Assembly was divided into three groups of people with differing attitudes toward the revolution. One group, the constitutional monarchists, believed that the revolution had gone far enough. They considered a limited monarchy under middle-class control the ideal form of government. They were *conservatives*—that is, they did not want to change ex-

isting conditions. Another group wanted to abolish the monarchy and set up a republic under middle-class control. They were *radicals,* advocating far-reaching changes. A third group, the *moderates,* had no extreme views. They sided with conservatives or radicals, depending on the situation.

In the hall where the Legislative Assembly met, conservatives sat on the right, moderates in the center, and radicals on the left. Since that time, this placement of political parties has become traditional in France. The terms *right, center,* and *left* are often used to designate shades of political opinion.

The Assembly was frequently deadlocked on domestic issues, but it united in facing a foreign threat brought by Emperor Leopold II of Austria and King Frederick William II of Prussia. In August 1791 these two monarchs had proclaimed that European rulers should restore the monarchy in France as it had been. Actually they did not plan to move against France. (Prussia was busy planning the Second Partition of Poland.) But each group in the French Legislative Assembly hoped that a successful war would increase its influence. Only a few farsighted men feared that war would lead to military dictatorship. There was little opposition when the Assembly forced Louis XVI to declare war on Austria in April 1792. Soon afterward an army of Austrian and Prussian troops invaded France.

The end of the monarchy. In Paris the invasion by Austrian and Prussian armies touched off mass uprisings. A group of radicals seized control of the city government and set up an organization called the Commune. This body menaced the lives of the royal family and threatened the Assembly with violence unless it abolished the monarchy. On August 10, 1792, the Assembly by order of the Commune voted to suspend the office of king. Troops marched on the royal palace, massacred many of the king's guards, and imprisoned Louis XVI and his family. A date was set for the election of delegates to a National Convention. They were to draw up another new constitution for France.

Thus the brief constitutional monarchy ended

amid great danger and confusion. In the midst of a foreign war, France faced a national election and a complete change of government. Riots broke out in many areas. Lafayette, commander of the army, could not accept the new situation; he gave up his command and fled to the Austrian Netherlands. There, despite the fact that he had always supported Louis XVI, he was arrested as a revolutionary and was held in Austrian prisons for five years.

CHECKUP

1. What were the most important accomplishments of the National Assembly?

2. "The revolutionaries had been more skillful in overthrowing the Old Regime than in creating a workable government to replace it." Explain.

3. Describe the political make-up of the Legislative Assembly.

4. IDENTIFY: *émigrés, départements,* flight to Varennes, Commune.

3   Violence and war paved the way for Napoleon Bonaparte

It had been determined that the delegates to the National Convention should be elected by *universal manhood suffrage*—that is, every man could vote, regardless of whether he owned property. Although there were thus some 7 million qualified voters in France, only 10 percent cast their ballots. Many stayed away from the polls in fear; those who did vote were often threatened unless they voted for candidates known to oppose the monarchy.

France under the National Convention

The National Convention held its first meeting in September 1792. The delegates, like those in the Legislative Assembly, were divided into three main groups. This time, however, there were no monarchists. On the right sat the Girondists, so called because many of them came from the province of Gironde in southwestern France. On the left were the Jacobins, members of a radical, mostly middle-class political club of that name. Among the most powerful Jacobins were Georges Jacques Danton and Maximilien Robespierre (ROHBZ·pih·air). Between the two groups was a large number of delegates who at first had no definite views but came to favor the Jacobins as the Convention proceeded. The Convention also included some extreme radicals, who wanted a republic representing all the people, not just the middle class. Their most important leader was a Parisian doctor, Jean Paul Marat.

The National Convention governed France by dictatorial methods for three years. As soon as it met, it proclaimed the end of the monarchy and the beginning of a republic. Besides its official function of drawing up a new constitution, it had to assume many of the responsibilities of government. It had to suppress disorder and revolt at home, and wage war against foreign invaders.

The National Convention tried King Louis XVI on charges of plotting against the security of the nation. By a small majority vote, he was declared guilty and sentenced to death. He was beheaded by the guillotine January 21, 1793.

Exporting the revolution. When the National Convention met in September 1792, encouraging news helped to dispel the uncertainty and confusion in France. Under its new general, Charles François Dumouriez (du·moo·RYAY), the French army had inflicted defeats on the Austrian and Prussian forces and stopped the invasion.

These French military victories were followed by a French invasion of the Austrian Netherlands and the capture of Brussels. Joyful over these victories, the National Convention declared that the French armies would liberate all the peoples of Europe from their autocratic rulers.

The French decision to export the ideas of liberty, equality, and fraternity by force of arms alarmed the rest of Europe. Great Britain, the Dutch Netherlands, Spain, and the kingdom of Sardinia joined Austria and Prussia in an alliance against France, which came to be called the First Coalition. Even in France there were many who doubted the wisdom of trying to spread ideas with bayonets.

"The Death of Marat," 1793

It is hardly surprising that the art of France reflected the shattering changes brought by the revolution. In subject, in mood, and in technique, this work by Jacques Louis David contrasts sharply with that of Boucher on page 405.

The Jacobin leader Jean Paul Marat was stabbed to death by Charlotte Corday as he was bathing. She had been convinced by the Girondists that he was a cruel tyrant. (Marat suffered from a painful skin disease and could find relief only by sitting in a warm bath.)

Because of its bizarre circumstances, Marat's assassination was not a conventional subject for a painting. But David—himself a revolutionary who at one time presided over the Convention—was a great artist and succeeded in creating a moving and forceful painting. In Marat's hand is a letter from his assassin. The knife that she plunged into his chest lies on the floor. The painting's stark drama is highlighted by David's simple inscription, "To Marat."

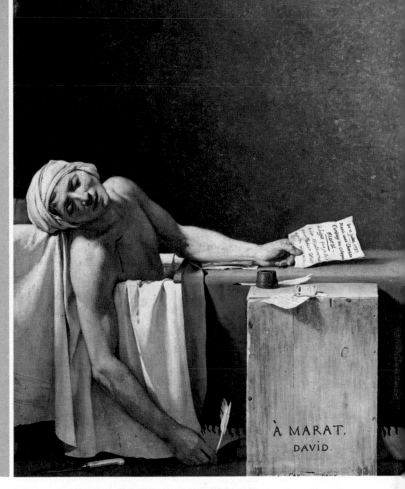

The French commander, Dumouriez, deserted to the Austrians early in 1793, after several military defeats. For a time the enemies of France were successful. French troops were driven out of the Austrian Netherlands, and France itself was again invaded.

Desperate measures

In 1793 the Convention took extreme steps to meet the dangers faced by France. It set up the Committee of Public Safety to direct the army in crushing foreign invaders. It also established a court called the Revolutionary Tribunal, which sought out and tried "enemies of the revolution."

The Committee of Public Safety met danger from the outside by adopting conscription—the draft. All men between eighteen and forty-five were liable to military service. The new national army was led by a competent man, Lazare Nicolas Carnot. Under Carnot, called the "Organizer of Victory," the French army took on a new spirit. It was an army of loyal, patriotic young men. Its officers were men of all classes who proved their ability and daring. For the first time the talents and ability of an entire nation, and all the classes, were called upon to fight a war.

Despite the optimism of the army, France's troubles were far from over. Jacobins, including Danton and Robespierre, controlled the Convention. Soon they arrested many of the Girondist delegates, and others fled from Paris to outlying districts, where they stirred up rebellion. A young woman from Normandy, influenced by Girondist propaganda, journeyed to Paris and assassinated Marat. The general unrest was intensified by a food shortage.

The Reign of Terror. To meet the danger of opposition and revolt within France, the Conven-

411

tion, under Robespierre's direction, instituted a program to suppress all opposition. It was known as the Reign of Terror and lasted from September 1793 to July 1794. According to one delegate: "What constitutes the Republic is the complete destruction of everything that is opposed to it."

The Revolutionary Tribunal conducted swift trials and handed down harsh sentences. Many people were arrested, tried, and executed on mere suspicion. The method of execution was beheading by the guillotine, which had become the symbol of the times.

Marie Antoinette, widow of Louis XVI, was among the first to be executed. Peoples of all classes, suspected of disloyalty to the revolution, were guillotined by the hundreds. The Girondist leaders were also executed. Antoine Lavoisier, the famous chemist, was condemned because he had once been concerned with tax collection. The Tribunal sent him to death with the words: "The Republic has no need of genius."

Danton and Robespierre persecuted not only the moderate members of the Convention but also the extreme radicals, the followers of Marat, who wanted a republic representing all the people. Many of them were led to the guillotine. There is a widely held, but incorrect, idea that the Reign of Terror was directed against the nobility. Among those executed were as many bourgeois as nobles and clergy combined, and nearly three times as many peasants and laborers as people from the other classes.

In the spring of 1794, Danton felt that the Reign of Terror had accomplished its purpose and should be relaxed. But Robespierre became ever more fanatical; he accused Danton of disloyalty to the revolution, and Danton and his followers were executed. As he mounted the scaffold, Danton is reported to have said, "Show my head to the people; they do not see the like every day."

For a hundred days, Robespierre ruled with an iron hand, carrying out a policy of suppression that aroused fear even among his supporters. Finally, the members of the Convention called a halt. In July 1794, Robespierre himself was arrested and then guillotined. The Reign of Terror was ended. The moderates, or what remained of them, were again in control.

Work of the National Convention

In spite of the dangers and difficulties of the time, the Convention brought about many reforms in France. It began the organization and arrangement of all French laws into a single code. It provided for a national system of public education. It abolished slavery in the French colonies.

The Convention did away with the law of primogeniture, under which only the oldest son could inherit his father's property. It also adopted the metric system, an efficient system of weights and measures based on the decimal system. The metric system is now used in many parts of the world, and by scientists almost everywhere.

Meanwhile the citizen army under Carnot was winning victories. By 1795 the French had driven the invaders out of France and had conquered territory as far east as the Rhine River. Even more important, the hostile coalition had begun to break up. Spain, Prussia, and the Dutch Netherlands had withdrawn; Great Britain, Austria, and Sardinia were on the defensive. However, the French paid a heavy price for victory. At home the spirit of militarism made it possible for the Convention to use the army to crush opposition of any sort. Abroad the French army was so haughty in victory that it aroused opposition among the peoples it "liberated."

In 1795 the Convention took up the task of drafting still another constitution for France. In October, just as it was to go into effect, there was an uprising in Paris. It was quickly suppressed by troops under the leadership of a relatively unknown general named Napoleon Bonaparte.

The Directory

The new constitution written by the National Convention in 1795 called for a republican form of government. Voting was restricted to property owners; thus, as under the National Assembly, control was back in the hands of the middle class. There was a legislature of two houses. The executive branch, which controlled the government, consisted of five men chosen by the legislature.

These five men were called Directors; therefore, the government created by the Constitution of 1795 is known as the Directory.

The Directory governed France for four years. It was unsatisfactory in many ways. As a "middle-of-the-road" government, it satisfied neither the radicals nor conservatives. Middle-class control proved as inefficient as control by privileged nobles. The government was made up of weak, corrupt, and selfish men. The Directors quarreled among themselves and were unable to agree on solutions to the problems of France. The Directory soon became as unpopular as the Old Regime. It repeated history by going bankrupt and paved the way for military dictatorship.

Napoleon Bonaparte

The Directory did encourage good leadership in the French army. The continuing war with Great Britain, Austria, and Sardinia provided opportunities for able military leaders. The years 1795–1799 saw the rapid rise of the young general whose suppression of a Paris uprising had permitted the Directory to be established.

Napoleon Bonaparte was born in 1769 of Italian parents on the Mediterranean island of Corsica, a French possession. In his youth he attended military school in France and graduated as an artillery officer. He served in the revolutionary armies and became a general at the age of twenty-four. As you have read, he defended the National Convention against the rioting Parisians in 1795. The following year, he was put in command of the French army fighting in northern Italy against the Austrians and Piedmontese (people from the Piedmont region of the kingdom of Sardinia).

Napoleon was a short man, vain, domineering, and overwhelmingly ambitious. He was a superb organizer and administrator in both political and military affairs. Above all, he was a military genius who ranks among the great generals of all time. He was especially skillful in the rapid movement of troops, and in massing forces at critical points on the battlefield—two techniques that gave him superiority over the older, slower army tactics of his opponents.

Napoleon quickly showed his ability in Italy.° The French army was small, weak, and poorly equipped. Within weeks, however, he had so organized and inspired it that he forced the Sardinians to make peace. Other minor members of the anti-French alliance—the Italian states of Parma, Modena, and Naples, and the Papal States—soon sued for peace also. Napoleon defeated the Austrians twice, and in 1797 forced them to sign a humiliating peace treaty. France gained control of all of northern Italy, which had been under Austrian domination.

The Near Eastern campaign. Napoleon became so popular in France that the Directors were worried about their own security. Napoleon, on the other hand, was seeking new conquests to keep his name before the French people. When he proposed to weaken the British by cutting off their trade with Egypt and the rest of the Near East, the Directory quickly consented, since such a campaign would remove him from Paris.

The Near Eastern campaign was a disaster. British forces destroyed the French fleet near Alexandria and thus cut the French army off from home. Napoleon left his army to its fate and secretly returned to France. He concealed the true situation in Egypt (which was possible before the days of rapid communication) and made exaggerated claims of victories in the Near East.

Napoleon became the popular hero of the time. However, his reputation and popularity could not change the facts; France was in a truly dangerous situation. The British had organized a Second Coalition against France, including Great Britain, Austria, and Russia. French armies were driven out of Italy, and French control over the other conquered states was slipping.

Napoleon's seizure of power. Many Frenchmen, including some of the Directors, believed that Napoleon was the one man who could restore order at home and win victory abroad. A plot was organized to overthrow the government and place Napoleon in power. In 1799, three of

---

° Because of the dominant role played by Napoleon beginning in 1796, the wars fought by France from this time until 1815 are generally known as the Napoleonic Wars.

the Directors resigned and the other two were arrested. Troops with fixed bayonets surrounded the meeting place of the two legislative houses and forced most of the delegates to leave. Those that remained turned the government over to Napoleon and two of his fellow plotters.

This sort of seizure of power by force is called a *coup d'état* (koo day·TAH), meaning literally a "stroke of state." Napoleon himself said later: "I found the crown of France lying on the ground, and I picked it up with a sword."

CHECKUP

1. Describe the three main groups in the Convention.

2. What was the Reign of Terror? Who were some of its victims?

3. What were the weaknesses of the Directory?

4. What circumstances made Napoleon's *coup d'état* possible?

5. IDENTIFY: universal manhood suffrage, Marat, Committee of Public Safety, Revolutionary Tribunal, conscription, metric system.

4 Napoleon built an empire by wars and conquests

The *coup d'état* of 1799 made Napoleon dictator of France. The government which he set up kept the outward form of a republic, but Napoleon was the real ruler. Under one title or another, and under several constitutions, he ruled France as a military dictator from 1799 until 1814. He had such great influence on France and the rest of Europe that this period is known as the Napoleonic Era, or the Age of Napoleon.

The people of France were willing to accept Napoleon's dictatorship as long as he promised them security. Napoleon, in turn, did not try to abolish the results of the revolution. The ideals of the Declaration of the Rights of Man remained. Serfdom and feudal privileges were not restored, and the land which the peasants now owned remained theirs. But liberty meant only freedom of opportunity. It was not liberty from control, because Napoleon believed that the people should obey orders given by a leader.

The Consulate

Napoleon found time to reorganize and centralize the administration of France. To begin with, he gave France its fourth government in the ten years since 1789. Napoleon's government, designed to give him unlimited power, was known as the Consulate because the executive branch was made up of three Consuls. He took the title of Consul from the chief executive of the Roman Republic in an attempt to appeal to popular admiration for ancient Roman strength and virtues.

Real power was concentrated in the hands of Napoleon as First Consul. He had command of the army and navy, the right to appoint and dismiss all officials, and the right to propose all new laws. The legislature was powerless. There were several assemblies, but none had any real authority.

Napoleon submitted the constitution of his new government to the people for a vote, a procedure known as a *plebiscite* (PLEB·uh·site). They were allowed only to vote yes or no and could not make any changes. When asked what was in the new constitution, Napoleon replied haughtily, "There is Bonaparte." The vote showed a vast majority in favor of the new constitution—of "Bonaparte."

Napoleon is usually remembered as a military leader. But his work as a statesman was more important, and much of it was more lasting. Under Napoleon's direction, scholars completed the revision and organization of the laws begun by the National Convention. They drew up codes of criminal law and commercial law. They arranged civil laws in an orderly system called the Napoleonic Code. The Napoleonic Code was widely copied and forms the foundation of many European legal systems.

Napoleon wanted a central, national financial institution, so he established the Bank of France. Although the bank was privately owned, it was closely supervised by the government. The government also set up a system of public education as planned by the National Convention. It included elementary schools, high schools, universities, and technical schools. These were all supervised and directed by a central agency called the University of France.

The Civil Constitution of the Clergy of 1790 had begun a long quarrel between the Roman Catholic Church and the government of France. Napoleon ended the conflict by an agreement with the pope in 1801. It gave the Catholic Church a favored position in France, but it did not abolish the religious toleration guaranteed by the Declaration of the Rights of Man.

Napoleon as emperor

Napoleon soon moved to increase his power even more and to make it permanent and hereditary. In 1802 a new constitution, which made Napoleon First Consul for life, with increased powers, was approved by plebiscite. Two years later the French people voted in favor of still another constitution which declared France an empire. Napoleon Bonaparte was named Emperor Napoleon I.

The new empire (called by modern historians the First French Empire) was inaugurated by the coronation of Napoleon in the Cathedral of Notre Dame in Paris. One part of the elaborate ceremony was significant. The pope had come to Paris to crown the new emperor. However, when the time came for him to place the crown on Napoleon's head, Napoleon took the crown from the pope's hands and placed it on his own head. Thus, he demonstrated that the power and authority which he held were all his own and were not given to him by anyone.

As emperor, Napoleon continued to show his three great skills: as an organizer, as a diplomat, and as a military genius.

He reorganized the French army and improved military discipline and the method of selecting officers. The army was still raised by conscription, but Napoleon was able to create in the drafted men a tremendous sense of patriotism and loyalty to him. The common soldier was made to feel his own importance. "Every soldier carries a field marshal's baton in his knapsack," Napoleon

Napoleon, feared and hated by millions during his lifetime, dines greedily upon the world in the cartoon above. Napoleon slices off Europe while an English statesman spears the ocean. Within a few years of Napoleon's death, most Frenchmen had forgotten the hardships and wars of the Napoleonic Era. Some regarded Napoleon as a kind of saint (although he was not recognized as such by the Roman Catholic Church). Below, St. Napoleon sits astride his horse as the patron of warriors.

said, meaning that every man could win promotion if he was capable and daring.

Napoleon also engaged in some shrewd and skillful diplomacy. In 1799 he had convinced Russia to desert its allies, Great Britain and Austria, and make peace with France. He had then persuaded other European countries to form a league of armed neutral states against Britain. After this came a military action against the Austrians, who had already been weakened by the withdrawal of Russia. By 1801, Austria was compelled to ask France for peace. The French, however, could not win as complete a victory against the British because Great Britain was fighting on the seas, where it was stronger than France. Both sides, though, were weary of war. In 1802 a peace treaty was signed between Great Britain and France.

For a time it looked as though Napoleon would keep his promises to the French people: peace with military glory, firm and steady government, and economic prosperity. However, Napoleon soon began to raise and drill troops again. It was widely believed that he planned to invade and conquer the British Isles. In 1803 he had sold the North American territory of Louisiana (which Spain had ceded to France in 1800), to the United States for $15 million. He used much of the money for military preparations.

War with the Third Coalition

Even if Napoleon had been willing to stop in 1802 with the gains he had made in Europe, he might have been forced into war. France had expanded far beyond its "natural boundaries." Everywhere, men wanted to throw off French control. The British knew that Napoleon's ambition threatened their commerce, their empire, and their control of the seas. French domination of the Austrian Netherlands, which had been secured in 1794, gave Napoleon bases from which he might be able to launch an invasion of Britain.

Great Britain declared war on France in 1803 and in 1805 organized a Third Coalition against Napoleon. Austria, Russia, and Sweden allied themselves with Great Britain; Spain was allied with France. Napoleon planned to strike at the heart of British power by defeating the British navy and then invading Great Britain. But in 1805 a British fleet led by Admiral Horatio Nelson defeated a combined French and Spanish fleet near Cape Trafalgar off the southern coast of Spain. Nelson was killed, but the French and Spanish fleets were almost completely destroyed. It was only in battles on land against Austria and Russia that Napoleon was successful.

The Continental System. Despite the defeats they had inflicted upon him, Napoleon had nothing but contempt for the British, whom he called "a nation of shopkeepers." He believed that if they lost trade and profits, they would be willing to make peace on his terms. Therefore, in a change of strategy, he ordered a blockade of the British Isles. This blockade was called the Continental System because Napoleon held control over so much of the continent of Europe. Napoleon forbade the importation of British goods into any country under French control and tried to force other European countries to stop buying British products.

The British responded with a blockade of France. A series of British orders forbade ships of neutral countries to trade with France or its allies unless they first stopped at a British port to get a license. Napoleon, in turn, decreed that the French would seize any neutral ship which obeyed the British order.

Neutral nations were thus placed in an awkward position. If they disregarded the British order, their ships might be captured by the British. But if they obeyed the British, their ships would be seized by the French. The United States was especially hard hit, for it depended to a great extent on trade with both the British Isles and the continent of Europe. Both France and Britain interfered with American shipping, but British ships did the most damage. This conflict over trade between Britain and the United States was one cause of the War of 1812 in America.

The British and French blockades differed in their effectiveness. The British fleet made Britain's blockade of the continent at least partly effective. The French blockade of Great Britain, however, existed largely on paper because Napoleon did not have enough ships to enforce it. Europeans needed British manufactured goods. They also needed the products that British ships brought to Europe from all over the world. The French orders caused discontent everywhere, even in France. Prices rose and smuggling became common.

Although the British blockade was hurting France, British leaders were not satisfied with the effects of the blockade alone. They wanted the complete military defeat of Napoleon.

Once more Napoleon proved himself the master general. His strategy was to strike his enemies one at a time, before they could unite effectively. In December 1805, Napoleon smashed the combined forces of Russia and Austria at Austerlitz, a town in the Austrian Empire north of Vienna. Prussia soon signed a treaty with France, and the Third Coalition broke up. Britain still remained a danger, although British armies could not harm Na-

poleon much. Prussia led a Fourth Coalition against France in 1806, but Napoleon's troops were again victorious.

The reorganization of Europe

By 1808, Napoleon completely dominated Europe. Austria and Prussia had been forced to sign humiliating peace treaties, and Russia allied itself with France. Napoleon ruled the Austrian and Dutch Netherlands and Spain, and forced Denmark and the Papal States into alliances. To stop the possibility of any Russian gains, Napoleon formed the territory that Prussia had taken from Poland into a Grand Duchy of Warsaw (see map, page 419), which he gave to his ally, the king of Saxony.

Various treaties since 1795 had given France the right to intervene in the hundreds of small German states. Napoleon made several territorial settlements. He organized the most important states into the Confederation of the Rhine, with himself as Protector. He abolished the Holy Roman Empire and forced its emperor to take the lesser title of emperor of Austria. All of the small states of northern Italy were unified into the kingdom of Italy and were made dependent on Napoleon. He placed many of his relatives on the thrones of the conquered countries.

CHECKUP

1. What were Napoleon's chief accomplishments as First Consul? as emperor?

2. Why did Britain declare war on France in 1803?

3. What was the Continental System? How did the British react to it? How successful were the British and French blockades?

4. IDENTIFY: Consulate, plebiscite, Nelson.

5. LOCATE: Cape Trafalgar, Austerlitz, Grand Duchy of Warsaw, Confederation of the Rhine.

5 European nations united to bring an end to Napoleon's rule

The changes Napoleon made in Europe were not confined to enlarging his empire and reorganizing the territories he conquered. Wherever the French army went, the Napoleonic Code was put into

effect; feudalism and serfdom were abolished; the modernized methods of the French army were introduced.

Without intending to, the French also instilled

a spirit of nationalism in the people they conquered. At home the events of the revolution and the stirring words of the Declaration of the Rights of Man had produced feelings of patriotism and loyalty—not for local regions but for France. People thought of themselves as Frenchmen with a country and ideals worth fighting for. Now these same nationalistic feelings of loyalty and patriotism appeared among the conquered peoples —not, of course, for France but for their homelands.

At first the French were received as liberators, but they soon came to be regarded as foreign invaders. Taxes in the conquered countries increased steadily to pay the costs of war and occupation. Troops were quartered in private homes. In every country, people wanted to get rid of the French occupation forces and to govern themselves.

The Continental System also helped to stir up feelings against French rule. It was violated everywhere. The more it was violated, the more harshly and persistently Napoleon insisted on its enforcement. Persons who protested against it or who were caught violating it paid dearly, regardless of their rank or position. When Napoleon's brother Louis, ruler of the Netherlands, was negligent in stopping smuggling, Napoleon dismissed him and combined the Netherlands directly with his empire of France. Even the pope was placed under arrest when he expressed disapproval of the French blockade.

Napoleon was master of Europe and in a seemingly unconquerable position (see map, opposite). Time was working on the side of his enemies, however. The constant wars had sapped French manpower. To get the large armies he needed, Napoleon drafted men from all the conquered countries. Often they served unwillingly. The patriotic, revolutionary spirit of the earlier French army was gone.

Besides, the armies of his opponents were improving. The generals who opposed Napoleon had learned his methods of rapid movement and massing of troops. Other nations, especially Britain and Prussia, had learned how to raise, equip, and drill large bodies of troops.

The loss of Spain

Trouble broke out in the Iberian Peninsula when Portugal, whose prosperity depended on trade with Great Britain, refused to observe the Continental System. Then, in 1808, the Spanish revolted against Napoleon's brother Joseph, the king of Spain. Britain sent an army under Arthur Wellesley (the future Duke of Wellington) to help the Spanish and Portuguese patriots. In spite of everything Napoleon did, he could not suppress the Spanish uprising or drive out the British army. Napoleon's forces were harried by guerrilla (guh-RIL·uh) troops. *Guerrilla* is the Spanish word for "little war" and describes a kind of unofficial warfare fought by volunteers behind the lines.

The Peninsular Campaign, as it was called, lasted six years. Although Napoleon continued to control the government of Spain, the campaign was a steady drain on French manpower at a time when it was badly needed elsewhere. (In 1809, however, Napoleon was still able to put down a war begun against him by Austria—the result of a Fifth Coalition of his enemies.)

In 1812 the Spanish, with British aid, captured Madrid and drove out the French king. They then proceeded to draw up a new constitution that provided for limited monarchy and a one-house legislature, abolished the Inquisition, and limited the right of the Church to own land. The Spanish revolt and the new constitution showed two things: the tremendous influence of the French Revolution, and the rising spirit of nationalism and opposition to Napoleon.

Catastrophe in Russia

Czar Alexander I of Russia viewed Napoleon's domination of Europe with alarm and distrust. Establishing the Grand Duchy of Warsaw under Napoleon's protection looked like a springboard for an attack on Russia. The French continental blockade broke up a long-established exchange of Russian grain and raw materials for British manufactured goods. Gradually, enforcement of the blockade was relaxed in Russia. In 1812, Alexander I announced that trade with Britain would be renewed.

Inefficient as it was, the blockade was Na-

NAPOLEON'S EMPIRE IN 1810

French Empire	States allied with Napoleon
States controlled by Napoleon	Independent European states

✕ Battle sites

poleon's only way of striking at the British. For the czar, an ally, to ignore it openly was intolerable. Napoleon decided to invade Russia, and he exerted pressure on all parts of his empire to supply soldiers.

When finally assembled, Napoleon's army totaled 600,000 men. But it was vastly different from the enthusiastic, loyal, and patriotic armies of the early French Empire. Fewer than half of the soldiers were French; the larger part of the "Grand Army" was composed of conscripts—Danes, Germans, Dutch, Balkan Slavs, Italians, Swiss, and Poles—who were fighting because they were forced to.

In May 1812, Napoleon began his march eastward at the head of his international army (see map, page 419). The Russians used an effective strategy: they "made distance their ally." Instead of meeting the French in open battle on the vast plains of western Russia, the Russian army retreated slowly, drawing Napoleon's army deeper and deeper into the country. As they retreated, the Russians burned or otherwise destroyed everything that might be of value to the invaders. (This is called a "scorched-earth" policy.)

The Russians left behind them bands of guerrilla troops to harass the French by hit-and-run tactics and by destroying their supplies. The French had to leave behind increasing numbers of troops to hold towns and guard their supply lines.

In mid-September the French army reached and captured Moscow, but it was a hollow victory. The Russian winter was about to set in. The Russians had stripped the city, and fires added to the destruction. So many buildings in Moscow were burned that there were not enough winter quarters for the French troops. The supply line from France was long and in danger of being broken. Napoleon decided to lead his army back.

Napoleon's retreat from Moscow was one of the greatest military disasters of all time. The Russian winter was exceptionally severe. Plagued by snow and bitter cold, the Grand Army had to pass again through the devastated country. Both the Russian army and the guerrillas harassed the retreating French without mercy. French discipline broke down and there were many desertions. When the army reached Prussia in December, it had lost four fifths of its men. The Russian army followed the French and invaded Napoleon's empire, and the Prussians joined in the attack.

Final defeat

Everywhere in Western Europe, people were rising to throw off French rule and join the invading Russians. Napoleon abandoned his army and hurried to France to raise new forces to defend his empire. He was able to gather a new army of hastily drilled conscripts, but he faced overwhelming odds. Prussia, Austria, Great Britain, and Sweden joined Russia in a new alliance to invade France.

Napoleon tried his old strategy of striking before his enemies could unite, but this time he was too late. In October 1813, an allied army met Napoleon in the "Battle of the Nations" at Leipzig, in Saxony. The new French army was decisively defeated and Napoleon retreated into France. The allies captured Paris in March 1814, and forced Napoleon to abdicate. He gave up all claims to the throne of France for himself and his family. He was granted a pension and the small island of Elba off the western coast of Italy. He agreed to remain there for the rest of his life and was allowed to rule as a sovereign.

The victorious allies agreed that the boundaries of France should be the same again as those of 1792, before the great expansion began. They restored the Bourbon monarchy to the throne in the person of Louis XVIII,° brother of the executed Louis XVI.

Napoleon's return and the Hundred Days

Napoleon had no intention of spending the rest of his life on the island of Elba. There were many people in France who wanted him back, and he began at once to plot his return. He escaped from Elba and landed in France on March 1, 1815.

Napoleon had only a small group of men with him at first. But the troops sent against him by the Bourbon king deserted to their beloved emperor. Everywhere, resistance collapsed; Louis XVIII fled the country. On March 20, Napoleon entered Paris in triumph. (Then began the period that is called the Hundred Days.) To avoid war, he announced that France gave up all claims to territories formerly conquered.

Napoleon hoped that disputes among the allies over the division of territory (about which you will read in the next chapter) would keep them from opposing his return. But he was mis-

° **Louis XVIII:** The brother of Louis XVI had lived in England during the revolution. He and other royalists regarded the son of Louis XVI as King Louis XVII, though, of course, he had never been crowned. Historians are not sure what happened to the young son of Louis XVI. He may have died in prison a year or two after his father was executed. According to other stories, he escaped and lived in obscurity the rest of his life.

taken. The combined armies of Prussia, Great Britain, and the Dutch Netherlands, under the command of the Duke of Wellington, began to move toward France. Napoleon once more raised a French army to meet them.

On June 18, 1815, the allied and the French armies met at Waterloo in the Austrian Netherlands. The battle that followed decisively ended the career of Napoleon. (From this battle we get the expression "to meet one's Waterloo.") The French were badly defeated. Again Napoleon abdicated, and again the Bourbon monarchy was restored.

Napoleon surrendered to the British, asking to be allowed to take refuge in England. The British were unwilling to take such a chance. They sent the fallen emperor to live under constant guard on the lonely, dismal island of St. Helena in the South Atlantic. Here Napoleon died in 1821.

As the years passed, there grew up a legend of Napoleon. People forgot the wars and the failures and remembered only the glories and achievements. Napoleon was transformed from a vain, ambitious, despotic dictator into the "Little Corporal," the "Good Emperor," the "true patriot of the revolution."

Effects of the revolution and Napoleon

The twenty-six years between 1789 (when the French Revolution began) and 1815 (when Napoleon was finally overthrown) were a short time as history goes. Yet these years brought sweeping changes to the Western world. Trends and influences that began then spread far and wide and still continue to influence the course of history.

In France the ideas of the revolution—liberty, equality, and fraternity—were so well established that they could not be abolished completely, even with the restoration of the monarchy under the Bourbons. The idea of popular sovereignty—the belief that the real power of government rests with the people—became firmly entrenched. The French people believed that a strongly centralized government, responsible for the welfare of the people, would give them education and economic security, protection of their rights, equality before the law, and religious toleration.

These ideas were spread all over Europe by the French armies and conquests. In Germany, Italy, and Spain, feudalism and serfdom were abolished and the fundamental ideas of the Napoleonic Code were established. The ideas of equality, of religious toleration, and the rights of the people to have a voice in their government were like seeds scattered over Europe.

Other countries, influenced by French ideas on the one hand and seeking to express their own nationalism on the other, began to make changes. Governments in Austria, Prussia, and elsewhere tried to undertake reforms, to reorganize, and to make their operations more efficient in order to regain control of their own national affairs. In Germany and Italy, where Napoleon combined many small states, there grew up a desire for real national unity. The various national groups in the Austrian Empire—the Czechs, Hungarians, Slavs, and Italians—craved independence and self-government. The Slavs of the Balkan states wanted to throw off Ottoman rule. The French invasion of Russia aroused a strong feeling of patriotism there, as well as a liberal movement among the younger army officers.

The French Revolution and the Napoleonic Era brought another development that profoundly influenced mankind: the so-called "nation in arms." The wars of the 1500's and 1600's had been fought by comparatively small armies of mercenary soldiers. The revolutionary era introduced conscription so that every able-bodied man was liable to service in the army. Most modern wars were to be fought not by professionals but by all the men of a nation.

CHECKUP

1. What ideas were spread by Napoleon's invasions?

2. Why did Napoleon declare war on Russia? How did his Russian campaign end?

3. What was the battle of Waterloo? What happened to Napoleon afterward?

4. IDENTIFY: guerrilla troops, "Grand Army," "scorched-earth" policy, "Battle of the Nations," Louis XVIII, the Hundred Days, "nation in arms."

5. LOCATE: Leipzig, Elba, Waterloo.

CHAPTER REVIEW

Chapter 19   The French Revolution and Napoleon Affected All Europe   (1774—1815)

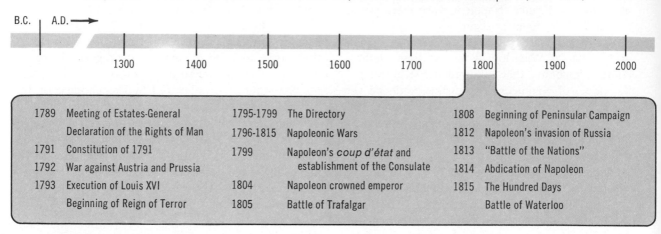

1789	Meeting of Estates-General	1795-1799	The Directory	1808	Beginning of Peninsular Campaign
	Declaration of the Rights of Man	1796-1815	Napoleonic Wars	1812	Napoleon's invasion of Russia
1791	Constitution of 1791	1799	Napoleon's *coup d'état* and	1813	"Battle of the Nations"
1792	War against Austria and Prussia		establishment of the Consulate	1814	Abdication of Napoleon
1793	Execution of Louis XVI	1804	Napoleon crowned emperor	1815	The Hundred Days
	Beginning of Reign of Terror	1805	Battle of Trafalgar		Battle of Waterloo

CHAPTER SUMMARY

The Old Regime of France—an absolute monarchy, with three Estates—was repressive and inefficient. Beginning in the mid-1700's, discontent grew.

Unwilling to make real financial reforms, King Louis XVI summoned the Estates-General. When he insisted on retaining old voting procedures, the Third Estate met separately, proclaimed itself a National Assembly, and took the Tennis-Court Oath to write a new constitution. The king's calling of troops led to widespread riots; the Bastille was captured and the "Great Fear" swept the countryside.

The National Assembly adopted the Law of the Fourth of August, the Declaration of the Rights of Man, and the Civil Constitution of the Clergy. It also wrote the Constitution of 1791, creating a limited monarchy. Invasion by Austrian and Prussian troops, however, touched off riots that ended this monarchy.

The National Convention, which ruled France for three years, proclaimed a republic and executed the king. Threatened by new invasions, it set up the Committee of Public Safety, which organized a conscripted army, and the Revolutionary Tribunal, which suppressed domestic opposition with the Reign of Terror. France was later ruled by the Directory. It was inefficient and corrupt, and was overthrown by Napoleon.

Napoleon ruled France as a military dictator. His reforms included the Napoleonic Code, the Bank of France, and a system of public education. Highly ambitious, he extended French control over much of Europe. After his defeat at Trafalgar, he waged economic war through the Continental System.

By 1808, Napoleon dominated Europe. The Peninsular Campaign, however, was a steady drain. A French invasion of Russia ended in catastrophe. Defeated at the "Battle of the Nations," Napoleon abdicated and went to Elba. He soon escaped, but his enemies defeated him again at Waterloo.

The ideas of the French Revolution became firmly rooted in France and were spread throughout Europe. Two other developments were increased nationalism and the concept of the "nation in arms."

QUESTIONS FOR DISCUSSION

1. During the early days of the French Revolution, parish priests generally supported the common people while the higher clergy generally supported the nobles. How do you explain this fact?

2. The French Revolution came suddenly and violently. By what means could Louis XVI have forestalled it?

3. The wars that France had to fight against most of Europe were partly responsible for the rise of Napoleon. Why is it that war often leads a nation to military dictatorship?

4. The Spanish used guerrilla warfare against Napoleon's forces. How is guerrilla fighting conducted? Why is it effective even against modern armies?

PROJECTS

1. Write an essay demonstrating that the Reign of Terror was an outgrowth of extremist positions.

2. Write an editorial for an English newspaper on the news that Napoleon has left Elba and returned to France.

3. Make a list of the permanent effects of the French Revolution and the Napoleonic Era.

4. Draw a poster advocating revolution in Louis XVI's France.

CHAPTER 20

Reaction Dominated Europe as Latin America Won Freedom

The Napoleonic Era left the world a conflicting legacy. There was great material damage and destruction from the long period of warfare. Statesmen of the victorious nations faced difficult problems in deciding what to do with the Europe that Napoleon had created. It was a vastly different Europe from that of 1789. Ruling families had been driven from their thrones and nobles had been forced into exile. States had been shuffled about and combined to suit Napoleon. The Old Regime in France was dead and other absolute monarchies had suffered greatly.

The Europe of 1815 was also different because of new and vital forces that were to dominate the coming century—nationalism and liberalism. These two ideas can be regarded as keys to much that happened in the 1800's. Understanding them will help you understand the many complex events you will be studying in the next several chapters.

As you have read, nationalism is a feeling of loyalty and patriotism toward one's nation. Such a simplified definition, however, compresses much history into a few words. Actually several factors work together to develop the feeling of nationality among a people. One factor is the sense of shared experiences, dangers, and problems. Another is pride in accomplishments. A common race helps, but it is not necessary, as in the case of the United States. A common language also helps, but again is not necessary: the Swiss have a strong feeling

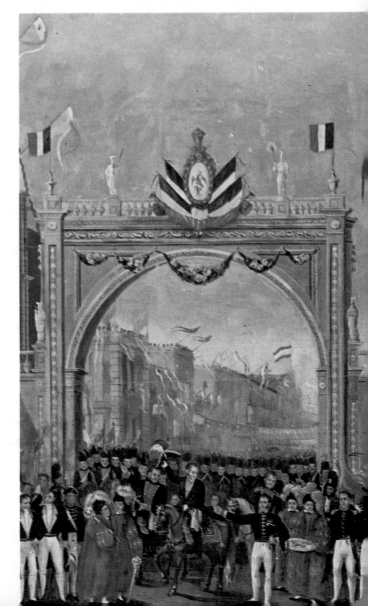

Mexicans celebrating their independence in 1821

of nationalism, although Switzerland has three official languages—French, German, and Italian.

A common government sometimes helps develop national feeling, but this feeling may exist without it. When Poland was divided among Russia, Prussia, and Austria, the Polish people continued to think of themselves as a nation. On the other hand, various peoples who lived in the Austrian Empire had the same government, but thought of themselves as separate nations.

Nationalism has been important in shaping the modern world. It can be carried to such extremes, however, that it is dangerous. When a people thinks only of its own rights, aims, and desires, it acts selfishly and disregards others. Nationalism can lead to jealousy, rivalry, and war. Extreme nationalism is called chauvinism (SHOH·vun·iz·um), after Nicholas Chauvin, a fanatically patriotic soldier in Napoleon's armies. When chauvinism prevails, it is almost impossible for nations to work together peacefully.

Like nationalism, liberalism has no simple definition. It has meant different things at different times. In Europe in the 1800's, it was a movement aimed chiefly at securing individual freedom—freedom of thought, religion, and economic opportunity. Above all, liberals hated the tyranny of absolute rule. Thus they worked to secure constitutions and other legal safeguards to limit governmental authority and protect civil liberties.

Liberalism grew out of the Enlightenment, particularly the writings of men like Locke and Rousseau. Liberals were also strongly influenced by the political revolutions of the late 1700's, with their ideals of liberty, equality, and fraternity. Most liberals of the 1800's, however, were moderates of the middle class who feared mob rule as much as they disliked autocracy. Unlike the liberals of the 1900's, they did not believe in the democratic ideal of political participation by all citizens. Instead, they felt that voting should be limited to men of property and education.

THE CHAPTER SECTIONS:

1. The great powers readjusted boundaries and suppressed revolts (1815–1829)

2. Spain established a rigid colonial society in Latin America (1500–1800)

3. Revolutions brought independence to Latin American nations (1800–1840)

1 The great powers readjusted boundaries and suppressed revolts

In September 1814, while Napoleon was living in exile on the island of Elba, the leading statesmen of Europe gathered in Vienna, capital of the Austrian Empire, to restore peace and order to Europe. About 700 diplomats attended the Congress of Vienna at one time or another, representing every European country except the Ottoman Empire. Six ruling monarchs were present.

The Congress of Vienna was interrupted in 1815 by the return of Napoleon from exile. As you have read, the powers united quickly against him and, after the Hundred Days, defeated him for the final time at Waterloo. Then the deliberations at Vienna were resumed.

The great powers

Despite the presence of many notable men, the real decisions at the Congress of Vienna were made by only a few. The four great powers that had done the most to defeat Napoleon were Great Britain, Austria, Russia, and Prussia. These countries were represented by outstanding leaders: Lord Castlereagh (KAS·ul·ray), foreign secretary of Great Britain; Prince Klemens von Metternich, chief minister of Austria and chairman of the conference; Czar Alexander I of Russia; and King Frederick William III of Prussia.

It is not usual in peace conferences for the losers to have much of a role. However, the representative of defeated France was soon playing an important part at the Congress of Vienna. He was the French diplomat Charles Maurice de Talleyrand. This shrewd, unscrupulous old man was a master at changing sides, and he had wielded great influence from the days of the Estates-General through the reign of Napoleon. At the Con-

The Congress of Vienna was strongly influenced by the keen intellect and shrewd diplomacy of Metternich, left. Born to a noble Austrian family in 1773, Metternich as a young man was horrified at the excesses of the French Revolution and the Napoleonic Era. Hating liberalism and disorder in government, he used his position as chairman of the Congress to encourage a firm and conservative balance of power among the great nations. One view of the Congress, below, shows Metternich, standing at left, introducing to assembled diplomats the English Duke of Wellington, commander of the forces that finally defeated Napoleon at Waterloo. Talleyrand is seated with his arm on the table, at right. A more satiric view of the meeting, above, depicts the major powers weighing nations like bales of bodies. Lesser nations wait in the background like scavengers to see what scraps will be left for them.

gress of Vienna, he was the foreign minister of the restored Bourbon king, Louis XVIII.

Talleyrand urged that settlements should be based on the principle of legitimacy. This meant that all the former ruling families (that is, the legitimate rulers) should be restored to their thrones. As you have read, the Bourbon monarchy was restored in France. Bourbon rulers also returned to power in Spain and Italy.

Territorial settlements

The winning powers soon began wrangling among themselves over the division of spoils. The two most difficult problems concerned Poland and the German state of Saxony. From Prussia's Polish territory, as you recall, Napoleon had created the Grand Duchy of Warsaw, which he gave to his faithful ally, the king of Saxony. Russia now demanded all of this territory. Prussia was willing to agree, provided that the king of Saxony be deposed and Saxony be given to Prussia.

This arrangement was opposed by both Great Britain and Austria. Britain did not want to see Russia become too strong. Austria feared that the addition of Saxony might make Prussia too powerful in German affairs. For a time, war seemed to threaten. Then, Talleyrand was admitted to the conference. He suggested the compromise that settled the argument. Prussia received part of Saxony; most of what had been the Grand Duchy of Warsaw went to Russia, with a small portion going to Prussia (see map, opposite page).

The Dutch Netherlands, one of Napoleon's early conquests, received the Austrian Netherlands and became the single kingdom of the Netherlands. To compensate for this loss, Austria was given the northern Italian states of Venetia and Lombardy. Austrian Hapsburgs were also placed at the head of the north Italian states of Parma, Modena, and Tuscany.

In addition to gaining the largest share of the Grand Duchy of Warsaw, Russia had acquired Finland as a result of war with Sweden. Since Sweden had fought Napoleon, it was compensated by receiving Norway, formerly a Danish possession. Denmark was thus punished for cooperating with Napoleon. Prussia, in addition to

its share of Saxony and Poland, received an area along the lower Rhine River.

The reason for all this territorial reshuffling was to set up a ring of strong states around France so that it could not again threaten the peace of Europe. The feelings of the people involved were not considered when regions changed hands. Territories were parceled out as if they were uninhabited deserts.

Although Britain did not receive territory in continental Europe, it did gain possession of many holdings overseas. Britain had seized most of these during the wars. They included several of the French West Indies and the island of Malta in the Mediterranean Sea. From the Danish the British gained Helgoland, an island in the North Sea. From the Dutch they took Cape Colony in Africa and what became British Guiana in South America.

France was stripped of its conquests, and its boundaries were fixed as they had been in 1792. In addition, it had to pay a large indemnity—compensation to other nations for damages it had inflicted on them. France also had to pay for forts which the victorious nations maintained on the French borders.

Reaction, absolutism, and nationalism

The first few years after the Napoleonic Era have been called a time of *reaction,* a time when those in authority wanted to return to the conditions of an earlier period. Reactionaries are extremists who not only oppose change, but generally would like to turn the clock back to the time before certain changes occurred.

In Europe after 1815, reaction took the form of attempts by the victors to restore conditions to what they had been before the upsets and revolutions had taken place.

In Spain, Naples, and the states of northern Italy, the reinstated rulers abolished the constitutions that had been adopted during Napoleon's rule. They returned to absolutism as if nothing had ever happened.

Switzerland alone was allowed to retain its constitutional republican government, but had to promise that it would always remain neutral in

EUROPE IN 1815
after the Congress of Vienna
——— Boundary of the German Confederation

European wars. This neutrality was guaranteed by the European powers. Many nationalistic groups were disappointed. Some Italians had hoped for a united Italy. This hope was not fulfilled. To make matters worse, many Italian states were placed under a hated foreign rule. The desire of the Polish people for national independence was also blocked, nor was there self-government for national groups living in the Austrian Empire.

The German desire for national unity came closer to fulfillment. Napoleon had consolidated many of the German states into the sixteen-member Confederation of the Rhine. Now more states, including Prussia, were added to form the German Confederation, with thirty-nine members. Austria dominated this Confederation, since the Confederation's Diet was always presided over by an Austrian delegate.

Alliances among the great powers

The four allies that had finally defeated Napoleon—Great Britain, Austria, Russia, and Prussia—agreed in November 1815 to continue their coalition, which became known as the Quadruple Alliance. The chief purpose of the alliance was "to guarantee Europe from dangers by which she may still be menaced"—that is, revolutionary movements. Members of the alliance agreed to see that France carried out the terms of the peace treaty and to hold periodic conferences to keep the major powers in agreement on matters that concerned them all.

Czar Alexander I of Russia doubted that peace could be maintained and revolutions prevented simply by alliances. He was a firm believer in absolute monarchy. However, he believed just as firmly that monarchs should be guided by Christian moral principles, with a strong sense of duty toward their subjects. Shortly before joining the Quadruple Alliance, he had urged that all rulers should pledge themselves to rule as Christian princes by signing an agreement called the Holy Alliance. It had been signed by all the rulers of Europe except the king of England, the Turkish sultan, and the pope, who refused to be instructed in Christian principles by the czar, an orthodox Catholic.

If the rulers who signed the Holy Alliance had lived up to its high ideals, the history of the next fifty years might have been different. But they had agreed to the Holy Alliance only to humor the idealistic czar and had little intention of following its principles. Castlereagh scoffingly called it "a piece of sublime mysticism and nonsense."

Out of the practical Quadruple Alliance grew what was called the Concert of Europe—a form of international government by concert, or agreement. It was aimed at maintaining peace and the status quo (a Latin phrase meaning roughly "the condition in which things exist"). In this case, of course, the status quo was the balance of power established by the Congress of Vienna.

The first of the periodic conferences provided for by the Quadruple Alliance was held in 1818. France, having fulfilled the terms of the peace settlements, was restored as a full member of the European family of nations and was admitted to the Quadruple Alliance to make it a Quintuple Alliance. Although these various alliances were relatively short-lived, the Concert of Europe lasted until 1848, and the principles on which it was based came into play again several times later in the 1800's. The statesmen at Vienna, although ignoring popular national and liberal movements, did give Europe something very valuable—peace and order. After the Vienna settlements, there was no major war among the great powers for almost forty years.

Metternich and repression

For thirty years after the Congress of Vienna, Prince Metternich, chief minister of Austria, influenced Europe so strongly that the time is sometimes known as the Age of Metternich. Metternich was a reactionary and believed that absolute monarchy was the only good government. He looked with fear and horror at liberalism, constitutions, and such ideals as freedom of speech, the press, and religion. He believed the best way to handle such ideas was to suppress them completely.

Metternich's aims were simple: to prevent war or revolution and to preserve absolutism. At home in Austria, he had little difficulty in achieving these aims. He set up an efficient system of secret police to spy on revolutionary organizations and individuals. Liberals were imprisoned, fined, or exiled.

Because Austria controlled the German Confederation, Metternich was able to persuade the rulers of most German states to adopt the same methods. Hapsburg rule in northern Italy made sure that no revolutionary movements would succeed there. In France the restored Bourbon king, Louis XVIII, had to move cautiously in domestic affairs; he was quite willing, however, to join in suppressing revolutions elsewhere.

Metternich turned the Concert of Europe into an instrument for suppressing liberal ideas and revolutions everywhere in Europe. Whenever there was a threat to the status quo, representatives of the five powers gathered to discuss ways of handling it. Austria, Russia, and Prussia went further; they agreed to act together to put down any attempt at revolution anywhere.

Great Britain could not agree to this last step. It opposed interfering where liberal popular movements were attempting to overthrow absolute rulers. Britain itself had a representative government, and the British people (though not their rulers) sympathized with other peoples in their struggles for similar governments. More important, Britain was a trading nation. Meddling with other countries was not good for British commerce. Under the influence of George Canning, who became foreign secretary in 1822, Britain withdrew from the Quintuple Alliance that same year.

The Metternich system in operation

For a time the Metternich system operated successfully. When discontent flared up among German university students in 1819, Metternich called together the leaders of the larger states of the German Confederation at Carlsbad in Bohemia. At his insistence they adopted measures known as the Carlsbad Decrees. Students and faculty members of the universities were placed under strict watch. Newspapers and periodicals were rigidly censored.

In spite of repression, there were several underground movements that opposed the status quo. In 1820 a revolt in Spain forced King Ferdinand VII to restore the constitution he had abolished. The four continental members of the Quintuple Alliance were alarmed and, despite British protests, sent a French army to Spain. In 1823, Ferdinand was restored to full power.

The Spanish revolt inspired other uprisings in 1820. In Naples, revolutionaries forced the ruler to grant a constitution. This revolt was soon put down by an Austrian army. In Portugal, too, the ruler was forced to accept a constitution. A few years later, however, he abolished it and assumed absolute power.

In 1821 the Greeks revolted against the harsh, brutal rule of the Ottoman Turks. Influenced by Metternich, European rulers refused Greek pleas for aid. However, many individuals came to the support of the Greeks, either as volunteers or by sending arms. (One of these volunteers was Lord Byron, the English poet, who died in Greece in 1824.) Finally, the nations that had usually sided with Metternich—Russia, Britain, and France—brought pressure on the Ottoman sultan. By the Treaty of Adrianople in 1829, Greece became an independent state, while the Serbs and Rumanians, to the north in the Balkan Peninsula, received some rights of self-government.

Greek independence was the first real failure of the Metternich system in Europe. It showed that the sense of nationalism encouraged by the French Revolution could not be suppressed forever.

CHECKUP

1. What is nationalism? What factors help create it? How would you define liberalism as a movement of the 1800's?
2. Explain, with examples, the principle of legitimacy as it operated at the Congress of Vienna.
3. What was the Quadruple Alliance? the Holy Alliance?
4. Why is the period after 1815 called the Age of Metternich? What were Metternich's aims?
5. IDENTIFY: chauvinism, Talleyrand, reactionaries, Concert of Europe, status quo, Carlsbad Decrees, Treaty of Adrianople.

2 Spain established a rigid colonial society in Latin America

You will remember from Chapter 15 that several European nations established colonies in southern North America, Central America, and South America. This region, from the northern border of Mexico southward to the tip of South America

and including the West Indies, is called Latin America (see map, page 431). Most of it was settled by the Spanish and Portuguese, whose languages are derived from Latin. Even though the Latin American colonies were far away from

Europe, they were controlled and strongly influenced by the mother countries of Spain and Portugal for over 300 years.

The land

Latin America is about 8 million square miles in area. Perhaps this figure will mean more to you when you realize that Brazil alone is almost as large as the United States.

Vast rivers reach deep into the heart of South America. The Orinoco, the Amazon, and the La Plata, with their tributaries, make up some of the world's most extensive river systems.

Latin America has many rugged and impressive mountains. The Andes Mountains extend along most of the western coast of South America. There is a great variety of climate: dry semi-desert areas in Mexico and along the west coast of South America; steaming rain forests in Central America and northeastern South America; rolling, grassy plains called pampas in southeastern South America; and the llanos (LAH·nohs), flat, treeless plains in northern South America. Throughout Latin American history, geographic features such as mountain ranges and rain forests have tended to isolate communities from each other and to prevent unity.

As you learned in Chapter 13, the Western Hemisphere was first inhabited by people whom the Europeans called Indians. Latin America was the home of the highest Indian civilizations—those of the Mayas, Aztecs, and Incas—and had a greater Indian population than regions to the north. For these reasons, Indian influence has always been stronger there than in the north.

Brazil, as you know, was settled by the Portuguese; you will read about its progress in the last section of this chapter. Almost all the rest of Latin America was colonized by the Spanish. Eventually Spanish possessions in the New World were divided into four parts, called viceroyalties because each was ruled by a viceroy (see inset map, page 436). Spanish claims in North America and most of Central America, including the West Indies, formed the viceroyalty of New Spain, governed from Mexico City, the former Aztec city of Tenochtitlán. (New Spain also included the Philippine Islands in the Pacific Ocean.) Southern Central America and northwestern South America made up the viceroyalty of New Granada, with its capital at Bogotá. The viceroyalty of Peru, ruled from Lima, included most of the Pacific coast. The rest of the Spanish Empire was part of the viceroyalty of La Plata, governed from Buenos Aires. (The southernmost part of South America was not included in any viceroyalty.)

Spanish society in Latin America

Spanish society in the New World was based on classes as in Europe. At the top were the officials who were born in Europe and were appointed to high government office—the viceroys and lesser officials. They received many benefits and took for themselves a large share of the wealth of the colonies they administered. They lived luxuriously. Their hope was always to build up a great fortune and return home to Europe to live in comfort and idleness for the rest of their lives. Most of the higher clergy were also born in Europe and belonged to this upper class.

Next below the ruling class were the white people of Spanish descent who had been born in the colonies and regarded the New World as their home. These colonial-born whites were called creoles. Many were ambitious, often well-educated, owners of farming estates and mines. Most of the lower clergy were creoles. The creoles resented rule from abroad through the viceroys. They regarded the viceroys and other appointed officials as foreigners, who had come to the Americas only to get rich and had no real interest in the region.

Below the creoles were the people of mixed white and Indian blood, called mestizos, most of whom were farmers or laborers. At the bottom of the social scale were the slaves—some Indians, mostly Negroes, with some mixture of the two.

The Roman Catholic Church was an important force in Latin American society. Many churchmen held high political office, and the government gave a great deal of financial support to the Church.

The Church helped spread European civilization in the New World. It carried on missionary

NORTH AMERICA

SIERRA MADRE OCCIDENTAL

Rio Grande

GULF OF MEXICO

MEXICO

WEST INDIES

CENTRAL AMERICA

CARIBBEAN SEA

ISTHMUS OF PANAMA

Magdalena R.

Lake Maracaibo

Orinoco R.

M T S.

LLANOS

Rio Negro

EQUATOR

Amazon River

SOUTH

BRAZILIAN

HIGHLANDS

São Francisco R.

ANDES

Lake Titicaca

AMERICA

Paraguay R.

Salado R.

Paraná R.

Uruguay R.

ANDES MTS.

PAMPAS

Rio de la Plata

Strait of Magellan

CAPE HORN

ATLANTIC

PACIFIC OCEAN

OCEAN

PHYSICAL REGIONS OF LATIN AMERICA

0   1000   2000 miles

work among the Indians and founded schools. In 1551, as you have read, the Spanish established the first universities in the Western Hemisphere: one in Mexico City and one in Lima. The first printing press in the Americas was set up in Mexico City in the 1530's to print religious books.

Capitals such as Mexico City and Lima were larger and more cosmopolitan than most North American cities. Townspeople enjoyed plays, operas, bullfights, and numerous religious festivals.

The economy

Many Spaniards came to the Americas hoping to make a quick fortune and return home. But far more settled permanently in the New World. As you know, Spain's most important revenue came from gold and silver, mined mainly in Mexico and Peru. But the permanent colonists in the Americas soon turned to agriculture. They introduced crops they had known in Europe, such as sugar cane and citrus fruits. They also cultivated plants that were native to the New World—corn, potatoes, tobacco, and cacao (used to make chocolate). Vast herds of cattle roamed the plains areas of Mexico and the llanos and pampas of South America.

The basic economic unit of colonial Latin America was a self-sufficient farming estate that resembled a medieval manor. Many such estates were given as royal grants to court favorites. The owners were usually absentee landlords—that is, they did not live on their estates. Overseers managed the estates and supervised the workers. Often the overseers were inexperienced and brutal.

It was difficult to find enough workers for mines and farms because many Spaniards felt that physical labor was degrading. Europeans enslaved the native Indians, but forced labor and new diseases brought death to thousands of them. In the Peruvian mines, the Indian death rate was as high as 90 percent.

In the early 1500's, only a few years after the discovery of America, the first Negro slaves from Africa arrived in the West Indies. Each year thereafter, thousands of Negroes were captured in Africa and shipped to Latin America to work as slaves in mines and on farming estates.

Growing discontent

For almost 300 years, Latin America changed very little. As in France during the Old Regime, there were privileged classes: rulers, wealthy landowners, and the clergy. Below them were the workers, mostly oppressed and unhappy.

Gradually, however—also as in France—discontent began to grow. The creoles in particular resented their foreign-born rulers and the fact that they were barred from high government positions.

The colonists also disliked the rigid restrictions of the Spanish mercantile system. Like Great Britain, Spain regarded its colonies as a source of raw materials and a place to sell finished products. It opposed the development of local industries that might make the colonies more self-sufficient. Trade restrictions specified that all goods had to be transported in Spanish ships, and forbade the colonists to trade with North America.

The economic system, like that of pre-revolutionary France, brought wealth to a few and poverty to most. The government imposed heavy taxes, and the Church collected numerous tithes.

By the late 1700's, unrest was widespread in the Latin American colonies. It fed upon news and ideas from North America and Europe. The people of Latin America learned about the American Revolution and the French Revolution. Spain tried to suppress such information in order to keep a firm hold on its colonies without having to contend with revolutions and ideas of freedom. But while ideas traveled slowly, they did travel. Latin Americans read the writings of Locke, Rousseau, and Jefferson. They learned that people elsewhere believed in freedom for all men and they, too, began to think about such ideas.

CHECKUP

1. Name and describe the social classes of the Spanish colonies in Latin America.
2. What were the main sources of discontent in the Spanish colonies?
3. IDENTIFY: pampas, llanos, viceroyalties, absentee landlords.
4. LOCATE: Latin America, New Spain, New Granada, Peru, La Plata, Bogotá, Lima, Buenos Aires.

3 Revolutions brought independence to Latin American nations

By the early 1800's, the situation in Spain's American colonies was ripe for revolution. There had been uprisings in several of the Spanish viceroyalties in the 1780's, but they were put down. The only successful revolt that began before 1800 took place on the island of Hispaniola, in the West Indies. The French owned the western part of the island and the Spanish the eastern part (see inset map, page 436).

An uprising that began in 1791 eventually came under the leadership of a former Negro slave, Dominique Toussaint L'Ouverture. He won control of the island by 1801. A veteran French army, sent by Napoleon and aided by the Spanish, captured Toussaint, who died in prison. However, the French were weakened by malaria and yellow fever and were attacked by rebel forces under another former slave, Jean Jacques Dessalines. The French suffered such heavy casualties that they had to give up the island in 1803.

The island was proclaimed the independent nation of Haiti in 1804. The eastern portion, Santo Domingo, eventually was regained by Spain and did not become independent of Spain until 1821. (Today this eastern portion is known as the Dominican Republic.)

Mexico and Central America

As you have read, Napoleon conquered Spain in 1808 and put his brother on the throne. In the following years the country was the scene of savage fighting in the Peninsular Campaign. Even after Napoleon's defeat at Waterloo, Spain was weakened by internal troubles. These circumstances provided the Spanish colonists in the Americas with a golden opportunity, since Spain was not in a position to offer much resistance to independence movements.

One of the first important uprisings in Spanish territory was proclaimed by a Mexican priest, Miguel Hidalgo, in 1810. He advocated the independence of Mexico from Spain and promised reforms such as the abolition of slavery and a fairer distribution of land.

After some early victories, Hidalgo was captured and executed in 1811. Another priest, José Morelos, assumed leadership, but he was captured and shot in 1815. Other men took charge of the rebellion, and the viceroy of New Spain was forced to grant independence to Mexico in 1821.

Although they had achieved independence, the Mexican people lacked experience in how to use it wisely. The liberating general, Augustín de Iturbide, soon proclaimed himself emperor of Mexico and established an expensive court that put the country deeply in debt before Iturbide was forced to abdicate. Even after Mexico declared itself a republic in 1824, conditions were unsettled for many years.

The example of Mexico was followed in Central America. There the chances of successful rebellion seemed poorer. There were fewer people and Spanish control was stronger. Nevertheless, revolts began in 1821 and soon spread throughout the whole region, which became independent in a short time.

The new countries formed in Central America were briefly part of Iturbide's Mexican empire. By 1823, however, representatives from Guatemala, El Salvador, Honduras, Nicaragua, and Costa Rica met to form the United Provinces of Central America. This union had a federal constitution, an elective president, and an assembly, but it fell apart in a few years and the individual nations had to solve their own problems.

Independence in New Granada

The real strongholds of the Spanish colonial empire were the viceroyalties in South America. In New Granada, independence was won under the inspired leadership of Simón Bolívar, known as the "George Washington of South America."

Bolívar was born in the city of Caracas, the son of a wealthy creole family. He was educated in Europe, where he traveled widely, seeing and studying the effects of the French Revolution. He returned home in 1807 and soon became a leader in the independence movement.

Latin America suffered under the harsh and despotic rule of Spain and Portugal for centuries. Much of the hard physical labor necessary for the prosperity of the mother countries was done by slaves. At right, Negroes in Brazil wash for diamonds; their white masters sit over them with whips in hand. The struggles for freedom and independence were ably commanded by men like Simón Bolívar, above, and José de San Martín. In freeing the viceroyalty of Peru, San Martín was aided by a Chilean patriot, Bernardo O'Higgins. The two men are shown below with their troops.

Bolívar and another revolutionary, Francisco Miranda, led a revolt against the Spanish in 1810. It was unsuccessful, and the leaders had to flee. Miranda led a force against the Spanish in 1812, but he was captured and later died in prison. Bolívar was able to seize the city of Caracas in 1813, but the viceroy of New Granada gathered an army that defeated the revolutionists and forced Bolívar into exile. He fled to Jamaica, where he was able to secure help for a new attempt to free Venezuela, as his native country now called itself.

Beaten again in 1815, Bolívar determined to attack the Spanish in what is now Colombia. In 1819 he set out from Venezuela with a small army, crossed the Andes, and defeated the Spanish at Boyacá, thus freeing much of New Granada. Bolívar was hailed as "the Liberator" and was made president, with almost absolute power, of Great Colombia. This new nation included the areas known today as Colombia, Venezuela, Ecuador, and Panama.

Freedom for La Plata and Peru

The forces of independence in the viceroyalty of La Plata had not been idle. By 1810, creole rebels in Buenos Aires had seized control of the government. In 1816 they declared independence for the United Provinces of La Plata, later named Argentina. Meanwhile the states of Paraguay and Uruguay had become independent.

However, the Spanish were strongly entrenched in the large viceroyalty of Peru. Rivalries among the creole rebels helped the Spanish. The creoles could not agree on the kind of government they wanted; some favored a monarchy, while others preferred a republic.

José de San Martín, a creole born in Argentina, was convinced that genuine independence could not last while Spain was still in possession of the viceroyalty of Peru. He decided that the best way to get at the Spanish was to strike first at the southern region, where there was already much unrest among the people. At Mendoza, Argentina, San Martín gathered an army, which made an incredibly difficult crossing of the Andes Mountains. It overcame strong Spanish resistance

to free the southern part of the viceroyalty, known as Chile, in 1818.

In Chile the patriots raised an army and a considerable force of ships for the final struggle to gain Peru. The campaign lasted until 1821, when independence forces captured Lima, the capital, and proclaimed Peru an independent republic under San Martín, who was honored as the "Protector of Peru."

Bolívar, moving his troops south to help in the liberation movement, met with San Martín in 1822. San Martín decided that leadership should not be divided and resigned his command to let Bolívar take full charge of the liberation movement in South America.

After several more years of hard fighting, the entire region of Peru was cleared of Spanish forces. By 1825 the northern territory of Upper Peru, which had been part of the viceroyalty of La Plata, had become an independent republic, named Bolivia in honor of Bolívar.

Brazil

Brazil, largest of the Latin American colonies, was the last one on the continent of South America to win independence. It was achieved without bloodshed.

Brazil had been ruled by a governor general appointed by the king of Portugal. Social and economic conditions in Brazil had been similar to those in the Spanish viceroyalties. When Napoleon's army invaded Portugal in 1808, the royal family fled to Brazil and settled in Rio de Janeiro. From there King John VI ruled the colony and still claimed to rule the homeland. Even after the overthrow of Napoleon, John stayed in Brazil. But Portugal wanted him back, and the colony wanted him gone. Finally, in 1821, John VI returned to Portugal, leaving his son, Dom Pedro, in charge of the Brazilian government.

The people of Brazil had been influenced by the independence movement in neighboring Spanish colonies. The departure of the Portuguese king gave them their opportunity. Brazilian patriots asked Dom Pedro to become ruler of an independent Brazil, and he willingly consented. A constitutional assembly met and established a con-

NEW NATIONS IN LATIN AMERICA
about 1825

LIBERATED TERRITORY
Formerly Spanish
Formerly Portuguese
Formerly French
× Battle site

0   500   1000   1500 miles

UNITED STATES

MEXICO

GULF OF MEXICO

PACIFIC OCEAN

BAHAMAS (Br.)

WEST INDIES

CUBA (Sp.)

SANTO DOMINGO
PUERTO RICO (Sp.)

Mexico City

BRITISH HONDURAS
HONDURAS
GUATEMALA
EL SALVADOR
NICARAGUA
COSTA RICA
PANAMA

JAMAICA (Br.)
HAITI

CARIBBEAN SEA

UNITED PROVINCES OF CENTRAL AMERICA

TRINIDAD (Br.)

ATLANTIC OCEAN

Caracas
Boyacá ×
VENEZUELA
Bogotá
COLOMBIA
Quito
ECUADOR

GREAT COLOMBIA

GUIANAS (Br.) (Du.) (Fr.)

BOLÍVAR

PERU
Lima

BRAZIL

BOLIVIA
La Paz
Sucre

SAN MARTÍN

PARAGUAY
Asunción

Rio de Janeiro

ARGENTINA

URUGUAY

Mendoza
Santiago
Buenos Aires
Montevideo

CHILE

PATAGONIA (UNEXPLORED)

Strait of Magellan

NEW SPAIN

Mexico City
CUBA
HISPANIOLA
(Br.)
(Br.)
WEST INDIES

ATLANTIC

NEW GRANADA
Bogotá
GUIANAS
(Br.)

PACIFIC OCEAN

BRAZIL

Lima
PERU

LA PLATA

Rio de Janeiro

Buenos Aires

OCEAN

LATIN AMERICA ABOUT 1790

Spanish
Portuguese
French
British
Dutch

stitutional empire under Dom Pedro as Emperor Pedro I. In 1822, Brazil proclaimed its independence from Portugal, and Portugal recognized the independence of its former colony.

Thus almost all of Latin America had become independent by 1825 (see map, opposite). Only in Cuba, Jamaica, Puerto Rico, the Guianas, British Honduras, and a few small islands did European rule continue.

The Monroe Doctrine

At the very beginning of their national existence, the new nations of Latin America found themselves in danger. In 1823, after Ferdinand VII had been restored to his Spanish throne by a French army, he asked the Quadruple Alliance to help him regain his American colonies. However, two circumstances prevented this from happening: (1) Great Britain objected. The British had built up a profitable trade with independent Latin America and feared that it would be lost if the region were restored to Spain. (2) The United States also opposed European intervention in the New World—not only in Latin America, but also along the northwestern coast of North America, which Russia was trying to reserve for itself.

The British foreign secretary, George Canning, proposed a joint British-American declaration opposing foreign intervention, but the United States preferred to act alone. In 1823, President James Monroe sent a message to Congress that was a "hands-off" notice to the nations of Europe concerning the Americas.

In this statement, which came to be known as the Monroe Doctrine, Monroe said that the United States would not interfere in Europe's affairs, or in the affairs of any existing European colonies in the Western Hemisphere. However, no more colonies were to be established in the Western Hemisphere. The United States announced that it would oppose any attempts to establish new colonies, to add territory to existing colonies, or to interfere with any of the American governments. President Monroe was trying to protect not only the newly independent nations of Latin America but the United States as well.

Metternich and other European leaders blustered and denounced the Monroe Doctrine. But no nation of Europe tried to defy it or test it. The combination of both British and United States opposition discouraged any European power from meddling in Latin American affairs. The new nations of Latin America remained independent.

Common ties but no union

Simón Bolívar had dreamed of a great federal United States of South America, like that of the English-speaking states of North America. The patriotic San Martín had tried to help bring this union about by unselfishly withdrawing from his position of leadership in Peru in favor of Bolívar.

The people of Latin America had common ties that seemed to make such a union possible. The white settlers shared a common cultural heritage and religious faith. Spanish was spoken almost everywhere except in Brazil, where the people spoke Portuguese. In spite of these ties, the dream of Latin American unity did not become a reality. Everywhere there were rivalries and jealousies. Geographical barriers kept regions separate. Independence did not bring social reforms, and class differences continued.

By the time Bolívar died in 1830, Great Colombia had split into separate nations, and conflicts had broken out among other Latin American countries. "I have plowed the sea," Bolívar said shortly before he died, saddened by the impermanence of what he had done. By 1840 the region south of the United States had broken up into seventeen independent, sovereign nations.

CHECKUP

1. Who is known as the "George Washington of South America"? Why?

2. What were the accomplishments of San Martín? Why did he resign his command?

3. What circumstances prevented the Spanish from regaining their American colonies? State the main provisions of the Monroe Doctrine.

4. IDENTIFY: Toussaint L'Ouverture, Hidalgo, Miranda, John VI, Dom Pedro.

5. LOCATE: Haiti, Santo Domingo, Caracas, Great Colombia, Mendoza, Rio de Janeiro.

CHAPTER REVIEW

Chapter 20   Reaction Dominated Europe as Latin America Won Freedom   (1500—1840)

B.C. | A.D. ➡

| 1300 | 1400 | 1500 | 1600 | 1700 | 1800 | 1900 | 2000 |

1551	Founding of first universities in America	
1791	Beginning of revolt in Haiti	
1814-1815	Congress of Vienna	
1815	Formation of Holy Alliance	
	Formation of Quadruple Alliance	
1816	Argentine independence declared	
1818	Chile proclaimed independent	
1819	Carlsbad Decrees	
	Victory of Bolívar at Boyacá; freedom for New Granada	
1821	Independence of Mexico	
	Beginning of Greek revolt	
1822	Independence of Brazil	
1823	Monroe Doctrine	
1829	Treaty of Adrianople	

CHAPTER SUMMARY

Nationalism and liberalism were two great forces that influenced the post-Napoleonic world. They played only a small role at the Congress of Vienna, however. Diplomats met there to restore legitimate rulers to power and reshuffle territories in order to prevent further aggression by France. Reactionary leaders disappointed nationalist hopes for self-government in Italy, Poland, and Austria, although the German Confederation was a step toward unity.

Both the Quadruple Alliance and the Holy Alliance grew out of the Congress of Vienna. So did the Concert of Europe, which tried to maintain the status quo.

Metternich, who dominated Europe for years, worked to suppress liberal and nationalistic movements that threatened absolutism. He succeeded in Germany, Italy, and Spain, but failed in Greece.

Metternich failed too in Latin America. Spain had ruled most of the region for centuries. In its four viceroyalties, colonial society was based on fixed classes. There were many great farming estates, owned by absentee landlords, where slaves did much of the work. Discontent grew among creoles and those who disliked Spain's mercantile policy.

The first Latin American colony to wage a successful revolt was Haiti. Not long afterward, Mexico gained its freedom. Five Central American colonies tried unsuccessfully to unite. In South America, Bolívar worked tirelessly to free the viceroyalty of New Granada. After a successful revolt in La Plata, San Martín invaded Chile and Peru, finally overcoming Spanish resistance. In Brazil (a Portuguese colony), independence came peacefully.

Although Spain wanted to regain its colonies, it was opposed by both Britain and the United States.

The American President issued the Monroe Doctrine, a "hands-off" notice to European powers.

Revolutionary leaders hoped for federal union in Latin America, but divisive forces proved too strong. By 1840 there were seventeen sovereign states there.

QUESTIONS FOR DISCUSSION

1. Why is it correct to say that the European liberals of the 1800's would be considered reactionaries today?

2. The Congress of Vienna restored monarchies and suppressed liberal and nationalistic aspirations; on the other hand, it preserved peace and order in Europe for many years. Do you think a long period of peace justified the policies that were pursued by the Congress of Vienna? Explain.

3. As a trading nation, Britain withdrew from the Quintuple Alliance. Is it necessarily true that a country without alliances has more opportunities for trade?

4. Why did Spain try to keep the ideas of the Enlightenment, the American Revolution, and the French Revolution from spreading to Latin America? Are there countries in the contemporary world that try to prevent the free flow of ideas? Do you think they can succeed? Explain.

5. Why were the Latin American countries, unlike the former English colonies of North America, unable to form a federal union?

PROJECTS

1. Write a short essay explaining why the Metternich system was destined to fail.

2. As a citizen of the United States, write a letter to a pro-revolutionary friend in Latin America at the time of the revolts there, giving him encouragement.

CHAPTER 21

The Industrial Revolution Transformed the Modern World

You have studied the great political revolutions that changed England, the Americas, and France in the 1700's and 1800's. Men in Europe and the Americas struggled for the right to be considered as individuals, to be equal before the law, and to have a voice in their own governments. All citizens of free nations today can trace their freedom of action and thought to the turmoils of the Age of Revolutions.

Freedom of action and thought, or the desire to gain them, are important characteristics of the contemporary world. Our century is also strongly influenced by science and technology. Science is concerned with man's understanding of nature. Technology concentrates on the way nature can be made useful for mankind.

You have read about the growth of science, beginning with the Scientific Revolution of the 1500's and 1600's and continuing with the work of men like Newton. Technology became a dominant factor in Western life in the 1800's, with what is called the Industrial Revolution.

The Industrial Revolution was a sweeping change in the way goods were produced. For centuries, manufacturing was carried on mainly by the handicraft system—that is, goods were made by hand, usually by skilled laborers. Beginning about 1750, more and more goods were produced by machines. This development was possible largely because older sources of power—animals,

Curious spectators watching an early train in Germany

wind, and water—were harnessed more efficiently, and because a new power source—steam—came into use.

The Industrial Revolution led to a host of related changes. Factories took the place of home workshops. Capitalists grew in numbers and importance. Trade, transportation, and communications were stimulated. Vast cities grew up almost overnight.

These developments took place first in England, then spread gradually to other countries. France, Germany, and the United States were substantially industrialized by the late 1800's. Russia did not undergo its Industrial Revolution until after 1918, and countries like China and India are still working to become industrialized.

Countries that have not yet experienced industrialization are usually called undeveloped or underdeveloped nations.

THE CHAPTER SECTIONS:

1. The Industrial Revolution began in England (1700–1850)

2. Transportation and communications improved as industrialism spread (1760–1870)

3. The Industrial Revolution affected many aspects of society (1750–1850)

4. Living and working conditions gradually improved (1776–1890)

5. Socialism offered radical solutions to the problems of industrialism (1800–1860)

1 The Industrial Revolution began in England

The Industrial Revolution began in England because of a combination of conditions that existed there. What economists call the *factors of production*—that is, the basic sources of wealth—were favorably balanced. These factors may be summarized as: (1) land, (2) labor, (3) capital, (4) management, and (5) government.

Land, to the economist, includes all the natural resources. Thus England was favored because it had a good supply of coal and some iron ore. Excellent harbors aided trade, and rivers provided water power and inland transportation.

England also had a good labor supply. Workers were available chiefly because of changes in agriculture, about which you will read shortly.

Capital, too, was readily available. Many Englishmen had grown wealthy from trade since the time of the Commercial Revolution. They had surplus funds to invest in new enterprises.

England possessed advantages in terms of management—the men who bring together land, labor, and capital. As you read in Chapter 17, English society was not rigid. It was not dishonorable for young men from the gentry and middle class to go into business. There was also an opportunity for men of the lower class to rise in business.

The English government also supplied a necessary factor of production. It favored commercial interests and provided stability that stimulated expansion.

In addition to all these factors of production, there was a large demand for goods. The British Isles and British colonies overseas provided an ample market, and there were also trade opportunities in many other parts of the world. The British navy and merchant fleet were the best in the world.

The agricultural revolution

The revolution in industry was preceded and made possible by a revolution in agriculture. It, too, began in England.

You have read about the enclosure movement, the fencing off of common land into individual holdings. This movement continued in the 1700's and had two chief results. (1) As large landowners added to their holdings, small owners either became tenant farmers or gave up farming and moved into the cities. (2) Since land did not have to be farmed in common, agreement among numerous farmers was not necessary and experimentation was easier.

Among the first experimenters were men whom

we would call "gentlemen farmers." One of them was Jethro Tull, who lived in the early 1700's. He was bothered by the wastefulness of sowing seed broadcast—that is, scattering it by hand on top of the soil and over a wide area. He invented what he called a seed drill, with which seeds could be planted in the soil in regular rows.

Experiments showed Tull that crops grew better if the weeds were removed and the soil between the rows of plants was pulverized regularly. To do this work, he invented a cultivator that could be drawn by horses.

Viscount Townshend, who was also an English gentleman farmer, found a way to avoid the fallow-field practice, in which a certain percentage of a farmer's fields remained unplanted each year. By repeated experiments, he learned that soil fertility could be preserved by alternating crops of different kinds. This system, called crop rotation, has become a basic principle of modern farming. Townshend also urged farmers to plant such root crops as turnips, which could be stored and used to feed livestock during the winter. He was so enthusiastic about turnips that he became known as "Turnip" Townshend.

Improvements in machinery further reduced farm labor and increased production. For example, iron plows replaced wooden ones. An American blacksmith added a further improvement by inventing an iron plow in three parts so that a broken part could be replaced at small cost.

Scientific agriculture speeded up the movement of small farmers to the cities. The new techniques and machines were often expensive, and small farmers could not afford them. Then too, as mechanization increased, fewer farm laborers were needed.

The cotton textile industry

The first manufacturing process to undergo mechanization was the production of cotton textiles. Cotton came first for several reasons. It was well adapted to mechanization. The cotton industry grew up after the decline of craft guilds and therefore was not subject to guild restrictions. There was a huge market for cotton cloth both in England and abroad. As you study the developments that took place, note how interrelated the changes were—how one invention led to others in a kind of chain reaction.

Cotton cloth had been imported into England since the late Middle Ages. It was both popular and expensive. In the 1600's, businessmen began importing raw cotton and employing English spinners and weavers to make it into cloth. This industry was an example of the domestic system, with men and women working in their homes. Although production increased, it still could not meet the demand.

The first new development came in the loom for weaving. A loom is set up with a series of threads from top to bottom, called the woof. A shuttle containing the thread running the other way (the warp) is pushed back and forth across the loom. It is a slow process. In 1733 a clockmaker named John Kay invented the flying shuttle, a cord mechanism that moved the warp thread more rapidly through the loom. Now the weavers could weave faster than the spinners could spin on their simple spinning wheels, and there came a demand for more thread. Prizes were offered for a better spinning machine.

A poor English workman, James Hargreaves, won the prize in 1764 with a machine that he named the spinning jenny in honor of his wife. This machine could produce eight times as much thread as a single spinning wheel. Five years later, Richard Arkwright improved the process with a machine called the water frame because it was driven by water power.

The jenny and the flying shuttle were small, hand operated, and relatively inexpensive; they could be used in workers' homes as part of the domestic system. The water frame, though, was large, costly, and operated by water power. Arkwright, therefore, opened a spinning mill and, within a decade, employed several hundred workers. It was the beginning of the modern factory system.

Ten years later, Samuel Crompton combined the best features of the spinning jenny and the water frame in another machine, the spinning mule. Now there was so much thread that the weavers fell behind.

In 1785 an English clergyman, Edmund Cartwright, met the need with a power loom in which the shuttle was automatically operated by water power. With this loom, one man could weave as much cloth as 200 hand-loom operators. At about the same time, a cylindrical press was invented for the rapid printing of colored patterns on cotton cloth.

With all these improvements, cotton cloth was cheaper to produce and sell. As the price went down, the demand increased, and so did the need for raw cotton. In 1701, England imported 1 million pounds of cotton; in 1802; it imported 60 million pounds.

Most of the imported raw cotton came from the southern United States. At first, cotton had not been profitable there because of the difficulty of removing the seeds to prepare it for market. By hand, one man could clean only a pound of cotton a day. Then, in 1793, Eli Whitney invented the cotton gin, a machine that could do the work of fifty men. Aided by Whitney's invention, the southern United States met the demands of the English textile manufacturers and became the cotton-producing center of the world.

Steam engines

The early machines of the Industrial Revolution were driven by water power. It was a great improvement over human, animal, and wind power, but it did have drawbacks. A factory had to be located beside a stream or river, preferably near a natural waterfall or a place where a dam could be built. This location might not be near transportation, raw materials, a labor supply, or markets. In addition, water power was not constant, but was likely to vary with the seasons. A new source of continuous, dependable, portable power was needed. All of these desirable features were found in steam.

The power contained in steam had been observed by men since ancient times. It was not until 1712, however, that Thomas Newcomen, an English engineer, produced the first successful steam engine. Newcomen engines were used to pump water from mines. They were more powerful and dependable than water wheels, but they were very crude machines, slow and expensive to operate.

In the 1760's, James Watt, a Scottish instrument maker and engineer, studied the Newcomen engine, devised several ways of improving it, and in 1769 produced the modern steam engine. The Watt engine was quickly adapted for use in driving the new spinning and weaving machines.

As a result of Watt's invention, steam displaced water as the major power source, and the Industrial Revolution moved forward at a faster pace. The steam engine was by far the most important invention of the Industrial Revolution.

Iron and steel

The increasing number and variety of machines brought a great demand for iron to make them. England had produced iron from early times with wood or charcoal as fuel. Then it was discovered that coal worked even better. Iron and coal became the twin raw materials of modern industry, and England had these materials in abundance.

Many an early steam engine blew up because the iron used in its construction was too weak to withstand high pressures. A stronger, harder material was needed. This was steel—iron with certain impurities removed. The existing process for making steel was slow and expensive, and the metal remained a luxury item until the 1850's. During that decade an American, William Kelly, and an Englishman, Henry Bessemer, discovered a new way of making steel. The Bessemer process reduced the cost so much that steel became what it is today, the basic material of our industrial civilization.

Industrialization in other fields

Using steam engines and iron and steel, English manufacturers quickly introduced power-driven machinery in many industries. The production of shoes, clothing, ammunition, and furniture became mechanized. So did printing and paper-making. Machines were used to cut and finish lumber, to process foods, and to make other machines.

Some new inventions and processes had important by-products (secondary products that re-

An Early Sewing Machine

The invention of the sewing machine in the 1800's, stimulated by revolutionary changes in the textile industry, had a tremendous impact on both home and industry. Shortly after it was invented, the "iron seamstress" became the most widely advertised and distributed product in the world. Dealers in sewing machines were among the first to promote installment buying and guaranteed service. As a result, the new machines were purchased by many households. They virtually ended the traditional bondage of women to the needle.

The early machine at right is a graphic reminder that industrial design has often lagged behind technological progress. When faced with the task of creating new "packages" for new inventions, designers have frequently based them on traditional forms or—as in this case—adorned them with traditional decorations. The cherubs and dragonfly have a certain charm, but no meaningful relationship to sewing. These decorative elements actually made the machine difficult to operate, and later models were simplified.

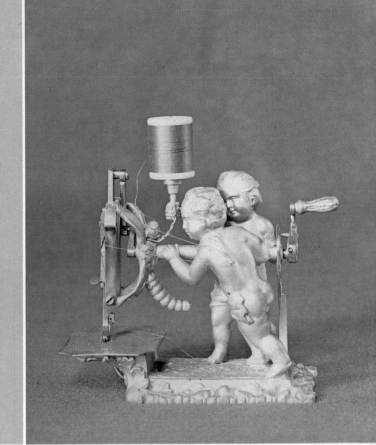

sult from manufacturing something else) which developed into separate industries. Coke, made from coal, improved the smelting of iron. Then it was discovered that the gases driven off from the coal in making coke would burn to give light. During the 1830's, gas was piped into London and burned in street lamps. By the 1850's, gas was used for lighting streets and homes in hundreds of cities throughout the Western world.

Another new industry of the 1800's was the production of rubber. It was first used to make waterproof shoes and coats, but they became sticky in warm weather. In 1839, after years of experimenting, Charles Goodyear of the United States discovered a process for "curing" rubber to make it more elastic and usable. He mixed the raw rubber with sulfur and then heated it. His method, called vulcanizing, became the basis of the modern rubber industry.

Still another industry grew up after 1850, when men discovered how to use what had formerly been a nuisance. Crude oil, or petroleum, had been known for many years. During the 1850's, men learned that it could be distilled to produce paraffin, lubricating oil for machinery, and kerosene for lighting and heating.

CHECKUP

1. What was the Industrial Revolution? Why did it begin in England?

2. How did the enclosure movement lead to changes in agriculture? What were the principal effects of the agricultural revolution?

3. Summarize the contributions to the cotton textile industry of Kay, Hargreaves, Arkwright, Crompton, Cartwright, and Whitney.

4. IDENTIFY: Tull, Townshend, crop rotation, Newcomen, Watt, by-products, vulcanizing.

2 Transportation and communications improved as industrialism spread

When the Industrial Revolution began, land transportation hardly differed from what it had been during the Middle Ages. Roads were little more than deeply rutted trails, thick with dust in dry weather, deep with mud when it rained. Fifty miles was a day's uncomfortable journey for a passenger in a stagecoach. Packhorses and clumsy wagons were used to carry heavy goods.

Moving men and goods

The changes of the Industrial Revolution made better transportation necessary. Raw materials had to be carried to factories and finished products to market. A Scot, John McAdam, worked out a new way of building roads. First came a road-bed of large stones, then layers of carefully selected smaller stones. These roads were called macadam roads. Macadamized roads are still constructed, although modern road builders use asphalt to bind the smaller stones together.

Both England and Western Europe had extensive networks of rivers that could be used as water highways. Some canals had been dug to connect them, but many more were constructed after people began using locks, which regulate the level and flow of water. The period from 1760 to 1850 was a great era of canal building. Canals furnished cheaper and slightly faster transportation than roads; however, they soon met with competition from a new form of transportation.

Watt's steam engine also offered many possibilities for new means of transportation. If the steam engine could turn a wheel to run a machine, why could it not turn a wheel to move itself? In 1814, George Stephenson, an English engineer, perfected a moving engine, or locomotive, that propelled itself by steam and ran on rails. In 1829, Stephenson's famous engine, the *Rocket,* pulled a string of cars from Liverpool to Manchester at the speed of 29 miles an hour. Networks of railroads were soon built throughout the Western world. Almost continuous improvements—steel rails, air brakes, more comfortable coaches, and special cars for different kinds of freight—made railroad transportation fast, safe, and cheap.

Many men tried adapting the steam engine to ships, but credit for doing this successfully is usually given to an American, Robert Fulton, who established the first regular inland steamboat service. His boat, the *Clermont,* was launched on the Hudson River in 1807 and at once began regular trips between New York City and Albany. Steamboats soon appeared on many of the rivers and lakes of the world.

In 1838 the *Great Western,* operating by steam alone, crossed the Atlantic Ocean in fifteen days. Regular steamboat traffic across the Atlantic was developed by Samuel Cunard of Great Britain, whose Cunard Line still operates. The steamship, like the railroad, was improved over the years. Ships were built of iron and steel instead of wood. Goods were moved more quickly and cheaply all over the world.

The communications revolution

Science played only a small role in the invention of textile machinery, the steam engine, the locomotive, and the steamship. These were the work of amateur inventors and engineers, and did not come from the laboratory of the scientist. It was in communications that scientific and technical developments began to be linked. The development of rapid communication is also an example of the international character of science.

From early times, men had observed electricity and its connection with magnetism, but they had not put their knowledge to much practical use. For one thing, no one had found a way to provide a steady flow of electric current. Around the year 1800, an Italian, Alessandro Volta, was able to build the first battery, a device which provided a steady current of electricity. Soon afterward, André Ampère of France worked out laws governing the magnetic effect of an electric current.

The work of Volta and Ampère was put to practical use by Samuel Morse of the United States. He sent electrical impulses over a wire, which made a machine click. Morse worked out

The Industrial Revolution depended on a close relationship among many different products and processes. The hand-driven spinning jenny, right, represented an advance over the spinning wheel, but production increased even more with power-driven jennies. One observer wrote of seeing a boy, tending two such machines, who produced more thread than 600 women could spin with wheels. Without improved transportation to haul raw materials and finished products, industrialization would not have been possible. Robert Fulton's *Clermont,* below, could make good progress against both wind and current. Early iron works were often built close to a railroad, as shown at bottom.

a system of dots and dashes, the Morse code, by which these clicks could be translated into letters of the alphabet. By 1844, Morse's telegraph had become a practical instrument, and telegraph wires were stretched out across continents. Ideas could then travel at the speed of electricity.

Men soon began experimenting to find a way to carry electrical impulses under the sea by using cables—telegraph wires that were heavily insulated to protect them from water. Early in the 1850's, England was connected with continental Europe by a cable from Dover to Calais. However, the problem of spanning the great distance of the Atlantic Ocean presented enormous difficulties. It was not until 1866 that Cyrus Field and a group of enterprising Americans finally laid a cable across the Atlantic Ocean. Soon afterward, all the continents were joined by cables.

The spread of industrialism

The revolutionary changes in agriculture, industry, transportation, and communications did not have much effect on continental Europe for several years. There were various reasons for the delay. Many European countries lacked raw materials and large, accessible markets. England, in order to keep its monopoly on new methods, forbade the exportation of machines and the emigration of skilled workers. The wars of the French Revolution and the Napoleonic Era also slowed European development.

France, after a late start, did develop some industry, especially in textiles, iron, and mining. The French government helped this development in two ways. It levied high tariffs to keep out foreign manufactured goods, and it encouraged railroad building. But France did not become as completely industrialized as Britain. Its fertile farm lands, owned mostly in small peasant holdings, remained important in the French economy.

Industry grew slowly in the German states because they were not united. Efficient government as a factor of production was lacking. Although some factories were established in the middle 1800's, real industrialization had to await the unification of Germany. You will read about this unification in Chapter 23.

While German industry lagged, agricultural progress there was stimulated by a chemistry professor, Justus von Liebig. After numerous studies, he reached the conclusion that soil is a combination of chemicals which supply the nourishment for plant growth. Poor soil is poor because it lacks certain chemicals. If these can be added, the soil will grow good crops. Liebig's book, published in 1840, made agriculture truly scientific.

It was in the United States that English inventions and methods were most eagerly adopted. The United States had everything that was needed for industrial development: national unity, a vast country with rich natural resources, rapidly increasing population, inventive genius, and a willingness to adopt, to adapt, and to take chances. Many canals and railroads were built. Industry moved west as transportation developed: the steel industry to Pittsburgh and the Great Lakes, the manufacture of farm machinery to Chicago. By 1869 the continent had been spanned by a railroad. By 1870 the United States was second only to Great Britain as a manufacturing nation.

Closely allied to the growth of American industry were revolutionary changes in farming. You have already read about Whitney's cotton gin and how it enabled the southern states to supply raw material for the English cloth industry. Another invention was a machine for harvesting grain, patented by Cyrus McCormick in 1834. The McCormick reaper, drawn by horses, freed many farmers from the slow, backbreaking work of cutting grain with a sickle or a scythe. The invention of the reaper was followed by other devices, such as the mechanical thresher for separating the grains of wheat from their stalks and hulls.

CHECKUP

1. What were four important steps in the improvement of transportation during the Industrial Revolution?

2. Explain and illustrate the statement: "Science played only a small role in the invention of textile machinery, the steam engine, the locomotive, and the steamship. . . . It was in communications that scientific and technical developments began to be linked."

3. Why was there a delay in the spread of the Industrial Revolution to continental Europe?

4. Why was the United States able to make such rapid progress in the development of its industry?

5. IDENTIFY: locks, Stephenson, *Rocket*, Fulton, *Clermont*, Liebig, McCormick.

3 The Industrial Revolution affected many aspects of society

For centuries, men had worked at home or in their fields. They were generally self-employed, owning their own tools and producing much of their own food. With the Industrial Revolution, this situation changed. The new machines, which were large and expensive, were owned by capitalists and operated in factories by men who worked for wages. The location of factories was determined by the need for power, raw materials, and markets. Often laborers had to move their homes in order to be near the factories where they worked.

The factory system introduced a new phase in the development of capitalism. Most earlier capitalists were merchants, who bought, sold, and exchanged goods. This phase of capitalism is sometimes called commercial capitalism. The capitalists of the Industrial Revolution were more involved in producing and manufacturing goods; therefore the capitalism of this period is often known as industrial capitalism.

Starting a factory required a great deal of capital. Some individuals were able to raise enough money to become owners during the early Industrial Revolution. There were also partnerships of two or more individuals, sometimes doing business on a large scale. Another common form of business organization was the joint-stock company (page 333).

Population and city growth

For centuries before 1750, the population of Europe had grown very little. When the Industrial Revolution began, it totaled about 140 million people. But by 1850, only a hundred years later, it stood at 266 million. The greatest population growth took place in such industrialized regions as England and Western Europe. The greater population resulted not so much from an increased birth rate as from a decreasing death rate.

One reason for the decrease was the greater food supply resulting from improvements in farming. Another was new knowledge of disease prevention and cure, about which you will read in a later chapter.

Changes in agriculture, industry, and transportation, with the resulting increase in trade, produced another striking result—the rapid growth of cities. The greatest spur to city growth was the factory system. Many early factories were located in already established cities, which grew tremendously. The population of Manchester, England, for example, grew from 25,000 in 1772 to 455,000 in 1851. When factories were located in rural areas, cities grew up around them. Urban (city) living became the typical way of life for increasing numbers of people.

Social classes

The Industrial Revolution caused several changes in social classes. In the first place, the capitalist-employer group grew in numbers and importance. The world had known capitalist employers before. You have read about capitalist merchants, shipowners, and bankers in medieval and early modern times. Now their number was increased by thousands of factory owners, many of whom became quite wealthy.

Most early industrial capitalists managed their factories themselves. Arkwright, for example, raised money, built factories, installed machines, hired workmen, bought raw cotton, superintended operations to see that the work was properly done, and sold the finished product.

As time passed and the factory system became more complicated, capitalists tended to leave the active work of superintending and management (except the raising of capital) to hired employees. Thus appeared the managerial group—neither owners nor laborers. As managers, they gave or-

Living and working conditions during the early Industrial Revolution were intolerable by modern standards. The young boy above—undernourished, unsmiling, uneducated—probably worked in this glass factory twelve to fourteen hours a day, six days a week. At the end of their long day, laborers went home to working-class slums like the one below. Rows of tenement houses, each with its tiny back yard and reeking chimney, were crowded with families. Such conditions slowly began to improve when workingmen, as at right, became organized in unions and demanded reforms.

ders and were paid a monthly or yearly salary. They were set apart from the ordinary workers, who obeyed orders and received an hourly or daily wage.

Almost all the managerial group, as well as factory owners and stockholders, came from the middle class. The upper classes continued to gain their wealth from the ownership of land. Many aristocrats, especially in the early days, looked down on business and businessmen. In a way, the Industrial Revolution was the triumph of the middle class over the aristocracy. It put vast wealth into the hands of the bourgeois, who in time gained political power as well.

Another increasingly important group was made up of the factory workers of the cities, the proletariat. It was a new class of workers, who had to sell their labor because they had no property or tools of their own and who received low wages because they had few skills. Skilled workers found that factory owners did not want or need their skills because the factory system put a premium on unskilled labor. Women and children would accept lower wages than men. They were also especially useful in spinning mills because they were more skillful than men in tying threads when they broke.

In time other workers entered the factories. Many small farmers, tenants, and farm laborers moved to the cities, as you have read. Gradually, too, skilled artisans had to take factory jobs, where their special skills were of no advantage. Only a few artisans, such as shoemakers and tailors, remained independent.

Working conditions

In the early days of the Industrial Revolution, working conditions were poor. Long hours were the rule, often from sunrise to sunset. A working day fourteen to sixteen hours long was considered normal for men, women, and children alike.

Factories were uncomfortable places, noisy, dirty, and poorly ventilated. The air was hot and steamy in summer, cold and damp in winter. Sanitary facilities were primitive. Early machines had no safety devices and serious injuries were frequent. Accident insurance or any other form of compensation for injury was unheard of.

Wages were low. In England as late as 1867 the average weekly wage for laborers ranged from $5.00 to $9.00. Wages for women and children were much lower. Conditions in the United States were somewhat better because labor was scarcer.

Perhaps the worst feature of early industrialization was child labor. It was common for children of five to be employed in cotton mills and mines. Conditions in coal mines were particularly bad. Women and children pulled carts in tunnels where the roof was too low for a donkey to pass through. Women worked on their hands and knees. Children who fell asleep at their tasks were beaten.

Living conditions

If life in the mines and factories was hard and monotonous, life in the workers' homes was not much better. Working people lived in cramped and crowded tenements, with as many as a dozen people to a room. As late as 1840, one out of every eight working-class families in Manchester lived in a cellar. Food was poor and recreation almost nonexistent.

Urban factory workers also had to face a condition that had seldom troubled farm workers. At times there would be difficulty in selling all the goods of the fast-moving machines. As sales income decreased, employers would cut production, reduce wages, and lay off workers. The threat of unemployment became a terrible nightmare for the factory worker. There was no unemployment insurance to tide him over a crisis. Unless he could find private charity, he faced starvation.

Although the laboring classes suffered during the Industrial Revolution, there is no doubt that their living standard was considerably improved when cheap goods produced in the factories became available to them. During the 1800's, also, real wages (wages measured in terms of what they will buy) increased rapidly.

One must be careful, too, in making comparisons. Conditions during the early Industrial Revolution were shocking, indeed, compared to living and working conditions today. Compared to conditions in rural areas or nonindustrial cities at the same time, however, they were not so bad. The lower economic classes, whether peasants or artisans, had always worked long and hard. They had always suffered from periodic famines and epidemics. And women and children had always worked hard, especially in rural areas.

Some historians believe that industrialization always brings hardship to some social class—usually the lowest one. It is difficult to raise a nation from a state of underdevelopment to the level of an industrial society. Sacrifices must be made to achieve this goal.

The laboring classes of Britain and the United States suffered when their countries were being industrialized. (We see the same sort of sacrifices being made in the world today in a country like Russia.) Only after the early period did all classes begin to share the benefits. But if you were a child pulling coal cars in a mine or tending a textile machine, your job would not become more pleasant if you were told that *eventually* the men and women in your social class would have a higher standard of living and better working conditions.

CHECKUP

1. Why did the population of Europe grow rapidly after 1750?

2. What social classes became more important as a result of the Industrial Revolution?

3. What do you consider to be the best feature of the Industrial Revolution? the worst? Explain.

4. IDENTIFY: commercial capitalism, industrial capitalism, real wages.

 Living and working conditions gradually improved

You may wonder why governments did not pass laws to end abuses in mines and factories and protect the workers. The answer has to do with certain theories that became widespread as the Industrial Revolution progressed.

Economic theories

During the Enlightenment, a group of economists attacked the ideas of mercantilism. They believed there were certain natural laws that governed economic life. Any attempt to interfere with these natural economic laws was certain to bring disaster. The views of these economic thinkers were best stated by Adam Smith, a Scot, in his book *The Wealth of Nations,* published in 1776.

Smith reasoned that all business and economic activity is regulated by two natural laws—the law of supply and demand and the law of competition. In any business, prices (and therefore profits) will be fixed by the workings of supply and demand. If an article is scarce and there is a great demand for it, people will pay a high price for it. Thus profits from its sale will rise. When this happens, men with money will invest it to produce more of the scarce article. Soon there will be a plentiful supply.

Now each manufacturer will face competition.

In order to get people to buy his product, he must either reduce the price or improve the quality, or both. If too many manufacturers enter the same business, the price will go down so far that some manufacturers will not make enough money to cover their costs. Some may be forced out of business entirely. This will generally happen to the least efficient businesses—the ones that are so poorly organized and managed that their production costs are high. When such manufacturers have to quit, the supply of the article will decrease and the price will go up. Then the capable, efficient, and well organized producers will make a reasonable profit.

Thus, Adam Smith argued, every man should be free to do what he thought best for himself—to go into any business he wanted and to operate it for his own greatest advantage. The result would be beneficial to everyone. Laborers would have jobs, investors and owners would make profits, and buyers would receive better goods at lower prices. Smith's system was one of completely free enterprise.

Smith's ideas were appealing to industrialists because the forces he outlined were supposed to work automatically. In fact, he argued that if anything interfered with the absolutely free working of supply and demand and competition, the system could not work well. Laws and regulations, like those under mercantilism, were thought of as interfering with the workings of natural laws.

Malthus and Ricardo. Smith's ideas received strong support from the writings of two other men, Thomas Malthus and David Ricardo. Malthus was an Anglican clergyman who became a professor of economics. In his book *An Essay on the Principle of Population,* published in 1798, he wrote that the greatest obstacle to human progress was the increasing population. People, he said, multiplied more rapidly than the food supply increased, despite such checks as famines, epidemics, and wars. Human misery and poverty were therefore inevitable.

David Ricardo was an English businessman who built up a large fortune early in life and then was elected to the House of Commons. He, too, wrote that working-class poverty was inevitable. In his book *Principles of Political Economy and Taxation,* published in 1817, Ricardo said that labor was like all other commodities— cheap when plentiful and expensive when scarce. Population was increasing as Malthus had predicted. This meant that wages would inevitably be forced down to the lowest possible level, just enough to allow workers to avoid starvation. If wages were increased, workers would have more children, increasing the supply of workers and thus driving wages down again. This idea became known as the "iron law of wages."

Malthus and Ricardo painted a grim picture for the worker, condemned to inevitable poverty and suffering by unchangeable laws. Small wonder that the new social science of economics came to be known as the "dismal science."

Laissez faire. The writings of economists supported early industrialists in doing what they wanted to do anyway—buy labor, like any other commodity, as cheaply as possible. Economic theories also indicated that governments should not interfere with the operations of business. This attitude was summed up in the French phrase *laissez faire* (les·ay FAIR), meaning "let do"— that is, leave things alone.

Laissez faire had a great appeal for employers, factory owners, and businessmen in general. They were pioneers, facing keen competition; there were more failures and bankruptcies than successes. Factory owners worked as hard as their employees did and took far greater financial risks. Because of these risks, they regarded themselves as public benefactors and felt morally justified in operating their companies just as they saw fit. The less they paid for raw materials and labor, the higher would be their profits in proportion. Most of these profits would be invested in new enterprises, creating more jobs and more goods.

The theory of laissez faire was put into practice in England during the 1800's. Formerly either the government or the guilds had regulated the quantity and quality of goods produced, the hours and wages of workers, and the qualifications of apprentices and masters. In the middle 1800's, most of these regulations were discontinued. Tariffs, which had been used to regulate foreign trade, were abolished and free trade became the rule. Other European countries and the United States adopted many of the features of laissez faire economics, though not as completely as Britain.

Factory laws

You can see that wages, hours, and conditions of labor for a factory worker depended entirely on market conditions. As time went on, more and more people became concerned about this situation, and they worked to bring about improvements by law. The first attempts to improve working conditions by legislation were made in Great Britain, where industrialism was more widespread than elsewhere. Workers themselves played little part in this political movement since they could not vote or be represented in Parliament until 1867. (Indeed, many middle-class factory owners were not represented until 1832.)

The passage of factory laws was aided by conflict between the landowning aristocracy, represented by the Tory Party, and middle-class factory owners. The middle class wanted repeal of the tariffs on imported raw materials and foodstuffs. Cheaper raw materials meant lower costs of production, while cheaper food would reduce the cost of living, so employers could pay lower wages.

The Art of Social Protest

When the abuses that accompanied industrialism aroused reformers, artists were among those who took up the cause of the working classes. The lithograph above, by the Swiss artist Théophile Steinlen, is an example of social protest in art. He dramatizes the gap between rich and poor by showing a fat, cigar-smoking capitalist, left, gloating over the misery of a downtrodden family symbolically yoked to a plow.

Tory landowners were willing to lower tariffs on some raw materials, but they were bitterly opposed to any change in the so-called Corn Laws—laws that set tariffs on imported grain and thus protected their own crops from foreign competition. (In British usage, the word *corn* is a general term for cereal grains, such as wheat.) Suspicious of the swift rise of the middle-class businessmen, whom they regarded as newly rich upstarts, and irritated by their demands for repeal of the Corn Laws, the Tories were willing to help factory workers against factory owners.

As you might expect, the earliest laws dealt with the employment of women and children. The Factory Act of 1819 showed how far the movement had to go. It prohibited the employment of children under nine years of age in cotton mills.

Children between the ages of nine and eighteen were limited to twelve hours of work a day. In 1833 this law was applied to all textile factories. No children under nine were to be employed. Children from the ages of nine to thirteen were limited to nine hours daily; children from ages thirteen to eighteen to twelve hours a day.

Nine years later, another law forbade the employment in mines of all women and girls and of boys under ten years old. A great advance came in 1847 with the passage of the Ten Hours Act, which established a ten-hour day for women and children under eighteen in textile factories. Since it was not profitable to run the factories without women and children, the ten-hour day became general for all textile workers.

Growing interest in reform

As time went on, more and more people realized the need for change. Reforms were urged by humanitarians. (A humanitarian is a person who works to promote human welfare.) Clergymen preached against what they considered to be the un-Christian selfishness of businessmen.

Influential writers did much to make people aware of appalling conditions in mines and factories. Novels by the great English writer Charles Dickens were especially important. *Dombey and Son* (1848) and *Hard Times* (1854) both attacked selfish businessmen. In *David Copperfield* (1849–1850) Dickens described his own wretched boyhood experiences as a worker in a warehouse. Essayists and critics like Thomas Carlyle and John Ruskin denounced the materialism of their times—the obsession with money and the neglect of spiritual values.

The philosopher John Stuart Mill, although a believer in laissez faire, was critical of the economic injustices and inequalities of English society. He thought that the government should intervene to protect working children and improve housing and factory conditions. In a famous essay, *On Liberty,* published in 1859, he wrote that a government should promote the welfare of its citizens. "A state which dwarfs its men," he said, "will find that with small men no great thing can really be accomplished."

The union movement

The early factory laws were not very effective. They were not strictly enforced, and they did not solve all the workers' problems. For example, they did not deal with wages. It seemed clear that any improvements in this field had to come through the efforts of the workers themselves. To be successful, they had to act together in unions.

Organizing unions was not easy. English law regarded workmen's associations as illegal "conspiracies in restraint of trade." When workers tried to unite anyway, employers were successful in getting Parliament to pass laws against "unlawful combinations." An act of 1800 stated that persons who combined with others to demand higher wages, shorter hours, or better working conditions were liable to imprisonment. In time, efforts on behalf of the workers began to make headway. In 1824, the laws against "unlawful combinations" were repealed. In 1825, Parliament passed an act that permitted laborers to meet in order to agree on wages and hours.

In the 1840's, many workers joined the Chartist movement, about which you will read in Chapter 25. When it failed, they worked harder to strengthen labor unions. The National Association for the Protection of Labour was formed in 1845 and helped persuade Parliament to allow peaceful picketing. In the 1870's, Parliament passed laws legalizing the strike—refusal by a group of laborers to work, in order to enforce some demand.

In France, the labor movement followed a similar path, although it made slower progress. French trade unions were outlawed in 1791, but they began to emerge in the 1820's. It was not until 1884 that they were completely legalized. In Germany, workmen's associations came into existence in the 1840's. The movement grew so fast during the late 1800's that the government became alarmed. It banned all unions in 1878 with a law that remained in effect until 1890.

Once workers had gained the legal rights to form unions and to strike, they could deal with employers on more equal terms. Gradually, factory owners granted unions recognition—that is, they agreed that union representatives could speak and bargain for all the members. Union and management met to negotiate wages, hours, and working conditions. If the bargainers could agree, they wrote their agreements into a contract, to last for a fixed period of time. This whole process of negotiation is called collective bargaining.

If employers refused to recognize unions, or if the negotiators could not agree on terms, workers would then strike. In the early period of the labor movement, strikes were fairly common. In time, agreements by negotiation became more frequent.

CHECKUP

1. According to Adam Smith, how did the law of supply and demand and the law of competition work? What conclusion did he draw from these laws?

2. Why did the ideas of Smith, Malthus, and Ricardo appeal to industrialists?

3. Can you see any weaknesses in Malthus' theory of population or Ricardo's "iron law of wages"?

4. Why were British landowners in Parliament willing to pass laws regulating factory practices?

5. IDENTIFY: laissez faire, Corn Laws, humanitarian, Dickens, Mill, strike, collective bargaining.

5 Socialism offered radical solutions to the problems of industrialism

Many people were disturbed by the fact that the great wealth produced by the Industrial Revolution was so unevenly distributed. A few people became enormously rich, while many remained in utter poverty. Some reformers became convinced that laissez faire capitalism was not the best economic system, and that neither laws nor labor unions could do enough to remedy inequalities. They thought that a better distribution of wealth could be achieved only by changing the way in which the means of production were owned and operated. The means of production include everything used to produce and exchange goods—land, mines, railroads, factories, stores, and banks.

Socialism

Some reformers of the 1800's advocated a political and economic system called *socialism*. It was based on the belief that the means of production should be owned publicly (or socially) and should be operated for the welfare of all the people. Under capitalism the means of production are owned by private citizens and operated by them for their own private profit. Socialists wanted to establish an economic system that would do away with the profit motive and competition. They believed that everyone had a right to share in the profits of industry.

Utopian socialists. The early socialists were called utopian socialists because they tried to work out detailed schemes for model communities and to persuade people to join in setting them up. (You will remember that Thomas More described a model community in his *Utopia*.) Utopian socialists believed that men could live at peace with each other if they lived in small cooperative settlements, owning all the means of production in common and sharing the products.

Various utopian schemes were advocated in the early 1800's, many by French reformers such as Charles Fourier (foo·RYAY). In Britain the most influential utopian socialist was a Welshman, Robert Owen.

Owen, who lived from 1771 to 1858, left school as a boy and went to work. He was extremely successful in understanding business and in handling people, and he soon became manager of a cotton mill. Eventually he became both owner and manager of a large mill in New Lanark, Scotland, which employed over 1,500 people.

Owen believed that if people lived in a good environment, they would cease to act selfishly. As a factory owner, he felt responsible for the welfare of his workers and devoted much time and money to making their lives happier and more secure. He built good homes for them, paid them decent wages, and established a store where they could buy food at cost. He also set up schools for their children. This sort of care, in which someone in authority treats those under him as if they were his own children, is called *paternalism*.

Owen believed, however, that workers should not be completely dependent on their employers' paternalism. He encouraged them to form unions. He also established cooperative communities in both Great Britain and the United States. Owen's best-known settlement was at New Harmony, Indiana. Like most utopian communities, it suffered from internal conflicts and disbanded after a few years.

Karl Marx and "scientific socialism"

Some thinkers were impatient with utopian socialism, which they felt was too idealistic and impractical. The most important of such critics was Karl Marx, who was born in Prussia in 1818. Marx was a journalist, whose radical political views made him unpopular in his own country. Forced to leave, he eventually settled in London, where he lived until his death in 1883.

In 1848, with a fellow German, Friedrich Engels, Marx published the *Communist Manifesto,* a pamphlet outlining his ideas. Marx believed that all the great movements of history had been formed by economic conditions—a belief known as *economic determinism*. According to Marx, there are two basic classes in every society: the owners of the means of production and the workers. He wrote that all history is the story of the struggle between these classes.

The kind of society in each period of history is determined by those who own the means of production. If workers wage a successful revolution against the owners, a new class comes into power and the nature of society changes as well. Thus, for Marx, the French Revolution represented the uprising of the middle class, or bourgeoisie, against the privileged feudal aristocracy. The triumph of the bourgeoisie gave rise to capitalism, and society changed accordingly.

Capitalism, said Marx, was a necessary stage in the development of mankind, but it, too, would change. He believed that the Industrial Revolution had launched another struggle, this one between the bourgeoisie and the workers, or proletariat.

Marx argued that all wealth is created by labor. Under capitalism, he said, labor receives only a small fraction of the wealth it creates. Most of

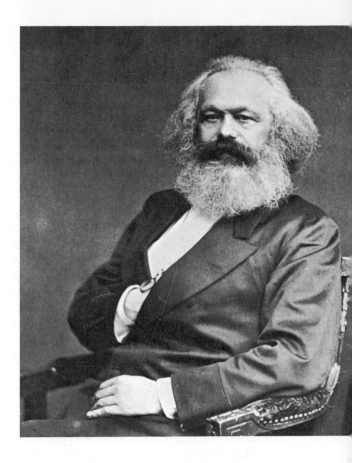

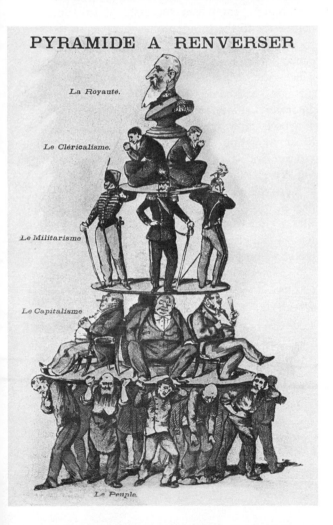

PYRAMIDE A RENVERSER

La Royauté.

Le Cléricalisme.

Le Militarisme

Le Capitalisme

Le Peuple.

Early socialists were in conflict on many issues, but agreed that cooperation rather than competition would end economic and political inequality. Robert Owen, above left, tried many reforms that were much in advance of the social conscience of his time. He did not, however, oppose private ownership and operation of industries. Karl Marx, above, was impatient with the idealism of reformers like Owen. Marx advocated the complete reorganization of society. *The Communist Manifesto* ended with these words: "The proletarians have nothing to lose but their chains. They have a world to win. Workingmen of all countries, unite!"

Agreeing with Marx, socialists in Belgium saw their social structure as a "Pyramid to Overturn." The cartoon at left shows the working classes bending under the load of capitalists, army, clergy, and, above all, the king. Social injustice aroused people throughout the world, but did not bring about violent revolutions.

455

the wealth goes to the bourgeois owners in the form of profits. As a result of this inequality, Marx held, the capitalist system necessarily suffered from increasingly severe depressions, because laboring people lacked money to buy the output of factories. He thought the time would soon come when capitalist society would be divided into a few capitalists and a vast mass of proletarians. The proletarians, gathered together in cities, would suffer poverty and unemployment.

In these circumstances the proletarians in the most advanced and industrialized nations would unite, seize power by force in a revolution, and establish socialism. Since many people would not be ready to accept socialism, the workers would have to control the government. Marx referred to this phase as the "dictatorship of the proletariat." After a period of education, people would become experienced in living and working together cooperatively. Then force would no longer be needed and the state would "wither away." It was this last stage, characterized by a truly classless society, that Marx called pure communism.° He believed that it was the inevitable outcome of human history. Everyone would contribute what he could and receive what he needed. Said Marx: "From each according to his abilities, to each according to his needs."

Marx called his variety of socialism "scientific socialism" because he thought he was describing objective laws of historical development—that is, laws that would work inevitably. (It was he and Engels who coined the term *utopian socialists* for earlier, more idealistic thinkers.) Marx elaborated many of his ideas in *Das Kapital* (German for "capital"), analyzing capitalism in detail.

Socialism after Marx

Socialists began to form political parties to put their ideas into practice in the mid-1800's. Many

---

° **communism:** In Marx's time the terms *communism* and *socialism* were used in many different ways. For Marx and Engels, a communist was one who believed that men could live cooperatively without being forced to do so. Today, as you will read later, a communist is usually someone who believes that a cooperative society in Marx's sense cannot be introduced without a violent revolution.

of these parties were influenced by the ideas of Marx and Engels. Marxist, or radical, socialists generally believed that revolution was necessary to overthrow the capitalist system.

Another group of socialists, though influenced by Marx, believed that socialism could come gradually by education and through the democratic form of government. These moderate socialists believed that when enough people were educated about socialism, they would elect socialist representatives to their government. When socialists had won a majority in the legislature, the government would take over the means of production peacefully. The owners would be paid, and the government would then operate the means of production in the public interest.

Marx believed that workers had to unite in order to fight capitalism successfully. In 1864 he helped found the International Workingmen's Association, called the First International. This organization failed for various reasons—one of which was Marx's overbearing and dictatorial manner—and came to an end in 1876. A Second International was formed in 1889, after the death of Marx. However, it was torn by quarrels between moderate and radical socialists and could not survive as an international organization during World War I.

You will read in later chapters about socialist parties in various European countries, and about Marxist ideas as they were put into practice in Russia and elsewhere during the 1900's. (See also the chart on page 807.)

CHECKUP

1. What are the essential features of socialism?

2. According to Marx, what determines the kind of society that exists at any one time? How does society change? Give an example.

3. Why did Marx think capitalism would inevitably fail?

4. What is meant by: utopian socialism? "scientific socialism"? moderate socialism?

5. IDENTIFY: means of production, Fourier, Owen, paternalism, Engels, *Communist Manifesto, Das Kapital,* First International.

CHAPTER REVIEW

Chapter 21 The Industrial Revolution Transformed the Modern World (1700—1890)

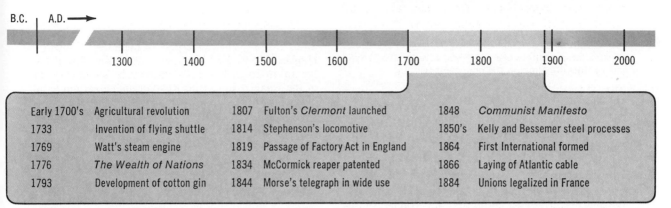

Early 1700's	Agricultural revolution	1807	Fulton's *Clermont* launched	1848	*Communist Manifesto*
1733	Invention of flying shuttle	1814	Stephenson's locomotive	1850's	Kelly and Bessemer steel processes
1769	Watt's steam engine	1819	Passage of Factory Act in England	1864	First International formed
1776	*The Wealth of Nations*	1834	McCormick reaper patented	1866	Laying of Atlantic cable
1793	Development of cotton gin	1844	Morse's telegraph in wide use	1884	Unions legalized in France

CHAPTER SUMMARY

The Industrial Revolution—the production of goods by machinery in factories—changed the world. It began in England because of that country's favorable balance of the factors of production. It was preceded by an agricultural revolution characterized by increased production and the movement of farm workers to the cities.

In the cotton textile industry, the first to be mechanized, each invention stimulated others in an interacting process. Basic to the Industrial Revolution was the replacement of water power by steam power. Almost as important was the development of better methods of making steel. As industrialism spread, it gave rise to new industries based on gas, rubber, and petroleum.

Transportation improved with better roads, networks of canals and railroads, and the use of steam power in ships. Rapid communication became possible with the telegraph and cable. The Industrial Revolution spread slowly in France and Germany, more quickly in the United States.

The technological developments of the Industrial Revolution had profound effects. Population increased and cities grew rapidly. The middle class gained importance, as did the proletariat. In the new factories and growing cities, conditions were often bad.

Improvements were slow in coming, largely because of the economic theory of laissez faire. The writings of Smith, Malthus, and Ricardo encouraged industrialists to do what they pleased. With Tory help, however, some factory laws were passed. Humanitarians and writers also aided working people.

In spite of such reforms, some people maintained that only socialism would bring real improvements. Utopian socialists advocated small cooperative settle-

ments. Marx's "scientific socialism," predicting the inevitable overthrow of capitalism, advocated proletarian revolution that would eventually lead to the pure communism of a classless society. Marxist socialists believed in violent revolution. Moderate socialists thought that socialism could be achieved peacefully through democratic methods.

QUESTIONS FOR DISCUSSION

1. Today there are still many underdeveloped nations in Asia, Africa, and Latin America. Why do you think they are trying hard to become industrialized?

2. In order to industrialize an undeveloped area, roads or railroads are often built before anything else is done. Would you consider this the best way to industrialize an area? Explain.

3. What provisions do you think child labor laws should have today?

4. Today there is much concern over the "population explosion." Do you consider this a proof of Malthus' theories? Explain.

5. Karl Marx predicted that capitalist societies would be faced with inevitable revolutions. For what reasons has this not happened in the United States?

6. It has been claimed that the Industrial Revolution created a new man—the industrial worker, or proletarian. In what respects is this claim valid?

PROJECTS

1. In a short essay try to explain why Karl Marx was such an influential thinker.

2. Write an editorial for a newspaper in which you either defend or attack completely free enterprise.

3. Make a chart of early inventors listing their names, the names of their inventions, and the purpose of the inventions.

For additional bibliographical information on the books cited in these projects, see the Basic Library (page xviii) and Further Reading on the opposite page.

INDIVIDUAL PROJECTS

1. Write an essay discussing the influence of such Enlightenment thinkers as John Locke and Jean Jacques Rousseau on the American Declaration of Independence. For your essay consult Eisen and Filler, *The Human Adventure,* Vol. 1, "The Inalienable Rights of Man" and "The Sovereignty of the People."

2. A wealth of human interest stories and dramatic accounts of the American Revolution can be found in *American Heritage.* Use one of the following articles as a basis for a short class report: "General Clinton's Dumbbell Code," April 1959; "We Shall Eat Apples of Paradise," June 1959; "Francisco, the Incredible," October 1959; "Captor of the Barefoot General," August 1960; "A Near Thing at Yorktown," October 1961; "Jack Jouett's Ride," December 1961; "Private Yankee Doodle," April 1962; "A Sword for George Rogers Clark," October 1962; "Pater Patriae as Pater Familias," April 1963; "The Last Days and Valiant Death of Nathan Hale," April 1964.

3. Write an essay on one of the following aspects of the French Revolution: (1) the causes and the start of the revolution, (2) the foreign reaction and the foreign threat to the French Revolution, (3) the Reign of Terror, (4) the changes in France caused by the revolution. Consult the unit bibliography for appropriate books.

4. Write a report on the causes, leaders, ideas, and results of the Latin American revolutions of the early 1800's. Discuss the extent of European and North American influence on Latin America at that time. Read one of the following books: Bailey, *Famous Latin American Liberators;* Baker, *He Wouldn't Be King;* Peck, *The Pageant of South American History.* Also consult Copeland and Lamm, *The World's Greatest Speeches,* "Simón Bolívar: Address at Angustora."

5. Write a paper on one of the aspects of the Industrial Revolution, such as the cotton industry or the factory system, and discuss its effects on society at that time. For your essay read Eisen and Filler, *The Human Adventure,* Vol. 2, "Child Labor in the Fac-

tories" and "The Liverpool-Manchester Railway"; Hughes and Fries, *European Civilization,* "Child Labor in an English Textile Factory," "Social Aspects of the English Industrial Revolution," and "On Conditions in the English Industrial Centers in 1848."

6. Karl Marx's ideas are still in the news. Consult the *Readers' Guide to Periodical Literature* for current magazine articles on Marx's relevance to the communist countries.

GROUP PROJECTS

1. Form a panel in which each student is to report to the class on one aspect of the Enlightenment — science, religion, or social thought. The students should point out the ways in which the Enlightenment was a break with the past, and its influence on today's world. Each panelist should read one or two chapters in Gay, *The Age of Enlightenment,* and be prepared, after having given a report on these chapters, to answer questions from the class.

2. Three students should conduct a " Who am I? " program, using quotations from John Locke, Voltaire, Baron de Montesquieu, Jean Jacques Rousseau, George III, Samuel Adams, Patrick Henry, Thomas Jefferson, George Washington, and Benjamin Franklin. The students should take turns reading the quotations to the class; after identification, the quote should be discussed briefly. Select your quotations carefully from such sources as Bartlett, *Familiar Quotations,* and Seldes, *The Great Quotations.*

3. Three students can prepare a series of oral reports on Napoleon I. Each student should read one of the books on Napoleon listed on the opposite page. The first report should deal with Napoleon's rise to power and his domestic reforms; the second with how he controlled and influenced Europe; and the third with Napoleon's defeat. At the end of these reports, the three students might, as a panel, answer class questions about the Napoleonic Era.

4. Prepare a debate on the following topic: Industrialization has made government control of economic life necessary.

5. A committee of students may prepare a bulletin-board display on the Industrial Revolution. Pictures should illustrate the new inventions, such as the steam engine, while cartoons could depict child labor and other problems created by the Industrial Revolution.

Further Reading

BIOGRAPHY

Anthony, H. D., *Sir Isaac Newton*. Macmillan.*

Bailey, Bernadine, *Famous Latin-American Liberators*. Dodd, Mead.

Baker, Nina B., *He Wouldn't Be King: The Story of Simón Bolívar*. Vanguard.

Berlin, Isaiah, *Karl Marx: His Life and Environment*. Oxford Univ. Press.*

Castelot, André, *Queen of France*. Harper & Row. A biography of Marie Antoinette.

Cunliffe, Marcus, *George Washington: Man and Monument*. New American Library.*

Ludwig, Emil, *Napoleon*. Pocket Books.*

Markham, F. M. H., *Napoleon and the Awakening of Europe*. Macmillan.*

Maurois, André, *Adrienne: The Life of the Marquise de Lafayette*. McGraw-Hill.

Oman, Carola, *Lord Nelson*. Verry.

Padover, Saul K., *Jefferson*. New American Library.*

Smart, C. A., *Viva Juarez!* Lippincott.

Thompson, J. M., *Leaders of the French Revolution*. Barnes & Noble.

——, *Robespierre and the French Revolution*. Macmillan.*

Warner, Oliver, *Nelson and the Age of Fighting Sail*. Harper & Row.

Wedgewood, C. V., *The Life of Cromwell*. Macmillan.

NONFICTION

Ashton, T. S., *The Industrial Revolution: 1760–1830*. Oxford Univ. Press.*

Esposito, V. J., and J. R. Elting, eds., *A Military History and Atlas of the Napoleonic Wars*. Praeger.

Gay, Peter, *The Age of Enlightenment*. Time-Life.

Gershoy, Leo, *The French Revolution, 1789–1799*. Holt, Rinehart and Winston.*

Hartman, Gertrude, *Machines and the Men Who Made the World of Industry*. Macmillan.

Herold, J. C., *The Horizon Book of the Age of Napoleon*. Harper & Row.

Horizon eds., *The French Revolution*. American Heritage.

Mantoux, P. J., *The Industrial Revolution in the Eighteenth Century*. Macmillan.

May, Arthur, *The Age of Metternich, 1814–1848*. Holt, Rinehart and Winston.*

Morgan, Edmund S., *The Birth of the Republic, 1763–1789*. Univ. of Chicago.

Morris, Richard B., *The Peacemakers: The Great Powers and American Independence*. Harper & Row. Peace of Paris of 1783.

Palmer, R. R., *Twelve Who Ruled*. Atheneum.* Reign of Terror.

Peck, Anne M., *The Pageant of South American History*. McKay.

Pope, Dudley, *Decision at Trafalgar*. Lippincott.

Robiquet, Jean, *Daily Life in France Under Napoleon*. Macmillan.

Spencer, Cornelia, *More Hands for Man*. Hale. Life in England during the Industrial Revolution.

Van Doren, Carl, *The Great Rehearsal*. Viking.* The American Constitution.

Webster, Charles, *The Congress of Vienna*. Barnes & Noble.

Williamson, Hugh R., *The Day They Killed the King*. Macmillan. Execution of Charles I.

Worcester, Donald E., *The Three Worlds of Latin America: Mexico, Central America, South America*. Dutton.

HISTORICAL FICTION

Carpentier, A., *Explosion in a Cathedral*. Little, Brown. Set in the Caribbean during the French Revolution.

Costain, Thomas B., *Ride with Me*. Pocket Books.* Napoleonic Wars.

Dickens, Charles, *David Copperfield*. Dell.*

——, *A Tale of Two Cities*. Dell.* French Revolution.

——, *Hard Times*. Bantam.*

Forester, C. S., *Lord Hornblower*. Little, Brown. Sea battles in the Napoleonic Era.

Hardy, Thomas, *The Trumpet Major*. St. Martin's.* England during expected Napoleonic invasion.

Hawes, Charles B., *The Dark Frigate*. Little, Brown. England in Cromwell's time.

Roberts, Kenneth, *Arundel*. Fawcett.* American expedition against Quebec in 1775.

——, *Rubble in Arms*. Fawcett.* American victory at Saratoga.

——, *Oliver Wiswell*. Fawcett.* Tory side of the American Revolution.

Sabatini, Rafael, *Scaramouche*. Bantam.* French Revolution.

Sprague, Rosemary, *Fife and Fandango*. Walck. Peninsular Campaign in Spain.

Tolstoy, Leo, *War and Peace*. Dell.*

Trease, Geoffrey, *Victory at Valmy*. Vanguard. French Revolution.

Uslar Pietri, A., *The Red Lances*. Knopf. Venezuela during war of independence.

* Paperback.

The London Gazette
Published by Authority.

From Saturday March 11, to Tuesday March 14, 1786.

AT the Court at St. James's, the 13th Day of March, 1786.
Whitehall, March 11, 1788.

UNIT

SIX

THE AGE OF

An election rally in the main square of Florence, Italy. In March of 1860 the people of Tuscany and several other regions of Italy voted overwhelmingly to join with Sardinia, the leading state in the struggle for Italian independence. The feeling for national unity was strong throughout much of Europe in the late 1800's and early 1900's.

460

UNIFICATION AND NATIONALISM

CHAPTER 22

France Underwent Many Upheavals During the 1800's

For centuries, beginning in the Middle Ages, European rulers had steadily increased their power and prestige. Royal families such as the Tudors, the Bourbons, the Hohenzollerns, and the Romanovs constantly worked to build, extend, and consolidate the nations they ruled. Eventually their powers became absolute and they could do very much as they pleased.

The power of kings was reinforced by religious authority. Since the days of Charlemagne, representatives of the Church had crowned monarchs and anointed them with holy oil. Wrote Shakespeare: "Not all the water in the rough rude sea can wash the balm from an anointed King." According to the theory of divine right, the king was actually God's representative on earth and was responsible only to God.

You have read how conditions began to change in the 1600's and 1700's. The rationalist spirit of the Enlightenment cast doubt on the superhuman qualities of kings. England restricted royal power and created a limited constitutional monarchy, with sovereignty in the hands of a representative parliament. The French went further, with a violent revolution that abolished the monarchy altogether. As Napoleon redrew the map of Europe, creating and destroying monarchies to suit himself, kings began to seem like any other men.

Many of the monarchs who were restored to

Armed Parisians during the revolt of 1830

their positions after the Congress of Vienna were met with uprisings and revolts that toppled them rudely off their thrones in a matter of months. An American diplomat in Britain in the 1840's wrote that "The world is growing weary of that most costly of all luxuries, hereditary kings."

One difficulty was that monarchs clung fiercely to the past and seemed unable to adjust to change. It was said of the Bourbons that they had learned nothing and forgotten nothing. At a time when the Industrial Revolution was overturning society, most kings continued to act as if they ruled simple agricultural communities. At a time when nationalism and liberalism were sweeping Europe, kings stubbornly refused to liberalize their governments. Said one French ruler: "I would rather hew wood than be a king under the conditions of the king of England." It could be said that the people of Europe needed leadership to help them cope with new and complex forces, and that royalty failed to provide it.

And yet, the idea of monarchy was not completely out of favor. Throughout the 1800's, many people continued to feel that it was the best kind of government. They thought that a monarch provided a continuous link with the history of a nation. They believed that it was wrong to set up completely new societies with no regard for the past. Such a view was expressed by a French conservative and monarchist, who wrote: "My country is everything, I am nothing. My king is her symbol, the nobles are her true knights, the Church is her guide and tutor. Let me then die for king and nobles and Church and country."

THE CHAPTER SECTIONS:

1. Revolutions upset France in 1830 and 1848 (1814–1848)
2. Louis Napoleon ruled the Second French Empire (1848–1869)
3. After defeat in war, France established the Third Republic (1869–1914)

1   Revolutions upset France in 1830 and 1848

Prince Metternich of Austria was able to suppress liberal movements for many years. He did not succeed everywhere, as you have learned. The Latin American colonies of Spain and Portugal won and kept their independence. In the Balkan Peninsula, Greece won independence from the Ottoman Empire, and the Serbs and Rumanians gained some self-government. However, these changes took place only on the fringes of Europe, or far distant from it. In the heart of the continent, Metternich was able to preserve his system through the 1820's.

The overthrow of Charles X

In 1814 the Bourbon family had been restored to the throne of France in the person of King Louis XVIII. Louis, who was glad to be king and did not want to upset things, retained many of the reforms established between 1789 and 1815. He retained the bank of France, the state-supported schools, and the Napoleonic Code. He accepted a constitution that limited his power.

This constitution set up a legislature to assist in governing the country, although only wealthy people could vote to elect its members.

When Louis XVIII died in 1824, he was succeeded by his brother, Charles X. Charles was an ardent believer in absolute monarchy. As soon as he became king, he pledged that *émigrés* whose estates had been seized and sold to the peasants would be repaid in full for their losses by the government. This was a very unpopular policy. It meant taxing all the people for the benefit of the emigrant nobles who had opposed any progress or democracy in France.

Charles abolished most of the liberal provisions of the weak constitution which his brother had accepted and tried to restore many features of the Old Regime. Such moves were certain to cause trouble in France. In the years since 1789, the nation had gone too far toward self-government and learned too much about throwing off autocratic rule to accept these changes peacefully. In July 1830 a revolt broke out and spread throughout the country. Charles X was forced to abdicate.

The French revolt of 1830, a major blow to the Metternich system, inspired revolutions elsewhere. Uprisings in Italy failed, but one in the former Austrian Netherlands succeeded.

The Congress of Vienna had given the Austrian Netherlands to the Dutch Netherlands. It was not a happy union, for the Dutch had little in common with the Belgians (the people of the Austrian Netherlands). The Dutch had their own language; the Belgians spoke Flemish or French. The Dutch were Calvinist Protestants; Belgians were Roman Catholics.

Two months after the French rebellion in 1830, Belgians in Brussels revolted against their Dutch rulers and proclaimed Belgian independence. Their attempt was successful for two reasons: (1) Both the British and the French approved Belgian independence and refused to intervene. (2) Austria and Russia, which might have intervened, were busy elsewhere. The Dutch resisted Belgian independence for several years, but in 1839 they gave in and signed a treaty recognizing Belgium as an independent monarchy under Leopold I (who had become king in 1831).

Louis Philippe, the "Citizen King"

The leaders of the French revolt of 1830 were sure that they wanted to be rid of Charles X, but could not agree on the kind of government they wanted after he was gone. Those who favored a republic were not strong enough to win. Finally a compromise was reached. All groups agreed on the choice of another king. He was Louis Philippe, Duke of Orléans, who belonged to a branch of the Bourbon family but had a record of liberal beliefs.

Louis Philippe was in a delicate position. He was a king, but an elected king. From the experience of Charles X, he knew that he could be deposed if he did not have the support of the majority of the French people. Therefore, he tried hard to please them and called himself the "Citizen King."

The group that benefited most during the reign of Louis Philippe was the upper middle class. After the revolt of 1830, the suffrage was broad-

ened so that it included the 200,000 wealthiest citizens. Many of these were newly rich manufacturers. Under Louis Philippe, workers were forbidden to organize, and labor unions were outlawed. High tariffs were placed on imported goods. The tariffs benefited the owners of industries because foreign-made goods were kept out of France, but the tariffs resulted in higher prices for domestic goods.

Louis Philippe's foreign policy also pleased the middle class. He began to build a new colonial empire, especially in North Africa. (You will read about this empire in Chapter 26.)

While the French middle class generally favored Louis Philippe, he faced opposition from other quarters. Two groups of monarchists opposed him. One group, the believers in legitimacy, thought that only the direct descendant of Charles X could be the rightful king. The other group, the Bonapartists, wanted to revive the empire of Napoleon, for by now the wars, miseries, and oppressions of the Napoleonic Era were forgotten. Napoleon had become a legend as the ruler who had made France glorious.

At the other extreme from the monarchists were the republicans. They believed that France should become a republic and grant political rights and make social changes to benefit all the people. Most French workers felt this way. They disliked Louis Philippe's antilabor measures and the high prices that resulted from his tariff policy.

Roman Catholics were also displeased with Louis Philippe. The higher clergy and many devout Catholics disliked the separation of Church and state. This policy, begun during the French Revolution and continued by Napoleon, was kept in force under Louis Philippe.

The revolutions of 1848

By 1848 there was widespread opposition to the regime of Louis Philippe, and great desire for change. Trouble began over a matter that was important because it involved the democratic principle of free speech. In February, opponents of the government organized meetings where they spoke out against official policy. Louis Philippe then issued a decree prohibiting the final meeting.

The publication of the decree led to riots in Paris. The disorders did not seem serious until the National Guard, summoned to restore order, joined the rioters. The disturbances grew until Louis Philippe was compelled to abdicate and flee to England.

The people of Paris set up a temporary government to restore order. Its members represented many points of view, but the majority of the members favored a republic; thus the Second French Republic was proclaimed in 1848. (The First Republic had lasted from 1792 until 1804, when Napoleon became emperor.) There was much disagreement, however, over what kind of republic the second one was to be.

The most vigorous and active group in the temporary government was the city working class, the proletariat. Many proletarian leaders believed in socialism. France at this time was suffering from an economic depression. There was much unemployment, especially among the proletariat. The socialist members of the temporary government urged the establishment of "national workshops" to give people work. It was the first appearance in modern times of the idea that the government has a responsibility to do something about unemployment.

The national workshops were supposed to be regular business enterprises where unemployed men could find useful and productive work. It was hard, however, to find useful jobs for the workshops to handle without competing with and injuring privately owned businesses. Therefore, the national workshop scheme turned into a charity instead of a sound business venture, and the work offered was often useless and degrading.

The Second Republic, employing universal manhood suffrage, held elections in April to choose a National Assembly that would write a constitution for a permanent government. They showed that the people of rural France were far more conservative than those of the cities. For one thing, the peasants had little interest in the national workshops and did not want to be taxed to support them. When the new National Assembly met in June, conservative members in the majority voted to stop the program of national workshops.

HISTORY THROUGH ART

"The Gleaners" by Millet

"This art offends me and disgusts me," said the French director of fine arts about the work of Jean-François Millet. Millet not only rejected the popular romanticized style of his day—the 1850's and 1860's—but also used peasants and workers as his subjects. Gleaners are the poorest peasants, who gather the leavings from a field after reaping; here they appear noble and dignified. That "The Gleaners" seems sentimental and idealized today is evidence of constantly changing tastes and values in art.

Violent rioting broke out in Paris. Fearing a widespread revolution, the Assembly allowed army officers to assume power. For three days Paris was a battlefield, but the army was too strong for the workers. The rebellion was crushed and its socialist leaders were imprisoned, exiled, or executed. (Among those who fled France at this time was Karl Marx.) The effort to assist unemployed workers in France had lasted less than six months.

The Second Republic and Louis Napoleon

In organizing the Second Republic, the National Assembly tried to steer a moderate course. To the workers it promised social reforms. To the liberals it guaranteed freedom of the press, reforms in the courts, and abolition of slavery in French colonies. To the Catholics it pledged

465

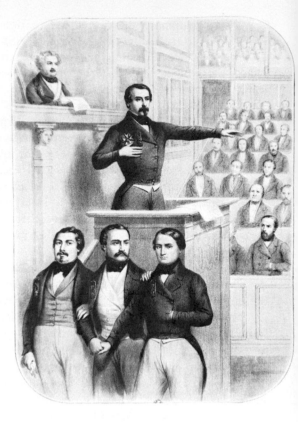

The Second Republic was born amid riots and discontent. In February 1848 a mob of Parisians invaded the royal palace and seized the king's throne, which they carried in triumph through the streets. Finally they set it on fire, above, in the square where the Bastille had once stood. Ten months later, in the Chamber of Deputies, Louis Napoleon took the oath of office as president, right.

greater cooperation with the Church. The peasants, who owned their own land and feared excessive taxes, were assured that private property would be respected.

The constitution provided for a republican form of government with a president, to be elected by all the people. He would serve for a four-year term and was not eligible for a second term. There was a single legislative body, consisting of representatives elected by universal manhood suffrage.

In December 1848, there was an election of officials for the new government. The man who was elected president was not one of the men who helped to create the Second Republic. Instead, by an overwhelming vote, the people chose as their leader Louis Napoleon Bonaparte, nephew of the first Napoleon.

Louis Napoleon had spent most of his early life in exile, because the restored Bourbons did not want any Bonapartes stirring up the people

of France. While in Italy, Louis Napoleon had belonged to a revolutionary society called the Carbonari. Twice he had returned to France to take part in unsuccessful *coups d'état*. After the second failure he was imprisoned but managed to escape to England. Throughout this period he worked tirelessly to spread the legend of the glory of his uncle, Napoleon Bonaparte.

Louis Napoleon did not return to France until after the uprising of 1848 had taken place. No one knew just what he stood for politically. Nevertheless, he got four times as many votes as the next candidate. Thus the first president of the Second French Republic was a man with an illustrious name whose real political opinions were unknown.

CHECKUP

1. Which class of people benefited most during the rule of Louis Philippe? What government policies favored them?

466

3. Which was the most active group in the temporary government of the Second Republic? How did they try to solve the problem of unemployment? What difficulties did they encounter?

4. What did the National Assembly of the Second Republic pledge to do for the various groups of France?

5. IDENTIFY: Charles X, Leopold I, the "Citizen King."

2 Louis Napoleon ruled the Second French Empire

It was soon clear that Louis Napoleon wanted to be more than a president. He began to work for the support of various groups in France. Like his uncle, he did everything he could to gain the backing of the army. To win support from French Catholics, he helped the pope by putting down an attempt by Italian patriots to set up a republic in Rome. He also repealed certain laws so that the Catholic Church could have more control of French education.

Louis Napoleon favored the middle class by encouraging the development of manufacturing. At the same time he tried to keep the favor of the workers by generous promises and by a program of public works that gave employment to many. To the peasants he spoke of his devotion to the principle of private property and of the prosperity he had brought them through better transportation and larger markets. A new bank provided funds for agricultural improvements.

In addition to all this, Louis Napoleon was able to pose as a champion of democratic rights. In 1851 the legislature passed a law that *disfranchised* many city workers—that is, deprived them of the right to vote. Louis Napoleon vetoed the bill and insisted that the legislature restore universal manhood suffrage. When he was refused, he dissolved the legislature and assumed autocratic powers. At the same time he issued a decree giving voting rights to all Frenchmen of legal age. Thus he was able to pose as a defender of the people. Meanwhile, however, he limited criticism of his actions by a strict censorship and by driving his critics out of France.

Establishing the empire

Louis Napoleon now employed the plebiscite, a device which his uncle had also used. The French people were asked to approve a plan whereby Louis Napoleon would be given power to draft a new constitution for the Second French Republic. Most people thought of him as their champion and believed that he was defending law and order. The vote was almost twelve to one in favor of his plan.

The new constitution retained Louis Napoleon as president and extended his term to ten years. A Council of State appointed by the president was given lawmaking powers. This meant that the president really controlled the legislature through his power of appointment. The long term of ten years gave him a chance to build up his power and popularity.

Under the new constitution, Louis Napoleon held real power, but he was still not satisfied. He wanted the outward show as well. He was determined to follow in the footsteps of his uncle, and Napoleon I had been an emperor.

In 1852 there was another plebiscite on still another constitution. By cleverly handling the votes, Louis Napoleon gained the consent of the French people to allow him to drop the title of president and take the title Emperor Napoleon III. (As with Louis XVIII, the omitted number kept up a pretense—in this case that the son of Napoleon I had been Napoleon II.)

As emperor of the Second French Empire, Louis Napoleon held unlimited power. He had won it partly because of his famous uncle. (Some men scornfully called the nephew "Napoleon the Little.") He had been elected president of the Second French Republic mainly because no one knew exactly what he stood for. By clever political juggling he had been able to abolish the constitution of the Second Republic and substitute another that made him emperor. He now had the title as well as the power to act, and people waited to see what he would do.

Napoleon III: "All things to all men"

Napoleon III was opposed by several groups. Monarchist believers in legitimacy thought of him as a pretender, not entitled to be a king. Republicans were unhappy because he had brought about the end of the Second Republic.

There were other groups that would join the opposition if their demands were not satisfied. French Catholics, middle-class businessmen, workers, and peasants—all expected him to live up to the promises he had made when he was seeking support as president. And since some of these groups wanted things that others opposed, it was clear that almost anything the emperor did would arouse opposition from some group.

In such a situation a ruler whose position is shaky has to make a decision. Should he try to please everyone, even though pleasing one group on a certain issue might antagonize another? Or should he select those groups that would make him strong enough to hold real power, favor them, and with their support overcome all opposition?

Napoleon III chose the first way. He continued to steer a middle course: he balanced favors given to one group with favors to another. His favors to the aristocracy were extended to the old Bourbon aristocracy as well as to the descendants of those who had supported Napoleon I. To win the Catholics he cooperated with the Church both at home and abroad. To win the middle class he encouraged the building of railroads and levied high tariffs to protect the new industries. Even though such tariffs increased the cost of living, Napoleon III was able to pose as the friend and supporter of labor. He continued his program of public works, building roads, canals, and harbors. He beautified Paris with magnificent public buildings, monuments, and wide, lovely boulevards. This program created many jobs and also satisfied the people's love of beauty and display. Because of his projects, Napoleon III was called by his admirers "the workingman's emperor."

On the surface the Second Empire looked like a democracy. There was a constitution and a legislative body elected by universal manhood suffrage. But in reality, France was under a new style of absolutism. The legislature could pass only those laws proposed by the emperor. The legislature had no power over spending. It could not question the emperor's ministers.

People suspected of opposing the government could be imprisoned or exiled without trial. Newspapers were strictly censored; a paper that criticized the emperor or his government was warned twice, then suppressed. There was no freedom of speech. Liberal professors in the universities were discharged. Organized opposition to the government of Louis Napoleon was almost impossible.

The Crimean War

In order to quiet discontent at home, Napoleon III tried to win glory abroad. At the beginning of his reign, the new French emperor's chief foreign problem involved Russia. Czar Nicholas I considered Louis Napoleon an upstart and was slow to recognize him as the real ruler of France. Napoleon's aim in foreign affairs was to win the cooperation of Great Britain in his opposition to Russia. His chance to do so came about through the weakening Ottoman Empire.

Called by many "The Sick Man of Europe," the once great Ottoman Empire fully justified that nickname. The government was weak, corrupt, and inefficient. The various Christian minorities under Turkish rule in the Balkans ° were unhappy and dissatisfied. Nationalism was strong among them, and they looked toward freedom and independence.

Because of earlier agreements, Russia claimed the right to protect all Orthodox Christians living under the rule of the Ottoman Turks; France was the protector of Roman Catholics. In the 1850's both Russia and France claimed jurisdiction over certain holy places in Palestine. Napoleon III took a firm stand against Russian demands and won an alliance with Great Britain, which feared Russian expansion toward the eastern Mediterranean.

The Ottoman Turks, backed by France and Great Britain, resisted Russian claims in the Palestine dispute. In 1853 the three allies went to

° **Balkans:** the countries of the Balkan Peninsula—today Rumania, Yugoslavia, Bulgaria, Albania, Greece, and that part of Turkey which lies in Europe. In the 1850's, most of this area, except for Greece, belonged to the Ottoman Empire.

The Crimean War was the first war to be covered by photographers and newspaper reporters. The notorious mismanagement was therefore chronicled and illustrated for all the world to see. In the early part of the war, lack of sanitary facilities for the care of the sick and wounded led to an alarming mortality rate. After repeated requests, Florence Nightingale was allowed to reorganize a military hospital, and frontline assistance was also made available. At right, a nurse aids a wounded soldier. The largest expeditionary force that had ever set out for war overseas—57,000 men—was assembled for the siege of Sebastopol. Below is the French and British camp before the city. Tactics and strategy for the siege were discussed in a council of war by representatives of Britain, Turkey, and France, bottom left. At bottom right are British cavalry officers.

war against Russia. War was not officially declared until March 1854, and full-scale fighting did not begin for another six months. It took place mostly in the Crimea, and the war is therefore known as the Crimean War.

The Crimean War has been called "the most unnecessary war in history." On both sides the hostilities were conducted with inefficiency and waste. The famous poem "The Charge of the Light Brigade," by the English poet Alfred Lord Tennyson, described one tragic event of the war, when a brigade of 600 horsemen, blindly following orders, charged across a valley and were cut to pieces by enemy fire. The most memorable military action was the eleven-month siege of the Russian naval base at Sevastopol in the southern Crimea. Almost the only constructive result of the war was the establishment of modern field hospitals and professional nursing of the wounded, the work of Florence Nightingale of England.

After two years of fighting, with huge losses on both sides from battle and disease, Russia was defeated. It had to give up its claim to protect the Christians in the Ottoman Empire. It was also forbidden to build up a navy in the Black Sea. The Ottoman Empire was to be "protected" as a member of the European family of nations.

As the nation which had most desired the Crimean War, France won glory but little else. Certainly none of the peace terms benefited France. In fact, supporting the Turks was bound to mean trouble in the future. In spite of all efforts to bolster the shaky Ottoman Empire, it was growing continually weaker. Russia, on the other hand, made a quick recovery from the war and was gradually gaining in strength.

Intervention in Mexico

Napoleon III now turned to the building of the French colonial empire. In North Africa he took advantage of a native revolt to strengthen French rule over Algeria. In 1859, French engineers began the construction of the Suez Canal. In the Far East, Napoleon established French control over Cambodia, thus beginning a move into Indo-China. But his most important effort was in the Western Hemisphere.

A military dictatorship in Mexico was overthrown in 1861 in a revolt led by Benito Juárez (HWAH-rays), who was then elected president. Juárez announced that his new government would not repay money which former Mexican governments had borrowed from European bankers. To force payment of the loans, Great Britain, Spain, and France sent troops to Mexico to take charge of the collection of customs (import taxes) so that the loans would be repaid. In a short time, Britain and Spain reached agreement with Juárez and withdrew their troops.

Napoleon III, however, saw an opportunity to set up a new colony, and kept the French troops in Mexico. In 1863, French forces overthrew the Juárez government. Napoleon III installed an emperor, the Archduke Maximilian, brother of the emperor of Austria.

The Mexicans hated Maximilian and he was kept in power only by French troops. The United States vigorously protested this violation of the Monroe Doctrine by France, but could do little more at the time, since it was fighting the Civil War. After the Civil War ended in 1865, however, the United States sent an army to the Mexican border and then asked Napoleon III when he would withdraw his troops.

The combination of the American warning and a possible war with Prussia caused Napoleon III to waver. His Mexican adventure collapsed entirely when French troops were defeated by Mexican forces under Juárez. Finally the French abandoned Maximilian, who was captured and executed by the Mexicans in 1867.

CHECKUP

1. By what steps did Louis Napoleon become emperor of France?
2. How did Napoleon III try to be "all things to all men"?
3. What were the chief causes of the Crimean War? the results?
4. Why did Napoleon's attempt to make a colony of Mexico fail?
5. IDENTIFY: "the workingman's emperor," "The Sick Man of Europe," Florence Nightingale, Juárez, Archduke Maximilian.

3 After defeat in war, France established the Third Republic

By 1869, Napoleon III faced extensive opposition in France. He was blamed for the ruinous venture in Mexico. He had meddled in Italian affairs (page 495), antagonizing not only the Italians but also republicans and Catholics in France. French liberals had not forgiven Napoleon for destroying the republic. Elections held in 1869 showed strong opposition by both conservatives and liberals.

The Franco-Prussian War

Napoleon III decided to try to regain the support of all groups in France by another bold and risky venture. Prussia at this time was working to unite all the German states under its leadership, as you will read in Chapter 23. By opposing this unification, Napoleon could gain the support of almost all Frenchmen because Prussia was universally disliked in France.

This scheme was risky, however, and might lead to war. In such an event, France could not count on any outside help because the emperor's foreign policy had antagonized most of Europe. To make matters worse, the man virtually at the head of the Prussian government and directing its foreign policy was Otto von Bismarck, one of the shrewdest diplomats and most outstanding statesmen in Europe. Bismarck considered Napoleon III "the greatest unrecognized mediocrity in Europe" (meaning that nobody realized how weak and unimportant he was), and knew that the French emperor was no match for him.

While Napoleon hoped that Prussia would back down and war would not be necessary, Bismarck had decided that war with France was necessary to achieve German unification. When two nations reach such a point, only a slight excuse for war is needed. It came soon from an unexpected part of Europe.

A revolution in Spain had driven out the reigning Queen, Isabella II, and the Spanish were looking for a new ruler. In 1870 they offered the throne to a German, Prince Leopold, cousin of the king of Prussia. Leopold was not impressed and refused the offer. But Bismarck persuaded the Spanish to renew the offer and Leopold to accept it.

Napoleon III took a strong stand against this development. If Leopold accepted the invitation, Prussia and Spain would be ruled by the same family, the Hohenzollerns (just as they had both been ruled by Hapsburgs in the time of Emperor Charles V). Urged on by members of his court, Louis Napoleon dispatched strong notes to Prussia and Spain, asking that Leopold again turn down the offer.

Leopold did withdraw, and the French emperor won an easy diplomatic victory. But he decided to gamble on a further move, intended to discredit the Prussian royal family thoroughly. He insisted that King William I of Prussia pledge publicly that no member of the Hohenzollern family would ever be a candidate for the Spanish throne.

The Ems dispatch. The French ambassador delivered the French demand to King William at a resort known as Ems. The king's reply was somewhat vague and indefinite. The ambassador, not satisfied, asked for another meeting to discuss the matter. The Prussian king replied that since he was returning to Berlin, he would be unable to see the ambassador again at Ems.

Bismarck received a dispatch from the king at Ems summarizing his meeting with the French ambassador. Bismarck decided to use it to trick Napoleon III into declaring war on Prussia. He altered it slightly and made it sound as though the king had dismissed the ambassador offensively and with contempt. Then Bismarck released the so-called Ems dispatch to the public through the newspapers.

The Ems dispatch became public on July 14, Bastille Day, the great French national holiday when patriotic feeling was at its highest. The French people were outraged. Napoleon III had been willing to go to the brink of war, but he had not really wanted it. Now he was helpless to prevent it. On July 19, 1870, the French legislature declared war on Prussia by an overwhelming vote of 246 to 10.

French defeat. The French army showed appalling inefficiency and confusion from the very start of the Franco-Prussian War, as it is called. There were disastrous French defeats. Although ill at the time, Napoleon III went to the front in the province of Alsace to take command of the army. At the battle of Sedan, with a force of 80,000 men, he fell into the enemy's hands. The nephew of Napoleon I became a common prisoner of war.

Immediately after the capture of Napoleon III, the Legislative Assembly proclaimed the fall of the Second French Empire and the establishment of a Third Republic. The new government tried to defend the nation but was cut off when Paris was besieged by the Prussians. A republican leader, Léon Gambetta, escaped from Paris in a balloon, but he was able to do little to rally the rest of the country. Paris finally fell in January 1871, and the war was over.

France under German domination

In the Treaty of Frankfort, Bismarck dictated harsh terms to the defeated country. France had to give up its claims to Alsace and the eastern part of Lorraine. It also had to pay an indemnity of 5 billion francs (about 1 billion dollars) within three years; German troops were to occupy northern France until the indemnity was paid. Bismarck thought that France would not be able to pay the indemnity for many years, if ever, and thus that German forces would control France indefinitely.

Bismarck permitted the election of a National Assembly in February 1871 to decide whether France wanted to resume the war, or on what terms the country was willing to sign a peace treaty. During the election campaign the republicans urged renewal of the war. The monarchists took the position that France was already defeated and should negotiate with the conquerors. About 70 percent of the elected delegates were monarchists—not because the French people were overwhelmingly monarchist but because they overwhelmingly wanted peace.

As in the days of the revolutions of 1848, the people of Paris were strongly republican. They had fought almost alone to defend the city against the Prussians and were angered by the terms of the peace treaty, which had not yet been approved by the National Assembly. They knew that the majority of its members were monarchists who did not favor a republic.

In March the socialists and radical republicans of Paris, supported by the National Guard, set up a municipal council to govern the city. It was called the Commune, like the Paris government established in 1792 during the French Revolution. The Communards, as members of the Commune were called, proposed a program to socialize France: decentralization of the government, separation of church and state, and replacement of the regular army by a national guard. Wide discontent among the Communards led them to stage a violent and revolutionary uprising in Paris. Troops sent by the National Assembly entered Paris and fought several bitter and bloody battles with the Communards. Finally, in May, the forces of the Commune were defeated and its leaders were executed, imprisoned, or exiled. That same month the National Assembly approved the Treaty of Frankfort.

The monarchists had a large majority in the National Assembly, but they were themselves divided into three groups. One favored giving the throne to the grandson of Charles X (a Bourbon). A second group, about equal in number, wanted the grandson of Louis Philippe (of the House of Orléans). A third group, the Bonapartists, much smaller than the others, wanted to restore Napoleon III.

While the monarchists argued, the republicans gained seats in the National Assembly and were able to rule the nation as a conservative republic. One thing all of the members were agreed upon: the indemnity imposed by Germany should be paid as soon as possible. The government was able to borrow money to pay the sum that Bismarck had thought to be a crushing burden, and German soldiers left France in September 1873.

Crisis and uncertainty

Although the Third Republic of France was set up in 1870, after the fall of Napoleon III, the quarreling factions were unable to agree on a con-

"The Shop Window" by Eugène Atget

Photography was developed in the 1800's (see page 631), and much pioneering work was done by the French. For many years, photography was regarded as a clever device—a "mirror with a memory"—for depicting people and places. (As you have read, the earliest documentary photographic reporting dates from the Crimean War.) Gradually, however, it came to be recognized as an art in itself.

An outstanding artist with the camera was Eugène Atget of France. In the early 1900's, he determined to photograph everything in and around Paris that he felt was artistic or picturesque. In "The Shop Window," with its reflection of buildings and a tree, every detail stands out with amazing clarity. This photograph beautifully illustrates the power of the camera to evoke a moment of vanished time.

stitution until 1875. Finally the assembly passed a group of laws known as the Constitution of 1875, which made France officially a republic. It was, as one French statesman said, "the form of government which divided France the least."

The president, who could not be a member of the legislature, was to be elected by it for a term of seven years. His ministers, who formed the cabinet, had to approve his actions and were responsible for government policy. The constitution did not specifically provide for a premier, or prime minister, but the position soon became established. The Senate was to be elected by an indirect system, while members of the Chamber of Deputies were to be elected by universal manhood suffrage. Although Paris was the capital of France, the legislators were afraid of the Paris mobs; therefore they settled on Versailles as their meeting place.

During the 1880's, France faced many problems, most of which were created by groups represented in the legislature. One group wanted to make war on Germany in revenge for the Franco-Prussian War of 1870. Another group was hostile to the Catholics. Still another backed French expansion overseas, along the lines begun by Napoleon III. The conservative republicans managed to steer a course that avoided extremes; legislation encouraged education and legalized trade unions. But the nation was not stable financially, and many people were out of work.

In the 1890's the nation was rocked by a financial scandal as a result of the failure of the Panama Company, which had been formed to build a canal across Panama. Ferdinand de Lesseps, the man who was responsible for the building of the Suez Canal, had been its president, and

(continued on page 476)

Paris Besieged and Liberated

Beautified by Napoleon III, Paris basks in the sunlight, below. This painting by Claude Monet captures the spacious beauty for which the "City of Light" is noted. In the background rises the dome of the Pantheon, burial place of French heroes. When the Franco-Prussian War came, Paris was besieged for four months, maintaining contact with the rest of Europe by balloon and carrier pigeon. At right is the aircraft in which Gambetta escaped in his futile attempt to rally the countryside to the city's aid.

Defeat was a humiliating experience for the French. In the drawing at left, Honoré Daumier—a political satirist and an ardent republican—shows France as a woman weeping over her dead on a battlefield that seems to stretch into eternity. After 1871 a liberated Paris soon returned to its pleasure-loving ways. In the joyous work by Pierre Renoir at far right, a lighthearted couple dances in an outdoor cafe.

thousands of Frenchmen had invested in it. Its failure was due to dishonesty and mismanagement, but the government was endangered because of accusations of bribery made against a number of legislators.

Still another threat to the republic came from extremists of the labor movement. There were clashes between workers and troops. *Anarchists,* who believed in the abolition of all governments by force, set off bombs and attempted to assassinate public figures, including the president.

The Dreyfus case. The most serious danger to the Third Republic began in 1894 and lasted into the next century. An attempt to betray French military secrets to Germany was uncovered. A Jewish officer, Captain Alfred Dreyfus, was accused, convicted, and sentenced to life imprisonment in the French penal colony on Devil's Island, off the coast of South America. Evidence soon came to light which indicated that Dreyfus had been falsely convicted. But the French army would permit no criticism of its actions, and it was supported by monarchists, many Catholics, and anti-Semites (people who dislike Jews).

Although the real traitor was discovered, he was cleared by the army. Émile Zola, a famous French novelist, wrote an open letter, *"J'Accuse"* ("I Accuse"), in which he placed the blame for this national scandal on the army and its supporters. He was tried but fled to England. Even though many of the men responsible for the false charges against Dreyfus confessed, it was not until 1906 that his name was cleared.

The Dreyfus case was important because it led to a clash between the two major groups in France —the right, composed of those who had condemned Dreyfus and supported the army, and the left, which championed his cause.

Continuing difficulties

After the Dreyfus case, French republicans planned several reforms. Steps were taken to end the favored position of the Roman Catholic Church in France, a situation that had been established under Napoleon I in 1801. In 1905, Church and state were officially separated; France was to have complete religious freedom.

France was disturbed internally by strikes and labor troubles in the early 1900's. There were also crises in Morocco, which brought France and Germany into disagreement. But Great Britain and France, long enemies, had come closer together and in 1904 had signed an alliance. It settled many of their disputes and united them as allies against Germany and Austria.

You have seen that the government of the Third French Republic was often in danger of collapsing. One reason for this instability was the large number of political parties, usually from ten to fifteen. They ranged from the monarchists on the far right to radical socialists on the far left. There were also a number of "splinter groups," smaller divisions within the important parties. No one party ever had complete control of the French government. It was necessary for parties to unite temporarily, or form coalitions, in order to get anything accomplished. When a coalition collapsed, a new effort would have to be made to establish a majority.

The Chamber of Deputies could not be dissolved by the premier when he was defeated in a vote, but only by the president with the consent of the Senate. In practice this was rarely done, so that deputies could vote to overturn the premier and his ministry without having to campaign for re-election themselves. This they did with little apparent hesitation.

CHECKUP

1. How did Napoleon III hope to regain the support of all his opponents in France? How did the throne of Spain play a part in his plans?

2. Give the terms of the treaty that ended the Franco-Prussian War. Why did Bismarck believe German forces would control France indefinitely? How long did German control last?

3. Why did France not remain a monarchy after the defeat of 1871?

4. What problems did France face in the late 1800's and early 1900's? What were the governmental weaknesses of the Third French Republic?

5. IDENTIFY: Prince Leopold, Ems dispatch, Communards, anarchists, Dreyfus, splinter groups, coalitions.

CHAPTER REVIEW

Chapter 22 France Underwent Many Upheavals During the 1800's (1814–1914)

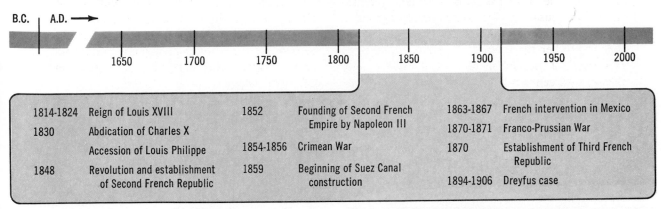

1814-1824	Reign of Louis XVIII	1852	Founding of Second French Empire by Napoleon III	1863-1867	French intervention in Mexico
1830	Abdication of Charles X			1870-1871	Franco-Prussian War
	Accession of Louis Philippe	1854-1856	Crimean War	1870	Establishment of Third French Republic
1848	Revolution and establishment of Second French Republic	1859	Beginning of Suez Canal construction	1894-1906	Dreyfus case

CHAPTER SUMMARY

Louis XVIII, who became king of France after the overthrow of Napoleon, accepted moderate reforms. But his successor, Charles X, tried to restore the Old Regime, and the French revolted, forcing him to abdicate. Soon afterward, the Belgians also rebelled and succeeded in establishing their independence from the Netherlands.

The reign of Louis Philippe, chosen king after Charles X, benefited the upper middle class but aroused opposition from other forces, and he, too, was forced to abdicate. Parisians set up a temporary government, proclaimed the Second French Republic, and created national workshops. A conservative National Assembly abolished the workshops and crushed the ensuing Parisian uprisings.

French voters chose as president Louis Napoleon Bonaparte. By cleverly winning the support of many different factions, he soon became Emperor Napoleon III, creating the Second French Empire. Still posing as a defender of the people, Napoleon III turned the government into an autocracy and suppressed opposition.

Louis Napoleon involved France in dubious foreign ventures. The country gained little in the Crimean War. In Mexico, efforts to rule through a puppet emperor, Maximilian, failed because of Mexican and American opposition. Most disastrous was the Franco-Prussian War, into which Bismarck maneuvered Napoleon III. The French were defeated, Napoleon was captured, and the Second Empire was abolished.

The Third French Republic had a shaky beginning, with the rising of the Paris Commune, suppressed by the army. Other problems included a scandal involving the Panama Canal Company, the Dreyfus case, labor disputes, and political instability.

QUESTIONS FOR DISCUSSION

1. Under Louis Philippe, a group that benefited greatly were the capitalists, who generally favored a laissez-faire economic policy. Were high tariffs on imported goods consistent with this policy? Explain why or why not.

2. At what point in French history did the idea appear that government has a responsibility to do something about unemployment? Do you agree that governments today have this duty? Justify your position pro or con.

3. Louis Napoleon gave all Frenchmen of legal age the right to vote. However, in view of his strict censorship and persecution of his critics, how meaningful was the right to vote in France? Besides voting, what is at least one other factor that is absolutely necessary to maintain a democratic system of government?

4. Why did the large number of political parties in the Third French Republic frequently threaten its existence? What advantages are there to a two-party system, as exists in the United States, over a multi-party system?

PROJECTS

1. It was said of the Bourbons that they had learned nothing and forgotten nothing. Write a short essay indicating the new forces in the world that the Bourbons ignored.

2. Write a campaign speech of Napoleon III in which he appeals to several different groups of French voters.

3. Draw a cartoon illustrating the phrase "Napoleon the Little."

4. Draw a poster calling Frenchmen to arms against the Prussian enemy during the Franco-Prussian War.

CHAPTER 23

Germany Became a United and Powerful Nation

On February 2, 962, Otto I was crowned emperor of the Holy Roman Empire. On August 6, 1806, Francis II, prodded by Napoleon, dissolved the empire and resigned the imperial title. Eight and a half centuries had not been enough time to create a strong, unified state for the German people.

Why the German people were unable in this long time to form an enduring union is a great historical mystery. The Germans had a common language, kingship, and history. Vigorous, intelligent rulers like Otto I, Henry IV, Frederick Barbarossa, and Frederick II were several times on the verge of achieving strong central government, but all of them eventually failed. The imperial decree of 1356, which put the election of the emperor into the hands of seven electors, recognized the decentralization of the government. The Treaty of Westphalia in 1648, by granting German rulers independence from the Holy Roman Empire, made German decentralization part of international law.

The result was an empire with a fantastic number of political divisions. In 1648 the total was estimated at 1,800! Many of these divisions were tiny territories, ruled by knights, and might contain no more than 300 people. Some were free cities, such as Hamburg and Bremen. There were many other regions controlled by hereditary dukes or princes whose families had ruled since the early

The coronation of William I as king of Prussia

Middle Ages. Some of these were quite small; the Principality of Waldeck, for example, had a total area of 433 square miles and was only about 20 miles wide. At the opposite extreme were the vast territories of the Hohenzollerns and such large states as Hanover, Saxony, Bavaria, and Württemberg.

Almost every one of these German states insisted on maintaining its own laws, coinage, army, and tariffs. Elaborate palaces were built to imitate the splendors of Versailles. The sovereign, no matter how petty, was an absolute ruler. His chief aim—often his only aim—was to preserve his realm exactly as it had always been.

Most German rulers taxed their subjects heavily. Another way they could make money was to offer their troops as mercenary soldiers to other nations. You will remember that Great Britain needed additional forces to fight the American Revolution. The ruler of Hesse-Cassel did a brisk business supplying them. But of the 19,400 Hessian soldiers he "exported," 7,500 lost their lives in a distant land, fighting a war probably few of them understood.

The famous German poet Johann Wolfgang von Goethe (GUHR·tuh) noted that in his birthplace of Frankfort, there stood a Roman Hall that contained portraits of all the Holy Roman Emperors. In the late 1700's, the townspeople began to worry because space was running out. When Francis II became emperor in 1792, his portrait occupied the last empty place. As it turned out, Napoleon solved Frankfort's problem neatly by putting an end to the Holy Roman Empire during the reign of Francis.

Not all of Germany's problems could be solved so easily. But after the time of Napoleon, the long delayed process of centralization and consolidation went forward with great speed. In the 1870's, a united and powerful Germany took its place in the European family of nations.

THE CHAPTER SECTIONS:

1. Prussia became the leading state in the German Confederation (1786–1863)

2. Out of three wars, Prussia created a united German Empire (1863–1871)

3. Industrialization and socialism created problems for Germany (1871–1914)

1   Prussia became the leading state in the German Confederation

You have read how Prussia was built up into a strong and prosperous state during the 1700's as a result of efficient rule by Frederick William I and his son Frederick the Great. The reigns of these men extended from 1713 to 1786. They were followed by two weak rulers, who allowed most of Prussia's power to be lost.

The Napoleonic Era

Frederick William II, king from 1786 to 1797, helped to form the First Coalition of Prussia, Austria, Great Britain, Spain, the Dutch Netherlands, and the kingdom of Sardinia against the revolutionary government of France. Prussia was defeated in 1795 and had to give up all of its claims to territories west of the Rhine River.

Ten years later, Frederick William III, king until 1840, allowed himself to be drawn into the Third Coalition against Napoleon. Prussian armies were disastrously defeated, and the peace that followed almost wiped Prussia out of existence.

Napoleon dominated Prussia from 1806 until 1812. In addition to seizing Prussian lands and forming new states from them—which he gave to his relatives and allies—he imposed restrictions on Prussia. The Prussian army was limited in size. The country had to pay a large indemnity, support an army of occupation within its territory, and contribute soldiers to the French armies.

These restrictions actually helped Prussia by stimulating patriotic demands for national revival. Prussians wanted to get rid of the French and to regain the greatness and power they had enjoyed under Frederick the Great. They demanded reforms that would rebuild the nation. These demands resulted in the abolition of serfdom and the removal of medieval class distinctions that still prevailed. The government improved education and the system of levying and collecting taxes.

The strength of Prussia had long rested on its army, which the French had now restricted in size. But the Prussians found a clever way to get around the restrictions. All able-bodied men were drafted and required to serve short army terms. During this time they received intensive military training. They were then placed in the reserves, and a new group of men was drafted into the regular army. Thus there were trained men who were not really part of the army but who could be called into active service when needed. Technically Prussia observed the limits placed on its standing army by the French, and at the same time kept available a large force of trained men.

Napoleon's territorial changes in Germany also worked in Prussia's favor. Austria had been Prussia's strongest rival. An Austrian Hapsburg had held the position of Holy Roman Emperor since the 1400's, thus giving Austria a vague claim over the German states. Now that the Holy Roman Empire was abolished and Napoleon had reorganized and consolidated many German states into the Confederation of the Rhine, Prussia found it easier to influence them.

In addition, Napoleon's rule stimulated nationalism in the German states as it had throughout Europe. Some of Germany's greatest thinkers and writers were active during the period of the French Revolution and Napoleon. Frederick the Great himself had despised the German language and usually wrote and spoke French. Now Germans were beginning to appreciate their language, their past, and their traditions.

German nationalism favored Prussia more than Austria. The population of Prussia was mostly German. In Austria, although the Germans ruled, they were a minority. There were many other nationalities, including Hungarians, Rumanians, Italians, and Slavs. Most of them wanted independence from Austria so that they could establish their own national governments.

The revived Prussian state, with its reborn army, was strong enough to play a major part

in the final struggle against Napoleon. Prussian armies fought in the "Battle of the Nations" and at Waterloo, and Prussia earned the right to be one of the four great powers represented at the Congress of Vienna and to be a member of the Quadruple Alliance.

In 1815 the Congress of Vienna, as you read earlier, turned Napoleon's Confederation of the Rhine into the German Confederation, with additional members that included Prussia. The Congress gave Prussia much important territory, including two thirds of Saxony and an area along the lower Rhine River. Prussian lands now stretched almost unbroken from Russia to the Rhine and beyond (see map, page 427). The government was well organized and efficient, with a strong economy. The population included some Poles and other Slavs, but the overwhelming majority of the people were of Germanic origin.

German unity

Some Germans realized that, at a time when other European nations were large and powerful, disunity kept the German states weak. German writers and thinkers looked back to the days of great German heroes, such as Frederick Barbarossa, and thought that a united Germany would restore the grandeur and power of ancient times. Many university professors supported this movement. Students formed societies to work for German unity. Some of the believers in German unification wanted a constitutional monarchy. Others favored a republic.

Opposition to German unity came from several sources. You will remember that Metternich wanted to keep the German states disunited so that Austria could maintain its influence over them. Austria preferred to retain the German Confederation as a loose union under Austrian leadership. France also wanted to keep Germany weak and divided. The royal families and nobility of the German states did not want to lose their social position and privileges, nor did government workers want to lose their jobs. The religious division of Germany was a major problem, too. Prussia and northern Germany were Protestant; the south German states were Catholic.

"Two Men Looking at the Moon"

Many artists were filled with the nationalistic spirit that flooded Europe during and after the Napoleonic Era. Caspar David Friedrich, who painted the work at right, was a patriotic German. He admired German art of the Middle Ages and deliberately included in his paintings some of its common motifs. Among these were gnarled and twisted trees, like the one here. This brooding nighttime scene, with its air of melancholy, is typical of the Romantic Movement (see page 650). Romanticism emphasized the past and thus was especially appealing to Germans, who, in the early 1800's, were taking a new interest in their national traditions and customs.

The Zollverein

The first step toward German unity came in the economic field. The movement of goods from one German state to another was greatly hindered by the tariffs that each state charged on goods coming in from the outside. There were even tariffs on goods shipped from one Prussian possession to another. The tariffs, of course, increased the prices of goods and reduced the amount that was sold.

The drive for freer movement of goods was begun by the aristocratic landowners, or Junkers (YOONG·kurs), of Prussia, who wanted to sell their farm products more widely. In 1818 they persuaded the king of Prussia to abolish all tariffs within his territories. Beginning the next year, Prussia made treaties with other German states, thus setting up a customs union called the Zollverein. By 1844 it included almost all the German states except Austria.

The Zollverein benefited its members by making prices lower and more uniform. It encouraged the spread of the Industrial Revolution in Germany by providing a wide, free market for goods produced within the German states and by offering tariff protection against foreign competition. Both production and consumption increased. Uniform systems of weights, measures, and currency were adopted. Businessmen became strong advocates of German unification.

The establishment of the Zollverein had no immediate political effects, and the various states of the German Confederation continued to act independently of each other. However, by making their economies dependent on each other, it furnished a sound basis for later political union. Prussia, as the leader of the movement for a customs union and as the strongest industrial state, increasingly became the economic and political leader. Austria, which was not a member of the Zollverein, was increasingly considered to be outside "the real Germany."

The revolutions of 1848 had only limited success in the German states. In Berlin, below, mobs overcame guards at the palace of the Prussian king, who then granted concessions. Soon afterward the Frankfort Assembly began its meetings, one of which is depicted at right. The Assembly's work came to nothing. Disheartened liberals fared little better under Bismarck, above, whose autocratic policies again drove them underground.

The revolutions of 1848

In the years after the Congress of Vienna, there were strong nationalistic and democratic movements within the states of the German Confederation. You will recall that Metternich, with his Carlsbad Decrees of 1819, was successful in thwarting a liberal, democratic movement among German university professors and students. Driven underground by the decrees, these groups continued to work in secret for limited constitutional monarchies with democratic rights.

In the revolutionary year of 1848, the uprisings in France touched off political agitation in much of Germany. Everywhere there were demands for constitutions establishing representative, democratic governments. In general, German rulers agreed to these demands, and there was little bloodshed except for a disturbance in Berlin. After several revolutionists had been killed there, King Frederick William IV was humiliated by being made to wear the colors of German liberalism (black, red, and gold) and to honor the men who had been slain.

Elections were held in most of the German states for representatives to a National Assembly which would meet at Frankfort to try to unify Germany. The Frankfort Assembly met for a year, beginning in May 1848. Almost all of its members were professional men, with a high proportion of lawyers and judges. The representatives spent a great deal of time discussing and arguing, but finally wrote a constitution setting up a national parliament under an emperor. They elected Frederick William IV to the position.

The Prussian king, however, turned down the Assembly's offer and, by political maneuvering, managed to destroy almost all of its work. He did grant his own people a constitution, but it did not limit his power very much. By 1850 the situation was much as it had been before the revolutions of 1848.

Bismarck and Prussian strength

William I became king of Prussia in 1861. He immediately had trouble with the Prussian parliament, which had been controlled by a liberal majority for several years. In 1862, William called upon Otto von Bismarck, a conservative Junker statesman, to direct the political course of Prussia as minister president (prime minister) of the cabinet. Bismarck accepted.

Bismarck was antidemocratic and opposed the idea of a parliament. He believed strongly that Prussia was predestined to lead the German people to unity. He was willing to help this destiny come about by using trickery, bribery, or military force. A monarchist, he served William I to the best of his great abilities. Bismarck was intelligent and well educated. Unlike many Junkers, he kept informed about conditions in other countries. He studied foreign developments carefully and was able to put his knowledge to good use.

Bismarck had great contempt for idealists, whom he regarded as mere talkers, not men of action. He once said of German policy that it could not be carried out by "speeches, shooting-matches, and songs, but only through blood and iron."

For years, Bismarck was virtually the ruler of Prussia and had the thorough cooperation of the king and the two generals in charge of the army, Count Helmuth von Moltke and Count Albrecht von Roon. They agreed that it was necessary to reorganize the Prussian army and strengthen it even more. First, however, an increase in taxes was needed.

The Prussian parliament refused to appropriate the money for a military expansion program. Bismarck simply dismissed the parliament and collected the taxes without parliamentary authorization, paying no attention to the protests of the liberals. His plan was to stop the criticism with military victories.

Bismarck, Von Moltke, and Von Roon proceeded to make the Prussian army a great war machine. The old, slow muzzleloading guns were replaced by breechloading rifles that fired faster and more accurately. Everything possible was done to make the military force operate like an efficient machine. Military strategists tried to plan for every possible situation the Prussian army might encounter in the field so that it could counteract and overcome whatever tactics or maneuvers the enemy tried. For example, if a bridge were blown up to delay Prussian forces, Prussian engineers would be ready with the parts of a bridge to fit that exact spot. Military planning on such a detailed scale had seldom been attempted before.

CHECKUP

1. How did events of the Napoleonic Era tend to work for the benefit of Prussia?

2. What groups of people favored German unity? What forces opposed it?

3. "... by making their economies dependent on each other, it [the Zollverein] furnished a sound basis for later political union." Explain the meaning of this statement.

4. In the movement to unify Germany, what were the differences in ideas and methods between the liberals and Bismarck?

5. IDENTIFY: Junkers, Frankfort Assembly.

 ## Out of three wars, Prussia created a united German Empire

Bismarck had to overcome two major obstacles to increase the power and size of Prussia. First, he had to drive Austria out of its position of leadership in the German Confederation. Second, he had to overcome Austria's influence over the south German states, which he considered the major opponents to Prussian leadership. Bismarck went at these objectives carefully. Instead of attacking Austria directly, he chose a roundabout way.

The Danish War

On the border between Denmark and Germany lay two small states, the duchies of Schleswig and Holstein (see map, page 486). The population of Holstein, which had been part of the German Confederation since 1815, was entirely German. Schleswig's population was a mixture of Germans and Danes. The duchies were ruled by the Danish king under a constitution which provided that they were separate from Denmark. In 1863, King Christian IX came to the Danish throne. At the insistence of many Danes, he proclaimed a new constitution that tried to annex Schleswig to Denmark.

Both Prussia and Austria protested against the new Danish constitution. Acting together, they demanded that it be revoked. When Denmark refused, Prussia and Austria declared war against Denmark. Denmark had hoped for help from France and Great Britain, but neither acted. In 1864, after three months of fighting, the small country went down to defeat.

The peace treaty gave the two duchies to Prussia and Austria jointly. Austria demanded that the two duchies form a single state within the German Confederation. Prussia opposed this settlement. After bitter wrangling, it was decided that Prussia should administer Schleswig, and Austria should administer Holstein.

The Seven Weeks' War

Now Bismarck moved to drive Austria out of the German Confederation. He prepared the way by a series of skillful diplomatic actions. First, he persuaded Napoleon III of France to remain neutral if war developed between Prussia and Austria. In return for French neutrality, France demanded certain territory held by the south German states. Bismarck persuaded Napoleon to put these demands in writing. On the other hand, Bismarck's promises to Napoleon were oral, not written, and were very vague.

Bismarck's next step was to form an alliance with the new nation of Italy (which you will read about in the next chapter). In return for fighting against Austria, Italy was to receive the Austrian territory of Venetia. Then, by various complicated moves, Bismarck provoked Austria into declaring war on Prussia in 1866.

Austria had as allies several German states, including Bavaria, Saxony, and Hanover. But it had not counted on the superb training and preparation of the Prussian army. In fact, Prussia's conduct of the war came as a surprise to the whole world. Prussian forces moved by train

When Prussian troops entered the largest city of Holstein after the Danish War, they received an enthusiastic welcome. The citizens flew Prussian flags and gathered to cheer.

wherever railroad tracks were available, and used the telegraph to keep in communication. Prussian initiative led to victory over Austria in only seven weeks.

The Treaty of Prague ended the so-called Seven Weeks' War in the summer of 1866. Austria approved the dissolution of the German Confederation and surrendered its rule of Holstein to Prussia. The Italians gained Venetia.

Many Prussians wanted Bismarck to crush Austria completely and seize the south German states, which had fought on the side of Austria.

However, Bismarck was a shrewd diplomat. He wanted Austria out of the German Confederation, but not as a permanent enemy. And he wanted the south German states to join Prussia willingly, not by force. There were no seizures of territory and no indemnities. Considering the completeness of the Prussian victory, the Treaty of Prague provided a lenient peace. This, too, was part of Bismarck's plan.

In north Germany the situation was different. Here Prussia had everything to gain and nothing to lose. The duchies of Schleswig and Holstein,

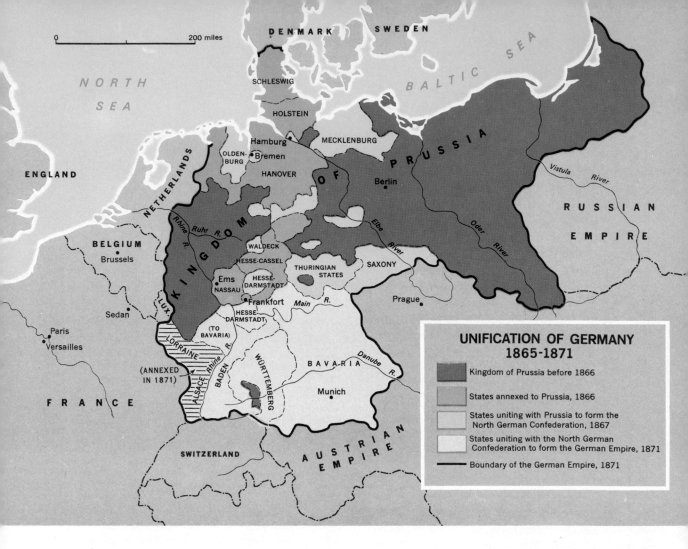

UNIFICATION OF GERMANY
1865-1871

Kingdom of Prussia before 1866

States annexed to Prussia, 1866

States uniting with Prussia to form the
North German Confederation, 1867

States uniting with the North German
Confederation to form the German Empire, 1871

Boundary of the German Empire, 1871

the states of Hanover, Hesse-Cassel, and Nassau, and the free city of Frankfort were all added to Prussia. Now Prussia included a large part of the land and population of Germany (see map, this page). The remaining states north of the Main River were allowed for a time to remain independent; but in 1867 they were united with Prussia into a North German Confederation. Each state had self-government, but the king of Prussia was hereditary president of the Confederation. As the largest state, with the most powerful industry and army, and with the greatest number of representatives, Prussia dominated the legislature of the Confederation.

Only the three southern states of Bavaria, Baden, and Württemberg and the southern part of Hesse-Darmstadt remained outside the sphere of Prussia's influence. If they could be persuaded to join Prussia, German unity would be complete. But Catholic and Austrian influence was strong there; it would take some great outside danger to persuade the states to unite willingly.

The Franco-Prussian War

You will remember that Bismarck had a low opinion of Napoleon III and decided that war with France would benefit Prussia and all Germany. You have read about Bismarck's shrewd diplomacy in bringing it about—the "doctoring" of the Ems dispatch and its release to the press at a crucial time. He was just as shrewd in persuading the south German states to fight on the side of Prussia. When France declared war on Prussia in 1870, Bismarck showed the leaders of the south German states the 1865 document in which Napoleon III had demanded their territory for France. He persuaded them that their greatest danger was from France, not Prussia. He thus converted the states from rivals into allies against France and secured their help in winning a Prussian victory.

The Franco-Prussian War was short but decisive. No outside nation made any move to help France. The Prussian army was superbly trained and equipped and ably led. Within a few months the French were totally defeated.

Bismarck had been lenient with Austria when it was conquered because many of its people were Germans and he did not want them as enemies. He had no such feeling about France. As you have read, France was occupied by German troops, lost Alsace and part of Lorraine, and had to pay a huge indemnity.

Formation of the German Empire

For Germany the peace was not as important as an event that took place before the treaty was signed. On January 18, 1871, representatives of the allied German states met in the Hall of Mirrors of the palace of Versailles near Paris. There they issued an official proclamation declaring the formation of the German Empire, which included all of the German states except Austria (see map, opposite). The capital of the empire was to be Berlin, capital of Prussia.

William I of Prussia was proclaimed German emperor. Bismarck was elevated to the position of chancellor, or chief minister, of the German Empire. Because of his policy of "blood and iron," he was often called the "Iron Chancellor."

The new German Empire was not all that Bismarck desired. He was forced to make many compromises in order to accomplish his purpose. Much as he disliked constitutions, he accepted one that united the twenty-five German states in a federal form of government. Each state had its own ruler as well as the right to handle its own domestic matters, including public health, education, law enforcement, and local taxation.

THE UNIFICATION OF GERMANY

1815 German Confederation formed

1862 Bismarck became prime minister of Prussia

1864 After Danish War, Schleswig turned over to Prussian administration

1866 Prussian victory in Seven Weeks' War resulted in dissolution of German Confederation and Prussian annexation of several north German states

1867 North German Confederation established

1870 Southern German states joined Prussia in Franco-Prussian War

1871 All German states (except Austria) united to form German Empire

The imperial government was given control of all common problems such as national defense, foreign affairs, tariffs, and commercial matters. At the head of the imperial government was the emperor, called the Kaiser, who was also king of Prussia. He was not, as Bismarck would have liked, an absolute monarch, but he had tremendous power. He could appoint the chief executive officer, the chancellor, who was responsible to him. The emperor commanded the army and navy and controlled foreign policy. He could declare a defensive war on his own authority; he could wage an offensive war with the consent of the upper house of the legislature.

The legislative branch of the government was composed of two houses. The *Bundesrat* (BOON-dus·raht), a federal council, was the upper house. It was composed of fifty-eight members, who were appointed by the rulers of the various states. The emperor (as king of Prussia) appointed seventeen of these members, and since fourteen votes could block a change in the constitution, he could thus defeat any amendment that he wanted to.

The *Reichstag* (RYKS·tahk), or legislative assembly, was the lower house of the German legislature. Its nearly 400 members were elected by universal manhood suffrage. The Bundesrat drew up all the bills for consideration by the Reichstag and could veto its actions. The Bundesrat and the emperor acting together could dismiss the Reichstag. There was little chance that the Reichstag would pass any liberal democratic laws to upset the status quo.

The German constitution strongly favored Prussia in imperial affairs. The king of Prussia had become emperor of Germany. Prussia had the greatest number of delegates in the Bundesrat. As the most populous state, it also had the largest number of delegates in the Reichstag.

Prussia itself was still governed under the conservative constitution adopted in 1850. This constitution placed power in the hands of the king and the Junkers. Thus, with Prussia in control, there was little chance that the German Empire would adopt democratic measures.

In the establishment of such new nations as the United States, nationalism and democracy had gone together. At first glance this also seemed to be true of the new Germany. It had a constitution and a federal form of government. Closer inspection showed that this appearance was misleading. Germany was nationalistic but not democratic. It was aristocratic. Nationalism and democracy had been completely separated in the formation of the German Empire.

CHECKUP

1. Prussia fought three wars to unite Germany. Name them and tell what each accomplished.

2. How did Bismarck persuade the south German states to accept Prussian leadership in Germany?

3. Name the powers held by the emperor of the new German Empire.

4. "Nationalism and democracy had been completely separated in the formation of the German Empire." Explain.

5. IDENTIFY: Treaty of Prague, Iron Chancellor, Kaiser, Bundesrat, Reichstag.

3 Industrialization and socialism created problems for Germany

Because Bismarck could not get the absolute monarchy he wanted, he tried to achieve it in roundabout ways. However, in the years after 1871, he had to accept many compromises to make the German political system work. As Germany increased steadily in wealth and power, it had many new needs. And even though its constitution did not give the people many powers, they did have a voice which had to be respected.

Opposition to Bismarck

In spite of rigid control by the aristocratic Prussians, the new German imperial government soon ran into difficult political problems. Dissatisfied groups formed political parties that opposed Bismarck's policies. Some wanted the imperial government to be more liberal and democratic and to enact social reforms. Others feared Bismarck's military policy and the ever-growing army and navy.

Deputies from the south German states, especially from Bavaria, often raised issues involving the federal principle. They resented the interference of the imperial government in what they considered local and domestic affairs. They thought their own state governments should deal with such matters.

Relations with the Roman Catholic Church presented special problems. In 1864, Pope Pius IX had issued a "Syllabus of Errors" denouncing liberalism, religious toleration, and secular education (education controlled by the government instead of by the Church). Six years later a Vatican council proclaimed that the pope was infallible (incapable of error) in matters of faith and morals. The long-standing claim of the pope to administer Church property seemed like foreign interference in German domestic affairs. Bismarck came to feel that the Catholic Church was a threat to the German Empire. The fact that the south German states were Catholic made this feeling stronger. In 1872, diplomatic relations between the imperial government and the papacy were broken off. Then there began what was called the *Kulturkampf* (German for "war of civilization")—a bitter struggle between the Roman Catholic Church and the German government.

Germany adopted strict measures to control the Catholic clergy and Catholic schools. The Jesuits were expelled; all the Catholic clergy were to be Germans, educated in German schools. Clergymen who opposed these measures were imprisoned or banished. This religious policy stirred up a hornet's nest of opposition. A Catholic party was formed to oppose the *Kulturkampf* and to work for other changes. Many non-Catholic liberals also joined the opposition. By 1880, Bismarck began to modify the *Kulturkampf,* both because he needed the support of the Catholic party, and because he thought that the menace from Catholicism was no longer real. Diplomatic relations were re-established with the papacy, the laws against Catholics were repealed, and by 1887 the *Kulturkampf* was at an end.

Industrial development

German unification brought about increased industrial development. The Zollverein, beginning in 1819, had aided industrialization, and political unification after 1871 helped it further. The victory over France brought with it not only the rich iron mines of Lorraine but also a billion dollars in gold for capital.

The government owned the railroads of Germany and managed them so as to promote industrial development. A system of canals provided cheaper, though slower, transportation. Germany was rich in natural resources. North of Lorraine were the great coal deposits of the Ruhr Valley. A tremendous steel industry grew up in this area because of the availability of iron and coal.

In one way, the fact that industrial development came later in Germany than in Great Britain and France proved to be an advantage. German industries could use the best methods and most improved machinery developed elsewhere. German scientists worked out further changes and improvements.

Under Bismarck's leadership, the government helped industry in many ways. Money and banking laws became uniform throughout the empire. Postal and telegraph services, the means of communication by which so much business is conducted, were centralized. A high-tariff policy was adopted to protect German industries from foreign competition.

The government encouraged German industrialists to form huge organizations called cartels. In a cartel, all the producers in a single industry, such as steel or chemicals, unite to fix prices, limit production, and divide markets. Thus they try to eliminate competition through a monopoly. With all of these influences at work, Germany rapidly became an industrial nation, exporting manufactured goods and importing food and raw materials. By 1900 it was threatening the positions of leading producers of steel and machinery, such as Great Britain and the United States. Germany was also rivaling these nations for leadership in world trade.

Agriculture did not decline in Germany as industry increased. Through the application of scientific methods and the use of fertilizers, produced by the rapidly developing chemical industry, even the poor, sandy, shallow soil of northern Germany was made quite productive. Like its manufactures, German farm goods were protected by tariffs.

Berlin increasingly became the center of the new empire. Connected with all parts of Germany by rail and canal, it grew into a major commercial city with a rapidly expanding population.

Socialism in Germany

With the growth of German industry, there was a change in the social pattern of German life. Cities increased greatly in population, and a class of factory workers appeared. German workers, like those in other nations, wanted decent wages, hours, working conditions, and security against accidents, sickness, old age, and unemployment. Some people believed that the cartels, which favored the capitalists, meant lower wages for workers and higher prices for consumers. Many men thought that these various problems needed government action and that the government should pass laws to benefit workers and regulate industry.

Socialist reformers went even further, advocating government ownership of all major industries. German socialists banded together in 1869 to form the Social Democratic Workingmen's Party. The party grew quickly, with most of its members coming from the ranks of the city workers. In 1871 it was able to elect two members to the Reichstag. By 1877 that representation had increased to twelve.

Even if the Social Democrats had had a much greater representation, they could have done very little. The Reichstag was powerless to pass any laws that the Bundesrat opposed. And since the Bundesrat represented the hereditary rulers, there was little chance that it would propose or pass any such laws as the socialists wanted. But the Reichstag made a good public platform for socialist members to air their grievances and complaints, and to make promises of what they would do if they had the power.

Bismarck's anti-socialist campaign

By 1877 the Social Democrats polled half a million votes. Every gain in socialist voting strength, every demand for reform alarmed Bismarck. The old chancellor decided to use all of his weapons to fight the socialists. His opportunity came in 1878, when there were two attempts to assassinate the emperor. Neither of the would-be assassins had any connection with socialism, and Bismarck knew this. However, he took advantage of the public excitement to accuse the Social Democrats of plotting the attempts. The emperor and the Bundesrat dissolved the Reichstag and called for new elections. There was a widespread campaign against socialists and their ideas.

The election had almost no effect on Social Democratic representation in the Reichstag, but Bismarck was able to push through laws aimed at repressing the socialists. It was made unlawful to spread socialist ideas through newspapers, books, or pamphlets. Socialists were forbidden to hold public meetings.

Despite such restrictive laws, the socialists continued their efforts. By 1884, Social Democratic representation in the Reichstag had increased to twenty-four despite the restrictions. As he did in the *Kulturkampf,* Bismarck had to examine his tactics and see how to achieve what he wanted against growing opposition.

Since repression had failed, the Iron Chancellor decided to try something else. He decided that the reforms the socialists proposed were less dangerous than a powerful socialist political party which might later make even more radical demands. If the government granted reforms, people would have less reason to join the socialists and the party would lose strength.

Bismarck's new policy was called "stealing the socialists' thunder." He said that he wanted to pass laws that would help the workingmen so that the Social Democrats "will sound their bird call in vain." Beginning in 1883, he put through several reforms that were both wise and farseeing. First came insurance against sickness, then insurance against accidents, paid for by the employer. Other laws limited hours and provided for certain holidays from work. The final step was an act that provided for payments to workers when they were physically disabled or too old to work.

Germany thus adopted a pioneering program of government-directed social reforms. The reforms did not wipe out socialism in Germany, but they did remove many of the workers' fears and grievances. German social legislation was later copied in many other industrial nations.

Bismarck's foreign policy

Bismarck's foreign policy was based largely on German armed might. He once declared: "We Germans fear God, but nothing else in the world." Even after unification, Germany glorified military strength. Conscription was adopted throughout the German Empire. The army constantly increased in size and used the most modern weapons and equipment. Professional military men held important positions in nonmilitary branches of the government as well as in the army. However, although the army was strong in Germany, the country was less belligerent after it had been

490

unified. Until 1890, when Bismarck fell from power, Germany sought peace rather than war.

Bismarck analyzed the European situation thus: his greatest worry was that some day Germany might have to fight a war on two fronts—eastern and western—at the same time. Therefore, he did not want France and Russia to become allies. He worked to keep up the friendship between the Hohenzollerns and the Romanovs of Russia. Austria he considered a natural ally, even though Prussia had displaced Austria as the leader of Germany. The Iron Chancellor promoted friendship between Hohenzollerns and Hapsburgs.

Prussia had helped Italy gain Venetia in 1866, an action that had brought Germany the friendship of Italy. Bismarck strengthened this friendly relationship and Germany and Italy became allies. In 1882, Bismarck succeeded in forming an alliance—officially called the Triple Alliance—made up of Germany, Austria, and Italy.

The resignation of Bismarck

Bismarck's beloved Kaiser William I died in 1888. His son reigned only a few months before he died, and was succeeded in turn by his son, William II. The young monarch and the old chancellor soon disagreed violently. William II felt that Bismarck was too powerful and that, by ignoring the imperialistic race for colonies, about which you will read in Unit 7, he had failed to promote Germany's interests. Bismarck felt that the young emperor was taking away the powers which the chancellor had exercised wisely for years. He also feared that William was too rash and undisciplined to use his considerable authority with wisdom.

In 1890, Bismarck, who had thought himself indispensable to Germany, was forced to resign, which he did with a great feeling of bitterness. Although he and William II were later reconciled personally, Bismarck did not serve Germany again.

William II set out to build up Germany's colonial empire. He also urged the passage of new laws to help workers so that he became known as the "Labor Emperor." He increased the size and

In a cartoon symbolizing Bismark's resignation, the chancellor, as the pilot, leaves the ship signifying Germany; William II sneeringly looks on.

strength of the German army and began to build up the German navy. This move brought Germany into conflict with Great Britain, which considered that it alone ruled the seas. New agreements with neighbor nations were signed, and, by 1914, Germany was stronger than ever before.

CHECKUP

1. What were three problems faced by the German Empire in the 1870's and 1880's?

2. What were the major factors in the rapid industrial development of Germany?

3. Describe the chief social reforms adopted under Bismarck.

4. IDENTIFY: *Kulturkampf*, cartels, Social Democratic Workingmen's Party, Triple Alliance.

CHAPTER REVIEW

Chapter 23   Germany Became a United and Powerful Nation   (1786–1914)

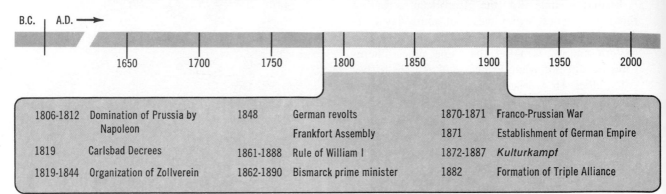

1806-1812	Domination of Prussia by Napoleon	1848	German revolts	1870-1871	Franco-Prussian War
			Frankfort Assembly	1871	Establishment of German Empire
1819	Carlsbad Decrees	1861-1888	Rule of William I	1872-1887	*Kulturkampf*
1819-1844	Organization of Zollverein	1862-1890	Bismarck prime minister	1882	Formation of Triple Alliance

CHAPTER SUMMARY

For centuries, Germany was divided into many states varying widely in area and population. Prussia, one of the strongest states, came under Napoleon's control in the early 1800's. French domination stimulated Prussian nationalism, and a reorganized Prussian army helped to defeat Napoleon.

Although many Germans wanted unity, it was opposed by Austria, France, and several of the lesser German states. The Zollverein did much to unify Germany economically, but little came of the revolutions of 1848 and the Frankfort Assembly.

New leadership took over when Bismarck became prime minister of Prussia. He modernized the army and became virtual ruler. To exclude Austria while uniting the other German states, Prussia fought three wars. The Danish War resulted in Prussian control of Schleswig and in Austrian control of Holstein—a troublesome settlement. Two years later, Prussia defeated Austria in the Seven Weeks' War.

In the Franco-Prussian War, Bismarck gained the support of the south German states, and Prussia won a decisive victory. It resulted in the unification of the German states into the German Empire, with William I of Prussia as Kaiser and Bismarck as chancellor.

In the new German Empire, much power was wielded by the Kaiser. Prussia virtually controlled both the Bundesrat and the Reichstag. Bismarck faced difficulties, however. His *Kulturkampf* was a failure. Industrialization, aided by political unification, French spoils, and government encouragement, bolstered socialist strength. As the party won more votes, Bismarck tried first repressive measures and then a broad program of social reforms.

Bismarck believed in a strong army, but pursued an essentially peaceful course. Aiming to avoid a two-front war, he negotiated the Triple Alliance of Germany, Austria, and Italy. Soon afterward, however, he clashed with the new emperor, William II, and was forced to resign.

QUESTIONS FOR DISCUSSION

1. Bismarck as chancellor of Germany was responsible solely to the emperor. In Britain the prime minister is responsible to Parliament. Why is there such a vital difference between these two arrangements?

2. Bismarck was well informed about conditions in other countries. How did this knowledge help him? Would you vote for a presidential candidate in the United States if he did not know about foreign affairs? Explain.

3. Instead of encouraging the Franco-Prussian War in order to unify Germany, why didn't Bismarck simply conquer the south German states that held out against unification? Why do you agree, or disagree, with Bismarck on his decision?

4. How successful was the Social Democratic Workingmen's Party in Germany? Although followers of Marx, most German socialists did not advocate revolution. Would you support the existence of such a socialist party in the United States? Explain your position.

PROJECTS

1. Write a letter to Bismarck telling him why it would be a mistake to demand a large indemnity from France after the Franco-Prussian War.

2. Make a diagram of the government of the German Empire and explain why it could not be considered a democracy.

3. Draw a map of central Europe showing Prussia in 1860 and the territories acquired under Bismarck. Indicate from which country the Prussians won each territory.

Problems Beset Italy, the Ottoman Empire, and Eastern Europe

Around the mid-1800's, the political methods and ideas of many Europeans changed. In the early part of the century, the men who wanted to improve conditions did so with noble aims for reforming society. But few of them had much practical experience in the world of politics. Many had a kind of mystical faith in the future and thought that their causes would win wide support simply because they represented right and justice. In Poland and Germany, for example, liberals expected mass uprisings when revolutions broke out. They were bitterly disappointed when the peasants, most of whom were ignorant or afraid, refused to join their cause.

Even when liberal or nationalistic revolts succeeded, their leaders often could not hold on to their gains. They had no clear ideas of what to do once they had gained power. Thus they tended to split into various groups and to waste their strength in futile quarrels.

Political life in the later 1800's was dominated by men of a different kind. They were not idealists but realists. They believed in facing life as it was, not as it should be. The revolutions of 1848 were important in bringing about this change. Revolutionaries found that idealism was not enough to solve the difficult problems of changing a political system and governing a nation. Such men studied their countries and their political institutions as well as the people and their

Executing Hungarian patriots after the 1848 revolt

social problems in order to chart practical courses for the future. They learned to balance groups against each other and did not hesitate to use dishonest or unscrupulous means to achieve their goals. Principles were sacrificed and promises were broken if it seemed necessary or advantageous. Politics became a matter not of idealistic aims but of compromise.

This policy became known by a German word, *Realpolitik* (ray·AHL·poh·lih·TEEK), which means "practical, or realistic, politics." It could be practiced by men within a nation, or by one nation toward others. In the latter case, it was often accompanied by threats of force or by force itself. You have read about Bismarck's actions that resulted in the creation of a united Germany.

They were examples of *Realpolitik*. While the liberal idealists of the Frankfort Assembly had failed to create a united Germany, Bismarck, with "blood and iron," had succeeded. Many other statesmen of the late 1800's used *Realpolitik* to get what they wanted, and it has continued to be an important factor in political life up to the present time.

THE CHAPTER SECTIONS:

1. Italy was united, but difficulties continued (1831–1911)

2. In central Europe, interest was focused on the Balkans (1848–1913)

3. In spite of some reforms, Russia remained a rigid autocracy (1850–1905)

 Italy was united, but difficulties continued

The conquests of Napoleon I had given the Italian Peninsula something resembling unity for a few years. Italians, inspired by liberal and national ideals, had overthrown many rulers of the Italian states. But after the Congress of Vienna, Italy was again divided. Lombardy and Venetia were annexed by Austria; the rest of Italy was divided into several large and small states. Most of them were dominated by Austria, and most were ruled by reactionaries who tried to wipe out any advances made during the Napoleonic Era.

Early movements for unification

Italian nationalism became a strong force in the early 1800's. Many thinkers and writers fostered interest in Italy's traditions. This nationalistic movement, which aimed toward liberation and unification, became known as the Risorgimento (ree·sawr·jee·MEN·toh), Italian for "resurgence." Because nationalists could not work openly, they formed secret societies. An early group of this sort was the Carbonari. One of its most famous members and a man who had great influence on later Italian history was Giuseppe Mazzini.

Mazzini, born in 1805, had a vision of a united Italy, and to this vision he devoted his entire life.

He was charming, intense, and eloquent. His ideal of nationalism became almost a religion with him and many of his fellow patriots.

Mazzini was imprisoned and then exiled for his part in an unsuccessful uprising against Sardinia in 1830. He issued a call in 1831 for all Italian patriots to join a new movement, Young Italy, to spread the ideals of the Risorgimento among the Italian people. Mazzini called Young Italy "a brotherhood of Italians who believe in Progress and Duty."

In 1848, liberal and nationalistic rebellions in several of the Italian states helped to spark the revolution in France. Sardinia, the Kingdom of the Two Sicilies, and Tuscany were forced to grant constitutions to their subjects, and Austrian rule was overthrown in Lombardy and Venetia. Revolutionaries seized Rome in 1849 and set up a republic that was governed by Mazzini himself and two other leaders. All of these movements except one soon failed. The former rulers were restored, the constitutions were revoked, and Mazzini had to flee the country once more. Only Sardinia kept its constitution and its independence.

Despite the failure of the revolts of 1848 and 1849, Italian patriots continued their efforts.

They were now agreed on their principal aim, a united Italy. But they did not agree on how to achieve unity, or the ideal form of government after unification had succeeded.

Three groups had differing ideas: (1) Many Italians, especially the Catholic clergy, wanted a federation of Italian states headed by the pope. (2) Liberals wanted an Italian republic. They opposed federation, partly because the papacy had turned against liberalism after 1849. (3) Another group wanted a constitutional monarchy under the king of Sardinia.

Cavour in Sardinia

The kingdom of Sardinia, as you have read, included not only the island of Sardinia but also the mainland regions of Savoy, Piedmont, and Nice (see map, this page). It was the only state in northern Italy not dominated by Austria. Its constitution provided for a parliament, whose elected representatives had a considerable voice in the government. Its king, Victor Emmanuel II, was sympathetic to liberal aims.

However, it was not the king of Sardinia but his chief minister, Cavour, who actually led the nation. Count Camillo Benso di Cavour, born in 1810, was an aristocrat, well educated and widely traveled. He edited a nationalist newspaper in 1847, took part in the revolutions of 1848, and in 1852 became premier of Sardinia.

Cavour disliked absolutism and admired the English system of parliamentary government. He wanted Italy to be both united and industrialized. Cavour hoped to make Sardinia both strong and liberal so that it could become a leader among the forces of nationalism in Italy.

Unlike the idealistic Mazzini, Cavour made skillful use of *Realpolitik*. He reorganized and strengthened the army. He helped to establish banks, factories, and railroads, encouraged shipbuilding, and negotiated treaties with other countries to increase trade. Under the slogan "a free church in a free state," he tried to reduce the influence of the Roman Catholic Church in politics. The politically powerful Jesuit order was expelled from the country.

Cavour also brought Sardinia to the notice of

UNIFICATION OF ITALY • 1858-1870

Kingdom of Sardinia before 1859

From Austria to Sardinia in 1859

Added to Italy in 1866

Added to Italy in 1870

Added to Sardinia in 1860 to form the Kingdom of Italy

the larger European powers in 1855, when he joined France and Great Britain in the Crimean War against Russia. The idea of this small state's taking part in such an undertaking amused many people. But Sardinia's participation enabled it to take part in the peace conference at Paris in 1856, which increased its standing in European affairs.

Napoleon III and war with Austria

Since Austrian control of part of northern Italy was the greatest obstacle to Italian unity, Cavour searched for allies against Austria. You will remember that Napoleon III was seeking ways to increase French prestige. Cavour proposed an alliance of France and Sardinia against Austria. Napoleon was at first reluctant to take this step, fearing that it would antagonize the pope and the French Catholics. However, he hoped that, with Austria driven out of Italy, France could dominate a weak confederation of Italian states. Ca-

495

vour, on the other hand, believed that with Austria out of Italy, the other Italian states would join Sardinia and make a strong alliance against both France and Austria.

Cavour and Napoleon made a secret agreement in 1858. Napoleon agreed that if Austria declared war on Sardinia, France would send troops to help drive the Austrians out of Lombardy and Venetia. In return for this help, Cavour promised to give the regions of Nice and Savoy to France.

In 1859, Cavour began to mobilize Sardinia—that is, make preparations for war. Fearing that he planned to attack Austria, the Austrian emperor played directly into Cavour's hands by arrogantly demanding that the military buildup be stopped in three days. At that period, mobilization and demobilization took a long time, and such a demand was impossible to meet. Cavour, secretly delighted, firmly rejected Austria's attempt to interfere in the affairs of Sardinia. Austria declared war.

At first the war also went according to Cavour's plans. The combined Sardinian-French forces quickly drove the Austrians out of Lombardy and marched on into Venetia. Patriots in Tuscany, Modena, and Parma overthrew their Austrian rulers and asked to be annexed to Sardinia.

This was more than Napoleon III had planned on. He did not want a strong, united Italy any more than he wanted a united Germany. He was afraid that if the war lasted a long time, Prussia, for its own ends, might help Austria. In July 1859, only three months after the war began, he broke the agreement with Cavour by signing a secret armistice with Austria. According to its terms, Sardinia received Lombardy, but Austria kept Venetia. Hapsburg rulers were restored to Tuscany, Modena, and Parma.

This was a severe setback for Cavour and the Italian nationalists. Napoleon III had delivered only half of his side of the bargain, but he insisted on receiving his full price—Nice and Savoy. Fearing to lose his half-victory, King Victor Emmanuel II agreed to the French terms.

The Italian people refused to give up their aims. Popular feeling ran far ahead of governmental caution. Rebellions in Parma, Modena, and Tuscany again expelled the royal houses and set up popular temporary governments. The people of Romagna, a province in the Papal States, also revolted. When elections were held in all these areas, the votes were overwhelmingly in favor of joining Sardinia.

Napoleon III was completely opposed to any such arrangement. For a time there was a chance of war between France and Sardinia in which the Italians would try to regain Nice and Savoy. Then, in 1860, Cavour made another agreement. France was to keep Nice and Savoy; in return, Sardinia was to be allowed to annex Parma, Modena, Tuscany, and Romagna. Although it was difficult for Italians to give up Nice and Savoy, they thus took a long step toward Italian unity.

Garibaldi's Red Shirts

The lower half of the Italian Peninsula, together with the large island of Sicily, made up what was called the Kingdom of the Two Sicilies. It was ruled by a harsh Bourbon king, Francis II. Earlier revolts there had been unsuccessful; but it now became the target of the Italian nationalists, and a man with a long history of devotion to Italian freedom led the way.

Giuseppe Garibaldi was born in Nice in 1807. As a youth, he joined Mazzini's Young Italy movement, and in 1834 had to flee for his life. He lived for several years in Latin America. Returning to Italy, he fought in the revolutions of 1848. Forced to flee again, he lived in the United States for several years, returning once more to Italy in 1854.

With financial assistance secretly furnished by Cavour, Garibaldi recruited an army of 1,100 men. They were called Red Shirts because of the uniform they wore into battle. In the spring of 1860, Garibaldi and his Red Shirts invaded the island of Sicily, where they were welcomed by the people. Crossing to the mainland, Garibaldi and his forces seized Naples, the capital city, and drove Francis II and his forces north to the border of the Papal States.

Garibaldi now planned to continue his march northward and capture Rome and then Venetia.

496

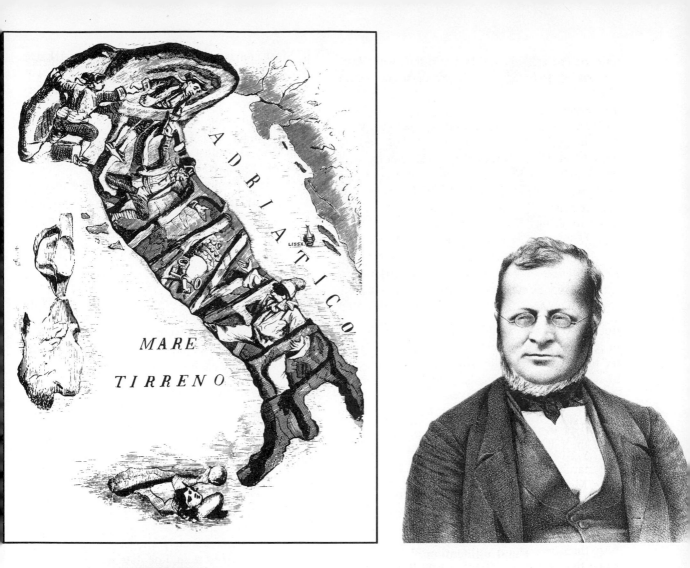

The unification of Italy was achieved largely through the efforts of Count Cavour, above, and Giuseppe Garibaldi, left. Cavour welded together the states of northern Italy, while Garibaldi liberated Sicily and the south. Although the kingdom of Italy was proclaimed in 1861, the nation could not be truly unified so long as the Papal States did not belong. This situation was ingeniously portrayed in the cartoon above left, published in 1866. The letters *LO STIVALE*, Italian for "the boot," are worked into the drawing. Three figures in the north, clasping hands, reach toward a harlequin with outstretched hand in the south. (This clown figure is a traditional symbol for Naples.) The Papal States, represented by the pope's crown and keys, prevent the hands from joining. This division was mended in 1870 when the Papal States became part of Italy.

497

THE UNIFICATION OF ITALY

1848 Sardinia granted a constitution

1852 Cavour became premier of Sardinia

1859 Lombardy ceded to Sardinia

1860 Sardinia lost Nice and Savoy, gained Parma, Modena, Tuscany, and Romagna

Garibaldi took Sicily and Naples

1861 Kingdom of Italy proclaimed

1866 Italy gained Venetia

1870 Rome became capital of united Italy

But Cavour was afraid that France or Austria might enter the conflict, and that Garibaldi might try to set up a republic. An army was sent south to stop Garibaldi's advance, and most of the territory of the Papal States was annexed to Sardinia. Cavour left the city of Rome under the control of the pope.

In the fall of 1860, Garibaldi and Cavour met in Naples. Garibaldi was reluctant to abandon his plan for conquest of the entire Italian Peninsula. But Cavour persuaded him to agree to the establishment of the kingdom of Italy, with Victor Emmanuel II of Sardinia as its ruler.

Final unification

Elections were held everywhere in Italy in 1860 except in Venetia and Rome. The people voted overwhelmingly for national unity under the king of Sardinia. Representatives met at a parliament in the city of Turin in February 1861 and confirmed Victor Emmanuel II as king of Italy "by grace of God and the will of the nation." Cavour died four months later, worn out from his labors to create a united Italy.

The new kingdom included every part of Italy except Venetia, which still belonged to Austria, and the western part of the Papal States around the city of Rome, ruled by the pope (see map, page 495). European governments now had only two choices: to recognize the new state or to fight

it. Most embarrassed of all was Napoleon III. He did not make war on the new country, but he sent French troops to Rome to prevent the Italian nationalists from seizing it.

The unification of Italy was not complete in 1861, but the end was in sight. By allying itself with Prussia against Austria in the Seven Weeks' War of 1866, Italy was able to gain Venetia. When the Franco-Prussian War broke out in 1870, Napoleon III had to recall his troops from Rome. The Italians entered the city, and the citizens of Rome voted overwhelmingly for union with Italy. That same year, Rome was proclaimed the capital of the kingdom of Italy.

The pope protested bitterly but ineffectively. He shut himself up in the Vatican palace, saying he would remain "the prisoner of the Vatican" until the Papal States were restored to him. Relations between the papacy and the Italian government were difficult for many years.

Problems of united Italy

Italy was politically united; however, many problems remained. Few Italians were experienced in self-government, and graft and scandal were common. The various regions of the country remained jealous of their own traditions and independence. There was tension between the north, which became industrialized, and the agricultural south. In Sicily, local strong men—organized in a secret society known as the Camorra, or Mafia—formed a kind of state within the state, which the central government was powerless to control.

The leaders of Italy admired what Bismarck had done in Germany and hoped to follow a similar course in their own country. Within a few years, Italy had the third largest navy and the third largest merchant marine in the world.

Italy's buildup of military and naval strength was achieved by taxing its people heavily. This led to unrest, and there were peasant uprisings—particularly in Sicily—in the 1890's. Looking for victories to build the country's prestige, Italy engaged in unfortunate colonial ventures in Africa, about which you will read in Chapter 26. A brief war against the Ottoman Empire in 1911 cost a great deal of money and brought Italy little in return. There were strikes and riots all through Italy during the next several years in protest against taxes and governmental inefficiency.

CHECKUP

1. Who was Mazzini and what was his place in Italian history?

2. What were three chief plans for Italian unity?

3. Trace the steps toward Italian unification as they occurred in the following years: 1852, 1858, 1859, 1860, 1866, 1870.

4. IDENTIFY: *Realpolitik*, Carbonari, Young Italy, Risorgimento, Red Shirts, Camorra.

5. LOCATE: Kingdom of the Two Sicilies, Tuscany, Venetia, Piedmont, Nice, Modena, Romagna.

2 In central Europe, interest was focused on the Balkans

"When France sneezes, all Europe catches cold," a statesman said in 1848. He was describing how uprisings in France had set off revolts in almost every other European nation. The Austrian Empire was no exception.

In Vienna there were clashes between demonstrators and the army. Emperor Ferdinand ordered Metternich to resign; Metternich did so and fled the country. Later in 1848, Ferdinand himself abdicated and the throne went to Franz Josef I, who was only eighteen years old.

In Hungary, too, there were uprisings. The people of this region, one of the largest parts of the Austrian Empire, were discontented. Most of them were Magyars, who spoke their own language and maintained a distinctive culture. There was a strong nationalist movement aimed at making the Magyars dominant in Hungary and freeing the region from Austrian domination.

The Hungarian patriot Louis Kossuth led the revolt in 1848. For a time it looked as though Hungary would gain its independence, and in 1849, Kossuth was elected "responsible governor-president" by the Hungarian Diet. A few months later, however, the revolutionists were defeated by Austria and Russia. (Czar Nicholas I offered his help because he was afraid that the revolt might spread to Russian Poland.) Kossuth fled the country.

Formation of the Dual Monarchy

For almost twenty years, Austria managed to keep liberalism and nationalism from becoming major issues. But after Austria's defeat by Prussia in 1866, Hungarian demands for freedom became more insistent. Austria tried to solve this problem in 1867 by forming the Dual Monarchy—also called Austria-Hungary—in which the Hungarians shared power with the Austrians.

The Dual Monarchy had a common monarch, Franz Josef I, whose title was Emperor of Austria and King of Hungary. There were three joint ministries: war, finance, and foreign affairs. Austria and Hungary each had its own parliament. That of Austria met at Vienna, that of Hungary at Budapest. Each could deal with all matters except those in the three common fields.

From an economic standpoint, the Dual Monarchy was a practical arrangement. The various parts of the empire fitted together into one economic unit. Hungary was chiefly agricultural, furnishing raw materials and food. Austria was strongly industrial, producing manufactured goods. Each furnished a market for the other.

There were, however, many problems. Austria, because of its manufacturing interests, wanted high protective tariffs. Hungary, as a farming region, favored low tariffs and freer trade. Nor did the formation of the Dual Monarchy solve the problem of nationalities. The Austrian Germans and the Hungarian Magyars were masters in what were almost separate national states. The other national minorities in both Austria and Hungary —the Czechs, Serbs, Croats, Rumanians, Poles, and Italians—did not benefit very much. They continued to agitate for self-government.

There were also problems in the common army over command and language. The Austrians spoke German; the Hungarians spoke Magyar, which had been declared the official language of Hun-

Between 1819 and 1848, almost every country in Western Europe underwent some form of political uprising. You have read about many of these movements in Chapters 20, 22, 23, and 24. The chart below summarizes some of the most important revolts of this period.

Year	Location	Event	Outcome
1819	German states	Student unrest	Carlsbad Decrees issued
1820	Spain	Revolt forced king to restore suspended constitution	King returned to full power by French army
1820	Naples	Revolutionaries forced ruler to grant constitution	Revolt put down by Austrian army
1820	Portugal	Ruler forced to accept constitution	King eventually restored to absolute power
1821	Greece	Rebellion against rule of Ottoman Turks	After pressure by Russia, Britain, and France, Ottomans granted Greece independence in 1829
1830	France	Revolt against King Charles X	Charles deposed and Louis Philippe chosen king
1830	Belgium	After revolt against Dutch rule, independence proclaimed	Independence recognized in 1839
1848	France	Riots in Paris forced Louis Philippe to abdicate	Second Republic established
1848	Italian states	Uprisings led to granting of constitutions in Sardinia, Kingdom of Two Sicilies, and Tuscany, and overthrow of Austrian rule in Lombardy and Venetia	Former rulers restored and all constitutions revoked except for that of Sardinia
1848	German states	Political agitation centered on demands for constitutions establishing representative governments	Frankfort Assembly met and drafted constitution, but Prussian king undid most of Assembly's work
1848	Austrian Empire	Uprisings in Vienna forced Metternich to resign, while Hungary tried to gain independence.	Emperor Ferdinand abdicated in favor of Franz Josef I, and Hungarians were defeated

gary and was now known as Hungarian. There were also various Slavic languages.

You have read how Bismarck, to strengthen Prussia and form a united Germany, declared war on Austria in 1866. Defeat in the Seven Weeks' War forced Austria out of positions of power in Germany and Italy. To compensate for this, the Dual Monarchy tried to gain influence and territory in the Balkans, a region controlled chiefly by the Ottoman Empire.

The Ottoman Empire

As you have read, the Ottoman Turks controlled a vast empire. By the late 1600's, it included the North African coast, Egypt, western Asia, southern Russia, the Balkan Peninsula, and Hungary (see map, page 352). Then Ottoman power gradually declined. By 1700 the Austrians had regained Hungary, and from that time on the Ottoman Turks were on the defensive.

The Ottoman government was completely autocratic, a combined military and political organization. The sultan was a commander in chief, controlling both governmental and religious affairs, and checked only by the sacred laws of Islam. Early sultans had been responsible rulers. Later sultans turned to the pleasures of palace life and left both army and government affairs to lesser officials.

Government officials, from the vizier (chief minister) down, were both administrators and military commanders, for the army was the government. Power rivalries, favoritism, bribery, and corruption existed everywhere.

Provincial government was poor. Governors, called pashas or beys, gave little consideration to the welfare of their subjects. Their chief responsibility was to collect revenue and manpower for the central government. Pashas gained and held office by bribery. They farmed out tax collection and paid themselves well from the revenues.

Economic and social weaknesses. Turkish rulers did little to improve agriculture, maintain irrigation, or build roads, hospitals, and schools. The tax system discouraged both agriculture and industry, and production declined. Most peasants planted only enough land to produce a crop that they could harvest quickly and hide from the tax collector.

Ottoman rule did not endear the Turks to their subject peoples. Many of the people of the empire were Christians or Jews. In strictly religious matters the Turks granted toleration to non-Moslems under their own religious leaders. However, if Jews or Christians were rebellious or plotted with neighboring enemy powers, the Turks slaughtered them unmercifully.

Discontent in the Balkans

In the early 1800's, discontent in the Balkan area of the Ottoman Empire was increased by the rise of nationalism. The Balkan region was the home of many peoples—Serbs, Bulgarians, Rumanians, and Greeks (see map, page 502).

The Turks, a landholding and governing minority, tried to suppress nationalistic movements. During the 1820's, as you have read, the Greeks and Serbs revolted. Aided by outside powers, Greece gained independence in 1829, and Serbia achieved some self-rule. Encouraged by these successes and by the evident weakness of the Turks, Serbia and Greece tried to gain more territory. Rumanians and Bulgarians also wanted self-rule.

Foreign countries intervened for their own selfish ends in the struggles between the Turks and these nationalist groups. Russia supported Balkan nationalists for several reasons. The Russians were Slavs, like the Bulgarians and Serbs in the Balkans. The Russians were Orthodox Christians, as were many of the discontented Balkan groups. But more important was the fact that if the Ottoman Empire collapsed, Russia might gain control of the water route from the Black Sea to the Mediterranean.

The Russian drive toward the Mediterranean caused the British to give their support to the crumbling Ottoman Empire. Great Britain did not want the Russians in the Mediterranean where they might challenge British sea power.

It was a curious alignment of nations. The Russian government was autocratic, but it championed the cause of freedom and independence of the Balkan peoples. Democratic Britain supported the autocratic Turks in suppressing freedom.

The Congress of Berlin

In 1875, revolts broke out in several Turkish provinces in the Balkans. Two years later, Russia took up the cause of the rebels and declared war on the Ottoman Empire. The Turks were defeated and forced to sign the Treaty of San Stefano in 1878. It granted independence to Rumania, Montenegro, and Serbia. It also created a large Bulgaria, which Russian troops were to occupy for some years. The enlarged Bulgaria extended far enough south to give Russia a seaport on the Aegean Sea.

Other European powers were alarmed by the

501

DECLINE OF THE OTTOMAN EMPIRE · 1683-1913

Territory lost by the Ottoman Empire, 1683-1913

The Ottoman Empire in 1913

New boundaries of 1913, after the Balkan Wars

sudden increase of Russian influence in the Balkans. Before the Treaty of San Stefano could go into effect, a group of nations, led by Great Britain and Austria, forced the Russians to consent to an international conference at Berlin to rewrite the treaty.

All the major European powers met at the Congress of Berlin in 1878. It approved the following terms: Serbia, Montenegro, and Rumania were to retain their independence. Bulgaria was to have self-government, but its area was reduced in size and kept within the Ottoman Empire—thus removing Russia's access to the Aegean Sea. Austria was to govern Bosnia and Herzegovina, but was not permitted to annex them.

The British were given the right to occupy and

administer the island of Cyprus, long held by the Turks. The Turkish sultan still officially ruled the island, but Great Britain actually took it over. The use of Cyprus as a naval base increased Great Britain's power in the eastern Mediterranean and was a move to keep Russia bottled up.

Other nations continued to reduce both the size and the power of the Ottoman Empire. France, Great Britain, and Italy seized parts of its African territory, as you will read in Chapter 26. In 1908, Bulgaria became completely independent. In the same year, Austria broke the agreement of the Congress of Berlin by annexing Bosnia and Herzegovina outright. In 1912, Italy seized several islands in the southeastern Aegean Sea, including Rhodes. The island of Crete was the scene of revolts in 1896 and 1905, which resulted in a degree of self-government and, finally, annexation by Greece in 1913.

The Balkan Wars

In 1912 and 1913, two wars fought in the Balkans resulted in the further alteration of boundaries and increased international tensions. Turkish misrule and the desire to liberate fellow nationals within the Ottoman Empire brought Bulgaria, Serbia, Greece, and Montenegro into a Balkan League. These countries wanted to take and divide among themselves the Balkan territories of the Ottoman Empire. In 1912 the Balkan League declared war on the Turks and quickly defeated them. The Balkan allies, however, could not agree on the partition of the Turkish territories in the Balkans, and hostilities broke out again in 1913. This time, Serbia, Greece, Montenegro, Rumania, and the Ottoman Empire turned upon and defeated Bulgaria.

As a result of the first war, Serbia gained a seaport on the Adriatic and Albania became independent. Bulgaria claimed considerable territory in the central Balkans and along the Aegean Sea. As a result of the second war, however, Austria forced Serbia to give the Adriatic seaport to Albania. Bulgaria suffered humiliating territorial losses to Serbia and Greece and was left with only a small outlet on the Aegean.

By the end of 1913, the territory of the Ottoman Empire in Europe had shrunk until it included only the city of Constantinople and a small region that gave it control of the vital water route from the Black Sea to the Mediterranean (see map, opposite page).

CHECKUP

1. When was the Dual Monarchy formed? What were its strengths and weaknesses?

2. How did the following factors contribute to the decline of the Ottoman Empire: its system of government, both central and local? its economy? its rule of other peoples?

3. How was the Ottoman Empire reduced in size between 1878 and 1913?

4. IDENTIFY: Kossuth, Franz Josef I, pashas, Balkan League.

5. LOCATE: Bosnia, Herzegovina, Montenegro, Serbia, Rumania, Bulgaria, Albania, Cyprus.

③ In spite of some reforms, Russia remained a rigid autocracy

By the mid-1800's, Russia had the largest territory and population of any European nation. It had weaknesses, too. Industrial development, which so strengthened the West, lagged behind in Russia. Most of its extensive natural resources were undeveloped. Another weakness was the fact that despite its size, Russia was mostly landlocked. Either its ports were frozen for much of the year, or the exits from the seas were controlled by other countries. This situation accounted for persistent Russian efforts to win unrestricted access to the Mediterranean Sea, past Constantinople and the Dardanelles. These efforts, as you have read, led to conflicts with the Ottoman Empire.

There was another problem. Russia was by no means a nation like Britain or France. The huge Russian Empire included a great variety of peoples and national groups. Most people in the European part of Russia belonged to one of three related groups: (1) the Great Russians, living in central and northern Russia; (2) the Ukrainians (sometimes called the Little Russians), living in the south; and (3) the White Russians, living in the west. They all belonged to the Orthodox Church. Scattered throughout the empire were smaller racial, national, and religious groups speaking many languages. Many of them, such as the Poles and Finns, had been conquered by the Russians and did not like Russian rule.

Russian domestic and foreign policies

The domestic program of the czars was designed to keep Russia an autocracy. The liberal movement that influenced other European nations so strongly in the 1800's made little progress in Russia. The czar held autocratic power over the sprawling Russian Empire. However, political developments in Western Europe were bound to have some effect. Western influence had been felt in Russia since the time of Peter the Great. Improved transportation and communication made this influence stronger still. Nationalistic ideas appealed to the Russian minorities, especially to the strongly patriotic Poles and Finns. Liberalism, by the early 1800's, began to attract some of the educated members of the aristocracy.

The czars, faced with problems caused by restless nationalities and liberal ideas, met them with harsh measures. There was strict censorship of speech and press, enforced by secret police, the army, and government officials. The czars rejected all demands for a constitution and a lawmaking body. In the 1830's, Nicholas I, czar from 1825 to 1855, began a program of "Russification." This policy meant that non-Russian peoples in the empire were compelled to use the Russian language, accept the Orthodox religion, and adopt Russian customs and culture.

The foreign policy of the Russian rulers was twofold. (1) In the Balkans they backed what was called Pan-Slavism—the union of all Slavic peoples under Russian leadership. (2) Elsewhere they pressed the program of expansion that was begun under the first czars: eastward into Asia and southward toward the Ottoman Empire. Russian expansion received a setback with its defeat in the Crimean War, when it lost both territory and privileges.

Alexander II and reforms

Alexander II became czar in 1855. Although basically conservative and autocratic, he was easily influenced by public opinion. At this time liberal reformers were agitating against serfdom, and Alexander turned his attention to the problem.

Serfdom had come late to Russia and was not firmly established there until it had almost disappeared in Western Europe. By the mid-1800's, however, it was in effect almost everywhere in Russia. Millions of peasants were bound to the land and could not leave unless so ordered by

government officials or permitted to do so by the nobles who owned the land.

Toward the middle of the 1800's, liberal reformers began to receive some support in their campaign against serfdom from a new group of people, the middle-class industrialists. As industries were established, factory owners began to urge that the serfs be freed. The industrialists were not inspired by liberal ideas, but simply needed workers for their factories.

Alexander II appointed committees to study the problem of serfdom. In 1861 he issued an Emancipation Edict that freed all the serfs. The terms of the edict also provided that the government would buy part of the land owned by the nobles and sell small tracts to the serfs.

Emancipation did not actually improve conditions very much for the serfs. The land was sold to them in small strips and at high prices. Peasants could not afford enough land to allow them to earn the payments for the land, pay the taxes, and still live. Therefore they had to rent additional land from landlords. Rents were high. Some peasants, unable to secure land, moved to the towns and cities and there provided a source of cheap labor for the factories.

Alexander II attempted other liberal reforms. Beginning in 1864, each province of European Russia was allowed to have an assembly of nobles and of delegates elected by townsmen and peasants. These assemblies levied local taxes and controlled public health, schools, relief for the poor, and some public works.

Alexander also reformed the courts. Civil and criminal cases, which were formerly tried secretly by administrative officials, were now tried by juries in open courts. However, political offenders accused of plotting against the government were still tried in secret. Alexander also established some schools.

Alexander II gained a considerable reputation as a liberal reformer, but his policies did not please everyone. Reactionaries opposed them and tried to convince the czar that such actions endangered the position and privileges of the ruler and the nobles. Liberals considered Alexander's reforms as only modest first steps and pointed out the

The Revolution of 1905

In the late 1800's and early 1900's Russia suffered from widespread misery and grave discontent. Peasants on farms and workmen in cities labored long hours in miserable surroundings for scant pay. Their plight is starkly illustrated in the painting above, which dates from the 1870's. Men dressed in rags and harnessed to a yoke like animals tow a barge upstream. Revolt came in 1905, but was ruthlessly crushed. Below right, czarist troops fire into a crowd of revolutionary workers in St. Petersburg.

need for further changes. Radicals were even more critical.

Radicals and reaction

Radical political activity in Russia was carried on by several groups. The Nihilists (NY·uhl·ists), were active in the 1860's. They wanted to abolish the whole political and social structure and build a completely new Russia. They wanted to keep nothing that depended on faith instead of reason. This idea gave them their name, which came from the Latin word *nihil,* meaning "nothing."

Another group, the Populists, urged their followers to live among peasants as teachers and doctors. Some believed that all the large estates should be seized and the land divided among the peasants. The government seized and arrested many Populists. Numerous Russian radicals then turned to violent action, joining a movement known as the People's Will. They favored the use of terrorism—bombings and assassinations of high officials—to force the government to grant their demands.

Radical activity frightened Alexander II, and

he turned to repressive measures in the late 1860's. Gradually, however, he became convinced that additional changes were necessary. In 1881 he signed a decree creating a commission to prepare reforms. Ironically, on that same day he was assassinated by a terrorist.

The assassination of Alexander II put a definite end to liberal reforms and led to another intensive campaign of reaction. Under Alexander III (czar until 1894) and his successor, Nicholas II, censorship, control of the church and of education, spies and informers, imprisonment and exile were used to stamp out any trace of liberalism. "Russification" was intensified. Jews were severely persecuted and frequently murdered in massacres called pogroms (poh·GRUMS). Finns, Poles, and other minorities were oppressed under the slogan "One Czar, One Church, One Language."

The attempt to preserve the old order met with much opposition, both open and underground. The development of industry in Russia produced a class of city workers who wanted the right to form unions and to strike. Middle-class industrialists wanted a voice in the government. Liberals and radicals were more determined than ever to gain reforms. The attempt of the Russian government to suppress all of these varied aims produced an explosive situation. Terrorism increased. Socialists, who had founded the Social Democratic Labor Party in 1898 as a moderate organization, grew more and more radical in the demands they made.

The Revolution of 1905

In 1904 and 1905, Russia fought a war with Japan in the Far East, as you will read in Chapter 27. To the surprise of the world, the Russians were badly defeated by the small, recently Westernized Japanese nation. Russia's defeat revealed that its government was corrupt and inefficient as well as autocratic, reactionary, and oppressive. This revelation provided the spark for all the discontented groups in the country.

The result was the Revolution of 1905. Workers struck and held demonstrations, merchants closed their stores, and industrialists shut down their factories. Lawyers refused to plead cases and

servants deserted their employers. Nicholas II faced a crisis. Russian autocracy had to yield or perish. He reluctantly decided to yield.

The czar issued a decree called the October Manifesto. It guaranteed individual liberties and provided for the election, by limited suffrage, of a parliament called the Duma. No law was to be valid without the approval of the Duma. These measures ended the strikes and the revolution.

The peace treaty with Japan was signed in 1905, and after this the czar's government was in a better position to deal with its critics at home. Two sessions of the Duma were dismissed because members insisted that the czar's ministers be responsible to the Duma. Then the qualifications for voting were changed so that only large landowners could vote. The result was a more conservative Duma, and one more cooperative with the czar.

The revolutionary movement of 1905 failed to achieve more impressive results for three chief reasons: (1) The army remained loyal to the czar. (2) The French, bound to Russia by a military alliance, lent money to support the Russian government. (3) The revolutionary groups split—a familiar story. Moderates of the middle class, frightened by radical demands, withdrew. Radicals disagreed among themselves. Workers lost heart and deserted their leaders.

The reactionaries learned nothing from the Revolution of 1905. Revolutionary leaders were hunted down and imprisoned, exiled, or executed. All the repressive measures were used as before. The government of Russia remained just about what it had been—an absolute monarchy.

CHECKUP

1. What were the most important aims of Russian foreign policy?

2. What two groups favored the abolition of serfdom in Russia? Did emancipation improve the condition of the serfs? Why or why not?

3. Why did the Russian revolutionary movement of 1905 fail?

4. IDENTIFY: "Russification," Nihilists, Populists, terrorism, October Manifesto, Duma.

CHAPTER REVIEW

Chapter 24 Problems Beset Italy, the Ottoman Empire, and Eastern Europe (1831–1913)

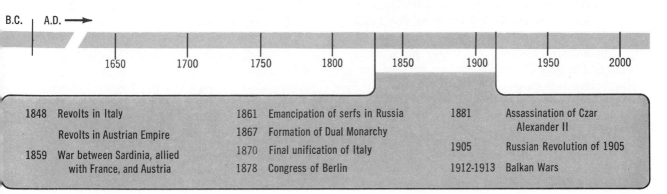

B.C. | A.D. ⟶

| 1650 | 1700 | 1750 | 1800 | 1850 | 1900 | 1950 | 2000 |

1848	Revolts in Italy	1861	Emancipation of serfs in Russia	1881	Assassination of Czar Alexander II
	Revolts in Austrian Empire	1867	Formation of Dual Monarchy		
1859	War between Sardinia, allied with France, and Austria	1870	Final unification of Italy	1905	Russian Revolution of 1905
		1878	Congress of Berlin	1912-1913	Balkan Wars

CHAPTER SUMMARY

In Italy, as in Germany, Napoleonic domination stimulated nationalism. But revolts—inspired by the Risorgimento and idealistic leaders like Mazzini—failed in 1830 and in 1848–1849.

Beginning in the 1850's, the movement for Italian unification was led by Cavour, who as chief minister of Sardinia used *Realpolitik*. He formed an alliance with Napoleon III, and France and Sardinia defeated Austria. Sardinia gained Lombardy and, after further revolts, four north Italian states in exchange for Nice and Savoy.

After Garibaldi's success in Sicily and Naples, the kingdom of Italy was formed. By 1870, Italy was a unified nation. However, the new country was plagued by regionalism, unrest over taxes and military spending, and unwise colonial ventures.

Central Europe, too, faced serious problems. Austria's formation of the Dual Monarchy made sense economically but left minority groups dissatisfied. In the declining Ottoman Empire, corruption was widespread and government was inefficient. Discontent in its Balkan territories led to interference by European nations. Russia's defeat of the Turks and resulting gains alarmed other European powers, who met at the Congress of Berlin to revise the treaty. Two Balkan Wars juggled boundaries further.

Russia in the 1800's exhibited many weaknesses. Industrial development lagged, there were few ports, and the people were disunited. Although serfdom was abolished, the peasants gained little. Nor did the granting of local self-government and court reforms please everyone. Nihilists, Populists, and other radicals pressed for sweeping reforms. The assassination of Czar Alexander II intensified government repression, but opposition continued. The Revolution of 1905, sparked by Russia's defeat in war with Japan,

forced Czar Nicholas II to promise individual liberties and an elected Duma. Soon, however, conservatives became entrenched again and Russian absolutism continued.

QUESTIONS FOR DISCUSSION

1. Can you think of some instances in recent United States history in which *Realpolitik* has come into play?

2. The Metternich system collapsed in 1848. Was the collapse caused by the activities of rebels and reformers? Was it due to the fact that the system ran counter to the spirit of the times? Explain.

3. When the new Italian kingdom made Rome its capital, what was the reaction of the Pope? Why was the relationship between church and state in Italy bound to cause trouble?

4. As the Ottoman Empire declined, its Balkan possessions offered a temptation for other nations to interfere. Can you think of similar areas in the world today? How are powerful countries handling them?

5. Germany and Italy were unified at about the same time; their populations were approximately equal. Germany immediately became a great power, but Italy did not. Why do you think this happened?

6. Do you think building a unified nation was more difficult in Russia than in Britain, France, or Germany? Why or why not?

PROJECTS

1. Write a short essay evaluating the roles played by Mazzini, Cavour, and Garibaldi in unifying Italy.

2. Write a letter to Czar Nicholas II explaining why you think it is a mistake to return to oppressive measures after issuing the October Manifesto.

3. Draw a map showing the territories that made up a united Italy by 1870.

The English-Speaking Peoples Developed Democratic Nations

In the latter 1800's, reaction and absolutism prevailed in the Dual Monarchy of Austria-Hungary, the Ottoman Empire, and Russia. In Western Europe, the situation was different. France, as you have seen, preserved a republic, shaky as it sometimes was. Smaller nations, such as Switzerland, Belgium, and the Netherlands, were also organized along constitutional lines. Some conservatives and reactionaries claimed that liberal institutions would work successfully only in small nations like these. But developments during the 1800's in several large and powerful countries—Great Britain, new nations within its empire, and the United States—showed that this was not true. In these English-speaking nations, self-government flourished and democracies came into being.

A democracy is essentially a nation in which the people control the government. When all the citizens meet together to discuss and vote on matters of mutual concern—usually in a small society—it is called *direct democracy*. (The Greek city-state of Athens functioned in this way.) Larger societies usually have *representative democracy;* the people elect representatives to make and enforce the laws that regulate their lives.

Democracy is based on the ideal that every individual is a person of inborn dignity and worth. His rights cannot be taken from him, but must be observed and protected by his fellow citizens. He is entitled to fair and just treatment under

Delegates arriving for a discussion of Canadian union

the law. He should have the opportunity to develop his abilities and to share in the rewards of life in his society.

To be sure that his rights and liberties are protected by his government, each individual in a democracy has an equal voice in that government. In fact, he *is* the government. Government is his creation and his servant. Its very existence depends on the "consent of the governed." Democratic government exists only to serve the individual citizen. It regulates, controls, and judges the actions of people only to make sure that they do not violate the rights of others. Each citizen gives up some of his rights to complete freedom of action so that all citizens may have both freedom and security.

These are the *ideals* of a democracy. The best of democracies often fall short of their ideals, but the right of citizens to seek peaceful improvement is the great distinction of a democratic society.

There is no magic inherited by English-speaking peoples that gives them the secret of democracy. Over the centuries the British gained experience in ruling themselves through representative bodies. It was natural that those who left their homeland to set up communities elsewhere should preserve their traditions in government as well as their English language and customs. You will remember that the Americans who rebelled against British rule in 1775 did so to secure, among other things, the "rights of Englishmen." Slowly but surely these rights were broadened and protected as the basis of democratic governments in several parts of the world.

THE CHAPTER SECTIONS:

1. Great Britain changed peacefully to a democracy (1832–1911)

2. Canada, Australia, and New Zealand became self-governing dominions (1770–1910)

3. The United States emerged as a major power (1791–1900)

1 Great Britain changed peacefully to a democracy

Great Britain was one of the first European nations to do away with divine-right monarchy. The Glorious Revolution of 1688 made Parliament the real ruler of the country. As you have read, Britain became a limited constitutional monarchy with executive power vested in a cabinet led by the prime minister. The government, however, was not a democracy because all the people did not have a chance to participate in it. It could be said that, throughout the 1700's and into the next century, Great Britain was an aristocracy controlled chiefly by the nobility and the wealthy landowners.

Voting restrictions

Theoretically the House of Commons represented the British people in the government. Members of Commons were elected by the voters of their districts, but the right to vote was severely restricted in several ways:

(1) Only property owners and a few other privileged people could vote.

(2) Catholics, Jews, and Dissenters (non-Anglican Protestants) could not hold political office.

(3) Voting in elections was done openly instead of by secret ballot. This system encouraged bribery and the influencing of voters.

(4) The boundaries of election districts, or boroughs, had not been changed since 1664. In some districts, called "rotten boroughs," the population had decreased or even disappeared, but the districts still sent members to Commons. On the other hand, some areas that had greatly increased in population, such as the industrial cities, had no representation in Parliament at all.

(5) In some boroughs the choice of a representative was completely controlled by the nobles, who were members of the House of Lords. These were called "pocket boroughs" because in each of them the noble had the representative "in his pocket," meaning that the representative would vote as he was told to by the noble.

(6) Only men who owned considerable prop-

erty could be elected to the House of Commons. Representatives received no salary. Thus a man who was not a large landowner could not be elected, and a man without a large income could not afford to serve.

The Reform Bill of 1832

As time went on, the middle class and workers began to demand reforms. For a while the upper classes were able to postpone reforms. Many Englishmen had become fearful of political change because of the French Revolution, especially the Reign of Terror. Then from 1793 to 1815, British involvement in wars with France served as an excuse for delaying action.

After the defeat of Napoleon, Britain, like continental Europe, went through a period of reaction. Even long-established civil liberties were seriously threatened, and the right of *habeas corpus* was suspended. Reformers who once might have tried to gain the support of the king could find no help there. George III was insane for several years before he died in 1820. His son, George IV, was an incompetent monarch who was widely disliked. Near the end of his reign, in 1829, one piece of reform, the Catholic Emancipation Act, was passed. It permitted Roman Catholics to be elected to Parliament if they recognized the Protestant monarch as the true ruler of Britain.

Demands for voting reform increased. Several times the House of Commons passed bills to give more people the right to vote, and to reapportion election districts more fairly. Each time the House of Lords refused to pass the bill. Finally the Whigs, who came to power in 1830, forced William IV, who became king that same year, to announce that he would create as many new lords as necessary to give the bill a majority in the House of Lords. To avoid this move, the lords grudgingly gave in and passed the bill in 1832.

The Reform Bill of 1832 took representation in Commons away from the rotten boroughs and pocket boroughs and gave it to the new industrial cities. Scotland was also given a larger representation in Parliament. Property qualifications for voting were lowered so that about one out of

every thirty Englishmen could now vote. As a result, parliamentary power came more into the hands of the owners of factories and banks, the merchants, and the shipowners.

The Whig Party, which had forced the passage of the Reform Bill of 1832, had the support of the new voters. Since many voters favored even more liberal reforms, the party changed its name and became the Liberal Party. The Tory Party of the large landowners had opposed the reforms and was reluctant to go any further. It became known as the Conservative Party.

Social and economic change

Although there were no important political reforms for several years after 1832, there were vital social and economic developments. In 1833, Parliament passed an act that provided for the gradual abolition of slavery throughout the British colonies. All children under the age of six were declared free; all children over six years of age were to be free within seven years.

The Liberal Party soon forced the adoption of other reforms. You have read about some of the factory legislation of this period. The government took a timid first step toward free public education by giving financial support to private and church schools. Imprisonment for debt was abolished.

William IV died in 1837. Since he had no male heirs, the throne went to his eighteen-year-old niece, Victoria. She said, early in her reign, "I will be good." She interfered very little in the government and allowed her prime ministers a free hand. She was to reign for more than sixty years, until 1901, a period so outstanding in British history that it became known as the Victorian Era.

The Corn Laws. For many years, as you have read, Britain's Corn Laws set very high tariffs on imported grain. By raising prices on imports, the Corn Laws protected expensive British grain against competition from cheaper foreign crops. British landowners benefited because they could sell their grain at high prices; this situation, however, was a hardship for workingmen and laborers who had to buy grain products or starve.

The Victorian Era is aptly named because of the indelible stamp left upon Western thought and manners by Queen Victoria, right. She was spirited and self-assured, but nevertheless established the amicable relations between Parliament and the British royal family that have endured ever since. Married to the handsome Prince Albert and mother of nine children, she set an example of happy but highly proper family life that endeared her to her subjects. For the last thirty years of Victoria's reign, English politics were dominated by Gladstone of the Liberals, below, and Disraeli of the Conservatives, below right. Victoria usually thought Gladstone too pompous, but was shocked at the vulgarity of his making political speeches from trains, as shown here. The statue of Disraeli portrays him in the traditional costume of the Order of the Garter.

In 1846, after a bitter fight, a bill was forced through Parliament repealing the Corn Laws. Grain could now be imported into Britain free of tax. The repeal of the Corn Laws was the first step Britain took in the direction of free trade.

Chartism and political reforms. The year of European revolutions, 1848, saw the failure of an attempt at further political change in Britain. Beginning in the 1830's, a group known as the Workingman's Association petitioned Parliament to adopt reforms such as universal manhood suffrage and the secret ballot. These proposals were made in a document called "A People's Charter," and those who advocated them were known as Chartists.

Chartist conventions were held in 1839, 1842, and 1848. Although their proposals were relatively mild, the Chartists were denounced as men who threatened the very foundations of society. In 1848 the British authorities were worried that revolution might occur in Britain as it had on the continent. But the Chartists were not united in their aims, and the movement died out.

Despite the failure of the Chartist movement, almost all of the reforms its members advocated were eventually adopted. Workingmen continued

512

to agitate for voting rights, and were joined by many others who favored more democratic government. Leaders of both the Conservative and Liberal parties came to realize that reforms might gain the gratitude and the votes of the new voters.

In 1867 a second Reform Bill was passed. It was more sweeping than the first, and almost doubled the electorate. By lowering property qualifications, the second Reform Bill extended the vote to most city industrial workers. Some groups were still left out: household servants, members of the armed forces, agricultural workers, and all women. However, the addition of new voters made further reforms possible.

Disraeli and Gladstone

The period between 1866 and 1894 was dominated by two men who were entirely different in character and outlook. One was Benjamin Disraeli, a leader of the Conservative Party, who served twice as prime minister. He was witty, shrewd, and greatly interested in British foreign affairs and the enlargement of the empire. The other was William Gladstone, who, as leader of the Liberal Party, was prime minister four times. He was most concerned with British domestic and financial matters. Devout and cautious, he was a great contrast to Disraeli. He was so pompous and formal that Queen Victoria once complained: "Mr. Gladstone addresses me as if I were a public meeting."

Disraeli's first term as prime minister, in 1868, was short; but during his second ministry, from 1874 to 1880, Britain gained control of the Suez Canal and Queen Victoria became Empress of India. These were major concerns of the Conservative Party.

The Liberal Party was more occupied with the "Irish Question." In 1801, Ireland and Great Britain had been joined by the Act of Union into the United Kingdom of Great Britain and Ireland. The Irish were poorly represented in the British Parliament, however, and the people—most of them Roman Catholics—resented having to pay taxes to help support the Anglican Church.

The Irish hated British rule, especially the absentee landlords who owned much of the land.

Several times in the mid-1800's, famine swept Ireland when the potato crop failed. Many Irish had abandoned their homes and emigrated to the United States. Those who remained wanted new land laws and home rule—that is, self-government. Gladstone tried unsuccessfully to get home-rule bills passed. During the 1890's, it was the Conservatives who made concessions to the Irish so that the Irish Question was less troublesome for a few decades.

In 1872, Britain adopted the secret ballot, which meant that a man could vote as he chose, without being afraid that he might suffer because someone disapproved of his politics. This move also reduced bribery, which had been common.

In 1884 the Liberals took the lead in pushing through Parliament the third Reform Bill, which gave the vote to most agricultural workers. In the following year the Redistribution Bill divided Britain into electoral districts that were approximately equal in population.

The early 1900's

During the late 1800's and early 1900's, the union movement grew stronger in Britain. Socialism, too, won many followers. In 1884, a group of intellectuals founded the Fabian Society, a moderate organization aimed at "reconstructing society in accordance with the highest moral possibilities." At first the Fabians worked through the established political parties, but in 1906 they helped found a new organization, the British Labour Party.

In 1905 the Liberal Party came to power. Under Herbert Asquith, prime minister from 1908 to 1916, the Liberals adopted extensive social welfare legislation. Laws provided for child care, old-age pensions, better housing, and health and unemployment insurance. These changes meant that the government had to spend more money, and that taxes must be increased to raise it.

To meet the costs of the new program, the budget of 1909 called for changes in taxation that increased the tax burden of the wealthy. Opposition to the budget was so strong in the House of Lords that the Liberals decided to deprive the lords of their power to block reforms. The Par-

ISOLDE

HISTORY THROUGH ART

"Isolde" by Aubrey Beardsley

Much of the art of the Victorian Era was sentimental and fussy. People admired paintings that told a story or illustrated a moral. A counter trend of the late 1800's was Art Nouveau (French for "new art"). This style was characterized by a philosophy of "art for art's sake" and by undulating lines that imitated natural forms. Aubrey Beardsley was an English illustrator whose designs typify the sophistication of Art Nouveau. Although his work was highly artificial, its boldness and originality had a strong influence on many other artists.

liament Bill of 1911 took away the lords' power to veto tax and appropriation bills and allowed them only to delay the passage of other bills. The lords were bitterly opposed and passed the act only after George V, who had become king in

513

1910, threatened to create enough new Liberal lords to pass it.

Within a month after the passage of the Parliament Bill, Liberals and workingmen gained another goal for which they had long worked. Parliament passed a law giving members of the House of Commons a salary of 400 pounds a year (about $2,000). Today this seems like a small amount, but it was a good salary then. It meant that a person without an independent income could now afford to serve in Parliament.

2 Canada, Australia, and New Zealand became self-governing dominions

You have read about the beginnings of the British Empire during the 1500's and 1600's. As time went on, this empire came to consist of two chief kinds of possessions: (1) colonies, where a relatively small number of British ruled a large native population, and (2) sovereign states, where British settlers and their descendants ruled themselves in comparative independence. You will read more about Britain's colonial possessions in Unit 7. This section deals with three of the most important sovereign states—Canada, Australia, and New Zealand.

Canada

In 1791, as you read in Chapter 18, the British Parliament passed the Constitutional Act, dividing Canada into two provinces: Upper Canada and Lower Canada (see map, opposite). This act was an attempt to settle the differences between French Canadians in Lower Canada and British settlers in Upper Canada. But it did not really satisfy either group. British Canadians wanted even more self-government and the French resented British rule.

During the 1830's, discontent was increased by poor economic conditions, including a business depression, unemployment, and crop failures. In 1837 there were uprisings both by the French in Lower Canada and the British in Upper Canada. The French Canadians tried to establish an independent French republic, whereas the British Canadians sought greater freedom from British

officials. Neither revolt was successful, and both were soon put down.

The Durham Report. In 1838 the British government sent a new governor general, Lord Durham, to Canada. A leader of the Liberal Party, he had helped to write the Reform Bill of 1832. Now he was given broad powers to try to relax the tense situation in Canada. He was also instructed to survey Canadian conditions and make recommendations to Parliament.

Lord Durham treated the Canadians so leniently that he was severely criticized in Britain. He resigned after holding office only five months. In 1839, however, he submitted a report to Parliament with a basic principle that was to guide all later British colonial policy—that if Great Britain granted self-government to colonies like Canada, it could hold them in the empire.

The Durham Report recommended that the two Canadas be reunited into one province and that it be granted responsible government with a single elected legislature and an executive council responsible to that legislature. The British governor general could exercise power only in emergencies. The report also recommended that the British government aid immigration to Canada, build a railroad to help unite and develop the country, reform the tax and judicial systems, and expand education.

In 1840 the British Parliament carried out the recommendations of the Durham Report in the Act of Union. This act joined Upper and Lower

Canada and created a parliament in which each region had equal representation. Between 1846 and 1848 the British enlarged the powers of the Canadian parliament and granted self-government to the people of Canada.

Creating the dominion. The union of Upper and Lower Canada did not work well in every respect. Each region was jealous and suspicious of the other. Their equal strength in the parliament resulted in many deadlocks. A way out came in 1864 when the eastern colonies of New Brunswick, Nova Scotia, and Prince Edward Island were considering a federal union. Delegates from Canada and the colonies met in the city of Quebec. They recommended a plan of federation, which the British Parliament approved as the British North America Act of 1867. It created the Dominion of Canada with the provinces of Ontario (formerly Upper Canada), Quebec (formerly Lower Canada), Nova Scotia, and New Brunswick.

In 1869, Canada purchased a huge area, including the present Northwest Territories, from the Hudson's Bay Company—a private trading company in Canada (see map, page 516). Because the Canadians feared that the United States would try to annex all or part of this vast area, they quickly created the province of Manitoba out of a segment of it. British Columbia and Prince Edward Island became provinces during the 1870's, thus bringing the number of provinces in the Dominion up to seven.

By the terms of the British North America Act, each province kept its own legislature to deal with domestic affairs. The federal parliament, which dealt with common problems, met in Ontario at the Dominion capital, Ottawa. Dominion government was a parliamentary democracy with a cabinet based on the British model. The political parties in Canada—Liberals and Conservatives—were similar to those in Britain, and the party in power appointed the premier, who exercised much the same influence as the prime minister in Great Britain.

Canada did not become completely independent through the British North America Act. It was part of the British Empire and recognized

CANADA IN 1800

the British sovereign; her representative, the governor general, had the power of veto (although it was rarely used). The British government exerted a definite and strong influence over Canada's foreign relations.

Other developments. During the remainder of the 1800's, Canada was largely concerned with internal affairs. The Canadian Pacific Railway, extending from coast to coast, was completed in 1885. This and other railway lines helped open up the vast expanses of western Canada to immigration, and thus to farming and manufacturing. The provinces of Alberta and Saskatchewan were formed and joined the Dominion in 1905.°

Another factor in the development of western Canada was the discovery of gold in the Klondike region. During the late 1890's, thousands of prospectors went to the area searching for gold. Primarily because of the Klondike Gold Rush, there was a large enough population to organize the Yukon Territory in 1898.

There were several revolts in Canada, some by Indians in Manitoba opposing government encroachment on their land, and others by Canadian Irish who hoped to help Ireland gain freedom from Britain. All of these rebellions were easily put down, often without force or bloodshed. However, bad feeling between British and French Canadians continued to trouble the nation:

° In 1949, Newfoundland and its dependency, Labrador, became the tenth province of the Dominion of Canada.

515

Boundary and fishery disputes with the United States occurred several times, but were submitted to arbitration and settled peaceably by treaties. The two nations, sharing a common heritage from Great Britain, were in most cases far more interested in peace than in war. The boundary between the two became famous as a symbol of how two major nations could exist peacefully side by side. Stretching for 3,000 miles from the Atlantic to the Pacific oceans, it is the longest unfortified boundary in the world.

Australia

Australia is a huge island, a continent in itself, yet it remained unknown to the rest of the world for centuries. The European explorers who sailed into the Pacific Ocean in the 1500's missed it entirely. The Dutch discovered it in the early 1600's and named it New Holland, but considered it too poor a land to colonize or trade with. Captain James Cook, an Englishman on a scientific expedition for the navy, sailed along the eastern shore of Australia in 1770. He named the region New South Wales because of its resemblance to southern Wales, and claimed it for Great Britain.

Before the American Revolution, Britain had sent many convicts to America. After the loss of its thirteen American colonies, Britain decided to use Australia as a penal colony. The first shiploads of convicts arrived in New South Wales in 1788, and soon the town of Sydney was founded on the southeast coast. Free settlers arrived shortly

THE DOMINION OF CANADA TODAY

Territory purchased from the Hudson's Bay Company, 1869

Boundary established by treaties, 1783-1846

0   1000 miles

afterward. Land grants were made to them, and land was also available to convicts who had served their time, gained their freedom, and wished to stay on in Australia.

The early 1800's were a lawless period, with clashes among immigrants, ex-convicts, and gangs of escaped convicts called bushrangers. In addition, many of the aborigines (ab·uh·RIJ·uh·neez) —the original inhabitants of Australia—were hunted down and exterminated as if they were animals.

Explorations by the British revealed that New South Wales was only part of a large continent, much of which was desert but some of which was fertile and could be developed. Sheep and cattle raising became an important industry. In 1829 the British, alarmed by French explorations along the coasts, laid formal claim to the entire continent of Australia. By 1836 the additional colonies of Tasmania, Western Australia, and South Australia had been organized. The colony of Victoria was formed in 1851, and Queensland in 1859 (see map, this page).

The discovery of gold in 1851 in the new colony of Victoria brought a flood of immigrants to Australia. Soon the colonial legislatures began to pass acts that restricted the right of immigration to white persons. This "White Australia" policy antagonized many nations, particularly in the Orient, but it was maintained so strictly that only a few immigrants from countries other than Great Britain were admitted to Australia as permanent settlers.

For several decades, each Australian colony was independent and self-governing. Their legislatures were modeled after the British Parliament, except that both the upper and lower houses were elective. (In New South Wales the members of the upper house were appointed for life.) It was not until the 1890's that the Australian colonies began seriously to consider uniting into a federal union as protection against the imperialism of European nations. Discussions went on for ten years. Finally, in 1901, the Commonwealth of Australia was created. (Although Australia did not use the term, it was considered, like Canada, to have *dominion status*.)

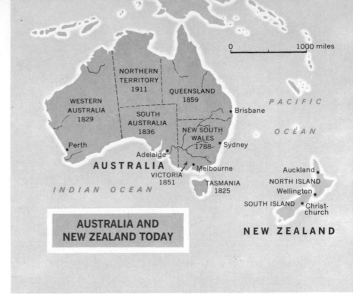

AUSTRALIA AND NEW ZEALAND TODAY

Because of strong influence exerted by local trade unions and the Labor Party, Australia adopted a great deal of social legislation. It included bills establishing old-age pensions, compulsory arbitration of labor disputes, and wage-fixing boards.

New Zealand

Like Australia, the islands of New Zealand, to the southeast, were first discovered by the Dutch and later rediscovered by Captain Cook. Early development there was carried on by private companies in the 1820's and 1830's. In 1840, British sovereignty was established through a treaty with the Maori (MAH·oh·ree) chieftains, who were the native rulers of the islands. A few years later the British Parliament gave New Zealand a constitution, and the islands became a self-governing colony.

Disputes over land brought the British settlers into conflict with the native inhabitants, and several Maori wars were fought in the 1840's and 1860's. In other respects the development of New Zealand was similar to that in Australia. There was a discovery of gold in 1861 and the establishment of immigration restriction acts. New Zealand became the first country in the world to adopt woman suffrage when it gave women the right to vote in 1893. In 1907, New Zealand joined the British Empire as a dominion.

517

1. Trace the steps by which Canada achieved self-government.

2. Why do you think Canada was able to achieve independence without a revolution?

3. IDENTIFY: Klondike Gold Rush, Cook, aborigines.

4. LOCATE: New Brunswick, Prince Edward Island, Ontario, Quebec Province, Manitoba, British Columbia, Ottawa, Alberta, Saskatchewan, New South Wales, Tasmania, South Australia, Victoria.

 ## 3 The United States emerged as a major power

In 1788, when the Constitution of the United States was ratified, the new nation consisted of thirteen states along the Atlantic coast and additional territories that stretched westward to the Mississippi River. Its population totaled about 4 million people. Most of them lived in farming communities in the eastern part of the country.

The young nation was born at a time when Europe was in turmoil, and most Americans wanted to stay out of European affairs and develop their nation in peace. They did this so successfully that, during the next hundred years, the territory of the United States grew to almost four times its original size, and its population increased to 60 million. By 1900 the United States was ready to take its place among the great nations of the world.

Territorial and political growth

You have read that many European powers in the 1500's and 1600's expanded overseas and set up colonies. The United States, in contrast, expanded overland, within the continent of North America. In governing the territories gained by expansion, the United States differed significantly from European governments. The new nation was determined to expand without acquiring any colonies, in the usual sense of the word. As you have read, the Northwest Ordinance of 1787 provided that the Northwest Territory would be divided into states that were to be admitted into the Union on a basis of equality with existing states. It provided for orderly expansion and the natural movement of democratic ideas into new territories.

Even before the Revolutionary War, it was clear that the American people would not remain clustered along the Atlantic seaboard. During the late 1700's and early 1800's, pioneers on horseback, in wagons, and on foot moved around and through the Appalachian Mountains into the land between the mountains and the Mississippi River. There they carved farms out of the wilderness and set up trading posts that eventually became cities. Eleven new states joined the Union between 1791 and 1821.

You have read about Napoleon's sale of the vast territory of Louisiana to the United States in 1803. Extending westward from the Mississippi River roughly to the Rocky Mountains, the so-called Louisiana Purchase almost doubled the size of the United States. In 1819 the United States also purchased Florida from Spain (see map, opposite page).

In 1836, American settlers in Mexican territory to the south of the Louisiana Purchase declared themselves independent and set up the Republic of Texas. The United States annexed Texas in the 1840's, and war with Mexico resulted. The United States won the Mexican War, gaining not only Texas but also the Mexican Cession—a huge region that became the states of Utah, Nevada, California, and parts of Arizona, Colorado, New Mexico, and Wyoming. In 1846 Americans signed a treaty with Britain by which they gained control of the so-called Oregon Country, which became the states of Oregon, Washington, Idaho, and parts of Montana and Wyoming. Thus, by 1850, the relatively new nation stretched from coast to coast and from Mexico to Canada. With the Gadsden Purchase in 1853, additional territory was added to the southwest.

The principles of the Northwest Ordinance were applied to all these additions. Men could settle in the new territories, secure in the knowledge that

TERRITORIAL GROWTH OF THE UNITED STATES TO 1860

---------- Present-day state boundaries

——— Boundary established by treaties, 1783-1846

their civil rights were protected, and that, when the population was large enough to justify it, their territories would be admitted to the Union as equal states.

During the next fifty years, settlement caught up with territorial acquisitions. The discovery of gold in California in 1848 led to the Gold Rush— a flood of migrants to the Pacific coast in search of quick wealth. Cattle ranchers, farmers, and miners settled in the plains and mountains of the western United States.

As the United States grew in size, it also became more democratic. In the early days of the country, some states had limited the right to vote to those who owned property. But the new states farther west imposed no such qualifications, and

they were gradually dropped in most eastern states. During the presidency of Andrew Jackson in the early 1830's, many changes were made. Public education became more widespread; an increasing number of political offices became elective instead of appointive; political candidates came to be chosen by party conventions rather than by small groups of legislators. Foreign visitors spoke of the "general equality of conditions" and the "great democratic revolution" taking place in the United States.

The slavery question

Although the United States had a unified federal government, it was not free from *sectionalism* —a kind of rivalry among the various sections

CAUTION!!
COLORED PEOPLE
OF BOSTON, ONE & ALL,

You are hereby respectfully CAUTIONED and advised, to avoid conversing with the

Watchmen and Police Officers of Boston,

For since the recent ORDER OF THE MAYOR & ALDERMEN, they are empowered to act as

KIDNAPPERS
AND
Slave Catchers,

And they have already been actually employed in KIDNAPPING, CATCHING, AND KEEPING SLAVES. Therefore, if you value your LIBERTY, and the *Welfare of the Fugitives* among you, *Shun* them in every possible manner, as so many *HOUNDS* on the track of the most unfortunate of your race.

Keep a Sharp Look Out for KIDNAPPERS, and have TOP EYE open.
APRIL 24, 1851.

The Civil War was caused largely by the bitter conflict over slavery. The institution had already been abolished in the territories of most European nations. The medallion at top was made in 1768 for the Slave Emancipation Society of England. In the United States, abolitionists found the English experience helpful to their cause. The sign above was posted by Boston abolitionists. When war came, the North profited from its overwhelming advantage in material resources. Below, Northern soldiers stand beside a heavy and powerful cannon. Artillery of this sort had to be transported on a specially constructed railroad track.

of the country. During the early 1800's, three chief sections took shape: the Northeast, a region of growing cities and industry; the South, an area of many large farms, especially cotton plantations; and the West (at that time the land between the Appalachians and the Mississippi), a frontier region of small, independent farmers.

With these different ways of life, it is not surprising that men from each of these sections should have held very different views on such issues as internal improvements at federal expense, tariffs, banking and currency, and public lands. As time went on, however, the greatest single issue dividing the sections was that of slavery.

Negro slavery had existed in the American colonies almost from the beginning. The Constitution accepted slavery as legal, but left its regulation up to the states. In states where it existed, it could be abolished only by action of the state itself. Some states had taken such action chiefly for economic reasons. Slavery had been abolished in the Northeast and West, where it was not profitable or necessary. It remained and increased in the South, where it was thought necessary, especially after the cotton gin made cotton a profitable crop. In the southern states the principal crops, cotton and tobacco, were thought to require slave labor.

Both cotton and tobacco were crops that exhausted the soil. Southerners needed new lands, the unsettled lands of the territories, to which they could move when their soil was exhausted. Thus the question arose: should slavery be permitted in the territories? Southerners argued that Congress did not have the power to prohibit it. Northerners and Westerners argued that it did. A growing number of people came to advocate abolition—the ending of slavery everywhere in the United States.

As the 1800's wore on, the slavery question led to bitter sectional quarrels. Twice southern states threatened to *secede*—that is, to withdraw from the Union. Each time compromises were arranged so that secession was avoided. Then, in 1860, the United States elected as President Abraham Lincoln, who led the newly formed Republican Party.

The Republicans had pledged to prevent the spread of slavery into the territories.

Secession and war

Shortly after the results of the election were known, South Carolina seceded, and was soon followed by other states. They formed the Confederate States of America, with Jefferson Davis as president. Eventually eleven southern states joined the Confederacy.

President Lincoln and Congress maintained that the Constitution did not give a state the right to secede. They declared the act of the Southerners a rebellion, which it was the duty of the United States government to suppress. Efforts to compromise proved useless. War came in 1861 and lasted four years.

The Civil War was the most costly conflict in which the United States had been involved up to that time. It has also been called the first modern war because it introduced new and lethal devices such as explosive shells, ironclad warships, and the Gatling gun, a forerunner of the machine gun.

Although European nations opposed slavery, many tended to favor the Confederacy in the Civil War. Industrial and commercial interests looked forward to the weakening of their business competitors in the Northeast. The British needed Southern cotton and frequently aided Confederate ships by letting them use British ports, in spite of strong Northern protests. Napoleon III of France, as you have read, took advantage of the conflict to intervene in Mexico.

As time went on, it became clear that the agricultural South lacked the industries and railroads necessary to supply its armies. By 1865 its men were hungry and in rags, its land devastated by Northern troops. The Confederacy surrendered in April 1865. The Union was preserved.

In January 1863, President Lincoln had issued the Emancipation Proclamation, freeing slaves in those parts of the country that were "still in rebellion against the United States." Later, three amendments to the Constitution freed all the slaves, gave them citizenship, and granted them the right to vote. Thus the doctrine of the equality of all men before the law was strengthened.

This 1860 photograph of Abraham Lincoln illustrates the President's description of himself: "I am in height six feet four inches, nearly."

521

Most immigrants arrived in America with only a few personal possessions. Here a group waits at Ellis Island in New York Harbor, the "Gateway to the New World."

The Union was saved only at a tragic cost. The North and South together had lost nearly half a million men. Families had been torn apart as brother fought against brother. Nor did freedom solve the problems of the former Negro slaves. The war left deep scars on the nation that were to remain for a long time.

The late 1800's

The period from 1865 to 1900 was one of phenomenal growth in the United States. You have read about American industrialization and the factors that made it possible. Cities doubled and tripled in size, and railroads crisscrossed the nation to bind them together.

One important factor in the growth of the United States was immigration. For many decades, most immigrants came from England and Scotland. In the middle 1800's, two other regions sent a heavy wave of immigration: (1) Ireland, which suffered severe potato famines; and (2) Germany, where the revolutions of 1848 caused many liberals to flee.

The late 1800's saw heavy immigration from southern and eastern Europe, especially Italy, Russia, and Austria-Hungary. The United States, which absorbed more immigrants than any other country in the world, became known as a "melting-pot" where diverse nationalities blended with relatively little friction.

By 1900 the United States seemed to offer unlimited possibilities for economic and financial expansion. You will read in Chapter 28 about the foreign policy of the nation in the late 1800's and early 1900's.

CHECKUP

1. Explain and give examples of the various ways in which the territory of the United States was expanded.

2. In the United States, settlement moved from east to west, but democratic practices moved west to east. Explain.

3. Why did Southerners consider it so important for slavery to be permitted in the territories? How did this issue lead to the Civil War?

4. IDENTIFY: Gatling gun, Emancipation Proclamation, "melting-pot."

5. LOCATE: Louisiana Purchase, Texas Annexation, Mexican Cession, Oregon Country, Gadsden Purchase.

CHAPTER REVIEW

Chapter 25 The English-Speaking Peoples Developed Democratic Nations (1770–1911)

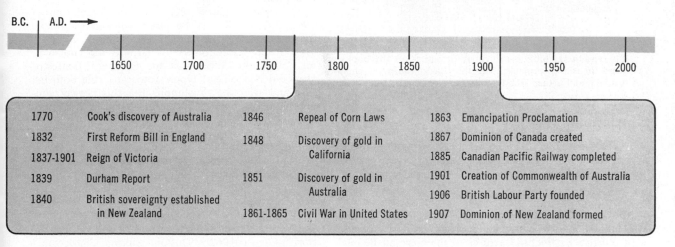

1770	Cook's discovery of Australia	1846	Repeal of Corn Laws	1863	Emancipation Proclamation
1832	First Reform Bill in England	1848	Discovery of gold in California	1867	Dominion of Canada created
1837-1901	Reign of Victoria			1885	Canadian Pacific Railway completed
1839	Durham Report	1851	Discovery of gold in Australia	1901	Creation of Commonwealth of Australia
1840	British sovereignty established in New Zealand			1906	British Labour Party founded
		1861-1865	Civil War in United States	1907	Dominion of New Zealand formed

CHAPTER SUMMARY

Although Great Britain had become a limited constitutional monarchy, the right to vote was severely restricted. Finally, in 1832, Parliament passed the Reform Bill, equalizing representation and lowering property qualifications for voting. Other reforms included the abolition of slavery, the passage of factory legislation, and the repeal of the Corn Laws. Although the Chartist movement failed, many Chartist measures were adopted.

Disraeli and Gladstone dominated the late 1800's, when Britain expanded its empire and further broadened the suffrage. In the early 1900's the Liberals adopted extensive social legislation and reduced the power of the House of Lords.

Several British possessions gained independence. Discontent in Canada led to the Durham Report, which established Britain's basic colonial policy. In the 1840's, Canada gained self-government. After its organization as a dominion, it increased in size, its growth stimulated by a cross-country railroad and the discovery of gold in the west.

Australia began as a British penal colony, but livestock raising and the discovery of gold attracted other settlers. Its several separate colonies united in 1901 to form a dominion within the British Empire. New Zealand, originally developed by private companies, came under British sovereignty in 1840 and joined the British Empire as a dominion in 1907.

Another English-speaking nation, the United States, expanded greatly during the 1800's with the Louisiana Purchase and the acquisition of Florida, the Mexican Cession, and the Oregon Country. However, the country was divided by sectionalism and the slavery question. The result was a tragic civil war, in which the Union defeated the Confederacy. The postwar period saw great industrial growth and immigration.

QUESTIONS FOR DISCUSSION

1. What is the difference between direct democracy and representative democracy? What are the advantages and disadvantages of each?

2. What were the "rotten boroughs" in England, and how were they dealt with in the Reform Bill of 1832? Do you approve of the United States Supreme Court decisions in the 1960's calling for reapportionment of voting districts in order to achieve the principle of "one man, one vote"?

3. The British Conservatives fought the Reform Bill of 1832 with all the means at their disposal. Once it was passed, however, they accepted it. Do you think it is a good idea, after a change in administration, for the new party to accept most of the legislation passed by previous administrations? Explain.

4. How did the immigration policies of the United States and Australia differ during the 1800's? With which policy do you agree?

PROJECTS

1. Write an editorial for a liberal British newspaper, attacking the various voting restrictions that existed in the early 1800's.

2. Draw a map of the southwestern Pacific area showing the major cities and territorial divisions of Australia and New Zealand.

3. Draw a map showing the territorial acquisitions of the United States, with the date and the method of acquiring each one.

STUDY IN DEPTH

UNIT SIX

For additional bibliographical information on the books cited in these projects, see the Basic Library (page xviii) and Further Reading on the opposite page.

INDIVIDUAL PROJECTS

1. Nationalism has shaped much of history. Write an essay in which you define the characteristics of nationalism and discuss some of its manifestations in the 1800's. For your essay consult Eisen and Filler, *The Human Adventure,* Vol. 2, "The Dedication of Young Italy" and "Cavour and the Emperor Napoleon III Plan a War"; Hughes and Fries, *European Civilization,* "Fichte Lectures to the German People on Nationalism"; Peterson, *Treasury of the World's Great Speeches,* "Charles Stewart Parnell Demands Home Rule for Ireland."

2. Prepare an oral report on either Halasz, *Captain Dreyfus,* or Schechter, *The Dreyfus Affair.* Focus your report on these questions: What was the position of the army in the Third French Republic? How did the French press react to the Dreyfus case? What part was played by Émile Zola and the French intellectuals? What was the final outcome of the Dreyfus case? What was its significance?

3. Prepare a class report on the revolutions of 1848 in Europe. Investigate the causes, events, and results of the various revolutions that occurred throughout Europe. Consult the following readings: Eisen and Filler, *The Human Adventure,* Vol. 2, "The Paris Workers in Revolt—June 1848" and "The Revolution of 1848 in Berlin"; Stearns, *Pageant of Europe,* "Louis Blanc's Account of the Failure of the Workshops"; Peterson, *Treasury of the World's Great Speeches,* "Alexis de Tocqueville Feels 'A Gale of Revolution in the Air'"; Snyder and Morris, *A Treasury of Great Reporting,* "A February Revolt Brings a Republic to France, but the Bloody Strife of the July Days Forecasts Its Early Doom."

4. Prepare an oral report on the tactics of Bismarck's *Realpolitik.* Be sure to give a number of examples of the chancellor's application of *Realpolitik* to the issues confronting him. For references see Eisen and Filler, *The Human Adventure,* Vol. 2, "Bismarck's Formula for Success," "Prussia's Reluctance to Wound Defeated Austria," and "Bismarck Edits a Telegram from His Monarch"; Peterson, *Treasury of the World's Great Speeches,* "Bismarck Recommends the Values of Blood and Iron" and "Bismarck Pleads for a Bigger Arms Budget." For a more detailed account read either Morrow's or Taylor's biography of Bismarck.

5. Prepare an oral report on the Revolution of 1905 in czarist Russia. Be sure to answer the following questions: What were the grievances of Father Gapon and his followers? What was the course of the revolution? What was the October Manifesto? How did Nicholas II typify autocratic rule both before and after the revolution? For this project consult the books on Russian history listed on the opposite page.

6. Informative articles about the American Civil War can be found in *American Heritage.* Read one of the following articles and use it as the basis for a class report: "Prison Camps in the Civil War," August 1959; "The Bloodiest Man in American History," October 1960; "Lincoln and the Telegraph," April 1961; "Lest We Forget," August 1961; "Bull Run Russell," June 1962; "Sherman: Modern Warrior," August 1962; "DuPont Storms Charleston," June 1963; "A Civil, and Sometimes Uncivil, War," October 1964; "So Eager Were We All," June 1965.

GROUP PROJECTS

1. A committee of students can prepare two charts on nationalism for the classroom bulletin board. One chart should show the successes and failures of nationalistic uprisings between 1815 and 1850, indicating the countries, dates, events, outcomes, and leaders involved. A second chart might show how and where each of the following helped to build nationalism: (1) wars, (2) national leaders and heroes, (3) railroad building and development of resources, (4) colonies, (5) common language and literature, (6) schools.

2. Organize a debate on the topic: National states are no longer the best form of political organization. This debate should be between one group of students who believe in some kind of international government, and another group that holds that traditional national states are best for political order in the world.

3. An interesting "You Are There" program can be created about Garibaldi's exploits in Sicily. Several students should prepare the program on tape and include an interview with Garibaldi or one of his soldiers describing some of the military engagements. Parts of a speech given by Garibaldi should also be included. A book of interest for this project is Trease, *A Thousand for Sicily,* and shorter pieces such as Copeland and Lamm, *The World's Great Speeches,* "Giuseppe Garibaldi: To His Soldiers"; Snyder and Morris, *A Treasury of Great Reporting,* "Garibaldi and His Thousand Redshirts Win Palermo."

Further Reading

BIOGRAPHY

Blake, Robert, *Disraeli*. St. Martin's.

Cooper, L. U., *Young Victoria*. Roy.

Davenport, Marcia, *Garibaldi: Father of Modern Italy*. Random House.

Flexner, Marion W., *Drina, England's Young Queen*. Coward-McCann. Queen Victoria.

Guérard, Albert, *Napoleon III*. Knopf.

Halasz, Nicholas, *Captain Dreyfus*. Grove.*

Mack Smith, Denis, *Garibaldi*. Knopf.

McLeod, R. A., *Cavour and Italian Unity*. Exposition.

Magnus, Philip, *Gladstone: A Biography*. Dutton.

Maurois, André, *Disraeli*. Modern Library.

Morrow, Ian F. D., *Bismarck*. Macmillan.

Mosse, W. E., *Alexander II and the Modernization of Russia*. Macmillan.

Nolan, Jeannette C., *Florence Nightingale*. Messner.

Parris, John, *Lion of Caprera: A Life of Garibaldi*. McKay.

Sandburg, Carl, *Abraham Lincoln: The War Years and The Prairie Years*. Dell.*

Strachey, Lytton, *Queen Victoria*. Harcourt Brace Jovanovich.*

_____, *Eminent Victorians*. Putnam.*

Taylor, A. J. P., *Bismarck*. Knopf.

Warner, Oliver, *Captain Cook and the South Pacific*. Harper & Row.

Woodham-Smith, Cecil, *Florence Nightingale*. Avon.*

NONFICTION

Artz, F. B., *France Under the Bourbon Restoration, 1814–1830*. Russell & Russell.

Creighton, Donald, *The Story of Canada*. Houghton Mifflin.

Gibbs, P. B., *The Battle of the Alma*. Lippincott. Crimean War.

Karpovich, Michael, *Imperial Russia, 1801–1917*. Holt, Rinehart and Winston.*

Kohn, Hans, *Basic History of Modern Russia*. Van Nostrand.*

Leslie, R. F., *Reform and Insurrection in Russian Poland*. Oxford Univ. Press.

Mazour, Anatole G., *Rise and Fall of the Romanovs*. Van Nostrand.*

Moorehead, Alan, *Cooper's Creek*. Dell.* Exploration in Australia.

Nazaroff, Alexander, *The Land of the Russian People*. Lippincott.

* Paperback.

Peck, Anne M., *Pageant of Canadian History*. McKay.

Petrie, C. A., *The Victorians*. McKay. Life in England during the Victorian Era.

Price, M. Phillips, *A History of Turkey: From Empire to Republic*. Hillary House.

Rosenberg, Arthur, *Imperial Germany: The Birth of the German Republic 1871–1918*. Beacon.*

Schechter, B., *The Dreyfus Affair*. Houghton Mifflin.

Trease, Geoffrey, *A Thousand for Sicily*. Vanguard.

Werstein, Irving, *The Franco-Prussian War: Germany's Rise as a World Power*. Messner.

Williams, Roger L., *The World of Napoleon III*. Macmillan *

Wolf, John B., *France, 1814–1919: The Rise of a Liberal-Democratic Society*. Harper & Row.*

Woodham-Smith, Cecil, *The Great Hunger*. New American Library.* Famine in Ireland.

_____, *The Reason Why*. Dutton.* Crimean War.

HISTORICAL FICTION

Born, Edith de, *Felding Castle*. Knopf. Austria during Franz Josef's time.

Crane, Stephen, *Red Badge of Courage*. Bobbs-Merrill.* American Civil War.

Dickens, Charles, *Life and Adventures of Nicholas Nickleby*. Dodd, Mead.* England's neglect of public education.

Eden, Dorothy, *Lady of Mallow*. Ace Books.* Victoria's England.

Fowler, Helen M., *The Blazing Straw*. Macmillan. Republicans in Ireland.

Giono, Jean, *The Straw Man*. Knopf. Revolution in Italy in 1848.

Hugo, Victor, *Les Miserables*. Fawcett.* Life of the poor in France during the 1800's.

Lampedusa, Giuseppe di, *The Leopard*. New American Library.* Sicily during the unification of Italy.

Macken, Walter, *The Silent People*. Macmillan. Irish fight against the British.

Mann, Thomas, *Buddenbrooks*. Random House.* Story of family life in both pre- and post-unification Germany.

Marshall, Alan, *I Can Jump Puddles*. World. Life of the Australian pioneers.

Priestley, Harold, *John Stranger*. Roy. Victorian England.

Sadoveanu, Mihail, *Tales of War*. Twayne. Balkan resistance to the Ottoman rulers.

Singer, I. B., *The Magician of Lublin*. Bantam.* Life of Jews in Poland.

Wibberley, Leonard, *Kevin O'Connor and the Light Brigade*. Farrar, Straus & Giroux. Crimean War.

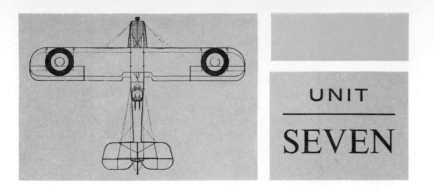

UNIT
SEVEN

WESTERN IMPERIALISM

Bowed down before massed Allied flags—symbolic of the powers that opposed him in World War I—the German Kaiser sinks to defeat, his sword broken. Propaganda posters, such as this one from France, were used by both sides to boost morale and raise funds for the war effort.

526

AND WORLD WAR

CHAPTER 26

Imperialism Transformed the Continent of Africa

European explorers crossing a river in Africa

Beginning in the late 1400's and continuing into the 1700's, as you have read, European nations extended their power to far parts of the world. Explorers, traders, and missionaries traveled to distant places they had not known before.

Soon the earliest travelers were followed by settlers and government officials, who established colonies in many places for the benefit and glory of European nations. An important factor in these ventures, you may recall, was mercantilism, which held that colonies added considerably to a nation's wealth.

In the late 1700's, European interest in empire building declined. Great Britain and France lost colonies in North America. A French economist wrote that colonies, once they matured, were like ripened fruits dropping from the tree. In addition, the French Revolution and Napoleonic Wars kept attention focused on European affairs for many years. Further, during the early 1800's, much capital that had formerly been invested in colonies was used instead to finance the industrialization of Europe.

Political movements in Europe also diminished the interest in empires. The drive toward democratic governments, attempts to gain national unity, labor and land reforms—all these movements occupied time and attention.

The diminished interest in empire building showed in several ways in the early 1800's. In accordance with the principles of laissez-faire economics, trade with colonies was opened to the ships of all nations, not just to those of the mother country. Rarely did European nations attempt to annex new colonies. Great Britain, having learned a bitter lesson in the American Revolution, granted a large degree of self-government to Canada and other territories.

Then the situation changed. Beginning about 1870, and continuing until the outbreak of World War I in 1914, many nations became involved in a new kind of empire building called *imperialism*. By the end of this period, European nations, the United States, and even Japan had brought most of the world under their control.

This unit tells that story and shows how imperial rivalries became an important cause of World War I. This chapter tells how imperialism engulfed almost all of the enormous continent of Africa. Although the story focuses first on North Africa, then moves down the west coast and up the east coast, imperialistic control was actually extended over widely separated parts of the continent at the same time.

THE CHAPTER SECTIONS:

1 Several different forces stimulated imperialism

In Chapter 15 you read about the era of exploration and discovery that resulted in the overseas empires of Portugal, Spain, and other European countries. This expansion was related to mercantilism and appealed mainly to adventurers, merchants, and bankers. The imperialism of the late 1800's had different origins and often involved the emotions—if not the active participation—of a whole people.

Reasons for imperialism

Imperialism arose out of a complex mixture of political, economic, and social forces. Historians do not agree on which ones were most important, or even that all of them were valid. Whether or not the reasons were good ones, however, many people believed in them. They acted on their beliefs by trying to create new empires or enlarge older ones.

Desire for self-sufficiency. After 1850 the Industrial Revolution picked up speed as new sources of power, new machinery, and new industries were developed. Increased industrial production spurred the demand for traditional raw materials such as iron and coal, and created a need for new ones—manganese and tungsten for steel alloys, copper for the electrical industry, rubber for a variety of uses. Industrialization also brought rising standards of living in Europe and the United States, with increased demands for such tropical products as coffee, tea, and spices.

None of the industrialized nations had all of these products. But no industrial nation wanted to be dependent on another for its raw materials. In the thinking of the late 1800's and early 1900's, the ever-present possibility of war made it seem necessary for an industrial nation to control the source of its raw materials lest it find itself at the mercy of an enemy.

Need for new markets. After 1870, the technique of mass production, about which you will read in Chapter 31, made it possible to turn out goods in enormous quantities. Indeed, goods now had to be produced in large quantities to make production profitable. Only when the new and expensive machinery was used to full capacity could it pay for itself and make profits for its owners.

People in Europe and the United States, even with their rising standards of living, could not buy all the things being produced. Industrialists began to look abroad for new markets, especially in Asia, Africa, and Latin America, regions that were not industrialized.

It was believed that people in these areas would buy manufactured goods if they knew about them and could get them. It was even argued that the customs of these people might be changed to create new markets. Articles were written telling how busy European and American factories would be, and how much profit they would earn, if only the Chinese could be persuaded to add one inch to their shirts, or, better still, if only the people of central Africa could be persuaded to wear shirts at all.

Many people urged that industrialized nations should control their new markets abroad, just as they controlled the sources of their raw materials. Industrialists wanted their governments to guarantee them exclusive rights to sell in these markets, just as they were demanding protective tariffs to assure their exclusive markets at home.

Investing surplus capital. The Industrial Revolution produced large profits and created immense fortunes for owners of industry. Wealth increased tremendously (in the United States twelve times over between 1850 and 1900), and it became concentrated in the hands of relatively few people.

Wealthy people looked for places to invest their money profitably. Undeveloped regions promised large profits, though with many risks. Companies sent out prospectors to find minerals that could be mined profitably. Banks lent money to local rulers in undeveloped areas to build railroads, establish plantations, and open mines.

The special risks of investment abroad often brought demands for protection. Foreign-owned mines, plantations, and factories were sometimes attacked and damaged by discontented natives. Those who had invested money demanded that their governments protect their investments. Governments put pressure on native rulers or sent troops. Thus, economic imperialism often led to political imperialism—the establishment of a colony.

Outlets for population. Industrialization was accompanied, as you have read, by a rapid growth of population. Industrial development created many jobs but, in Europe, not enough to employ all the new job seekers. As a result, people left Europe in great numbers for the more thinly settled regions of the United States, Latin America, Africa, and Australia.

Nationalists regretted seeing the emigrants leave because they often became naturalized citizens of the countries where they settled. Ties with the former homeland weakened and finally disappeared. How much better, the nationalists thought, if emigrants could go to colonies. There they would still be loyal subjects under the political control of the mother country.

Many new colonies were unsuited for settlement by Europeans or were already heavily populated. But these considerations did not trouble the patriots.

Nationalism. Nationalism, a strong force throughout the 1800's, was particularly powerful in the period from 1870 to 1914. Nationalists argued that colonies added to the strength and prestige of the nation. For one thing, armies were growing larger, and colonies came to be considered a source of military manpower. Gurkhas and Pathans, the fighting men of Nepal and Afghanistan, joined Australians and New Zealanders to build up British armies. The Senegalese, a Negro people of West Africa, fought loyally for the French.

A large navy was just as necessary as a large army—even more so when widely scattered colonies and far-ranging merchant ships had to be protected. The steam-powered navies of the late 1800's had to stop for supplies more often than earlier sailing fleets. For many years, steam-powered ships burned coal. Thus the range of a steamship was "from coal to coal." The coaling station, a place where warships and merchant ships could refuel, became highly important in war and commerce. Equally important were far-flung naval bases, where warships could be stationed, armed, provisioned, and repaired, as well as refueled. Tiny islands with nothing to recommend them but strategic location became important as coaling stations or naval bases. Often they were objects of fierce competition among naval powers.

Imperialism appealed to people's desire for national glory and prestige. Germany and Italy, which did not become united nations until the late 1800's, felt that they had to build up colonial empires in order to compete with long-time colonial powers such as Britain, France, and the Netherlands. However, it is interesting to note that the British, who already had a large empire, entered the imperialistic race for colonies as enthusiastically as the Germans or Italians. National "honor" would not allow them to watch territorial prizes go to rival nations.

Missionary motives. The urge to spread the Christian religion, as you know, had been influential in the colonial expansion of the 1500's and 1600's. Roman Catholic missionaries had carried on their work since that time, and they increased their activities in the period of imperialism. There were also an increasing number of Protestant missionaries.

Besides spreading the gospel, missionaries did other important work. Education became a regular missionary activity. Trained men and women went out from Europe and America as medical missionaries. Knowledge of medicine, hygiene, and sanitation spread with knowledge of Christianity.

The "white man's burden." Closely related to the missionary motive was the idea that the people of advanced Western nations had a duty to transmit Western ideas and techniques to more "backward" people. People were considered "backward" if they were pagans, or if their culture was different from that of the West.

The British poet Rudyard Kipling wrote a famous poem that urged members of his race to "take up the white man's burden." He meant the obligation of carrying Western civilization to those he considered less fortunate. The French spoke of their "civilizing mission." Naturally, the people of each industrial nation considered its civilization and culture to be the highest, and therefore the one most suited to be taken to the "backward" peoples of the earth.

Opponents of imperialism scoffed that the only burden the white man wanted to take up was the burden of colonial wealth, which he wanted to carry back home as fast as possible. Such opponents, however, were a minority with little influence in their countries.

HISTORY THROUGH ART

Carved and Painted African Mask

Comfortable in their prejudices, Europeans of the imperialist era regarded most African art as "primitive" and "barbaric." Missionaries, especially, scorned it since so much of it was associated with African religious rituals. (The mask above, made by a tribe in the western Sudan, was probably worn by a dancer in rites to insure crop fertility.) For this very reason, however, much African art survived; missionaries would often confiscate objects as trophies after having converted their African owners to Christianity.

531

The nature of imperialism

You have now read about the major forces that stimulated imperialism. As you continue to read this unit, and indeed throughout the rest of this book, watch these forces at work and think about their consequences.

Were the new colonies, for example, really worth what they cost? Imperialism created bitter rivalries among the imperial powers and hatred among the colonized. Rivalries led to the building of larger armies and navies at great cost. Colonial rivalries were an underlying cause of World War I, whose staggering costs must also be taken into account. Much of the suspicion and hatred among nations today had its roots in imperialism.

In the beginning, imperialism was not actively planned by governments. Usually it began with the work of individuals: merchants, explorers, scientists, or missionaries. Sometimes one of these individuals was abused by the natives. His government then sent soldiers to protect him. Often the soldiers established themselves permanently. Soon, government officers appeared, and a new colony came into being.

Loans to native rulers were often the entering wedges of imperialism. When the local rulers spent the money recklessly, as they often did, they found themselves heavily in debt and were forced to grant economic privileges. Economic privileges often led to political control.

Some terms used in connection with imperialism need explanation. Originally a *colony* was a settlement established by citizens of a country in another region. Ancient Greek colonies and British colonies in North America were like this. During the imperialistic era, however, a colony came to be an area in which a foreign nation gained total control over a given region and its native population. It was gained by discovery, settlement, or conquest, and was annexed, becoming a part of the empire.

In a *protectorate,* the native ruler kept his title, but officials of the foreign power "pulled the strings." The "protecting" power kept out other foreign nations. In a *condominium,* two nations ruled a region as partners. A *concession* was the grant of economic rights and privileges in a given area. Concessions were given to foreign merchants or capitalists who wanted to trade, to build railroads, or to develop mineral deposits and other natural resources. A *sphere of influence* was a region where one nation had special, sometimes exclusive, economic and political privileges that were recognized by other nations.

CHECKUP

1. Why did European interest in colonies decline between the late 1700's and the late 1800's?
2. Name and explain four motives behind imperialism that were related to the Industrial Revolution.
3. What were three other motives for seeking colonies?
4. Why did Germany and Italy get a late start in the race for colonies?
5. IDENTIFY: coaling station, protectorate, condominium, concession, sphere of influence.

2 European imperialists gained control of North Africa

North Africa, as you have read, knew many conquerors, including the Romans, the Byzantines, and the Arabs. In the 1800's, most of the region was part of the Ottoman Empire, although Turkish control in many areas was weak.

The French in Algeria

For a long time, expert Moslem seafarers, called the Barbary pirates, had been operating off the coast of North Africa. The term *Barbary* means "of the Berbers." The Berbers, as you recall, were a people of North Africa who were converted to Islam during the 600's. The North African coast along which the pirates lurked was called the Barbary coast. Four Moslem states—Morocco, Algiers, Tunis, and Tripoli—made up the so-called Barbary States. (These countries are now called Morocco, Algeria, Tunisia, and Libya.) The swift sailing ships of the Barbary pirates had taken a heavy toll of Mediterranean

North African Musicians

The French artist Eugène Delacroix visited North Africa in the 1830's, traveling on an official mission with Louis Philippe's ambassador to the sultan of Morocco. The French had just acquired Algeria and were also interested in neighboring regions of Africa. In a sense, Delacroix was ahead of his time, just as French imperialism preceded by several decades that of most Western countries. His journey to North Africa was an unusual one in an era when most painters traditionally spent their formative years studying in Rome. The journal he kept at this time abounds in excited descriptions of the new sights and sounds he was experiencing.

The water-color sketch at right shows two Moroccan musicians. Together with Delacroix' many other sketches and paintings of life in North Africa, it stimulated in Europeans a fascination with the more exotic aspects of Arab culture.

shipping, including, during the early 1800's, some ships of the United States.

The operations of the Barbary pirates gave France an excuse to intervene in North Africa. Unlike other European nations, the French were interested in imperial expansion early in the 1800's; they wanted to compensate for the loss of French prestige after the defeat of Napoleon in 1815.

The French complained about the Barbary pirates to the Algerian ruler, the dey, and received what they considered an insulting reply. In 1830 a French force occupied Algeria, arrested the dey, and settled down to stay. For more than forty years, the French had to fight against almost continuous rebellions and widespread violence, but, economically, the struggle was worth the price. Algeria was a rich land, especially along the coast. Many French people and other Europeans moved in, taking over the best land and running the businesses. Algeria became an exporter of farm products, wine, and meat, playing an important part in French economic life.

French seizure of Tunisia

East of Algeria lies Tunisia, a small country with a long past. Its capital, Tunis, grew up near the once-formidable Carthage, rival of ancient Rome. Tunisia was part of the Ottoman Empire, but weakly held. The seizure of Tunisia illustrates two characteristics of imperialism: the dangerous rivalry among the imperial powers, and the method of using loans and "incidents" to gain territory.

Tunisia was a poor and backward country. Its Turkish ruler, called the bey of Tunis, was a lavish spender for his own pleasures and carefree about finances. When the revenue from the country did not support his style of living, he borrowed money from European bankers. When the loans were due, he borrowed more. Finally the bankers refused further loans. Then the French government, seeing a chance to gain influence, lent him money.

The bey did not learn from experience. His carefree spending continued. When the French loan was due, he raised taxes, which were already

533

FRANCE

ATLANTIC
OCEAN

PORTUGAL SPAIN

ITALY

OTTOMAN EMPIRE

Strait of Gibraltar → Algeciras
Tangier
SP. MOROCCO
Algiers
Tunis
MALTA (Br.)
MEDITERRANEAN SEA
CYPRUS (Br.)

MADEIRA IS. (Port.)

MOROCCO
Agadir ATLAS MTS.
TUNISIA
Tripoli
Alexandria
Cairo
SUEZ CANAL

CANARY ISLANDS (Sp.)

ALGERIA

LIBYA (TRIPOLI)

EGYPT

ARABIA

RÍO DE ORO

S A H A R A

Aswan
Nile R.
RED SEA

CAPE VERDE ISLANDS (Port.)

FRENCH WEST AFRICA
Timbuktu

Senegal R.
Niger R.

Lake Chad

EQUATORIAL AFRICA

ANGLO-EGYPTIAN
Omdurman Khartoum
SUDAN
(Condominium)
Fashoda

ERITREA
Aduwa
FR. SOMALILAND
BR. SOMALILAND

Dakar
GAMBIA
SENEGAL

Niger River

NIGERIA

Addis Ababa
ETHIOPIA (Independent)

PORT. GUINEA
FRENCH GUINEA

DAHOMEY
TOGO

IT. SOMALILAND

SIERRA LEONE
Monrovia LIBERIA (Independent)
IVORY COAST
GOLD COAST
Lagos

CAMEROONS

Ubangi R.

UGANDA

BRITISH EAST AFRICA

EQUATOR

FERNANDO PO (Sp.)
RIO MUNI

Congo River

BELGIAN
CONGO

Lake Victoria

IMPERIALISM IN AFRICA
to 1914

French		German
British		Portuguese
Italian		Spanish
Belgian		

FRENCH CONGO
Brazzaville

Ujiji

GERMAN
EAST AFRICA

ZANZIBAR (Br.)

Lake Tanganyika

ANGOLA

L. Mweru

L. Bangweulu

Lake Nyasa

NYASALAND

Mozambique

RHODESIA
Zambezi R.

MOZAMBIQUE
(PORT. EAST AFRICA)

MADAGASCAR

GERMAN
SOUTHWEST
AFRICA

Victoria Falls

BECHUANALAND

TRANSVAAL

UNION OF SOUTH AFRICA

INDIAN

OCEAN

ORANGE FREE STATE
NATAL

Cape Town CAPE COLONY
CAPE OF GOOD HOPE

0 2000 miles

heavy. This tax policy brought a rebellion against the bey and furnished the incident that gave the Europeans their chance. The French government demanded that the bey's creditors create a commission to restore order and reorganize Tunisia's finances. The commission, formed in 1869, included representatives of the British, French, and Italian governments.

All three of these nations wanted Tunisia. Italy, in the process of being united and already eager for colonies, had encouraged many Italians to emigrate to Tunisia. In a complicated series of negotiations, France and Britain reached an agreement, which was announced in 1878 at the Congress of Berlin. The French were to have a free hand in Tunisia, and the British could occupy the island of Cyprus, in the eastern Mediterranean. Italy, new, poor, and inexperienced at the diplomatic game, had nothing to trade and was ignored in these deals. The Tunisia incident resulted in many years of bad feeling on the part of Italy toward France.

In 1881, border raids into Algeria by Tunisian tribes provoked a further incident. France sent in troops and forced the bey of Tunis to make Tunisia a French protectorate. The bey remained ruler in name, but the real ruler was the major French official, called the resident-general.

French rule brought certain improvements to Tunisia: public order, roads, schools, industries, and sound finances. Native Tunisians received some benefits, but, as you might guess, the lion's share went to Frenchmen. Religious differences, local pride, and a rising spirit of nationalism inspired many Tunisians to keep working for independence.

Rivalry over Morocco

Imperialistic ventures were often linked in a sort of chain reaction. A gain in one place led to a demand for a move somewhere else. France first took Algeria. Then it seemed necessary to take Tunisia to protect French interests in the east. Then France felt it needed Morocco to protect its interests to the west.

Notice on the map, opposite, the strategic location of Morocco. It lies to the south of the narrow Strait of Gibraltar, the entrance to the Mediterranean Sea. It borders on both the Mediterranean Sea and the Atlantic Ocean. The water brings cooling breezes, while the Atlas Mountains cut off hot winds from the Sahara desert. The climate is pleasant and the soil is rich.

Strategic location and riches made Morocco a tempting prize for imperialists, but this in itself was a sort of protection. So many European countries wanted the country that each one was afraid to take it because doing so might touch off an explosion. Also, the Berbers of Morocco were a warlike people. They had ruled Spain for centuries, and had defended Morocco against attempted conquest.

By the early 1900's, however, France was willing to take risks for the rich prize of Morocco. It tried to proceed with great caution. French officials made diplomatic deals with Britain, Italy, and Spain, promising to support each in its ambitions elsewhere in return for support in Morocco. Somehow, though, France overlooked Germany. Kaiser William II was a fierce imperialist and a rash diplomat, which Bismarck had not been. Learning of France's moves, he publicly proclaimed that the sultan of Morocco was an independent sovereign in whose lands all foreign powers were to enjoy the same rights.

So great was the international tension that it was decided to call a conference of the great powers to try to settle the Moroccan controversy peacefully. The conference was held in 1906 at Algeciras (al·juh·SIHR·us), in southern Spain.

The Algeciras Conference was a diplomatic victory for France. Delegates decided that Moroccan finances should be placed under the control of an international bank in which France held major control. The Moroccan army was to be led by officers of three European nations, France being the strongest. The conference also ruled that Algerian-Moroccan frontier police were to be French, and that the internal Moroccan police would be controlled by France and Spain. Germany was shut out completely, except that merchants and investors of all countries were to have equal rights in Morocco.

Now France, still moving cautiously, could

take advantage of various incidents, including uprisings of Moroccans, to gain complete control. One French move to "restore order" stirred up Germany again. In 1911, Kaiser William sent the German gunboat *Panther* to the Moroccan port of Agadir "to protect German lives and property." This Agadir Incident, which brought Europe close to war, was settled when France bought off Germany with a piece of land in tropical Africa and reaffirmed the promise of equal trading rights for all nations in Morocco. Except for the small northern strip of Spanish Morocco, which was acquired by Spain, and the city of Tangier, which was placed under international control, rich Morocco became, like Tunisia, a French protectorate.

Egypt and the Suez Canal

The ancient land of Egypt had been part of the Ottoman Empire for centuries. By the mid-1800's, when the empire was crumbling, the Turkish viceroys in Egypt, called khedives (kuh-DEEVZ), had become almost entirely independent. They still paid some tribute to the Ottoman sultan, but they were absolute rulers in Egypt.

In 1854 a French company, headed by Ferdinand de Lesseps, gained a concession to build a canal through the Isthmus of Suez. Almost half the stock of the company was bought by the Egyptian government. Individual Frenchmen bought most of the rest. The canal was completed in 1869 (see map, page 534).

Within a short time the Egyptian government fell into financial difficulties. The khedive, Ismail Pasha, was an enthusiastic admirer of Western ways. He began a program of extensive improvements in the country, far greater than its revenues could pay for. Like the bey of Tunis, Ismail had very expensive habits himself and little concern with financial management. When money was scarce he had two solutions: borrow the money and raise taxes. Between 1869 and 1879, he increased the foreign debt of his government by more than twenty times. Finally, foreign banks refused to lend him more money.

Ismail's solution was to sell Egypt's stock in the Suez Canal. This was an opportunity for the British. They were very eager to control the canal because it was, and still is, a vital link in the trade route between Britain and India, Australia, and New Zealand. In 1875, on the advice of Prime Minister Benjamin Disraeli, the British government bought the Egyptian stock and thus became the largest single stockholder in the canal. The British holdings were so large and the rest of the stock so widely scattered among private investors that the British gained virtual control of the canal.

Ismail soon spent the British money and his government went bankrupt. The next event was both familiar and threatening. To solve the financial problem, Egypt's creditors set up an international commission, with representatives from Great Britain, France, Austria, and Italy. The commission controlled Egypt's borrowing abroad and carefully checked its revenues and spending. When a serious crop failure in Egypt reduced the tax revenue, the British and French decided to take drastic steps.

British control over Egypt. Now came the familiar imperialist pattern. An Egyptian rebellion provided the necessary incident. In 1882 the British and French sent a combined fleet toward Alexandria, but the French withdrew and the British proceeded alone. They bombarded Alexandria, landed troops, and soon occupied the entire country. There they remained, claiming that they must safeguard the Suez Canal, their main route to India. The Egyptian government remained outwardly independent, but real control was in British hands.

British rule brought certain benefits to Egypt. Finances were put on a sounder basis. In 1902 the building of a storage dam at Aswan and an extensive irrigation system placed more land under cultivation. Courts became more efficient and less corrupt. Forced labor and degrading forms of physical punishment were abolished. These improvements, however, reached only a few people.

Egyptian aristocrats disliked British rule even though they benefited from it. This, too, became a familiar imperialist pattern. The longer the British remained, the stronger grew nationalist feeling against them, and the more the British

Imperialism in Egypt was intensified by the building of the Suez Canal. Digging the canal required thousands of workers, some of whom are shown above during the last few days of work. Ferdinand de Lesseps, caricatured at left as a Samson whose strength has pushed apart the earth, hoped the canal would contribute to world peace, but it became instead a source of friction. Below is a drawing of one of the many conferences at which the British guaranteed token independence to Egypt.

feared to pull out and risk their control of the Suez Canal.

Italy in North Africa

When Italy had agreed to be neutral in Morocco, France was to be neutral in Tripoli, the North African region lying to the west of Egypt. This region, mostly desert, belonged to the Ottoman Empire, but Turkish control was weak. The region had almost no economic value, but, as one diplomat put it, when Italy came to the table, only the crumbs were left. So Italy decided to eat the crumbs.

First Italy secured guarantees of neutrality from several European powers in addition to France. Then, in 1911, on a flimsy excuse, it declared war on the Ottoman Empire. Italy received an unpleasant shock, for the Turks showed surprisingly strong resistance. The war, which had been planned as a short one, dragged on for over a year. Trouble in other parts of the Ottoman Empire and pressure from European powers finally made the Turks yield.

Italy took Tripoli as a colony and renamed it Libya. It was a profitless victory. Except for a narrow strip along the coast, the land was barren. The population was small, but the people violently opposed Italian rule. As a result, the Italian government had the military expense of keeping the country pacified for many years.

CHECKUP

1. How did the French gain Algeria? Tunisia? Morocco?
2. How did the British win control of the Suez Canal? How did they become virtual rulers of Egypt?
3. IDENTIFY: Barbary pirates, dey, bey, Algeciras Conference, Agadir Incident, khedives, Ismail Pasha.
4. LOCATE: Algeria, Tunisia, Tunis, Morocco, Suez Canal, Libya.

 Several European nations carved up western and central Africa

You read in Chapter 12 about sub-Saharan Africa, the vast land south of the Sahara desert. Various African kingdoms and empires flourished there at one time, but most of them had vanished or declined by the late 1500's.

In the 1500's and 1600's, the first great period of European colonization, several nations established trading posts on the east and west coasts of sub-Saharan Africa. These were small settlements only, with vague boundaries. The British, French, Portuguese, and Spanish all had such posts (see inset map, page 534). The slave trade was their most profitable activity. When most European countries abolished the slave trade early in the 1800's, European interest in sub-Saharan Africa died down.

Since Europeans had merely clung to the coasts of sub-Saharan Africa, it is perhaps understandable that their maps should show the vast interior of Africa as *Terra Incognita* (Latin for "unknown land"). This was not an unknown land to Arab traders, who had crisscrossed large parts of it for centuries. Nevertheless, to European imperialists of the latter 1800's, any prior development of Africa south of the Mediterranean fringe was of no consequence. Africa was a fruit tree ripe for the picking.

Sub-Saharan imperialism

The division of sub-Saharan Africa into colonies is a good example of how imperialism worked in undeveloped regions. Early European explorers pushed into the interior, hacking their way through rain forests and crossing the savannas. They discovered that there were regions in Africa where white men could live—regions rich in business opportunities. There was trade with the natives for desirable products, such as ivory. There were minerals to be mined and other resources to be developed with cheap native labor. Control could be held by small military forces.

Explorers and other early arrivals sent back reports which influenced other people to follow them. Sometimes the Europeans met with resistance and violence from the natives. Then European soldiers appeared, followed by government officials to protect the interests of their citizens. Soldiers and officials were usually followed by builders, engineers, and technicians to open mines and build roads, railroads, bridges, and dams. Then the region would be exploited and developed for the benefit of the developers.

Sub-Saharan Africa illustrated imperialism in another way: not many Europeans settled in the newly opened regions. Usually a few Europeans controlled large native populations, sometimes using native troops whom they trained and equipped. Even in South Africa, where European settlement was heaviest, the proportion of white settlers to natives was very small.

French possessions

Since the 1600's, France had held a small island at the very tip of the "bulge" of western Africa. Using this as a base, the French worked inland along the Senegal River in the region known as Senegal. It was not until the 1800's, however, that systematic development took place. Frenchmen explored the western part of the vast Sudan region and took possession of the ancient city of Timbuktu. Along the coast, commercial settlements were made in French Guinea, the Ivory Coast—so called from its abundance of elephants—and Dahomey. The city of Dakar was founded in 1857.

The French posts in Senegal, French Guinea, the Ivory Coast, and Dahomey were separated by the coastal possessions of other nations. Therefore the French worked tirelessly to link their seaports by inland possessions. From the coast they pushed inland with small military forces. They either overcame native opposition by force or secured tribal agreements that allowed them to enter the interior peacefully.

By 1900 the French had laid claim to a vast area called French West Africa (see map, page 534). Since it included much of the Sahara, its size did not necessarily mean wealth. However, there were products of great value in some parts of the region, and the numerous French seaports provided outlets for them.

While some Frenchmen were establishing claims in the Sudan and along the southern coast of the African "bulge," others staked out claims farther south. Pierre de Brazza explored the northern Congo basin and, in 1880, founded the city of Brazzaville on the lower Congo River. His explorations formed the basis for another French colony along the northwestern banks of the Congo and Ubangi rivers, which was known as the French Congo.

For a time the French hoped to extend the French Congo to reach the watershed of the Nile River, far to the northeast. They failed in this attempt, as you will see, but did gain control of a large region to the north, adjoining French West Africa. Together with the French Congo, this region became known as French Equatorial Africa.

The Gold Coast and Nigeria

The British too had interests along the southern coast of the "bulge" of western Africa. East of the Ivory Coast was an area known as the Gold Coast because of its gold mines. The region was first settled by the Portuguese in the late 1400's. Their possession was untroubled until other Europeans discovered that the Portuguese were mining gold there. In the scramble that followed, the Portuguese were ousted by the Dutch who, in turn, were replaced by an English trading company.

During the 1600's and 1700's, trade in slaves became more important and profitable than trade in gold. The slaves were usually prisoners of war sold to the merchants by the Ashanti, a confederation of native tribes who controlled the region. Although the slave trade was abolished in 1807, the British remained, and the government took over control from the various private trading companies that had become established there.

Throughout the 1800's the British held the coast and were continually pushing into the interior, often clashing with the Ashanti. By 1901, however, Britain had annexed all the territory of the Ashanti and had made the Gold Coast a British colony.

The British were responsible for improvements in transportation, education, and sanitation, although it was the natives themselves who brought about a great improvement in the standard of living through the development of the cacao industry. The rapid spread of cacao farming brought prosperity to the country and helped to bring it closer together politically.

To the east of the Gold Coast was Nigeria, which took its name from the Niger, one of the great rivers of tropical West Africa. Control of this river meant control of a vast region with rich resources. As early as the 1500's, the British had been in the area to trade for slaves. In the 1790's a Scottish physician named Mungo Park traveled almost the whole length of the river. Other British explorers reached the Niger after a hazardous journey across the Sahara from Tripoli.

In 1861 the British annexed the port city of Lagos and pushed steadily inland. For a time there was sharp rivalry with a French company, but the British were able to unite with it and control it. Eventually the British government bought out the company and made Nigeria a protectorate.

The Belgian Congo

In the mid-1870's, Henry Stanley, a British journalist who had been active in East Africa, set out to explore the Congo River basin. He began his journey from central Africa with 3 white men and 356 natives. After tremendous hardships, he arrived at the mouth of the Congo almost three years later with only 82 Africans.

Stanley tried to interest the British government in the vast area he had explored, but failed. He then turned to King Leopold II of Belgium, who wanted the region. After much national and international maneuvering, Leopold established his authority there, declaring it was his duty "to open to civilization the only part of our globe where it has not yet penetrated, to pierce the darkness which envelops whole populations."

Thus a territory of some 900,000 square miles became Leopold's personal property, not a colony of Belgium. It had rubber and ivory but needed capital for development. Leopold formed a corporation and sold stock.

The development of the Belgian Congo was extremely profitable, although in their haste for quick profits, the Belgians carelessly destroyed rubber trees without replanting for the future. However, there was other wealth in gold, diamonds, palm oil, coffee, cotton, and timber.

But "piercing the darkness" was disastrous for the natives. Whole regions were set aside as absolute monopolies for the corporation. Africans were ruthlessly uprooted from their villages and forced to work for the white man. Conditions in the Belgian Congo became an international scandal, arousing so many protests that in 1908 King Leopold transferred his colony to the Belgian government.

The Germans in West Africa

For some years after the unification of Germany in 1871, Chancellor Otto von Bismarck showed little interest in colonies because he doubted their value. German industrialists wanted Germany to take territories in Africa and elsewhere, but Bismarck was cool to their suggestions. In the mid-1880's he yielded. Once in the scramble, Germany went the whole way. After Kaiser William II forced Bismarck to resign in 1890, Germany drove even harder for its "place in the sun"—for colonies and empire.

A German explorer raised the German flag in Togo, on the southern shore of the African "bulge." To the southeast a German merchant negotiated with a native chieftain in the region of the Cameroons and began to push inland. Farther south, below Angola, Germans began to establish themselves in what became known as German Southwest Africa (see map, page 534). Neither France nor Great Britain welcomed the arrival of the Germans in West Africa. By cleverly playing them against each other, however, Germany was able to overcome their opposition and to gain a firm foothold in its three West African colonies.

Although Germany's African possessions were as large as the homeland, the Germans really got what was "left over." Togo and the Cameroons consisted of tropical rain forests. They were thinly populated and could not provide many workers. Both water and labor were scarce in German Southwest Africa. The climate was fa-

European influence in Africa took many forms. The first people to come were usually explorers, like the British journalist Henry Stanley, above left. They were often followed by men whose chief aim was to exploit both the natural and human resources of an area. The two natives below left were bound in chains because they refused to work for European agents. Teachers and missionaries tried to moderate such brutal mistreatment and to shoulder "the white man's burden." A European teacher in German Southwest Africa, above, gives lessons under the stern and watchful portraits of the Kaiser and his wife. Below, a Protestant missionary baptizes converts in a river in the Belgian Congo.

vorable for white settlement, but the natives clung to their land, and it was costly to dislodge them.

The Germans planned to make Southwest Africa a land of cattle ranches. However, German officials and ranchers were so arrogant and overbearing that in 1893, and again from 1903 to 1907, the native Hottentots and Hereros rebelled. They were ruthlessly crushed. The Germans lost 5,000 lives and a great deal of money; the Hereros were reduced in number from 80,000 to some 15,000 starving people. The resulting labor shortage greatly reduced the value of the colony.

Other West African regions

In the scramble for West African territory, Spain acquired two colonies: a narrow strip along the northwest coast called Río de Oro, and Río Muni, just south of the Cameroons. Spain also held the Canary Islands in the Atlantic and the island of Fernando Po off the coast of the Cameroons. Portugal held two territories: Portuguese Guinea, south of Senegal on the "bulge," and Angola, the oldest colony in Africa.

By the early 1900's the entire west coast of Africa and vast regions of the interior had been divided up among imperialist powers, with one important exception—Liberia.

Freed Negro slaves from the United States, under the protection of the American government, settled at Monrovia, (named after President James Monroe) in 1822. The Republic of Liberia became independent in 1847. It was a rare political experiment: a Negro republic of former slaves. The republic had many economic difficulties, which at times made its continued independence doubtful. There is little question that it would have ended as the protectorate of some ambitious European colonial power if the United States had not helped Liberia maintain independence. American diplomatic pressure discouraged European attempts to take over the small republic.

CHECKUP

1. How did colonization usually occur in sub-Saharan Africa?

2. How and by whom was the Congo basin exploited?

3. IDENTIFY: *Terra Incognita,* Ashanti, Mungo Park, Hottentots, Hereros.

4. LOCATE: Dakar, French West Africa, French Equatorial Africa, Gold Coast, Nigeria, Lagos, Belgian Congo, Cameroons, German Southwest Africa, Río de Oro, Río Muni, Liberia.

4 Imperialism engulfed southern and eastern Africa

Southern and eastern Africa, like western Africa, contained several coastal settlements established by Europeans in the great era of exploration that began in the late 1400's. Little was known of the interior, however, until the 1800's.

South Africa

European settlement in South Africa began in 1652, when Cape Town was established by the Dutch. Many Dutch people settled there, where they were known as Boers (BOHRZ). The Boers were hardy, thrifty pioneers—farmers who founded homes, rather than wandering explorers or hunters. They built up Cape Colony, which was profitable as well as strategically located (see map, page 534).

During the Napoleonic Wars, the British seized Cape Colony, which was recognized officially as a British possession at the Congress of Vienna. The Boers disliked foreign rule. Many of them left Cape Colony and moved north and east during the 1830's. There they carved out three colonies: Natal, on the southeast coast; the Orange Free State, to the west; and the Transvaal (meaning "across the Vaal River"), to the north. Within a few years, after a clash between the British and Boers, Natal became a British colony. Most of the Boers of Natal then moved into the Transvaal. By the 1850's the Boer republics of the Orange Free State and the Transvaal had won British recognition of their independence, but not for long.

542

Cecil Rhodes. The expansion of British power in South Africa is largely the story of one man, Cecil Rhodes. He arrived in Cape Colony from England in 1870, a sickly clerk of modest means and education. That same year diamonds were discovered on the northern border of Cape Colony, and Rhodes established a successful claim. He soon showed a great talent for business and a genius for organization. Within ten years a corporation formed by Rhodes gained a complete monopoly of South African diamond production. The discovery of gold in the Transvaal in 1886 was another opportunity for Rhodes' organizing talent. By the mid-1890's, Cecil Rhodes had become wealthy.

Rhodes was a firm believer in the superiority of British culture, which he thought would in time prevail throughout the world.° His greatest dream for Africa was a railroad running from Cape Colony, in the south, all the way to Cairo, in the north, through a chain of British colonies. He began to work for the northward expansion of Cape Colony. The first step was the establishment of a protectorate over Bechuanaland (bech-oo·AH·nuh·land), an unclaimed region west of the Transvaal. Next, Rhodes organized the British South Africa Company, which gained control of a huge territory north of Bechuanaland and the Transvaal; this territory was named Rhodesia, after Rhodes.

For Rhodes, the two independent Boer republics, the Orange Free State and the Transvaal, remained roadblocks in the path of "progress." The Transvaal was especially so. After the discovery of gold there, prospectors and miners rushed into the area from Cape Colony. The Boers deplored this gold rush as an invasion of their territory and property rights. They were deeply religious people and regarded the miners as godless, lawless, and destructive, though a

---

° In his will, Cecil Rhodes provided a fund for scholarships to Oxford University for students from the British Empire, the United States, and Germany. His purpose in instituting the famous Rhodes Scholarships was to help prepare the way for the peaceful union under British leadership of all Anglo-Saxon peoples (that is, the English and Germanic peoples, who were distantly related).

profitable source of revenue. With others, Rhodes began to plot the overthrow of the Transvaal government. In 1895 one of his associates organized a raid for this purpose, but it failed.

The Boer War. Relations between the British and the Boers now became openly hostile. The Transvaal allied itself with the Orange Free State and sought protective alliances with the Netherlands and Germany. The Boers passed high tariffs and other laws discriminating against the British. Grievances were allowed to pile up until they resulted in a war between the British and the Boers. The Boer War began in 1899 and lasted almost three years.

The Boers fought bravely. As underdogs they had the sympathy of much of the world. In the end, however, British might prevailed. The Transvaal and the Orange Free State were annexed as colonies of the British Cape Colony. The British permitted the Boers to continue using their own form of the Dutch language, called Afrikaans (af-rih-KAHNZ), in their schools and courts. No indemnities were imposed, and the British even granted money to help people rebuild their farms. Within five years, keeping a promise made at the time of the peace, the British granted limited self-government to the two Boer states.

In 1908, Cape Colony, Natal, the Transvaal, and the Orange Free State drew up a federal constitution. In 1910, after the British Parliament had approved the constitution, they united in the Union of South Africa, a British dominion.

Portuguese East Africa

Up the east coast from the Union of South Africa, Portugal strengthened and extended its control over a large region called Portuguese East Africa, or Mozambique. Portuguese explorers and traders had appeared along the coast of this area in the early 1500's, not long after they had rounded the tip of Africa on their way to India and the Far East. They had established a trading fort at the town of Mozambique as early as 1508. For nearly 400 years, the Portuguese held this east coast seaport for trade, especially the slave trade. In the late 1800's, when the slave trade was ended, the Portuguese built roads and

The Boer War

From their first encounter in South Africa, in the early 1800's, a strong antipathy arose between the British and the Boers—the descendants of the Dutch East India Company employees who arrived in 1652 under the command of Jan van Riebeeck, left. The discovery of gold and diamonds in the late 1800's aggravated the situation. A flood of English-speaking foreigners came to seek their fortunes in mining and were repeatedly denied political rights in the Boer republic of Transvaal. The resulting tensions, coupled with other British demands, helped to provoke the Boer War. Above, Boer troops line up in trenches. Accompanied by mounted units, British infantrymen, below, cross a river by lifeline. Although the British were superior in numbers and organization and soon gained the upper hand in the war, Boer guerrillas prolonged the bitter conflict for two years.

railroads into the interior, opened mines, and established prosperous plantations for growing cotton, tobacco, coffee, and tea.

German, British, and French rivalries

One of the most important of all the explorers of Africa was David Livingstone, a Scottish missionary who spent over thirty years in East Africa. After establishing a post in Bechuanaland in 1841, he explored much of the area to the north. His discoveries included the Zambezi River, Victoria Falls, and Lakes Mweru and Bangweulu (see map, page 534).

When, in the 1860's, Livingstone seemed to have disappeared in the interior, a young newspaperman named Henry Stanley was sent to look for him. (It was this same Stanley who later explored the Congo basin.) Stanley set out in 1869 and finally found Livingstone two years later at the small settlement of Ujiji on Lake Tanganyika. His greeting—"Dr. Livingstone, I presume?"—became famous, and his successful search did much to publicize the possibilities for imperialistic development in Africa.

Although the British had been the first to explore the region east of Lake Tanganyika, it was the Germans who claimed the region officially. In the 1880's a German adventurer named Karl Peters used bribery and threats of force to persuade some chieftains in the area to sign agreements placing themselves under his protection. Returning to Germany, he persuaded the German government to recognize the agreements and to establish a protectorate over the area in 1885.

Germany's announcement of its new protectorate, called German East Africa, annoyed the British and French, both of whom had plans for this area. However, the three nations were able to reach an agreement. Germany and Britain recognized France's claim to the large island of Madagascar, in the Indian Ocean. A narrow coastal strip north of German East Africa was recognized as a British sphere of influence. The British moved into the interior from this strip to create the protectorate of British East Africa (see map, page 534).

German East Africa proved to be the most attractive of Germany's African possessions, and Germans settled there in some numbers. Despite its potential, it never paid its way as a business venture, but it did block the British dream of a Cape-to-Cairo railroad.

North of German East Africa and west of British East Africa lay the rich territory of Uganda, which was coveted by both Great Britain and Germany. After the natives rebelled and overthrew their ruler, ambitious Germans from German East Africa hurried to Uganda and occupied its capital. They signed an agreement with the deposed ruler, placing him and his country under the "protection" of Germany. At that time, however, the German government was negotiating with the British to get the strategic island of Helgoland in the North Sea. In return for Helgoland, the British received Uganda, the island of Zanzibar, and favorable border adjustments elsewhere in Africa.

Italy in East Africa

Italy, as you have read, entered the colonial race late. By the time it turned to imperialism, the desirable regions were taken. When it became interested in the east coast of Africa in the 1890's, all that remained were an uninviting region of Somaliland on the Indian Ocean, and an equally unattractive desert region along the Red Sea called Eritrea. The Italians obtained leases to these two regions from various local rulers. Thus, for the moment, Italy satisfied its imperialistic urges with two strips of desert coastline that proved to be an annual drain on the Italian economy.

There was a chance, however, to expand into the interior. Touching each of the new coastal colonies was an interior region, Ethiopia, ruled by a native emperor. The French were trying to get a concession for a railroad in Ethiopia. When the Italians began to make moves in that direction, the French persuaded the emperor to cancel a treaty he had made with Italy. Seizing this incident as a pretext, the Italians invaded Ethiopia from neighboring Eritrea. However, the Ethiopian army had been trained and equipped by the French. To the amazement of the world, and especially the Italians, the invading army was decisively defeated at the battle of Aduwa in 1896. The Italians withdrew from Ethiopia and recognized its independence.

Thus Ethiopia joined Liberia as one of the two sovereign, independent states in Africa, each recognized by the Western powers. Such recognition was a rare experience for a "backward" country in the imperialistic era.

Anglo-Egyptian Sudan

The Sudan, as you have read, is a vast geographic region of savannas south of the Sahara, stretching from the Atlantic Ocean to the Nile Valley and beyond. In the imperialistic era, the term *Sudan* also referred to a specific eastern part of this region south of Egypt. It was inhabited by Arabs and various native tribes, many of whom were excellent fighters. Egypt claimed the Sudan, having conquered it in the early 1800's.

After Great Britain established control over Egypt in 1882, the Sudan became important to the British for two reasons. First, the upper Nile River flows through the Sudan (see map, page 534). Control of the region would afford a chance to build dams for irrigation and to control the flow of water in the lower Nile. Second, control of the Sudan would be a step toward the British dream of a Cape-to-Cairo railroad. (At this time the Germans had not yet secured German East Africa.) France also wanted the Sudan, both because of its possessions farther west and because it already had a toehold on the Red Sea (French Somaliland) and wanted to extend its territory inland.

In the 1880's, the British and Egyptians sent a force under a British general, Charles Gordon, to put down a native revolt in the Sudan. They were besieged for ten months at Khartoum on the Nile River, and Gordon was killed just two days before reinforcements arrived. Nevertheless, both Britain and France still regarded the Sudan as a prize worth the risk of war, and both continued their efforts to gain possession of it.

In the 1890's, Britain ordered another military force to move southward along the Nile

from Egypt. Under General Herbert Kitchener, these troops defeated a Sudanese army at Omdurman, then moved farther south.

Meanwhile the French sent one expedition from French Somaliland, which never arrived, and another from the French Congo, under Major J. B. Marchand. Marchand's two-year journey with a small Senegalese force was a daring one through some 3,200 miles of tropical rain forest. In July 1898 he reached Fashoda, on the upper Nile River, and raised the French flag.

The British force reached Fashoda in September, and Kitchener insisted that the French flag be lowered and the British and Egyptian flags be raised. There was tension, which was relieved when both officers decided to ask their governments for instructions.

Since neither government really wanted war, they negotiated a peaceful settlement of the Fashoda Incident. The French were willing to recognize the British as masters of the Sudan. In return, the French received the northern part of French Equatorial Africa and recognition of all their possessions in French West Africa.

Great Britain and Egypt established a condominium in the Sudan, known as the Anglo-Egyptian Sudan. There was little doubt, however, which nation held the upper hand. Under British management the region made progress. But it was still imperial rule, and the people preferred freedom.

CHECKUP

1. What groups came into conflict in South Africa? How was the conflict settled? What adjustments followed?

2. How did the island of Helgoland in the North Sea play a part in the division of Africa?

3. Give two reasons why the British wanted the Sudan. Why did the French want it? What was the settlement?

4. IDENTIFY: Rhodes, Afrikaans, Livingstone, Peters, Fashoda Incident.

5. LOCATE: Natal, Orange Free State, Transvaal, Bechuanaland, Rhodesia, Ujiji, German East Africa, Madagascar, Uganda, British East Africa, Anglo-Egyptian Sudan.

CHAPTER REVIEW

Chapter 26   Imperialism Transformed the Continent of Africa   (1830–1914)

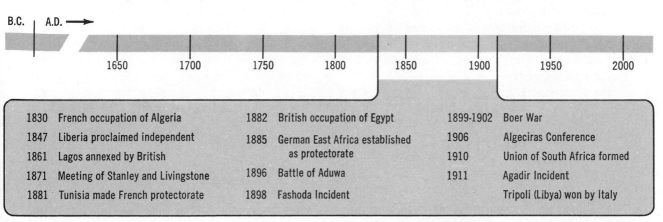

B.C. | A.D. →

1650	1700	1750	1800	1850	1900	1950	2000

1830	French occupation of Algeria	1882	British occupation of Egypt	1899-1902	Boer War
1847	Liberia proclaimed independent	1885	German East Africa established	1906	Algeciras Conference
1861	Lagos annexed by British		as protectorate	1910	Union of South Africa formed
1871	Meeting of Stanley and Livingstone	1896	Battle of Aduwa	1911	Agadir Incident
1881	Tunisia made French protectorate	1898	Fashoda Incident		Tripoli (Libya) won by Italy

CHAPTER SUMMARY

After a decline of interest in colonies, European nations became involved in a new kind of empire building—imperialism—in the late 1800's. It arose from a need for self-sufficiency, new markets, and places to invest surplus capital and settle excess population. Nationalism, missionary motives, and the "white man's burden" were also important factors. Although imperialistic ventures were usually initiated by individuals, governments cooperated in establishing colonies, protectorates, and spheres of influence.

In North Africa, France occupied first Algeria and then Tunisia. When conflict arose over Morocco, a conference was held at Algeciras, where France won a diplomatic victory. After the Agadir Incident, which almost led to war, Morocco, too, came under French domination. Egypt's financial difficulties allowed Britain to extend control over the Suez Canal and eventually over Egypt itself. Italy, a latecomer, took Libya from the Turks.

Sub-Saharan Africa typified imperialistic methods, with early explorers followed by soldiers, government officials, and developers. In western Africa, France gained French West Africa, the French Congo, and French Equatorial Africa. Britain took the Gold Coast and Nigeria. King Leopold II of Belgium held the Belgian Congo personally at first, but scandals forced him to turn it over to the Belgian government. Germany, Spain, and Portugal also held territories in West Africa; by 1900, Liberia—under American protection—was the only independent nation in the area.

In southern Africa, Britain dominated Cape Colony, but conflicts arose with Boer settlers. After British victory in the Boer War, the Union of South Africa was formed as a British dominion.

Imperialistic rivalries in East Africa were bitter. Portugal, Britain, and Germany all claimed sizable territories, with Italy—defeated by independent Ethiopia—again gaining relatively undesirable regions. A confrontation between France and Britain at Fashoda resulted in British control over the Sudan.

QUESTIONS FOR DISCUSSION

1. Do you think American aid programs of today have anything in common with the "white man's burden" concept of imperialism? Explain and comment.

2. How was it possible for a relatively small number of Europeans to hold large African populations in check, even during open revolts? What had happened in Europe that gave Europeans their superiority? Do Europeans still wield such superior power today?

3. How does a study of imperialism in Africa help explain why many Africans today hate or at least distrust Europeans and the West generally? Do you think such feelings are justified?

4. Do you think Germany should have followed Bismarck's advice concerning imperialism rather than the policy of William II? Justify your answer.

5. What are the differences and similarities between the colonization that began in the 1500's and the imperialism of the period from 1870 to 1914? Does imperialism still exist today?

PROJECTS

1. Make a list of the forces that stimulated imperialism and explain each one of them.

2. Draw a cartoon on the theme of the "white man's burden."

3. Draw a map of Africa in 1914 showing European colonial possessions there.

CHAPTER 27

Imperialist Powers Gained Control of the Far East

While European nations were carving up Africa, their new drive for colonial empires also penetrated into much of Asia. In India, China, Korea, and Southeast Asia, they sought and gained colonies, concessions, and spheres of influence.

As a setting for imperialist penetration, Asia differed in certain ways from Africa. Most of Africa was thinly settled. Although there had been several native kingdoms, they no longer existed at the time of the imperialistic era. Most Africans lived a fairly simple tribal existence, some in small villages, others as nomads who followed their livestock from one area to another.

Asia, on the other hand, was thickly settled by people whose complex civilizations went back to the dawn of history. Asians had been overrun by various invaders through the centuries but had usually "swallowed up" their conquerors and gone on living in traditional ways.

In one important respect, however, Africa and Asia were alike when the imperialists moved in. Europe and the United States had been industrialized; Africa and Asia had not. Europeans and Americans had steamships, for example, that could go far up the rivers of Asia's ancient lands. They had tools and weapons—especially weapons—that were far superior to anything the people of Asia knew about. Imperialism could be imposed on Asia by force, and it was.

A figure symbolizing China watches in horrified anger as foreign troops stream past the Great Wall

There were also differences in the nature of imperialism within Asia. In India (as in Africa) Western powers took control of governments and exercised authority. To be sure, they exploited the regions they controlled. Along with authority, however, they also assumed certain responsibilities. They protected the region from outside attack and stopped internal wars. And they did take some, though not much, responsibility for the people who lived in the regions they controlled. In China this was not so. The imperialist powers took on authority but no obligations. They did not protect the country from war, nor did they promote the welfare of its people.

The major exception to imperialist domination was Japan. When it was exposed to Western military power in the 1800's, Japan hastily underwent technological and political revolutions in order to resist imperialism. Its "crash program" succeeded so well that Japan soon became an imperialist nation itself and joined the Western nations in bringing most of the Far East under imperialist domination.

THE CHAPTER SECTIONS:

1. The British secured firm control over India (1700–1914)

2. Japan, formerly isolated, became a powerful modern nation (1853–1900)

3. Foreign powers began to extend their influence over China (1839–1898)

4. China and Southeast Asia fell under imperialist domination (1880–1912)

1   The British secured firm control over India

The strong forces of imperialism that swept outward from Europe in the 1800's brought important and fateful changes to India. In that vast subcontinent, however, with its ancient civilization and huge population, the changes were not abrupt as they were in so many parts of Africa. Rather, they were intensifications of European influence that had been present in India for centuries.

European traders in India

You have read how India was important to European traders during the age of exploration. The Portuguese set up several trading posts along India's western coast and enjoyed a near-monopoly on trade with India and the East Indies for about a hundred years.

Then, in the 1600's, after the decline of the Portuguese Empire, England and France formed trading companies that established bases in India. The British East India Company, as you have read, gained footholds at Bombay, on the northwest coast; Madras, on the southeast coast; and Calcutta, to the northeast in the delta of the Ganges River. The French company settled at Pondicherry, south of Madras.

The British and French companies in India were interested in commercial profits, not in ruling Indian colonies. They traded in luxury goods that brought high prices in Europe, such as silk, jewels, indigo, tea, pepper, and other spices. They used armed guards or soldiers only to protect their property. There were just a few Englishmen and Frenchmen in India.

British-French rivalry

Early in the 1700's the Mogul Empire dissolved into anarchy, leaving a *power vacuum* in India—that is, a situation where no one was in control. Britain and France, which opposed each other in Europe and North America, each tried to rush into the vacuum by making alliances with rival Indian states.

French affairs in India were directed by Joseph François Dupleix, a clever administrator. He met his match in Robert Clive, who had begun his career as a minor clerk with the British East India Company and then became an officer with the company's military forces. When the French menaced Madras in 1751, Clive, with great daring and only a few troops, captured an important military post nearby. French troops were diverted

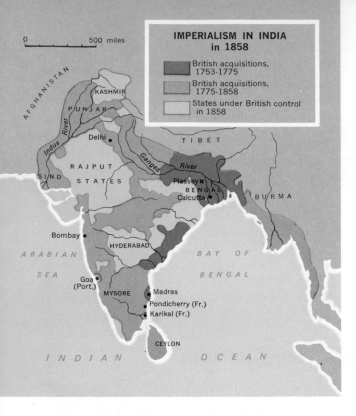

IMPERIALISM IN INDIA
in 1858

- British acquisitions, 1753-1775
- British acquisitions, 1775-1858
- States under British control in 1858

0   500 miles

AFGHANISTAN · KASHMIR · PUNJAB · SIND · RAJPUT STATES · Indus River · Delhi · TIBET · Ganges River · Plassey × · BENGAL · Calcutta · BURMA · Bombay · HYDERABAD · ARABIAN SEA · BAY OF BENGAL · Goa (Port.) · MYSORE · Madras · Pondicherry (Fr.) · Karikal (Fr.) · CEYLON · INDIAN OCEAN

from Madras to attack him, but he held out successfully until reinforcements arrived.

British-French rivalry in India came to a head during the Seven Years' War (1756–1763). The British trading post at Calcutta lay within the important Indian state of Bengal (see map, this page), whose ruler was allied with the French. Troops of the Bengal ruler captured Calcutta, imprisoned 146 British, and locked them up overnight in a small jail cell that has since been called the "Black Hole of Calcutta." By the next morning, 123 of the prisoners had died of suffocation.

When Clive heard this news, he pushed northward from Madras with his troops, recaptured Calcutta, and set out to conquer all of Bengal and dethrone its ruler. In a major battle at Plassey in 1757, he and his troops were successful. Clive then appointed a new ruler and brought all of Bengal under control of the British East India Company. In 1761 the British also took Pondicherry.

Although the Treaty of Paris in 1763 restored Pondicherry to the French, from this time on most of India lay open to the control or influence of the British East India Company. The French and Portuguese held only a few small trading posts. The Mogul Empire had disintegrated into hundreds of small states, none of which was strong enough to resist the British East India Company.

Expansion of British authority

After the capture of Bengal, the British government became uneasy at the thought of a commercial company's controlling the lives of millions of Indian people. In the 1770's the British government assumed the right to appoint the company's highest official, called the governor general. For all practical purposes, however, the company was free to earn profits as it could and to use its own officials and troops as it chose.

For a long time the British East India Company had been dealing with what was left of the Mogul Empire, employing many Indians in company positions. In the late 1780's came a change that had long-lasting effects. The British government appointed Lord Cornwallis, a few years after his defeat at Yorktown in the American Revolution, to be governor general of India.

One of Cornwallis' first actions was to clean up widespread corruption among company employees. For this purpose he created a governing civil service of company officials who were forbidden to have any part in the company's commercial activities. Believing that Indian employees were responsible for some of the corruption, Cornwallis ordered that Indians be excluded from all important company positions. Indian resentment over this discrimination festered for years.

As time went on, the British were drawn deeper into the quicksands of Indian political rivalries. Although official policy wavered, the general tendency during the early 1800's was for the British East India Company to extend its power into more and more areas.

Several strong Indian states engaged in constant jealous rivalries and even warfare. The British took advantage of such warfare until they won control of these regions. Religious hatred between Hindus and Moslems, as well as the caste system, prevented Indians from uniting against the foreigners. The British usually did not need to employ any of their own troops. Instead, when actual fighting was necessary, they made use of native troops, called sepoys, who were trained and led by British officers.

By 1857 the British East India Company ruled about three fifths of the subcontinent directly. It ruled most of the rest indirectly through its control over native princes. Britain also controlled the island of Ceylon, which it had seized during the Napoleonic Wars.

Until about 1830, the British made no attempt to impose their way of life on India. In the 1830's, however, English became the language of instruction in Indian schools, and pupils studied the literature, history, and science of Western civilization.

The British also enforced several reforms. Slavery and the killing of infant girls were prohibited. The ritual suicide known as suttee was declared illegal. Thuggee, a semi-religious cult that required its members to commit murder and robbery, was suppressed. (It is from this cult that we get our word *thug*.)

The Sepoy Rebellion

India in the mid-1800's presented the strange spectacle of a huge land, with millions of people and an ancient civilization, controlled by a foreign commercial corporation. British population in India had grown rapidly and by this time included British wives and families. Many of the British officials copied the autocratic habits of the Indian rulers they had replaced.

Many Indians resented the autocratic rule of British officials as well as their increasing tendency to impose Western ways of life upon India. The sepoys were particularly dissatisfied because they had been forced to fight for the British in numerous campaigns in faraway Afghanistan and Burma. In 1857 they mutinied.

The immediate cause of the Sepoy Rebellion involved a new kind of rifle that the British East India Company issued in 1857. The cartridges for this rifle had been greased to make the bullets slide more easily through the barrel. In order to load his rifle, the sepoy had to bite off part of the cartridge. According to rumors, the cartridges were greased with the fat of cows and pigs. To the Hindu the cow is sacred; to the Moslem the pig is taboo. Sepoy forces included both Hindus and Moslems. Thus, biting the cartridge would violate religious customs of both groups.

Agitators were able to whip up existing resentments by claiming that the company had purposely tried to insult the two religions. With help from the Indian populace, the sepoy troops staged a widespread and bloody mutiny against their British masters.

The Sepoy Rebellion almost drove the British out of India, but the rebellion was finally suppressed by troops sent from England. In 1858, Parliament dissolved the British East India Company and transferred rule of India to the British Crown, or government. A viceroy was sent to replace the governor general and, in 1877, Queen Victoria was proclaimed Empress of India.

British imperialism in India

Although after 1858 India was ruled directly by the British government, conditions did not change much. British India made up about three fifths of the subcontinent (see map, opposite). The rest consisted of over 550 states, headed by native princes. The British government, through its viceroy, controlled their right to make treaties and declare war, either with foreign countries or with one another. Great Britain also regulated their internal affairs when it seemed necessary.

To control India, both British and native, the British government used the old Roman device of "divide and rule." It granted favors to those princes who cooperated with imperial rule and dealt harshly with those who did not. It treated Hindus and Moslems equally, but did little to ease religious hatred.

The British were interested chiefly in profitable trade in India. To get it, they maintained public order by ending the many local wars and massacres. They set up efficient governmental administration and guarded against foreign invasions. They built roads, bridges, railroads, factories, hospitals, and schools. They tried to improve agricultural methods, health, and sanitation.

The British in India were a great puzzle to the natives, who attributed British power to their non-vegetarian diet and their fair complexions to alcohol. A representative of the British East India Company, above, holds a durbar, a kind of royal reception. The English enjoyed the luxury of being waited on. Below, a foppish gentleman is groomed for the day by five servants. In the cartoon at right, Prime Minister Disraeli appears as Aladdin, offering "new crowns for old" as he exchanges Queen Victoria's British crown for the crown of India.

Naturally, many of these improvements helped the Indians. But other effects of British rule were harmful. The Indian handicraft industry almost disappeared. British cotton mills made cloth so cheaply that it could be transported to India and sold for less than the product of Indian hand weavers. Local artisans had to search for work in the cities or gain a miserable livelihood from farming small plots of land.

During the late 1800's and early 1900's, British rule in India had created a situation where the peoples of two alien cultures lived side by side with almost no warm human contacts. The British had imposed themselves above Indian society as a superior race, a sort of super-caste—socially, at least. The British formed exclusive social circles wherever they settled. Their clubs were open to any European but closed to any Indian, no matter how distinguished. Posted everywhere—in railway carriages and waiting rooms and even on park benches—were signs reading "For Europeans Only." For generations all Indians, including English-educated Brahmans, were insulted, humiliated, degraded, and subjected to contemptuous treatment by the British.

The rise of Indian nationalism

Although the British did not mingle socially with the Indians, Western civilization had a powerful impact on India. For one thing, it led to a serious conflict of values. India was a land of primitive agriculture and handicrafts in isolated villages. Both Hinduism, with its ancient caste system, and Islam, which regulated behavior by the unchanging precepts of the Koran, stressed age-old customs and respect for tradition.

Western culture emphasized material progress and political change. British discrimination against Indians injured their pride in their ancient civilization. Indians, especially educated Indians, regarded Europeans as materialists and money-grubbers who cared little for the higher values of mind, soul, and spirit.

British education had a profound effect on India. In earlier days, only Brahmans were educated, mainly to read and ponder the sacred Sanskrit writings. Indian merchants might have some simple schooling in reading, writing, and mathematics. All women and men of the lower castes were uneducated. During the 1800's the East India Company, the British government, missionaries, and private individuals started schools and colleges in India. They educated only a small percentage of the people, but, among other things, they taught them about nationalism and the liberal ideals of democracy. Indian scholars could, and did, condemn British imperialism by using quotations from British writers. Many Indians came to believe in socialism.

A movement for Indian self-rule began in the late 1800's. The Indian National Congress held its first meeting in 1886. Not all Indian nationalists agreed on the same approach. Some, especially those who had been educated in British schools and universities, wanted to advance toward independence gradually and by democratic methods. They also wanted to keep certain aspects of Western culture and industry that they thought could benefit India. Others wanted to break all ties with Great Britain and to sweep away all Western influence. They wished to revolt not only against Western culture but also against Islam.

The views of this second group alarmed Indian Moslems. They were a minority in the land, and British rule protected them from discrimination and violence. They feared that if British rule were removed, their future might be in danger. The Moslems were therefore much less enthusiastic about driving out the British than were the Hindus. In 1906 they formed the Moslem League to protect their interests. The independence movement gathered strength very slowly, and the British kept India under a tight rein.

CHECKUP

1. What important decision was made by Lord Cornwallis?
2. What were the causes of the Sepoy Rebellion? the results?
3. List the beneficial and harmful effects of British rule in India.
4. IDENTIFY: power vacuum, Clive, "Black Hole of Calcutta," thuggee, Indian National Congress, Moslem League.

As the surge of imperialism swept across Africa and India in the late 1800's and early 1900's, it was bound to reach the Far East, especially China. But one part of the Far East did not succumb to Western imperialism—Japan. Japan, indeed, became a competitor of the Western powers in the carving up of China and other parts of the Far East.

Earlier chapters told how Japan, after nearly a century of contact with Portuguese traders and missionaries, expelled all foreigners in the early 1600's. In 1638, with the aid of Dutch naval vessels, the Japanese destroyed the last Portuguese stronghold. Japan, ruled by shoguns of the Tokugawa family, then retreated into isolation. After 1715 it permitted just two Dutch merchant ships to stop and trade each year at an island in the harbor of Nagasaki.

The end of Japanese isolation

To help maintain Japanese isolation, the government refused shelter to storm-driven ships of other nations. Shipwrecked sailors were treated harshly. Such treatment of American whaling and merchant ships finally brought an end to Japanese isolation.

In 1853, United States President Millard Fillmore sent a naval force to Japan under Commodore Matthew Perry. Perry had orders to negotiate a commercial treaty that would open Japanese ports to American trade as well as guarantee the safety of American sailors. He presented a letter from President Fillmore, urging the treaty, and said he would return for an answer the following year.

In Japan there was controversy over the decision. Some powerful leaders favored military resistance and continued isolation. Others believed that Japan could not hold out. The latter prevailed. The shogun reluctantly agreed to negotiate when Perry returned in 1854.

The negotiations were attended by colorful ceremonies, symbolic of the two contrasting cultures. The Japanese gave the Americans beautiful silk, lacquer ware, and other articles exquisitely made by hand. The Americans presented the Japanese with guns, a telegraph set, and a model railroad train on which dignified Japanese officials took rides with their loose robes flying.

The negotiations led to the Treaty of Kanagawa in 1854, a turning point in Japanese history. Two Japanese ports were opened to Americans, both for shelter and trade. Such ports were known as treaty ports. The treaty also provided for better treatment of shipwrecked sailors. Within two years Japan signed similar treaties with Great Britain, Russia, France, and the Netherlands. They opened several Japanese seaports where representatives of foreign nations had the right to live, trade, purchase naval supplies, and establish consulates (diplomatic offices which protect a nation's business interests in a foreign country).

At first, conservative Japanese isolationists held out successfully against any real contacts with the outsiders. Foreign consuls were ignored, and contacts with foreign traders were kept to a minimum. It took patience and tact to win greater favors, trust, and understanding. The United States consul general, Townsend Harris, was equal to the task. With patience, honesty, and sincerity, he gradually gained the confidence of Japanese officials. In 1858 his success led to another treaty in which the Japanese and United States governments agreed to exchange diplomatic representatives. Now more American consuls were admitted and more treaty ports were opened. Tariff regulations were written. Foreigners living in Japan were given the right to observe their own religious ceremonies. Similar treaties with other nations soon followed.

The decision to modernize

The end of isolation brought Japan face to face with a great decision. Should Japan resist Western influence, by force if necessary? Or should the nation try to become strong in the only way the imperial powers would respect—by westernizing and industrializing?

The decision was not made without a struggle. In the 1860's a civil war broke out between pro-shogun and pro-emperor forces. Both groups attacked the foreigners. A combined naval force from the fleets of Great Britain, France, and the Netherlands then entered southern Japanese ports, put down the rebellion, and forced the rebels to pay an indemnity. In 1867 a group of young, progressive daimio overthrew the shogun and gave complete authority to the emperor. Japan became an absolute monarchy in fact as well as in theory. The emperor took the name Meiji (MAY·JEE), meaning "enlightened peace," for his reign. It lasted until 1912 and is often called the Meiji Era.

The young Japanese daimio persuaded the emperor that Japan must take the road toward westernization and industrialization. The decision was carried through in the most thorough fashion. Japan invited foreign experts to help modernize transportation and communications, set up modern industries, and reorganize the legal and political systems. Commissions of Japanese scholars went abroad to study American and European governments, armies, navies, and school systems.

Spectacular industrial development took place during the Meiji period. The Japanese copied the best methods, machines, and techniques to be found in Great Britain, Germany, and the United States. Quickly they mechanized their textile manufacture and developed a steel industry. They expanded shipbuilding and foreign trade. Japanese cities were linked by railroads, the telegraph, and the telephone. Banking also developed rapidly. In thirty-five years the Japanese almost duplicated the industrial development that had taken 150 years in the West.

The Japanese set up a complete system of universal compulsory education that soon abolished illiteracy almost entirely. Girls were educated in home management. Boys received technical and industrial training. All were strongly imbued with loyalty to the emperor.

In light of Japan's later history, it is revealing to know what models the Japanese followed in their program of modernization. In military matters they copied the German ideas of universal

HISTORY THROUGH ART

"Père Tanguy" by Van Gogh

Soon after Perry's trip to Japan, European artists "discovered" Japanese prints when some were used for wrapping a package sent to Paris. Among those who admired the Japanese sense of line and freedom from traditional perspective was Vincent van Gogh. In his portrait of the art dealer Père Tanguy, painted in the 1880's, he used Japanese prints as a colorful background for the stiff but appealing figure of his friend. (Tanguy was a kindly man who lent money to many poor artists.) The painting is fittingly symbolic of two worlds that were just beginning to know each other.

military training and strict army organization. British naval officers helped organize and train the Japanese navy. In industrializing, the Japanese copied Britain, Germany, and the United States.

New Japanese government

The greatest dilemma was government. The Japanese wanted to keep a divine, supreme emperor. At the same time they wanted to give at least the appearance of democratic, constitutional government. They found an almost perfect model in the constitution of the German Empire. A Japanese constitution was drafted by an appointed commission. Its draft was accepted by the emperor and proclaimed in 1889. The people were not given a chance to vote on it.

The emperor remained the sacred descendant of the gods. His orders were superior to any acts of the legislature. He appointed and could remove his own group of advisers, called the Cabinet of Ministers. There was a two-house legislature: a house of peers, or lords, whose positions were mostly hereditary, and an elected house of representatives. Neither house could consider any legislation that was not presented by the cabinet.

As a further safeguard against any "excess of democracy," the emperor had absolute veto power over all laws passed by the legislature. He alone could negotiate treaties; these did not have to be approved by either house. He could summon the legislature at his pleasure and dissolve the lower house when he pleased. He commanded the armed forces and could declare war and make peace. He was supposed to act only on the advice of his cabinet, but, of course, he alone appointed and removed cabinet members.

An ominous feature of the new constitution was the powerful role of the military. The emperor was supreme commander. He was advised in military and naval matters by a Supreme War Council and Supreme Navy Council of top-ranking officers. They recommended to the emperor the army and navy officers who should serve as minister of war and minister of the navy. The military forces were in no way controlled by the civil government. In fact, the contrary was often true. If the ministers of war and navy disapproved of a government policy, they might resign and force all the other ministers to resign.

Such was the government that controlled the destiny of Japan after 1889. It was filled with contradictions. It was an absolute monarchy with a constitution. It copied democratic institutions but was not democratic. It had a legislature that could not initiate legislation, declare war, make peace, or draft treaties.

The first meeting of the Japanese legislature, in 1890, was a historic occasion. Both houses met with the emperor, who is shown here, top center, in the place of honor.

Problems of modernization

The Meiji Era in Japan was truly remarkable. Probably no other nation in history has set out so systematically to investigate, copy, and quickly adapt to another culture. However, modernization caused internal problems in Japan, for many Western ideas conflicted with long-held Japanese customs and traditions. These conflicts created psychological problems among the Japanese people. And there were other problems, too.

As in Europe, industrialization and scientific development produced a sudden increase in Japan's population. Cities grew rapidly. Every inch of land capable of being farmed was put to use. Individual landholdings grew smaller and smaller and were farmed by intensive methods. This meant that the work was done by hand, as we might cultivate a small garden. Even so, the food supply did not increase as rapidly as the population.

There was, indeed, a surplus of population—more people than the land would support, more people than could possibly find jobs. Therefore, Japanese people began to emigrate to Korea, to the island of Formosa (or Taiwan), and to Hawaii and other islands of the Pacific. Many came to the United States.

In time, the United States, Canada, and Australia passed laws restricting immigration. The United States, for example, completely prohibited the immigration of Japanese, as well as Chinese, while still permitting the immigration of Europeans. As proud people, both Japanese and Chinese resented this discrimination.

Japanese industrial development created another problem. The islands lacked almost all of the raw materials needed in modern industry, so they had to be imported. The only way for a nation to pay for its imports is by selling its own goods abroad. Since Japan needed imported food as well as industrial raw materials, it had to export or die.

In exporting goods Japan met with restrictions, just as it did in its export of people. Many countries passed tariff laws to protect their own home markets against Japanese competition. They argued that Japanese manufactured goods were cheap because Japanese labor was cheap, which was true. A nation as poor as Japan then was cannot pay high wages or maintain high standards of living.

CHECKUP

1. Why did Commodore Perry go to Japan? What did he achieve there?

2. Name four powers held by the emperor of Japan under the constitution of 1889.

3. What problems did westernization bring to Japan?

4. Compare Japan's adoption of Western culture with its earlier adoption of Chinese culture.

5. IDENTIFY: treaty ports, consulates, Harris, Meiji.

3 Foreign powers began to extend their influence over China

When you last read about China, that vast land with its large population and ancient civilization was under the rule of the Ming dynasty, which came to power in 1368. Proud of Chinese traditions and scornful of foreigners, the Ming rulers resisted Portuguese traders who appeared there in the early 1500's, permitting them to set up a trading post only at Macao.

Isolation under the Manchus

Like so many dynasties before it, that of the Ming finally collapsed. It was succeeded in 1644 by the Manchu dynasty. The Manchus were related to the Jurchen, the barbarian people who had ruled northern China during the Sung dynasty. However, they had been living for a long time in Manchuria, where they learned to admire and respect Chinese traditions. Thus they tended to follow the policies of their predecessors, the Ming, including resistance to foreign trade and influence. All ports except Canton were closed to foreign traders.

The Manchu dynasty was to rule China until 1911, but it began to weaken as early as the

1800's. The age-old cycle was being repeated. Land was concentrated in a few hands. The masses of Chinese were wretchedly poor. Debts from loans and taxes forced peasants to become tenant farmers and finally bandits. Warlords and bandits gained control of large areas and weakened the central government. China was still almost wholly agricultural. There had been no Industrial Revolution there to produce the manufactured goods, weapons, and means of transportation and communication that were giving the West its rising standard of living.

In the early 1800's the Chinese people were isolated from one another as well as from foreigners. The days of good transportation and communication within China were gone. Each village was an isolated community with little or no knowledge of the rest of the world.

Cracks in China's isolation

The first crack in Chinese isolation occurred as a result of trouble with Great Britain. British merchants at Canton had developed a profitable trade by bringing in opium from India and selling it throughout southern China. The trade, of course, caused severe physical and moral damage among the Chinese. The Chinese authorities were also worried about the drain on China's silver supply. They demanded that opium sales be stopped and that all opium cargoes be turned over to them.

There was an exchange of demands between the British and Chinese governments. The so-called Opium War broke out in 1839 and lasted for three years. The British won when they secured control of an important region near Nanking.

In the treaty of 1842 that ended the Opium War, China was compelled to give the island of Hong Kong to the British and to open Amoy, Foochow (now Minhow), Ningpo, and Shanghai to foreign trade. These ports, together with Canton, were the first Chinese treaty ports (see map, opposite page). No tariff of more than 5 percent could be charged on British goods. A further provision stated that British subjects in these ports were to be governed by British, not Chinese, laws

and were to be tried in British courts. This exemption of foreigners from the laws of the nation where they live or do business is called *extraterritoriality*.

Great Britain could not hold its privileged, monopolistic position in China for long. France and other Western powers, including the United States, soon demanded and received similar trade treaties with similar provisions of extraterritoriality. These treaties were not negotiated with China; China was forced to sign them. Among the Chinese they came to be called "unequal treaties."

In demanding these treaties, the Western powers were not attempting to take territory in China. They were content to let the Manchus struggle with their own warlords and other internal problems. Instead, they were trying to establish secure trade relations.

Rebellion and its aftermath

The intrusion of the Western powers into China was made easier by an event that occurred in China itself. In the mid-1800's, southern and central China were torn by a rebellion that threatened to overthrow the Manchu dynasty. The rebel leader, a southern Chinese influenced by Christian teachings, claimed to be the younger brother of Jesus, charged with the mission of establishing a new dynasty—the Taiping, or "Great Peace." His ideas attracted many followers.

When the government tried to suppress the Taiping movement, it turned into a political rebellion. It lasted from 1850 to 1864 and caused great destruction in southern China and the Yangtze Valley. With the aid of some regional armies and foreign adventurers, the Manchus suppressed the rebels.

Both the Manchu dynasty and the country were weakened by the Taiping Rebellion. To raise money, the government established a system of internal tariffs. These tariffs handicapped trade without much helping the central treasury because tariff collectors stole most of the money. The treasury was further weakened when foreigners took over the collection of foreign customs duties in Chinese ports.

During the Taiping Rebellion the Manchus

IMPERIALISM IN THE FAR EAST TO 1914

British	Dutch
French	Russian
German	Japanese
Portuguese	United States

Major Chinese treaty ports
after 1842 underlined

were unable to protect foreign citizens as Western governments had demanded. In 1856, war with Britain again broke out, and British forces, with French aid, again defeated the Chinese.

The Manchus were forced to sign another "unequal treaty," which opened additional treaty ports on the coast and along the Yangtze River. The Chinese permitted the British to open an

559

embassy in the Manchu capital, Peking. Soon there were also embassies of the other foreign powers at Peking. The Chinese government pledged protection for Christian missionaries and their converts. Great Britain took possession of a small section of the Chinese mainland opposite Hong Kong. In separate treaties, Russia received territory north of the Amur River and east of the Ussuri River, bordering the Sea of Japan. In the southern part of this territory, Russians founded the port of Vladivostok and established a naval base there (see map, page 559).

The Sino-Japanese War

Japan, as you know, was rapidly adopting a number of Western practices and ideas. Now Japan decided to try imperialism.

The territory that most interested Japan was the nearby peninsula of Korea. Korea had long been a dependency of China. Korean authorities had to refer all matters involving foreign relations to the Chinese emperors. No foreigners were allowed in the country. But it was clear that this Korean isolation could not last long. Russia, France, and the United States were all interested in gaining trade privileges there. Fearing that a Western-controlled Korea might threaten its safety, Japan began to demand privileges in the Korean peninsula.

Japan maintained that Korea was independent, while China still claimed Korea as a dependency. Out of this confusion, Japan secured a treaty that opened some Korean ports to Japanese trade. China then allowed the Koreans to make similar treaties with six Western nations.

Japan used many methods to increase its influence in the Korean peninsula. In 1894 a rebellion broke out in Korea. Both Japan and China sent armed forces to put it down. It was an explosive situation, and it exploded. There was a short war, called the Sino-Japanese War. Early in 1895 the seeming giant, China, was defeated by the seeming pygmy, Japan.

The Japanese now forced China to sign a treaty. In addition to trade privileges, the Japanese wanted territory. By the Treaty of Shimonoseki in 1895, China was compelled to recognize the complete independence of Korea. China also had to cede to Japan the great island of Formosa and the nearby Pescadores. In another provision of great importance, China ceded to Japan the strategic Liaotung Peninsula on the southern coast of Manchuria. At the tip of the Liaotung Peninsula, which juts into the Yellow Sea, was the excellent harbor of Port Arthur. Finally, China also had to pay Japan an indemnity amounting to 150 million dollars.

Russian plans in Manchuria and Liaotung

No Western power was pleased with the Treaty of Shimonoseki, and Russia was especially displeased. Russia wanted no strong power in Korea, close to its naval base at Vladivostok. Also, Russia had plans of its own for Manchuria, including the Liaotung Peninsula. To understand them, look again at the map on page 559.

Notice that the northern border of Manchuria follows the long, curving line of the Amur River. Notice also that Manchuria's eastern border is the Ussuri River. As you recall, territory north of the Amur and east of the Ussuri had been given by China to Russia in the aftermath of the Taiping Rebellion. At the southern tip of the eastern Russian territory locate Russia's seaport and naval base, Vladivostok. Notice also that Manchuria extends northward to Siberia. Notice finally the Liaotung Peninsula.

In 1891 the Russians had begun a gigantic project: the building of a railroad from western Russia all the way across Asia to Vladivostok. If this Trans-Siberian railroad had to follow the Amur River line, it would be 350 miles longer than if it could cut straight across Manchuria to Vladivostok. The Manchurian route also presented fewer engineering difficulties in the form of rivers and mountains. Russia also hoped to link its Trans-Siberian railroad to the Liaotung Peninsula by a line from Harbin, in central Manchuria, to Port Arthur, at the tip of the Liaotung Peninsula.

With these plans afoot, Russia was more than willing to "aid" China in keeping Japan off the Asiatic mainland. France, which had recently concluded an alliance with Russia, was also willing to help. Germany, eager to get on better terms with Russia and perhaps to weaken the Russo-French alliance, also offered its services. In a joint note, Russia, France, and Germany "advised" the Japanese government to withdraw from the Liaotung Peninsula.

The Japanese were furious, but they were not ready to face such an array of force. They gave the Liaotung Peninsula back to China in return for an increased indemnity. France and Russia gave China further "aid"—a loan to help pay the indemnity to Japan.

The price of European "aid"

There was a catch, of course, in all of this "aid" to China. China had to pledge that no foreign power would receive any special rights in Chinese financial affairs unless France and Russia received them, too. Great Britain and Germany hastened to make similar loans with similar provisions.

Beginning in 1896, there were still more bills for China to pay. France demanded and received special trading privileges and the right to develop mineral resources in southern China. It also received a 99-year lease to the territory of Kwangchowan and the right to build a railroad linking southern China with the French protectorate in Indo-China (page 566). Germany was given a 99-year lease to the port of Tsingtao and surrounding territory on the south shore of the Shantung Peninsula, which juts into the Yellow Sea. Germany also received mining rights and permission to build a railway in Shantung. Britain would not be left out. It negotiated for more trading privileges in the Yangtze Valley and the right to build a naval base at Weihaiwei on the north shore of the Shantung Peninsula. This base was to balance the German base at Tsingtao.

Russia, organizer of the "aid," presented the highest bill. It demanded and received the right to lease a tax-free right of way for its railroad across Manchuria—to be called the Chinese Eastern Railway. It also received permission to "maintain order" along the Manchurian route and certain other extraterritorial privileges. In effect, northern Manchuria would be under Russian economic and military domination. In a further and secret treaty, Russia and China formed an alliance for mutual aid in case either should become involved in war with Japan.

When the Germans and British seized their bases in the Shantung Peninsula, Russia demanded entry to the Yellow Sea, too. The Russians forced China to lease to them the southern part of the Liaotung Peninsula, including the important base at Port Arthur. Russia also was given the right to build a branch of the Chinese Eastern Railway from Harbin to Port Arthur.

The fury of the Japanese can be easily imagined. They had been forced by the Western powers to give up the spoils of their victory and now had to watch those spoils being divided up.

CHECKUP

1. List the main provisions of the treaty that ended the Opium War.

2. What was the Taiping Rebellion? What results did it have?

3. State the price charged for "aid" to China by France, Germany, and Russia after the Sino-Japanese War.

4. IDENTIFY: Manchus, extraterritoriality, "unequal treaties," Treaty of Shimonoseki, Trans-Siberian railroad.

5. LOCATE: Canton, Hong Kong, Amoy, Foochow, Ningpo, Shanghai, Vladivostok, Formosa, Liaotung Peninsula, Port Arthur, Harbin, Tsingtao, Shantung Peninsula, Weihaiwei.

④ China and Southeast Asia fell under imperialist domination

Up to about 1900 the imperialist powers had operated mainly along the Chinese coast and up the Yangtze River. Then they began to carve the interior of China into spheres of influence.

The United States watched this new development with some concern because it did not want its merchants to be excluded from Chinese trade. In 1899 the American government appealed to

Foreign Domination of China

The end of Chinese isolation began in 1839 with the Opium War. A French caricature, left, exaggerated the issue when it pictured an Englishman, backed by troops, saying to China: "You must buy this poison. We want you to deaden yourself so completely that we'll be able to take all the tea we want to drink with our beefsteak." The Sino-Japanese War brought further foreign control with the loss of the Liaotung Peninsula and strategic Port Arthur, which the Japanese attacked in 1894, above. Vexed at these and other intrusions upon their independence, patriotic Chinese fought back in the Boxer Rebellion. At right, a stalwart Chinese guard beats back a Japanese attack on Peking. But the Chinese were defeated and their lands dismembered by foreign powers. At far right, Manchurian refugees leave their homes in 1910 after the secret partition of Manchuria between Russia and Japan.

the powers interested in China to recognize what it called the Open Door Policy. According to this policy, no nation would claim exclusive trading rights, and all nations could have equal rights to trade anywhere in China. The interested powers agreed, but their agreement did not mean much. No nation wanted to be exposed before the world as the only one to refuse, but none really intended to observe the Open Door Policy.

The Boxer Rebellion

By 1900 the fate of China seemed to be sealed. The Chinese had been unable to forestall the numerous grants of special privileges to the foreign powers, but resented what had happened.

In 1898 the aging Manchu dowager empress (widow of an earlier ruler) forced her nephew, the emperor at that time, to give up the throne so she could take it for herself. Partly to stop Chinese attacks on the Manchus, she did every-

thing she could to stir up hatred for foreigners, especially the missionaries. Within a year there were widespread attacks on foreigners in every part of China. The attacks were led by members of a patriotic society called the "Righteous Fists" (known in English as "Boxers"). Foreigners who could do so fled to the protection of their embassies at Peking. There they were besieged by an army of angry Chinese.

Despite their jealousies and rivalries, the imperialist nations were determined to protect their common interests and teach China to respect their power. Acting jointly for once, Great Britain, France, Germany, Russia, Japan, and the United States sent a combined army to China. They relieved the besieged embassies and put down the rebellion in 1901. Then they imposed heavy penalties, including payment of a large indemnity and the right to maintain garrisons of foreign troops at Peking and along the railroad to the coast.

This move completed the domination of China by foreign powers. Had it not been for the rivalries among the imperialists, they would have divided China politically then and there. However, they realized that, because of location, Russia and Japan would be in a position to benefit most from the actual breakup of China. As it was, Russia took advantage of the rebellion to move 100,000 troops into Manchuria. Thus, all agreed to be contented with the indemnity and other penalties without taking territory.

The Russo-Japanese War

The Boxer Rebellion had an important indirect effect. It sharpened the rivalry between Japan and Russia and brought on a war between them.

When most foreign troops were withdrawn from China after the rebellion, the Russians lingered on in Manchuria, despite promises to leave. Japan regarded this Russian hesitation with dis-

pleasure. It looked on Manchuria as a future Japanese sphere of influence. Despite several protests by the Japanese government, the Russians were in no hurry to depart. The Japanese prepared to force them out.

In 1902, Japan signed an alliance with Great Britain. Each agreed that the other had the right to defend its special interests in China, Manchuria, and Korea against the aggression of any third power. The two powers agreed to remain neutral if either of them became involved in a war with a single power, but to aid each other if a third power joined the conflict. The alliance was aimed at Russia, although, of course, it carefully did not say so.

The Anglo-Japanese alliance meant great prestige for Japan. Japan no longer stood alone but now had the support of a first-class European power. The Japanese put increased pressure on Russia. They demanded the withdrawal of Russian troops; they also proposed that they would leave Manchuria to Russia if Russia would leave Korea to Japan. The Russians reluctantly agreed to negotiate, but they were slow. Early in 1904, without any declaration of war, Japan launched a sneak attack on the Russian naval force at Port Arthur and sank a number of ships. The Russians later sent part of their Baltic fleet all the way around Africa to Asia, but it, too, was defeated by the Japanese navy. The Japanese army marched northward through Korea and reached Manchuria. Another force landed on the Liaotung Peninsula and forced its way inland.

Russia was handicapped in this war. The Russians were fighting 5,000 miles from their source of supplies. Russian public opinion was divided; probably a majority of the people opposed the war. The czar's government mismanaged the war.

Japan had the advantage of better preparation, the people's united support of the war, and being closer to the fighting. However, the Japanese victories were costly, especially as the Russians fell back farther inland. Japan's struggling economy was seriously strained and there was danger that it would collapse entirely. The Japanese government therefore requested Theodore Roosevelt, President of the United States, to act as mediator in bringing about peace negotiations. In 1905 a treaty ending the Russo-Japanese War was signed at Portsmouth, New Hampshire.

In the Treaty of Portsmouth, Russia turned over to Japan its lease on the Liaotung Peninsula, including Port Arthur, and control of the southern branch of the Chinese Eastern Railway. It recognized that Japan's interests and rights in Korea were greater than those of any other power. Russia agreed to withdraw all troops from Manchuria, except for railway guards, and Manchuria was restored to China. Instead of paying an indemnity, Russia turned over to Japan the southern half of the Russian island of Sakhalin, north of Japan, and gave the Japanese special fishing rights along the Siberian coast.

Later, in a secret agreement, Japan and Russia divided Manchuria into two spheres of influence—the northern half to Russia, the southern half to Japan. Japan also promised not to interfere with Russia's ambitions in Outer Mongolia; Russia, in return, promised not to interfere with Japan's control of Korea. Three years later, in 1910, Japan proclaimed the annexation of Korea and renamed it Chosen. There were no protests. In 1912, Outer Mongolia, aided by Russia, declared its independence (see map, page 559).

Overthrow of the Manchus

Among the Chinese there arose increasing demands for a change. Many of the leaders of the movement were Chinese who had been educated in Western Europe or the United States. They wanted not only the overthrow of the Manchus but also a complete break with "Old China." Influenced by Western ideas, they wanted constitutional, democratic government, with freedoms guaranteed by a bill of rights. They also wanted industrialization.

The Manchus themselves saw the need for change. They tried to make some reforms, but these were too little and too late. In 1911, rebellion spread through southern China. In a last desperate gesture, the ruling Manchus decreed the establishment of a constitutional monarchy, but they were too late.

Negotiations between the Manchus and the revolutionary leaders soon broke down, for the revolutionaries would accept nothing but a republic. Heading those who favored a republic was Sun Yat-sen, who had lived in the United States, attended school in Hawaii, and studied medicine in Hong Kong. He believed that much of Old China would have to go so that a New China could face the world on equal terms. Sun Yat-sen founded the Kuomintang (KWOH·MIN·TANG), Chinese for "Nationalist People's Party."

In February 1912, the Manchus were forced to abdicate. The Kuomintang proclaimed the Chinese Republic, based on what Sun Yat-sen called "The Three Principles of the People": "The People's Government, The People's Rights, The People's Livelihood." Briefly expanded, these principles foresaw for China: (1) political unification and the ending of foreign influence; (2) a gradual change to democratic government with full personal liberties and rights for all; and (3) economic

The overthrow of the Manchus, inspired by Sun Yat-sen, below, was the end of a long dynasty. The dowager empress, above, would have fumed had she known that the revolutionaries were snipping off men's braids, above right, symbol of the old order.

improvements, including land reforms and industrialization. The revolution and the republic opened a new and turbulent era in Chinese history, about which you will read in later chapters.

Imperialism in Southeast Asia

East of India and south of China lies a large peninsula that thrusts southward from the mainland of Asia (see map, page 559). This peninsula, along with many islands in the Indian Ocean and Pacific Ocean, is known as Southeast Asia.°

° **Southeast Asia:** The region consists of the present-day countries of Burma, Thailand, Laos, Cambodia, North Vietnam, South Vietnam, Malaysia, and Indonesia. (The Philippine Islands—about which you will read in Chapter 28—are sometimes considered part of Southeast Asia, too.)

Southeast Asia was strongly influenced by India, especially the religious teachings of Hinduism and Buddhism. Several powerful empires flourished there at various times. You have read how, in the late 1400's and early 1500's, the East Indies were the principal target of European traders who were searching for pepper and other spices so highly prized in Europe at that time. In the seaports of the islands and the nearby mainland, Portuguese and, later, Dutch merchants enjoyed a rich and active trade until the early 1800's, but they largely ignored the areas inland from the sea.

In the 1800's and early 1900's, imperialism came to Southeast Asia as it did to nearby India and China. In addition to spices, the area became an important source of the world's tea and coffee, and later of such valuable subsoil wealth as tin and oil. For the imperialists, there were rich prizes to be won in Southeast Asia.

British successes. The kingdom of Burma, on the eastern border of India, was naturally of interest to the British imperial power in India. Several wars involving the British and Burmese were fought in the 1800's until, by 1886, all of Burma came under British control and was administered as part of British India.

At the tip of the Malay Peninsula is the island of Singapore. The British moved onto this island, then uninhabited, in the late 1700's. Throughout the 1800's they gradually pushed their influence northward to include large parts of the peninsula up to the southern borders of Siam (today known as Thailand). They also created a city at Singapore, which became an important naval base in the British Empire and one of the world's busiest seaports.

Great Britain also gained control of two other island regions. One was the northern part of the island of Borneo, which became a British protectorate in the 1880's. The other was the southeastern portion of New Guinea. (Germany ruled the northeastern part of the island.)

French gains. The eastern part of the mainland of Southeast Asia contained several small, weak nations that were under Chinese influence and that paid annual tributes to the government of China.

Beginning in the late 1700's, French merchants gained trading rights at seaports on the South China Sea. Gradually, French influence expanded. In the latter 1800's, French imperialists forced China to give up its influence in the area, and the French became the dominant power in what became known as French Indo-China.

Siam. The kingdom of Siam was better organized and ruled than were other parts of Southeast Asia. The British on the Malay Peninsula and the French in Indo-China nibbled at the borders of Siam, but left the kingdom largely independent. To maintain their independence, Siamese rulers skillfully maneuvered British interests against French interests. The British and French finally decided that an independent Siam was a useful buffer state between their possessions.

The Dutch East Indies. The Dutch East India Company, formed in 1602 to exploit the island possessions of the Netherlands, was highly successful for a long time. By the late 1700's, however, it had become corrupt and inefficient. In 1798 the Netherlands revoked the company's charter and made the Dutch East Indies (also called the Netherlands East Indies) a royal colony, reorganizing its administration.

The Dutch East India Company had used a system of forced labor in the East Indies that was little short of slavery. The Dutch government somewhat improved working conditions for the natives. By the late 1800's, several native revolts led the government of the Netherlands to make basic reforms in the administration of its richest imperial possession.

CHECKUP

1. State the causes and results of the Boxer Rebellion.
2. Summarize the chief results of the Russo-Japanese War.
3. What were Sun Yat-sen's aims for the Chinese Republic?
4. IDENTIFY: Open Door Policy, Treaty of Portsmouth, Kuomintang.
5. LOCATE: Sakhalin, Malay Peninsula, Singapore, Siam, Borneo, New Guinea, French Indo-China.

CHAPTER REVIEW

Chapter 27 Imperialist Powers Gained Control of the Far East (1700–1914)

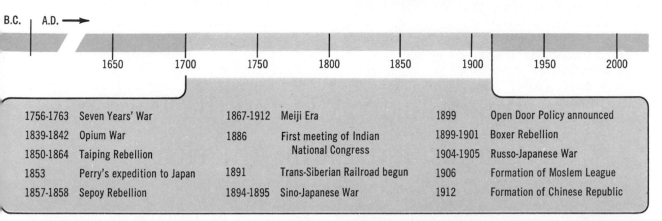

1756-1763	Seven Years' War	1867-1912	Meiji Era	1899	Open Door Policy announced
1839-1842	Opium War	1886	First meeting of Indian National Congress	1899-1901	Boxer Rebellion
1850-1864	Taiping Rebellion			1904-1905	Russo-Japanese War
1853	Perry's expedition to Japan	1891	Trans-Siberian Railroad begun	1906	Formation of Moslem League
1857-1858	Sepoy Rebellion	1894-1895	Sino-Japanese War	1912	Formation of Chinese Republic

CHAPTER SUMMARY

As the Mogul Empire declined in the early 1700's, India became the scene of British-French rivalry, resolved by British victory in the Seven Years' War. After 1763 the British East India Company controlled most of the country. When Indian discontent culminated in the Sepoy Rebellion, the British government assumed direct control of India. British rule brought several improvements but fostered Indian nationalism. Nationalists worked through the Indian National Congress and the Moslem League.

Japan, isolated until the 1800's, came under Western influence when the United States and European powers forced the opening of several treaty ports. After a civil war and a demonstration of Western strength, progressive daimio overthrew the shogun and made the emperor the real ruler. The ensuing Meiji Era was noted for rapid industrialization and the establishment of a new government.

Like Japan, China had been isolated for centuries. Chinese isolation, however, was ended by a conflict—the Opium War—and a series of humiliating treaties and settlements. Western powers first gained trading privileges and, after the Taiping Rebellion, actual territories. Japanese victory in the Sino-Japanese War gave Westerners an excuse to intervene further and gain additional territories.

The Open Door Policy advocated by the United States won lip service only, but the rival powers did act jointly to suppress the Boxer Rebellion. This uprising stimulated rivalry between Russia and Japan, who fought a war in which the Japanese were victorious. In 1911, dissatisfied with their rulers, the Chinese overthrew the Manchus. Under the leadership of Sun Yat-sen and the Kuomintang, they established the Republic of China the following year.

Imperialism was also a strong force in Southeast Asia. The British ruled Burma and much of the Malay Peninsula, while the French controlled Indo-China, and the Dutch retained most of the East Indies. By the late 1800's only Siam remained free.

QUESTIONS FOR DISCUSSION

1. What were the basic characteristics of the two cultures that met in India after the British began to control the subcontinent? Which of these do you think might have been the cause of friction?

2. While Japan industrialized in approximately thirty-five years, it took much of the West about two hundred years to become fully industrialized. How was it possible for the Japanese to make such rapid advances?

3. In what respects did the military have great power in Japan after 1889? Was this a healthy situation? Would you ever approve of a government controlled by the military? Justify your answer.

4. What was the attitude Europeans generally held toward Asians? Why do you think the victory of the Japanese in the Russo-Japanese War surprised the West and pleased many Asians?

PROJECTS

1. Write a dialogue that takes place in the 1800's between a British officer and a patriotic Indian on the topic of imperialism.

2. Write a letter to a British newspaper condemning the opium trade carried on by British merchants in southern China.

3. Draw a map of China showing its major cities and the areas that were lost to foreign control between 1842 and 1914. In each case indicate the foreign country that was involved.

CHAPTER 28

Imperialism Affected the Pacific Islands and Latin America

Few parts of the world were not influenced in one way or another by the surge of imperialism in the late 1800's and early 1900's. You have read how imperialist nations partitioned Africa and took over much of Asia. Scattered throughout the Pacific Ocean were thousands of islands to attract the attention of imperial powers. And there were, as well, many special temptations in Latin America.

Imperialism in these regions brought the United States into the foreground as an imperialist power. For several decades after the announcement of the Monroe Doctrine in 1823, the United States had been rarely involved in affairs beyond its borders. It had been preoccupied with its own internal development, with the Civil War, and with industrialization.

There were a few exceptions. Between 1846 and 1848, it fought a war with Mexico and won vast territories in what is now the southwestern region of the United States. In 1854, as you have read, Commodore Matthew Perry persuaded Japan to open several of its ports to trade. Soon afterward, Russia wanted to dispose of Alaska; in 1867 the United States bought it for about 7 million dollars and made it a territory. In that same year, Americans occupied the Midway Islands, halfway across the Pacific Ocean. Midway became important as a cable station and as a supply base for both naval and merchant ships.

American naval victory in the Spanish-American War

Not until the late 1800's, however, did Americans become actively interested in imperialism. Then many of them began urging that the country should join other nations in the race for imperial possessions. Their arguments were familiar ones: the need for markets, the need for places to invest surplus capital safely, and—in spite of the rich natural resources of the United States—the need for raw materials.

The forces of nationalism were strong, too. During the late 1800's the United States Navy expanded, and Americans were proud to learn that their naval forces were putting on a brave display in seaports around the world. Then, too, many people in the United States were stirred by the missionary motive and by the idea of the "white man's burden." When, as you will read, an opportunity arose to take the Philippine Islands, President William McKinley said, "There was nothing left for us to do but to take them all, and to educate the Filipinos, and uplift and civilize and Christianize them. . . ."

For these reasons and others, the United States and many of its citizens were poised, in the late 1800's, to join other imperialist nations in the rivalry for territory and influence.

THE CHAPTER SECTIONS:

1. Several nations annexed islands in the Pacific Ocean (1840–1914)

2. Unsettled conditions in Latin America led to American intervention (1889–1898)

3. The United States became increasingly involved in Latin America (1898–1917)

1 Several nations annexed islands in the Pacific Ocean

Only a few of the islands and island groups in the Pacific were economically attractive to the imperialist powers. These few areas had large native populations that could be taught to want and buy manufactured goods. Some of the areas had fertile soil that could be taken over and made into rich plantations. In others there were subsoil minerals to be exploited. Imperialism in most of the Pacific islands, however, was based on another motive—the need for coaling stations and naval bases.

In the days of sailing ships, captains might stop at almost any populated island in the Pacific to buy meat, vegetables, and fruit, and to get fresh water. Otherwise, they could sail for months on end with the wind in their sails. As sailing ships gave way to steamships in the late 1800's, dependable coaling stations became an urgent necessity. A steamship did not have to wait for favorable winds, but it did need to refill its coal bunkers. Thus, with the coming of steam power, coal freighters (called colliers) fanned out over the Pacific to replenish coal supplies at coaling stations.

Naval bases also became a necessity. On sailing ships, the ship's carpenter and crew could repair almost anything that broke down or wore out. The power machinery of a steamship, on the other hand, was so heavy and complicated that it could be repaired or replaced only by massive equipment and trained workmen at special naval bases.

Since the imperialist powers were rivals in the Pacific, as elsewhere, none was willing to trust the other for its coal supplies and naval repairs. Each of the powers, therefore, sought out its own Pacific islands.

European powers in the Pacific

You have read how the English explorer Captain Cook rediscovered Australia and New Zealand in the late 1700's. He and other explorers, from France and the Netherlands, also sailed to many of the smaller Pacific islands. Missionaries went out to Christianize and educate the natives, and some small settlements were made.

The French were among the first actually to annex territory. They laid claim to the Marquesas Islands and established a protectorate over Tahiti and the other Society Islands in the 1840's. Shortly afterward they took over New Caledonia and used it as a penal colony for several decades. However, in the Pacific, as in Africa and much of Asia, the heyday of imperialism did not begin until the 1870's. In 1876, only 57 percent of the Pacific islands were owned by Western powers. By 1900, 98 percent of the islands were controlled by imperialist nations (see map, this page).

During the imperialistic era, Great Britain took the Fiji Islands, established a protectorate over the Gilbert Islands and some of the Solomons, and annexed the Cook Islands to New Zealand. With France, it took possession of the New Hebrides Islands in 1896. These islands became a condominium in 1906.

Germany acquired some of the Solomons in the 1880's, but later transferred all but two to Britain. The Germans also established a protectorate over the Marshall Islands. In 1899 they bought the Caroline Islands and the Mariana Islands (except for Guam) from Spain.

The Samoan Islands

The most serious rivalry over territory in the Pacific area involved the Samoan Islands. Here the United States played a major role. American interests in Samoa had been developing for a number of years. In 1878, Americans gained the right to use the harbor city of Pago Pago on the island of Tutuila as a trading post, coaling station, and

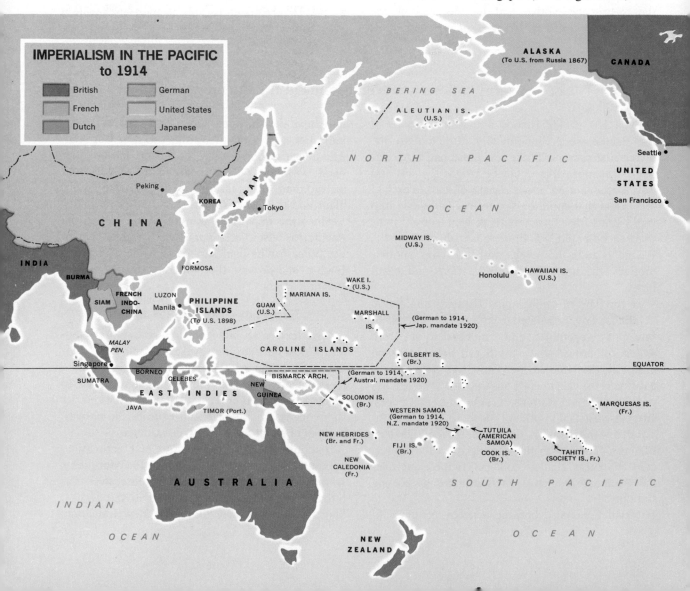

IMPERIALISM IN THE PACIFIC
to 1914

- British
- French
- Dutch
- German
- United States
- Japanese

naval base. Great Britain and Germany secured similar rights in other parts of the Samoan Islands.

For a number of years, rivalry among the three foreign nations for control of the Samoan Islands was so intense that they almost came to blows. To forestall further trouble, the three nations set up a system of joint control in 1889, but it did not work.

In 1899 a solution was worked out by treaty. Great Britain, preoccupied with the Boer War, withdrew its interests. The United States established firm control over Tutuila and six other small islands whose combined area was only about 75 square miles; these possessions became known as American Samoa. Germany gained control of all the other islands in the Samoan group, eventually called Western Samoa. Since the major value of American Samoa lay in the naval base at Pago Pago, the area was placed under the control of the United States Navy.

The Hawaiian Islands

Far more important to the United States than its Samoan possessions were the Hawaiian Islands (see map, opposite). This group of eight principal islands had fertile soil, good rainfall, and a mild climate. Foreign traders and missionaries, including Americans, had begun settling there in the 1820's, but interfered little with the government and economy of the natives. After 1865, however, businessmen from the United States and other foreign nations began to develop sugar cane and pineapple plantations on the islands.

The native rulers of the Hawaiian Islands resented foreign influence and announced that they intended to bring an end to it. American planters then prevailed upon the United States minister in the islands to call ashore a force of American marines. Native troops, ill-prepared to match this show of force, refused to fight. By 1893 the foreign businessmen, supported by American marines, were in control of the islands.

American planters then asked the United States government to annex the Hawaiian Islands. At first there was a loud outcry in the United States against this naked use of American military force

on behalf of business interests far outside the nation's borders. However, the American planters kept up their pressure and were successful in 1898, when the United States annexed the islands. Unlike imperialist nations elsewhere, however, the United States made the Hawaiian Islands a territory, which meant that they were legally entitled, in due time, to become a state of the federal Union.

The Philippines, Guam, and Wake Island

Since the 1500's and 1600's, the Philippine Islands and Guam in the western Pacific Ocean had been parts of Spain's far-flung empire. In 1898 the United States declared war on Spain, as you will read in the next section. Most of the fighting took place in Cuba and Puerto Rico, but the first United States military action against Spain took place in the Pacific.

When war was declared, United States naval forces in the western Pacific moved quickly into the harbor of Manila, capital of the Philippine Islands, and destroyed a small Spanish fleet stationed there. Within a few months, American land forces, supported by Filipino revolutionists, closed in upon the land side of Manila and defeated its Spanish garrison. With the collapse of Spanish power at Manila, the entire Philippine Islands came under the control of the United States. At about this time, American forces also occupied Guam, a small, Spanish-held island east of the Philippines (see map, opposite).

Under the treaty of 1898 that settled the war between the United States and Spain, the United States retained control of Guam and the Philippine Islands. Guam, small and weak, quickly became an important American naval base.

The Philippine Islands confronted the United States with a more complex problem. The combined area of the islands was about 115,000 square miles. Of the more than 7,000 islands, most were very small, uninhabited specks in the ocean. But a few, including Luzon with the capital of Manila, were large and heavily populated.

Some Filipinos welcomed the Americans and even fought with them against the Spaniards. But most of the native population, having smarted

Women of Tahiti

European interest in the foreign and far-away was expressed not only in the work but also in the life of the artist Paul Gauguin. Originally a stockbroker and "Sunday painter," he left France to live in Tahiti. There he lived among the natives and learned to speak their language. He painted "Two Tahitian Women on the Beach" about 1891. Gauguin admired the culture of these island people and tried to represent their gentleness and simplicity in this art. In Tahiti he wrote, "I am escaping the artificial, I am penetrating nature." Thus he helped create the image of "the romance of the South Seas," which generally had little resemblance to the reality of coaling stations, pineapple plantations, and foreign businessmen.

under Spanish rule for centuries, saw little advantage in changing one foreign master for another. Under a leader named Emilio Aguinaldo, Filipino natives fought thousands of American troops for three years, hoping for independence. The Filipinos were finally defeated in 1902.

American businessmen were quick to take advantage of the wealth of the Philippines, but the United States government and many of its citizens were uneasy over the role of the United States as an imperialist power in the far Pacific. Accordingly, a government for the Philippine Islands was created in which the governor and an executive council were United States citizens, but in which there was a legislative assembly elected by the Filipinos. The islands were promised their independence when the United States was satisfied that they could govern themselves and resist the domination of other foreign powers. In the meantime the United States helped the Filipinos to build schools and roads, improve health and sanitation, and develop foreign trade.

Besides acquiring the Philippine Islands and Guam, the United States also took possession of Wake Island in the central Pacific. Thus the United States acquired another link in a chain of island possessions running from its west coast across the vast distances of the Pacific Ocean all the way to the Far East.

CHECKUP

1. Why were the Pacific islands important possessions?

2. Explain briefly how the United States gained the following: (a) American Samoa, (b) Hawaii, (c) the Philippines.

3. Were there any differences between the Pacific imperialism of the United States and that of the European powers? Explain.

4. LOCATE: Alaska, Midway Islands, New Caledonia, Guam, Wake, and these island groups: Marquesas, Society, Fiji, Gilbert, Solomon, Cook, New Hebrides, Caroline, Marshall, Mariana, Samoa, Hawaii.

2 Unsettled conditions in Latin America led to American intervention

Imperialism in the Americas was different from that in the Pacific. Canada and the United States, of course, were strong enough to resist any imperialist thrust. Latin America, however, was weaker and thus more tempting. Behind the shield of the Monroe Doctrine, the Latin American nations were in general protected by the United States from outright occupation by European powers. But they were subject to economic interference as outsiders sought out markets and raw materials. And the United States itself became increasingly involved with its neighbors south of the Rio Grande.

Problems in Latin America

Most of the nations of Latin America, you will recall, gained independence from Spain and Portugal in the early 1800's. They were, however, poorly prepared for self-rule. Educated creoles formed less than one fifth of the population. Most other Latin Americans—mestizos, Indians, and Negroes—were ignorant and illiterate. Some lived in primitive ways that had changed little for centuries.

Independence brought little change in social conditions. The Roman Catholic Church, the official religion in most Latin American countries, wielded considerable power and influence. Land was still owned in huge estates, and the landowners kept almost all of their former privileges. The mass of the people had no land and lived in wretched poverty as tenant farmers.

The governments of most Latin American countries were taken over by the creoles. They were inexperienced in ruling because they had been kept out of all the important positions during Spanish control. They were as haughty and overbearing toward the masses as the Spanish governors had been in colonial days.

The majority of Latin American nations became republics in name only. Many were ruled by military dictators who allied themselves with the wealthy landowners. There were frequent boundary disputes, family feuds, and struggles between rival groups seeking power. These conflicts brought destruction to the countryside and death to the inhabitants. Governments often succeeded each other not by election but by revolution or *coup d'état.*

The Pan American Union. During the 1800's, various nations of the Americas held several conferences to settle common problems. These meetings, however, usually involved only a few countries. The first one that aimed at including all the Western Hemisphere republics met in Washington, D.C., in 1889; the only independent American nation not present was the Dominican Republic. The following year the delegates formed the International Bureau of American Republics, which in time became known as the Pan American Union.

The chief object of the Pan American Union was to promote peaceful cooperation. Subsequent conferences dealt with such subjects as disease control and the regulation of commerce. Often, however, measures passed by conference delegates were not ratified by member nations and so did not become law. Because the Pan American Union lacked force, its effectiveness was limited.

Economic imperialism

The unsettled conditions throughout much of Latin America were an open invitation to economic imperialism. As the pace of the Industrial Revolution increased, factories in the United States and Western Europe needed more and more raw materials. Latin America was rich in many of these. To secure them, a foreign industrialist would approach the ruler in a Latin American country and pay a large sum of money for the right to produce and export certain raw materials.

Economic imperialism penetrated still further into Latin America when governments there borrowed money from foreign banks and private lenders. Often the government that had borrowed the money was later overthrown in a revolution and the new government would refuse to pay its debts. Generally the new government gave a reason that was true enough: the money had not really gone to the country but into the pockets of the former ruler and his supporters.

Loans that were not repaid frequently led to intervention by the foreign powers. European lenders would persuade their governments to bring pressure to get payments. Sometimes warships were sent and troops were landed to compel payment. A typical method was to take over the collection of the customs—the principal tax—and hold out enough money to pay the debts.

American intervention

Throughout most of the 1800's, the United States had little to do with its neighbors to the south. One exception involved Mexico. In 1865, as you have read, the United States threatened to send an army to aid Benito Juárez in his fight against Emperor Maximilian and the forces of Napoleon III of France. This threat by the United States was in line with the Monroe Doctrine; French military control of Mexico clearly violated the Monroe Doctrine.

In 1895 the United States intervened in a dispute between Great Britain and Venezuela. Early in the 1800's, Britain had acquired British Guiana, on the northern coast of South America (see map, opposite). On a number of occasions, Britain had tried to push the boundary of British Guiana westward into territory that was also claimed by Venezuela.

Venezuela then asked the United States for support in its demand that the border dispute be submitted to arbitration. When Britain refused, the American secretary of state boldly declared: "Today the United States is practically sovereign" in the Western Hemisphere. President Grover Cleveland insisted on arbitration. Finally, Great Britain, then involved with the Boers in South Africa, gave in and the dispute with Venezuela was settled. Once more the United States had championed the cause of a weak Latin American nation against powerful European interests.

Trouble with Spain

Only in 1898 did the United States become deeply involved in Latin American affairs. Its involvement grew out of disputes with Spain.

The main cause of tension between Spain and the United States was Cuba (see map, opposite), a Spanish colony in the West Indies. For many years the Cubans had been discontented with Spanish rule. There were several rebellions, which the Spanish government suppressed with great difficulty. Many United States citizens and corporations had invested money in Cuba, especially in railroads and in sugar plantations and refineries. When another rebellion broke out in 1895, American property was destroyed and the American government protested.

The destruction of American property was only one reason for the tense relations; there were three others. First, many Americans felt sympathetic toward Cuba's desire for independence and indignant over Spanish ill-treatment of the Cuban rebels. These sentiments were stirred up by anti-Spanish speeches and writings by Cubans who had settled in the United States and by sensational stories in American newspapers relating Spanish atrocities in Cuba. Second, rising American indignation over Cuba was fanned into flame early in 1898 by publication of a private letter in which the Spanish minister to the United States wrote critically of President McKinley. Third, this indignation had not entirely died down when an American battleship, the *Maine,* was blown up in the Cuban harbor of Havana. The *Maine* had been sent to Havana to protect American citizens and their property. No one knew who or what had caused the explosion, but people in the United States assumed that the Spaniards were to blame.

Probably no single one of these reasons—not even the sinking of the *Maine*—would have been a sufficient cause for war. All of them together, however, fused into an explosive popular demand in the United States for a declaration of war on Spain.

The Spanish-American War

Spain showed some willingness to come to terms with the United States over Cuba. President McKinley and his cabinet did not want war. But American leaders felt unable to resist the rising

IMPERIALISM
IN THE CARIBBEAN · 1898-1917

United States and possessions
British possessions
French possessions
Dutch possessions

popular demand for aggressive measures. Congress declared war in April 1898.

The United States officially declared that it was fighting only for the independence of Cuba and had no intention of taking the island for itself. This statement was adopted at the insistence of members of Congress who opposed rising American imperialism.

The Spanish-American War has been called "brief, glorious, and inexpensive." The result was never much in doubt. Fighting took place in the West Indian islands of Cuba and Puerto Rico and also, as you have read, in Spanish possessions in the Pacific—the Philippine Islands and Guam. After being defeated in all of these places and on the sea, Spain was unable to continue fighting and asked for peace. A treaty was signed in December 1898.

By the terms of the peace treaty, Spain surrendered claim to Cuba and ceded Puerto Rico and the Pacific islands of Guam and the Philippines to the United States. One by-product of the war was the sudden popularity of a future American President, Theodore Roosevelt. Roosevelt had resigned a high government position to become the leader of a dashing group of volunteer cavalrymen called the Rough Riders. American newspapermen gave great publicity to the exploits of this group and their leader.

Cuba as an American protectorate

When peace was restored, the United States observed its promise not to take Cuba as a colony. It recognized Cuba's independence, helped restore order, and set up a republican government.

There were strings attached, however. The

575

The Spanish-American War came, one American said, because opinion leaped "from quiet inquiry to hot impatience." American newspapers helped to inflame the public. Publishers discovered that sales skyrocketed when they published sensational stories and pictures of Spanish "atrocities" in Cuba. At left is the front page of the New York *Journal* of February 17, 1898 (two days after the sinking of the *Maine*), offering a reward of $50,000 for "The Detection of the Perpetrator of the Maine Outrage." These methods worked well: circulation rose enormously and American feeling reached a fever pitch.

As soon as war was declared, 200,000 men volunteered for service. To most American youths, war was a romantic escapade, arousing emotions like those expressed by Theodore Roosevelt: "It will be awful if the game is over before we get there." Volunteers leaving Washington for Cuba, below left, were given rousing farewells. In spite of poor training and antiquated equipment, the United States quickly defeated Spain. Below, American troops man trenches at San Juan Hill, near Santiago, Cuba.

United States insisted that the Cubans include the so-called Platt Amendment in their new constitution. This amendment gave the United States the right to intervene in Cuba to protect the independence of the island and to maintain an orderly government. Cuba also promised not to make any treaties that might weaken its independence and not to borrow money from any foreign power unless it could be repaid out of ordinary government revenues. This limitation on borrowing was imposed to keep foreign powers from using debt as an excuse to move in on Cuba.

Another provision of the Platt Amendment allowed the United States to have an unlimited number of coaling and naval stations in Cuba. This indefinite number was soon reduced to one naval base at Guantánamo Bay.

Thus, although Cuba did not become an American colony, it did become a protectorate of the United States. Americans did much to rebuild the country, but there was continued resentment toward United States interference in Cuban affairs.

CHECKUP

1. "Independence [in Latin America] brought little change in social conditions." Explain.

2. What methods did imperialist powers use to gain entry into Latin America?

3. What were the causes of the Spanish-American War? the results?

4. IDENTIFY: Pan American Union, Rough Riders, Platt Amendment.

5. LOCATE: Mexico, Venezuela, British Guiana, Cuba, Havana, Puerto Rico, Guantánamo Bay.

3   The United States became increasingly involved in Latin America

The Spanish-American War showed that the United States had assumed new importance as a world power. Even though Spain was, by this time, one of the weaker European countries, the easy American victory dramatized America's growing strength.

When the peace treaty came before the United States Congress for ratification, there was a long debate that revealed much opposition to the taking of colonies and protectorates. Finally, however, the treaty won the necessary two-thirds vote. Apparently a majority of Americans now approved a policy of imperialism. In the election of 1900, President McKinley and his supporters in Congress were re-elected by large margins. (His Vice-President was Theodore Roosevelt of Rough Rider fame. When McKinley was assassinated in 1901, Roosevelt became President.)

Governing American possessions

The United States' pledge of independence for Cuba did not apply to the other areas it had won from Spain. Americans insisted on keeping control of Puerto Rico, Guam, and the Philippines, for which the United States paid Spain 20 million dollars.

The United States government still insisted that it would avoid political or military alliances with other nations. However, with colonies and protectorates in two oceans, it could no longer be as isolated as it had been in the past. As President Theodore Roosevelt said, " In foreign affairs we must make up our minds that . . . we are a great people and must play a great part in the world. It is not open to us to choose whether we will play that part or not. . . . All we can decide is whether we shall play it well or ill."

Americans were now responsible for the welfare of peoples of different races, languages, religions, and cultures in places far from their shores. They had to find ways of governing and defending them.

The American Congress adopted several different ways of governing the new areas under its control. Alaska, which, as you recall, was purchased from Russia in 1867, and Hawaii became territories, privileged in due time to become states of the Union. Cuba, as a protectorate, could govern itself but was limited by the terms of the Platt Amendment.

In Puerto Rico, as in the Philippine Islands, the government consisted of an appointed governor and executive council who were United States citizens and a legislative assembly elected by the local people. Some form of independence was foreseen for both areas when they and the United States government could agree that they were ready to manage their own affairs.

The small, sparsely inhabited islands of the Pacific that came under United States control were directly governed by the United States government. Local inhabitants had no direct voice in their own government, but the United States built schools and roads, and in other ways tried to improve their standards of living.

The Panama Canal

In addition to governing its new and far-flung areas, the United States was also obliged to defend them. The major problem of defense came to light during the Spanish-American War.

Before the war the American battleship *Oregon* had been stationed on the Pacific coast. When war became likely, this ship was needed to strengthen American forces in the Caribbean Sea. It had to go at high speed all the way around South America, a distance of over 11,000 miles. The United States realized that it would either have to build two complete navies to protect its empire or find some easier and quicker way to move warships between the Atlantic and Pacific oceans.

A canal across the Isthmus of Panama had long been talked about. The same French company that built the Suez Canal had also tried unsuccessfully to build a canal across Panama. The United States government now began negotiating for permission and a right of way to build a canal.

First, the United States arranged with the British to be released from an earlier treaty which pledged that any canal should be built jointly by Great Britain and the United States. Next, Americans bought the rights of the French company. Then they began to negotiate with Colombia for a lease to a strip of land across the isthmus in Panama, at that time a province of Colombia (see map, page 575).

In these latter negotiations, the United States struck a snag. After a treaty had been negotiated, the Colombian senate adjourned without ratifying

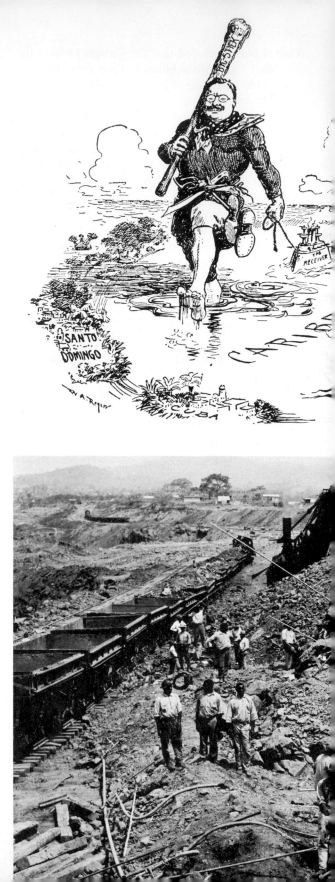

Imperialism in Latin America

The building of the Panama Canal was an enormous task. At left, workmen drill holes for dynamite to blast out a section of earth and rock. During construction of the canal, the United States became increasingly involved in Latin American affairs. Roosevelt believed that in foreign affairs the United States should "speak softly and carry a big stick." In the cartoon at upper left he shoulders his "big stick" as he wades through the Caribbean Sea towing United States ships that symbolize American roles in the area.

Roosevelt's somewhat paternal attitude toward Latin America masked a deep concern for the enormous American investments in the area. The Roosevelt Corollary, formulated partly to protect these interests, was used often in the years following its announcement. When Pancho Villa, above, killed American citizens on American soil, President Wilson invoked its spirit in ordering the United States Army to pursue him into Mexico.

579

it. There was great indignation in the United States. People felt that Colombia was trying to bargain for more money. The United States government investigated a possible canal route through Nicaragua.

There was also indignation in the province of Panama. The people of the province were eager to have the canal built there because it promised them great benefits. When negotiations between the United States and Colombia seemed to break down, the people of Panama began a revolution to gain independence from Colombia.

American warships stationed at Panama prevented Colombian troops from moving in to suppress the revolt, and the revolution succeeded. The United States then quickly recognized the independence of Panama. In 1903 a treaty between the two governments was drawn up and speedily ratified, giving the United States all the rights necessary to build a canal across Panama.

The building of the Panama Canal was one of the world's greatest engineering projects. It would probably have been impossible to build without power shovels and other new machines that had recently been invented. Medical science, too, played a vital part. Cuban and American scientists had discovered that mosquitoes carry yellow fever, a disease that had done much to cause the French to fail in their effort to build a canal across Panama. By wiping out the mosquitoes, Americans controlled the disease and thereby enabled the men to work in Panama.

Advantages of the canal. The Panama Canal was opened in 1914. It shortened the sea route from New York to San Francisco by over 5,000 miles, and the sea route from New York to the new territory of Hawaii by 4,400 miles. Fleets in the Atlantic and Pacific could now be quickly combined into one unit when necessary. Commercially the canal was also very useful. It was open to the merchant ships of all nations upon payment of toll charges. The shorter distances lowered the operating costs of a ship many times more than the toll it paid to use the canal.

The Panama Canal had an important effect on the attitude of the United States toward the countries in Central and South America bordering on the Caribbean Sea. Formerly this region had been a sleepy backwater of the world, a dead end of commerce. The canal made it an important trading area of the world.

The Roosevelt Corollary

When the United States occupied Puerto Rico and established a protectorate over Cuba in 1898, it was dealing with areas that had been Spanish colonies for many years and that had not known independence since before the time of Columbus. In 1903, when the United States supported the revolution in Panama and gained the Panama Canal Zone, it was interfering in the affairs of Colombia, an independent, self-governing nation. Such interference occurred several times in the next few years.

The Dominican Republic, controlled by dictators for decades, fell into almost complete anarchy in the early 1900's. The nation owed a total of 32 million dollars to the United States and several European countries. When the European countries threatened to use force to collect the money owed to them, President Roosevelt intervened.

The United States would have objected to such happenings in the Western Hemisphere at any time after the Monroe Doctrine. In the early 1900's, however, there was the added fear that a strong European power with a foothold in the Caribbean region could threaten the Panama Canal or the sea lanes leading to it. Therefore the United States adopted a new policy toward Latin America.

In 1904, President Roosevelt's annual message to Congress included a passage on Latin America. His statement became known as the Roosevelt Corollary to the Monroe Doctrine—that is, a natural consequence of the earlier announcement.

Roosevelt said that if any situation threatened the independence of any country in the Western Hemisphere, the United States would act as an "international police power" to prevent a foreign country from stepping in. In practice this meant that if a Latin American country were threatened by revolution, or if nonpayment of debts brought threats from abroad, the United States would establish a protectorate over that country.

Application of the Corollary. This is just what happened in the Dominican Republic. In 1905 the United States took over the collection of customs. Americans collected the taxes and supervised the spending of money. Then they saw to it that the country's foreign debts—including, of course, those owed to American banks and other investors—were paid. Roosevelt did not want to take the Dominican Republic outright. He said: "As for annexing the island, I have about the same desire . . . as a gorged boa constrictor might have to swallow a porcupine wrong-end-to." But difficulties continued and, in 1916, marines were sent in; they occupied the Dominican Republic for eight years.

The United States also became involved in Nicaragua. After the dictator who had been ruling fled the country, the United States sent in marines to restore order in 1912. They occupied the country off and on until 1933.

In Haiti, orderly government broke down early in the 1900's. By 1914, French investors were strongly pressing their claims. It was also rumored that Germany was seeking control of a naval base in Haitian territory. The American President at that time, Woodrow Wilson, was anxious to avoid European penetration of the Caribbean area and landed marines in Haiti in 1915. They remained there for nineteen years.

In 1917 the United States purchased three of the Virgin Islands, east of Puerto Rico, from Denmark. With this purchase the United States added another base to assure its control over the Caribbean.

Mexico was torn by a revolution that first broke out in 1910. Americans had invested billions of dollars in the country and were deeply troubled by the violence and bloodshed. Marines temporarily occupied Veracruz in 1914, after the arrest of some American sailors. Two years later, a bandit named Pancho Villa raided a New Mexican town, killing several people. United States troops were sent into Mexico to find and punish Villa. Bad feeling between the two countries mounted, and for a time there was a threat of full-scale war. Only when American troops withdrew in 1917 did tensions ease.

The "Colossus of the North"

It can be seen that in the Panama Canal dispute and later involvements in Latin America, the United States acted not only to protect weak nations from interference by strong European powers, but to serve its own interests as well. For the latter reason, especially, there arose in Latin America a deep distrust of the United States— the "Colossus of the North," as Latin Americans called it.

The United States wielded tremendous influence over much of Latin America through a policy known as "dollar diplomacy." It was so named by its critics and was a major cause for Latin American resentment of the United States. American businessmen and bankers, sometimes encouraged by the United States government, lent money to Latin American countries. When these countries failed to repay the loans, the United States government intervened to "protect the investments of its citizens." Often marines were sent in or the United States supervised local elections.

United States investments frequently brought benefits to Latin American countries. Tax money, honestly administered, was used to build roads and schools and improve medical and sanitary facilities. Probably the countries were never better governed or less troubled by wars, revolutions, and financial crises. Yet Latin Americans did not always welcome these benefits. They resented the fact that the influence of the United States, especially in the Caribbean area and Central America, was supreme.

CHECKUP

1. Why was the Panama Canal important?

2. How did the United States apply the Roosevelt Corollary? What effect did its actions have on Latin Americans?

3. United States policy toward Cuba, the Philippines, the Panama Canal, and the Caribbean region has been called an example of the "chain reaction" of imperialism. Comment on this statement.

4. IDENTIFY: *Oregon*, Roosevelt Corollary, "Colossus of the North," "dollar diplomacy."

5. LOCATE: Canal Zone, Colombia, Dominican Republic, Nicaragua.

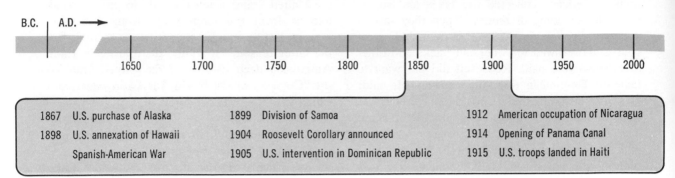

B.C. | A.D. ➞

1650   1700   1750   1800   1850   1900   1950   2000

1867	U.S. purchase of Alaska	1899	Division of Samoa	1912	American occupation of Nicaragua
1898	U.S. annexation of Hawaii	1904	Roosevelt Corollary announced	1914	Opening of Panama Canal
	Spanish-American War	1905	U.S. intervention in Dominican Republic	1915	U.S. troops landed in Haiti

CHAPTER SUMMARY

During the late 1800's, as sailing ships gave way to steamships, Pacific islands became valuable as coaling stations and naval bases. France, Britain, Germany, and the United States all established claims in the area. Rivalry over the Samoan Islands was resolved when they were divided between the United States and Germany. Hawaii, settled by American planters, became an American territory after the landing of United States marines there. The United States also gained the Philippines, Guam, and Wake.

In Latin America, a haughty but inexperienced privileged class governed the poor, uneducated masses. Military dictatorships and revolutions were common. Unsettled conditions left the countries vulnerable to economic imperialism. The United States intervened to aid Mexico and Venezuela against European powers, but became more directly involved when it went to war with Spain. The Spanish-American War—provoked by the desire to protect American investments, sympathy for Cuban independence, and the sinking of the *Maine*—resulted in an American victory. After the war (in which the United States also gained Puerto Rico), Cuban independence was recognized, but the island remained an American protectorate.

The Spanish-American War revealed the need for a United States canal across the Isthmus of Panama. When Colombia delayed negotiations, Panama rebelled, receiving help and speedy diplomatic recognition from the United States. The United States then received authority to build the Panama Canal.

As the Caribbean area grew in importance, President Theodore Roosevelt issued the Roosevelt Corollary, expanding the Monroe Doctrine and sanctioning American intervention in America to prevent European expansion. In the early 1900's, American influence became dominant in Latin America with the occupation of the Dominican Republic, Nicaragua, and Haiti. Although United States rule often brought improvements, Latin Americans resented the "Colossus of the North."

QUESTIONS FOR DISCUSSION

1. Do you consider the actions of the United States in the Pacific and the Caribbean after 1898 typical of imperialism? Justify your answer.

2. By the late 1800's the Pacific islands and the countries of Latin America were "fair game" to the imperialist nations. However, no great power would have then attempted imperialistic practices in the United States, even though it had been independent only a half century longer than most Latin American nations. How do you account for the difference?

3. Several times in the Pacific and in Latin America the United States government provided military forces on behalf of business interests. To what degree do you approve of this kind of action?

4. What was the attitude of the American people toward war with Spain in 1898? Should a President follow a popular demand for war, even though he might not favor such an action?

PROJECTS

1. Write a short essay in which you either defend or criticize United States imperialism.

2. Make a list of the various territories that the United States gained during its imperialistic ventures, and explain how each possession was obtained.

3. Draw a cartoon showing the sinking of the *Maine,* attempting to heighten the desire for war in the United States.

4. From an anti-imperialist point of view, draw one of the following: (1) a cartoon showing Spanish treatment of Cubans before 1898; (2) a cartoon showing American soldiers fighting Filipino natives after 1898.

World War I Drastically Altered the Course of History

In the early 1900's, many people believed that the world was on the verge of a long era of prosperity and peace. They thought that scientific and industrial progress would create a better life than man had ever known, and that widespread education would prepare the masses to govern themselves with wisdom and moderation.

During the late 1800's, many international organizations were founded to further cooperation among nations. The Red Cross was established to provide care for the victims of disaster, whether in peace or wartime. The Universal Postal Union set postal rates for member countries and made communication among the peoples of the world easier. A further symbol of international cooperation was the revival of the Olympic games, which had not been held since ancient times.

Philanthropists—men interested in the welfare of the human race—gave of their time and money to bring nations closer together. Alfred Nobel, the Swedish inventor of dynamite, contributed part of his large fortune to set up the Nobel Peace prizes, awards for outstanding contributors to the cause of peace. Andrew Carnegie, an American financier, built a Palace of Peace at The Hague, in the Netherlands, for international conferences.

Efforts were made to try to limit armaments. Representatives of several nations met at The Hague, in 1899 and again in 1907, for disarmament talks. Even as nations met to discuss

An American soldier fighting in France

peace, however, they prepared for war. Although they cooperated in some fields, they continued to fear and distrust one another. In 1910 an Englishman wrote a book "proving" that war was impossible; it was clear, he said, that the winners would suffer as much as the losers. As if in answer, a book published by a German the following year stated that war was not only a "biological necessity," but that Germany must strike the first blow.

Whether or not it was a "biological necessity," war did break out three years later. But the Englishman was right, too, because by the time the war was over, most of the victors had indeed suffered as much as the vanquished.

The war that began in the summer of 1914 was different from any previous war. It involved nations all over the world and was fought on battlefields from the plains of central France to Africa and the Near East. The war dragged on for more than four years, causing incredible property damage and taking the lives of more soldiers than any previous war.

The people of the time rightly called it the Great War; because we have known one other such conflict more recently, we know it as World War I.

THE CHAPTER SECTIONS:

1. Conflicting national interests set the stage for war (1882–1914)

2. Fighting broke out in the Balkans and spread rapidly (1914)

3. The nations of the world fought a new kind of war (1914–1917)

4. After defeating the Central Powers, the Allies drafted peace terms (1917–1919)

5. A "new Europe" was created, but many problems remained (1919–1920)

1   Conflicting national interests set the stage for war

Some historians have called the years before 1914 a period of "international anarchy," meaning that each nation in Europe pursued policies without regard for the wishes or interests of its neighbors. Since 1815, when the Congress of Vienna met after the Napoleonic Wars, relations among European powers had been more or less harmoniously regulated by the Concert of Europe. Beginning in the late 1800's, however, cooperation among nations was made difficult by the growth of intense nationalism and imperialistic rivalries. In this anarchic situation, the great powers built up their military strengths and formed secret alliances to protect themselves.

Nationalism

Nationalism has been defined as the feeling among a group of people that they belong together, bound by the ties of a common culture, a common history, and common problems. After the French Revolution and the Napoleonic Wars, national groups tried to unite under governments controlled by the people themselves. Nationalism and liberalism were thought to be natural allies. By the late 1800's, however, partly because of the success of *Realpolitik,* the nationalistic movement became more chauvinistic and less liberal. For instance, the German people had been successfully united under a national government that was far from democratic.

The desire to unite all the people of a nation under a single government had explosive possibilities in a Europe whose nationalities were so mingled. Two examples will illustrate the dangers. (1) In the Balkans, the Slavic kingdom of Serbia, once part of the Ottoman Empire, was eager to bring the Slavs of neighboring regions under its rule. Austria feared an independent Slavic state in the Balkans, and thus opposed Serbia's ambition. Russia, on the other hand, was anxious to expand its own influence at the expense of Austria; thus Russia supported Serbia's claims. (2) In France, after 1871, there was a strong desire to regain the French-speaking (and iron-producing) provinces of Alsace and Lorraine that France had lost to Germany in the

"The Philosopher's Conquest"

A sense of ominous foreboding pervades this work by Giorgio di Chirico, who painted it in the same year that World War I began in Europe. The cannon and cannon balls are obvious symbols; it is said that Chirico, who was living in Paris at the time, was moved by the sounds of artillery being drawn through the streets. In spite of the clock and the puffing locomotive, time seems to stand still. There are mysterious objects—two artichokes in the foreground, a sailing ship in the distance. The sense of unreality is heightened by the absence of human forms, except those suggested by a shadow at the right, and by the painting's curious title. Chirico was one of the earliest surrealists (see page 658). Whatever his intention, his work could be said to symbolize the uneasiness that many Europeans felt on the eve of war.

Franco-Prussian War. Such conflicting aspirations caused tension and made it difficult to settle international disputes peacefully.

Imperialism

As you have read, the imperialist nations came to the brink of war several times in the scramble to partition Africa among themselves. In 1898, Great Britain and France almost exchanged blows over the Sudanese village of Fashoda. Germany and France narrowly avoided war over their rival claims to Morocco on two occasions between 1905 and 1911. Each incident was settled by makeshift compromises that usually left one or more of the participants dissatisfied.

In the Far East, the rival ambitions of Russia and Japan had already produced a war, but it was limited to the two nations. Imperialistic rivalries in China continued to be dangerous to the peace.

The declining Ottoman Empire threatened to be the source of still further conflicts between im-

perialist nations. Its weakness offered temptations to Great Britain, Russia, France, Austria, and Italy, each eager for a share of the spoils.

Militarism

The thinking of many European leaders in the years before World War I was dominated by militarism—the glorification of armed strength and the belief that international problems can best be solved by the use of force. Both nationalism and imperialism depended on a strong army and navy. The nation that was militarily strong usually got what it wanted, as Prussia showed in its wars with Denmark, Austria, and France. The weaker nations lost out, as Italy learned on several occasions.

Because of the widespread reliance upon armed strength, army officers increasingly influenced decisions made by civilian government officials. The influence of private citizens was weakened, even in democratic nations like Britain.

The most obvious case of army influence on

politics was in Germany. In the late 1800's, Germany developed the general staff, an organization made up of the best trained and most brilliant officers. Their duty was to perfect the organization, equipment, and training of the army and to prepare plans for any war that might possibly come. In effect, they could dictate government policy.

Another military innovation on which Germany relied was a reserve force maintained through conscription. You have read how Prussia developed this kind of force when its standing army was reduced in size by Napoleon.

Most European nations in the 1800's, following Prussia's lead, began to build reserve armies of men who were conscripted, given military training, and then returned to civilian life. These men, using arms and equipment kept at convenient places throughout the country, were subject to call at any time and received periodic "refresher" training. If a nation mobilized by ordering its reserves into active service, other nations would begin to mobilize for their own protection. It was a process that was hard to stop once it had begun. European military leaders had a maxim: "Mobilization means war."

The armaments race. As the international situation became increasingly tense, each European nation felt it necessary to keep its armed forces stronger than those of any potential enemy. Thus an armaments race began. Standing armies were increased in size and equipped with new and more destructive weapons. Large sums were spent for the fortification of national boundaries. In the 1890's, Germany began to build up a large and modern navy to rival that of Great Britain. Germany's example was followed by France, the United States, Japan, and Italy.

Great Britain traditionally depended upon its navy rather than upon its army, and for many years it had followed a policy of maintaining a navy equal in size to the combined navies of the two next strongest powers. Germany's attempt to rival the British on the sea was certain to lead Britain into increasing its navy still more.

The armaments race was very expensive and resulted in higher taxes. Each government justi-
fied the higher taxes by appealing to its civilian population in two ways: pride in the nation's strength and the desire for security and protection. At the same time that manufacturers of armaments were growing rich, taxpayers were being deprived of the peaceful benefits their taxes could otherwise provide. The armaments race was, for most people, a race without prizes, and, in a tense world, an extremely dangerous one.

The system of alliances

During the late 1800's the balance of power in Europe was changed by the unification of Germany and Italy. Germany, especially, created an entirely new situation. Instead of a group of relatively weak states divided into rival groups, there appeared a unified German Empire under the leadership of Prussia. It was militarily strong, had rapidly developing industries, and was led by a diplomat, Otto von Bismarck, who was both ruthless and skillful.

The Triple Alliance. Bismarck's primary aim in foreign policy was to keep France isolated and without allies so that it would not seek revenge for its defeat in 1871. In order to achieve this goal, Bismarck formed the Dual Alliance with Austria-Hungary in 1879. In 1882, as you have read, he made it the Triple Alliance by including Italy. Both were "defensive" alliances: each country promised to come to the assistance of the others if they were attacked.

Italy's joining this alliance was a strange move. For many years, Austria had been Italy's most hated enemy. Austria's territory included the cities of Trieste and Fiume, which Italy had long desired. Austria also held the province of Tyrol, which contained the famous Brenner Pass, the chief invasion route from the north into Italy. Despite these facts, Italy's disappointment over France's recent seizure of Tunisia led it to join the Triple Alliance. Bismarck considered Italy a weak link in the Triple Alliance. However, the forging of the alliance did isolate France.

To keep France isolated, Bismarck also tried to maintain friendly relations with Great Britain and Russia. Britain was much more interested in overseas expansion than in events on the continent of

cau
the
ho
an
ha
pu
of
Bo

cer
cau
Sho
pow
con

Th
san
In
All
a c
avo
ing

and
Stra
was
Bri
enta
eve

flic
keg
riva
S
com
cou
wou
as
the
lock
zeg
as

Military preparation was an overriding preoccupation among Western nations in the early 1900's. "There is only one master in this country, and I am he," said Kaiser William II. He liked to display his power in military parades and maneuvers. Above, in greatcoat and spiked helmet, he takes part in his favorite pastime—reviewing his elite troops, then the most powerful in the world. The United States, which had not taken an active role in the European wars of the 1800's, needed training in wartime tactics. A British soldier, right, instructs Americans in digging and fortifying trenches. When war was declared, millions of men were mobilized. Below, French reservists leave Paris on their way to the front.

Archduke Franz Ferdinand, heir to the Austrian throne, is shown here with his wife. Their assassination on June 28, 1914, "lit the fuse" that set off World War I.

pire into the Triple Alliance and thereby extend German influence in the Balkans.

Germany also planned to build a railroad from Berlin through the Balkans to Constantinople and on to Baghdad, near the Persian Gulf. The British regarded the proposed Berlin-to-Baghdad railroad as a threat to their Mediterranean-Red Sea "lifeline" to India. They feared that such a railroad would provide a better route to India than the British route through the Suez Canal. They also feared strong competition for trade in the Near East. The Russians were afraid that Germany would become a strong protector of the Ottoman Empire, and that Russia's chances of gaining Constantinople and the Straits would thus decrease. Germany secured the first concessions to construct the Berlin-to-Baghdad railroad in 1902. The railroad was built in sections and was

still in the early stages of construction in 1914.

Germany's actions in the Balkans complicated an already confused situation. The chief result was something Bismarck had carefully avoided— the strengthening of ties between Great Britain and Russia. Both countries were determined to resist German expansion in the Balkans. Austria, on the other hand, gained Germany as a strong supporter for its opposition to Balkan nationalism.

Assassination at Sarajevo

The spark that touched off the explosion of the Balkan "powder keg" and led to war came on June 28, 1914. On that day the heir to the Austrian throne, Archduke Franz Ferdinand, and his wife were visiting Sarajevo (sah·rah·YEH·voh), the capital of Bosnia and Herzegovina, on a mission of good will. As the two drove through the streets in an open automobile, a young man rushed forward and fired a revolver, killing both the archduke and his wife.

The assassin was a member of one of the many secret societies of Serbian nationalists. Its members included high government officials. There is no evidence that the Serbian government itself had any part in the plot, although the prime minister of Serbia had general knowledge of it.

Franz Ferdinand was probably chosen for assassination because of his position on the question of Slavic independence. He had wanted to change the Dual Monarchy of Austria-Hungary into a triple monarchy by creating a semi-independent Slavic state under Austrian guidance. The Serbian nationalists were violently opposed to this idea because they wanted to unite the Slavs under their leadership.

The assassination brought to a head the long struggle between Serbia and Austria. The Austrian government was determined that the troublesome Serbs should be punished. But before Austria acted, it made sure of German support in case the Russians should try to protect their fellow Slavs in Serbia. Germany promised to back Austria in anything Austria did. The Austrian government made sure of the support of all parts of the empire. Then it presented the Serbian government with an ultimatum. An ultimatum puts forth the final terms offered for a settlement; if the ultimatum is rejected, negotiations are ended.

War between Austria and Serbia

In its ultimatum, Austria demanded that the Serbian government officially condemn all anti-Austrian propaganda, suppress all anti-Austrian publications and societies, eliminate all anti-Austrian books and teachers from Serbian schools, and dismiss any officials who had promoted anti-Austrian propaganda. Serbia might have agreed to these conditions. Austria made other demands, however, that were certain to be unacceptable to the Serbian government: Austrian officials must be allowed to help in suppressing the propaganda, and Austrian judges must be allowed to sit in judgment of those accused of the crime at Sarajevo. All of these terms had to be accepted within

forty-eight hours or Austria would declare war.

The reply of the Serbian government was mild and conciliating. Serbia accepted all the terms except the last two, but expressed willingness to submit the entire dispute to an international court recently created at The Hague. However, not counting on Austria to be reasonable, the Serbian government also ordered mobilization of all troops. It was a wise step. In spite of the mildness of the Serbian reply, Austria declared war on Serbia on July 28, after the time limit on the ultimatum had elapsed.

Germany, Russia, and France

All attempts to get Austria to continue negotiations were in vain. Germany hesitated but continued to support Austria. When it was certain that the Austrians would attack Serbia, Russia prepared to defend Serbia by mobilizing troops along the Russian-Austrian border. Expecting Germany to join Austria, Russia also sent troops to the German border. Germany immediately demanded that Russia cancel mobilization within twelve hours or face war. Russia did not submit to this ultimatum and Germany declared war on Russia on August 1, 1914. Convinced that France was prepared to side with Russia and hoping to gain a military advantage by swift action, Germany declared war on France two days later.

Now the position of Great Britain became highly important. Understandably, the British did not want a European war. If one came, they wanted to stay out of it if possible. Few British leaders thought that neutrality was possible, however. What was needed was something to stir the British people and make them willing to go to war. Germany itself provided the excuse.

The entry of Great Britain

The neutrality of Belgium had been guaranteed by the great powers in 1839, shortly after Belgian independence. Under the terms of this guarantee, Belgium agreed to stay out of any European war and not to help any of the belligerents (warring nations). The other powers agreed not to attack it. However, Belgium's location was of great importance to Germany's military plans. It is on the flat European coastal plain and has borders on both France and Germany.

Since the late 1800's, Germany's daring foreign policy had made it necessary for the German general staff to plan for Bismarck's nightmare— a two-front war against France and Russia. The general staff counted on the efficiency of Germany's army to mobilize, strike, and knock France out of the war before the Russians could attack from the east. However, the Franco-German border was mostly hilly, wooded country, heavily fortified by both countries. If the Germans could smash into France at the lightly fortified Franco-Belgian border, they might be able to capture Paris before French mobilization could be completed. Thus the Germans planned to drive into France across the open plain of Belgium.

As soon as the German government had declared war on France, it sent an ultimatum to Belgium, demanding that German troops be permitted to cross Belgian territory. The British protested, insisting that the guarantee of neutrality be observed. The German foreign minister replied that surely Britain would not fight a war over "a scrap of paper." The Germans marched into Belgium on August 4, 1914; Great Britain declared war on Germany later that day.

Other participants

Japan declared war later in August, siding with Great Britain in accordance with the terms of the Anglo-Japanese alliance of 1902. Great Britain was reluctant to accept this help, but it had no choice. Japan hoped to destroy the German Pacific fleet, which was stationed at the leased base of Tsingtao, on the Shantung Peninsula. This action would help Britain, to be sure, but there was another side to the coin. Japan had its own plans for the Far East. The war was a golden opportunity which the Japanese quickly seized. They captured the German base of Tsingtao and then the entire Shantung Peninsula.

Within six weeks after the assassination at Sarajevo, all the nations of the Triple Alliance and the Triple Entente were at war except Italy. The Italian government took the position that the Austrians and Germans were the aggressors;

therefore the Triple Alliance, a defensive treaty, did not require Italy to help them. It declared itself neutral. Whatever Italy could hope to gain from the war—the Tyrol region and the cities of Trieste and Fiume—had to come at the expense of Austria. There was little chance that Austria would give them up, but its opponents might offer them as spoils of victory.

Italy remained neutral for nine months, during which time each side bargained desperately for its aid. Finally, secret treaties were drawn up among Great Britain, France, Russia, and Italy, dividing the spoils of war in case of victory over Germany and Austria. In May 1915, Italy entered the war against its former allies, Germany and Austria.

In the meantime, Germany had negotiated to win other allies. In November 1914, the Ottoman Empire had plunged into the war on the side of Germany and Austria. This was a serious blow to the other side. The Turks were not a strong military power, but they occupied a strategic position. Control of Constantinople and the Dardanelles bottled up Russia's Black Sea fleet, just as German control of the entrance to the North Sea bottled up the Russian Baltic fleet. Furthermore, Russia lacked the industry to allow it to fight a modern war very long without help from its allies. The Turks' decision made it impossible for such help to reach Russia through the Mediterranean and Black seas. Germany also made tempting offers to Bulgaria, and in October 1915 that nation entered the war on the side of Germany.

CHECKUP

1. What were the chief aims in the Balkans of the following nations: Serbia? Russia? Great Britain? Germany?

2. Why did the British regard the Berlin-to-Baghdad railroad as a threat?

3. What event can be said to have "lit the fuse" in 1914, setting off the war? Why was it probably done?

4. Why did Belgium play a strategic role in the outbreak of World War I?

5. IDENTIFY: "powder keg of Europe," propaganda, ultimatum, belligerents.

3 The nations of the world fought a new kind of war

The nations that marched to war in the summer of 1914 thought that the conflict would be brief and decisive. Each side expected to win a quick victory. They were wrong. The fighting dragged on for four years. During that time it became clear that this was a war unlike any in history.

The opposing sides

Germany, Austria-Hungary, Bulgaria, and the Ottoman Empire became known as the Central Powers. Notice on the map on page 594 that they formed an almost solid block of territory from the North Sea to the Persian Gulf. Their closeness to each other geographically was one advantage, and there were others. Germany was superbly prepared, and its army was excellently organized and trained. It was equipped with superior weapons and fought in enemy territory rather than on its own soil. Germany's industry and transportation system were geared to war. Its lines of communication with its allies were far better than those of its enemies.

Britain, France, Russia, and their partners in the war became known as the Allied Powers, or the Allies. Although they did not have the geographic advantages of the Central Powers, they had more manpower and a greater industrial potential. They also controlled the seas; therefore, they could obtain food and raw materials more easily and could blockade and attempt to starve the Central Powers.

As a result of diplomatic maneuvers, Greece and Rumania joined the Allies in 1916. Eventually there were thirty-two countries on the Allied side. Many of them, however, joined late in the war and made only token contributions.

Innovations in warfare

World War I was an industrialized war. Weapons were produced with the same efficiency that industrialists had learned to apply to other products in peacetime. All the industries of the warring powers were organized to aid in the war effort.

One of the most important weapons of World War I was the machine gun. Largely because of its effectiveness, land armies often found any advance difficult and costly. To protect themselves from the machine gun's raking fire and from artillery bombardments, men dug extensive systems of trenches, where they might live for weeks or even months.

Both sides used weapons that had never been used before. In 1916 the British introduced the tank, an armored means of transport, mounted with guns, that enabled troops to break through enemy lines. However, many British military authorities were opposed to the tank, and its fullest possibilities were not realized. Another new weapon was the airplane, only recently invented (as you will read in Chapter 31). Airplanes in the early 1900's were neither very maneuverable nor very fast. They were used primarily for observing troop movements, and only occasionally were there so-called dogfights between planes. However, both sides used them for dropping explosives. Germany sent dirigibles (a large, early form of blimp) to bomb London, but with little effect.

Germany was the first nation to make extensive use of submarines, and its U-boats (undersea boats) did serious damage to Allied shipping. The Germans were also the first to use poison gas, which the Allies later adopted. However, gas lost much of its effectiveness after the development of the gas mask.

World War I was a war of the people. Except for the wars of the French Revolution, European wars traditionally had been fought by professional soldiers who worked simply for their pay and rations. World War I was fought by vast citizen armies. Those who could not fight worked at home to help the war effort. To stir the enthusiasm of the people, governments made wide use of propaganda. Newspapers and popular magazines portrayed the enemy as brutal and subhuman, while praising national aims and achievements.

593

The war from 1914 to 1916

The German attack on France, launched through Belgium in August 1914, nearly succeeded. By September, German troops reached the Marne River, almost at Paris (see map, opposite page). However, the French stood fast. Reserves were moved out from Paris by every means of transportation available, even city taxicabs. The French army counterattacked, the Germans were forced to withdraw, and Paris was saved. This battle of the Marne, which lasted from September 5 to 12, changed the entire nature of the war. Germany's hope of a swift victory was ended and both armies settled in for a long fight. Both armies dug long lines of trenches on the so-called western front that stretched from the Swiss border through Germany, France, and Belgium to the shores of the North Sea.

On the eastern front the Russians completed mobilization much more quickly than the Germans had expected. One Russian army moved westward toward Budapest, the capital of Hungary. Another moved through East Prussia, threatening the important seaport of Danzig.

In late August a German force met this second Russian army in a fierce battle at Tannenberg, in East Prussia (see map, this page). The Russians were driven back after suffering a humiliating defeat. Soon afterward the Germans launched an offensive in the east and drove the Russians completely out of Germany and eastward into Russian Poland.

WORLD WAR I IN EUROPE · 1914-1918

Central Powers
Allied Powers
Neutral nations
✕ Battle sites

It was clear that Russia's greatest weakness was lack of equipment. In 1915, Britain and France decided on a daring venture to try to get aid to Russia: an attempt to force their way through the Dardanelles and capture Constantinople. It was thought at first that battleship bombardment of the fortifications of the Straits would result in the surrender of Constantinople. After five days of bombardment, troops were landed on the Gallipoli Peninsula to try to establish a beachhead. The Turks, supervised by German officers, resisted stubbornly, and after eight months of fighting, the attempt was given up. The Gallipoli campaign cost the Allies a total of 145,000 men killed and wounded.

Naval warfare. Unable to reach quick victory on land, Britain decided to blockade the North Sea in an effort to keep merchant ships from reaching Germany. Originally the blockade was meant to keep raw materials for war equipment from the Germans, but gradually the blockade became an attempt to starve out the German people and ruin their economy.

Germany also used the naval blockade. Employing a fleet of submarines, Germany tried to force Britain to surrender by stopping the importation of needed foodstuffs and munitions. In May 1915, a German submarine sank, without warning, the British passenger liner *Lusitania* off the coast of Ireland. Of the 1,200 lives lost, more than 100 were American. The American President, Woodrow Wilson, sharply warned Germany that another such incident would not be tolerated. Germany used submarine warfare only sparingly for the next two years, not wishing to provoke the neutral Americans into entering the war on the side of the Allies.

In May 1916 the only large naval battle of the war was fought off the coast of Jutland, in the North Sea. Neither side could claim total victory, but the German navy retired into the Baltic Sea, where it stayed until the end of the war.

The war of stalemate

By 1916 the war had reached a stalemate. No naval battles were expected while the German fleet remained in the Baltic Sea. On land there

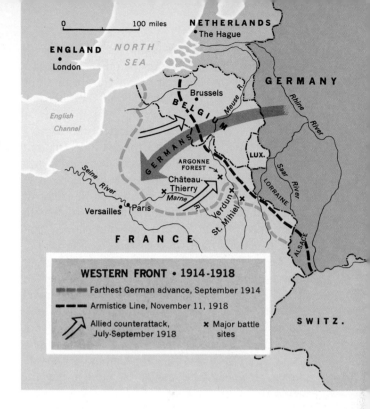

WESTERN FRONT · 1914-1918
▬▬▬ Farthest German advance, September 1914
▬ ▬ ▬ Armistice Line, November 11, 1918
➤ Allied counterattack, July-September 1918
× Major battle sites

was the futile standoff of trench warfare. Each side learned that it could not break through the other's line of trenches. Each side learned that, no matter how ghastly the cost, few important gains could be made. A small area of land on the western front changed hands over and over, costing both sides thousands of lives. The conflict had become what is called a war of attrition—a slow and painful wearing-down process in which one side tries to outlast the other.

The most famous example of this sort of warfare was at Verdun, in northeastern France (see map, this page). The Germans attacked Verdun in February 1916. They did not expect to capture the town, but did expect the French to defend it to the last man. In this way Germany hoped to use the Verdun offensive to bleed the French army to death. After six months of fighting, however, the Germans gave up. Germany had lost 330,000 men to France's 350,000.

The role of the United States

When World War I began in 1914, the United States immediately declared its neutrality. Many

Americans followed the course of the war with interest, favoring one side or the other, but almost everyone felt that the war was a European affair in which the United States should not become involved.

However, the war soon affected the United States considerably. As the strongest industrialized neutral nation, the United States became a supplier of food, raw materials, and munitions. The United States government insisted on the right of American citizens and business firms to trade with either side without interference, but agreed that if an American ship were carrying contraband—war materials supplied by a neutral to a belligerent nation—the goods might be seized. The United States insisted on the right of its citizens to travel in safety on ships of any nation, neutral or belligerent. As a neutral, the government could not lend money to either side. No effort was made, however, to stop banks, corporations, or private citizens from buying bonds of foreign governments or selling goods on credit.

At the beginning of the war, American investors and businessmen were dealing with both sides. But as the British blockade of Germany tightened, American trade became more and more one-sided. Soon the United States was trading only with the Allies, who were paying for most of the goods with borrowed American money.

American entry into the war. British propaganda was far more successful in impressing Americans than was Germany's. Graphic stories of German atrocities—brutal crimes of war, often committed against defenseless civilians—stirred up American feelings. Many of these stories were untrue, but since the United States depended largely upon British sources for war news, they were widely believed.

Early in 1917 the issue of American involvement was settled. In January the German foreign minister, Alfred Zimmerman, sent a secret telegram to the German ambassador in Mexico, instructing him to attempt to draw Mexico into the war on Germany's side. In exchange for Mexican participation, Germany promised Mexico the return of some parts of the southwestern United States that were lost by Mexico in 1848. The

596

World War I

Like all modern conflicts, World War I stimulated the development of new and "improved" methods of destruction. The airplane, upper left, was first used in combat. The Browning machine gun, upper right, was especially deadly. So was poison gas, against which the soldiers shown here wear masks to protect themselves. The German 5.9-inch howitzer, lower right, was the most lethal artillery weapon of the war.

There are many accounts of heroism and glory from World War I, but most of it was utter misery for the people who lived through it. At lower left, probably after waiting weeks or even months in the slimy mud of trenches, foot soldiers are about to follow their leader "over the top" to attack the enemy. Some of these men will live; others will die instantly. Those who are seriously wounded will be lucky if, after dark, medical corpsmen on foot can find them and carry them off on stretchers. The walking wounded, like the British soldiers at left, will make their painful way back from the front lines to a field hospital. Civilians shared the sufferings of war to a greater extent than ever before. At right is a German town after Russian forces had passed through and burned it in 1914.

British intercepted the telegram, decoded it, and sent it on to Washington. Publication of the Zimmerman telegram in American newspapers enraged public opinion.

Also in January, Germany, faced with extreme food and munitions shortages at home, decided that the war must be brought to a conclusion before all hope of victory was gone. Germany decided to resume unrestricted submarine warfare, taking the chance that the United States would not enter the war, or that Britain could be defeated by the German blockade before the United States had time to mobilize.

In March 1917 the autocratic czarist government of Russia was overthrown by a revolution whose leaders promised to establish a constitutional government. (You will read about this revolution in Chapter 34.) It was also expected that the revolution would force Russia to withdraw from the war. In any case, after the fall of the czar's government, all of the major Allied Powers were liberal democracies. Americans would more readily accept a war in which the lines were drawn between democratic and nondemocratic nations.

On April 2, 1917, President Wilson appeared before Congress to ask for a declaration of war against the Central Powers. He said that "The world must be made safe for democracy." On April 6, Congress voted, by an overwhelming majority, to enter the war on the side of the Allies.

It was not until the spring and summer of 1918 that troops of the newly drafted and trained American army arrived in Europe in large numbers. Meanwhile the hard-pressed Allied troops had to hold on. American entry into the war, however, gave the Allies a needed morale boost.

CHECKUP

1. Name the principal Central Powers; the principal Allied Powers. What were the advantages of each side?

2. What were some important new weapons and military techniques introduced in World War I?

3. How was the United States as a neutral power affected by World War I? What factors led to its entry into the war?

4. IDENTIFY: *Lusitania,* war of attrition, contraband.

5. LOCATE: Marne River, Tannenberg, Gallipoli Peninsula, Jutland, Verdun.

4 After defeating the Central Powers, the Allies drafted peace terms

President Wilson's statement of America's aim in entering the war—to make the world "safe for democracy"—was lofty and idealistic. Late in 1917, however, a serious blow hurt the Allies' morale. In November there was a second Russian revolution in which the Communist Party seized control. In March 1918, in the Russian town of Brest-Litovsk, the new Russian leaders signed a separate peace treaty with Germany. Meanwhile they published the terms of the secret treaties signed by the Allies when Italy entered the war. The revelation that their governments were fighting for bits of land made the war seem shoddy to many people on the Allied side.

The Fourteen Points

The British Prime Minister, David Lloyd George, tried to undo the bad impression by stating more idealistic aims in a speech to Parliament. But it was President Woodrow Wilson who best expressed what many people thought the Allied aims should be. This he did in the so-called Fourteen Points, which he announced in a speech to Congress in January 1918. There were six points of a general nature (points 1–5 and 14), and eight points that dealt with specific countries and regions, such as Russia, Belgium, Alsace-Lorraine, and the Balkans.

The six general proposals may be summarized as follows:

(1) No secret treaties. All treaties should be openly negotiated and all made public.

(2) Freedom of the seas for all nations, in peace and war.

(3) The removal of all economic barriers (tar-

"Armistice Night," painted by the American artist George Luks, gives a vivid impression of the joyful celebrations that marked the end of World War I.

iffs); equal opportunity for trade among all nations.

(4) Reduction of national armaments "to the lowest point consistent with domestic safety."

(5) Fair adjustment of all colonial claims. The interests of the people of a region were to be considered equally with those of the nation claiming title to the territory.

(14) "A general association of nations," which would guarantee political independence and protection to large and small states alike.

The Fourteen Points caught the imagination of people everywhere as a statement of aims worth fighting for. They raised the morale of Allied fighting men. Copies dropped behind the German lines made the German people more willing to surrender. Some historians feel, however, that Wilson made a serious mistake. He did not use his influence during the war, when it was greatest, to get the Allies to agree definitely to the Fourteen Points and to renounce their secret treaties.

Defeat of the Central Powers

The collapse of the Russians allowed the Germans to withdraw troops from the eastern front and to stage a huge offensive on the western front during the spring and summer of 1918. It was their last desperate gamble to break through the Allied lines, capture Paris, and end the war before the Americans could turn the tide. The German submarine blockade was failing. American troops and supplies were reaching Britain and France in increasing numbers.

The German offensives of 1918 lasted until mid-July. They failed by a very narrow margin. In May the Germans reached the Marne River, only 37 miles from Paris. But by this time more than 250,000 Americans were landing in France every month. Under a newly organized joint command, headed by the French general Ferdinand Foch (FOHSH), the Allied forces stopped the Germans in June at Château-Thierry (see map, page 595). In July the Allies began to counterattack. A final Allied push in September, at St. Mihiel

599

and in the Argonne Forest, proved successful, and the German armies were forced back to the borders of Germany.

At the same time, things were going badly for the Central Powers in the Near East and the Balkans. Bulgaria, seeing little hope for victory or for aid from its allies, caved in first, in September. The Turks soon followed, suing for peace. By November a revolution in Austria-Hungary brought the old empire to an end. Austria and Hungary formed separate governments.

The Kaiser's government in Germany also fell as a result of the war. Woodrow Wilson had said that he would deal only with a government that truly represented the German people. Certain German generals, wishing to end the war before Germany itself was invaded, pressed the Kaiser to form a representative government to sue for peace. Many Germans, however, looked upon the Kaiser himself as an obstacle to peace, and on November 9 he was forced to abdicate. A republic was proclaimed, and two days later the war ended.

On November 11, 1918, the chancellor of the new German Republic signed an armistice. An armistice is not a peace treaty; it is an agreement to stop fighting until a treaty can be drawn up. However, the terms of the armistice that Germany had to sign left no doubt that it had been defeated. Germany had to cancel the severe and humiliating peace treaty that it had forced the Russians to sign. It had to surrender all its submarines and a large part of its surface fleet. It had to release all war prisoners and turn over certain munitions that might make additional fighting possible.

The peace conference at Paris

After the armistice in November 1918, the Allies faced the task of arranging peace terms. The announced ideals of the Allies—self-government for all peoples and a world of lasting peace—raised the hopes of men and women everywhere. But it was Woodrow Wilson (whose Fourteen Points were accepted as worthy goals by people in both the defeated and the victorious countries) who best expressed the almost universal longing for peace and democracy.

President Wilson had written and spoken of a peace conference in which both sides would be represented and which would write a treaty fair to all. But the war had caused such bitterness and had been so costly, in terms both of human lives and of property, that the former enemies could not sit down together as if nothing had happened. The Allies had won the war, and in spite of Wilson's protests, it was the Allies alone who wrote the terms of peace.

Delegates of the victorious nations met in Paris in January 1919 to write the peace treaties. It was a large gathering. Almost all of the Allied Powers sent representatives. Russia, which was now in the midst of a civil war, was the only Allied Power not invited.

Nor were the defeated powers represented at Paris. The victors decided to work out the terms among themselves and call in representatives of the defeated powers only to accept the terms. The Allies also decided that a separate treaty should be written for each of the defeated Central Powers; since Austria and Hungary now had separate governments, five different treaties were to be drawn up.

Technically, the work of writing the treaties was done by the representatives of all the victorious nations. In fact, however, the work had been done in advance, behind the scenes, by the representatives of the four most powerful Allies: Great Britain, France, the United States, and Italy. The leaders of the Big Four, as they were called, were Prime Minister David Lloyd George of Britain; Premier Georges Clemenceau (klem-un·SOH) of France; President Woodrow Wilson of the United States; and Premier Vittorio Orlando of Italy.

Problems facing the peacemakers

The political situation in much of Europe was confused. Three great empires—Germany, Austria-Hungary, and Russia—had fallen by 1919. They were no longer hereditary monarchies, but republics. A fourth empire, that of the Ottoman Turks, was tottering. Nationalist groups pressed their claims in many areas of Europe—Russia, Germany, Austria, Hungary, and the Ottoman

Empire. Each group wanted independence, self-government, and unity within the borders of a single nation. Nationalism was strong in colonial possessions, too. The Arabs, the Egyptians, and the Indians all desired independence and self-rule.

The victorious nations had many territorial demands that were difficult to reconcile. France wanted, above all, security from German attack in the future. It insisted on the return of Alsace and Lorraine, which had been guaranteed in the Fourteen Points. In addition, it demanded that the French boundary be extended to the Rhine River so that France would gain the Rhineland—territory on the west bank of the Rhine that had formerly belonged to Germany. France also demanded the valley of the Saar River, which had valuable deposits of coal.

Italy claimed the Tyrol and Trieste in accordance with the secret treaties it had made in 1915. It also claimed Fiume, although this city had not been promised in the secret treaties. Lloyd George, Wilson, and Clemenceau were willing to give in on the Tyrol, but Wilson steadfastly opposed giving Fiume to Italy. The controversy over this point became so bitter that Orlando left the conference and went home in disgust. The Big Four then became the Big Three.

Great Britain wanted all of Germany's African colonies. It also demanded that the German navy be destroyed and that Germany be prohibited from building warships. Belgium requested two small portions of German territory along its borders.

During the war, Japan had occupied the German-held Marshall, Caroline, and Mariana islands as well as Tsingtao and most of the Shantung Peninsula. It now demanded permanent ownership of all these regions. Japan also asked that the powers recognize its "special position" in China. This meant, in effect, that in any further seizure of Chinese territory, Japan was to have the first choice and largest share. There was a

Woodrow Wilson looked dignified and determined as he set out from his Paris hotel for a meeting of the peace conference at Versailles.

bitter fight over the Japanese demands, and Japan threatened to follow Italy's example and withdraw from the conference. To keep Japan at the conference, Wilson gave in on Shantung.

Another problem was that of reparations—payment for war damages. In the west the war had been fought principally on French and Belgian soil. Four years of trench warfare had devastated a wide strip of land. Who should pay for restoring the land? Did war damages include damage to property only, or should they also include payment of pensions to wounded veterans, widows, and orphans?

Finally, there was the problem of a world organization to keep the peace, a League of Nations. This was the last of Wilson's Fourteen Points, and while it had more widespread appeal than any other, many European political leaders were skeptical about its chances for success.

The peace: justice or vengeance?

Very early in the conference, two conflicting viewpoints appeared. The British, French, and Italian governments had given lip service to the Fourteen Points, but they had never given up the aims stated in the secret treaties, written at the time Italy entered the war on the side of the Allies. You will remember that in these treaties the Allies agreed to divide the spoils of war—territories to be taken from the Central Powers—among themselves after the war. Thus the idea of a "peace of justice" came to be represented by the Fourteen Points, whereas the idea of a "peace of vengeance" was represented by the terms of the secret treaties.

It would have been difficult to write a "peace of justice," even if everyone had wanted one. Woodrow Wilson believed that it was possible, and he reasoned that only such a peace could be lasting. Unless all countries, including the defeated powers, were treated justly, the treaties would only create new problems and stir up new hatred and desires for revenge. In time, he thought, these would surely lead to another war.

Many people, however, disagreed. The war had left much bitterness, hatred, and longing for revenge. Among the victors there was a strong feeling that the defeated must be taught a lesson. Only by harsh treatment, they reasoned, could Germany and Austria be taught the penalty for starting a war. Some went further and argued that Germany should be divided up and disarmed completely. This sort of feeling was especially strong in France. Twice within fifty years, Frenchmen had seen their country overrun, occupied, and devastated by the Germans. Belgians also had good reason to hate the Germans. The Germans had invaded and devastated Belgium in violation of a treaty promise. The peace treaty, the Belgians felt, should make it impossible for Germany ever to do these things again.

CHECKUP

1. What were the six general proposals of Wilson's Fourteen Points? What effect did they have?

2. What were five main problems faced by the peacemakers?

3. Why did Wilson believe in a "peace of justice"? Summarize the arguments of those who opposed him.

4. IDENTIFY: Foch, armistice, Big Four, reparations.

5   A "new Europe" was created, but many problems remained

As you have read, separate treaties were made with each of the Central Powers. The most famous was the Versailles Treaty with Germany.

The Versailles Treaty

In May 1919, representatives of the new German Republic were called in, presented with a peace treaty, and told to sign it. The Germans complained bitterly that the treaty did not follow the Fourteen Points. They objected especially to two features: (1) The treaty made Germany admit that it alone was guilty of starting the war and therefore must pay reparations. (2) Since the total amount of reparations had not been agreed

EUROPE AFTER WORLD WAR I 1923

TERRITORIES LOST:

By Germany
By Austria-Hungary
By Bulgaria
By Russia
By the Ottoman Empire

——— Boundaries of 1923

upon by the victors, Germany was being asked to sign a "blank check." In spite of their protests, the Germans had no choice but to sign. This they did on June 28 in the famous palace built by Louis XIV at Versailles, near Paris.

In the Versailles Treaty, Germany acknowledged its "war guilt" and its liability to reparations payments. Germany would pay 5 billion dollars within two years and an unnamed sum later. In 1921 the Allies set the total bill at 33 billion dollars. The treaty also provided for the formation of the League of Nations and for numerous territorial adjustments (see map, this page).

Alsace and Lorraine were returned to France.

Germany agreed not to fortify the Rhineland, which was to be occupied by Allied troops for an unspecified period of time. The Saar Valley was to be administered by the League of Nations for fifteen years, during which time all of the coal mined in the area was to go to France in part payment of reparations. At the end of fifteen years, the people of the region were to vote on whether to continue under the League, to become part of France, or to rejoin Germany.

Germany was also required to give Belgium the territory it demanded, and to cede part of Schleswig to Denmark. Germany also lost considerable territory on its eastern borders.

A large area was given back to the restored nation of Poland. This region, which cut East Prussia off from the rest of Germany and also gave Poland an outlet to the Baltic Sea, was called the Polish Corridor. Danzig, on the northern coast of the Corridor, became a free city, administered by the League of Nations.

All of Germany's colonies were divided among the victors, who were to supervise them on behalf of the League of Nations. Britain received German East Africa (renamed Tanganyika), part of the Cameroons, and part of Togo. German Southwest Africa went to the Union of South Africa. Part of Togo and part of the Cameroons went to France. In the Pacific the German-held islands north of the equator went to Japan. Those south of the equator went to Australia and New Zealand. Japan also took Tsingtao and Germany's rights to the Shantung Peninsula.

Germany had to abolish conscription and was forbidden to maintain a reserve army. The famous general staff was disbanded. The manufacture of heavy artillery, tanks, military airplanes, and poison gas was forbidden. There were to be no battleships larger than 10,000 tons and no submarines at all.

Thus the treaty makers tried to make sure that Germany would be, if not a peace-loving nation, then certainly a peace-keeping one. However, although the provisions regarding Germany were strict, the means of enforcing them were not.

Austria-Hungary

You will remember that the Dual Monarchy split in two as the war was ending. Thus separate treaties were arranged with Austria and Hungary.

Austria was recognized as an independent republic. It lost the southern Tyrol and the city of Trieste to Italy. The new nation had 6 million people, 2 million of whom lived in its capital, Vienna. It was said that Austria became "a capital without a country." It could not grow enough food for its people, nor supply its industries with adequate raw materials. Austria rapidly sank into a state of financial crisis and poverty.

Hungary lost a great deal of territory. It became landlocked, and although it remained pri-

marily an agricultural nation, it could produce barely enough food to feed its citizens.

Two new nations were created out of the old Dual Monarchy. One was Czechoslovakia, in central Europe. It included the Slavic peoples called Czechs, Slovaks, and Ruthenians. The other was Yugoslavia, in the western Balkans. It united the old kingdoms of Serbia and Montenegro, the former provinces of Bosnia and Herzegovina, and part of the Adriatic coast.

The Ottoman Empire

Like the other Central Powers, Bulgaria was penalized by the victors; it was reduced in size and lost its outlet to the Aegean Sea, which went to Greece. The Ottoman Empire, however, paid an even higher price for being on the losing side. The treaty, signed in 1920, was severe.

The island of Cyprus, a British possession since 1878 and annexed in 1914, was formally recognized as a British colony. The Dodecanese Islands in the Aegean Sea were given to Italy. The region of Thrace, on the European mainland, went to Greece, as did the city of Smyrna, on the coast of Asia Minor. Constantinople and the Straits remained in Turkish hands, but were to be unfortified and controlled by an international commission. (As you will read in Chapter 33, a later treaty restored some of these losses to the Turks.)

The sultan had to give up all claims to land in North Africa, including Egypt and the Anglo-Egyptian Sudan. Several new nations—Palestine, Trans-Jordan, and Syria (including Lebanon)— were eventually created out of former Turkish territory along the eastern Mediterranean Sea (see map, page 603). Turkish territory still farther east became the country of Iraq. None of these countries, however, was independent. Palestine, Trans-Jordan, and Iraq went to Great Britain under the supervision of the League of Nations. Syria and Lebanon were to be administered by France. In Arabia, the kingdom of Hejaz was recognized as independent.

Unsolved problems

If you compare the maps on pages 594 and 603, you will see four new nations along the Baltic Sea, in what was previously Russian territory. They were Finland, Estonia, Latvia, and Lithuania. In 1918 they had declared their independence from Russia, and they were recognized by the victorious powers at the end of the war.

You have read how the peace treaties created a new Poland. Much of its territory came from Russia. Russia also lost the province of Bessarabia, in the southwest, to Rumania.

Russia, a former Allied power, actually lost more territory than Germany did. There were two reasons for this: (1) Russia had withdrawn from the war late in 1917 and signed a separate treaty with Germany. (2) The Western European powers feared that the revolution in Russia would spread westward. It was therefore decided to isolate Russia from Western Europe by creating a ring of buffer states around Russia's western boundaries. Such harsh treatment of a former Allied power seemed bound to cause trouble.

Another serious problem was left unsolved by the treaty makers. The attempt to unite members of each European nationality under their own government did not always succeed. For example, there were 250,000 German-speaking Austrians in the Tyrol, which was now partly under Italian rule. There were Germans in Danzig and in the Polish Corridor. There were also 3 million former Austrian subjects—a German-speaking group called Sudeten Germans—in Czechoslovakia.

To meet the problem of national minorities— people living under governments controlled by foreign nationalities—all five treaties contained clauses in which each government pledged to treat fairly any such group within its borders. Each minority group was guaranteed certain rights, to be protected by the League of Nations.

The League of Nations

In helping to draft the peace settlement, President Wilson had made several compromises with the ideals he had stated in his Fourteen Points. He realized that the treaties failed in many respects to provide a "peace of justice." He consoled himself, however, with the thought that the new League of Nations would be able to remedy the injustices.

While the treaty settlements were being worked out, a special commission, including Wilson, wrote the covenant (constitution) of a League of Nations. This covenant was adopted by the Paris conference and included as part of the Versailles Treaty.

According to the covenant, the League of Nations had two main aims: to promote international cooperation, and to maintain peace by the peaceful settlement of disputes and by reducing armaments. It was to include all independent, sovereign nations. It was to function through three main agencies: an Assembly, a Council, and a Secretariat. The League was to work closely with a related but independent body, the Permanent Court of International Justice, or World Court.

The Assembly was to be a sort of lower house. It was to be composed of representatives of all member nations. Regardless of size, each nation was to have one vote. The Council, an upper house, was to be composed of nine member nations (later increased to fifteen). Its five permanent members were to be Great Britain, France, Italy, Japan, and the United States. The additional seats on the Council were to be filled by rotation from among the smaller nations. The Secretariat, a staff composed of expert advisers and clerical workers, was to manage the routine business of the League.

The League provided a way for trying to deal with the problems created by imperialism in so-called "backward" regions of the world. Until the people of an area were considered ready for independence, the League took the area in trust— that is, took over responsibility for it. It assigned the area as a *mandate* to the government of an advanced nation to administer. The administering nation was pledged to prepare the people for independent self-government, not to fortify the territory, and to make annual reports to the League concerning its progress.

Peace-keeping measures. The members of the League of Nations accepted an obligation not to resort to war; they promised to submit any disputes to arbitration. Arbitration could be carried on by the World Court, or by special boards or commissions set up for a particular case. The covenant also provided that if a member broke his pledge to submit to arbitration, or went to war, the League could impose penalties on that member. Possible penalties included breaking diplomatic relations, imposing economic sanctions (refusal to buy anything from or sell anything to the offending member), blockade, or, as a last resort, the use of military force.

Although the League of Nations had been Wilson's idea, the United States never became a member of the organization. Because the covenant was a part of the Versailles Treaty, its adoption depended on ratification of the treaty by the United States Senate. Some senators disapproved of the League itself, while others wanted changes in the peace settlement. Because of this opposition, and Wilson's unwillingness to make any compromises, the treaty—and thus the League of Nations—failed to pass the Senate. Technically, the United States remained at war with the Central Powers until 1921, when it signed separate treaties with them.

Thus the League of Nations began without the membership and support of the United States, its principal creator and by then the most powerful nation in the world. President Wilson prophetically stated that if the United States did not join, the war would have to be fought again.

The new organization held its first meeting at Geneva in November 1920. Forty-two member nations were represented. Germany was not allowed to join the League until 1926, and Russia did not become a member until 1934. By 1935 there were sixty-two members.

Costs of the war

The costs of World War I stagger the imagination. Each of the belligerent nations suffered enormous and lasting effects from the years of fighting. Reliable estimates indicate that over 8 million people lost their lives in battle. Many more were wounded, and millions were crippled for life.

Militarily, Russia was the most severely hit, losing more than 2 million men. Germany lost almost that many, and France and its colonies lost nearly 1½ million. Austria-Hungary counted 1¼ million dead after the war, and Britain almost

1 million. American lives lost numbered 115,000.

For the first time in history, the loss of life among the civilian population was almost as great as that among the armed forces. Naval blockades, artillery and aerial bombardments, famine, disease, and political violence all took their toll. The destruction of property was appalling. One historian has estimated that the total cost to all the warring powers was 400 billion dollars.

Other costs of World War I are harder to estimate. The period immediately afterward was one of political, economic, and social confusion. Hunger, unemployment, and disease encouraged political unrest.

Another cost that cannot be measured is the loss to civilization itself. The legacy of social unrest, lingering hatred, and future human suffering cannot be accurately described. A journalist wrote in 1938: "Spiritually and morally, civilization collapsed on August 1, 1914—the civilization in which people now middle-aged grew up, a culture which with all its shortcomings did give more satisfaction to more people than any other yet evolved. Young people cannot realize how the world has been coarsened and barbarized since 1914; they may feel the loss of security into which their parents were born, but they cannot appreciate how much else has been lost; even we who once had it cannot recall it now without an effort." °

° From "We Lose the Next War" by Elmer Davis in *Harper's Magazine,* March 1938, p. 342.

CHECKUP

1. Summarize the provisions of the Versailles Treaty concerning (a) reparations, (b) Germany's colonies, and (c) German military power.

2. Name six nations that lost territory by the peace treaties, and six nations that gained territory. What nations were created in Europe?

3. How did the peace settlement create problems with regard to Russia? national minorities?

4. What were the aims of the League of Nations? its main agencies? What provisions did it make for peace-keeping?

5. LOCATE: Czechoslovakia, Yugoslavia, Bessarabia, Finland, Estonia, Latvia, Lithuania.

CHAPTER REVIEW

Chapter 29 World War I Drastically Altered the Course of History (1882–1920)

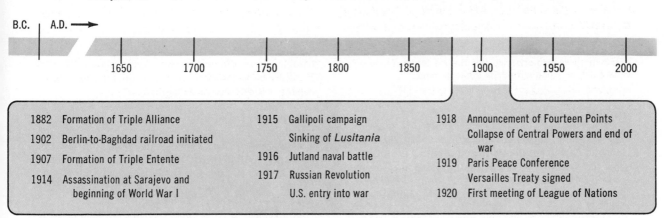

B.C. | A.D. ➞

1650 1700 1750 1800 1850 1900 1950 2000

1882	Formation of Triple Alliance
1902	Berlin-to-Baghdad railroad initiated
1907	Formation of Triple Entente
1914	Assassination at Sarajevo and beginning of World War I
1915	Gallipoli campaign
	Sinking of *Lusitania*
1916	Jutland naval battle
1917	Russian Revolution
	U.S. entry into war
1918	Announcement of Fourteen Points
	Collapse of Central Powers and end of war
1919	Paris Peace Conference
	Versailles Treaty signed
1920	First meeting of League of Nations

CHAPTER SUMMARY

In the early 1900's, despite efforts to bring nations closer together, the forces of nationalism, imperialism, and militarism led to extreme international tension and an intense armaments race. A system of rival alliances further complicated the situation.

The spark that set off World War I occurred in the Balkans, when the heir to the Austrian throne was assassinated by a Serbian nationalist. Austria soon declared war on Serbia, and within six weeks most of the major nations of Europe (plus Japan) were at war.

Both the Central Powers and the Allies had distinct advantages; advanced technological innovations included the use of machine guns, tanks, airplanes, submarines, and poison gas. After initial advances on both sides, the war reached a stalemate with thousands of troops bogged down in trenches.

In 1917, after the Russian Revolution, the United States entered the war. President Wilson's Fourteen Points aided Allied morale, and American troops helped turn the tide of battle. The collapse of the Central Powers followed soon afterward.

When the Allies met in Paris to draft peace treaties, their representatives faced difficult problems involving territorial demands, reparations, and the establishment of a new world organization. Two conflicting viewpoints—justice versus vengeance—aggravated their difficulties.

In the Versailles Treaty, Germany was forced to acknowledge its war guilt, promise reparations, cede several territories, and limit its military forces. Separate treaties recognized Austria and Hungary as independent nations, and created Czechoslovakia and Yugoslavia. The Ottoman Empire and Russia both lost territory. The new League of Nations was created to promote cooperation and peace, but it was weakened by the United States' refusal to join.

QUESTIONS FOR DISCUSSION

1. Which of the causes of World War I still threaten world peace today? Justify your selections.

2. President Wilson said that, "The world must be made safe for democracy." Do you think democracy did make gains as a consequence of World War I?

3. What did Wilson's Fourteen Points have to say about secret treaties? What are the advantages, or disadvantages, of treaties that are openly negotiated?

4. Do you think it was an error of the Allies at the end of World War I not to invite the defeated Central Powers to the peace negotiations? Explain.

5. It has been said that the seeds for another war were sown with the settlements made after World War I. Why do you agree or disagree?

PROJECTS

1. Tell the story of the outbreak of World War I as it might have been told by a contemporary Frenchman, German, Englishman, and American.

2. Make a list of the underlying causes of World War I, and briefly explain each one.

3. Draw a cartoon depicting the balance of power between the Triple Alliance and the Triple Entente.

4. Draw a poster for either Britain or Germany, to be used as propaganda in the United States before it entered World War I.

5. Draw a map of Europe including (1) the route of the German attack on France in 1914, (2) the main fighting fronts of the war, and (3) the location of the North Sea blockade.

6. Draw a political map of Europe after the peace settlements ending World War I.

607

STUDY IN DEPTH

UNIT SEVEN

For additional bibliographical information on the books cited in these projects, see the Basic Library (page xviii) and Further Reading on the opposite page.

INDIVIDUAL PROJECTS

1. For the classroom bulletin board draw a large map of Africa in 1914 showing, by the use of color, how Africa was divided among European colonial powers. Palmer, *Historical Atlas of the World,* and Shepherd, *Shepherd's Historical Atlas,* should be used for this exercise.

2. India became a prized British colony. Write a report tracing the steps by which Britain gained possession of India and describe the Indians' reactions to British control. Read the following: Eisen and Filler, *The Human Adventure,* Vol. 2, "The Sepoy Rebellion" and "The Growth of National Feeling in India"; Hughes and Fries, *European Civilization,* "The Process of English Imperialism in India."

3. Prepare an oral report on the opening of Japan to the West by Commodore Perry. Explain the reasons for Japan's isolation, Perry's motives for the journey, and the reception Perry's party received upon its arrival in Japan. Read in Eisen and Filler, *The Human Adventure,* Vol. 2, "The Closing of Japan" and "The Opening of Japan." Also consult two pertinent articles in *American Heritage:* "When Perry Unlocked the 'Gate of the Sun,'" April 1958, and "Meeting with the West," August 1963.

4. Sun Yat-sen, the father of the revolution of 1911 in China, spoke of "The Three Principles of the People." Tape one of Sun Yat-sen's lectures, play it to the class, and lead a discussion on the meaning and content of the speech. For this exercise use Peterson, *Treasury of the World's Great Speeches,* "Sun Yat-sen Takes Up the Yellow Man's Burden."

5. Write an essay on one of the following aspects of the Spanish-American War: (1) the origins of the war, (2) public opinion at the outset of the conflict, (3) a major battle of the war. Consult the following sources: Freidel, *The Splendid Little War,* and *American Heritage,* "The Needless War with Spain," February 1957; "The Enemies of Empire," June 1960; "The Sham Battle of Manila," December 1960; "How We Got Guantanamo," February 1962.

6. What were the causes of World War I? The following questions should serve as a guide for your report: What conflicts were caused by imperialistic rivalries? Where in Europe was nationalism causing trouble? How did militarism aggravate conditions in Europe? How did the system of alliances among European nations create tensions?

7. World War I was a new kind of war, fought with new kinds of weapons. Report to the class on trench warfare and the weapons used in the war. Consult: Snyder and Morris, *A Treasury of Great Reporting,* "Will Irwin Denounces the Germans of World War I for Using Poison Gas at Ypres," "H. G. Wells Unveils the Tank"; Werstein, *1914–1918: World War I Told with Pictures.*

8. Prepare an oral report on the formation of the League of Nations. Discuss Woodrow Wilson's part in this and his hopes for its success. Read the following selections: Copeland and Lamm, *The World's Great Speeches,* "Woodrow Wilson: The League of Nations"; Stearns, *Pageant of Europe,* "The Treaty of Versailles and the Covenant of the League of Nations"; Peterson, *Treasury of the World's Great Speeches,* "President Wilson Goes to the People in Behalf of the League of Nations."

GROUP PROJECTS

1. Four or five students should organize a panel discussion on imperialism. Items that should be researched and discussed are the economic reasons for imperialism, the "white man's burden," national pride, means of control of foreign territory, and imperialistic rivalries. Panelists should answer questions from the class at the end of the discussion.

2. Three students might work together as a panel and present to the class a series of reports on the peace settlement after World War I. The reports should discuss Wilson's Fourteen Points, the Versailles Treaty, and the German reaction to the peace treaty. After the reports the panel should answer questions from the class. The following sources should be consulted: Eisen and Filler, *The Human Adventure,* Vol. 2, "The Allies Impose Terms upon the Germans"; Stearns, *Pageant of Europe,* "The Armistice (November 11, 1918): From Wilson 'The Fourteen Points'"; Hughes and Fries, *European Civilization,* "The Treaty of Versailles."

3. Organize a debate on the following topic: War creates more problems than it solves. Was this true of World War I? Do you think this would apply to a world war today?

Further Reading

BIOGRAPHY

Ascherson, Neal, *The King Incorporated*. Doubleday. King Leopold II of Belgium.

Benét, Laura, *Stanley, Invincible Explorer*. Dodd, Mead.

Benz, Francis E., *On to Suez! The Story of De Lesseps and the Canal*. Dodd, Mead.

Buck, Pearl S., *The Man Who Changed China: The Story of Sun Yat-sen*. Random House.

Cowles, Virginia, *The Kaiser*. Harper & Row. William II.

Eaton, Jeanette, *David Livingstone: Foe of Darkness*. Morrow.

Edwardes, Allen, *Death Rides a Camel*. Julian Press. Sir Richard Burton, African explorer.

Garraty, John A., *Woodrow Wilson*. Knopf.

Harlow, Alvin Fay, *Andrew Carnegie*. Messner.

Jackson, J. H., *Clemenceau and the Third Republic*. Macmillan.*

Lockhart, J. C., and C. M. Woodhouse, *Cecil Rhodes*. Macmillan.

Meyer, Edith Patterson, *Dynamite and Peace: The Story of Alfred Nobel*. Little, Brown.

Payne, Robert, *Lawrence of Arabia*. Pyramid.* British colonel who led the Arabs against the Ottoman Empire during World War I.

Pringle, Henry F., *Theodore Roosevelt*. Harcourt Brace Jovanovich.*

Smuts, J. C., *Jan Christian Smuts: A Biography*. Morrow.

Williams, Beryl, and Samuel Epstein, *William Crawford Gorgas: Tropic Fever Fighter*. Messner.

NONFICTION

Baldwin, Hanson W., *World War I*. Grove.*

Barnett, Correlli, *The Swordbearers: Supreme Command in the First World War*. New American Library.*

Bocca, Geoffrey, *La Légion: The French Foreign Legion and the Men Who Made It Glorious*. Crowell-Collier.

Collier, Richard, *Great Indian Mutiny*. Dutton. Sepoy Rebellion.

Congdon, Don, ed., *Combat: World War I*. Dell.*

Falls, Cyril, *The Great War: 1914–1918*. Putnam.*

Fleming, Peter, *The Siege at Peking*. Harper & Row. Story of the Boxer Rebellion.

Freidel, Frank, *The Splendid Little War*. Dell.* Spanish-American War.

* Paperback.

Furneaux, Rupert, *The Zulu War*. Lippincott.

Hirsch, Phil, ed., *World War I*. Pyramid.* Twelve true stories.

Lafore, Laurence, *The Long Fuse: An Interpretation of the Origins of World War I*. Lippincott.*

Moorehead, Alan, *The Blue Nile*. Dell.*

———, *The White Nile*. Dell.*

Pitt, Barrie, *1918: The Last Act*. Ballantine.* End of World War I.

Reynolds, Quentin, *They Fought for the Sky: The Dramatic Story of the First War in the Air*. Holt, Rinehart and Winston.

Roosevelt, Theodore, *The Rough Riders*. New American Library.*

Sellman, R. R., *The First World War*. Criterion.

Spencer, Cornelia, *The Land of the Chinese People*. Lippincott.

———, *Made in India*. Knopf.

Tuchman, Barbara, *The Guns of August*. Dell.* Outbreak of World War I.

———, *The Proud Tower*. Macmillan. The world from 1890 to 1914.

Werstein, Irving, *1914–1918: World War I Told with Pictures*. Pocket Books.*

HISTORICAL FICTION

Achebe, Chinua, *Things Fall Apart*. Obolensky. Tribal life in a Nigerian village in the 1800's.

Buck, Pearl, *The Good Earth*. Pocket Books.* Peasant life in China.

Chauncy, Nan, *Devil's Hill*. Watts. Pioneer life in Tasmania.

Dessi, Giuseppe, *The Deserter*. Harcourt Brace Jovanovich. World War I in Italy.

Doolittle, Hilda, *Bid Me to Live*. Grove. American expatriate in England.

Forster, E. M., *A Passage to India*. Harcourt Brace Jovanovich.* India during the colonial period.

Hemingway, Ernest. *A Farewell to Arms*. Scribner.* World War I.

Huggins, Alice M., *The Red Chair Waits*. Westminster. China in transition.

Malgonkar, Manohar, *The Princess*. Viking. The old order and the new democracy in India.

Mazzetti, Lorenza, *The Sky Falls*, McKay. Story of an Italian boy during World War I.

Remarque, Erich, *All Quiet on the Western Front*. Fawcett.* Young German soldier in World War I.

Small, S. H., *Dangerous Duty*. Walck. Engine-room boy accompanies Commodore Perry to Japan.

Werfel, Franz, *The Forty Days of Musa Dagh*. Pocket Books.* Turkish persecution of Armenians during World War I.

THE GROWTH OF

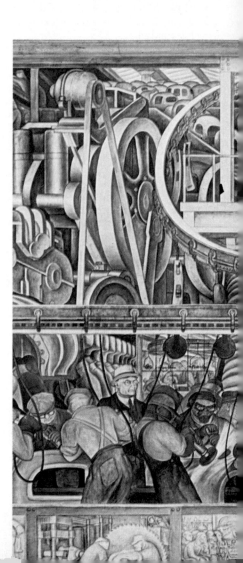

In the 1930's a Detroit museum commissioned the well-known Mexican artist Diego Rivera to paint a mural on one of its courtyard walls. Fittingly, the main panel—a portion of which is reproduced at right—showed the manufacture of automobiles, the chief industry of Detroit. In the foreground are workmen sanding a car, assembling a chassis, and welding. Behind them, rows of steering wheels and tires move along conveyor belts and a group of visitors watches. Above, men work on an engine and on car bodies. The interplay of men and machinery so vividly and forcefully portrayed here became a major concern with the growth of modern science and technology.

SCIENCE AND TECHNOLOGY

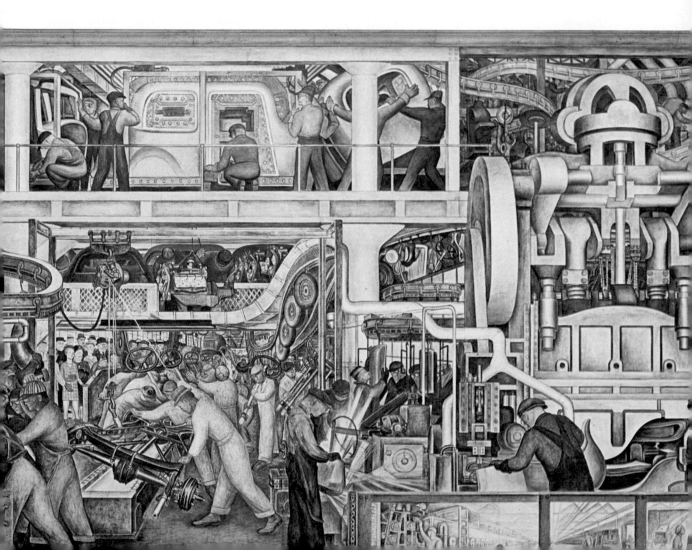

30

Scientists Explored the Nature of Matter and Man

In the century or so between the battle of Waterloo and the Versailles Treaty, the world changed enormously. The Industrial Revolution, new methods of communication, and increased trade brought the various parts of the world closer together. The imperialistic race for colonies and a world war transformed the political balance of power.

Tremendous changes were also going on in the realm of ideas. You have read about the force of such concepts as liberalism and nationalism, and how they affected people during the 1800's. At the same time, the pursuit of knowledge was unlocking the forces of nature. The findings of science in the 1800's and early 1900's were to make incredible changes in every facet of daily life and to bring the far reaches of the earth even closer together.

The scientists of the 1800's did not set out to transform the world; they were looking for answers to questions about the nature of matter and of life. These scientists worked out of intellectual curiosity or love of learning, for there were not many ways to make a living from science.

During the middle and later 1800's, this situation was almost completely changed as science and the scientist found their places in society. Universities and colleges were the first organizations to employ scientists, where they became important as teachers. After about 1870, industry

An English physicist in his laboratory

also provided a place for the scientist who could solve industrial problems by using scientific knowledge, as you will see in the next chapter. Only then could large numbers of scientists earn a living while carrying on scientific activities.

From about 1800 on, science developed so rapidly that it began to divide into special branches. In 1800, for example, a man might work in both chemistry and physics; by 1900 he was either a chemist or a physicist, and he probably specialized further in one particular aspect of his subject. New sciences came into being. Scientific methods were extended to new fields of inquiry. The social sciences, those dealing with man and society, made their appearance.

The solving of practical problems by the use of science is known as applied science. The search for new scientific knowledge and the development of theories or mathematical formulas that explain or relate known facts in new ways is called pure science. It is with pure science that this chapter deals.

THE CHAPTER SECTIONS:

1. The physical sciences revealed the composition of matter (1803–1930)

2. The biological sciences uncovered the nature of life (1803–1909)

3. Several sciences contributed knowledge about man and society (1835–1920)

1 The physical sciences revealed the composition of matter

The physical sciences are those that deal with the inanimate (nonliving) aspects of nature. They include astronomy, geology, physics, and chemistry. The most significant developments in the physical sciences during the 1800's and early 1900's centered on the atomic theory.

Background of the atomic theory

According to modern atomic theory, all matter in the universe is made up of very small particles called atoms. The arrangement and structure of these atoms, and their chemical combinations, account for the different properties, or characteristics, of the materials we find in the world.

The atomic theory, like many other scientific ideas, can be traced back to the speculations of some Greek philosophers, such as Democritus, about whom you read in Chapter 6. Although these thinkers believed that all material substances could be broken down into atoms, they offered no experimental or mathematical proofs for their belief. For many centuries, atomism was merely one of several philosophical theories about physical reality.

With the Scientific Revolution in the 1500's and 1600's, and its shift from speculation to investigation, the atomic theory began to become part of science. A famous atomist of that time was

the great English scientist Isaac Newton. He convinced his followers that the atomic view of nature was a help to science even though it could not yet be supported by experimental proof or mathematical demonstration.

The atomic theory in chemistry

John Dalton, an English chemist and schoolteacher, was the first scientist to obtain convincing experimental information about the atom. In 1803 he outlined a method for "weighing" atoms. It was impossible, of course, to weigh the minute, invisible atoms individually. Dalton overcame this difficulty by learning the relative weights of atoms of different elements as they combined to form chemical compounds.

He reasoned that if one atom of one element combines with one of another to form a tiny basic particle of a compound, then the ratio in which measurable amounts of the two elements combine must reflect the relative weights of their atoms. After studying the ratios of elements in various gases, Dalton assigned an arbitrary weight of 1 to the lightest element, hydrogen, and expressed the weights of other elements in relation to it. Thus oxygen, which proved to be sixteen times as heavy as hydrogen, had an atomic weight of 16, and so on. (Dalton himself did not

The "Science" of Cubism

Since classical times—when the Greeks worked out rules governing correct proportions—some artists in almost every era have tried to base their work on scientific principles. In the early 1900's, painters developed cubism, an attempt to reduce natural forms to their basic geometric shapes, and to present different aspects of objects (for example, both front and side views) in one painting. Georges Braque, a leading cubist, painted "Violin and Jug" in 1910. Both objects are shown as though the artist had walked around them and noted down many different planes and angles in a seemingly jumbled but actually well-organized composition. Theoretically, we know more about the objects because we see them from two different angles at once. The absence of strong colors accentuates the mathematical precision of the painting.

arrive at this figure of 16, partly because his measurements were not accurate. However, other scientists quickly saw the value of his methods and determined the correct atomic weight for oxygen and for many other elements.)

Because he was the first scientist to provide definite information about the individual atoms, John Dalton is called the father of modern atomic theory. Through his work, scientists came to see that the atomic theory provided a simple basic framework that explained many known facts about matter and pointed the way to discovering others. It also provided a means of describing chemical compounds by formulas.

During the 1800's, many scientists explored the paths opened up by Dalton, and much was learned about the atom. Once the atomic weights of all known chemical elements were determined, scientists discovered that if the different elements were listed in the order of their atomic weights, then elements having similar properties appeared with some regularity. Several scientists tried to arrange these known elements in a chart or table that would place similar elements together in groups, or families.

In 1869 a Russian chemist, Dmitri Mendeleyev, produced the first workable classification of the elements. Mendeleyev's Periodic Table, somewhat modified today, is a familiar part of every chemistry textbook. His original table showed gaps that led to the later discovery of natural elements unknown at that time. Then, in the 1900's, the table provided suggestions leading to the creation of synthetic elements not found in nature.

The atomic theory in physics

Although modern atomic theory had its origin in the study of chemistry, it soon became part of physics (the science of matter and energy). This began to occur when scientists studying heat and gases explained their findings with a new theory of atoms in motion.

During the 1700's, most men believed that heat was a fluid substance, called caloric, capable of flowing in and out of a body of matter. But investigators of the 1800's found many things about heat that such a theory did not explain. For instance, if heat was a fluid, why did it have no mass or weight?

Scientists began to think of heat as the result of the motion of a body's atomic particles. In a cold body—ice, for example—the motion of the atoms is relatively restricted. In a hot body—such as hot water—the atoms move much more vigorously, bouncing into one another. If water is heated to its boiling point, the atoms move extremely fast and the water is turned into a gas-water vapor.

The physicists of the 1800's concentrated their attention on the particles that composed gases. They assumed that these particles, called molecules, were made up of several small, hard atoms, which they pictured somewhat like billiard balls. The molecules of gas, traveling through space, struck one another and thus moved in jagged paths. By making these assumptions, and using mathematics, physicists were able to account for the temperature and pressure of gases in a variety of situations. Thus the atomic theory became a part of physics, later to become a much more basic part, as it had become in chemistry.

The structure of the atom

The billiard-ball view of the atom was useful and simple, but it proved to be an inaccurate guide in understanding the world of matter. Physicists were soon convinced that material substances were more complex and mysterious than they had suspected. In 1895 a German physicist, Wilhelm K. Roentgen, was passing electricity through a vacuum within a glass tube; he noticed that a fluorescent substance on a table nearby glowed brightly when the electric current was switched on in the tube. Roentgen immediately concluded that the tube was sending out a new form of ray. Soon he discovered that the rays penetrated many substances, including human skin and tissue, and would leave an impression on a photographic plate. Because he did not know what caused this powerful penetrating radiation, Roentgen named the rays X-rays. They had a twofold influence on the growth of science. X-rays became an important tool for workers in medicine, and they raised new questions about the material world.

Two years after Roentgen's discovery of X-rays,

an English physicist, J. J. Thomson, probed further into the nature of matter. In 1897 he discovered the electron, a tiny particle that had a negative electrical charge. He announced that it was more than a thousand times lighter than the smallest known atom, and he suggested that all atoms contained electrons. Therefore, subatomic particles (that is, particles inside atoms), rather than atoms, must be the true building blocks of the material universe.

While the electron was being reluctantly accepted by the majority of physicists, a French team of chemists, Pierre and Marie Curie, provided new evidence that atoms were not the simple, indivisible particles that had been pictured by Dalton and others. The Curies, in experimenting with uranium and radium, found that these elements threw off powerful rays containing tiny particles of matter. While this was taking place, the chemical nature and atomic weight of uranium and radium were changing. All of this activity meant that the atoms of these elements were constantly and spontaneously disintegrating and releasing energy. This process is called radioactivity. Elements that undergo it are called radioactive elements.

Rutherford. Thomson's electrons and the Curies' disintegrating atoms were fitted together by Ernest Rutherford of Britain to form a new picture of the atom. Rutherford bombarded very thin sheets of gold with particles emitted by radioactive elements. He expected that the particles would go completely through the gold sheets. But 1 out of 10,000 particles bounced back. He concluded that the gold atom was mostly space that allowed the particles to pass through, yet contained something extremely small which repelled the few particles that bounced back.

Rutherford's experiments led him to present a new model, or description, of the atom. At the center was an extremely small and heavy nucleus, or core. About this nucleus whirled electrons in circular orbits. The atom was no longer thought of as a solid, spherical piece of matter.

Even the small nucleus of the atom was not indivisible. Rutherford bombarded the nucleus with heavy particles from radioactive elements

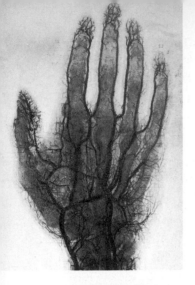

Exploring Matter and Energy

Like many major scientific advances, the discovery of the X-ray by Wilhelm Roentgen, center left, was accidental. The invisible ray, which provided new insights into the structure of the atom, was discovered when Roentgen happened to leave a fluorescent object exposed in a room. When it started glowing, he reasoned that there must be a cause for the phenomenon and started experimenting by photographing many objects, including the hand at left. At about the same time, the Curies, studying the nature of matter, accidentally discovered that some elements emitted energy in the form of rays. Marie Curie, shown below in her laboratory, won two Nobel prizes for her experiments with radioactive elements but remained puzzled by the relationship of matter to energy. Albert Einstein, bottom right, provided the equation that clarified this relationship. The photograph of a uranium atom, bottom left, gave visual evidence that nuclear reaction, producing energy, took place within the atom.

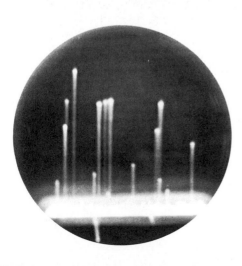

and found that it contained still smaller particles, which he called protons. In the bombardment of atoms, some of the bombarding particles may be absorbed. When this occurs, the atoms being bombarded are transformed into an unstable heavier element, which disintegrates. For example, in 1919, Rutherford bombarded nitrogen atoms with small, high-energy particles from radioactive elements and produced oxygen and hydrogen.

Rutherford thus made three important contributions to physics. First, in giving us the nuclear model of the atom, he founded nuclear physics. Second, he produced the first man-made atomic disintegration. Third, he was the first to change one chemical element, by experimental means, into another.

The atom described by Rutherford was modified by scientists who followed him. He had thought in terms of two subatomic particles—electrons and protons—but his successors discovered another, the neutron, and eventually more than thirty elementary particles. In their attempt to refine the model of the atom, they found it necessary to make some fundamental changes in the simple model advanced by Rutherford. Scientists still hold to Rutherford's basic idea of a tiny nucleus around which electrons move. But the more they have explored the nucleus and the orbital electrons, the more complex they have found the atom to be.

Planck and Einstein

In 1900 the German physicist Max Planck overturned the then common belief that energy was continuous and that it could be divided into any number of smaller units. Planck proved that energy could only be released in definite "packages," which he called *quanta* (the plural of *quantum,* the Latin word for "how much"). Planck's quantum theory formed the basis for a completely new approach to the study of matter and energy.

In 1905 an extraordinary young German scientist, Albert Einstein, published three papers that revolutionized physics. In one of them, he extended Planck's quantum theory to light. In a second paper, Einstein developed his equation $E = mc^2$. According to this equation, E (energy)

is equal to m (mass) multiplied by c^2 (the speed of light times itself). This formula means that a small amount of mass can be transformed into a tremendous amount of energy.

In a third paper, Einstein examined some of the basic concepts and ideas of mechanics and developed his special theory of relativity. He concluded that: (1) No material particles can move faster than the speed of light. (2) Motion can be measured only relative to some particular observer. Thus it does not make sense to speak of absolute motion, space, or time.

Einstein's special theory of relativity and his general theory of relativity—announced eleven years later—overturned long-held ideas. Isaac Newton and the scientists who had followed him thought of the material universe in terms of the three dimensions of length, breadth, and depth. They claimed that all material particles move toward one another because they possess a power of attraction called gravity. Einstein declared that all events occur not only in the three dimensions of space but also in a fourth dimension—time. This he called the space-time continuum. Gravity, he said, is not a property of matter, but a property of the space-time continuum.

Nuclear energy

In continuing the work of Rutherford, physicists have paid special attention to the nucleus, the central core of the atom. Neutrons and protons are tightly packed together in atomic nuclei and cannot be separated without great difficulty. In order to split the nuclei of atoms, atomic scientists have bombarded them with subatomic particles, as Rutherford first did in 1919. To do this, scientists have built gigantic particle-accelerators. These are machines designed to accelerate subatomic particles to speeds great enough to smash apart the tightly packed nuclei of atoms at which the subatomic particles are aimed.

The scientists who first studied the results of atom smashing were surprised to find that some part of the mass (material substance) of the atom was missing after its nucleus had been smashed. They were unable to account for the missing mass until they applied Einstein's equation, $E = mc^2$.

same processes produced all other living things. Charles Darwin, in one comprehensive theory, was thus able to advance an explanation for the variety and history of the plants and animals on earth.

Darwin's theory had a great impact on scientists. It set them gathering evidence to prove or disprove it—in the records of fossils as well as in the study of living organisms. It stirred up controversy because it placed man in the animal kingdom, an idea many people did not like. And it led, as you will see, to notions of progress and perfectability that were applied, often falsely, in fields far from science.

Genetics

Darwin left an important question unanswered: why were the offspring not like their parents? That is, how did variation (on which natural selection acted) come to be? Unknown to Darwin, during his lifetime a monk in Austria, Gregor Mendel, had been quietly gathering evidence about inherited variation. Mendel was the founder of genetics—the study of the ways in which inborn characteristics of plants and animals are inherited by their descendants. He did much of his work in the 1860's and 1870's, although scientists did not know about it until later.

Mendel worked in a quiet monastery garden, breeding pea plants. He took tall plants and short plants and mated them. The result was not medium-sized pea plants but all tall plants. Then Mendel fertilized these tall offspring with their own pollen, and was surprised to find that they produced a mixed generation of short and tall plants. In some way, shortness had been hidden away in the tall plants. Being a careful experimenter, Mendel counted the talls and shorts produced and discovered that there was a constant, simple ratio of talls to shorts.

From this experimentation Mendel concluded that inborn characteristics were not necessarily blended or mixed together, but were inherited as if they were associated with some kind of particle. For example, tall plants could carry, and pass on to the next generation, the particles for shortness. Mendel never discovered the actual

particles that were responsible for the inheritance of the inborn characteristics of his plants, but assumed that they existed because his experimentation pointed to their existence.

Later biologists went beyond Mendel's work and learned more about the nature of the particles involved in his experiments. They studied closely the formation of new plant and animal cells. Walther Flemming of Germany first described how cell division took place. He was also the first to observe threadlike bodies in cells that were dividing to form new cells. These bodies were later named chromosomes.

Biologists studying chromosomes soon learned that: (1) Each cell in a given organism has the same number of chromosomes; in man, for example, each cell has 46 chromosomes. (2) When reproductive cells divide, the new cells contain half the usual number of chromosomes. In 1902 an American biologist, Walter S. Sutton, concluded that the chromosomes were the particles involved in Mendel's experiments. The joining of cells during reproduction forms a new cell that now has the normal number of chromosomes. This newly formed cell is made up of chromosomes donated by the parent cells and will finally develop into an individual that shares, in some fashion, the characteristics of both.

Because a human being, for example, has far more characteristics than there are chromosomes in a cell, it soon became necessary to suppose that any given characteristic must be associated with a very small portion of a chromosome. In 1909, this small division of the chromosome was named the gene. It remained for future scientists to explore the possibility that the atom is as important to the gene, the cell, and the theory of evolution as it is to inanimate matter.

CHECKUP

1. How did the work of Oken, Brown, Schleiden, Schwann, and Virchow contribute to our knowledge of cells?

2. How did Lamarck's theory of evolution differ from that proposed by Darwin?

3. IDENTIFY: genetics, Flemming, chromosomes, gene.

620

Darwin, Mendel, and Freud were pioneers in the search for a fuller understanding of mankind. Charles Darwin, above, was chosen at the age of twenty-two to serve as official naturalist with a British scientific expedition that sailed from England in 1831. For five years he studied plants, animals, and fossils along the coasts of South America and on the islands of the Pacific. From these studies came his monumental theory of evolution. Gregor Mendel, upper right, spent most of his life as a monk in an Austrian monastery studying the inborn characteristics of garden peas. He published his findings in 1866, but the importance of his work was not realized until thirty-five years later. Sigmund Freud, at right, was a man of great industry, learning, and eloquence. Though firmly convinced of the correctness of his theories, Freud took a rather pessimistic view of mankind. He wrote: "I have not the courage to rise up before my fellow-men as a prophet, and I bow to their reproach that I can offer them no consolation."

3 Several sciences contributed knowledge about man and society

As this chapter moved from the physical to the biological sciences, you read that it was more difficult to study living beings than to study inanimate objects. Even greater difficulties arise when the subject matter concerns the complexities of human behavior.

The social sciences

The social sciences are those that study man as a member of society. The subjects with which they deal are old and familiar—man's economic development, political institutions, history, and relations with his fellow men. But the idea of making them objective and factual—that is, social *sciences*—was a new one in the 1800's. For example, the study of politics dates back to Plato and Aristotle, and was the subject of such thinkers as Machiavelli, Locke, and Rousseau. In the 1800's, however, it became known as political science, and men tried to study law and government as objectively as possible.

Another social science, economics, began with Adam Smith, about whom you read in Chapter 21. But not until the later 1800's did economists begin to collect and arrange masses of statistics in order to test their theories.

Like political science, history dates back to the Greeks. It too, however, underwent change in the 1800's. Influenced by nationalism, many scholars wrote histories detailing the accomplishments and glories of their native countries. Historical writing was based more and more on systematic inquiry and careful organization of material. Historians began a massive search for the evidence of the past contained in documents, diaries, letters, and other sources. New interpretations of man's history began to emerge from the evidence discovered. Among the greatest historians of the 1800's were Leopold von Ranke of Germany, Thomas Macaulay of England, and George Bancroft of the United States. The French philosopher Voltaire was noted for his attention to social and intellectual history. He influenced many historians to concentrate less on wars and great men and devote more time to the masses of

men and how they lived. Later historians, influenced by Darwin, tried to see historical events in terms of evolution.

One social science that first emerged in the 1800's was anthropology, the study of man's cultures. You have already read about some of the dramatic discoveries in the field of archeology (a branch of anthropology): Champollion's use of the Rosetta Stone to read Egyptian hieroglyphics and Rawlinson's decipherment of cuneiform writing. It was also in the 1800's that men realized how old the earth was and how long man had lived on it. They found prehistoric cave paintings, discovered Egyptian, Sumerian, and Assyrian remains, and excavated such buried cities as Troy and Mycenae.

Sociology. Another social science that first appeared in the 1800's was sociology, the study of man's relationships with his fellow man. This branch of the social sciences was initiated by the Frenchman Auguste Comte. More than any other social science, sociology tried to adapt the methods and theories of the various biological sciences.

Herbert Spencer, an early sociologist, believed that Darwin's theory of evolution could be used as the basis for studying human communities. Darwin, as you know, claimed that nature selected certain individuals and permitted others to perish. Spencer applied this doctrine of natural selection to society in his *Principles of Sociology,* three volumes published in 1877–1896. If you study society, he said, you will find superior men who are well adapted to it. In exercising their "natural rights," these men also contribute to the progress of mankind as a whole. At the same time, society will contain inferior men—the poor, the lazy, the stupid, the criminal—who contribute nothing.

Spencer wrote that society, like the plant and animal worlds, had evolved from lower to higher forms through natural selection and survival of the fittest. This means that for progress to continue, inferior men should not be helped in any way. If they were permitted to die out, then society would be made up exclusively of superior men. This application of Darwin's theory came to be known as Social Darwinism.

Spencer's ideas were never very widely accepted in England. They found their home in the United States, where leaders of big business and some important sociologists welcomed them. Spencer's theory of social progress through natural selection became for a time a powerful force in American social thought. It was later rejected when sociologists discovered that it was impossible to divide mankind into two groups—the superior and the inferior.

Social scientists realized that they could not get quick results by borrowing wholesale from the other sciences. Fortunately, not all sociologists followed the path of Herbert Spencer. There were others who believed that sociology could become a science not by borrowing theories but by using scientific methods—observing closely, gathering facts, and basing theories on these facts. This group had its beginnings in the work of a Belgian mathematician of the early 1800's, Adolphe Quételet (kay·TLEH). He carefully compiled information on such topics as crime, births, and deaths and produced detailed statistical tables. However, many people consider that the first truly scientific work in the field of sociology was a study of suicide by a French scholar, Émile Durkheim, published in 1897.

Psychology

Closely related to the social sciences (and considered by some scholars to belong to this category) was psychology, another new science of the 1800's. Psychology is the study of the human mind—how it works and how it affects man's behavior. Although its origins can be traced back to Greek thinkers, it was long considered a branch of philosophy because it was not experimental.

Two philosophers of the 1600's formulated important theories about the working of the mind. René Descartes (day·KART) of France thought that the human mind was best studied as merely another organ of the body and not as some special soul or spirit independent of the body. John Locke of England (whose political theories you read

"Anxiety" by Edvard Munch

"We should stop painting interiors with people reading and women knitting. We should create people who breathe and feel and suffer and love." So said Edvard Munch, a Norwegian artist of the late 1800's. With his interest in men's deepest feelings—especially their undefined fears and tensions—Munch mirrored in art what many psychologists were investigating in science. "Anxiety" shows a ghostly procession of people with mask-like faces, fear blotting out all their individuality. The painting could be said to echo Munch's statement: "I hear the scream in nature."

about in Chapter 17) tried to explain how the mind came to have its thoughts and ideas. Locke believed that the mind of a newborn infant was like a blank sheet of paper on which his various experiences made impressions. These impressions, linked together, or associated, in the mind, were the source of the growing individual's thoughts.

For a century and a half after the time of Descartes and Locke, men spun theories about the nature of man's mind. Then in the mid-1800's, a number of scientists in Germany determined to make psychology an experimental science like biology. Ernst Weber conducted experiments measuring man's ability to sense small differences in the weight of light objects and found that his results could be expressed in a precise mathematical formula. Hermann von Helmholtz studied man's perceptions of sound and color and explained them in terms of the physical structure of the eye and ear.

Wilhelm Wundt opened the first psychological laboratory in 1879. There, investigators attempted to analyze their own conscious experiences in the way that chemists break down chemical compounds into their elements.

Pavlov. Darwin's theory of evolution made a strong impact on psychology. Among other things, it influenced psychologists to study animal behavior and to relate their findings to man. The most famous of these early experimenters was a Russian biologist, Ivan Pavlov, who discovered the conditioned reflex in the 1890's. Psychologists had long known that certain behavior was automatic. A child does not have to be taught to pull his hand away from fire, but removes it automatically. In the same way, a dog does not have to be taught to salivate (water at the mouth) when he eats his food. This kind of involuntary response to a stimulus is called reflex action.

Pavlov proved, by experiments with dogs, that certain reflex actions could be conditioned, or taught, to an animal. First he offered food to a dog; the dog salivated. Second, he rang a bell each time the food was presented to the dog. The animal salivated and also began associating the sound of the bell with food. Finally, he offered no food to the dog but rang the bell. The dog salivated when the bell was rung. It had been conditioned to salivate when it heard the bell. As a result of his researches, Pavlov believed that all habits, and even mental activity, are chains of conditioned reflexes.

Pavlov's dogs had been conditioned to respond in a certain way to a certain stimulus. This stimulus-response pattern of behavior was quickly developed by an American psychologist, John B. Watson, and others into a whole system of psychology called behaviorism. They explained all human behavior in terms of the responses of the nervous system to the stimuli of the environment. The behaviorists, as they were called, were interested only in the observable, measurable response of the animal to some definite stimulus—food, sound, light.

Freud. Another explanation of human behavior was developed by the Austrian physician Sigmund Freud (FROID) in the early 1900's. Whereas Wundt had studied the conscious mind, and the behaviorists refused to study the mind at all, Freud introduced the revolutionary concept of the unconscious—that is, the mental processes of which a person is unaware—as a determining factor in man's behavior. He had hypnotized certain mentally disturbed patients and had found that under hypnosis they could remember past experiences they could not otherwise recall. Freud believed that early experiences had led to their illness, and he treated them by gradually bringing the disturbing memories, fears, and conflicts to the level of consciousness. To do this he studied their dreams and encouraged them to talk about whatever came to their minds. Then he interpreted their dreams and thoughts to show what lay beneath them in the unconscious mind. This process of revealing and analyzing the unconscious is called psychoanalysis. Freud discussed his theory of psychoanalysis fully in a book titled *A General Introduction to Psychoanalysis,* which was published in 1920.

Although details of Freud's theories were later discarded or challenged in the light of increasing knowledge, much of his basic theory and method formed the foundation of psychiatry, the study and treatment of mental illness.

CHECKUP

1. How did the study of politics, economics, and history change in the 1800's?

2. What is sociology? Summarize Spencer's theory of Social Darwinism.

3. How did Pavlov's proof of the conditioned reflex influence the thinking of the behaviorists?

4. How did Freud's theories conflict with those of the behaviorists?

5. IDENTIFY: anthropology, Quételet, Durkheim, Descartes, Wundt, reflex action, psychoanalysis.

CHAPTER REVIEW

Chapter 30   Scientists Explored the Nature of Matter and Man   (1803–1930)

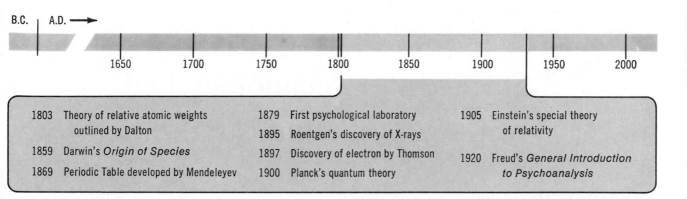

1803 Theory of relative atomic weights outlined by Dalton	1879 First psychological laboratory	1905 Einstein's special theory of relativity
1859 Darwin's *Origin of Species*	1895 Roentgen's discovery of X-rays	
	1897 Discovery of electron by Thomson	1920 Freud's *General Introduction to Psychoanalysis*
1869 Periodic Table developed by Mendeleyev	1900 Planck's quantum theory	

CHAPTER SUMMARY

Pure science developed rapidly in the 1800's. The physical sciences were transformed by the atomic theory. Knowledge of the atom was contributed by chemists Dalton and Mendeleyev and furthered by physicists Roentgen, Thomson, and the Curies. Rutherford's model of the atom marked the founding of the science of nuclear physics. The study of matter and energy was revolutionized by the brilliant work of Einstein. In 1905 he announced his application of Planck's quantum theory to light, described the transformation of matter into energy, and outlined his special theory of relativity. Later physicists, working with the nucleus, built huge particle accelerators to smash atoms.

In the biological sciences, progress was made in three important fields. Cell theory profited from the work of Oken, Brown, Schleiden, Schwann, and Virchow. The theory of evolution advanced by Darwin had an enormous impact on scientists and laymen. And the new science of genetics, founded by Mendel, answered many questions about biological inheritance.

The social sciences that had long been developing —political science, economics, and history—became more scientific. New ones included anthropology and sociology. Spencer's Social Darwinism tried to apply Darwin's theory to human communities, while the work of Quételet and Durkheim was based on close observation and carefully gathered data.

Another new science was psychology. German scientists did important work in this field, as did a Russian, Pavlov. One school of psychology based on his work was behaviorism. It was challenged by a great Austrian, Freud, who introduced the idea of the un-conscious and developed a psychiatric treatment known as psychoanalysis.

QUESTIONS FOR DISCUSSION

1. In the past, scientists found it hard to make a living, while today they are in a favored position in this regard. How do you explain this fact? What does it indicate about the contemporary world?

2. What is the difference between applied science and pure science? If you were president of a large company dealing with scientific products, would you invest your company's money in pure science? Why or why not?

3. Leonardo da Vinci, in addition to his work as an artist, mastered almost all the scientific knowledge of his day. Why would this be impossible for a present-day scientist?

4. Knowledge of the physical and biological sciences has increased more rapidly than understanding of psychology, sociology, or political science. Do you see any problems resulting from this situation? Explain.

5. What is a scientific theory? Is knowledge in science always final? What do you think constitutes scientific truth?

6. What did Social Darwinism teach? How would you evaluate its teachings?

PROJECTS

1. Make a chart listing fifteen people discussed in this chapter, together with their discoveries in the fields of physical science, biological science, and the social sciences.

2. Write a short essay analyzing the potential promise and peril of man's use of nuclear energy.

CHAPTER 31

Science and Technology Led to Large-Scale Industrialization

"The Bridge," by Joseph Stella

The Industrial Revolution of the 1700's was, as you read in Chapter 21, a technological revolution in which the use of machinery and the factory system increasingly replaced the production of goods by hand. As this system of production continued to grow and spread during the 1800's, scientific knowledge was also growing at a rapid rate.

For almost a century after Watt and Lavoisier, industry and science grew side by side but independently. Beginning about 1870, however, the findings of pure science were applied to manufacturing. The result was a new wave of industrial growth that produced the scientific industry and the industrial science that are characteristic of today's world.

A typical feature of large industrial organizations today is the industrial research laboratory. The modern industrialist hires scientists to assist industry in the production of a better or cheaper product. A research chemist may be asked to develop a more powerful gasoline or a strong new plastic material. A research physicist may be given the job of creating a new electrical lighting system or of improving the telephone communication network. A research biologist may work on a new vaccine for a drug company or on a new baby food for a food processor.

One of the first industrial research laboratories was founded in Germany during the 1880's. The leaders of the German chemical industry created the research laboratory in order to use the latest chemical discoveries in the manufacture of dyes, fertilizers, drugs, and explosives.

In the United States the electrical industry provided the first research laboratories. One of the earliest was the laboratory the inventor Thomas Edison set up for himself. "Inventions to order" was Edison's slogan, and businessmen brought their problems to him to be solved. Bell Laboratories, founded in the late 1800's by the American Telephone and Telegraph Company, was among the first American industrial research laboratories. The General Electric Company founded its research laboratory in 1900.

The industrial laboratory had advantages for both the scientist and the firm that hired him. It gave the scientist financial security. In return he helped solve the company's scientific problems, and he usually gave the company the right to patent any inventions or processes he developed.

This meant that for seventeen years the company had the exclusive right to manufacture and sell such products.

As science became more important to industry, universities expanded their science departments and added research laboratories where scientists explored the outer limits of scientific knowledge for its own sake. Governments put scientists to work on practical problems having to do with navigation, natural resources, agriculture, and the weather. Science and the scientist took leading places in industrial nations.

THE CHAPTER SECTIONS:

1. Science and invention fostered rapid industrial advance (1831–1930)

2. Industrial growth produced the giant business enterprise (1870–1920)

3. Industrialization in some countries had effects in all (1850–1930)

1   Science and invention fostered rapid industrial advance

After 1870 the application of science to industrial problems had particular impact in three directions: (1) the development and use of new sources of power, (2) the creation of new products and materials and the improvement of old ones, and (3) inventions that provided rapid communication over long distances.

Electricity for power and light

As you know, the early Industrial Revolution depended largely on the use of steam power to run machines. As industry grew during the 1800's, businessmen were always on the lookout for new and better sources of power. In the 1870's a tremendous new power source—electricity—was developed by applying the findings of pure science to the needs of industry.

The scientific key to the problem was a discovery made by an English scientist, Michael Faraday, in 1831. From the work of Ampère and other scientists, he knew that electricity could produce magnetism; he wanted to find out whether

magnetism could produce electricity. He found that by moving a magnet through a coil of wire, he could produce an electric current in the wire.

Faraday had been interested chiefly in exploring the nature of electricity. Other men took his discovery and used it to develop the dynamo, or electric generator. Driven by a steam engine or by water power, the dynamo transformed mechanical power into electrical energy, which in turn could be used to run machinery in factories.

English and American inventors kept trying to make use of another scientific discovery about electricity—that a current passing through certain kinds of wire caused the wire to glow. Here was a possible source of light for city streets, homes, and factories. Electric light bulbs were first produced in 1845, but they burned out in a very short time. In 1879, Thomas Edison, sending a current through a carbon filament, made a bulb that glowed for two days before burning out. In a few years, after further improvements, lighting by electricity replaced gas light.

To make electricity practical, it had to be carried from the place where it was generated to the place where it would be used. After much work on the problem, Edison developed a successful central powerhouse and transmission system that was put into effect in 1882 in New York City, London, and Milan.

The electrical industry grew by leaps and bounds. Waterfalls, such as Niagara Falls, were tapped to run huge dynamos, whose hydroelectric power was sent long distances through wires. Tremendous dams were built in many countries to provide artificial sources of water power for hydroelectric systems. The use of electricity became a measure of whether a region was "advanced" or "backward."

As electricity came to be produced and transmitted on a large scale in the late 1800's, electric motors replaced steam engines in factories. Where hydroelectric power was not available or was too expensive, steam engines turned the generators at central powerhouses.

The internal-combustion engine

The electric motor had one limitation—it had to be connected with its power supply. Therefore it was not very useful for moving vehicles. Electric railways were used in big cities in the form of subways and streetcars, but they were impractical for long distances. Thus for some years steam engines continued to pull trains, and horses continued to draw carriages and wagons.

Then an engine was invented that could use a portable fuel supply of gasoline or oil. It was called the internal-combustion engine because the combustion, or burning, of fuel took place inside a closed cylinder. (In the steam engine, combustion takes place outside the cylinder.)

The first practical internal-combustion engines were used in France in the 1860's to run pumps and printing presses. But they used street-lighting gas as fuel, which meant that they, too, were tied to their source of power.

Automobiles. In the late 1800's, several European inventors worked on gasoline engines that would drive self-propelled vehicles. (The word *automobile* was first used for such vehicles in

1876.) Pioneers in this field included Gottlieb Daimler and Karl Benz of Germany and Louis Renault of France. The first successful gasoline-powered automobile in the United States was built by Charles and Frank Duryea in 1893. Three years later, the American inventor Henry Ford produced his first automobile.

These early automobiles were handmade and very expensive. In 1909, Ford began producing an automobile that was inexpensive, dependable, and easy to manufacture. This was the famous Model T Ford. Within eighteen years, Ford's factory manufactured 15 million of them.

The diesel engine. In 1892 a German engineer, Rudolf Diesel, invented an economical oil-burning engine. It was heavy, but it produced more power from less fuel, and it proved useful in powering vehicles hauling heavy loads. In 1925 the first diesel locomotive went into service and began to replace the steam locomotive on the railroads of the world. The diesel engine was also used in ships and in trucks hauling heavy loads.

Airplanes. Since the 1700's, men had used balloons, which are lighter than air, to float above the earth. Beginning in the 1800's, inventors tried to devise a heavier-than-air machine that would actually fly—an airplane. Many early planes were models and were not designed to carry people. The first men to succeed in flying an airplane in powered, sustained, controlled flight were Wilbur and Orville Wright of the United States. They achieved this flight at Kitty Hawk, North Carolina, in 1903. It lasted 12 seconds and covered 120 feet.

The Wright brothers' achievement was another instance of the combination of science and technology. The Wrights succeeded where other men had failed because they studied aerodynamics (the principles governing the movement of air around objects) and used the internal-combustion engine to drive their plane through the air.

From the Wright brothers' modest beginning, an important airplane industry developed. World War I transformed the plane from a novelty into a military weapon. After the war, it began to be used commercially. In the 1920's, its chief use was for carrying mail, with a few passengers. In

Transportation and communications profited from an outburst of creative inventiveness in the late 1800's and early 1900's. Several men in Europe and America experimented with automobiles. Among them was Karl Benz of Germany, shown at right with a passenger in an 1887 model of his auto. A wealth of inventions sprang from the mind of Thomas Edison, who characterized genius as "one per cent inspiration and ninety-nine per cent perspiration." Below, he works in his laboratory at Menlo Park, New Jersey. His restless energy led him to explore almost every phase of modern technology, justly earning him the title of "the wizard of Menlo Park." Using the discoveries of Marconi and others, inventors developed radio in the 1900's. The earliest broadcasting stations, like the one at bottom, were shrouded with cloth draperies in a primitive effort to make them soundproof.

the 1930's, improved planes and better schedules encouraged passenger travel. Airports were built at major cities, and in the late 1930's, passenger planes began to fly across the Atlantic.

Petroleum and chemicals

The internal-combustion engine, like the steam engine, was a technological advance embodying no new scientific principles. But its fuels, gasoline and oil, were part of another industrial success story in which science and technology combined.

Until its use in the internal-combustion engine, gasoline was a waste product from the refining of petroleum to produce kerosene for lighting. Then, around 1900, natural gas and electric lights began to replace kerosene, and the newly invented automobile increased the demand for gasoline. Kerosene became the relatively useless by-product and gasoline the major source of profit.

In the early days, a hundred gallons of crude (unrefined) oil produced only eleven gallons of gasoline. Oil producers could not keep up with the increasing demand for gasoline without producing huge quantities of unwanted kerosene and other waste products. Scientists were put to work to solve the problem, and by the 1930's, they had succeeded in developing ways to produce proportionately more gasoline and less kerosene from crude oil.

The modern chemical industry had begun in 1856, when William Perkin, an eighteen-year-old English chemist, accidentally produced the synthetic (artificial) dye mauve. Before Perkin's discovery, all cloth-dyeing materials were extracted from plants, animals, or minerals. Perkin's mauve was made from aniline, which in turn was derived from coal tar, a waste product formed in the production of coal gas.

German industrialists, using Perkin's discovery as a springboard, developed not only a whole range of aniline dyes but many other products synthesized from coal tar and other substances. The Germans soon led the world in the production of chemicals. World War I, by cutting off exports from Germany, stimulated the development of chemical industries in other countries, especially in the United States.

Metallurgy and the steel industry

Metals also benefited from scientific discoveries. The extraction and processing of metallic ores became a science known as metallurgy.

The Industrial Revolution of the 1700's and early 1800's made steel a basic industry on which all others depended. Bessemer's process of steel-making depended on the use of iron ore containing very little phosphorus. Where deposits of such ore were available, as in the United States, huge steel-making industries sprang up. Where they were not available, as in Great Britain, the Bessemer process was not so effective. In the late 1800's, however, scientists developed the open-hearth furnace, which enabled manufacturers to use lower-grade ores.

Metallurgists learned new ways to remove impurities from iron. They also developed various steel alloys, adding other metals to steel to give it greater hardness, strength, or other desirable qualities. Improvements in steel led to its use as a building material. Structural steel was first employed in the United States in the 1870's. During the next decade, builders constructed the first skyscraper, a ten-story insurance company building in Chicago.

New means of communication

The modern communications industry developed out of the theoretical work of a small group of scientists in the 1800's. The application of their discoveries and founding of new industries was usually carried on by other men.

You have read how Morse built on the work of Ampère and Volta in developing the telegraph. In a similar way, Alexander Graham Bell made use of the discoveries of Faraday in inventing the telephone. In the 1870's, several men were attempting to send the human voice over a distance by means of an electrical circuit. Bell, the only one of these inventors to succeed, was an American teacher of the deaf. In 1876 he patented the telephone.

Telephones are useless if only a few people rent them. Bell and the men who had financed his early experiments formed the Bell Telephone Company in 1880 to create a telephone network

Charlie Chaplin in "Modern Times"

Mechanization created feelings of uneasiness in a great many people. Among them was the brilliant comedian Charlie Chaplin. Ironically enough, he used the new mechanical invention, the movie, as the vehicle for his satire. "Modern Times" was released in 1936. Chaplin not only starred in the film but also wrote, produced, and directed it. The movie depicts him—in his usual role as a gentle tramp—at work in a huge factory. Here he is shown tightening bolts on an endless assembly line. In pursuit of one neglected bolt, he knocks other workers over, upsets the entire factory routine, and ends a captive of the machinery.

Film Stills Archive, The Museum of Modern Art

to join the instruments together. In 1885, long-distance lines were put into service to supplement and link the various regional networks.

The telegraph and telephone depend on wires strung between instruments. A way to send messages through space without wires was developed in 1895 by a young Italian inventor, Guglielmo Marconi.

Marconi's invention was based on the work of two earlier scientists, James Clerk Maxwell of Great Britain and Heinrich Hertz of Germany. Maxwell, a follower of Faraday, had made a mathematical study of electricity and magnetism, and in 1864 he predicted the existence of invisible electromagnetic waves that travel through space with the speed of light. In the 1880's, Hertz not only proved that such waves did exist, by transmitting and receiving them, but also measured their length and velocity.

Marconi invented instruments for sending and receiving these radio waves, as they came to be called, and his wireless telegraph soon proved itself valuable for ship-to-ship and ship-to-shore communication. In 1901 he sent the first wireless-telegraph message across the Atlantic Ocean.

The invention of the vacuum tube in 1904 made possible a receiving set that could pick up radio waves carrying music and the human voice. Regular commercial radio broadcasting began in 1920, when station KDKA of Pittsburgh started its operations. The British Broadcasting Corporation (BBC) was formed in 1923. In the next twenty years, radio became a major communications medium in many parts of the world.

Several other inventions in the field of communications took shape in the late 1800's and early 1900's. The first practical phonograph was invented by Edison in 1877, although sound recordings were not very accurate until the 1920's. The first photographs were made in the early 1800's. For many years, however, photography was a difficult and time-consuming process, since it required long exposures on glass plates. Only after 1888, when George Eastman of the United States introduced his Kodak—which used a roll of film and exposed portions of it for a fraction of a second—could the average person enjoy owning and using a camera.

631

Using this same sort of flexible film, Edison developed an early type of motion picture in the 1890's. By 1927, when sound was added to the motion picture, movies had become one of the most popular forms of entertainment.

CHECKUP

1. What is the purpose of the industrial research laboratory? In what fields were early industrial research laboratories created in Germany? in the United States?

2. What developments made electricity a new source of power?

3. What is an internal-combustion engine? How was it put to use?

4. What developments in petroleum research, chemicals, and metallurgy fostered industrial growth?

5. IDENTIFY: Daimler, Model T, Diesel, Wright brothers, aerodynamics, Bell, Marconi, Eastman.

2 Industrial growth produced the giant business enterprise

The rapid growth of industry brought many changes to the factory and to business enterprise. Some of these changes dated back to the early Industrial Revolution; others came about as science transformed industry from 1870 on.

Mass production

One development was mass production—a system of manufacturing large numbers of items exactly alike. It was much faster, and therefore cheaper, than making items one at a time, and it had other advantages.

Prior to industrialization, products such as firearms were handmade by master craftsmen and their apprentices. Each firearm would be produced by one man. It would be fashioned, part by part, by the craftsman as he taught his apprentices the craft of making guns. The finished product might be a masterpiece of individual craftsmanship. But it had one major flaw. Each part was made to operate in that weapon alone and could not be transferred to another—even a similar one made by the same craftsman. Furthermore, the apprentices had to work many years until they mastered all the skills necessary to manufacture a completed firearm. This system produced a small number of handmade items that were expensive and difficult to repair.

Division of labor. Industrialization changed the craftsman system. Instead of relying on a master and his apprentices, factory owners hired large numbers of unskilled laborers, divided the manufacturing process into a series of simple steps, and then assigned a step to each worker. This process, a form of division of labor, produced a large number of items in a given length of time and therefore lowered the cost. The use of machinery aided the division of labor, since machines performed many of the steps.

Interchangeable parts. The American inventor Eli Whitney used division of labor in making muskets in the early 1800's. In Whitney's factory, some men worked on musket barrels, others on trigger mechanisms, and still others on the wooden stocks.

An essential part of Whitney's system was the use of interchangeable parts for his firearms. He designed machinery that could be operated by unskilled workmen and yet turn out identical, interchangeable parts. It was this development that made division of labor possible in a product made of several parts that had to fit together. Whitney's system resulted in the speedy production of a large number of muskets that were inexpensive and could be easily repaired. If part of a musket broke, it could be replaced by a part that was identical.

Other manufacturers quickly realized the usefulness of interchangeable parts, and Whitney's principle was widely adopted. The increasing use of precision power tools after 1900 was of great importance in the making of interchangeable parts for complex products.

The assembly line. Division of labor and the system of interchangeable parts were two essential elements of mass production. A third element

632

was the assembly line. Until the late 1800's, the actual assembling of separate parts into a final product was done at a central point and was a slow and inefficient process. Then manufacturers devised the assembly line, which made use of a conveyor belt that carried the unfinished products past each worker in turn. As each item passed a worker, he performed his special task. This saved his time and energy, increasing the number of times per hour he could perform his task.

Chicago meat packers of the 1890's were some of the earliest users of the assembly-line technique. Hogs or cattle, hanging from a moving chain, were carried past a series of meat cutters, each trained to carry out one portion of the butchering operation.

Henry Ford saw great potentialities in the mass-production system. By applying it to the making of automobiles, he founded one of the largest industries in the United States. In 1913, Ford assembly-line workmen were producing automobiles at the rate of one every ninety-three minutes. The frame of the automobile was carried along on a conveyor belt from one worker to the next. Each man made his small contribution to the finished product by adding one or more of the 5,000 interchangeable parts that constituted the Ford Model T. Mass production lowered the price of automobiles and made them available to most American families.

If automobiles could be mass-produced, so could thousands of other items. Following the lead of Ford, American and European industrialists began to mass-produce clothing, furniture, and heavy machinery. Because mass production usually lowered the cost of an item, more and more people in the industrialized nations were able to buy more and more things and enjoy a higher standard of living.

The corporation

Mass-production methods could not be used to any extent by small companies having few workers. Nor could small companies afford to buy the machinery necessary for large-scale production, hire the engineers and managers to plan production, and employ scientists for research. These things required great amounts of capital. Companies with sizable capital could also save by buying raw materials in large quantities at lower prices. They could even own sources of raw materials, such as mines and forests.

As the scale of business enterprises grew during the 1800's, therefore, the corporation became the dominant form of business organization. Corporations were similar to the joint-stock companies of the Commercial Revolution. Individuals bought shares of stock, elected directors to decide policies and hire managers, and received dividends according to the number of shares they owned.

In a joint-stock company, however, shareholders were responsible for the company's debts. If a company went bankrupt, a man who had invested only a few dollars might have to contribute thousands to pay off creditors. In a corporation, the shareholder's liability, or financial responsibility, was limited to the amount he had invested. For this reason, corporations could attract greater numbers of investors.

In the late 1800's, the size of corporations increased greatly both in the amounts of capital invested and in the size of the manufacturing establishment or group of enterprises. When the American financier J. P. Morgan and his associates formed the United States Steel Company in 1901, the new company had a capital investment of a billion dollars. It was only the first of many billion-dollar corporations. Banks and other financial institutions played an increasingly important role in forming and operating large corporations. For this reason, capitalism from the late 1800's on is often called finance capitalism.

Increasing the size of a corporation did not solve all its problems. A large manufacturing enterprise could produce goods at a lower cost than a small one. To get lower costs, however, it had to operate at full capacity, turning out goods in as great a quantity as possible. There was then the problem of selling the goods.

If a number of corporations were producing the same products, competition became very keen. If they tried to sell their products by cutting prices, the smaller and less efficient businesses suffered. Often they had to sell out to larger firms.

Mass production of goods took many different forms, but was almost always based on three ideas: division of labor, so that each workman could become efficient and speedy in performing one single operation; interchangeable parts, so that the objects produced in this way could be easily fitted together; and the assembly line, which saved time by bringing the job to the workman.

Such ideas are seen at work in the three different industries pictured here. At right, women stuff pickles into bottles—one phase of an operation that included the pickling itself, sterilizing, and sealing. Below, workmen slaughter pigs, dip them in scalding water to remove the bristles, and begin the butchering process. So efficient was this that one firm proudly claimed: "We use everything but the squeal."

Above, the chassis of Model T Fords move along an outside track to a point where bodies will be lowered onto them and bolted down. When completely assembled, right, the cars are cranked up, given a quick test run, and loaded onto freight cars to be delivered to an eager American market.

As a result, although the size of individual corporations increased steadily, the number of individual corporations decreased just as steadily. The world had entered an era of "big business." In 1927, almost half the wealth and income of corporations was owned by 200 companies.

Not only were there fewer corporations, but many that did survive were controlled by a single individual owning more than half the stock. In the United States, such men included John D. Rockefeller of Standard Oil and Andrew Carnegie of Carnegie Steel.

Monopolies

Even the giants found that competition was not the blessing that Adam Smith had proclaimed —at least, not to the owners. Competition that reduced selling prices also reduced profits to the stockholders. Therefore, corporations tried to avoid competition by getting together to create monopolies. (A monopoly, as you have read, has complete control of a commodity, a service, or a market.) In this way they could control competitive production and fix prices to insure maximum profit to the stockholder. The consumer had to pay these prices or go without the goods. Monopolies could also keep wages down, or force down the prices the corporations paid for raw materials and supplies.

Monopolies became especially common in Germany (where they were known as cartels) in the decades before World War I. Sometimes industries in different countries formed international cartels to fix world prices or to control raw materials or markets.

Business and government

The expansion of industry and the growth of powerful corporations became the concern of governments because national well-being was involved. Different countries handled the situation in different ways, according to their history, traditions, and special circumstances.

In the United States, where the tradition of limited government authority was strong, the trend in the 1800's was for the government to leave business alone. This policy of noninterfer-

Monopoly, sitting among its enormous profits, greedily demands and receives more tribute.

ence allowed the giant business firms to do pretty much as they pleased.

In some European countries the government played a more active role. This was true in Germany, for example. You have read how Bismarck, eager to make the country as rich and powerful as Great Britain and France, encouraged the growth of cartels in the chemical industry, among others.

Some monopolies make economic sense. It would be ridiculous, for example, for competing companies to string several sets of telephone wires across a country, or for a subscriber to call one friend on one company's lines and another friend on another's. One large centralized system is not only economical but essential. An enterprise of this sort is called a natural monopoly. Natural monopolies include such public utilities as the telephone, telegraph, electric power, natural gas, and transportation systems.

Where such industries began as private enterprises, most governments left ownership to the stockholders of the monopolistic corporation, but stepped in to regulate rates, routes, resources, safety conditions, and other matters of public concern. In many countries, however, the governments built and owned transportation, communications, and power systems.

During the 1800's and early 1900's, most nations followed a laissez-faire policy toward monopolies that were created by corporations simply to control prices or markets in the interest of the corporations. The United States was the only major nation to try to control monopolies (or trusts, as they were generally called there). In 1890, Congress passed the Sherman Antitrust Act, which, although not generally effective until after World War I, did enable the government to break up the Standard Oil Company—Rockefeller's trust —in 1911.

During World War I, governments became involved in economic activities as they attempted to mobilize national resources for the war effort. In Russia, after the second revolution, the government actually took over the ownership of all industries. Although few other countries took such extreme steps, the general tendency in the years after World War I was toward greater and greater government regulation of business.

CHECKUP

1. What three things are necessary for mass production? What is its chief advantage?
2. What is the principal difference between a joint-stock company and a corporation? Why was this difference an advantage to the growth of industry?
3. IDENTIFY: finance capitalism, natural monopoly, Sherman Antitrust Act.

Industrialization in some countries had effects in all

It is no wonder that people living in the late 1800's and early 1900's believed in progress. The world was changing more rapidly than it ever had before. And the rate of change continued to increase over the years.

News and travel

One of the greatest changes after 1850 was in the ease with which news, people, and goods could travel from one part of the world to another. In 1850, most people knew little of the world beyond the farm or town where they lived. By the early 1900's, the world was brought to their doorstep by inventions like the telegraph, telephone, and wireless.

An older means of communication, the newspaper, profited from increased mechanization. New inventions made printing fast and cheap. Among these inventions were the linotype, which set type by machine instead of by hand, and the electrically powered rotary press. By the 1930's, newspapers were even carrying up-to-the-minute news pictures from far-off places, transmitted by wireless.

Radio broadcasts brought news of the outside world to even the remotest rural areas. Radio also made it possible for one man's voice to reach millions of people at once. Government leaders of the 1900's made skillful use of this means of mass communication.

Transportation systems grew enormously after 1850. By World War I, railroads crisscrossed North America, Western Europe, the British dominions, and Japan. Transcontinental systems were constructed or planned. The Trans-Siberian railroad, the longest in the world, reached from Moscow to Vladivostok. A railroad line crossed South America through the high Andes Mountains. You have read about British plans for a Cape-to-Cairo railroad in Africa and German attempts to build a line from Berlin to Baghdad. Though neither line was ever completely finished, parts were put into use.

After World War I, the automobile began to take the place of the railroad for passenger travel in many regions. Networks of hard-surface roads were built, reaching beyond the railroads into remote places. Trucks began to compete with the railroads for freight, and the swift-flying airplane for passengers.

Ships were larger, more numerous, and faster. The diesel engine and high-powered steam turbine replaced less powerful steam engines. After World War I, oil replaced coal as fuel for both steam-powered and diesel-powered ships. Three major canals were built to shorten shipping routes. Two of these were the Suez Canal, connecting the Mediterranean and Red seas, and the Panama Canal, across the Isthmus of Panama. In Europe, the Kiel Canal, completed in 1895, shortened by 300 miles the trip between the North Sea and the Baltic Sea.

Most of the few unexplored regions of the world were mapped in the early 1900's. In 1909 the American explorer Robert E. Peary became the first man to reach the North Pole; a Norwegian, Roald Amundsen, discovered the South Pole in 1911. Amundsen was the first to navigate the Northwest Passage to the Pacific, which explorers had been seeking since the 1500's.

Differences in industrial growth

Science and industry produced rapid changes, but not at the same speed all over the world. In fact, one of the results of industrialization was that some parts of the world advanced far ahead of others in material development so that there were much greater differences in ways of life than ever before. In medieval times, for example, the life of the average European was not very different from that of the average Chinese. But by the 1900's, industrialization had given the European more to eat and wear, better material surroundings, and greater freedom to move about and change jobs, while the life of the Chinese remained similar in many ways to that of his medieval ancestors.

As you read in Chapter 21, Great Britain first led the world in industrialization. Other Western European countries, notably Belgium and France, followed. The United States was second only to Britain as an industrial nation by 1870. After unification, Germany caught up rapidly. Italy, however, lagged behind because it lacked the necessary resources. Most of central and eastern Europe was also backward industrially.

Japan, discussed earlier, was the first Asian country to begin large-scale industrialization. In other parts of Asia, technological progress was slower. India developed a textile industry in the 1880's and built up iron, steel, and chemical industries during World War I. But on the whole, India remained a poor agricultural nation, with only a few large manufacturing cities. China, too, was rural and poor. In much of Africa, South America, and Southeast Asia, the economy remained rural and, in many places, primitive.

By the late 1800's, it seemed clear to anyone looking at Western Europe, the United States, or Japan, that industrialization brought a nation wealth and power. A wealthy nation could afford a strong fighting force, and it could make its influence felt wherever it bought its raw materials or sold its manufactures. This strength made other nations envious or fearful. As a result, many nations, instead of importing foreign products, learned foreign methods of production and built competing industries.

International trade

Mass production requires mass consumption, often in worldwide markets. This problem became important with the great increase of production resulting from the application of science to industry. The industrial nations produced more goods than they could consume. Nor was any nation completely self-sufficient in raw materials. Thus international trade became more important than ever before.

International trade involved not only the buying and selling of goods, but also the investment of capital. Before World War I, Great Britain was the largest single investor nation, owning 20 billion dollars' worth of stocks and bonds in foreign countries, including the United States. France also invested heavily abroad, especially in the Americas. For example, French capital was instrumental in building the Santa Fe Railroad.

You have read about laissez-faire economics, and how this theory influenced Great Britain and several other nations to adopt a policy of free trade. In the late 1800's, however, many nations became dissatisfied with free trade and abandoned it. The following example will help to show why and how this came about.

In the early years of industrialization, the Brit-

This cartoon illustrates "The Grand Old Game of Tit for Tat" that characterized international tariff agreements. Each country wanted to export its goods without having to import competing goods from other countries. Realizing the impossibility of such an arrangement, France and Belgium, at rear, and Germany, at right, offer to import American products in return for a promise that the United States will take their exports (symbolized here by wine and beet sugar). Uncle Sam, with great confidence in the huge "U.S. Home Market" in which to sell American products, refuses them. In the late 1800's, when this cartoon was made, the highly productive United States depended almost entirely on domestic sales. This policy was to change in the next century.

ish steel industry prospered by exporting its products to the rest of the world. But when Germany developed its own steelworks in the late 1800's, the situation changed.

To begin with, Germany placed a high tariff on imported British goods to make their prices higher than those of German products. This was known as a protective tariff because it protected the German producer from British competition and guaranteed him at least the German market for steel. Then, as German steel manufacturers developed efficient production methods, they began to compete with Britain for the trade of other countries. Thus Britain, having lost the German market, also began to lose other markets.

Tariff walls. The same thing happened with other products, and in other countries. More and more producers entered the field, and more and more tariffs were imposed to help them. A nation whose products were excluded from another country by a high tariff would retaliate with a high tariff of its own on imports from that country. Eventually many countries had erected so-called tariff walls—high tariffs on long lists of imports.

The net effect of tariff walls was to restrict trade between nations. Not only did they limit the sale of the product taxed, but they reduced all trade. For example, if Great Britain's exports of steel fell off as the result of another country's tariff on steel, Britain could not import as much from other countries. If you multiply Britain by other countries and steel by other products, you will see that a tariff wall could deny to producers the mass markets they needed abroad, even though it protected them from foreign competition.

A tariff wall even interfered with trade inside a country. Without tariffs, an individual consumer could buy cheaper foreign products and have money left over to spend on other things, which would help not only that consumer but also the firms from which he bought the extra goods.

So a paradox arose. On the one hand, national rivalries, fears, and the interests of special groups erected tariff walls and other barriers to free trade. On the other hand, communications, transportation, and trade brought the various parts of the world closer together, and industry developed on a scale that demanded world markets and free access to raw materials.

Depressions

Because of economic interdependence, what happened in one country could have effects all over the world. This was particularly true of depressions.

A depression is a period when business activity declines, and there is much unemployment and economic hardship. The Industrial Revolution had brought with it alternate periods of prosperity and depression (a pattern known as the business cycle). It is usually difficult to pinpoint the cause of a drop in business activity. But it is easy to see that in an industrialized country, trouble in one spot can spread rapidly to others.

Say, for example, that one large firm begins to cut its orders of raw materials and lay off workers. The suppliers of materials may have to reduce their operations. The workers must reduce their spending or find other jobs. The income of the grocer and the landlord is then reduced. Workers compete with each other for jobs, and wage rates may fall. The effects go on spreading. People begin to worry about the future. Panic may ensue, and the economy may grind to a near stop.

When science and technology brought about the era of large-scale production for mass markets, and huge investments of capital in foreign countries became common, the problem of depressions became international. A depression spreads from one country to another just as it does from one business to another. This happened after World War I, when the end of the fighting brought war industries to a halt. And it happened again in the 1930's, which brought the most serious depression the world had yet known.

CHECKUP

1. How did changes affect newspaper communication and shipping in the late 1800's and early 1900's?

2. What nations were most industrialized by the 1900's? Which areas lagged behind?

3. What are tariff walls? What effects did they have?

4. IDENTIFY: Peary, Amundsen, depression, business cycle.

CHAPTER REVIEW

Chapter 31 Science and Technology Led to Large-Scale Industrialization (1831–1930)

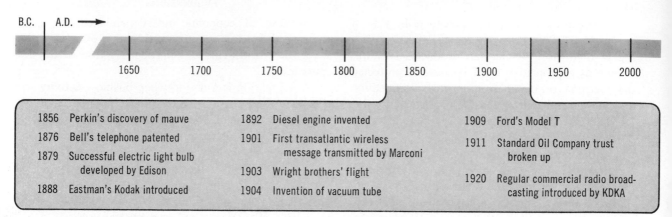

B.C. | A.D. ➝

1650   1700   1750   1800   1850   1900   1950   2000

1856	Perkin's discovery of mauve	1892	Diesel engine invented	1909	Ford's Model T
1876	Bell's telephone patented	1901	First transatlantic wireless message transmitted by Marconi	1911	Standard Oil Company trust broken up
1879	Successful electric light bulb developed by Edison	1903	Wright brothers' flight	1920	Regular commercial radio broadcasting introduced by KDKA
1888	Eastman's Kodak introduced	1904	Invention of vacuum tube		

CHAPTER SUMMARY

After about 1870 the application of science to manufacturing produced a new wave of industrial growth. New sources of power became important. Faraday's discoveries were applied by Edison and others to produce electric power and light. The development of the internal-combustion engine made possible such self-propelled vehicles as the automobile, the railway locomotive, and the airplane.

New and improved products included gasoline, various synthetic substances, and better steel alloys. Rapid communications were furthered by the telephone, the wireless telegraph, and the radio, while advances in photography led to the motion picture.

Along with new inventions and products went new ways of doing business. Mass production—based on the division of labor, interchangeable parts, and the assembly line—transformed several industries. It was most useful in large companies; the corporation, whose system of limited liability attracted many shareholders, became the dominant form of business organization. As corporations grew larger, monopolies were formed to avoid competition. National governments became increasingly involved in business, in some cases encouraging cartels, in others regulating or even building industries.

Rapid industrialization had worldwide effects. Improved transportation and communication linked people more closely, but differences in industrial development made some parts of the world—Western Europe, the United States, and Japan—wealthier and more powerful than less advanced nations. International trade, more important than ever before, was restricted by tariff walls. At the same time, economic interdependence increased, and depressions had far-reaching repercussions.

QUESTIONS FOR DISCUSSION

1. Beginning in the late 1800's, a region that had electricity was considered "advanced," while a region without it was thought to be "backward." Why should this be the case? Can you apply this same distinction today?

2. How did the assembly line change working conditions? Do you think mass production necessarily leads to boredom or a lack of creativity? Would such factors influence your decision to become an assembly-line worker in a large factory? Justify your position.

3. In some countries, like the United States, natural monopolies are run by huge private corporations under government control; in many other countries they are operated by the government itself. Explain which system you prefer.

4. If you could return to the 1870's or 1880's, what familiar things would you miss? Are there any unpleasant features of the present day which would disappear?

5. New methods of transportation and communication are said to have "shrunk the world" by making it easier for people to travel and to keep informed of what is happening in distant localities. Show that this has both benefited and harmed humanity.

PROJECTS

1. Write a short essay on the nature of big business, including a discussion of some of its outstanding features.

2. Make a chart of ten people and their inventions or discoveries which advanced civilization between 1831 and 1930. Distinguish between contributions that were original and those that continued the work of others.

CHAPTER 32

Industrialized Nations Underwent Rapid Change in Many Fields

You have read how the discoveries of pure science in the 1800's and early 1900's overturned traditional concepts about man and the universe. These discoveries, and others, were applied to industry to improve products and processes. New industries grew up. Transportation and communication underwent new change. Giant business enterprises were formed, and the nations of the world became more dependent on each other than ever before.

It is understandable that the changes in industrialized societies should affect almost every aspect of men's lives. Chapter 21 described how the Industrial Revolution of the 1700's and early 1800's affected daily life—how the factory system changed basic patterns of working, how men flocked to cities to live, how society changed with the growth of an urban proletariat and a strong middle class of managers and entrepreneurs.

These trends continued in the later 1800's and became more widespread in the 1900's. Probably the most characteristic feature of this period of history was the rapidity of change. It is hard for us today to realize how many of the things we take for granted are relatively new. In less than a hundred years, science and industry have given us the automobile, the airplane, the telephone, the radio, and television. Our homes and public buildings are lighted by electricity and kept warm with central heating systems. Phonograph

Workers and their families in a city slum

"Cliff Dwellers" (detail) by George Wesley Bellows. Los Angeles County Museum of Art

World War I. Robert Frost's poems, most of them set in New England, used familiar forms and stressed traditional moral values.

CHECKUP

1. Briefly explain the Romantic Movement, especially as it was related to the age of revolutions and to nationalism. Show how it was reflected in the work of three writers.

2. What is realism in writing? How was it illustrated by the work of Ibsen? Balzac? Twain?

3. Why is Zola an important literary figure?

4. Name four famous novelists of the early 1900's and one work by each.

 4 Musicians and artists developed many varied styles

Music, painting, sculpture, and architecture, like literature, echoed the spirit of the times in which they were created. In the visual arts, trends such as experimentation and rapidly changing styles were especially noticeable.

Music

In music, as in literature, the 1800's began with a shift to romanticism that reflected the tumult of the revolutionary years. Musicians of the 1700's had written rather formal music in the classical style. In the revolutionary and Napoleonic period, the German composer Ludwig van Beethoven (BAY·toh·vun) began to write music that was emotional and personal and reflected the upheaval of the times. He did not abandon traditional forms but gave them greater force and expressiveness by such techniques as abrupt contrasts of tempo and rhythm. Especially in his nine great symphonies, he brought to music the romantic spirit of the age.

The Romantic Movement led to a great outpouring of music, especially in Austria and Germany. Franz Schubert is famous for his songs, many of them settings of German poems. Robert Schumann composed many works for a new instrument, the piano, and also wrote many songs. He and Felix Mendelssohn brought to music the lyric quality of romantic poetry, as in Mendelssohn's "Songs Without Words." One of the greatest German romantic composers was Johannes Brahms. He wrote symphonies and concertos that were classical in form but, like Beethoven's, used the full resources of the orchestra to produce rich, intensely emotional music.

Romanticism flourished in other countries as well. The Polish-born Frédéric Chopin (SHOH-pan) wrote a whole literature of graceful and romantic piano pieces. Franz Liszt of Hungary used native folk songs and dances in his lively orchestral rhapsodies. He also developed the tone poem, a kind of symphonic music based on a literary or philosophical theme. In Russia, Peter Ilich Tchaikovsky (chy·KAHF·skee) wrote orchestral works full of melody and emotion. Often his works were built around stories, such as the fairy tale of the *Nutcracker,* the romance of *Romeo and Juliet,* and the defeat of Napoleon at Moscow in the *1812 Overture.* He and such other Russian composers as Modest Moussorgsky—known for his opera *Boris Godunov*—developed a distinctive music that made much use of Russian folk themes.

One of the greatest operatic composers of the 1800's was Giuseppe Verdi of Italy. His best known works, such as *La Traviata* and *Aïda,* include some of the most beautiful and expressive music ever written for the human voice.

While Verdi worked within traditional forms, the German Richard Wagner (VAHG·nur) developed new ones. He called his operas "music dramas" and tried to unite all the elements—singing, orchestral music, dancing, costumes, and scenery—to create overwhelming theatrical effects. The music flowed from beginning to end without interruption for solos. An intense German nationalist, Wagner based many of his plots, including *Siegfried* and *Tristan and Isolde,* on German myths. He greatly enlarged the orchestra, setting a precedent for most later composers.

Experiment and change. Several composers of the late 1800's and early 1900's followed in the general tradition of romantic music, as influenced by Wagner, and are sometimes called post-romantics. Gustav Mahler of Austria used vast orchestras and choruses in his lengthy tone poems *Death and Resurrection* and *The Song of the Earth*. Richard Strauss, a German, is known for tone poems like *Till Eulenspiegel's Merry Pranks* and his opera *Der Rosenkavalier*.

Another trend, however, was to break away from older styles. Claude Debussy of France developed unusual harmonies and rhythms in trying to create delicate impressions of clouds, sea, or moonlight.

More revolutionary was Igor Stravinsky of Russia. In such compositions as his ballet *The Rite of Spring,* first performed in 1913, he wrote in two or three keys at once. Arnold Schönberg of Austria discarded the conventional eight-tone musical scale completely, using a twelve-tone scale and writing music without a dominant key, called atonal music.

These developments were not unlike the literary experiments of Joyce and Eliot, and had somewhat the same effect, producing a limited audience. It is not hard to see such music as a reflection of the conflicts and uncertainties of the early 1900's, or as a protest against the standardization of life that industrialization brought about.

In the United States there grew up a distinctive form of syncopated, improvised music known as jazz. It is not known how jazz began, but southern Negro musicians played an important role in its development; some of the elements of jazz may have been brought by slaves from Africa. The harmonies and rhythms of jazz influenced one of the most famous American composers, George Gershwin. He was known especially for his folk opera *Porgy and Bess*.

Painting and sculpture

Painting and sculpture followed patterns similar to those in literature and music, with some variations. Romanticism and realism were brief movements, followed quickly by experimentation that was intensely individualistic. There was less nationalism than in literature or music, more "art for art's sake." Like writers and musicians, paint-

ers and sculptors were often rebels, consciously or unconsciously, against the materialism and mechanization of an industrial world.

While Germans and Austrians dominated the world of music in the 1800's and early 1900's, the French were the outstanding painters and sculptors. In the 1820's and 1830's, romantic painters, like romantic writers, used subjects from the past and depicted episodes bursting with action and drama. Such a painter was Eugène Delacroix (DEL·uh·krwah) of France. John Constable and J. M. W. Turner in England, both landscape painters, reflected the romantic interest in nature. Their work had color and vitality, partly because they often went outdoors to paint instead of working in their studios.

The kind of realism that portrayed real people and everyday life in the industrial age characterized the works of the French artists Gustave Courbet and Honoré Daumier. Another kind of realism was attempted by a group of French painters known as impressionists. Their aim was to give vivid impressions of people and places as they might appear in a fleeting glance. To do this, the impressionists studied the science of light and color perception and experimented with small patches of different colors placed side by side to create shimmering effects. Claude Monet and Pierre Auguste Renoir were leading impressionists.

New directions. Impressionism in painting flourished in the 1860's and 1870's. It did not last long, but it influenced music and poetry. It also marked a turning point in painting, away from the faithful rendering of scenes and people that had been characteristic since the Renaissance. Beginning in the late 1800's, experimentation was popular. Form, design, color, and emotion became more important than subject matter. Realism was left to the camera, and painting became intensely individualistic.

Paul Cézanne's landscapes and still lifes emphasized the solid forms of objects he painted. Paul Gauguin (go·GAN), who left Europe to live in Tahiti, stressed color and simple, flat design. So did Henri Matisse, who painted many decorative scenes of southern France. The Dutch painter
(*continued on page 658*)

Music, Painting, and Sculpture

Artistic styles underwent rapid and constant change throughout the 1800's and 1900's. The three musicians pictured at left—Beethoven, Wagner, and Stravinsky—represent three major trends that succeeded each other in little more than a century. The romantic Beethoven, a tormented and difficult genius, has been characterized by one writer as "the first musician to write in the first person singular." Wagner was painted by Renoir at the end of his long and stormy career as an innovator in opera. Stravinsky's unusual techniques sometimes led to riots among concertgoers; the sketch at left is by Picasso.

Romanticism in painting stressed boldness and emotion. Turner painted "Burning of the Houses of Parliament," below left, after sketching the actual event in 1834. The cool regularity of Cézanne's "Bridge," below, exemplifies this painter's interest in form for its own sake.

Sculpture, like the other visual arts, moved from the realistic to the abstract. When first exhibited, Edgar Degas' charmingly awkward "Young Dancer," right, disconcerted viewers with her real gauze skirt and silk hair ribbon. Forty years later, Constantin Brancusi rendered a "Bird in Space," below right, with a single polished bronze shaft.

Vincent van Gogh (van GOH) expressed his own intense emotions with thick blobs of pure color, swirling brush strokes, and distorted perspective. Edgar Degas, Henri de Toulouse-Lautrec, and Édouard Manet painted scenes of Paris and Parisians, each in his own distinctive way. Paris became a center for artists from every land.

The French sculptor Auguste Rodin also broke with tradition. He used irregular surfaces for heightened effect. Some of his statues included unworked portions of the marble from which they were carved, giving his work a deliberately unfinished quality.

In painting after 1900, distinct trends in experimentation arose. One was cubism, led by Pablo Picasso and Georges Braque. The cubists took the basic geometrical forms Cézanne had emphasized—cone, cylinder, and sphere—and added cubes and flat planes. They painted objects in terms of these forms, often showing them in several aspects at the same time so that their original appearance could hardly be determined.

Another group were the surrealists, who attempted to symbolize the unconscious. Their paintings, usually done in careful realistic detail, contained dreamlike collections of objects in fantastic settings, whose meanings were difficult to unravel. The best-known surrealists were Salvador Dali of Spain and Giorgio di Chirico of Italy.

The trend away from realism became increasingly pronounced. As Picasso said: "Nature and art, being two different things, cannot be the same thing. Through art we express our concept of what nature is not." In abstract painting, objects in the real world were distorted or simplified to emphasize certain qualities. In nonobjective painting, artists abandoned any attempt to picture objective reality.

Architecture

Romanticism in architecture expressed itself first in the so-called Gothic revival of the mid-1800's. The British Houses of Parliament, American churches and college buildings, and other public structures were built in the Gothic style.

Then the technological revolution of the late 1800's stimulated new styles that made use of structural steel. Architecture began to express the age of technology instead of borrowing styles from past ages. The American Louis Sullivan was a leader in the new architecture. Not only did he help to develop the skyscraper, but he also developed a doctrine called functionalism, which held that the form of a building should be dictated by the use to which it was put, rather than by prevailing fashions.

His pupil Frank Lloyd Wright adopted Sullivan's ideas and added his own, especially the concept that buildings should be related to their environment. In the Middle West, his prairie houses, as they were called, were low buildings with long horizontal lines. In the 1920's, Wright went to Tokyo, where he built the Imperial Hotel. Adapting it to its location, he floated it on a cushion of mud instead of anchoring it rigidly to rock. It was the only large building in Tokyo that survived a severe earthquake that occurred in 1923.

European architects also developed a new style of architecture in the 1900's. Influenced by Sullivan and Wright, a group of architects that included the Swiss Le Corbusier and the German Walter Gropius developed a functional architecture called the international style. The style was plain and severe, depending for its beauty on uncluttered lines, good proportions, and unbroken expanses of steel and glass. It could be said that while modern literature, art, and music were moving away from the everyday, industrial, technological world, architecture deliberately and enthusiastically embraced it.

CHECKUP

1. Name three romantic composers; for what type of music was each known? What innovations did Wagner bring to music?

2. Name and describe briefly two important schools of painting of the early 1900's.

3. How did the technological revolution influence architecture? Who were some leading American and European architects of the 1900's?

4. IDENTIFY: Verdi, Stravinsky, atonal music, impressionists, abstract painting.

CHAPTER REVIEW

Chapter 32 Industrialized Nations Underwent Rapid Change in Many Fields   (1796–1940)

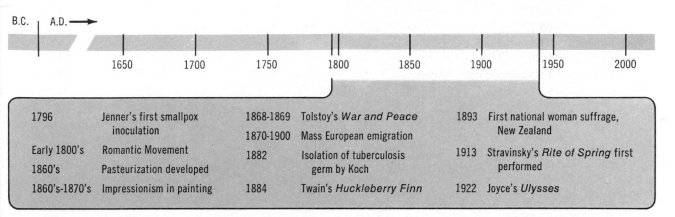

1796	Jenner's first smallpox inoculation	1868-1869	Tolstoy's *War and Peace*	1893	First national woman suffrage, New Zealand
Early 1800's	Romantic Movement	1870-1900	Mass European emigration		
1860's	Pasteurization developed	1882	Isolation of tuberculosis germ by Koch	1913	Stravinsky's *Rite of Spring* first performed
1860's-1870's	Impressionism in painting	1884	Twain's *Huckleberry Finn*	1922	Joyce's *Ulysses*

CHAPTER SUMMARY

In industrialized nations, many aspects of life changed rapidly in the 1800's. The population increased as more was learned about diseases and their prevention. Discoveries by Jenner, Pasteur, Lister, and Koch were landmarks in medical science. New drugs were developed, and researchers discovered the importance of a balanced diet and how to make it possible for more people. Two important population movements took place. One was a mass migration away from Europe. The other was a shift to the cities.

Many social changes occurred. The status of women improved. Universal, compulsory education won gradual acceptance. Organized religion was influenced by positivism and similar philosophies. As the number of religious sects grew, toleration increased, and gradually church and state were separated in many nations.

The arts reflected the rapid changes in society. Literature in the early 1800's was dominated by the Romantic Movement, which appealed to sentiment and glorified emotion. Mid-century writers, such as Flaubert, Tolstoy, and Balzac, turned to realism. In the 1900's, experimentation with new techniques was exemplified in the works of Proust, Joyce, Mann, and Kafka.

Music, too, had its Romantic Movement, with Beethoven paving the way for such composers as Schubert, Schumann, Chopin, and Tchaikovsky. Among the giants of the 1800's were Verdi and Wagner. In the next century, new techniques were developed by Stravinsky and Schönberg.

In painting, romanticism and realism flourished briefly before yielding to an intensely individualistic period marked by such experimental styles as cubism, surrealism, and abstract art. Architecture, with its adoption of functionalism and development of the international style, seemed one of the few arts to embrace the modern industrial world.

QUESTIONS FOR DISCUSSION

1. Advances in medical science have enabled more people to live longer. What are some of the problems that have resulted?

2. When Pasteur's theories were first announced, they met with great opposition. Most new ideas of scientists today meet with less opposition. Can you account for this change?

3. Man has greatly increased his mobility, and there is a constant movement of people from one area to another, especially in the United States. In what ways has this mobility influenced American life?

4. Should government—local, state, or national—give assistance to medical researchers, writers, artists, or musicians? In each case explain your answer.

5. Has the gain of equal rights by women in politics, education, and business improved society? Explain.

6. Should education be free and compulsory for all? Should the kind of education and the learning age be the same for all students? Justify your answer.

PROJECTS

1. Make a list of the great contributors in the field of health. Place at the top the name of the individual you think made the greatest contribution. Tell why you rate this person first.

2. Make a sketch of a modern building that you know and admire.

3. Draw a cartoon showing some of the problems of modern cities.

For additional bibliographical information on the books cited in these projects, see the Basic Library (page xviii) and Further Reading on the opposite page.

INDIVIDUAL PROJECTS

1. After reading Untermeyer, *Makers of the Modern World,* De Kruif, *Microbe Hunters,* or a biography of a scientist or inventor listed on the opposite page, prepare either a written or an oral report on one of the following: Charles Darwin, Louis Pasteur, Thomas Edison, Max Planck, Henry Ford, Wilbur and Orville Wright, Marie Curie, Guglielmo Marconi, Albert Einstein. Your report should focus on the motivation of your subject and the significance of his work.

2. Write a report on one of the discoveries or inventions discussed in the text. Your paper should be written from a historical point of view, showing how certain theories and discoveries developed from one stage to the next. *Life* has published a series of books in its Nature and Science Library that should be consulted for your report. Especially useful volumes in the *Life* series are Ralph Lapp, *Matter,* and Ruth Moore, *Evolution.*

3. Advances in transportation have greatly reduced traveling time. Draw a diagram for the bulletin board illustrating the comparative Atlantic crossing times by boat from Europe to North America in 1640, 1840, 1940, 1950, and today. Draw a companion diagram for the Atlantic crossing by airplane in 1940, 1950, and today.

4. In the United States a number of individuals—Vanderbilt, Rockefeller, Carnegie, and Ford among them—created and controlled enormous industries. Prepare an oral report on one of these early industrialists. Your report should discuss the reasons for the success of the particular man you are investigating. Read Hoyt, *The Idea Men,* Weisberger, *Captains of Industry,* and Josephson, *The Robber Barons.* Also consult *American Heritage,* "Epitaph for the Steel Master," August 1960; "Faces from the Past— J. P. Morgan," February 1963; "A Set of Mere Money-Getters?" June 1963; "The Grand Acquisitor," December 1964.

5. Prepare a class report on the "population explosion." Show the rate of population increase since 1800, discuss why this increase was possible, and what dangers it has brought to the world. For magazine articles consult *Readers' Guide to Periodical Literature.*

6. Prepare a newscast from Kitty Hawk, North Carolina, at the time of the Wright brothers' successful airplane flight. For reference consult: Eisen and Filler, *The Human Adventure,* Vol. 2, "The Flight at Kitty Hawk"; Snyder and Morris, *A Treasury of Great Reporting,* "The World's First Airplane Flight Is Reported Exclusively by the Norfolk *Virginia-Pilot.*"

7. Make a scrapbook showing the development of architecture from around 1800 to today. For this project collect photographs from magazines. Write captions for each picture giving the style of architecture and the material and methods used in the building. As a reference consult Watterson, *Architecture.*

8. In industrialized nations, increasingly more people live in cities. This tremendously rapid growth of urban centers has been the cause of many problems that every city must face today. If possible, arrange to interview a city official to discuss urban problems. Also collect newspaper and magazine articles on urban problems. Report your findings to the class and be prepared to answer questions.

9. Prepare an oral report on the history and development of the automobile. You should consider the following questions: What did early automobiles look like? What significant improvements have been made? What changes has the automobile brought to our lives? You might illustrate your report with a bulletin-board display.

GROUP PROJECTS

1. A group of students might present a musical program to the class. Selections by some of the composers mentioned in Chapter 32 should be obtained on records. A different student should introduce each piece of music with a short discussion of the life of the composer and the particular piece of music about to be heard by the class.

2. Organize a panel discussion on the accomplishments and prospects of science and technology. The emphasis of the discussion should be on the influence of science and technology on society. In preparing for the discussion, the panelists should do considerable outside reading.

3. A group of five students might form a panel to discuss the various artistic movements of the 1800's and early 1900's. Each student should investigate and report on a different movement—romanticism, realism, impressionism, cubism, surrealism. The reports should be illustrated with prints from your local museum or reproductions from magazines. Panelists should consult the Basic Library and the bibliography on the opposite page for pertinent readings.

Further Reading

BIOGRAPHY

Beckhard, A., *Albert Einstein.* Avon.*

Charnley, Michael V., *Boys' Life of the Wright Brothers.* Harper & Row.

Clemens, Samuel Langhorne, *The Autobiography of Mark Twain.* Washington Square.*

Curie, Eve, *Madame Curie.* Pocket Books.*

De Kruif, Paul, *Microbe Hunters.* Harcourt Brace Jovanovich.* Sketches of twelve great scientists.

Farmer, Laurene, *Master Surgeon.* Harper & Row. Biography of Joseph Lister.

Goss, Madeleine, *Beethoven: Master Musician.* Holt, Rinehart and Winston.

Hays, Wilma Pitchford, *Eli Whitney: Founder of Modern Industry.* Franklin Watts.

Jacobs, Herbert, *Frank Lloyd Wright: America's Greatest Architect.* Harcourt Brace Jovanovich.

Josephson, Matthew, *Edison.* McGraw-Hill.*

Latham, Jean Lee, *The Story of Eli Whitney.* Harper & Row.

———, *Young Man in a Hurry: The Story of Cyrus Field.* Harper & Row.

Moore, Ruth, *Charles Darwin.* Knopf.

Pearson, Hesketh, *Sir Walter Scott: His Life and Personality.* Harper & Row.

Stone, Irving, *Lust for Life.* Pocket Books.* Vincent van Gogh.

Untermeyer, Louis, *Makers of the Modern World.* Simon & Schuster.*

Wecter, Dixon, *Sam Clemens of Hannibal.* Houghton Mifflin.* Mark Twain.

NONFICTION

American Heritage, eds., *The American Heritage Book of Flight.* American Heritage.

Asimov, Isaac, *The Search for the Elements.* Basic Books.

Burlingame, Roger, *Machines That Built America.* New American Library.*

Butterfield, Herbert, *The Origins of Modern Science.* Macmillan.*

Canaday, John, *Mainstreams of Modern Art.* Simon & Schuster.

Davis, Lance E., *Growth of Industrial Enterprise, 1860–1914.* Scott, Foresman.*

Gardner, Martin, ed., *Great Essays in Science.* Washington Square.*

Handlin, Oscar, *The Uprooted.* Grosset & Dunlap.* Immigration to the United States.

* Paperback.

Hofstadter, Richard, *Social Darwinism in American Thought.* Beacon.*

Hoyt, Edwin P., *The Idea Men: How Their Ingenuity Spurred America's Growth.* Meredith.

Huyghe, René, ed., *Larousse Encyclopedia of Modern Art.* Prometheus Press.

Josephson, Matthew, *The Robber Barons.* Harcourt Brace Jovanovich.*

Kennedy, John Fitzgerald, *A Nation of Immigrants.* Harper & Row.*

Lapp, Ralph, *Matter.* Time-Life.

Meyer, Jerome S., *World Book of Great Inventions.* World.

Moore, Ruth, *Evolution.* Time-Life.

Ramsey, Frederic, Jr., and Charles Edward Smith, eds., *Jazzmen.* Harcourt Brace Jovanovich.*

Riis, Jacob A., *How the Other Half Lives.* Hill & Wang.* Indictment of slum life.

Ross, Frank Jr., *Modern Miracles of the Laboratory.* Lothrop, Lee & Shepard.

Schlesinger, Arthur M., *Rise of the City, 1878–1898.* Macmillan.

Steffens, Lincoln, *Shame of the Cities.* Hill & Wang.* Corruption in American industrial cities.

Sullivan, Louis H., *Autobiography of an Idea.* Dover.* Statement by an American architect.

Weisberger, Bernard A., and Allan Nevins, *Captains of Industry.* Harper & Row.

Wright, Frank Lloyd, *On Architecture.* Grosset & Dunlap.*

HISTORICAL FICTION

Cather, Willa, *My Antonia.* Houghton Mifflin.* Novel about the American West.

Davenport, Marcia, *Valley of Decision.* Houghton Mifflin.* Rise of the steel industry and unions.

Dreiser, Theodore, *The Financier.* Dell.*

Gogol, Nicolai, *Dead Souls.* Penguin.* Rich and humorous novel about Russian swindler in the 1800's.

Llewellyn, Richard, *How Green Was My Valley.* Macmillan.* Story of a mining town in Wales.

Lewis, Sinclair, *Arrowsmith.* New American Library.* Story of a research doctor.

Norris, Frank, *The Octopus.* Bantam.* Abuses of railroad monopolies in California.

Roth, Henry, *Call It Sleep.* Avon.* Story of European immigrants in New York.

Sinclair, Upton, *The Jungle.* New American Library.* Factory life in Chicago.

Verne, Jules, *Around the World in Eighty Days.* Dell.*

Zola, Émile, *Germinal.* Doubleday.* Life in the French mines.

DICTATORSHIPS

The years after World War I were characterized by the rise of several strong dictatorships. The most threatening was that of Adolf Hitler in Germany. He is shown at left, facing the members of the Reichstag as they extend their arms in the Nazi salute. The eagle and swastikas above the podium, symbols of the Nazi Party, add to the theatrical effect so often used by totalitarian regimes to bolster their appeal.

662

AND DEMOCRACIES

CHAPTER 33

Democracy Faced Severe Tests After World War I

Parade of the victorious Popular Front in France

World War I, according to Woodrow Wilson, was fought to make the world "safe for democracy." In 1919 it seemed as if this aim had been achieved. The Western democracies had won the war. The new nations created at the Paris peace conference each established democratic governments. Older nations, such as China, that underwent governmental change during this period also announced democratic goals.

It soon seemed, however, that many of the new governments had been set up more in imitation of Western governmental systems than out of any deep devotion to democratic principles. Most of the people who administered them had no experience in democratic government. Social and economic troubles multiplied, and serious signs of weakness began to appear.

Even the older and more experienced democracies felt the strain of the postwar years. Although Great Britain, France, and the United States remained democracies, important changes occurred in these nations as well.

For one thing, most postwar democratic governments took a more active role in economic matters. Before World War I, many people had felt that governments should leave the economy in the hands of businessmen. Traditional theories of free enterprise demanded nearly complete separation of government and business.

But the war had led many nations to adopt a

planned economy—governmental regulation and direction of national resources to achieve a definite goal. Since government regulation of the economy had worked well in wartime, some people reasoned that peacetime economic problems could also be solved by increasing the power of the government over privately owned businesses.

Demobilizing the armed forces led to widespread unemployment and competition for jobs. As a result, organized labor put pressure on governments to help solve workingmen's problems. Some men had made sizable fortunes during the war. Those who had experienced economic hardship, however, demanded a more equal distribution of the wealth.

Farms and factories had produced in great quantity to fill wartime needs. When the needs lessened after the war, markets could not be found for the goods the farms and factories were able to produce.

During the war, many women took jobs outside their homes. They also began to take a more active role in political affairs. In most of the democracies, women had been given the right to vote by the end of World War I. Most people saw woman suffrage as a step toward more complete democracy, but some were convinced that it would upset the traditional family structure.

Social and economic problems like these raised serious questions about the future of democracy everywhere. In some nations, the postwar situation led to impatience with the democratic process itself as a means of solving problems.

THE CHAPTER SECTIONS:

1. France emerged from World War I victorious but unstable (1919–1938)

2. The British Empire adjusted to the postwar era (1919–1937)

3. Democratic experiments fared poorly in eastern Europe and Asia (1918–1935)

4. A worldwide depression began in the United States (1919–1935)

1   France emerged from World War I victorious but unstable

During the four years of World War I, northern France had been a battleground. At war's end, cities lay in ruins, farmhouses had been destroyed, and the land itself was scarred with trenches and pitted with shell holes. Allied troops and supplies had passed through western France on their way to the front. Wharves needed replacing; railroads and roads were worn out. Most tragic of all was the loss of lives. A large percentage of the young men of France had been killed during the war.

In spite of its losses, France seemed to enter the postwar period with many advantages. It had regained Alsace and Lorraine, and had won as mandates some territories of the Ottoman Empire and a share of Germany's colonies. It could claim the coal of the Saar Valley for fifteen years and had a chance of getting the territory permanently if the inhabitants should then vote to join France. Its former enemy, Germany, was limited in military strength and had to pay reparations.

The Third French Republic had been born in the strife-torn year of 1870. It had lasted longer than any other French government since 1789, but it often seemed in danger of collapse. At the end of World War I, struggles among the various factions in French politics continued.

Because of the great number of political parties and splinter groups, coalition governments were always necessary. In countries such as France, where there are more than two major political parties, parliamentary government often runs into trouble. In order to get a majority in parliament, two or more parties have to combine to form coalition cabinets. Such governing coalitions may hold together only a short time. In France, in the seventy years between 1870 and 1940, there were 106 different cabinets, or ministries. Thus the average life of a French government cabinet was less than a year.

French government was actually a little less shaky than it looked. The overthrow of a ministry seldom resulted in a general election that would result in a completely new membership in the Chamber of Deputies. It simply meant a reshuffle of cabinet positions among the leaders of the political parties. Often the same coalition of parties would be able to form a new cabinet with a new man as premier and the other positions reshuffled. It was like a game of musical chairs. A large bureaucracy of civil servants kept their jobs regardless of the party in power. They could be counted on to keep things going when cabinets fell.

The short life of most French cabinets, however, made it difficult for any political group to carry out a long-range, planned political program. More dangerous to the political health of France was the fact that many elements, particularly monarchists on the extreme right and communists on the extreme left, were opposed to democracy itself.

Financial troubles

France had managed to reduce its debt, but it still owed money that it had borrowed during and after the war from its citizens and from the United States. Inflation took its toll, too. In 1913 the French franc was worth about twenty cents in American money. By 1926 it had fallen to two cents, and two years later was "stabilized" at four cents. This meant that anyone who had bought French government bonds in 1913 had lost 80 percent of the money he had invested.

The finances of the Third Republic had always been shaky. Although the French tax rate was the highest in Western Europe, revenues were not adequate because landowners and industrialists were able to avoid paying their share of taxes. The burden fell mostly on industrial workers and the lower middle class, those least able to pay.

Since taxes did not produce enough revenue, France tried to solve its problems by borrowing—selling bonds—or by printing more paper money. These moves were inflationary, making the value of the money go down and prices go up. Economically, such moves were suicidal, but politically they were painless.

The expenses of the French government continued to be high for several reasons. The number of civil servants increased during and after the war. The government had to repair damaged areas and pay interest on its heavy debt. Most important, perhaps, was military security.

The Maginot Line. Twice in less than fifty years, France had been invaded by Germans. Frenchmen seemed willing to make many sacrifices to prevent this from happening again. The French army was rebuilt. A series of steel and concrete fortifications nearly 200 miles long was built along the frontiers of Germany and Luxembourg. This fortification was named the Maginot (MAZH-uh-noh) Line, after the statesman who planned it. Since trench warfare had been the basic feature of World War I, the French planned to make their defenses impregnable so that the country could never again be invaded by land from the east. The French were preparing to fight the last war over again.

Enormous sums of money were devoted to the construction of the Maginot Line. This system gave French civilians and military planners a dangerous illusion of security. French military forces were trained and equipped for another war of stalemate, rather than for a war of movement.

International affairs

The instability of the French government during the 1920's and 1930's caused France to lose much of its former prestige. France seemed an unreliable ally because it was weak financially and lacked a consistent foreign policy.

In July 1922, Germany informed the Allies that it could not afford to continue to pay reparations on schedule. Great Britain was willing to negotiate the problem with Germany, but France was not. In January 1923, assisted by Belgium but over British objections, France marched troops into the Ruhr Valley, the source of most of Germany's coal and iron. France intended to occupy the area and operate Germany's steel mills there until it had collected the money Germany owed. The German workers refused to cooperate, German telegraphers refused to handle French messages, and German shopkeepers refused to deal with the French. The French attempt ended in failure and the troops were soon withdrawn.

In 1925 the political situation in Europe seemed to be improving. In that year, representatives of Great Britain, France, Germany, Belgium, Italy, Czechoslovakia, and Poland met at Locarno, Switzerland, where they signed a number of treaties known together as the Locarno Pact. The delegates to the conference pledged their countries to the peaceful settlement of all future disputes. The existing Franco-German boundaries were guaranteed. France signed mutual assistance treaties with both Poland and Czechoslovakia. Germany was invited to join the League of Nations.

However, France's protective alliances began to show serious weaknesses. By the mid-1930's, Belgium canceled its defensive alliance with France and declared itself neutral in any future war. France's prewar ally, Russia, was now under a communist government. France and Russia formed an alliance, but it was a shaky one. France's wartime ally, Italy, was now under a militarist dictatorship, and its old opposition to France reappeared. France, in keeping with its aim of encircling Germany, made postwar alliances with Yugoslavia and Rumania as well as with Poland and Czechoslovakia. But these relatively weak nations, although they shared France's mistrust of Germany, were undependable allies.

Only Great Britain was left for France to depend on. But, as you will see, British foreign policy during the 1920's and 1930's was not entirely consistent, either. Postwar France seemed to lose all sense of direction and to drift wherever British policy carried it.

Political unrest

In 1934 a financial scandal involving a highly placed French government official caused violent protests, especially from the extreme right. In

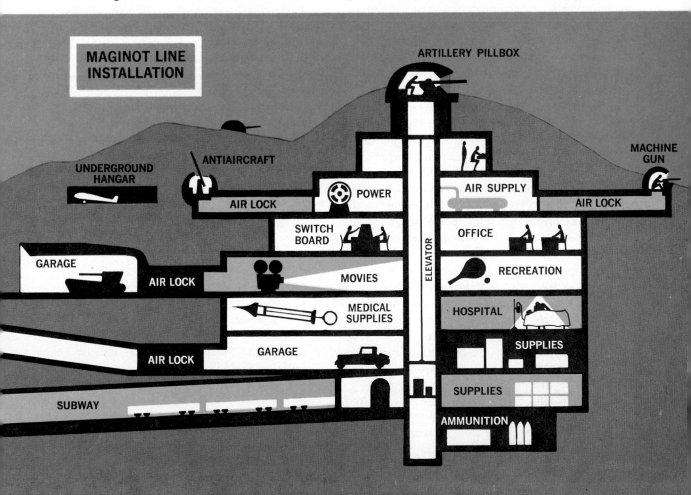

HISTORY THROUGH ART

Dada, The Art of Surprise

The horrors of World War I drove many artists to despair. One group launched an international movement in protest against the civilization that had led to the war. They called this movement Dada and announced that "Art is nonsense." A Swiss, Mèret Oppenheim, created the fur-covered cup, saucer, and spoon at left. Like other Dada objects, its incongruity was aimed at shocking complacent observers out of tired thinking and into a new self-awareness.

Coll., The Museum of Modern Art, New York. Purchase

February, riots broke out in Paris. Many of the rioters demanded an end to the republican form of government and called for a strong military dictatorship to "discipline" the country and reunite the opposing parties under a nationalistic regime.

The trade unions responded to this threat from the right by calling a general strike a week later. (This is a collective refusal of essential workers in various industries to continue working until their demands are met.) Shortly thereafter the parties of the left—socialists and communists—organized a coalition government in an attempt to restore political stability to France.

The name which this coalition took was the Popular Front.° Its leader, Léon Blum, a socialist, was elected premier in 1936. United for the moment against the threat of a right-wing *coup d'état,* Blum's government carried out many far-reaching reforms.

The Popular Front first persuaded the leaders of industry to grant an immediate pay raise to all workers. A forty-hour week was established, and workers were to be given vacations with pay. The government promised its protection to labor-union organizers and set up machinery for the

° **Popular Front:** This term was subsequently used in various other countries to denote a coalition of leftist parties, especially one formed to counteract strong right-wing opposition.

arbitration of labor disputes. The Bank of France was put under public control and the armaments industry was partially nationalized.

Price rises soon offset the benefits of wage increases, and industrialists proved less than cooperative in carrying out their part of the bargain. Blum's ministry lasted only about a year, but for this brief period, France had a government with the power and determination to act.

After the fall of the Popular Front, the French working classes were hard hit. The forty-hour week was abolished in 1938. The workers protested by organizing sit-down strikes, with workers staying at their jobs but refusing to work. Severe antilabor legislation followed. France remained a democracy, but the French people were bitterly divided and fearful of German military power, which was reviving at an alarming rate.

CHECKUP

1. Summarize French losses and gains as a result of World War I.

2. What were the causes of French financial difficulties after World War I? How did the French government try to solve them?

3. Why did France move troops into the Ruhr Valley? What were the results of its action?

4. IDENTIFY: planned economy, Maginot Line, Locarno Pact, general strike, Popular Front.

668

2 The British Empire adjusted to the postwar era

Like France, Great Britain seemed to have won a great victory in World War I. But, as in France, the cost had been great.

You will recall that, as a result of the war, Great Britain gained several mandates, some from Germany and some at the expense of the Ottoman Empire. Germany was no longer to be feared as a naval power. Temporarily, at least, Germany would also be less of a rival in industry and world trade.

Britain had not suffered the destruction that continental European countries had. But there were heavy losses among the merchant ships on which so much of British prosperity depended. There was also the huge cost in human lives.

Economic problems

Britain, like France, faced grave economic difficulties after World War I. There was a heavy war debt, owed both to people at home and to the United States. Taxes were extremely heavy, but were based mostly on ability to pay. It could be said that British taxes during this period achieved what revolutions did elsewhere: the reduction of large fortunes and the breaking up of great estates.

British industry and trade suffered after World War I. The coal mines, on which much of Brittain's industry depended, were beginning to give out, and the remaining seams of coal were narrow and of poor quality. British factories were run down. Machinery was worn out or inefficient compared with newer American or Japanese machines. During the war the United States and Japan had taken over many of the British world markets. These markets were now hard to regain. Several new nations adopted a policy of *economic nationalism*—that is, they tried to improve their own economic well-being, through tariff walls and similar restrictions, without consideration for other countries. This policy, too, damaged British trade. Yet Britain had to sell abroad to pay for needed imports of food and raw materials. It had to export or die.

Labor unrest. By 1921, 2 million workers were out of work and had to be supported by the government. Labor unions fought hard to keep the high wages and full employment of the war years, but industrialists fought just as hard to resist the unions' demands. The result was serious labor unrest.

In 1926 the coal miners went on strike. Their action led to a general strike. Soon almost half of Britain's 6 million unionized workers had left their jobs. The government, however, declared a state of emergency and sent soldiers and sailors to replace the striking workers. The general strike failed and the miners went back to work. The Trades Disputes and Trade Unions Act of 1927 imposed strict controls on unions and declared general strikes illegal.

Throughout these troubles, Britain remained faithful to the principles of constitutional government. Some radicals proposed anti-democratic solutions to their country's problems, but voters overwhelmingly rejected such measures.

Discontented workers found their spokesman in Ramsay MacDonald, leader of the Labour Party. After 1922 the Labour Party grew in strength. The Liberal Party declined rapidly because it could not attract working-class members. MacDonald formed a coalition with the Liberal Party and was elected prime minister in 1924 and again in 1929. Through moderate reforms, such as the extension of unemployment benefits and old-age insurance, Great Britain avoided the sort of social unrest that toppled democratic institutions elsewhere in Europe during the postwar years.

British possessions

Although the British Empire was larger as a result of the war, it had many weaknesses. From all over the world came demands from colonial peoples for more freedom, for self-government, or for complete independence.

Ireland. The first really serious trouble came close to home, in a country that had been ruled by Britain for centuries. Ireland had never been happy under British rule. During the late 1800's, Britain had given Ireland a degree of self-government, but not enough to satisfy most Irish. They wanted complete independence.

During World War I, when Britain was busy elsewhere, Irish nationalists rose up in the Easter Rebellion of 1916. The British put down the rebellion, but fighting broke out again in 1918. For years the Irish Republican Army fought British troops in a bloody and bitter struggle. (The British were called "Black and Tans" because of their uniforms.)

In 1921 the British gave in and signed a treaty. The following year, southern Ireland became the Irish Free State, a self-governing dominion with loose ties to the mother country. Six counties in the north of Ireland chose to remain in the United Kingdom, with representatives in the British Parliament. This region is known as Northern Ireland.

In 1937 the Irish Free State adopted a new constitution and the name Eire (AIR·uh). Eamon De Valera was elected its first prime minister. Twelve years later, Eire became completely independent, calling itself the Republic of Ireland.

The division of the island was religious as well as political. The Republic of Ireland is Roman Catholic; Northern Ireland is mostly Protestant. The split continued to trouble relations between Britain and Ireland.

Egypt. Although technically under Turkish rule, Egypt had been controlled by the British since 1882. In 1914, when the Ottoman Empire joined the Central Powers, Britain declared Egypt independent and set it up as a protectorate. In 1922 this protectorate was formally ended, although, because of its interests in the Suez Canal, Britain continued to exert influence through the Egyptian king.

During the 1920's and early 1930's, an independence movement grew strong in Egypt. In 1936 the British and Egyptian governments reached an agreement. In the previous year, as you will read later, Italy had invaded Ethiopia. The British needed Egyptian support, and they agreed to help Egypt become a member of the

League of Nations. The two nations pledged to help one another in time of war. Egypt agreed that Great Britain should hold military control of the Suez Canal for twenty years. With this agreement, Egypt became completely independent; it joined the League in 1937.

Western Asia. In the peace settlements after World War I, Great Britain had received as mandates Trans-Jordan, Iraq, and Palestine, all formerly part of the Ottoman Empire.

The spirit of nationalism had made Arabs discontented under the Ottoman Empire. They were equally unhappy under British control. In Iraq, discontent led to many uprisings. By 1930 the British recognized the kingdom of Iraq as an independent nation but kept some rights there, especially concessions in the country's rich oil fields.

Palestine was important to the British because of its strategic location and because a vital oil pipeline from Iraq ended at the Palestinian port of Haifa.

The British were in an embarrassing position in Palestine. In 1917, during the war, the Jewish chemist Chaim Weizmann had turned over to the British government a formula for making an important ingredient of high explosives. Weizmann was a leader in Zionism, a movement to resettle Jews in Palestine. In gratitude to him, and to secure Jewish support for the Allies, the British diplomat Arthur Balfour told Zionist leaders that the British would "view with favor" the creation of a Jewish "national home" in Palestine. Nothing, however, was to threaten the civil and religious rights of non-Jews in Palestine.

This so-called Balfour Declaration was cautiously worded because, in order to gain Arab support against the Turks, the British had also promised to aid the formation of an independent Arab state that might include Palestine.

With the British holding mandates in the Near East after the war, both Jews and Arabs wanted Britain to fulfill the promises it had made. Existing hatred between Arabs and Jews was intensified. Heated disputes arose over places of worship claimed by both groups. There were also conflicts over the number of Jews allowed to enter Palestine.

670

Great Britain's postwar troubles were acute both at home and abroad. In 1924, Ramsay MacDonald, below, formed Britain's first Labour government, but it was weak and lasted only a few months. In 1926, a strike of miners, left, brought on a general strike, which led to strict control of unions. Abroad, British "Black and Tans" maintained martial law in Ireland. At lower left, a detachment surveys Dublin from a rooftop. In India, nationalism found its spokesman in Mohandas Gandhi, shown lower right on his way to a meeting with British officials.

India. The largest British colony, India, had entered World War I on the side of the Allies, contributing important support in both men and money. In return, Britain had promised India a greater degree of self-government.

Any settlement for India had to satisfy many conflicting groups. British conservatives opposed giving up this important part of the British Empire. Native princes, many of whom were almost absolute rulers in their domains, also favored the status quo. Many groups in India were hostile to one another. There was bad feeling between Hindus and Moslems, and wide gulfs between upper-caste and lower-caste Hindus. Indian nationalists demanded complete self-government.

The chief spokesman for Indian nationalism was Mohandas Gandhi, who in 1920 became leader of the Indian National Congress—India's most important political party. He was not only a political leader but was also revered as a spiritual force. The Indians called him Mahatma, meaning "the saintly one."

Gandhi wanted complete self-government for India. He also urged Indians to give up Western ways and to strengthen their ancient culture and religion. Gandhi developed an approach—based partly on the New Testament and Hindu scriptures—that he called "nonviolent noncooperation." This technique was a form of *passive resistance,* or *civil disobedience*—the peaceful refusal of citizens to cooperate with their government in order to win concessions from it.

Among other things, Gandhi's program included refusal to buy British goods and to pay taxes. He and many of his followers were put in prison, but the jails could hold only limited numbers. The British found this form of resistance difficult to deal with.

In 1935, after many conferences and investigations, Britain granted India a federal constitution with more self-government, but not dominion status. The British viceroy still controlled India's defense and foreign affairs. Discontent continued.

The Statute of Westminster

Even in those parts of the British Empire that already had almost complete self-government,

there were demands for greater independence. In Canada, Australia, New Zealand, and the Union of South Africa, Britain still appointed a governor general. He had a veto power over laws, although he did not use it. Britain also controlled foreign policy.

Now these dominions demanded complete self-government. The British showed a genius for accommodation, adjustment, and acceptance of the political realities of life. They gave in without a struggle.

In 1931 an act of the British Parliament, called the Statute of Westminster, recognized Canada, Australia, New Zealand, and South Africa as completely independent. They were considered equal partners with the United Kingdom in a very loose organization called the British Commonwealth of Nations. Members of the Commonwealth were considered completely self-governing. The British Parliament had no power to make laws for them or interfere in their affairs. However, each member agreed to declare its loyalty to the British monarch and to recognize its cultural ties with Great Britain.

Over the years, several British colonies became independent and joined the Commonwealth. Membership was made attractive by favorable trade arrangements with the mother country. This informal arrangement worked remarkably well for both Great Britain and the regions that had formerly been its colonies.

CHECKUP

1. What economic problems faced the British in the postwar period?
2. Why was Palestine important to the British? What was the Balfour Declaration, and why was it issued?
3. What is the British Commonwealth of Nations? What are the obligations of its members?
4. Both Great Britain and France faced serious financial problems in the postwar period. Compare the methods by which each nation tried to meet its problems. What were the results of the measures taken in each country?
5. IDENTIFY: economic nationalism, Easter Rebellion, Zionism, Gandhi, passive resistance.

Democratic experiments fared poorly in eastern Europe and Asia

In countries that had had little previous experience with democracy, attempts of the people to govern themselves fared badly in the postwar years. In general, their imitation of the Western democracies was limited to scientific and technical matters. Attempts to "transplant" the basic institutions of democracy did not succeed.

Eastern Europe

Conditions in eastern Europe after World War I were not favorable to democracy. The newly established nations, which stretched from the Baltic Sea to the Adriatic Sea, lagged far behind the Western democracies in industrial development. The economy of much of the region had been manorial for centuries, and serfdom existed in some areas until the mid-1800's. At the time of World War I, the economy was still mainly agricultural. Most of the land was owned by a few wealthy aristocrats.

In some of the new countries, the large estates of the aristocrats were broken up and given to the peasants. But most of the peasants were too poor to buy the necessary equipment, fertilizer, and seed to make their farms productive. The farms, in any case, were usually too small to be run efficiently.

Most of the new eastern European countries tried to industrialize and turned to economic nationalism to protect their industries. As a result, trade among them was difficult. High tariffs proved self-defeating because goods produced by the new industries could not be sold to neighboring countries at a reasonable profit.

Most of the people of eastern Europe were poorly educated and had no experience in self-government. Quarreling political groups, unfamiliar with parliamentary methods, often tried to turn their opponents out of office by force. Impatience with the slowness of the democratic process caused unrest in times of crisis. There were bitter conflicts among aristocrats, military men, the middle class, and peasants.

These economic, social, and political problems led to much instability. Finland, the Baltic States (Estonia, Latvia, and Lithuania), and Czechoslovakia managed to sustain democratic regimes, but few other nations in eastern Europe succeeded in doing so. Three examples will illustrate what happened.

Austria. The Austria created after the war was a small country with only 6 million inhabitants. Many Austrians wanted *Anschluss,* or union, with Germany, but the peace treaties forbade it. By 1920 a constitutional assembly created a constitution for Austria. The government was to be federal with a president and a parliament. The system, however, was quite complex, and the Austrians could not make it work. Austria's economic weakness and a constant struggle between socialists and conservatives weakened the democratic regime. In 1922 a reactionary Catholic priest became chancellor of Austria. The country became less democratic and the Church began to take control of the government.

Hungary. The new country of Hungary was declared a republic in November 1918. In the following year, Béla Kun, a Hungarian communist who had participated in the revolution in Russia, overthrew the republic and tried to establish a communist regime modeled on Russia's new government. He planned to break up the large estates and distribute land to the peasants, but he was bitterly opposed by the aristocrats who owned the land.

A counterrevolution of aristocrats and army officers seized power and attempted to restore the Hapsburg monarchy. Although the new government declared Hungary to be a monarchy, the Allies would not permit the Hapsburgs to return to power. Technically a monarchy, Hungary was ruled by Admiral Nicholas Horthy, a reactionary representative of the military class. Within two years, Hungary had gone from a democracy to a military dictatorship. Under Admiral Horthy's rule, landlocked Hungary was called "a kingdom without a king ruled by an admiral without a fleet."

Poland. Soon after the war a constitutional assembly met in Poland. It adopted a democratic constitution closely modeled on that of the Third French Republic. However, bitter opposition from both the right and the left prevented the new government from operating effectively. In 1926, Poland followed the example of Hungary and turned to military dictatorship. Dictator Marshal Josef Pilsudski, like Admiral Horthy in Hungary, represented the aristocracy and the military.

Turkey under Mustafa Kemal

You have read about the harsh terms of the peace treaty that was forced upon the Ottoman Empire after World War I. For some time a group of Turkish nationalists, called the Young Turks, had been trying to reform the weak, inefficient, and corrupt Turkish government. Discontent over the terms of the treaty brought Turkish unrest to a head. The result was a revolution in 1922 led by an able and energetic leader, Mustafa Kemal. The revolutionists demanded that the treaty of 1920 be canceled and a new one written. The European powers agreed, wishing to avoid further unrest.

By the new treaty, written in 1923, the Turks regained eastern Thrace, Smyrna, and full control of Constantinople (now Istanbul). The Straits were still to be left unfortified and were to be administered by a commission of the League of Nations. They were to be open to the vessels of all nations in peace and to neutral vessels in wartime.

The revolution led by Mustafa Kemal put an end to the Ottoman Empire and established the Republic of Turkey. The capital was moved from Constantinople to Angora (now Ankara) in Asia Minor (see map, page 603). The government was to be a Western-style parliamentary democracy with a strong executive. Kemal became the first president.

Kemal wanted Turkey to become a progressive nation, modeled on the industrialized powers of the West. He ordered his subjects to adopt Western dress. The fez, the traditional hat of Turkish men, was prohibited. He insisted that all Turks adopt family surnames, like Europeans. He himself was given the name Atatürk, meaning "father of the Turks." Women received the right to vote. Polygamy was abolished. For the first time the Moslem religion was separated from political affairs, and there was an attempt to lessen its influence over the people.

Perhaps more important still, Turkey adopted the Western calendar, the metric system of weights and measures, and the Roman alphabet. This last change made it possible for many more people to learn to read and write because the Roman alphabet was far easier to use than the difficult Arabic script. Atatürk also began a program of economic development. The government paid subsidies to farmers and aided new industries.

Modernizing Persia

The ancient country of Persia also underwent change after World War I. Before the war it had been divided into British and Russian spheres of influence, with a zone in the center where either could have concessions. After the war the country was torn by civil wars and the conflicting ambitions of the British and the Russians. In 1925 an army officer, Reza Khan, deposed the ruling shah and took power as Reza Shah Pahlavi. In foreign policy he was anti-Russian. Domestically he followed a policy much like that of Kemal Atatürk, introducing Western industries and customs. In 1935 the name of the country officially became Iran.

Although there was a limited, constitutional monarchy, much power remained in the hands of the large landowners. Reza Shah suppressed political parties and strictly controlled the press and education.

Troubles in China

You have read how the Manchu dynasty was overthrown in 1912, when the Kuomintang (Nationalist People's Party) proclaimed a republic. The Republic of China, however, existed mainly on paper. The Kuomintang, led by Sun Yat-sen, controlled a small region around Canton, in southern China. The rest of the country was divided up among various warlords. The official capital of China was still Peking, in the north.

Upheavals followed World War I as nation after nation tried to adjust its ancient ways of life to the realities of the postwar world. Mustafa Kemal, above, reviews his troops in 1923 after their successful revolution in Turkey. In China, Chiang Kai-shek, left, became the leader of Nationalist forces, which drove the opposing communists on the "Long March." At left, below, mules carry dismantled artillery pieces to Shensi province; peasants at right hold primitive handmade spears as they rest on the march.

The Nationalists, as members of the Kuomintang were called, asked for help from foreign powers to overthrow the warlords and establish the Republic of China as a strong central government. The United States, Great Britain, Japan, and other powers remained indifferent to the plea. The only country that offered help was Russia, now under a communist government. It sent technical and political advisers to help reorganize the Kuomintang and build up an army. Chinese communists cooperated with the Kuomintang; they also began to organize factory workers and peasants.

Sun Yat-sen died in 1925. Leadership of the Nationalists was taken over by a young general, Chiang Kai-shek. The Nationalist army grew in strength. In 1926 it moved against the warlords of the north and seized Hankow. Two years later the Nationalists occupied Peking, which they renamed Peiping.

Although the Kuomintang was expanding the area under its control, disagreements began to divide its membership. A left wing of the party, composed of socialists and communists, wanted to put more power in the hands of peasants and workers. A conservative right wing opposed radical change, especially land reform. Chiang Kai-shek became leader of this right wing.

In 1927, before the northern offensive was completed, Chiang expelled the left-wing members of his party and sent the Russian advisers home. He then set up a Nationalist government in Nanking.

The leaders of the left wing took whoever would follow them into Kiangsi province, in southeastern China, where they set up their own government. It was modeled on the Russian communist regime and was called the Chinese Soviet Republic. This group was attacked repeatedly by the Nationalists and finally forced to evacuate Kiangsi. In a famous "Long March," lasting nearly two years, this left-wing group traveled some 6,000 miles west and north, re-establishing the Chinese Soviet Republic in northern Shensi province in 1935. This region, with its town of Yenan, became their headquarters in the long civil war that followed.

Chiang Kai-shek's regime. Chiang's government at Nanking was a one-party government with Chiang as virtual dictator. He and his followers wanted a strong China with an efficient government, but they were not much interested in democracy. In general, although they tried to westernize and industrialize China, they wanted to keep much of its traditional political system without changing it.

Attempts to industrialize were hampered because of lack of capital. Much government revenue was spent on maintaining the army because the Chinese feared Japanese aggression. The control of many of China's natural resources by foreign powers also hindered economic development. Most foreign powers were unwilling to give up the special privileges they had held since the era of imperialism.

By 1937 the area of China under Nationalist control had made progress despite many obstacles. The Nationalists had begun a program of building roads and of repairing, rebuilding, and extending railroads. They improved finances and reformed the educational system.

However, because the Nationalists needed the backing of landowners and merchants, they failed to deal with two ancient problems. No changes were made in the age-old system of land ownership, nor in the method of collecting taxes in the provinces. You may recall that these were two continuing problems that had plagued Chinese dynasties through many centuries. Because of peasant discontent, the communist government in Shensi was able to win support and build up an army.

CHECKUP

1. What changes and reforms were made by Mustafa Kemal?

2. Summarize briefly the history of the Kuomintang between 1912 and 1927.

3. What obstacles did the Nationalists meet in trying to industrialize China?

4. IDENTIFY: *Anschluss,* Kun, Horthy, Pilsudski, Young Turks, Reza Shah Pahlavi, Chinese Soviet Republic, "Long March."

4   A worldwide depression began in the United States

Like France and Great Britain, the United States had fought on the victorious Allied side in the war. Unlike them, it had fought for only about a year. It had been separated from the battlefields by the Atlantic Ocean, and there had been no devastation of American land. Naturally, the United States emerged from the war in a very different situation than did its allies.

At the end of World War I, the United States was much stronger economically than it had been in 1914. Both industry and agriculture had expanded tremendously, and there was a boom, as a sudden increase in prosperity is called. The war had created great wealth, although many felt that it was less evenly divided than ever. Wages had increased, but prices had gone up even more. There was considerable inflation; prices had more than doubled between 1913 and 1920.

Postwar isolation

The United States emerged from the war as the apparent successor to Britain as a world leader. It had tipped the balance in favor of the Allies and had taken a strong role in drawing up the peace settlement. The most dramatic indication of America's new position, however, was financial. In 1914 the United States had owed about 4 billion dollars to foreign governments and businessmen. In 1919, conditions were reversed; foreign governments owed the American government about 10 billion dollars. Much more was owed to individual Americans who had bought foreign bonds.

However, the refusal of the United States to join the League of Nations indicated that it did not want the responsibility of world leadership. Americans seemed to want to sit back and enjoy their new-found prosperity and avoid entanglement in European affairs.

This was the era in American history often referred to as the "Roaring Twenties" because of the fast pace of life and sometimes frantic pursuit of pleasure. It was the era when jazz won popularity, movie stars became public idols, and Charles Lindbergh gained fame overnight for piloting an airplane alone across the Atlantic Ocean.

America and the world economy

In the middle 1920's, it seemed to many people as if the world economy had completely recovered from the war. Agricultural and industrial production soared, and profits were enormous.

But there were flaws in the system that were overlooked. For one thing, the wages paid to labor did not keep pace with the increase in productivity. There was not enough money in the hands of consumers to buy everything that was produced. Profits were either reinvested in new machinery and additional factories or paid out to wealthy stockholders. Increased use of labor-saving machinery not only stimulated production but also reduced employment.

The agricultural economy was not healthy. American farmers had greatly increased their production during the war to help feed the Allies. Now that outlet was closed. The demand for food, in economists' terms, is inelastic because it cannot go beyond a certain point within a certain market area. The average family, no matter how much money it has, can consume only so much food and no more. The use of modern machinery and methods led to serious overproduction of food, and prices fell. This was especially true in the wheat market, where production far outstripped consumption in the 1920's.

Another flaw in the system was economic nationalism. The operation of the world market demanded a free flow of goods from one country to another. But industrial nations set up tariff walls in the 1920's, hoping to protect their expanding industries from outside competition. Home markets could not consume all that was being produced, and high tariffs made it difficult for foreign buyers to drain off the surplus.

The United States raised its tariffs to the highest level in its history. It insisted upon American dollars in exchange for goods sold abroad, but high tariffs made it hard for European countries

The Great Depression began in the United States and was probably worse there than elsewhere. Of the estimated 30 million jobless people around the world in 1932, 12 million of them were in the United States. Countless businesses, like the one at left, went bankrupt. In New York City, below, hundreds of hungry men stand in snow and rain to receive a little soup and bread. The desperate problems of the depression were compounded for thousands of Midwestern Americans by devastating dust storms. Relentless winds swept over drought-ridden land, burying millions of acres under tons of drifting dust. Poverty-stricken families piled their possessions into trucks and cars and moved away. At bottom left, Oklahoma farmers and their families head for California. When they could find no jobs, the government built makeshift camps for them. At lower right, "Okies" gather around an outdoor stove.

to sell goods in America. If they could not sell goods *to* the United States, there was no way for them to acquire dollars to purchase goods *from* the United States. American banks and businessmen were willing to lend money to Europeans so that they could buy American goods, but this practice did not provide a solid base for international trade. It merely created more indebtedness, and European nations already had heavy war debts.

Millions of Americans were speculating in the stock market—that is, making risky investments in stocks in the hope of quick, high profits. Prices of stocks sold through the New York Stock Exchange rose to high levels, and many investors did make large profits. The trouble was that much of the money invested in the stock market had also been borrowed. Frequently the only security the borrowers had to offer was money that they expected to make in the future, for everyone expected the prices of stocks to rise indefinitely.

The Great Depression

In October 1929, a wave of panic swept the investors in the New York Stock Exchange, and within a few hours the stock market collapsed completely. No one was willing to buy stocks while the prices were declining and, as a result, most of the stocks on the exchange became virtually worthless. Vast fortunes were swept away. Hundreds of American banks, factories, mining companies, and business firms went bankrupt.

The collapse of the New York stock market was the beginning of a worldwide depression, called the Great Depression. Some of the most reliable European banks were forced to close their doors. By 1932 there were more than 30 million workers unemployed and hungry in countries all around the world. Germany stopped paying reparations. The Allied nations ceased debt payments to the United States.

The strange thing about depression poverty was that it was poverty in the midst of plenty. The prices of goods fell very low, but goods could not be sold because people simply did not have the money to buy. Manufactured products piled up in warehouses and farm crops rotted. Some coun-

tries tried to force prices higher by destroying surpluses. Canada burned part of its wheat crop. Brazil dumped coffee into the sea. European exports and imports declined over 60 percent in three years, and United States trade went down 68 percent.

The United States responded to the depression by raising its tariffs even higher than before and by cutting off American loans to Europe. Germany and Austria wanted to establish a customs union to aid their economies, but several European nations opposed the project and it was forbidden by the World Court. In every case, it appeared, the immediate response to the depression made recovery more difficult.

In 1933 an International Monetary and Economic Conference met in London, but it failed to promote greater financial cooperation among the industrial nations. Most of these countries had already decided upon economic nationalism as the proper answer to depression.

Results of the Great Depression

Great Britain tried to induce full employment and stimulate production by making low-interest loans to its industries. Besides raising its tariffs against foreign goods, Britain tried to find a solution for depression problems within the Commonwealth. In 1932, at a conference in Ottawa, Canada, Britain devised a system of "imperial preferences" by which British dominions agreed to apply low tariffs to one another's products. In a period of international economic uncertainty, the British Commonwealth attempted to become economically self-sufficient.

France, which was less industrialized than Great Britain, was hit less hard by the depression. However, French trade declined, unemployment increased, and industrial production dropped sharply. The uncertainty of the depression years caused even greater political instability in France than the postwar troubles had created. In 1933 alone there were four changes of government.

Elsewhere in the world the depression caused unrest and violence. In Germany, as you will read in the next chapter, it helped destroy the postwar republican government. Representative governments survived the shock of severe depression only where democratic traditions were strong.

The New Deal. The United States had lagged behind most other industrial nations in social legislation. There was no unemployment insurance and little in the way of government relief programs. When the depression came, American workers had to rely on their private savings, if any, and on charity provided by private organizations. People stood in so-called bread lines to receive a bowl of soup or a plate of stew. Some earned money by selling apples in the streets.

Under President Herbert Hoover, the federal government tried to remedy conditions, but the measures adopted were not far-reaching. Hoover believed that prosperity was "just around the corner."

Elections brought a new President, Franklin D. Roosevelt, to office in 1933. He immediately embarked upon a program of relief and reform that was called the New Deal. The government first made grants of money to the states for direct relief—food, shelter, and clothing for the needy—and began a program of public works to provide employment.

Roosevelt's emergency relief program was followed by a sweeping reform of America's economic system. Banks and stock exchanges were put under strict regulation. A Social Security Act, passed in 1935, provided for unemployment and old-age benefits. A forty-hour work week and minimum wage levels were established. The federal government, which had earlier remained neutral or sided with the industrialists in labor disputes, guaranteed workers the right to establish unions.

The federal government also tried to relieve the desperate situation of farmers by paying them to take land out of production and to plant soil-building crops. Later the government adopted a program of buying and storing surplus farm crops. Another federal program of far-reaching economic and social significance was the Tennessee Valley Authority (TVA), established in the valley of the Tennessee River and its tributaries. The government built a series of multipurpose dams, intended to generate cheap electricity, help prevent floods and soil erosion, improve navigation, and provide recreation.

In Latin America the Roosevelt administration tried to undo the legacy of ill will and suspicion created by the American policy of intervention. Roosevelt fostered a program—begun in the 1920's—called the Good Neighbor Policy, which stressed mutual cooperation and noninterference in Latin-American affairs. The United States joined with other American nations in an agreement, the Montevideo Pact, which declared that "No state has the right to intervene in the internal or external affairs of another state." As proof of its good intentions, the United States signed a treaty with Cuba canceling the Platt Amendment, withdrew its troops from Haiti, and surrendered its right to interfere in Panama.

The Roosevelt administration also tried to revive world trade. The Trade Agreements Act, passed in 1934, allowed the President to make special agreements with foreign countries. If a foreign nation lowered its tariff rates on some American products, the President was empowered to lower American tariff rates on some of that country's products. With measures such as this, United States foreign trade began to recover.

Under the New Deal the United States government was more deeply involved than ever before in the welfare of the individual citizen. It attempted in many ways to restore prosperity. But the causes of the depression were too deeply rooted to be cured completely even by such an ambitious program as the New Deal. The economic hardships caused by the Great Depression were not fully overcome until the United States once more mobilized for war in the late 1930's.

CHECKUP

1. How did postwar conditions in the United States compare with those in Europe?

2. What conditions helped bring on the Great Depression?

3. What was the New Deal? Give specific examples of its measures.

4. IDENTIFY: boom, "Roaring Twenties," speculating, "imperial preferences," Good Neighbor Policy, Trade Agreements Act.

CHAPTER REVIEW

Chapter 33   Democracy Faced Severe Tests After World War I   (1918–1938)

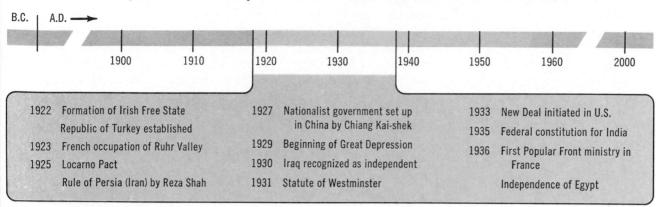

1922	Formation of Irish Free State	
	Republic of Turkey established	
1923	French occupation of Ruhr Valley	
1925	Locarno Pact	
	Rule of Persia (Iran) by Reza Shah	

1927   Nationalist government set up
          in China by Chiang Kai-shek
1929   Beginning of Great Depression
1930   Iraq recognized as independent
1931   Statute of Westminster

1933   New Deal initiated in U.S.
1935   Federal constitution for India
1936   First Popular Front ministry in
          France
          Independence of Egypt

CHAPTER SUMMARY

After World War I, many democratic nations experienced serious problems. France, which had suffered severe war losses, was plagued by an unstable government and financial difficulties. Heavy military expenditures were necessary for the Maginot Line. A system of alliances was aimed at isolating Germany, but many of France's allies were weak.

Britain was hurt by the war and by economic nationalism, but the newly important Labour Party took measures to head off serious trouble. The British Empire, however, began to disintegrate. Ireland, Egypt, and Iraq won independence. Palestine was a trouble spot because of conflicts between Arabs and Jews. Partial self-government failed to satisfy Indian nationalists. Demands for greater independence in the dominions led to the Statute of Westminster, establishing the British Commonwealth of Nations.

Finland, the Baltic States, and Czechoslovakia remained democracies, but conditions elsewhere in eastern Europe were less favorable. Beset with weak economies and other problems, Austria, Hungary, and Poland soon set up repressive or dictatorial regimes. In both Turkey and Persia (Iran), strong leaders introduced social reforms and economic improvements.

China, although technically a republic, underwent internal strife. The Kuomintang under Chiang Kai-shek fought to create a united country but soon expelled left-wing members, who established a rival Chinese Soviet Republic. Civil war between Nationalists and communists resulted.

The United States, the strongest world power after World War I, chose to remain isolated politically and economically. Overproduction of food, unwise foreign trade policies, and speculation led to a stock market crash and a worldwide depression. Although

the New Deal introduced economic and social reforms, the Great Depression continued through the 1930's.

QUESTIONS FOR DISCUSSION

1. Democracy seems to be a commodity that is difficult to export. Why do you think this is true?

2. France, Great Britain, and the United States each faced serious problems after World War I. Rate the three nations as to how well you think each handled its problem. Defend your rating.

3. Explain how nationalism could be a force for progress in Turkey and a creator of problems in Palestine and Ireland.

4. During the era after World War I, many governments were faced with general strikes. Why can such strikes be very effective? Would you advocate a general strike in some particular situation in order to gain political action?

5. What were some of the new roles assumed by the government during the New Deal? Do you support the increase in government power over the welfare of the individual citizen? Justify your position pro or con.

6. If you had been a military adviser in France, what arguments would you have used to persuade the French government that the Maginot Line was impractical?

PROJECTS

1. Write a short essay on the causes of the Great Depression.

2. Write an editorial for an American newspaper advocating government aid to Sun Yat-sen's government.

3. Draw a cartoon showing the pros and cons of economic nationalism.

34

Totalitarian Dictatorships Came to Power in Europe

You have read about totalitarianism, the system in which the government controls almost every aspect of an individual's life. Ancient Sparta was totalitarian; its rulers tried to exert total control over their people. Over the centuries, various states used totalitarian methods. In the period after World War I, however, totalitarianism became especially powerful and dangerous as it was established in several nations. This chapter will deal with Russia, Italy, and Germany, whose totalitarian regimes influenced the entire world.

Each of the modern totalitarian nations has had a dictator—a man who holds almost absolute power over the country. As you have read, there were dictators in the Roman Republic. They were appointed to rule during times of emergency and were allowed to hold office for a specific length of time. Modern totalitarian dictators, however, stay in office until they die or are overthrown by rivals.

Modern totalitarianism is also different from earlier forms of dictatorship in that it relies on ideologies—doctrines that attempt to answer all of men's questions and problems. In this sense, modern totalitarian theories are like twisted forms of religion.

Totalitarian dictatorship often takes root and thrives in countries where people can see no other way out—where life seems to offer only poverty, hunger, disease, and hopelessness. People will ac-

Burning books, a common practice in dictatorships

cept a dictatorship, or allow one to be established, when they think that their problems cannot be solved in any other way.

Dictatorship, of whatever kind, is a complete denial of the democratic ideal. In a dictatorship it is the state, the government, which must be served and which must succeed. The rights and dignity of the individual citizen must be sacrificed to the welfare of the state. You can see the absolute and fundamental difference: In a democracy the government is the servant of the people and exists for their welfare. In a dictatorship the people exist for the welfare of the state. To be sure, the totalitarian state usually promises the citizen material things, such as food and clothing. But to get them the citizen must be willing to give up many fundamental rights, liberties, and beliefs.

The totalitarian dictatorship is a police state. That is, the dictator controls the armed forces and the police and uses them to destroy opposition. People are arrested without warrants and punished without trials. Secret police spy on all citizens, and the fear thus created prevents opposition from forming.

The dictator relies on propaganda as well as on force to control the people. Unfriendly newspapers and magazines are suppressed. Newspapers and broadcasting are used skillfully to create public support. With no public opposition permitted, the people are told only what the dictator wants them to hear.

The two major forms of totalitarianism in the period since World War I have been communism and fascism. Both have relied on similar means of repression and used similar means of propaganda. In their origins and in their goals, however, the two have differed widely. Watch for these differences as you read how Russia became a communist dictatorship and how fascist dictatorships came to power in Italy and Germany.

THE CHAPTER SECTIONS:

1. The czarist regime of Russia collapsed and Bolsheviks took over (1914–1921)

2. Russia tried to build a society according to Marxist theory (1921–1938)

3. Mussolini imposed a fascist dictatorship in Italy (1918–1934)

4. The Nazi Party, under Adolf Hitler, seized control of Germany (1918–1936)

1 The czarist regime of Russia collapsed and Bolsheviks took over

Russia, which had been torn by revolutionary disturbances throughout the 1800's, faced continuing problems in the early 1900's. The Revolution of 1905, discussed earlier, had brought changes that were more apparent than real. The elected legislative body, the Duma, had little power. The czar remained an almost absolute ruler. The Russian people were denied the democratic rights and civil liberties that they had been promised. Citizens who sought further reforms joined secret societies, which often expressed their members' frustration in violence.

There were also grave economic problems. Russia was far behind Western European countries in its industrial development and agricultural methods. For example, in 1914 only 1½ percent of Russia's people were industrial workers, compared with 40 percent of Great Britain's popula-

tion. For their part, the Russian peasants were unhappy with the results of their emancipation. Debts, taxes, and rents kept them in poverty.

The fall of the monarchy

The Russo-Japanese War of 1904–1905 had shown Russia's weakness. World War I exposed it still further. There were not enough railroads or good roads. Russian industry could not adequately equip and supply the army. When the Ottoman Empire entered the war on the side of the Central Powers, Russia was cut off from outside supplies.

The Allies had counted heavily on the Russian "steamroller"—the great masses of men in the Russian armies. When the war came, Russian troops proved to be poorly equipped and badly led. Russian soldiers were courageous, but courage was not enough. Behind the army was an inefficient and corrupt government, completely unfit to deal with the problems of modern warfare. Nevertheless, for over three years, Russian troops held back more than half the troops of the Central Powers. During this period, 1,700,000 Russians were killed, 5 million were wounded and crippled, and more than 2 million were taken prisoner by the enemy. If the Russians had not fought so well, the Allies might have lost the war.

By the spring of 1917, the Russians were weary of hardships and disheartened by the appalling casualties they had suffered. They had lost all faith in their government. Strikes and street demonstrations broke out in Petrograd (as St. Petersburg had been called since 1914). Czar Nicholas II ordered them put down by force. When the Duma demanded reforms in the government, Nicholas ordered the Duma dissolved.

In the past the government had always been able to use the army against disturbances such as those in Petrograd. Now, however, the soldiers joined the rioters. The uprising spread from the capital to the countryside. Unable to depend on the army, the government was helpless.

The Duma, encouraged by the army's disobedience, refused the czar's order to disband. Czar Nicholas, who was at army headquarters near the front lines when the disturbances broke out, tried to return to the capital, but he was prevented from doing so by officers of his own army. On March 15, 1917, unable to control his subjects or his army, Nicholas II abdicated. The 300-year-old Romanov monarchy was ended.

The Bolsheviks

A liberal provisional government was set up to rule Russia until a constitutional assembly could be elected to decide upon a permanent system of government. While the provisional government tried to restore order, a rival force was working for change in Russia. It was the Petrograd Soviet (or council) of Workers' and Soldiers' Deputies.

The Petrograd Soviet had been quickly organized when the disorders began in Russia. It was modeled on similar organizations that had participated in the Revolution of 1905. The Petrograd Soviet was composed chiefly of moderate socialists, called Mensheviks, but contained a small number of radical socialists, known as Bolsheviks. Most of the prominent Bolsheviks lived outside of Russia, having been exiled in 1905.

Other soviets similar to the one in Petrograd were soon established throughout Russia. They won much support, for their program was more attractive than that of the provisional government. They called for immediate peace, land reforms, and the turning over of factories to the workers. The provisional government was divided on these issues and wanted to postpone as many decisions as possible until an elected constitutional assembly could be convened. The soviets were hesitant to rebel against the provisional government, fearing that they lacked adequate popular support. At the same time the provisional government was powerless to govern. These two groups jockeyed for position while the rest of the country was fast moving toward chaos.

Lenin. On April 16, 1917, the leader of the Bolsheviks, N. Lenin,° returned to Russia from exile in Switzerland. The German government, hoping to weaken Russia further by adding more fuel to the growing revolution, had helped Lenin and some of his followers pass through Germany. Lenin's first act, once back in Russia, was to insist that all governing power be turned over to the soviets.

Lenin was an extremely intelligent and forceful man. He came from the ranks of the lower nobility, and had studied law. After his older brother had been executed by the czarist police as a revolutionary, Lenin became a fanatical rebel. He was a devoted socialist and also a shrewd politician.

Lenin was a radical socialist who believed in revolution. He modified Marxism, however, partly because of conditions in Russia. As you have read, there was little industry in Russia; thus the Russian proletariat formed a small class. Lenin

---

° **Lenin:** Lenin was born Vladimir Ilyich Ulyanov, but assumed the name N. Lenin as a young man. It is not known what, if anything, the *N* represented.

The Russian Revolution of 1917 broke out in Petrograd, then the capital of Russia. Russian soldiers, right, joined civilian revolutionaries in taking over the city. As the revolution quickly spread, Bolsheviks—most of whom had been exiled after the Revolution of 1905—sped back to Russia to take part. Their leader, Lenin, harangues a crowd, middle right. He led his faction to victory partly by ordering the storming of the Winter Palace in Petrograd, below, where the moderate government had its headquarters. Lenin then redirected Marxist thinking and more than anyone else laid the foundations of the present Soviet Union. In May 1918, Czar Nicholas II and his family, who had been captured and imprisoned in Siberia, lower right, were taken into the cellar of a building and shot as White armies approached.

Russian Socialist Realism

Once in power, the Russian communists enforced an important belief: that artists, like everyone else, should work for the benefit of society. They condemned art as an end in itself and fostered "socialist realism." Artists were to glorify the revolution and the proletariat, and to paint in a realistic style. Art was judged according to how well it met these standards. "An Honored Steelmaker and His Team," by G. Gorelov, is a typical example of modern Russian painting. The idealized faces of the workmen, the posed determination with which the group at right stares into the future, even the carefully depicted machinery in the background—all these elements are meant to impress the viewer and inspire him to work for the glory of the Soviet Union.

believed that if left to work spontaneously, the forces of history might not move in the direction Marx had predicted. Lenin advocated the use of a small group of devoted Marxists, who would train the working class to become a revolutionary force and manipulate events in order to bring about pure communism. Lenin's adaptation of Marxism formed the basis of what we now know as Russian communism.

Lenin's slogan, "Land, Peace, and Bread," reached the heart of the masses in 1917. He also promised immediate favorable laws for city factory workers. But the Bolsheviks still did not control the soviets.

In June 1917, delegates from all the soviets in Russia met in a congress. The more moderate socialists outnumbered the Bolsheviks by more than five to one. The congress appointed a Central Executive Committee to speak for all the soviets. Since the Bolsheviks could not command a majority of the soviets, they worked hard to control the Central Executive Committee.

During the summer the war continued to go badly for Russia. Food shortages and inflation added to the misery of the Russian people. By September the Bolsheviks had gained control of the Central Executive Committee. They claimed that only the soviets, as the true representatives of the Russian people, were entitled to govern Russia.

On November 7, 1917, the Bolsheviks overthrew the provisional government and seized control of Russia. This revolution is often called the second Russian revolution (the first having been in March), or the Bolshevik Revolution. The following spring the Bolsheviks renamed themselves the Communist Party.

Civil war

At the end of 1917, the situation in Russia was confused. The communists still did not have complete control of the country. First they signed separate peace treaties with each of the Central Powers—Germany, Austria-Hungary, Bulgaria, and the Ottoman Empire. The communists were anxious to make peace on any terms, especially since Russia's army was exhausted from three years of bitter fighting. Therefore the treaties were harsh toward Russia, and it lost a sizable amount of territory.

After making the peace settlements, the new regime turned its attention to internal problems. The communists faced much opposition within Russia, not only from former aristocrats and other reactionaries, but also from middle-class liberals and the Mensheviks. In scattered groups, under various leaders, they tried to overthrow the communists in a civil war. The communists had adopted the symbolic color of European revolutionary socialism—red—as their color. They were therefore called the "Reds." Those who opposed the communists were called the "Whites" in the civil war.

The civil war, which began in December 1917, lasted almost three years, adding to the devastation begun by World War I. The Red Army—as the forces of the new government were called—and the several White armies fought many battles and left an appalling trail of destruction.

The Allies had been angered by the separate treaties that the new Russian government had signed. There was also fear among the Western democracies that the revolution would spread if the communists gained control of Russia. (One of the main doctrines of Marxism was that the workers' revolution must be worldwide, or it could not succeed anywhere; this was known as the doctrine of world revolution.) Therefore the Allies aided the White forces with arms and money.

Several of the Allies even sent small forces of troops to help overthrow the communist government. Late in 1917, the Japanese had seized Vladivostok, which they held until 1922. In 1918, French and British troops landed at Murmansk and seized Archangel. American troops landed in Siberia.

The Allies helped prolong the civil war, but they could not change the result. By 1921 the communists had completely defeated the White forces. The communists did not forget Allied intervention and the Allies' attempt to overthrow the communist government. Much of their later hostility toward the Western democracies can be traced to this intervention.

The communists in control

As soon as they had seized power in 1917, the communists began to reorganize Russia's system of government. The capital was moved from Petrograd to Moscow. A cabinet, the Council of People's Commissars, was hastily formed. It was headed by Lenin. A National Congress was also established. This huge body was made up of over a thousand representatives from the soviets. Officially the National Congress was the sovereign legislative body of the nation. In fact, however, real power rested with the People's Commissars.

In 1922 the country was given a new name, the Union of Soviet Socialist Republics (U.S.S.R.). This name indicated that the power in Russia was to be in the hands of the soviets, the revolutionary councils of workers and soldiers. The guiding economic system was to be socialism. Politically, the country was to be divided into separate republics, which were to be joined in a federal union. Eventually there were sixteen of these republics in the U.S.S.R.°

In 1922, when the civil war ended, the communists took complete control of the devastated country. The czar and his family had been executed in 1918. Many nobles and members of the middle class were also executed in a "Red Terror" similar to the Reign of Terror of the French Revolution. Many other lives had been lost in battle, in raging epidemics of typhus, or through starvation. Agriculture had declined until it was a struggle for the peasants to raise enough to keep alive. City people faced starvation. The transportation system was ruined. Of the small number of prewar industrial factories, only 13 percent remained. The hoped-for revolutions in other countries had not taken place.

Between 1918 and 1921, Soviet leaders had followed a policy known as War Communism. Although they nationalized all the Russian industries, their social and economic measures were not based on a long-range plan. Whatever food could be seized from the peasants, whatever industrial commodities could be produced, had been distributed on a basis of need. The first need was that of the Red Army. Civilians were left to do without, possibly to starve, because the main concern of the Soviet government was to save the revolution. Now, with peace at hand, the communist leaders had to develop a program to build their "new society" in Russia.

° **U.S.S.R.:** From this time on, it is correct to speak of the Soviet Union and the Soviet people. However, the terms *Russia* and *Russians* also continued in common use to refer to the U.S.S.R. and its people.

CHECKUP

1. What are the chief characteristics of a modern totalitarian dictatorship?

2. After the March 1917 revolution in Russia, what two groups struggled for power? On what questions did they disagree?

3. How did Lenin modify Marxism?

4. What caused the civil war in Russia? How long did it last? Why did the Allies intervene?

5. IDENTIFY: Petrograd Soviet, Mensheviks, Bolsheviks, doctrine of world revolution, "Red Terror," War Communism.

2 Russia tried to build a society according to Marxist theory

The problems of trying to build a socialist society in Russia were many and complex. Russia is a huge country whose people represent many nationalities and speak over a hundred different languages. In 1921 there were vast differences in civilization and culture, too. In European Russia lived people thoroughly in tune with modern ideas and society. On the far peninsula of Kamchatka, in the Pacific, there were tribes just emerging from Stone Age culture.

Communism in Russia

The communist leader Joseph Stalin had a favorite saying, "Facts are stubborn things." In trying to build a society based on Marxist theory, Soviet leaders faced tremendous contradictions between theory and reality—"stubborn facts."

Karl Marx, you will recall, had developed his "scientific socialism" in terms of the Western capitalist nations, which were already industrialized in the late 1800's. After industry had been built up through the capitalistic profit system, Marx expected the workers to revolt and take over ownership of the factories. But in Russia a socialist revolution had occurred before the country was industrialized. The "stubborn fact," the economic reality, was that there were almost no industries to nationalize and no wealth to share. Arguments over how to divide the results of production were meaningless when there was little industrial production.

Marx had foreseen a revolution led by the proletariat, who would also control the new government. In Russia, however, the "stubborn fact" was that the revolution had been carried out by a minority, the Bolsheviks, who continued in power. The proletariat formed a small, relatively

insignificant group. Like the majority of Russians, they were uneducated and poorly equipped to govern a nation.

Lenin, the head of the Soviet government, was a devoted Marxist, but he was also a practical man. He realized that to build a socialist society, Russia needed fewer theories and more farms, factories, mines, and trained workers. It needed thousands of schools and better houses for its people. These things could be produced only by money and hard work.

There was not much money in the Soviet Union of 1921. The government had confiscated Russian savings, but the amount was not enough to restore the economy of the country.

The needed capital had to come from abroad. Foreigners, however, would not be willing to invest their savings in a country that offered no interest and might confiscate the capital. Nor would Russian workers and peasants be willing to work if they knew that what they produced would be taken from them. If Russia were to attract capital and industrialize, compromise seemed necessary.

The New Economic Policy

Lenin decided that it was necessary to take "one step backward" before Russia could take "two steps forward." Departing from strict Marxist theory, he announced what was called the New Economic Policy (NEP). This system allowed some free enterprise in order to stimulate Russia's economy.

The NEP permitted individuals to buy, sell, and trade farm products. The major industries—oil, mining, steel, and the railroads—remained under government ownership and management. Smaller businesses and home industries could be privately owned and operated for profit. Foreign capital was welcomed for the development of state industries, and investors were promised a high rate of return. Foreign technicians were invited to come to Russia, with the promise of high salaries.

While Lenin attempted to build up Russia's industries, agriculture remained a problem. Russia's farm lands, which had been seized from the wealthy landlords during the revolution, were divided among the peasants. The government tried to persuade them to pool their land into large collective farms where they could share the scarce modern farm machinery. But the great majority of peasants stubbornly held on to their small strips of land and stuck to the old ways of farming.

Stalin in power

Lenin died in 1924, and there followed a struggle for power among the high officials of the Communist Party. The main contestants in the struggle were Leon Trotsky and Joseph Stalin. Trotsky, born Lev Bronstein, was a brilliant party organizer who had played an important role in the Bolshevik Revolution of November 1917. He had almost single-handedly created the Red Army that defended the communist regime in the civil war. Joseph Stalin came from Georgia, in the Caucasus region of Russia. (He changed his last name from Dzhugashvili, basing his new name on *stal,* the Russian word for "steel.") He had studied for the priesthood but was expelled from the seminary and became a revolutionist. Under Lenin, Stalin had risen to the position of secretary general of the Communist Party.

One issue in the dispute between Trotsky and Stalin concerned the future of the revolution. Trotsky followed the strict Marxist belief that the revolution, to be successful, had to take place all over the world. Stalin, on the other hand, broke with accepted doctrine and advocated "socialism in one country"—Russia. After socialism had been successful in Russia, said Stalin, the revolution would spread to the rest of the world.

The struggle between the two factions was bitter, savage, and merciless. By 1928, as a result of a series of betrayals and assassinations, Stalin was securely in power. Trotsky went into exile. (He was later murdered in Mexico, probably on Stalin's orders.) Stalin was not as intelligent or as broadly educated as Lenin had been, nor was he nearly as flexible in his thinking. He was, however, shrewd and ruthless. Under his leadership, Russia became a police state, a nation ruled by terror and intimidation. Some historians date the beginning of true totalitarianism in Russia from 1928, the year Stalin assumed complete power.

In 1928, Stalin announced the end of the NEP and the return to a completely controlled economy such as Russia had experienced under War Communism. The economic controls of the period from 1918 to 1921 had been emergency measures. Stalin's goal was to make the planned economy a permanent feature in Russia.

The Five-Year Plans

Russian economists were put to work developing a master plan of economic growth. The result of their work was the first Five-Year Plan, published in 1928. Industrial, agricultural, and social goals were established for the next five years. Detailed plans were drawn up for agriculture and industry. There were also plans for expanding the educational system, for building more hospitals, and for constructing more housing.

The resources of backward, agricultural Russia were stretched to the breaking point to enable the country to become a modern, industrialized society. Heavy industries were vastly expanded at the expense of consumer goods—those products, such as food and clothing, that satisfy human needs. The Russian people, Stalin said, had to make great sacrifices in their personal lives so that Russia could grow strong. Stalin employed fear of renewed intervention by the Western democracies to speed the process. He said, "We are in a race. We are from fifty to a hundred years behind the advanced countries. We must run through the distance in ten years. Either we do this, or they will crush us."

The planners hoped that collective farming with modern machinery would produce enough food for the Russian people, with a surplus for export. Money from these exports would help pay for the expansion of industry. Therefore the future of Russia as an industrial nation depended on a rapid increase in farm production. All farms were to be merged into collectives. Peasants had to join or suffer severe consequences. Hundreds of thousands of the wealthier peasants were executed when they attempted to withhold their lands from collectivization. Others were imprisoned or exiled.

The first Five-Year Plan was successful in most industries, and about 70 percent of the most productive farm land was collectivized. Still, there were defects. The quality of goods produced was

This official photograph of Joseph Stalin masks his cruel and dictatorial personality.

often poor. There were still not enough railroads. Grain, oil, and timber were often in short supply.

A second Five-Year Plan was begun in 1933. It was even more comprehensive than the first. Again the program called for increases in heavy industries. But as a reward for the work and sacrifices of the people, the production of consumer goods was also increased. The second Five-Year Plan, however, had to be revised because of the international situation. In 1933, as you will read, Adolf Hitler came to power in Germany. Increasingly his foreign policy showed him to be a threat to the Soviet Union. In 1936, Stalin canceled the consumer-goods program in order to increase the production of military supplies.

Russia as a police state

As time went on, Soviet leaders admitted that the state was not "withering away" in accordance with Marx's prediction, that it was, in fact, maintained by force. Many years would have to pass, they said, before the classless society of pure communism could be attained. For the time being, Russians would be rewarded according to their work, not according to their needs. Thus, although the Soviet Union was considered by most people to be a communist state, Stalin and other leaders described it as a socialist dictatorship of the proletariat.

Police state tactics were not new in Russia. The czars had used secret police and spies to maintain their absolute rule. Stalin used similar tactics. Under his rule, the Russians were still ruled by fear. People had to conform, to agree, to express no opinion at all, or to express only the "party line," the policy of the Communist Party.

The Soviets had disestablished the Orthodox Church and seized its property; religious worship was ridiculed, and children were taught atheism. Artists, writers, and musicians were ordered to produce "socialist realism" in the service of the state. Their works were subject to rigid control and censorship.

The actual membership of the Communist Party was always small—possibly $2\frac{1}{2}$ million out of the more than 200 million people of the Soviet Union. The top places in government and industry always went to party members, who had special privileges. However, admission to the party was difficult. Members had to accept party orders without question and were expected to make any sacrifices necessary.

In 1936, Stalin proclaimed a new constitution for the U.S.S.R. This "Stalin Constitution," as it was called, preserved the essential framework that had existed in Russia under Lenin. The parliamentary body was to be called the Supreme Soviet and was to meet twice every year. While in recess, its authority was to reside in the Presidium, a small committee elected by the Supreme Soviet. Executive and administrative authority was vested in the Council of People's Commissars (later renamed the Council of Ministers).

On paper the Soviet government was representative, democratic, and parliamentary. In fact, however, most power lay in the hands of the Politburo (Political Bureau) of the Communist Party. As head of the party, Stalin controlled the Politburo.

Stalin's personal dictatorship gradually grew harsher. In 1934, following the assassination of a high party official, Stalin began a purge, or "purification," of party members disloyal to him. Through public trials, intimidation, and brutality, he began to rid the party of all members who would not submit to his will. The purge reached its height between 1936 and 1938. It has been estimated that by 1938, nearly 8 million persons had been arrested. For those not important enough to be given a formal trial, arrest was usually followed by deportation, imprisonment in forced labor camps, or execution.

The Comintern. Soviet foreign policy during the 1920's and 1930's was contradictory. On the one hand, the new communist government wanted to be accepted by the established nations of the world. On the other hand, it supported the Third, or Communist, International (often called the Comintern), an organization that Lenin had founded in 1919 to help spread the revolution throughout the world. The Comintern continued to agitate for the overthrow of the governments of the capitalist democracies.

There were communist parties in many lands. The leaders of these parties looked to Moscow for their orders. The Comintern worked through these parties to arouse workers and urge rebellion. Such open calls to rebellion caused fear, suspicion, and hostility in the outside world.

Although many tensions remained, both the Soviet Union and the Western democracies began to accept the status quo by the mid-1930's. Since it appeared unlikely that communism could overthrow democracy in the West, or that the democracies would overthrow Stalin's dictatorship in Russia, it seemed necessary for both sides to learn to live together.

CHECKUP

1. How did conditions in Russia in 1921 contradict Marxist theory?
2. What was the New Economic Policy?
3. What economic policies did Stalin institute?
4. How did Stalin suppress opposition to his regime?
5. IDENTIFY: Trotsky, consumer goods, "Stalin Constitution," Comintern.

3 Mussolini imposed a fascist dictatorship in Italy

Italy's postwar problems were complicated and seemingly insoluble. There was the basic problem of a poor land with a large population. There was not enough food to supply the needs of the people, and the country lacked the raw materials to support industries. The soil of Italy had begun to wear out even in the days of the Roman Empire. Little had been done since then to improve it.

The war and its aftermath took their toll in Italy as elsewhere. There was heavy loss of life, a crushing burden of debt, unemployment, and inflation. There were labor troubles, including many violent strikes. Various groups promised solutions of all kinds, from reactionaries on the right to communists on the left. The Italian government, a constitutional monarchy, seemed paralyzed and helpless to meet the pressing needs of the situation. Like France, Italy had a coalition government that was able to remain in power only by doing nothing.

Mussolini and fascism

One man who did offer positive actions for Italy was Benito Mussolini. Mussolini, the son of a blacksmith, had been a socialist as a young man and had edited a socialist newspaper. His ideas had brought him a term in jail and a period in exile. During World War I, his views changed. He became an extreme nationalist and was expelled from the Italian Socialist Party. When Italy remained neutral at the outbreak of war, Mussolini advocated entrance on the Allied side. After Italy joined the Allies, he enlisted in the army and was wounded in battle.

When Mussolini returned from the war, he began to organize his own political party. He called it the Fascist Party, and its doctrine, fascism. The words *fascist* and *fascism* come from the Latin word *fasces*. In ancient Rome the fasces was a bundle of rods bound tightly around an ax; it symbolized governmental authority. The various groups of the nation, Mussolini said, should be bound together like the rods of the fasces. He defined fascism as "the dictatorship of the state over many classes cooperating."

Mussolini found his first followers among demobilized soldiers and discontented nationalists. His first program advocated many liberal and even moderately socialist ideas, while expressing complete opposition to revolutionary socialism and communism.

Gradually, however, the fascists attracted another following. Wealthy landowners and businessmen, especially large manufacturers, were attracted by the anti-communist program. They gave the fascists much financial support. Professional men also joined. There was strong support among the lower middle classes, grievously hurt by inflation, and among the unemployed.

Realizing the appeal of strong anti-communism, Mussolini began to emphasize that part of his program. Fascism began to stand for the protection of private property and of the middle class.

Mussolini promised to prevent a proletarian revolution, but at the same time offered the industrial working class full employment and social security. He stressed national prestige; Italy would gain all its war aims, and there would be a return to the glories of the Roman Empire.

Mussolini's rise to power

The Fascist Party began a violent campaign against its opponents, especially socialists and communists. Rowdy groups, called *squadristi,* broke up strikes and political meetings, destroyed labor-union headquarters, and assaulted anyone who spoke up against them. The squadristi also drove properly elected socialist officials from office. This violence was carried on, they said, because the government could not defend the nation from these left-wing enemies within. The fascists adopted a black shirt as their uniform and thus were called Black Shirts. The more confusion and discontent there was in Italy, the stronger they became.

In October 1922, Black Shirt groups from all over Italy began to converge on Rome. They claimed that they were coming to defend Italy against a communist revolution. Liberal members of the Italian parliament insisted that the king declare martial law and suppress the fascist squadristi. When he refused, the cabinet resigned. Conservative advisers persuaded the king to appoint Mussolini as the premier and ask him to head a coalition government. Mussolini requested emergency powers to deal with Italy's pressing problems. The parliament granted his request, but his emergency powers were to remain in force for only a year.

Mussolini had often criticized democracy as a weak and ineffective form of government. Once in office, he began to destroy democracy in Italy and set up a fascist dictatorship. Fascists were appointed to all official positions both in the central government and in the provinces. A new election law was passed, providing that the party receiving the most votes would automatically gain two thirds of the seats in the Chamber of Deputies, the lower house of parliament. An election under the new law was held in 1924. Fascist

Communism and fascism are alike in many respects, relying on dictatorships maintained by force and on other totalitarian measures. However, there are important differences between the two forms of government. Several of these are summarized below.

Communism	Fascism
Seeks international revolution	Is extremely nationalistic
Appeals to working class and peasants	Appeals to middle and upper classes
Promises a classless society	Promises to preserve existing classes
Is based on a socialist economy	Is based on a capitalist economy
Promises eventual abolition of government control	Intends for government control to be permanent
Is violently anti-fascist	Is violently anti-communist

squadristi controlled the voting places; not surprisingly the fascists won the election. Once they had their majority in the Chamber of Deputies, they voted "decree powers" to Mussolini—that is, his decrees would have the force of law. He took the title *il Duce* (DOO-chay), Italian for "the leader."

Italy as a police state

Now all the trappings of dictatorship began to appear. Opposition parties were wiped out by intimidation, kidnaping, assault, and murder. Local democratic governments in towns and cities were abolished and were replaced by officials appointed from Rome. Freedom of speech, press, and assembly were suspended, as was trial by jury. Free labor unions were abolished and strikes were outlawed. Labor unions were reorganized under the control of the government. Police, both uniformed and secret, were everywhere and spied on people in all walks of life.°

Mussolini became commander in chief of the

° This form of anti-communist, one-party government, in which rigid state control is maintained by force and censorship, came to be known generally as fascism. There were fascists and fascist parties in countries outside of Italy, although they usually took other names.

army, navy, and air force, and head of the police. The powers of both the Senate and the Chamber of Deputies were reduced. They could consider only laws which il Duce introduced. Although Mussolini allowed the king to reign as a figurehead, real power was concentrated in the hands of the Grand Council of the Fascist Party. This council was made up of some twenty of the leaders. At the head of the council was Mussolini. The government, controlled by the Fascist Party, regulated every phase of the life of the people. The individual had to serve the state. The slogan "Believe! Obey! Work!" appeared on billboards and posters everywhere.

The corporate state. Mussolini worked out a complicated plan for governing Italy. The nation was to be like a huge corporation. All groups within it were to work together for the good of the nation under the direction of il Duce.

Mussolini claimed that geographic representation, in which members of a parliament represent the people of a specific region, was outmoded in modern industrial society. In its place he introduced representation for each occupation and profession. The principal economic activities, such as agriculture, transportation, manufacturing, and commerce, were formed into syndicates that were

693

like corporations. (Thus Italy was called a corporate state.)

By the 1930's there were twenty-two of these syndicates in Italy. In each, representatives of management, labor, and the government met to establish wages, prices, and working conditions. The national syndicates were united and controlled by a Ministry of Corporations, which was headed by Mussolini himself. All strikes were forbidden. Labor disputes were arbitrated by the government. Labor unions and capitalists alike were subjected to the will of Mussolini's government. Private property was left in the hands of its owners, and profits were allowed. Unlike the communist revolution in Russia, the fascist revolution did not destroy social classes. Its aim was to end social unrest by another means. All parts of the society were forced to cooperate with one another for the welfare of the nation.

At the top of the entire system was the fascist dictator, Mussolini. He attempted to symbolize the new, strong Italy by such feats as lifting heavy cornerstones into place at the dedication of new buildings and publicly jumping through flaming hoops.

Violence and brutality against any opposition remained a part of Italian life, but the fascist government did solve some problems. It reduced unemployment. Industry and agriculture improved and became more prosperous. The government began a great program of public works—buildings, schools, roads, and land improvement. The famous Pontine Marshes at the mouth of the Tiber River, a source of malarial mosquitoes since Roman days, were drained and turned into farm land.

Education was strengthened. School attendance was made compulsory to the age of fourteen. In 1913, 40 percent of the Italian people had been illiterate. By 1939, this figure was reduced to 25 percent. The education aimed at making good fascists. Children studied lessons that taught the doctrines of fascism, the virtues of il Duce, the glories of Italy, and the evils of those who denied Italy its "rightful claims."

The army and navy were greatly increased. This program of building up armaments achieved a double purpose. It added to the military strength of Italy and helped to reduce unemployment. War was advertised as a glorious, patriotic adventure.

But this picture of prosperity and efficiency had dark shadows. Mussolini's program was costly, and the treasury of the Italian government was never well filled. The already low standard of living of the people went down even more. Italy's old problems remained—there were too many people, not enough food, and too few natural resources. The expanded armed forces also placed a heavy financial burden on the economy.

CHECKUP

1. What were some of the problems of postwar Italy?
2. Trace Mussolini's rise to power.
3. What was the corporate state?
4. IDENTIFY: squadristi, Black Shirts, il Duce.

4   The Nazi Party, under Adolf Hitler, seized control of Germany

In November 1918, Germany was declared a republic. The following year, an assembly met in the city of Weimar and drafted a constitution that made Germany a federal republic, known as the Weimar Republic.

The Weimar Republic

Germany's new government had a president and a two-house parliament. The president and members of parliament were elected by universal suffrage. In the upper house, the Reichsrat, the seventeen states of the federal republic were represented. In the lower house, the Reichstag, political parties were represented directly according to the number of votes they received—a system called *proportional representation*. A prime minister, called the chancellor, was appointed by the president.

The Weimar Republic was not popular with the German people, however. The revolution of

1918, which deposed the Kaiser, had not been a mass uprising of the sort that usually overthrows governments. Instead, it had been carried out by the German General Staff, men who were eager to end the war and arrive at an armistice before the German army was destroyed and Allied troops had an opportunity to occupy Germany.

Woodrow Wilson had announced that he would deal only with a government elected by the German people; thus a republic had been created. Many Germans, however, opposed republican government. Moreover, the Weimar representatives had signed the humiliating Versailles Treaty, which made the republic even more unpopular. Later political agitators were to attack the Weimar Republic bitterly and castigate the so-called "November criminals" who, they said, had surrendered while there was still a chance of German victory.

Many of the difficulties of the Weimar Republic reflected the economic, social, and political problems that affected all of Europe after World War I. Unemployment was high. Inflation reached fantastic proportions. In 1913 a German mark was worth about twenty-five cents. In 1923 it took one trillion marks to equal twenty-five cents. Imagine that you had had savings of 500,000 marks ($125,000) in 1913 and left this amount in the bank for ten years. When you went to draw it out in 1923, you would have received a single bill worth less than a penny.

Within the first year of its existence, the Weimar Republic faced two attempted revolutions. In Munich, the capital of the state of Bavaria, a communist government took over and attempted to withdraw Bavaria from the federal union. Later, in Berlin, a right-wing group tried to overthrow the republic and to elevate men of its own choosing to power. The republic was powerless to defend itself and, in both cases, was forced to rely on temporary alliances with anti-republican groups.

The Bavarian communist revolt was put down by members of the "free corps"—private right-wing armies made up of demobilized soldiers who were loyal only to their own generals. The attack on the republic in Berlin was defeated when members of the legal government, fleeing the city, called a general strike. The workers of Berlin left their jobs, paralyzing the city and making it impossible for the right-wing rebels to establish themselves in power.

The Nazis and Hitler

One of the many anti-republican political parties formed in Germany after World War I was the German Workers' Party. In 1920 the party, attempting to broaden its appeal, changed its name to the National Socialist German Workers' Party. It became known as the Nazi Party, from the first two syllables of the word national (pronounced nah·tsee·oh·NAHL in German). The party was not, as its name might indicate, a working-class group. Rather, it was extremely nationalistic and violently anti-communist. It was a fascist party and, like many such parties at the time, it attracted a wide assortment of discontented and bitter people. Promising to protect Germany from communism, it also, in time, attracted the support of wealthy businessmen and landowners.

One of the first Nazi recruits was an ex-soldier named Adolf Hitler. Hitler was born in Austria in 1889, the son of a minor government official. As a young man, he had gone to Vienna, where he was unsuccessful as an artist and worked for a while at various odd jobs. In Vienna, a cosmopolitan city in which many Jews had risen to respected positions in business, the arts, and the professions, Hitler became violently anti-Semitic.

Hitler served in the German army in World War I. He later moved to Munich, where he joined the Nazi Party. In 1923, Hitler took part in a Nazi uprising in Munich. It failed and he was sentenced to prison. While there, he wrote *Mein Kampf (My Struggle)*, a rambling, hate-filled book that became the "Bible" of the Nazi movement. After his release from prison, Hitler became the leader of the Nazis.

Hitler was a gifted, hypnotic orator, and in the confused political and economic situation of the postwar period, his emotional speeches attracted many enthusiastic listeners. The frustration, self-

(continued on page 698)

Fascist dictators mobilized for war long before it came. In Italy, boys were trained to arms from the age of six. Above a group parades before Mussolini. At lower left, Mussolini breaks ground for a new train terminal in Rome, part of his vast railroad modernization program. At lower right, he addresses his troops during maneuvers. On the opposite page, a poster addressed to women (*Frauen*) urges them to persuade their unemployed husbands to vote for Hitler. The German dictator is shown upper right in Nazi military uniform. Below, a German anti-aircraft battery practices as planes fly in formation overhead. In 1938, the two dictators rode together through Rome, lower right.

"The Tightrope Walker" by Paul Klee

The Nazis, like the communists in Russia, believed that much of modern art did not serve their goals. In 1937 they organized an exhibit of "Degenerate Art," which included abstract paintings, works by Jews, and African sculpture. In the show were seventeen paintings by Paul Klee, a pacifist violently opposed to Nazism. The water color above typifies his humor, imagination, and deliberately childlike style—qualities that won him an enthusiastic following elsewhere but were not greatly admired in totalitarian Germany.

pity, and hatred expressed by Hitler both in his speeches and in *Mein Kampf* reflected the feelings of many other Germans of his day.

Hitler's program tried to appeal to almost every element in the German population. To farmers he promised land reforms. To the workers he offered better working conditions, social legislation, nationalization of big business, and the abolition of unearned profits. There was a heavy emphasis on German nationalism. Hitler promised to repeal the Versailles Treaty, especially the "war-guilt" clause. He said that he would restore Germany to equality in armaments and regain all its lost territory and colonies to build a "Greater Germany." Like Mussolini, he promised protection against communism.

To these promises, Hitler added another, and uglier, policy—his garbled racial doctrine. According to this doctrine, the Germans, as "Aryans" (an incorrect use of the word, as you will remember from your earlier reading), were the "master race." All other peoples were inferior. Slavs, such as Poles and Russians, were fit only to serve Aryan masters. The Negro race Hitler considered hardly human, and he regarded Jews with special hatred. Frustrated people with twisted minds often seek out scapegoats to blame for their own failings. Hitler raised this trait to the level of national policy.

Hitler's rise to power

Throughout the 1920's, Nazi strength was low. Inflation had gradually been curbed. Despite the problems of the Weimar Republic, the German people seemed willing to give it a chance to prove itself. Then came the Great Depression. The hardships it brought led to a great increase in Nazi strength.

In the election of 1930, many middle-class voters turned to the Nazis. These voters saw their savings destroyed; many of them were afraid of a communist revolution. Two years later the Nazis won 230 seats in the Reichstag. They became the largest single party in the parliament but did not have enough votes to form a government by themselves.

In January 1933, when it appeared that no

other party could successfully form a government, the president of the republic, Paul von Hindenburg, appointed Hitler chancellor. Hitler formed a coalition government, but soon called for a new election to widen the Nazis' margin of power in the Reichstag. A few days before the election, the Reichstag building was set on fire. Hitler blamed the fire on the communists and, making use of public fear of a communist revolution, gained 44 percent of the votes in the election.

The Nazis still lacked a majority in the Reichstag, but by intimidating the parliament with the Nazis' private army—called Storm Troopers, or Brown Shirts—Hitler was granted emergency powers to deal with the alleged communist revolt. He used these powers to make himself a dictator. Within a few months, opposition to Hitler was made illegal.

The Nazi program in action

Once in power, Hitler began to turn Germany into a police state. Opposition parties and labor unions were ordered to disband. All government was centralized under the Nazi Party. The Gestapo, a secret-police force, was given much power. Hitler, who often modeled his policies on Mussolini's, took the title *der Führer* (FYOOR·ur), German for "the leader." Opposition newspapers were suppressed, and the government controlled all radio stations. The penalty for broadcasting without government permission was death. Schools were strictly controlled and students were taught only what agreed with Nazi doctrine.

Liberals, socialists, and communists were thrown into large prisons called concentration camps. Members of the so-called "inferior races" were subjected to increasingly severe persecutions. This policy was applied with special harshness to the Jews, who were deprived of many of their rights, publicly humiliated, and even murdered by Storm Troopers. German courts dealt leniently with persons accused of offenses against Jews. Jews were forced to live in segregated areas and to wear yellow stars of David (the six-pointed star that is a symbol of Judaism). This policy was later carried to a monstrous extreme, as you will read in Chapter 36.

Like Mussolini, Hitler promised to restore the glories of his country's past. He called his regime the Third Reich; *Reich* is the German word for "empire." (The first had been the Holy Roman Empire, and the second was the German Empire of the Hohenzollerns.) He promised the Germans that the Third Reich would last a thousand years.

Germany's racial superiority, Hitler claimed, justified expansion of its borders to take *Lebensraum* (LAY·buns·rowm)—German meaning "living space"—from the Slavs of eastern Europe. Such expansion would necessitate a large and well-equipped army. Germany, which had been secretly rearming since the 1920's, now began to defy openly the disarmament provisions of the Versailles Treaty.

In 1936, after three years of rearmament, Hitler was ready to try out both his own strength and the readiness of Germany's former enemies—the Allied Powers—to resist his aggressive moves. According to the Versailles Treaty, the Rhineland, Germany's territory on the French side of the Rhine River, was to be left unfortified. In the spring of 1936, Hitler's army marched into the Rhineland (see map, page 713). France sent a note of protest; the other powers did nothing.

Encouraged by his unexpected success in the Rhineland, Hitler sought an alliance with Mussolini in order to have support for future aggressive moves. In the fall of 1936, the fascist and Nazi dictators formed an alliance, which they called the Rome-Berlin Axis. An axis is a line that passes through an object and around which that object revolves. In typical boastful fashion, the dictators meant that the world revolved around the "axis" between Rome and Berlin.

CHECKUP

1. Discuss the chief problems faced by the Weimar Republic in the 1920's.

2. What were the main features of Hitler's program?

3. How did the following factors aid Hitler in his rise to power: the Great Depression? the Reichstag fire? the Storm Troopers?

4. IDENTIFY: proportional representation, Nazi Party, *Mein Kampf*, Third Reich, *Lebensraum*, Rome-Berlin Axis.

CHAPTER REVIEW

Chapter 34 Totalitarian Dictatorships Came to Power in Europe (1914–1938)

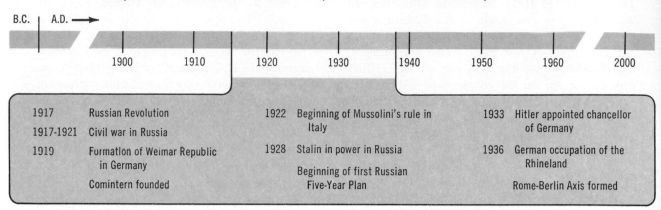

1917	Russian Revolution	1922	Beginning of Mussolini's rule in Italy	1933	Hitler appointed chancellor of Germany
1917-1921	Civil war in Russia	1928	Stalin in power in Russia	1936	German occupation of the Rhineland
1919	Formation of Weimar Republic in Germany		Beginning of first Russian Five-Year Plan		Rome-Berlin Axis formed
	Comintern founded				

CHAPTER SUMMARY

Totalitarian regimes came to power in several European countries after World War I. In Russia, huge war losses revealed governmental inefficiency and corruption, and helped lead to the overthrow of the monarchy. A moderate provisional government struggled for control against soviets of workers and soldiers. The Bolsheviks (communists), under Lenin, in turn overthrew the moderate government late in 1917.

The communists were victorious in a three-year civil war. They wanted to make the new U.S.S.R. a Marxist state but had to modify communism with the New Economic Policy. After a power struggle following Lenin's death, Stalin emerged as dictator of Russia. He adopted a planned economy and initiated a Five-Year Plan to modernize industry, agriculture, and social services. Although many goals were met, the Russian police state became increasingly oppressive.

In postwar Italy, coalition governments were powerless to solve basic problems. Mussolini, leader of the new Fascist Party, won power, overcame opposition by violence, and turned Italy into a dictatorship. In Mussolini's corporate state, fascists dominated the government. Some improvements were made, but there were no individual rights, and the country remained poor.

Germany's Weimar Republic, blamed for the harsh peace terms of the Versailles Treaty and for postwar inflation, was attacked by both leftists and rightists. Hitler, who became leader of the anti-democratic Nazi Party, won many followers by appealing to German resentment and pride.

Nazi strength was increased by depression hardships, and Hitler came to power in 1933. His fascist police state soon eliminated most opposition. Particularly harsh treatment was reserved for "inferior" races, especially Jews. Hitler rearmed Germany, marched into the Rhineland, and—with Mussolini—formed the Rome-Berlin Axis.

QUESTIONS FOR DISCUSSION

1. Can you give an explanation of the fact that many people in Russia, Italy, and Germany were ready to accept dictatorship? Would it be possible for a dictator to take over the United States? Explain.

2. Lenin won the support of the Russian masses with his slogan, "Land, Peace, and Bread." What does this say about conditions in Russia in 1917? Do you think Lenin would have gained more supporters if he had promised political freedom to the Russian people? Justify your answer.

3. Would you advise underdeveloped countries in Africa and Asia to follow the Russian example of Five-Year Plans? Why or why not?

4. Why did wealthy businessmen and landowners in Italy and Germany support fascism? Why are wealthy businessmen often welcome members in a political party?

5. What was the official policy toward education in fascist Italy and Nazi Germany? In what ways does education in the United States serve the state?

PROJECTS

1. Write a short speech for Mussolini, stressing his promises for the Italian people.

2. Write a short dialogue between a supporter of the Weimar Republic and a member of the Nazi Party.

3. Draw a campaign poster for the Nazi Party before 1933.

4. Draw a cartoon satirizing Hitler's racial teachings.

Local Aggressions
Destroyed the Uneasy Peace

By the 1930's the nations of the world were once more divided into opposing camps. One group included the nations that were generally satisfied with the World War I peace settlement. The other group consisted of dissatisfied nations that wanted changes. Mainly, it was the democracies that wanted to preserve the status quo, and the dictatorships that wanted change. With each passing year, international relations grew more strained.

The League of Nations tried valiantly to preserve the peace. But it suffered from two serious weaknesses. First, its membership was incomplete. The United States never joined, and the Soviet Union was not admitted until 1934. The absence of these world powers proved a definite handicap to the League's effectiveness.

Another, more basic, weakness was that the League was composed of sovereign, independent states. It could not make laws for its members, but could only recommend certain actions. Whether the recommendations were carried out depended on whether the member nations wanted to do so.

Although the League had serious shortcomings, it performed many valuable services during the 1920's and 1930's. It offered expert advice to countries suffering from economic problems and helped arrange loans among its members to prevent bankruptcy. It settled a dispute between

Japanese soldiers with prisoners in Manchuria

Britain and Turkey over the boundaries of Iraq, and a controversy between Germany and Poland over Silesia. The League also engaged in humanitarian work. It aided the return of war prisoners and refugees after World War I and carried on relief work in areas suffering from famine.

Because of the political weakness of the League, however, the major powers began to hold diplomatic conferences outside the world organization. The first of these meetings was held in 1921 and 1922 in Washington, D.C. Nine of the powers interested in the Far East (excluding the Soviet Union, which was not invited) attended this Washington Naval Conference. Several treaties resulted. One, the Five-Power Treaty, provided for a ten-year "naval holiday," during which no warships would be built. It also established a ratio for naval strength that would give the United States and Britain equality, Japan three fifths as much tonnage, and France and Italy 1.67 as much tonnage as the United States and Great Britain. The participating nations also signed a Nine-Power Treaty, agreeing to take no further territory from China and to maintain the Open Door Policy.

The most optimistic of the postwar diplomatic conferences was held in 1928 at Paris. The American secretary of state, Frank B. Kellogg, and the French foreign minister, Aristide Briand, drafted a treaty condemning war as a means of settling international disputes. Eventually, more than sixty nations signed the Kellogg-Briand Pact. War was thus made "illegal," but no one had yet found a way to make it impossible.

THE CHAPTER SECTIONS:

1. Japan and Italy made the first aggressive moves (1925–1936)
2. Civil war in Spain led to intervention by foreign powers (1936–1939)
3. Hitler annexed Austria and Czechoslovakia (1938–1939)
4. Hitler's attack on Poland marked the beginning of World War II (1939)

1 Japan and Italy made the first aggressive moves

Peace was preserved throughout the 1920's by a series of conferences and informal diplomatic arrangements. In the 1930's, however, it became clear that such makeshift arrangements would no longer be effective.

Militarism in Japan

You have read how Japan underwent a vast program of modernization in the late 1800's. It changed its government and also began to industrialize and seek foreign markets. As an industrial country, Japan needed a readily available source of raw materials. As a densely populated nation, it needed room for its population to expand.

The Paris peace settlement had given Japan control over former German concessions on the Shantung Peninsula, and a mandate over the Marshall, Caroline, and Mariana island groups. These new territories relieved some of the pressure of Japan's rapid wartime industrialization, but the need for additional markets, raw materials, and space still existed.

During the 1920's, Japan followed a moderate foreign policy. It voluntarily gave its holdings on the Shantung Peninsula back to China. It also signed the Five-Power Treaty, the Nine-Power Treaty, and the Kellogg-Briand Pact.

At the same time, liberal politicians in Japan tried to make the government more democratic. In 1925, for instance, Japan adopted universal manhood suffrage. But for all its apparently liberal laws, Japan was still far from democratic. The Japanese Diet, or parliament, had strictly limited powers. The emperor was outwardly an absolute ruler; the cabinet was responsible to him and ruled in his name. The constitution of 1889, however, required that representatives of the army and navy sit in the cabinet, and no government could be formed without their cooperation. Civilian authorities had almost no control over the activities of the armed forces. Furthermore, the in-

Military invasions by Italy and Japan were preludes to World War II. Mussolini decreed that "the Italian character must be formed through fighting." Ethiopia was the means. Above left, Italian soldiers with a modern machine gun mow down primitively armed Ethiopians. An Ethiopian leader and troops wearing tribal regalia, above right, surrender to the invading Italian forces. In the Far East, Japan used an accidental skirmish in Manchuria to touch off major hostilities against China. A Japanese armored unit, below left, moves along a railroad in its pursuit of Chinese troops. Below right, a Chinese woman huddles in the ruins of Hankow.

dustrialization of Japan had put much political power in the hands of the industrialists and large landowners. Thus, military leaders and people of great wealth, rather than the Japanese voters, determined the policies of the government.

Japan's economic problems increased during the 1920's. China, which was also trying to industrialize, set up high tariffs that hurt Japan. Overcrowding in Japan was made worse when other countries restricted immigration; the United States shut its doors completely to Japanese immigrants in 1924. The worldwide depression that began in 1929 brought additional burdens.

All these difficulties played into the hands of the military leaders, who constantly urged the use of force to solve Japan's problems. These militarists, many of whom belonged to the old samurai class, urged taking the mandated islands as outright possessions. They insisted on a larger army and a stronger navy for Japan. They also cast longing eyes on the Chinese province of Manchuria as a region for possible Japanese expansion. The militarists in Japan advocated a Japanese "Monroe Doctrine for Asia," which would allow Japan to control the Far East.

In 1930, Japan's liberal prime minister, Yuko Hamaguchi, was fatally shot. Political disorder followed, and within two years the government of Japan was controlled by the militarists.

Japan's attack on Manchuria

In September 1931, there was a mysterious explosion near Mukden, Manchuria, which damaged a Japanese-controlled railroad. Without warning and without the consent of China, Japanese troops occupied Mukden. The Republic of China appealed to the League of Nations for help. The Japanese delegate to the League stated that the occupation of Mukden was purely a local matter and warned the League not to interfere. Japan claimed that it was not declaring war on China, nor conquering its territory, but merely "suppressing banditry." This incident began a conflict between Japan and China that was to continue, off and on, until 1945. Japan, however, never referred to it as a war but always as the "China Incident."

The League of Nations sent an investigating commission, headed by Lord Lytton of Great Britain, to Manchuria. At the same time, Japan continued its conquest. In 1932 it declared Manchuria to be an independent nation, under the name Manchukuo (MAN·CHOO·KWOH). Its ruler was the former Manchu emperor. In reality he was a puppet of Japan who danced when the Japanese pulled the strings.

After nine months the Lytton Commission advised the League not to recognize Manchukuo's independence and recommended that the region be restored to China. When the League voted on this recommendation, only Japan voted against it. As a result of its diplomatic defeat, Japan withdrew from the League of Nations. Some historians regard Japan's successful aggression against China in Manchuria as the actual beginning of World War II.

The lesson seemed clear. The League of Nations was too weak to check a definite act of aggression by a great power. The major nations, especially Britain and France, were willing to join in condemning aggression, but they did not press for any further action, such as economic sanctions. Thus it appeared that the League would take no strong action against aggressor nations, and that such nations could withdraw from the League and follow any policy they wanted. The League suffered a great loss of prestige. Japanese aggression, unchecked, started a chain reaction that led to the collapse of peace in the West as well as in the East.

War in China

Japan pressed further demands on China, announcing its intention to extend its influence to China Proper and not merely to outlying regions. Early in 1937, Chiang Kai-shek and the Chinese communists agreed to halt their civil war and form a common front against Japan in northern China. It was probably this agreement that influenced Japan to begin a full-scale war against China.

In July 1937, Japanese and Chinese troops clashed near Peiping, the former imperial capital. Japanese armies captured Peiping and at once began to move southward. China resisted the invasion of Japanese troops, but its armies were inferior to Japan's.

By 1939 the Japanese occupied about a fourth of China (see map, this page), including all its seaports, the Yangtze Valley as far as Hankow, and many cities in the interior. Still the Chinese refused to give up. Wherever they had to fall back, they followed a scorched-earth policy, burning villages and destroying crops in order to prevent these resources from falling into enemy hands. They moved their capital far up the Yangtze River to Chungking. Everywhere they fought a guerrilla war, cutting off Japanese supplies and making lightning raids behind the Japanese lines.

The war was an enormous drain on both countries. By 1939, Japan had lost a million troops in China and spent 10 billion dollars. Chinese losses were uncountable.

The United States and the European powers continued to play a cautious role. The United States pursued a policy of neutrality, prohibiting the sale of munitions to either side. But private companies in the United States and Britain continued to sell vital scrap iron and gasoline to the Japanese. They sold to China, too. A trickle of supplies went overland from the south by railroad from Rangoon through Mandalay to Lashio, and from there along the Burma Road to Kunming and on to Chungking. Another trickle came overland from Russia.

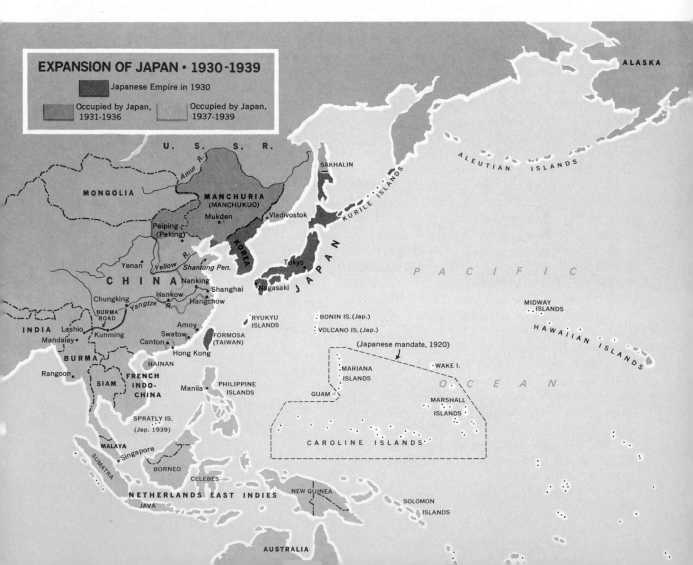

EXPANSION OF JAPAN · 1930-1939

Japanese Empire in 1930

Occupied by Japan, 1931-1936

Occupied by Japan, 1937-1939

Italy's defeat of Ethiopia

You have read of the rise to power of Mussolini and the Fascist Party in Italy. Like the militarist leaders of Japan, Mussolini sought to solve his country's economic problems by overseas expansion. The object of his ambitions was Ethiopia, one of the few independent nations in Africa. Chapter 26 told how Ethiopians had defeated an Italian army in 1896. Mussolini was determined to reverse this humiliating defeat for the glory of his "new Italy."

As in Manchuria, a border incident provided the pretext for aggression. In December 1934, an Italian border patrol in Italian Somaliland clashed with an Ethiopian border patrol. There was every indication that the Italians had provoked the incident. Mussolini at once ordered Italian forces in Eritrea and Italian Somaliland to invade Ethiopia to "restore order."

Ethiopia was poorly prepared to resist such an invasion and asked the League of Nations for protection. Emperor Haile Selassie was a dignified but pathetic figure as he appeared before the League Assembly and appealed to the members to stop the aggression.

Here was an even clearer test than Manchuria, for Ethiopia was an independent government and a League member. As with Manchuria, however, selfish national interests weakened League action. Neither Britain nor France had much enthusiasm for strong action by the League. The United States offered no help. The League made a mild effort to bring the dispute to arbitration. In October 1935, Mussolini replied with an all-out campaign to conquer and colonize Ethiopia.

The League then declared Italy an aggressor and applied economic sanctions. The sanctions were sweeping enough, but observance was half-hearted. League members continued to sell oil, coal, and other minerals to Italy. Other countries, including Germany, traded freely with Italy. The United States would not sell munitions to either belligerent nation, but—as in the case of the Sino-Japanese war—private corporations continued to sell basic raw materials, especially oil, to the aggressor nation.

In a long war, Italy might have been weakened and forced to give in to the demands of the League. But the Ethiopian army was not equipped to make it a long war. Its soldiers fought barefooted with rifles and spears, while the Italians used the most modern techniques, including poison gas and bombing. The Italians entered the Ethiopian capital, Addis Ababa, in the spring of 1936. Mussolini then declared Ethiopia a part of the Italian Empire and proclaimed King Victor Emmanuel III the emperor of Ethiopia.

The League of Nations was forced to admit a second defeat. It had imposed sanctions, but did not enforce them. It had offended Mussolini without hampering him. The hopes of successful peace keeping that had been raised earlier served to deepen the cynicism that followed the League's failure. During the summer of 1936, it called off the sanctions on Italy. In 1937, Italy withdrew from the League.

The Rome-Berlin Axis, which you have read about, was formed in the same year that Italy took Ethiopia. Shortly afterward, Japan signed the Anti-Comintern Treaty with Germany. The two nations pledged themselves to work together to prevent the spread of Russian communism. Italy soon endorsed the Anti-Comintern Treaty. Japan and the two Axis Powers—Italy and Germany—had learned from experience that the democracies were apparently unwilling to go to war to prevent aggression unless their own territory was threatened. This viewpoint, of course, was almost certain to result only in bolder aggressive moves in the future.

CHECKUP

1. Describe some of the accomplishments of the League of Nations during the period of the 1920's and 1930's.

2. What conditions in Japan helped pave the way for militarist control?

3. How was the League of Nations put to the test by aggressions in Manchuria and Ethiopia? How successfully did it meet these crises?

4. IDENTIFY: Five-Power Treaty, Nine-Power Treaty, Kellogg-Briand Pact, "China Incident," Lytton Commission, Anti-Comintern Treaty.

5. LOCATE: Manchukuo, Chungking, Burma Road.

2 Civil war in Spain led to intervention by foreign powers

Spain had lagged far behind the rest of Western Europe during the 1800's. It was a poor country. Much of the land was barren, and there were few mineral resources. There was some industry, but the economy was mainly agricultural. Much of the land was owned in large estates by the nobility. The Catholic Church, the established church, was wealthy and powerful. It controlled the educational system.

The early 1900's

The government of Spain was a constitutional monarchy, with the king's power limited by an elected parliament called the Cortes. Politically, the country was unstable. Throughout the early 1900's, the nation was troubled by violent strikes, political assassinations, military plots, and separatist movements in the provinces. There were several radical parties, including socialists, communists, and anarchists.

Many radical movements were directed against the Church. Opponents felt that it was too conservative and used its great power and influence to prevent needed political, social, and economic reforms. They found it very difficult, however, to criticize the Church on these grounds without being accused of heresy and attacks on the faith.

In the period after World War I, the disordered conditions in Spain grew worse. In 1923, General Miguel Primo de Rivera led a revolt and established a military dictatorship. The king, Alfonso XIII, remained as a figurehead, but Primo de Rivera was the actual ruler. He admired Mussolini and adopted many fascist techniques—censoring the press, controlling education, and suppressing opposition parties.

The Spanish Republic

Primo de Rivera depended upon the support of the army. He lost this support by 1930 and was forced to resign. The following year, because of growing republican sentiment, King Alfonso abdicated and Spain became a republic.

A general election chose a constitutional assembly. This assembly was dominated by liberal republicans, who wrote a democratic constitution. Spain was to be ruled by a one-house Cortes, with a president, premier, and cabinet responsible to it. Elections were to be by universal suffrage. There was to be freedom of religion. Church and state were to be separated, and education was to be secular.

The government was given much control over industry and property, and tried to put reforms into effect rapidly. Land taken from the Church and the nobles was given to landless peasants. Clergymen were barred from teaching in schools and were no longer paid by the government. Workers received many benefits—shorter hours, better wages, the right to organize, and a voice in the management of business.

These sweeping reforms antagonized conservatives both in Spain and abroad. Bitter opposition arose over the limitations on Church authority, the seizures of land, and the new rights of laborers. Many people, including most of the officers of the army, wanted to return to a monarchy.

Shortly after the establishment of the republic, conservatives organized a fascist party called the Falange (FAY·lanj), Spanish for "phalanx." The Falange was determined to preserve the power of the army, landowners, and the Church, regardless of whom the voters might elect to office.

However, the most extreme radicals—communists and anarchists—wanted even more drastic changes. To achieve them, and to prevent a feared seizure of the government by the conservatives, the radicals stirred up strikes and riots, which the government suppressed by force. Successive elections produced more conservative governments and slowed down changes.

Civil war

In February 1936 a Popular Front government was elected. The Spanish Popular Front, like the Popular Front in France, represented a coalition of left-wing working-class parties united in their

The Spanish Civil War was a grim foreboding of World War II. At the front, upper left, a Loyalist soldier falls to the ground, killed instantly by machine-gun fire. In a city, above, civilians gaze upward at aircraft, fearful of the bombs that may soon fall. Although anti-fascists of many kinds came to Spain to help the Loyalists, foreign aid tipped the balance in favor of the Nationalists, who had reinforcements and supplies from Germany and Italy. At far left, Franco greets the German ambassador at a formal reception. Below, a French policeman leads defeated Loyalist troops across the border to safety.

opposition to fascism. Prominent rightists were jailed, and the Falange responded with acts of terrorism. Those in the Cortes who urged moderation quickly lost control of the situation. In July a conservative leader was assassinated. His murder was followed by army uprisings, led by Falangists, in Spanish Morocco, the Canary Islands, and Spain itself. Thus began a bitter civil war that was to last for almost three years.

The Falangist rebels, led by General Francisco Franco, called themselves Nationalists. Those who supported the republic were known as Loyalists, or Republicans. The Nationalists expected a quick victory because most army officers and many troops had joined the revolt. But Spanish workmen and peasants in large numbers came to the aid of the elected government. By the end of 1936, the Nationalists held most of the north and west of Spain. The Loyalists held the east and southeast, most of the northern coastline, and the capital city of Madrid.

Foreign aid. The Spanish Civil War soon became a small European war. Germany and Italy saw a fascist Spain as a link in their chain around France and as a threat to Britain. They helped the Nationalists with well-organized and fully equipped "volunteer" units. Soviet Russia was sympathetic to the republican government. Despite Russia's internal problems and the great distance from Russia to Spain, Russia was able to help the Loyalists by sending planes, technicians, and military advisers. This aid, however, was not nearly as extensive as that given to Franco by his fascist allies.

Unlike Mussolini and Hitler, who made no serious effort to take over the direction of the war from Franco, Stalin tried to manage the various groups—including socialists, anarchists, communists, and liberal republicans—who made up the Loyalist side. The communists who came to Spain, regardless of their country of origin, were disciplined and directed by the Comintern. They worked their way into positions of control and fought not only against the fascists but also against political enemies among their "allies," especially the Trotskyists (followers of the exiled Trotsky). For the non-communist Loyalists, the war became two wars—one against the fascists and one against the communists.

Volunteers from France, Britain, the United States, and other nations also went to the aid of the Spanish Republic. These anti-fascist volunteers became known as the International Brigade. The International Brigade, however, numbered only about 40,000, while Italy alone sent more than 50,000 trained troops.

Thus the Spanish Civil War brought into the open the struggle between fascism and socialism that was seething all over Europe in the 1930's. It also became a testing ground for new weapons and tactics.

France and Great Britain were afraid that the Spanish Civil War might spread to the rest of Europe and involve them. In September of 1936, at the suggestion of the French government, a Nonintervention Committee was established, representing twenty-seven nations. All agreed to a policy of nonintervention in Spain, with a blockade to stop the flow of volunteers and supplies. The blockade stopped most aid to the Loyalists, but not German and Italian aid to Franco. To Hitler and Mussolini this was one more proof that Britain and France would do nothing to stop aggression unless it involved their own territory.

Victory for Franco

The Spanish Civil War in 1937 was in a condition of stalemate. By the spring of 1938, however, the Nationalist forces had grown strong enough for a large-scale offensive. Franco's plan was to encircle Madrid, march east to Valencia, and thus split the Loyalist-held territory in two. The Republican government moved to Barcelona, from where it attempted to direct the Loyalist troops.

It was during the campaign to capture Madrid that one of Franco's generals used an expression that has since become common. He announced that he had four columns marching on Madrid, and a fifth column of people within the city, who would rise against the defenders when the right time came. Since then the expression *fifth column* has come into wide use to describe traitors within a country who aid its enemies.

HISTORY THROUGH ART

"Guernica" by Pablo Picasso

Although he lived in France, Picasso had been born in Spain and was keenly sympathetic to the Loyalist cause during the civil war. The painting above expresses his outrage over the needless German bombing of the town of Guernica, which had no strategic value. Using only blacks, grays, and whites, Picasso evokes anguish and horror with his distorted human and animal figures writhing in agony under a stark electric light.

Dissension among the Loyalists weakened their cause. The many radical parties often quarreled bitterly about aims and programs. But Barcelona and Madrid remained under Loyalist control until March 1939, when they fell to the Nationalists. With the fall of these two cities, the resistance to Franco crumbled.

The three-year war left Spain devastated. Over half a million people had lost their lives. Both sides had resorted to torture and brutality. Many years were to pass before the country could begin to recover from the economic destruction or forget the hatred caused by the war.

Spanish fascism

Soon after the end of the war, Franco set up a fascist government modeled on Mussolini's dictatorship in Italy. Like Mussolini, Franco became head of the state with unlimited power. He was responsible, as one decree said, "only to God and history." He too assumed a title—*el Caudillo,* Spanish for "leader." His party, the Falange, was the only one permitted. Its National Council, chosen by Franco, "advised" him on legislation.

The economic organization of Spain resembled that of fascist Italy, with syndicates, or corporations, organized by occupations and economic activities. Free elections and most civil rights were abolished. Under Franco's regime, the old ruling groups—the army, landowners, and the Roman Catholic Church—continued to hold positions of power. But even these former ruling groups, who had turned to fascist dictatorship to protect themselves from the lower classes, were now subject to the will of the dictator.

Although Spain had become a fascist dictatorship, it did not join the Rome-Berlin Axis. The nation had been so exhausted by the civil war that it probably would have been of little help to the Axis.

1. Why was much Spanish radical activity in the early 1900's directed against the Catholic Church?

2. State some of the democratic features of the Spanish Republic. What reforms were adopted?

3. What policy did Great Britain and France adopt toward the Spanish Civil War? What was the effect of this policy on Hitler and Mussolini?

4. IDENTIFY: Cortes, Primo de Rivera, Falange, Franco, Nationalists, Loyalists, International Brigade, fifth column, el Caudillo.

 Hitler annexed Austria and Czechoslovakia

As Germany grew increasingly stronger, Hitler's foreign policy became more aggressive. In 1933 he had taken Germany out of the League of Nations and announced his intention to rearm. In 1935, after an intense campaign of Nazi propaganda, the people of the Saar voted to return to German rule. In 1936, as earlier stated, Germany reoccupied the Rhineland and began to build fortifications there. Although most of these measures were clear violations of the Versailles Treaty, Britain and France failed to take any determined action against Germany.

Hitler's technique of aggression

Hitler became convinced that he could do almost as he pleased. He did not really want war, provided he could get what he wanted without it. But Hitler was willing to risk war in order to gain what he wanted. He believed that if he stood firm and seemed prepared to fight, his opponents would always back down at the last moment.

Hitler had a planned technique for conquest without actual war; it has been called a "war of nerves" because it played alternately on the fears and hopes of his opponents. The technique proceeded more or less as follows: In the nation to be attacked, a Nazi party was formed. It was organized among the German minority, if there was one, or it was formed among discontented people of the area and supported in every way by Germany.

Next, a stream of atrocity stories was circulated about the mistreatment of Germans in the area. German propaganda encouraged antiwar sentiments. Those who favored a strong stand against Hitler were branded as warmongers. Then Hitler would concoct a "crisis" of some kind, and

he would demand a "German solution to the question," usually involving a readjustment of territory in Germany's favor.

Finally, Germany would begin preparations for war by mobilizing reserves and shifting troops to the frontier. Any yielding by the victim became the first step toward complete control by a Nazi dictatorship. All pledges and promises were violated and soon the entire country was taken over.

Anschluss with Austria

As you have read, the peace treaties after World War I had left Austria in an impossible condition economically. The only hope for Austria's future seemed to lie in some sort of union with Germany. But *Anschluss* was prohibited by the treaties.

A Nazi party had been formed in Austria in the late 1920's. By the early 1930's, the Austrian government had become extremely conservative and a near-dictatorship, and did little to resist the Nazi inroads. By 1938, threats from both Hitler and Mussolini forced the Austrian government to include Nazi members in the cabinet. Once there, they began to "bore from within," weakening Austria's will to resist Hitler, while Germany stepped up pressure from the outside.

The Austrian chancellor offered to take a vote of the Austrian people on the question of *Anschluss,* but Hitler refused to permit it. The chancellor resigned, and a German army marched into Austria unopposed. In March 1938, Hitler proclaimed Austria a part of the Third Reich. The League of Nations took no action, although, as in the case of Ethiopia, one of its members had lost its independence. Britain and France sent protests to Hitler which he disregarded. But no stronger action was taken by the democracies.

The addition of Austria enlarged Germany's population, territory, and resources. It also increased Hitler's influence in Europe. Strategically, Germany had now penetrated the heart of central Europe and reached a common border with its ally Italy. A glance at the map, opposite, will show what the annexation of Austria did to Czechoslovakia, which Hitler had announced as the next step in his program of expansion. Germany now almost completely encircled the Czech republic. Nazi propaganda, however, claimed that Czechoslovakia had become "a dagger aimed at the heart of Germany."

Czechoslovakia and the Sudeten crisis

Around the western rim of Czechoslovakia, in a region known as the Sudetenland, lived more than 3 million Germans. This territory had been included in Czechoslovakia by the peace treaty because it is separated from Germany and Austria by a chain of mountains, which gave the new state a natural and defensible frontier. Czechoslovakia had fortified these mountains heavily, until they were a defensive line second only in Europe to France's Maginot Line. The addition of this region to Czechoslovakia was one instance where nationalism and the principle of self-determination of peoples had given way to the claims of defense.

The Czech government made efforts to protect the rights of the Sudeten Germans. They were allowed to use German in their schools and were given proportional representation in the parliament, the civil service, and the army. Still, many of the Sudeten Germans wanted to be united with Germany.

With the victory of Nazism in Germany, a Nazi party grew up among the Sudeten Germans. This party became a strong force in the Czech parliament. After 1935 the Nazis had more votes than any other party, although not a majority.

After the annexation of Austria, the Sudeten Nazis demanded a completely self-governing Sudetenland. Hitler took up the demand, ranting against Czech "oppression" of Germans. Many fictitious stories of discrimination and atrocities against the Sudetens were spread by Nazi propagandists. Riots broke out, and in September 1938, the situation became so critical that the Czech government placed the country under military law. The Sudeten Nazi leader fled to Germany.

When the Czechoslovakian Nazi party was threatened with suppression, Hitler announced that the German army would invade Czechoslovakia to protect Germany's "Sudeten brothers" and return them to their "fatherland." The Sudetenland would be annexed to Germany. Without its heavily fortified mountain region, Czechoslovakia would be defenseless against Germany. Germany mobilized its army and sent troops to the frontier. The world waited tensely to see what action Czechoslovakia's allies would take.

Czechoslovakia was a League member, but membership had proved no protection to Ethiopia and Austria. However, the Czechs had other resources—defensive alliances with both France and the Soviet Union. The Soviet alliance provided that Russia would aid the Czechs only on condition that France did.

France turned to Great Britain for support. Britain, however, urged France to be patient. The French did not want to go to war over Czechoslovakia and welcomed the offer of Neville Chamberlain, the British prime minister, to send a personal representative to investigate and "advise" the Czech government. The British representative advised the Czechs to make every possible concession to avoid war. The result was increased independence for the Sudetens.

Hitler was still not satisfied and began to increase Germany's military preparations. Chamberlain then asked Hitler for a face-to-face talk to discuss Germany's demands. He made two trips, on September 15 and 22, 1938, to visit Hitler in Germany. On his second visit, Hitler demanded that the Sudetenland be returned to Germany. If not, he said, he would invade it and take it.

Appeasement at Munich

As tensions mounted in Europe, Hitler unexpectedly suggested a conference, to be attended by himself, Chamberlain, Mussolini, and Edouard Daladier, the premier of France. The conference would begin on September 29 at Munich, and the participants would try to settle the Czech problem peaceably. Conspicuously absent from the meeting were (1) the U.S.S.R., which was, with France, pledged to defend Czechoslovakia, and (2) a representative of Czechoslovakia itself. Russia was not invited because Hitler wanted to split the U.S.S.R. from the West.

At Munich, Chamberlain and Daladier, eager to avoid war at any cost, accepted Hitler's demand that the Sudetenland be annexed to Germany. The policy they followed—attempting to preserve peace by yielding to the demands of an aggressor—is known as appeasement. (Since 1938, the name Munich has become symbolic of appeasement and surrender.) Chamberlain and Daladier promised to use their influence to force Czechoslovakia to yield to Hitler's terms. Upon his return to England, Chamberlain happily showed a waiting crowd the agreement signed at

**AGGRESSIONS LEADING TO WORLD WAR II
1935-1939**

Axis Powers   Axis-controlled lands,
                   September 1, 1939

Munich, exclaiming, "This means peace in our time."

Soon after the Munich conference, France announced that it would not honor its alliance with Czechoslovakia or come to its aid. Germany began to occupy the Sudetenland. The small country of Czechoslovakia, deserted by its allies, was now left defenseless.

Hitler, in speaking of the Sudetenland, said, "This is the last territorial claim I shall make in Europe." Poland and Hungary, however, soon seized Czechoslovakian territories along their borders, claiming that they were inhabited by Poles and Hungarians. In March 1939, Hitler made the Czech area of Czechoslovakia a German protectorate. He then declared the remainder of the country an independent state called Slovakia, but soon seized that too.

Thus, within a period of six months, an independent republic, the last democracy in central Europe, and the most prosperous of the nations formed after World War I, was wiped completely from the map of Europe. The League of Nations was compelled to cross another name from its list of members.

CHECKUP

1. What were three aggressive steps taken by Hitler between 1933 and 1936?

2. What were the most important results of the German *Anschluss* with Austria?

3. Describe the steps in Hitler's "war of nerves" technique. Show how they were applied in Czechoslovakia.

4. IDENTIFY: "a dagger aimed at the heart of Germany," appeasement, "peace in our time."

4 Hitler's attack on Poland marked the beginning of World War II

The fall of Czechoslovakia in March 1939 marked the high point of Hitler's diplomatic victories and bloodless conquests. Germany was now the strongest and most strategically located power in continental Europe. The Rome-Berlin Axis completely upset the balance of power and the hope for peace through collective security—that is, peace through the joint action of nations banded together to prevent aggression.

Memel and Albania

While Hitler was in the process of annexing Czechoslovakia, he was also making moves toward Lithuania. Hitler's quarrel with Lithuania involved the former East Prussian seaport city of Memel (see map, page 713). Germany had surrendered Memel to the Allies in the Versailles Treaty. The city had been taken by Lithuania in 1923. After study, the League of Nations recommended, and Lithuania agreed, that Memel should be recognized as part of Lithuania, but be given considerable self-government.

After Hitler came to power, a Nazi party sprang up among the Germans in Memel. They demanded that the city be annexed to Germany; naturally,

Hitler echoed these demands. The Lithuanian government took oppressive measures against the Memel Nazis. In 1935 the predominantly German population of Memel gave the Nazis a majority in the city government. After Germany and Hungary had taken what was left of Czechoslovakia, Hitler increased his demands on Lithuania. In March 1939 the pressure became too great and Lithuania ceded the city of Memel and adjacent territory to Germany.

Still another area lost its independence in the spring of 1939. Mussolini, once a model for other dictators, had by now become the imitator of Hitler. In April 1939 he invaded Albania, on the east coast of the Adriatic Sea. The Italians took the country in a few days. The king of Italy, who had recently become emperor of Ethiopia, gained an additional title—king of Albania.

Preparations for war

By the summer of 1939, British and French leaders had no illusions about the peaceful intentions of the fascist dictators, and they began to prepare for war. In France the premier was given dictatorial powers to speed wartime preparations.

In Britain, Neville Chamberlain rushed through Parliament a huge armaments program and a conscription law. France already had a defensive alliance with Poland. Britain announced that it, too, would help Poland if Germany attacked it.

France also had a nonaggression treaty with the Soviet Union. Britain and France now approached Russia, suggesting a mutual alliance against Germany. Stalin, however, was suspicious of the Western democracies. Until this time, the U.S.S.R. had been excluded from all major decisions in Europe and the rest of the world. The Soviet leaders feared that the Western powers would welcome a chance to turn Hitler loose on them.

Because of their suspicions, and to further their own plans, the Russians insisted that any mutual assistance pact they signed with Britain and France also had to guarantee the independence of Poland, Finland, and the Baltic countries of Estonia, Latvia, and Lithuania. They also wanted a military alliance of Russia and all these states so that they could act instantly if Germany attacked any of them.

This arrangement sounded reasonable enough, but it brought instant protests from the nations involved. All but Lithuania had common borders with Russia. A common military agreement would mean that, in case of a German attack, Russian armies would move into their countries to meet the Germans. All of them, especially Poland, dreaded such protection. They were afraid that they might never be able to get rid of the protectors. For this reason the negotiations dragged on till they reached a stalemate.

The Hitler-Stalin Pact

At the same time that Stalin was negotiating with Great Britain and France, he was carrying on secret negotiations with the German foreign minister. In August 1939 the Western democracies received a tremendous shock. Hitler proudly announced that Germany and the Soviet Union had signed a nonaggression treaty. Moscow soon confirmed the announcement.

The reasons for such an agreement between openly declared enemies were not immediately apparent. However, many historians believe that neither side expected the treaty to be a lasting one, and that Hitler and Stalin were simply playing for time. Hitler wanted to assure himself of Russian neutrality while he dealt with France and Great Britain. Stalin apparently hoped that Hitler would find himself bogged down in the west, giving Russia adequate time to prepare for its eventual encounter with Germany.

Publicly, the Hitler-Stalin Pact pledged Germany and Russia never to attack each other, and to remain neutral if the other were involved in war. Secretly, however, the two dictators agreed to divide eastern Europe into spheres of influence. Germany was to take western Poland. Russia was given a free hand in the Baltic States, in eastern Poland, and in the province of Bessarabia, which it had lost to Rumania in 1918. There was little doubt of the meaning of the pact. The Western nations had lost a possible ally in the east, and Germany had a pledge of Russia's neutrality. It was a tremendous military advantage, which Hitler was quick to use.

Danzig and the Polish Corridor

The crisis that finally touched off World War II began in Poland. Hitler's dispute with Poland involved the Polish Corridor, the strip of territory cut through Germany to allow Poland to reach the seaport of Danzig (see map, page 713). Danzig, a free city protected by the League of Nations, was to be a port for both Germany and Poland.

Danzig had its own elected two-house legislature. The executive was a commissioner appointed by the League. He also served as chief justice, but appeals from his decisions could be made to the League Council or to the World Court. The port of Danzig was controlled by a commission made up of equal members of Poles and Germans, with a neutral chairman. Poland was guaranteed free use of the port and free trade between Poland and Danzig.

Danzig offered Hitler an unequaled chance to put his technique of aggression into practice. There was a heavy German population. The city had been "torn from the fatherland." The commis-

Hitler's aggressive methods brought a large part of Europe under his control without fighting. At Munich, above, he meets with Chamberlain. There, Britain and France abandoned the Sudetenland to Germany. At right, Hitler drives triumphantly through a Sudeten town. The Russian drawing below savagely attacks aggressions of this sort, picturing the German swastika, tipped with daggers, grinding remorselessly over a pile of skulls. As it turned out, Hitler was prepared for ruthless war. The time came in 1939 when Hitler's armored columns and warplanes streaked across the Polish border in a new kind of "lightning war." At far right, Polish cavalry try to stop German tanks. Warsaw, lower right, was smashed.

sioner was a foreigner. The despised Poles were given rights in the city and its port.

A strong Nazi party sprang up in Danzig, encouraged by propaganda and financial help from Berlin. By 1937 it had won control of the city government, using the usual Nazi tactics where they seemed necessary. The city government took actions and issued demands that made relations with Poland increasingly difficult and the position of the League commissioner almost impossible.

After he secured Austria and Czechoslovakia, Hitler stepped up his campaign against Poland. The Nazis demanded the return of Danzig to the fatherland. Hitler started a propaganda campaign claiming that the Poles were mistreating the Germans in the Polish Corridor. Within a week after signing the nonaggression pact with Russia, Hitler demanded a "German solution" to the Polish question: Danzig must be returned to Germany, and the Germans must be allowed to occupy a strip through the Corridor. Messages flew back and forth between Germany and Poland, but neither of the two countries would change its stand.

On the morning of September 1, 1939, Hitler declared that Danzig was annexed to the Reich. At the same time, without warning, his air force made a massive attack on Poland, while Nazi troops, led by tank columns, struck across the border. Two days later, Great Britain and France kept their promises to Poland and declared war on Germany. Within forty-eight hours the unannounced attack on Poland became the beginning of World War II. In the next chapter you will learn how the war spread from Europe to all the world.

CHECKUP

1. How did France and Great Britain prepare for war in the summer of 1939?

2. Why did France, Great Britain, and Russia fail to sign an alliance against Hitler?

3. What was the Hitler-Stalin Pact? What may have been Hitler's and Stalin's reasons for signing it?

4. By what steps did Hitler seize Danzig and the Polish Corridor?

CHAPTER REVIEW

Chapter 35   Local Aggressions Destroyed the Uneasy Peace   (1921–1939)

1921-1922	Washington Naval Conference	1935	Saar returned to Germany	1938	*Anschluss* of Germany and Austria
1928	Kellogg-Briand Pact	1936	Italian defeat of Ethiopia		Munich conference
1931	Japanese attack on Manchuria	1936-1939	Spanish Civil War	1939	Hitler-Stalin Pact
	Republic of Spain established	1937	Japanese invasion of China		German invasion of Poland

CHAPTER SUMMARY

The League of Nations failed to stop aggressions after World War I because of basic weaknesses: its membership was incomplete, and it could only recommend action. Japan was the first aggressor. Despite wartime gains, the nation had serious economic problems which played into the hands of the military. When the Japanese occupied Manchuria and created the puppet state of Manchukuo, the League demanded restoration of the area to China, but without success. Soon, Japanese armies invaded China, beginning a war that was to last for several years.

Following Japan's example of attacking a weaker nation, Italy invaded Ethiopia. The League imposed economic sanctions, but feeble enforcement and Ethiopian weakness made Italian victory possible.

Spain, meanwhile, was the scene of internal conflicts. After the country became a republic, it adopted sweeping reforms that were opposed by conservatives. Many of these formed a fascist party, the Falange. Soon Falangist forces—the Nationalists—rebelled against the republic under Franco's leadership. Germany and Italy aided Franco, while Russia and other foreign volunteers helped the Loyalists. Within three years the republic was overthrown, and Franco set up a fascist state modeled after Italy.

Hitler became increasingly aggressive. After his success in the Saar and the Rhineland, he used a "war of nerves" technique to annex additional territories. First came *Anschluss* with Austria. Then he moved against Czechoslovakia, with the Sudetenland as his object. When Czechoslovakia called on its allies for help, they met at Munich and yielded to Hitler.

The next areas to fall to the Axis were Memel—taken from Lithuania by Germany—and Albania, which fell to Italy. Britain and France tried unsuccessfully to draw Stalin into an alliance; he instead signed a nonaggression treaty with Hitler. The latter,

using Danzig and the Polish Corridor as an excuse, launched a "war of nerves" on Poland. It culminated in September 1939, when German armies invaded Polish territory and set off World War II.

QUESTIONS FOR DISCUSSION

1. Do you agree that the absence of the United States from the League of Nations weakened the organization?

2. Opponents called the League of Nations (as its opponents call the United Nations today) a "supergovernment." How accurate do you consider this description? Explain your answer.

3. Why did smaller countries in the League of Nations usually favor stronger measures against aggressors than did the great powers?

4. How did Mussolini gain control over Ethiopia? Why do you think Italians were enthusiastic about Mussolini's exploits in Africa, while most people in the world were outraged by them? Should a citizen criticize his country when he feels it has adopted the wrong policy? Explain.

5. Name three points at which aggressive dictator nations might have been stopped during the 1930's. Explain why other nations, including the United States and the Soviet Union, followed a policy of appeasement.

PROJECTS

1. Write a short essay pointing out why the policy of appeasement toward Hitler failed.

2. List the countries that fell to totalitarian rule in the period between the two world wars, and give reasons why.

3. Draw a cartoon condemning fascist aggression.

4. Draw a map of Europe showing the territorial expansion of fascist Italy and Nazi Germany up to World War II.

The Allies Defeated the Axis in World War II

Some historians refer to the years between 1919 and 1939 as the Twenty-Year Truce. They regard World War II as a continuation of World War I and as an attempt to settle problems left unsolved at the Paris peace conference. In many ways the two world wars were similar. Both began in eastern Europe and spread rapidly. In both, Germany fought on two fronts. And, finally, both wars resulted in German defeats at the hands of an alliance led by Western democracies.

But there were also many differences between the two world wars. World War I had been a war of stalemate and attrition. World War II was a war of swift movement. Hitler's invasion of Poland on September 1, 1939, set the example for the new kind of warfare. The German attack on Poland was called a *Blitzkrieg*—German for "lightning war." Hitler used more than a million men in the assault. Dive bombers screamed down to drop explosives on cities below. Artillery was motorized for rapid movement. Panzer units— tanks and armored trucks—attempted to divide the enemy forces into small groups, encircle them, and destroy them or force them to surrender. In this war of swift movement, trench fighting was a thing of the past.

Another difference between the world wars was the extent of civilian involvement. Although World War I had caused extensive hardship behind the lines, civilians during World War II suffered to

Japanese planes bombing the Philippines

an extent undreamed of in 1918. Bombers hit railroads and bridges to disrupt the transport of war materials to the front. This kind of bombing was to be expected. But fleets of planes also bombed nonstrategic targets in order to spread panic and break the morale of civilians. This kind of systematic destruction, carried on by both sides, reached staggering proportions.

World War II was also more truly a *world* war than World War I had been. In World War I the fighting, with only a few exceptions, was confined to Europe. In World War II it took place not only in Europe but also in Africa, in Asia, and on islands in the Pacific Ocean.

After Japan joined the Rome-Berlin Axis in 1940, there were three Axis Powers—Germany (including Austria), Italy, and Japan. Later in the war, Hungary, Rumania, Bulgaria, and Finland also sided with the Axis. The most important Allies were Britain, the United States, the Soviet Union, and China. The Free French and the governments-in-exile of conquered countries (such as the Netherlands) were also Allies. The Allies eventually numbered over forty-five countries.

THE CHAPTER SECTIONS:

1. German forces quickly overran Western Europe (1939–1941)

2. Russia and the United States were drawn into the war (1941–1942)

3. The tide of battle turned against the Axis Powers (1942–1943)

4. Victories over Germany and Japan brought the war to an end (1943–1945)

1   German forces quickly overran Western Europe

While Germany was attacking Poland in September 1939, France moved its army up to the Maginot Line, the chain of fortifications guarding France's eastern frontier (see map, page 723). British forces crossed the English Channel and landed on the northern coast of France, and the British navy blockaded Germany's ports. The Germans massed troops behind the Siegfried Line, the system of fortifications they had built in the Rhineland. Although German submarines had begun to sink merchant ships—both enemy and neutral—there was little action on the western front. Newspapers began to speak of the "phony" war, or "sitzkrieg," in Western Europe. Many people still hoped that an all-out war could be avoided.

Russian moves westward

As the Germans marched into western Poland, the Soviet army massed on the Russian-Polish border. Then, in accordance with the secret provisions of the Hitler-Stalin Pact, the Russians moved into eastern Poland. In this Fourth Partition, Poland once more disappeared from the map. The Russians then took the Baltic countries of Estonia, Latvia, and Lithuania. Diplo-matic pressures from Moscow had previously given the Russians land, sea, and air bases in these Baltic nations. Annexation to the Soviet Union soon followed.

Russia tried the same tactics in Finland, but there the story was different. When the Russians asked to have bases in Finland, the Finns rejected the demands. On November 30, 1939, Russia attacked Finland. The Finns appealed to the League of Nations, which expelled the Soviet Union for its aggression against a member nation. (The Soviet Union became the only country ever to be expelled from the League for aggression.) The Finns fought bravely for three months, but their resistance crumbled in March 1940. They were forced to cede territories in southern and eastern Finland to the Soviet Union. The Finnish-Soviet border was also demilitarized— that is, troops and military equipment were removed from it.

Scandinavia and the Low Countries

On April 9, 1940, the "phony" war ended with a sudden German invasion of Denmark and Norway. Hitler had prepared the way in Scandinavia by sending in Germans as workmen to secure the services of native collaborators.° Fifth columnists seized power plants and radio stations, disrupting transportation and communications and aiding the Nazi invasion. In a single day, German troops seized several of Norway's strategic North Sea ports. Both Denmark and Norway were under German control by the end of April.

The reasons for Hitler's invasion of these countries soon became clear. By seizing them, Germany secured an outlet to the Atlantic and made certain that it would not be bottled up in the Baltic Sea as had happened in World War I. The long Scandinavian coastline—especially that of Norway with its fiords (inlets bordered by rocky cliffs)—gave Germany excellent bases for submarines. There were also many good sites for airfields. Shipping to France and Britain was thus put in grave danger.

The British realized that Hitler posed an immediate threat to their safety. Neville Chamberlain, whose appeasement policy had proved so unsuccessful, was forced to resign as prime minister. He was succeeded by Winston Churchill, a statesman who had attacked appeasement and warned against the Nazi menace to Europe.

Hitler, meanwhile, continued his attack. He intended to take as much territory as possible before his opponents could mount an offensive against him. On May 10, 1940, German panzer units invaded the Low Countries—the Netherlands, Belgium, and Luxembourg. Luxembourg fell in one day, the Netherlands in five days. When the city of Rotterdam delayed the Nazi advance by resisting the German army, Hitler ordered his air force to attack. Even while a surrender was being negotiated, Nazi bombers leveled the heart of the great Dutch city. Belgium surrendered at the end of May.

Hitler's forces were now in a position to outflank France's Maginot Line. The German panzers drove westward, toward the English Channel.

° **collaborators:** persons who assist their country's enemies, or who willingly work with enemy occupation forces. In Norway, Germany was aided by Major Vidkun Quisling, a Norwegian army officer who betrayed his country and became the head of a puppet regime under Nazi control. During World War II, therefore, collaborators were often called "quislings."

British, Belgian, and French troops at Dunkirk, a seaport in northern France, were cut off from the major French force to the south. Outnumbered and with no room to maneuver, the encircled troops could only surrender or withdraw. They chose to withdraw. The British air force was able to gain momentary control of the air to defend the trapped forces from bombing attacks. Every available ship and boat in England—including fishing craft and rowboats—was ordered to Dunkirk. Between May 27 and June 4, some 340,000 men were safely transported across the channel to England.

The evacuation of Dunkirk was, of course, a military defeat for the Allies. The British army had been driven from the continent, leaving its equipment behind. But the success of the astounding rescue operation at Dunkirk helped raise British morale considerably. On June 4, Churchill addressed one of his most stirring speeches to the British people. "We shall defend our island," he said, "whatever the cost may be. We shall fight on the beaches, we shall fight on the landing grounds, we shall fight in the fields and in the streets, we shall fight in the hills; we shall never surrender."

The fall of France

After Dunkirk the French were left to fight alone on the continent. The Maginot Line was now useless. Having overrun Belgium, the Germans were in a position to attack France from the north, where few fortifications had been built.

Germany began its offensive against France early in June 1940. The French fought a desperate, losing battle. Their army was not trained or equipped for the new kind of war. Northern France was a scene of utter confusion. Civilians, carrying whatever goods they could save, blocked roads attempting to flee southward. German planes bombed and machine-gunned the fleeing refugees, spreading panic and disorder.

Mussolini, taking advantage of France's weakness, declared war on France and Britain on June 10, and Italian forces invaded southern France. In President Roosevelt's words: "The hand that held the dagger has struck it into the back of its neighbor." On June 14 the Germans entered Paris, and French armed resistance collapsed. Rather than surrender, the French cabinet resigned.

There were, however, some Frenchmen who were willing to surrender. The aged Marshal Henri Pétain, a hero of World War I, formed a government and assumed dictatorial powers. The man who became his vice premier, Pierre Laval, had long urged cooperation with Hitler. Late in June the Pétain government signed an armistice with Hitler and Mussolini. The armistice terms were severe. German troops were to occupy northern France, including Paris, and a strip of territory along the Atlantic coast southward to Spain. The costs of the occupation were to be paid by France. The French navy was to be disarmed and kept in French ports. Pétain's government moved to the city of Vichy, in the south. Thus France was divided into Occupied France and Vichy France (see map, opposite page). The Vichy government also controlled most French possessions in North Africa and the Near East. It became symbolic of appeasement, surrender, and fascism.

Some Frenchmen who wanted to continue to fight against the Germans escaped to Africa or to England. Under the leadership of General Charles de Gaulle, they formed the Provisional French National Committee—called the Free French government—with its headquarters in London.

Within France itself there grew up an underground, or resistance movement, members of which worked secretly to oppose the German occupation forces. Members of the French underground were called Maquis (mah·KEE)—a French term for scrubby undergrowth, common in the areas where resistance fighters hid. Similar resistance movements developed in most of the countries that were occupied by Germany. Members engaged in sabotage, blowing up bridges, wrecking trains, and cutting telephone and telegraph lines. Underground fighters needed great courage. When they were discovered by the Germans, they were usually tortured and executed.

The Battle of Britain

After the fall of France, French generals predicted that Great Britain would "have her neck wrung like a chicken's in three weeks." (Churchill later commented: "Some chicken! Some neck!") Hitler began scattered bombing raids on Britain, which gradually increased in intensity. These attacks were part of his plan, called Operation Sea Lion, to weaken and then invade and conquer the British Isles.

With Great Britain poorly prepared for war, Hitler appealed to "reason and common sense" in Britain, offering to negotiate a peace settlement. He was rebuffed by Churchill, and Germany stepped up the air attacks on Great Britain, striking centers of civilian population as well as railroad and industrial targets. The period of the heaviest attacks, from August through November 1940, is known as the Battle of Britain.

German bombers blasted British cities with explosives and fire bombs. London was bombed continually during September and October; in November, the city of Coventry was burned practically to the ground. The aim was to lower morale and destroy the people's will to fight. But the British doggedly dug out of the ruins and fought on. They were well defended by fighter planes of the Royal Air Force.

British planes, though fewer, were better in quality than the German planes. They were piloted by daring and skillful fliers—volunteers from France, Belgium, Poland, and Czechoslovakia, as well as British members of the Royal Air Force. British planes also had the advantage of radar, a new tracking device that enabled pilots to detect enemy aircraft even at a great distance. During the summer and fall of 1940, they took a heavy toll of German planes. Of these fighter pilots, Churchill said, "Never in the field of human conflict was so much owed by so many to so few."

The Germans continued night bombing raids for almost two years. At the same time British bombers made increasingly heavy raids on German cities. By the middle of 1941, air warfare had become a stalemate. However, because of Germany's blockade of British shipping from European ports, there was a chance that Britain could be starved out. This might have happened, except for the United States.

WORLD WAR II IN THE WEST
1939-1945

Chief Axis Powers

Maximum area of Axis control

→ Allied advances

✕ Battle of the Bulge

Maginot Line

▲▲▲▲ Siegfried Line

–·–·– Boundaries of September 1, 1939

Neutral or non-belligerent nations <u>underlined</u>

United States involvement

The determination of the United States to remain neutral in future wars was clearly expressed in the Neutrality Act of 1937, which forbade Americans to sell war equipment to belligerent nations. When war in Europe broke out in 1939, opinion in the United States was divided. Many people felt that Nazi Germany was a threat not only to Europe but to civilization itself. Others believed that Europe's wars were no affair of the United States.

As the war progressed, the United States gradually became more involved. The Neutrality Act of 1939 allowed the sale of munitions to belligerent nations, but only on a cash-and-carry

(continued on page 726)

Early Days of the War

The Allied cause seemed almost hopeless when Hitler's Blitzkrieg slashed through France. The invaders captured countless French soldiers like the one at left, whose exhaustion contrasts with the jaunty grin of his German captor, and stranded British forces on the beaches at Dunkirk, below. Before trying to invade England, Hitler sent hordes of aircraft on continuous bombing raids to destroy British fortifications, smash cities, and undermine the British will to resist. At right, rescue workers pull a woman out of her demolished home after a raid on London during the Battle of Britain. At far right, Londoners bed down in a subway station that has been converted into an air-raid shelter.

Hitler failed to defeat the British, largely because the RAF doggedly fought off German aircraft until British land forces could be trained and help could arrive from the United States. At middle right, fuselage markings show that this British pilot has been notably successful in shooting down enemy planes. In August 1941, President Roosevelt and Prime Minister Churchill, lower right, met at sea to formulate the Atlantic Charter.

basis. In spite of German submarine attacks, the British still controlled the sea routes between the United States and Great Britain. Thus this law, in effect, permitted the sale of arms only to Britain. After the disaster at Dunkirk and the fall of France, American sympathies for Britain increased. In September 1940, President Roosevelt, by executive agreement, transferred fifty old American destroyers to Great Britain in exchange for long-term leases on British naval and air bases in Newfoundland, the British West Indies, and British Guiana. In that same month, Congress passed the first national conscription law ever adopted by the United States in peacetime.

Early in 1941, Churchill appealed to the United States: "Give us the tools, and we will finish the job." In March, Roosevelt was authorized by Congress to supply war materials to Britain on credit. This measure was known as the Lend-Lease Act. The direction of America's involvement was clear to everyone. In May 1941 a German submarine sank an American merchant ship. Roosevelt retaliated by freezing all German and Italian assets in American banks—that is, making it impossible for them to be used.

The Atlantic Charter

Because they wanted to avoid the secret-treaty incidents of World War I, Roosevelt and Churchill decided to announce the war aims of the democracies. In August 1941 they met on board a British battleship off the coast of Newfoundland and drew up a statement called the Atlantic Charter.

Among its provisions were these: (1) Neither nation sought any territorial gains. (2) No territorial changes were to be made unless approved by the people concerned. (3) All people had the right to choose their form of government. (4) All nations should have equal rights to trade and obtain raw materials. (5) There should be economic cooperation to ensure everyone a decent standard of living. (6) Peace should bring all men security and freedom from want and fear. (7) There should be freedom of the seas. (8) All nations should give up the use of force.

By the fall of 1941, the United States Navy was waging an undeclared war on German submarines. The United States had moved far away from its neutrality of 1937. The only remaining restrictions were those prohibiting American merchant ships from being armed or entering war zones. In November 1941, Congress abolished these restrictions. The United States, as a non-belligerent ally, was now giving the British "all aid short of war."

CHECKUP

1. What was the "phony" war? What advantages did Germany gain by seizing Norway and Denmark?

2. Why was the Maginot Line useless in June 1940? What were the "three Frances" after the French were defeated?

3. How did the United States move from the position expressed in the Neutrality Act of 1937 to giving Great Britain "all aid short of war"?

4. IDENTIFY: Blitzkrieg, panzer units, collaborators, Maquis, Battle of Britain, Atlantic Charter.

5. LOCATE: Siegfried Line, Rotterdam, Dunkirk, Coventry, Vichy France.

2 Russia and the United States were drawn into the war

By the fall of 1940, Germany held almost all of Western Europe. It controlled the Atlantic coastline from the tip of Norway to Spain, and its submarines were allowed to use Spanish ports. Spain, because of its civil war, was not able to join the fighting, but neither was it neutral. Franco called the country a "non-neutral non-belligerent." The Axis also controlled much of the western Mediterranean coastline—an important advantage.

In September the Japanese government joined the Rome-Berlin Axis as an ally of Hitler and Mussolini. This move strained Hitler's "master race" doctrine with its contempt for non-Caucasians. He proved equal to the situation, however, by announcing that the Japanese were "yellow Aryans."

Great Britain still held some bases: Gibraltar, on the southern coast of Spain; the islands of Malta and Cyprus, in the Mediterranean; and Alexandria, in Egypt. Some British troops were also stationed in Palestine and Egypt, where they protected the Suez Canal.

Eastern Europe and the Mediterranean

Mussolini, once the senior partner in the Axis alliance, hoped to build a Mediterranean empire for Italy. His attack on France in June 1940 had proved Italy's military weakness. Although the French defenders had been vastly outnumbered, Italian advances were slow and costly. In the fall of 1940, Mussolini sent his troops into British Somaliland, Egypt, and Greece.

The Greeks routed the invading Italian army. The British stopped the advance into Egypt. In their counterattack, the British took Tobruk, a port city in Libya. The invasion of British Somaliland also failed, and a counterattack drove the Italians out of Ethiopia as well. Emperor Haile Selassie was restored to his throne.

Not until Hitler turned his attention to the Balkans did Axis fortunes in the east improve. Germany seized Rumania, which it needed for the rich oil fields there. In March 1941, German pressure on Bulgaria resulted in the occupation of that country by German troops. (By November 1941, Rumania, Bulgaria, and Hungary had allied themselves with Germany.)

In April 1941, Hitler invaded Yugoslavia after failing to persuade the Yugoslavian government to allow German troops to march through the country to Greece. In less than two weeks, Yugoslav resistance was crushed.

Next came Greece. Despite stubborn resistance by the Greeks, aided by British and other Allied troops, the German panzers prevailed. The British withdrew to the island of Crete. Now the Germans used a new technique. German troops were parachuted into Crete, and by the end of May, the British were forced to abandon the island and move to Egypt. Thus Germany controlled the entire Balkan Peninsula except the city of Istanbul and the Straits (see map, page 723). In June, Germany and Turkey signed a treaty assuring Turkish neutrality.

The German victories in Greece and Crete enabled Hitler to launch the next move in his giant strategy—a huge pincers movement against the Suez Canal. One part of the Axis force was to come by way of North Africa, the other through Syria, Iraq, Trans-Jordan, and Palestine. The rich oil fields of the Near East would also give Hitler a considerable advantage in the war.

Hitler hoped that political pressure would force Turkey to allow German troops to pass through the country. The Germans prepared the way with Nazi parties and fifth columnists. They thought that pressure on the Vichy government would easily gain them the French mandate of Lebanon. The plan did not succeed, however. Turkey, in spite of great pressure, remained neutral. The British and Free French held Iraq and, in July 1941, drove the Vichy French out of Syria. One month later, Allied forces also occupied Iran.

Meanwhile the Germans had moved forces across the Mediterranean to North Africa by air and in ships that broke through the British blockade. Throughout 1941, Italian and German troops led by General Erwin Rommel—the "Desert Fox" —fought the British in Libya. In the summer of 1942, Rommel's forces drove the British out of Libya and back into Egypt. At El Alamein, only 70 miles from Alexandria (see map, page 723), the German offensive began to run down for lack of supplies. The British made a stand, and Rommel remained stalled at El Alamein.

Germany's attack on Russia

The Russians regarded the German victories in the Balkans with unconcealed alarm and anger. They considered the Balkans, especially Rumania and Bulgaria, as their sphere of influence.

A Soviet-German conference took place in Berlin in November 1940. The Russians demanded that Bulgaria, Istanbul, and the Straits be an exclusively Soviet sphere of influence. Hitler suggested instead that Germany should have all of Europe, and that Russia should establish a sphere in Asia which would provide an outlet to

Russians near Stalingrad search for their dead among civilians slain by the Nazis. The city was completely destroyed during the many months of fighting.

the Indian Ocean. These suggestions, of course, were totally unacceptable to Stalin.

On June 22, 1941, the war entered a new phase. Without a declaration of war, German armies invaded the Soviet Union. The Germans were soon aided by Hungarians, Italians, Rumanians, and Finns (Finland had allied itself with Germany). Franco sent a division of troops from Spain. Hitler had opened a new, 2,000-mile front. Churchill declared that, although he did not admire communism, any nation that fought the Nazis was an ally and should receive help. The United States declared its willingness to give Lend-Lease aid to the Russians.

As in World War I, getting aid to Russia was extremely difficult (see map, page 723). The sea route across the Mediterranean, and through the Straits and the Black Sea, had to run the gantlet of submarine and air attacks from Italy and the Balkans. The route through the Baltic Sea was impossible. There were two Russian ports, Mur-

mansk and Archangel, in the Arctic. Convoys to them had to pass the long, Axis-held coast of Norway under constant plane and submarine attack. A new route, therefore, was developed from the Persian Gulf across Iran by train and truck to southern Russia. It became a lifeline for supplies from Britain and the United States.

The Russian defense. The initial force of the Nazi panzer columns was tremendous. Everywhere the Russian armies were driven back. Within a very short time, Moscow and Leningrad (as Petrograd had been called since 1924) were under siege. There, however, the attack bogged down. Instead of winning the expected easy victory, the German armies found themselves face to face with a strong and resourceful enemy.

The Russians used the same scorched-earth tactics against Hitler that their forefathers had used against Napoleon. The retreating armies and civilians carried away what they could and destroyed everything else. The territory gained by the Germans was more a hindrance than a help. Many Russian soldiers remained behind, hiding out in swamps and forests and making guerrilla attacks on railroads, bridges, and trains.

Hitler had expected the Russians to surrender after a short campaign. The Russian stand at Leningrad and Moscow wrecked his timetable. When the short Russian autumn came, Hitler faced the same decision Napoleon had had to make: should he retreat or should he stand? Hitler chose to stand.

Soon the Germans had to face a new enemy—what the Russians call Generals Frost and Mud. The Nazi troops were poorly equipped for the bitterly cold Russian winter. The Russians chose the winter for a counterattack, especially to relieve pressure on Moscow. For the first time in World War II, the Germans had to retreat.

Nevertheless, the year 1941 ended with the Germans deep in Russian territory. In spring 1942 they struck southward, aiming to cut the supply line from Iran. One German spearhead drove toward the city of Stalingrad. Another drove toward the Caucasus, the oil-producing region of Russia (see map, page 723).

The southern German army drove deep into the Caucasus toward the Caspian Sea. Fighting fiercely, the Russians stopped the Germans before they reached their goal—the port of Baku. North of the Caucasus the Russians were forced back until they reached Stalingrad.

"New Order" and "Final Solution"

The invasion of Russia was part of Hitler's master plan for the creation of a "New Order" for Europe. Europe was to be organized into a single political and economic system, ruled from Berlin and dominated by the "Aryan race." According to this plan, Russia was to serve Germany as a producer of food and raw materials. An official economic plan issued by the German government stated: "There is no doubt that . . . many millions of people will be starved to death if we take out of the country the things we need." This did not concern the Führer. Russians were Slavs and therefore, according to Nazi ideology, "racially inferior."

Another aspect of Hitler's plan for a "New Order" went into effect as the Germans continued their offensives. The persecution of racial minorities had always been an aspect of Nazi policy. In 1941, Hitler ordered the annihilation of the entire Jewish population of Europe. The Nazis called this program the "Final Solution" of the "Jewish problem." This unbelievably barbaric goal was possible in Hitler's Germany because so many people had accepted the insane Nazi theories about "Aryan" racial superiority.

Jews by the thousands from Germany and from countries occupied by the Germans were transported to eastern Germany and Poland, where they were herded together in concentration camps. Among the most infamous were Dachau and Buchenwald in Germany, and Treblinka and Auschwitz in Poland. Some inmates were used as slave laborers. Most, however, were murdered by poison gas, or shot, sometimes hundreds at a time. In some Western European countries, especially Denmark, efforts were made to protect native Jews from the Nazis. In the east, however, a long tradition of anti-Semitism made the Nazi program more devastating.

The Final Solution was made possible by the confusion of the wartime situation, but it did not further the German war effort. The Final Solution, in fact, damaged the war effort. Jewish workers were removed from the labor force by the extermination policy. Soldiers, railroads, and vital equipment were committed to the program, and the expense was great. It is estimated that, by the time the Nazi government fell, its leaders had murdered 6 million European Jews. Nearly as many non-Jews, including Slavs, Gypsies, and resistance workers, were also murdered.

Japanese aggressions in the Pacific

The attack on Russia caused the withdrawal of many German troops from the western front. Hitler postponed Operation Sea Lion, his plan to invade Britain. Germany's attack on Russia therefore aided the Allies because the Germans had to fight a war on two fronts, much as they had done in World War I.

A second major source of assistance in the

"Ya usin' two blankets or three?"

Willie and Joe: The War as It Was

There was little illusion among those at the front in World War II. They knew that fighting was a grim business and that the heaviest burdens, as always, would fall to the common enlisted man. In the American army, this was the G.I. (from the words "Government Issue," a term used by the quartermaster's department). Probably the best-known G.I.'s of the war were Willie and Joe, two characters created by the American cartoonist Bill Mauldin. His incisive pen-and-ink drawings captured the ironic wit of the foxhole. They appeared in an army newspaper and delighted soldiers and civilians alike.

Unshaven and cynical, Willie and Joe typified the Americans' determination to finish the war and get back home. Here the incongruity of the question points up the doggedness of the combat infantryman, who hangs on to life's trivia in order to keep his sanity. This same sort of understatement in the face of misery is apparent in Mauldin's wry comment on life up front: "It's a little better when you can lie down, even in the mud."

struggle against the Axis came in December 1941, when the United States joined the war. The United States was drawn into the conflict not as a direct result of the situation in Europe but because of events in the Pacific area.

You have read about Japanese militarism and aggression in the 1930's. Like Germany, Japan had a master plan for domination. It wanted to control a large area and coordinate all its resources for Japan's benefit. A Japanese propaganda campaign stressed "Asia for the Asiatics" and spoke of eastern Asia and the Pacific as the Greater East Asia Co-Prosperity Sphere—a region that would be dominated by Japan.

Early in 1939, with the situation in Europe growing increasingly tense, Japan saw a long-awaited chance. Its first move was to take the island of Hainan and some small islands off the coast of French Indo-China, thus cutting the British route from Hong Kong to Singapore (see map, page 705). Neither France nor Britain was able to stop this move.

After the fall of the Netherlands and France, Japan made further aggressive moves. The Japanese government declared the Netherlands East Indies to be under Japanese "protective custody." Japanese pressure forced the Vichy government to allow French Indo-China to become a Japanese protectorate. Britain was forced to close the Burma Road. In September 1940, as discussed earlier, Japan formed an alliance with Hitler and Mussolini. The United States met these Japanese moves in three ways: protests against violations of the Nine-Power Treaty, aid to Chiang Kai-shek, and an embargo on the sale of oil and scrap iron to Japan. It had already moved a large part of its Pacific fleet to Hawaii.

During 1941, relations between the United States and Japan grew steadily worse. Japan and the Soviet Union signed a five-year nonaggression treaty. An even more militaristic government came to power in Japan under Premier Hideki Tojo. Late in 1941 the Japanese sent a special representative to Washington, D.C., to confer.

American entry into the war

On December 7, 1941, while Tojo's representative was still in Washington, the Japanese launched a sneak attack on the United States naval base at Pearl Harbor, Hawaii, using aircraft and submarines. Several American ships were sunk, and others were badly damaged. The American dead totaled over 2,300.

On December 8, 1941, Congress declared war on Japan, as did the British Parliament. Three days later, Germany and Italy declared war on the United States, and Congress replied in kind. Thus the United States became a full-fledged belligerent in World War II.

The Japanese were quick to take advantage of American unpreparedness. On the same day as the attack on Pearl Harbor, Japan began aerial attacks on the Philippines. Americans in the Philippines had known for some hours of the bombing at Pearl Harbor. For reasons that have never been explained, the planes of the American air force, on which much of the defense against invasion depended, were carefully drawn up in formation on the airfield. They were "sitting ducks" to the attacking Japanese.

Soon afterward the Japanese landed on Luzon. Within a month, they had captured the American island outposts of Guam and Wake. In less than three months, the mainland areas of Burma, Thailand, and Malaya, including the mighty British fortress of Singapore, had been added to Japan's conquests. The Japanese went on to conquer a vast island empire: most of the Netherlands East Indies, the Philippines, and the Gilbert Islands. Australia remained as the last stronghold of resistance in the southwest Pacific, but it could be supplied only over a long route from Hawaii. Japanese landings on New Guinea and the Solomon Islands threatened even this supply line (see map, page 735).

CHECKUP

1. What gains did the Germans make in southeastern Europe in 1941?

2. What was Hitler's strategy in the Near East? How well did it succeed? Explain.

3. How did Britain and the United States get help to Russia? How did the Russians defend themselves against German attack?

4. IDENTIFY: "non-neutral non-belligerent," "yellow Aryans," Rommel, Generals Frost and Mud, "New Order," "Final Solution," Greater East Asia Co-Prosperity Sphere.

5. LOCATE: Tobruk, El Alamein, Murmansk, Archangel, Stalingrad, Baku, Hainan, Pearl Harbor, Malaya, Gilbert Islands.

3 · The tide of battle turned against the Axis Powers

Representatives of twenty-six nations met in Washington, D.C., in January 1942 to unite in the common purpose of defeating the Axis. Chief among these nations were Great Britain, the Soviet Union, and the United States. Other nations —in Europe, Asia, and the Americas—contributed what they could to the alliance. Each nation pledged to use all its resources to defeat the Axis, not to sign a separate peace, and to abide by the provisions of the Atlantic Charter.

During the war years that followed, the leaders of the Allied nations—particularly Roosevelt, Churchill, and Stalin—met frequently to discuss the conduct of the war and plans for the peace to follow. Conferences were held during 1943 in Casablanca, Morocco; Quebec, Canada; Moscow, Russia; Cairo, Egypt; and Teheran, Iran.

The battle of Stalingrad

The German summer offensive of 1942 had pushed the Russians back to Stalingrad (see map, page 723). There a tremendous battle, the most spectacular of the war, was fought for six months. Suffering terrible losses, the Germans penetrated the city, but the Russians did not retreat. They defended the city street by street and house by house. Every foot of ground the Germans took was gained at huge cost.

In November 1942, the Russians began a counterattack, encircling the German troops in the city. Although Hitler ordered his trapped forces to fight to the death, what was left of his army in Stalingrad surrendered on January 31, 1943. The heroic and successful defense of Stalingrad was a crucial turning point in the war. The Germans never completely recovered from this defeat.

After Stalingrad the Russian army never gave up the initiative. Throughout 1943 they forced German troops in Russia to retreat steadily. By 1944 the Germans had fallen back into Poland. For Russia, the victory over the Nazi invaders was won at a staggering cost.

The war in North Africa

While the Russians were defending Stalingrad, the Allies were making progress in North Africa. Late in the summer of 1942, Allied reinforcements were rushed to El Alamein, where British troops were under German attack. In a decisive battle in October, troops under British General Bernard Montgomery routed Rommel's force. The Germans were pushed westward across Libya into Tunisia.

In November 1942, American and British forces under American General Dwight Eisenhower landed in Morocco and Algeria. Admiral Jean Darlan and the Vichy French resisted the first landings, but a truce was soon arranged. As a result of this truce, the Vichy government was subjected to increased Nazi control, and German troops occupied Vichy France, in addition to northern France.

Eisenhower's forces pushed eastward from Morocco and Algeria into Tunisia as Montgomery's army moved westward. Rommel's army was thus trapped between the two. The campaign was hard-fought, but by the middle of May 1943, the Germans in North Africa were forced to surrender. Italy's African empire disappeared; the French colonies in Africa were held by the Free French. The Suez Canal was controlled by the Allies, and the Mediterranean was made more secure for Allied naval operations.

The invasion of Italy

Throughout 1942, Stalin had made constant demands that the British and Americans open a second front in Europe to relieve the German pressure on Russia. The Allies argued that they were not ready, and that an attack before they were fully prepared would be too dangerous to risk. In 1942 the United States—the mainstay of Allied industrial might—was still in the process of turning its economy to wartime production. Stalin suspected that the Western powers hoped that Germany and Russia would destroy each other.

When North Africa was secured by the Allies, Stalin renewed his demands for a landing in Europe. Churchill insisted upon an attack on what he called the "soft underbelly of the Axis"—Italy and the Balkans. In July 1943, Allied armies from North Africa landed on the strategic island of Sicily. Resistance was strong, but the island was taken in little more than a month. Then the Italian mainland was bombed in preparation for a landing.

In Italy, Mussolini was forced to resign, and Marshal Pietro Badoglio (bah·DOH·lyo) became premier. His first act was to dissolve the Fascist Party. When the Allied army landed on the southwestern Italian mainland in September 1943, the Italians surrendered unconditionally. They then declared war on Germany. The Italian government was recognized as a "co-belligerent" (one who fights the same enemy, but is not an ally).

German troops in Italy continued to resist the Allied advance with skill and determination. The battle to establish a second beachhead at Anzio, on the central Italian coast, was one of the fiercest of the war. The advance up the peninsula was slow, every gain paid for by the lives of Allied soldiers. For example, at Monte Cassino—the famous monastery established by St. Benedict—the Germans held out for three months. Mussolini retreated with the Germans, a virtual prisoner.

Sea and air attacks

Meanwhile, the Battle of the Atlantic was being won. This conflict between German and Allied ships had begun in the spring of 1940. An enormous number of Allied ships were sunk by German submarines. By the fall of 1943, convoys of troop and supply ships from the United States were well protected by destroyers and other es-

The Allied counterattack against the Axis Powers was worldwide. Above, at El Alamein in 1942, British troops capture a survivor of a German tank crew. Within a year, all German forces in North Africa had surrendered. Meantime, halfway around the world, American forces were perfecting techniques that would permit them to start driving the Japanese back toward their homeland. One technique was amphibious warfare, as at left, with troops storming ashore from landing craft that could draw up into the shallow water off island beaches. Another method, below, was to destroy the Japanese navy with carrier-based planes and PT (from "patrol torpedo") boats. At lower left, American engineers use elephants to help clear a portion of the Burma Road.

cort ships and by planes based both on land and on aircraft carriers. New scientific devices, such as sonar—a tracking device employing sound waves—were perfected to locate submarines. The "wolfpacks" of Nazi submarines became the hunted instead of the hunters.

Allied air attacks against Germany and the occupied countries rose steadily in intensity. At first the Allies, operating from bases in the British Isles and using pinpoint bombing—bombing aimed at specific targets—concentrated on strategic sites. Later they began to bomb civilian areas as well, hoping to weaken both the ability and the will of the Axis Powers to fight. Almost every German city was bombed; some, like Hamburg, were almost wiped out. Industries in occupied countries were bombed also.

The war in the Pacific

The Japanese advance in the Pacific received its first check in May 1942. A Japanese fleet thrusting toward Australia was defeated by American and Australian air and naval forces in the five-day battle of the Coral Sea. Soon afterward a larger Japanese fleet, pushing eastward to try to capture the Midway Islands, northwest of Hawaii, was met by an American fleet. In the crucial battle of Midway, fought from June 3 to June 6 chiefly by carrier-based planes, the Japanese were defeated. With these two victories, the United States Navy began to turn the tide in the Pacific.

To divert attention from their threat to the Midway Islands, the Japanese landed at Kiska and Attu in the Aleutian Islands and bombed the American naval base at Dutch Harbor. These actions represented the high point of the Japanese advance.

To realize how immense this operation was, look at the map on the opposite page. The Midway Islands are over 2,500 miles away from the Japanese homeland. Dutch Harbor is almost as far. The northern tip of Australia is nearly 1,000 miles farther from Japan. In 1942, all the intervening seas were held by the Japanese navy. Many of the islands were occupied by Japanese troops and protected by Japanese planes.

Early in August 1942, to protect the Australian supply line, American marines landed on the Solomon Islands, seizing the airfield on Guadalcanal. This jungle island was so important that four times in the next four months the Japanese launched savage attacks on the American forces. All were repulsed, with terrible losses on both sides.

The American offensive. In 1943 the Allied nations took the offensive in the Pacific. Sea, air, and land forces of the United States, aided by forces from Australia and New Zealand, waged a long series of battles to drive the Japanese entirely out of the Solomon Islands. In the central Pacific, Tarawa—one of the Gilbert Islands—was captured after a savage fight. In the Aleutians, American forces regained Attu and Kiska.

The Allies adopted a strategy called "island-hopping." Certain Japanese-held islands were captured, while others were by-passed and left helpless for lack of supplies. Defenders of one of the greatest Japanese bases, Truk, in the Caroline Islands, were thus left without supplies and cut off from their own forces.

The American navy had been greatly enlarged and by 1944 was stronger than the Japanese navy. That year saw the addition of many aircraft carriers, the new backbone of the fleet. The army and marine corps were now large enough for new Pacific offensives.

During 1944 the Americans cleared the Japanese from the Marshall Islands, New Guinea, and the Marianas. Saipan and Tinian, in the Marianas, became bases for long-range bombing attacks on Japan. In October 1944, an American army under General Douglas MacArthur landed at Leyte in the central Philippines. Shortly after the landing, the Japanese fleet suffered a crushing defeat in a great air and sea fight, the battle of Leyte Gulf. After six months of hard fighting, the entire Philippine archipelago was recovered.

China and the Burma Road. In China the war from 1940 to 1943 had been a deadlock. In 1944 the truce between Chiang Kai-shek and the Chinese communists broke down. Each side accused the other of fighting it rather than the Japanese. Undoubtedly both sides were to blame. It seemed clear that China would not be able or willing to make much of an offensive because the China

WORLD WAR II IN THE EAST · 1941-1945

Maximum area of Japanese control

Allied advances   Allied air attacks

U.S.S.R. (Neutral until Aug. 8, 1945)

ALASKA

MONGOLIA

MANCHURIA
(MANCHUKUO)

Peiping
(Peking)   Port
Arthur

CHINA

INDIA

Chungking   Nanking

Shanghai   Nagasaki

BURMA
ROAD

Lashio   Kunming

BURMA

THAI-
LAND
(SIAM)

FRENCH
INDO-
CHINA

HAINAN

Hong
Kong

FORMOSA
(TAIWAN)

LUZON

PHILIPPINE

ISLANDS

LEYTE

MALAYA

Singapore

SUMATRA

BORNEO

CELEBES

NETHERLANDS   EAST   INDIES

JAVA

INDIAN   OCEAN

AUSTRALIA

0   2000 miles

SAKHALIN

KURILE IS.

KOREA   JAPAN

Hiroshima   Tokyo

RYUKYU IS.

OKINAWA

IWO JIMA

SAIPAN
GUAM
TINIAN

MARIANA
ISLANDS

CAROLINE ISLANDS

TRUK

NEW GUINEA

SOLOMON
ISLANDS

GUADALCANAL

CORAL
SEA

ATTU   ALEUTIAN ISLANDS   Dutch
KISKA   Harbor

1943

PACIFIC   OCEAN

WAKE I.

MIDWAY   HAWAIIAN ISLANDS
ISLANDS   1942

Pearl Harbor

MARSHALL
ISLANDS

TARAWA

NAURU   GILBERT
ISLANDS

1943

1944

1942-43   1942

coast and the Burma Road—China's principal
supply routes—were still in Japanese hands.

The Burma Road might have been reopened
if Britain had been able to get assistance from
India. Here, however, it ran into difficulties resulting from (1) the Indian independence movement, and (2) Hindu-Moslem hostility within
India. In return for military help, Britain offered

India dominion status after the war. But Gandhi
and the Indian National Congress demanded immediate self-government. The Moslems demanded a separate, independent state if India
were granted self-government. When Britain refused immediate self-government, Gandhi and his
followers continued their program of civil disobedience and urged nonresistance to Japan.

735

1. What were the turning points of the war in (a) Russia? (b) North Africa? (c) the Pacific?

2. Why did Stalin want a second front? Describe the circumstances under which it was launched.

3. IDENTIFY: Montgomery, "soft underbelly of the Axis," Badoglio, sonar, pinpoint bombing, "island-hopping."

4. LOCATE: Anzio, Coral Sea, Kiska, Attu, Dutch Harbor, Guadalcanal, Tarawa, Truk, Saipan, Tinian, Leyte.

4 Victories over Germany and Japan brought the war to an end

By 1943 the Axis Powers had dipped deeply into their supplies of both manpower and war materials. On the Allied side, the United States—which had escaped direct attack on its mainland—had successfully turned its huge industrial potential to the manufacture of war goods. The joint Allied command was now ready for the final push that would win the war.

Victory in Europe

As the Allies were fighting their way through Italy in late 1943, plans were being made for another, and more important, invasion of Europe. Roosevelt and Churchill revealed their plans for the opening of this second front to Stalin at Teheran in November 1943. The invasion, called Operation Overlord, was "aimed at the heart of Germany and at the destruction of her armed forces." The landing was to be made on the beaches of the narrow, heavily wooded French peninsula of Normandy (see map, page 723), the same beaches from which William the Conqueror had invaded England in 1066.

The long-awaited landing came on June 6, 1944 (D-Day in military terminology). The initial attack involved 175,000 men and many tons of equipment. The men and material were transferred across the English Channel in one of the most daring invasion operations in military history. Within a month, more than a million men had landed in France. The Germans had expected a landing in France, but the exact location of the assault had successfully been kept secret. German forces were rushed to Normandy to meet the Allied invasion, but were outnumbered. Hitler had been forced to draw upon young and inexperienced combat troops by 1943, while the Al-

lies had large resources of trained American manpower to employ in Operation Overlord.

The Germans tried two defenses: (1) to bottle up the Allies on the Normandy peninsula, and (2) to strike at Britain with two newly developed weapons in an attempt to break British morale. These weapons were the V-1, a pilotless flying bomb, and the V-2, a more advanced pilotless missile that employed rocket propulsion. These bomb raids on Britain caused much destruction, and ceased only when Allied forces captured the launching sites that the Germans had built for the bombs in France and Belgium. Had the development of such missiles come earlier in the war, Germany's chances of success would no doubt have been improved.

After heavy fighting, Allied troops broke out of Normandy and moved into northern France. At the same time, Allied forces landed on the Mediterranean coast of France and fought their way northward. On August 25, 1944, Allied troops entered Paris. By September they faced the strongly fortified Siegfried Line along Germany's western frontier.

The drive from the east. In June 1944 the Russians began a major drive against Germany from the east. By the end of 1944, the Red Army had taken the nations of Finland, Estonia, Lithuania, Latvia, Rumania, Bulgaria, and Albania. The British aided in driving the Germans from Greece. Yugoslavia had earlier been liberated with the help of partisan (guerrilla) troops under Marshal Tito. By far the heaviest Russian fighting, however, was in Poland. By July 1944, Russian troops were approaching Warsaw.

Some German generals advised Hitler to surrender, and some field commanders laid down their arms in the face of the Allied advances. But Hitler refused to concede defeat. In July 1944, several German generals tried unsuccessfully to assassinate Hitler. The job of defeating Germany would have to be completed by force.

The drive from the west. The Americans pierced the "unconquerable" Siegfried Line in October after five weeks of fighting. The Allies took port cities in France and Belgium, easing the problem of supplying the Allied forces. The Allies cleared Alsace and Lorraine of German troops and prepared to continue the attack.

The Germans had strength for one desperate counterattack. Just before Christmas in 1944, they drove a 50-mile wedge into Allied lines in Belgium. After a costly ten-day battle—the Battle of the Bulge—the Allies turned back the German drive. At the same time, the Russians had mounted a large-scale attack in the east. In three weeks they advanced 265 miles into German territory.

The Allies then pushed beyond the Siegfried Line and moved eastward. American troops found an undestroyed bridge at Remagen and were able to push across the Rhine quickly. American and British columns from the west and Russians from the east slashed the crumbling German army into smaller and smaller bits. In early spring 1945, German defenses collapsed.

The Russian and American armies made their first contact at Torgau on April 25, 1945. It was agreed that the Russians should take Berlin.

At the end of April, the German army in Italy surrendered unconditionally. Italian guerrillas pursued and captured Mussolini. The ex-dictator was shot and his body displayed in public, hanging upside down, before jeering crowds. On May 1, news came that Hitler had committed suicide during the struggle for Berlin. The following day the Russians captured the battered and devastated city. Within a week the German high command surrendered unconditionally. May 8, 1945, was V-E Day—the day of victory in Europe.

The defeat of Japan

The Pacific war continued. The main islands of Japan could now be reached by long-range bombers from Saipan, and systematic raids on Japanese industrial cities began early in 1945. However, the Allies needed still closer islands as fighter bases and emergency landing fields.

The first move was into a group of islands about 750 miles directly south of Tokyo. American marines landed on the small volcanic island of Iwo Jima (see map, page 735), which they captured after a month of the bitterest fighting of the war. Okinawa, largest of the Ryukyu Islands, was taken after more desperate fighting. Japanese resistance became stronger as their home islands were approached. At Okinawa, nearly 250 ships were damaged by suicide attacks of fanatical Japanese pilots who crashed their planes, loaded with explosives, into the ships. These suicide attacks were called kamikaze attacks, after the "Great Wind" that had saved Japan from Chinese-Mongol attack in 1281.

Despite such bitter resistance, the Allies continued the intensive bombing of Japan. Japanese ports were effectively blockaded—especially by Allied submarine fleets—and the Japanese navy was immobilized. Nevertheless, the Japanese government refused to surrender. Actual invasion of the Japanese islands seemed the only way to insure an Allied victory. There were also Japanese armies in Korea and Manchuria. It was possible that, even with their home islands conquered, these troops might continue their resistance.

Yalta and Potsdam

Roosevelt and Churchill hoped to persuade Stalin to bring Russia into the war in the Pacific. Before the defeat of Germany, Russia had been completely occupied in defending itself, and it considered the war against Japan as the business of the United States.

In February 1945, Roosevelt and Churchill met with Stalin at Yalta, in southern Russia. The Big Three, as the Allied leaders were called, agreed that Germany should be temporarily divided and occupied by troops of the victorious powers, including France. The liberated areas of Europe were to have democratically elected governments. Russia was to enter the war against

(*continued on page 740*)

Allied Victory

On the damp, overcast morning of June 6, 1944, the greatest armada in history crossed the English Channel to assault the continent of Europe. American, British, and Canadian troops poured ashore along a 60-mile front in Normandy, France. At left, German prisoners are marched along the beach by their Allied captors.

Not until Allied forces had penetrated deep into Hitler's Europe did the extent of Nazi atrocities become fully known. Battle-hardened veterans, accustomed to violent death in many forms, were sickened by what they saw in the concentration camps they liberated. At Buchenwald, below left, they found heaps of bodies awaiting burial.

In the Far East, victory was not assured until the United States dropped atomic bombs on Hiroshima and Nagasaki, causing enormous destruction and thousands of deaths. Walking amidst the devastation that was once Hiroshima, below, is a victim of the bomb.

At right is a view of the official Japanese surrender on board the battleship *Missouri* at anchor in Tokyo Bay. The document was signed by two Japanese representatives and by generals and admirals of the Allied nations.

Japan. As compensation, it was to receive Japanese territories, including southern Sakhalin and the Kurile Islands. Russia was to be granted a lease on Port Arthur, and, with China, was to operate the Chinese Eastern Railway.

Another conference was held in July 1945 at Potsdam, near Berlin. By this time, important changes had taken place in the world situation. President Roosevelt had died and had been succeeded by his Vice-President, Harry S. Truman. Winston Churchill's Conservative Party had fallen from power in Britain, and Clement Attlee, of the Labour Party, was prime minister.

Most important, however, was the fact that the United States had produced a workable atomic bomb. Scientists from many nations—including refugees from fascism, such as Enrico Fermi of Italy—had worked to harness the enormous energy released by the splitting of atoms, and had succeeded in creating the most destructive weapon known up to that time. With this weapon in the American arsenal, it would not be necessary for the Allies to invade Japan. At the Potsdam Conference, Truman, Attlee, and Stalin decided to issue an ultimatum to Japan, demanding surrender. (They also made various decisions regarding peace settlements in Europe, as you will read in Chapter 38.)

The Japanese government refused to surrender. On August 6, 1945, a single American bomber dropped an atomic bomb on the Japanese city of Hiroshima. The bomb exploded with the force of 20,000 tons of TNT. Some 80,000 persons were killed, and more than half of Hiroshima was destroyed. Two days later, Russia declared war on Japan. Russian armies swept into Manchuria, where they met little resistance. On August 9, a second and even more powerful atomic bomb was dropped on the city of Nagasaki. The following day, Japan sued for peace, asking only that the emperor be allowed to keep his throne. The Allies agreed on condition that he be subject to the orders of the Supreme Allied Commander in the Pacific, General Douglas MacArthur. On September 2, 1945 (known as V-J Day), the official Japanese surrender documents were signed aboard the American battleship *Missouri* in Tokyo Bay.

Costs of the war

World War II, to a much greater extent than World War I, was a war of movement and of machines. Military casualties, however, were still enormous. Battle losses of the Soviet Union have been estimated at 7 million lives, although an accurate count has never been made. Germany lost 2¼ million men in battle, and Japan's total loss—civilian and military—was nearly 1½ million. Lives lost by Great Britain, France, and the United States numbered in the hundreds of thousands. The suffering of millions of others—murdered in German concentration camps and gas chambers, uprooted by the ravages of war, or injured in combat—is incalculable.

As the war progressed, the destructiveness of weapons and tactics increased. More shocking, perhaps, is the fact that increased brutality and destructiveness were accepted more and more easily by the civilian populations of the belligerent nations. At the beginning of the war, the German bombing of Rotterdam and of British cities caused a wave of horrified protest throughout the world. Attacks from the air on helpless civilians were considered the height of needless and savage brutality.

By 1943, however, Allied air attacks on Axis civilian centers were accepted simply as part of modern warfare. The destruction of Hamburg and the atomic bombings of Hiroshima and Nagasaki did not bring any great public protest. In the words of one historian, World War II "was, as never before, a war between whole nations, and women and children figured very high among the death rolls." By 1945, the killing of thousands of civilians had come to be accepted as a normal practice of war.

CHECKUP

1. How did the Allies attack France? What defense measures did Germany take?

2. What was the fate of Mussolini? of Hitler?

3. What were the chief decisions made at Yalta and Potsdam?

4. IDENTIFY: D-Day, Tito, Battle of the Bulge, V-E Day, V-J Day.

5. LOCATE: Remagen, Torgau, Iwo Jima, Okinawa.

CHAPTER REVIEW

Chapter 36   The Allies Defeated the Axis in World War II   (1939–1945)

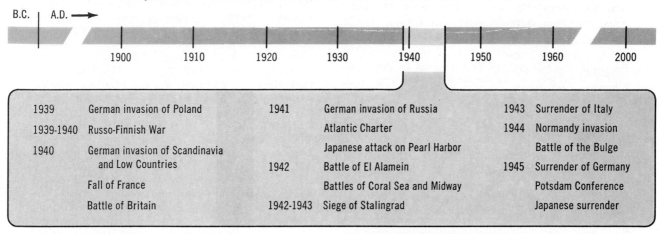

1939	German invasion of Poland	1941	German invasion of Russia	1943	Surrender of Italy
1939-1940	Russo-Finnish War		Atlantic Charter	1944	Normandy invasion
1940	German invasion of Scandinavia and Low Countries		Japanese attack on Pearl Harbor		Battle of the Bulge
	Fall of France	1942	Battle of El Alamein	1945	Surrender of Germany
			Battles of Coral Sea and Midway		Potsdam Conference
	Battle of Britain	1942-1943	Siege of Stalingrad		Japanese surrender

CHAPTER SUMMARY

In the first two years of World War II, the German Blitzkrieg overran Poland, Denmark, Norway, the Low Countries, and France. Russia meanwhile seized the Baltic States and defeated Finland. Although Dunkirk was a military disaster, the British, led by Churchill, stood fast through the dark days of the Battle of Britain.

Germany then turned to the Balkans and North Africa, making significant gains. The war entered a new phase when the Germans attacked Russia and drove deep into its territory. This invasion was part of Hitler's master plan for a "New Order," a Europe dominated by "Aryans." So was the "Final Solution" of the "Jewish problem," which resulted in the murder of about 6 million European Jews.

In the Pacific, Japan continued its aggression in China and also seized several Allied possessions. Its surprise bombing of Pearl Harbor brought the United States into the war on the side of the Allies. Japan rapidly conquered a vast Pacific empire.

The tide of battle turned in 1942, with Allied counterattacks in Russia and North Africa, and naval victories in the Pacific. Next came the invasion and surrender of Italy and the American strategy of "island-hopping" in the Pacific.

After the Allied landing in Normandy, Germany was attacked from both east and west. In the spring of 1945, Hitler committed suicide as the Allies reached Berlin, and the Germans surrendered. In spite of heavy bombardments, Japan continued to hold out until atomic bombs were dropped on Hiroshima and Nagasaki. Then, as Russia swept into Manchuria (a strategy agreed upon at Potsdam), Japan also surrendered and the war was over.

QUESTIONS FOR DISCUSSION

1. How did the German Blitzkrieg differ from warfare in World War I? How do you envision a war fought with today's most modern weapons?

2. Why must World War II be considered a total war? Do you think the bombing of nonstrategic targets, such as residential areas in cities, was justified? Explain.

3. In what way was the evacuation of British troops at Dunkirk a success? How important is the morale of a people and its army in a modern war?

4. Do you think the atomic bombings of Hiroshima and Nagasaki were justified? Defend your position.

5. In what respects was the United States following a policy of isolationism before the outbreak of World War II? Do you think the United States should have become a belligerent in the war before 1941? Explain your position.

6. How did the underlying causes of World War I differ from those of World War II?

7. What were the provisions of the Atlantic Charter? Explain whether the United States should continue to uphold these ideals.

PROJECTS

1. Write a short essay explaining why it was necessary to defeat Hitler.

2. As a reporter for an American newspaper, write a news article describing the bombing of Rotterdam by the Germans during World War II.

3. Draw a cartoon depicting the similar fate that Napoleon's and Hitler's armies met in Russia.

4. Draw a map of Europe showing the advance of Hitler's armies during 1939 and 1940.

STUDY IN DEPTH

UNIT NINE

For additional bibliographical information on the books cited in these projects, see the Basic Library (page xviii) and Further Reading on the opposite page.

INDIVIDUAL PROJECTS

1. Compare the westernization of Turkey by Atatürk with that of Russia by Peter the Great two hundred years earlier.

2. Draw a series of cartoons for the bulletin board showing the plight of a nation during the Great Depression. For ideas for your drawings read Eisen and Filler, *The Human Adventure*, Vol. 2, "Hunger and Unemployment in Britain."

3. What was Lenin's role in the Bolshevik Revolution? Report your findings on this question to the class. Read Eisen and Filler, *The Human Adventure*, Vol. 2, "Lenin Rules in the Kremlin," and one of the biographies of Lenin by Fischer or Shub listed on the opposite page.

4. Hitler's speeches often brought his audiences to mass hysteria. Write a speech that Hitler might have made before World War II and put it on tape. You should include in the speech such topics as Hitler's view of race, *Lebensraum*, unemployment, communism, nationalism, use of force, the Versailles Treaty, party organization, and democracy. Play the speech to the entire class and lead a discussion of its contents. The following sources should be used for this project: Copeland and Lamm, *The World's Great Speeches*, "Adolf Hitler: Germany's Claims"; Eisen and Filler, *The Human Adventure*, Vol. 2, "Hitler's Theories"; Peterson, *Treasury of the World's Great Speeches*, "Hitler Takes Full Responsibility for the Blood Purge."

5. Munich has become the symbol of appeasement. In an essay, define appeasement, discuss what happened in Munich in 1938, and give your own opinion of a policy of appeasement—does it have merit or will it always lead to disaster? Original sources are: Stearns, *Pageant of Europe*, "The Policy of Appeasement"; Copeland and Lamm, *The World's Great Speeches*, "Neville Chamberlain: The Munich Agreement"; Eisen and Filler, *The Human Adventure*, Vol. 2, "Appeasement in Munich"; Peterson, *Treasury of the World's Great Speeches*, "Prime Minister Chamberlain Returns in Triumph from Munich."

6. The attack on Pearl Harbor by Japan brought the United States into World War II as a belligerent.

Prepare a special newscast originating in Hawaii a day after the bombing of the American fleet in Pearl Harbor. Record the newscast on tape and play it to the class. Consult the following sources for information: Copeland and Lamm, *The World's Great Speeches*, "Franklin Delano Roosevelt: For a Declaration of War Against Japan"; Eisen and Filler, *The Human Adventure*, Vol. 2, "The Japanese Attack Pearl Harbor"; Peterson, *Treasury of the World's Great Speeches*, "Roosevelt Asks for a Declaration of War Against Japan"; Snyder and Morris, *A Treasury of Great Reporting*, "Three Newspaper Accounts of 'A Date Which Will Live in Infamy'"; *American Heritage*, "Pearl Harbor: Who Blundered?" February 1962.

7. Interview someone who participated in World War II, asking the following questions: What was your role in the war? Where were you located during the war? Did you know why you were fighting—did you have reasons? What were some unusual experiences you had during the war? How do you feel about war?

8. The Allied heads of state held several meetings during World War II. In a written report, summarize the agreements that were made during these conferences. See Eisen and Filler, *The Human Adventure*, Vol. 2, "Plans for Victory and Peace"; Hughes and Fries, *European Civilization*, "The Teheran Conference" and "The Yalta Conference"; Stearns, *Pageant of Europe*, "Defining the Peace Terms and Plans for Post-War Security."

GROUP PROJECTS

1. Organize a debate on the following topic: The United States was wise to drop the first atomic bomb.

2. Perhaps the most evil aspect of Nazi policy was the systematic extermination of nearly 12 million people. After World War II, many Nazi war criminals excused their behavior on grounds that they were loyal German citizens simply following orders. Do you think this is justifiable? Do you believe that, in a military situation, all orders should be obeyed, even if a subordinate may consider them immoral? Organize a debate on these issues. Participants in the debate should read extensively, including: Eisen and Filler, *The Human Adventure*, Vol. 2, "Nazi War Crimes"; Snyder and Morris, *A Treasury of Great Reporting*, "Two Foreign Correspondents Describe the Nazi Death Factories" and "Jerusalem 1961: The Eichmann Trial Recalls the Faces of Six Million Dead"; Stearns, *Pageant of Europe*, "Man's Inhumanity to Man." Also consult *Readers' Guide to Periodical Literature* for relevant magazine articles and the unit bibliography for pertinent books.

Further Reading

BIOGRAPHY

Ayling, S. E., *Portraits of Power*. Barnes & Noble.* Biographies of leading political figures of the 1920's, 1930's, 1940's.

Baker, R. M., *Chaim Weizmann: Builder of a Nation*. Messner.

Bullock, Alan, *Hitler, A Study in Tyranny*. Bantam.*

Burns, James MacGregor, *Roosevelt: The Lion and the Fox*. Harcourt Brace Jovanovich.*

Deutscher, Isaac, *The Prophet Armed: Trotsky 1879–1921*. Random House.*

_____, *Stalin: A Political Biography*. Oxford Univ. Press.

Fermi, Laura, *Mussolini*. Univ. of Chicago.

Fischer, Louis, *Gandhi*. New American Library.*

_____, *The Life of Lenin*. Harper & Row.*

Frank, Anne, *Anne Frank: The Diary of a Young Girl*. Pocket Books.* Story of a girl and her family persecuted by Nazis.

Gorham, Charles O., *The Lion of Judah: A Life of Haile Selassie I, Emperor of Ethiopia*. Farrar, Straus & Giroux.

Halperin, William, *Mussolini and Italian Fascism*. Van Nostrand.*

Kinross, Lord, *Atatürk*. Morrow.

Macleod, Iain, *Neville Chamberlain*. Atheneum.

Shub, David, *Lenin*. New American Library.*

Wibberley, Leonard, *The Complete Life of Winston Chuchill*. Farrar, Straus & Giroux.

Young, Desmond, *Rommel, the Desert Fox*. Harper & Row.*

NONFICTION

Benoist-Mechin, Jacques, *Sixty Days That Shook the West*. Putnam. Hitler's invasion of France.

Bliven, Bruce, Jr., *The Story of D-Day: June 6, 1944*. Random House.

Blond, Georges, *The Death of Hitler's Germany*. Pyramid.*

Churchill, Sir Winston, *The Second World War*. Golden Press.

Crossman, Richard, ed., *The God That Failed*. Bantam.* Six famous men tell of their disillusionment with communism.

Flender, Harold, *Rescue in Denmark*. Macfadden-Bartell.* Rescue of Jews.

Footman, David, *Civil War in Russia*. Praeger.

Goldston, Robert, *The Russian Revolution*. Bobbs-Merrill.

* Paperback.

Hersey, John, *Hiroshima*. Bantam.* Interviews with six survivors of the atomic bomb.

Lord, Walter, *Day of Infamy*. Bantam.* Pearl Harbor attack.

Middleton, Drew, *Sky Suspended*. McKay. Battle of Britain.

Moorehead, Alan, *The Russian Revolution*. Bantam.*

Reynolds, Quentin, *The Battle of Britain*. Random House.

Rumpf, Hans, *The Bombing of Germany*. Holt, Rinehart and Winston.

Shannon, David, *The Great Depression*. Prentice-Hall.*

Shirer, William L., *The Rise and Fall of the Third Reich*. Fawcett.*

Snyder, Louis L., *The War*. Dell.*

Taylor, A. J. P., *From Sarajevo to Potsdam*. Harcourt Brace Jovanovich.

Teall, Kaye M., *From Tsars to Commissars*. Messner.

Toland, John, *The Last 100 Days*. Random House. World War II.

HISTORICAL FICTION

Fenner, Phyllis R., ed., *No Time for Glory: Stories of World War II*. Morrow.

Forester, C. S., *The Ship*. Little, Brown. A warship during a naval engagement.

Hemingway, Ernest, *For Whom the Bell Tolls*. Scribner. Spanish Civil War.

Hersey, John, *A Bell for Adano*. Bantam.* Occupation of an Italian village by American troops.

_____, *The Wall*. Pocket Books.* Resistance to the Nazis by the Jews of the Warsaw ghetto.

Koestler, Arthur, *Darkness at Noon*. New American Library.* Russian police state.

Lewis, Elizabeth F., *To Beat a Tiger*. Holt, Rinehart and Winston. Life in China during the Japanese occupation.

MacInnes, Helen, *Above Suspicion*. Harcourt Brace Jovanovich. Espionage in Nazi Germany.

Michener, James A., *Tales of the South Pacific*. Pocket Books.* World War II stories.

Orwell, George. *Animal Farm*. New American Library.* A satire on revolution and communism.

Remarque, Erich, *The Night in Lisbon*. Harcourt Brace Jovanovich. A refugee from Germany is pursued by the Nazis.

Shute, Nevil, *Most Secret*. Ballantine.* British intelligence during World War II.

Silone, Ignazio, *Bread and Wine*. New American Library.* Italy under fascism.

Wouk, Herman, *The Caine Mutiny: A Novel of World War II*. Doubleday.*

743

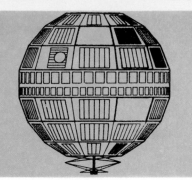

THE CHANGING

At a steel mill in central India, workers laboriously carry earth on their heads while excavating for a new addition to the factory. The contrast between modern technology and ancient, backbreaking methods of toil is only one of the many contradictions that perplex the people of today.

WORLD SINCE 1945

CHAPTER 37

The United Nations
Was Organized to Preserve Peace

The events of the years between the two world wars showed the ineffectiveness of the League of Nations as a peace-keeping agency. World War I and World War II showed, however, that other methods of keeping the peace—militarism, alliance systems, and pious pledges with no method of enforcement—were equally ineffective.

Events of the 1930's and 1940's proved that once a major war broke out, it was almost impossible for a great power to remain neutral. The only real hope for lasting peace seemed to be some sort of collective security through an international organization.

Shortly after the United States entered World War II, President Roosevelt referred to the nations allied against the Axis as the United Nations. This name became official on January 1, 1942, when twenty-six nations signed the "Declaration by United Nations." This document set forth their war aims, roughly the same as those expressed in the Atlantic Charter.

Plans for an international organization were discussed throughout the war by the Allied leaders. Beginning in August 1944, representatives of Britain, the Soviet Union, China, and the United States met at Dumbarton Oaks, a magnificent mansion in Washington, D.C., to draft a provisional charter for an organization to be known as the United Nations. This would be a new organization, although it had the same name as the

Delegates at the United Nations General Assembly

wartime alliance. In February 1945 the proposed charter was discussed by the Big Three—Roosevelt, Churchill, and Stalin—at Yalta. There they agreed on voting procedures to be followed in the United Nations and set the time and place for the first General Assembly, at which the final Charter would be drawn up.

In April 1945, representatives of fifty nations met in San Francisco. After two months, they agreed to a final version of the charter, which was then submitted to the governments of those nations for their ratification. Within four months, fifty-one ° nations had accepted the Charter. It went into effect October 24, 1945.

In ratifying the Charter, member nations agreed to the following purposes of the United Nations: (1) to maintain peace and security; (2) to promote equal rights and the self-determination of peoples; (3) to develop international cooperation; and (4) to encourage respect for human rights and fundamental freedoms without distinction as to race, sex, language, or religion.

THE CHAPTER SECTIONS:

1. The United Nations was created to give a voice to all nations (1942–1970's)

2. Many problems threatened the effectiveness of the United Nations (1945–1970's)

1 The United Nations was created to give a voice to all nations

Like the League of Nations, the United Nations (UN) was organized by the victorious powers after a world war. However, because both the United States and the Soviet Union were members from the beginning, the UN reflected the true power structure of the world more accurately than the League had done.

The United Nations is composed of six main organs—the General Assembly, the Security Council, the International Court of Justice, the Economic and Social Council, the Trusteeship Council, and the Secretariat. There are also several related boards, commissions, and specialized agencies (see chart, page 749).

The General Assembly

The General Assembly is made up of representatives of all the member nations, each of which is entitled to five delegates, five alternates, and as many advisers as it wishes. The large number of representatives makes it possible for nations to be represented on the various committees, where much of the work of the Assembly is done.

The Assembly is given the duty of drawing up the UN budget and assessing each nation's share of the cost. It elects the temporary members of the Security Council, and the members of the Economic and Social Council. Acting with the Security Council, the General Assembly elects the Secretary-General and the judges of the International Court of Justice. It receives and considers the reports of the various agencies of the United Nations. The Assembly may consider and discuss any problem that relates to world peace unless that problem is already being considered by the Security Council.

When a matter is brought to a vote in the General Assembly, each member nation has one vote. On procedural matters (those that involve comparatively routine details), a simple majority vote is needed. On substantive matters (matters of substance, or importance), a two-thirds vote is required. Nations may also abstain (not vote).

The Security Council

The Security Council is made up of representatives of fifteen member nations. Five of them (usually called the Big Five) are permanent members: the United States, Great Britain, the Soviet Union, France, and China.° Ten are tem-

° **China:** At first, Nationalist China, or Taiwan. On October 25, 1971, the Assembly voted to seat the representatives of the People's Republic of China (Communist China) and to expel Nationalist China.

° **fifty-one:** Poland, which had lacked a government in April 1945, had one by October.

porary members that are elected for two-year terms by the General Assembly and cannot be reelected immediately. Each member nation on the Council has one representative and one vote.

The chief responsibility of the Security Council is to maintain peace, settle disputes among nations, and prevent or resist aggression. When the Council is considering a dispute, it may get more information by asking questions of the parties involved or, with their consent, by sending representatives to investigate. After the dispute has been discussed, the Council usually urges the disputing nations to meet and work out their own solution. Sometimes it appoints mediators to aid the negotiations. The Council may suggest some kind of compromise, or it may send the case to the International Court of Justice for decision. Only when these peaceful measures have been tried and have failed, and when the Council believes that a threat to the peace still remains, can it use force.

The Council can order United Nations members to break diplomatic relations with an offending nation. It can also call for economic sanctions against the offender, such as an embargo on the sale of goods, or a boycott on buying goods. Finally, it can ask the members to provide the armed forces and facilities that may be necessary to stop armed aggression.

It is important to understand the voting of the Security Council. It takes nine of the fifteen votes to adopt any measure. On procedural matters the votes of any nine will pass a resolution. But on substantive matters, a negative vote by any of the five permanent members can override an affirmative majority and defeat any proposal. Thus any one of the Big Five may prevent the Council from taking an important action by voting against it. This is the much-discussed veto power. If more than one of the Big Five votes against a measure, it is not considered a veto.

The veto was included in the Charter at the insistence of both the United States and the Soviet Union. Many people believe that the Soviet Union has abused the veto. In the first twenty years of the Council's operation, the U.S.S.R. used the veto power more than a hundred times. Among the other Big Five members, only eight vetoes were cast during the same period. In recent years, however, the United States has used the veto several times.

The International Court of Justice

The International Court of Justice (also called the World Court) is made up of fifteen judges elected by the Security Council and General Assembly for terms of nine years. They are elected as individuals who are distinguished jurists, not as representatives of governments.

The jurisdiction of the Court is limited in three ways: (1) It hears only cases involving governments or agencies of the United Nations. It does not deal with cases of individuals or groups of people. (2) It accepts only cases that are legal disputes involving international law. Thus it is prevented from considering political disputes, or disputes which come within the domestic jurisdiction of a nation. (3) It cannot consider a case unless all the parties are willing to have the Court try it. For example, between 1954 and 1960 the United States filed suits against the Soviet Union, Hungary, and Czechoslovakia to recover damages for the shooting down of American planes. In each case the defendant refused to accept the Court's jurisdiction. Under the Charter the Court could only dismiss the cases.

The restrictions on the Court and the unwillingness of nations to allow certain cases to be tried limit its usefulness. It has, however, settled disputes involving such matters as territories, fisheries, and rights of nationals in foreign countries.

The Trusteeship Council

The Trusteeship Council is a body set up to deal with colonies and trust territories—former mandates of the League of Nations that had not yet become independent. These territories were voluntarily placed under the United Nations trusteeship system by the mandate powers. The Charter also allows colonial powers to place colonies (which the Charter calls non-self-governing territories) under trusteeship. By the early 1970's none had yet done so.

Each trustee nation signs an agreement with the United Nations, promising to maintain order,

THE UNITED NATIONS AND RELATED AGENCIES

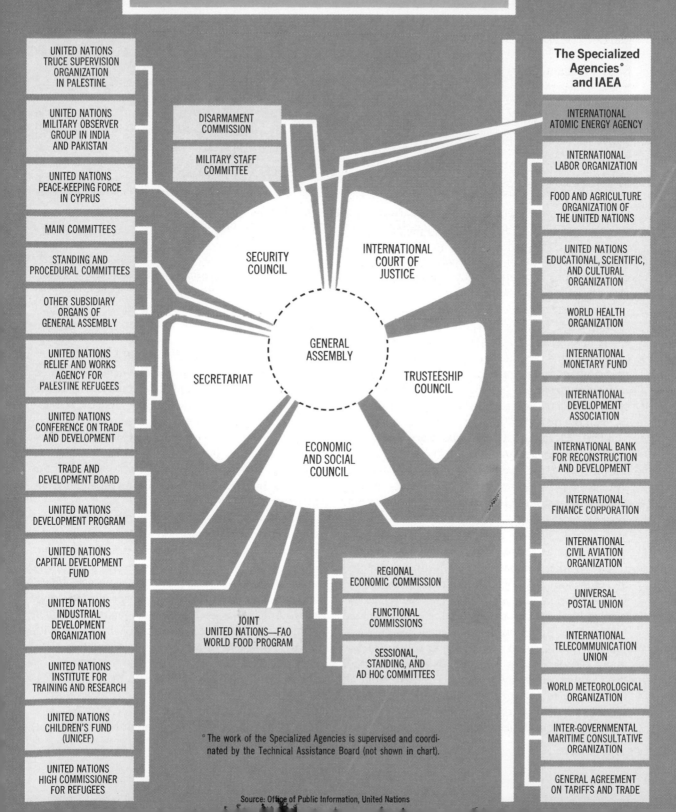

UNITED NATIONS TRUCE SUPERVISION ORGANIZATION IN PALESTINE

UNITED NATIONS MILITARY OBSERVER GROUP IN INDIA AND PAKISTAN

UNITED NATIONS PEACE-KEEPING FORCE IN CYPRUS

MAIN COMMITTEES

STANDING AND PROCEDURAL COMMITTEES

OTHER SUBSIDIARY ORGANS OF GENERAL ASSEMBLY

UNITED NATIONS RELIEF AND WORKS AGENCY FOR PALESTINE REFUGEES

UNITED NATIONS CONFERENCE ON TRADE AND DEVELOPMENT

TRADE AND DEVELOPMENT BOARD

UNITED NATIONS DEVELOPMENT PROGRAM

UNITED NATIONS CAPITAL DEVELOPMENT FUND

UNITED NATIONS INDUSTRIAL DEVELOPMENT ORGANIZATION

UNITED NATIONS INSTITUTE FOR TRAINING AND RESEARCH

UNITED NATIONS CHILDREN'S FUND (UNICEF)

UNITED NATIONS HIGH COMMISSIONER FOR REFUGEES

DISARMAMENT COMMISSION

MILITARY STAFF COMMITTEE

SECURITY COUNCIL

INTERNATIONAL COURT OF JUSTICE

SECRETARIAT

GENERAL ASSEMBLY

TRUSTEESHIP COUNCIL

ECONOMIC AND SOCIAL COUNCIL

JOINT UNITED NATIONS—FAO WORLD FOOD PROGRAM

REGIONAL ECONOMIC COMMISSION

FUNCTIONAL COMMISSIONS

SESSIONAL, STANDING, AND AD HOC COMMITTEES

The Specialized Agencies° and IAEA

INTERNATIONAL ATOMIC ENERGY AGENCY

INTERNATIONAL LABOR ORGANIZATION

FOOD AND AGRICULTURE ORGANIZATION OF THE UNITED NATIONS

UNITED NATIONS EDUCATIONAL, SCIENTIFIC, AND CULTURAL ORGANIZATION

WORLD HEALTH ORGANIZATION

INTERNATIONAL MONETARY FUND

INTERNATIONAL DEVELOPMENT ASSOCIATION

INTERNATIONAL BANK FOR RECONSTRUCTION AND DEVELOPMENT

INTERNATIONAL FINANCE CORPORATION

INTERNATIONAL CIVIL AVIATION ORGANIZATION

UNIVERSAL POSTAL UNION

INTERNATIONAL TELECOMMUNICATION UNION

WORLD METEOROLOGICAL ORGANIZATION

INTER-GOVERNMENTAL MARITIME CONSULTATIVE ORGANIZATION

GENERAL AGREEMENT ON TARIFFS AND TRADE

° The work of the Specialized Agencies is supervised and coordinated by the Technical Assistance Board (not shown in chart).

Source: Office of Public Information, United Nations

In a conference room at United Nations headquarters in New York City, a special committee of the Trusteeship Council meets to discuss problems of racial discrimination.

to foster free political institutions, to develop education, to protect native rights, and to guarantee free speech and worship.

The Trusteeship Council has a varying number of members. The Big Five are represented. Each trustee nation has a seat. Then, to insure fair consideration and action, there is an equal number of members from nontrustee nations.

It might be said that the purpose of the Trusteeship Council was to work itself out of existence by helping its trust territories to become independent. Eleven trust territories were placed under the trusteeship system in 1945. By 1973 there was only one, the Pacific islands of the Marshalls, the Carolinas, and—with the exception of Guam—the Marianas (administered by the United States).

The Secretariat

The Secretariat consists of clerical and administrative workers, advisers, and technical experts, all of whom are permanent employees of the United Nations organization. The Secretariat is headed by the Secretary-General. He is nominated by the Security Council and elected by the General Assembly for a term of five years. He has many responsibilities. He attends all meetings of the Council and the Assembly. He carries out all tasks assigned to him by the proper agencies. He reports annually to the General Assembly on the progress of the United Nations.

The Secretariat is divided into several departments, each under an assistant secretary-general. Each member of the Secretariat pledges to serve the interests of the United Nations and to take no orders from his own or any other government.

The Economic and Social Council

The Economic and Social Council was created to improve economic and social conditions. It has eighteen members, elected by the General Assembly for three-year terms. Each member has one vote, and there is no veto. The Council may recommend action, but it must depend on the good will and self-interest of nations, along with the force of public opinion, for its recommendations to be accepted and carried out.

The Council has set up a number of commissions to make recommendations on definite subjects, such as population, transportation and communication, human rights, the status of women, and the narcotics traffic. It has set up a technical assistance program to help underprivileged countries. And it has created, or associated with it, a number of specialized agencies, each dealing with a single problem or a related set of problems.

Specialized agencies. There are a number of specialized agencies (see chart, page 749). Although they are linked to the United Nations through the Economic and Social Council, each agency has its own charter, organization, budget, and membership. Members of the United Nations are not required to belong to the specialized agencies; under certain conditions, nonmembers of the United Nations may belong to a specialized agency.

The work of the specialized agencies is supervised and coordinated by the Technical Assistance Board, which has one main aim: to help nations help themselves. It gives assistance only when aid is requested by a government, and works mainly in underdeveloped countries.

A good example of the coordinated work of technical assistance and the cooperation of the receiving government took place in India in the 1950's. For centuries, India has had problems supplying its people with food. For various reasons, less than half the land of the subcontinent is cultivated. One area at the base of the Himalaya Mountains has rich soil, but it was a rain forest that swarmed with malarial mosquitoes. At the request of the Indian government, Technical Assistance Board officials agreed to a combined project there.

The World Health Organization supplied a Greek expert on malaria and a British public-health nurse. The Food and Agriculture Organization sent in experts to work with Indian agricultural specialists. Supplies and equipment were provided by the United Nations Children's Fund (UNICEF), which also carried on a mother-and-child health program. The Indian government used tractors and bulldozers to clear the jungle. As soon as part of the land was cleared, people began moving in from other parts of India. The malaria rate was reduced considerably. A whole new region was rendered productive, and a step taken to lower the starvation rate in India.

One of the best-known specialized agencies is the United Nations Educational, Scientific, and Cultural Organization (UNESCO). It was founded to encourage education and stimulate greater international exchange of knowledge.

The International Bank for Reconstruction and Development (often called the World Bank), another of the specialized agencies, was established to help finance the rebuilding of devastated areas and to help underdeveloped regions.

One agency not connected with the Economic and Social Council is the International Atomic Energy Agency (IAEA). It works directly with the General Assembly and the Security Council to promote peaceful uses of atomic energy.

CHECKUP

1. What are the four purposes of the United Nations?

2. Summarize the membership, principal functions, and methods of voting of (1) the General Assembly and (2) the Security Council.

3. IDENTIFY: International Court of Justice, Trusteeship Council, Secretariat, Economic and Social ·Council.

2 Many problems threatened the effectiveness of the United Nations

Politically, from the beginning, the United Nations faced serious problems, many stemming from a split that developed among the Allies. On one side were the democratic and other non-communist countries, led by the United States, Great Britain, and France. On the other were the communist dictatorships and their satellites (smaller, dependent nations), led by the Soviet Union and Communist China. The democratic and other non-communist countries were often called the West, or the free world. The communist bloc, centered in eastern Europe and parts of Asia, was known as the East, or the communist world. The conflict between East and West was called the Cold War.

Armaments control

The Charter of the United Nations expressed the eagerness of member nations to relieve the world's people of the crushing burden of armaments. It directed the Security Council to make plans for the regulation and reduction of armaments. A Disarmament Commission was established.

The United Nations

To carry on and direct the many UN activities, thousands of officials and workers from all over the world gather at the permanent headquarters in New York City, upper left. Above, in 1973, Secretary-General Kurt Waldheim of the UN addresses a group of Americans meeting to celebrate United Nations Day. Among the UN's many other functions is the promotion of economic well-being and education. At left, a French expert employed by the United Nations instructs apprentices in Morocco as part of a program to help modernize the country's leather industry. One of the UN's most effective leaders was America's Ralph J. Bunche, Under-Secretary for Political Affairs, who died in 1971. Below, on a mission to the Middle East, Bunche greeted refugees on the island of Cyprus.

To be successful, the Disarmament Commission (at first, the members of the Security Council plus Canada) had to reach agreement on three related problems: how to prevent nuclear warfare; how to reduce and destroy the existing supply of nuclear weapons; how to make sure that no more nuclear weapons were built.

The most difficult problem to negotiate was that of inspection. The United States insisted on complete inspection, to see that existing weapons were not hidden and that new ones were not secretly produced. The Soviet Union denounced this idea as a proposal for spying. First, the Russians said, agree to outlaw the production and use of atomic weapons, then destroy those in existence. After that, methods of inspection could be discussed.

On this point the disarmament negotiations became stalled. Meanwhile, the armament race continued. Both sides developed atomic weapons, then even more powerful hydrogen bombs. They produced long-range guided missiles, capable of carrying nuclear warheads from continent to continent. They developed MIRV ° missiles with more than one warhead, each capable of being aimed at a different target. They developed missiles that could be fired from submerged submarines that were driven by atomic power. The three original nuclear powers (the United States, the Soviet Union, and Great Britain) were increased to five by the addition of France and Communist China.

Some progress toward disarmament or arms limitation was made:

(1) Antarctica was neutralized and demilitarized. Nuclear explosions were prohibited. (December 1959)

(2) The United States, Great Britain, and the Soviet Union agreed to stop testing nuclear weapons anywhere except underground. (August 1963). Neither France nor China signed this agreement.

(3) A General Assembly resolution agreed to prevent the spread of the arms race to outer space. (October 1963)

° **MIRV:** Multiple independently targeted re-entry vehicle.

(4) Under the Nuclear Non-proliferation Treaty (N.P.T.), nations without nuclear weapons agreed not to produce or receive them. The nuclear powers agreed to share with other nations the peaceful benefits of atomic research, and to work toward arms limitation and disarmament. (May 1968)

(5) The United States and the Soviet Union agreed to prohibit the installation of fixed nuclear weapons on the seabed outside the three-mile limit. (October 1969)

(6) In the Strategic Arms Limitation Talks (SALT), anti-ballistic missile (ABM) sites were limited to two in the United States and two in the Soviet Union. An interim agreement limited both land- and sea-based launchers. (May 1972)

There was still a long way to go. The 1972 SALT agreements placed no curb on converting warheads in launchers or submarines to MIRV missiles. There was no limit on the number of missile-carrying aircraft. The quantity of missiles and launchers left to each side was enough to wipe out civilization. Still, it was encouraging to see progress. SALT talks continued in an atmosphere which took it for granted that atomic warfare was unthinkable.

Increased membership

The founders of the United Nations hoped that all countries would eventually belong to the organization, and provided a way for them to be admitted. Recommendation of a new member is made by the Security Council, where it is subject to a veto. Admission is by a two-thirds vote of the General Assembly.

Nine new members had been admitted by 1950, when the Cold War intervened. For five years no new members survived the Security Council admission process. In 1955 the deadlock broke; by 1973 there were 135 members.

Most of the new members were nations of Asia and Africa. In 1945 Asian and African members had numbered only thirteen. In 1973 the combined Asian and African membership constituted more than half the total of 135 members. The balance of power in the UN shifted significantly. In the beginning the West could almost always

UNICEF and Children's Art

Only in relatively recent times has children's art merited serious attention. Appropriately, UNICEF has given it a wide audience by using it on the calendars and Christmas cards it sells to raise funds. (UNICEF is financed entirely by voluntary contributions.) "In the Zoo" was painted by an eight-year-old Czechoslovakian girl and won a prize in an international children's art contest held annually in India.

get the two-thirds vote needed to pass a resolution in the General Assembly. Now the West controls only about one-fourth of the votes.

The new balance of power affected General Assembly action in at least two ways. First, most of the new members tried to remain neutral in the East-West struggle. Neutralists formed a majority of the membership. Second, most of the new members were former colonies, only recently independent. They were likely to act together on matters that seemed to involve imperialism, colonialism, or racism.

In 1971 Communist China (the People's Republic of China) was admitted to the United Nations, and Taiwan (Nationalist China) was expelled. This action climaxed an effort to seat the People's Republic that began in 1950 when the communists gained control of mainland China. The United States had announced that it would support action to seat the People's Republic, but would resist any attempt to expel the Nationalists. However, in 1971, the United States was unable to prevail on this issue, as it had always done before.

It now seemed likely that other excluded nations would be admitted to the UN. East and West Germany were admitted in 1973. North and South Korea and North and South Vietnam were still outside but their admission seemed closer.

Peace-keeping and finance

Between 1946 and 1973, United Nations peace-keeping forces were sent to twelve trouble spots throughout the world. Large-scale forces were used for combat in Korea. Small observer groups supervised cease-fires or truces. Medium-sized forces tried to keep local conflicts from expanding, or to keep order. Such forces were sent to the Suez region, the Congo, and Cyprus. These actions caused serious financial problems, as you will read.

In 1956, when Egypt occupied the Suez Canal, Israeli, British, and French forces invaded Egypt. French and British vetoes prevented Security Council action. Under Uniting for Peace ° procedures, the General Assembly met in emergency session. It called for a cease-fire, but to no avail. It then created the United Nations Emergency Force (UNEF) to act as a buffer between the hostile forces, and to supervise the withdrawal of the invaders. It later supervised borders and insured observance of armistice terms. The costs

° **Uniting for Peace procedures:** If the Security Council is blocked by a veto in time of crisis, any seven members of the Council, or a majority of members of the General Assembly, can call an emergency session of the Assembly. The Assembly can then recommend collective measures, including the use of armed forces. These procedures were adopted at the time of the invasion of South Korea by the North Koreans.

of UNEF were met partly by contributions and partly by special assessments levied on members.

In 1960, when the Republic of the Congo became independent of Belgium, it dissolved into anarchy. The Congo government asked for help from the United Nations. The Security Council authorized the Secretary-General to provide military assistance. Between 1960 and 1964 the situation in the Congo was stabilized by nearly 20,000 UN troops. To meet these costs, the General Assembly again set up a special account outside the regular UN budget and made special assessments on members.

Several members refused to pay the special assessments for UNEF and the Congo, despite the fact that the International Court ruled them legal and binding. The refusals brought a financial crisis. By 1964 the United Nations had a deficit of 113 million dollars and unpaid assessments of 112 million dollars. In the early 1970's this debt still hung over the organization.

Another financial problem arose in an effort to help developing nations get capital for economic growth. Developed countries have large percentages of the world's capital and small percentages of the world's population. Underdeveloped countries have just the reverse. This unequal distribution contributes to world unrest.

The United Nations Development Program (UNDP), trying to raise the large amounts of capital needed for more equitable distribution, asked the developed countries to contribute one percent of their Gross National Products (GNP) ° for this purpose. Contributions, including those of the United States, regularly fell short.

From the beginning, the United States has been the major contributor to the overall budget of the United Nations. In 1971, however, the General Assembly voted to reduce the United States' share from 31.5 percent to 25 percent.

Environmental conference

In June 1972 the world's first environmental conference was held at Stockholm, Sweden. All the member nations of the United Nations were

° **Gross National Product (GNP):** The total value of all goods and services produced within a nation.

represented except the Soviet Union, which declined to attend because East Germany (not then a member) was not invited.

It became evident that positions of the developed and underdeveloped countries on environmental problems differed widely. The developed nations were concerned about such problems as industrial pollution of air and water, diminishing natural resources, and the rapid growth of world population. The underdeveloped nations were determined to have industries, even at the risk of pollution. They also refused to accept interference in their population policies.

The conference adopted Earthwatch, a global network of 100 stations to monitor atmospheric pollution. There were also to be ten stations in remote areas to assess global climate changes. The whole system was to be coordinated by the World Meteorological Organization. The conference also set up a new environmental organization, the Governing Council for Environmental Programmes, to supervise a special environmental fund set at 100 million dollars over five years.

The conference, by an overwhelming vote, fixed a ten-year moratorium on the killing of whales. It lacked authority to enforce this moratorium, but the action did strengthen the International Whaling Commission, which had some authority.

Questions of population, diminishing natural resources, and the generation and consumption of power were sidestepped at the conference. Still, a start had been made toward dealing with environmental problems of concern to all the nations of the world.

CHECKUP

1. What were the main problems facing the UN Disarmament Commission? What major difficulty hindered disarmament negotiations? Why?

2. How did the balance of power in the United Nations change after 1955? How did the change influence the West? UN voting? General Assembly action?

3. Why have financial problems resulted from UN peace-keeping operations?

4. What steps toward environmental control did the UN Environmental Conference take? What problems were avoided? Why?

CHAPTER REVIEW

Chapter 37   The United Nations Was Organized to Preserve Peace   (1942–1970's)

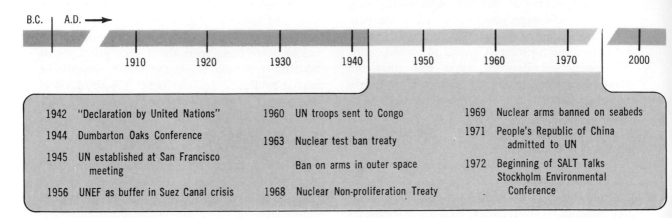

1942 "Declaration by United Nations"	1960 UN troops sent to Congo	1969 Nuclear arms banned on seabeds
1944 Dumbarton Oaks Conference	1963 Nuclear test ban treaty	1971 People's Republic of China admitted to UN
1945 UN established at San Francisco meeting	Ban on arms in outer space	1972 Beginning of SALT Talks Stockholm Environmental Conference
1956 UNEF as buffer in Suez Canal crisis	1968 Nuclear Non-proliferation Treaty	

CHAPTER SUMMARY

The United Nations, planned during World War II, was established in 1945. It has six main organs: (1) the General Assembly, which draws up the UN budget, receives agency reports, and considers problems relating to world peace; (2) the Security Council, charged with maintaining peace through negotiation, economic sanctions, or armed force; (3) the International Court of Justice, made up of fifteen judges elected by the Security Council and the General Assembly; (4) the Trusteeship Council, which supervises colonies and trust territories; (5) the Secretariat, made up of clerical and administrative workers, headed by the Secretary-General; and (6) the Economic and Social Council, created to improve economic and social conditions. Associated with it are several specialized agencies supervised by the Technical Assistance Board.

The UN faced serious problems, many arising from the split between Western and communist nations. Attempts to reduce armaments and control nuclear weapons became deadlocked over the problem of inspection. However, several international agreements were reached.

The UN approached the goal of universal membership. Most new members were African or Asian. They frequently voted together on matters concerning colonialism or racism. Most of them were neutrals in foreign affairs.

Peace-keeping brought financial difficulties. Some member nations refused to pay assessments for UN forces sent to Suez and the Congo. Unpaid assessments brought near bankruptcy.

An environmental conference was held in Stock-

holm. It set up stations to monitor atmospheric pollution, others to assess climate changes. It created a new environmental organization, but disagreed about more questions than it agreed upon.

QUESTIONS FOR DISCUSSION

1. What are the chief weaknesses of the United Nations? Can they be eliminated? Explain.

2. Would you favor taking power from the Security Council and giving it to the General Assembly? Justify your answer.

3. One of the powers of the Security Council is to call for economic sanctions against a country. Why is it difficult to implement such a measure, even when it is passed by the Council?

4. Which of the many UN activities do you consider to be the most important contribution to world peace? Justify your answer.

5. The United States spends much more on its defense budget than on the United Nations. Which do you think is a better guarantee for peace, the UN or an up-to-date American defense system? Explain your choice.

PROJECTS

1. Winston Churchill said the arms race led to a "balance of terror." Draw a cartoon using Churchill's statement as a theme.

2. Draw a map of the world and show where the UN has undertaken peace-keeping operations, indicating with what strength these missions were carried out.

CHAPTER 38

Europe Recovered from the War and Took Steps Toward Union

World War II left Europe devastated. Cities were ravaged, rural areas laid waste, industries destroyed, transportation and communication systems wrecked. Such widespread destruction had never before been known. Millions of refugees were displaced. They had to be cared for, returned to their homes, and given employment. Orderly transition to peacetime government was another problem facing Europe in 1945.

The most immediate need, however, was to prevent famine and epidemic disease. The Allied nations had foreseen the needs of the postwar period and, in November 1943, had formed a United Nations Relief and Rehabilitation Administration (UNRRA). The chief purpose of this temporary organization—in which forty-four nations participated—was to provide emergency aid for the war-torn nations of Europe and Asia. Nations that had escaped invasion were asked to contribute 1 percent of their national income for 1943 to the relief project. All the Allies made efforts to help UNRRA, but the largest contributions were made by the United States, Great Britain, and Canada.

Between 1945 and 1948, when it was disbanded, UNRRA gave aid to twenty-five countries with a total population of about a billion people. Its most important work was in Greece, Poland, Yugoslavia, Czechoslovakia, Austria, and Italy. Homeless people were fed and clothed; medical

Clearing rubble from Coventry Cathedral in England

care was given to the sick and wounded; hospitals were rebuilt. Reconstruction was begun on roads, railroads, bridges, and factories. Farmers received seed and livestock.

UNRRA's program was an excellent example of international cooperation. Yet in the midst of such cooperation, discord among the victorious powers began to grow. The United States and the Soviet Union emerged as the two strongest nations in the postwar world. Relations between the two had never been friendly, but they had united to defeat the common German enemy. After the war, their antagonisms revived. Mutual suspicion and hostility led to the so-called Cold War—a conflict between communist and Western nations that was waged by political and economic means rather than with weapons. The Cold War shaped and colored almost all events in Europe and throughout the world until the late 1960's. As the wartime alliance fell apart, Russia sought to dominate all of eastern Europe. The Soviet army, which had marched into eastern Europe as an army of liberation, became an army of occupation. Travel, communication, and cooperation between East and West became difficult. As Winston Churchill said in 1946, "From Stettin in the Baltic to Trieste in the Adriatic, an iron curtain has descended across the Continent."

THE CHAPTER SECTIONS:

1. The victors attempted to settle Europe's political problems (1943–1955)

2. The Cold War led to a vast program of American aid (1947–1961)

3. Cooperative ventures aided the economic recovery of Western Europe (1945–1970's)

4. Europe moved from Cold War to détente (1947–1970's)

 The victors attempted to settle Europe's political problems

At the Yalta Conference in 1945, Churchill, Roosevelt, and Stalin had agreed that both Germany and Austria were to be divided into four zones. The United States, Russia, Great Britain, and France would each be responsible for the administration of one zone in each country. The two capitals, Berlin and Vienna, were also to be divided into four zones, to be administered separately by the four Allies. Supervision of the occupied regions was to be in the hands of an Allied Control Council, composed of military leaders of the occupying armies. Decisions of this council had to be unanimous.

At the Potsdam Conference, later in 1945, Stalin, Attlee, and Truman agreed that the World War II peace treaties should be written by a Council of Foreign Ministers representing Russia, Britain, the United States, France, and China. All decisions made by the Council had to be satisfactory to all its members.

Problems of peace-making

When the war in Europe was over, occupation zones were set up (see map, opposite), and the Allied Control Council and Council of Foreign Ministers began their work. Such arrangements were practical as long as the Allies remained on friendly terms. As the postwar hostility between East and West grew, however, unanimous decisions by the councils became more and more difficult to reach.

The governments of the United States, the Soviet Union, and Great Britain had survived the test of war. Elsewhere, however, changes had to be made. In Italy, by a plebiscite held in June 1946, the monarchy was abolished and a republican form of government was set up. In France, after the Allied liberation in August 1944, a provisional government headed by General Charles de Gaulle ran the country until 1946. Late that year, a Fourth French Republic was proclaimed.

Much of the rest of Europe was in a state of flux. Germany's eastern European allies were occupied and ruled by Russian armies. National governments had to be restored in Poland and Czechoslovakia. The monarchy in Greece was tottering. The future of both Germany and Austria seemed uncertain.

758

Postwar treaties

Early in 1947, after months of debate and disagreement, the Council of Foreign Ministers reached agreement on a treaty with Italy. The defeated nation renounced all claims to countries that it had invaded during the war. Italy also ceded the Dodecanese Islands in the Aegean Sea to Greece, and small areas along its western boundary to France (see map, this page).

The city of Trieste, on the Adriatic coast, caused an especially difficult problem. Trieste had a mixed population of Italians and Yugoslavs. The 1947 treaty established a Free Territory of Trieste as an independent, neutral area, guaranteed by the Security Council of the United Nations. This settlement proved unsatisfactory to Marshal Tito, who was the communist dictator of Yugoslavia. In October 1954 a new agreement was reached, dividing the Free Territory of Trieste. Italy received the city itself and pledged to maintain a free port. Yugoslavia received an adjacent area. Each side promised to respect the rights of national minorities that were located in its territory.

The Council of Foreign Ministers also drew up treaties with Rumania, Hungary, Bulgaria, and Finland. The terms of these treaties were similar. The defeated countries had to return territory they had taken, and their prewar boundaries were changed. They had to pay reparations to nations that their armies had invaded. Their armed forces were reduced in size.

Negotiating treaties with Germany's minor allies was difficult because of the East-West ideological split. For the same reason, agreement over Austria proved to be almost impossible. The four-way occupation of the country continued for years without any agreements on peace terms. It was not until 1955, ten years after the war ended, that a treaty with Austria was finally negotiated and signed.

Austria had been occupied, first by the Germans, then by the Allies, for a total of seventeen years. The treaty of May 1955 made it once more a "sovereign, independent, and democratic state." The treaty forbade political or economic union between Austria and Germany in "any form

**TERRITORIAL CHANGES IN EUROPE
1945-1948**

■ Territorial changes after World War II

▢ Soviet occupation zones

▢ Occupation zones of Western powers

---- International boundaries after World War II

whatsoever." Austrian boundaries were defined as those that existed on January 1, 1938.

German settlements

It had taken ten years to reach an agreement over Austria. In the early 1970's, more than twenty-five years after the war, no final agreement had been reached on Germany.

On the map on this page you can see the division of Germany into four zones of occupation.

759

Notice that Berlin is in the eastern, or **Soviet,** zone. The city itself was divided into four occupation sectors. Supplies for the city had to pass through Soviet-held territory.

The end of the war found Germany a devastated country, with its territory greatly reduced in size. At the Potsdam Conference the Allies had agreed that Poland's western boundary should be fixed temporarily at the line of the Oder and Neisse rivers, thus including part of prewar Germany in Poland. Stalin tried to have the Oder-Neisse line accepted as permanent, but the British and Americans insisted that the final decision be made at the peace conference. This transfer of territory to Poland stripped Germany of a large farming area that had formerly produced a fourth of its food supply. Poland also took part of East Prussia, and the Soviet Union took the rest.

The postwar population of Germany was constantly increased by Germans who had formerly lived outside the boundaries of prewar Germany. Czechoslovakia, for example, insisted that the Sudeten Germans, the cause of Hitler's invasion of Czechoslovakia, must leave the country. The Russians adopted the same policy toward Germans in East Prussia and in the Baltic States.° Poland followed suit, expelling Germans from the area of prewar Poland as well as from the territory taken from Germany after the war.

Although these moves were not surprising in view of prewar troubles with German minorities, the burden of housing, feeding, and employing these refugees in shrunken postwar Germany created a serious problem.

German industry. The immediate problem of keeping Germany peaceful was easily solved. The Allied Control Council moved swiftly to disband all German land, air, and sea forces. The German General Staff, with all its military schools and institutions, was abolished. German industry was forbidden to manufacture big guns, tanks, or airplanes—even private or commercial planes. The plan was to make sure that Germany could not rearm. All industrial plants and equipment

° **Baltic States:** Although Russia had annexed the Baltic States in 1940 and continued to regard them as part of the Soviet Union after the war, the United States did not recognize the annexation.

that could be used for war production were to be dismantled.

This plan proved difficult to enforce. There was, first of all, the complex question of what constituted a war industry. A factory that manufactures tractors may easily be converted to the production of tanks. A steel plant may turn out armor plate as well as steel beams.

There was an even more basic problem. In their zone the Russians began by dismantling industrial plants and shipping them east to replace Russian factories destroyed during the war. They changed their policy, however, as they came to realize that they would soon have to support millions of unemployed workers. They allowed the factories to remain, but took as reparations part of the goods produced.

In the western zones a similar economic problem arose. An agricultural Germany, with only light industries, could not support the German population. There seemed to be only two alternatives—either allow Germany to industrialize fully, or face the prospect of having to feed and support the German population indefinitely.

The British and Americans gradually moved toward a more lenient treatment of Germany and its industries. This policy was violently opposed by the French, who had good reason to fear the industrial power of Germany.

The Allied Control Council, therefore, found it increasingly difficult to reach unanimous decisions regarding German industry. Meetings of the Council of Foreign Ministers became a series of violent accusations, counter-accusations, and name-calling. After one such meeting in 1948 failed to reach agreement on a single vital issue, the Council adjourned indefinitely.

War trials and denazification

The military occupation of Germany revealed to the world the full extent of the horrors of German concentration camps. As you have read, the Nazi policy of extermination led to the death of millions of people. More than 6 million of the estimated 10 million Jews living in Europe had been killed by the Nazis. Many had died of disease and starvation in concentration camps; many others had been shot, hanged, or suffocated in gas chambers. Some were subjected to horrible tortures, serving as subjects for so-called "scientific" experimentation on the human body. The Nazi victims also included almost 6 million non-Jewish Europeans—Poles, Czechs, Russians, Yugoslavs, Dutch, French, and Gypsies.

Beginning in November 1945 and continuing for almost a year, a special international court met at Nuremberg, Germany, to try major Nazi leaders who had taken part in these murders, and had been captured. Hitler was dead, and some of his highest officers had escaped to Spain and Latin America. But many of the top leaders had been captured. The court tried twenty-two of the principal Nazi leaders for "conspiracy to wage aggressive war," "crimes against the peace," and "crimes against humanity" in the extermination camps, the slave-labor camps, and in the conquered countries. Twelve were sentenced to death, seven to life imprisonment, and three were acquitted. The court also declared the Nazi Party a criminal organization.

The Nuremberg trials were unprecedented. For thousands of years the conduct of warfare had been governed by rules, customs, and conventions (certain kinds of international agreements).

However, this was the first time that leaders of a country were brought to trial for starting a war. The trials were widely criticized on the grounds that there was no legal precedent for punishing the leaders of a defeated nation. Some people argued that in trying only Germans and not possible war criminals of other nations, the court was violating accepted ideas of justice. Others felt that the trials were an act of vengeance on the part of the victorious powers.

Defenders of the trials argued that, although the court was specially created, the laws by which it acted did exist, uncodified, in various Hague conventions, League of Nations agreements, and international treaties. In addition, it was thought that the trials would help preserve peace and forward the development of international law. They did in fact lead to the United Nations adoption in 1948 of a convention against *genocide*—the systematic extermination of an entire people or national group.

Trials of other war criminals continued for many years in postwar Germany. Hundreds of ex-Nazis were prosecuted—not only high-ranking officers but also camp guards, minor officials, and doctors who had taken part in medical "experiments." They were convicted of murder, the use

The Nuremberg trials were purposely held in a city famous for its great Nazi Party rallies. In the witness box, below left, sits Hermann Goering, wartime head of the German Air Force.

of slave labor, and violation of the laws of war concerning the treatment of war prisoners and civilians.°

The Allies also pursued a policy of removing former Nazis from positions of authority in government, industry, and education. They set up denazification courts, before which suspected Nazis had to appear and try to clear themselves. Difficulties soon appeared, however. The German economy had broken down almost completely, and its rebuilding required technically skilled leaders, many of whom had been Nazis. In addition, there was no agreement as to what degree of connection with the Nazi Party justified purging nor on uniform application of the policy in the four occupation zones. By 1948 the denazification courts had almost ceased to function.

CHECKUP

1. What were the problems of peace-making in postwar Europe?

2. What were the main terms of the Austrian peace treaty?

3. How was the situation of postwar Germany complicated by the problem of population? the problem of industrial plants?

4. IDENTIFY: UNRRA, Cold War, Allied Control Council, Council of Foreign Ministers, Nuremberg trials, genocide.

2 The Cold War led to a vast program of American aid

Difficulties between East and West over the writing of the treaties and over the government of occupied Germany grew increasingly severe during the postwar years. It was feared that the communists, led by the Soviet Union, planned to take over all of Europe. As the strongest democratic nation, the United States became the leader of the non-communist nations.

The Soviet satellites

During the war, as the Russians fought their way toward Germany, the Red Army liberated and occupied Poland and Germany's eastern allies—Rumania, Bulgaria, and Hungary. The Russians set up communist-controlled governments in all of these countries. In Albania and Yugoslavia, governments were set up by local communists who had led native resistance groups.

The Allies had promised the peoples of these countries free elections in which they could choose their governments. Local communists, however, eliminated all opposition, and elections were rigged in their favor. By 1947, all of these nations had become communist dictatorships. They came to be known as Soviet satellites because, like planets circling the sun, they were dependent on the Soviet Union. In matters of both domestic and foreign policy, the satellite states were subordinated to Russia.

It became clear, after the war, that the Russians were still intent upon fostering communism throughout the world. Beyond its satellites, Russia used the Communist Information Bureau (Cominform) to stir up dissension and revolution wherever and whenever it could. Local communist parties were willing partners in this plan.

United States leadership

As the Cold War developed, it became increasingly clear that if communist expansion was to be stopped, the United States would have to take the lead. As the strongest major power and the sole possessor of atomic weapons at that time, the United States had both the military and the economic strength to supply and defend the free world.

The rest of the Western powers were exhausted. France and Italy had to reorganize economies and governments. Great Britain had spent almost all its strength in the war. It had domestic problems as well as difficulties throughout the empire.

° In 1961 the trial of Adolf Eichmann, a former Nazi official, attracted worldwide attention. He had escaped to South America but was seized there by secret agents of the government of Israel. Eichmann was tried before a special Israeli court in Jerusalem, where he was accused and convicted of being the chief agent of Hitler's policy of mass extermination of the Jews. Eichmann was hanged in 1962.

The Truman Doctrine. The United States emerged as leader of the West early in 1947. Great Britain had been giving the Greek government large-scale military and financial aid to suppress a communist-supported rebellion. In spite of a large United States loan, Britain was almost bankrupt. The British government announced that it could no longer defend the eastern Mediterranean region. The Western powers feared that Greece, Turkey, and western Asia—with its rich oil resources—might fall to communism.

The United States decided to take action. In March 1947, President Truman, speaking before the American Congress, announced what came to be called the Truman Doctrine. The United States, Truman said, considered the continued spread of communism a menace to democracy. The United States would not try to stamp out communism where it existed, or in any country that freely chose communism. It would, however, use its money, materials, technical knowledge, and influence to help countries threatened by communism if they asked for help. (This approach is often referred to as the "containment" policy because it aimed to "contain," or restrict, the spread of communism.)

Truman further declared that the United States would "support free peoples who are resisting attempted subjugation by armed minorities or by outside pressures." Truman asked Congress to appropriate 400 million dollars to help defend Greece and Turkey from communist aggression. After a United Nations investigating committee reported that neighboring communist countries were helping the Greek rebels, the United States Congress granted this request. With American financial and technical aid, the Greek government put down the rebellion. Thus the policy of "containment" scored an important victory.

The Marshall Plan. Although UNRRA provided emergency relief at the end of World War II, by 1947 Europe's most pressing need was more economic aid. To be effective, the aid would require a coordinated effort on a continent-wide scale. European nations would have to help themselves, but they would also need outside help.

In 1947, United States Secretary of State

HISTORY THROUGH ART

Modern Stained-Glass Windows

Rebuilding Europe after the war was an enormous task, especially when it involved the restoration of historic landmarks. One of these was the heavily damaged church of St. Foillan in Aachen, a German industrial city and the ancient capital of Charlemagne. Originally built in the 1100's, the church was reconstructed after a fire in the 1600's. When St. Foillan was again rebuilt, it included new stained-glass windows in abstract style. Their rich colors and timeless beauty furnished ample proof of the adaptability of traditional art forms to contemporary design.

763

George C. Marshall suggested a new policy that formed the basis for legislation adopted the following year by Congress. The European Recovery Program (often called the Marshall Plan) stipulated that the United States was prepared to give the needed aid to Europe on certain terms. The European countries were to: (1) confer and determine their needs on a continental basis; (2) show what resources they could put into a common pool for economic rebuilding; (3) end inflation and stabilize their currencies; and (4) try to remove trade barriers so that goods could flow freely throughout the continent.

Eventually, sixteen European nations worked out plans for the European Recovery Program. Congress appropriated 17 billion dollars to carry out the program for its first four years. The American offer of aid was extended to the Soviet Union and its satellites but was rejected.

The United States Congress looked upon the money spent on European recovery as a sensible investment. There were, of course, humanitarian motives—the desire to relieve suffering. But the program was also motivated by what is called enlightened self-interest—looking out for oneself in a way that also benefits others. American farmers and manufacturers, paid by the United States government, sent surplus goods to Europe. The United States thus helped to avert a depression at home, which might have resulted from overproduction in the postwar years. European countries were helped to become self-supporting again and to become customers for American goods.

The Cold War in central Europe

Events in Czechoslovakia show how Russia operated in the Cold War. Prewar Czechoslovakia had been the most democratic of all the central European countries. The postwar government was democratic, too, although it included many communist officials. Czechoslovakia was not occupied by the Russian army, but it had common borders with Poland, Hungary, Austria, and Germany—which were occupied—and with the Soviet Union. The Czechoslovakian government tried to maintain friendly relations with both the Western democracies and the communists. The difficulties

of this task increased as the Cold War progressed.

In February 1948, national elections in Czechoslovakia showed a decline in the communist vote. A few weeks later, shortly after the death of the Czech foreign minister, the communists held an election in which the voters were offered a single list of communist-approved candidates. The communists wrote a new constitution, which the president of Czechoslovakia refused to sign. In June he resigned, to be succeeded by a communist, who approved the revised constitution. Thus Czechoslovakia became a full-fledged member of the Soviet-dominated communist bloc of eastern Europe.

Czechoslovakia could have been saved only by war, which the Western powers were not willing to risk. At the end of World War II, the United States had demobilized rapidly. Great Britain's forces were spread throughout the world. The Russians, however, still had many divisions under arms.

Only one break appeared in the iron curtain that divided East and West. During the spring of 1948, there was a disagreement between Stalin and Marshal Tito of Yugoslavia. Tito objected to Soviet domination, announcing that Yugoslavia would follow an independent course. By June 1948 the split became definite, and Yugoslavia was expelled from the Cominform.

The Yugoslav situation presented a dilemma for the West. Tito maintained stoutly that he was a communist, and he ran Yugoslavia as a dictatorship. But he had broken with the Soviet Union. The Western powers decided that Tito should be given aid cautiously, as long as he continued to oppose the Soviet Union.

The division of Germany

By 1948, joint government in Germany was becoming impossible. Economically the country was in great difficulty. In the Western zones the problem was complicated by the constant stream of German refugees from the Soviet zone.

The three Western occupying powers began discussions aimed at uniting their zones in the hope of solving at least the economic problems. In response, in June 1948 the Russians stopped

EUROPEAN ALLIANCES · 1945-1970's

Members of NATO in Europe, 1955
(Iceland also a member)

Communist nations (all except Yugoslavia
bound by the Warsaw Pact)

Neutral
nations

all land and water traffic into Berlin from the west. They refused to allow trucks, barges, and trains to pass the checkpoints at the borders. Thus West Berlin was threatened with starvation.

Although the Western powers had been unwilling to come to the aid of Czechoslovakia, they acted swiftly during the Berlin blockade. The United States and Great Britain organized an airlift to supply West Berlin by plane. The 2 million inhabitants of the western sectors of the city received their daily supplies of food and coal in this

fashion. In a short time the airlift operated so efficiently that raw materials were being supplied to West Berlin factories. The Soviet Union lifted its blockade of the city in May 1949.

Meanwhile the Western occupying powers announced that if no peace treaty with Germany were written, they would allow the Germans in their zones to write a constitution and set up a democratic government. The western Germans held a constitutional assembly at Bonn and set up a government. On May 23, 1949, the Federal

Children greet a plane bringing a precious cargo of food and fuel to Berlin during the blockade of 1948–1949. At the peak of the airlift, a plane landed every minute at Berlin's airport.

Republic of Germany was proclaimed, with its capital at Bonn. However, West Germany was still under the control of the combined Western occupation authorities. The Western powers also unified their sectors of Berlin and permitted the democratic election of a municipal government.

In October 1949 a provisional communist government, the German Democratic Republic, was established in the Soviet zone of Germany. This region became known as East Germany (see map, page 765). Although the Soviet Union and its satellites recognized the German Democratic Republic as the legitimate government of East Germany, the United States, Great Britain, and France did not. Nor, of course, did the Soviet Union and its satellites recognize the new government of West Germany.

Conflict over Berlin

In the years after 1948, Berlin remained one of the main trouble spots of the East-West struggle. With American aid, West Berlin made an astonishing recovery from the devastation of war. In East Berlin, recovery was slow and halting. West Berlin became a center for radio broadcasts to the communist bloc. Both sides claimed—probably correctly—that the other side used its sector of Berlin as a center for espionage. From the communist point of view, one of the worst features of West Berlin was that it served as an escape hatch for discontented citizens of East Germany

and other satellite countries. There was a steady flow of refugees—as many as 3,000 daily.

In 1961 the situation in Berlin took a grave turn. In order to stop the flow of refugees, the East German government built a massive wall of concrete, topped by barbed wire, along the entire boundary line dividing the city. Certain crossing points were left open, but they were strictly guarded at all times. Neither East Berliners nor West Berliners were allowed to cross the line without special authorization.

The building of the Berlin wall brought a sharp crisis with many protests and counterprotests. The United States sent additional troops to Berlin and renewed earlier promises that American troops would remain in the city to defend the rights of its inhabitants. The flow of refugees to the west was greatly reduced; East German guards shot at anyone trying to escape. The wall became a symbol of world tensions.

Both before and after the building of the Berlin Wall, the West German government successfully provided housing and jobs for refugees from East Germany and from other nations of eastern Europe. The economic growth of West Germany continued at a rapid pace. The German automobile industry, for example, made impressive advances and became a strong competitor of the American industry. The West German currency, the mark, became the most stable currency in Europe.

1. What countries became Soviet satellites after World War II? Why were they called this?

2. What were two major actions taken by the United States in the late 1940's to stop communist expansion in Europe?

3. Summarize briefly events in Czechoslovakia in the late 1940's.

4. Why was the Berlin airlift necessary? How was it carried out?

5. IDENTIFY: Cominform, "containment" policy, enlightened self-interest.

3 Cooperative ventures aided the economic recovery of Western Europe

One of the most outstanding characteristics of postwar Europe was its economic recovery. In a comparatively short time, the rubble of bombed cities was cleared away, industries returned to full production, and roads, rail lines, and bridges were rebuilt. In West Germany the rate of recovery was so rapid that many people referred to the "German miracle."

There were also important political changes, particularly in the older, more established democracies like Great Britain and France. Although these nations no longer wielded power as great as they had in the 1700's and 1800's, their role in shaping opinion and in influencing younger nations was still important.

Great Britain after the war

You have read how, in 1945, Winston Churchill and the Conservative Party were defeated and Clement Attlee, head of the Labour Party, became the British prime minister.

The Labour Party was a moderate socialist party whose leaders made many changes in the British economic and social systems. Railroads, utilities, coal mines, and the Bank of England were nationalized. Welfare measures included one extending free education to the age of sixteen and another providing free medical care for everyone. Great Britain became a *welfare state*—that is, one in which the government undertakes primary responsibility for the individual and social welfare of its citizens.

Great Britain faced many severe economic problems after the war. Its industrial equipment was outdated and inefficient. In addition to many workers killed in the war, the country had lost, and continued to lose, scientific and managerial workers, many of whom migrated to Canada, Australia, and the United States. Valuable colonies and possessions had been lost, and the cost of the nation's remaining overseas commitments was a heavy burden. In 1960 the British withdrew from Cyprus in the Mediterranean Sea. By the 1970's Great Britain was prepared to abandon all its remaining bases east of the Suez Canal. British problems in Northern Ireland also continued.

Despite its many problems, Great Britain began, in the 1950's, to experience favorable economic development. The government reduced unemployment, stabilized its currency, improved housing conditions, and raised the general standard of living.

The Fifth French Republic

Postwar France also faced severe problems. Economic recovery was slow in spite of Marshall Plan aid. The French Empire was crumbling; in North Africa and Southeast Asia, as you will read in later chapters, there were bitter and costly struggles. Among France's many bickering political parties, none were able to form a lasting coalition to run a stable government. Finally, in 1958, the French legislature, under pressure from army leaders, authorized General Charles de Gaulle to write a new constitution and to rule by decree until the new constitution was ratified. Thus, the Fourth French Republic collapsed without a struggle.

The new constitution, which was approved by French voters in October 1958, created the Fifth French Republic. Under the new constitution, much power was concentrated in the hands of the president. He appointed the prime minister. He could dissolve the legislature and assume dictatorial powers in times of national emergency. He could, through the prime minister, enact laws unless a majority of the National Assembly opposed them.

The first president of the Fifth Republic was General de Gaulle. He concluded France's colonial warfare and established stability at home. This stability was attained, however, at a high cost to the French taxpayer.

In foreign policy, de Gaulle was a staunch nationalist. He believed that Europe could prosper only under a system of national states. He opposed British and American influence in Europe, and believed that Germany must be kept divided and weak. He hoped to maintain cordial relations with the Soviet Union and Poland as a check on possible German aggression in the future. He insisted that France must test nuclear devices in the atmosphere.

After several years, conditions within France became less stable than de Gaulle had planned. In 1968 violent riots shook the nation. Militant students demanded educational reforms. Strikes for higher wages and better working conditions spread rapidly throughout industrial areas. To meet the crisis, de Gaulle dissolved the National Assembly and called for a general election.

Departure of de Gaulle. To win a favorable vote, de Gaulle acknowledged the need for social improvements in France. When re-elected, he approved a 15 percent increase in workers' wages. This concession strained the finances of the country without increasing industrial production. The result was rising inflation that cut deep into the workers' recent wage increases. De Gaulle's popularity declined. When his further proposals for reform were defeated in a national referendum, in April 1969, the seventy-nine-year-old president resigned. His successor, George Pompidou, announced that he would follow a middle-of-the-road policy at home and abroad.

European economic cooperation

In the early 1950's the French proposed that the six nations producing most of Western Europe's steel and coal unite all their facilities and production. The European Coal and Steel Community (ECSC) was formed in 1952 by France, West Germany, Italy, and the so-called Benelux

countries (Belgium, the Netherlands, and Luxembourg). A central authority was set up to regulate production and prices, and members agreed not to charge each other tariffs on coal or steel. A remarkable feature was that the ECSC was free of national control.

In 1958 the same six nations took another important step toward economic union by establishing the European Economic Community (EEC) —usually called the Common Market. The treaty provided that in three stages, over a fifteen-year period, tariffs and import quotas among the six member nations would gradually be abolished. A common tariff would be placed on goods coming into the Common Market from outside. There was to be a European Investment Bank, with capital contributed by the member governments. Its purposes were to finance projects beyond the means of a single nation and to help build up industries in the less developed areas of the member nations, such as southern Italy.

At the same time the six nations also created the Atomic Energy Community (Euratom). Each of the members agreed to share information on the peaceful uses of atomic energy.

In the 1960's, Greece, Turkey, and many of the newly independent African states became associate members of the European Economic Community. As such they did not have the right to vote, but were entitled to other privileges and could eventually join as full-fledged members.

The Common Market made steady progress toward European economic unity in the 1960's. In 1967 it adopted a five-year plan to provide greater price and wage stability and more uniform tax levels among member countries. Also in 1967 the EEC merged with the European Coal and Steel Community and the Atomic Energy Community. The three communities set up a single European Commission with headquarters in Belgium, a step toward greater economic unity.

Effects of the Common Market

The members of the European Economic Community found it relatively easy to reduce internal industrial tariffs. By the mid-1960's, tariffs on industrial goods moving from one member country

"He says hello"

Postwar Europe quickly set about the huge job of reconstruction. Two Germans, above, supervise the rebuilding of Dresden. The Cold War created worldwide tensions and in many ways impeded European recovery. The cartoon at left satirizes the United States and Russia, who can transmit even the simplest message only through diplomatic underlings. The Marshall Plan provided Europe with vital economic aid. A shipment of flour is lowered into the hold of a ship, below left. Military defense against Russia also seemed necessary. For this purpose, the nations symbolized by the hats, below, signed the Atlantic Pact creating NATO.

to another had been reduced to 30 percent of their starting level. Early in 1965 the European Commission approved a plan to eliminate all industrial tariffs by mid-1967 instead of the originally planned date of 1970.

Agreements on a common agricultural policy were the most difficult to reach. It took five years of hard bargaining, complicated by a seven-month French boycott of the organization, before a compromise was reached in 1966. The agreement resulted in higher farm prices and a rise in food costs for consumers. It was hoped, however, that the accord would eventually lead to increased and more efficient production, with a corresponding decline in food prices.

During the first seven years of EEC, trade among the member states increased 66 percent and trade with nonmember states increased 50 percent. During that same period, world trade as a whole increased only 46 percent. The figures on industrial production are almost as striking. In the Common Market region, industrial production increased 38 percent. In the United States, it increased 23 percent, while in Great Britain it increased only 18 percent.

The social results of the EEC were also significant. The movement of workers from country to country became increasingly free. Eventually, it was planned that social security rates, pensions, and other payments would be uniform among the member nations. A worker from one Common Market country would be completely free to get a job in any other.

The communist response. In 1949, several communist nations joined to form their own common market, the Council for Mutual Economic Assistance (Comecon). Its members were the Soviet Union, Poland, East Germany, Czechoslovakia, Hungary, Rumania, Bulgaria, Albania, and Mongolia. (Albania was excluded in 1961.) Over the years, China, North Vietnam, North Korea, and Yugoslavia sometimes attended Comecon meetings as observers.

The main purpose of Comecon was to coordinate industrial development and trade within the Soviet bloc. The organization tried to integrate the economies of the member states and to expand trade with the capitalist countries.

Comecon was far less successful than its counterpart, chiefly because it lacked trading flexibility. Trade was conducted on a nation-to-nation and balanced basis. Thus, Bulgaria would sign an agreement with Poland, providing for an exchange of a certain amount of Bulgarian products for products of about the same value received from Poland. No money would change hands; deliveries from one country would be checked off against deliveries from the other.

Comecon members found this system cumbersome and unsatisfactory. Some also objected to plans under which they were to supply raw materials while other members—especially the Soviet Union—did the manufacturing.

Effects on the United States. Europe had always been an important customer for American manufactured products and foodstuffs. Alarm at the possibility of losing this market to the EEC produced two kinds of action in the United States. First, many American corporations hurried to build factories or to buy shares in corporations located in the Common Market countries in order to avoid the proposed tariff walls. Second, the United States Congress passed a new Trade Expansion Act, giving the President power to cut American tariffs in bargaining with other countries for tariff cuts on American goods.

Great Britain and the EEC

For nearly fifteen years Great Britain was not a member of the European Common Market. Whether it should become a member or not was a complicated issue. On the one hand, if Britain remained outside the Common Market, British influence in European affairs would decline and Britain would suffer economically. On the other hand, if Britain joined the Common Market it would have a serious effect upon such nations as Australia and New Zealand in the British Commonwealth of Nations, from whom Britain had imported most of its agricultural products for many years. As a Common Market member, Britain would have to place a tariff on the agricultural products of all non-member countries, including the Commonwealth nations.

Despite such problems, British pride was hurt when Britain's application to join the EEC was twice rejected, once in 1963 and again in 1967, by Charles de Gaulle. De Gaulle, you recall, wanted to diminish Anglo-American influence on the continent of Europe. In explaining his vetoes of British membership in the Common Market, he argued that integrating the economies of Great Britain and the continent would be too difficult.

In 1969, after de Gaulle retired, Great Britain was invited to join the EEC. But by that time, the British economy had improved. Arguing against membership, Prime Minister Harold Wilson insisted that Britain could now stand on its own feet. Other critics argued, rightly, that British consumers would pay higher prices for food. In effect, they would be subsidizing inefficient European farmers when they might be getting less expensive food from non-European nations, in-cluding nations of the British Commonwealth.

Great Britain was still willing to join the EEC, but only under "reasonable conditions." Debate and negotiations continued until 1973, when Great Britain finally became a member of the European Economic Community.

CHECKUP

1. What changes did the Labour Party make in Great Britain?

2. What problems did the Fourth French Republic face? What were the characteristics of the Fifth French Republic?

3. What were the arguments for Great Britain's joining the Common Market? the arguments against?

4. IDENTIFY: welfare state, EEC, Comecon, de Gaulle.

4 Europe moved from Cold War to détente

Although Europe benefited from increased economic cooperation in the postwar years, political crises frequently arose. Most of these stemmed from the division of Europe into communist and non-communist blocs.

Cold War rivalries

The Soviet threat in the immediate postwar years brought a surprising degree of unity in Western Europe, considering the region's long history of nationalistic rivalries. In 1947 Great Britain and France signed a treaty of military alliance. The communist seizure of Czechoslovakia in 1948 brought further steps. Britain, France, and the Benelux countries signed a fifty-year treaty pledging economic and military assistance if any were attacked. The treaty also created a Council of Europe (to go into effect in 1949), which many people hoped would be the nucleus of a federal parliament for Europe. They hoped that Western Europe might some day have a federal government similar to that of the United States. The Council's original members were Britain, France, the Benelux countries, Denmark, Sweden, Norway, Italy, and Ireland. Several other nations joined the Council later.

NATO. Meanwhile the United States continued to take a keen interest in European affairs. With the Russian takeover of satellite nations in eastern Europe, many people feared a Soviet push to the west. Indeed, Churchill later said that it was only fear of American atomic bombs that had prevented Russia from overrunning Western Europe. Increasingly the Western nations recognized the need to develop ground forces to deter a Soviet drive.

In April 1949, a mutual defense pact, providing for creation of the North Atlantic Treaty Organization (NATO), was signed by twelve nations: the United States, Great Britain, France, Italy, Portugal, Norway, Denmark, Iceland, Canada, and the Benelux countries (see map, page 765). Greece and Turkey joined in 1952, West Germany in 1955. The signers agreed that an attack on one should be considered an attack on all. In such an event, all members would meet immediately to plan united action.

The United States Senate ratified the NATO

Three Europeans who made history were Pope John XXIII, Charles de Gaulle, and Nikita Khrushchev. John XXIII became pope in 1958 and almost at once called for a council that modernized the Roman Catholic Church. De Gaulle made France again a force to be reckoned with in world affairs. Khrushchev's shrewd peasant stubbornness was often difficult to deal with, but his regime maintained peace with the West and raised the standard of living in the U.S.S.R.

treaty in July 1949. It was the first United States defense treaty with European nations since 1778, when the American government had signed an alliance with France. For the first time in its history, the United States pledged itself, during peacetime, to go to war in support of European allies should war break out.

NATO, however, was only a mutual-defense treaty and did not provide for a standing army. Two events were instrumental in strengthening the alliance. One was the explosion, in the fall of 1949, of the first Russian atomic bomb. Western scientists had predicted that the Russians would eventually develop atomic weapons, but the speed with which they did so came as a shock. The second event was the communist invasion of South Korea in 1950, about which you will read in Chapter 40.

In 1954 the NATO nations drew up a detailed plan of defense. Among other things, it provided that: (1) West Germany was to be restored to full sovereignty and allowed an army of 500,000 men. (2) A Western European Union would be formed in which the armies of Germany and Italy would be combined with those of NATO mem-

bers. (3) West Germany was to be granted full membership in NATO.

Under this plan, each member nation was to contribute troops to an ever-ready NATO force that would include about 750,000 men. The plan also called for some 4,000 aircraft and extensive naval commitments.

Not all the goals set in 1954 were reached. The expenditures required for such a large standing army would probably have slowed economic reconstruction, reduced standards of living, and increased taxes among the NATO members. Consequently, NATO members came to rely increasingly on American nuclear weapons rather than upon the proposed divisions of ground troops.

The Warsaw Pact. The Soviet response to a strengthened NATO was immediate. In May 1955, in Warsaw, Poland, the Soviet government held a meeting of representatives of the European communist bloc—the Soviet Union, Poland, East Germany, Czechoslovakia, Hungary, Rumania, Bulgaria, and Albania. (Yugoslavia was the only European communist country that did not take part.) These nations adopted a twenty-year agreement, called the Warsaw Pact, by which each nation pledged in the event of war to furnish troops in proportion to its population. The satellites pledged about 1½ million men. Added to the vast manpower of the Soviet Union, the Warsaw Pact provided the communist bloc with a potentially formidable force of troops.

You will notice that, within ten years after World War II, a diplomatic revolution had occurred. The United States and Russia, allies in World War II, had become adversaries. West Germany and Italy, former Axis powers, had become allies of the Western democracies.

Relations with the Soviet Union

Joseph Stalin, the Soviet dictator, died in 1953. As is often the case in dictatorships, a power struggle occurred in the Russian government after Stalin's death. Gradually, Nikita Khrushchev (kroosh-CHAWF) emerged as head of the Soviet Communist Party. By March 1958, Khrushchev had outmaneuvered his rivals and become premier.

Soviet foreign policy shifted often during the years after Stalin's death. At times it was violently anti-Western; at other times Soviet leaders spoke of their desire for "peaceful coexistence"—harmony between East and West. The general trend seemed to be less threatening than it had been under Stalin, but the atmosphere of the Cold War continued for many years. The Cold War was marked chiefly by strained relations between the world's superpowers, the Soviet Union and the United States. These nations held opposing views about political, economic, and social organization. They struggled for influence in many parts of the world. By the late 1960's and early 1970's, neither side was prepared to abandon its basic beliefs, but each came to feel that its interests could be better served by negotiations than by confrontations. Thus, the Cold War gradually gave way to a period of détente—that is, to relaxation of international tensions.

Summit conferences. After Stalin's death, many people in the West urged their leaders to test the Soviet desire for peaceful coexistence. They hoped that if the leaders of the major world powers could meet face to face, general agreement could be reached. These meetings came to be known as "summit conferences" because the highest officials of each participating country were present.

In July 1955, the heads of government of the United States, Great Britain, France, and the Soviet Union met at Geneva to discuss four important problems: (1) the unification of Germany, (2) European security, (3) disarmament, and (4) East-West cultural exchange and freedom of travel. Some progress was made on the fourth point, but none on the first three.

In September 1959, Premier Khrushchev paid a thirteen-day visit to the United States, during which he met with President Eisenhower. This meeting led to optimism about a second summit conference, to be held in Paris in May 1960.

Shortly before the Paris conference was to open, however, a United States high-altitude reconnaissance plane, of a type known as the U-2, was shot down over the Soviet Union while on a photographic mission. This U-2 incident doomed the conference to failure. Thereafter, for several years, summit conferences held little prospect for success in relieving world tension.

In 1964 Premier Khrushchev was deposed. Aleksei Kosygin became Premier, but major power in the Soviet Union was now held by Leonid Brezhnev, First Secretary of the Communist Party. In 1967 Kosygin traveled to the United States for talks with President Johnson, but little was accomplished. Finally, when Cold War tensions were easing in the early 1970's, President Nixon and Secretary Brezhnev held important conversations in both Moscow and the United States.

Satellite rebellions. Outwardly, in the postwar years, the communist bloc seemed a solid, firmly knit group of nations, united by a common ideology and purpose. But the satellites had once been independent national states, some with long-standing antagonisms toward Russia.

Yugoslavia's growing independence from Russia after 1948 aroused envy among Russia's satellites. "Titoism" became a kind of goal for some people in the satellite countries. In 1953, a revolt by East German workers had to be put down by Soviet tanks and troops. In 1956, Poland threat-

Many people in Czechoslovakia hoped in 1968 that their nation might soon enjoy more freedom and independence. Their hopes were shattered when Soviet forces occupied the country.

ened revolt and gained a small amount of independence in domestic policy.

In 1956 Hungary revolted. For a time the rebels controlled all of western Hungary. Soviet troops were at first withdrawn but later returned and bloodily suppressed the revolt. No help for the rebels came from the Western powers.

In 1968 Czechoslovakia, under Alexander Dubcek (DOOB·chek), began a program of reforms, promising civil liberties, democratic political reforms, and a more independent political system. Within six months, Warsaw Pact troops, chiefly from the Soviet Union, invaded Czechoslovakia. They seized the reform leaders and replaced them with "safe" men.

The satellite rebellions weakened Soviet prestige in Western Europe; the communist parties in both France and Italy assumed greater independence from the Soviet Union. The rebellions also seemed to prove several things. First, many people in the satellites accepted Soviet domination unwillingly. Second, the troops from satellite countries, promised in the Warsaw Pact, might prove of little help to the Soviet Union in case of war. Finally, the Soviet Union was determined to maintain control over its east European satellites at all costs.

Weakening alliances

During the late 1950's, many NATO members became discontented with the organization for several reasons: (1) The alliance had grown increasingly dependent on nuclear weapons, which could be used only when the President of the United States gave permission. This meant, in effect, that the United States controlled the defense of Europe. (2) Because of the growing strength of Western Europe, and problems of the Soviet Union in its own sphere, Western leaders felt that the Russians would not risk a push to the west and that the NATO force was no longer a military necessity. (3) With the development of long-range missiles, Europeans feared that the Soviet Union could occupy Europe while threatening to destroy American cities, and that the United States might not risk its own destruction in order to defend Western Europe.

Chief among those who questioned America's intentions was President de Gaulle of France. He wanted a loosely united Europe—ultimately to include the eastern European satellite nations— all under the leadership of France. In 1966 he announced that France would withdraw its forces from NATO, and demanded that the United States give up the NATO bases it held in France.

No other European leader went quite so far as de Gaulle in challenging American involvement in Europe. However, leaders in other NATO countries were also reluctant to furnish troops, and were displeased about their lack of control over NATO's nuclear weapons.

As the 1970's began, NATO faced an uncertain future. European members, particularly West Germany, feared that the organization might disband entirely and that the United States might withdraw its forces from Europe. Meanwhile the future of NATO's rival, the Warsaw Pact, appeared equally uncertain. Rumania and Albania, two of the original members, had ceased to cooperate with the organization. The Soviet Union even suggested that NATO and the Warsaw Pact disband simultaneously. When the Warsaw Pact nations met in March 1969, the members recommended calling a full European conference to settle remaining postwar problems. The suggestion brought a favorable response in a number of countries.

In September 1969, Maurice Schumann, the French Minister of Foreign Affairs, declared that the foreign policy of France aimed at ending the division of Europe into blocs. A month later, Poland urged the formation of a collective system of security in Europe to replace existing military groupings.

In the early 1970's, several developments helped to relax tensions in Europe. Here, Leonid Brezhnev of the Soviet Union and Willy Brandt of West Germany discuss an agreement.

Dissatisfaction also became apparent in the communist world. There was increasing bitterness between the Soviet Union and Communist China, caused in part by rivalry for the leadership of world communism. Soviet attempts to mold the eastern European satellites into a tight economic union were not very successful, as you have read. Like NATO, the Warsaw Pact drew increasing criticism from its members. Rumania, playing a role similar to that of France, advocated greater independence for the smaller member nations.

Germany: "One Nation, Two States"

Throughout the postwar period, Germany remained divided—or, as the Germans preferred to say, "One Nation, Two States." National unification remained a lingering idea and for years remained the chief postwar problem. The Berlin Wall, as you have read, became a permanent feature of the German landscape, sealing off East Berlin from West Berlin. The question of free access to West Berlin, which was entirely surrounded by East Germany, continued to be a disturbing issue.

During the 1950's and 1960's East Germany, like West Germany, made impressive economic progress and became, technologically, one of the most advanced members of the communist bloc. East Germany also became important militarily. For these reasons, neither the Western allies, particularly France, nor the communist countries, particularly the Soviet Union, favored German unification. Both sides bitterly recalled the role of a single, strong Germany in the first and second World Wars.

For West Germany, relations with the Soviet Union remained the most difficult foreign policy problem. A new government that came to power in October 1969, headed by Chancellor Willy Brandt, promised a more flexible attitude toward the Soviet Union, but it found Moscow most cautious. The Soviet Union continued to insist upon three severe conditions: (1) West Germany must grant full recognition to East Germany; (2) it must abandon West Berlin; (3) it must accept the existing boundary between East Germany and Poland.

These conditions were not all acceptable to West Germany and its allies, but some improvements in German-Soviet relations were made. In November 1969 the Brandt government agreed to sign the Nuclear Non-proliferation Treaty. This treaty, you recall, said that nations without nuclear weapons would not produce nor receive them from nuclear powers. The treaty was severely criticized by the opposition to the Brandt government. The opponents argued that West Germany might be defenseless in a nuclear war, particularly if NATO collapsed.

In 1973, under Brandt's guidance, West Germany ratified a treaty establishing formal relations with East Germany. Other agreements provided for economic relations and cultural exchanges between East and West Germany. It was also agreed that West German planes might fly to Japan over Siberia, with landings in West Berlin. In return the Soviet Union was granted landing rights in West Berlin.

Also in 1973 Leonid Brezhnev of the Soviet Union visited West Germany, where he signed another significant document. This agreement called for a ten-year period of economic cooperation between West Germany and the Soviet Union and provided for a joint commission to supervise the exchange of raw materials, skills, and manufactured goods. Under the agreement, West Germany had the right to represent West Berlin.

Shortly after this event, Czechoslovakia and West Germany signed an agreement to dispose of all problems still remaining from the Munich Pact of 1938 in a manner "satisfactory to both sides." Some bitter hatreds of World War II were eased when West Germany declared that the Munich Pact had been "immoral."

CHECKUP

1. What diplomatic revolution occurred within ten years after World War II?

2. What satellite rebellions took place? What did they seem to prove?

3. What changes came over the two systems of alliances?

4. IDENTIFY: summit conference, NATO, Warsaw Pact, Dubcek, "One Nation, Two States."

CHAPTER REVIEW

Chapter 38 Europe Recovered from the War and Took Steps Toward Union (1943–1970's)

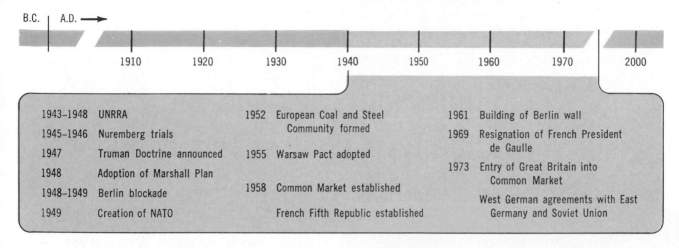

1943–1948	UNRRA
1945–1946	Nuremberg trials
1947	Truman Doctrine announced
1948	Adoption of Marshall Plan
1948–1949	Berlin blockade
1949	Creation of NATO

1952	European Coal and Steel Community formed
1955	Warsaw Pact adopted
1958	Common Market established
	French Fifth Republic established

1961	Building of Berlin wall
1969	Resignation of French President de Gaulle
1973	Entry of Great Britain into Common Market
	West German agreements with East Germany and Soviet Union

CHAPTER SUMMARY

Before the end of World War II, UNRRA was created to prevent famine and disease. Such cooperative efforts were hindered by the antagonisms of the Cold War. Conflict between East and West made peace settlements difficult. Although diplomats soon completed treaties with Italy and four other German allies, the Austrian treaty took ten years to negotiate.

Germany was divided into four zones and occupied. An influx of refugees created problems, as did the question of German industry. Many Nazi leaders were tried, but denazification was soon abandoned.

The creation of satellite nations and establishment of the Cominform revealed Soviet plans to spread communism throughout the world. The United States, as the strongest Western nation, gave help through the Truman Doctrine and the Marshall Plan. In central Europe the communists seized Czechoslovakia, whereas Yugoslavia broke with the Russians. When the latter blockaded Berlin, a Western airlift supplied the city. Soon afterward, Germany was divided into West and East Germany.

Great Britain adopted moderate socialism and gave up its empire peacefully. A military coup overthrew the inept Fourth French Republic and led to the Fifth Republic, with de Gaulle as president.

Western Europe adopted several cooperative economic ventures, including the Coal and Steel Community, the Common Market and Euratom. Lower industrial tariffs produced a manufacturing and trade boom. After a long delay, Great Britain joined the Common Market. The communist-sponsored Comecon had only limited success.

The Soviet threat resulted in the formation of (1) the Council of Europe and (2) NATO, originally a mutual-defense pact but later maintaining a joint army. Soviet Russia responded with the Warsaw Pact. Summit conferences failed to settle East-West difficulties. Satellite rebellions, especially in Hungary and Czechoslovakia, indicated opposition to Soviet domination. Because so many refugees were leaving East Berlin, the Russians built the Berlin wall.

NATO and the Warsaw Pact weakened as the two sides later moved toward détente.

QUESTIONS FOR DISCUSSION

1. Do you agree with the idea that there are "crimes against humanity" for which people should be tried? Explain.

2. Why is it that Western Europe made great economic strides after receiving economic aid, while other parts of the world receiving such aid today make relatively slow progress?

3. Do you think the expansion of the Common Market into a politically united Europe is a desirable goal? Justify your position.

4. Do you consider Brandt's "move to the East" a wise one? Why or why not?

PROJECTS

1. Make a chart of some of the chief political and economic events in Europe after 1945. Arrange them in three columns: (1) existing situation or communist action, (2) Western reaction, and (3) communist counteraction. In preparing the chart, give dates and follow chronological order.

2. Draw two political cartoons of the Berlin wall, one from a Western point of view, the other from a communist point of view.

Colonies in Africa and the Middle East Gained Independence

In Africa and the Middle East,° nearly 230 million people won independence in the two decades after World War II. A number of factors combined to foster independence. Growing nationalism within the colonial areas inspired rebellion against outside rule. World War II weakened the hold of European nations on their colonies. The United Nations fostered respect for racial, national, and individual integrity. Freedom for colonial peoples was a part of this ideal.

The imperialist powers themselves stimulated independence. In order to develop the resources of a colony, Europeans often linked parts of it together and with outside areas. After the war the British and French, especially, began to prepare their colonies for self-government by promoting representative institutions and encouraging local political parties.

The advance toward independence by 230 million people was, of course, impressive. Yet the newly independent nations faced many grave problems in their first years of freedom. Representative government, which had developed gradually over many centuries among Western nations, was relatively new to the former colonial areas. In many cases, political experience and qualified leaders were lacking. The level of education in

° **Middle East:** This term generally refers to the countries of southwestern Asia west of Pakistan, as well as Egypt and the island of Cyprus.

African leaders on the day of Nigerian independence

most of the new nations was low; in some parts of Africa scarcely 3 percent of the people could read and write. The supply of physicians, teachers, and skilled workers was inadequate. Old loyalties to tribes or ruling families complicated the formation of political parties.

The boundaries of the new nations were often artificial, having been drawn by the imperialist powers in the 1800's for their own convenience. In some cases, people of similar racial or cultural backgrounds were separated. In other cases, hostile peoples with little common heritage were grouped together. Many of the new nations were not viable—capable of existing and developing normally—especially from an economic point of view. As colonies, they had been integrated into the economic systems of the imperialist nations. Once independent, they often lacked the proper balance of industry and agriculture required for successful economic growth.

African nations made several attempts to cooperate with each other in various ways. The most successful of such attempts involved only a few nations in regional alliances. A more ambitious effort was started in 1963 when thirty African states agreed to form the Organization of African Unity (OAU). Deep conflicts among leaders of the African nations stood in the way of effective action, and by the early 1970's the accomplishments of the OAU were not impressive.

THE CHAPTER SECTIONS:

1. Sub-Saharan Africa faced several kinds of problems (1948–1970's)

2. Dangerous tensions arose in Egypt and the Middle East (1945–1970's)

3. Other North African nations gained independence (1951–1970's)

1 Sub-Saharan Africa faced several kinds of problems

Africa south of the Sahara exhibited the problems of newly independent states perhaps better than any other region. Independence came very rapidly. Indeed, many people believed that it came before the people were ready. But, ready or not, Africans demanded *uhuru*—freedom—and they got it. In 1914 only Liberia and Ethiopia were fully independent. By the mid-1960's there remained only three African colonies of considerable size, Spanish Sahara and Portuguese Angola and Mozambique (see map, page 781).

Independence came quite easily, and with good prospects of successful development, to some of the African states south of the Sahara. Others, however, experienced great strife and turmoil. The difference rested partly on the willingness of imperialist governments to grant independence, and partly on their past colonial policies. In countries where native Africans had been used in the lower offices of the colonial government—thus creating a nucleus of trained civil servants around which to build a new government—the transition to independence was relatively smooth.

Another factor was the population itself. Almost 800 languages and dialects are spoken in sub-Saharan Africa, and only a few are common to large areas. There are many tribes, with different customs and traditions.

Still another factor was the number of white settlers. If they were in control and feared native African rule, they opposed independence or tried to control the new governments.

Most of the new states in sub-Saharan Africa were small in population. At least three fourths of the mineral resources were still owned and operated by foreign countries. Many small nations had few natural resources at all. Most of the African states needed a great deal of economic help from outside countries to operate their governments and develop their economies. Perhaps most importantly, the people had much to learn about the duties of independence.

Three examples—the Congo, Nigeria, and South Africa—will serve to illustrate some of the problems faced by independent African nations after World War II.

The Congo (Zaire)

The Congo ° went through severe trials in its struggle for independence. The Belgian government, which had administered the Congo since 1908, had improved housing, education, roads, sanitation, and health. Native workers were given the opportunity to work at relatively skilled, high-paying jobs—but not in government.

Independence. After World War II a strong movement for independence began in the Congo. In the 1950's, native nationalists demanded that the Congolese receive the right to choose their own government. When the Belgians arrested native leaders, rioting broke out. Finally the Belgians gave in. General elections were held in 1960. Patrice Lumumba, leader of the extreme nationalists, became premier, and his major rival, Joseph Kasavubu, became president.

The Congo became independent as the Democratic Republic of the Congo in June 1960, but its problems were far from over. The new republic was made up of many different tribal and language groups. There was a fierce struggle to control the new government. The Cold War became a factor in this conflict. Lumumba had communist support, while some Western nations favored Kasavubu.

In July 1960, soldiers in the Congolese army mutinied against their Belgian officers. Encouraged by the military, native tribesmen began slaughtering white settlers and missionaries. Many whites, fearing for their lives, began to leave the country. Their departure increased the disorder, for they were the professional and government workers.

Attempts at secession increased the turmoil further. The most important of these involved the mining province of Katanga, whose leader, Moise Tshombe, set up an independent government. His army was led by Belgian mercenaries.

° **Congo:** Two African nations (both of which became independent in 1960) took the name Congo. One, formerly the French Congo, is known officially as the Republic of the Congo. The other, formerly the Belgian Congo, was known officially as the Democratic Republic of the Congo until 1971, when it became the Republic of Zaire. It is this African country to which the single term Congo usually refers.

The Congo moved rapidly toward anarchy. Lumumba was held prisoner by the Tshombe regime in Katanga, where he was murdered following an alleged escape.

United Nations intervention. Civil war and governmental chaos were complicated by foreign intervention. The United Nations Security Council called on Belgium to withdraw its troops from Katanga. It also authorized the UN Secretary-General, Dag Hammarskjöld (HAHM·ar·shoold), to provide a United Nations force to restore and maintain order in the Congo. This force, the ONUC, was composed mainly of troops from other African nations. It was sent into the Congo in the summer of 1960.

The UN force came under attack from almost all factions in the Congo dispute. In an effort to strengthen the central government and restore order, Hammarskjöld then arranged a personal meeting with Tshombe in Northern Rhodesia. Although Hammarskjöld was killed in a plane crash on his way to the meeting, Tshombe and the United Nations soon agreed to a cease-fire and an exchange of prisoners.

Hammarskjöld's successor as Secretary-General, U Thant of Burma, ordered the ONUC to expel all foreigners from Katanga and restore order in the province. Execution of the order brought some heavy fighting, but, by the beginning of 1963, Tshombe's army was defeated and he went into exile.

Continuing difficulties. UN troops remained in the Congo until mid-1964, maintaining law and order and ending the most dangerous of the Congolese secessionist movements. After they withdrew, there was more trouble. Revolts by small bands of primitively armed men broke out in several provinces. President Kasavubu's government seemed unable to cope with the situation, and his army could not quell the revolts.

Kasavubu's solution was to invite Tshombe to return from exile and become premier in a "government of national reconciliation." Tshombe accepted the offer, announcing that the new government would unite all political factions.

The primitive rebel bands began to receive aid from other African countries, especially those in

NATIONALISM IN AFRICA
AFTER WORLD WAR II

Independent nations

Colonies of European nations
at the end of 1968

0   1000 miles

which communists had influence. Because the Congolese army was unable to put down these revolts, Tshombe hired white mercenary troops. It was a drastic step for an African leader, and it brought him condemnation throughout Africa. In 1965, Kasavubu removed him from office, but soon after was overthrown himself by an army general, Joseph Mobutu.

Leadership of the Congo was not clearly es-

tablished for several years. In 1967, when Tshombe was fleeing into exile, his plane was hijacked and forced to land in Algeria. The Algerian Supreme Court ruled that Tshombe be extradited, or sent back, to the Congo, where he was under a sentence of death for his part in the Katanga secession. The court's ruling was not carried out, however, and Tshombe remained in prison in Algeria until his death in 1969. In 1970

781

The Congo

Formerly a Belgian colony, the Congo attained freedom amid problems and strife. Riots, bloodshed, martial law, and intertribal warfare accompanied independence. At left, Congolese natives flee Leopoldville, hoping to relocate in an area free from the horrors they have been experiencing. Intertribal jealousies were aggravated by Belgians, trying to retain mining interests, and by communists, trying to subvert the new government. UN forces drawn from twenty-two countries were moved in to try to establish orderly government. Below, UN Secretary-General Dag Hammarskjöld reviews troops in Leopoldville. A UN soldier and local police, bottom, patrol the streets of Elizabethville.

Mobutu was elected president of what became, in the following year, the Republic of Zaire.

In the 1970's the Republic of Zaire began gradually to recover from the political chaos and civil wars of the 1960's. The resources of the nation are many. Zaire produces about 6 percent of the world's copper and nearly 50 percent of its cobalt. Other minerals include gold, silver, manganese, and uranium. The nation's tropical forests could produce many valuable products. Given peace, time, capital, and education, the Congolese people may attain more prosperous lives.

Nigeria

Another African nation that gained its independence after World War II is the Republic of Nigeria. Nigeria, with more than 60 million people, is one of the most populous nations of West Africa. It is also one of the richest, especially in its daily output of about 2 million barrels of oil. As a former British colony, Nigeria became independent in 1960 and joined the British Commonwealth of Nations. The original constitution set up a federation of four regions in which each region had a large degree of local independence. It was hoped that this loose plan of government would prevent warfare among the various tribes and serve as a model for other African states. Time proved these hopes false, both in Nigeria and elsewhere in Africa.

Serious trouble broke out in Nigeria in 1966. At that time a military government took over, bringing to an end a period of coalition government in which the northern region had dominated. The new government established twelve new states in place of the original four regions. In 1967 the former eastern region, home of the powerful Ibo tribe, seceded from the federation and declared itself the Republic of Biafra. At once a bitter civil war broke out between the central government and the new republic.

Biafra. The new nation of Biafra fared badly in the fighting. Nigerian troops seized and blockaded Biafra's ports, cutting off the struggling state from trade with other countries. Step by step, Nigerian forces pressed the Biafran army into a narrow area in the southeast, where the rebels became isolated from the outside world. By the end of 1969, Biafra held less than a fourth of its former eastern region. Trapped in a narrow strip of African scrubland, seven and a half million Biafrans faced slow starvation. With further resistance hopeless, Biafra surrendered in January 1970.

Throughout the fighting, Nigeria maintained that the war with Biafra was a purely domestic problem—a rebellion to be suppressed by national forces. Nigerian officials regarded any aid to the besieged Biafrans as interference in the internal affairs of Nigeria, and a violation of the principle of sovereignty accepted by the Organization of African Unity. For this reason most African nations refused to recognize Biafra. Since even food relief was regarded as hostile aid, the rebel population underwent incredible suffering.

Despite Nigerian hostility, several nations and international organizations tried to send aid to the Biafrans. Because of the blockade, however, food and medical supplies could be sent only by air. With very little aid arriving, disease and starvation claimed the lives of about two million Biafrans.

The Nigerian conflict had grave consequences for both sides, delaying Nigeria's industrial and social development. The war casualties drained the population of its most productive labor; a million men, mostly Ibos or Biafrans, died in battle or of starvation. In the early 1970's, however, there were signs that the military government was restoring stability at home and regaining a position of leadership among African nations. General Yakubu Gowon, head of the government, promised to try to restore civilian government by 1976. (See picture, page 784.)

South Africa

The African country best fitted to give industrial leadership and aid to new African nations in the postwar years was the most unpopular because of its racial policies. The Union of South Africa was the only African nation that had had an industrial revolution. There was an iron and steel industry and other manufacturing. South African mines produced about three fourths of

Nigeria's rising leadership in Africa was shown in 1973 when General Gowon addressed the UN General Assembly as chairman of the OAU. He is shown here with his wife and with UN Secretary-General Kurt Waldheim.

the world's supply of gold; other important minerals included diamonds, uranium, tin, platinum, chrome, and asbestos. The country also exported meat, wool, and sugar.

The burning issue in South Africa was the race problem. In the 1960's, with the total population of the country at about 16 million, approximately 3 million whites firmly controlled 11 million African Negroes. (There were also about 500,000 Asians and 1½ million "coloreds"—people of mixed heritage.) Of the whites, about 60 percent were Afrikaners, of Boer or German descent; roughly 40 percent were of British descent.

Until 1948, South Africans of British descent played a major role in the government, which, in general, maintained a moderate racial policy. In that year, however, Afrikaner nationalists came to power and proceeded to carry out a policy of race separation known as *apartheid* (uh·PART·hyt) —the Afrikaans word for "apartness."

Apartheid entailed the physical separation of South Africa's whites from its Africans, Asians, and coloreds. Africans were promised "tribal homelands" where they could exercise considerable self-government, but by the early 1970's only one such homeland had been established. Most Africans, Asians, and coloreds were forced to live in restricted areas, usually in or near cities. South Africa's vital economic and strategic resources were monopolized by whites. Black Africans had no political rights, while those of Asians and coloreds were severely curtailed.

Apartheid, which carried racial discrimination to a point hardly known elsewhere, led to much criticism. In 1961, after disagreements with Great Britain over its policies, the Union of South Africa withdrew from the Commonwealth of Nations, proclaiming itself the Republic of South Africa. Secretary-General U Thant of the United Nations, speaking before a meeting of the Organization of African Unity, strongly condemned apartheid and accused the South African government of blocking the peaceful evolution of a society based on justice and racial equality. The United Nations itself, however, was divided on the issue. Some members questioned whether the UN could force members to give equal civil rights to all their citizens. They felt that such action might be interference in the domestic affairs of a nation, which the UN charter forbids.

The United Nations did adopt resolutions condemning apartheid and recommending that member nations place embargoes on South Africa's shipping. Such efforts accomplished little. In 1969 the coloreds of South Africa were granted the right to form their own Representative Council with jurisdiction over such things as education and social welfare. During an economic boom and labor shortage in the early 1970's, blacks were permitted to take some jobs from which they had formerly been excluded. But blacks continued to be without any political rights, while the rights of Asians and coloreds remained strictly limited.

1. What factors stimulated the drive toward independence in Africa and the Middle East? What conditions caused problems for the new nations in developing their governments and economies?

2. What was the policy of the Belgian government toward its colony of the Congo? What happened after independence?

3. Describe the South African policy of apartheid.

4. IDENTIFY: OAU, Zaire, Ibo, Biafra, Gowon.

2 Dangerous tensions arose in Egypt and the Middle East

After World War II, affairs throughout northern Africa were strongly influenced by hostilities that arose in Egypt and the neighboring Middle East. In the early 1970's this area continued to be extremely dangerous to world peace.

Egypt, like so much of the underdeveloped world, came under the control of European imperialist nations in the 1800's and early 1900's. After World War I the people of the region grew increasingly dissatisfied with foreign control. A basic factor in their dissatisfaction was the growing force of Arab nationalism.

The Arabs, as you have read, spread out from their homeland in Arabia to conquer much of North Africa and the Middle East. Today their descendants constitute what is often called the Arab world—countries dominated by Arabic-speaking Moslems, from Morocco in western Africa through Iraq and Saudi Arabia in western Asia (but excluding both Israel and Turkey).

The Arab world is a vast territory with about 70 million inhabitants. Although its rich oil deposits are important, it is generally a poor region of sandy deserts and barren plateaus. Arab nationalism appealed to the pride and ancient heritage of its people and aimed toward some kind of union of all the Arab peoples.

In 1945, Egypt, Saudi Arabia, Yemen, Syria, Lebanon, Trans-Jordan, and Iraq formed the Arab League to promote cooperation. In later years, Libya, Sudan, Morocco, Tunisia, Kuwait, and Algeria also joined (see map, page 786). The Arab League made little progress toward its goals. Although the Arab nations were linked by religious and cultural ties, several forces kept them apart. There were disputes over boundaries, going far back into Arab history. Family feuds and dynastic rivalries were a problem, too. In practice, the Arab League seemed to be united on only one issue—opposition to Israel.

Egypt

Egypt had become completely independent from Great Britain in 1936. After independence, however, there was continued discontent over the Egyptian king's extravagance, government corruption, and delays in promised reforms. People felt humiliated by the poor showing the Egyptian army made in a war against Israel in 1948–1949 that you will read about later. In 1952, a group of army officers under General Mohammed Naguib led an uprising that forced the king to abdicate. In 1953, Egypt was declared a republic and Naguib became president. A power struggle ensued, and within two years Colonel Gamal Abdel Nasser became the dominant power. Although he was elected president in 1956 and the forms of democratic government continued to be observed, he controlled Egypt as a military dictatorship.

Egypt had emerged from World War II as the strongest Arab country. Under Nasser, Egypt attempted to lead the Arab world. Like other leaders of emerging states, Nasser played East against West in the Cold War in order to get economic and military aid from both sides. For example, when the United States proved reluctant to sell arms to Egypt, Nasser obtained them from Czechoslovakia in exchange for Egyptian cotton.

The Suez crisis. Nasser negotiated with the United States, Great Britain, and the World Bank for loans to build a dam at Aswan, on the upper Nile River. The dam was a gigantic undertaking, estimated to cost about 1.3 billion dollars. When completed it was expected to increase the arable land of Egypt by about 25 percent. In July 1956, in reproof to Nasser for his arms agreement with

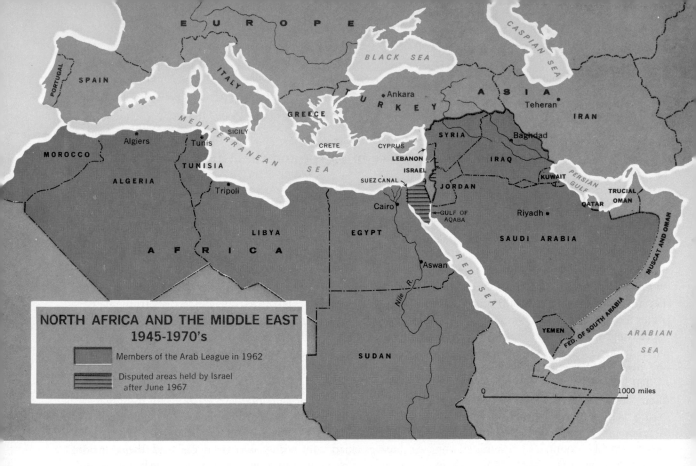

NORTH AFRICA AND THE MIDDLE EAST
1945-1970's

Members of the Arab League in 1962

Disputed areas held by Israel
after June 1967

Czechoslovakia, the United States and Great Britain announced that they were withdrawing their offers of loans to build the dam. The World Bank also withdrew its offer.

Nasser's reaction was immediate. On July 26, 1956, he announced that Egypt was taking over the Suez Canal Company and would operate the canal. He said that stockholders would continue to be paid, but that profits would be used to build the Aswan Dam. He also announced that the Soviet Union had promised technical help in building the dam.

Egyptian nationalization of the Suez Canal raised many problems. There was a possible threat to Europe's oil supply, most of which was shipped from oil fields in the Middle East through the canal. The industrialized nations of the West depended so heavily on this oil that France and Britain feared its loss would cripple their transportation services and cause their factories to

shut down. Equally serious, from the viewpoint of the West, was the prospect of increased Soviet influence in the sensitive Middle East.

The Egyptian moves were especially alarming to the new state of Israel. Relations between Israel and the neighboring Arab states, especially Egypt, had been most unfriendly. Egypt had refused to allow Israeli ships or ships of other countries with cargoes bound for Israel to pass through the Suez Canal, even though an international agreement of 1888 required that the canal be kept open to ships of all nations.

Egypt's seizure of the Suez Canal in 1956 brought tensions to a head. United Nations efforts at mediation failed. Israel, in a lightning invasion, seized the Gaza Strip—an Egyptian-administered coastal district adjoining Israel's southern border. The Israelis then defeated the Egyptians in the Sinai Peninsula and advanced toward the canal.

Great Britain and France, in secret agreement

with Israel, sent an ultimatum demanding a cease-fire. They insisted that Egypt consent to temporary British-French occupation of the canal. When Egypt refused, Britain and France seized the Mediterranean end of the canal, driving back the Egyptian army. Both sides sank ships in the canal to block it.

United Nations intervention. When British and French vetoes prevented the Security Council from acting, Uniting for Peace procedures were applied. The General Assembly demanded a cease-fire and withdrawal of the invading forces. It also authorized the United Nations Emergency Force (UNEF) to patrol the cease-fire line.

The three invading nations faced much pressure from hostile world opinion. In the General Assembly the United States voted against them. The Soviet Union threatened to help Egypt militarily. Even in Israel, Britain, and France, people criticized the attack. After three days of fighting, the invaders agreed to a cease-fire.

UN Secretary-General Hammarskjöld formed the UNEF and moved it to the war area with amazing speed. Britain and France withdrew their troops. The Israelis tried to gain Egypt's agreement to their use of the canal, but failed. Then they, too, withdrew. But hostilities between Egypt and Israel were far from being solved.

Palestine, the new state of Israel

You will recall that both Arabs and Jews laid claim to the ancient land of Palestine. Jews thought of it as their homeland because of Biblical tradition, and had been encouraged in their expectations by the Balfour Declaration of 1917. Arabs, too, believed they had a promise of British support for an Arab state that would include Palestine. In addition, they maintained that they had lived on the land for centuries, and thus had more right to it than the Jews.

Zionism grew stronger after World War I, and many Jews settled in Palestine. Nazi persecutions brought thousands more. They bought land from the Arabs and established businesses in the cities. Some Palestinian Arabs showed opposition, but Jews had little difficulty buying land.

European Jews, especially, carried with them the civilization of the modern world. Most Palestinian Arabs, on the other hand, lived in an almost feudal culture. A few wealthy landlords owned most of the land, while the peasants lived in poverty and ignorance.

Jewish knowledge of modern techniques of agriculture, industry, commerce, and science gave the Jews in Palestine a relatively high standard of living, which caused envy and discontent among the Arab peasants. Ruling families were faced with demands for a better way of life. The Arabs began to demand that Jewish immigration be halted, or they would stop it by force. Both Arabs and Jews criticized the British.

In 1947 the British turned the problem over to the United Nations General Assembly and announced that they would withdraw from Palestine the following year. The Assembly recommended that Palestine be partitioned into an Arab state and a Jewish state. In 1948 the Jews proclaimed the region allotted to them—western Palestine—as the Republic of Israel (see map, page 786). Chaim Weizmann became its first president and David Ben-Gurion the first prime minister.

Arab leaders were angered by the establishment of a Jewish nation on land they claimed, and war broke out as soon as British troops withdrew. The armies of Syria, Lebanon, Iraq, Trans-Jordan, and Egypt attacked Israel with the announced aim of driving the Israelis into the sea.

To the surprise of many, Israeli troops made quick gains, although greatly outnumbered by the Arabs. In 1949 a UN mediator, Ralph Bunche of the United States, persuaded the belligerents to sign an armistice. (It was then that Trans-Jordan, which had been allotted eastern Palestine as well as its original territory across the Jordan River, changed its name to Jordan.)

Tensions remained, however, and border incidents continued. The Arab states refused to grant Israel legal recognition and imposed economic boycotts on the country. Arab nationalists, such as Nasser, stimulated anti-Jewish feeling as a means of uniting the Arab states. The Suez crisis of 1956 made the situation more explosive than ever.

Other problems plagued the new state of Israel. About a million Arabs had fled the country at the outbreak of war and had been interned in refugee camps in the Gaza Strip, Lebanon, Syria, and Jordan. Israel would not let them return, claiming that they would overburden the already crowded country. Most Arab countries refused to integrate them fully into their populations; only Jordan would accept the refugees as citizens. Israel came into conflict with Syria and Jordan over its plan to divert water from the Jordan River to irrigate the Negev desert in southern Israel. Syria and Jordan, claiming that Israel was not a legally constituted nation, threatened to divert the water before it reached Israel. Israel in turn threatened to destroy any diversion dams that might be built.

In spite of all these difficulties, the new state of Israel made much progress. Considerable economic aid came from American grants and loans and from German reparations in compensation for the mass destruction of Jewish lives and property during World War II. Jewish refugees from every continent were welcomed and provided for. Collective farms (the best known form of which is called the kibbutz) proved successful in turning former desert areas into productive land. With vast public works programs and other developments, Israel's standard of living became the highest in the entire Middle East.

Continuing hostilities. After the Suez crisis of 1956, you recall, the United Nations arranged an uneasy truce and sent a peace-keeping force to patrol the cease-fire lines along the Israeli-Egyptian border. Although tension between Israel and Egypt continued, the truce remained unbroken until 1967.

In May 1967, at Egypt's demand, the UN withdrew its peace-keeping force. At the same time, Egypt closed the Gulf of Aqaba, at the head of the Red Sea, to Israeli shipping, thereby threatening Israel's economic existence. As a further threat to Israel, Egypt reached a military agreement with Jordan that placed Jordanian troops under Egyptian command.

With its Arab neighbors mobilizing for war, Israel decided to strike. On June 5, 1967, Israeli planes attacked airfields in Egypt, Syria, Jordan, and Iraq. Within a few hours, the Arabs were left virtually without air power. By the end of the sixth day, Israel was completely victorious.

Late in 1967, after the UN had arranged another cease-fire, it sent Gunnar B. Jarring of Sweden to the Middle East as a special envoy to try to find a peace formula. But both parties remained unyielding. The Arabs refused to grant legal recognition to Israel. The Israelis refused to withdraw from recently won territory or to negotiate indirectly. The territory involved this time included the Jordanian section of the city of Jerusalem, the Golan Heights in Syria, the Gaza Strip, and the Sinai Peninsula.

In the fall of 1973, fighting erupted again. Powerful Egyptian forces crossed the Suez Canal to attack Israeli defense positions in the Sinai Peninsula and Syrian forces struck across the Israeli-Syrian border. Quickly mobilizing, Israeli troops drove the Syrians back toward the Syrian capital, encircled Egyptian forces on the east bank of the Suez Canal, and crossed the canal to occupy Egyptian land on the west bank. After 2½ weeks of fierce fighting, the UN succeeded in establishing an uneasy cease-fire agreement.

In the weeks that followed, worldwide tensions were heightened when several Arab oil-producing states reduced, or cut off completely, their shipments of oil to major industrialized nations in an effort to force concessions from Israel. Finally, Israel and several of the Arab states agreed, for the first time in their long history of hostility, to meet face to face and try to negotiate their differences. Late in 1973 a meeting began in Geneva, Switzerland.

CHECKUP

1. What is the Arab world? What factors led to its unity? To its disunity?

2. What factors led to the Suez Crisis of 1956 and how was it resolved?

3. What was the Six-Day War? What territories did the Israelis insist on keeping afterward?

4. IDENTIFY: Arab League, Nasser, Aswan, UNEF, Bunche, Jarring, Waldheim.

Nationalism created tensions in the Middle East and North Africa. Arab nationalism had a strong impact in specific crises. Nasser of Egypt—his portrait carried by an admirer, above—won wide popularity when he seized the Suez Canal. Arabs were also united in their fierce opposition to Israel. Over a quarter century, Arab-Israeli hostility erupted in warfare four times, as shown in the cartoon, lower right. Even between wars, Israel kept constant guard on its frontiers, as shown in the picture, upper right, where two armed Israelis, one a woman, keep watch against invaders. Below, in 1973, Israeli guns are shelling Syrian positions.

25-Year War

©1973 HERBLOCK

3 Other North African nations gained independence

Westward from Egypt along the Mediterranean Sea are the newly-independent nations of Libya, Tunisia, Algeria, and Morocco. All of these Arabic-speaking nations have assisted Egypt in its confrontations with Israel.

Libya

Libya gained its independence in 1951 and became a constitutional monarchy under King Idris I, a former tribal leader. Although the country is mainly desert, it has a fertile coastal strip where olives, dates, citrus fruits, wheat, and barley are grown. But beginning in the late 1950's, the discovery and development of oil fields began to overshadow agriculture in Libya's economy. By 1969 the country was the world's fourth largest oil producer. By 1972 Libyan income from taxes on foreign oil companies reached two billion dollars annually.

Libya's growing oil prosperity in the 1960's brought progress in education and a higher standard of living for many of the Libyan peoples. But the new wealth from oil also increased corruption and allowed a few families and government officials to become very rich. These inequities in the distribution of wealth contributed to instability. The result was political unrest.

End of the monarchy. In 1969, while the seventy-nine-year-old king Idris I was in Turkey, a group of young Libyans overthrew the government and announced the formation of the Libyan Republic. The change of government in Libya raised important questions for the future. The Western world watched anxiously, since Libya had important oil contracts with the United States and West Germany, as well as military agreements with Great Britain and the United States.

At first the new government promised to respect the rights of foreign oil companies and to honor Libya's existing treaty obligations. But the government came under pressure from Libyan students and others to close foreign military bases, take over foreign economic interests, and play a more active part in the Arab struggle against Israel.

In October 1969 the new government asked the United States and Great Britain to evacuate their military bases on Libyan soil by the early 1970's. In November 1969 the government decided to nationalize all foreign banks in the country. In the early 1970's it moved toward greater control over all foreign oil companies operating within Libya. In 1973 it took over several American-owned oil companies and informed the others that they would have to pay more for Libyan oil.

The new Libyan Republic, headed by a young military officer, Muammar el-Qaddafi, represented a new generation of nationalist Arabs. He had strong anti-West feelings, and was even stronger anti-Israel. His government began to provide about 200 million dollars annually to Egypt in subsidies and loans. He also favored a close union with Egypt. Negotiations for this purpose began in 1972. The two countries agreed to a merger at some future time. As an ardent pan-Arabist, Qaddafi favored the merging of Egypt and Libya as soon as possible. President Anwar Sadat of Egypt had reservations about the speed with which the union might be achieved.

Algeria

For many years a strong independence movement had stirred the native peoples of Morocco, Tunisia, and Algeria. After World War II the French made gradual and grudging concessions, first in Morocco and then in Tunisia. In 1956 France recognized both territories as independent, sovereign nations. Morocco became a kingdom ruled by a sultan. In 1957 Tunisia declared itself a republic and elected Habib Bourguiba (boor·GEE·buh) as its first president.

In Algeria the situation proved far more explosive. The region had been French since 1830. About four fifths of its 10 million inhabitants were Arab or Berber Moslems. The other inhabitants, the *colons* (French for "colonists"), were Europeans or of European descent. Most of them were French. The French had made many improvements in Algeria's transportation, agricul-

Even after Algerian independence was proclaimed in 1962, die-hard forces of the Secret Army Organization (OAS) tried to maintain their resistance. In this picture, troops and security officers of the new government are searching for hideouts of OAS forces in Algiers.

ture, industry, health, and education. However, most of the benefits went to the colons.

Guerrilla war. After World War II, Algerian nationalists pressed for a greater voice in their own government. There were two groups of Algerian nationalists: moderates, who wanted home rule within the French federal system, and radicals, who demanded complete independence from France. Radicals had formed the National Liberation Front (FLN, from its name in French). In 1954 they launched a destructive guerrilla war, which the French were unable to suppress.

In 1958, as you have read, French army leaders insisted that General de Gaulle be made head of the French government. They thought he would push the Algerian war to a successful fin-

ish for France. They were disappointed.

In 1960, de Gaulle gave the Algerians three choices, to be voted upon in a plebiscite: (1) complete independence, (2) self-government and ties to France, or (3) continuation as a part of France.

Extremist French army officers and colons then formed the Secret Army Organization (OAS, from its name in French). They used terrorism to prevent reconciliation between colons and Moslems. OAS forces provoked Moslem riots so that the French army could rule by martial law. They also assassinated Frenchmen who favored peace; there were even unsuccessful attempts on the life of de Gaulle.

Peace negotiations. The negotiations between French and Algerian representatives were long and difficult. Finally, in 1962, the two sides reached a settlement. France agreed to accept the result of a plebiscite in Algeria. If Algerians voted for independence, France would help establish order and give tariff and other commercial advantages as well as loans for economic aid. Algeria promised to respect the rights of French citizens and to pay for confiscated property.

The Algerian plebiscite was held on July 1, 1962. The vote was overwhelmingly for independence. Two days later Algeria officially seceded from France and became a sovereign state.

Independent Algeria

The new state faced formidable economic difficulties. The country was in chaos. Many colons were afraid of persecution and left the country. Among them were civil servants, professional men, and skilled workmen. There was also serious unemployment among Algerian workers, most of whom were unskilled.

Land that had been abandoned by the fleeing colons was turned over to Moslem peasants. The position of these peasants improved somewhat. But peasants still working the former Moslem lands were as miserably poor as ever. About 85 percent of the country's commercial and industrial enterprises were still privately owned by French citizens. The remaining enterprises were nationalized, but the inexperience of their workers proved a serious handicap.

Once independent, Algerians had to decide upon a form of government for their country. Some favored much local self-rule; others preferred a strongly centralized authority. The latter group was led by Ahmed Ben Bella and supported by an army group led by Colonel Houari Boumedienne. After some fighting, Ben Bella's group gained control and he became premier. Within two years, leaders of all opposing factions were imprisoned or exiled.

Ben Bella proclaimed Algeria a socialist state. He accepted economic aid from both East and West, but generally took an anti-Western stand. His agents tried to stir up rebellion against pro-Western governments in other parts of Africa.

Ben Bella's policies were not successful. He did not win favor with many African leaders, most of whom feared his attempts at subversion. Nor did his proclaimed socialism and threats to nationalize all industry seem to solve Algeria's problems. He made no move against French-owned industry. In 1965 he was overthrown by a military *coup d'état* led by Colonel Boumedienne, who assumed control of the government. The government of Boumedienne remained relatively stable. Several plots against the new head of state were crushed. Former President Ben Bella remained a government prisoner.

Under Boumedienne, the Algerian government moved in the late 1960's and early 1970's to fulfill the hopes of the land-hungry peasants and idle factory workers. Large landed estates were broken up and industrial workers were put in charge of factories, especially those abandoned by the French. Nearly a third of the government budget was spent on industrial development. The oil refining industry, taken over by the government, expanded with the completion of a pipeline across the Sahara Desert. The production of chemical fertilizers and liquid gas added to the economy. The country's chief exports were oil, iron ore, wine, citrus fruits, and tobacco.

Despite this economic progress and new educational programs, three out of five Algerian workers remained unemployed and only 26 percent of the people were literate. In 1968 a prolonged drought followed by severe floods slowed the nation's economic progress. In return for substantial aid, Algeria granted the Soviet Union the right to establish a strategic military base on the Algerian shore of the Mediterranean Sea.

CHECKUP

1. Who was Muammar el-Qaddafi? What new policies did he adopt?

2. Why was it difficult to reach a peaceful settlement of the Algerian problem in the 1950's? How did the country gain independence?

3. What policies has Boumedienne followed in Algeria?

4. IDENTIFY: Idris I, colons, FLN, Ben Bella, Bourguiba.

CHAPTER REVIEW

Chapter 39 Colonies in Africa and the Middle East Gained Independence (1945–1970's)

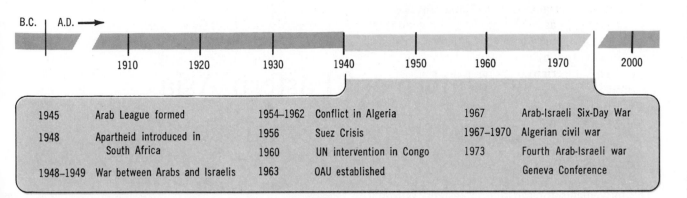

1945	Arab League formed	1954–1962	Conflict in Algeria	1967	Arab-Israeli Six-Day War
1948	Apartheid introduced in South Africa	1956	Suez Crisis	1967–1970	Algerian civil war
		1960	UN intervention in Congo	1973	Fourth Arab-Israeli war
1948–1949	War between Arabs and Israelis	1963	OAU established		Geneva Conference

CHAPTER SUMMARY

Newly independent nations in Africa and the Middle East faced grave problems, including political inexperience, inadequate education, tribal and racial conflicts, and economic backwardness.

In Africa, freedom came more easily to some countries than others. The Congo was unprepared for independence. Rivalries among leaders, secession threats, and foreign interference necessitated intervention by a UN force. In Nigeria, secession of Biafra brought civil war and terrible massacres. South Africa presented a different kind of problem with apartheid producing a threatening racial situation that brought protests from several other nations.

Arab states formed the Arab League to promote cooperation, but divisive forces prevailed. After an uprising in Egypt, Nasser emerged as a military dictator and a strong Arab leader. After Israel gained its independence, it was attacked by Arab armies. When Nasser seized the Suez Canal, Britain, France, and Israel invaded Egypt. Worldwide pressure, exerted mainly through the United Nations, resulted in withdrawal of the invaders. In the Six-Day War, Israel defeated the Arabs and kept strategic territory. Constant tension over this territory led to a fourth war between Arabs and Israelis.

Another Arab nation, Algeria, was the scene of violent disturbances for several years. The French army put de Gaulle in power; peace negotiations were finally successful and Algeria became independent, with a tendency toward socialism.

Libya, with new oil riches, was taken over by a military dictator who sought merger with Egypt.

QUESTIONS FOR DISCUSSION

1. Nationalism in Africa may be considered as one of the consequences of European imperialism. Do you think nationalism is good for Africa? Explain your point of view.

2. Should Belgium be held responsible for the chaos that resulted in the Congo after it gained its independence? Give reasons for your position.

3. Do you agree with the policy of an embargo on trade with the Republic of South Africa?

4. Why were the colons in Algeria—particularly the members of the OAS—so opposed to Algerian independence?

5. Many national leaders, including those in Africa and the Middle East, play off East against West to gain economic aid from both blocs. Do you think this is a legitimate way to obtain economic help? Should the United States refuse aid to countries that also accept aid from the communist nations? Justify your answer.

6. Why did Nasser become a hero to many Arabs after he seized the Suez Canal?

7. What do you think would help lessen tensions between Arabs and Israelis? Do you see any hope for such an easing of tensions?

PROJECTS

1. Write a short essay on the United Nations' role in the Congo and in the Suez crisis.

2. Write an imaginary editorial for a pro-Arab newspaper, denouncing Israel as a trouble maker in the Middle East.

3. As an Israeli, write a letter to a friend in the United States, describing some of the many advances that your country has made.

4. Draw a cartoon criticizing South Africa's policy of apartheid.

40

The Nations of Eastern Asia
Suffered from Internal Conflicts

The movements for self-rule in eastern Asia that had begun decades earlier came to fulfillment after World War II. Between 1947 and 1962 the vast colonial empires of Great Britain, France, and the Netherlands fell apart and were replaced by native governments. Viewed from the West, it was the twilight of imperialism; viewed from the East, it was the dawn of independence. Few of these transitions to independence were accomplished peaceably. Even India, from which Britain voluntarily withdrew, became the scene of bitter warfare in its first years of independence.

In some ways, however, India was more fortunate than other former colonies in Asia. During their years of colonial rule, the British had recruited and trained Indian civil servants. These administrators were able to run the government efficiently and honestly once independence was gained. As early as 1935, Britain had also granted India a constitution and an elected legislature. Thus the workings of parliamentary democracy were familiar to many Indians.

The French and Dutch colonies in Asia had not been so carefully prepared for self-rule. When independence came, power frequently became concentrated in the hands of dictators or groups of generals. Exploitation, which once benefited foreign rulers, now benefited a native ruling class. Peasants and workers were no better off for having been freed from foreign rule.

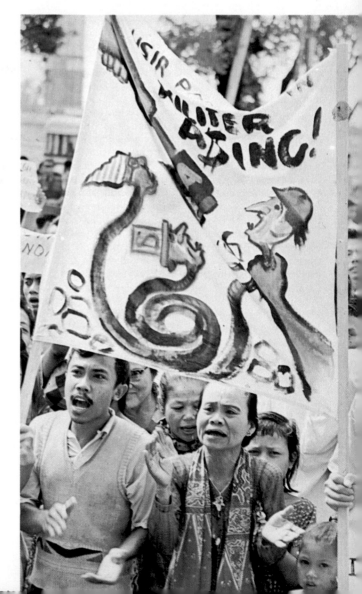

Indonesians supporting withdrawal from the UN, 1965

The newly independent Asian nations had much in common. Most were weak politically, economically, and militarily. They needed outside help badly, but many were suspicious of possible demands that might be tied to this help. They were suspicious because they did not want to exchange their hard-won independence for dependence on either side in the Cold War.

After World War II, eastern Asia became a battleground for armed conflicts arising out of the Cold War. The Western powers that fought these wars claimed that they were preventing the further spread of communism in Asia. However, many people in Asia saw Western involvement in the wars as a revival of Western imperialism. Communist propagandists succeeded in making use of genuine native discontent to spark conflicts. Many men—Asian, American, and European—died in these confusing and inconclusive wars. Although the heyday of European imperialism in eastern Asia had ended, the region had not yet become the peaceful and productive region envisioned by the early leaders of its independence movements.

1 India, Pakistan, and Bangladesh became independent nations

Indian neutralism during World War II hindered the Allied cause and convinced the British that India should be granted full independence. In 1947, after negotiations, the British, Hindus, and Moslems agreed to divide the subcontinent along religious lines. Moslems received two widely separated areas in the north, to be called Pakistan. Hindus controlled the rest, India. Both new countries became dominions in the British Commonwealth of Nations.

India's government and leadership

After three years as a dominion, India became a federal republic with an elected president and parliament. The president was the official head of state, but the prime minister and cabinet, chosen by the parliament, wielded the executive power. States and subdivisions merged into larger areas.

Jawaharlal Nehru, the first prime minister, served from 1950 until his death in 1964. A wealthy Brahman, educated at Cambridge University in England, Nehru had become a lawyer. Falling under Gandhi's influence, he had devoted himself entirely to the independence movement.

As prime minister, Nehru favored Western, scientific modernism. His main goals were: (1) unity of India, overcoming the dividing forces of language, caste, and regional interests; (2) a secular state free of religious interference; (3) economic planning, in a socialist but non-communist pattern; (4) a democratic government; (5) neutralism in foreign affairs. After Nehru's death, his policies were carried forward by his daughter, Mrs. Indira Gandhi, who became prime minister in 1966.

Social and economic problems

Religious riots continued, and the caste system caused problems. Language was especially difficult. There are fifteen major and fifty-five minor Indian languages, plus dialects. English is most widely spoken. The constitution of 1950 made English the official language for fifteen years. Thereafter, Hindi, spoken by 40 percent of the people, was to become official. When the time came in 1965, riots and strikes against the language change forced the government to adopt English as as alternate language indefinitely.

Under Nehru, India developed a *mixed economy,* in which some industries are privately owned and some are owned by the government. The government planned all phases of economic

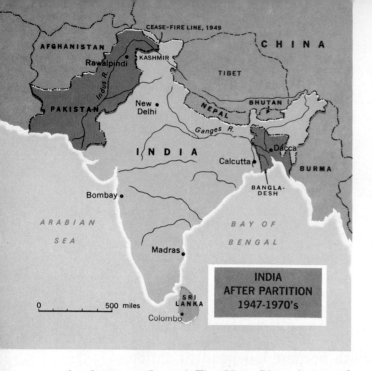

CEASE-FIRE LINE, 1949

AFGHANISTAN

Rawalpindi

KASHMIR

CHINA

TIBET

BHUTAN

PAKISTAN

New Delhi

NEPAL

Indus R.

Ganges R.

Dacca

BANGLA-DESH

Calcutta

BURMA

Bombay

INDIA

ARABIAN SEA

BAY OF BENGAL

Madras

SRI LANKA

Colombo

0   500 miles

INDIA AFTER PARTITION 1947-1970's

development. Several Five-Year Plans increased both industrial and agricultural production, but from pitifully small beginnings.

Many economic problems stemmed from the ever-growing population. India has 15 percent of the world's population on 2 percent of the world's land area. A population of 350 million in 1947 had increased to 550 million by the early 1970's. Government attempts to encourage smaller families met resistance from the Indians' age-old pride in large families.

It is almost impossible for a Westerner to comprehend the depth of poverty in India. Millions of people live on the verge of starvation. Probably 100 million people lack regular employment. Millions in the cities are homeless and sleep lying in the streets.

Foreign relations

Partition left India and Pakistan a thorny problem in the northern state of Kashmir (see map this page). India claimed Kashmir because the ruling prince, a Hindu, chose to join India. Pakistan claimed Kashmir because 85 percent of its people were Moslems. Border fighting was uneasily settled in 1949 by a United Nations cease-fire line. In 1957 India annexed part of

Kashmir. Pakistan protested, and more border incidents threatened the peace. In 1966, at the invitation of the Soviet Union, the prime ministers of the two countries met to discuss the problem. They agreed to withdraw their troops behind the cease-fire line and to negotiate a settlement later.

In world affairs, India tried to cultivate friendship with both the Communist and Western blocs, and with the uncommitted countries. Relations with China, cordial at first, became strained in 1959 when the Chinese moved into Tibet. A revolt took place in Tibet, after which the Dalai Lama (dah·LYE LAH·muh), Tibet's major religious-secular leader, fled to India along with some of his followers. In 1960 discovery of a Chinese-built base and a strategic road in territory claimed by India brought protests and border skirmishes. The Chinese invaded northeastern India, winning easy victories and making their way to the Indus-Ganges plain. There they declared a cease-fire and withdrew.

The Pakistan and Chinese conflicts forced the Indian government to spend on its military forces much money it would have preferred spending on its economic system.

Pakistan

Until 1971 Pakistan was composed of two unequal, widely separated parts. West Pakistan included the Indus River valley, site of India's earliest civilization. East Pakistan (now Bangladesh) was in the Ganges Delta. With only 15 percent of the land area, it had over half of the population. Between the two halves lay a 1,000-mile wide wedge of Indian territory.

With nearly 100 million people in 1947, Pakistan was the world's most populous Moslem state. The population increased rapidly after 1947. Development of an economically viable nation was hampered by lack of natural resources and geographic separation. Like India, Pakistan was troubled by poverty, illiteracy, and differences in language and culture. Trouble with India led to large defense spending, which hurt the economy. Much military and economic aid came from the United States.

Problems in India were aggravated by the partition of the subcontinent in 1947. Mass migrations, upper right, were often accompanied by violence that made age-old difficulties even harder to bear. Child labor has existed for centuries; above, a little girl spreads rice to dry in the sun. Poverty, too, has always plagued India; below, old people beg along a roadside. In foreign affairs, India bore heavy defense costs. At lower right, Nehru appears with his daughter, Mrs. Indira Gandhi, who later became prime minister.

At first a dominion, Pakistan became a parliamentary republic in 1956, and a military dictatorship under General Ayub Khan in 1958. It began as a strongly pro-Western nation and was an original member of the Southeast Asia Treaty Organization (SEATO)—an eastern counterpart of NATO—which was formed in 1954 to help prevent the forceful spread of communism in Southeast Asia. Pakistan's Western aid was viewed with concern by India. However, when the Chinese invasion brought Western aid to India, Pakistan protested. It then became friendlier to China.

In 1965 Ayub Khan had himself elected president of a "guided democracy," but opposition to his rule grew. There were demands for economic reforms, direct elections, democratic government, and greater autonomy for East Pakistan.

Bangladesh

In 1969 Ayub was forced to resign, handing over authority to the army chief-of-staff, General Yahya Khan. In 1971 civil war broke out between West and East Pakistan after Yahya Kahn refused to convene a new assembly in which elected members from East Pakistan would have outnumbered those from West Pakistan. The power-ful West Pakistan army met stout resistance from ill-prepared East Pakistan forces. Fighting broadened into war between India and Pakistan, in which India was successful. Pakistan surrendered in East Pakistan and accepted a cease-fire in West Pakistan. The new nation of Bangladesh was created to replace East Pakistan.

In 1973, India, Pakistan, and Bangladesh signed a peace settlement. They agreed to an exchange of prisoners of war and the repatriation of people who chose to live either in Pakistan or in Bangladesh. Pakistan pledged to recognize the independence of Bangladesh.

Bangladesh is a small and weak state, very heavily populated. There is a jute industry and agriculture, but little else. Located in the delta of the Ganges, it is often flooded.

CHECKUP

1. List the main points of Nehru's program for India.

2. What were some of the domestic problems facing India after independence?

3. How did the trouble between West and East Pakistan turn out?

4. IDENTIFY: Nehru, Hindi, mixed economy, Kashmir, Bangladesh.

② Communists won control of China and North Korea

Fighting between Nationalist and Communist Chinese broke out even before World War II ended. The communists rapidly gained the upper hand. The Nationalists suffered wholesale desertion and the capture of armies. In 1949 Chiang Kai-shek and the Nationalists fled to the island of Taiwan, leaving the mainland to the communists. The United States, which had tried to prevent the defeat with military equipment and advisers, refused to recognize the new government of mainland China, and worked to keep it out of the United Nations.

Chinese government and economy

The People's Republic of China was a one-party dictatorship. Communists held all key posts in government and in the armed forces. Executive power rested with a committee of the Political Bureau of the Communist Party, a group of seven men headed by Mao Tse-tung. Under this committee, a pyramid of bureaus and committees spread over the country, controlling every phase of Chinese life.

China had been devastated by more than thirty years of war. The people were miserably poor and had suffered periodic epidemics and famines. The currency was inflated, farms lay destroyed, industry and transportation had almost ceased to function.

By 1953 China had recovered enough to be ready for its first Five-Year Plan. The Soviet Union gave some help in the form of loans, but

China under communism became an entirely different nation from the loosely organized, family-centered society that it had been for centuries. Radical communist ideas reached into almost every aspect of Chinese life. Family life remained strong, but nearly all children attended school or nurseries while both parents worked under various kinds of communal organization. At right, workers on a rural commune harvest a rich crop like flax for making textiles. Lacking much modern machinery, millions of hand laborers all over China constructed enormous flood control and irrigation systems, as in the building of a canal below. Thus, by the 1970's, China had gone far toward solving its age-old problems of famine and devastating floods. The leader of this vast transformation in China was the communist dictator, Mao Tse-tung. Mao is shown in the center above with his second in command, Foreign Minister Chou En-lai, as they greet Prime Minister Tanaka of Japan during an official visit to China in 1972. Relations between China and the non-communist nations improved after enmity arose between China and the Soviet Union.

most of the capital came from China itself. Land was confiscated. Some was given to peasants, who later formed collective farms. Some was operated as state farms.

Despite droughts, floods, peasant opposition, and poor planning, the first Five-Year Plan showed gains in agricultural and industrial production. A second Five-Year Plan, the Great Leap Forward, was then announced. In some places, huge rural *communes* were established, in which men, women, and children lived in separate barracks. The men and women worked in the fields in large groups under strict supervision. They were also expected to develop local industries.

Three successive crop failures, poor planning, and peasant resentment toward completely communal living conditions led to abandonment of this plan. The communes were kept as administrative units, but families now lived in their own homes in China's countless small villages. Men and women still worked in the large fields of the communes, but each family also had a small plot of land where it could raise some of its own produce. Many communes also developed successful small industries.

During the early 1960's, under these modified communal arrangements, agriculture recovered and became successful. Large industries in the cities were also successfully organized along modified communal lines. In 1964 the Chinese demonstrated their technological and industrial progress when they detonated their first nuclear device.

From 1966 to 1968, China was torn by a political struggle called the Great Cultural Revolution. It was difficult for an outsider to know what was happening, but it was clear that a struggle for power was taking place within the Communist Party. After two years of turmoil, peace was restored by the army. Mao Tse-tung survived as China's leader, with Chou En-lai as his second in command, but many places in the Party organization remained vacant until the Party Congress in 1973.

When the Cultural Revolution had quieted, the country resumed its agricultural and industrial progress. In the 1970's, Westerners who visited China found no signs of want or starvation. Food in short supply was rationed. Everyone who could, worked; children were cared for in schools or in nurseries. Although housing was in short supply, it was carefully rationed. Everyone received medical care, possibly from a "barefoot doctor" (a partly trained person). Fully trained professionals were available in hospitals throughout the country. The people seemed hard-working and contented. The cities were clean and orderly.

Foreign relations

The Soviet Union and the People's Republic of China began as allies who were united by a common political faith, common economic interests, and a military and economic alliance. However, they soon disagreed over Marxism and foreign policy.

Russian leaders believed that world communism could be achieved by scientific and economic successes. Capitalist versus communist wars were not inevitable; coexistence was possible. Because nuclear weapons made victory impossible, disarmament was desirable. Each communist country should produce only those things it could produce best; all should integrate production into a single economic unit. Production should be stimulated by wage increases and incentives.

Chinese leaders believed that power came from revolutions. Communists must support "national wars of liberation." Peaceful coexistence was impossible in the long run. Disarmament was both undesirable and dangerous. The Russians, they said, had abandoned true Marxism and become renegades. They held that each communist country should develop its own economy; none should dominate. Wage increases and incentives would restore the forces of capitalism.

At first this Chinese-Soviet struggle was confined to bitter public speeches, and to conflicts for leadership among the communist countries and the underdeveloped nations. Later there were border skirmishes along the Chinese-Soviet border, especially in the region of Sinkiang where the Chinese had their nuclear facilities. Both sides stationed troops along the border. There were indications that the Soviets were encouraging new settlements along the Siberian borders of China.

Mao Tse-tung's policies toward the world as a whole were arrived at by deciding who was the main enemy, then building a united front of all possible forces to resist that enemy. For two decades there was no question that the main enemy was the United States. China's main fear was United States military power in Indo-China, Japan, and Taiwan. But United States withdrawal of military forces from Vietnam took place while Soviet threats along the northern border of China increased.

As their relations with the Soviet Union grew worse, the Chinese gave hints of willingness to come to terms with the United States. In 1972, after much diplomatic maneuvering, both open and secret, President Nixon visited China. Arrangements were made to exchange news representatives and for businessmen and private citizens to visit each other's country. Thereafter, diplomatic representatives were exchanged. This was not full diplomatic recognition, but close to it. In 1971, as you have read, the People's Republic of China had been admitted to the United Nations. Before these events occurred, however, there was a long period of Cold War tensions and confrontations in the Far East. The first serious confrontation took place in Korea.

The Korean War

By agreement, at the end of World War II the Soviet Union occupied northern Korea and the United States occupied southern Korea. The dividing line was the thirty-eighth parallel of latitude (see map, page 806).

Each occupying power organized the government in its zone. A United Nations commission was sent to supervise elections for a government to rule the entire peninsula. The Russians would not allow the commission into their zone, and elections, held in 1948, took place only in the south. The result was the Republic of Korea, known as South Korea, with Syngman Rhee as president. At the same time a People's Democratic Republic, known as North Korea, was created in the north. Its president was Kim Il-sung. The United Nations recognized South Korea as the legal government, while communist countries recognized only North Korea.

In June 1950 the North Korean army invaded South Korea. The Security Council of the United Nations, meeting in emergency session, declared North Korea an aggressor and called on United Nations members to furnish troops or supplies to resist the aggression.

The war that followed was a seesaw affair. The United Nations army, commanded by American General Douglas MacArthur, was driven far to the south. Then, reinforced, UN troops fought their way back to the thirty-eighth parallel. The United Nations then agreed reluctantly to allow UN forces to cross into North Korea, but they were ordered to stop south of the Yalu River, the border between North Korea and Manchuria. As United Nations troops neared the Yalu, Communist China entered the war on the side of North Korea, driving the UN forces south of the thirty-eighth parallel again.

In a few months the UN troops again advanced northward to the parallel. A controversy then arose over whether to bomb the bases in Manchuria from which Chinese planes attacked and from which the Chinese army was supplied. MacArthur insisted that the bases be bombed and the coast of China blockaded. United States President Truman and the General Assembly of the UN opposed such moves, fearing that the Soviet Union would come to China's assistance and that a third world war might result. When MacArthur continued to advocate these policies, Truman removed him from his post.

Under MacArthur's successor, General Matthew Ridgeway, United Nations forces fought their way slowly up the peninsula. In July 1951, armistice negotiations were started.

The armistice. After two years of negotiations, the armistice was signed in July 1953. With a few minor changes, it fixed the border again at the thirty-eighth parallel. It provided that a peace conference be held within three months, but the conference never took place and no peace treaty was signed. Thus the Korean War came to an inconclusive end, with the peninsula still divided.

The Korean War

United Nations action in Korea served notice that Western nations would not stand aside, as they had before World War II, while aggressions took place. Nineteen member nations eventually contributed troops to the United Nations force. Advancing over a snow-covered hill in South Korea, above, a UN patrol cautiously moves forward during a search for communist troops. At left below, American soldiers round up North Korean and Chinese prisoners. Injured and ragged refugees, below right, flee from a war zone.

During the remainder of the 1950's and 1960's, Korea's story was one of border incidents and attempts by each side to infiltrate the other. Each side worked to establish its own economy, and for a long time neither seemed willing to do anything to bring the two sides together. In 1972, however, they agreed to try to reunite the divided country. An agreement was signed fixing the composition and functions of a North-South Coordinating Committee to work for independent and peaceful unification. The work of the committee might be long and hard, but at least the two sides were trying to negotiate their differences.

CHECKUP

1. In the People's Republic of China, what was the first Five-Year Plan? The Great Leap Forward? The Cultural Revolution? What was the outcome of the Cultural Revolution?

2. What were the principal disagreements between the People's Republic of China and the Soviet Union?

3. Summarize the course of the Korean War. What gains and losses resulted?

4. IDENTIFY: Political Bureau, Great Leap Forward, Chou En-lai, Kim Il-sung, North-South Coordinating Committee.

3 The island nations of Asia attempted to become self-sufficient

The island nations of eastern Asia—Japan, Taiwan, the Philippines, Indonesia, and Malaysia—lie in a great arc along the Pacific coast (see map, page 806). Except for Japan, each has been a colony. Some former colonies won independence peacefully, some by painful struggle.

The occupation of Japan

After World War II, Japan lost all the territory gained during its earlier period of expansion. Its large and growing population was now confined to the home islands. The country still needed to import food and raw materials, and most of the industries that had produced export goods to pay for these imports had been damaged or destroyed. Countries invaded by Japan claimed reparations.

After its defeat, Japan was occupied by American troops under General MacArthur, who became the country's virtual ruler. The first aim of the occupation was demilitarization. It was planned that the war industries that remained should be taken as reparations and divided among the countries Japan had invaded.

Taking factories for reparations created the same difficulties in Japan as in Germany. Unless the victors wished to support them indefinitely, the Japanese had to be allowed to support themselves. To do this, industries were necessary. The United States insisted that the payment of reparations be postponed indefinitely.

The occupation's second aim was to create a peaceful and democratic government. Under MacArthur's supervision, the Japanese adopted a new constitution in 1947. This so-called "MacArthur constitution" provided for a parliament, the Diet, to be elected by universal suffrage. Executive power rested with a premier and a cabinet responsible to the Diet. War was prohibited, and armed forces were limited to those needed for police purposes. The emperor remained, but he had little power and was no longer considered divine.

In 1951, Japan and 48 other nations signed the World War II peace treaty. Japan formally renounced its claims to Korea, Taiwan, the Pescadores, southern Sakhalin, the Kurile and Ryukyu islands, and all special rights in China. The Japanese pledged to settle all disputes peacefully and to pay reparations for war damages. The continued presence of American troops was assured by two American-Japanese treaties. One was a mutual-defense alliance; the second allowed American forces to use bases in Japan until the nation was able to defend itself.

Postwar developments

Prewar Japan had been the most industrialized of the Asian nations. Although the destruction of many factories and loss of its Asian possessions hurt its economy, Japan's postwar recovery was rapid and impressive. Within a few years, agriculture was so improved that the country became almost self-supporting in food. Farms became larger and more efficient as smaller, less productive farmers gave up farming and moved to the cities.

In the postwar years, Japan also developed large and efficient industries that produced products of high quality. Before the war, Japanese goods had been known for low prices and poor quality. Postwar products—photographic, optical, electronic, and automotive—could compete with any in the world, in quality as well as in price.

Japan entered the 1970's as Asia's leading industrial power. Outstripping all other nations in shipbuilding and electronics manufacturing, Japan had become the world's third-ranking industrial nation. The country's economic leaders faced a growing problem in finding markets for a rapidly expanding volume of production. The problem arose partly from the fact that Japan could not exploit its logical market, the Asian mainland, because of Communist China. Nevertheless, Japan enjoyed general prosperity. Efforts to solve the prewar population problem met with considerable success. The birth rate declined markedly. As much of the rural population moved to the cities, Japan became a truly urbanized, industrialized society.

The United States was Japan's best customer and principal supplier. The trade balance favored the United States for many years. Japanese attempts to increase sales in the United States met with boycotts by American importers and pressure for "voluntary export controls." In the late 1960's and early 1970's, however, the balance of trade swung heavily in favor of Japan. The United States increased its pressure for export controls and for abolition of controls making it difficult to import into Japan. The United States joined other nations in successfully bringing pressure for an upward revaluation of Japanese money.

Postwar prosperity did not benefit every Japanese equally, but much wealth did seep downward. Two far-reaching social changes occurred. (1) Women received greater legal, political, and social freedom. (2) The authority of the family, traditionally the center of all Japanese life, de-clined. Japanese youths were freed from much of the parental authority of earlier days.

The Cold War led to a reversal of Japan's international position. Occupation policy had limited the armed forces and military production of Japan and required a constitutional promise to renounce war. The communist victory in China and the stalemate in Korea changed American attitudes. It now seemed necessary for Japan to be able to defend itself and aid the West in case of war in Asia. Japan was therefore urged to increase its armed forces.

The Japanese were not eager to rearm. Many of them feared a return of the military domination of prewar days. They preferred to spend their money building peacetime industries, expanding exports, and raising living standards. The United States therefore supplied money to help rebuild Japan's armed forces as well as its industries.

Political life and foreign relations

Japanese political life continued to reflect important disagreements over the nation's domestic and foreign policies. The conservative democratic party consistently controlled the national parliament, but socialist and other left-wing parties were loud in their criticism of the governments. They severely criticized the government for signing the mutual security pact with the United States, a measure scheduled for review in 1970. Government critics denounced the presence of American bases on Japanese soil and insisted on the return of Okinawa to Japan. They also protested the visits of American nuclear-powered vessels to Japanese ports.

Relations with the United States continued to be friendly. In 1968 the United States returned the Bonin and Volcano islands, including Iwo Jima, to Japan. In November 1969 President Nixon and Prime Minister Eisaku Sato met and reached an agreement whereby the island of Okinawa was to be returned to Japan in 1972. The United States was to retain military bases on the island for the security of both countries but was to remove all nuclear weapons. The two leaders also discussed the eventual return of the Ryukyu island chain to Japan.

The close United States–Japanese relations were shaken during later years of the Nixon administration. When President Nixon reestablished relations with mainland China in 1971, the Japanese were dismayed because they had not been given advance information, which hurt the ruling party in an election then being held. They also resented the new economic pressures put upon them by the United States and other nations. By the 1970's Japan had become the greatest industrial power in Asia, as well as the third greatest in the world. It had been a faithful ally of the United States since World War II. To some Americans it seemed a diplomatic blunder for the United States to treat Japan in such an offhand fashion.

Taiwan

When the Nationalists were driven from China in 1949, they established themselves on the large island of Taiwan, about a hundred miles from the Chinese mainland. Their government, called the Republic of China, was democratic in appearance, but in reality was a one-party dictatorship under Chiang Kai-shek.

The Republic of China (often called Nationalist China) held China's permanent seat on the United Nations Security Council until the People's Republic of China was admitted to the UN in 1971. The admitting resolution expelled the Nationalists from the UN, but they had withdrawn from the organization beforehand.

The United States had given aid to Chiang Kai-shek for many years, and had kept troops and a fleet based on Taiwan. In the new agreements with the People's Republic of China, the United States promised to withdraw its troops from Taiwan "as soon as the tension in the area was reduced."

The Philippines

In 1934, after agitation in both the Philippines and the United States, the United States Congress passed an act granting independence to the Philippines. Freedom was delayed by World War II and by Japanese occupation of the islands, but on July 4, 1946, an independent Republic of the Philippines was proclaimed, with a constitution

HISTORY THROUGH ART

Japanese Advertising Poster

Postwar Japan, in spite of strong American influence, maintained and guarded many of its ancient traditions. Two of these, the art of print-making and the tea ceremony, are represented in the poster above. Bold yet subtly colored, it illustrates the superb graphic technique of the Japanese, whose prints have influenced artists and advertising throughout the world. The purity and sophistication of the poster are well suited to the product it advertises: "Tanko, the Magazine About Tea for Devotees of the Tea Cult."

similar to the Constitution of the United States.

The two nations remained closely linked. The United States kept Philippine military bases under ninety-nine-year leases and gave the Philippines preferential tariff treatment. It contributed large sums of money to repair war damage and help rebuild the islands' economy. Philippine foreign policy was strongly pro-Western. The new republic joined SEATO and signed a mutual-defense treaty with the United States.

In the early 1970's, peace in the Philippines was threatened by communist-led guerrillas and

by a revolt of Moslems. Proclaiming the need to deal vigorously with these and other problems, President Marcos declared martial law and took several other steps that led the Philippines a long way toward one-man rule.

Indonesia

You have read about the Netherlands East Indies, administered by the Dutch for many years. This archipelago of some 3,000 islands includes

Sumatra and Java (see map, opposite). The Dutch also controlled parts of Borneo and New Guinea.

During World War II the Netherlands East Indies were occupied by the Japanese. After the war, Achmed Sukarno led a nationalist independence movement in armed resistance against Dutch return. After a bitter struggle the United Nations intervened to secure a cease-fire. In 1949 the Netherlands granted independence to the islands. They became the Republic of Indonesia, with Sukarno as president.

Indonesia faced problems similar to those of many other newly independent countries—few trained civil servants or competent business administrators, a high rate of illiteracy, and many political parties. Political power was concentrated in the heavily populated island of Java, where the capital, Jakarta (formerly Batavia), was located.

Indonesia experienced fifteen years of poor government under Sukarno. The economy of the country slowed almost to a standstill. Wild and reckless government spending brought the nation near to bankruptcy. Adventurism in foreign policy was unsettling. In 1966 General Suharto, in a coup, took over the central government. The government remained weak, inefficient, and corrupt, but the economic condition of the country slowly improved.

Malaysia and Singapore

In 1963, Malaya, Singapore, and British (northern) Borneo, which had all become independent of Great Britain, united to form the Federation of Malaysia. The new nation faced difficult problems. Externally, the Philippines claimed part of northern Borneo, while Sukarno proclaimed that Malaysia was a British scheme to maintain colonialism and "encircle" Indonesia. Internally, the federation was threatened by a clash of peoples and cultures. In the nation as a whole there were more Malays than Chinese, with a small percentage of other ethnic groups, including Indians. Singapore, however, had a large majority of Chinese. Most Malays were uneducated, easy-going farmers. The Chinese were city dwellers, technically able and economically aggressive. Malays controlled the federation government; the Chinese controlled most of the business and the wealth.

Fearing that the Chinese might increase their political influence, the Malays forced Singapore to secede from the federation in 1965. Then, in 1969, serious riots broke out in Malaysia. Malay mobs threatened to eliminate the Chinese and Indians from any part in political life, and possibly to drive them out of the country. The Chinese retaliated by raising the price of goods and by refusing loans to farmers. The Malays could not run the economy by themselves. The important rubber industry was badly affected. Malaysia's continued survival was threatened.

CHECKUP

1. What were the two chief aims of American occupation forces in Japan? In each case, what were the results?

2. How did Japan's economy improve after World War II? What problem remained?

3. When did the Philippines become independent? What links remained between it and the United States?

4. LOCATE: Japan, Indonesia, Malaysia, Taiwan, Singapore.

4   Continental Southeast Asia became a battleground of the Cold War

Continental Southeast Asia consists of the nations of Burma, Thailand, Laos, Cambodia, North Vietnam, and South Vietnam (see map, page 806). All of these nations were independent by 1954, but the sense of nationalism remained weak. Populations were divided by tribal and religious differences. Governments, controlled by the wealthy, were often inefficient and corrupt and commanded little loyalty from the people they ruled. Although the region was fertile and rich in minerals, its people had a low standard of living. A so-called double revolution—against foreign influence and against exploitation by rich natives—gained momentum in the area after World War II.

Burma

Since before World War II, British-held Burma had been important as the starting point of the Burma Road, over which supplies moved to China. Japanese armies invaded Burma in 1942 and held it until war's end. After the war the Burmese did not want the British back, nor did the British try to return. In 1948, Burma was declared an independent republic.

The new nation faced difficulties: lack of a strong central government, few trained civil servants, tribal and political fighting, and communist attempts to seize the country. The first premier, U Nu, headed a coalition government that restored order and made reforms in land distribution, agriculture, education, and public health.

Democratic government did not last long. The coalition that had pacified the country broke up into bickering groups. In 1958 the army took over the government and proceeded to suppress uprisings, cut living costs, and eliminate corruption.

Geographic position made neutralism necessary for Burma. The government accepted help from the United States, the Soviet Union, China, and Japan, but refused to take sides in the East-West conflict. It declined to join SEATO.

Thailand

Thailand (formerly Siam) had never been a European colony. In World War II it was occupied by Japan. Under Japanese pressure, Thailand declared war on Great Britain and the United States and became a Japanese ally. Later it renounced the alliance and was the first former Axis ally to be admitted to the United Nations.

The strains of the war and postwar years brought many governmental changes. In 1958 the army took control, establishing a military dictatorship. The Thai government was strongly pro-Western. It was one of the three Asian members of SEATO and received military and economic aid from the United States. During the Vietnam War the United States bombed other parts of Southeast Asia from bases in Thailand. Thai troops fought in Cambodia on the Allied side. When United States forces were withdrawn from Vietnam, some troops and many aircraft went to bases in Thailand.

The French in Indo-China

You have read how the French became the dominant power in the eastern part of Southeast Asia, a region that became known as French Indo-China. During World War II, some French collaborators welcomed the Japanese. In 1945, however, the Japanese invaders expelled the French completely and set up three "independent" kingdoms—Laos, Cambodia, and Vietnam.

Unlike the British in Burma, the French tried to return after the war. The League for the Independence of Vietnam (the Viet Minh), led by a long-time communist, Ho Chi Minh, resisted French return. At first Ho and the French agreed that Vietnam should be a free (but not completely independent) state associated with France. This arrangement led to conflicts. In 1946, war broke out between the French and the Viet Minh.

Ho and his followers set up a government in the north; the French set up a puppet emperor in the south. The northern Democratic Republic of Vietnam was recognized and supported by the communist bloc; South Vietnam was recognized and supported by France, Great Britain, and the United States.

The French fought a long and costly war against Viet Minh forces, which were aided by Communist China. The French received military supplies from the United States. In May 1954 the Viet Minh crushingly defeated a French army at Dienbienphu, and France agreed to negotiate.

The Geneva Agreements. Between May and July in 1954, delegates from North and South Vietnam, Cambodia, Laos, Communist China, France, Great Britain, the United States, and the Soviet Union met at Geneva to work out arrangements for the future of Indo-China. According to the so-called Geneva Agreements, Laos was to remain independent. All foreign troops were to withdraw, but a communist-dominated group, the Pathet Lao, was left in control of two northern

PREDICTIONS OF KARL MARX

Karl Marx, as you read in Chapter 21, made several predictions about the future. He based these on history as he saw it and on the industrialized societies of the late 1800's. Events have not worked out as Marx thought they would, and neither communism nor capitalism developed as he foresaw. The column on the left, below, summarizes some of Marx's predictions. The column on the right, based on today's vantage point, shows what happened.

Marx predicted	What happened
Capitalist society would undergo increasingly severe depressions until wealth would be concentrated in the hands of a few capitalists, with a vast mass of suffering proletarians.	Capitalism has been more flexible than Marx predicted. Although there have been depressions, the rich have not grown richer and the poor poorer. In capitalist nations—the United States and most of Western Europe—wealth has been distributed more and more equitably, with workers receiving an increasingly larger share of the profits and standards of living constantly rising.
The proletarians in industrially advanced nations would unite and seize power by force in a revolution.	Communist revolutions have occurred in industrially backward nations, such as the Soviet Union and China. And they have been carried out by small groups of highly trained and disciplined revolutionists, not by the masses.
After a period characterized by a "dictatorship of the proletariat," the state would "wither away."	In such communist countries as Russia and China, there is no "dictatorship of the proletariat," but rather a dictatorship tightly controlled by a small minority of the Communist Party. The state shows little sign of "withering away."
Under communism, a truly classless society would come into existence. People would contribute what they could, and receive what they needed.	In communist countries, important party members, scientists, engineers, and other professionals enjoy higher incomes, better housing, and more privileges than other citizens. The children of these privileged people have a better chance for higher education.

provinces. Cambodia was recognized as independent and, by stubborn insistence, avoided being divided. Neither Laos nor Cambodia could make foreign alliances.

Vietnam was divided into two zones at the seventeenth parallel (see map, page 806), with Ho Chi Minh in control of the north. There was to be an election in 1956 to choose a government to unite the country.

South Vietnam and the United States were the only nations that refused to sign the Geneva Agreements. The Vietnamese opposed any continued partition. The United States felt that the terms represented a surrender to the communist bloc.

The two Vietnams

The Geneva Agreements of 1954 meant a victory for Ho Chi Minh. North Vietnam had most of the industry and minerals of the region and enough good land to be almost self-sufficient in food. With Chinese and Soviet help, the North Vietnamese rebuilt and expanded industry.

South Vietnam was in chaos. A newly formed government faced a shattered economy, many refugees from the north, a disorganized army, and fighting among political and religious factions, several of which had private armies.

The head of the new government was Ngo Dinh Diem (NOH DIN ZIM), member of a wealthy family. He disarmed the private armies and restored order. With American help he reorganized and strengthened the army. His was a "strong man" government. He outlawed the Communist Party, tried to suppress all other opposition, and showed little interest in reform or in winning support in the country. He refused to hold the elections called for.

The resumption of war. In 1959, war broke out again, waged by guerrillas called the Viet Cong. Many of them were southern peasants. These peasants, who sided with Ho Chi Minh's communist government, were taken north, trained in guerrilla warfare, and then returned south. They were fierce fighters, skilled in sudden attacks, ambushes, and terrorism.

The warfare was also political. The Viet Cong offered land reform, neutralism, and peace. By persuasion and terror, they won either active peasant support or passive acceptance.

Ngo Dinh Diem met both internal dissatisfaction and the Viet Cong danger with harsher repression. In November 1963 there was a *coup d'état* in which Diem was assassinated and his government was replaced by a military group. In the next three years, nine different military groups ruled South Vietnam.

American involvement. The involvement of the United States in the Vietnam War began almost imperceptibly and grew by slow stages, without a declaration of war or much information to the American people. President Eisenhower sent military and economic aid. President Kennedy continued this policy, and also sent American "advisers" to the South Vietnamese. As the guerrilla war increased in intensity, so did American commitments. American "advisers" went into battle with the South Vietnamese troops.

American troop strength began to reach significant size under President Johnson when Americans went openly into battle. Different reasons were given for the American presence: that the Chinese must be stopped from expanding; that the spread of communism must be halted; that, according to the "domino theory," if South Vietnam fell, other nations of Southeast Asia would fall, one by one; that the North Vietnamese were invading South Vietnam territory as aggressors.

In 1965 President Johnson ordered air attacks on North Vietnam and the country was subjected to heavy bombing. At the same time, the President was making both open and secret peace proposals to the North Vietnamese.

Opposition grew in the United States to American participation in the war. In the Senate a group of opposition leaders tried and failed to stop the war effort by cutting off funds. Peace marches, sit-ins, and teach-ins took place throughout the country.

In 1967 President Thieu and Vice President Ky were elected in South Vietnam, amid widespread reports of fraud. Thieu and Ky brought to an end the succession of "revolving door" governments.

In January 1968 the North Vietnamese and Viet Cong staged a big offensive, overturning many village governments and threatening several South Vietnamese cities, including Saigon. On March 31, President Johnson announced a limited halt to the bombing of North Vietnam and stated that he would not again be a candidate for the Presidency. Soon thereafter came an agreement with the North Vietnamese to begin negotiating. A peace conference met in Paris, but soon became deadlocked.

President Nixon was elected on a pledge to end the war. He soon announced a limited withdrawal of American troops. Complete withdrawal, he said, would take place on a scheduled, but secret, timetable. The Paris peace talks remained deadlocked. In 1970 the President announced an invasion of Cambodia and resumed the bombing of North Vietnam. American anti-war demonstrations increased.

During 1971 and 1972, troop withdrawals left only 25,000 American troops in South Vietnam. However, there were increased bombings of Laos, Cambodia, and North Vietnam. The President also announced the mining of North Vietnam's coastal waters.

In 1973, during secret talks between representatives of the United States and North Vietnam, agreement was reached for a cease-fire and the end of the war in South Vietnam. The United

810

The South Vietnam War

In South Vietnam the United States and its allies, mainly the South Vietnamese, were trying to stop aggression by the North Vietnamese. But it was an extremely difficult and complex effort. There were seldom any clearly defined battle zones as in previous wars, and villagers had to be protected in countless areas where fighting might break out at any moment. At left, a Vietnamese family hauling rice in an ox cart pulls aside to let a column of tanks pass by. The Viet Cong and their North Vietnamese allies usually fought from hideouts in jungles, caves, and hillsides. Below, American helicopters and ground troops search for enemy guerillas. In 1973, after talks between Le Duc Tho of North Vietnam and Henry Kissinger of the United States, above right, the United States withdrew its troops from South Vietnam.

American troops are here shown boarding an airplane in South Vietnam for return to the United States. After the troops left, fighting resumed between North and South Vietnam.

States withdrew its remaining troops. American prisoners of war held in North Vietnam came home. However, United States air forces withdrew only to Thailand, and the fleet remained along the coast. American bombing in Cambodia continued until Congress outlawed it. There was no clearcut ending of the war, and sporadic fighting continued in South Vietnam. The United States continued to supply aid. In 1975 South Vietnam fell to the Viet Cong, and the long war finally came to an end.

Controversy over the Vietnam War, and over the part played in it by the United States, would continue for many years. North and South Vietnam, as well as Laos and Cambodia, were widely devastated. Countless refugees were homeless.

There had been millions of casualties and the expenditure of billions of dollars. The United States had been torn by savage disagreements at home and severely criticized abroad.

CHECKUP

1. How was Thailand involved in the Vietnam War?

2. What were the chief provisions of the Geneva Agreements?

3. What reasons were given for United States participation in the war?

4. What extensions of the war took place under President Nixon?

5. IDENTIFY: U Nu, Ho Chi Minh, Viet Cong, "domino theory."

812

CHAPTER REVIEW

Chapter 40 The Nations of Eastern Asia Suffered from Internal Conflicts (1945–1970's)

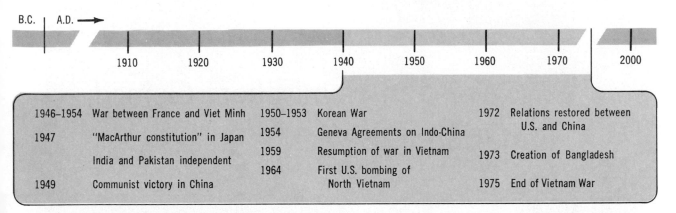

1946–1954	War between France and Viet Minh	1950–1953	Korean War
1947	"MacArthur constitution" in Japan	1954	Geneva Agreements on Indo-China
	India and Pakistan independent	1959	Resumption of war in Vietnam
		1964	First U.S. bombing of North Vietnam
1949	Communist victory in China		

1972 Relations restored between U.S. and China

1973 Creation of Bangladesh

1975 End of Vietnam War

CHAPTER SUMMARY

Many Asian colonies became independent after World War II. India, under Nehru, adopted a mixed economy but could make few gains because of its constantly growing population. Foreign affairs were complicated by conflicts with Pakistan and China. Pakistan faced similar domestic problems; in addition, it was separated into two parts. Attempted democracy gave way to military dictatorship. After civil war, East Pakistan became Bangladesh.

In China a communist victory overthrew the Nationalists. A dictatorship under Mao Tse-tung made drastic changes in China's economy. Disagreements with Russia led to serious competition for communist world leadership and to restoration of relations with the United States.

Korea was divided after the war. When communist North Korea invaded South Korea in 1950, it was repulsed by UN forces and an armistice was eventually signed.

Japan, occupied by the United States, lost its wartime territorial gains but underwent remarkable agricultural and industrial recovery. However, the problem of finding export markets remained. Two other island nations—Taiwan and the Philippines—were closely linked with the United States.

Indonesia under Sukarno suffered from economic mismanagement and belligerent foreign ventures. He was deposed and Suharto became the ruler. The new Federation of Malaysia was endangered by cultural and economic differences.

Southeast Asia experienced serious difficulties. Burma became a military dictatorship, neutral in the Cold War. Thailand, also a dictatorship, was strongly pro-Western. In Indo-China, France waged a long war and was defeated by the communist-led Viet Minh. The Geneva Agreements neutralized Laos and Cambodia, and divided Vietnam, but war broke out again a few years later. In the 1960's the United States became increasingly involved in the Vietnam war. It fought there for ten years and then withdrew.

QUESTIONS FOR DISCUSSION

1. Nehru began a program of modernization for India that emphasized industrialization. What objectives was he hoping to reach?

2. How do you explain the fact that, although untouchability has been outlawed in India, it has not disappeared?

3. Many underdeveloped countries, including India, have adopted a mixed economy. Explain whether you think there is any merit in this kind of economic organization.

4. Why must the future development of India and Communist China be considered of great importance to Asia?

5. Why do you think some people in the world favor Russia's policy of peaceful coexistence, while others support China's policy of national wars of liberation?

6. What is your position on the United States government's policy in Vietnam?

PROJECTS

1. Write a short essay explaining what the American attitude should be toward the conflict between China and the Soviet Union.

2. As an Indian, write a letter to the editor of an American newspaper in favor of India's policy of neutrality.

The Western Hemisphere Gained Importance in World Affairs

In your study of world history, you have read how the people of first one region and then another wielded power and influence—among them the Egyptians of the Nile Valley, the Assyrians in the Fertile Crescent, the Chinese under the Han dynasty, and the Romans of the empire period. With the beginning of the modern era, the focus of power shifted to Western Europe. Through such great movements as the age of exploration, the Industrial Revolution, and the imperialism of the late 1800's, the European impact was worldwide.

By the mid-1900's this situation had changed. As one historian wrote: "In 1945 the great powers of Europe were still thought to be decisive factors in world affairs. Since then, the old continent has become far less important. Today the rivalry between two superpowers, the United States and Russia, determines the fate of the rest of the world. At the same time the rise of the former colonial regions to independence has introduced a wholly new element into the international balance of power...."

You have read about the East-West rivalry of the Cold War and about the new nations of Africa and Asia. Throughout these discussions you have read from time to time about the important role played by the United States. It is now appropriate to study the United States itself in the years after World War II, in order to understand better

Technicians working inside a guided missile

how and why it came to play so prominent a role in world leadership.

It is well to remember, however, that the United States is not alone in the Western Hemisphere. It has often overshadowed its neighbors —Canada to the north, Latin America to the south—in power and prestige, but the importance of these other nations of the Western Hemisphere in world affairs has also constantly increased since World War II.

1   Unstable economic and political conditions disturbed Latin America

During and just after World War II, the nations of the Western Hemisphere entered into several mutual defense pacts. Inter-American cooperation went a step further in 1948, at Bogotá, Colombia, when delegates from the twenty-one countries of the Pan American Union met and founded the Organization of American States (OAS). Each member was represented on the Council, the policy-making body. Regular conferences were to be held at five-year intervals, with special meetings and conferences when needed.

This move represented a continuation of the Good Neighbor Policy, through which the United States sought cooperation with its southern neighbors. Stresses in the postwar era, however, often made it difficult to live up to this ideal.

Economic problems

World War II brought prosperity, full employment, and a somewhat higher standard of living to parts of Latin America. After the war the situation changed. There were several one-crop countries (those in which the economy depended almost entirely on the production and export of one crop, such as coffee or sugar). These countries and others needed industry, but industrialization needed capital. The Latin American countries tried to attract capital from United Nations agencies—the World Bank, the UN Special Fund—and from foreign investors. They had scant success.

Latin Americans mainly blamed the United States because, out of its vast program of foreign aid, relatively little went to Latin America. Their complaint was justified, but much blame also rested with Latin America's own wealthy ruling class. Such people avoided paying taxes needed for education and public welfare. Many chose to invest their money abroad rather than risk it at home. United States aid was frequently misused through governmental inefficiency or corruption.

The Alliance for Progress. In 1960 the United States established a Special Progress Fund from which loans could be made to Latin American governments for land and tax reforms, and for building schools, hospitals, and roads. In 1961 the Fund was expanded into a ten-year project known as the Alliance for Progress. Its goals were, among others, improved housing, education, and sanitation, tax reforms, and gradual reduction of tariffs and trade barriers. Aid was to be increased in countries that made progress, decreased in countries that did not. Costs were to be divided equally between the United States and Latin America.

The Alliance was expected to score great successes, but for many reasons it did not. Land reforms and social changes came slowly. Rapid population growth made worse such problems as health, education, and housing.

President Nixon promised modifications in United States policy toward Latin America. He wanted the relationship to become more of a mutual partnership, less dominated by the United States. However, the amount of financial aid he promised was less than the amounts of previous years, and less than Latin Americans had hoped for. In 1971, while trying to equalize American exports and imports, he included Latin American nations under a 10 percent surcharge on imports to the United States. Since Latin America was already importing much more from the United States than it was exporting, Nixon could have excluded Latin American goods from the import surcharge, but he did not. He did make a change in the policy of "tied" aid—the requirement that American aid be spent only for American goods and shipped in American ships. He allowed aid funds to be spent in Latin America as well as in the United States.

Government instability

Latin America consisted of democratic as well as dictatorial governments. In many countries, small groups overthrew democratic governments —especially where election results displeased them—and took over themselves. These groups, called *juntas,* usually consisted of military officers closely allied with conservative landholders and businessmen.

Sometimes support and encouragement of the juntas came from outside. In the 1950's the United States was accused of helping to overthrow a liberal government in Guatemala, which it claimed was communist. In 1963 a military group took over the government in the Dominican Republic from a liberal, popularly elected president. When a revolt later broke out among left-wing forces, the United States sent in troops. After negotiations, an election was held and a conservative was elected president.

The United States was widely criticized in both these cases for by-passing the Organization of American States and the United Nations, and for helping to overthrow legitimate governments. Its defenders replied that the OAS had been asked to act, but had refused. They said that the United States should not allow a communist government to take over a strategically located country.

However, the overthrow of a Latin American government did not usually need help from the outside. In 1964 the Brazilian army rebelled against a leftist-oriented government, and took over. It set up a tightly organized rule, with

censorship, purge of elected legislative bodies, and torture of political prisoners. It still held power ten years later.

In 1973 Uruguay, which had long been praised as an example of democratic government, fell to a military junta. The country had been in economic and political turmoil for years. Groups of guerrillas, the Tupemaros, had terrorized Uruguay, capturing industrial leaders, local and foreign, and holding them for ransom. The army was called on to wipe out the guerrillas, which it did. The military forces then demanded more power in the government. In July 1973 the president, a conservative, dissolved Congress and replaced it with a twenty-member Council of State, headed by himself.

Argentina. Argentina, which had been ruled by a military junta, was permitted to hold elections in 1973. The country had severe problems, including an economic crisis brought on by the highest inflation in the world and by an almost total loss of foreign capital reserves. Radical guerrillas robbed banks and kidnapped Argentine and foreign businessmen, holding them for ransom. Strikes and riots disturbed the country.

Hector Campara was chosen president in the 1973 election. He stated that he was only a stand-in for Juan Perón, who had been dictator of Argentina until he was ousted in 1946. Campara soon resigned. In a new election, Perón became president. Whether the seventy-seven-year-old leader would be able to control the inflation, strikes, and urban terror was uncertain.

Chile. Salvador Allende was elected president of Chile in 1970, the first democratically elected president running on a Marxist platform in a non-communist country. Allende was one of the founders of the Chilean Socialist Party and had served his country in several elective and appointive offices. He pledged nationalization of major foreign firms in mining, banking, and communications, as well as a strong program of land reform.

Allende nationalized the copper industry, took over the operations of International Telephone and Telegraph Company (I.T.T.), and established diplomatic relations with the communist

Latin American nations struggled to solve their problems in various ways. In Cuba, Castro's rebels were supplied, above left, by local farmers. United States citizens were shocked when Castro declared himself a communist; upper right, he stands before a picture of Karl Marx. The United States sometimes intervened with troops in attempts to preserve order. In the Dominican Republic, below left, local women pass in front of a Marine tank. More peaceful influence was exerted through the Alliance for Progress and UNESCO. Below right, UNESCO aid supports the work of solar energy technicians in Mexico.

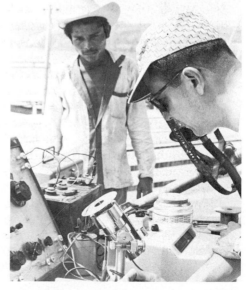

government of Cuba. But the country was torn by strikes and riots, ravaged by inflation, and short of food. In 1973 a revolt against Allende broke out. Doctors, dentists, and nurses went on strike, protesting the inflation, which had soared 235 percent in the past year. Truck drivers and copper miners also went on strike, paralyzing the nation's economy. In the midst of the chaos, a Chilean military junta seized the government and took over management of the nation. Allende died, probably by suicide. Thus ended the first freely elected Marxist government and also, at least for a time, a long tradition of democratic government in Chile.

Cuba

In 1959 Fidel Castro led a successful revolt against the dictatorship of Fulgencio Batista in Cuba, seized the island nation, and set up a communist government. The government confiscated privately owned industries and land. Some land was given to peasants, some operated as collectives.

American property was confiscated with only vague promises of repayment. Cuba's relations with the Soviet Union became friendly. It became evident that, in Castro's Cuba, communism had won a foothold in the Western Hemisphere. Castro tried, by subversion, to spread revolution to other Latin American countries.

The United States government took several actions. It broke diplomatic relations. It boycotted Cuban products, and tried to persuade its OAS and NATO allies to do so. It helped a group of Cuban exiles to invade Cuba at the Bay of Pigs, a disastrous failure.

When American intelligence services learned, in 1962, that the Soviet Union was sending nuclear missiles to Cuba, and building missile sites there, a serious crisis arose in relations between the United States and the Soviet Union. After a tense confrontation, the Soviet leaders agreed to dismantle the bases and remove the missiles. The United States agreed not to invade Cuba.

The Cuban standard of living remained low in the 1960's and 1970's, but Castro's government proved to be stable, free from corruption, and strongly dictatorial. Its attempts at subversion in Latin America were unsuccessful and were given up. Anti-Americanism remained strong. In economic policy the government leaned increasingly on the Soviet Union. In foreign policy, after a period of freedom, Cuba more and more followed the Soviet lead.

Mexico

Not all Latin American nations have become dictatorships. One that has not is Mexico. Since a popular revolution in 1911 and adoption of a revolutionary constitution in 1917, Mexico has had an honorable record of elected presidents.

Presidents Obregon and Calles in the 1920's started a program of agrarian reform—that is, the breaking up of large estates and distribution of the land among poor farmers. In the 1930's President Cárdenas continued the program of agrarian reform and also put into effect other basic reforms of the Mexican Revolution, including a closely controlled national economy and government ownership of the oil and railroad industries. Later governments took over the electrical power and telephone industries while continuing the program of agrarian reform.

Mexico has usually cooperated in the foreign policies of the OAS and the United States, but not always. It has, for example, maintained diplomatic relations with Cuba under Castro, although these relations became strained beginning in 1969 when Cuba granted political asylum to hijackers of a Mexican plane.

Although Mexico is among the leaders of the Latin American nations in economic growth, a great spurt in population has raised problems. Industrialization has produced a prosperous middle class, but many urban workers remain desperately poor and there are still millions of landless farmers. However, the Mexican government has tried to ease these conditions by social and economic reforms and by continuing to distribute land.

CHECKUP

1. What blame rested with the Latin American ruling class for the area's failure to industrialize?

2. What criticism fell upon the United States for the overthrow of Latin American governments? How did its defenders reply?

3. Describe how juntas took over two Latin American governments.

4. What actions did the government of the United States take against Castro's government in Cuba? With what success?

5. IDENTIFY: OAS, one-crop country, Alliance for Progress, "tied" aid, Perón, Allende, Cárdenas.

2 Canada became a vital area of the modern world

Canada was relatively isolated for many years before World War I, but was brought actively into world affairs by the two world wars. After World War II, Canada became a vigorous supporter of the United Nations and an important member of NATO. It loaned almost 4 billion dollars to other countries after World War II, and welcomed thousands of refugees from Europe.

Economic growth

Canada experienced considerable economic development after World War II. Much of the country remained basically agricultural. Production of crops such as wheat, barley, flax, and feed grains provided a surplus for export. At first this surplus was a problem, but world shortages during the 1960's and 1970's brought large purchases by China and the Soviet Union. Most of the surplus disappeared.

Canada's industries also grew after World War II. The large Canadian forest areas provided many wood products. The wood pulp and paper industries expanded, selling most of their paper to the United States for newspapers. Development of electric power and improvement of transportation stimulated the mining of iron, coal, uranium, and—especially—greater production of oil and gas. Aircraft, electrical, textile, and automobile industries sprang up in the provinces of Quebec and Ontario. Much of the capital for this industrial development was furnished by the United States.

Relations with the United States

For more than a century Canada has had close relations with the United States. During and after World War II this relationship was strengthened, especially in military and economic affairs.

Canadian national defense relies heavily on the United States. The United States and Canada have a Permanent Joint Defense Committee. Together they built a line of radar installations across the Arctic, called the Distant Early Warning (DEW) Line. They also established the North American Air Defense Command.

Close economic cooperation between Canada and the United States produced the St. Lawrence Seaway, which opened a 2,400-mile waterway linking the Great Lakes and the Atlantic Ocean. The Seaway enables ocean-going ships to reach every port on the Great Lakes. Another important cooperative venture was made possible by the Columbia River Treaty, signed in 1961. It provided for joint development of the Columbia River basin. Completion of the project will double the water-storage capacity of the Pacific Northwest.

There were also problems in the economic relations between the two countries. Canadians became uneasy because many Canadian industries were owned or controlled by Americans, either as branches of American corporations or through large stock purchases. Canadians feared that too many decisions affecting their welfare might be made by people mainly interested in the welfare of their corporations.

A recent problem is the balance of trade between the two nations. The balance had been steadily favorable to the United States until, in the 1970's, it tipped to favor Canada. To regain its favorable balance, the United States might decrease its imports of Canadian manufactured goods and increase its imports of oil, gas, electricity, ores, and other primary materials. But such actions might increase Canadian unemployment and threaten the unity of Canada as a single nation.

INDIAN OCEAN

INDIA

INDONESIA

CHINA

ASIA

U. S. S. R.

EUROPE

AFRICA

AUSTRALIA

PHILIPPINES

ARCTIC OCEAN

NORTH POLE

PACIFIC OCEAN

ATLANTIC OCEAN

NEW ZEALAND

CANADA

NORTH AMERICA

UNITED STATES

VENEZ.

BRAZIL

CUBA

SOUTH AMERICA

COL.

MEXICO

CENTRAL AMERICA

PERU

ARGENTINA

CHILE

ANTARCTIC CIRCLE

TROPIC OF CAPRICORN

EQUATOR

TROPIC OF CANCER

ARCTIC CIRCLE

THE WESTERN HEMISPHERE IN RECENT WORLD AFFAIRS

Western defense system (nations allied under NATO, CENTO, SEATO, OAS, and other treaties)

Communist nations

•••••• Distant Early Warning (DEW) Line

Separatism

Canada has, from far back, been the home of two different groups—Canadians of French descent and Canadians of British descent. They have lived side by side, but have remained essentially separate. Both have clung to their language, religion, and traditions.

In the balance of trade threat, British and French Canada might stand together, saying to the United States: "If you want our electricity, oil, and iron ore, you must take our manufactured goods." However, Canadian political unity was

weak enough, and the economic interests of some provinces sufficiently opposed to one another, that the provinces might try to negotiate their own separate trade arrangements with the United States.

During the 1960's a French-Canadian separatist movement grew especially strong in the province of Quebec. The most extreme group, the Quebec Liberation Front, wanted complete independence. Even moderate French Canadians of the Quebec Party complained of discrimination in government and industry.

Quebec politics were being reshaped by three forces: urbanization, modernization, and secularization. The society became increasingly city-dwelling, with pressing needs for industrialization and jobs. An ambitious and outspoken middle class demanded that they, not the British, should control the economy as well as the government of Quebec. Finally the state, not the church, was seen as the force needed to preserve French culture.

At an election late in 1973, the Quebec Party —the more moderate party in the province— strongly outpolled the Quebec Liberation Front. It was expected that the Quebec Party would not press for outright independence but would try to re-negotiate the status of Quebec within the Canadian federation. In any event, the federation will be subjected to many stresses in coming years—some from Quebec, some from other provinces, and some from the United States.

CHECKUP

1. How did the Canadian economy develop after World War II?

2. Why did some Canadians fear American investment in Canada?

3. What three forces have reshaped Quebec politics in recent years? What may be the result?

4. IDENTIFY: DEW Line, St. Lawrence Seaway.

3 The United States faced many problems in the postwar years

Harry S. Truman became President of the United States in 1945 when Franklin D. Roosevelt died. Truman was elected in his own right in 1948, and served until 1953. He was President when the United States began the European Recovery Program, took part in the Berlin airlift, helped form NATO, and played a leading role in the Korean War.

Truman's successor, Republican Dwight D. Eisenhower, referred to himself as a "dynamic conservative." Domestically, he carried on many of the reforms of his predecessors. He tried also to reduce the cost of government and to strengthen private initiative in the economy. In foreign affairs Eisenhower brought the Korean War to an end. During his administration, SEATO was created in an attempt to halt communism in the Far East, while the Eisenhower Doctrine provided resistance to communism in the Middle East.

John F. Kennedy, a Democrat, served as President only from 1961 to 1963. It was he who solved the Cuban missile crisis. He also initiated the Alliance for Progress and the Peace Corps. Kennedy introduced into Congress a broad program of domestic legislation that he called the New Frontier. He was assassinated before much of his legislation had been passed by Congress. Lyndon B. Johnson then became President, and

was elected as President in his own right in 1964.

Johnson's domestic program aimed at creating what he called the Great Society. It included much of Kennedy's domestic legislation, along with many new ideas. In foreign affairs Johnson was chiefly concerned with the war in Vietnam.

President Richard M. Nixon, a Republican, took office in 1969 and was re-elected in 1972. The Democrats controlled Congress, so Nixon's domestic program was largely stifled. In foreign affairs he established friendly relations with China and the Soviet Union. He also withdrew American troops from Vietnam.

The economy

After World War II the American economy reached new peaks of productivity, with huge new industries and much construction. The 1940's and 1950's had no depression but did have several recessions (periods of temporary business slowdown and increased unemployment). The 1960's had no recession, but, toward the end, inflation became a problem.

The 1970's began with a recession. The country slowly pulled out of it, but was left with high unemployment and bad inflation. The Nixon administration tried many solutions, most of them tending toward protectionism (using government means to reduce imports). It adopted export controls, stopped converting dollars into gold, adopted a temporary surcharge on imports, and persuaded foreign trading partners "voluntarily" to hold down their sales of steel and textiles to the United States. At this time most major nations were making some moves toward dismantling trade barriers. Many economists believed that American protectionism was self-defeating.

Too many American dollars had gone abroad in three ways: paying for wars; paying for businesses bought abroad by American firms; spending by American tourists. Individuals and corporations abroad speculated against the dollar. They would sell dollars and buy the currency of a nation considered strong—the currency of Switzerland or West Germany, for example. Trying to halt the speculation, the Nixon administration stopped converting dollars into gold. Then it devalued the dollar (reduced the amount of gold which the dollar called for) twice in fourteen months. But pressure continued against the dollar in the world's money markets.

Political problems

Many of the American successes of the postwar world were long-term; many of the defeats and setbacks were immediately obvious and frustrating. Some Americans tried to explain their frustrations by a "conspiracy theory." If the United States, the most powerful nation in the world, could not contain communism, they said, it was because our leaders were "soft on communism." According to advocates of the "conspiracy theory," Roosevelt, Truman, and Eisenhower, among others, conspired to "deliver America to the communists."

Senator Joseph McCarthy of Wisconsin was the most dramatic spokesman for the "conspiracy theory." Between 1950 and 1954 he questioned the loyalty of many government officials, and built up a large following. In 1954 a Senate committee investigated McCarthy's conduct and found his charges groundless. The Senate then censured him for "conduct unbecoming to a Senator." His influence collapsed.

The racial question. Black Americans freed from slavery during the Civil War had been officially granted civil rights but in fact had not received them. In many regions, both North and South, black people were prevented from voting and from obtaining decent education, jobs, and housing. Dissatisfaction grew, especially after World War II. Organizations like the Urban League and the National Association for the Advancement of Colored People (NAACP) worked to find employment and to secure civil rights for black Americans by legal action and lobbying.

A turning-point came in 1954. Then, in the case of *Brown v. Board of Education of Topeka,* the United States Supreme Court unanimously declared unconstitutional state laws requiring black children to attend separate schools. States having such laws were ordered to integrate their schools "with all deliberate speed."

This important decision encouraged the black civil rights movement. There was mass action against discrimination in public transportation, hotels, restaurants, and places of amusement. Dr. Martin Luther King, Jr. was a prominent black leader. Influenced by Gandhi, he advocated non-violent methods: boycotts, marches, and sit-ins. Dr. King was awarded the Nobel Peace Prize in 1964. In 1968 he was assassinated.

The years after 1964 saw many civil rights protests. In 1967, the United States experienced the worst disorder in the nation's history when severe riots occurred in more than fifty cities, accompanied by looting and burning. Again, after the murder of Dr. King in 1968, rioting took place in many cities.

During the Johnson administration, Congress passed several civil rights acts and a number of other laws to aid Black Americans and other minorities. The Nixon administration was less active in the field of civil rights.

Student unrest. During the middle 1960's the United States, like many other countries, was troubled by widespread unrest among college students. Beginning in 1964 at the University of California in Berkeley, strikes, confrontations, sit-ins, and the seizure of buildings disturbed campuses across the country. Black students demanded "black studies" taught by black profes-

The United States faced several pressing domestic problems in the 1950's and 1960's. The career of Senator Joseph McCarthy, left, was a lesson in vigilance against demagogues. While enjoying general prosperity, Americans became aware of pockets of poverty and tried to do something about them. At lower right, the local office of a government agency operates in New York City to help young Puerto Ricans. The most searching American self-appraisal came with the civil rights movement, led by such men as Martin Luther King, above. In August 1963, over 200,000 supporters of equal rights marched peacefully in Washington, D.C., lower left, to bring attention to their cause.

sors in separate, black-controlled departments. Minority students demanded more liberal admissions policies, with tutoring help where needed. Students, white as well as black, complained of lack of communication, absence of student voice in policy decisions, outmoded courses, and ineffective teaching methods. They revolted against the military draft. In addition, the more radical students revolted against many basic values of American society.

Most colleges and universities tried to meet the student demands. Congress and state legislatures were less cooperative, however. Some of them passed restrictive laws, and many appropriated a smaller amount of money to be used for higher education.

The withdrawal of American troops from Viet-nam and abolition of the draft seemed to put an end to the campus revolt.

The turnaround in foreign affairs

A diplomatic barrier to international unity began to be lifted in February 1972, when President Nixon made a historic visit to the People's Republic of China. He talked with Chinese officials, including Premier Chou En-lai and Chairman Mao Tse-tung, about easing relations between the United States and Communist China. A joint communique after the meetings indicated agreement on the need for increased contacts between the two nations and their peoples, and on eventual withdrawal of American troops from Taiwan.

In May 1972, President Nixon became the first

The hopes of people everywhere for lasting world peace became brighter in 1972 when relations between the United States and its long-time adversaries, the Soviet Union and the People's Republic of China, were improved. In these pictures, President Nixon of the United States shakes hands with Premier Chou En-lai of China during their meeting in Peking (left), and with Communist Party Secretary Brezhnev of the Soviet Union, in Moscow (right).

Americans as Innovators

The first art movement to grow up in the United States totally independent of European influence was abstract expressionism. It flourished in the 1950's and New York was its center. Artists of this school swirled, dribbled, and even threw paint on canvas to create exciting, vibrant compositions in which recognizable objects had completely disappeared. Some people saw this art as a reflection of a world turned upside down by war, automation, and atomic weapons. Others regarded it as a sort of modern romanticism, with the artists expressing extremely personal emotions that could only be guessed at by the onlooker. Franz Kline, a leading abstract expressionist, painted "Henry H. II," at left, in 1959–1960.

American President to visit the Soviet Union. While there he talked with Communist Party Secretary Brezhnev, Premier Kosygin, and other Soviet officials. During the visit the two nations signed an arms control treaty (page 753), an agreement on health cooperation, an environmental research pact, and an agreement on technological cooperation. At the end of the visit, the signing of a joint declaration of principles and a joint communique seemed to signal an improvement in relations between the two countries.

The moves by President Nixon toward China and the Soviet Union took the world by surprise. In general, the reaction was favorable. In each case, the initial move was followed by a period of increased friendly activity that was generally conceded to be a hopeful sign in the search for world peace and for more friendly relations among all nations. The first severe test for the new spirit of détente came in 1973 when, as you have read, warfare broke out again in the Middle East between Israel and the Arab nations.

Watergate

In July 1972, during the presidential election campaign, the Democratic headquarters in the Watergate office and apartment complex in Washington, D.C., were burglarized. The burglars were trying to photograph documents and to install listening devices.

A federal grand jury indicted seven defendants. Five pleaded guilty; two stood trial and were convicted. The trials were postponed until after the election, which President Nixon won by carrying forty-nine states.

In January 1973 the "Watergate case" began to break open with increasing charges of illegal and unethical practices committed by officials of the Nixon re-election campaign. The Senate demanded that the Justice Department prosecutors of the case be replaced by a special prosecutor, which was done. The Senate also set up a special committee to hear testimony on Watergate and related matters. Its purpose was to learn the facts about the 1972 election, and to recommend new election laws to Congress. Several law suits were filed against the Committee to Re-elect the President.

The testimony before the Senate Committee brought out a sordid picture. The burglary itself was perhaps less important than the attempt to cover it up, which implicated members of the White House staff. Also implicated was the use of funds for the re-election—some illegally given,

825

some illegally used, and some, apparently, given for special favors to be done by the government. Also of concern were certain "dirty tricks" used against Democratic contenders.

It was uncertain whether the President had known of the planned break-in; he denied it. It was also uncertain whether, for a long time, he had known of the coverup. The people of the nation were shocked and dismayed.

Their shock had not ended. In the fall of 1973, Vice-President Spiro Agnew, amid charges of bribe-taking while Governor of Maryland, resigned his Vice-Presidency and pleaded "no contest" to an indictment for income tax evasion. Under provisions of the twenty-fifth amendment to the Constitution, President Nixon nominated as the new Vice-President, and Congress confirmed, Gerald Ford, Republican minority leader of the House of Representatives.

As 1973 ended, the American people were split among those who thought that President Nixon should resign, those who thought he should be impeached, and those who thought he should serve out his second term. Faced with probable impeachment, President Nixon resigned in August 1974, and Vice-President Ford became President.

CHECKUP

1. What policies did the Nixon administration follow in trying to solve the nation's economic problems?

2. What was the conspiracy theory as applied to American foreign policy?

3. What are civil rights? What methods did Black Americans use to achieve them in the period after World War II?

4. What was the turnaround in American foreign policy? How was it received in the world?

5. IDENTIFY: New Frontier, Joseph McCarthy, *Brown v. Board of Education of Topeka,* Martin Luther King, Jr., Watergate, Spiro Agnew.

4   The United States played a leading role in science and technology

You have read how science and technology led to the large-scale industrialization that characterized the Western world and Japan in the late 1800's and early 1900's. This trend continued in the later 1900's. Although scientists and technologists of many nations made important contributions, the wealth and resources of the United States enabled it to play a leading role in developing new ideas and making them available to large numbers of people.

The Atomic Age

Of all the developments spurred by the needs of World War II, none was as important as the atomic bomb. People speak of the Atomic Age that was ushered in when the United States exploded two atomic bombs over Japan in 1945.

Attempts to limit the production of atomic bombs began when peace was signed. But an armaments race also began. Nuclear weapons testing produced dangerous fallout. Demands by people throughout the world brought a test bomb treaty in 1963 that was signed by the United States, the Soviet Union, and Great Britain, but not by France and China. You have read of other attempts to limit the wartime use of atomic power (page 753).

Atomic energy has many peacetime uses. The invention of the nuclear reactor—a device that releases and controls the energy stored in atoms—made it possible to run dynamos, generate power, and provide power for ships and submarines. Atomic energy has many uses in medicine. In the United States, atomic blasts have been used to release natural gas. Work went forward on "breeder reactors" which create more fuel than they consume, and on the production of energy by fusion.

All uses of atomic energy bring problems. Disposal of atomic waste is a particularly difficult one. Some of the material loses radioactivity fairly quickly. Some, however, remains radioactive for hundreds and even thousands of years.

Space exploration

Both the United States and the Soviet Union developed several kinds of guided missiles, with constantly increasing explosive power, maneuverability, and range, during the Cold War period. But the so-called Space Age began in 1957, when the Soviet Union sent its first artificial satellite, Sputnik I, into orbit around the earth. The Russian achievement jolted the United States into a crash program to try to equal and surpass it.

The first achievements were made by Russia. They included the first rocket to the moon, in 1959; the first rocket to go around the moon, sending back pictures of the "dark side," in 1959; the first manned orbital flight, in 1961; the first space vehicle to carry more than one person, in 1964.

After a slower start, the United States equaled, if not surpassed, the Soviet achievements. Its first manned orbital space flight took place in 1962; many followed. The United States has also carried out a wide variety of unmanned satellite programs. The Tiros series photographed the earth's cloud cover and traced the origins of cyclones and hurricanes. The Echo, Telstar, and Syncom series were communications relays. The Mariner series probed toward other planets. The Ranger series photographed the moon.

On July 20, 1969, American astronauts Neil Armstrong and Edwin Aldrin stepped from their spacecraft, Apollo II, onto the dusty surface of the moon—a dramatic proof of America's progress in science and technology. The astronauts explored the moon's surface, performed scientific experiments, and returned triumphantly to earth bearing a load of moon rocks. A number of other Apollo flights followed.

In 1973 the United States established a space shuttle. A large space vehicle, the Skylab, was put into orbit. Then a smaller vehicle, Apollo, with a crew of three astronauts, was sent to link up with it. After nearly two months in space, the astronauts returned to earth, while Skylab stayed in orbit, awaiting other crews.

The costs of space research and development are enormous. It is estimated that during the early 1970's the United States had already spent 40 billion dollars on the moon program alone. Many people protested, saying that the money could better be spent on medical research, education, and relief for the needy. Others doubted the value of manned flights, since instruments are usually more accurate than human observers.

Both American and Soviet governments continued to commit vast sums to space research. In addition to propaganda victories, advocates of space research listed other gains: (1) Military advances included reconnaissance satellites. (2) Industrial gains included increased capacity for worldwide communication and by-products such as lightweight plastics and new metals and alloys. (3) Scientific advances included better weather forecasting and enormous gains in the science of astronomy.

International scientific cooperation

The International Geophysical Year (IGY) lasted from 1957 until the end of 1958. Some 8,000 scientists from 64 nations took part. Rockets and artificial satellites measured the radiation of the sun. Observations were made of the sediment at the bottom of oceans, and of tides and currents and their effect on climate. Investigations in the polar regions gathered data about the effect of these areas on weather, and measured the melting rate of glaciers.

The Committee on Space Research of the IGY worked toward international communication with space vehicles, the exchange of space data, and agreements to avoid contaminating other planets. The United Nations set up a Committee on the Peaceful Uses of Outer Space.

The "green revolution"

The late 1960's brought good news about world food supplies. The Philippine International Rice Institute and the Rockefeller International Maize and Wheat Improvement Center, in Mexico, developed new, high-yielding seeds for low-growing rice and wheat. Combining the new seed with greater use of fertilizers and improved irrigation techniques, India in 1968 produced a wheat crop 35 percent greater than its previous

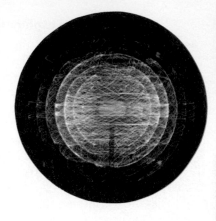

Science and technology made extraordinary progress in the years following World War II. Among man's most spectacular achievements were those involving space travel and exploration. At left is the liftoff of an American Atlas rocket. It is topped with an Agena satellite. The photograph below, taken by the crew of an American spacecraft, is a view of India and Ceylon from a distance of about 540 miles above the earth's surface. Yuri Gagarin, a Russian, was the first man to circle the earth in a spaceship. The celebration held in Moscow in his honor is shown on the opposite page, bottom left.

Much of modern science is based on nuclear physics. Above, a model of an atom—greatly enlarged—indicates its constant motion. Harnessing atomic energy holds great promise. Britain's first atomic energy plant, right, is used to generate electricity. Sailors, far right, admire the first French nuclear submarine, launched in 1967. This powerful ship can stay submerged and hidden for months without having to surface for fuel. Although nations have been secretive about their military progress, many cooperated in the International Geophysical Year. Below, far right, an American astronaut performs exterior work on Skylab while floating in space.

record. Pakistan expected to be self-sufficient in food within a year or two. In 1970 Dr. Norman E. Borlaug, Director of the Wheat Improvement Center, developer of the wheat seed, received the Nobel Peace Prize.

Such improvements seldom come without costs. The "green revolution" required more irrigation, mechanization, and commercial fertilizers, and more education in new ways of planting and of controlling insects. It was found that the rice, for example, grew well only if large amounts of fertilizer were used; that its lush foliage attracted insects; that its short, stiff straw made it hard to harvest; and that it was susceptible to several rice diseases. Nevertheless, it was an improvement, one that dealt with one of the world's severe problems—the threat of famine.

Other developments

World War II stimulated developments in the field of transportation. The use of jet propulsion enabled planes to fly great distances, faster than the speed of sound. The helicopter was especially useful in difficult terrain or densely populated regions.

New technological developments stimulated the growth of industries. One was the aircraft industry. Another, the electronics industry, included the manufacture of radios, television sets, and computers. Another industry centered on the manufacture of synthetic products, including fibers, such as nylon, and a whole range of plastics.

In medicine, a major step toward understanding genetics was the synthesis of a single gene of yeast by Har Gobind Khorana in the early 1970's. Research in this field would, it was predicted, reveal secrets of heredity that are presently unknown to scientists. Another study produced favorable results in the drug treatment of leukemia, a blood disease formerly considered incurable. Chemists also unraveled the chemical structure of an antibody molecule, a step toward better understanding of immunity. An American and a British chemist won Nobel Prizes for this feat.

Ease of communication, a gift of the new technological developments, served also to point up the vast differences between "have" and "have

not" nations. The people of advanced nations like the United States became concerned over the "revolution of rising expectations" among peoples of underdeveloped nations in Latin America, Africa, and Asia.

The world's productive capacity is concentrated in the northern hemisphere, mainly in the United States, Europe, and Japan. Much of the world's raw materials—oil, copper, tin, natural rubber, bauxite, coffee, timber—are held by underdeveloped countries, most of them in the southern hemisphere. Achieving a fair distribution of raw materials and of finished goods among the world's peoples is one of the many difficult challenges that lie ahead.

The prospect before us

And so you have reached the end of the book, but not the end of the story. History is a tale that never ends. Each day's headlines bring reports of new developments. If they were really new—with no connection to anything that existed before—the world would be impossible to understand. But the new grows out of the old and is built upon it. Knowing what has gone before, you are better able to understand what happens next.

Ours is a dangerous world, but an endlessly interesting one. Signs of danger are plentiful, but so are signs of progress. Mankind fears war, but also hopes for victory over disease and hunger. Those who understand the interests and challenges of the world have a great responsibility to help achieve the peace upon which, in our times, all of humanity depends.

CHECKUP

1. When did the Atomic Age begin? What peacetime uses of atomic energy were developed?

2. What event launched the Space Age? What were some of the scientific programs of American satellites?

3. What objections were made to space research programs? How did their advocates defend them?

4. What was the "green revolution"? In what ways did it fall short of being a perfect solution?

5. IDENTIFY: nuclear reactor, IGY, Skylab.

CHAPTER REVIEW

Chapter 41   The Western Hemisphere Gained Importance in World Affairs   (1940–1970's)

1948	OAS founded	1958	First U.S. artificial satellite	1962	Cuban missile crisis
1952	First U.S. hydrogen bomb	1959	Castro to power in Cuba	1967	Riots in American cities
1954	*Brown vs. Topeka*		St. Lawrence Seaway completed	1969	U.S. astronauts land on moon
1957	Sputnik I orbited by Russia	1961	Alliance for Progress initiated	1972	Nixon visits China and U.S.S.R.
1957–1958	International Geophysical Year		Columbia River Treaty signed	1973	Watergate and Agnew scandals

CHAPTER SUMMARY

Inter-American cooperation was furthered by the formation of the OAS. Latin America was troubled by economic problems and only partly helped by the Alliance for Progress. Many countries, including Brazil and Uruguay, were controlled by dictators or military juntas. Allende, elected president of Chile, worked to establish a Marxist state there but was overthrown by military forces. Castro set up a communist regime in Cuba. Russian aid to Cuba brought a grave Soviet–United States confrontation in 1962.

Postwar Canada enjoyed a manufacturing and mining boom. The Canadians feared being too dependent, economically, on the United States. Trade balance with the United States was a problem, but a strong separatist movement among French Canadians was more serious.

The American economy reached new peaks of productivity, but poverty, recessions, inflation, and the shrinking value of the dollar were serious problems. McCarthyism won many followers, but was quickly discredited. The Supreme Court's school desegregation decision led to many civil rights campaigns. The United States established relations with China and friendlier relations with the Soviet Union. The Watergate and Agnew scandals created grave troubles.

The United States and the Soviet Union competed in the Space Age. The United States placed men on the moon in 1969. The synthesis of a single gene of yeast and the chemical structure of antibodies were important biochemical discoveries. Many new developments offered both threats and promises. The "green revolution" promised to help relieve the threat of widespread famine; its need for chemical fertilizer threatened the environment.

QUESTIONS FOR DISCUSSION

1. What recent evidence has there been of both cooperation and friction among the nations of the Western Hemisphere? How can the United States further improve relations in the Americas?

2. How has Castroism helped Cuba? How has it hurt Cuba?

3. There is considerable inequality in the distribution of wealth in the United States. Is this situation desirable, or should there be a change? Justify your position.

4. A number of countries have learned how to make atomic bombs, and more will probably be able to do so in the future. Why is this a dangerous trend?

5. In what ways does the civil rights movement affect the position of the United States abroad?

6. The historian Arnold Toynbee said that a civilization advanced or declined according to the way it responded to the challenges it faced. What do you consider to be the four greatest challenges the United States faces in today's world? In what way, if any, do you think the American response to each challenge could be improved?

7. The present placement of productive capacity and of raw materials is said to predict that the world of the future will be different. In what ways will it be different? How might this problem be met?

PROJECTS

1. As a Canadian, write a letter to an American friend explaining why some Canadians are concerned about American investments in your country.

2. Write an editorial for a newspaper of the early 1950's attacking McCarthyism.

3. Draw a cartoon picturing the situation of Castro in Cuba or Perón in Argentina.

831

For additional bibliographical information on the books cited in these projects, see the Basic Library (page xviii) and Further Reading on the opposite page.

INDIVIDUAL PROJECTS

1. Report to the class on the Common Market. Be sure to discuss how and why the Common Market was formed, its present agreements, and its hopes and prospects for the future. Consult *Readers' Guide to Periodical Literature* and read the chapter on the Common Market in Gunther, *Inside Europe Today*.

2. Write a paper on the policy of apartheid as practiced in the Republic of South Africa today. The following questions should be investigated and answered in detail: What is the origin and racial make-up of the population in the Republic of South Africa? How does the government defend apartheid? By what means does the government enforce apartheid? How do other African nations react to this racial policy? How does the rest of the world react to apartheid? Consult *Readers' Guide to Periodical Literature*.

3. Prepare a report on automation, focusing on how it operates and what consequences it has for future employment. Consult *Readers' Guide to Periodical Literature* for recent magazine articles.

4. President Kennedy initiated the Alliance for Progress in Latin America. One student should report to the class on the aims of the Alliance and another student should report on the success with which these aims are being fulfilled. Hughes and Fries, *European Civilization*, "Alliance for Progress" and *Readers' Guide to Periodical Literature* should be consulted.

5. Prepare a series of bar graphs illustrating comparative economic conditions in the world today. There should be a different graph for population, income per person, caloric consumption, and industrial output. The bars of the graph should represent a key country on each continent. For information consult Boyd, *An Atlas of World Affairs*, Steinberg, *The Statesman's Year-Book*, and the *Oxford Economic Atlas of the World*.

6. Prepare an oral report on the Peace Corps. Find out how it got started, why people join it, what it does, and in what areas it is active. The report should be followed by a class discussion on the merits of the Peace Corps. For information consult *Readers' Guide to Periodical Literature* and write to the Peace Corps, Washington, D.C. 20525.

7. Write a paper analyzing the problems of general disarmament and reviewing the progress of disarmament since World War II. Information can be found in Copeland and Lamm, *The World's Great Speeches,* "Bernard Mannes Baruch: Control of Atomic Weapons" and "Dwight David Eisenhower: Peaceful Use of Atomic Energy"; Eisen and Filler, *The Human Adventure,* Vol. 2, "A Partial Ban on Nuclear Testing"; Hughes and Fries, *European Civilization*, "International Control of Atomic Power."

GROUP PROJECTS

1. Four students should form a panel, each discussing one of the speeches on the UN given below. A general class discussion should follow the panel's presentation. The speeches in Copeland and Lamm, *The World's Great Speeches*, are "Oswaldo Aranha: A New Order Through the United Nations," "Pierre Mendes-France: The Search for International Cooperation," "Dag Hammarskjöld: Values of Nationalism and Internationalism," and "Eleanor Roosevelt: The United Nations as a Bridge."

2. Six students should organize a debate on the subject: Resolved, that the emerging African nations would have done better to remain as colonies.

3. A committee of students might present a "You Are There" program on the Suez crisis of 1956. The Arab-Israeli conflict, the control of the Suez Canal and the financing of the Aswan Dam should be discussed. In addition, imaginary interviews with Nasser, Ben-Gurion, and Eden should be held. Developments in Washington, Moscow, Paris, and at the United Nations should also be considered. For information consult *Readers' Guide to Periodical Literature* and the bibliography on the opposite page. Also read Eisen and Filler, *The Human Adventure*, Vol. 2, "Israel Becomes an Independent State" and "The Leadership of Nasser."

4. Four students should form a panel to report on Latin America, with each panelist concentrating on one country. A discussion comparing the problems and hopes of Latin American countries should follow the individual reports. For this exercise read the following articles in *National Geographic:* "Mexico in Motion," October 1961; "Brazil, Ôba!" September 1962; "Venezuela Builds on Oil," March 1963; "Flamboyant Is the Word for Bolivia," February 1966.

Further Reading

BIOGRAPHY

Alexander, Robert J., *Prophets of the Revolution.* Macmillan. Latin American leaders.

Apsler, Alfred, *Fighter for Independence: Jawaharlal Nehru.* Messner.

Cathcart, Helen, *Her Majesty the Queen, the Story of Elizabeth II.* Dodd, Mead.

Cousins, Norman, *Dr. Schweitzer of Lambaréné.* Harper & Row.

Dean, Vera M., and H. D. Harootunian, *Builders of Emerging Nations.* Holt, Rinehart and Winston.

Kugelmass, J. Alvin, *Ralph J. Bunche: Fighter for Peace.* Messner.

Levine, I. E., *Champion of World Peace: Dag Hammarskjöld.* Messner.

MacLeish, Archibald, *The Eleanor Roosevelt Story.* Houghton Mifflin.

Macridis, Roy C., ed., *De Gaulle: Implacable Ally.* Harper & Row.*

St. John, Robert, *Ben-Gurion.* Doubleday.

Schlesinger, Arthur M., Jr., *A Thousand Days: John F. Kennedy in the White House.* Houghton Mifflin.

Severn, William, *Adlai Stevenson, Citizen of the World.* McKay.

Smith, Leslie, *Harold Wilson.* Scribner.

NONFICTION

Abernathy, Robert G., *Introduction to Tomorrow.* Harcourt Brace Jovanovich.

Berger, Morroe, *The Arab World Today.* Doubleday.*

Bowles, Cynthia, *At Home in India.* Harcourt Brace Jovanovich.

Eichelberger, C. M., *UN: The First Twenty Years.* Harper & Row.

Ellis, Harry B., *The Common Market.* World.

Fairbank, John K., *The United States and China.* Viking Press.

FitzGerald, Frances, *Fire in the Lake: The Vietnamese and Americans in Vietnam.* Little, Brown.

Goldman, Eric F., *The Crucial Decade and After: America, 1945–1960.* Random House.*

Griffin, Ella, *Africa Today.* Coward-McCann.

Gunther, John, *Inside South America.* Harper & Row.

Halberstam, David, *The Best and the Brightest.* Random House.

* Paperback.

Lamb, Beatrice P., *India, a World in Transition.* Praeger.*

Leckie, Robert, *Conflict.* Avon.* The history of the Korean War.

Levin, Meyer, *The Story of Israel.* Putnam.

Logan, Rayford W., and Irving S. Cohen, *American Negro: Old World Background and New World Experience.* Houghton Mifflin.

McClellan, G. S., ed., *The Two Germanies.* Wilson.

Mehdevi, Anne Sinclair, *Persia Revisited.* Knopf.

Rama Rau, Santha, *This Is India.* Harper & Row.

Reischauer, Edwin O., *Beyond Vietnam: The United States and Asia.* Vintage.

Sanders, Ronald, *Israel: The View from Masada.* Harper & Row.

Shaplen, Robert, *The Lost Revolution: The U.S. in Vietnam.* Harper & Row.*

Smith, Datus C., *The Land and People of Indonesia.* Lippincott.

Snow, Edgar, *Other Side of the River.* Random House. Red China today.

Terrill, Ross, *800,000,000, The Real China.* Atlantic: Little, Brown.

Theobald, Robert, *The UN and Its Future.* Wilson.

Trease, Geoffrey, *This Is Your Century.* Harcourt Brace Jovanovich.

Ulam, Adam B., *The Rivals: America and Russia since World War II.* Viking.

Velen, Elizabeth and Victor, eds., *The New Japan.* Wilson.

Vining, Elizabeth G., *Return to Japan.* Lippincott.

Wallbank, T. Walter, *Contemporary Africa: Continent in Transition.* Van Nostrand.*

HISTORICAL FICTION

Ambler, Eric, *State of Siege.* Knopf. British engineer is caught in an Indonesian rebellion.

Le Carré, John, *The Spy Who Came in from the Cold.* Dell.* Espionage on both sides of the iron curtain.

Markandaya, Kamala, *Nectar in a Sieve.* New American Library.* Indian setting.

Michener, James A., *The Bridge at Andau.* Random House. Hungarian revolution in its early days.

Orwell, George, *Burmese Days.* New American Library.* A British community is torn over the application of an Indian physician to join a club.

Paton, Alan, *Cry, the Beloved Country.* Scribner.* Story of a Negro priest in South Africa.

Reggiani, Renee, *The Sun Train.* Coward-McCann. Poor Sicilian family resettles in northern Italy.

Shute, Nevil, *On the Beach.* New American Library.* Imaginary atomic war.

Wunsch, Josephine, *Passport to Russia.* McKay. American girl in Russia.

	EUROPE	NEAR EAST	AFRICA	ASIA	AMERICAS
1,750,000 B.C.					
			O L D S T O N E A G E		
			East Africa man		
				Peking man Java man	
	Neanderthal man Cro-Magnon man				Migrations across Bering Strait
			M I D D L E S T O N E A G E		
4000 B.C.			N E W S T O N E A G E		

	ITALY	GREECE	TIGRIS-EUPHRATES VALLEY	WESTERN FERTILE CRESCENT	ASIA MINOR
4000 B.C.			Copper in use		
		Neolithic culture on Crete and Aegean Islands			
		Ionian and Achaean invasions	Sumerians		
			Babylonians		
					Hittite migration into region
	Indo-European invasions	Cretan civilization	HAMMURABI'S code		
			Hittite invasion	Hebrews in Palestine	Hittite Empire
		Dorian invasion		Phoenicians	
1000 B.C.	Latins	Age of Kings		SOLOMON	
	Etruscans	HOMER	Assyrians		
		Control by nobles	Chaldeans	Israel conquered by Assyrians	Rule by Persia
500 B.C.	Latins conquer Etruscans	Age of Tyrants	ZOROASTER	Judah conquered by Chaldeans	
	Roman Republic established	Golden Age	Persians		
		PERSIAN WARS			
		Age of PERICLES			
		PELOPONNESIAN WAR			
400 B.C.					
		Conquest by PHILIP OF MACEDON			
300 B.C.		E M P I R E O F A L E X A N D E R T H E G R E A T —			
	PUNIC WARS	Hellenistic Age			
200 B.C.					
		Conquest by Rome			Western portion conquered by Rome
100 B.C.	CIVIL WAR				
	JULIUS CAESAR				
	AUGUSTUS				
0				BIRTH OF CHRIST	

Chronology of Historical Events

By coordinating the dates, along the sides, with the areas, across the top, you can see what was happening in various parts of the world at the same time—for example, that the Latins came into Italy during the Greek Age of Kings. For ease of reading, certain features are high-lighted. All names of persons appear in bold-face type, such as **CONFUCIUS**; rulers and important political leaders are printed in blue, such as **JULIUS CAESAR**. Important wars and revolutions also appear in boldface type (printed in red), such as **PUNIC WARS**.

EGYPT	AFRICA	INDIA	CHINA	THE AMERICAS	
Copper in use	Neolithic culture				4000 B.C.
Egypt united under **MENES**		Indus Valley civilization			
Old Kingdom		Aryan invasion			
Middle Kingdom		Vedic Age	Hsia dynasty		
Hyksos rule Empire **AMENHOTEP**		Epic Age	Shang dynasty Chou dynasty		
Assyrian domination	Nok culture	Magadha rule Persian invasion	**CONFUCIUS**		1000 B.C.
Persian domination	Cush	**GAUTAMA BUDDHA**	**LAO-TZU**		500 B.C.
					400 B.C.
		ALEXANDER'S invasion		Mayan culture	
		Maurya Empire **ASOKA**			300 B.C.
		Andhra dynasty in Deccan	Ch'in dynasty Great Wall		200 B.C.
		Greco-Bactrian Empire	Han dynasty **WU TI**		
					100 B.C.
Conquest by Rome					0

835

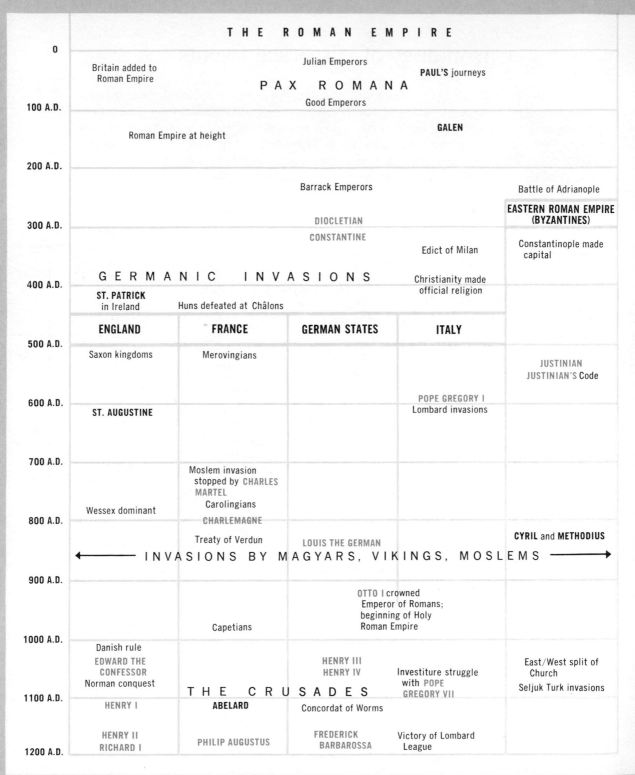

THE ROMAN EMPIRE

0		Julian Emperors	
	Britain added to Roman Empire	PAX ROMANA	PAUL'S journeys
100 A.D.		Good Emperors	
	Roman Empire at height		GALEN
200 A.D.			
		Barrack Emperors	Battle of Adrianople
			EASTERN ROMAN EMPIRE (BYZANTINES)
300 A.D.		DIOCLETIAN	
		CONSTANTINE	Constantinople made capital
		Edict of Milan	
	GERMANIC INVASIONS	Christianity made official religion	
400 A.D.	ST. PATRICK in Ireland	Huns defeated at Châlons	

	ENGLAND	FRANCE	GERMAN STATES	ITALY	
500 A.D.	Saxon kingdoms	Merovingians			JUSTINIAN JUSTINIAN'S Code
600 A.D.	ST. AUGUSTINE			POPE GREGORY I Lombard invasions	
700 A.D.		Moslem invasion stopped by CHARLES MARTEL Carolingians			
800 A.D.	Wessex dominant	CHARLEMAGNE Treaty of Verdun	LOUIS THE GERMAN	CYRIL and METHODIUS	

←——— INVASIONS BY MAGYARS, VIKINGS, MOSLEMS ———→

	ENGLAND	FRANCE	GERMAN STATES	ITALY	
900 A.D.			OTTO I crowned Emperor of Romans; beginning of Holy Roman Empire		
1000 A.D.		Capetians			
	Danish rule EDWARD THE CONFESSOR Norman conquest	THE CRUSADES	HENRY III HENRY IV	Investiture struggle with POPE GREGORY VII	East/West split of Church Seljuk Turk invasions
1100 A.D.	HENRY I	ABELARD	Concordat of Worms		
	HENRY II RICHARD I	PHILIP AUGUSTUS	FREDERICK BARBAROSSA	Victory of Lombard League	
1200 A.D.					

RUSSIA	AFRICA AND MIDDLE EAST	INDIA	CHINA	JAPAN	THE AMERICAS	
		Kushan Empire				0
						100 A.D.
Slav settlements			Six Dynasties			200 A.D.
	Aksum	Gupta rule	Hun invasion			300 A.D.
	Vandal invasions					400 A.D.
	Zimbabwe	Hun invasions	Sui dynasty	Buddhism introduced from China		500 A.D.
	MOHAMMED'S Hegira	HARSHA Rajput era Chalukya dynasty in Deccan	Tang dynasty	First envoys to China Great Reform		600 A.D.
	Moslem expansion from Spain to India Ghana	Indus Valley conquered by Moslems	LI PO TU FU	Great Treasure	Toltecs in Mexico	700 A.D.
Kievan state			Diamond Sutra	Fujiwara control	Catastrophe strikes Mayan civilization	800 A.D.
	RHAZES		Sung dynasty			900 A.D.
YAROSLAV THE WISE	AVICENNA Islam imposed on western Sudan Rise of Turks	Beginning of Moslem invasions		The Tale of Genji		1000 A.D.
			Chin dynasty in north	Minamoto control Shogunate established		1100 A.D. 1200 A.D.

	ENGLAND	FRANCE	GERMAN STATES	ITALY	SPANISH PENINSULA	RUSSIA	OTHER EUROPEAN STATES
1200 A.D.	**JOHN** Magna Carta		**FREDERICK II**	**INNOCENT III** **ST. FRANCIS OF ASSISI**			
						Mongol rule of Russia	
1250 A.D.	**SIMON DE MONTFORT** vs. **HENRY III**			**ST. THOMAS AQUINAS** **DANTE**			
	Growth of royal courts	**PHILIP IV**		**BONIFACE VIII**			
1300 A.D.			Hanseatic League	Babylonian Captivity		Rise of Moscow **IVAN I**	
	HUNDRED YEARS' WAR						
	B E G I N N I N G O F R E N A I S S A N C E						
1350 A.D.	**CHAUCER**			**BOCCACCIO**			
	WYCLIFFE			Great Schism			
1400 A.D.				Council of Constance	**PRINCE HENRY** launches Portuguese voyages		**HUSS**
		JOAN OF ARC					**VAN EYCKS**
1450 A.D.	**WARS OF THE ROSES**		**GUTENBERG**	**LEONARDO** **MICHELANGELO** **RAPHAEL** **TITIAN**	Marriage of **FERDINAND** and **ISABELLA**	**IVAN III**	**ERASMUS**
	HENRY VII Tudors	**LOUIS XI**		**MACHIAVELLI**		Mongols overthrown	**DÜRER**
1500 A.D.	**HENRY VIII** Act of Supremacy	**RABELAIS**	**LUTHER'S** 95 Theses		**CHARLES I (V)** **MAGELLAN'S** voyage		**CALVIN'S** *Institutes* **COPERNICUS**
				Council of Trent	Jesuit order founded	**IVAN IV (THE TERRIBLE)**	
1550 A.D.	**ELIZABETH I**		Peace of Augsburg		**PHILIP II**		**BRUEGHEL**
	Defeat of Armada	**HENRY IV** Edict of Nantes			Portugal ruled by Spain	Cossack expansion eastward	Dutch revolt against Spain
1600 A.D.	**SHAKESPEARE** Stuarts		**KEPLER**				Dutch E. India Company organized
	← T H I R T Y Y E A R S ' W A R →			**GALILEO**			
	CIVIL WAR **CROMWELL**	**LOUIS XIV**	Treaty of Westphalia				
1650 A.D.	Restoration						
	Glorious Revolution	Edict of Nantes revoked				**PETER I (THE GREAT)**	
	B E G I N N I N G O F E N L I G H T E N M E N T						
1700 A.D.	W A R O F S P A N I S H S U C C E S S I O N					St. Petersburg built	
	GEORGE I						
		MONTESQUIEU	**MARIA THERESA**				
1750 A.D.	B E G I N N I N G O F I N D U S T R I A L R E V O L U T I O N						
	WATT'S steam engine	**ROUSSEAU** **LOUIS XVI** **FRENCH REVOLUTION**	**FREDERICK THE GREAT**			**CATHERINE THE GREAT**	Partitions of Poland
1800 A.D.							

BYZANTINE EMPIRE	AFRICA	INDIA	CHINA	JAPAN	OTHER EASTERN AREAS	THE AMERICAS	
							1200 A.D.
Constantinople captured by Crusaders	Mali Benin Timbuktu center of learning	Delhi sultans			Mongol Empire **GENGHIS KHAN**	Toltecs defeated by Aztecs	
							1250 A.D.
Constantinople regained by Byzantines Empire reorganized			**KUBLAI KHAN** Yüan dynasty **POLOS'** visit	Mongols repulsed by "Great Wind"			
							1300 A.D.
Ottoman Turks in Asia Minor	**MANSA MUSA**			Ashikaga control		Incas in South America Aztec power at height	
							1350 A.D.
		FIRUZ SHAH	Ming dynasty				
		TAMERLANE'S invasion Mongol rule					1400 A.D.
Constantinople captured by Turks			Foreign contacts ended				1450 A.D.
OTTOMAN EMPIRE		Delhi sultans					
						COLUMBUS discovers America	
	DIAS' voyage around Cape of Good Hope Songhai Portuguese in Angola, Mozambique, Zanzibar	**DA GAMA'S** voyage Mogul Empire	Portuguese in Macao		Portuguese in E. Indies	**CORTÉS PIZARRO**	1500 A.D.
SULEIMAN I				Portuguese traders and missionaries **NOBUNAGA**			1550 A.D.
		English in Madras, Bombay, Calcutta **SHAH JEHAN**	Manchu dynasty	Tokugawa control Isolation begun Dutch at Nagasaki	Dutch in E. Indies	Jamestown Quebec Plymouth	1600 A.D.
	Dutch establish Cape Colony	Taj Mahal French in Pondicherry	Boundary treaty with Russia			Louisiana claimed for France	1650 A.D.
							1700 A.D.
							1750 A.D.
		French defeated Rule by British E. India Company			Australia, New Zealand discovered by **COOK,** settled by British	**AMERICAN REVOLUTION** Constitutional Act in Canada	1800 A.D.

	ENGLAND	FRANCE	GERMAN STATES	ITALY	RUSSIA	OTHER EUROPEAN STATES
1800 A.D.	←		N A P O L E O N I C W A R S			→
		NAPOLEON in power	Confederation of the Rhine		NAPOLEON'S invasion repulsed	
			CONGRESS OF VIENNA			
		Bourbons restored	German Confederation		Holy Alliance	
1820 A.D.	Factory Act		Carlsbad Decrees	Rising in Naples		Revolt in Spain
	Development of railroads	Revolution overthrows	Zollverein		NICHOLAS I "Russification"	Greek revolt
		CHARLES X		Revolt in Sardinia		
	Reform Bill of 1832	LOUIS PHILIPPE		Young Italy movement		Belgian independence
	VICTORIA					
1840 A.D.	Chartists					
	Corn Laws repealed	Second Republic	*Communist Manifesto*	Widespread rebellions; war against Austria		
		NAPOLEON III: Second Empire	Frankfort Assembly	METTERNICH ousted from Austria	ALEXANDER II	
	CRIMEAN WAR					
	DARWIN'S				Emancipation of serfs	
1860 A.D.	*Origin of Species*	Impressionists	BISMARCK In power	Unification and independence of Italy		
	Second Reform Bill	PASTEUR	GERMAN EMPIRE	Dual Monarchy of AUSTRIA-HUNGARY	TOLSTOY	
		FRANCO-PRUSSIAN WAR			MENDELEYEV'S Periodic Table	
	Suez Canal acquired	Third Republic		VERDI		
			Congress of Berlin	MENDEL		
1880 A.D.					ALEXANDER III	Serbia, Montenegro, Rumania recognized as independent
	Third Reform Bill		← Triple Alliance →		Trans-Siberian railroad	
		DREYFUS case	ROENTGEN	FREUD	MARCONI'S wireless	NICHOLAS II
	THOMSON	CURIES		Bosnia, Herzegovina annexed		
1900 A.D.		Cubism	EINSTEIN	War with Ottomans	WAR WITH JAPAN Revolution of 1905	Algeciras Conference
	Labour Party	Triple Entente	W O R L D W A R I			BALKAN WARS
			GERMANY	AUSTRIA	Bolshevik Revolution under LENIN	Czechoslovakia, Yugoslavia, Baltic States formed
1920 A.D.			Weimar Republic		NEP	
	Irish Free State	Occupation of Ruhr		Fascist march on Rome	STALIN in power	Locarno Pact
				MUSSOLINI		
	Statute of Westminster	Popular Front	HITLER to power *Anschluss* with Austria		Purge at height	SPANISH CIVIL WAR
1940 A.D.			W O R L D W A R I I			Soviet satellites in eastern Europe
		Fourth Republic	U N I T E D N A T I O N S		Cominform	
	NATO formed		Nuremberg trials	Republic created		Hungarian revolt
	Colonies lost		East and West Germanies established		Warsaw Pact	
		Fifth Republic DE GAULLE		Treaty with Allies	Sputnik I	
1960 A.D.		Common Market	Berlin wall		Break with China	
		DE GAULLE resigned				Czechoslovak revolt
	Common Market		East-West treaties		East-West *détente*	
1980 A.D.						

AFRICA AND MIDDLE EAST	INDIA	CHINA	JAPAN	OTHER EASTERN AREAS	NORTH AMERICA	LATIN AMERICA	
				Dutch E. Indies made royal colony	Louisiana Purchase	Haiti independent Spanish-American colonies win independence	1800 A.D.
							1820 A.D.
French in Algeria	Westernization begun				MONROE DOCTRINE	Brazil free	
		OPIUM WAR			Durham Report		1840 A.D.
Liberia independent Boer republics	SEPOY REBELLION	TAIPING REBELLION WAR WITH BRITAIN	Arrival of **PERRY**	French take Marquesas, Tahiti	**MORSE'S** telegraph MEXICAN WAR		1860 A.D.
Suez Canal completed Wholesale seizure of			Shogunate ended Meiji Era Westernization	Wholesale seizure of Pacific islands and Southeast	Dominion of Canada **EDISON**	French in Mexico: MAXIMILIAN	1880 A.D.
African lands by Britain, France, Belgium, Germany, Italy **BOER WAR**	Indian National Congress	SINO-JAPANESE WAR BOXER REBELLION	Imperial constitution	Asian countries by France, Britain, Germany, U. S. Commonwealth of Australia	First skyscraper Sherman Antitrust Act SPANISH-AMERICAN WAR	Pan American Union	1900 A.D.
Moroccan crisis Agadir Incident	Moslem League	Chinese Republic	RUSSO-JAPANESE WAR	Dominion of New Zealand	**WRIGHT BROTHERS** ROOSEVELT Corollary	Panama revolution	
W O R L D W A R I ⟶			Korea annexed			Panama Canal opened	1920 A.D.
ATATÜRK Persia ruled by REZA SHAH Italy defeats Ethiopia	Passive resistance under GANDHI	**CHIANG KAI-SHEK** Japanese invasion	Invasion of Manchuria		Stock market crash; Great Depression		1940 A.D.
W O R L D W A R I I ⟶		CIVIL WAR					
Arab League UN intervention in Congo, Suez	Independence for India and Pakistan Chinese invasion	Communists control mainland; Nationalists retreat to Taiwan	First atomic bomb, Hiroshima **"MACARTHUR constitution"**	KOREAN WAR French defeat in Indo-China U. S. intervention in Vietnam	TRUMAN Doctrine **MARSHALL** Plan *Brown vs. Topeka* St. Lawrence Seaway	O A S CASTRO revolution in Cuba Alliance for Progress	1960 A.D.
SIX-DAY WAR FOURTH ARAB-ISRAELI WAR	Independence for Bangladesh	Communists in UN; Nationalists out	Great industrial power	U.S. withdrawal from Vietnam	U.S. space pro-grams Watergate scandals	Overthrow of Marxists in Chile	1980 A.D.

EUROPE

ARCTIC OCEAN

NORTH POLE

ARCTIC CIRCLE

ATLANTIC OCEAN

EUROPE

BARENTS SEA

KARA SEA

LAPTEV SEA

EAST SIBERIAN SEA

BERING SEA

ALEUTIAN ISLANDS

PACIFIC OCEAN

Verkhoyansk

Igarka

Yenisei R.

Irtysh River

Omsk

Moscow

UNION OF SOVIET SOCIALIST REPUBLICS (U.S.S.R.)

RUSSIAN SOVIET FEDERATED SOCIALIST REPUBLIC

SIBERIA

Lena River

Chita

Lake Baikal

Irkutsk

Ulan Bator

MONGOLIA

GOBI DESERT

Khabarovsk

Amur River

SEA OF OKHOTSK

SAKHALIN

KAMCHATKA PEN.

KURILE IS.

Vladivostok

Harbin

MANCHURIA

SEA OF JAPAN

JAPAN

Tokyo
Yokohama
Osaka

RYUKYU IS.

KOREA
NORTH KOREA
SOUTH KOREA
Seoul

YELLOW SEA

Peking

Yellow R.

Nanking
Shanghai

EAST CHINA SEA

Taipei
TAIWAN

PHILIPPINE SEA

PAPUA NEW GUINEA

CORAL SEA

AUSTRALIA

Manila

PHILIPPINES

Quezon City

URAL River

URAL MTS.

CASPIAN SEA

Aral Sea

KAZAKH S.S.R.

L. Balkhash

UZBEK S.S.R.

Tashkent

KIRGHIZ S.S.R.

TADZHIK S.S.R.

TURKMEN S.S.R.

TIEN SHAN

KUNLUN MTS.

TIBET

Lhasa

HIMALAYA MTS.

BHUTAN

NEPAL
Katmandu

CHINA

Wuhan

Yangtze R.

Chungking R.

Chungking

Mekong R.

BURMA

Rangoon

BANGLADESH

Calcutta

BAY OF BENGAL

THAILAND
Bangkok

LAOS
Vientiane

NORTH VIETNAM
Hanoi

HAINAN

SOUTH VIETNAM
Saigon

CAMB.
Pnom-Penh

Canton

Hong Kong (Br.)

SOUTH CHINA SEA

FEDERATION OF MALAYSIA

Kuala Lumpur

Singapore

SUMATRA

BORNEO

CELEBES

INDONESIA

JAVA SEA

Jakarta

Bandung

JAVA

TIMOR

Moscow

TURKEY
Ankara

Istanbul

CYPRUS

LEB.

ISRAEL

SYRIA

JORDAN

Disputed

MEDITERRANEAN SEA

BLACK SEA

CAUCASUS MTS.

Tehran

Baghdad

IRAQ

KUWAIT

IRAN

PLATEAU OF IRAN

Persian Gulf

QATAR

TRUCIAL OMAN

MUSCAT AND OMAN

Muscat

SAUDI ARABIA

Riyadh

Mecca

Medina

RED SEA

YEMEN
Sanaa

SOUTH YEMEN
Aden

ARABIAN SEA

New Delhi

Rawalpindi

AFGHANISTAN
Kabul

PAKISTAN

Karachi

Indus R.

INDIA

Ganges R.

Bombay

Madras

SRI LANKA
Colombo

INDIAN OCEAN

AFRICA

TROPIC OF CANCER

EQUATOR

1000 miles

ASIA

PAGE 843

NORTH AMERICA

PAGE 844

SOUTH AMERICA

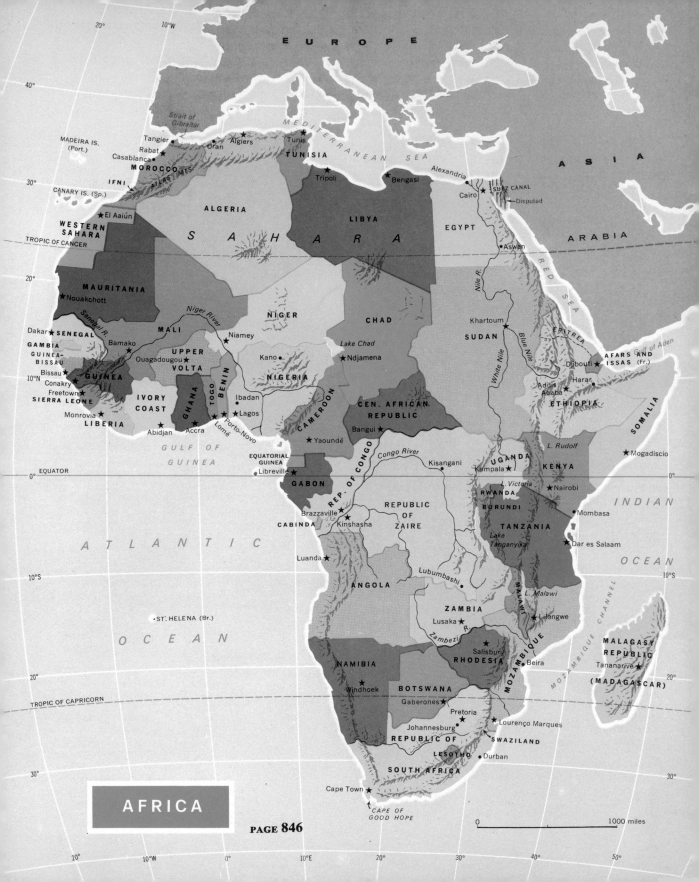

AFRICA

PAGE 846

INDEX

Italicized page numbers preceded by *c, m,* or *p* refer to a chart (*c*), map (*m*), or picture (*p*) on the page.

Boldface page numbers **(74)** are pages on which a definition is given.

Pronunciations, indicated by phonetic respellings in parentheses, are based on Funk and Wagnalls *Standard College Dictionary,* published by Harcourt Brace Jovanovich, Inc.

Brahma, 165
Brahmans, 66, 162, 164, 165, 553
Brahms, Johannes, 654
Brancusi, Constantin, *p657*
Brandenburg, *m238*, 239, *m338*, 345, *m346*, 349, *m475*, 357–58
Brandt, Willy, *p775*, 776
Braque (BRAHK), Georges, *p614*, 658
Brazil: early exploration and colonization, *m318–19*, 320, *m326–27*; independence, 435, *m436*, 437; during Great Depression, 679; government of, 816; and Cuba, 816; today, *m820*, *m845*
Brazza, Pierre de, 539
Brazzaville, *m534*, 539
Bremen, 223, *m225*, 478, *m486*
Breslau (BRES·low), *m225*
Brest-Litovsk, *m594*
Brest-Litovsk, Treaty of, 598, 600
Brezhnev, Leonid, 773, *p775*, 776, *p824*, 825
Briand, Aristide, 702
Brisbane, *m517*
Britain: Phoenician trade with, 50; in Roman Empire, 137–38, *m137*, 141, 195; barbarian invasions of, *m156*, 157, *m194*, 195. *See also* England; Great Britain.
British Columbia, 515, *m516*
British Commonwealth of Nations, 672, 770, 783, 784, 795
British East Africa, *m534*, 545
British East India Company, 549–51. *See also* English East India Company.
British Empire, 669–70, 672
British Guiana, 426, *m436*, 574, *m575*. *See also* Guyana.
British Honduras (Belize), *m436*, *m575*, *m844*
British North America Act, 515
British Somaliland, *m534*, 727
Brittany, 208, *m209*, *m236*, 237
bronze, 12, 21, 73
Brown, Robert, 618
Brown Shirts, 699
Brown v. Board of Education of Topeka, 822
Browning, Robert, 652
Brueghel (BROY·gul), Peter, 297, *p298*
Bruges (BROOZH), 223, *m224–25*, 229
Brunswick, *m225*
Brussels, 410, *m419*, 464, *m595*
Brutus, Marcus, 136
bubonic plague, 643
Bucephala, *m103*
Bucharest (BOO·kuh·rest), *m502*, *m759*, *m765*
Buchenwald (BOOK·un·wald), 729
Budapest, 499, *m502*, 594, *m603*, *m723*, *m765*
Buddha (BOOD·uh), 161, *p161*, 166, *p172*, 173
Buddhism: teachings of, 166; spread

of, 167–68, *m167;* and Asoka, 169; decline of, in India, 171; in China, 178, 271; in Japan, 277; and *no* plays, 280
Buenos Aires (BWAY·nus EYE·riz), 430, 435, *m436*
Bulgaria: converted to Christianity, *m205*, 247; independence, 501–02, *m502;* and Balkan Wars, 503; in World War I, 592, 593, *m594*, 600; after World War I, *m603*, 604; in World War II, 720, *m723*, 727, 736; after World War II, 759, *m759;* as communist nation, 762, *m765;* joins Comecon, 770; joins Warsaw Pact, 772–73; today, *m842*
Bunche, Ralph, *p752, 787*
Bundesrat (BOON·dus·raht), 487–88
Burgundians, *m156*, 157, 189, *m245*
Burgundy, 208, *m209*, *m236*, 237
Burma: Buddhism in, *m167*, 168, 169; visit of Marco Polo, *m274*, 314; British in, 551, *m559*, 566; in World War II, 731, *m735*, 808; independence, *m806*, 807, 808; today, *m843*
Burma Road, 705, *m705*, 730, 734–35, *m735*, 808
Burundi, *m781*, *m846*
bushido, 279
Bushmen, *p14*
business cycle, 639
Byelorussian (byeh·luh·RUSH·un) Soviet Socialist Republic, *m842*
by-products, 442–43
Byron, Lord, 650
Byzantine Empire: history and culture of, 245–48, *m246*, *p248*, *p249*, 250; Vikings in, *m194;* and Crusades, 217–18, *m218*, *m219*, 220; and medieval trade, 222–23, *m224–25;* and Turks, 255; and Mongols, *m274*
Byzantium (bih·ZAN·shih·um), *m84*, 92, *m97*, *m156*, 245. *See also* Constantinople.

Cabinda, *m781*, *m846*
Cabinet, British, 376, 377
Cabot, John, *m318–19*, 324
Cabral (kah·VRAHL), Pedro Alvarez, *m318–19*, 320
Cadiz, 51, *m51*
Caesar, Julius, *p132*, 135–36
caesar, official in late Roman Empire, 154
Cairo, *m224–25*, *m251*, 254, *m723*, *m781*, *m786*
Calais (KAL·ay), 235, *m236*
Calcutta, 325, *m326*, 549, 550, *m550*, *m796*
calendar: development of, 13, 15; Egyptian, 32; Sumerian, 40; Chinese, 73; Caesar's reform of, 135–36; Moslem, 251; Mayan, 282; Aztec, *p285*
Calgary, *m516*
Calicut, *m224–25*, *m318–19*

Caligula (kuh·LIG·yuh·luh), Roman emperor, 137
caliph, 253
caliphates, 254
Calles, Plutarco E., 818
calligraphy (kuh·LIG·ruh·fee), 74
Calvin, John, *p306*, 308
Calvinism: origins and spread of, 308, *m309;* in Netherlands, 340; and Thirty Years' War, 345; in England, 368, 370, 371, 374
Cambodia, *m167*, 168, 276, *m806*, 807, 808, 809, 810, 812, *m843*
Cambyses (kam·BY·seez), Persian king, 47
Cameroon, *m781*, *m846*
Cameroons, *m534*, 540, 604
Camorra, 498
Campara, Hector, 816
Canaanites (KAY·nun·ites), 54, *m54*
Canada: early exploration, *m318–19*, 325, *m326–27*, 329; in 1700's, *m388*, 393, 399; development in 1800's, 514–16, *m515;* immigration laws, 557; and Commonwealth status, 672, 679; after World War II, *m516*, 767, 819–21; joins NATO, 771; separatism, 820–21; today, *m844*
Canadian Pacific Railway, 515, *m516*
canals: in early civilizations, 13; in ancient Egypt, 20, 32; in Tigris-Euphrates Valley, 36; during Industrial Revolution, 444; and trade, 637
Canal Zone, *m575*, *m844*, *m845*
Canary Islands, *m326–27*, *m534*, 709, *m846*
Canning, George, 429, 437
Canossa, *m205*, 212
Canterbury, 197, *m197*, *m205*
Canterbury, archbishops of, 196
Canton, *m271*, 272, *m272*, *m318–19*, *m326–27*, 558, *m559*, 674
Canute (kuh·NOOT), Danish king, 198
Cape Colony, 425, *m534*, 542–43
Cape Horn, *m318–19*, *m431*
Capet, Hugh, 208
Capetians, 207–08
Cape-to-Cairo railroad, 543
Cape Town, *m534*, 542
Cape Verde Islands, *m318–19*, 320, *m326–27*, *m534*
capitalism: in Middle Ages, 226–27; industrial, 447, 449; and socialism, 454, 456; finance, 633, 635; and communism, *c809*
Caracas, 433, *m436*
Cárdenas, Lázaro, 818
Caribbean Sea, 316, *m318–19*, *m431*, *m436*, *m575*
Carlsbad, *m427*
Carlsbad Decrees, 429
Carlyle, Thomas, 452
Carnegie, Andrew, 583, 635
Carnot (kahr·NOH), Lazare Nicolas, 411, 412

Caroline Islands, 570, *m570,* 601, 702, *m706,* 734, *m735,* 750
Carolingians, 191–92, 193
Carpathian Mountains, 258, *m259*
carrack (KAR·uk), **316**
Carroll, Lewis, 652
cartels, 489
Carthage (KAHR·thij): Phoenician colony, 51, *m51, m84;* and Rome, *m128,* 129–30, *m131, m138;* and Vandals, *m156;* in Byzantine Empire, *m246*
Cartier (kahr·TYAY), Jacques, *m318–19,* 329
cartographers, 313
Cartwright, Edmund, 442
Casablanca, 731
Cascade Range, 385, *m386*
Caspian Sea, and early pasturelands, 11, *m12;* and Hittites, 42, *m42;* and Persian Empire, 47, *m48;* and Alexander's empire, *m103;* and Moslem Empire, *m251;* and early Russia, 258, *m259, m354;* and Mongol Empire, *m274;* and Ottoman Empire, *m352;* and Middle East, *m786*
Cassius, Gaius, 136
caste (KAST) **system,** 164, 166, 269, 550
Castiglione (kahs·teh·LYOH·nay), Baldassare, 294
Castile-León, 237, *m237*
castle, 200, 202–03, *p221*
Castlereagh (KAS·ul·ray), **Lord,** 424, 427
Castro, Fidel, *p817,* 818
cathedral, 152, 234
Catherine of Aragon, queen of England, 309–10
Catherine II (the Great), czarina of Russia, 353–55, *m353, p356,* 382
Catholic Church. *See* Roman Catholic Church.
Catholic Emancipation Act, 510, *c512*
Cato the Elder, 130
Caucasus, *m723,* 729
Caucasus Mountains, 11, *m37,* 46, *m48,* 85, *m138,* 258, *m259*
Cavaliers, in England, 371
Cavour (kah·VOOR), Camillo Benso di, 495–96, *p497,* 498
Caxton, William, 300
Cayuga Indians, 286
Celebes (SEL·uh·beez), *m318–19,* 321, *m326–27, m559, m570, m735, m806*
cell theory, 618
Celts, 195
censors, in Roman Republic, 127
center, political position, **409**
CENTO. See Central Treaty Organization.
Central African Republic, *m781, m846*
Central America. *See* Latin America.

central Asia, *m1, m177,* 260
Central Powers, 593–96, *m594,* 598–600, 606
Central Treaty Organization (CENTO), *m820,* 821
centuries, in Roman Republic, 126
Ceylon: and India, *m60,* 61; Buddhism in, *m167,* 169; in age of exploration, *m318–19;* Portuguese in, 322; and imperialism, *m550,* 551; independence, *m796*
Cézanne (say·ZAHN), Paul, 655, *p657,* 658
Chad, *m781, m846*
Chad, Lake, *m256,* 258, *m534*
Chaeronea (ker·uh·NEE·uh), battle at, *m103,* 104
Chaldeans (kal·DEE·unz), 45, 46, *m47, p49,* 50, 53
Châlons (shah·LAWN), battle at, *m156,* 158
Chalukya dynasty, 266
Chamberlain, Neville, 712, 713, 715, *p716,* 721
Champagne, province, 208, *m209,* 223, *m224*
Champlain, Samuel de, 329
Champollion (shan·paw·LYAWN), Jean François, 21
Chandragupta I, Gupta ruler, 171
Chandragupta II, Gupta ruler, 171
Chandragupta Maurya, 168–69
Changan, 178, *m178,* 270, *m271*
Chao K'uang-yin, Sung ruler, 271
Chaplin, Charlie, *p631*
chariot races, Roman, 143
Charlemagne (SHAHR·luh·mayn), 191–92, *m191, p193*
Charles I, king of England, 370–71, *p372,* 373
Charles I, king of Spain. *See* Charles V, Holy Roman Emperor.
Charles II, king of England, 374, 376, 385
Charles IV, Holy Roman Emperor, 239, *p240*
Charles V, Holy Roman Emperor, 306, 309, 333, 337–39, *p341*
Charles VII, king of France, 236
Charles X, king of France, 463–64
Charles the Bald, Frankish king, 192, *m192*
Charles the Bold, duke of Burgundy, 237
Charles Martel, 190
Charleston, 385–86, *m388, m389*
Chartist movement, 453, 512
Chartres (SHAHR·tr'), *m205,* 234
Château-Thierry (shah·TOH-tyeh-REE), battle at, *m595,* 599
Chaucer (CHAW·sur), Geoffrey, 232
Chauvin (shoh·VAN), Nicholas, 424
chauvinism (SHOH·vun·iz·um), **424**
chemical industry, 630, 830
chemistry, 233, 379, 613–14

Chiang Kai-shek (CHYAHNG KY-SHEK), *m675,* 676, 704, 730, 734, 798, 805
Chicago, 446, 630, 634
Chichén-Itzá (chee·CHEN-eet·SAH), 283, *m283*
child labor, 449, 452
Children's Crusade, 220
Chile, 284, *m326–27,* 435, *m436,* 816, 817, *m820, m845*
China: prehistoric man in, 6, *m7;* earliest civilization, 11–13, *m12,* 58–59; physical regions, 66–67, *m67, p68–69,* 70; pattern of dynasties, 70–71; Hsia dynasty, 71–72; Shang dynasty, 72–74, *m73,* 76, *p76;* arrival of Buddhism, *m167,* 168, 169; Chou dynasty, 175–76, *m175,* 179; Ch'in dynasty, 176–77, *m176,* 178; Han dynasty, 177–78, *m177;* Six Dynasties period, 178, 179; early culture, 179–80, *p181,* 182; medieval trade, *m224–25;* Moslem trade with, 254; Mongols in, 261–62, 274–75, *m274;* Sui dynasty, 270; Tang dynasty, 270–71, *m271,* 279; Sung dynasty, 271–72, *m272;* Chin dynasty, 272, *m272;* Yüan dynasty, 274–75; Ming dynasty, 275–76, *m276;* in age of exploration, *m318–19,* 321, *m326–27;* and Russian boundary treaty, 330; Manchu dynasty, 557–64; in age of imperialism, 557–64, *m559, p562–63;* republic established, 564–65; after World War I, 601·02; under Kuomintang, 674, 676; war with Japan, 704–05, *m705;* in World War II, 720, 734–35, *m735,* 740, 746; and nuclear weapons, 753; and UN, 754; and Comecon, 770; Soviet relations, 776, 800–01; invasion of Tibet and India, 796; communist regime in, *p799,* 800–01, *m806;* in Korean War, 801; relations with U.S., 801, 805, 824, 825; and Geneva Agreements, 808; today, *m843. See also* Nationalist China.
Ch'in dynasty, 176–77, *m176,* 178
Chin dynasty, 272, *m272,* 274
Chinese Eastern Railway, *m559,* 561, 564, 740
Chinese language, 74
Chinese Soviet Republic, 676
Chios, *m97*
Chirico (KEE·ree·koh), Giorgio di, *p585,* 658
chivalry, 203
Chopin (SHOH·pan), Frédéric, 654
Chou (JOE) **dynasty,** 175–76, *m175,* 179
Chou En-lai, *p799,* 824, *p824*
Christ. *See* Jesus Christ.
Christchurch, *m517*
Christian IX, king of Denmark, 484
Christianity: rise of, 148–49, *m149,* 151–53, 155; in early Middle Ages,

197, 203–08, *m205;* Crusades, 217–20, *m218,* 221; in later Middle Ages, 239, 241–42; Reformation, 304–05, 307–11

Christian Scientists, 649

chromosomes, 620

Chungking, 70, *m559,* 705, *m705, m735*

Churchill, Winston: becomes prime minister, 721; on Dunkirk evacuation, 721; on Battle of Britain, 722, *p725;* and Atlantic Charter, 726; and wartime conferences, 731, 736, 737, 740, 747; and invasion of Italy, 732; on Cold War, 753, 758, 771

Church of England, *m309,* 310, 368, 371, 374, 512

Chu Yüan-chang, Ming ruler, 275–76

Cicero, 144

Circus, Roman, 143

Cisalpine Gaul, 125, *m125, m128,* 129, *m131,* 134, 135, *m137*

cities: beginnings of, 13; founded by Alexander the Great, 106, 119; patriarchal, 152; medieval, 227–29, 232–34; and industrialization, 447, 644, 646

city-states: defined, **37;** Sumerian, 37; Phoenician, 50; in Shang China, 72; ancient Greek, 88–89; Sparta, 94–95; Athens, 95–98; Greek leagues of, 101, 106; Aryan, 162; Italian, 213–14, 222

Civil Constitution of the Clergy, 407, 415

civilization, 11

civil liberties, 374

civil rights, 822

civil service, Chinese, 177, 180, 270, 276

Civil War, in U.S., 521–22

Claudius, Roman emperor, 137–38, *p139*

Cleisthenes (KLYS·thuh·neez), 97

Clemenceau (klem·un·SOH), Georges, 600, 601

Cleopatra, 135, 136

Clericis Laicos, papal bull, 240

Clermont, ship, 444, *p445*

Clermont, 217, *m218*

Cleveland, Grover, 574

Clive, Robert, 549–50

Clovis, Frankish king, 189–90

coal industry, 442, 669, 768

coaling stations, 530, 569

coalitions, 476

Cochin, *m326–27,* 329

coke, 443

Colbert (kawl·BAIR), Jean Baptiste, 347, 348, 349

Cold War, 751, 762–66, 771–76, 785, 795, 804, 807–12

Coleridge, Samuel Taylor, 274, 650

collaborators, 721

collective bargaining, 453

collective farms: in U.S.S.R., 689–90; in Communist China, 800; in Cuba, 818

collegia (kuh·LEE·jih·uh), Roman, **154**

Cologne, *m224, m238,* 239

Colombia, 435, *m436, m575,* 578, 580, *m820, m845*

Colombo, *m796*

colonies: Phoenician, 51, *m51;* Greek, 92; in age of exploration, 321–27, 329–30, 332–34; in North America, 385–89, 391–95, 397–99; and imperialism, **532;** after World War I, 604, 778; and UN, 748, 750, 778

colonus, 143

Colophon, Greek settlement, *m99*

Colosseum, *p139,* 143

Columbia River Treaty, 819

Columbus, Christopher, 316, *m318–19,* 320

Comecon. *See* Council of Mutual Economic Assistance.

Cominform, 762, 764

Comintern, 691

Commercial Revolution, 330, 332–34

Committee of Public Safety, 411

Commodus, Roman emperor, 153

common law, 211

Common Market. *See* European Economic Community.

Commonwealth, Cromwell's, 373

Communards, 472

communications, modern, 830

communism: Marx and, 454, 456, *c807;* in Russia, 684, 686–91; and fascism, *c693;* in China, 676, 798, 800–01; in postwar Europe, 762–66, 770, 771, 772–74, 776; in Asia, 795; in Korea, 801; in Vietnam, 808–09, 810; in Guatemala, 816; in Chile, 816, 818; in Cuba, *p817,* 818; in Middle East, 821

Communist China. *See* China.

Communist Manifesto, 454

Communist Party, in U.S.S.R., 686–91

compass, 315

competition, law of, 450

compurgation, 199

computers, 830

Comte, Auguste, 622, 649

concentration camps, 699, 729, 760

Concert of Europe, 428

concession, 532

Concord, 394

Concordat of Worms, 213

condominium, 532

Confederate States of America, 521

Confederation of the Rhine, 417, *m419,* 480

Confucius, 161, 179, 180, 182

Congo, Democratic Republic of the, 754, 755, 780–81, *p782,* 783. *See also* Belgian Congo; Zaire.

Congo, Republic of the, 780, *m781, m846*

Congo River, 256, *m256, m534,* 539

Congress of Berlin, 501–02, 535, 589

Congress of Vienna, 424, 426–28

Conrad III, Holy Roman Emperor, 219

conscription: in French Revolution and Napoleonic Era, 411, 419, 421; in Prussia, 480; in German Empire, 490; before World War I, 586; in Britain, 715; in U.S., 726

Conservative Party, Great Britain, 510, 512–13, 740, 767

Constable, John, 655

Constance, *m205,* 242, 300

Constance Missal, 300

Constantine, Roman emperor, 155, *p155, p249*

Constantinople: founding of, 155, *m156;* and Christianity, *m149,* 152; Byzantine capital, 245, *m246,* 247, 248, 249, 250; and Crusades, 218, *m218,* 220, *c220;* and medieval trade, 222, *m224–25, m259;* and Mongols, *m274;* Ottoman capital, 255, 351, *m352, m502,* 503, 589; and World War I, 592, *m594,* 595; after World War I, 604, 674

Constitutional Act, 399, 514

Constitutional Convention, in U.S., 398–99

constitutional monarchy, 377–78

constitution: defined, **373;** Cromwell's, 373; British, 377–78; U.S., 398–99; French (revolutionary), 407, 409; establishing Directory, 412–13; Napoleonic, 414; establishing Third French Republic, 472–73; German, 483, 487–88; Japanese, 556; Cuban, 577; "Stalin," in U.S.S.R., 691; establishing Fifth French Republic, 767; "MacArthur," in Japan, 803; Philippine, 805

Consulate, in France, 414–15

consuls, in Roman Republic, 127

containment policy, U.S., 763

Continental Congress: First, 393–94; Second, 394–95, 397–98

Continental System, 416–17, 418–19

Convention, National, 409, 410, 411, 412

Cook, James, 516, 517

Cook Islands, 570, *m570*

Cooper, James Fenimore, 650

cooperative communities, 454

Copernicus, Nicholas, 301, 302, 378

Copley, John Singleton, *p394*

copper, 11–12, 21

Coral Sea, *m735*

Coral Sea, battle of the, 734

Corbusier, Le, 658

Corday, Charlotte, 411

Cordova, *m246, m251,* 254

Corinth, *m84, m99,* 102, *m103, m149*

Corn Laws, 452, 510, 512

ME

Fifth French Republic, 768
Fiji Islands, 570, *m570*
Fillmore, Millard, 554
Finland: ruled by Sweden, 352, *m354;* acquired by Russia in 1800's, 426; independent after World War I, *m603,* 605; government of, 673; war with Russia, 720; in World War II, *m723,* 728, 736; after World War II, 759, *m759, m765;* today, *m842*
First Coalition against France, 410
First French Empire, 415
First International, 456
Fiume (FYOO·may), 586, 592, 601, *m603*
Five-Power Treaty, 702
Five-Year Plans: in U.S.S.R., 689–90; in India, 796; in China, 798, 800
Flanders, 208, *m209,* 223, *m224–25,* 235, *m236,* 297
Flaubert (floh·BAIR), Gustave, 652
Fleming, Alexander, 644
Flemish language, 340, 464
Flemming, Walther, 620
Florence, 293, 294, 296, *p460–61, m495*
Florida, 323, *m326–27,* 387, *m388,* 392, *m392,* 397, *m519*
Foch (FOHSH), Ferdinand, 599
folk art, 387, *p387*
Foochow, 558, *m559*
Ford, Henry, 628
Formosa, 557, *m559,* 560, *m570, m735. See also* Taiwan.
Forum, Roman, *p139*
Fourier (foo·RYAY), Charles, 454
Fourteen Points, 598–99, 601, 602, 605
Fourth French Republic, 720, 758, 767–68
Fra Angelico, 296
France: Cro-Magnon man in, 9; as part of Gaul, 125; invaded by Germanic tribes, 156; ruled by Franks, 189–91; Charlemagne's empire, 191–92, *m191;* invaded by Vikings, 194–95, *m194;* growth of, under early Capetians, 208–09, *m209;* and Crusades, 217, *m218;* and medieval trade, 223, *m224–25;* in Hundred Years' War, 235–36, *m236;* in later Middle Ages, 237, *m238,* 241; during Renaissance, 294–95; and Reformation, 308, *m309,* 311; early exploration and colonization, *m318–19, m326–27,* 329; under Henry IV, 342–43; under Richelieu, 343; and Thirty Years' War, 345, *m346;* under Louis XIV, 347–50, *m351;* in late 1700's, 360; during Enlightenment, 380, 382; in French and Indian War, 392, *m392;* and American Revolution, 395, 397; and French Revolution, 401–13, *c416;* under Napoleon, 413–21, *m419;* at Congress

of Vienna, 424, 426, *m427;* and Greek independence, 429; Industrial Revolution in, 446, 453; revolution of 1830, 463–64; under Louis Philippe, 464; revolution of 1848, 464–65; under Napoleon III, 465–72, 495–96; and Franco-Prussian War, 471–72, 486–87; under Third Republic, 472–73, 476; at Congress of Berlin, 502; imperialism in Africa, 532–33, *m534,* 535–36, 539, 545, 546; imperialism in Asia, 549–50, 558, 559, *m559,* 561, 562, 566; imperialism in the Pacific, 569–70, *m570;* before World War I, 584–85, 586, 588, *m588;* in World War I, 591–600, *m595;* at Paris Peace Conference, 600–05; after World War I, 665–68; during Great Depression, 679; at Washington Naval Conference, 702; and Spanish Civil War, 709; in World War II, 717, 721–22, *m723,* 730, 736, 737; and UN, 747, 751, 755; and nuclear weapons, 753, 825, 826; after World War II, 758, *m759,* 762, 767–68; joins ECSC, 768; and EEC, 768, 770, 771; and Council of Europe, 771; and NATO, 771, 772, 775; summit conferences, 773; Suez crisis, 786–87; and Algeria, 790–92; and Indo-China, 808–09; today, *m842*
Franche-Comté, *m346,* 349
Francis II, Holy Roman Emperor, 478, 479
Francis II, king of Sicily, 496
Francis of Assisi, St., 207
Franciscans, 207, 242
Franco, Francisco, *p708,* 709–10, 726, 728
Franco-Prussian War, 471–72, 474, 486–87, 585
Frankfort, *m224,* 482, 485, *m486*
Frankfort, Treaty of, 472
Frankfort Assembly, *p482,* 483
Franklin, Benjamin, 379, *p381, p396,* 397
Franks, *m156,* 189–92, 194
Franz Ferdinand, archduke of Austria, 590–91, *p590*
Franz Josef I, emperor of Austria, 499
Frederick I, king of Prussia, 358
Frederick II, Holy Roman Emperor, 214
Frederick II (the Great), king of Prussia, 358, *p359,* 360, 382, 480
Frederick Barbarossa, Holy Roman Emperor, 213–14, 219
Frederick William of Brandenburg, 357–58
Frederick William I, king of Prussia, 358
Frederick William II, king of Prussia, 409, 479

Frederick William III, king of Prussia, 424, 479
Frederick William IV, king of Prussia, 483
Free French, 722, 727
French Congo, *m534,* 539. *See also* Congo, Republic of the.
French East India Company, 329
French Equatorial Africa, *m534,* 539, 546
French Guiana, *m436, m845*
French Guinea, *m534,* 539
French and Indian War, 360, 392
French Indo-China. *See* Indo-China.
French language, 145, 198, 229, 348
French Revolution: background, 401–02, 404–05; course of, 406–07, 409–13; effects of, 421, 432, 647; Marx on, 454
French Somaliland, *m534,* 546
French West Africa, *m534,* 539, 546
French West Indies, 426
frescoes, 85
Freud (FROID), Sigmund, *p621,* 624, 653
Friedrich, Caspar David, *p481*
Frost, Robert, 653
Fuggers (FOOG·urz), banking family, 333
Fujiwara family, 279
Fulton, Robert, 444

Gabon, *m781, m846*
Gadsden Purchase, 518, *m519*
Gagarin, Yuri, *p828–29*
Galen, 144, 174, 233
Galilee, Sea of, *m54, m149*
Galileo, 302, *p303,* 304, 311
Gama, Vasco da, 316, *p317, m318–19*
Gambetta, Léon, 472, 475
Gambia, *m534, m781, m846*
Gandhara, 169
Gandhi (GAHN·dee), Indira, 795, *p797*
Gandhi, Mohandas, *p671,* 672, 735, 795, 822
Ganges River, 59–60, *m60, m167, m171, m266, m269, m550, m796*
Ganges Valley, 59–60, 61, 162, 166
Gao, *m256,* 258
Garibaldi, Giuseppe, 496, *p497,* 498
Gascony, 208, *m209,* 210, 235, *m236*
gasoline, 628, 630
Gatling gun, 521
Gauguin (go·GAN), Paul, *p572,* 655
Gaul: area, 125, *m125, m128;* Hannibal in, *m131;* under Roman rule, 135, *m137,* 141; invaded by Germanic tribes, *m156,* 156–57; Hun attack on, 158; conquered by Franks, 189
Gauls, *p132*
Gautama Buddha. *See* Buddha.
Gaza Strip, 786, 788

857

General Assembly, UN, *p746,* 747, *c749,* 753, 754, 755, 787

General Electric Company, 627

General Staff, German, 586, 604, 695, 760

genetics, 620, 830

Geneva, New York, 387

Geneva, Switzerland, 308, 606, *m765*

Geneva Agreements, 1954, 808–09

Genghis Khan (JEN·giz KAHN), 261, *p261,* 274–75, *m274*

Genoa (JEN·oh·uh), 218, *m218,* 222, 223, *m224–25,* 293, 315, *m318–19*

genocide (JEN·uh·syd), **761**

geocentric theory, 302

George I, king of England, 377

George II, king of England, 377, 385

George III, king of England, 392–93, 395, 510

George IV, king of England, 510

George V, king of England, 513–14

Georgia, U.S. state, 385, *m388, m519*

Georgia, Russian province, 689, *m842*

German Confederation, 427–28, *m427,* 480–81, 484–85

German East Africa, *m534,* 545, 604

German Southwest Africa, *m534,* 540, 542, 604

Germanic tribes, 134, *m137,* 156–58, *m156,* 189, 195

Germantown, 387

Germany: Neanderthal man in, 6, 9; as part of Gaul, 125; Germanic tribes, 134, 156–58, *m156;* Vikings in, *m194,* 195; St. Boniface in, *m205,* 206; in Holy Roman Empire, 211–14, 238–39, *m238;* medieval trade, 222–23, *m224–25;* during Renaissance, 294–95, 297, 300; and Reformation, 304–05, 307, *m309;* Thirty Years' War, 345–46, *m346;* and Louis XIV, 349, *m350;* rise of Brandenburg (Prussia), 357–58, 359; during French Revolution and Napoleonic era, 409, 410, 417, *m419,* 420, 421, 479–80; revolts in early 1800's, 429; in Industrial Revolution, 446, 453; attitudes toward unity, 480; formation of Zollverein, 481; revolutions of 1848, 483; Frankfort Assembly, 483; unification under Bismarck, 471–72, 483–87, *m486, c487;* formation of German Empire, 487–88; in late 1800's, 488–91, 635, 639; and imperialism, 530–31, *m534,* 535–36, 540, 542, 545, *m559,* 561, 562, 566, 570–71, *m570;* formation of Triple Alliance, 491, 586, 588–89, *m588;* militarism in, 585–86; in Balkans, 589–90; in World War I, 591–96, *m594, m595,* 598–600, 606; peace settlements, 600–05, *m603;* and League of Nations, 606, 667, 702; under Weimar Republic, 694–95; French occupa-

tion of Ruhr, 666–67; signs Locarno Pact, 667; and customs union with Austria, 679; rise of Hitler, 695, 698–99; Anti-Comintern Treaty, 706; and Spanish Civil War, 709; aggressions leading to World War II, 711–15, *m713;* attack on Poland, 717; in World War II, 719–40, *m723;* postwar problems, 758–62, *m759;* division of, 764–66, 776. For period after 1949, *see* East Germany; West Germany.

Gershwin, George, 655

Gestapo (guh·STAH·poh), 699

Ghana (GAH·nuh), kingdom of, *m256,* 258

Ghana, republic of, *m781, m846*

Ghent, 223, *m224–25,* 229

Ghori, Mohammed, 266

G.I., 730

Gibraltar, 349, *m350, m723,* 727

Gibraltar, Rock of, 253

Gibraltar, Strait of, 51, *m51, m534,* 535

Gilbert Islands, 570, *m570,* 731, 734, *m735*

Giotto (JAH·toh), 296

Girondists (juh·RAHN·dists), **410,** 411, 412

Giza, *p17, m27,* 29

glaciers, 6, *m7*

gladiators, *p142,* 143–44

Gladstone, William, *p511,* 512–13

Glorious Revolution, 375

Gluck (GLOOK), Christophe, *p381*

Goa, *m318–19,* 321, *m326–27, m550*

Gobi Desert, *m67, p68,* 70, *m224–25*

Goethe (GUHR·tuh), Johann Wolfgang von, 479, 650

Golan Heights, 788

gold: and Spanish Empire, 324, 432; and Commercial Revolution, 332; Klondike Gold Rush, 515; discovery of, in Australia, 517; California Gold Rush, 519; discovery of, in Transvaal, 543

Gold Coast, *m534,* 539–40

Golden Horde, 262, 267, *m267, m274,* 275, 330

Good Hope, Cape of, *m256,* 316, *m318–19, m326–27,* 329, *m534*

Good Neighbor Policy, 680, 815

Goodyear, Charles, 443

Gordon, Charles, 546

Gorgon, *p93*

Gothic architecture, *p231,* 234

Gothic revival, 658

Goths, *m156*

Governing Council for Environmental Programmes, 755

government: beginnings of, 10, 13; in ancient Egypt, 23; in Fertile Crescent, 37, 39, 41, 45, 47, 54–55; of Aryan tribes, 65; of Shang China, 72; in ancient Greece, 88–89, 92–94, 95, 96–98, 106; in Hellenistic period,

119; of Romans, 126–27, 130–31, 135–37, 140, 154–55; in early China, 176–77; Confucius on, 179; Lao-tzu on, 180; under Charlemagne, 192; in medieval Europe, 198–200, 204, 206–07, 234; in Moslem Empire, 254; in feudal Japan, 279–81; in early modern Europe, 336, 366–67, 375–78; and Enlightenment, 379–80, 382; in American colonies, 387–89, 394–95, 397–99; under Old Regime in France, 402; in revolutionary period, 407, 409–10, 412; under Napoleon, 414–15; monarchy in modern times, 462–63; modern democracy, 508–09; democracies after World War I, 664–65; modern totalitarianism, 682–83

Gowon, Yakubu, 783, *p784*

Gracchus (GRAK·us), Gaius, 134

Gracchus, Tiberius, 134

Grand Army, of Napoleon I, 419–20

Grand Canal, China, 270, *m271, m274, m275*

Grand Canyon, 323

grand jury, 210

Granicus, battle of, *m103,* 104

gravitation, law of, 378

Great Britain: formation of, 349, 376; and wars in late 1700's, 360; American colonies and Revolutionary War, 384–99, *m398;* and Canada, 399; and French Revolution, 410, 412, 413; and Napoleon, 416–18, 420–21; at Congress of Vienna, 424, 426–28, *m427;* and revolts of early 1800's, 429, 437; and Industrial Revolution, 439–54; agricultural revolution, 440–41; in Crimean War, 468, 470; intervention in Mexico, 470; at Congress of Berlin, 502; growth of democracy in, 508–10; during Victorian Era, 510, 512–13; in early 1900's, 513–14; and dominions, 514–17; imperialism in Africa, *m534,* 535–36, 539–40, 542–43, 545–46; imperialism in Asia, 549–51, *m550,* 553, 558–59, *m559,* 561–63, 566; imperialism in Pacific, 569–71, *m570;* dispute with Venezuela, 574; and armaments race, 586; in Triple Entente, 588–89, *m588;* in World War I, 591–600, *m594,* 606; at Paris Peace Conference, 600–05; and League of Nations, 605; industry and trade, 637, 639; after World War I, 669–72; signs Locarno Pact, 667; at Washington Naval Conference, 702; and Spanish Civil War, 709; and German aggressions, 711–14; preparations for war, 714–15; in World War II, 717, 720–22, *m723,* 726–28, 729–32, 735–37, 740; and UN, 746–47, 751; and nuclear weapons, 753, 825; and UNRRA, 757–58; after World War II, 758–60,

m759, 762, 763, 765, m765, 767; and EEC, 768, 770–71; and Council of Europe, 771; and NATO, 771–72; and 1955 summit conference, 773; and South Africa, 784; Suez crisis, 785–87; and Palestine, 787; and India, 794, 795; and Burma, 808; and Geneva Agreements, 808–09. *See also* Britain; British Commonwealth; England.
Great Colombia, 435, *m436*, 437
Great Cultural Revolution, 800
Great Depression, *p678*, 679–80
Greater East Asia Co-Prosperity Sphere, 730
Great Lakes, 329, *m386*, *m388*, 391, 398, *m516*, *m519*, 819
Great Leap Forward, 800
Great Reform, in Japan, 279
Great Schism (SIZ·um), 241–42
Great Society, 821
Great Treasure, in Japan, 279
Great Wall of China, 176, *m176*, *m177*, *p181*, *m271*, *m272*, *m274*, *m276*, *p548*
Greco-Bactrian Empire, 169, 170
Greece: physical regions, *p82*, 83–84, *m84*, *m97*; Phoenicians in, *m51*; earliest civilization of, 84–87, *m85*; migrations to, 85, 87; colonies, *m84*; early city-states, 88–89, 92–97; Persian Wars, 98–101, *m99*; in Age of Pericles, 101, 102; Peloponnesian War, 102; Spartan rule, 102; Theban rule, 102; conquest by Philip of Macedon, 103–04; and Alexander the Great, *m103*, 104–06; culture of, during Golden Age, 108–18; Hellenistic culture, 118–21; Roman conquest of, 130, *m137*; Christianity in, *m149*, 151; barbarian invasions of, *m156*; and Byzantine Empire, 245, *m246*; and Ottoman Empire, *m352*; independence, 429; and Balkan Wars, *m502*, 503; in World War I, 593, *m594*; after World War I, *m603*, 604; in World War II, *m723*, 727, 736; after World War II, 757, 758, *m759*; U.S. aid to, 763; and NATO, *m765*, 771; and Cyprus, 767–68; and EEC, 768; today, *m842*
Greek alphabet, *p22*, *m52*
Greek language, 119
Greek Orthodox Church, 247
Greenland, *m7*, 195, *m326–27*, *m844*
Gregory I, pope, 197, 204
Gregory VII, pope, 212–13
Grimm brothers, 650
Gropius, Walter, 658
Guadalcanal, 734, *m735*
Guadeloupe, *m326–27*, *m575*
Guam, *m570*, 571, 575, 731, *m735*, 750
Guantánamo Bay, *m575*, 577
Guatemala, 433, *m436*, *m575*, 816, *m844*

guerrilla (guh·RIL·uh), **418**
Guiana, *m326–27*
guilds, 228, 232
Guinea, *m781*, *m846*
gunpowder, 272
Gupta Empire, 170–71, 173–74
Gurkhas, 530
Gutenberg, Johann, 300
Guyana (formerly British Guiana), *m845*

habeas corpus, **374**
Habeas Corpus Act, 374
Hades (HAY·deez), 89, 92
Hadrian, Roman emperor, 138, *p139*
Hadrian's Wall, *m137*, 141, *m156*
Hague (HAYG), The, 583, 591, *m594*
Haifa (HY·fuh), 670
Haile Selassie (HY·lee suh·LAS·ee), 706, 727
Hainan (HY·NAHN), *m559*, 730, *m735*, *m806*
Haiti (HAY·tee), 433, *m436*, *m575*, 581, 680, *m844*
Halicarnassus, *m97*
Halley's comet, 182
Hamburg, 223, *m224–25*, 478, *m486*, *m723*, 734
Hammarskjöld (HAHM·ar·shoold), Dag, 780, *p782*, 787
Hammurabi (hah·moo·RAH·bee), Babylonian ruler, 41, *p44*
Hammurabi's code, 41, *p44*, 55
Han dynasty, 177–78, *m177*, 813
Han River, 177, *m177*
Hancock, John, 393
Hangchow, *m271*, 272, *m272*, *m274*, 315, *m559*
Hanging Gardens of Babylon, 46
Hankow, *m559*, 676, 705
Hannibal, 130, *m131*
Hanoi, *m806*
Hanover, *m350*, 357, 479, 484, 486, *m486*
Hanoverian dynasty, 377
Hanseatic League, 223, *m225*
Hapsburg family: early growth of, 239; and Charles V, 337–39, *m338*; and Netherlands, 340; and Thirty Years' War, 345–46, *m346*; and Treaty of Utrecht, 349, *m350*; and Maria Theresa, 357; and Italy, 426, 496
hara-kiri (HAR·uh-KIR·ee), **281**
Harappa, 61–62, 64
Harbin, *m559*, 560, 561
Hardy, Thomas, 653
Hargreaves, James, 441
Harold, Saxon king, *p196*, 198
Harris, Townsend, 554
Harsha, 265
Hartford, 384, *m388*
Harvey, William, 304
Hastings, *m209*
Hastings, battle at, 198

Hatshepsut (ha·CHEP·soot), Egyptian queen, *p26*, 27
Hattusas, 42, *m42*
Havana, 574, *m575*
Hawaii: Japanese in, 557; in age of imperialism, *m570*, 571, 580; in World War II, 731, *m735*; today, *m844*
Hawkins, John, 324
Haydn (HYD·n), Franz Joseph, *p381*
Hebrew language, 52
Hebrews. *See* Jews.
Hegira (hih·JY·ruh), **251**
Hejaz, *m603*
Helen of Troy, 89
Helgoland, 426, *m426*, 545
heliocentric theory, **301**
Heliopolis (hee·lee·AHP·uh·lis), *m27*, 32–33
Hellas, 94
Hellen, Greek hero, 94
Hellenes, **94**
Hellenistic Age, 119–21
Hellespont, *m97*, 98, *m99*, 100
Helmholtz, Hermann von, 624
helots (HEL·uts), **94**–95
Hemingway, Ernest, 653
Henry I, king of England, 210
Henry II, king of England, 210
Henry III, king of France, 211, 212
Henry IV, Holy Roman Emperor, 212–13
Henry IV, king of France, 308, 342–43, *p344*, 368
Henry VII, king of England, 235
Henry VIII, king of England, 309–10, 366, 367, 368, *p369*
Henry the Navigator, prince of Portugal, 316
Hera, Roman goddess, 92, 128
Hercules, Greek hero, *p100*
Hereros, 542
heresy, **207**
Hermes (HUR·meez), Greek god, *p91*, 92, *p113*
Hero, Greek scientist, 121
Herodotus (hih·RAHD·uh·tus), 18, 47, 99, 100, 118, 168
Hertz, Heinrich, 631
Herzegovina (hur·tsuh·goh·VEE·nuh), 502, *m502*, 589, 590, 604
Hesse-Cassel, 395, 479, 486, *m486*
Hesse-Darmstadt, 486, *m486*
Hessians, 395, 479
Hidalgo, Miguel, 433
hierarchy (HY·uh·rahr·kee), Church, 203–04
hieratic (hy·uh·RAT·ik) **script**, **21**
hieroglyphic (hy·ur·uh·GLIF·ik) **writing**, **21**, *p22*
High Renaissance, 296–97
Himalayas (hih·MAHL·yuz), 59, *m60*, 61, 170, *m171*, *m266*, *m269*
Hinayana Buddhism, 167–68
Hindenburg, Paul von, 699
Hindi, 793

Indra, Aryan god, 65

indulgences, 304–05, 311

Indus-Ganges plain, 59–60, 61, 174, 796

Indus River: early civilization along, 11, *m12,* 13, *m60,* 61–64; Aryan invasions, *m60,* 64; and Persians, 47, *m49;* and Alexander the Great, *m103,* 104; and Moslems, 266, *m266*

industrial design, 443

industrial research, 626–27

Industrial Revolution: defined, **439–40;** background, 440–41; early development, 441–45; spread of, 446; effects, 447–50; and economic measures, 452–53; and socialism, 453–56; and imperialism, 529

industry: in Middle Ages, 228; and mercantilism, 334; Industrial Revolution, 439–56; and imperialism, 529–30; and World War I, 593; in late 1800's and early 1900's, 626–39; European, after World War II, 768, 770–71; Latin American, 815; Canadian, 819; U.S. after World War II, 821–22; and modern technology, 826, 830

inflation, 368

Innocent III, pope, 214, 219–20

inoculation, 174, 642

Inquisition, 207, 311, 339, 340, 418

Institutes of the Christian Religion, 308

Intercontinental Ballistic Missiles (ICBM's) and MIRV's, 753, 826

interdict, 204

internal-combustion engine, 628

International Bank for Reconstruction and Development (World Bank), 751, 785, 786, 815

International Brigade, 709

International Bureau of American Republics, 573

International Court of Justice, 748, 755

International Geophysical Year (IGY), 827

International Monetary and Economic Conference, 679

International Telephone and Telegraph Company, 816

International Whaling Commission, 755

Intolerable Acts, 393

inventions: Stone Age, 10, 12; in ancient Egypt, 21, 32; Sumerian, 40; in Hellenistic Age, 121; of Chinese, 272, 274; in Renaissance, 300–04; in Industrial Revolution, 441–46; in late 1800's and early 1900's, 627–32

Invincible Armada, 325, 339

Ionian Sea, *m97, m99*

Ionians, 85, 87, 95–96

Iran: modernization of, 674; in World War II, *m723,* 728, 729; today, *m786, m843.* See also Persia.

Iran, plateau of, 46, *m843*

Iraq (ih·RAK): creation of, *m603,* 604; as British mandate, 670; and League of Nations, 702; in World War II, *m723,* 727; joins Arab League, 785, *m786;* war with Israel, 787, 788; today, *m843*

Ireland: Vikings in, *m194,* 195; Christianity in, 197, *m205,* 206; and Reformation, *m309,* 311; rebellions in 1600's, 371, 373, 374; "Irish Question," in 1800's, 512–13; independence, 669–70; in World War II, *m723;* joins Council of Europe, 771; today, *m842*

Irian Jaya (formerly New Guinea), *m806, m843*

Irish Free State, 670

iron: earliest uses, 12–13; in ancient Egypt, 20; Hittite use of, 42, 43; in Industrial Revolution, 442; modern metallurgy, 630

Iroquois Indians, *m283,* 286

irrigation: beginnings of, 13; in ancient Egypt, 18, 20, 32; in early China, 70, 71, 72, 182

Irving, Washington, 650

Isabella, queen of Castile-León, 237–38

Isabella II, queen of Spain, 471

Isis, Egyptian goddess, 33, 151

Islam (iss·LAHM), 251, *m251,* 253. *See also* Moslems.

Ismail Pasha, ruler of Egypt, 536

Israel, kingdom of, *m54,* 55

Israel, republic of: Suez crisis and invasion of Egypt, 786–87; independence, 787–88, *p789,* 825; wars with Arabs, 786–88; today, *m843*

Issus, battle at, *m103,* 104

Istanbul, 674, *m723*

Italian language, 145, 229, 232

Italian Peninsula, 83, *m84,* 123–24

Italian Somaliland, *m534,* 706

Italy: physical regions, 123–24, *m125;* Phoenician colonies in, *m51;* Greek settlements in, *m84,* 124–25; Etruscans in, 124–25, *m125;* Latins in, 124–25, *m125;* Roman Republic, 125–36, *m128, m131;* Roman Empire at height, 136–45, *m138;* Christianity in, *m149, m205;* Roman Empire in decline, 153–59, *m156;* Ostrogoths in, *m245;* conquered by Justinian, 245, *m246;* Lombards in, 191, *m191,* 204; invasions, 800–1000 A.D., *m194;* in early Holy Roman Empire, 212–14, 238–39; and Crusades, *m218;* medieval trade, 222, 223, *m224–25;* Renaissance in, 293–94, 296–97; and Scientific Revolution, 300–02, 304; and age of exploration, 315, *m318–19;* during French Revolution and Napoleonic

Era, 413, 417, *m419,* 421; after Congress of Vienna, 426, 427, *m427,* 429; unification of, 494–96, *m495,* 498–99, *c498;* and imperialism, 530–31, *m534,* 535, 538, 545–46; seizure of Aegean islands, *m502;* joins Triple Alliance, 491, 586, 588, *m588;* in World War I, 592, *m594;* after World War I, 600, 601, *m603,* 604, 605; at Washington Naval Conference, 702; signs Locarno Pact, 667; Mussolini and fascism, 691–94; forms Rome-Berlin Axis, 699; invades Ethiopia, 706, *m713;* and Spanish Civil War, 709; invades Albania, *m713,* 714; in World War II, 720, 721, *m723,* 727, 732; after World War II, 757, 758, 759, *m759,* 762; postwar alliances, *m765,* 768, 711–72; today, *m842*

Iturbide (ee·toor·VEE·thay), Agustín de, emperor of Mexico, 433

Ivan I, Russian ruler, 262

Ivan III, Russian ruler, *p261,* 262, 351

Ivan IV (the Terrible), czar of Russia, 351

Ivory Coast, *m534,* 539, *m781, m846*

Iwo Jima, *m735,* 737, 804

Jackson, Andrew, 519

Jacobins, 410

Jagatai, Empire of, *m267, m274,* 275

Jakarta, *m806,* 807

Jamaica, 435, *m436,* 437, *m575, m844*

James I, king of England, 368, *m369,* 370, 376, 384

James II, king of England, 374–75, 376, 380

Jamestown, 325, *m326–27,* 384, 386, *m388*

janizaries (JAN·uh·zer·eez), 255

Janus, Roman god, 128

Japan: physical regions, 276, *m277;* Buddhism in, *m167,* 168; early history, 277, 279; in feudal period, 279–81; early culture, 281; medieval trade, *m224–25;* in age of exploration, 321, *m326–27,* 329; modernization of, 554–57; and imperialism, *m559,* 560–61, 563–64; in World War I, 592, 601; at Paris Peace Conference, 601–02; and Versailles Treaty, 604; and League of Nations, 605, 704; after World War I, 702, 704, *m705;* war with China, 704–05; signs Anti-Comintern Treaty, 706; joins Rome-Berlin Axis, 720, 726–27; and World War II, 720, 729–31, 734–35, *m735,* 737, 740, 808, 826; after World War II, 803–05; today, *m843*

Japan, Sea of, *m67, m277, m559,* 560

Japanese language, 322

Jarring, Gunnar B., 788

Java: prehistoric man in, 6, *m7;* Buddhism in, *m167,* 169; and early exploration, *m318–19, m326–27,* 329; and imperialism, *m559;* and World War II, *m735,* 807. *See also* Indonesia.

Java man, 6, *m7*

jazz, 655, 677

Jefferson, Thomas, 394, 432

Jenner, Edward, 642, 643

Jerusalem, *m54,* 55, 148, *m149,* 152, *m251,* 313, 788

Jerusalem, Kingdom of, 218–19, *m219*

Jesuits (Society of Jesus), 311, 489, 495

Jesus Christ, 148, 149, *p150, p152*

Jews: in ancient Egypt, 28, 32–33, 53–54; settle in Palestine, 54; early kingdoms, 54–55; defeat and captivity, 47, 55; law, 55–56; Bible, 56; Judaism, 56; and Jesus, 148; in Middle Ages, 227; in Spain, 238, 324, 339; Dreyfus case, 476; in Ottoman Empire, 501; Russian pogroms, 506; in Britain, 509; emigration from Europe, 644; Zionism and resettlement of Palestine, 670; and Hitler, 695, 698, 699; World War II persecution, 729; and war crimes trials, 760–62. *See also* Israel.

Jidda, *m224–25,* 250, *m251*

Jimmu, emperor of Japan, 277

Joan of Arc, 236

John, king of England, 210–11, 214

John VI, king of Portugal, 435

John XII, pope, 212

John XXIII, pope, *p772*

John of Jandun, 242

Johnson, Lyndon B., 773, 810, 821, 822

joint-stock company, **333,** 386, 447, 633

Jordan, *m786,* 787, 788, *m843. See also* Trans-Jordan.

Jordan River, 53, *m53, m149,* 788

joust, **203**

Joyce, James, *p651,* 653

Juárez (HWAH·rays), Benito, 470, 574

Judah, kingdom of, *m54,* 55

Judaism (JOO·dee·iz·um), 56

Julian Emperors, *c136,* 137–38

Junkers (YOONG·kurs), **481,** 483, 488

Juno, Roman goddess, 128

juntas, 816

Jupiter, Roman god, 128

Jurchen, 272, 274, 557

Justinian, Byzantine emperor, 245, *m246,* 248, *p249*

Justinian's Code, *p249,* 250

Jutes, *m156,* 157, 195

Jutland, battle of, *m594,* 595

Kafka, Franz, 653

Kaifeng, 271, *m272*

Kaiser, 137

Kalahari Desert, 256, *m256*

Kalidasa, Indian dramatist, 171, 173

Kamakura, *m277*

Kamchatka, *m326–27,* 688

Kami, Japanese gods, 277

Kamikaze (kah·mih·KAH·zee), 280

kamikaze attacks, 737

Kanagawa, Treaty of, 554

Kanishka, Kushan king, 170

Kansu, 175, *m175, m176*

Karakorum, 261, *m274*

Karikal, *m550*

karma, **165,** 166

Kasavubu, Joseph, 780, 781

Kashgar, *m224–25*

Kashmir, *m550,* 796, *m796*

Kassites, 43

Katanga, 780, 781, *m781*

Kay, John, 441

Kazakh (kah·ZAHK) **Soviet Socialist Republic,** *m843*

Keats, John, 650

Kellogg, Frank B., 702

Kellogg-Briand Pact, 702

Kelly, William, 442

Kemal, Mustafa. *See* Mustafa Kemal.

Kennedy, John F., 810, 821

Kent, 197, *m197*

Kenya, *m781, m846*

Kepler, Johann, 302, 378

Khanbalik (Peking), *m274*

Khartoum, *m534,* 546

khedives (kuh·DEEVZ), **536**

Khitan, *m271,* 271–72

Khorana, Har Gobind, 830

Khrushchev (kroosh·CHAWF), Nikita, *p772,* 773

Khufu (KOO·foo), pharaoh of Egypt, 29

Khyber Pass, 59, *m60*

Kiangsi, 676

Kiel Canal, 637

Kiev (kee·EV), *m193,* 222, *m224–25,* 259, 260, 262, *m274, m354*

Kim Il-sung, 801

King, Martin Luther, 822, *p823*

King James Version, 370

King's Friends, 393, 397

Kinsai (Hangchow), *m274,* 315

Kipling, Rudyard, 531

Kirghiz (kir·GEEZ) **Soviet Socialist Republic,** *m843*

Kiska, 734, *m735*

Kissinger, Henry, *p811*

Kitchener, Herbert, 546

Kitty Hawk, 628

Klee (KLAY), Paul, *p698*

Kline, Franz, *p824*

Klondike, 515, *m516*

Klondike Gold Rush, 515

knights, 203, 211, 237

Knossos (NAHS·us), 85, *m85, p86*

Knox, John, 308, 368

Koch, Robert, 643, *p645*

Kodak, 631–32

Koran, *p252,* 253

Korea: Buddhism in, *m167,* 168; and Han Empire, *m177;* and printing, 274; invasion by Japanese, 280; and imperialism, *m559,* 560, 564; Korean War, 801, *p802, m806;* and Japan, 803; today, *m843*

Korean War, 801, *p802, m806*

Kosciusko (kahs·ees·US·koh), Thaddeus, 395

Kossuth, Louis, 499

Kosygin, Aleksi, 773, 825

Kshatriyas (KSHAHT·rih·yuz), **164**

Kublai Khan, 274–75, *m274,* 314–15

Kukulcan, Mayan god, 283

Kulturkampf (kool·TOOR·kahmpf), **489,** 490

Kun, Béla, 673

Kunlun Mountains, *m67*

Kunming, 705, *m705, m735*

Kuomintang (KWOH·MIN·TANG), 564, 674, 676

Kurile (KOO·ril) **Islands,** *m735,* 740, 803, *m806*

Kushan Empire, 170, 173, 174

Kuwait (koo·WITE), 785, *m786, m843*

Kwangchowan, *m559*

Ky, Nguyen Cao, 810

Kyoto, *m277,* 279, 321

Kyushu, 276, *m277,* 321

Labor Party, Australia, 517

labor unions, 453

Labour Party, Great Britain, 513, 669, 740, 767

Labrador, 516, *m516*

Laconia, 94, 95, *m97*

Ladoga, Lake, 259, *m259*

Lafayette, Marquis de, 395, 406, 410

Lagos, *m534,* 540

laissez faire (les·ay FAIR), **451,** 637

Lamarck (lah·MARK), Jean Baptiste, 619

Lancaster family, 235

Land of Goshen, 53

language: written, 14–15; and nationalism, 423–24

Laos, 565, *m806,* 807, 808–09, 810, 812, *m843*

Lao-tzu (LOW·DZU), 179–80

La Paz, *m436*

La Plata, 430, 435, *m436*

La Plata River, 430, *m431*

lares (LAIR·eez), Roman spirits, 128

La Rochelle, 343, *m346*

La Salle, Robert de, *m318–19,* 329

Lashio, 705, *m705, m735*

Latin America: defined, **429;** physical regions, 430, *m431;* Indians in, 282–86, *m283;* in age of exploration, 316, *m318–19,* 320, 322–27, *m326–27,* 329; colonial period, 430, 433, *m436;* gains independence, 434–35, *m436,* 437; and imperialism, 573–75, *m575,* 577–78, 580–

81; after World War II, 815–16, *p817*, 818, *m820;* today, *m845*
Latin language, 145
Latins, 124, 125, *m125*
latitude, 314
Latium (LAY·shee·um), 124, 125, *m125*
Latvia: created, *m603,* 605; government of, 673; before World War II, 715; seized by Russia, 720, 736; after World War II, *m759,* 760, *m765*
Latvian Soviet Socialist Republic, *m842*
Laval, Pierre, 722
Lavoisier (lah·vwah·ZYAY), Antoine, 379, 412
law: Babylonian, 41; Hittite, 42–43; Jewish, 55–56; ancient Greek, 96, 97; Roman, 126, 140, 250; in Byzantine Empire, 250; feudal, 199; medieval Church, 204, 206–07; in England, 211; Russian, 260; in China, 276; in Japan, 279; under Napoleon, 414; international, 748
lay investiture, 207, 212–13
League for the Independence of Vietnam (Viet Minh), 808
League of Nations: formation and organization of, 605; peace-keeping measures, 605–06; membership, 606, 701; mandates, *m603, 705;* weaknesses of, 701–02; work of, 701–02; and Japanese aggression in Manchuria, 704; and Italian aggression in Ethiopia, 706; and Germany, 711; and Czechoslovakia, 712; expels U.S.S.R., 720; and UN, 747
Lebanon (LEB·uh·nun): part of Syria, 604; as French mandate, 727; joins Arab League, 785, *m786;* war with Israel, 787, 788; today, *m843*
Lebanon Mountains, 50, *m54*
Le Duc Tho, *p811*
Leeuwenhoek (LAY·vun·hook), Anton van, 379
left, political position, **409**
Legalists, in China, **176**
Legislative Assembly, in France, 407, 409
Leibnitz, Gottfried Wilhelm von, 378–79
Leipzig, *m419,* 420
Lena River, *m326–27*
Lend-Lease Act, 726
Lenin, N., 684, *p685,* 686, 688–89, 691
Leningrad, *m723,* 728, 729, *m765*
Leo X, pope, 304
Leonidas, king of Sparta, 100
Leopold, Hohenzollern prince, 471
Leopold I, king of Belgium, 464
Leopold II, emperor of Austria, 409
Leopold II, king of Belgium, 540
Lepidus (LEP·uh·dus), Roman general, 136, 137

Lesbos, *m97*
Lesotho, *m781, m846*
Lesseps, Ferdinand de, 473, 476, 536, *p537*
letters of credit, 333
lettre de cachet (LEH·truh duh kah-SHAY), **402**
Leviathan, 380
Lexington, 394
Leyte, 734, *m735*
Leyte Gulf, battle of, 734
Liaotung (LYOW·DOONG) **Peninsula,** *m559,* 560, 561, 564
liberalism: defined, **424;** suppression of, 428–29; and *Realpolitik,* 493–94; and education, 647
Liberal Party, Great Britain, 510, 512, 513, 514, 669
Liberia, *m534,* 542, 779, *m781, m846*
liberum veto, **355**
Libya: ruled by Italy, *m534,* 538; in World War I, *m723,* 727, 732; joins Arab League, 785, *m786;* independence, *m781,* 790; republic, 790; union with Egypt proposed, 790; today, *m846*
Liebig, Justus von, 446
Lima, *m326–27,* 430, 432, 435, *m436*
Lincoln, Abraham, 520–21, *p521*
Lindbergh, Charles, 677
Li Po, Chinese poet, 270
Lisbon, *p317, m326–27, m419, m765*
Lister, Joseph, 643
Liszt, Franz, 654
literature: Hebrew, 56; Aryan, 64–65; Greek, 89, 117–18; Roman, 144–45; early Indian, 162, 171, 173; Chinese, 182; medieval, 229, 232; Japanese, 281; during Renaissance, 293–95; of Enlightenment, 380, 382; and reform, 452; trends in 1800's and 1900's, 650, 652–54
Lithuania: about 1500, *m238;* and Poland, *m259,* 262; after World War I, *m603,* 605; government of, 673; before World War II, *m713,* 714, 715; seized by Russia, 720, 736; after World War II, *m759,* 760, *m765*
Lithuanian Soviet Socialist Republic, *m842*
Liu Pang, Han ruler, 177, 179
Livingstone, David, 545
Li Yüan, Tang ruler, 270
Lloyd George, David, 600, 601
Locarno Pact, 667
Locke, John, 380, 394, 399, 432, 623
Lombard League, 214
Lombards, *m156,* 191, *m191,* 204, 245, *m246*
Lombardy, 191, 213, 222, 426, *m427,* 494, *m495,* 496
London: in early English history, *m197;* and medieval trade, *m224–25;* population of, 229, 644; and

Renaissance printing, 300; and street lighting, 443, 628; in World War I, *m594, m595;* and International Monetary Conference, 679; in World War II, *m713, m723*
longitude, 314
Long March, *p675,* 676
Long Parliament, 371
Lorraine: in 1721, *m350;* and Germany, 472, *m486,* 487, 489; French desire for, 584–85; and World War I, *m595,* 598; after World War I, 601, 603, *m603;* in World War II, 737
Lothair, Frankish king, 192, *m192,* 237
Louis VII, king of France, 219
Louis IX, king of France, 275
Louis XI, king of France, 236–37
Louis XIII, king of France, 343
Louis XIV, king of France, 329, *p336,* 347–50, 376, 402
Louis XV, king of France, 350, 402
Louis XVI, king of France, *p403,* 404–07, *p408,* 409–10
Louis XVII, son of Louis XVI, 420
Louis XVIII, king of France, 420, 426, 428, 463
Louisiana, territory, *m326–27,* 329, *m388,* 391, 392, *m392, m398,* 416
Louisiana Purchase, 518, *m519*
Louis the German, Frankish king, 192, *m192*
Louis Napoleon. *See* Napoleon III.
Louis Philippe, king of France, 464–65
Louis the Pious, Frankish king, 192
Louvois (loo·VWAH), Francois, 348, 349
Loyalists, in American Revolution, 393, 399
Loyalists, in Spanish Civil War, 709, 710
Loyang, *m177, m271*
Loyola, St. Ignatius, 310–11
Lübeck, 223, *m225*
Lucca, *m495*
Luks, George, *p599*
Lumumba, Patrice, 780
Lusitania, 595
Luther, Martin, 305, *p306,* 307
Lutheranism, 307–08, *m309*
Luxembourg, *m595,* 721, *m723, m765,* 768, 771, *m842*
Luzon, *m570,* 571, 731, *m735*
Lyons, *m218, m224–25*
Lytton, Lord, 704
Lytton Commission, 704

Macao (muh·KOW), *m318–19,* 321, *m326–27,* 557, *m559*
MacArthur, Douglas, 734, 740, 801, 803
Macaulay, Thomas, 622
MacDonald, Ramsay, 669, *p671*

Menes (MEE·neez), ruler of Egypt, 23, *p26*

Mensheviks, 684, 686

mercantilism, 333–34; in France, 342, 347; in England, 373, 374; in British colonies, 391; in Spanish colonies, 432; attacked, 450

Mercia, 195, *m197*

Meroveg, 189

Merovingians, 189–90

Mesolithic Age, 9

Mesopotamia, defined, **36,** *m37;* conquered by Alexander the Great, *m103,* 104; in Roman Empire, *m137;* in Moslem Empire, *m251,* 252; Ottoman Turks in, 256

Messiah, 148

Messina, Strait of, *m125, m128,* 129, *m131*

mestizos, 430, 573

metallurgy, 630

Methodius, Byzantine missionary, 247

metics, 96, 109

metric system, 412

Metternich, Prince Klemens von: at Congress of Vienna, 424, *p425;* and revolts in early 1800's, 428–29; denounces Monroe Doctrine, 437; and France, 464; and Germany, 480, 483; resignation, 499

Metz, 338, *m338,* 345, *m346*

Mexican Cession, 518, *m519*

Mexican War, 518

Mexico: Indians in, 283–84; *m283;* in age of exploration, *m318–19,* 322–23; in Spanish Empire, 322–23, *m326–27,* 430, *m431,* 432; independence of, 433, *m436;* French intervention in, 470; war with U.S., 518; U.S. intervention in, 581; and World War I, 596, 598; government of, 818; and Cuba, 818; today, *m820, m844*

Mexico, Gulf of: and early explorations, *m318–19, m326–27,* 329; and physical regions in U.S., 385, *m386;* and North American colonies, *m383, m392, m398;* and Latin America, *m431, m436;* and territorial growth of U.S., *m519;* and imperialism, *m575*

Mexico City, *m318–19, m326–27,* 430, 432, *m436*

Micah, Hebrew prophet, 56

Michael, archangel, *p202*

Michelangelo Buonarroti (my·kul-AN·juh·loh bwaw·nar·RAW·tee), 297, *p298,* 311

Middle Ages: defined, **189;** feudalism, 198–200; manorial system, 200, *p200, p201,* 202; life of nobility, 202–03; the Church during, 203–08; Crusades, 217–22; revival of trade, 222–27; growth of towns, 227–29; language and literature, 229, 232;

universities, 232–33; philosophy, 233; science, 233; art and architecture, 233–34

Middle East, *m1,* **778**

Middle Stone Age, 9

Midway, battle of, 734

Midway Islands, 568, *m570,* 734, *m753*

migration, 36

Milan: in late Roman Empire, 154; and Christianity, *m149,* 150–51; in Lomard League, 213–14; in Renaissance, 293; under Spanish rule, 337, *m338;* under Austrian Hapsburgs, 349, *m350;* and unification of Italy, *m495*

Miletus, *m97,* 98

Mill, John Stuart, 452

Millet (mee·LEH), Jean-Francois, *p465*

Minamoto family, 279

Ming dynasty, 275–76, *m276,* 557

Minhow, 558

Minorca, *m350*

Minos (MY·nus), king of Crete, **84**

Mirabeau, Count de, 405

Miranda, Francisco, 435

missiles, guided, 736, 753, *p814,* 826–27

missionaries: Buddhist, sent out by Asoka, 169; in Ireland and England, 197; sent out by Gregory I, 204; Byzantine, 247; and European colonization, 321; in Latin America, 430, 432; and imperialism, 531, 560, 562, 569, 571

Mississippi River: and American Indians, *m283,* 286; and early explorations, 323, *m326–27,* 329; and physical regions of U.S., 385, *m386;* and North American colonies, *m388,* 391, 392, *m392,* 397, *m398;* and Quebec Act, 393; and Northwest Territory, 398; and westward expansion, 518, *m519*

Missouri, ship, *p739,* 740

Missouri River, 385, *m386, m519*

Mobutu, Joseph, 781, 783

Model T Ford, *p633*

Modena, 413, 426, *m427, m495,* 496

Mogul Empire, 269–70, *m269,* 549

Mohammed, 251, 253

Mohawk Indians, 286

Mohawk River, 385, *m386,* 397

Mohenjo-Daro, *m60,* 61–62, *p63,* 64

Moldavian Soviet Socialist Republic, *m842*

Molière, 347

Moltke, Helmuth von, 483

monarchy, 89, 462–63

monasticism, 204–06

Monet (moh·NEH), Claude, *p474,* 655

money: in ancient Sparta, 95; in Middle Ages, 223, 226, 227; and Commercial Revolution, 332

Mongolia, 11, *m12,* 70, 261, 770, *m806, m843*

Mongols: as central Asian nomads, 260–61; under Genghis Khan, 261; in Russia, 262; empire in 1294, *m274;* in China, 274–75; in India, 267, *m267*

monks, 205–06

monopolies, 635–36

monotheism (MAHN·uh·thee·iz·um), **27,** 56, 165

Monroe, James, 437, 542

Monroe Doctrine: proclaimed, 437; violated by France, 470; and U.S. in Latin America, 573; Roosevelt Corollary to, 580–81

Monrovia, *m534,* 542

monsoon, 61

Montana, 518, *m519*

Monte Cassino, monastery, 205, *m205, m723,* 732

Montenegro, 501, *m502,* 503, *m603,* 604

Montesquieu (mahn·tus·KYOO), Baron de, 380, 381, 399, 404, 405

Montevideo, *m436*

Montevideo Pact, 680

Montezuma, Aztec ruler, 322

Montfort, Simon de, 211

Montgomery, Bernard, 732

Montreal, *m326–27,* 329, *m388,* 394, *m515, m516*

Moors, 237, 238, 253–54, 324, 339

More, Thomas, 295, 454

Morelos, José, 433

Morgan, J. P., 633

Mormons, 649

Morocco: Barbary pirates in, 532–33, *m534;* European rivalry over, 535–36; and British-French *entente,* 588; in World War II, *m723,* 732; independence, 780; joins Arab League, 785, *m786;* today, *m846*

Morse, Samuel, 444, 446

mosaics, 248

Moscow: rise of, *m259,* 262; princes of, 351, *m354;* and Napoleon, 419–20, *m419;* becomes capital of Russia, 687; in World War II, *m723,* 728–29

Moses, 32–33, 54, *p298*

Moslem League, 553

Moslems: Mohammed and Islam, 251, 253; invasions and conquests, *m194,* 212, *m251,* 253–54; government, 254; economy and trade, *m224–25,* 254; culture, 233, 254; rise of Turks, 217, 255; in India, 266–67, *m266,* 269; and Sepoy Rebellion, 551; Moslem League, 553; in Cyprus, 767; and Arab world, 785; and partition of India, 795; in Pakistan, 796; in Philippines, 806

Mosul, 222

motion pictures, *p631,* 632

Mound Builders, *m283,* 286

x

865

Moussorgsky, Modest, 654
Mozambique (moh·zam·BEEK), m318–19, 321, m326–27, m534, 543, 545, 779, m781, m846
Mukden, 704, m705
Munch, Edvard, p623
Munich, 695, 712–14, m713, 776
Murasaki Shikibu, Lady, 281
Murmansk, m723, 728
Muscat and Oman, m843
Mussolini, Benito: rise of, 691–94, p696, p 697; invasion of Ethiopia, 705; and Spanish Civil War, 709; at Munich conference, 712–14; invasion of Albania, m713, 714; in World War II, 721, 727; resignation, 732; captured and hanged, 737
Mustafa Kemal, 674, p675
Mweru (MWAY·roo), Lake, m534
Mycenae (my·SEE·nee), 85, m85, 87, p87
Myron, Greek sculptor, 112
Mysore, m550

Nagasaki, m277, m326–27, 329, 554, m559, m735
Naguib (nah·GEEB), Mohammed, 785
Nalanda, m171, 173
Namibia (formerly South-West Africa), m781, m846
Nanhai, m177
Nanking, 276, m276, 558, m559, 676, m735, m806
Nantes (NAHNT), m309, m346
Naples, city, m426, 429, m495, 496
Naples, Kingdom of, m238, 337, m338, m346, 349, m350, 357, 413, m419
Napoleon I (Bonaparte): background, 413; suppresses Paris uprising, 412, 413; Near Eastern campaign, 413; seizure of power, 413–14; as First Consul, 414–15; as emperor, p401, 415–20, p415, m419; defeat, 420–21; effects of, 421
Napoleon II, 467
Napoleon III (Louis Napoleon): and Second Republic, 465–67, p466; as emperor, 467–68, 472; and Franco-Prussian War, 471–72, 486–87; and Italy, 495–96, 498
Napoleonic Code, 414, 417, 421
Napoleonic Wars, 413
Nara, m277, 278
Narbada River, m168, 170, m171, 174, 265, m266, m269
Nassau (NAH·sow), 486, m486
Nasser, Gamal Abdel, 785–86, 787
Natal, m534, 542
National Assembly, France, 405–07, 409
National Association for the Advancement of Colored People (NAACP), 822
National Convention, France, 409–12
nationalism: beginning of, in Middle

Ages, 234; and Church, 239, 241; during Napoleonic Era, 418, 421; growth of, in 1800's, 423–24, 426–28; and Realpolitik, 493–94; and imperialism, 530–31; and World War I, 584–85; and education, 647; and Romantic Movement, 650; in Africa and Middle East, 778–92, m781; in Asia, 794–98
Nationalist China (Taiwan), 746, 747, 754, 798, 805, m806, 824
Nationalists, Spanish Civil War, 709–10
National Liberation Front, Algeria, 791
national minorities, 605
NATO. See North Atlantic Treaty Organization.
naturalists, 652–53
natural law, 380
natural rights, 380
Nauru (nah·OO·roo) Island, m735
Navarre, 237, m237
Navigation Act, 373, 391
Nazareth, 148, m149
Nazis (NAH·tseez): rise of, in Germany, 695, 698–99; and Hitler's technique of aggression, 711; in Austria, 711; in Czechoslovakia, 712; in Memel, 714; in Danzig, 717; and wartime extermination policy, 729; after World War II, 761–62
Neanderthal (nee·AN·dur·tahl) man, 6, m7, p8, 9
Near East, 1
Nebuchadnezzar (neb·yoo·kud·NEZ-ur), Chaldean ruler, 46
Negev desert, 788
Negroes: in early sub-Saharan Africa, 255–58, p257; in American colonies, 386; in Latin America, 430, 432, p434; and U.S. Civil War, 519–21, p520; in age of imperialism, 538–46, p541; and jazz, 655; Hitler on, 698; in modern Africa, 777–82; civil rights movement in U.S., 822, p823; "black studies," 822, 824
Nehru, Jawaharlal (NAY·roo, juh-WAH·hur·lahl), 59, 795, p797
Nelson, Horatio, 416
Neolithic Age, 9–10
Neolithic Revolution, 10
Nepal, 530, m796, m843
Nero, Roman emperor, 138, 151
Nerva, Roman emperor, 138
Netherlands: part of Gaul, 125; Germanic invasions, 156; ruled by Franks, 189; as Burgundian possession, m236, 237; defined, 237; about 1500, m238; and Reformation, 308, m309; in age of exploration, m318–19, 324, m326–27, 327, 329; independence, 340, 345, m346; and Glorious Revolution in England, 375; and American Revolution, 395, 397; and French Revolution, 410,

412; and Napoleon, 418; and Congress of Vienna, 426, m427; and imperialism, 554, m559, 566, m570; in World War II, 721, m723; joins EEC, 768; joins NATO, m765, 771; and Council of Europe, 771; in Southeast Asia, 794, 806–07; today, m842
Netherlands East Indies. See Dutch East Indies.
Neutrality Act: of 1937, 723; of 1939, 723, 726
New Amsterdam, m326–27, 329, 374, 387, m388
New Brunswick, m515, 515, m516
New Caledonia, 569–70, m570
Newcomen, Thomas, 442
New Deal, 680
New Delhi, m796
New Economic Policy (NEP), 688–89
New England, 325, 387, m388, 389
Newfoundland, m318–19, 324, m326-.27, 329, 349, 515, m516
New France, m388, 391
New Frontier, 821
New Granada, 430, 435, m436
New Guinea: in age of exploration, m318–19, 321, m326–27; and imperialism, m559, 566, m570; in World War II, 731, 734, m735. See also Irian Jaya; Papua New Guinea.
New Harmony, 454
New Hebrides, 570, m570
New Holland, 516
New Netherland, 387
New Order, under Hitler, 729
New Orleans, m326–27, m388, 391, 392, m392, m398
New South Wales, 516, m517
New Spain, 430, 433, m436
New Stone Age, 9–10
New Sweden, 387
New Testament, 56
Newton, Isaac, 378–79, p381, 382, 613, 617
New York City, 329, m388, m389, 628, 644
New Zealand: discovery and development of, 517, m517; and imperialism, m570; and Versailles Treaty, 604; and immigration, 644; and woman suffrage, 647; in British Commonwealth, 672, 770; in World War II, 734
Nicaea, m103
Nicaragua, 433, m436, m575, 581, m844
Nice (NEES), 349, m350, 495, m495, 496
Nicholas I, czar of Russia, 468, 499, 504
Nicholas II, czar of Russia, 506, 598, 684, p685, 687
Nicomedia, 154
Niger, m781, m846

Pago Pago (PAHNG·oh PAHNG·oh), 570–71

Paine, Thomas, 397

painting: prehistoric, *p8,* 9; Egyptian, *p19,* 29, 32; Hebrew, *p55;* Cretan, 85, *p86;* Greek, 100, *p100,* 112, *p113;* Roman, *p145;* early Christian, *p150;* medieval, *p186–87, p188, p190, p201, p213, p216;* Renaissance, *p292, p295,* 296–97, *p298–99, p332, p369;* in India, *p172,* 173, *p264, p331, p552;* Chinese, 272, *p273;* Japanese, *p278, p331;* American Indian, *p331;* in 1700's, *p381, p394, p403, p411;* in 1800's, *p401, p462, p465, p474–75, p481, p513, p533, p555, p572,* 655, *p656–57,* 658; in 1900's, *p585, p599, p610–11, p614, p623, p626, p641,* 658, *p686, p698, p710, p825*

Pakistan: formation of, 795, *m796;* Kashmir dispute, 796; government and economy, 796, 798; civil war, 798; today, *m843*

Palatinate (puh·LAT·uh·nayt), *m238,* 239

Paleolithic (pay·lee·oh·LITH·ik) **Age,** 5–6, 9

Palestine: physical regions, 50, 53, *m54;* early Hebrews, 53–54; Hebrew kingdoms in, 55; Jewish law, literature, and religion, 55–56; in Roman Empire, *m137;* and Christianity, 147–48, *m149;* and Crusades, 217–22, *m218;* and medieval trade, 222, *m224–25;* in Byzantine Empire, 245, *m246;* Moslem conquest of, *m251,* 253; and Crimean War, 468, 670; British control of, *m603,* 604, 670; Jewish resettlement in, 670; in World War II, *m723,* 727; independence of, 787. *See also* Israel.

Pan American Union, 573, 815

Panama: independence, 435, *m436;* and Panama Company, 473, 476; and Panama Canal, *m575,* 578, 580; and Montevideo Pact, 680; today, *m844*

Panama, Isthmus of, 282, *m283, m318–19,* 320, *m431,* 578

Panama Canal, 578, *p578–79,* 580

Panama Company, 473, 476

Pankhurst, Emmeline, *p648*

P'an Ku, Chinese hero, 71, 76

Pan-Slavism, 504, 589

Panther, ship, 536

papacy. *See* popes.

papal bull, 240

papal line of demarcation, *m318–19,* 320

Papal States: creation of, 191, *m191, m192;* pope as ruler, 206, 212, 239; and Holy Roman Empire, 212, 213, 214; expansion of, 241; and Na-

poleon, 413, 417, *m419;* and Italian unification, *m495,* 496, 498

paper, 21, 300

Papua New Guinea, *m806, m843*

Papua, Territory of, *m843*

papyrus (puh·PY·rus), **21**

Paraguay, *m436, m845*

Paraguay River, *m431*

Paraná River, *m431*

pariahs (puh·RY·uz), **164**

Paris, Trojan prince, 89

Paris: in Charlemagne's empire, *m191, m192;* and growth of France, 208, *m209, m236;* and medieval trade, *m224–25;* population of, 229, 644; during French Revolution, 406, 407, 409, 412; during Napoleonic Era, 415, *m419,* 420; during revolutions of 1848, 465; under Napoleon III, 468, 472, *p474–75;* in World War I, 594, *m594, m595,* 599; and peace conference (1918), 600–02, *m603;* in World War II, 721–22, *m723,* 736

Paris, Treaty of, 1763, 392, 550

Paris, Treaty of, 1783, 396

Paris Peace Conference, 600–06

parish, 152

Park, Mungo, 540

Parliament, in England: early development of, 211; during Hundred Years' War, 235; under Tudors, 367; under Stuarts, 368, 370–71; and English Civil War, 371, 373; under Cromwell, 373; under Charles II, 374; after Glorious Revolution, *p372,* 375–78; and reforms in 1800's, 509–10, 512–13; Parliament Bill of 1911, 513–14

Parliament Bill, 513–14

Parma, 213, 413, 426, *m427, m495,* 496

Parthenon, 112, *p113*

pashas, 501

Passover, 54

Pasteur (pahs·TUR), Louis, 642–43, *p645*

Patagonia, *m436*

Pataliputra, 168, *m168*

paternalism, 454

Pathans, 530

Pathet Lao, 808–09

Patna, 168

patriarchs, 152

patricians (puh·TRISH·unz), **125**

Patrick, St., 197, *m205,* 206

Patriots, in American Revolution, **393**

Paul, St., 149, *m149,* 151

Paul III, pope, 311

Paul VI, pope, 311

Pavlov, Ivan, 624

Pax Romana, 139, 140–41, 143–45, 147, 153

Pax Sinica, 178

Peace of Augsburg, 307, 345

Peace of God, 200

peaceful coexistence, 773, 800

Pearl Harbor, 731, *m735*

Peary, Robert E., 637

Pechenegs, *m259,* 260

pedagogue (PED·uh·gahg), **110**

Pedro, Dom (Pedro I, emperor of Brazil), 435–36

Peiping (BAY·PING), 704–05, *m705, m735. See also* Peking.

Peking: medieval trade, *m224–25;* Chin dynasty capital, 272, *m272;* in Mongol Empire, *m274;* early guidebook to, 314; as treaty port, *m559,* 560; in Boxer Rebellion, 562; in 1900's, 674, 676, *m806. See also* Peiping.

Peking man, 6, *m7*

Peloponnesian War, 102

Peloponnesus (pel·uh·puh·NEE·sus), 85, 87, 92, 94, *m97, m99,* 102

penates (puh·NAY·teez), Roman spirits, 128

penicillin, 644

Peninsular Campaign, 419, 433

People's Democratic Republic, 801. *See also* North Korea.

People's Republic of China. *See* China.

Pepin II, Frankish ruler, 190

Pepin III, Frankish ruler, 190–91

Pergamum, *m97*

Pericles (PER·uh·kleez), 101–02, 109, 114, 117

Pericles, Age of, 101, 109

Perkin, William, 630

Permanent Court of International Justice, 605

Permanent Joint Defense Committee, 819

Perón, Juan, 816

Perry, Matthew, 554

Persepolis, *p49, m103*

Persia: defined, **46;** early history and culture, 46–48, *m48, p49,* 50; wars with Greece, 98–101, *m99;* and Peloponnesian War, 102; and Alexander the Great, *m103,* 104, 106; and India, 166, 168; medieval trade, *m224–25;* Islam in, *m251,* 253, 254; Mongols in, 262; and Ottoman Empire, *m352;* modernization of, 674. *See also* Iran.

Persian Gulf: and early Fertile Crescent, 35, 36, *m37;* medieval trade, 222, *m224–25,* 254; and World War I, 590, 593; and World War II, *m723,* 728

Persian Wars, 98–101, *m99*

Persis, 46, *m48*

perspective, 296, *p296*

Peru: Incas in, 284, 286; Spanish in, *m318–19,* 323, *m326–27;* viceroyalty of, 430, 432, *m436;* independence, 435, *m436;* today, *m845*

Pescadores (pes·kah·DOH·rays) **Islands,** *m559,* 560, 803, *m806*

Pétain (pay·TAN), Henri, 722

Peter, Apostle, 204

Peter I (the Great), czar of Russia, 351–53, m354, p356

Peters, Karl, 545

Peter's Pence, 204

petit (PET·ee) **jury, 210**

Petition of Right, 370, 378

Petrarch (PE·trark), Francesco, 294

Petrograd, m603, 684

petroleum industry, 443, 630

phalanx (FAY·langks), **103**

pharaoh (FAIR·oh), **23**

Phidias (FID·ee·us), 112

Philadelphia, m388, m389, 393, 397

Philip Augustus, king of France, 208, 210, m218, 219

Philip of Macedon, 103–04, 108

Philip II, king of Spain, 325, 339–40, p341

Philip IV, king of France, 236, 240, 275

Philip V, king of Spain, 349

Philippines: in age of exploration, m318–19, 320, 322, m326–27; in viceroyalty of New Spain, 430; and U.S., m559, 569, m570, 571–72, 575, 577–78; in World War II, 731, 734, m735; joins SEATO, 805; independence, 805–06, m806; today, m843

Philistines, 54, m54

philosophy: defined, **114;** ancient Greek, 114–15, 117; Hellenistic, 119–21; in early China, 179–80; in Middle Ages, 233; in Renaissance, 293–94; during Enlightenment, 379–80, 382; in late 1800's, 647, 649

Phoenicia (fuh·NEE·shuh), 50–53, m51, m52, m54, m84, m137

phonograms, 15

phonograph, 631

photography: development of, 631–32; first use in war, 469, p469; as art, 473, p473; in space, 827, p828

physics: in Hellenistic period, 121; in Renaissance, 302, 304; in modern times, 614–15, 617–18

Picasso, Pablo, p656, 658, p710

pictograms, 15

Picts, 157, m157

Piedmont, 349, m350, 413, 495, m495

Piero della Francesca, p295

Pilsudski (peel·SOOT·skee), Josef, 674

Piraeus (py·REE·us), 96, m97, 101

Pisa (PE·sah), 218, m218, 222, m224–25

Pisistratus (py·SIS·truh·tus), 96, 97

Pittsburgh, 446, 631

Pius IX, pope, 488

Pizarro, Francisco, m318–19, 323

Plains Indians, 286

Planck, Max, 617

Plassey, battle at, 550, m550

Plataea (pluh·TEE·uh), m99, 101, 168

Plato (PLAY·toh), 115

Platt Amendment, 577, 680

Platte River, m386

plebeians (plih·BEE·unz), **125–26**

plebiscite (PLEB·uh·site), **414**

Pliny the Elder, 174

Plutarch, 144–45

Pluto, Greek god, 92

Plymouth, 325, m326–27, 384, m388

Poe, Edgar Allan, 650, 652

pogroms (poh·GRUMS), 506

poison gas, 593, 604, 729

Poitiers (pwah·TYAY), 190, m191, 235, m236

Poland: medieval trade, m224–25; Mongols in, 262; union with Lithuania, 262; Calvinism in, 308, m309; Counter-Reformation in, 311; partitions of, 353–55, m355; and Napoleon, 417, m419; after Congress of Vienna, 426, m427; nationalism in, 493, 499, 503, 504; in World War I, 594, m594; independence, m603, 604, 605; signs Locarno Pact, 667; postwar government, 674; German aggression in, m713, 715, 717; in World War II, 717, 719, 720, m723, 729, 736; after World War II, m759, 760, 761; as communist nation, 762, m765; joins Comecon, 770; and Warsaw Pact, 772–73, 774; revolts in, 773–74; today, m842

polis, 88–89

Polish Corridor, m603, 604, 605, m713, 715, 717

Politburo, 691

Polo, Marco, m274, 275, 314–15, p317

polytheism (PAHL·ih·thee·iz·um), **27**

Pompey, Gnaeus, 134–35

Pompidou, George, 768

Ponce de León (PON·say day lay·ON), Juan, m318–19, 322

Pondicherry, m326–27, 329, 549, m550

Pontifex Maximus, 128

Pontius Pilate, p150

Pope, Alexander, 378

popes: early importance in Church hierarchy, 204; alliance with Franks, 190–91; political role in Middle Ages, 206–07; and Holy Roman Empire, 212–14; and Crusades, 217–20; Babylonian Captivity, 241; Great Schism, 241–42; and Reformation, 304–05; and Counter-Reformation, 310–11; under Napoleon, 418; and Kulturkampf in Germany, 488–89; and unification of Italy, 498

Popular Front, France, 667–68

Popular Front, Spain, 707, 709

popular sovereignty, 382

population: in prehistoric times, 13; in Greek city-states, 88–89; in late Roman Empire, 153, 154; in medieval towns, 229; and Industrial Revolution, 447; Malthus on, 451; and

imperialism, 530; growth, in late 1800's, 642, 644, 646

Populists, in Russia, 506

Po River, 124, m125, m131, 191, m191

Port Arthur, m559, 560, 564, m735, 740

portolanos, 314

Portsmouth, m388, 564

Portugal: medieval trade, m224–25; and early Spain, 237, m237; in age of exploration, 316, m318–19, 320; overseas empire, 321–22, m326–27, 329; Spanish rule of, 339; and Napoleon, 418; revolt in early 1800's, 429; and Brazil, 435, m436, 437; and imperialism, m534, 542, 543, 545, m550, 557, m559; in World War I, m594; in World War II, m723; joins NATO, m765, 771; today, m842

Portuguese East Africa, m534, 543, 545. *See also* Mozambique.

Portuguese Guinea, m534, 542, m781, m846

Portuguese language, 145, 322, 437

Poseidon (poh·SY·dun), Greek god, 92

positivism, 649

Potomac River, 385, m386

Potsdam Conference, 737, 740, 758, 760

potter's wheel, 21

pottery: early Chinese, 73; Cretan, p88; ancient Greek, p100, 112; Wedgwood, p379

Praetorian (prih·TAWR·ee·un) **Guard, 140,** 153, 159

praetors (PREE·turz), in Roman government, 127, 140

Pragmatic Sanction, 357, 360

Prague (PRAHG), m205, m603, m759, m765

Prague, Treaty of, 485

Prajapati (prah·JAH·put·ih), Indian god, 65

Praxiteles (prak·SIT·uh·leez), 112, p113

prefectures, in Roman Empire, **154**

prehistoric man, 5, 6, m7, p8, 9–10

prehistoric time, 5

Presbyterian Church, 308, m309, 368, 371, 373

presbyters (PREZ·buh·turz), **308**

Presidium, 691

Prester John, 314, 316

Pride's Purge, 371, 373

priest, 203–04

Priestley, Joseph, 379

primogeniture, 412

Prince, The, 294

Prince Edward Island, m515, m516

Principia, 378

printing: in early China, 272, p273, 274; in Renaissance Europe, 300, p303; in late 1800's, 636

privateers, **340**
proconsuls, in Roman Republic, 131
procurators (PRAHK·yuh·ray·turz), in Roman Empire, 140
proletariat (proh·luh·TAIR·ee·ut), **449**, 456, 688, *c807*
propaganda, **589**
prophets, Jewish, **56**
proportional representation, **694**
proprietary colonies, 388–89
propthasia, *m103*
protectionism, **821–22**
protectorate, **532**
Protectorate (Cromwell's), 373
Protestant Episcopal Church of America, 310
Protestantism: Reformation, 305, 307–11, *m309;* under Louis XIV, 349; in Stuart England, 370; and German unification, 480; growth of sects, 649
Proust (PROOST), Marcel, 653
Provence, *m236,* 237
Providence, *m388*
Prussia: and Treaty of Utrecht, 349, *m350;* and rise of Hohenzollerns, 357–58; under Frederick the Great, 358, 360; and partitions of Poland, 356, *m356;* during French Revolution, 409; and Napoleon, 417, *m419,* 420, 479–80; at Congress of Vienna, 424, 426, *m427;* joins Quadruple Alliance, 428; and German unification, 480–81, 483–87, *m486;* in German Empire, 487, 488; Polish Corridor through, *m713,* 715
psychiatry, **624**
psychoanalysis, **624**
psychology, **623**–24
Ptolemy (TAHL·uh·mee), Alexandrian scientist, 144, 233, 314
Ptolemy, rulers of Egypt, 22, 106, 135
publicans, in Roman Republic, 131
Pueblo Indians, 286
Puerto Rico (PWER·toh REE·koh): in age of exploration, *m318–19,* 322, *m326–27;* as Spanish colony, *m436,* 437; and Spanish-American War, 571, 575, *m575;* under U.S. control, 577–78; today, *m844*
Pulakesin II, Indian king, 266
Pulaski, Casimir, 395
Punic Wars, 129–30, *m131*
Punjab, *m550*
purdah, **269**
Puritans, in England, 368, 370, 371
Pylos, *m85,* 86
pyramids: in Egypt, *p17,* 18, 23, 29, 33; in America, 282, 283
Pyrenees Mountains, 83, *m84, m131,* 191, *m191, m251*
Pythagoras (pih·THAG·ur·us), 117

Qaddafi, Muammar el-, 790
Qatar (KAH·tar), *m786, m843*

Quadruple Alliance, 428, 437, 480
quantum theory, **617**
Quebec, city, *m326–27,* 329, *m388,* 392, 394, 515, *m515, m516,* 731
Quebec, province, *m516,* 819, 820–21
Quebec Act, 393
Queensland, 517, *m517*
Quemoy (kih·MOI), *m806*
Quételet (kay·TLEH), Adolphe, 623
Quetzalcoatl (ket·sahl·koh·AT'l), Indian god, 283
Quintuple Alliance, 428, 429
Quisling, Vidkun, 721
quislings, **721**
Quito (KEE·toh), *m436*

Ra, Egyptian god, 33
Rabban Sauma, 275
Rabelais (RAB·uh·lay), François, 295
rabies, 643
radar, **722,** 819
radio, 631, 636
radioactivity, **615**
radium, 615
railroads: early, *p439,* 444, *p445;* in U.S., 446, 521; in Canada, 515, *m516;* Cape-to-Cairo, 543; Trans-Siberian, *m559,* 560; Chinese Eastern, *m559,* 561, 564; in late 1800's, 636; in World War II, 728, 729
rajah, **162**
Rajputs (RAHJ·pootz), 265–66, *m266, m550*
Raleigh, Walter, 324
Ramadan, **253**
Ramayana (rah·MAH·yuh·nuh), 162, 171, 173
Rameses II, pharaoh of Egypt, 28
Rangoon, 705, *m806*
Ranke (RAHNG·kuh), Leopold von, 622
Raphael, 297, *p299*
Ratisbon, *m218*
Rawalpindi, *m796*
Rawlinson, Henry C., 39, 622
realism: defined, **117;** in Greek drama, 117; in Renaissance painting, 296; in literature of 1800's, 652; in painting of 1800's, 655, 658
Realpolitik (ray·AHL·poh·lih·TEEK), **493–94,** 584
recession, **822**
Red Cross, 583
Redistribution Bill, 513
Red Sea, *m20, m27,* 29, 54, *m224–25,* 254, *m534, m786*
Red Shirts, 496, 498
Red Terror, **687**
Reformation, 304–10, *m309*
Reform Bill of 1832, 510, 514
Reform Bill (second), of 1867, 512
Reform Bill (third), of 1884, 513
Reformed Church, 308, *m309,* 340
Regina, *m516*
regular clergy, **205**

Reichsrat (RYKS·raht), 694
Reichstag (RYKS·tahk), 487–88, 490, 694, 698–99
Reign of Terror, 411–12
Reims (REEMZ), 231, 234
relativity, Einstein's theories of, 617
religion: earliest beliefs, 6, 9; of Egyptians, 27–28, 33; of Sumerians, 40; of Babylonians, 42; of Persians, 47–48, 50; of Phoenicians, 51; of Aryans, 64–65; of Shang Chinese, 74, 76; of Greeks, 89, 92; of Romans, 127–28; in early Africa, 257; of American Indians, 283; and imperialism, 531; and science, 647, 649; growth of toleration, 649. *See also* Buddhism; Christianity; Hinduism; Islam; Judaism; Shinto.
reliquary (REL·uh·kwer·ee), *p206*
Remagen, *m723,* 737
Renaissance (REN·uh·sahns): defined, **292–93;** origin of, 293–94; literature of, 294–95; art of, 296–97, *p292, p295, p296, p298–99, p369;* and science, 300–02, 304
Renault, Louis, 628
Renoir (ruh·NWAHR), Pierre Auguste, *p475,* 655, *p656*
reparations, **602,** 665, 760, 802
republic, **125**
Republicans, in Spanish Civil War, 709–10
Restoration, in England, 373–74
Revere, Paul, *p394*
revolution: defined, **10;** Marx on, 456. *See also* American Revolution; French Revolution; Russian Revolution (of 1905, of 1917).
revolutions of 1848: in France, 464–65; in Germany, 483; in Italy, 494; in Austria, 499, *c500*
Reza Shah Pahlavi, 674
Rhazes (RAY·zeez), 254
Rhee, Syngman, 801
rhetoric (RET·uh·rik), 111
Rhineland, **601,** 603, 699, *m713*
Rhine River: and Roman Empire, 137, *m137,* 141; and barbarian invasions, *m156, m194;* in Holy Roman Empire, *m338, m346, m350;* and Prussia, 479, 480; and unification of Germany, *m486;* in World War I, *m594, m595, m603;* in World War II, *m713,* 737. *See also* Rhineland.
Rhodes (ROHDZ), *m84, m97,* 119, *m137,* 144, 502, *m502*
Rhodes, Cecil, 543
Rhodesia, *m534,* 543, *m781, m846*
Rhodes Scholarships, 543
Ricardo, David, 451
Richard (the Lion-Hearted), king of England, 208, 210, *m218,* 219
Richelieu (ree·shuh·LOO), Cardinal, 343, *p344,* 345
Ridgway, Matthew, 801

samurai (SAM·oo·ry), **278**, 281

San Martín (san mahr·TEEN), José de, *p434*, 435, *m436*, 437

San Salvador, island, 316, *m318–19*

Sanskrit, 65

San Stefano, Treaty of, 501–02

Santa Sophia, church of, 248, *p249*, 250

Santo Domingo, *m436. See also* Dominican Republic.

Sarai, 262, *m274*

Sarajevo (sah·rah·YEH·voh), 590–91, *p590, m594*

Saratoga, battle of, 397

Sardinia, island: Phoenician settlements on, 51, *m51, m84;* Greek settlements on, *m84;* as Carthagenian territory, *m128*, 129; as Roman possession, 129, *m131, m137;* and Christianity, *m149;* in Byzantine Empire, 245, *m246;* Moslem invasions of, 194, *m194;* ruled by Hapsburgs, 337, *m338, m345;* in World War II, *m723*

Sardinia, kingdom: after Treaty of Utrecht, 349, *m350*, 357; and French Revolution, 410, 412, 413; and unification of Italy, 494–96, *m495*, 498

Sardis, 47, *m48, m99*

Saskatchewan, 515, *m516*

satellites, artificial, 827

Sato, Eisaku, 804

Saudi (sah·oo·dee) **Arabia,** *m603, m723*, 785, *m786, m843*

Saul, Hebrew king, 55, 58

Savoy, 349, *m350*, 495, *m495*, 496

Saxons, *m156*, 157, 191, *m191*, 195, 197, *m197*, 198

Saxony, *m338, m346, m350*, 357, 360, *m419*, 426, 480, 484–86, *m486*

Scandinavia, 156, 194, 223, 720–21

Schiller, Friedrich von, 650

Schleiden, Matthias, 618

Schleswig (SHLAYS·vikh), 484–85, *m486*, 603, *m603*

scholasticism, 233

Schönberg, Arnold, 655

schools. *See* education.

Schubert, Franz, 654

Schumann, Maurice, 775

Schumann, Robert, 654

Schwann, Theodor, 618

science: in ancient Egypt, 32; Sumerian, 40; in ancient Greece, 117; Hellenistic, 121; Roman, 144; in Gupta India, 174; in early China, 182; in Middle Ages, 233; Moslem, 254; during Renaissance, 300–02, 304; during Enlightenment, 378–80; in 1800's and early 1900's, 612–21; and industry, 626–31; and religion, 647, 649; after World War II, 826–30

Scientific Revolution, 300–02, 304

Scipio (SIP·ee·oh), Roman general, 130

scorched-earth policy, 420

Scotland: Celts in, 195; and Christianity, *m205;* about 1500, *m238;* Calvinism in, 308, *m309;* and England, in 1600's, 368, 371, 373; becomes part of Great Britain, 376; and Reform Bill of 1832, 510; today, *m842*

Scots, *m156*, 157

Scott, Sir Walter, 650

sculpture: prehistoric, 9, *p11;* Egyptian, *p24, p25, p26*, 29, *p31;* Sumerian, *p38, p39;* Assyrian, *p43, p44;* Indus Valley, *p58;* ancient Chinese, *p75, p76;* Greek, *p91, p93, p108*, 112, *p113;* Hellenistic, *p120;* Etruscan, *p126;* early Christian, *p152;* late Roman, *p155;* of early India, *p161, p164, p169;* medieval, *p193, p206, p226*, 233, 234; early African, *p257;* Renaissance, *p298;* in 1900's, *p651*, 655, *p657*, 658

SEATO. *See* Southeast Asia Treaty Organization.

Second Coalition against France, 413

Second Continental Congress, 394–95, 397–98

Second French Empire, 467–68, 470–72

Second French Republic, 465–67

Second International, 456

Secret Army Organization, Algeria, 791, *p791*

Secretariat, League of Nations, 605

Secretariat, UN, 747, 750

Secretary-General, UN, 750, 755

secret ballot, 513

secular clergy, 204–05

Security Council, UN: organization and voting, 747–48; and Secretary-General, 750; and Disarmament Commission, 751, 753; and new members, 753, 754; and peace-keeping operations, 754–55, 780, 787, 801

Sedan, *m486*

Sedan, battle of, 472

segregation, in U.S., **824**

Seleucus (sih·LOO·kus), Hellenistic ruler, 106

Seljuk (sel·JOOK) **Turks,** 217, *m259*

Semitic (suh·MIT·ik) **languages,** 52

Senate, in Roman Republic, 126, 130–31, 135, 136

Seneca (SEN·uh·kuh) **Indians,** 286

Senegal, 530, *m534, m781, m846*

Senegal River, *m534*, 539

Seoul (say·OOL), *m559, m806*

Separatists, 368, 370, 371, 373

Sepoy Rebellion, 551

seppuku (SEP·POO·KOO), **281**

Serbia: independence, 501, 502, *m502;* in Balkan Wars, 503; and World War I, 589–91, *m594;* as part of Yugoslavia, 604

Serbs, *m205*, 247, 429, 499, 501

serfdom: defined, **200, 202;** decline

of, 228–29; in England, 235; in France, 237, 406; in Russia, 351, 353, 382; abolition during Napoleonic Era, 421; Russian emancipation, 504

Sevastopol (sur·VAS·tuh·pohl), *p469*, 470, *m502*

Seven Cities of Cibola, 323

Seven Weeks' War, 484–86, 498, 500

Seven Years' War, 360, 392, 550

Severus, Septimius, Roman emperor, 153

Seville, *m194, m224–25, m251*, 323, *m326–27*

sewing machine, 443, *p443*

Shah, Firuz, Delhi sultan, 267

Shah Jehan, Mogul emperor, 269

Shakespeare, William, 295

Shang dynasty, 72–76, *m73*

Shanghai, 558, *m559, m735, m806*

Shangtu, 274, *m274*

Shantung Peninsula, *m559*, 561, 592, 601, 604, 702

Shelley, Percy Bysshe, 650

Shensi, 676

Sherman Antitrust Act, 636

Shih Huang Ti (SHIR HWAHNG tee), Chin ruler, 176–77, 182

Shikoku, 276, *m277*

Shimonoseki, Treaty of, 560

Shinto, 277

ship money, 370, 371

ships: Phoenician, 50; Cretan, 85; Greek, 110; Carthaginian, 129; Roman, in Punic Wars, 129; medieval, *p216;* improvement of, in age of exploration, 315–16; later improvements, 444, 636–37; and coaling stations, 530, 569; submarines in World War I, 593; limiting tonnage, 604, 702; in World War II, 726, 732, 734

shogun, 279

Siam, *m559, 566, m570, m806. See also* Thailand.

Sian, 177, *m177, m271*

Siberia, *m259, m326–27*, 330, *m559*, 560, 687, 801, *m843*

Sibir, *m326–27*

Sicilies, Kingdom of the Two, 214, *m427, m495*, 496

Sicily: Phoenician colonies in, 51, *m51, m84;* Greek colonies in, *m84*, 92, 124–25, *m125;* Carthaginian settlements in, *m128*, 129; ruled by Rome, *m131;* and Christianity, *m149;* Vandals in, 245, *m245;* Moslems in, 194, *m194*, 212; Normans in, 214; Frederick II in, 214; as Hapsburg possession, 337, *m338, m346;* ruled by Austria, 349, *m350*, 357; in 1810, *m419;* and unification of Italy, *m495*, 496; in late 1800's, 498; in World War II, *m723*, 732. *See also* Sicilies, Kingdom of the Two.

Sidon (SYD'n), 50, *m51, m54, m84*

Siegfried Line, 720, *m723,* 736, 737
Sierra Leone, *m534, m781, m846*
Sihanouk, Norodom, 809
Silesia, *m350,* 360, 702
Silk Route, *m177,* 178, *m224–25*
simony (SY·muh·nee), **207,** 311
Sinai, Mount, 54
Sinai Peninsula, 52, *m52,* 54, *m54,* 788
Singapore, *m559,* 566, *m570, m705,* 730, 731, *m735, m806,* 807
Sinkiang, 67
Sino-Japanese War, 560
Si (SHEE) River, *m67,* 70, 176, *m176, m271,* 321, *m559*
Siva, Indian god, *p164,* 165
Six Dynasties, China, 178, 270
Skylab, 827, *p829*
slavery: in ancient Egypt, 29; Sumerian, 39; Assyrian, 45; of Hebrews, 47, 53–54, 55; Jewish law on, 56; in ancient Greece, 92, 94–95, 96, 97, 98, 109, 110, 119, 121; Roman, 131, 133, 141, 143, 158; in Moslem Empire, 253; in colonial U.S., 387; abolished in French colonies, 412; in Latin America, 430, 432; abolished in British colonies, 510; and U.S. Civil War, 519–21; and Liberia, 542
slave trade: and Portugal, 316; and Britain, 349; and colonial U.S., *m389,* 391; in Africa, 538, 539, 540, 543
Slavs: invasions of Europe, 194, *m194,* 245, *m246;* converted to Christianity, 247; in Russia, 259; in Austria, 480; in Balkans, 589; emigration of, 644; and Hitler, 698, 729
Smith, Adam, 450–51, 622
Smyrna, *m603,* 604, 674
Social Contract, 382
Social Darwinism, 622–23
socialism: defined, **454;** utopian, 454; Marx and, 454, 456; radical, 456; moderate, 456; in France, 465; in German Empire, 489–90; in czarist Russia, 506; and Fabian Society in Britain, 513; and Russian Revolution, 684, 686; in U.S.S.R., 687, 688, 689, 690; in Italy, 692; and Spanish Civil War, 709; in Britain after World War II, 767
socialist realism, **686,** *p686*
Social Security Act, 680
sociology, 622–23
Socrates (SAHK·ruh·teez), 114–15, *p116*
Sofia, *m502, m723, m765*
Solomon, Hebrew king, 54, 55
Solomon Islands, 570, *m570,* 731, 734, *m735*
Solon, 96, 97, 110
Somalia, *m781, m846*
sonar, 734

Song of Roland, 232
Songhai, *m256,* 258
Sophia, princess of Hanover, 376, 377
sophistry (SAHF·is·tree), **111**
Sophists, **111,** 114, 115
Sophocles (SAHF·uh·kleez), 118
South Africa, Republic of, *m781,* 783–84, *m846*
South Africa, Union of, *m534,* 542–43, 604, 672, 783–84
South America. *See* Latin America.
South China Sea, *m167, m271, m559,* 566, *m806*
Southeast Asia, *m1,* 6, **565,** 566, 767, *m806,* 807–12
Southeast Asia Treaty Organization (SEATO), 798, 805, 808, *m820,* 821
South Korea, 754, 772, 801, 802, *m806, m843*
South Vietnam, 754, *m806,* 807, 808, 809–10, *p811,* 812, *p812, m843*
South-West Africa. *See* Namibia.
South Yemen, *m786, m843*
sovereignty (SAHV·run·tee), **367**
Soviet Union. *See* Union of Soviet Socialist Republics.
Space Age, **827**
space exploration, 827, *p828–29*
Spain: Phoenician colonies in, 51, *m51, m84;* Greek settlements in, *m84;* Carthaginian settlements in, *m128,* 129; and Punic Wars, 130, *m131;* ruled by Rome, *m131, m137,* 141; Christianity in, *m149,* 204; barbarian invasions, *m156,* 157, *m245;* in Justinian's empire, 245, *m246;* and Charlemagne, *m191;* Moslems in, *m194, m218, m251,* 253–54; medieval trade, 223, *m224–25;* unification of, 237–38, *m237;* exploration, 315, 316, *m318–19,* 320; overseas empire, 322–24, *m326–27,* 429–32; domination of Europe, 337–40, *m338;* War of Spanish Succession, 349; in North America, *m388,* 389, 392, *m392,* 395, *m398;* and French Revolution, 410, 412; cedes Louisiana to France, 416; and Napoleon, 418, *m419,* 421; Bourbon restoration, 426; 1820 revolt, 429; South American colonies gain independence, 433–37; cedes Florida to U.S., 518, *m519;* intervention in Mexico, 470; and Franco-Prussian War, 471; imperialism in Africa, *m534,* 535, 542; Spanish-American War, 571–72, 574–75; in early 1900's, 707; Spanish Civil War, 707, 709–10, *m713;* fascism in, 710; in World War II, *m723,* 726, 728; today, *m842*
Spanish-American War, 571–72, 574–77, 578
Spanish Civil War, 707–10, *m713*
Spanish language, 145, 229, 437

Spanish Morocco, *m534,* 536, 709
Spanish Netherlands, 340, *m346,* 357
Spanish Sahara, 779, *m781, m846*
Sparta: history and government of, 94–95, *m97;* in Persian Wars, *m99,* 100; in Peloponnesian War, 102; rule of Greece by, 102
Spencer, Herbert, 622–23
sphere of influence, **532**
Spice Islands (Moluccas), *m318–19,* 321, *m326–27,* 329
spinning jenny, 441, *p445*
Spirit of the Laws, 380, 399
splinter groups, **476**
Sputnik I, 827
squadristi, **692**
squire, in chivalry, **203**
stained glass windows, *p231,* 234, *p763*
Stalin, Joseph: quoted, 688; rise to power, 689–90; *p690;* dictatorship of U.S.S.R., 690–91; and Spanish Civil War, 709; Hitler-Stalin Pact, 715; World War II conferences, 731, 736, 737, 740, 747, 758; and second front, 732; disagreements with Tito, 764; death of, 773
Stalingrad, *m723,* 729, 731–32
Stamp Act, 393
Stanley, Henry, 540, *p541,* 545
star-chamber procedures, **370**
Statute of Westminster, 672
St. Basil, cathedral of, *p356*
steam engine, 121, 442, 628
steel industry: early development of, 442; in U.S., 446; in late 1800's, 630; and international trade, 637, 639; in Ruhr Valley, 666; in postwar Europe, 768
Steinlen, Théophile, *p452*
Stella, Joseph, *p626*
Stephenson, George, 444
Steuben, Baron von, 395
St. Helena, island, 421, *m846*
St. Lawrence River, 329, *m386, m388,* 391, *m515*
St. Lawrence Seaway, 819
St. Mihiel, battle at, *m595,* 599
Stockholm, *m224–25;* environmental conference, 755
Stoics, 120
Stone Age, 5–10
Stonehenge, *p4*
Storm Troopers, **699**
St. Peter's Church, 297, 304
St. Petersburg, 353, *m354, m419, m427, p505,* 684
Strategic Arms Limitation Talks (SALT), 753
Strauss, Richard, 655
Stravinsky, Igor, 655, *m656*
strike, **453**
Stuarts, 366, 368
student unrest, 822, 824
stupa, *p163,* **173**
stylus, 39

submarines: in World War I, 593, 595, 598, 599; limitation of, 604; in World War II, 720, 721, 726, 728, 732, 734, 737

Sudan, region, **255–56,** *m256,* 539

Sudan, country, *m781,* 785, *m786, m846. See also* Anglo-Egyptian Sudan.

Sudetenland (soo·DAYT'n·land), 712–14, *m713*

Sudraka, Gupta king, 173

Sudras, 164

Suez, Isthmus of, 20–21, *m20,* 24, *m27,* 35, *m37, m54,* 536

Suez Canal: construction of, *m534,* 536, *p537;* and British control over Egypt, 536, 538, 670; in World War II, *m723,* 727, 732; Egyptian seizure crisis, 754–55, 785–87; today, *m846*

suffrage: in ancient Athens, 96, 97; in Roman Republic, 125; in England during 1700's, 376; in early U.S., 399; during French Revolution, 410; under Directory, 412; and liberals of 1800's, 424; in France during 1800's, 464, 467; in German Empire, 487–88; in Britain during 1800's, 509–10, 512, *c512,* 513; woman, 517, 647, 648; in India, 792; in Japan, 802

Sugar Act, 393

Suharto, General, 807

Sui dynasty, 270

Sukarno, Achmed, 807

Suleiman I, Ottoman sultan, 352

sulfonamides, 644

Sulla, Lucius Cornelius, 134

Sullivan, Louis, 658

Sully, Duke of, 342

Sumatra, *m167, m318–19, m326–27,* 329, *m559, m735, m806,* 807

Sumer, 37, *m37, m42,* 53, 61

Sumerians, *p2–3,* 37–40

Summa Theologica, 233

summit conferences, 773

Sung dynasty, 271–72, *m272*

Sun Yat-sen, 564, *p565,* 674, 676

supply and demand, law of, 450

surgery, 643

Surinam (formerly Dutch Guiana), *m845*

surrealism, *p585,* **658**

suttee, 171, 551

Sutton, Walter S., 620

Sweden: Vikings in, 194; medieval trade, *m224–25;* about 1500, *m238;* and Lutheranism, 308; about 1560, *m338;* and Thirty Years' War, 345, *m346;* war with Russia, 352; in North America, 387; and Napoleon, 416, 420; acquires Norway, 425, *m426;* in World War II, *m723;* joins Council of Europe, 771; today, *m842*

Swiss Confederation, *m236, m238, m338*

Switzerland: as part of Gaul, 125; Reformation in, 308; independence, 345, *m346;* and Napoleon, *m419;* and nationalism, 423–24; neutrality guaranteed, 426–27; in World War II, *m723;* today, *m842*

Sydney, 516–17, *m517*

Syracuse, Sicily, *m84,* 92, 93

Syria: defined, **25,** *m27;* in Persian Empire, *m48;* and Phoenicia, 50, *m54;* conquered by Alexander the Great, *m103,* 104; ruled by Rome, 137, *m137, m156;* Christianity in, *m149, .m205;* medieval trade, 222, *m224–25;* in Justinian's empire, *m246;* ruled by Moslems, *m218,* 246, *m251,* 253; Ottoman Turks in, 255; after World War I, *m603,* 604; in World War II, *m723,* 727; joins Arab League, 785, *m786;* wars with Israel, 787, 788; today, *m843*

Syrian Desert, 53, *m54, m137,* 141

Tacitus, Cornelius, 144, 156–57

Tadzhik (tah·JEEK) **Soviet Socialist Republic,** *m843*

Tahiti, 569, *m570*

Taiping Rebellion, 558–59

Taiwan (TY·WAHN), *m559, m735,* 803, *m806. See also* Formosa; Nationalist China.

Taj Mahal (TAHZH muh·HAHL), 269

Tale of Genji, p278, 281

Talleyrand, Charles Maurice de, 424, 426

Tamerlane, 267, *m267, p268*

Tanaka, Kakuei, *p799*

Tanganyika, 604

Tanganyika, Lake, *m256, m534,* 545

Tang dynasty, 270–71, *m271,* 279

Tangier, *m224–25, m251,* 254, *m534,* 536

Tannenberg, battle at, 594, *m594*

Tanzania, *m781, m846*

Taoism (DOW·iz·um), 179–80

tariffs: defined, **334;** and mercantilism, 334; under Louis XIV, 347; and free trade in Britain, 451; under Louis Philippe, 464; and Zollverein, 481; in German Empire, 489; and British Corn Laws, 510, 512; against Japanese competition, 557; tariff walls, 639; and economic nationalism, 669; and Great Depression, 677, 679; and Common Market, 768–70

Tarik, Moslem general, 252

Tarquin family, 124

Tarsus, 149, *m149*

Tasmania, *m517,* 517

Taurus Mountains, *m20*

taxes: in ancient China, 71; in Roman Republic, 131; in Roman Empire, 153–54, 159; in Charlemagne's empire, 192; medieval Church, 204; under Capetian kings, 209; and

Philip IV, 241; under Charles I, 370; in American colonies, 391, 393; under Old Regime in France, 402, 404; in France after World War I, 666; in Britain after World War I, 669

Taxila, 168, *m168,* 173, 174

Tchaikovsky (chy·KAHF·skee), Peter Ilich, 654

Technical Assistance Board (UN), 751

technological unemployment, 830

Teheran (teh·uh·RAHN), *m723,* 736, *m786*

telegraph, 444, 446

telephone, 630–31

telescope, 302, *p303*

television, 827, 830

Tell el Amarna, *m27,* 28

Ten Commandments, 54, 56, 148

Ten Hours Act, 452

Tennessee Valley Authority (TVA), 680

Tenniel, John, *p652*

Tennis-Court Oath, 406

Tennyson, Alfred, Lord, 470, 652

Tenochtitlán (tay·nohk·tee·TLAHN), 283, *m283,* 284, *m318–19,* 322, 430

test-ban treaty, August 1963, 753, 826

Tetzel, Johann, 304–05, *p306*

Teutonic Knights, 220, *m238*

Thailand (TY·land): Buddhism in, *m167,* 168; and World War II, 731, *m735,* 807; after World War II, *m806,* 807, 808, 812; today, *m843. See also* Siam.

Thebes, Egypt, 25, 27, *m27,* 28, *m42, m45, m48, m256*

Thebes, Greece, *m97, m99,* 102

Themistocles (thuh·MIS·tuh·kleez), 100, 111

theocracy (thee·AHK·ruh·see), **308**

Theodosius, Roman emperor, 152

Thermopylae (thur·MAPH·uh·lee), battle at, *m99,* 100

Thieu, Nguyen Van, 810

Third Coalition against France, 416, 417

Third French Republic, 472–73, 476, 665–68

Third International (Comintern), 691

Thirty Years' War, 345–46, *m346*

Tho, Le Duc, *p811*

Thomson, J. J., 615

Thrace, *m48, m97,* 98, *m99,* 100, *m103, m603,* 604, 674

Thucydides (thoo·SID·uh·deez), 102, 118

thuggee, 551

Thutmose III (thoot·MOH·suh), pharaoh of Egypt, *p26,* 27

Tiberius, Roman emperor, 137

Tiber River, 124, 125, *m125*

Tibet, *m67,* 70, *m167,* 169, 173, 314, 796, *m796, m843*

Tierra del Fuego, 282, *m283, m845*

Pact, 772–73; satellite rebellions, 773–74, *p774;* relations with Communist China, 776, 800–01; and West Germany, 776; Korea and, 801; and Geneva Agreements, 808–09; and Cuba, 818; U.S. relations improved, 825; and space exploration, 827, *p828–29;* today, *m842, m843.* Before 1917, *see* Russia.

Union of Utrecht, 340

United Arab Republic (U.A.R.). *See* Egypt.

United Kingdom, *m419,* 512, *m842.* *See also* Great Britain.

United Nations (UN): organization of, 746–48, *c749,* 750–51; and disarmament, 751, 753; membership, 753–54; in Cyprus, 754; in Korea, 754, 801; problems of peacekeeping, 754–55; in Egypt, 754–55, 786, 787; in Congo, 754–55, 780; financial problems, 755; environmental conference, 755; UNRRA, 757–58; and South Africa, 784; Arab-Israeli hostilities and, 786, 787, 788; and Kashmir, 796; and Indonesia, 807; and outer space, 827

United Nations Children's Fund (UNICEF), 751, 754

United Nations Development Program (UNDP), 755

United Nations Disarmament Commission, 751, 753

United Nations Educational, Scientific, and Cultural Organization (UNESCO), 751, *p817*

United Nations Emergency Force (UNEF), 754–55, 787

United Nations Relief and Rehabilitation Administration (UNRRA), 757–58, 763

United Nations Special Fund, 815

United Provinces of Central America, 433, *m436*

United States: physical regions, 385, *m386;* colonial history, 386–89, *m388, p390,* 391, *m392;* declares independence, 391–95; Revolutionary War, 395, 397; establishes independent government, 397–99; proclaims Monroe Doctrine, 437; and Industrial Revolution, 446; opposes French in Mexico, 470; growth of, 518–19, *m519;* sectionalism and slavery, 519–21; Civil War, 521–22; and immigration, 522, 557; and Liberia, 542; and imperialism in Pacific, 569–72, *m570;* and imperialism in Latin America, 573–75, *m575,* 577–78, 580–81; in World War I, 595–96, 606, 698–99; and League of Nations, 606–07; industrial growth, 632–33, 635–36; suffrage and education, 647; postwar economy and Great Depression, 677, 679; New Deal, 680; in Russian civil war, 687; postwar dip-

lomatic conferences, 703; and World War II, 726, 730–31, 734, 740, 826; and establishment of UN, 746–47; and armaments control, 753, 826; in postwar Europe, *m759,* 762–66; EEC effects on, 770; and NATO, 771–72, 774–75; summit conferences, 773; Aswan dam loan and Suez crisis, 785–86, 787; and postwar Asia, 801, 803–07; and Geneva Agreements, 808–09; and Vietnam, 810, 812, *p812,* 821; and Latin America, 815–16, *p817,* 818; Canadian relations, 819; in world affairs in 1960's, *m820;* postwar domestic problems, 821–22, 824; foreign affairs in 1970's, 824–25; science technology of, 826–27, *p828–29,* 830; today, *m844*

Uniting for Peace resolution, UN, 754, 787

Universal Postal Union, 583

universities: development of, 232–33; science and, 612–13; growth of, 647

UNRRA. *See* United Nations Relief and Rehabilitation Administration.

U Nu, 808

untouchables, 164

Upanishads (oo·PAN·uh·shadz), 162, 165, 173

Ural Mountains, 258, *m259, m274, m326–27,* 330, *m354*

Urban League, 822

Urban II, pope, 217

Urbino, Duke of, *p295*

Urdu, 269, 793

Uruguay, *m436,* 816, *m845*

U.S. *See* United States.

U.S.S.R. *See* Union of Soviet Socialist Republics.

Ussuri River, *m559,* 560

usury (YOO·zhur·ee), **222**

U Thant (oo THAHNT), 780, 784

Utopia, 295, 454

utopian socialists, 454, 456

Utrecht (YOO·trekt), *m338*

Utrecht, Treaty of, 349, *m350*

Uzbek Soviet Socialist Republic, *m843*

V-1 bomb, 736

V-2 rocket, 736, 826

Vaisyas (VY·syuz), **164**

Valens, Roman emperor, 157

Vandals, *m156,* 157–58, 245, *m245*

van Eyck, Hubert, 297

van Eyck, Jan, 297

van Gogh (van GOH), Vincent, *p555,* 658

van Riebeeck, Jan, *p544*

Varuna, Aryan god, 65

vassal, feudal, **199**

Vedas, 64–65

Vedic Age, 64–66

Venetia (vuh·NEE·shee·uh), 426, *m427,* 484, 485, 494, *m495,* 496, 498

Venezuela (ven·uh·ZWAY·luh), 435, *m436,* 574, *m575, m845*

Venice: in Crusades, *m218,* 219–20; and medieval trade, 222, *m224–25,* 315; and Renaissance, 293, 297; and Marco Polo, *m274,* 314; and unification of Italy, *m495*

Venice, Republic of, *m238*

Ventris, Michael, 86–87

Verdi, Giuseppe, 654

Verdun, 338, *m338,* 345, *m346,* 595, *m595*

Verdun, Treaty of, 192, *m192*

Vergil, 144, 232

Versailles (vur·SY), city, *m350, m419, m486, m603*

Versailles, palace, 347–48, *p348,* 405, 487, 603

Versailles Treaty, 602–04, 605, 606, 695, 698, 699, 711

Vesalius, Andreas, *p303,* 304

Vespucci (ves·POO·chee), Amerigo, 320

Vesta, Roman goddess, 128

Vesuvius, Mt., *m125,* 145

veto, 127

viceroyalties, Latin America, 430, *m436*

Vichy France, 722, *m723,* 727, 730, 732

Victor Emmanuel II, king of Sardinia and Italy, 495, 496, 498

Victor Emmanuel III, king of Italy, 706, 714

Victoria, ship, *m318–19,* 320

Victoria, queen of England, 510, *p511,* 512, 551, *p552*

Victorian Era, 510

Vienna: in Crusades, *m218;* defeat of Turks at, 338; Congress of Vienna, 424, 426, *m427;* 1848 revolt, 499; and Duel Monarchy, 499; Hitler in, 695; occupied after World War II, 758, *m759*

Viet Cong, 810, *p811*

Viet Minh, 808

Vietnam, *m806,* 808, 809–10, *p811,* 812, *p812,* 821, *m843*

Vikings, 194–95, *m194,* 197, 223, *m224–25,* 259–60, *m259*

Villa (VEE·yah), Pancho, *p579,* 581

Virchow (FIR·khow), Rudolf, 618

Virgin Islands, *m575,* 581

Vishnu, Hindu god, 165

Visigoths, 156, *m156,* 157, 245, *m245*

Vistula River, 258, *m259, m355, m486*

Vladivostok (vlad·uh·vahs·TAHK), *m559,* 560, 687

Volga River, 259, *m259, m274, m354*

Volta, Alessandro, 444

Voltaire, *p381,* 382, 401, 404, 405, 622

voting. *See* suffrage.

Wagner (VAHG·nur), Richard, 654, *p656*

Wake Island, m570, 572, 731, m735
Waldeck, Principality of, 479, m486
Waldheim, Kurt, p752, p784
War Communism, 687, 689
War of the Austrian Succession, 360
War of 1812, 417
War of the Spanish Succession, 349, 392
warlords, in China, **71**
War of the Roses, 235
Warsaw, m355, m603, m713, p716–17, m723, 736, m759, m765, 772
Warsaw, Grand Duchy of, 417, m419, 426, m427
Warsaw Pact, m765, 772–73, 774, 775, 776
Washington, George, 385, 393, 395, p396
Washington Naval Conference, 702
Watergate, 825–26
Waterloo, battle at, m419, 421, 424, 480
Watling Island, 316, m318–19
Watson, John B., 624
Watt, James, 442
Wealth of Nations, The, 450
weapons: Hittite, 42; Assyrian, 43; Shang Chinese, 72; and Crusades, 220; and decline of feudalism, 235; Byzantine Greek fire, 247; improvement of, in early modern times, 337; and interchangeable parts, 632; in American Civil War, 521; and Sepoy Rebellion, 551; in World War I, 593, p596–97; in World War II, 736, 740; atomic, 751, 753, 771, 772, 776, 826
Weber, Ernst, 624
Wedgwood, Josiah, 379
Weihaiwei (WAY·HY·WAY), m559, 561
Weimar (VY·mahr), m603, .694
Weimar Republic, 694–95, 698
Wei River, 175, m175, m176
Weizmann, Chaim, 670, 787
Wellington, New Zealand, m517
Wellington, Duke of, 421, p425
Wessex, 195, 197, m197
West Berlin, 765, 766, p766, 776. *See also* Berlin.
Western Ghats (GAWTS), 60, m60, 61
West Germany, m765, 764–66, 767, 768, 771, 772, 773, 775, 776, m842
West Indies: discovery of, m318–19, 320; colonization of, 322, 323, m326–27, 329; and mercantilism, 334; and trade, 389, m389, 391; in vice-royalty of New Spain, 430, m436, m575
West Irian. *See* Irian Jaya.
West Pakistan. *See* Pakistan.
Westphalia, Treaty of, 345–46, m346, 357, 478
Whigs, 374, 510
White Lotus Society, 275
Whitney, Eli, 442, 632
William I (the Conqueror), king of

England, p196, 198, 208, 209–10, 736
William I, king of Prussia and German Kaiser, 471, p478, 483, 487, 491
William II, German Kaiser, 491, p526–27, 535, 536, 540, p587, 588, 589, 600
William IV, king of England, 510
William of Orange, king of England, 375, 376, 380
William Rufus, king of England, 210
William the Silent, Dutch leader, 340
Wilson, Woodrow, 581, 595, 598–99, 600, 601, p601, 605, 606, 695
Witan, in early England, 197
Wittenberg, 305, m309
Worcester, 384
Wordsworth, William, 650
World Bank. *See* International Bank for Reconstruction and Development.
World Court, 605, 679, 715
World Health Organization (WHO), 751
World Meteorological Organization, 755
World War I: causes of, 584–86; and alliance systems, 586, 588–89, m588; start of fighting, 589–91; participants, 591–93; weapons, 593; course of, 594–95, m594, m595, p596–97; role of United States, 595–96, 597; Fourteen Points, 599; defeat of Central Powers, 599–600; peace terms, 600–05; establishment of League of Nations, 605–06; costs of, 606; compared to World War II, 719–20
World War II: aggressions leading to, 711–15, m713, p716, 717; participants in, 720; early days of, 720–22, m723, p724–25; U.S. involvement in, 723, 726; Axis victories in, 726–27; invasion of Russia, 727–29; Japanese aggressions, 729–30; U.S. entry in, 731; Axis losses in, 731–32, 733; in Pacific, 734–35, m735; Allied victory in, 736–37, p738, 739; costs of, 740; European recovery from, 757–58; postwar European settlements, 758–62, m759; postwar Japan and, 803–05
Worms (VORMS), m205, 212, 307, m309
Wright, Frank Lloyd, 658
Wright, Orville, 628
Wright, Wilbur, 628
writing: invention of, 15; Egyptian, 21, p22; Sumerian, 39; Babylonian, 41–42; Phoenician, 51–52, m52; Aramean, 52–53; of Indus Valley people, 62–63, p62; Chinese, 74, p75; Cretan, 86–87; Greek, p22, 119; Mayan Indian, 282
Wundt (VOONT), Wilhelm, 624
Württemberg, 486, m486
Wu Ti, Han ruler, 177–78
Wycliffe (WIK·lif), John, 242

Xavier (ZAY·vee·ur), Francis, 321
Xenophon (ZEN·uh·fun), 114
Xerxes (ZURK·seez), Persian king, 47, 99–100, m99
X-ray, 615, p616

Yahweh, 54, 56, 89
Yahya Kahn, 798
Yajur-Veda, 65
Yakutsk, m326–27, 330
Yalta, m723, 737
Yalta Conference, 737, 740, 747, 758
Yalu River, 801, m806
Yang Chien, Sui ruler, 270
Yangtze River, 67, m67, p69, 70, 175, 559, m559, 561, 705
Yaroslav I (the Wise), Russian king, 260
Yedo, m277, 281
Yellow River (HWANG Ho): early civilizations along, 11, m12, 13; and geography of China, 67, m67, 70; and Hsia dynasty, 71–72; and Shang dynasty, 72, m73; and Chou dynasty, 175, m175; and medieval trade, m224–25; and Mongol rule, m274, 275
Yellow Sea, m67, 175, m175, m559, 560, 561
Yemen (YEH·mun), 785, m786, m843
Yenan, 676, m705
Yenisei River, m259, 260, m326–27
Yoga, 165
York family, 235
Yorktown, m388, 397
Young Italy, 494
Young Turks, 674
Yüan dynasty, 274–75
Yucatán peninsula, 282–83, m283
Yugoslavia: created, m603, 604; alliance with France, 667; in World War II, m723, 727, 736; territorial changes after World War II, m759; as communist nation, 764, m765, 770, 772, 773; today, m842
Yukon Territory, 515, m516

Zaire, m781, p782, 783. *See also* Congo, Democratic Republic of.
Zama, battle at, 130, m131
Zambezi River, 256, m256, m534, 545
Zambia, m781, m846
Zanzibar, m318–19, 321, m326–27, m534, 545
Zara, m218, 219–20
Zen Buddhism, 271, 280
Zeno, 120
Zeus (ZOOS), Greek god, p91, 92, 94, 112, 128
ziggurat (ZIG·oo·rat), p38, 40
Zambabwe, m256, 257–58
Zimmerman, Alfred, 596
Zionism, **670**, 787
Zola, Émile, 476, p651, 653
Zollverein (TSAWL·fer·ine), 481, 489
Zoroaster (zoh·roh·AS·tur), 48

ACKNOWLEDGMENTS Positions are shown in abbreviated form as follows: *t*—top, *c*—center, *b*—bottom, *l*—left, *r*—right.

Key: Art Reference Bureau, Art Ref.; The Bettmann Archive, Bettmann; Bibliotheque Nationale, Paris, BN; British Museum, BM; Brown Brothers, BB; Culver Pictures, Inc., Culver; Freelance Photographers Guild, FPG; Hirmer Verlag München, Hirmer; Library of Congress, LOC; The Metropolitan Museum of Art, MMA; New York Public Library, NYPL; Radio Times Hulton Picture Library, Hulton; Rapho-Guillumette, R-G; United Press International, UPI; Wide World, WW.

Unit I: 2–3 John Freeman, BM; 4 Tom Hollyman, Photo Researchers; 8 *tl, bl* "Merveilles du Tasili N'Ajjer" Jean-Dominique Lajoux; *tr* Ralph Solecki, Columbia Univ.; 2 *c* Musée des Antiquités Nationales St. Germain-en-Laye; *br* Max Parrish & Co., London; 11 Photo Veronese Paris, Permission SPADEM 1973 by French Reproduction Rights, Inc.; 14 *tl* Claudia Andujar, R-G; *tr* Irven DeVore, Harvard Univ.; *b* Stanley Washburn, Berkeley, Calif.; 17 Eliot Elisofon; 19 Duncan Edwards, FPG; 22 BM; 24 R. J. Segalat, Louvre; 25 *See p. iv;* 26 *tl* Art Ref.; *c* MMA, Excavations 1929–30, Rogers Fund, 1931; *r* MMA, Gift of Edward S. Harkness, 1914; *b* Staatliche Museen, Berlin; 30 Eliot Elisofon; 31 *tl* MMA, Excavations, 1919–20, Rogers Fund supplemented by contribution from Edward S. Harkness; *tr* Louvre; *b* BM; 32 *See p. iv;* 35 By courtesy of Iran Bastan Mus.; 38 *tl* MMA, purchased, 1886, funds from various donors; *tr* Oriental Institute, Univ. of Chicago; *br* Drawing after Victor Place; 39 John Freeman, BM; 43 R. J. Segalat, Louvre; 44 *tl, bl* Louvre; *tr, br* BM; 49 *tl, tr* Oriental Institute, Univ. of Chicago; *b* Staatliche Museen, Berlin; 55 *t, b See p. iv;* 58, 62 Josephine Powell, Rome; 63 *t* Prehistoric, Harappa Culture, Clay figures: dog, cart with wheels, oxen, man, Courtesy Mus. of Fine Arts, Boston; *c* National Mus. of Pakistan; *b* Frances Mortimer, R-G; 68–69 *t* Howard Sochurek, NYC; *bl* Marc Riboud, Magnum; *bc* Ronny Jacques, Photo Researchers; *br* Henri Cartier-Bresson, Magnum; 75 *tl, tc* Academia Sinica, Taiwan; *tr, b* Coll. Dr. Paul Singer; 76 Cleveland Mus. of Art, John L. Severance Fund, Purchased from the J. H. Wade Fund. **Unit II:** 80–81 Robert Emmett Bright, R-G; 82 R. G. Hogler from Photo Hogler, Bregenz, Austria; 86 *l* FPG; 87 *tl, bl* Hirmer; *r* R. G. Hogler from Photo Hogler, Bregenz, Austria; 88 Josephine Powell, Rome; 90 *t* Erich Lessing, Magnum; *b* Staatliche Museen, Berlin; 91 *tl* BM; *tc, tr* Erich Lessing, Magnum; *b* John Freeman, BM; 93, 100 Hirmer; 105 *tl* R. J. Segalat, BN; *bl* MMA, Gift of Alexander Smith Cochran, 1913; *r* Pierpont Morgan Library, Alexander Magnus MS Vol. II, St. Petersburg, 1887, pl 4 (from a facsimile); 108 Roloff Beny, Rome, Courtesy Time-Life Inc., National Archaeological Mus., Athens; 113 *tl* Raymond V. Schoder, S.J., Antiken Kleinkunst, Munich; *tc* Raymond V. Schoder, S.J.; *tr* Raymond V. Schoder, S.J., Mus. Olympia; *b* Don Renner, Fanwood, N.J.; 116 *bl* Alinari–Art Ref.; *br* Louvre; *tl* BM; 120 MMA, bequest of Walter C. Baker, 1972; 123 Roger Wood, London; 126 MMA, Purchase 1940, John Pulitzer bequest; 132 *l* West Point Mus. Coll.; *tr* Uffizi, Scala; *br* Roger Viollet, Paris; 133 Corning Mus. of Glass; 139 *tl* Thames & Hudson, BM; *br, tr* Numismatic Soc. of America; *bl* Hirmer; *b* George Holton, Photo Researchers; 142 *t* Raymond V. Schoder, S.J., Museo Nazionale, Naples; *c* Pierre Belzeaux, R-G; *b* Raymond V. Schoder, S.J., Leptis Magna; 145 MMA, Purchase 1903, Canessa, Rogers Fund; 147 Robert Emmett Bright, R-G; 150 Hirmer; 152 Oscar Savio, Musei Capitolini, Rome; 155 Hirmer; 161 Madanjeet Singh; 163 *t, b See p. iv;* 164 Cleveland Mus. of Art, John L. Severance Fund, Purchased from the J. H. Wade Fund; 169 Mus. of Oriental Art, Rome; 172 Madanjeet Singh; 181 *br* Stern, Black Star; *bl* Coll. Dr. Paul Singer; *tl* Ex Richard C. Rudolph Coll.; *tr* John Freeman, BM. **Unit III:** 186–87 R. J. Segalat, Louvre; 188 Reproduced by Gracious permission of Her Majesty Queen Elizabeth II; 190 Biblioteca Apostolica Vaticana; 193 Giraudon; 196 *t* From the Bayeux Tapestry by Charles H. Gibbs-Smith, published by Phaidon Press, London, Photo Victoria and Albert Mus.; *l* BM; *cr* J. Allen Cash, London; *b* Pierre Belzeaux, R-G; 200 Cliff Line; 201 *l* Universitatsbibliothek, Heidelberg; *r-1* BM; *r-2, r-3, r-4,* R. J. Segalat, BN; 202 Edita S. A., Lausanne, Institut fur Denkmalpflege; 206, 213 Giraudon; 216 Bodleian Library, Oxford; 221 *t* Pierpont Morgan Library, M.638, folio 20v; *c* BN; *b* Aerofilm Ltd., London; 226 Schuler Verlag, Stuttgart; 230 *l* Dmitri Kessel, Paris; *t* Houvet, Chartres; *b* BN; 231 *l* Alinari–Art Ref.; *r* Simonet, R-G; 240 *tl* BN; *tr* Banque de Paris & des Pays-Bas Bruxelles; *b* John Freeman, Lambeth Place Library, London; 244 NYPL; 248 Giraudon; 249 *t, br* Erich Lessing, Magnum; *bl* Photo Gabinetto Fotografico Nazionale, Rome; 252 *tl* By courtesy of Iran Bastan Mus.; *bl* Courtesy of the Smithsonian Institution, Freer Gallery of Art, Washington, D.C.; *r* Norman Kotker, NYC; 257 De Antonis, Rome, BM; 261 *t* Coll. of the National Palace Mus., Taipei, Taiwan, Rep. of China; *b* Hulton; 264 John Freeman, India Office Library and Records; 268 *tl* Ullstein Bilderdienst, Berlin; *tr* Mansell; *b* BM; 273 *l* Cleveland Mus. of Art, John L. Severance Coll.; *tr* (detail) Chinese and Japanese Special Fund, Courtesy Mus. of Fine Arts, Boston; *br* BM; 278 *tl* Mus. Yamato Bunkakan, Nara, Japan; *tr* Tokugawa Reimeikai Foundation; *br* Kyoto National Mus., Courtesy Jingo-ji; 280 Sakamoto, Kongo Family Coll., Tokyo; 284 Courtesy Mus. of Primitive Art; 285 *tl* Carlos Saenz, Museo Nacional de Antropologia, Mexico; *by* Museo Nacional de Antropologia y Arqueologia, Lima, Courtesy Peruvian Embassy; *r* Theodore Kurz, NYC. **Unit IV:** 290–91 Rudolf Jankel Coll., NYC; 292 Giraudon; 295 Uffizi; 296 Editions Gallimard, Paris; 298 *l* Erich Lessing, Magnum; *b* Kunsthistorisches Mus., Vienna; 299 *t* MMA, Gift of J. Pierpont Morgan, 1916; *br* Albertina, Vienna; 301 R. J. Segalat, Institut de France, Paris; 303 *br* Giraudon; *tl, bl* NYPL; *tr* Alinari–Art Ref.; 306 *tl, tr* Lutherhalle, Wittenburg; *bl* MMA Harris Brisbane Dick Fund, 1941; *br* Giraudon; 313 LOC; 317 *tl* Bodleian Library, Oxford; *tr* BM; *br* NYPL; 323 David H. H. Felix, Philadelphia; 328 *t* John Freeman, BM; *bl* NYPL; *br* BM; 331 *tl* Biblioteca Apostolica Vaticana; *tr* Victoria and Albert Mus.; *b* Suntory Art Mus., Tokyo; 332 Giraudon; 336 Van der Veen, R-G; 341 *r* Marburg–Art Ref.; *l* Reproduced by permission of the Trustees of the Wallace Coll.; *b* Culver; 344 *tl* Mansell; *tr* Bulloz; *b* Culver; 348 Archives Photographiques, Paris; 356 *tl* William Froelich, NYC; *tc* Sovfoto; *tr* A la Vielle Russie, NYC; *bl* NYPL; *br* NYPL; 359 *t, b* Giraudon. **Unit V:** 364–65 R. J. Segalat, BN; 366 Photo John Freeman, National Portrait Gallery; 369 *tl* Corsini–Art Ref.; *tr* Hulton; *bl* National Portrait Gallery; 372 *tl* National Maritime Mus., London; *tr* The Duke of Buccleuch and Queensberry; *br* Mansell; *bl* BM; 377 MMA, Whittlesey Fund, 1956; 379 Coll. Byron Born, NYC; 381 *tr* Bonnefoy, R-G; *cl* John Freeman, The Royal Society, London; *c* MMA, Gift of William H. Huntington, 1883; *cr* Kunsthistorisches Mus., Vienna; *b* Theatermuseum, Clara-Ziegler Stiftung, Munich; 384 Yale Univ. Art Gallery; 387 Mass. Hist. Soc.; 390 *t* Phelps Stokes Coll., NYPL; *c* Mass. Hist. Soc.; *b* N.Y. State Hist. Assn., Cooperstown; 394 Gift of Joseph W., William B. and Edward H. R. Revere, Courtesy Mus. of Fine Arts, Boston; 396 *b* Hist. Soc. of Penna.; *tl, tr* LOC; 401 Napoleon in his Study (no. 1374) Jacques-Louis David, Samuel H. Kress Coll., National Gallery of Art, Washington, D.C.; 403 *tl* MMA, Bequest of Isaac D. Fletcher, 1917; *l* Giraudon; *bl* NYPL: 405 *See p iv;* 408 *br* Louvre; *bl* R. J. Segalat, BN; *tr, tl* Giraudon; 411 Musée Royaux des Beaux Arts, Brussels; 415 *t* Print Division, NYPL; *b* BN; 423 Museo Nacional de Historía, Mexico; 425 *t* NYPL; *c* Nationalbibliothek, Vienna; *b* Hist. Pictures Service, Chicago; 434 *tr* Mansell; *b* Pan American Union; 439 *See p. iv;* 443 Smithsonian Institution; 445 *t* Richard Graber, Merrimack Valley Textile Mus.; *c* NYPL; *b* LOC; 448 *t* Granger Coll.; *bl* NYPL; *br* Bettmann; 452 Print Division, NYPL; 455 *tl* Hulton; *tr* NYPL; *bl See p. iv.* **Unit VI:** 460–61 Bruno Novarese, Museo di Firenze Com' Era; 462 Giraudon; 465 Louvre; 466 *l, r* R. J. Segalat; 469 *All* Gernsheim Coll., Univ. of Texas; 473 *See p. iv;* 474 *tl* Coll. Otto Hieronymi, NYC; *bl* Allen Memorial Art Mus., Oberlin College; 475 *l* Gernsheim Coll., Univ. of Texas; *r* Purchased, Picture Fund, Courtesy Mus. of Fine Arts, Boston. 478 Landesgalerie, Hannover; 481 Staatliche Kunstsammlungen Dresden-Germaldegalerie Neue Meister; 482 *tl* BB; *tr* Goethe House, NYC; *b* Bettmann; 485 Culver; 491 NYPL; 493 Editions Robert Laffont, Paris; 497 *tl* Biblioteca del Risorgimento, Florence; *tr* Oscar Savio, Rome; *b* Deutsche Fotothek, Dresden; 505 *All* Novosti Press Agency, London; 508 Confederation Life Coll., Toronto; 511 *tl* Hulton; *bl* Gernsheim Coll., Univ. of Texas; *br* National Portrait Gallery; 513 Courtesy of Fogg Art Mus., Harvard Univ., Grenville L. Winthrop Bequest; 520 *t* Coll. Byron Born, NYC; *c* NYPL; *b* Univ. of Penna. Library; 521 LOC; 522 Bettmann. **Unit VII:** 526–27 West Point Mus. Coll.; 528 NPYL; 531 Elisofon; 533 R. J. Segalat, BN; 537 *tl* Bettmann; *tr* Editions Robert Laffont, Paris; *b* Coll. Herbert Brooks Walker; 541 *tl* Hulton; *tr, bl* BB; *br* UPI; 544 *t, b* Hulton; *c* Fehr Coll., Cape Town; 548 Roger Viollet, Paris; 552 *t* National Army Mus., London; *br* NYPL; *bl* India Office Library and Records; 555 André Held, Ecublens; 556 Bradley Smith, N.Y.; 562 *l, r,* 563 *l* Ullstein-Birnback/Photoworld; *r* Roger Viollet, Paris; 565 *tl* Ullstein-Birnback/Photoworld; *tr* Roger Viollet, Paris; *br* Hulton; 568 Vt. Development Assn.; 572 Giraudon; 576 *tl* N.Y. Hist. Soc. *bl* LOC; *br* Culver; 578–579 *tl* Granger Collection; *tr* BB; *b* Panama Canal Co.; 583 Smithsonian Institution; 585 Art Institute of Chicago; 587 *t* Culver; *bl* Hulton; *br* National Archives; 590 Librairie Larousse; 596–97 *All* Imperial War Mus.; *except cr* Ullstein Bilderdienst, Berlin; 599 Coll. Whitney Mus. of American Art, N.Y., anonymous gift. 601 UPI. **Unit VIII:** 610–11 Detroit Institute of Arts, Gift of Edsel B. Ford; 612 Reproduced by courtesy of the Royal Institution of Great Britain; 614 Kunstmuseum, Basel; 616 *tl* Deutsches Mus., Munich; *cf* Bettmann; *cr* Culver; *bl* Fritz Goro, Time/Life Picture Agency; *br* Ernst Haas, Magnum; 621 *tl* National Portrait Gallery; *tr* BB; *br* Bettmann; 623 Munch-Museet, Oslo; 626 detail, Coll. of the Newark Mus.; 629 *t* Deutsches Mus., Munich; *c* Photoworld; *b* RCA; 631 Film Library, Mus. of Modern Art; 634 *t* Ford Motor Co.; *c* H. J. Heinz & Co.; *b* LOC; 635 N.Y. Hist. Soc.; 638 NYPL; 641 Los Angeles County Mus. of Art; 645 *t* Bettmann; *bl* Nicolas Bouvier, Geneva; *br* BB; 648 *tl* MMA; *bl* Photoworld; *r* Culver; 651 *tl* Photo Musée Rodin, Permission SPADEM 1973 by French Reproduction Rights, Inc.; *tr* NYPL; *bl* Louvre; *br* Gisele Freund, Paris; 652 Harbrace; 656 *tl* Rudolf Jankel Coll., NYC; *tc* Musée de l'Opera, Paris; *tr* Permission SPADEM 1973 by French Reproduction Rights, Inc.; *b* Cleveland Mus. of Art, John L. Severance Coll.; 657 *t* MMA, Bequest of Mrs. H. O. Havemeyer, 1929, the H. O. Havemeyer Coll.; *bl* Giraudon; *br* Philadelphia Mus. of Art, Louise and Walter Arensberg Coll. '50-134-14. **Unit IX:** 662–63 UPI; 664 Keystone; 667 Cliff Line; 668 *See p. iv;* 671 *tl* Photoworld; *tr* Keystone; *bl* Bettmann; *br* Thompson Newspaper Ltd., London; 675 *tl* Ullstein-Birnback/Photoworld; *tr* Hulton; *bl, br* Harrison Forman; 678 *t* LOC; *c* UPI; *bl, br* FSA Coll., NYPL; 682 Cornell Capa, Magnum; 685 *l* Sovfoto; *tr* Keystone; *cr* NYPL *br* Culver; 686 Sovfoto; 690 WW; 696 *t* BB; *bl, br* UPI; 697 *All* James Huntley Coll., London, *except br* WW; 698 Photo Klee-Stiftung, Berne, Permission Cosmopress and SPADEM 1973 by French Reproduction Rights, Inc.; 701 Ullstein-Birnback/Photoworld; 703 *tl* UPI; *tr* WW; *bl Natori,* Black Star; *br See p. iv;* 708 *tl, tr, b See p. iv;* *c* UPI; 710 1937—On loan to Mus. of Modern Art, from artist, Picasso; 716 *tl* Ullstein-Birnback/Photoworld; *tr* WW; *bl* Picture Coll., NYPL; *br* UPI; 717 *tr* UPI; 719 Air Force Art Coll.; 724–25 *tl* Ultgeverej D.E., N.V. de Arbeiderspers, Amsterdam; *b* Culver; *cr See p. iv; br* UPI; 728 Sovfoto; 730 NYPL; 733 *t, c, bl* U.S. Army; *br* WW; 738 *t* U.S. Army; *bl* Photoworld; *br* Illustrated, Black Star; 739 U.S. Army. **Unit X:** 744–45 Brian Brake, Magnum; 746 Serge Larrain, Magnum; 750, 742 *all* U.N.; 754 UNICEF, Shankar Dillai Child Book Trust; 757 Sue McCartney, Photo Researchers; 761 U.S. Army; 763 Robert Sowers, NYC; 769 *tl, br* NYPL; *tr* FPG; *bl* WW; 772 *l* Elio Sorci, Globe Photos, Inc.; *c* Renée Falcke, R-G; *r* John Bryson, R-G; 774 WW; 775 UPI; 778 Marc Riboud, Magnum; 782 *t* London *Times,* Pictorial Parade; *c* Paris *Match,* Pictorial Parade; *b* U.N.; 784 UPI; 789 *tl* London *Times,* Pictorial Parade; *tr* WW; *bl* UPI; *br See p. iv;* 791 AFP from Pictorial Parade; 794 Harry Redl, Black Star; 797 *tl, br* Marilyn Silverstone, Magnum; *tr, bl See p. iv;* 799 *t* UPI; *c* Eastfoto; *b* Paolo Koch, R-G; 802 *t* UPI; *bl See p. iv; br* Hulton; 805 Coll., Mus. of Modern Art, Gift of the designer; 811 *tl* UPI; *tr, b* WW; 812 UPI; 814 General Dynamics; 817 *tl* Robert Henriques, Magnum; *tr* Henri Cartier-Bresson, Magnum; *bl* Andrew St. George, Magnum; *br* U.N.; 823 *tl* Harris-Ewing Photo Trends; *tr* Bruce Davidson, Magnum; *bl* Flip Schulke, Black Star; *br* WW; 824 *both* UPI; 825 Harry Davidson Coll., courtesy Sidney Janis Gallery; 828 *l, br* NASA; *tr* Erich Lessing, Magnum; 829 *tl* Charles Rotkin, Photography for Industry; *tr* Pictorial Parade; *bl* Marc Riboud, Magnum; *br* NASA. Chronology by Cliff Line.